THE JAMES FORD

An Annotated Catalog of Original Source Materials
Relating to the History of European Expansion
1400—1800

BELL LIBRARY

JAMES FORD BELL LIBRARY
UNIVERSITY OF MINNESOTA
1994

Copyright © 1994 by the James Ford Bell Library. All rights reserved
Printed and bound in the United States of America at
Printing and Graphics: University of Minnesota, St. Paul
ISBN 0-9601798-4-4

Published by the James Ford Bell Library
University of Minnesota, 472 Wilson Library, 309 19th Avenue South
Minneapolis, Minnesota 55455
(612) 624-1528
fax: (612) 626-9353

PREFACE

The James Ford Bell Library at the University of Minnesota is a reflection of its founder's fascination with the beginnings of things. A merchant with an insatiable curiosity about nature, commerce, mechanics, and science, he built a flourishing milling business at the watershed of central North America, and in the process wondered how it all began—who preceded him and his mercantile colleagues here. He found his way into earlier accounts of trading activity in the heartland of the continent by acquiring books from the sixteenth, seventeenth and eighteenth centuries—the writings of explorers, merchants, and missionaries. And when that was well begun he could not avoid the search for their predecessors and contemporaries who undertook similar work in other parts of the world.

It was a field too vast for one man to encompass, so in 1953 James Ford Bell turned his Library over to his alma mater, the University of Minnesota, which he also served as regent for many years. Here the collection he had gathered found its place in an outstanding research library and in an academic environment that would contribute to its growth and its success. Until his death in 1961, James Ford Bell continued a vigorous acquisition program for the Library, and he provided that it would have support subsequently through the James Ford Bell Foundation.

In its development since becoming a part of the University of Minnesota Libraries, this collection has not changed it scope materially. It consists of original source materials relating to the history of European expansion prior to 1800, with particular emphasis on the mercantile aspects. It includes related subjects such as the intellectual background to the Age of Discovery, the practical aspects of navigation and astronomy, laws governing international maritime trade, cartography, philosophical rationale accompanying colonial and commercial expansion, the development of Christian missionary enterprise abroad, and the uses of natural history for commercial purposes. A very substantial part of the Library consists of accounts of discovery, exploration, commerce, and travel outward from Europe to all parts of the world.

The Library's first catalog was Frank K. Walter and Virginia Doneghy, *Jesuit Relations and other Americana in the Library of James Ford Bell*, Minneapolis, University of Minnesota Press, 1950. In 1955 the University of Minnesota Press published a *List of Additions* which described briefly the acquisitions of the intervening years. Subsequently *Lists of Additions* were issued in 1961, 1967, 1970, and 1975. The complete catalog published by the G.K. Hall Company in 1981 included the holdings to the end of 1980. The present catalog is a record of the Library's holdings as of December 31, 1992. This catalog will be supplemented by a listing of acquisitions in *The Merchant Explorer*, an annual publication of the Library. This catalog does not incorporate materials held by the Department of Special Collections or other divisions of the University of Minnesota Libraries.

This catalog is the result of over forty years of acquisitions and cataloging efforts by the curators of the James Ford Bell Library, plus the outside cataloging done by several individuals from the Cataloging Department of the University Libraries. Vsevolod Slessarev and Frank Gillis were Assistant Curators of the Library. The first cataloger was Ms. Virginia Doneghy, co-author of the earliest catalog of the collection. After her retirement, Ms. Alice Stahl and Mr. Robert Olson cataloged for the Library. Beginning in 1976 Ms. Valerie Roberts undertook the cataloging, which she continued until her untimely death in 1990. The descriptions of the 1992 acquisitions for this catalog were done by Assistant Curator Brad Oftelie.

Many staff members and volunteers made this new complete catalog possible. For typing, Jane Rasmussen Riedel, who typed the 1981 catalog; word processing: Brian Hanson, Sara Shannon, Mary Whitehead, Vicki Zobel; checking the National Authority File: Brad Oftelie, Pete Opitz, Maria Marcich; proof reading: all of the preceding plus Chris Gable, Abigail Garner, Helen Feldman, and Margaret Hanson. In this Library we have sometimes spoken of this new catalog as "the Hanson Catalog," since Brian Hanson has done so much work for its publication, from setting up WordPerfect files to preparing the final format of the pages by using the QuarkXPress publishing system. We thank all of these people. In addition we are grateful to the James Ford Bell Foundation for a grant to help with the publication of the catalog.

JOHN PARKER, *Curator Emeritus*
CAROL URNESS, *Curator*

James Ford Bell Library
Wilson Library 472
University of Minnesota
309 19th Avenue South
Minneapolis Minnesota 55455
(612) 624-1528
fax: (612) 626-9353

FORMAT

The James Ford Bell Library holdings are listed by main entry, by author usually, but the works of unknown authorship are entered by title, and those by companies or government agencies have corporate entries. All entries in the catalog have been checked against the National Name Authority file, and are given in the form established by that file. Names of authors and the first words of other entries are indicated in bold type.

The arrangement is alphabetical, with a few exceptions. Government publications are arranged chronologically within the issuing agency. Where an author's work is available in several editions the chronological arrangement has been modified according to language.

The titles and imprints are in standard type. Most titles have been given as they appear on the titlepages. Some very long titles have been shortened, either by ellipses or at a point indicated on the titlepage by major punctuation. Imprint information not on the titlepage is indicated in brackets. In almost every case the place of publication has been modified to its modern form.

As in previous editions of the catalogs of the James Ford Bell Library, no attempt has been made to provide bibliographical descriptions for the holdings. This information is available from the catalog at the James Ford Bell Library, and questions about pagination, numbers of maps, etc. are welcomed by the staff. The item numbers given in this catalog, for example V12, replace the item numbers given in the 1981 catalog. Any inconvenience that this causes is worth suffering to avoid the confusion that would arise by trying to maintain the older item numbers and integrate new ones with them.

The annotations are short, but we hope informative. In some cases they refer only to the particular importance of an item to the scope of the James Ford Bell Library, so researchers should keep that in mind as they use the catalog. There are longer commentaries in the records of the James Ford Bell Library, and questions about particular items in the catalog are welcome. It is interesting to remember that the practice of writing an annotation for every title added to the Library originated with Mr. Bell himself, in his own collecting and in the early years of buying books for the Library. This practice has been maintained, and we are pleased to share some of its results through the short annotations in this catalog.

A

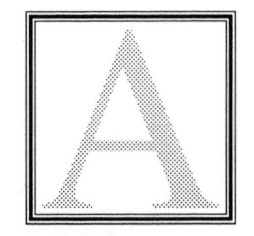

A.J.P. Carta que hum negociante portuguez escreve a hum seu amigo a esta capital, em que lhe relata a tomada de Bangalore, e os progressos das armas inglezas no paiz de Tipoo. Lisbon, Antonio Gomes, 1792.   A1
A newsletter describing the defeat of Tipu Sultan, Nawab of Mysore by Lord Cornwallis.

Aa, Pieter van der. De aanmerkenswaardige voyagien door Franc., Italianen, Deenen, Hoogduitsche en andere vreemde volkern gedaan na Oost en W. Indien. Leiden, Pieter van der Aa, 1706-07.   A2
Translations from original accounts of voyages to the East and West Indies by French, Italian, Danish, German, and other European explorers and merchants.

Aa, Pieter van der. De doorluchtige scheepstochten der Portugysen na Oost-Indien. Leiden, Pieter van der Aa, 1706-07.   A3
These narratives of Portuguese voyages to the East are translated from Barros.

Aa, Pieter van der. De wydberoemde voyagien an Oost-en W. Indien der Engelsen. Leiden, Pieter van der Aa, 1706-07.   A4
Translations of English voyages from a variety of sources.

Aa, Pieter van der. Der gedenkwaardige voyagien der Spanjaarden na West Indien. Leiden, Pieter van der Aa, 1706-07.   A5
Accounts of Spanish explorations and conquests in the West Indies, translated from the *Historia general* of Herrera y Tordesillas.

Aa, Pieter van der. Nouvel atlas, très-exact et fort commode pour toutes sortes de personnes ... Leiden, P. Van der Aa [1714].   A6
An atlas of 193 colored maps, portraying Europe, Asia, Africa, and America.

Aan 't volk van Nederland; of, Bewyzen en consideratien over de voordeelen der negotie met de Noord Americaanen. [n.p., ca. 1782]   A7
A collection of three pieces concerning Dutch trade, leading to the conclusion that peace with Britain and trade with the Americans was essential.

Aanmerkingen op de tegenwoordige toestand van zaaken tusschen Engeland en Holland. n.p., 1779.   A8
A commentary on Anglo-Dutch relations leading up to hostilities between them, from a Dutch point of view and taking into account commercial rivalries in many areas.

Aanmerkingen op den Brief, van eenen goeden Fries aan den Heer V.D.H. The Hague, H.H. van Drecht, 1779.   A9
A caution against offending Great Britain by continuing to trade with France.

Abbad y Lasierra, Iñigo. Historia geográfica, civil y política de la isla de S. Juan Bautista de Puerto Rico. Dala á luz Don Antonio Valladares de Sotomayor. Madrid, Don Antonio Espinosa, 1788.   A10
A systematic description and history of Puerto Rico, noting the presence of various European nationals there, its commerce, and giving a list of the bishops who served there.

[Abbot, George.] A briefe description of the whole worlde. London, For John Browne, 1608.   A11
The third edition of a geographical handbook, containing histories and descriptions of all known parts of the world.

[Abbot, George.] A briefe description of the whole world. London, For John Marriot, 1624.   A12
This sixth edition contains some rather recent additions, noting the beginnings of the Virginia colony, but nothing on New England. The establishment of the English factory in Japan is also mentioned.

Abbot, George. A briefe description of the whole world. London, T.H. for W. Sheares, 1636.
A13
Late edition of this popular geography, without significant changes in text.

Abeel, Johann, *et al.* [Account book for trade and general merchandising.] Manuscript. Albany and New York, 1694-1702. A14
The entries, which are written in Dutch, cover a variety of products including furs.

Abgenötiger, wogegründeter Gegen-Bericht der Königl. Dännemarckischen octroijrten Afrikanischen Guineischen ... Compagnie. Glückstadt, Melchior Rochen, 1665. A15
The Danish West African Company complains of the treatment received by them at the hands of agents of the Dutch West India Company, which had bases on the African coast.

[Abreu de Galindo, Juan de.] The history of the discovery and conquest of the Canary Islands. London, For R. and J. Dodsley and T. Durham, 1764. A16
Based on a seventeenth-century manuscript, this history deals most heavily with the fifteenth and sixteenth-century colonization of the islands, and includes information on the people, economy, and government.

Abreu y Bertodando, Felix Joseph de. Tratado juridico-politico, sobre pressas de mar. Cadiz, Imprenta Real [1746]. A17
This discourse on the Spanish law of prizes contains excerpts from treaties with other nations specifying the rights of each nation in such cases.

[Abreu y Figueroa, Fernando]. Sumario en hecho, y derecho de lo que resulta de los memoriales, y decretos que ha auido en la propuesta que el padre maestro Fray Fernando de Abreu y Figueroa hizo a su Magestad ... el año 1634 sobre retener los sinodos, o estipendios que paga en las Indias ... [n.p., ca. 1634]. A18
A summary of abuses of the American Indians inflicted under Spanish colonial administrators, with historical background going back to the time of Columbus.

An abridgement of the act for settling the government and trade of India. [India, ca. 1795.]
A19
The act here abridged provided for a considerable reorganization of the East India Company, and set forth policies regarding its trade.

Abschrifft ains Bryeffs von Constantinopel, auss wölchem man zu vernemen hatt, wölcher Gstalt der Gross Turck seine Priester und Doctores hat lassen umbringen, auss Ursachen, das sye bestendiger weyss bekant ... [Augsburg, M. Ramiger] 1539. A20
Translation of an Italian newsletter reporting persecution of Christians by the Turkish sultan.

The absolute necessity of laying open the trade to the East-Indies. London, For J. Williams, 1769.
A21
Contends that freedom for all Englishmen to participate in the East Indian trade will increase wealth and therefore cause a reduction in taxes.

An abstract of a letter from a person of eminency and worth in Caledonia to a friend at Boston in New England. Glasgow, Robert Sanders, 1699.
A22
A broadside containing an optimistic appraisal of the colony at Darien, predicting it would become "the best and surest mart in America."

Abstract of agreement between the Hudson's Bay Company and the Selkirk settlers. Manuscript on vellum roll. n.p. [ca. 1821-1822].
A23
Eight articles of agreement which bind the Selkirk settlers not to engage in the sale of spirituous liquors nor in the fur trade, and to transport all produce sold abroad in Company ships.

An abstract of the evidence delivered before a select committee of the House of Commons, in the years 1790 and 1791; on the part of the petitioners for the abolition of the slave trade. Edinburgh, For J. Robertson, 1791. A24
The abstract includes only evidence favorable to the cause of the abolitionists.

Abū Ma'shar. De magnis coniunctionibus. [Venice, Jacobum Pentium de Leucho, 1515.]
A25
The second edition of an astrology book written in the ninth century by an Arab scholar and translated in 1133 by John of Seville.

Abū Ma'shar. Introductorium in astronomiam. [Augsburg, Erhard Ratdolt, 1489.] A26
The first edition of an important astronomy text written in the ninth century. It includes material on the climate zones of the earth, geometric problems of the sphere, and other matter of geographical interest.

Abū Ma'shar. Introductorium in astronomiam. [Venice, Jacobus Pentius, 1506.] A27
The text of this edition follows closely that of the previous one. The illustrations also are similar, but are fewer in number and of inferior quality.

Académie royale des sciences, des lettres et des beaux-arts de Belgique. Mémoires sur les questions proposées ... Brussels, Antoine D'Ours, 1774. A28
One of the questions discussed was the nature of the economy and commerce of Belgium before the seventh century. It is treated by M. Du Rondeau.

[Acarete, du Biscay.] A relation of Mr. R.M.'s voyage to Buenos-Ayres. London, J. Darby, 1716. A29
An account of extensive travels in South America, with observations on trade and smuggling there. Dedicated to the directors of the South Sea Company.

[Accarias de Sérionne, Jacques.] Le commerce de la Hollande. Amsterdam, Changuion, 1768. A30
A description of Dutch commerce in America, the Levant, and the East Indies.

[Accarias de Sérionne, Jacques.] Hollands rijkdom, behelzende den oorsprong van den koophandel, en van den magt van dezen staat. Leyden, Luzac en van Damme, 1780-1783. A31
Under the editorship of Elie Luzac this edition becomes a new work, with extensive notes to the text and numerous appendices containing reprints of important documents in Dutch economic history.

[Accarias de Sérionne, Jacques.] Les intérêts des nations de l'Europe, dévélopés relativement au commerce. Leiden, Elie Luzac, 1766. A32
A general survey with discussion of the commerce of individual nations.

[Accarias de Sérionne, Jacques.] La richesse de la Hollande. Londres, Aux dépens de la Compagnie, 1788. A33
A history of Dutch commerce with discussion of the means whereby Dutch commercial prominence might be maintained or lost.

Accord tusschen de camers ende leven vande Noordsche Compia van Hollt., Zeelandt ... vande walvischvangen ... Manuscript. [Netherlands, 164-?] A34
Agreement between the chambers of Holland and Zeeland relative to their partnership in the Noordsche Compagnie engaged in whaling. Reference is made to earlier agreements dating between 1631 and 1634.

An account of several late voyages and discoveries to the south and north. London, For S. Smith and B. Walford, 1694. A35
Includes the voyages of Narborough, Tasman, Wood, and Martens.

An account of some transactions in the Honourable House of Commons ... relating to the late East-India Company. London, 1693. A36
Contains proposals for regulating the East India Company, the Company's replies and counter-proposals, and the charter granted to the Company by the crown in 1693.

Account of the duty on tin exported from anno 1610 to the year 1698. [n.p., ca. 1698.] A37
This history of the duties on tin and pewter was published in response to pewterers' complaints about being undersold by foreign pewter.

An account of the East-India Companies war with the Great Mogul. [London, ca. 1691.] A38
A condemnation of the Company's actions for starting a war which resulted in a five-year interruption of trade in India.

An account of the expedition to Carthagena, with explanatory notes and observations. London, For M. Cooper, 1743. A39
To this narrative about the unsuccessful and controversial attack on Cartagena by Admiral Vernon and General Weymouth is added a geographical description of the vicinity of Cartagena.

An account of the late application to Parliament, from the sugar refiners, grocers, &c. of the cities of London ... London, J. Brotherton, 1753. A40
Discusses evidence in support of allegations concerning the high price of sugar, suggesting that the price of sugar is high because of underproduction by the West Indian planters.

An account of the number of forts and castles, necessary to be kept up and maintained on the coast of Africa. n.p. [ca. 1720]. A41
A survey of the costs incurred in maintaining nine forts for the protection of the Royal African Company's trade.

An account of the number of Negroes delivered into the islands of Barbadoes, Jamaica, and Antego ... [London, 1709?]. A42
Statistics to prove the beneficial effects on the slave trade of the termination of the Royal African Company's monopoly.

An account of the Spanish settlements in America. Edinburgh, A. Donaldson [etc.] 1762. A43
A survey of Spain's position in the world, with particular emphasis on its commerce with the American colonies.

Aché, Anne Antoine, comte d'. Pieces indiquées dans le *Mémoire* imprimé de M. le comte d'Aché. Paris, [P.G.] Simon, 1766. A44
Sixty-two documents to support the position of the comte d'Aché against attacks made on his command of the French fleet in the Indian Ocean in 1758 and 1759.

Aché, Anne Antoine, comte d'. Réponse ... aux imputations faites ... par comte de Lally, par son mémoire ... intitulé *Tableau historique de l'expédition de l'Inde*. Paris, P.G. Simon, 1766. A45

A rebuttal to Lally's publication, chiefly concerning disagreement over the use of the French fleet at the time of the siege of Madras.

Aché, Anne Antoine, comte d'. Réponses ... Au mémoire du comte de Lally, intitulé: *Vraies causes de la perte de l'Inde.* Paris, Simon, 1766. A46

Another response by the comte d'Aché to accusations made by the comte de Lally regarding French losses to the British in India.

Acosta, José de. De natura novi orbis. Salamanca, G. Foquel, 1589. A47

The first edition of this highly popular book on the New World, written by a Jesuit priest who spent some seventeen years in various parts of New Spain.

Acosta, José de. Historia natural y moral de las Indias. Seville, Juan de Leon, 1590. A48

The first Spanish, and first complete, edition.

Acosta, José de. Historia naturale, e morale delle Indie. Venice, Bernardo Basa, 1596. A49

The first Italian edition, translated by Giovanni Paolo Gallucci.

Acosta, José de. Histoire naturelle et moralle des Indes, tant Orientalles qu' Occidentalles. Paris, Marc Orry, 1598. A50

The first French edition.

Acosta, José de. Histoire naturelle et morale des Indes, tant Orientales, qu' Occidentales. Paris, Adrian Tiffaine, 1616. A51

The second French edition.

Acosta, José de. Historie naturael ende moreal van de Westersche Indien. Enkhuizen, Jacob Lenaertsz, 1598. A52

This first Dutch edition was translated by Linschoten and used by De Bry in the preparation of the German edition.

Acosta, José de. Historie naturael en moreal van de Westersche Indien. Amsterdam, H. Laurensz., 1624. A53

The second edition of Linschoten's translation.

Acosta, José de. The naturall and morall histoire of the East and West Indies. London, V. Sims for Edward Blount and William Aspley, 1604. A54

The first English edition, translated by Edward Grimestone.

Acrelius, Israel. Beskrifning om de Swenska församlingars forna och näwarande tilstånd. Stockholm, Harberg & Hesselberg, 1759. A55

A history of New Sweden containing numerous documents relating to both civil and ecclesiastical affairs.

The act for permitting the free importation of cattle from Ireland, considered with a view to the interests of both kingdoms. London, For R. and J. Dodsley, 1760. A56

A proposal to encourage free importation of feeder cattle from Ireland to supply British needs economically and aid the Irish economy at the same time.

Acuña, Cristóbal de. Nuevo descubrimiento del gran rio del Amazonas ... Madrid, Imprenta del Reyno, 1641. A57

A description of the first navigation made down the Amazon from the Andes to the Atlantic Ocean. The purpose of the expedition was to determine the usefulness of the Amazon River as a trade route.

Acuña, Cristóbal de. Relation de la riviere des Amazones. Paris, Claude Barbin, 1682. A58

The earliest French edition of an account of the Amazon which was originally published in 1641. Contains an extensive discussion of the commercial importance of the river.

Adair, James. The history of the American Indians. London, For Edward and Charles Dilly, 1775. A59

An outstanding work on the American Indians, by an author who lived with them for many years. An appendix criticizes England's policies toward the colonies in matters of trade and taxation.

Adam, von Bremen. Chorographia Scandinaviae, sive descriptio vetustissima regionum & populoruum Aquilonarium, Sueciae, Daniae & Norwegiae. Stockholm, Reusnerianis, 1615. A60

This is the fourth part of Adam of Bremen's *Ecclesiastical History*. It describes the peoples and geography of Scandinavia and the islands of the North Atlantic, including Iceland, Greenland, and Vinland.

Adam, von Bremen. Historia ecclesiastica. Leyden, Plantin, 1595. A61

This ecclesiastical history, written by an eleventh-century historian and geographer, contains mention of Vinland and other Scandinavian colonies, as well as accounts of the Baltic trade.

Adams, Amos. A concise, historical view of the difficulties, hardships, and perils which attended the planting and progressive improvements of New England. London, For Edward and Charles Dilly, 1770. A62

This history is told in terms of colonial efforts at their own defense while being hampered by threats to their political and religous freedom by England.

Adams, John. Geschiedenis van het geschil tusschen Groot-Britannie en Amerika ... Amsterdam, W. Holtrop, 1782. A63

Adams explains the American position with respect to Great Britain with essays published in the *Boston Gazette* in 1775.

Adams, John. A memorial. To their High Mightinesses, the States General of the United Provinces of the Low-Countries. n.p., 1781.
A64
The ambassador of the United States urges close commercial relations with the United Netherlands.

Adanson, Michel. Histoire naturelle du Sénégal. Paris, Claude-Jean-Baptiste Bauche, 1757.
A65
A description and an account of travel in Senegal that contains observations on the climate, soil, products, etc., and includes an excellent map of the region.

Adanson, Michel. A voyage to Senegal, the isle of Goree, and the river Gambia. London, For J. Nourse, 1759.
A66
The first English edition, lacking the section in the French original entitled "Histoire des coquillages," but adding notes and a preface by the translator.

Adanson, Michel. Nachricht von seiner Reise nach Senegal und in dem Innern des Landes. Leipzig, Siegfried Lebrecht Crusius, 1773.
A67
One of two German editions issued in 1773; the editor and translator of this one was Johann Christian Daniel Schreber.

Adanson, Michel. Resa til Senegal. Upsala, J.F. Edman, 1795.
A68
An abridged Swedish translation.

Addington, Anthony. An essay on the sea-scurvy: wherein is proposed an easy method of curing that distemper at sea; and of preserving water sweet for any cruize or voyage. Reading, C. Micklewright, 1753.
A69
A view of the causes of scurvy aboard ship, and the means of preventing and of curing it in which salt water, spirit of salt, and vegetable diet figure prominently.

Addison, Lancelot. West Barbary, or A short narrative of the revolutions of the kingdoms of Fez and Morocco. Oxford, John Wilmot, 1671.
A70
In addition to the account of political events, this work contains descriptions of the geography, economy, and social life of North Africa, reflecting English commercial interests there.

An address to the inhabitants of Birmingham and its neighbourhood. n.p., 1793.
A71
A protest against the renewal of the charter of the East India Company, with its monopoly on East Indian trade.

An address to the merchants of Great Britain: or, A review of the conduct of the administration, with regard to our trade and navigation. London, For J. Roberts [1738].
A72
This defense of the government's peace policy argues that the national economy is better served by the encouragement of trade than by war.

An address to the Right Honourable L—d M—sf—d; in which the measures of government respecting America, are considered in a new light; with a view to His Lordship's interposition therein. London, For J. Almon, 1775.
A73
A perceptive and forceful argument against the usurpation of powers never intended for it by Parliament, urging the judiciary to redress the balance in the interest of the American colonies.

Adelung, Johann Christoph. Geschichte der Schiffahrten und Versuche ... des nordöstlichen Weges nach Japan und China ... Halle, J.J. Gerbauer, 1768.
A74
A history of attempts to find a northeast passage, including accounts of English, Dutch, Danish, Russian, and other navigations.

Adriaensen, Adriaen. Por Adrian Adrian Sen, de nacion Olandès. Con el señor Fiscal del Consejo Real de las Indias. [n.p., 1665]
A75
A legal process concerning sale of a ship by a Dutch citizen to a Spaniard, apparently without clear title to the ship.

The advantages and disadvantages which will attend the prohibition of the merchandizes of Spain. London, For J. Roberts [1740].
A76
An examination of Spanish imports into Britain finds that only dyestuffs should be admitted because they are essential to the woolen manufacture.

The advantages of peace and commerce; with some remarks on the East-India trade. London, For J. Brotherton and T. Cox, 1729.
A77
This discussion of the importance of trade introduces a concern for the growth of Russian interest in Asiatic commerce.

The advantages of the East-India trade to England ... London, For J. Roberts, 1720.
A78
Concerns the exporting of bullion in exchange for goods manufactured in India where labor costs were one-sixth as high as those in England.

The advantages of the revolution illustrated, by a view of the present state of Great Britain. London, For W. Owen, 1753.
A79
A review of the British economy, noting the progress of various industries since the revolution of 1688, the growth of colonial prosperity, and the general well-being of Great Britain.

Advantages which have accrued to the publick, and to the South-Sea Company, by the execution of the South-Sea scheme. [London] 1728.
A80

The Company's activities over an eight-year period are reviewed, and the conclusion reached that since it took no money out of the country, reduced interest on the national debt, and caused greater suffering to foreign than local investors it was a benefit to the nation.

Advertencias importantes a la total comprehension de la real voluntad de la Reyna Nuestra Señora en la formacion de la Compañia Española, para el commercio armado. [Valencia, 1669.]   A81

Concerns the formation of a Spanish commercial company which would employ armed merchant vessels.

Advis au roy, sur les affaires de la Nouvelle France. [Paris? 1626.]   A82

An appraisal of an unsatisfactory situation in New France with suggestions for its improvement. Includes a letter from M. Montz to Louis Hébert, both of whom took part in the early settlement of New France.

Advis pour les manufactures de France. Paris, 1627.   A83

Suggestions for the improvement of the French cloth trade.

Advys op de memorie van de herre resident van Vranckryck. n.p., 1648.   A84

Concerns European diplomatic affairs.

Advys op de presentatie van Portugael. Het eerste deel. n.p. [1648].   A85

The first of three parts, recommending that Portugal's offer of peace be accepted in the interest of the Dutch West India Company.

Aende ... commissarisen van Syn Majesteyt van Brittaingen ... Rotterdam, A. Leeuwen, 1661.   A86

Concerns a conference held by the ambassadors of England and the Netherlands relating to their respective East India companies.

Aenwysinge: datmen vande Oost en West-Indische Compagnien een Compagnie dient te maken ... The Hague, J. Veeli, 1644.   A87

"Proof that the East and West India Companies ought to be combined into one, together with twenty considerations on the traffic and commerce of these lands."

Aethicus Ister. Cosmographia. Basel, 1575.   A88

This is a collection of classical travels edited by Josias Simmler, including in addition to Aethicus the *Itinerarium Antonini*, the *Itinerarium* of Rutilius Claudius Namantianus, and the geography of Vibius Sequester.

Af-beeldinghe van d'eerste eeuwe der Societeyt Jesu. Antwerp, Inde Plantiinsche Druckeriie, 1640.   A89

The Dutch translation of the Latin edition of *Imago primi saeculi Societatis Jesu*. The emblem book includes extensive text and was published to celebrate the first one hundred years of the Society. The poems are by Adrien Poirters. Attributed to Jean de Tollenaere it is mainly the work of Johannes Bolland. Translated by Laurent Uwens.

Afhandling om nyttan för Sverige af handel och nybyggen I Indiera och på Africa. Stockholm, Peter Hesselberg, 1776.   A90

An advocate of Swedish colonization cites the experience of other European nations and urges Swedish enterprise in establishing a colony in West Africa, to trade to the West Indies also.

Agosti, Girolamo Oliviero. De imperio Romano, in pristinam gentem & dignitatem restituto, liber unicus. Eiusdem, De partitione orbis: libri quattuor. [Augsburg, Philippus Ulhardus, 1548.]   A91

Two poems in honor of Charles V., the second containing references to geography in both the eastern and western hemispheres, noting newly discovered areas.

Agostinho de Santa Maria, frei. Historia da fundaçaõ do real convento de Santa Monica da cidade de Goa, corte do estado da India, & do imperio Lusitano do oriente, fundado pelo illustrissimo, e reverendissimo senhor Dom Fr. Aleixo de Menezes. Lisbon, Antonio Pedrozo Galram, 1699.   A92

A history of an Augustinian convent originating in 1606. It includes a number of biographies of persons associated with the convent and an extensive biography of Aleixo de Menzes who was archbishop of Goa at the time the convent was begun.

Agostinho de Santa Maria, frei. Rosas do Japam, candidas açucenas, e ramalhete de fragrantes, & peregrinas flores, colhidas no jardim da Igreja do Japaõ ... Lisbon, Antonio Pedrozo Galram, 1709.   A93

An Augustinian chronicler describes the difficulties of Christian missions in Japan and in southeast Asia.

Agrell, Olof. Bref om Maroco. Stockholm, Johan A. Carlbohm, 1796.   A94

Eighteen letters dated from 5 September 1789 to 6 October 1791, commenting on economic and political matters in Morocco involving various European nations. The author was secretary to the Swedish consul in Morocco.

Agustin de Madrid, fray. Relacion del viage que hizo el abad Don Juan Bautista Sydot, desde Manila al Imperio del Japon, embiado por Nuestro Santissimo Padre Clemente XI. [n.p., 1717]   A95

An account of the papal embassy of Juan Battista Sidoti to Japan by way of the Philippines where Sidoti remained from 1704 to 1708. A major part of the work is the log of the ship which took Sidoti to Japan. The author was a member of the Discalced Franciscans who maintained a mission in the Philippines.

Ailly, Pierre d'. Imago mundi. Louvain, Johannes de Paderborn [ca. 1483]. A96
An important geography written without the influence of the Ptolemaic tradition. Its major contribution was the idea that the earth was somewhat bulged at the equator, and that Asia extended farther to the east than had previously been supposed. It is known to have had a strong influence on Columbus.

Aislabie, John. The speech of the Right Honourable John Aislabie, esq.; upon his defence made in the House of Lords, against the bill for raising money upon the estates of the South-Sea directors, on Wednesday the 19th of July 1721. London, Printed for J. Roberts, 1721. A97
Aislabie defends himself against accusations established in the House of Commons concerning his involvement in speculation in South Sea Company stock.

Aitzema, Lieuwe van. Verhael van de Nederlandsche vreede handeling. Amsterdam, Jacob Benjamin, 1653. A98
A history of Dutch foreign affairs between 1621 and 1648, frequently involving Dutch overseas trade.

Al molto rever. padre della Compagnia di Giesu. Tridenti, Superiorum permissu, 1702. A99
Collection of Jesuit letters from the Peking mission concerning the Chinese rites controversy. The letters date from the mid-1600s and continue up to the date of publication. All together they are a very good summary of Jesuit writings on the rites controversy.

Albertini, Francesco. Opusculum de mirabilibus novae & ueteris urbis Romae. [Rome, I. Mazochium, 1510.] A100
An account of the discoveries of Amerigo Vespucci appears in this history of Rome.

Alberto, Joaquim Antonio. Condiçoens, que S. Magestade. Lisbon, A.R. Galhardo, 1773. A101
A charter, with trading conditions listed, of a Portuguese merchant fleet planning to sail by February 1774. The charter is dated August 28, 1773 and signed by the directors Joaquim Antonio Alberto and Domingos Jorge Ferreira. The intended destination is India and China with stops in Madeira, Brazil and Mozambique.

Albertus, Magnus, Saint. De celo et mundō. [Venice, Joannem & Gregorius de Gregoriis fratres, 1495.] A102
A thirteenth-century astronomy in its second edition, describing the earth as a sphere and the heavens according to Ptolemy's system.

Albertus, Magnus, Saint. De natura locorum. [Vienna, H. Vietor & J. Singrenius, 1514.] A103
A treatise on climatology and meteorology in which the author states that the land to the south of the equator is habitable.

Albuquerque, Afonso de. Commentarios de Afonso Dalboquerque capitão geral & governador da India. [Lisbon, Joam de Barreyra, 1557.] A104
Albuquerque served as Portugal's second viceroy to India, his administration covering the period 1509-1515. His commentaries were edited by his natural son Braz. This is the first edition.

Albuquerque, Afonso de. Commentarios do grande Afonso d'Alboquerque. Lisbon, João de Barreira, 1576. A105
The second Portuguese edition.

Albuquerque, Afonso de. Commentarios do grande Afonso Dalboquerque capitão geral que foi das Indias Orientaes en temp do muito poderoso Rey D. Manuel o primeiro deste nome. Lisbon, Regia Officina Typografica, 1774. A106
This is the third Portuguese edition. Dedicated to the Marquis de Pombal, it was designed to stimulate patriotism and assist in the renaissance which Pombal was trying to bring about in Portugal.

Albuquerque, Afonso de. Held-dadige scheepstogt van Alfonso d'Albuquerque, na de Roode-Zee. Leyden, P. Van der Aa, 1706. A107
A history of the establishment of Portuguese supremacy in the East during the years 1509-15. An adaption from Barros.

Albuquerque, Francisco d'. Twee bysondere scheepstogten na Oost-Indien ... in het jaar 1503 en ... 1504. Leiden, P. Van der Aa, 1706. A108
An account of the fourth Portuguese fleet to be sent to India.

[Albuquerque, Matias de.] [Draft of a memorandum to King Phillip II of Portugal concerning political and military affairs in India.] Manuscript in Portuguese. n.p. [ca. 1603]. A109
The author of this memorandum served as viceroy of India from 1591 to 1596. His observations reflect continuing interest in the situation there.

Alcala, Marcos de. Vida maravillosa de San Martin de la Ascension y Aguirre, proto-martyr del Japon ... Madrid, Manuel Fernandez, 1739. A110
A collection of eulogies, documents and letters relative to the life of Martín de la Ascensión de Aguirre, a Franciscan missionary who served in Mexico, the Philippines and Japan in the sixteenth century.

Alcarotti, Giovanni Francesco. Del viaggio di Terra Santa. Novara, Heredi di Fr. Sesalli, 1596. A111

A narrative of travel to Jerusalem via Tripoli, noting mercantile, political, and military affairs en route. A guide for pilgrims is included, instructing in matters of clothing, food, money changing, etc.

Alcayaga, Estevan de. Miguel Ruiz en nombre de Estevan de Alcayaga y de Doña Maria de Lartaun su mujer ... Manuscript. [n.p., ca. 1589.] A112

A court document including records, evidence presented, and testimony in a litigation case concerning mining rights in Peru, and indicating the difficulties of mining there.

Alcazar y Zuniga, Andres de, *et al.* Señor ... nos hallamos en el reconocimiento de los indultos, y repartimientos hechos en Indias ... Seville, 1697. A113

Written by four deputies of commerce in the West Indies, this text concerns routes of navigation there.

Alcedo, Antonio de. Diccionario geográfico-histórico de las Indias Occidentales o América. Madrid, Benito Cano, 1786-89. A114

A comprehensive gazetteer of the Americas, giving geographical, historical, biographical, and other data particularly about the Spanish possessions.

Alcoforado, Francisco. An historical relation of the first discovery of the isle of Madera. London, For William Cademan, 1675. A115

The first English edition of the legendary discovery of Madeira by Lionel Machin and Anna d'Arfet in the fourteenth century, which according to the legend led the Portuguese to discover the island in 1420.

[Alcoforado, Francisco.] Relation historique de la découverte de l'isle de Madere. Paris, L. Billaine, 1671. A116

The first French edition.

Alcune riflessioni intorno alle cose presenti della Cina. [n.p., 1709.] A117

This series of twelve questions concerning the Chinese rites question has been attributed to both Tommaso Ceva and Carlo Ambrogio Cattaneo. It was prompted by publication in China of the papal decree of November 20, 1704 condemning the Chinese rites.

Alcuni casi ne I quali I vincoli sono utili al commercio in specie di seta e lana. n.p., 1791. A118

Relates to the effects of restriction upon foreign cloths on the trade in Italy.

Aldenburgk, Johannes Gregorius. West-Indianische Reisze, und Beschreibung der Beläg-und Eroberung der Statt S. Salvador in ... Brasilia. Coburg, Friderich Grüner, 1627. A119

An account of the Dutch occupation of Bahia in May 1624, and the recapture of the city the following year by the Portuguese. The author was a German officer in the service of the Dutch.

Aldrete, Bernardo. Varias antiguedades de España, Africa y otras provincias. Antwerp, Juan Hafrey, 1614. A120

This study by a Jesuit scholar is about equally divided between Spain and Africa. With respect to the latter, it notes classical, early Christian and Moslem history, and the development of Spanish and Portuguese colonies.

Alegambe, Philippe. Mortes illustres et gesta eorum de Societate Jesu. Rome, Typographia Varesii, 1657. A121

Contains biographical information relating to the missionary work of some 330 Jesuits.

Alègre, Jean. Table des principales rivieres du monde, et des principales villes par ou elles passent ... Paris, A. de Fer [ca. 1640]. A122

A broadside similar to the following item, with the rivers of the world located by country, and the major cities on them identified. The entire text is arranged within five circles.

Alègre, Jean. Table geographique divisée en six cercles, et tres commode pour apprendre toutes les principales parties du monde ... Paris, A. de Fer [ca. 1640]. A123

A geographical tool identifying the major political and geographical divisions of the earth, with their subdivisions, all arranged in six circles.

Alegrete, Manuel Telles da Sylva. De rebus gestis Joannis II, Lusitanorum regis, optimi principis nuncupati ad augustissimum regem Petrum II. Lisbon, Michael Manescal, 1689. A124

The reign of João II (1481-1495) was of major significance for Portuguese expansion overseas, encompassing the voyage of Dias, the eastward travels of Covilhão and Paiva, and closer relations with Ethiopia.

[Aleppo correspondence. Two manuscript letters dated 29 April 1484 and 19 September 1485, addressed to merchants in Tripoli.] A125

Both letters record the delivery of goods from one merchant to another and contain trade marks to identify the letters with the cases of goods being delivered.

[Alexandre, Noël.] Apologie des Dominicains missionnaires de la Chine. Ou réponse au livre du Pere Le Tellier, Jesuite, intitulé, Defense des nouveau Chrétiens; et à l'éclaircissement de P. Le Gobien de la même compagnie, sur les honneurs que les Chinois rendent à Confucius & aux morts ... Cologne, Heritiers de Corneille d'Egmond, 1699. A126

A statement of the Dominicans' case against two publications supporting Jesuit acceptance of Chinese rites in religious practice: Michel Le Tellier's *Defense des nouveaux Chrestiens* and Charles Le Gobien's *Histoire de l'édit de l'Empereur de la Chine*.

[Alexandre, Noël.] Conformité des ceremonies chinoises avec l'idolatrie grecque et romaine. Pour servir de confirmation à l'apologie des Dominicains missionaires da la Chine. Cologne, Heritiers de Corneille d'Egmond, 1700. A127
The author was a learned Dominican whose attempt to trace Chinese customs to Greece and Rome is coupled with an urgent plea that the Chinese rites controversy be settled quickly.

[Alexandre, Noël]. Conformité des ceremonies chinoises avec l'idolatrie grecque et romaine ... Cologne, Heritiers de Corneille d'Egmond, 1700. A128
This edition has some text in Latin, Italian, and Portuguese, the originals from which French translations in later editions were made.

[Alexandre, Noël.] Lettre d'un dottore di teologia dell' Universitá di Parigi dell' ordine de' predicatori, intorno alle idolatrie e superstizioni della China. Cologne, Eredi di Cornelio d'Egmond, 1700. A129
A collection of seven letters, two to Louis Daniel Le Comte, and five to Jean Dez, Provincial of the Jesuits; all letters relate to the Chinese rites controversy, presenting an anti-Jesuit point of view.

[Alexandre, Noël.] Lettre d'une personne de pieté. Sur un ecrit des Jesuites contre la censure de quelques propositions de leurs PP. Le Comte, Le Gobien, &c. touchant la religion & le culte des Chinois, faite par la Faculté de Théologie de Paris ... Cologne, Heritiers de Corneille d'Egmond, 1701. A130
An attack upon the Jesuit position with respect to the Chinese rites and upon the various writings which had defended their case against the censure of the Faculty of Theology at Paris.

[Alexandre, Noël]. Lettre[s] d'un docteur de l'ordre de S. Dominique sur les ceremonies de la Chine ... Cologne, Heritiers de Corneille d'Egmond, 1700. A131
A series of seven letters carrying the arguments of the opponents of the Jesuits with regard to the Chinese Rites controversy.

Alfonce, Jean. Les voyages avantureux. Poitiers, J. de Marnef [1559]. A132
The author of this travel narrative was the chief pilot in the expedition of Sieur de Roberval which went to Canada to support Cartier in 1542.

Alfraganus. Brevis ac perutilis compilatio Alfragani ... ad rudimenta astronomica est opportunum. Ferrara, Andreas Belfortis, Gallus, 1493. A133
The first edition of an authoritative work by a ninth-century Arabian astronomer. His writings on the sphere were the basis for much of Sacro Bosco's work, and they also influenced Dante's ideas on astronomy.

Algarotti, Francesco. Letters from Count Algarotti to Lord Hervey and the Marquis Scipio Maffei. London, For Johnson and Payne, 1769. A134
These twelve letters from 1739 to 1751 describe Russian trade with Europe and with China, and include comments on European military superiority in India, Admiral Anson's voyage, and the Anglo-French rivalry in North America.

Algarotti, Francesco. Letters military and political. From the Italian of Count Algarotti ... Dublin, P. Byrne, 1784. A135
The first Irish edition.

Algarotti, Francesco. Lettres du comte Algarotti sur la Russie. Neufchatel, La sociéte typographique, 1770. A136
The second French edition.

Algöwer, David. De mathesi Sinica amplissimae facultatis philosophicae indultu publice disputabunt ... respondens Joannes Matthias Has. Helmstad, Georg-Wolffgagni Hamii, 1702. A137
A doctoral dissertation by Johann Matthias Hasius, dealing primarily with the uses of mathematics in China for astronomical, military, and naval matters, and for preparation of the calendar.

[Alingham, William.] A short account of the nature and use of maps. As also some short discourses of the properties of the earth, and of the several inhabitants thereof. To which is subjoin'd, a catalogue of the factories and places now in possession of the English, French, Dutch, Spaniards, Portegueze and Danes, both in the East and West-Indies. London, Mount [etc.] 1698. A138
An elementary treatise on geography with instructions for measuring, mapping, using maps, and a listing of the colonial holdings of all of the European nations.

Alingham, William. A short account of the nature and use of maps. London, R. Janeway for Benj. Barker, 1703. A139
This edition has a completely revised text, and includes tables and diagrams not in the 1698 edition.

Alldridge, W. J. The universal merchant. Philadelphia, F. and R. Bailey, 1797. A140
Alldridge was an Englishman who settled in the United States and was a believer in the young country's principles, stating in his dedication that the "state, the professed objects of whose aim are, prosperity and happiness, must avoid war, encourage industry, cultivate virtue, and preserve good order at home." Banks, and coinage and business are major topics.

Allegatione per confirmare quanto si scrive nell' annotationi all' aviso di parnaso, al numero 57. Cavata dalla vita di F. Bartolome Dalla Casa, vescovo de Chiapa. Descritta da F. Michele Pio Bolognese ... Antopoli, Stamperia Regia, 1618. A141

A brief life of Bartolomeo de las Casas and commentary on his works.

Allen, Ira. The natural and political history of the state of Vermont, one of the United States of America. To which is added an appendix containing answers to sundry queries, addressed to the author. London, J.W. Myers and sold by W. West, 1798. A142

This is primarily a history of Vermont's claim to lands contested by New York. This is an early issue without the Appendix.

Allen, Robert. An essay on the nature and method of carrying on trade to the South-Sea. London, R. Mount, 1712. A143

A treatise on the need for further encouraging British trade to the South Sea.

Die allerneueste Staat von Siberien, einer grossen und zuvor wenig bekannten moscowitischen Provinz in Asien ... Nuremberg, Wolfgang Moritz Endters seel. Erben, 1725. A144

A description of Siberia with primary interest in natural history representing a variety of sources, and also informative of ancient and medieval knowledge of Siberia.

Allgemeine Historie der Reisen zu Wasser und Lande; oder Sammlung aller Reisebeschreibungen, welche bis itzo in verschiedenen Sprachen von allen Völkern herausgegeben worden ... In deutsche übersetzet ... Leipzig, Arkstee und Merkus, 1747-1774. A145

A massive collection of voyage and geographical literature, taken from Astley's English collection, the French of Prévost, and various other sources. Extensively illustrated with copper engravings.

Allgemeine Schatz-Kammer der Kauffmannschafft oder Vollständiges Lexicon aller Handlungen und Gewerbe so wohl in Deutschland als auswärtigen Königreichen und Ländern ... Leipzig, Johann Samuel Heinsius, 1741-1743. A146

A commercial dictionary with extensive descriptions of geographical and mercantile subjects.

Allison, Thomas. An account of a voyage from Archangel in Russia, in the year 1697. Of the ship and company wintering near the North Cape in the latitude of 71 ... London, D. Brown and R. Parker, 1699. A147

This writer was the captain of the *Ann* of Yarmouth, employed in the Russia Company's trade that sent ships up around Scandinavia to Archangel for Russian goods. The ship was caught in bad weather, and the crew spent the winter in the very northern part of Norway.

Almada, Andre Alvares d'. Relação e descripção de Guiné. Lisbon, Miguel Rodrigues, 1733. A148

Includes comments on the products, the fertility of the land, and tribal political relationships.

Almanach du commerce et des voyageurs, contenant l'indication des villes commerçantes de l'Europe. Paris, Duchesne [1774?]. A149

A handbook for merchants, with information on money, exchange, commercial regulations, etc.

Almeida, Francisco de. Roemrugte scheeps-togt van Francisco d'Almeida na Oost-Indien ... Leyden, P. Van der Aa, 1706. A150

A description, taken from Barros, of the exploits of the first Portuguese viceroy of India, whose naval victories over the Moslems established Portuguese supremacy in India.

Almeida, Manuel de. Historia geral de Ethiopia a alta, ou Preste Joam. Coimbra, Manoel Dias, 1660. A151

Written in collaboration with Balthazar Telles, this history of Ethiopia traces the progress of European influence there to about the middle of the seventeenth century.

Alós, Joachin de. [Manuscript report, signed, to the Marqués de Avilés concerning conditions in Paraguay.] Dated Valparaiso, 15 July 1799. A152

In a memorandum to the new governor, the Marqués de Avilés, former governor of Paraguay, describes conditions following the expulsion of the Jesuits.

Alphabetum Grandonico-Malabaricum sive Samscrudonicum. Rome, Congregationis de Propaganda Fide, 1772. A153

A text on the Grantha-Malabaric or Sanskrit alphabet prepared by the Congregation for the Propagation of the Faith for use among its missions.

Alsedo y Herrera, Dionisio de. Aviso historico, politico, geographico, con las noticias mas particulares del Peru, Tierra-Firme, Chile, y Nuevo Reyno de Granada. Madrid, Miguel de Peralta [1740]. A154

An account of events in the Spanish colonies in South America from 1535 to 1740, arranged chronologically by the tenures of the viceroys from Francisco Pizarro to Don Antonio Joseph de Mendoza.

Alsedo y Herrera, Dionisio de. Compendio historico de la provincia, partidos, ciudades, astilleros, rios, y puerto de Guayaquil en las costas de la Mar del Sur. Madrid, Manuel Fernandez, 1741. A155

A description of the province of Guayaquil in the viceroyalty of New Granada, with accounts of products and commerce, and a fine map of the town of Guayaquil.

Alströmer, Jonas. Sveriges vålstånd om det vil, förestält uti et tal då commercie-rådet Jonas Alström ... Stockholm, Lars Salvius, 1745.
A156
A survey in essay form of Swedish resources with an account of the sciences in Sweden at the time and suggestions for improving the Swedish economy.

Altamirano, Pedro Ignacio. Defensa juridica ... procedieron el Governador y oficiales reales de Cartagena. [Lima? ca. 1737.] A157
Concerns accusations against Spanish officials regarding illegal commerce.

Alvares, Francisco. Ho Preste Joam das Indias. [Coimbra?] Luis Rodriguez, 1540. A158
First edition of an account of Ethiopia by a priest who accompanied the Portuguese embassy led by Rodrigo de Lima there in 1520-27. The book was the earliest detailed description of Ethiopia published in Europe.

Alvares, Francisco. Historia de las cosas de Etiopia. Antwerp, Juan Steelsio, 1557. A159
The first Spanish edition.

Alvares, Francisco. Historia de las cosas de Ethiopia. Toledo, P. Rodriguez, 1588. A160
The third Spanish edition.

[Alvares, Francisco.] Historiale description de l'Ethiopie. Antwerp, Jehan Bellere, 1558.
A161
This first separate French edition is taken from the French translation of the first volume of Ramusio's collection, published in Lyon, 1556.

Alvares Solano do Valle, Manoel, ed. Commentaria ad fodinarum regimen. In quibus, quae de fodinis necessaria, ac utilia sunt ad controversias forenses decidendas, plené discutiuntur multaque alia obiter explanantur ... Lisbon, Antonii de Sousa à Sylva, 1739. A162
A collection of laws regulating mining in Brazil. The text is in Portuguese, the commentary in Latin.

Alvarez, Francisco, Asturian. Noticia del establecimiento y poblacion de las colonias Inglesas en la America Septentrional. Madrid, Antonio Fernandez, 1778. A163
A Spanish view of the English possessions in North America, noting the productions of each and their value to the mother country.

Amat y Junient, Manuel de. Manuscript copy of a letter to King Charles III of Spain. Manuscript in Spanish. [Lima, ca. 1773] A164

A copy of a response to a royal cedula of 24 July 1773 in which Charles III inquired about the rivers rising in Peru and flowing into Brazil.

Amati, Scipione. Relation und gründtlicher Bericht von dess Königreichs Voxu im japonischen Keyserthumb gottseliger Bekehrung. Ingolstadt, Elisabeth Angermayrin, 1617.
A165
An account of early Franciscan missions in Japan, the embassy from Japan to Rome in 1615, and a review of Franciscan missionary establishments in all parts of the world.

Amato, Giuseppe Carlo. Il microscopio de computisti, o sia economia prattica ... Palermo, Angelo Felicella, 1740. A166
A general commercial handbook for southern European countries, including a listing of fairs held in major cities.

Ameilhon, Hubert-Pascal. Histoire du commerce et de la navigation des Egyptiens. Paris, Saillant, 1766. A167
A history of ancient Egyptian commerce including voyages around Africa and to India.

America: or, An exact description of the West-Indies. London, R. Hodgkinsonne for E. Dod, 1655. A168
A description of the New World, with particular attention paid to food products and fibers to be found there.

Les Americains réunis à Paris, & ci-devant composant l'Assemblée générale de la partie françoise de Saint-Domingue, a l'Assemblée nationale. Paris, Imprimerie Nationale, 1791.
A169
A statement celebrating representation by St. Domingue in the National Assembly.

The American gazeteer. London, A. Millar [etc.] 1762. A170
Gives geography, climate, manufactures, and natural products of various parts of the New World.

American husbandry. Containing an account of the soil, climate, production and agriculture of the British colonies in North-America and the West-Indies; with observations on the advantages and disadvantages of settling in them, compared with Great Britain and Ireland. By an American. London, J. Bew, 1775. A171
A survey of agricultural possibilities, achievements and methods, with extensive observations on deficiencies in the management of American agriculture.

Amhurst, N. (Nicholas). The second part of an argument against excises. London, H. Haines, 1733. A172
An attack upon the proposed excise tax on wine and tobacco.

[Amhurst, N. (Nicholas).] Some farther remarks on a late pamphlet, intitled, *Observations on the conduct of Great-Britain.* London, For Richard Francklin, 1729. A173
Criticizes an earlier pamphlet for its soft line against the Spaniards in the West Indies. Contains also the *Postscript, in vindication of our West-India merchants against a late charge of theft and pyracy.*

Ami des noirs. Lettre a MM. les députés des trois ordres, pour les engager à faire nommer par les Etats-Généraux, à l'exemple des Anglois, une Commission chargée d'examiner la cause des noirs. [Paris? 1789?] A174
A strong argument for terminating the slave trade, citing English precedent in investigating the evils of the trade.

Amman, Jost. Eigentliche Abbildung desz ganzen Bewerbs der löblichen Kaufmannschafft ... und fürnehmsten Handelstädt. [Augsburg, ca. 1585.] A175
This large woodcut has been called an "Allegory of Trade." A massive scale balancing credits and debits dominates the center, while the city of Antwerp with its busy harbor is shown in the background and trading scenes are portrayed in the foreground.

Amstelophilus. Op de onafhankelykheid van Noord-America. [n.p., 1782] A176
A poem celebrating the outcome of the American Revolution.

Amsterdam (Netherlands). Exstract uyttet register der resolutien van den heeren burgermeesteren ... der stadt Amstelredamme. n.p., 1650. A177
Proposals advanced in 1639 for the beginning of an insurance company for the better protection of Amsterdam's commerce in the Mediterranean.

Amsterdam (Netherlands). Extract uyttet register der resolutien van den herren burgmeestern ... der stadt Amsteldamme. n.p., 1650. A178
Another edition of the preceding item, but with additional material relating to the necessity for close cooperation between the provinces of the Netherlands.

Amsterdam (Netherlands). Insinuatie en protest ... gedaan aan't Collegie ter Admiraliteyt. n.p., 1685. A179
A protest to the Admiralty against taxes which were considered disadvantageous to Amsterdam's commerce.

Amsterdam (Netherlands). Missive van heeren Burgemeesteren en regeerders ... houdende derzelver berigt op zeekere papieren door den Heer Ridder Jorke ... ter hand gestelt. Amsterdam, Pieter Mortier [1780]. A180
A statement concerning negotiations for a treaty of commerce between the city of Amsterdam and American representatives, discovered by the British when they captured an American ship.

Amsterdam (Netherlands). Propositie ende protest ... tegens het heffen van het last en veylgeldt. n.p. [1685]. A181
This protest against taxes levied by the government of Holland and West Friesland, contends that they will ruin commerce.

Amsterdam (Netherlands). Burgemeesters. Copye vande resolutie van de heeren burgemeesters ende raden tot Amsterdam. Op't stuck vande West-Indische Compagnie. n.p., 1649. A182
The affairs of the Dutch West India Company are discussed, and the views of the Burgomasters and members of the Common Council of Amsterdam are set forth.

Amsterdam (Netherlands). Burgemeesters. Copye vande resolutie van heeren burgemeesters ende raden tot Amsterdam. Op't stuck vande West-Indische Compagnie. n.p., 1649. A183
A variant of the previous item.

Amsterdam (Netherlands). Burgemeesters. Copye vande resolutie van heeren burgemeesters ende raden tot Amsterdam. Op't stuck vande West-Indische Compagnie. Utrecht, J. Havick, 1649. A184
Utrecht edition of the above item.

Amsterdams dam-praetje, van wat outs en wat nieuws en wat vreemts. Amsterdam, Jan van Soest, 1649. A185
A discussion of the Dutch-Portuguese conflicts in Brazil and Angola.

Amsterdams-praetjen tusschen Jan Dircxsen en Pieter Leunis, over de saecken van desen tegenwoordigen tijdt. Amsterdam, 1661. A186
A discussion of Anglo-Dutch negotiations in London, and the trade rivalries between the two countries in Africa and the East Indies.

Anania, Giovanni Lorenzo d'. L'universale fabrica del mondo. Venice, Aniello San Vito di Napoli, 1576. A187
A world geography in four parts, describing Europe, Asia, Africa, and the New World. In listing his sources the author shows familiarity with much of the most recent material.

Anania, Giovanni Lorenzo d'. L'universale fabrica del mondo, overo cosmografia. Venice, Muschio, 1582. A188
This edition includes five maps and lists some one hundred and seventy authorities on which the work is based.

Anatomia, ofte ont-ledinge roerende de saeken der Engelsche en Hollanders, in Amboyna. Amsterdam, S. van der Meulen, 1652. A189
An answer to the Dutch contention that an English conspiracy was the cause of the Amboyna Massacre.

Anburey, Thomas. Travels through the interior parts of America. London, For William Lane, 1789.   A190
    A series of seventy-nine letters by an English officer who observed many aspects of commercial life in America from Quebec to Virginia.

[Anburey, Thomas.] Journal d'un voyage fait dans l'intérieur de l'Amérique septentrionale. Paris, La Villette, 1793.   A191
    The second French translation, with notes by the translator-editor François Joseph M. Noël.

Ancher, Peder Kofod. Oeconomiske tanker til høiere efter-tanke. Copenhagen, C.G. Glasings Efterleverske, ved Nicolaus Møller, 1756-1757.   A192
    A discussion of the Danish economy from many aspects, in three parts. The second part was written by Balthazar Gebhardus van Obelitz, who like Ancher was a legal scholar and writer on political economy.

Anciens memoires de la Chine, touchant les honneurs que les Chinois rendent à Confucius & aux morts. Paris, Nicolas Pepie, 1700.   A193
    A collection of sixteen pieces dealing with the Chinese Rites controversy from a pro-Jesuit point of view.

The ancient trades decayed, repaired again: wherein are declared the several abuses that have utterly impaired all the ancient trades in the kingdom. London, T.N. to be sold by Dorman Newman and T. Cockerel, 1678.   A194
    A review of English commercial problems with particular emphasis on woolen and silk manufactures. The author proposes new regulations for the cloth industry and urges abandonment of some of the old ones.

[Anderson, Adam.] An historical and chronological deduction of the origin of commerce. London, A. Millar, 1764.   A195
    A general history of commerce, with particluar emphasis on British trade.

Anderson, Adam. Anderson's historical and chronological deduction of the origin of commerce. Dublin, P. Byrne, 1790.   A196
    This is the third edition of Anderson's work on the history of commerce. It has been extensively revised by William Combe and deals mainly with the British Empire. He illustrates his points with abstracts of treaties, acts of Parliament and pamphlets, as well as pertinent statistical information on prices, currency, populations, etc.

[Anderson, Aeneas.] An accurate account of Lord Macartney's embassy to China; carefully abridged from the original work: with alterations and corrections, by the editor, who was also an attendant on the embassy... London, For Vernor and Hood, 1795.   A197

    The anonymous editor of this abridged edition adds a brief note of his own, a portrait of the emperor, Tchien Loong, and omits the appendix, the glossary of Chinese words, as well as altering and shortening the text substantially.

Anderson, Aeneas. A narrative of the British embassy to China in the years 1792, 1793, and 1794. London, For J. Debrett, 1795.   A198
    The first published account of Lord Macartney's embassy to China, the first such embassy sent from England in the eighteenth century. The embassy failed in its purpose of arranging a commercial agreement with China, but books published about it gave Europeans good descriptions of China.

Anderson, Aeneas. A narrative of the British embassy to China, in the years, 1792-1793, and 1794. London, For J. Debrett, 1795.   A199
    The second edition.

Anderson, Aeneas. A narrative of the British embassy to China, in the years 1792, 1793, and 1794 ... New York, T. and J. Swords for Robers and Berry, 1795.   A200
    One of two American editions of this year.

Anderson, Aeneas. Berättelse om Ängelska beskickningen til China. Stockholm, Johan Pfeiffer, 1796.   A201
    A Swedish translation of a journal account of an embassy to China headed by George Macartney, which provided Europeans with descriptions of China.

Anderson, Aeneas. Relation de l'ambassade du Lord Macartney à la Chine. Paris, Denné, 1797.   A202
    The second French edition, translated from the second English edition.

Anderson, Aeneas. Relacion de la embaxada del Lord Macartney a la China en 1792, 93, y 94. Contiene las diversas particularidades de esta embaxada ... y puesto ahora en Castellano de la segunda edicion Francesa por M.B. Madrid, Torres y Brugada, 1798.   A203
    The only Spanish edition, based on the second French which is based on the second English edition.

Anderson, Johann. Nachrichten von Island, Grönland und der Strasse Davis, zum wahren Nutzen der Wissenschaften und der Handlung ... Hamburg, Georg Christian Grund, 1746.   A204
    This description of Greenland and Iceland concentrates primarily on natural history and commercial possibilities, with some attention also to the Eskimos of Greenland.

Anderson, Johann. Efterretninger om Island, Grønland og Strat Davis. Copenhagen, Gabriel Rothe, 1748.   A205

This Danish edition does not include the Eskimo vocabulary found in the German edition, but it adds Per Högström's account of Lapland, and material on Iceland.

Andrade, Antonio de. Novo descobrimento do gram Cathayo, ou reinos de Tibet ... no anno de 1624. Lisbon, Matteus Pinheiro, 1626.　　A206

The account of the first European travel to Tibet, undertaken by a Jesuit missionary from India who subsequently established a mission at Tsaparang.

Andrade, Francisco de. Cronica do muyto alto e muito poderoso rey destes reynos de Portugal Dom João III deste nome ... Lisbon, Jorge Rodriguez, 1613.　　A207

This is one of the major chronicles of Portuguese overseas expansion, covering the period 1521-1557.

Andreae, Johann Ludwig. Mathematische und historische Beschreibung des gantzen Welt-Gebäudes. Nürnberg, P. Lochner, 1718.　　A208

An eighteenth century history of astronomy and geography illustrated with twelve engraved plates of globes and astronomical instruments. Includes many tables of figures. Divided into three parts: physical geography, astronomy, and a general geographical description of the world.

Andrés del Espíritu Santo. Relacion de la fundacion de la provincia de S. Nicolas de Tolentino de los descalcos de la orden de N.P.S. Augustin. De sus conventos y doctrinas en las islas Philipinas. Manuscript in Spanish. [Manila, 1640.]　　A209

A history of the early years of the mission of the Descalced Augustinians in the ecclesiastical province of San Nicolas de Tolentino in the Philippines, apparently unpublished.

Anecdotes du ministere de Sébastien-Joseph Carvalho, comte d'Oyeras, marquis de Pombal, sous le regne de Joseph I, roi de Portugal. Varsovoe, Janos Rovicki, 1783.　　A210

An anti-Pombal account of his conflicts with Jesuits and other missionary groups, with major consequences for the missions in South America and in India.

Anghiera, Pietro Martire d'. De orbe novo decades. [Alcalá, Arnaldi Guillelmi, 1516.]　　A211

The first three *Decades*, recording the history of Spanish activity in the New World up to 1516. Also included is an account of the author's embassy to Egypt in 1501.

Anghiera, Pietro Martire d'. De nuper sub D. Carlo repertis insulis. Basel, Adam Petri, 1521.　　A212

This publication is frequently cited as a substitute for the lost first letter of Cortes.

Anghiera, Pietro Martire d'. De rebus oceanicis & orbe nouo decades tres ... Eivsdem praeterea Legationis Babylonicae libri tres ... Basel, apud Ioannem Bebelim, 1533.　　A213

This edition also contains an account of the author's embassy to Egypt.

Anghiera, Pietro Martire d'. De rebus oceanicis et novo orbe, decades tres ... Item eivsdem, De Babylonica legatione, libri III. Et item De rebvs aethiopicis ... Damiani a Goes ... Cologne, apud geruinium Calenium & haeredes Quentelios, 1574.　　A214

This edition includes numerous writings of Damião de Goes.

Anghiera, Pietro Martire d'. De orbe novo. Paris, Guillaume Auvray, 1587.　　A215

This edition was published by Richard Hakluyt, then living in Paris, and dedicated to Sir Walter Raleigh. It contains an outstanding map showing Drake's voyage and other Elizabethan discoveries, as well as the first use on a map of the name "Virginia."

Anghiera, Pietro Martire d', and Oviedo y Valdes, Gonzalo Fernandez de. Libro primo ... Libro secondo ... Libro ultimo del summario delle Indie Occidentali. Venice, 1534.　　A216

Contains abridged versions of the first three *Decades* of Peter Martyr, and the *Summario de la natural et general historia de l'Indie Occidentali.*

Anghiera, Pietro Martire d'. De nuovo orbe, or the history of the West Indies. London, T. Adams, 1612.　　A217

The first complete English translation of the eight *Decades* of Peter Martyr; the first three were translated by Richard Eden, the remaining five by Michael Lok.

Anghiera, Pietro Martire d'. Extraict ou recueil des isles nouvellement trouvee en la grand mer oceane. Paris, S. de Colines [1532].　　A218

The first part of this work is an abridgment of the *Decades*.

Anghiera, Pietro Martire d'. Opera. Legatio Babilonica Occeanea decas. Poemata. [Seville, Jacobus Cromberger, 1511.]　　A219

This work includes the author's account of his embassy to the Sultan of Egypt on behalf of Spain in 1501 and the first *Decade*, containing an account of Columbus's first three voyages.

Anghiera, Pietro Martire d'. Relationi ... delle cose notabili della provincia dell' Egitto. Venice, Giorgio de' Cavalli, 1564.　　A220

The first separate edition of the author's account of his 1501-2 embassy to Egypt to secure greater freedom for pilgrims en route to and from Palestine.

Anghiera, Pietro Martire d'. Opus epistolarum ... cui accesserunt epistolae Ferdinandi de Pulgar. Amsterdam, Danielem Elzevirium, 1670.　　A221

A collection of 813 letters reflecting a variety of Spanish diplomatic and other interests, including the early voyages to American and to India.

Anglés y Gortari, Matias de. Copia del informe que hizo en la villa de Potosy ... sobre los punctos, que han sido causa de las discordias suçedidas en la ciudad de la Assumpcion de la provincia del Paraguay. [n.p., ca. 1731]   A222
A report on civil unrest in Paraguay, with commentary on the Jesuit mission there and a recommendation for diminishing Jesuit temporal authority.

Anglés y Gortari, Matias de. Sommario di documenti autentici citati nel supplemento alle riflessioni e all' appendice de'Portoghesi. Genoa, 1760.   A223
A translation of the foregoing item with extensive annotation.

Anglicanus, *pseud.* The necessity and policy of the commercial treaty with France, &c. considered. London, For William Richardson, 1787.   A224
A defense of the treaty with France as a means of recovering commerce lost through the independence of the American colonies.

Angus, Charles and William. Letter book. Manuscript. Liverpool, 1779-1851.   A225
Records commercial transactions for the firm of Charles and William Angus, which owned part interest in two ships engaged in a variety of trading and shipping activities in many ports and areas of the world.

Anhang til Christian Jacob Lyckes Noget til publikum eller Forsvar for Etatsr. de Coninck og Reyersen, angaaende de sager, som de d. 27 Junii 1789 have tabt ved Høiesteret, indeholdende det den tydske oversaettelse vedføiede tillaeg med nogle anmerkninger af en jurist paa landet. Copenhagen, Johan Rudolph Thiele, 1789.   A226
An appendix to *En Kort efterretning om handels-expedition.*

Anjos, Manoel dos. Historia universal, em que se descrevem os imperios, monarquias, reinos, e provincias do mundo, com muitas cousas notaveis, que ha nelle ... Lisbon, Manoel Fernandes da Costa, 1735.   A227
A general history of Europe and Asia, with references to European overseas empires. The author lists 165 sources used in making this compilation.

Ankarcrona, Theodor. Tal om förbindelsen emellan landtbruk, manufacturer, handel ock siöfart. Hållit för Kongl. Svenska Vetenskaps Academien ... Stockholm, Lor. Lud. Grefing [1744].   A228
A speech demonstrating the relationship between agriculture, manufacturing, trade, and maritime commerce, presented to the Swedish Royal Academy, with negative comment by the secretary of the Academy, Jacob Faggot.

Anmärkningar wid the Tankar som v.B. nyligen låtit trycka om tobaks-planteringens nytta och skada. Stockholm, Kongl. Tryckeriet, 1748.   A229
A reply to *Tankar, om tobaks-planteringens nytta och skada,* urging that tobacco be considered for urban rather than rural production in Sweden.

Anmerckungen über die Aufführung abseiten Gross-Britanniens, in Absicht auf die Friedens-Handlung, und andre Staats-Geschäffte, ausserhalb Landes. n.p., 1729.   A230
A discussion of Anglo-Spanish conflicts in the West Indies and over the Ostend Company, translated from the English.

Annehmlicher Discurs von der Holländer Religion, samt andern obschwebenden Welt-Händeln. n.p., 1674.   A231
A review of the national interests of various European nations including the commercial aspirations of each.

The annual register, or A view of the history, politics, and literature for the year 1779. London, For J. Dodsley, 1796.   A232
A reprint of the 1780 issue which contained a proposal by Benjamin Franklin and Alexander Dalrymple that the benefits of European civilization be brought to the natives of New Zealand.

Ansaldi, Ansaldo. De commercio et mercatura discursus legales plerùmque ad veritatem editi. Rome, Dominici Antonii Herculis, 1689.   A233
The first edition of a basic text in commercial law, based primarily on the commercial life of Italian cities.

Ansaldi, Ansaldo. Discursus legales, de commercio, et mercatura ... Cum indice argumentorum, causarum, materiarum, & rerum opulentissimo. Geneva, Fratres de Tournes, 1751.   A234
While dealing largely with Italian trade, this treatise on commercial law also enunciates principles of general applicability.

Anselm, Saint, Archbishop of Canterbury. Opera & tractatus beati Anselmi archiepiscopi Cantuariensis ordinis Sancti Benedicti. [Nuremberg, C. Hochfader, 1491.]   A235
An appended chapter called "Imagine mundi" is a medieval geography probably based on the *Imago mundi* of Honorius Augustodunensis. It contains descriptions of the known regions of the world.

Anselm, Saint, Archbishop of Canterbury. Opuscula. [Basel, J. Amerbach, ca. 1497.]   A236
The third edition. Included in the text is the medieval geography *Imago mundi.*

Anstruther, Sir John. The speech ... at a very numerous and respectable court of proprietors of India stock. London, For John Stockdale, 1788.
A237
A defense of Warren Hastings, blaming the East India Company and other individuals within it for the troubles in Benares.

An answer to a calumny; with some remarks upon an anonimous pamphlet ... London, W. Wilkins, 1728. A238
A defense of the South Sea Company's slave trade in Jamaica, with observations on the causes of the decline in Jamaica's economy.

An answer to a late tract, entituled, *An essay on the East-India trade.* London, Tho. Cockerill, 1697. A239
The tract mentioned was by Charles Davenant who "argues for the importation and wear of East-India manufactories to be the highest improvement of our trade and navigation; the mistake whereof the following pages explode."

An answer to an invidious pamphlet, intituled, A brief state of the province of Pennsylvania. Wherein are exposed the many false assertions of the author or authors, of the said pamphlet ... and the several transactions, most grossly misrepresented therein, set in their true light. London, For S. Bladon, 1755. A240
A defense of the Quakers who in William Smith's *A briefe state of the province of Pennsylvania* had been held responsible for the poor state of the Colony's defenses.

An answer to reasons (so call'd) against the bill for exporting Irish linen ... [London, ca. 1710.]
A241
Concerns the proposal to permit exports of Irish linens duty-free to the American colonies.

An answer to the case of the old East India Company. London, K. Astwood, 1700. A242
An argument to the effect that the East India Company did not have a monopoly on the East Indian trade.

An answer to the considerations, occasioned by the Craftsman upon excise, so far as it relates to the tobacco trade. London, For E. Nutt, 1733.
A243
A critic of the proposed excise tax on tobacco contends that such a tax would be damaging to trade and ruinous to the planter in America.

An answer to the most material objections that have been raised against restraining the East-India trade. [London, ca. 1699.] A244
Arguments on behalf of free trade are challenged with contentions that local industry would suffer, particularly from East Indian goods.

An answer to the Observations on the Papers relative to the rupture with Spain. London, J. Hinxman, 1762. A245
A response to the views of John Wilkes who had alleged that the trouble with Spain arose out of matters not disclosed in the *Papers relative to the rupture with Spain.*

An answer to the reasons against an African Company ... London, 1711. A246
A pamphlet in response to criticism leveled at the joint-stock company by those who favored free trade.

An answer to the reply to the supposed treasury pamphlet. London, For John Stockdale, 1785.
A247
This is a response to *A reply to the treasury pamphlet* entitled *The proposed system of trade with Ireland explained*, in which increased free-trade relationships between Britain and Ireland are considered.

An answere to the Hollanders declaration, concerning the occurrents of the East-India. n.p., 1622. A248
A defense of English actions on Banda, and an attack upon Dutch statements about the English inciting the people of Banda to revolt.

[Anthoine de Saint-Joseph, Antoine-Ignace.] Essai historique sur le commerce et la navigation de la Mer-noire, ou Voyage et enterprises pour établir des rapports commerciaux et maritimes entre les ports de la Mer-noire et ceux de la Méditerranée ... Paris, H. Agasse, 1805. A249
An account of the author's travels in Russia with a view to developing French commercial relations there, noting recent diplomatic events that had opened the Black Sea to Mediterranean trade.

Anti-Brittannus. De heersch-en plonderzugt der Engelschen geroskamd: ter aanmoediging van regtschapen vaderlanders om die vermetelen kloekmoedig het hoofd te bieden. Straatsburg, Ernst Kletz, [1779]. A250
A poetic and patriotic piece condemning British greed and lust for power.

Anton Friedrich Büschings wöchentliche Nachrichten von neuen Landcharten, geographischen, statistischen und historischen Büchern und Sachen. Berlin, Haude und Spener, 1773-1788. A251
A weekly review of significant publications in history and geography, with strong emphasis on the voyage literature of the period.

[Antonio da Encarnação]. Relaçoēs summarias de alguns serviços que fizeram a Deos, e a estes reynos, os religiosos Dominicos, na partes da India Oriental nestes annos proximos passados. Lisbon, Lorenço Crasbeeck, 1635. A252

A report on the Dominican missions in the Indian Ocean and in Indonesia, with particular emphasis on the island of Solor.

Antunez y Acevedo, R. (Rafael). Memorias históricas sobre la legislacion, y gobierno del comercio de los Españoles con sus colonias en las Indias Occidentales. Madrid, Imprenta de Sancha, 1797. A253
A documentary history which examines the regulation of Spanish-American trade and includes reprints of twenty-three documents dating from 1529 to 1790.

Antwoord op de missive geschreven aen ... de Heeren Staten Generael ... n.p., 1659. A254
Concerns the negotiations between Sweden and Denmark and the restoration of free trade in the Baltic.

Antwoordt op seecker deens manifest ... Boxtehoe, 1644. A255
A reply to Danish protests against Swedish occupation of Jutland. The author notes the injustices of the Danes, particularly in constantly increasing toll charges.

Antwoordt op sekeren brief Evlaly. n.p., 1629. A256
Describes Dutch-Spanish hostilities in the West Indies.

Antwoort op een seker brief geschreven aen sijn vrient, dienende tot vervolgh van't Fransch en Munsters praetje. n.p. [1646]. A257
The anonymous author points out that the Dutch war with Spain is of no great significance, and that the emerging enemy in terms of commercial potential is France. The gains made by France in various parts of the world are indicated and discussed.

Anville, Jean Baptiste Bourguignon d'. Amérique Septentrionale publiée sous les auspices de Monseigneur le Duc d'Orleans prémier prince du sang. Paris, Chez l'auteur, 1746.
A258
This map is particulary distinctive for its portrayal of the Mississippi River valley and the river systems between the St. Lawrence and James Bay.

Anville, Jean Baptiste Bourguignon d'. Canada, Louisiane et terres angloises. Paris, Chez l'auteur, 1755. A259
The two northern sheets only of this map, based largely on Mitchell's map of the same year but with significant omissions and additions to justify French claims in America.

Anville, Jean Baptiste Bourguignon d'. [Collection of twenty-nine maps.] 1743-1767.
A260
This collection includes maps of both hemispheres, of the continents and subdivisions of them, and of the Roman empire.

Anville, Jean Baptiste Bourguignon d'. Mémoire de M. D'Anville ... sur la China. Pekin, et se trouve à Paris, Chez l'auteur, 1776.
A261
A commentary on the problems of mapping China, including interpreting Chinese place names, the linear measurement of the *li*, and a manuscript of the China coast brought back to Europe in the Dutch ship *Castricon*.

Anville, Jean Baptiste Bourguignon d'. Mémoires sur l'Égypte ancienne et moderne, suivis d'une description du Golfe Arabique ou de la Mer Rouge. Paris, Imprimerie Royale, 1766. A262
Includes ancient and modern maps of Egypt, with commentary on early and modern sources.

Anville, Jean Baptiste Bourguignon d'. Nouvel atlas de la Chine. The Hague, H. Scheurleer, 1737. A263
Contains forty-two maps, including the first printed map of Bering's route from Tobolsk to the Bering Strait.

Anville, Jean Baptiste Bourguignon d'. Proposition d'une mesure de la terre ... Paris, Chaubert, 1735. A264
This work reflects geographers' concern with the measurement of the variance in the length of a degree of arc at the equator compared to other points on the globe. D'Anville's measurements were all made in France.

Anville, Jean Baptiste Bourguignon d'. Traité des mesures itinéraires anciennes et modernes. Paris, Imprimerie royale, 1769. A265
A history of measurement by land and by sea from ancient times to the eighteenth century, including units of measurement used in India and China, all of which related to portraying distance on maps and charts.

Apian, Peter. Cosmographicus. Landshut, Joannes Weyssenburger, 1524. A266
The first edition of one of the most important cosmographies of the sixteenth century, which was to go through more than thirty editions before 1600.

Apian, Peter. Cosmographicus ... ac erroribus vindicatus per Gemma Phrysium. Antwerp, J. Grapheus [1529]. A267
The second edition.

Apian, Peter. Cosmographiae introductio. Ingolstadt, 1529. A268
An abridgement of the author's *Cosmographia*, probably made by the author. The diagrams are similar but in smaller size. The colophon bears the date 1532.

Apian, Peter. Cosmographicus liber. Antwerp, Arnoldum Birckman, 1533. A269
The second edition to contain the commentary by Gemma Frisius, it also includes a twenty-two page appendix by Gemma Frisius.

Apian, Peter. Cosmographicus liber. Antwerp, J. Grapheus for G. Bontius [1534]. A270
The same sheets as the previous edition, the only differences being in the title page and colophon.

Apian, Peter. Cosmographia. Antwerp, A. Berckmano, 1539. A271
This edition also contains the appendix by Gemma Frisius.

Apian, Peter. Cosmographiae introductio cum quibusdam geometriae ac astronomiae principiis ad eam rem necessariis. Venice, J. Antonium de Nicolinis de Sabio, 1541. A272
This edition is abridged in some parts, expanded in others, and rearranged (as compared with earlier editions).

Apian, Peter. Cosmographia. Antwerp, Gregorio Bontio, 1545. A273
Includes introductory matter not in the earlier editions, and concludes with the *Usus annuli astronomici* by Gemma Frisius.

Apian, Peter. La cosmographie. Paris, Vivant Gaultherot, 1551. A274
The second French edition.

Apian, Peter. Cosmographia. Antwerp, Haeredes Arnoldi Birckmanni, 1564. A275
This edition incorporates changes made in Latin editions from 1545 on.

Apian, Peter. Cosmographie oft beschrijvinghe der gheheelder werelt. Antwerp, Jan Verwithagen, 1573. A276
The fifth Dutch edition.

Apian, Peter. Cosmographia. Antwerp, C. Plantin, 1574. A277
Follows closely the text of the 1564 Antwerp edition, but with minor variations.

Apian, Peter. La cosmographia ... corregida y añadida por Gemma Frisio. Antwerp, Juan Bellero, 1575. A278
This Spanish edition contains excerpts from accounts of the New World by López de Gómara and Gerónimo Girava.

Apian, Peter. Instrumentum primi mobilis. Nuremberg, Jo. Petreium, 1534. A279
A description of an instrument designed to explain the *primum mobilis* of the universe. Included is the text of Jabir ibn Alfah's commentary on Ptolemy's *Almagest*.

Apian, Peter. Isagoge in typum cosmographicum. Landshut, Joannes Weyssenburger [1520]. A280
Probably the first geographical work of Apianus, this tract describes a map which is no longer extant.

Apollonius, Levinus. De Peruviae, regionis, inter Novi Orbis provincias celeberrimae, inventione: & rebus in eadem gestis. Antwerp, Joannem Bellerum, 1567. A281
Records the Spanish conquest of Peru and expeditions from Peru to the north, south, and east.

Apollonius, *Rhodius*. Argonautica, antiquis unà, & optimis cum commentariis. Frankfurt, Petri Brubacchii, 1546. A282
The classical account of the voyage of the Argonauts in quest of the golden fleece in its fourth Greek edition, this one being a reprint of the Aldine edition of 1521.

Apollonius, *Rhodius*. Argonauticorum libri quatuor, nunc primùm latinatate donati. Basel, Joannes Oporini, 1550. A283
This is the first Latin edition, the translation made by Johann Hartung.

An appeal from the hasty to the deliberative judgment of the people of England. London, For J. Debrett, 1787. A284
An appeal to continue support of the British position in India, even though the Hastings administration has been guilty of acts embarrassing to British citizens.

An appeal to the landholders concerning the reasonableness ... of an excise upon tobacco and wine. London, For J. Peele, 1733. A285
This tract advocates an excise tax on wine and tobacco, noting the taxes on other imports and reminding the reader that it is a luxury tax.

Appelböm, Harald. Memorie van Heer Appelboom, resident van zijne Coninlijcke Majesteyt van Sweeden. Delft, Jan Pietersz, 1655. A286
The Swedish ambassador to the Netherlands justifies the actions of his king in blockading the port of Danzig, where the Dutch had an active trade.

Appelböm, Harald. Versoek vande Herre Appelboom ... over de geruchte van een machtige vloot. n.p., 1656. A287
The ambassador warns the Dutch not to send a fleet to the Baltic to protect their trade.

An application of some general political rules, to the present state of Great-Britain, Ireland and America. In a letter to the Right Honourable Earl Temple. London, For J. Almon, 1766. A288
The main point of this tract is the "British safety, power and trade" are preeminent considerations in the debate over the taxation of the colonies for purposes of defense.

Après de Mannevillette, Jean-Baptiste-Nicolas-Denis d'. Le Neptune oriental, ou routier général des côtes des Indes orientales et de la China ... Paris, J. F. Robustel, 1745. A289

A navigational guide to the East Indies with twenty-five charts done by an official of the French East India Company.

Après de Mannevillette, Jean-Baptiste-Nicolas-Denis d'. Le Neptune orientale. Paris, Demonville; Brest, Malassis, 1775. A290

This second edition was expanded through the addition of numerous charts, and the preface was also expanded and brought up to date. Among the new charts are many by William de la Haye and Alexander Dalrymple.

Après de Mannevillette, Jean-Baptiste-Nicolas-Denis d'. Verhandeling over de zeevaart van Frankryk naar de Indiën. Amsterdam, Joannes van Keulen en Zoonen, 1769. A291

First Dutch edition of a pilot guide to the East Indies, with variations in text from the French original of 1745, and an introduction by the translator, P. Steenstra.

Après de Mannevillette, Jean-Baptiste-Nicolas-Denis d'. The East India pilot, or Oriental navigator. London, For Robert Sayer and John Bennett [1777-81]. A292

This English edition contains additions based upon Dutch and English East Indian navigational experience. It describes all of the coasts that might be encountered from Britain to the East Indies.

Après de Mannevillette, Jean-Baptiste-Nicolas-Denis d'. Mémoire sur la navigation de France aux Indes. Paris, Imprimerie Royal, 1768. A293

A route guide for French navigators to the East Indies.

Après de Mannevillette, Jean-Baptiste-Nicolas-Denis d'. Instructions sur la navigation des Indes Orientales et de la Chine, pour servir au Neptune oriental ... Paris, Demonville; Brest, Malassis, 1775. A294

A separately published text to the standard pilot guide for East India sailing, first published in 1745 and revised in 1775.

Après de Mannevillette, Jean-Baptiste-Nicolas-Denis d'. Supplément au Neptune oriental ... Paris, Demonville; Brest, Malassis, 1781. A295

Issued without the maps, this text is instructive in their use.

Après de Mannevillette, Jean-Baptiste-Nicolas-Denis d'. Supplément au Neptune orientale. Paris, Demonville; Brest, Malassis, 1781. A296

A supplement to the second edition of 1775 with additions and corrections based upon materials found among the author's papers after his death in 1780.

Aquaviva, Claudius. Epistola R.P.N. Claud. Aquaviva praepositi generalis Societatis Jesu, ad patres & frates eiusdem Societatis. Dillingen, J. Mayer, 1584. A297

This is the first edition of Aquaviva's letters which call for a renewal of the Jesuit spirit and emphasize the importance of the missions in the Far East. Includes a description of Japan and a statement of its significance to the Society.

Arabernas seder och lefnadssått. Öfversattning, med tillagde anmärkningar, som uplysa flera ställen af den Heliga Skrift. Upsala, Johan Edman, 1783. A298

A collection of information on Arabia, drawing heavily on Jean de la Roque and Laurent d'Arvieux with extensive commentary by the anonymous editor.

Aragon (Spain). Citizens. Oyd, que os hazen à saber, de parte, y por mandamiento de los illustrissimos señores ... n.p. [1686?]. A299

Merchants and other citizens here discuss the exclusion of French trade from Spain.

Aranda, Gabriel de. Vida, y gloriosa muerte del V. Padre Sebastian de Monroy, religioso de la Compañia de Jesus, que murió dilatando la fè alanceado de los barbaros en las Islas Marianas. Seville, Thomas Lopez de Haro, 1690. A300

The account of the martyrdom of Father Monroy is accompanied by a description of the Mariana mission of the Jesuits and of the islands and their people.

Arbuthnot, John. Tables of ancient coins, weights and measures, explain'd and exemplify'd in several dissertations. London, J. Tonson, 1727. A301

This work, first published in 1707, became the source for many economic treatises comparing the value of money and commodities between ancient and modern times. Adam Smith used Arbuthnot's estimates of comparative values. Includes a section on the navigation of the ancient world.

Archdale, John. A new description of that fertile and pleasant province of Carolina. London, For John Wyat, 1707 A302

A short history and survey of the colony by a former governor, in which he defends his actions and gives some future prospects.

Arckenholtz, Johan. Lettre aux auteurs de Journal encyclopedique de Liege au sujet des Remarques sur les Finnois ou Finlandois. Frankfurt & Leipzig, 1756. A303

A discussion of the origins of the Lapps in response to a publication indicating their ancestors were one of the tribes of Israel.

[Arckenholtz, Johan.] Otroliga nya tidender eller correspondence öfwer de Nya Swenska handels projecter. [Stockholm, 1731.]   A304
    A collection of seven tracts defending the privileges granted to the Swedish East India Company.

Arckenholtz, Johan. En wäns swar utur Stockholm, til sin gode wän uti Giötheborg. Stockholm, P.J. Nyström, 1734.   A305
    He worked for twelve years trading under the Company's auspices with bitter results. He concludes in this pamphlet that the whole of Sweden's wealth could be spent and all that would be left would be worn silks, cracked porcelain and empty tea pots.

[Arcq, Philippe-Auguste de Sainte-Foy, chevalier d'.] Histoire du commerce et de la navigation des peuples anciens et modernes. Amsterdam, Paris, Desaint & Saillant [etc.] 1758.   A306
    Describes the commerce of ancient civilizations, believing their example pertinent to contemporary problems.

Arcq, Philippe-Auguste de Sainte-Foy, chevalier d'. La noblesse militaire. n.p., 1756.   A307
    A reply to Coyer's *Noblesse commerçant*.

Ari Thorgilsson (*Frodi*). Schedae ara prestz froda um Island. Skalholt, H. Kruse, 1688.   A308
    The first printing of *The book of the Icelanders* which refers also to Vinland.

Aristotle. [Meteorologia.] Venice, J. and G. de Gregoriis, de Forlivio, 1491.   A309
    The second edition of a classic work on cosmography.

Aristotle. Meterologia Aristotelis eleganti Jacobi Fabri Stapulensis paraphrasi explanata ... Nuremberg, F. Peypuss, 1512.   A310
    This edition includes maps as well as illustrations. The newly discovered parts of the world are described, including the "new land of Americus ... said to be bigger than the whole of Europe."

Arlegui, José de. Chronica de la provincia de N.S.P.S. Francisco de Zacatacas. Mexico, Joseph Bernardo de Hogal, 1737.   A311
    A history of the Franciscan mission in northern Mexico, including numerous biographies of priests who served there.

Armour, James. A premonitor warning: or Advice, by a true lover of his country, unto all whose hands this may come. n.p., 1702.   A312
    A view of Scotland's economic situation on the eve of union with England, calling for a national bank of Scotland to provide needed capital.

[Arnauld, Antoine.] Histoire de Dom Jean de Palafox ... et des differens qu'il a eus avec les PP. Jesuits. n.p., 1690.   A313
    A biography of a controversial bishop of Angelopolis, Mexico, including many documents relative to his conflicts with the Jesuits.

Arnauld, Antoine. Vita del venerabile servo di Dio, Monsignor D. Giovanni di Palafox, vescovo d'Angelopoli e poi d'Osma ... Venezia, Giuseppe Bettinelli, 1761.   A314
    An abridged translation, with a new introduction for the Italian audience.

Arnold, Christoph. Wahrhaftige Beschreibungen dreyer mächtigen Königreiche, Japan, Siam, und Corea. Nuremburg, M. & J. Endters, 1672.   A315
    A series of narratives of travels to the Far East, chiefly by representatives of the Dutch East India Company.

Arnould, Ambroise-Marie. De la balance du commerce et des relations commerciales exterieures de la France. Paris, Buisson, 1791.   A316
    Contains an outline of French commercial history, with advice on means of improving the nation's trade.

Arnould, Ambroise-Marie. Systême maritime et politique des Européens, pendant le dix-huitième siecle; fondé sur leurs traités de paix, de commerce et de navigation. Paris, Anton Bailleul, 1797.   A317
    A comparative history of European nations, and the United States with respect to their commercial policies and the impact of wars and peace treaties upon them.

An arrest on the East India privatier, as per advice and copy sent to its commander Sr. J. C. from H. K. near Hamburgh. n.p. [1681].   A318
    A powerful indictment of the East India Company for its monopolistic control of eastern trade, urging the formation of a new East India Company. Sr. J. C. is Sir Josiah Child.

Arrian. Arriana & Hannonis periplus. Basel, Froben, 1533.   A319
    This work contains first editions of a Roman periplus of the Black Sea from the second century, and of the account of Hanno's African voyage. The texts of both are in Greek.

Arrian. Ponti Euxini & Maris Erythraei Periplus. Geneva, 1577.   A320
    The first Latin edition of *The periplus of the Black Sea*, a survey done for the Emperor Hadrian in 131 A.D. Also included is *The periplus of the Erythrian Sea*, wrongly attributed to Arrianus.

Arrian. Arriani Indica, das ist, indianische Geschicht- oder Reise- Beschreibung der Flotte

Alexanders, des Grossen. Hamburg, Christian Liebezeit, 1710. A321
The first German translation of the description of India and Persia based upon the expedition of Alexander the Great.

Arrian. Arrian's voyage round the Euxine Sea translated; and accompanied with a geographical dissertation, and maps. To which are added three discourses ... Oxford, J.Cooke, Cadell and Davies, 1805. A322
The first English edition, with extensive editorial commentary by the translator William Falconer and his son Thomas.

Arrian. Expeditionis Alexandri libri septem et Historia Indica Graec. et Lat. cum annotationibus et indice Graeco locupletissimo Georgii Raphelli. Amsterdam, Westenium, 1757. A323
The text is in Greek and Latin, with extensive editorial commentary and an index of 203 pages.

Arrivabene, Lodovico. Il magno vitei di Lodovico Arrivabene Mantoano. In questo libro, oltre al piacere, che porge la narratione delle alte cavallerie del glorioso vitei, primo rè della China ... Verona, Girolamo Discepolo, 1597. A324
A partially fictitious description used as the basis for a literary work of an instructive and moralizing character.

Arrowsmith, John. The Arctic shores of America, from Baffin Bay to Cape Bathurst, showing the coasts, rivers &c. explored by the officers of the several British expeditions, between 1818 & 1859. Principally in search of Sir John Franklin. London, J. Arrowsmith, 1859. A325
This map covers the area of arctic North America from 64 to 74 degrees, and contains extensive place name detail as well as considerable text and routes referring to the various British expeditions in the Northwest Passage area.

Arrowsmith, John. British North America. London, J. Arrowsmith, 1848. A326
Dedicated to and apparently done for the Hudson's Bay Company.

Arrowsmith, John. Map of the countries round the North Pole. London, J. Arrowsmith, 1859. A327
A polar projection extending as far south as 50 degrees north latitude.

Arsène, de Paris. Derniere lettre ... au R. P. Provincial des Capucins de la province de Paris. [Paris, 1613.] A328
A letter written to the provincial of the Capucin order in Paris, describing the Razilly colony on Maranhão, established in 1612.

L'arte del navigare con il regimento della tramontana e del sole; e la vera regola ed osservanza del flusso e reflusso del acque sotto breve compendio dell'arte del navigare. Manuscript. [Italy, ca. 1570.] A329
A compendium of navigation modelled on Pedro de Medina's *Arte de Navegar*, with most topics more briefly treated, but with some additional subjects not covered by Medina.

Arteta de Monteseguro, Antonio. Discurso instructivo sobre las ventajes que puede conseguir la industria de Aragon ... Madrid, La Imprenta Real, 1783. A330
A discussion of free trade between Aragon and Spanish America.

Arthus, Gotthard. Historia Indiae Orientalis. Cologne, Wilhelmi Lutzenkirch, 1608. A331
This collection of travels describing the East Indies and Africa was assembled by one of the translators of De Bry's famous collection of voyages.

Arthy, Elliot. The seaman's medical advocate: or, An attempt to shew that five thousand seamen are, annually during war, lost to the British nation ... through the yellow fever. London, Richardson and Egerton, 1798. A332
The author was a surgeon in the West African and West Indian merchant service, and he describes conditions which he believed caused large numbers of sailors in both merchant and naval ships to contract yellow fever.

Articles of the treaty signed at Seville in Spain, between their Catholick and Britannick majesties. With remarks on the said treaty. London, 1729. A333
The observations on the treaty of Seville are unfavorable, contending that Spain got what it wanted, and Great Britain received nothing it did not already have.

Asgill, John. A brief answer to *A brief state of the question, between printed and painted callicoes, and the woolen and silk manufactures*. London, For J. Roberts, 1720. A334
The second edition of a reply to a pamphlet by Defoe, contending that silk manufacture should not be considered a staple industry and pointing out the profit that comes to England from the trade in calicoes.

[Ash, Thomas.] Carolina; or a description of the present state of that country. London, Printed for W.C., 1682. A335
The first account of the English settlement of present-day Charleston.

[Ashley, John.] The British empire in America, consider'd. London, J. Wilford, 1732. A336
A Barbados planter pleads for restrictions to be placed on the trade between the French West Indies and the North American colonies in order to revive the economy of the British sugar islands.

Ashley, John. Memoirs and considerations concerning the trade and revenues of the British colonies in America. London, C. Corbett, 1740; and London, H. Kent, 1743. A337
A request for further legislative assistance and encouragement for the West Indies sugar colonies.

[**Ashley, John.**] The present state of the British sugar colonies consider'd. London [For J. Wilford] 1731. A338
Ashley gives the conditions which led to French supremacy in the sugar trade, cites comparative figures for Barbados and Martinique, and asks that trade restrictions be placed on foreign powers and the British North American colonies.

[**Ashley, John.**] Proposals offered for the sugar planters redress, and for reviving the British sugar commerce. London, J. Wilford, 1733. A339
The author discusses three proposals for reviving the trade of the British sugar colonies and gives historical tables on sugar production there.

[**Ashley, John.**] Some observations on a direct exportation of sugar, from the British islands. London, 1735. A340
This tract attempts to gain support for permitting free trade directly between British colonies and foreign countries, especially in the West Indies sugar trade.

[**Ashley, John.**] The sugar trade, with the incumbrances thereon laid open. London, J. Peele, 1734. A341
Requests that West Indian planters be allowed to export sugar and other products directly to foreign markets and that the duties on these be reduced.

Asiatische Compagnie (Emden, Lower Saxony, Germany). Information etendue de la compagnie octroyee par Sa Majeste prussienne, etablie a Embden sous le nom de Compagnie asiatique; Embden le 1 Juillet 1751. n.p., Francois Varrentrapp [1751]. A342
A statement of the conditions under which the company would engage in trade with China, noting directors, intended commodities to be traded, etc.

Asiatische Compagnie (Emden, Lower Saxony, Germany). Uitvoerig berigt van de geoctrojeerde Koninglyke Prussische Asiatische Compagnie. Na Canton in China tot Embden. n.p. [1751]. A343
Dutch version of the previous item.

The Assiento contract consider'd, as also, the advantages and decay of the trade of Jamaica and the plantations. London, F. Burleigh, 1714. A344
A review of the sugar, tobacco, and slave trade of Jamaica, noting potential causes of their decline.

Assiento, que se ha ajustado con el Capitan Don Gaspar de Andrada, tesorero, y administrador general de la Compañia Real de Guinea ... Sobre encargarse de la introducion de Negros en la America. [Madrid, 1699.] A345
A contract between Manuel Ferreyra de Carvallo and the Companhia Real de Guinea for supplying slaves to Spanish American colonies.

Association for promoting the discovery of the interior parts of Africa, London. Proceedings. London, C. Macrae, 1790. A346
This volume contains the reports of John Ledyard, the Association's first agent, who undertook explorations in Egypt, and of John Lucas who explored inland from the coast of Tripoli.

Association for promoting the discovery of the interior parts of Africa, London. Proceedings. London, W. Bulmer [etc.] 1810. A347
These *Proceedings* include communications from John Ledyard, William Lucas, Mungo Park, John Horneman and Henry Nicholls.

Atkins, John. A voyage to Guinea, Brazil, and the West Indies. London, For Caesar Ward and Richard Chandler, 1735. A348
Contains numerous references to commodities of the west coast of Africa and the West Indies.

[**Atkins, Sir Jonathan**] *supposed author.* An account of His Majesty's island of Barbados & ye government thereof. Manuscript. [Barbados, ca. 1678.] A349
Atkins was governor of Barbados from 1674 to 1680, and this report details information on the history, government, inhabitants, economy, and revenue of the island and its dependencies.

Atkinson, James. Epitome of the art of navigation, or, a short, easy, and methodical way to become a compleat navigator. London, J. Mount and T. Page, 1765. A350
First published in 1686, this work saw many editions, a number of which (including this one) were revised by William Mountaine. Includes a volvelle.

Atlas maritimus & commercialis; or, A general view of the world, so far as relates to trade and navigation. London, For James and John Knapton [etc.] 1728. A351
A two volume atlas, the first of which gives historical, geographical, nautical and commercial information. The second volume contains fifty-four folding charts with accompanying text giving sailing directions for various parts of the world.

Atwood, Thomas. Geschichte der Insel Dominica. Göttingen, Johann Christian Dieterich, 1795. A352

A general description of Dominica, its natural history, products, state of economic development, and population. Translated from the first English edition of 1789, with notes by the translator, George Friederich Benecke.

Auckland, William Eden, Baron. A fifth letter to the Earl of Carlisle from William Eden, esq. on population; on certain revenue laws and regulations connected with the interests of commerce; and on public economy. London, For B. White and T. Cadell, 1780. A353

A response to Richard Price's *Observations on the populousness of England and Wales* which goes beyond the issue of population into the economy generally, particularly trade and related revenues.

Auckland, William Eden, Baron. Four letters to the Earl of Carlisle. London, For B. White [etc.] 1780. A354

A fifth letter is added to this third edition. The letters concern public debt, credit, free trade, and other British commercial interests.

[Auckland], William Eden, Baron. The history of New Holland, from its first discovery in 1616 to the present time. 2d ed. London, John Stockdale, 1787. A355

A history of the exploration of Australia with details of the voyages of Dampier and Cook particularly, preceded by a preface describing the plans for establishing a British settlement at Botany bay just prior to the voyage of the first contingent of settlers.

Audiffredy, chevalier d'. Mémoire pour donner sommairement un idée générale de la Guianne, ou colonie de Cayenne. Manuscript. n.p. [ca. 1790]. A356

A general description of the land and productivity of Guiana, with a special interest in the production of annatto there.

Augustinians. Provincia de India Oriental. Lettera del padre vicario provinciale dell' ordine di Santo Agostino dell' India orientale, scritta a padri provinciale. Rome, Ludoulco Dozza, 1629. A357

A report on the progress of the Augustinians' missions in Persia and in India.

[Augy, d'.] Réflexions sur une lettre écrite le 16 Mai, par le sieur Peynier, à l'Assemblée générale de la partie française de Saint-Domingue, séance à Saint-Marc. [Paris, L. Potier de Lille, 1791.] A358

A portion of the debate concerning representative government in the French colony of Saint Domingue.

Aureus tractatus de contractibus. Manuscript. Ferrara, 1465. A359

A treatise on contracts for the instruction of notaries. It may have been written by Rudolphinus de Passageriis.

Ausführliche historische und geographische Beschreibung des ... landes Louisiana. Leipzig, J.F. Gleditschens seel. Sohn, 1720. A360

A description of Louisiana and the French commercial activity there.

Austin, Jonathan Williams. An oration, delivered March 5th, 1778, at the request of the inhabitants of the town of Boston: to commemorate the bloody tragedy of the fifth of March, 1770. Boston, B. Edes and T. & J. Fleet, 1778. A361

"The armies of Britian seem to be held up as a standing evidence, how far the spirit of tyranny and oppression can operate."

Autenticq verhael, van't gepasseerde in de Oost-Indische Compagnie tot Hoorn. Utrecht, L. Verhulst, 1671. A362

An account of matters considered in the meetings of the directors of the Dutch East India Company from May 12, 1670, to July 3, 1671.

Authentic papers relative to the expedition against the Charibbs, and the sale of lands in the island of St. Vincent. London, J. Almon, 1773. A363

A collection of documents relative to the British taking possession of St. Vincent Island following the Treaty of Paris, 1763, noting the hostility to British authority of the resident Caribs and the former slaves.

An authentick and faithful history of that archpyrate Tulagee Angria. With a curious narrative of the siege and taking of the town and fortress of Geriah, and the destruction of his whole naval force, by Admiral Watson and Colonel Clive ... London, For J. Cooke, 1756. A364

A history of the Angrias, notorious pirates on the coast of India for more than a century, containing also interesting details of the Indian commerce and the English East India Company's part in it.

Authentische Aktenstücke als Beiträge zur Statistik der dänischen Staaten. n.p., 1795. A365

Contains statistics on Denmark's overseas trade and tolls levied on shipping in the Sund.

Autograph letter, unsigned, to Messrs. Lane and Booth, dated Newport, Rhode Island, 8 February 1762. Manuscript in English. A366

The letter requests insurance for a ship sailing to Africa and the West Indies to collect and deliver a cargo of slaves.

Autos de las conferencias ... Sobre la diferencia ocasionada de la fundacion de una colonia, nombrada del Sacramento en la margen septentrional del Rio de la Plata. [Rome, ca. 1685.] A367

Documents and geographical information intended to resolve the problem of Portugal's proposed colony on the north shore of the Rio de la Plata which Spain claimed was within her sphere of influence.

Avendaño, Diego de. R. P. Didaci de Avendaño Societatis Jesu, Segoviensis ... Thesaurus Indicus : seu generalis instructor pro regimine conscientiae, in iis quae ad Indias spectant. ... Antwerp, Jacob Meurs, 1668. A368

A discussion of legal issues arising in the espiscopal tribunals of Spanish-American courts, showing the adaptation of tradtional law to the South American situation.

Avienus, Rufius Festus. Opera. Venice, Antonius de Strata, 1488. A369

The first edition of this collection of ancient geographical and astronomical knowledge brought together by Avienus, a fourth-century poet. Contains the *Description of the World* by Dionysius Periegetes, the *Phaenomena* of Aratus, and the *Ora maritima* which is the compiler's own work.

Avis à l'auteur de la lettre d'un bon patriote, sur le memoire, présenté aux Etats Generaux, le 9 avril 1779, par Mr. L'ambassadeur d'Angleterre. Amsterdam, van Harrevelt [etc.] 1779. A370

A British point of view published in an attempt to keep the Dutch out of the alliance with the French and the American colonies.

Avis des'interessé aux habitans des pays-bas, qui sont sous la domination du roy d'Espagne. n.p. [1644]. A371

The Dutch are urged to restore their predominance in maritime commerce, and they are warned that Spain intends to keep Dutch commerce restricted to areas north of the equator.

Avisos de diversas partes, en que se da relacion de muchas cosas acontecides, en los meses de junio, hasta el de setiembre, del presente año 1597. Barcelona, G. Graells y G. Dotil, 1597. A372

This is a four page newsletter informing the Spanish public on a variety of current topics including the fighting between Spain and France; the movement of the English, German and Dutch fleets; battles with the Turks; and the papal negotiations with the King of Persia. Finally, mention is made of the arrival of the Portuguese India fleet.

Avity, Pierre d'. Description generale de l'Amérique. Paris, D. Bechet et L. Billaine, 1660. A373

Particularly concerned with South America.

Avity, Pierre d'. The estates, empires, & principalities of the world. London, Adam Islip for Mathewe Lownes and John Bill, 1615. A374

The first English edition of an extensive world geography. Edward Grimestone, the translator, notes that he has altered the text considerably with additions and deletions.

Avity, Pierre d'. Les estats, empires, royaumes, principautez du monde. Lyons, Claude La Riviere, 1659. A375

This edition is based on the text which was current before revisions were made by F. Ranchin. It contains four maps of the continents apparently based on maps of J. Hondius issued by Janssonius in 1638.

L'avocat pour et contre, ou, Resumé historique et philosophique de tout ce qu'on a écrit sur la liberté du commerce des munitions navales; suivi de jugement des plaideurs. Brussels, 1779. A376

An examination from the Dutch perspective of issues in contention with the British, largely maritime matters, but including others which reveal Dutch support of the American Revolution.

Avril, Philippe. Travels into divers parts of Europe and Asia. London, T. Goodwin, 1693. A377

The first English edition.

Avril, Philippe. Voyage en divers etats d'Europe et d'Asie ... Paris, C. Barbin [etc.] 1692. A378

An account of five years travel in the East, with particular emphasis on trade routes into China.

Avril, Philippe. Voyage en divers états d'Europe et d'Asia. Paris, J. Boudot, 1693. A379

The second French edition.

Ayala, Juan de. [A letter to Ferdinand and Isabella of Spain.] Manuscript. [Spain, 1503.] A380

The author of this letter resided on Hispaniola for ten years, after which he wrote this series of suggestions and recommendations for the better government and management of the first Spanish colony in the New World.

Aymé, Jean-Jacques. Déportation et naufrage de J.J. Aymé ... avec quelques observations sur cette colonie et sur le Négres. Paris, Maradan [1800]. A381

An account of exile in French Guiana.

Aymé, Jean-Jacques. Narrative of the deportation to Cayenne, and shipwreck on the coast of Scotland ... London, J. Wright, 1800. A382

This description of the colony for political exiles at Cayenne presents a comparison with official descriptions of that place published by the French government.

Ayres, Philip. The voyages and adventures of Capt. Barth. Sharp and others, in the South Sea ... London, B.W. for R.H. and S.T., 1684. A383

Describes the adventures of English buccaneers on the west coast of South America.

Azevedo, Don Balthasar. Por don Antonio de Echeverz y Subiza ... alcalde provincial de la hermandad de Panama y Portovelo ... Panama, 1704.   A384
   A history of the slave trade between Panama and Africa.

Azevedo, Luiz Marinho de. Apologeticos discursos offerecidos a magestade del rei Dom Joam, Nosso Senhor, quarto de nome ... em defensa da fama, e boa memoria de Fernão d'Alburquerque do seu co[n]selho, & governador, que foi da India ... Lisbon, Manoel da Sylva, 1641.   A385
   A defense of Portugal's governor general of India, Fernão d'Albuquerque with respect to his support for Portuguese forces against the English in the Persian Gulf during the period 1615-1635.

B

Backman, Daniel Andreas. Med guds wälsignande näd och wederbörandes tilstand yttrade tankar om nyttan, som kunnat tilfalla wårt kjära fädernesland, af des nybygge i America, fordom Nya Swerige kalladt. Åbo, Jacob Merckel [1754].   B1
    A brief discussion of the products of New Sweden, including tobacco, indigo, and sassafras.

Bacon, Anthony. A short address to the government, the merchants, manufacturers, and the colonists in America, and the sugar islands, on the present state of affairs. London, G. Robinson, 1775.   B2
    Bacon worries that the growing dispute between Britain and the North American colonies will disrupt trade between North America and the West Indies. He lived for a time in the colonies, involved in trade.

Bacon de la Chevalerie, M. Observations, présentées a l'Assemblée de MM les électeurs de la partie du nord de Saint-Domingue ... le 27 janvier 1789, au Cap-François. [Paris, Quillau, 1789]   B3
    A statement of issues and agenda for representatives of St. Domingue to the Estates General.

Bacqueville de La Potherie, M. de (Claude-Charles Le Roy). Histoire de l'Amerique septentrionale. Paris, Jan-Luc Nion, & F. Didot, 1722.   B4
    This richly-illustrated four volume work by a French naval officer describes aspects of Anglo-French rivalry in the St. Lawrence and Hudson Bay areas, and also describes extensively the various Indian nations of New France.

[Baegert, Jacob.] Nachrichten von der amerikanischen Halbinsel Californien. Mannheim, Churfürstl. Hof- und Academie-Buchdruckerey, 1772.   B5
    A Jesuit missionary's observations on Lower California, based on seventeen years' residence there.

Baena Parada, Juan de. Epitome de la vida, y hechos de Don Sebastian dezimo sexto rey de Portugal. Madrid, Antonio Gonçalez de Reyes, 1692.   B6
    This biography of Sebastian relates largely to his death in the battle of Alcazar-Kebir, 1578, and includes considerable descriptive material on North Africa.

Baerle, Caspar van. Rerum per octennium in Brasilia ... Amsterdam, J. Blaeu, 1647.   B7
    A handsomely illustrated work which constitutes one of the major printed sources for the history of Dutch commercial and colonial enterprise in Brazil, with a biography of the governor, Johan Maurits.

Baerle, Caspar van. Brasilianische Geschichte. Cleve, Tobias Silberling, 1659.   B8
    The first German edition.

Baerle, Caspar van. Rerum per octennium in Brasilia at alibi gestarum ... historia. Editio secunda. Cleve, Tobiae Silberling, 1660.   B9
    This edition contains four essays on the natural history of Brazil by Willem Piso, not included in either the earlier Latin or German edition.

Baerle, Caspar van. Epistolarum liber. Amsterdam, Joannem Blaeu, 1667.   B10
    A collection of more than five hundred letters, written between 1639 and 1647, some dealing with the Dutch in Brazil.

Baers, Johannes. Olinda, ghelegen int landt van Brasil, inde capitania van Phernambuco ... geluckelijck verovert op den 16. Februarij Anno 1630. Amsterdam, For Hendrick Laurentsz, 1630.   B11
    An eyewitness account of the Dutch conquest of Portuguese Pernambuco, a victory which won temporary control of the richest region in Brazil for the Dutch West India Company.

Baert-Duholant, Charles-Alexandre-Balthazar-François de Paule, baron de. Tableau de la Grande-Bretagne, de l'Irlande, et des possessions angloises dans les quatre parties du monde. Paris, H. J. Janson, 1800. B12
A survey of Great Britain and the British Empire with particular emphasis on the commodities and trade of each of the colonies, including numerous statistics on exports and imports.

Baïf, Lazare de. Annotationes ... in quibus tractatur de re navali. Paris, Robert Estienne, 1536. B13
A short history of early navigation based on the writings of classical authors. Also included are Baïf's *De re vestiaria* and *De vasculis*. The text was edited by Charles Estienne.

Baïf, Lazare de. Annotationes in legem II de captivis & postliminio reversis, in quibus tractatur de re navali. Basel, H. Froben, 1537. B14
The second edition.

Baïf, Lazare de. Annotationes in legem II de captivis & postliminio reversis, in quibus tractatur de re navali. Basel, H. Froben, 1541. B15
The woodcuts in this edition closely follow those of the Paris, 1536 edition, but are of inferior quality.

Baïf, Lazare de. Annotations ... in quibus tractatur de re navali. Paris, Robert Estienne, 1549. B16
The illustrations in this edition are from the same blocks as those in the 1536 edition.

Baillio. Mémoire pour les citoyens Verneuil, Baillio jeune, Fournier et Gervais, déportés de Saint-Domingue. [Paris, Guilhemat, 1793.] B17
Accusations against the French official Sonthonax, with evidence, by a member of the *Amis de la Convention Nationale*.

Balbi, Gasparo. Viaggio dell' Indie Orientali. Venice, C. Borgominieri, 1590. B18
An account of a jewel merchant's travels in India and southeast Asia between 1579 and 1588.

Baldaeus, Philippus. Naauwkeurige beschryvinge van Malabar en Choromandel ... en het machtige eyland Ceylon. Amsterdam, J. Janssonius van Waesberge & J. van Someren, 1672. B19
Describes the major commercial cities and their trade, and also gives a history of European commercial activity there.

Baldwin, Samuel, of the Custom House, London. A survey of the British customs. London, For J. Nourse, 1770. B20
Tables and charts defining British customs.

Baldwyn, George Augustus, editor. A new, royal, authentic, complete, and universal system of geography. London, Alex Hogg [etc.] [1794] B21
A massive compilation of geographical information published in eighty parts, including considerable material on the most recent British voyages of exploration and discovery.

Balen, Matthys. Beschryvinge der stad Dordrecht. Dordrecht, Symon Onder de Linde, 1677. B22
Contains "charters of the staple" as far back as 1299, and material on the commerce of Dordrecht with other cities.

Ballarini, Francesco. Epilogo sacro de' successi, che' nella Chiesa di Dio dal principio del mondo sin' al presente anno 1610, sono occorsi, con la monarchia de sommi pontefici. Rome [Giacomo Mascardi, 1610]. B23
A history of papal supremacy among rulers, with brief reference to its power in non-European areas.

Ballesteros, Thomas de. Tomo primero de las ordenanzas del Peru. Dirigidas. Al rey nuestro senor en su real y supremo consejo de las Indias. Lima, Joseph de Contreras, 1685. B24
The laws of Peru, with particular emphasis on administration, relations with the Indians, and the mining industry.

Balthasar, Juan Antonio. Carta del p. provincial Juan Antonio Balthassar, en que da noticia de la exemplar vida ... el venerable p. Francisco Maria Picolo. [Mexico, 1752.] B25
Father Picolo was a missionary in the American southwest for forty-two years. In 1716 he participated in an important exploration northward from the mission base in California.

Banco di San Giorgio (Genoa, Italy). Appendice alle leggi delle compere di S. Giorgio. Genoa, Giuseppe Pavoni, 1607. B26
Thirty-two additions to the laws governing the Banco di San Giorgio. The Banco di San Giorgio of Genoa had its origins in that city's participation in extensive wars within Italy and in the necessity of defending its commercial bases in the Mediterranean and Black Seas early in the fifteenth century. The city's loans and indebtedness were converted into one fund, administered by the company.

Banco di San Giorgio (Genoa, Italy). De immunitatibus à magistratu divi Georgii, concessis liber. Genoa, Haeredum Hieronymi Bartoli, 1593. B27
The Bank of St. George was a powerful force in the economic life of Genoa. This volume records the privileges, most of them dated early in the sixteenth century, granted by the bank to various merchant groups and cities.

Banco di San Giorgio (Genoa, Italy). Leggi delle compere di S. Giorgio, dell' eccellentissi-

ma republica di Genova. Riformate l'anno MDLXVIII. Genoa, Giuseppe Pavoni, 1602.
B28
The Banco di San Giorgio was founded in 1407. This collection of its laws extends to 1568, covering many aspects of Genoese trade abroad.

Banco di San Giorgio (Genoa, Italy). Riforma, et giunta alle leggi di S. Giorgio. Genoa, Giuseppe Pavoni, 1605. B29
Twenty-eight revisions in the laws governing the Banco di San Giorgio between 1579 and 1601.

Bancroft, Edward. Remarks on the review of the Controversy between Great Britain and her colonies. New-London in New England, T. Green, 1771. B30
A criticism of an anonymously published pamphlet by William Knox and George Grenville concerning the American colonies' claims to constitutional rights.

Bandini, Angelo Maria. Vita e lettere di Amerigo Vespucci. Florence, Stamperia all' Insegna di Apollo, 1745. B31
This book is a starting point for modern students of the controversy over Vespucci's voyages.

Bank, Anthony van der. Sociëteit der Surinaamse handel ingerigt ter verbetering en daaruit volgende herstelling van de plantagiën in de colonie Surinaame. Amsterdam, Voor den autheur [ca. 1745]. B32
A review of production and administrative problems in the Dutch Surinam plantations, with particular reference to coffee and sugar production.

Baptista, Mantuanus. De patientia aurei libri tres. [Brescia, Bernardinus de Misintis, 1497.]
B33
Contains mention of discoveries of islands in the Atlantic, noting their size and the fact that they are inhabited. Because none of the ancient geographers knew of them, the author assumes that they have only lately been discovered.

Barba, Alvaro Alonso. The art of metals, in which is declared the manner of their generation, and the concomitants of them. London, For S. Mearne, 1674. B34
This work advises the reader how to discover mines of gold, silver, copper, iron, lead, and tin. It also gives the locations of mines operating in the New World.

Barba, Alvaro Alonso. Arte de los metales en que se enseña el verdadero beneficio de los de oro, y plata por azogue ... con el Tratado de las antiguas minas de España, que escribió Don Alonso Carrillo y Laso ... Madrid, Manuel Fernandez [1770]. B35
A description of the properties of metals, the means of refining and discovering them, indicating the location of many Spanish mines in the New World.

Barbados. Laws, etc. Acts, passed in the island of Barbados. From 1643 to 1762, inclusive; carefully revised, innumerable errors corrected; and the whole compared and examined, with the original acts. London, For Richard Hall, 1764.
B36
The most complete compilation of the laws of Barbados to this date, including regulations of commerce, slaves, immigration, transportation, and other matters pertaining to the island's economy and civil affairs.

Barbaro, Ermolao. Castigationes Hermolai in Plinium castigatissimae: quum vix post Romanas: caeteris tamen aduc impressis. Cremona, Carolum a Darleriis, 1495. B37
The third edition of corrections to the text of Pliny's *Natural History* and to Pomponius Mela's *De situ orbis*.

Barbe, Simon. Le parfumeur françois qui enseigne toutes les manieres de tirer les odeurs des fleurs, & à faire toutes sortes de composition de parfums. Lyon, Hildaire Baritel [etc.] 1698.
B38
A handbook on the products and methods used in the perfume industry, including various spices and drugs as well as tobacco.

Barbé-Marbois, François, marquis de. État des finances de Saint-Domingue, contenant le résumé des recettes & dépenses de toutes les caisses publiques, depuis le 10 novembre 1785, jusqu'au 1er janvier 1788. Paris, Imprimerie Royale, 1790. B39
The intendant of the French colony of Saint Domingue makes a detailed accounting of the colony's finances, including twelve tables of statistics covering all aspects of its administration for the two years after assuming office.

Barbé-Marbois, François, marquis de. État des finances de Saint-Domingue, contenant le résumé des recettes & dépenses de toutes les caisses publiques, depuis le 1er janvier 1788, jusqu'au 31 decembre de la même année. Paris, Imprimerie Royale, 1790. B40
A continuation of the previous item.

Barbé-Marbois, François, marquis de. Réclamation de M. l'intendant de Saint-Domingue. n.p. [ca. 1789]. B41
The intendant proposes to continue to enforce a royal law restricting foreign trade in Saint Domingue in spite of an order from the governor-general authorizing it.

[Barbé-Marbois, François, marquis de.] Réflexions sur la colonie de Saint-Domingue. Paris, Garnery, 1796. B42
A conservative point of view on the management of the commerce of Saint Domingue.

Barbeyrac, Jean. Defense du droit de la Compagnie hollandaise des Indes orientales. The Hague, T. Johnson, 1725. B43

A defense of the Dutch East India Company against the rights to the East India trade being asserted by the Ostend Company.

Barbier, Guillaume. Privilèges des foires de Lyon. Lyons, G. Barbier, 1649. B44
A compilation of laws, orders, privileges, etc., granted to the fair of Lyons from 1349 to 1563.

Barbosa, José. Epitome da vida do illustris. e excelentis. senhor D. Luiz Carlos Ignacio Xavier de Menezes, primeiro marquez do Louriçal. Lisbon, Antonio Isidoro da Fonseca, 1743. B45
The subject of this biography served as Portuguese viceroy of India for two terms, 1717-1722 and 1741-1742. He was actively involved in diplomacy and military action in various parts of the Indian Ocean.

[Barbosa, Vincente]. Compendio da relaçam, que veyo da India o anno de 1691 a el-rey N.S. Dom Pedro II, da nova missam dos padres clerigos regulares da divina providencia na ilha de Borneo. Lisbon, Manoel Lopes Ferreyra, 1692. B46
An account of a mission of the Theatine order in Borneo which lasted from 1687 to 1691.

Barbosa Machado, Ignacio. Fastos politicos, e militares da antigua, e nova Lusitania em que se descrevem as acçoens memoraveis, que na paz, e na guerra obrarão os Portuguezes nas quarto partes do mundo. Lisbon, Ignacio Rodrigues, 1745. B47
This is the only volume published of a history of events curiously arranged by the month and day on which they happened. The volume extends only through January and February. Entries are brief but with reference to more extended accounts of the events noted.

Barchewitz, Ernst Christoph. Allerneueste und wahrhaffte ost-indianische Reise-Beschreibung ... Chemnitz, J. Christoph & J. D. Stözeln, 1730. B48
The author, in the service of the Dutch East India Company, was governor of the island of Letti. He describes numerous East Indian islands and their products.

[Barcia Carballido y Zúñiga, Andrés Gonzáles de.] Ensayo cronologico, para la historia general de la Florida. Madrid, Nicolas Rodriquez Franco, 1723. B49
A general history of early exploration of North America, and the establishment of trading companies there and in the West Indies.

Barcia Carballido y Zúñiga, Andrés Gonzáles de. Historiadores primitivos de las Indias Occidentales, que juntò, traduxo en parte, y sacò à luz, ilustrados con erudìtas notas, y copiosos indices ... Madrid, 1749. B50
A collection of the early writings on Spanish America.

Barère, B. (Bertrand). La liberté des mers, ou le gouvernement anglais dévoilé. [Paris, 1798.] B51
A condemnation of British maritime policy as the enemy of freedom and of natural rights throughout the world.

Barère, B. (Bertrand). Rapport fait au nom du comité de salut public. [Paris, Imprimerie Nationale, 1794.] B52
A short report on the military strength of the Windward Islands.

[Baring, Sir Francis.] A hasty sketch of the conduct of the commissioners for the affairs of India. London, For J. Debrett, J. Walter, and T. Sewell, 1788. B53
This pamphlet reflects the intentions of a group of persons within the East India Company to contradict the findings and actions of a parliamentary committee investigating the company's affairs.

Baring, Sir Francis. The principle of the commutation-act established by facts. London, J. Sewell, 1786. B54
This discussion of taxes on tea and windows contains statistical data on the British tea trade as it was handled by the East India Company.

Barozzi, Francesco. Cosmographia in quatuor libros distributa. Venice, Gratiosi Perchacini, 1585. B55
In addition to the usual topics treated in cosmographies, this one contains an enumeration and discussion of the errors in Sacro Bosco's *Sphaera mundi*.

Barrême. Le grand banquier ou Le livre des monnoyes etrangeres reduites en monnoyes de France ... Paris, Denys Thierry, 1696. B56
A commercial handbook dealing primarily with exchange of currencies in twenty centers from Murmansk to Cadiz.

Barrême. Les tarifs et comptes faits du grand commerce. Paris, Denys Thierry, 1685. B57
A book of various European and Asiatic weights, measures, and coins, with conversion tables.

Barrère, Pierre. Nouvelle relation de la France Equinoxiale. Paris, Piget [etc.] 1743. B58
A description of the northern coast of South America, particularly French Guiana.

Barretto, Francesco. Relatione delle missioni, e Christianità che appartengono alla provincia di Malavar della Compagnia di Giesu ... Rome, Francesco Cavalli, 1645. B59
In addition to reporting on the missions on the Malabar coast Barretto describes the mission in Ceylon and also in Bengal and the Coromandel Coast.

[Barrington, Daines.] Instances of navigators who have reached high northern latitudes. [London, B. White, 1774.] B60

A paper read at a meeting of the Royal Society on May 19, 1774. The author believed in the existence of a navigable polar passage and cited accounts of earlier voyages to the north to support his case.

Barrington, Daines. Miscellanies. London, J. Nichols, 1781. B61

Includes a journal of a Spanish voyage to western North America in 1775.

Barrington, Daines. The probability of reaching the North Pole discussed. London, C. Heydinger, 1775. B62

Considers the value of a polar passage, giving proofs that the polar seas are open.

Barrington, George. A voyage to Botany Bay. London, C. Lowndes [1793]. B63

An account of a voyage on a prison ship, with observations on the beginnings of British settlement in the vicinity of Sydney. The author was an accomplished pickpocket and an interesting writer.

Barrington, George. Voyage a Botany-Bay, avec une description du pays, des moeurs, des coutumes et de la religion des natifs ... Paris, Desenne, [1798]. B64

This French edition, based upon the English edition of 1796, adds a brief preface on the life and character of Barrington.

[Barron, William.] History of the colonization of the free states of antiquity. London, For T. Cadell, 1777. B65

This study of ancient colonial empires was intended as a guide to Great Britain for settlement of disputes with her American colonies.

Barron, William. Histoire de la fondation des colonies des anciennes republiques, adaptée a la dispute présente de la Grande Bretagne, avec ses colonies americaines. Traduite de l'Anglais. Utrecht, J. van Schoonhoven, 1778. B66

This French translation was intended for a Dutch audience. It contains editorial material warning the Dutch against participation in the French alliance for assisting the American colonies.

Barros, André de. Vida do Apostolico Padre Antonio Vieyra. Lisbon, Officina Sylviana, 1746. B67

The subject of this biography was a Portuguese missionary who served in Brazil during the seventeenth century. The text relates particularly to events in Maranhão and Pernambuco.

Barros, João de. Asia ... dos fectos que os Portugueses fizeram no descobrimento y conquista dos mares y terras do Oriente. Lisbon, G. Galharde, 1552-53; J. de Barreira, 1563; Impresso Real, 1615. B68

The *Decades* of Barros are regarded as the most important source for the early history of the Portuguese explorations along the coast of Africa and into India. As treasurer and factor of India House in Lisbon, the author had access to the archives and documents necessary to such a history.

Barros, João de. L'Asia. Venice, Vincenzo Valgrisio, 1561. B69

The first two decades were all that appeared in this edition, taking the history of the Portuguese in India to 1515.

Barrow, Sir John. An account of travels into the interior of southern Africa, in the years 1797 and 1798. London, A. Strahan for T. Cadell jun. and W. Davies, 1801-1804. B70

This work comprises two volumes, the first of which describes the land, natural history, products, and peoples of South Africa. The second volume considers the region's importance as a strategic base and commercial emporium. Barrow accompanied Lord Macartney to South Africa on a diplomatic mission.

Barrow, Sir John. Voyage dans la partie méridionale de l'Afrique; fait dans les années 1797 et 1798. Paris, Dentu, 1801. B71

The first French edition.

Barrow, Sir John. Resa i det inre af Södra Afrika, åren 1797 och 1798. Strengnäs, A.J. Segerstedt, 1804. B72

This Swedish translation is by Per Olof Gravander.

Barrow, Sir John. Travels in China, containing descriptions, observations, and comparisons, made and collected in the course of a short residence at the imperial palace of Yuen-Min-Yuen, and on a subsequent journey through the country from Pekin to Canton. London, A. Strahan for T. Cadell and W. Davies, 1804. B73

The author had been private secretary to Lord Macartney, British ambassador to China, and his observations cover a wide range of subjects relating to the social, political and cultural life of China.

Barrow, Sir John. Voyage en Chine, formant le complément du voyage de Lord Macartney ... Suivi de la relation de l'ambassade envoyée, en 1719, à Peking, par Pierre premier, Empereur de Russie. Paris, F. Buisson, 1805. B74

Jean Henri Castéra's translation includes an extensive introduction and numerous translator's notes. The account of the embassy to Peking is John Bell's narrative.

Barrow, Sir John. Travels in China ... London, For T. Cadell and W. Davies, 1806. B75

The second English edition.

Barrow, Sir John. Reizen in China. Haarlem, François Bohn, 1807-1809. B76

The only Dutch edition, following the English closely in both text and illustrations.

Barrow, John, teacher of mathematics. Abrégé chronologique ou Histoire des découvertes faites par les Européens dans les differentes parties du monde ... Traduit de l'Anglois par M. Targe. Paris, Saillant [etc.] 1766. B77

An abridged translation of a work which first appeared in English in 1756, a history of discovery and exploration based largely on journals of travelers, but with interpretive material by the translator.

Barrow, John, teacher of mathematics. A new geographical dictionary. Containing a full and accurate account of the several parts of the known world ... London, J. Coote, 1759-1760. B78

A compendium of geographical and related information, including maps, plans and engravings depicting peoples, costumes, etc.

Barry, Claude. Au roy et à nos-seigneurs les ministres d'état. Mémoire enforme de trés-humble rémontrance des maire, consuls lieutenans pour le roy de la ville de Toulon ... contenant l'etat de ses manufactures, et de son commerce ... Manuscript. Toulon, 1704. B79

A petition from the mercantile community of Toulon, designed to restore the city's commerce to its former prosperity.

Barry, de. Lettre ... a M.G - - - . de l'Académie Royale des Sciences. Contenant l'état actuel ... de l'Isle de Malegache. Paris, Laurent Prault, 1764. B80

A general description of Madagascar, including comments on the people, products, climate, commerce, and slave trade.

Bartholomaeus, *Anglicus*. De proprietatibus rerum. Manuscript. Low Countries. Early 15th Century. B81

A fine manuscript based upon a thirteenth-century encyclopedia, containing sections on geography and natural history that are of particular interest.

Bartoli, Cosimo. Del modo di misurare le distantie, le superficie, i corpi, le piante, le provincie, le prospettive, & tutte le altre cose terrene, che possono occorrere a gli huomini. Venice, Francesco Franceschi Sanese, 1564. B82

An instruction book on surveying methods, based on both classical and contemporary sources, with particular emphasis on the use of the quadrant and on triangulation.

Bartoli, Daniello. Dell' historia della Compagnia di Giesu l'Asia descritta dal p. Daniello Bartoli ... parte prima ... Genoa, Benedetto Guasco, 1656. B83

While this work deals largely with the life and works of Xavier it does go beyond into the seventeenth century, noting missions in Japan, China, and islands of the East Indies.

Bartoli, Daniello. Dell'istoria della Compagnia di Giesu l'Asia. Rome, Varese, 1660-1667. B84

This is a complete 3 volume folio set of Bartoli's work on the history of the Jesuits in Asia. Volume one is the 3rd printing published Rome, Varese, 1667 and includes a printing of Bartoli's Missione al Gran Mogor. Volume two (Japan) is the first printing of 1660 and volume three (China) is the first printing of 1663.

Bartoli, Daniello. La geografia transportata al morale. Venice, Nicolò Pezzana, 1666. B85

A Jesuit author selects thirty geographical places as topics as the means to introduce moral and philosophical subjects.

Bartoli, Daniello. La geografia transportata al morale del padre Daniello Bartoli ... Venice, Iseppo Prodocimo, 1676. B86

The Jesuit author uses thirty geographical topics.

Bartoli, Daniello. Missione al Gran Mojor del p. Ridolfo Acquaviva della Compagni di Gesu, sua vita, e morte ... Bologna, Erede del Benacci [1672]. B87

The third edition.

Bartoli, Daniello. Missione al Gran Mogor del padre Ridolfo Aquaviva della Compagnie di Giesu: sua vita e morte ... Rome, Gio. Maria Salvioni, 1714. B88

A biography of Rodolph Aquaviva, one of the leaders of the Jesuit mission in India in the last quarter of the sixteenth century.

Bartram, William. Travels through North and South Carolina, Georgia, East and West Florida ... together with Observations on the manners of the Indians. Philadelphia, James and Johnson, 1791; London, reprinted for J. Johnson, 1792. B89

One of the most notable eighteenth-century descriptions of the natural history of North America, with frequent reference also to the social life of Indian nations, and observations on travel in the southern United States.

Bartram, William. Travels through North and South Carolina, Georgia, East and West Florida, the Cherokee country ... and the country of the Chactaws. Dublin, For J. Moore [etc.] 1793. B90

Classic account of a naturalist's travels to Florida, Georgia, and the two Carolinas, from 1774 to 1778.

Barzaeus, Gaspar. Epistolae Indicae, in quibus luculenta extat descriptio rerum nuper in India Orientali praeclaré gestarum à theologis Societatis Jesu ... [Dilingae, Sebaldum Mayer, 1563.] B91

The first collection of Jesuit letters from the East to be published in Latin, also the first collection of Jesuit letters to be published in Germany.

Basse, Jeremiah. A proclamation. Manuscript. Burlington, New Jersey, 25 May 1699.   B92

This proclamation is similar to those issued by governors of Jamaica, New York, and Barbados in that it prohibited trade between the English colonies and the Scottish settlement at Darien.

[Baston, Thomas.] Thoughts on trade, and a publick spirit. London, For the author, 1716.   B93

A severe criticism of England's commercial and social situation, with particularly harsh words for monopolistic overseas trading companies.

Batavia, de hoofdstad van neerlands o. Indien. Amsterdam, Petrus Conradi; Harlingen, V. van der Plaats, 1782-83.   B94

A history and description of the chief base of the Dutch East India Company.

Batavian Republic. Rapport van de Gecommitteerden tot de zaaken van de Oostindische Compagnie, aan de provisionele Repraesentanten van het Volk van Holland. Ingeleverd den 15 Juny 1795. The Hague, Ter's Lands Drukkery van Holland, 1795.   B95

A report on the affairs of the East India Company by the revolutionary government of the Netherlands.

Batavian Republic. Nationale Vergadering. Placaat. De Nationale Vergadering, representeerende het volk van Nederland, overwegende, dat het door de verandering van zaken in de Bataaffsche Republiek, noodzakelyk is geworden, een nieuw reglement te arresteeren, volgens het welk in dezen oorlog ... de pryzen of buit, welke op den vyand zullen veroverd worden ... The Hague, 's Lands Drukkery, 1796.   B96

Batavian Republic. Nationale Vergadering. Proclamatie. De Nationale Vergadering, representeerende het volk van Nederland, den Nederlanderen Heil en Broederschap! Het Britsche ministerie heeft, op den 3 dezer maand eene koninglyke proclamatie doen emaneeren, waarby de vrye vaart van Groot-Brittanje op Nederland wordt toegestaan, zoo wel als de uitvoer van alle koopmanschappen ... The Hague, 's Land Drukkery, 1796.   B97

In response to a British proclamation limiting free trade between the two countries, the Dutch here prohibit the importing of British goods.

Batavian Republic. Nationale Vergadering. Publicatie : De Nationale Vergadering, representeerende het volk van Nederland, allen den geenen, die deze zullen zien of haaren lezen: Heil en Broederschap! Dat wy in overweging genomen hebbende het gestatueerde by de placaaten van de Staaten Generaal, van den 19 Juny 1723, en den 24 September 1732, dat, namelyk, geen makelaars of anderen, wie het zouden mogen zyn, zullen mogen staan overassurantien, ten behoeven van eenige Compagnien ... den 3 November 1796. The Hague, 's Lands Drukkery, 1796.   B98

Concerns insurance on ships and goods of the East and West India Companies.

Batavian Republic. Nationale Vergadering. Publicatie : De Nationale Vergadering, representeerende het volk van Nederland, allen den geenen die deze zullen zien of haren lezen, Heil en Broederschap! Nademaal wy overwogen hebben de menigvuldige verongelykingen en beledigingen, door het ryk van Groot-Brittannie en deszelfs onderzaaten dezen staat aangedaan ... den 2 Mey 1796. The Hague, 's Lands Drukkery, 1796.   B99

Authorizes the issuing of letters of marque and reprisal against British ships.

Batavian Republic. Nationale Vergadering. Publicatie. De Nationale Vergadering, representeerende het volk van Nederland, alien den geenen die deze zullen zien of hooren leezen, Heil en Broederschap! doet te weeten: Dat wy in overweging heebende genomen de voordragt door het committé tot de zaaken van de marine ... tot het opheffen der surcheance ... op den ophef van de convoyen en licenten gëemeneert ... The Hague, 's Lands Drukkery, 1796.   B100

Batavian Republic. Nationale Vergadering. Publicatie. De Nationale Vergadering, representeerende het volk van Nederland, allen den geenen die deeze zullen zien of hooren lezen, Heil en Broederschap! doet te weeten: Dat het committé tot de zaken van de marine ter onzer kennisse heeft gebragt dat ... onzer publicatie van 28. September 1796 verkeerdelyk geinterpreteert en ten madeele van 's lands rechten op de convoyen en licenten misbruikt wordt ... The Hague, 's Lands Drukkery, 1796.   B101

Batavian Republic. Nationale Vergadering. Publicatie : De Nationale Vergadering, representeerende het volk van Nederland, allen den geenen die deze zullen zien of haren lezen, Heil en Broederschap! Nademaal wy overwogen hebben de menigvuldige verongelykingen en beledigingen, door het ryk van Groot-Brittannie en deszelfs onderzaaten dezen staat aangedaan ... den 2 Mey 1796. The Hague, 's Lands Drukkery, 1797.   B102

This proclamation extended the charter of the Dutch East India Company to 1799.

Batavian Republic. Nationale Vergadering.
Publicatie : De Nationale Vergadering, representeerende het volk van Nederland, aan hetzelve volk, medeburgers! Nadien wy bevanden hebben, dat in de eersten druk van het ontwerp van constitutie ... den 3 July 1797. The Hague, 's Lands Drukkery, 1797. B103
Relates to Dutch assets in the East and West Indies.

Batavian Republic. Nationale Vergadering.
Publicatie : De Nationale Vergadering, représenteerende het volk van Nederland, aan haare medeburgeren, Heil en Broederschap! Doet te weeten: alzo wy in overweging genamen hebben, dat het belang van de generaale geoctroyeerde O. I. Compagnie ... den 2 Augustus 1797. The Hague, 's Lands Drukkery, 1797. B104
A proclamation concerning the Dutch East India Company's monopoly on the tea trade.

Batavian Republic. Nationale Vergadering.
Publicatie. De Nationale Vergadering, representeerende het volk van Nederland, allen den geenen die dezen zullen zien en hooren lezen, Heil en Broederschap! doet te weeten: Dat wy in ervaring gekomen zynde dat de zydse bommen en pinken, welke des nagts de zee-stranden aandoen, dadelyk hunne inhebbende passagiers aan land zetten, en hunne goederen lossen ... The Hague, 's Lands Drukkery, 1797. B105

Batavian Republic. Nationale Vergadering.
Publication. Le directoire exécutif intermédiaire de la Republique Batave, fait savoir par la présente que le corps représentatif considérant. 1. Que quelques armateurs & autres bâtimens armés sous pavillon francais ont l'audace de poursuivre, d'arrêter & de prendre dans les bras de mer ... des vaisseaux bataves ... The Hague, Imprimerie nationale, 1798. B106

Batavian Republic. Staats-bewind. Publicatie. Het uitvoerend bewind der Bataaffsche Republiek, doet de weeten: Dat de publicatie den 1. Maart 1799 geëmandeerd opzichtelyk den transitoiren doorvoer van goederen over het grondgebied der Bataaffsche Republiek zynde geärresteerd geworden. The Hague, 's Lands Drukkerye, 1800. B107

Batavian Republic. Staats-bewind. Publicatie. Het uitvoerend bewind der Bataafsche Republiek, doet te weten: Dat het vertegenwoordigend lichaam op de wyze by de staatsregeling voorgeschreven overwogen hebbende, dat het by eene eventueele verandering van het tarif der inkomende en uitgaande rechten overeenkomstig de goede ordre en geregelde administratie zal zyn, dat naar bevind der noodzaaklykheid eener heffig op de inkomende Levantsche goederen ... The Hague, 's Lands Drukkery, 1800. B108

Batavian Republic. Staats-bewind. Publicatie. Het uitvoerend bewind der Bataafsche Republiek, doet te weten: Dat het vertegenwoordigend lichaam op de wyze by de staatsregeling voorgeschreven overwogen hebbende, dat by placaat van de voormalige Staaten Generaal ... van den 1 February 1791 is geaesteerd geworden voor den tyd van tien jaaren, eene belasting bekend onder den naam van het borkumsche vuur-en bakengeld daarin breeder omschreeven ... The Hague, 's Lands Drukkery, 1801. B109

Batavian Republic. Staats-bewind. Publicatie. Het Staats-bewind der Bataafsche Republiek doet te weten: Dat hetzelve, overwogen hebbende het verzoek, by requeste gedaan ... om den, hun toekomende, tol, thans te schenkenschans gevestigd, in twee comptoiren te mogen splitzen, en voor het vervolg te Arnhem en te Nymegen te heffen ... The Hague, Staats Drukkery, 1803. B110

Batavian Republic. Staats-bewind. Publicatie. Het Staats-bewind der Bataafsche Republiek doet te weten: Dat hetzelve, overwogen hebbende het verzoek, by requeste gedaan ... om den, hun toekomende, tol, thans te schenkenschans gevestigd, in twee comptoiren te mogen splitzen, en voor het vervolg te Arnhem en te Nymegen te heffen ... The Hague, Staats Drukkery, 1803. B111

Batavian Republic. Staats-bewind. Publicatie. Het Staats-bewind der Bataafsche Republiek, doet te weten: Dat het wegevend lichaam van het Bataafsch gemeenebest, goedegekeurd hebbende de voordragt, daartoe door het Staats-bewind an hetzelve gedan, is besloten: 1. Te verklaren ... concerneerende de vaart op de Strait van Gibralter ... The Hague, Staats Drukkerye, 1803. B112

Batavian Republic. Staats-bewind. Publicatie. Het Staats-bewind der Bataafsche Republiek doet te weten: Dat het wetgevend lichaam van het Bataafsch gemeenebest, goedgekeurd hebbende de voordragt, daartoe, door het Staatsbewind, aan hetzelve gedaan, by alteratie in zoo verre ... eerstelyk, dat in de havenen van deze republiek zullen worden toegelaten al zulke neutrale vaartuigen, die geladen zyn met Yzer ... The Hague, Staats-Drukkery, 1803. B113

Batavian Republic. Staats-bewind. Publicatie. Het Staats-bewind der Bataafsche Republiek doet te weten: Dat, het wetgevend lichaam van het Bataafsch gemeenebest goedgekeurd hebbende de voordragt, daar toe, door het Staatsbewind, aan hetzelve gedaan, is gestatuëerd, gelyk wordt gestatuëerd by dezen: Dat het vierde point van het 49 art. der Instructie voor den Zeeraad, ... van den 2 April 1802, in zoo verre wordt geältereerd ... The Hague, Staats-Drukkerije, 1804. B114

Batavus somnians de bello anglico-batavico. Amsterdam [ca. 1655]. B115
A survey of the results of the Anglo-Dutch War, with reference to English commerce in India, Africa, and America and to Dutch losses to the Portuguese in Brazil.

Baudartius, Willem. Memorien, ofte korte verhael der ghedenckweerdighste gescheidenissen van Nederlandt ... Arnhem, Jan Jansz., 1620. B116
A collection of reports and documents on important events in the Netherlands from 1610 to 1620. Included are broadsides dealing with regulation of commerce and reports of Dutch exploration.

Baudeau, M. l'abbé (Nicolas). Encyclopédie méthodique. Paris, Panckoucke; Liège, Plomteux, 1783. B117
An encyclopedia of commercial terms, types of merchandise, weights, coins, and major commercial centers.

[Baudeau, M. l'abbé (Nicolas).] Idées d'un citoyen sur la puissance du roi et le commerce de la nation, dans l'Orient. Amsterdam, 1763. B118
Proposals for nurturing and extending French trade to Africa and the East Indies.

Baudier, Michel. The history of the imperiall estate of the Grand Seigneurs. London, William Stansby for Richard Meighen, 1635. B119
This volume also includes *The history of the court of the king of China* by the same author which is descriptive of Chinese social customs as well as the political structure of the country.

Baudrand, Michel-Antoine. Dictionaire geographique universel. Amsterdam; Utrecht, François Halma, Guillaume van de Water, 1701. B120
A massive geographical dictionary including descriptions of a vast number of places with information on the economy, political situation and significance of each.

Baudrand, Michel-Antoine. Geographia ordine litterarum disposita. Paris, Stephanum Michalet, 1681-82. B121
A massive geographical dictionary with some 20,000 entries encompassing the entire world and both ancient and modern geographies.

Bawier, Franz Urban. Merckwürdige Reisen und Begebenheiten seine Kriegsdienste zu Lande Seefahrten nach Ost-und Westindien und endliche Wohlfarth von ihm selbst beschrieben. Frankfurt and Leipzig, Georg Peter Monath, 1752. B122
A narrative of mutiny, piracy, privation, and shipwreck during a voyage extending from 1710 to 1717.

Bayard de La Vingtrie, M. (Ferdinand-Marie). Voyage dans l'intérieur des États-Unis, a Bath, Winchester, dans la vallée de Shenandoah, etc., etc., pendant l'été de 1791. Paris, Batilliot Frères [etc.] 1798. B123
An account of travels through the middle and northeastern states with particular emphasis on the American social scene.

Beantwoordinge des koninckx van polen aengaende de ... Sweetsche wapenen. Middelburg, Jan vander Hellen, 1656. B124
A criticism of the Swedes for going to war against Poland in what appeared to be an attempt to dominate the commerce of the Baltic area.

Beatty, Charles. The journal of a two months tour; with a view of promoting religion among the frontier inhabitants of Pennsylvania. London, For William Davenhill and George Pearch, 1768. B125
This account of travels through western Pennsylvania in 1766 is rich in descriptions of frontier life and travel, as well as accounts of Indians of that area, and rumors about the Indians and the geography of the land farther west.

Beatty, Charles. Tagebuch einer zween monatlichen Reise, welche in der Absicht die Religion bey den Grenzeinwohnern von Pensilvanien zu befördern, und das Christenthum bey den Indianern ... unternommen worden ... Frankfurt & Leipzig, Joh. Georg Fleischer, 1771. B126
This German edition is the only non-English version. It includes some commentary by the translator in the footnotes.

Beaufoy, Henry. The substance of a speech of Henry Beaufoy, esq. to the British Society for extending the fisheries, &c. at their general court held on Tuesday, March 25, 1788. London, T. Cadell [etc.] 1788. B127
The speech contains extensive notes from the author's journal during his tour of the west coast of Scotland and adjacent islands seeking situations for fishery establishments which could absorb displaced tenants and provide them an alternative to emigration to America. Legislation establishing the Society is included.

Beaujour, Louis-Auguste Félix, baron de. Tableau du commerce de la Grèce. Paris, Imprimerie de Crapelet [1800]. B128
An economic survey of Greece with a view to increasing French trade there.

Beaumarchais, Pierre Augustin Caron de. Observations sur le mémoire justificatif de la cour de Londres ... London; Philadelphia, 1779. B129
This work by the famous playwright was part of the pamphlet war that flared over French support of the Americans in the Revolution.

Beaune, M. De. Lettre écrite en forme de relation à Monsieur d'Argenson ... en Fevrier, 1720. Manuscript. Louisiana, 1720. B130
A thirty-two page report on the situation in Louisiana which is highly critical of Bienville, and which advocates that the French interest themselves more actively in the Illinois region. This report was probably taken to France by Hubert. D'Argenson, who was president of the Council of Finance and Keeper of the Seal.

Beauplan, Guillaume Le Vasseur, sieur de. Beschreibung der Ukraine, der Krim, und deren Einwohner ... Aus dem Französischen übersetzt und nebst einem Anhange der die Ukraine, und die budziackische Tatarey betrift ... von Johann Wilhelm Moeller. Breslau, Wilhelm Gottlieb Korn, 1780. B131
A description of the region from Poland to the Black Sea by a resident of the Ukraine during the early decades of the seventeenth century. This German translation from the French includes the account of Prince Maximilian Emanuel of Würtemburg through much of the same area.

Beausobre, Louis de. Introduction générale à l'étude de la politique, des finances, et du commerce. Amsterdam, J.S. Schneider, 1765. B132
Describes the commerce of each European nation, and Europe's commerce with other parts of the world.

Beauvais-Raseau, de. L'art de l'indigotier. [Paris, L. F. Delatour] 1770. B133
A description of indigo, its uses, different types, and a detailed account of production processes used in the West Indies.

Beaver, Philip. African memoranda: relative to an attempt to establish a British settlement on the island of Bulama. London, For C. and R. Baldwin, 1805. B134
A history of the Bulama settlement, and attempt at a colony based on labor by freed Negroes, written by a naval officer who presided over the colony from its beginning in 1792 until its failure two years later.

Beawes, Wyndham. Lex mercatoria rediviva: or, The merchant's directory. London, For the author by J. Moore, 1752. B135
The first edition of a massive commercial handbook intended as a guide for English merchants.

Beawes, Wyndham. Lex mercatoria rediviva: or, The merchant's directory. London, For R. Baldwin and S. Crowder, 1761. B136
The second edition, updating the legislation passed by Parliament since the previous edition in 1752.

Becattini, Francesco. Storia della Crimea piccola Tartaria, ed altre provincie circonvicine soggetto delle recenti vertenze tra la Russia e la Porta Ottomana ... Venice, Leonardo Bassaglia, 1785. B137
The geography of Crimea and adjacent regions is included, with reference to the economic significance of some places.

Beckford, William. A descriptive account of the island of Jamaica. London, For T. and J. Egerton, 1790. B138
The author's major concern is with the sugar industry on the island, but he also comments on other industries and on the condition of slaves.

Beckford, William. Remarks upon the situation of the Negroes in Jamaica. London, For T. and J. Egerton, 1788. B139
A description of the conditions of West Indian slaves with a view to encouraging better treatment for them, on grounds of both humanity and economics.

Bedencken op de aggreatie des conincx van Spangien, gestelt in forma van tsamensprekinge tusschen swaer-hooft ende truert-niet. Buyten Embden, Johan van Oldersum, 1608. B140
A discussion of the rigors of Hapsburg control of the Netherlands, as peace was being considered.

Bedenckinge over d'antwoordt der heeren bewinthebbers vande Oost-Indische Compagnie. The Hague, Jan Veeli, 1644. B141
Proposals to unite the Dutch East and West India companies were opposed by the former. This tract attacks their attitude as unpatriotic.

Bedenkingen en antwoort op de vrymoedige aenspraek aen ... Den heere prince van Oranje ... Vlissingen, Geeraerdt de Laet, 1650. B142
The author takes exception to remarks of Maximillian Teelink of Middelburg on a number of subjects, including the West India Company.

Bedik, Petrus. Cehil Sutun, seu explicatio utriusque celeberrimi, ac pretiosissimi theatri quadraginta columnarum in Perside Orientis ... Vienna, Leopoldi Voigt [1678]. B143
An account of Persia by an Armenian Christian missionary.

Beeckman, Daniel. A voyage to and from the island of Borneo in the East-Indies. London, For T. Warner and J. Batley, 1718. B144
The author was the captain of a ship sent out to Borneo to re-establish the trade of the East India Company there.

Beer, Martinus. Geographiae veteris, & novae, enchiridion. Nuremberg, Michaelis & Joh. Frid. Endterorum, 1672. B145
An elementary geography text.

Beeston, Sir William. Copy of a letter to James Vernon. Manuscript. Jamaica, 21 March 1699. B146
The lieutenant governor of Jamaica writes the secretary of state about the Scots' settlement at Darien, their problems with the Spaniards, and other commercial and maritime matters.

Begouën, Jacques-François. Discours ... sur le commerce de l'Inde. [Paris, Imprimerie Nationale, 1790.] B147
A defense of monopoly in the East Indies, and a repudiation of free trade generally.

Behr, Johann von der. Diarium ... über dasjenige, so sich Zeit einer neun-jährigen Reise zu Wasser und Lande ... zugetragen. Jena, U. Spaltholtz, 1668. B148
A description of the East Indies by a Dutch official, who notes also the activities of the English and Portuguese there.

Behrens, Karl Friedrich. Histoire de l'expedition de trois vaisseux ... aux Terres Australes en MDCCXXI. The Hague, Aux depens de la Compagnie, 1739. B149
An account of the expedition of three ships sent into the South Pacific by the Dutch West India Company, noting the major products of the various islands.

Béjar, duque de. Practica representacion al Rey nuestro Señor de la Compañia de Gibraleon, Real, y Catholica, por ser su Magestad su Protector. [n.p, ca. 1720.] B150
A representation by the Duque de Bajar on behalf of a proposed Compañia de Gibraleon for the purpose of carrying on trade to the East Indies.

Beleña, Eusebio Buenaventura. Recopilacion sumaria de todos los autos acordados de la real audiencia y sala del crimen de esta Nueva España. Mexico, Don Felipe de Zuñiga y Ontiveros, 1787. B151
A summary of all the judicial decrees and decisions reached at trial or in the governor's court. It includes a number of royal proclamations and laws.

Belhaven, John Hamilton, Baron. A speech in Parliament ... on the affair of the Indian and African Company. Edinburgh, 1701. B152
Lord Belhaven attributes the failure of the Darien Colony to England's opposition to competition from Scotland in the New World.

Bell, John. Travels from St. Petersburg in Russia, to diverse parts of Asia. Glasgow, For the author by R. and A. Foulis, 1763. B153
The first edition of a diplomat's account of his experiences in travels to the Near and Far East, including a map of the route followed from Moscow to Peking.

Bell, John. Travels from St. Petersburg in Russia, to diverse parts of Asia. Dublin, For Robert Bell, 1764. B154
The first Irish edition.

Bell, John. Voyages depuis St. Petersbourg en Russie, dans diverses contrées de l'Asie. Paris, Robin, 1766. B155
The first French edition.

Bell, John. Journey of John Bell, esq. from St. Petersburgh to Pekin. With an embassy from His Imperial Majesty, Peter the Great, to Kamhi, emperor of China. Philadelphia, Joseph and James Crukshank, 1803. B156
An abridged version of Bell's account of his travels across Siberia and Mongolia to Peking, noting particularly the religious and social customs of Siberians and Mongolians, and events at the emperor's court in Peking.

Belleforest, François de. L'histoire universelle du monde. Paris, Gervais Mallot, 1570. B157
A general geography of the world, combining classical and modern information, and including commentary on geographical discoveries from various sources.

Belleforest, François de. L'histoire universelle du monde. Paris, Gervais Mallot, 1572. B158
The second edition.

Belleforest, François de. L'histoire universelle du monde. Paris, Gervais Mallot, 1577. B159
The third edition, with considerable additions to the edition of 1572.

Bellegarde, M. l'abbé de (Jean Baptiste Morvan). A general history of all voyages and travels throughout the Old and New World, from the first ages to this present time ... By Monsr. Du Perier. London, Edmund Curll, 1708. B160
This is primarily a history of early Spanish conquest in the New World.

Bellegarde, M. l'abbé de (Jean Baptiste Morvan). Histoire universelle des voyages faits par mer & par terre, dans l'Ancien, & dans le Nouveau Monde ... Amsterdam, Pierre Humbert, 1708. B161
The first volume of an intended series of travel narratives and commentaries on them. No more were published. The introduction is an interesting essay on the importance of travel and discovery in all periods of history.

Bellin, Jacques Nicolas. Description des débouquements qui sont au nord de l'isle de Saint Domingue. Paris, Didot, 1768. B162

A guide to the passages used in the return voyage from Saint Domingue including thirty-four maps and charts.

[Bellin, Jacques Nicolas.] Déscription géographique de la Guyane. Paris, Didot, 1763.
B163
A description of the French, Dutch, Spanish, and Portuguese colonies in northern South America.

Bellin, Jacques Nicolas. Description geographique des Isles Antilles possédées par les Anglois. Paris, Didot, 1758. B164
A description of the British West Indies, with twenty-two maps and views.

Bellin, Jacques Nicolas. Le petit atlas maritime ... Paris, 1764. B165
A five-volume atlas of maps and charts depicting various coastal areas, harbors, and other regions of interest to navigators.

Bellin, Jacques Nicolas. Recueil des memoires qui ont été publiés avec les cartes hydrographiques. [Paris, ca. 1755.] B166
The twenty separately-issued publications collected here describe recently-published maps, note their improvements over earlier maps, and cite sources consulted in making them.

Bellin, Jacques Nicolas. Remarques sur la carte de l'Amerique Septentrionale. Paris, l'Imprimerie de Didot, 1755. B167
A map of the northern part of North America accompanying a volume of descriptions of rivers, islands, etc.

Belloni, Girolamo, marchese. Del commercio dissertazione. Venice, Remondini, 1757.
B168
A mercantilist treatise by a prominent Italian writer on economics, describing the ways in which a state must regulate its economy for maximum benefit.

Belloni, Girolamo, marchese. Dissertation sur le commerce. The Hague, Aux Depense de la Compagnie, 1755. B169
The second French edition.

Belon, Pierre. Les observations de plusieurs singularitez & choses memorables, trouvees en Grece, Asie, Judée, Egypte, Arabie, & autres pays estranges. Antwerp, C. Plantin, 1555.
B170
The author of this popular book of Near Eastern travels includes commentary on the products of the Levant, such as porcelain, amber, cloth, rhubarb, etc.

Belon, Pierre. Les observations de plusieurs singularitez & choses memorables, trouvees en Grece, Asie, Judée, Egypte, Arabie, & autres pays estranges. Paris, Hierosme de Marnef & la veufue Guillaume Cavellat, 1588. B171

This edition adds illustrations not found in earlier printings.

Belon, Pierre. Plurimarum singularium & memorabilium rerum in Graecia, Asia, Aegypto, Judaea, Arabia, aliisq. exteris provinciis. Antwerp, Christopheri Plantini, 1589. B172
The first Latin edition, translated by Charles L'Ecluse.

Beltrami, Giacomo Constantino. La découverte des sources du Mississippi et de la Riviere Sanglante. New Orleans, Benj. Levy, 1824.
B173
Beltrami accompanied Major Stephen Long on his second expedition, up the Mississippi and into the Red River valley. Beltrami then explored in what is now northwestern Minnesota by himself. His account is flamboyant and imaginative.

Beltrami, Giacomo Constantino. A pilgrimage in Europe and America leading to the discovery of the sources of the Mississippi and Bloody River. London, For Hunt and Clarke, 1828.
B174
The first English edition.

Bembo, Ambrosio. Viaggio e giornale per parte dell' Asia di quattro anni incirca fatto. Manuscript. [Italy, ca. 1676.] B175
A manuscript account of travels in India, Persia, and Arabia by a young Venetian nobleman. The 315 page narrative is illustrated with forty-seven pen and ink drawings by Guillaume Grelot, a French artist who had traveled with Sir John Chardin.

Bembo, Marco. [Correspondence from Candia, Crete.] 1479-1482. B176
Bembo was a Venetian merchant, and this correspondence reflects his firm's trade in wine, cloth, hemp, and other commodities in the eastern Mediterranean.

Bembo, Marco. [Correspondence from Modon, Greece.] 1482-1484. B177
These letters from a Venetian agent at Modon report on a variety of commercial and political matters including exchange rates, restrictions placed by the Turks, quality of cloth being sold, shipment of slaves, etc.

Bembo, Pietro. Historiae Venetae, libre XII. Venice, Aldus, 1551. B178
A history of Venice, covering the period 1487-1513.

Benavides de Bazán, Juan de. [Petition to Philip IV of Spain.] Manuscript. n.p. [ca. 1628].
B179
The author was captain of the Spanish silver fleet captured by Piet Heyn in 1628. He pleads for his life, citing the poor condition of Spanish shipping as a major cause of his defeat.

Bencius, Francesco. Quinque martyres. Libri sex ... Venice, Muschius, 1591. B180

A poem in six cantos eulogizing Rodolfo Acquaviva and four companions who accompanied him to Salsette peninsula in India where they were martyred.

Bendish Family. Papers. Manuscript. England and the Levant, 1642-1710.   B181

This collection includes sixty-two manuscript letters, one printed broadside, and two letter books. These relate to Sir Thomas Bendish, who was England's ambassador to Turkey under Charles I and II, and to his heirs who continued the family business with particular interests in the Mediterranean and in America.

Benedictus XIV, Pope. Discours de notre très-saint pere le Pape Benoît XIV, sur la mort précieuse de Pierre Martyr, religieux de l'ordre de Saint-Dominique. Paris, Babuty, Quillau, 1748.   B182

An oration celebrating the life of Pedro Martir Sanz, a missionary to China who served there from 1713 to his death in 1747. He was made vicar apostolic of Fokien in 1738.

Benezet, Anthony. A caution to Great Britain and her colonies, in a short representation of the calamitous state of the enslaved Negroes in the British dominions. Philadelphia printed: London reprinted and sold by James Phillips, 1784.   B183

A reprint of one of the earliest anti-slave trade tracts, originally published in 1767.

Benezet, Anthony. Notes on the slave trade, &c. [Philadelphia, Enoch Story, 1783.]   B184

A review of the evils of the slave trade, its impact in Africa, and its negative effects on slave traders and slave owners in England and in America.

Benezet, Anthony. Some historical account of Guinea ... with an inquiry into the rise and progress of the slave-trade, its nature and lamentable effects. Philadelphia, Joseph Crukshank, 1771.   B185

A description of the geography, history, and commerce of Guinea. Includes excerpts from other works regarding the situation in West Africa, the development of the slave trade, and its particular relationship to the British American colonies.

Benezet, Anthony. Some historical account of Guinea. London, W. Owen, 1772.   B186

First printing in Great Britain of the preceding work.

Benezet, Anthony. Some historical account of Guinea, its situation, produce, and the general disposition of its inhabitants. With and inquiry into the rise and progress of the slave trade. London, J. Phillips, 1788.   B187

This fourth edition includes a biography of Benezet and an endorsement of his anti-slavery activities.

Benjamin, of Tudela. Itinerarium Benjamini Tudelensis. Antwerp, Christopher Plantin, 1575.   B188

The first edition of an account of travels to the Near East and Asia between 1160 and 1173 in which the commercial activity of various eastern cities is described.

Benjamin, of Tudela. Itinerarium D. Benjaminis, cum versione & notis Constantini L'Empereur. Leiden, Officina Elzeviriana, 1633.   B189

This is the only edition where the Hebrew text is reproduced next to a Latin translation.

[Bennet, John, merchant.] The national merchant. London, For J. Walthoe, 1736.   B190

A discussion of colonial policy, advocating economic development of England's colonies, but resisting commercial aspirations of colonists which conflicted with those of England.

Bennett, John. Two letters and several calculations on the sugar colonies and trade ... London, R. Montagu, 1738.   B191

An attempt to obtain modifications of British policy concerning trade, government, security, and defense in the West Indies.

Benson, Martin. A Sermon preached before the Incorporated Society for the Propagation of the Gospel in Foreign Parts; at their Anniversary Meeting in the Parish-Church of St. Mary-le-Bow, on Friday, February 15, 1739-40. London, For J. and H. Pemberton, 1740.   B192

This sermon responds to bringing Christianity and European civilization to the Indians.

Benyowsky, Maurice Auguste, comte de. Memoirs and travels ... London, G.G. J. and J. Robinson, 1790.   B193

The first edition of a Hungarian nobleman's account of his experiences in Siberia and Madagascar. Contains information on economic activity in Siberia, Alaska, and the northern Pacific as well as an account of an unsuccessful attempt to establish a settlement in Madagascar.

Benyowsky, Maurice Auguste, comte de. Reisen durch Sibirien und Kamtschatka über Japan und China nach Europa. Berlin, Christian Friedrich Voss & Sohn, 1790.   B194

The first German edition.

Benyowsky, Maurice Auguste, comte de. Lefnadslopp och resor, af honom sjelf beskrefne. I sammandrag med tilläggningar. Stockholm, Kongl. Ordens-Tryckeriet, 1791.   B195

This Swedish translation is a condensed version by Samuel Lorens Ödmann.

Benyowsky, Maurice Auguste, comte de. Voyages et mémoires de Maurice-Auguste, comte de Benyowsky ... contenant ses opérations militaires en Pologne, son exile au Kamchatka, son

evasion et son voyage à travers l'Ocean Pacifique ... Paris, Buisson, 1791. B196
This French edition does not include some of the material relative to Madagascar found in the English edition. Also, it does not include the illustrations.

Benzoni, Girolamo. La historia del mondo nuovo. Venice, Francesco Rampazetto, 1565. B197
The first edition of this Milanese observer's account of his experiences during fourteen years spent in the West Indies.

Benzoni, Girolamo. Novae novi orbis historiae. Geneva, Eustathius Vignon, 1578. B198
This first Latin edition contains an account of French exploration in the New World.

Benzoni, Girolamo. Der newenn Weldt und indianischen Königreichs, newe unnd wahrhaffte History, von allen Geschichten, Handlungen, Thaten, Strengem unnd ernstlichem Reigiment der Spanier gegen den Indianern ... Basel, Sebastien Henricpetri [1579]. B199
The first German edition.

Benzoni, Girolamo. Histoire nouvelle du Nouveau Monde. Geneva, E. Vignon, 1579. B200
This French edition by Urbain Chauvelton includes an account of the destruction by the Spaniards of the Ribaut settlement in Florida.

Benzoni, Girolamo. Novae novi orbis historiae. [Geneva] Eustathium Vignon, 1581. B201
The third Latin edition.

Berch, Anders. Åminnelse-tal, öfver ... Herr Henric Kalmeter. Stockholm, Lars Salvius [1752]. B202
A memorial address in honor of Henric Kalmeter, a member of the Swedish Commercial Council and a prominent adviser in matters concerning Swedish economy and commerce.

Berenger, Jean Pierre. Collection de tous les voyages faits autour du monde. Paris, Poinçot [etc.] 1788-89. B203
This nine-volume set contains accounts of twenty-five circumnavigations of the earth.

[Beresford, William.] A voyage round the world; but more particularly to the north-west coast of America: performed in 1785, 1786, 1787, and 1788, in the King George and Queen Charlotte, Captains Portlock and Dixon. London, Geo Goulding, 1789. B204
An account of sailing, trading and exploring on the northwest coast of North America, in the Hawaiian Islands and in China. Includes descriptions of Russian, Spanish, French, and English fur trade on the northwest coast of North America as well as European commerce with Macao and China.

[Beresford, William.] A voyage round the world; but more particularly to the north-west coast of America: performed in 1785, 1786, 1787, and 1788, in the King George and Queen Charlotte, Captains Portlock and Dixon. London, Geo. Goulding, 1789. B205
The second edition.

[Beresford, William.] Voyage autour du monde, et principalement a la côte nordouest de l'Amérique. Paris, Maradan, 1789. B206
The first French translation.

Beresford, William. Der Kapitaine Portlock's und Dixon's Reise um die Welt; besonders nach der nordwestlichen Küste von Amerika während der Jahre 1785 bis 1788 ... Berlin, Christian Friedrich Voss und Sohn, 1790. B207
This German translation by Johann Reinhold Forster omits four of the illustrations, the second appendix, and presents the map in a reduced scale. Extensive notes by Forster are added.

Berettari, Sebastiano. Josephi Anchietae Societatis Jesu sacerdotis in Brasilia defuncti vita. Lyons, Horatij Cardon, 1617. B208
A biography of José de Anchieta, a Portuguese missionary in Brazil from 1553 to 1597. It includes considerable description of Brazil and its people.

Berg, Marcus. Beskrifning öfwer Barbariska slafweriet uti keisaredömet Fez och Marocco. Stockholm, Lor. Ludv. Grefing, 1757. B209
An account of the two-year captivity of a Swedish sea captain who reports events in Morocco from 1755 to 1756.

Bergamo (Italy). Laws, etc. Statutorum mercatandiae mercator. Manuscript. Bergamo [1566]. B210
A collection of 109 statuutes regulating various aspects of Bergamo's commercial life.

Bergasse, Nicolas. Considérations sur la liberté du commerce. London, 1788. B211
A brief history of the carrying trade in France, with arguments against the licensing of a monopoly of it.

Berger, Friedrich Ludwig, Edler von. Gründliche Erweisung ... einer Ost-und West-Indischen Compagnie. Regensburg & Leipzig, Johann Conrad Peetz, 1723. B212
A defense of the Ostend Company's right to trade in the East and West Indies.

[Berger, Friedrich Ludwig, Edler von.] Vindiciae luculentae juris ac privilegii in Indias atque Africam navigandi, ibique commercia colendi, Belgii Austriaci incolis novissime con-

cessi. Leipzig, Friedrich Lanckischens Erben, 1724. B213
A justification of the Ostend Company, based on the writings of earlier historians and lawyers. The text is in both Latin and German.

Bergeron, Pierre de. Relation des voyages en Tartarie de Fr. Guillaume de Rubruquis, Fr. Jean du Plan Carpin, Fr. Ascelin & autres religieux de S. François & S. Dominique ... Paris, Veufue Jean de Heuqueville & Louys de Heuqueville, 1634. B214
In addition to accounts of religious embassies to eastern Asia, this work includes a treatise on the Tartars from a variety of sources and another on the Saracens and Mohammedans.

Bergeron, Pierre de. Voyages faits principalement en Asie. The Hague, J. Neaulme, 1735. B215
A collection of Asian travels from the twelfth to the fifteenth century.

[Bergier, Nicolas.] Archimeron; ou, Traicté du commencement des jours. Auquel est monstré le particulier endroit sur la rondeur de la terre & de la mer, ou le jour de vingt-quatre heures prend son commancement. Paris, Abraham Saugrain, 1617. B216
A treatise on the measurement of time and the need to have an acceptable point from which it can be said a day begins, with a recommendation similar to what has become the international date line.

Bergier, Nicolas. Histoire des grands chemins de l'empire romain, contenant l'origine, progrès & etenduë quasi incroyable des chemins militaires, pavez depuis la ville de Rome jusques aux extremitez de son empire. Brussels, Jean Leonard, 1728. B217
A discussion of all aspects of the Roman roads, their structure, usefulness, finance, etc. The volume includes a comparison of the Peutinger Table with the Antonine Itinerary, the former of which is reproduced in the volume.

Bericht der vergadering van zeventien, by de provisionele repraesentanten des volks van Zeeland, den 22 September 1795 gerequireerd op het decreet der provisionele repraesentanten des volks van Holland van den 15 derzelve maand ... Middelburg, Issac de Winter, 1795. B218
Zealand's response to Holland's decree of September 15, 1795 dissolving the management of the Dutch East India Company, replacing it with a committee.

Bericht van een liefhebber der waarheit aan sijn vriend, over de tegenwoordige toestant van saken. n.p., 1684. B219
A pamphlet expressing fear that Dutch trade on German rivers and in the Baltic will be interfered with in the event of war.

[Bering, Vitus Jonassen.] Diese Charte über Siberien nimt ihren Anfang zu Tobolsk ostwarts bis an die euserste Grentz von Sukotsky gemacht unter Commendo des Capt: Commandeurs Bering. Ao: 1729. B220
A manuscript map measuring 21½ x 51 inches, in brilliant colors, depicting the route followed by Bering in his first expedition to eastern Siberia in the years 1725-29.

Berkel, Adriaan van. Amerikaansche voyagien, behelzende een reis na Rio de Berbice, gelegen op het vaste land van Guiana. Amsterdam, Johan ten Hoorn, 1695. B221
A description of the Dutch settlements on the Berbice, Essiquibo, and Surinam rivers, noting the products natural to the region and reporting French and English interest in the area.

[Berkeley, George.] A proposal for the better supplying of churches in our foreign plantations, and for converting the savage Americans to Christianity. London, H. Woodfall, 1724. B222
A proposal to establish a seminary in Bermuda for training preachers recruited in the American colonies and for educating Indians to serve as missionaries among their own people.

Berkeley, George. A Sermon preached before the Incorporated Society for the Propagation of the Gospel in Foreign parts; at their Anniversary Meeting in the Parish-Church of St. Mary-le-Bow, on Friday, February 18, 1731. London, J. Downing, 1732. B223
This sermon deals with problems in the missions, including dissenting preachers. The annual report appended contains the usual reports of progress of the Society in North America.

[Berlemont, Noël de.] Colloquia et dictionariolum octo linguarum. Amsterdam, Henricus Laurentius, 1623. B224
A dictionary of eight European languages intended in part for the use of merchants.

Bernard, Sir Francis. Select letters on the trade and government of America. London, For T. Payne, 1774. B225
An argument against unreasonable regulation of colonial trade by England.

Bernard, François. Histoire abrégée des voyages de Mr. François Bernard, et de la captivité ou esclavage chez les sauvages du Canada. Manuscript. [Portugal, ca. 1780.] B226
This manuscript represents itself to be the reminiscences of a Swiss soldier in British service during the French and Indian Wars. Bernard was captured by the Indians, and was taken westward perhaps as far as the Lake Superior region.

Bernard, François, 18th cent. L'Afrique hollandaise; ou Tableau historique et politique de l'état originaire de la colonie du Cap de Bonne-Espérance comparé avec l'état actuel de cette colonie ... Hollande, 1783. B227
A brief history of the establishment of the Dutch colony in South Africa, with an account of its current administrative structure.

[Bernard, François, 18th cent.] Analyse de l'histoire philosophique et politique des établissemens & du commerce des Européens dans les deux Indes. Leiden, J. Murray, 1775. B228
An analysis and commentary on Raynal's *L'histoire philosophique et politique*.

[Bernard, Jacques, comp.] The acts and negotiations, together with the particular articles at large, of the general peace concluded at Ryswick. London, For Robert Clavel and Tim. Childe, 1698. B229
Includes a review of negotiations leading to the general peace, the terms of agreements, and ratification statements of various monarchs.

[Bernard, Jacques, comp.] Ryswykse vrede-handel, bestaande in autentike acten, memorien en antwoorden, dewelke in't Keiserrijk, Sweeden, Savoyen, ende in de Nederlanden zijn voorgevallen; mitsgaders alle de noodige stukken en documenten ... 'sGravenhaage, Gerrit Rammazeyn en Meyndert Uytwerf, 1700. B230
Documents leading to the Peace of Ryswick, translated from the French edition of the previous year.

Bernard, Jean Frédéric, comp. Recueil d'arrests et autre pièces pour l'établissement de la Compagnie d'Occident. Amsterdam, J. F. Bernard, 1720. B231
A collection of documents relating to the establishment of a French trading company in North America.

[Bernard, Jean Frédéric, comp.] Recueil de voyages au nord. Amsterdam, J. F. Bernard, 1725-38. B232
A ten-volume collection of accounts of voyages of exploration and trade, chiefly to the northern regions, but including also voyages to Louisiana, Korea, Turkistan, and elsewhere.

Bernard, Jean Frédéric, comp. Relations de la Louisiane, et du fleuve Mississipi. Amsterdam, J. F. Bernard, 1720. B233
A variant of the fifth volume of *Recueil de voyages au nord*, by the same author.

Bernier, François. Voyages de François Bernier contenant la description des etats du Grand Mogol, de l'Hindoustan, du royaume de Kachemire, &c ... Amsterdam, Paul Marret, 1709-10. B234
An account of political events in India and a description of that country based upon a twelve year residence there by a French physician who served the Grand Mogol, Aurangzeb.

Berno, Pierantonio. [Two copper engravings depicting the organization and structures housing the fair of Verona.] Verona, Pierantonio Berno, 1722. B235
One of these engravings is a bird's-eye view, the other a plan of the structure housing the fair of Verona.

Bernoulli, Jean, comp. Historisch-geographische Beschreibung von Hindustan. Berlin; Gotha, C. W. Ettinger, 1785-88. B236
A collection of geographical and historical information on India including material from Joseph Tieffenthaler, Abraham Duperron, and James Rennell.

Berquen, Robert de. Les merveilles des Indes Orientales et Occidentales, ou nouveau traitté des pierres precieuses & perles. Paris, C. Lambin, 1661. B237
A detailed description of the varieties, quality, and locations of various precious stones to be found in the East and West Indies.

Berredo, Bernardo Pereira de. Annaes historicos do estado do Maranhaõ. Lisbon, Francisco Luiz Ameno, 1749. B238
This chronicle was written by a governor of the Brazilian provinces which made up the "Estado do Maranhaõ." Its terminal date is 1718.

Berriman, William. A sermon preach'd before the honourable trustees for establishing the colony of Georgia in America ... London, For John Carter, 1739. B239
The trustees of the colony are urged to see to it that the material gains from the colony are applied to religious work, specifically to the conversion of the slaves and Indians.

Bertholon, M. l'abbé (Pierre). Du commerce et des manufactures distinctives de la ville de Lyon. Montpellier, Jean Martel, 1787. B240
A history of the rise and decline of Lyons as a center for silk manufacture. The decline is attributed to an excess of regulation on the industry.

Berthoud, Ferdinand. Les longitudes par la mesure du temps, ou, Méthode pour déterminer les longitudes en mer ... Paris, J.B.G. Musier, 1775. B241
An important work in the search for a means of determining longitude at sea, with a detailed description of an instrument developed by the author and the means of using it.

Bertius, Petrus. Tabularum geographicarum contractarum libri septem. Amsterdam, Jodocus Hondius, 1616. B242

This edition contains 221 maps, covering all parts of the known world, with brief text describing each area.

Beschreibung der spanischen Macht in America, nebst einem Anhange von der ... malouinischen, oder fälklandischen Inseln ... Nebst einer vollständigen Beschreibung der spanischen Handlung zwischen der Stadt Manila und dem Hafen Acapulco. Sorau, Gottlog Hebold, 1771. B243

The three parts are paged separately. The section on the Falkland Islands concerns the Anglo-Spanish conflict over them, and includes a map.

Beschryving der stadt Delft. Delft, Reinier Boitet, 1729. B244

This history of Delft contains information on that city's participation in the Dutch East and West India companies and other aspects of its commerce.

Best, George. A true discourse of the late voyages of discovery for finding a passage to Cathaya ... London, H. Bynnyman, 1578. B245

This is the only contemporary account of all three of Frobisher's voyages in search of the Northwest Passage to be written by one who participated in them. Includes a map of the areas explored.

The best and most approved method of curing white-herrings ... London, For J. Davidson, 1750. B246

Instructions for conducting a herring fishery in the Shetland Island waters.

Betagh, William. A voyage round the world. London, For T. Combes [etc.] 1728. B247

An account of Shelvocke's voyage, highly critical of that captain, with information on the trade in guano off the South American coast and mention of the metals in California.

[Bethel, Slingsby.] An account of the French usurpation upon the trade of England. London, 1679. B248

A comparison of French and English commerce. "Every nation is more or less considerable according to the proportion it hath of trade."

[Bethel, Slingsby.] The present interest of England stated. London, For D.B., 1671. B249

Contains many suggestions for the improvement of England's commerce.

[Bethel, Slingsby.] Engelands interest, ofte tegenwoordich waerachtigh belangh. n.p., 1672. B250

A translation of the English tract cited above, noting the advantages England holds over other nations with respect to trade.

Beughem, Cornelis à. Bibliographia historica, chronologica, & geographica novissima, perpetuo continuanda. Amsterdam, Janssonio-Waesbergios, 1685. B251

A bibliography of historical and geographical works in linguistic categories: Latin and Greek, French, Spanish and Portuguese, Italian, English, German, and Dutch.

Beuningen, Koenraad van. Missive ... over ende ter saecke van den ... vredehandel ... Leiden, Charles Pers, 1667. B252

In preparation for the Treaty of Breda, the Dutch consider the relative values to them of New Netherland, Cormantin on the Guinea coast, and the island of Pouleron.

Beverlandt, Johannes and Jan Adrianensz van der Goes. [Copy of a letter written from the Essequibo River, 30 September 1627.] Manuscript. [Netherlands, ca. 1628.] B253

A report on the problems of establishing a settlement in Guiana, noting troubles with the inhabitants, types of goods that were needed, ships that had recently departed for the Netherlands, and exploration being undertaken on the Essequibo River.

Beverley, Robert. The history and present state of Virginia. London, For R. Parker, 1705. B254

The first history of Virginia written by a native, this work has a high reputation as a vivid, comprehensive, and interesting picture of life there. It includes commentary on trade with the Indians.

Beverley, Robert. The history of Virginia ... London, For F. Fayram, J. Clarke and T. Bickerton, 1722. B255

The second English edition.

[Beverley, Robert.] Histoire de la Virginie. Amsterdam, Thomas Lombrail, 1707. B256

One of two French editions published in 1707. The text contains no significant additions, and illustrations are based on the English edition.

Beverwyck, Jan van. Spaensche Xerxes, ofte beschrijvinge, ende vergelijkinge van den scheep-strijdt tusschen de groote koningen van Persen, ende Spaengjen, teghen de verbonde Griecken, ende Nederlanders. The Hague, Isaac Burchoorn, 1640. B257

A general comparison of Dutch and ancient Greek trade.

Beyer, Hartmann. Quaestiones in libellum De sphaera Joannis de Sacro Busto, in gratiam studiosae ivventutis olim in Academia Witebergensi collectae. Frankfurt, Petri Brubachii, 1571. B258

The author uses the *Sphaera mundi* of Sacro Bosco as a basis for discussion of numerous problems in theoretical geography.

Bèze, Claude de. Letre du P. de Beze au Reverend Pere de La Chaize pur conserver à la veuve et au fils de feu Mr. Constance Ministre de Siam le bien qu'il a laissé dans le commerce de la Compagnie des Indes Orientales. n.p. [ca. 1689].　　B259
An account of the Siamese revolution of 1688 by a Jesuit who was there. It was written to the confessor of Louis XIV.

Bèze, Claude de. [Letter to Louis XIV concerning events in Siam, 1688.] Corrected draft. n.p., 1690.　　B260
A plea by a Jesuit prominent in French efforts in Siam prior to 1688 on behalf of the widow of France's agent, Constant Phaulkon, for the restoration of the family fortune to her.

Bézout, Etienne. Suite du cours de mathématiques, a l'usage des gardes du pavillon et de la marine: contenant le traité de navigation. Paris, Ph.-D Pierres, 1794.　　B261
A continuation of the author's *Cours de mathématiques*, this work makes the connection between mathematical theory and the practice of navigation, including pilotage, use of charts and nautical instruments.

Biard, Pierre. Relation de la Nouvelle France, de ses terres, naturel du païs, & des habitans, item, du voyage des peres jesuites ausdictes contrées, & de ce qu'ils y ont faict jusques à leur prinse par les Anglois ... Lyons, Louys Muguet, 1616.　　B262
This is the first Jesuit account of New France, based on a residence in Acadia beginning in 1611 and ending in 1613. It describes in detail the land, natural history, and people, and is an optimistic statement of France's possibilities there as well as for Christian missions.

Bible. Psalterium, Hebreum, Grecum, Arabicum, & Chaldeum, cum tribus Latinis interpretationibus & glossis. Genoa, P. P. Porrus, 1516.　　B263
This polyglot Bible contains a biography of Christopher Columbus, noting the effect of his discovery upon Spain and the newly found islands.

Bickerse beroerten, ofte Hollandtschen eclypsis, teghen den helderen dagheraedt der provintie van Hollandt. n.p., 1650.　　B264
This pamphlet began a controversy over the reasons for the decline of the Dutch West India Company. Bicker was the mayor of the Amsterdam, and since that city had not supported the company, some of its proponents blamed him for its weakened position.

Bickham, George. The British monarch: or, A new chorographical description of all the dominions subject to the king of Great Britain. London, G. Bickham, 1748.　　B265
This volume was produced entirely from copper engravings, including five maps and texts describing the British counties and the North American colonies.

Biet, Antoine. Voyage de la France equinoxiale en l'isle de Cayenne, enterpris par les François. Paris, F. Clouzier, 1664.　　B266
An account of an attempt by the French to colonize in northern South America, with a description of the region.

Bigges, Walter. Expeditio Francisci Draki equitis Angli in Indias Occidentales A.M.D.LXXXV. Leiden, Fr. Raphelengium, 1588.　　B267
An account of Drake's West Indian expedition of 1585-86, illustrated with four hand-colored maps by Baptista Boazio.

Bigges, Walter. A summarie and true discourse of Sir Frances Drakes West Indian voyage. London, Richard Field, 1589.　　B268
This English edition has a dedication to the earl of Essex by Thomas Cates, a participant in the expedition.

Bijnkershoek, Cornelis van. De lege Rhodia de jactu liber singularis. Et de dominio maris dissertatio. The Hage, Joannem Verbessel, 1703.　　B269
A dissertation on the sea law of Rhodes.

Bijnkershoek, Cornelis van. Opera omina, in quibus multa ex Romano veteri ... Edidit et praefatus est B. Philippus Vicat. Geneva, Marci-Michaelis Bousquet & Chapuis, 1761.　　B270
The collected works, many of them dealing with international law.

Bijnkershoek, Cornelis van. Traité de juge competent des ambassadeurs, tant pour le civil, que pour le criminel. Traduit du Latin ... par Jean Barbeyrac. La Haye, Thomas Johnson, 1723.　　B271
A discussion of the legal status of ambassadors in the country of residence, dealing incidentally with their participation in commerce.

[Billardon-Sauvigny, Edme.] L'une et l'autre ou la noblesse commerçante et militaire. Avec reflexions sur le commerce, & les moyens de l'encourager. Mahaon [i.e. Paris] Williams Blakeney, 1756.　　B272
A continuation of the debate begun by Gabriel François Coyer's *La noblesse commerçante*.

Billon de Canserilles. Les intérêts des princes et les règles infallibles de bien gouverner un etat. Manuscript. Paris, 1720.　　B273
A work of 490 pages which the author addresses to Louis XV of France. Noting his great experience in overseas trade, he proposes numerous policies to restore French commerce. Most are in the direction of free trade.

[Bindon, David.] A letter from a merchant who has left off trade to a member of Parliament. London, R. Willock, 1738.   B274
   An argument on behalf of a restrictive tariff on imported linens to encourage local manufacture.

Bing, Lars Hess. Beskrivelse over kongeriget Norge, øerne Island og Faerøerne, samt Grønland ... forsattet i alphabetisk orden af Lars Hess Bing ... Copenhagen, Gyldendals Forlag, 1796.   B275
   A gazetteer describing all of the territories ruled by Denmark.

Bingham, William. A letter from an American, now resident in London, to a member of Parliament, on the subject of the restraining proclamation, and containing strictures on Lord Sheffield's pamphlet, on the commerce of the American states. Philadelphia, Robert Bell, 1784.   B276
   A collection of three tracts dealing with the outcome of the American Revolution in terms of resuming trade relations, and the treatment of American Loyalists.

Biörenklou, Matthias. Copie van een brief ... waer in verhael worden alle de dinghen ... n.p., 1656.   B277
   Reports on the war between Sweden and Poland.

Bion, N. (Nicolas). L'usage des globes céleste et terrestre, et des spheres suivant les differens systemes du monde. Paris, Michel Brunet [etc.] 1728.   B278
   The fifth edition of a textbook of astronomy and geography.

Biondo, Michelangelo. De ventis et navigatione. Venice, Cominum de Tridino Montisferrati, 1546.   B279
   The latter parts of the book, titled "Nove navigationis doctrina" and "De navigatione oceani ad novum orbem," treat new methods used in navigation.

[Biron, Claude.] Curiositez de la nature et de l'art, aportées dans deux voyages des Indes: l'un aux Indes d'Occident en 1698.& 1699. & L'autre aux Indes d'Orient en 1701. & 1702. Avec une relation abregée de ces deux voyages. Paris, Jean Moreau, 1703.   B280
   Relating primarily to the East Indies, this is largely a compendium of information on the natural history, music, medicine, architecture and other aspects of Asia.

Bizzarri, Pietro. Pannonicum Bellum, sub Maximiliano II. Rom. et Solymano Turcar. Basel, Sebastian Henricpetri, 1573.   B281
   The second edition of this history of sixteenth-century wars against the Turks, containing one of the earliest accounts of French efforts in establishing a settlement in Florida.

Bizzarri, Pietro. Senatus populique Genuensis rerum domi forisque gestarum historiae atque annales: cum luculenta variarum rerum cognitione dignissimarum, quae diversis temporibus, & potissimum hac nostra tempestate contigerunt, enarratione. Antwerp, Christophori Plantini, 1579.   B282
   This history of Genoa includes references to the republic's eastern commercial outposts in the late medieval period, commercial rivalries in the Mediterranean, and a chapter on Columbus and his voyages to America.

Björck, Eric Tobias. Ett ömt fast än enfaldigt fahr-wäl, af en ringa herde för Christi späda hiord wid Christina strander in Pennsilvanien och America nedlagt, tå han efter siutton åhrs forlop. Stockholm, Kongl. Boktryckeriet, 1715.   B283
   Eric T. Björck was one of two pastors selected to go out to New Sweden in 1697. He served there until 1713, and this is a farewell poem written to his congregation there.

Björck, Tobias E. (Tobias Eric). Dissertatio gradualis, de plantatione ecclesiae svecanae in America. Upsala, Literis Wernerianis [1731].   B284
   An outline history of the Swedish church in America by the son of Eric Tobias Björck.

[Black, David, writer on commerce.] Essay upon industry and trade. Edinburgh, J. Watson, 1706.   B285
   An argument for strict regulation of trade, especially on the exporting of commodities in less than their final manufactured state.

[Black, William.] Remarks upon a pamphlet, intitled, *The considerations in relation to trade considered.* [Edinburgh, 1706.]   B286
   This pamphlet contends that possible gains accruing to Scotland through customs union with England would be offset by higher rates imposed upon Scottish trade.

[Black, William.] A short view of our present trade and taxes, compared with what these taxes may amount to after the Union. [Edinburgh, 1706.]   B287
   The author sees a setback to Scottish commerce through the proposed union with England due to higher rates that would result from the customs union.

[Black, William]. Some considerations in relation to trade, humbly offered to His Grace, Her Majesty's high commissioner and the estates of Parliament. [Edinburgh] 1706.   B288
   A statement of Scottish concerns over that nation's commerce if the union with England were to be accomplished.

[Black, William]. Some overtures and cautions in relation to trade and taxes, humbly offered to the Parliament. n.p., 1707.   B289

A consideration of economic problems the author feels need to be addressed as a result of the union of England and Scotland.

Blackford, Dominique de. Précis de l'état actuel des colonies angloises dans l'Amérique Septentrionale. Milan, Freres Reycends, 1771.
B290
Contains a description of the British-American colonies based largely on previously published sources, and a French translation of Benjamin Franklin's testimony before the House of Commons in 1766 relative to the Stamp Act of 1765.

Blackwell, Isaac. A description of the province and bay of Darian. Edinburgh, Heirs and successors of Andrew Anderson, 1699. B291
A propaganda pamphlet, advertising the wonders of Darien as an inducement to settlers.

Blaeu, Joan. Le grand atlas. Amsterdam, J. Blaeu, 1667. B292
The French edition of the *Atlas major*, a twelve-volume set containing nearly 600 hand-colored maps and plates.

Blaeu, Willem Janszoon. Institutio astronomica de usu globorum & sphaerarum caelestium ac terrestrium ... Amsterdam, Joh. & Cornelium Blaeu, 1640. B293
A popular astronomy text, first published in a Dutch edition of 1620, and particularly concerns instruction in the use of globes according to both the Copernican and Ptolemaic systems.

[Blanch, John.] An abstract of the grievances of trade which oppress our poor. Humbly offered to the Parliament. London, 1694. B294
A series of complaints chiefly concerning the woolen trade in which workers were badly paid and frequently unemployed.

[Blanch, John.] The naked truth, in an essay upon trade: with some proposals for bringing the ballance on our side. London, 1696. B295
A survey of English overseas trade, noting losses through the importing of East India cloths, and the harmful effects of monopoly in other aspects of the economy.

Blanckley, Thomas Riley. A naval expositor, shewing and explaining the words and terms of art belonging to the parts, qualities, and proportions of building, rigging, furnishing, & fitting a ship for sea. London, E. Owen, 1750. B296
The only edition of this naval dictionary, with over 300 engravings by Paul Fourdrinier. Apparently the book was influential as Falconer used it in his important work *Universal dictionary of the marine*.

Blefken, Dithmar. Islandia, sive populorum & mirabilium quae in ea insula reperiuntur accuratior descriptio. Leiden, Henrici ab Haestens, 1607. B297
The first edition of an account of trade and travel in both Iceland and Greenland, by a German preacher accompanying merchants from Hamburg in 1563.

Blefken, Dithmar. Scheeps-togt na Ysland en Groenland. Leiden, P. Van der Aa, 1706.
B298
This Dutch edition is part of Pieter Van der Aa's great collection of voyages and travels to all parts of the world.

Bleyswijck, Dirck van. Beschryvinge der stadt Delft. Delft, Arnold Bon, 1667. B299
Contains information on the relation of Delft to the Dutch East and West India companies.

Bligh, William. A narrative of the mutiny, on board His Majesty's ship *Bounty*; and the subsequent voyage of part of the crew, in the ship's boat. London, For George Nicol, 1790. B300
Bligh's account of the voyage of survival made by him and the eighteen men cast adrift by the mutineers on the *Bounty*.

Bligh, William. Relation de l'enlevement du navire le Bounty, appartenant au roi d'Angleterre, & commandé par le lieutenant Guillaume Bligh; avec le voyage subséquent de cet officier & d'une partie de son équipage dans sa chaloupe ... Paris, Firmin Didot; Amsterdam, Gabriel Dufour, 1790. B301
This French edition contains an extended introduction by the translator Daniel Lescallier, much of it dealing with discipline aboard ship.

Bligh, William. Resa i Söderhafvet åren 1788, 1789, 1790. Hans half-årige vistande på ön O-taheiti och hemresa från ön Timor till England. Nyköping, Joh. Pet. Hammarin, 1795. B302
This Swedish edition, apparently based on the 1793 German edition by Georg Forster, deals almost entirely with the voyage to Tahiti, and very slightly with subsequent events of the voyage.

Blin, François Pierre. Opinion ... sur les réclamations adressées à l'Assemblée nationale par les députés extraordinaires du commerce & des manufactures de France, relativement aux colonies. [n.p., 1790.] B303
A demonstration of the value of France's West Indian colonies with recommendations for their governance.

Blome, Richard. L'Amerique angloise, ou, Description des isles et terres du roi d'Angleterre, dans l'Amerique. Traduit de l'Anglois. Amsterdam, Abraham Wolfgang, 1688. B304
A translation of *The present state of His Majesties isles and territories in America*, published in 1687, with a brief introduction.

Blome, Richard. A geographical description of the four parts of the world. London, T.N. for R. Blome, 1670.   B305
    First edition of a popular geography based upon the work of Nicholas Sanson.

Blome, Richard. The present state of His Majesties isles and territories in America. London, H. Clark, 1687.   B306
    A report on the various American colonies, noting their resources, climate, and productiveness.

Blondeau, Etienne-Nicolas, editor. Journal de marine, ou Bibliothéque raisonnée de la science du navigateur. Brest, R. Malassis, 1778-80.   B307
    This journal was issued in sixteen parts between June 25, 1778, and December 20, 1780. It contains many essays of importance to seamanship, on subjects including laws, navigating techniques, naval architecture, and health and sanitation aboard ship.

Blondel Saint-Aubin, Guillaume. Le tresor de la navigation divise en deux parties ... Havre de Grace, Jacques Hubault, 1697.   B308
    A treatise on spherical geometry as it applies to problems of navigation, first published in 1673.

Blount, Sir Henry. A voyage into the Levant. London, I.L. for A. Crooke, 1636.   B309
    An account of a journey to Turkey, with descriptions of the commerce carried on by the Turks.

Bluett, Thomas. Some memoirs of the life of Job, the son of Solomon the High Priest of Boonda in Africa; who was a slave about two years in Maryland; and afterwards being brought to England, was set free, and sent to his native land in the year 1734. London, Printed for Richard Ford, 1734.   B310
    An account of the enslavement and eventual liberation of a member of an African royal family, illustrative of aspects of the slave trade in Africa and in America.

Blundeville, Thomas. M. Blundevile his exercises, containing eight treatises. London, John Windet, 1606.   B311
    Includes accounts of the circumnavigations of Drake and Cavendish as well as a description of a world map by Petrus Plancius.

Boazio, Baptisto. The famous West Indian voyadge made by the Englishe fleete of 23 shippes and barkes ... begon from Plimmouth in the moneth of September 1585 and ended at Portesmouth in Julie 1586 ... [n.p., ca. 1589.]   B312
    This map measures 41.7 x 55.3 cm. and is in contemporary coloring. It traces both the outward and return routes of the fleet.

Bodinier, Toussaint. [Contract agreement to employ and equip the ship *La Marie*, commanded by Capt. La Roux to fish off Newfoundland. Manuscript in French. St. Malo, 19 April 1775.]   B313
    The contract contains the signatures of officers and crew. It directs them to take tobacco as cargo if the fishing catch is unsatisfactory.

't Boeck der Zee-rechten. Inhoundende dat hoochste ende oudtste Gotlantsche water-recht dat de gemeene kooplieden ende schippers geordineert ende ghemaeckt hebben tot Wisbuy. Amsterdam, 1645-1716.   B314
    A collection of six editions of the *Zee-rechten* together with additional separately published laws relating to maritime affairs and commentaries on Dutch sea law.

't Boeck der Zee-rechten: inhoudende dat hooghste ende oudtste Gotlantsche water-recht, dat de gemeene koop-lieden ende schippers geordineert ende gemaeckt hebben tot Wisbuy: de zee-rechten gemaeckt by Keyser Karel ...: mitsgaders de schips-rechten ghemaeckt by de oude Hanze-steden: als mede de Instructie ende ordonnantie voor de Commissarissen van de zee-saken t'Amstelredam ... Middelburgh, François Kroock, 1664.   B315

Boecler, Johann Heinrich. Hannonis Periplus. Strassburg, J. Staedel, 1661.   B316
    A dissertation on the navigation of Hanno down the west African coast about 530 B.C.

Boemus, Joannes. Repertorium librorum trium ... de omnium gentium ritibus. [Augsburg, S. Grim & M. Wirsung] 1520.   B317
    The first edition of an account of the peoples of Europe, Asia, and Africa, with descriptions of their customs, including some account of their trade.

[Boemus, Joannes.] De situ ac moribus regnorum que hac praesentis Europae, charta continentur ... epitome. Nuremberg, Christopher Zelle [ca. 1530].   B318
    A very greatly condensed epitome.

Boemus, Joannes. Omnium gentium mores, leges, & ritus ex ultis clarissimis rerum scriptoribus. Antwerp, Joannis Steelsii, 1537.   B319
    This edition includes *De regionibus septentrionalibus* by Jacob Ziegler, in an abridged edition.

Boemus, Joannes. Mores, leges, et ritus omnium gentium. Lyons, Seb. Gryphium, 1541.   B320
    This edition is much expanded over the first one of 1520. It is the first Latin edition to bear this inverted version of the title.

Boemus, Joannes. Omnium gentium mores, leges, & ritus ... Antwerp, J. Steelsii, 1542.
B321
Second printing by J. Steelsius of this popular work.

Boemus, Joannes. Mores, leges, et ritus omnium gentium. [Geneva], J. Tornaesium, 1591.
B322
Added to this edition are Damiao de Góis's *Fides, religio, et mores Æthiopum* and selections from Joseph Juste Scaliger's work on Ethiopia.

Boemus, Joannes. Mores, leges, et ritus omnium gentium. Lyon, J. de Tournes, 1582. B323
A pocket size edition.

Boemus, Joannes. Recueil de diverses histoires touchant les situations de toutes regions et pays. Paris, Galiot du Pre, 1539. B324
The first French edition.

Boemus, Joannes. Gli costumi, le leggi, et l'usanze de tutte le genti ... Venice, M. Tramezino, 1542. B325
The first Italian edition.

Boemus, Joannes. Gli costumi le leggi, et l'usanze di tutte le genti. Venice, M. Tramezino, 1549. B326
The second Italian edition.

Boemus, Joannes. Gli costumi, le leggi, et lusanze di tutte le genti. Venice, Francesco Lorenzini, 1560. B327
This Italian edition includes the section on the New World by Girolamo Giglio, first published in 1558.

Boemus, Joannes. I costumi le leggi, et l'usanze di tutte le genti ... tradotti per Lucio Fanno ... Aggiuntoui di nuou il Quarto Libro, nelqua si narra i costumi, & l'usanze dell' Indie Occidentali ... da M. Pre. Gieronimo Giglio. Venice, Dominico & Alvise Giglio, 1565.
B328
This edition appears to be the first to add a fourth part.

Boemus, Joannes. The fardle of facions conteining aunciente manners, customes, and lawes, of the peoples enhabiting the two partes of the earth, called Affrike and Asie. London, Jhon Kingstone and Henry Sutton, 1555. B329
The first English edition, translated by William Watreman.

Boemus, Joannes. The fardle of facions conteining the aunciente maners, customes, and lawes, of the peoples enhabiting the two partes of the earth, called Affrike and Asie. London, John Kingstone and Henry Sutton, 1555. B330
The first complete English edition of the early version of this work.

Boemus, Joannes. The manners, lawes, and customes of all nations. London. George Eld, 1611.
B331
The first English edition of the complete text.

Boemus, Joannes. Historia moralis, das ist, warhafftige Erzelung aller vornemsten geistlichen unnd weltlichen Regimenten, mancherley Sitten und Gewonheiten, welche alle und jede Völker durch die gantze Welt, in Africa, Asia, Europa und America vorzeiten gehabt ... Frankfurt am Main, Ludwig Bitsch, 1604. B332
This German edition contains the four parts common to the later editions of Boemus' work, but the America section appears to be original with the translator-editor, Johann Homberg.

Bogaert, Abraham. Historische reizen door d'oostersche deelen van Asia. Amsterdam, Nicolaas ten Hoorn, 1711. B333
A doctor in the service of the Dutch East India Company recounts his travels to the East Indies, noting particularly the French-Dutch rivalry in Siam.

Bohn, Gottfried Christian. Neueröffnetes Waarenlager. Hamburg, Johann Carl Bohn, 1763. B334
A commercial dictionary identifying the origins, characteristics, and uses of numerous commodities.

Bohn, Gottfried Christian. Wohlerfahrener Kaufmann. Hamburg, Johann Carl Bohn, 1762.
B335
Reviews trade regulations and commercial policies of the major German cities and of all the European countries.

Boileau, D. (Daniel). An introduction to the study of political economy, or, elementary view of the manner in which the wealth of nations is produced, increased, distributed, and consumed. London, T. Cadell and W. Davies, 1811.
B336
Designed by the author as an introduction to Adam Smith's *Wealth of nations*. Boileau also wrote treatises on both the French and German languages.

Boileau Despréaux, Nicolas. Satire XII. sur l'equivoque. n.p., 1711. B337
A satire on ambiguity relating to the Jesuits and their adversaries in France.

[Boisguilbert, P. Le Pesant de (Pierre Le Pesant).] Le detail de la France. n.p., 1695.
B338
A survey of the causes of French commercial decline, with recommendations of lower taxes and more free trade as the means to recovery.

[Boisguilbert, P. Le Pesant de (Pierre Le Pesant).] Le detail de la France, sous le regne present. n.p., 1707. B339

A discussion of the causes of France's economic decline, with emphasis on the effects of the export of grain.

Boisseau, Jean. Description de la Nouvelle France. Paris, J. Boisseau, 1643. B340
A 13½ x 21½ inch map portraying North America from Greenland to Virginia and from the Grand Banks to Lake Huron.

Boisseau, Jean. Geographie eclesiastique. Paris, Jean Boisseau, 1640. B341
A broadside instructional device, illustrating ecclesiastical jurisdictions within the Roman Catholic church.

Boisseau, Jean. Table generalle des longitudes et latitudes des villes plus renommées du monde. Paris, Louis Boissevin, 1649. B342
A tool for the student of geography, this broadside contains six circles within which are located the major cities of the world in relationship to each other.

Boissise, Jean-Robert de Thumery, sieur de. Propositie van der Heere de Boysye. n.p., 1618. B343
A proposal to the Dutch by the French ambassador for joint action against pirates in the Mediterranean.

Boissy, Lieutenant de. Manuscript letter signed. Canton, 21 February 1699. B344
The author was the brother of Jourdan de Boissy, the merchant chiefly responsible for the voyage of the *Amphitrite*, the first French commercial ship sent to China. He describes commercial opportunities there.

Boitard, Louis Pierre, engr. British resentment or the French fairly coopt at Louisbourg. London, For T. Bowles and J. Bowles and Son, 1755. B345
A cartoon exhibiting British optimism for success in the forthcoming conflict with France, based on a minor naval engagement off Newfoundland.

Bolingbroke, Henry St. John, Viscount. The craftsman extraordinary. London, For R. Francklin, 1729. B346
A pamphlet discussing the effectiveness of the protection given English merchant ships in the West Indies.

Bolingbroke, Henry St. John, Viscount. A letter to Caleb d'Anvers, Esq., concerning the state of affairs in Europe. London, For R. Francklin, 1730. B347
This pamphlet shows concern for the security of Gibraltar and England's Mediterranean trade.

[Bollan, William.] Coloniae anglicanae illustratae: or, the acquest of dominion, and the plantation of colonies made by the English in America. With the rights of the colonists, examined, stated, and illustrated. London, 1762. B348

This first part of an intended larger work relates early geographical knowledge to Portuguese exploration down the west coast of Africa in the fifteenth century. The proposed work was intended as a justification of colonial rights.

[Bollan, William.] The Free Britons memorial, to all the freeholders, citizens and burgesses, who elect the members of the British Parliament. London, For J. Williams, 1769. B349
An argument supporting Parliament and the electors of members as the guardians of liberty, particularly as a restraint upon ministers and soldiers. The author is particularly concerned about threats to civil liberties in the American colonies.

[Bollan, William.] The importance, and advantage of Cape Breton. London, John and Paul Knapton, 1746. B350
A discussion about French and English contention over this island of strategic and commercial importance until the siege of Louisburg in 1745 when the English gained temporary supremacy.

Bollan, William. The petitions of Mr. Bollan, agent for the Council of the Province of Massachusetts Bay, lately presented to the two houses of Parliament ... London, J. Almon, 1774. B351
A petition urging the loyalty of Massachusetts to the crown, demonstrating past support for British military campaigns in America and contending that closing the port of Boston would have a destructive effect on the merchant community which was not responsible for events such as the Boston Tea Party.

[Bollan, William.] A succinct view of the origin of our colonies. London, 1766. B352
The author shows deep concern for the loss of American trade as conflicts with English policy appeared.

Bologna (Italy). Compagnia Dei Drappieri. Statuti della Compagnia ... reformati ultimamente l'anno MDLVI. Bologna, P. Bonardo, 1557. B353
Contains twenty-five chapters, with commentary on the principal statutes in existence at the time of publication.

Bologna (Italy). Compagnia Dei Drappieri. Della reduttione delli numeri necessarii alli partiti ... Bologna, Alessandro Benaccio, 1560. B354
A request for a reduction in the number of members necessary to make up a quorum in meetings of the company.

Bologna (Italy). Compagnia Dei Drappieri. Fabius Mirtus Archiepisc. Nazarenus Bonon. &c. Bologna, Jo. Baptistae Ferronij [1589]. B355
A collection of contracts and other official documents by members of the company.

Bologna (Italy). Compagnia Dei Drappieri. Riforma et ordini nuovi da osservarsi nel Conseglio et Compagnia de Drappieri. Bologna, Vittorio Benacci, 1594. B356
The first edition, giving additions, revisions, and modifications to statutes then in existence, with explanatory notes printed in the margins.

Bologna (Italy). Compagnia Dei Drappieri. All' Illmo. Sig. Consaloniero, & Illmo. Senato ... [Bologna, ca. 1650.] B357
A petition by the guild that the term "draper" be registered for its exclusive use.

Bologna (Italy). Compagnia Dei Drappieri. Riforma et ordini nuovi da osservarsi nel conseglio, e Compagnia de' Drappieri. Bologna, Gio. Battista Ferroni, 1667. B358
This is largely a reprint of material found in the 1594 edition, but with fewer marginal notes.

Bologna (Italy). Compagnia Dei Drappieri. Ordine, et provisione da osservarsi in fare le imborsationi de gli officij della Compagnia. Bologna, Gio. Battista Ferroni, 1668. B359
Concerns the selection of officers and other matters pertaining to the administration of the company.

Bologna (Italy). Compagnia Dei Drappieri. Jesus Maria. Antichissima, e cospicua è l'Università e Compagnia de Drappieri. Bologna, Manolissi, 1677. B360
A chronological list of statutes, papal bulls, and other documents relating to the history of the drapers' guild of Bologna.

Bologna (Italy). Laws, etc. Statuti, ed ordini per l'onoranda arte de' fabbricatori di tele detti comunemente tovagliari approvati dall' illustrissimo, ed eccelso Senato di Bologna nel di 15 Dicembre 1733. Bologna, Clemente Maria Sassi, 1734. B361
A collection of regulations governing cloth manufacture in Bologna.

Bologna (Italy). Merchants. Capitoli da osservarsi per li sensali, secondo la forma delli statuti del foro de' mercanti di Bologna. Bologna, Vittorio Benacci, 1618. B362
A set of revisions in Bologna's mercantile code, concerning brokers primarily.

Bologna (Italy). Merchants. Addizione a gli statuti del foro de' mercanti della citta' di Bologna. Bologna, Stamperia Camerale [1791]. B363
The merchants of Bologna were apparently in need of additional funds for their organization so they levied seven new or increased taxes on themselves.

Bolton, Morgan & Co. [Letters to Robert and William Heysham, merchants, London.] Manuscript. Lisbon and Madeira, 1697-1713. B364
The correspondence covers trade in grain, wines, cloth and other goods, and reflects commerce with the New World as well as with Europe.

Bolts, William. Considerations on India affairs. London, For J. Almon [etc.] 1772-75. B365
A series of arguments questioning the wisdom of the East India Company's management of Indian commerce and government, supported by numerous documents. The author was a former servant of the Company.

[Bolts, William.] État civil, politique, et commerçant du Bengale. Maestricht, J.E. Dufour, 1775. B366
Includes considerable material on the commerce of the East India Company in Bengal.

Bonardo Fratteggiano, Gio. Maria. La minera del mondo ... nella qual si tratta delle cose più secrete, e più rare de' corpi semplici nel mondo elementare, e de' corpi composti, inanimati, & animati d'anima vegatativa, sensitiva, e ragionevole ... Venice, Fabio & Agostin Zoppini Fratelli, 1585. B367
The *Dizionario Biografico degli Italiani* refers to this as a "gleaning of imaginary notices" on the natural history of the world.

Bond, Denis. A true and exact particular and inventory of all and singular the lands, tenements and hereditaments, goods, chattels, debts and personal estate whatsoever, of Denis Bond ... London, S. Buckley, 1732. B368
Bond was involved in a scandal concerning the management of the Charitable Corporation for the Relief of the Industrious Poor. See also the entry pertaining to this subject under Sir Robert Sutton.

Bonne, Rigobert and Nicolas Desmarest. Atlas encyclopédique, contenant la géographie ancienne, et quelques cartes sur la géographie du moyen âge ... Padua, 1789-90. B369
A collection of 140 maps including an introductory group which depicts the earth as it was known to the ancients.

Bonner, Thomas. [Autograph journal of a voyage to India aboard the *Expedition*.] Manuscript. January 24, 1615, to June 18, 1616. B370
This journal records the voyage of a fleet commanded by William Keeling which carried Sir Thomas Roe on his embassy to the Great Mogul and continued on down the west coast of India to Ceylon and eastward to Indonesia.

[Bonnet, J.-Esprit.] Reponse aux principales questions que peuvent être faites sur les États-Unies de l'Amérique, par un citoyen adoptif de la Pensylvanie. Lausanne, Henri Vincent, 1795.

B371

This description of life in the United States incorporates 137 questions of the type likely to be asked by intending immigrants, with answers provided in the main body of the text.

[Bonneville, Zacharie de Pazzi de.] De l'Amérique et des Américains, ou Observations curieuses du philosophe la douceur ... Berlin, S. Pitra, 1771. B372

Bonneville, a military engineer, here criticizes both de Pauw's *Recherches philosophiques sur les Américains* and his *Défense* ... . The work has been attributed to Pierre Poivre and Antoine-Joseph Pernety but Sabin, among others, attributes it to Bonneville.

Bonnus, Hermann. Chronica der ... Geschichte unde Handel der keyserliken Stadt Lübeck. Magdeburg, Hans Walther, 1559. B373

A history of Lübeck, describing commercial relations with Sweden, Denmark, Holland, England, and various German cities.

Bontekoe, Willem Ysbrandsz. Journael ofte ... Oost-Indische reyse. Hoorn, Isaac Willemsz., 1646. B374

A narrative of a voyage to the East Indies from 1618 to 1625, with particular emphasis on the commerce of Java.

Bontekoe, Willem Ysbrandsz. Journael ofte ... Oost-Indische reyse. Hoorn, Isaac Willemsz. voor Jan Jansz. Deutel, 1648. B375

This is the second Hoorn edition, containing additions to the Spitzbergen narrative of Dirk Albertsz Raven.

Bontekoe, Willem Ysbrandsz. Le voyage ... aux Indes Orientales. Amsterdam, Daniel du Fresne, 1681. B376

The only earlier French printing of this narrative is in Thevenot's *Relations de divers voyages*.

Bontier, Pierre, and Jean le Verrier. Histoire de la premiere descouverte et conqueste des Canaries. Paris, Michel Soly, 1630. B377

In addition to the account of the colonization of the Canary Islands by Jean de Béthencourt, this volume also contains Pierre Bergeron's *Traicté de la navigation*, a general history of European overseas expansion.

Boothby, Richard. A briefe discovery or description of the most famous island of Madagascar or St. Laurence in Asia neare unto East-India. London, E.G. for J. Hardesty, 1646. B378

This treatise was designed to interest English colonists in going to Madagascar, where a trading company was preparing to operate in competition with the East India Company.

Borba, Jozé de. Relaçaõ da viagem, que fez o excellentissimo, e reverendissimo bispo D. Fr. Joaõ de Faro para a sua Sé de Cidade da Ribeira Grande, Ilha de Sant-Iago de Cabo-Verde ... Lisbon, Miguel Manescal da Costa, 1741. B379

An account of a voyage of the Bishop of Cape Verde to his see, with some account of ecclesiastical events there to the time of his death.

Bordeaux (France). Armée patriotique bordelaise. Adresse de l'Armée patriotique bordelaise, a l'Assemblée nationale. [Bordeaux, Imprimerie de l'Armée patriotique bordelaise, 1790]. B380

A pamphlet pointing out the universality of slavery in warm climates, and the necessity of it in the French colonies in the West Indies.

Bordeaux (France). Chambre de Commerce. Extrait du registre des délibérations de la Chambre du commerce de la ville de Bordeaux. Paris, Imprimerie Nationale, 1791. B381

Contains addresses concerning the problems in the French colonies.

Bordone, Benedetto. Libro di Benedetto Bordone. Venice, Nicolo d'Aristotile, 1528. B382

The first edition of this book describing the islands of the world, including the West Indies, islands off the coast of Africa, and islands in the Indian Ocean.

Bordone, Benedetto. Isolario ... nel qual si ragiona di tutte le isole del mondo ... Ricorretto et di nuovo ristampato con la gionta del Monte del Oro novamente ritrovato. Venice, Francesco di Leno [1537]. B383

This edition contains three double-page maps, 109 maps in the text, and a diagram. It is the first edition to include the letter from the prefect of New Spain reporting the conquests of Pizarro.

Bordone, Benedetto. Isolario ... nel qual si ragiona di tutte l'isole del mondo. Venice, Federico Toresano, 1547. B384

The last edition of this well-known island book, including the letter describing Pizarro's conquests in Peru.

Borland, Francis. Memoirs of Darien. Glasgow, Hugh Brown, 1714. B385

A history of the Scots' colony at Darien with observations on the reasons for its failure, by one who went there with the settlers.

Borough, Sir John. An historical account of the royal fishery of Great Britain. London, E. Curll, 1720. B386

The account attempts to prove England's sovereignty over nearby seas, and cites the example of the Dutch to show what wealth can be gained from an active fishing industry.

Borrhaus, Martin. Cosmographiae elementa commentario. Basel, Joannem Oporinum, [1555]. B387
This is a more extensive edition of a commentary on the *Elementale cosmographicum* which evolved from lectures given by Borrhaus in the 1520s and was first published in Strassburg, 1539 and in some editions of Apianus's *Cosmographia*.

[Borrhaus, Martin.] Elementale cosmographicum, quo totius & astronomiae & geographiae rudimenta, certissimis brevissimisque docentur apodixibus. Paris, Gulielmum Cavellat, 1551. B388
An elementary text in cosmography and geography.

Borrhaus, Martin. Cosmographiae elementa commentatio. Basel, Joannem Oporinum, [1555]. B389
A commentary on the previous item by its author, incorporating additions to the text and a twelve-page introduction.

Borri, Christoforo. Relatione della nuova missione delli pp. della compagnia di Giesù, al regno della Cocincina. Rome & Bologna, Francesco Catanio, 1631. B390
A very early account of Cochin China by a missionary who accompanied the first mission there in 1618 and remained for four years.

Borri, Christoforo. Relation de la nouvelle mission ... au royaume de la Cochinchine. Lille, Pierre de Rache, 1631. B391
One of two French editions of the preceding work published in 1631.

[Bos, Lambert van den.] Leeven en daden der doorluchtighste zee-helden en ontdeckers van landen, deser eeuwen. Beginnende met Christoffel Columbus ... en eyndigende met den roemruchtigen admirael M. A. de Ruyter, Ridd. &c ... Amsterdam, Jan Claesz ten Hoorn, en Jan Bouman, 1676. B392
The first edition of a collection of biographies of explorers and naval heroes, including Spanish, Portuguese, English, Dutch, Italian and Arabian seamen. Portraits of many are included.

Bos, Lambert van den. Leben und Tapffere Thaten der aller-berühmtesten See-Helden, Admiralen und Land-Erfinder unserer Zeiten. Nuremberg, Christoph Endter, 1681. B393
The first German edition, containing material not published in the earlier Dutch editions.

Bos, Lambert van den. Tooneel des oorlogs, opgerecht in de Vereenigde Nederlanden; door de wapenen van de Koningen van Vrankryk en Engeland, ... Amsterdam, Jacob van Meurs en Johannes van Someren, 1675. B394
This chronicle of European war covering the period 1669-1674 includes numerous items concerning the East and West Indies, Russia, and Asia.

Bosanquet Family. Account book. Manuscript. n.p., 1684-1750. B395
A record of mercantile transactions of an active London firm with particular interests in the Levant. It contains comments on exchange, a wide variety of merchandise, and other mercantile matters.

Bosman, Willem. Nauwkeurige beschryving van de Guinese Goud-Tand-en Slave-Kust. Utrecht, Anthony Schouten, 1704. B396
An account of Dutch commercial activities in West Africa in the form of letters from Bosman to D. Havart in Rotterdam. Bosman was an employee of the Dutch West India Company.

Bosman, Willem. Naukeurige beschryving van de Goud- Tand- en Slavekust, nevens alle desselfs landen, koningryken, en gemenebesten. Amsterdam, Isaak Stockmans, 1709. B397
The second Dutch edition, with added illustrations of fortresses in Guinea, and two folding maps not in the first edition.

Bosman, Willem. A new and accurate description of the coast of Guinea. London, J. Knapton [etc.] 1705. B398
The first English edition.

Bosman, Willem. Voyage de Guinée, contenant une description nouvelle & très-exacte de cette côte ... Utrecht, Antoine Schouten, 1705. B399
The first French edition.

Bosman, Willem. Reyse nach Guinea. Hamburg, Samuel Heyl und Johann Gottfried Liebezeit, 1708. B400
The first German edition, translated from the Dutch edition.

Bosman, Willem. Viaggio in Guinea. Venice, Marcellino Piotto, 1752-54. B401
This Italian edition is a translation from the French edition.

Bossu, M. Nieuwe reizen naer Noord-Amerika ... Amsterdam, Steven van Esveldt, 1769. B402
The first Dutch edition of a work originally published in French in 1768, recounting the author's experiences in North America. He describes the Mississippi Valley, the area of the present southern states including Florida, and the West Indies.

Boston (Mass.). An appeal to the world; or A vindication of the town of Boston, from many false and malicious aspersions. Boston, Edes and Gill; London, For J. Almon, 1770. B403

The aspersions of disloyalty cast upon Bostonians by Governor Bernard in letters to the Ministry are here replied to, and his own motives and judgement in making them are called into question.

[Botelho, Nuno Álvares.] Relacion de la batalla que Nuño Albarez Botello, general de la armada de altobordo, del mar de la India, tuvo con las armadas de Olanda, y Ingalaterra en el Estrecho de Ormuz. Madrid, Bernardino de Guzman, 1626. B404
An account of Portuguese victories in the Persian Gulf over Dutch and English fleets in February, 1625.

Botero, Giovanni. De la ragione de stato, libri dieci ... Milan, Pacifico Pontio, ad instanza di Pietro Martire, 1598. B405
A socio-economic study of the state as a political entity with emphasis on contributing factors such as industry, agriculture, population and colonies. Reference is made to Spanish and Portuguese overseas empires.

Botero, Giovanni. Aggiunte di Gio. Botero Benese. Alla sua ragion di stato ... con una relatione del mare ... Pavia, Andrea Viani, 1598. B406
A supplement to his *De la ragione di stato*, with a section on the oceans which is of particular significance.

Botero, Giovanni. Relatione universale de' continenti del mondo nuovo. Rome, Giorgio Ferrari, 1595. B407
The New World part of Botero's geography, apparently issued separately, for it contains its own dedication, index, and collation. The geography was first published in an Italian edition of 1592, in four parts.

Botero, Giovanni. Le relationi universali. Venice, Agostino Angelieri, 1607-08. B408
A compendium of geographical knowledge first published in 1592. This Italian edition includes all four parts published in the original edition.

Botero, Giovanni. Le relationi universali. Venice, Alessandro Vecchi, 1612. B409
In six parts, the last two including essays on several subjects, among them a discourse on naming the island of Taprobane.

Botero, Giovanni. Le relationi universali. Venice, Alessandro Vecchi, 1618. B410
This edition includes illustrations depicting monsters and semi-human types based on Pliny and other fabulist authors.

Botero, Giovanni. Relationi universali ... Venice, Bertani, 1659. B411
A late edition of this popular universal geography.

Botero, Giovanni. Allgemeine Weltbeschreibung. Cologne, J. Gymnici, 1596. B412
The first German edition.

Botero, Giovanni. Theatrum principum orbis universi. Cologne, Lambert Andrea, 1596. B413
The first Latin edition of the second part of Botero's geography, containing twenty-one maps, and descriptions of areas in Asia.

Botero, Giovanni. Relaciones universales del mundo. Valladolid, Diego Fernandez de Cordova, 1603. B414
This Spanish edition contains the first two parts only, and these are entirely geographical in interest.

[Botero, Giovanni.] Relations of the most famous kingdoms and common-weales thorough the world. ... London, Printed for John Jaggard, 1611. B415
The third English edition.

Bottier, Jacques André. Pratique du commerce pour la facilité du négociant ... de l'Asie, de l'Afrique ... Turin, Guibert et Orgeas, 1780. B416
A handbook for international commerce.

Bottschaft des grossmechtigsten Konigs David, aus dem grossen und hohen Morenlend ... [Dresden, W. Stöckel, 1533.] B417
Contains a description of Ethiopia, a letter from the King of Portugal to Pope Clement VII concerning Ethiopia, and three letters from King David of Ethiopia.

Boturini Benaducci, Lorenzo. Idea de una nueva historia general de la America Septentrional. Madrid, Juan de Zuñigá, 1746. B418
A collection of information on many aspects of Aztec life and history, based upon the author's knowledge of the language and his collection of antiquities which is listed in an appendix.

[Boucher, Jonathan] A letter from a Virginian to the members of the congress to be held at Philadelphia on the first of September, 1774. n.p., 1774. B419
An attempt to dissuade the congress at Philadelphia from going forward with a non-importation agreement among the colonies.

Bougainville, Jean-Pierre de. Paralléle de l'expédition d'Alexandre dans les Indes avec la conquête des mêmes contrées par Tahmas-Kouli-Khan. n.p., 1752. B420
In this comparison of two conquests eastward from Persia into India, the author finds differences outweighing similarities.

Bougainville, Louis-Antoine de, comte. Voyage autour du monde. Paris, Saillant & Nyon, 1771. B421
The first account of Bougainville's circumnavigation, with descriptions and maps of places visited, including notes on the commerce of some little-known islands.

[**Bougainville, Louis-Antoine de, comte.**] Voyage autour du monde. Paris, Saillant & Nyon, 1772.   B422
> Includes also a translation of an account of the voyage of Banks and Solander, 1768-71.

Bougainville, Louis-Antoine de, comte. A voyage round the world ... in the years 1766, 1767, 1768, and 1769. London, J. Nourse and T. Davies, 1772.   B423
> The first English edition, translated by Johann Reinhold Forster who adds notes and commentary where he feels Bougainville needs correction.

[**Bougainville, Louis-Antoine de, comte.**] Voyage autour du monde, par la frégate du roi La Boudeuse et la flute l'Étoile, en 1766, 1767, 1768, & 1769. Neuchatel, Société Thypographique, 1773.   B424
> This edition does not include the maps.

Bougainville, Louis-Antoine de, comte. Reise um die Welt welche mit der Fregatte la Boudeuse in den Jahren 1766, 1767, 1768, und 1769 gemacht worden. Leipzig, Caspar Fritsch, 1772.   B425
> The first German edition.

Bougainville, Louis-Antoine de, comte. Reis rondom de weereldt. Dordrecht, Abraham Blussé en Zoon, 1772.   B426
> The first Dutch edition, containing Johann Reinhold Forster's comments on Bougainville's voyage, and Bougainville's rejoinders.

Bougard, R. Le petit flambeau de la mer, ou Le véritable guide des pilotes cotiers. Havre de Grace, P.J.D.G. Faure, 1770.   B427
> A popular pilot guide, devoted largely to Europe, but with some harbors and coast of Africa, India, and islands included.

Bouguer, J. (Jean). Traité complet de la navigation ... Paris, P. de Heuqueville, 1706.   B428
> A wide-ranging text on navigation theory and method, including geometry, logarithms, instruments, astronomy, tides, charts and journals.

Bouguer, M. (Pierre). De la mâture des vaisseaux ... Paris, Claude Jombert, 1727.   B429
> A mathematically-oriented work on the masting of ships.

Bouguer, M. (Pierre). De la mâture des vaisseaux, piece qui a concouru à l'occasion du prix proposé l'an 1727 par les messieurs de l'Academie Royal de Sciences. Paris, Claude Jombert, 1728.   B430
> The prize-winning essay of the French Royal Academy of Science, addressing the question of the best way to mast ships.

Bouguer, M. (Pierre). De la methode d'observer exactement sur mer la hauteur des astres. Paris, Claude Jombert, 1729.   B431
> The prize-winning essay for the French Royal Academy for 1729, being a response to their query about the best means to determine altitude of the stars at sea.

Bouguer, M. (Pierre). De la méthode d'observer en mer la declinasion de la boussole. Paris, Claude Jombert, 1731.   B432
> The prize-winning essay for the French Royal Academy for 1731, this treatise on the compass and magnetic variation includes construction of the compass and the author's theory for determining magnetic variation.

Bouguer, M. (Pierre). La figure de la terre. Paris, C. A. Jombert, 1749.   B433
> Written by a member of the La Condamine expedition of 1736, this book describes plant and animal life in Peru as well as scientific phenomena.

Bouguer, M. (Pierre). Justification des Memoires de l'Academie Royale des Sçiences de 1744. Et du livre De la figure de la terre. Paris, Charles-Antoine Jombert, 1752.   B434
> An explanation of methods of observation used by the La Condamine expedition to Peru in answer to questions raised by critics of the author's earlier publications.

Bouguer, M. (Pierre). Nouveau traité de navigation, contenant la théorie et la practique du pilotage. Paris, Hippolyte-Louis Guerin & Louis François Delatour, 1753.   B435
> The first edition of a standard text on navigation, addressing problems of triangulation, use of compass, sea charts, and instruments as well as the application of astronomy to navigation.

Bouguer, M. (Pierre). Nouveau traité de navigation, contenant la théorie et la practique du pilotage ... Revu & abrégé par M. l'abbé de La Caille ... Paris, H.L. Guerin & L.F. Delatour, 1760.   B436
> An abridged version of the 1753 edition.

Bouguer, M. (Pierre). Traité du navire, de sa construction, et de ses mouvemens. Paris, Ch. Ant. Jombert, 1746.   B437
> A thorough and largely theoretical treatment of all aspects of ship construction, including equipment, in relation to the maneuverablity of the ship.

Bouguier, Jean. Arrests de la cour decisifs de diverses questions. Paris, Edme Pepingué, 1647.   B438
> Contains a discourse on a proposed commercial company to carry on overseas trade, which reflects French thinking near the beginning of their formal extension of trade to America.

Bouillet. Traité des moyens de rendre les rivieres navigables. Paris, Estienne Michallet, 1693.

B439
Concerns plans for the development of French commerce through the improvement of river transportation.

Boulenger, Jean. Traite de la sphere du monde ... Paris, Jean Jombert, 1688.　　B440
The final edition of a popular textbook in astronomy first published in 1610.

Boulton, S. Africa, with all its states, kingdoms, republics, regions, islands, &ca ... and also a summary description relative to the trade and natural produce, manners and customs of the African continent and islands. London, Laurie & Whittle, 1794.　　B441
Based on d'Anville's map of Africa, this map is in two sheets which include considerable text of historical and geographical content. An inset map of the Gold Coast provides additional detail for that area.

Bourdon Desplanches, Louis Joseph. Projet nouveau sur la manière de faire utilement en France le commerce des grains. Brussels, et se trouve à Paris, Veuve Esprit, 1785.　　B442
Considers commercial restraints upon the grain trade and the merits of free trade in grain.

Le bourgeois politique et impartial d'Amsterdam, ou lettre d'un Hollandois a son correspondant de Marseille sur l'arrivee de la flotte russe dans la Mediterranée. Amsterdam, 1771.　　B443
An account of the trade between the Netherlands and Russia.

Bourges, Jacques de. Relation du voyage de monseigneur l'evéque de Beryte vicaire apostolique du royaume de la Cochinchine. Paris, Denys Bechet, 1666.　　B444
An account of a voyage to Thailand and Cochin China via Turkey, Persia, and India, with observations on the commerce, missionary establishments, and events of the voyage en route, and with detailed description of Thailand where a mission was being founded.

[Bourgoing, Jean-François, baron de.] Nouveau voyage en Espagne ... Paris, Regnault, 1788.　　B445
Contains information on Spanish overseas commerce, and on the Philippine Company.

Bourne, William. A regiment for the sea. London, T. Este for Thos. Wight, 1596.　　B446
The first book on navigation by an Englishman, first published in 1574. This edition has the added "Hidrographical discourse to show the passage unto Cattay five manner of waies, two of them known and three supposed."

Bouton, Jacques. Relation de l'establissement des François depuis l'an 1635, en l'isle de la Martinique. Paris, S. Cramoisy, 1640.　　B447
An early description of the French settlement on Martinique.

Bouvet, de Lozier. Addition au Memoires [to Compagnie des Indes Orientales]. Paris, Sept. 5, 1740.　　B448
This is an autograph copy of the original manuscript.

Bouvet, de Lozier. ALS to Jean Frédéric Phélypeaux, comte de Maurepas. Paris, Sept. 30, 1741.　　B449
Bouvet was an explorer of the southern oceans, and proposes to Maurepas and other officials that he be permitted to lead an expedition to establish a French commercial base on the island of Terra Australes de Espiritu Santo in the South Pacific.

Bouvet, de Lozier. Copies de lettree écrites à m. de F. [m. Orry de Fulvy]. Paris, April 22, 1741; June 10, 1741; July 15, 1741.　　B450
This is an autograph copy of the original.

Bouvet, de Lozier. Memoire [to m. Orry de Fulvy]. Paris, August 31, 1741.　　B451
This is an autograph copy of the original.

Bouvet, de Lozier. Memoire to m. Orry de Fulvy. Paris, August 9, 1741.　　B452
This is an autograph copy of the original.

Bouvet, de Lozier. Memoire [to m. Orry de Fulvy]. Paris, April 12, 1741.　　B453
This is an autograph copy of the original.

Bouvet, de Lozier. [Memoire to m. Orry de Fulvy]. [Paris] 8 February 1741.　　B454
This is an autograph copy of the original.

Bouvet, de Lozier. Memoire [to m. Orry de Fulvy]. Paris, Sept. 30, 1740 (i.e. 1741).　　B455
This is an autograph copy of the original.

Bouvet, de Lozier. Memoires [to the Compagnie des Indes Orientales]. Paris, January 1740.　　B456
This is an autograph copy of the original manuscript.

Bouvet, de Lozier. Troisieme memoire [to the Compagnie des Indes Orientales]. Paris, February 1, 1741.　　B457
This is an autograph copy of the original manuscript.

[Bouvet, Joachim.] Icon regia monarchae Sinarum nunc regnantis ex Gallico versa. n.p., 1699.　　B458
An account of the emperor of China, K'ang Hsi, representing him as a strong but just ruler who was tolerant of Christians and under whose rule Christianity would prosper.

Bouvet, Joachim. Istoria de l'imperador de la Cina presentata al re di Francia. Padua, Giuseppe Corona, 1710. B459
First Italian edition of an account of the emperor of China, K'ang Hsi, written by a Jesuit who had served him as royal mathematician.

Bouvet, Joachim. Manuscript Memoire. [Canton, 5 February 1699.] B460
An account of a visit to the "viceroy" by members of the *Amphitrite's* company to thank the emperor for the hospitality extended to this first French trading mission to China.

Bouvet, Joachim. Ristretto delle notizie circa l'uso della voce Cinese Sam-ti che significa supremus imperator ò vero Alti Dominus, e della voce Tien che significa Coelum ... [n.p., ca. 1699] B461
Bouvet enters the Chinese Rites controversy with a discussion of the Chinese concept of God and Heaven.

[Bowdoin, James] Opinions respecting the commercial intercourse between the United States of America and the dominions of Great Britain, including observations upon the necessity and importance of an American navigation act. Boston, Samuel Hall, 1797. B462
Bowdoin urges an American navigation act to give the United States greater equality in dealing with Great Britain.

Bowen, Emanuel. A complete atlas, or distinct view of the known world. London, For W. Innys [etc.] 1752. B463
A collection of sixty-nine maps, some of which are detailed maps of harbors, islands, and estuaries.

Bowens, Jacobus. Nauwkeurige beschryving der oude en beroemde zee-stad Oostende. Brugge, Joseph de Busscher, 1792. B464
This history of Ostend shows particular concern for the commercial development of the city, including material on the Ostend Company and on a maritime insurance company created in the late eighteenth century.

Bowles, Carington. Bowles's new and accurate map of the world, or terrestrial globe ... London, Carington Bowles [1783?]. B465
This large map shows the world in two hemispheres with the tracks of the circumnavigations of the late eighteenth century by Anson, Byron, Cook, etc. It also has a Mercator projection of the world along with various astronomical depictions, tables and rather extensive text.

Bowles, Carington. Bowles's new pocket map of the discoveries made by the Russians on the northwest coast of America. London, For the author [ca. 1770]. B466
A copy of Thomas Jefferys' map of 1761, which was in turn based on a map issued by the Russian Academy of Sciences in 1758.

Boyer, Paul. Veritable relation de tout ce qui s'est ... passé au voyage ... à l'Amérique Occidentale. Paris, Pierre Rocolet, 1654. B467
An account of a French colonial undertaking on Cayenne by Charles Poncet de Bretigny in 1643, together with an economic evaluation of the region.

Bracciolini, Poggio. De varietate fortunae liber IV. Manuscript. Italy, late 15th century. B468
Contains an account of the travels of Nicolo Conti, who traveled in the East for more than twenty-five years, and reported his travels to Poggio Bracciolini, papal secretary in the mid-fifteenth century.

Bracciolini, Poggio. Historia Fiorentina. [Venice, Jacopo de Rossi, 1476.] B469
The history of Florence primarily during the turbulent period 1350-1445.

Brand, Adam. Beschreibung der chinesischen Reise. Hamburg, Benjamin Schillern, 1698. B470
First edition of an account of a Russian embassy to China in 1692-94, containing descriptions of the caravan routes of inner Asia.

Brand, Adam. Relation du voyage de M. Evert Isbrand. Amsterdam, J. de Lorme, 1699. B471
The first French edition.

Brand, Adam. Seer aenmercklijcke land-en water-reyse ... uyt Muscouw na China. Tyel, Jan van Leeuwen, 1699. B472
The first Dutch edition.

Brand, Johann Arnhold von. Reysen durch die Marck Brandenburg, Preussen, Churland, Liefland, Plesscovien, Gross-Naugardien, Tweerien und Moscovien ... anbey eine seltsame und sehr anmerckliche Beschreibung von Siberien ... Wesel, Jacobs von Wesel, 1702. B473
An account of travels in the Baltic area and to Moscow in 1673, appending Albrecht Dobbin's narrative of travels in Siberia, both edited with extensive commentary by Henrich-Christian von Hennin.

Brandenburg (Electorate). Copie van een brief vande Keur-vorst van Brandenburg ... n.p., 1656. B474
The Elector of Brandenburg writes to the King of Poland, justifying his alliance with Sweden in the struggle for control of the Baltic trade.

Brandenburg (Electorate). Notificatie gedaen door de Heeren Daniel Weyman ende Johan Copes ... n.p., 1656. B475
Envoys of the Elector of Brandenburg state that their country joined forces with Sweden because of good Swedish offers and their inability to resist.

Brandewijns praetje. Over de Fransche saken tusschen blaeuwe kees, swarte jan, geele gerrit, en klaes sonder baerd. Antwerp, H. van Stavoren, 1657. B476
A discussion of naval hostility between the French and Dutch.

Brandt, Geeraert. Historie der vermaerde zee-en koopstadt Enkhuisen. Hoorn, Jacob Duyn, 1747. B477
A history of one of the important commercial cities of the Netherlands.

Brandt in Brasilien. [Netherlands?] 1648. B478
A pamphlet citing disadvantages of continued Dutch occupation of Pernambuco where rebellion continued.

Brant, Sebastian. Stultifera navis. J. de Olpe, 1497 [i.e. Nuremberg, G. Stuchs, ca. 1497]. B479
In this classic of German literature the author indicates a knowledge of the recent discoveries in the western Atlantic, although he scorns those who concern themselves with such matters.

De Brasilsche breede-byl; ofte t'samenspraek, tusschen kees jansz. Schott, komende uyt Brasil ... n.p., 1647. B480
This "Brazilian Broadaxe" is a criticism of the Dutch West India Company, presented in the form of a conversation among persons who had been in Brazil.

Brasilsche gelt-sack, waer in dat klaerlijck vertoont wort, waer dat de participanten van de West-Indische Compagnie haer geldt ghebleven is. Reciff in de Bree-Bijl [i.e. Netherlands] 1647. B481
An accusation of mismanagement against the directors of the Dutch West India Company in Brazil. Like the preceding item, it is written in the form of a conversation.

Brasyls schuyt-praetjen, ghehouden tusschen een officier, een domine, en een coopman. n.p., 1649. B482
A pamphlet critical of the Dutch West India Company and its management of affairs in Brazil.

Bravo, Francisco. Representacion, que hace a Su Magestad ... sobre el estado en que se halla actualmente el comercio del nuevo reyno de Granada. [Madrid, 1748.] B483
A discussion of the illicit commerce in gold and other commodities of New Granada with suggestions for improved regulations.

Bravo de Lagunas y Castilla, Pedro José. Voto consultivo, que ofrece al excelentissimo señor D. Joseph Antonio Manso de Velasco ... Lima, Calle del Tigre, 1755. B484
A treatise on the commerce of Peru and Chile, with particular emphasis on the grain trade.

Breeden-raedt aende Vereenichde Nederlandsche provintien. Antwerp, Francoys van Duynen, 1649. B485
A thorough condemnation of ghe government of colonies administered by the Dutch West India Company.

Brelin, Johan. Beskrifning öfver en äfventyrlig resa til och ifrän Ost-Indien. Upsala, Kongl. Acad. Tryckeriet, 1758. B486
An account of a voyage to the East Indies made in 1755-57 on behalf of the Swedish East India Company, with reports on the trade in Canton, Java, and Brazil.

Brereton, John. A briefe and true relation of the discovery of the north part of Virginia. London, George Bishop, 1602. B487
The second issue, describing an early English attempt at New England settlement, and including the "Inducements" of the elder Richard Hakluyt, written in 1585 and published here for the first time.

Brerewood, Edward. Enquiries touching the diversity of languages, and religions through the chiefe parts of the world. London, For John Bill, 1614. B488
Besides presenting the religions of the world and the areas dominated by them, Brerewood discusses the size and populations of little-known regions and even speculates on the size of the Great Southern Continent.

Brerewood, Edward. Enquiries touching the diversity of languages, and religions, through the chiefe parts of the world ... London, John Bill, 1622. B489
A close reprint of the 1614 edition, but with five pages added on the languages of Europe from Joseph Scaliger.

Brerewood, Edward. Recherches curieuses sur la diversité des langues et religions, par toutes les principales parties du monde. Paris, Oliver de Varennes, 1640. B490
The second issue of the first French edition, translated by Jean de La Montagne, and based on the second English edition.

Brescia (Italy). Laws, etc. Leges Brixianae. [Brescia, Angelus and Jacobus Britannicus, 1490.] B491
This collection of the laws of Brescia contains a section titled "Statuta Mercantie" which deals with more than a hundred aspects of the trade of the city. Fourteen manuscript pages deal with early sixteenth-century laws.

Brescia (Italy). Laws, etc. Liber pactorum daciorum inclytae civitatis Brixiae. Venice, Ioannem Patauinum, 1552. B492
Contains information on many commercial activities of Brescia.

Bressani, Francesco Giuseppe. Breve relatione d'alcune missioni de' PP. della Compagnia di

Giesù nella Nuova Francia. Macerata, Heredi d'Agostino Grisei, 1653. B493
Bressani was an Italian Jesuit who served in Canada, survived capture by the Iroquois, and published this narrative in Italian in the hope of broadening European interest in the Canadian mission of the Jesuits.

Breuning von Buchenbach, Hans Jacob. Orientalische Reyss ... in der Turkey ... Egypten, Arabien etc. Strassburg, Johann Carolo, 1612. B494
Describes many of the leading commercial cities of the Near East.

Brev fra u til z; til geinsvar paa det trykte brev fra z til u, angaaende de opkomne tvistigheder I det Kongelige Asiatiske Compagnie I Kiøbenhavn. Copenhagen, Hegelunds Forlag hos J.F. Schultz, 1785. B495
A response to Friedrich Buchwald's *Brev fra Z til U*, having to do with controversy within the Danish Asiatic Company.

Brev til en ven indeholdende stof til menneskekundskab eller procurator-conduite I anledning af en executions-forretning passeret 31 martii 1787 hos de herrer etats-raader de coninck & reyersen som directeurer for expeditionen med skibet *Enigheden*. Copenhagen, Gyldendals Forlag, 1787. B496
Relates to a lawsuit of the Danish Asiatic Company against a firm allowing French and British ships to use the Danish flag for private trade in the East Indies.

Breve noticia, que se da' ao publico para consolação dos Portuguezes dos successos, que acontecerão no estado da nossa India, desde o mez de Janeiro de 1759, até o de 1760. Lisbon, Pedro Ferreira, 1760. B497
An account of a portion of the war between the Mahrattas and the Portuguese in India, with a treaty signed July 26, 1759.

Breve raggvaglio di quanto è accaduto in Roma à sig: mandarini venuti co il p: Guido Tasciard della Compagnia di Giesù, inviato straordinario dal re di Siam dopo l' udienza havuta da N.S. Innocenzo XI. [Rome, Domenico Antonio Ercole, 1689.] B498
An account of the audience given December 23, 1688 by Pope Innocent XI to an embassy from Siam accompanied by several Jesuits.

Breve ristretto delle notizie gia dedotte circa l'uso delle tabelle colle parole Cinesi King-Tien coelum colito, presentato alla Sagra Congregatione del s. Officio, in settembre 1699. [n.p., 1699] B499
This pamphlet concerns the political aspects of the Chinese Rites controversy which was offensive to the emperor who had granted great freedom to the Jesuits to preach in China.

Brewster, Sir Francis. Essays on trade and navigation. London, T. Cockerill, 1695. B500
A series of essays advocating trade policies with respect to shipbuilding, regulation of imports, the fishing trade, the encouragement of foreign craftsmen to come to England, etc.

Brewster, Sir Francis. New essays on trade. London, For H. Walwyn, 1702. B501
Discusses English and Irish trade, and the advantages of a union between the two countries.

Breydenbach, Bernhard von. Peregrinatio in Terram Sanctam. Mainz, Erhard Reuwich, 1486. B502
An account of a pilgrimage to the Holy Land, with outstanding illustrations, and with information on various eastern peoples met en route.

[Bricaire de La Dixmerie, Nicolas.] Le sauvage de Taiti aux Français; avec un envoi au philosophe ami des sauvages. London; Paris, Lejay, 1770. B503
An early example of the "noble savage" literature, based on Bougainville's visit to Tahiti, the introduction being a description of Tahiti and its people.

Brickdale, John. [Letter to merchants in Rhode Island.] Manuscript. Cadiz, 1764. B504
The brothers Samuel and William Vernon ran one of the most successful businesses during the heyday of Rhode Island trading companies in the four decades before the American Revolution. Their primary trade was West Indian rum for African slaves, traded to the West Indies for molasses which was shipped to New England (the commercial triangle). In this letter from John Brickdale the Vernons are advised of trading conditions in Spain including prices of goods. Products mentioned include wheat, staves, salt and Barcelona handkerchiefs.

Brickell, John. The natural history of North-Carolina. With an account of the trade, manners, and customs of the Christian and Indian inhabitants. Dublin, James Carson for the author, 1737. B505
Much of the material included is taken directly from John Lawson, *The History of Carolina*, but Brickell makes significant additions, particularly with respect to the Indians and to the medicinal properties of plants.

A brief account of the great oppressions and injuries which the managers of the East-India company have acted on ... their fellow subjects. [London, ca. 1691.] B506
A leaflet containing thirteen accusations against the management of the East India Company.

A brief account of the privileges and immunities granted by the French king to the East India Company. London, Ambrose Isted, 1671. B507

A statement of the privileges accorded to the French East India Company, with further remarks by the king on the means he proposes to encourage trade in general.

A brief narrative of the Indian Charity-School in Lebanon in Connecticut, New England: founded and carried on by that faithful servant of God the Rev. Mr. Eleazar Wheelock. 2d ed. with an appendix. London, J. and W. Oliver, 1767.
B508
Written by Nathaniel Whitaker, this work is based largely on Eleazar Wheelock's *A plain and faithful narrative*, 1763.

Brief van een goed patriot, over de memoire, door den heere ambassadeur van Groot-Britannien aan h.H.M. De h.H. Staaten-géneraal gepresenteerd den 9 April 1779. Breda, F. Hollander [etc.] [1779].
B509
A rejection of the British ambassador's proposal that the Dutch abandon their connection with France in supporting the American rebellion.

Brief van een particulier burger van London, aan zijn vriend in een voornaam koopstad van Holland. n.p., 1688.
B510
Complaints by an Englishman about excessive governmental regulation and taxation of commerce.

Brief van eenen Utrechtschen heer, zich te Amsterdam bevindende, aan zynen vriend te Utrecht. Utrecht, Schoonhoven en Co. [1777].
B511
A letter discussing the sale of the assets of some Surinam planters.

Briefe auf einer Reise von Stade nach Madras in Ostindien und aus Ostindien geschrieben nach Stade. Bremen, Georg Ludewig Förster, 1789.
B512
Nineteen letters written by a German military officer in British service describing points visited between England and the Malabar coast of India.

Briefe über die jetzige Uneinigkeit zwischen den amerikanischen Colonien und dem englischen Parlament. Aus dem englischen. Hannover, 1776.
B513
A collection of thirteen letters reviewing the history of the controversy between Parliament and the American colonies. There does not appear to be an English edition.

Briet, Philippe. Parallela geographiae veteris et novae. Paris, Sebastiani Cramoisy et Gabrielis Cramoisy, 1648-49.
B514
A comparative geography, relating ancient concepts to modern knowledge. Although it is largely concerned with Europe, there are maps of the other continents and world maps.

Briève & fidèle exposition de l'origine, de la doctrine, des constitutions, usages et ceremonies ecclesiastiques de l'Eglise de l'Unité des Freres. n.p., 1758.
B515
A history of the Moravian Brethren describing their religious and social customs, and with plates illustrating missionary work among American Indians, Eskimos, and Afro-Americans.

[Brink, Carel Fredrik.] Nouvelle description du Cap de Bonne-Espérance. Amsterdam, J.H. Schneider, 1778.
B516
Contains a history of settlement of the Cape region, with descriptions of the land, people, natural products, etc.

Brion de la Tour, Louis. La Russie européene, conformément à l'atlas de cet empire ... Paris, Desnos, 1766.
B517
The map is from the *Atlas général, civil et ecclésiastique* published by Desnos in 1768.

Brisacier, Jacques-Charles de. Manuscript letter signed. Paris, 14 October 1686.
B518
A defense of Roman Catholic missions in the East Indies against attacks by Jansenist critics.

Briscoe, John. A discourse on the late funds of the Million-act, Lottery-act, and Bank of England. London, J. D. for A. Bell, 1696.
B519
Contends that these acts will ruin trade.

Brissot, Joseph Pierre. Lettre à m. Barnave, sur ses rapports concernant les colonies, les décrets qui les ont suivis, leurs conséquences fatales ... Paris, Desenne, Bailly, 1790.
B520
Criticism of a well-known French politician, both for his views and his actions regarding colonies.

Brissot, Joseph Pierre. Réplique à la première et dernière lettre de Louis-Marthe Gouy. Paris, Belen, Desenne, Bailly, 1791.
B521
Strong moral arguments against the practice of slavery, with quotes and a rebuttal of letters from a defender of it in Saint Domingue.

Brissot de Warville, J.-P. (Jacques-Pierre). A critical examination of the marquis de Chatellux's Travels in North America ... Philadelphia, Joseph James, 1788.
B522
A critical commentary on Chastellux's *Travels*, contending that his remarks about the democratic society in America had insulted the population there.

Brissot de Warville, J.-P. (Jacques-Pierre). De la France et des États-Unis; ou, de l'importance de la revolution de l'Amérique pour le bonheur de la France. London, 1787.
B523
A consideration of the opportunities for French-American trade following American independence.

Brissot de Warville, J.-P. (Jacques-Pierre). The commerce of America with Europe. New York, T. and J. Swords, 1795.
B524

A translation of *De la France et des États-Unis*.

Brissot de Warville, J.-P. (Jacques-Pierre). Discours ... sur les causes des troubles de Saint-Domingue, prononcé à la séance du premier décembre 1791. Paris, Imprimerie Nationale [1791]. B525
An analysis of events in Saint Domingue by one friendly to the cause of the Mulattoes who had attempted to gain by force assurance of their right to vote and to hold office.

Brissot de Warville, J.-P. (Jacques-Pierre). Mémoire sur les noirs d l'Amèrique septentrionale, lu à l'assemblée de la Société des amis des noirs, le 9 février 1789. Paris, Bailly & De Senne, 1789. B526
The president of the Société des amis des noirs of Paris upon returning from the United States reviews the status of slavery and the slave trade in each of the states with a view to encouraging the abolition of slavery.

Brissot de Warville, J.-P. (Jacques-Pierre). Nouveau voyage dans les États-Unis de l'Amérique Septentrionale, fait en 1788. Paris, Buisson, 1791. B527
A detailed survey of the social, political, and economic conditions in the United States in two volumes, with a third being a new edition of *De la France et des États-Unis*.

Brissot de Warville, J.-P. (Jacques-Pierre). Nieuwe reize in de Vereenigde Staaten van Noord-Amerika ... uit het Fransch vertaald, en met eenige ophelderingen en bijvoegselen vermeerderd. Amsterdam, Martinus de Bruijn [1794]. B528
The only contemporary Dutch edition, with notes added to the text by the translator.

Brissot de Warville, J.-P. (Jacques-Pierre). New travels in the United-States of America. London, For J.S. Jordan, 1797. B529
The first English translation. Volume two is entirely concerned with the trade of the United States and its possibilities for France.

Brissot de Warville, J.-P. (Jacques-Pierre). Nye reiser i Nordamerica i aaret 1788. Copenhagen, A. Soldins Førlag [1798]. B530
The first and only Danish edition, with notes by translator-editor Diedrich von Bulöw.

Brissot de Warville, J.-P. (Jacques-Pierre). Nya resa genom Nord-Americanska Fri-Staterna är 1788. Stockholm, Anders Jac. Nordström, 1799. B531
The Swedish edition is based upon the 1792 German translation of Johann Reinhold Forster, including his notes.

Brissot de Warville, J.-P. (Jacques-Pierre). Projet de décret relatif à l'emploi des troupes destinées pour Saint-Domingue. [Paris, Imprimerie Nationale, 1791.] B532
Troops were to be sent to Saint Domingue only as a condition for restoring order.

Brissot de Warville, J.-P. (Jacques-Pierre). Tableau de la situation actuelle des Anglois dans les Indes Orientales. Paris, Perisse, 1784. B533
A history of English East-Indian commerce since the founding of the East India Company.

[Brissot de Warville, J.-P. (Jacques-Pierre).] Testament politique de l'Angleterre. n.p., 1780. B534
A satirical attack on British policies regarding their colonies and their foreign trade, by a Frenchman sympathetic to the American revolutionary cause.

[Brissot de Warville, J.-P. (Jacques-Pierre).] Testament politique de l'Angleterre. n.p., 1680 [i.e. 1780]. B535
One of four editions published in 1780.

Britain's mistakes in the commencement and conduct of the present war. [London] For T. Cooper, 1740. B536
Describes England's policies before and during the first year of war with Spain.

The British fishery recommended to Parliament. Edinburgh, W. Cheyne, 1734. B537
A proposal to subsidize the British fishing industry, with a map indicating ports and fishing areas of particular interest.

British merchant. Le négotiant anglois, ou traduction libre du livre intitulé: *The British merchant, contenant divers mémoires sur le commerce de l'angleterre avec la France, le Portugal & l'Espagne*. Dresden, Freres Estienne, 1753. B538
Designed to explain Anglo-French commercial rivalry, this work includes an abundance of statistics and also reproduces many diplomatic documents.

The British merchant; or, commerce preserv'd: in answer to *The mercator, or commerce retriev'd*. London, For A. Baldwin, Ferd. Burleigh, 1713-14. B539
A complete run of an editorial-type newspaper published twice a week from August 7, 1713, to July 30, 1714, to contradict *The Mercator*, edited by Defoe, and to attack the treaty with France which would have admitted greater trade with France.

Brito, Bernardo Gomes de. Historia tragico-maritima em que se escrevem chronologicamente os naufragios que tiveraõ as naos de Portugal ... Lisbon, Congregaçaõ do Oratorio, 1735-[37]. B540

Brito, Fernando Pereira

A collection of reprinted accounts of Portuguese shipwrecks from the sixteenth and seventeenth centuries, relating principally to the loss of ships on the African coasts.

Brito, Fernando Pereira de. Historia do nascimento, vida, e martyrio do ven. Padre Joaõ de Britto da Companhia de Jesu, martyr da Azia, e protomartyr da missaõ de Madurey ... Coimbra, Real Collegio das Artes da Comp. de Jesu, 1722.
B541
A biography of Joaõ de Britto, Jesuit missionary to India, including sixteen of his letters from there.

Brito Freire, Francisco de. Nova Lusitania, historia da guerra Brasilica. Lisbon, Joam Galram, 1675. B542
A history of the war between the Dutch and Portuguese in Brazil by the admiral of the Portuguese fleet during this war.

Brito Freire, Francisco de. Viage da armada da Companhia do Commercio, e frotas do estado do Brasil. [Lisbon, Joam Galram, 1675.] B543
An account of a commercial voyage to Brazil in 1655, apparently a reprint of the 1657 first edition.

Briviesca de Muñatones, Diego. Parecer acerca de la perpetuydad de las encomiendas de Indios del Reyno del Piru. Que hizieron los tres comissarios iuezes, que al dicho reyno embio el Rey Don Felipe II ... [n.p., 161-?] B544
Controversial report of a judicial commission appointed by Philip II in 1556 to study the question of whether or not Spanish settlers in Peru should be given permanent rights over the Indian population there.

Broecke, Pieter van den. Korte historiael ende journaelsche aenteyckeninghe ... Amsterdam, Herman Jansz Brouwer, 1634. B545
An account of a voyage made for the Dutch East India Company along the coast of Africa and then to the East Indies, noting the commerce carried on en route.

Broecke, Pieter van den. Wonderlijcke historische ende journaelsche aenteyckeningh ... van Cabo Verde, Angola, Guinea, Oost-Indien. Amsterdam, J. Hartgerts, 1648. B546
Brief accounts of voyages undertaken between 1605 and 1630. The earlier voyages deal with contacts made by the Dutch along the African coast.

[Broekhuizen, Gotfried van.] Eduward Meltons, Engelsch edelmans ... zee- en land-reizen; door Egypten, West-Indien, Perzien, Turkyen, Oost-Indien, en d' aangrenzende gewesten. Amsterdam, Jan Ten Hoorn, 1681. B547
A collection of travels, possibly fictitious, including illustrations by Jan Luiken.

Broemmert, Willem. Dagregister gehouden door den Ondersturman Willem Broemmert onder t'gezag van den E. Capitn. Oloff Berg. Manuscript. South Africa, 11 February 1700.
B548
The author was second in command to Oloff Berg who led an expedition into Hottentot country to procure beef for the Dutch East India Company's station in South Africa. This is a journal of that expedition.

Broniowski, Marcin. Tartariae descriptio. Cologne, Birckmann, 1595. B549
A description of eastern Europe, Muscovy in particular, with numerous plates and maps.

Broome, Ralph. An examination of the expediency of continuing the present impeachment. London, John Stockdale, 1791. B550
A partisan of Warren Hastings discusses the merits of continuing the trial.

[Brosses, Charles de.] Histoire des navigations aux Terres Australes. Paris, Durand, 1756. B551
A history of exploration in the south Atlantic and Pacific oceans, including descriptions of sixty-seven voyages.

Brosses, Charles de. Terra Australis cognita: or, Voyages to the Terra Australis ... during the 16th, 17th & 18th centuries. Edinburgh, A. Donaldson, 1766-68. B552
This English edition has a preface by the editor, John Callander, on the value of discovering the imagined Southern Continent.

Brough, Anthony. Considerations on the necessity of lowering the exorbitant freight of ships employed in the service of the East-India-Company. London, For G. G. J. and J. Robinson, 1786. B553
The author, a merchant, asserts that if it is to discourage competition from merchants of other countries the East India Company must reduce freight costs, and he proposes to do this through the use of smaller ships which he believed held many advantages over craft then in use by the company.

Broughton, Thomas. Manuscript document signed. South Carolina, 12 May 1735. B554
A grant of 12,000 acres of land to Jean Pierre Purry, from a total of 48,000 reserved for him along the north shore of the Savannah River, for the purpose of settling a colony of Swiss emigrants. The grant includes a survey of the land. It is signed by James St. John, surveyor general, as well as Thomas Broughton, lieutenant governor of South Carolina.

[Broughton, William Robert.] Plan of the River Oregan, from an actual survey. London, A. Arrowsmith, 1798. B555
A detailed map of the Columbia river recording discoveries for about one hundred miles made by a member of Vancouver's expedition in 1792.

Broughton, William Robert. A voyage of discovery to the Pacific Ocean. London, T. Cadell and W. Davis, 1804. B556
A narrative of an expedition from England by Cape Horn to Hawaii, Japan, and the American Northwest coast in 1795-98.

Brouwer, Hendrick. Journael ... van de reyse ... naer de custen van Chili. Amsterdam, B. Jansz, 1646. B557
An account of a Dutch West India Company voyage to Chile, and also of the voyage of Marten de Vries to the north of Japan.

Brown, John, philomath. The description and use of the carpenters-rule: together with the use of the line of numbers (inscribed thereon) in arithmatick and geometry ... London, W.G. for William Fisher, 1662. B558
Among several devices described are dials, almanacs, nocturnals, quadrants and other instruments used in navigation.

[Brown, Robert.] Remarks on the Earl of Selkirk's observations on the present state of the Highlands of Scotland. Edinburgh, J. Anderson, 1806. B559
An argument against emigration of Scotch settlers to Canada because of the weaking effect it would have on Britain.

Browne, John. The merchants avizo. Very necessary for their sonnes and servants, when they first send them beyond the sea ... London, John Bill, 1616. B560
A handbook of instruction for the young merchant abroad, advising as to conduct, correspondence, merchandising, and keeping of accounts. First published in 1589, this is the fourth edition.

[Browne, Sir John.] Seasonable remarks on trade. With some reflections on the advantages that might accrue to Great Britain, by a proper regulation of the trade to Ireland. Dublin, S. Powell, 1728. B561
This writer recommends using the cheaper labor and goods of Ireland to enable British commerce to compete with the Dutch, and he traces the decline of the Russian trade to lower costs of goods and labor in France and the Netherlands. He also proposes developing trade between Ireland and Africa.

[Browne, Sir John.] Seasonable remarks on trade. With some reflections on the advantages that might accrue to Great Britain, by a proper regulation of the trade to Ireland. [Dublin] 1729. B562
A collection of five tracts relating to Ireland's economy and the means by which it might be improved as a more active participant in the commerce of the British Empire. The first tract is a reprinting of the preceding item. Two of the tracts are critical of Browne's views.

Browne, Montfort. [Identure for one thousand acres of land in West Florida, to Lawrence Sigu Des Roches.] Manuscript. n.p., 10 March 1774. B563
The land leased to Des Roches was on the east bank of the Mississippi in what is now West Feliciana Parish, Louisiana.

Browne, Patrick. The civil and natural history of Jamaica. London, For the author, 1756. B564
A complete and well-illustrated history of Jamaica with particular emphasis on natural products.

Browne, Richard. [Letter and manuscript document relating to a commercial voyage from England to Smyrna and return.] [London, ca. 1672.] B565
These manuscripts describe the details of a voyage from London to Smyrna, returning by Constantinople, Leghorn, Messina, and Malaga, with the ship being cast away on the return voyage to London, all of it relating to the claims of the surviving crew members.

Browne, William George. Travels in Africa, Egypt, and Syria, from the year 1792 to 1798. London, For T. Cadell [etc.] 1799. B566
This traveler was concerned with literary and architectural antiquities as well as current customs and the economies of the major cities in Egypt and the Levant. The account of Darfur, which includes a map, is the earliest Western description of that country.

Browne, William George. Reisen in Afrika, Aegypten und Syrien in den Jahren 1792 bis 1798. Leipzig, Gera, Wilhelm Heinsius, 1800. B567
The anonymous translator provides a twenty-six page preface and numerous notes to the text.

Bruce, James. Voyage aux sources du Nil, en Nubie et en Abyssine, pendant les années 1768, 1769, 1770, 1771, & 1772. Paris, Hôtel de Thou, 1790-1792. B568
One of the classic accounts of the upper Nile region in its first French edition, including also the account of William Paterson's travels in South Africa. Both works provide important illustrations of the natural history of Africa.

Bruce, James. Resa genom Abyssinien. I sammandrag med anmärkningar af Samuel Ödmann. Stockholm, Johan Pfeiffer, 1795. B569
This Swedish edition, an abridged translation by Samuel Lorens Ödmann, does not include illustrations or maps.

[Bruce, John.] Historical view of plans, for the government of British India and regulation of trade to the East Indies. [London] 1793. B570
A survey of the history of English East Indian affairs, with recommendations for the administration of East Indian territories and commerce for the future.

Bruce, Peter Henry. Des Herrn Peter Heinrich Bruce ... Nachrichten von seinen Reisen in Deutschland, Russland, die Tartarey, Türkey, Westindien u.s.f. ... aus dem Englischen ubersetzt. Leipzig, Johann Friedrich Junius, 1784.
B571

An account of military service in Russia and Turkey, with subsequent travels to the Bahamas and Carolina.

Bruce, Peter Henry. Memoirs of Peter Henry Bruce, esq., a military officer in the services of Prussia, Russia, and Great Britain. Containing an account of his travels in Germany, Russia, Tartary, Turkey, the West Indies, &c ... London, Printed for the author's widow, and sold by T. Payne and son, 1782.
B572

An account by a military officer of travels in Russia, the Bahamas and South Carolina, with observations on peoples, governments, economies, transportation, etc.

Bruel, Joachim van den. Historiae Peruanae ordinis eremitarum S. P. Augustini. n.p., Guilielmum Lesteenium, 1651-52.
B573

A history of the Augustinian order in Peru, including also material on the conquest of Peru.

Bruijn, Georg. Opmuntring til mine medborgere om deeltagelse i canal-handelen. [Copenhagen, Johan Friderik Schultz, 1784.]
B574

A description of the Schleswig-Holstein canal and its importance to Danish commerce.

Brulley, Augustin Jean. Discours historique sur la culture du nopal et l'éducation de la cochenille. Paris, Imprimerie du Lycée des Arts, 1795.
B575

Observations on early attempts to establish the cochineal industry in Saint Domingue with recommendations that it be undertaken as an aid in restoring the colony's economy.

Brulley, Augustin Jean. Précis des manoeuvres contre-révolutionnaires opérés dans la partie Française de Saint-Domingue. Paris, P. J. Duplain [1789].
B576

A discussion of the political situation in Santo-Domingo, with a plea to the National Assembly for careful consideration of the problems there. The author proposes a system of mortgages as the means to raise funds necessary to restore ruined plantations.

Brun, Antoine de, Baron de Aspremont. Brief aen hare Hoog Mogende ... Amsterdam, Dirck vander Cunst, 1647.
B577

The Spanish plenipotentiary at Munster urges the Dutch to make peace and to consider France the major threat to them.

[Brun, Antoine de, Baron de Aspremont.] Proposition, gedaen door den ambassadeur van Spagnie, aende Heeren Staten Generael. The Hague, Michiel Stael, 1650.
B578

The Spanish ambassador protests the seizure, by a ship of Groningen, of a Spanish trading ship returning from the Gambia River.

Brun, Antoine de, Baron de Aspremont. Vertoogh van Antoine de Brun, raedt ende ambassadeur van Sijne Majesteyt van Spagnien tot bevordering der aengevangen vrede-handlinge tot Münster. Dordrecht, J. Verhaghen, 1647.
B579

A pamphlet discussing issues relating to the Peace of Westphalia.

Bruni, Leonardo. Historia Fiorentina. Venice, Jacomo de Rossi, 1476.
B580

The first edition of a history of Florence written about 1427.

Bruton, William. Newes from the East-Indies. London, I. Okes, 1638.
B581

A description of a voyage to Bengal, with observations on that part of India.

Bruyn, Cornelis de. Reizen ... door de vermaardste deelen van Klein Asia. Delft, Henrik van Krooneveld, 1698.
B582

The first edition of this Dutch painter's account of his travels in the Levant over a period of twenty years. The book is beautifully illustrated.

Bruyn, Cornelis de. A voyage to the Levant: or, Travels in the principal parts of Asia Minor. London, For Jacob Tonson and Thomas Bennet, 1702.
B583

The first English edition.

Bruyn, Cornelis de. Cornelis de Bruins reizen over Moscovie, door Persie en Indie. Amsterdam, Rudolf en Gerard Wetstein, 1714.
B584

A richly detailed and well-illustrated account of the author's travels through eastern Europe and the Middle East.

Bruyn, Cornelis de. Voyages de Corneille Le Brun par la Moscovie en Perse, et aux Indes Orientales. Amsterdam, Freres Wetstein, 1718.
B585

The first French edition.

Bruyn, Cornelis de. Travels into Moscovy, Persia, and part of the East Indies. London, For A. Bettesworth [etc.] 1737.
B586

The first English edition.

Bruzen de La Martinière, M. (Antoine-Augustin). Introduction a l'histoire de l'Asie, de l'Afrique, et de l'Amerique. Amsterdam, Zacharie Charelain, 1735.
B587

A general history of the non-European parts of the world, particularly with respect to the expansion of European interests there.

Bry, Theodor de, Johann Theodor, Johann Israel, and Mathew Merian. Reisen im occidentalischen Indien, and Reisen im orientalischen Indien. Frankfurt, 1590-1630. B588
  The *Great* and *Small Voyages* of the De Bry family constitute two of the most important collections of voyages. They include German translations of the accounts of explorations to Asia, Africa, the East Indies, and the American continents.

Buache, Jean-Nicolas. Géographie élémentaire moderne et ancienne. Paris, D'Houry, 1772. B589
  A geographical textbook with its major emphasis on modern geography. It tends toward brief, factual, and practical notes on political, economic, and location information.

Buache, Philippe. Carte du Perou, pour servir à l'histoire des Incas et à celle de l'etat present de cette province. Paris, 1739. B590
  The map resulted from the La Condamine expedition of 1736-39, and in addition to showing the Peru-Ecuador area it shows the upper Amazon River and its tributaries.

Buache, Philippe. Considérations geographiques et physiques sur les nouvelles decouvertes au nord de la ... Mer du Sud. Paris, 1753-55. B591
  A collection of papers presented to the Académie Royale des Sciences, including maps portraying the various theories regarding the existence of a Northwest Passage.

The bubblers medley, or a sketch of the times being Europes memorial for the year 1720. London, Carington Bowles [1720]. B592
  A broadside lampoon of events surrounding the South Sea Bubble, in illustration and verse.

[Buchan, David Stewart Erskine, Earl of.] Letters of Albanicus to the people of England, on the partiality and injustice of the charges brought against Warren Hastings ... London, For J. Debrett, 1786. B593
  A series of five letters defending Hastings and attacking Burke, more on general principles than on the specific charges brought against Hastings.

Buckeridge, Nicholas. Manuscript letter-book. [1651-53.] B594
  Buckeridge was the agent of the Asada Association, a company of merchant interlopers who operated from the island of Asada off the coast of Madagascar.

Bucquoi, Jakob de. Aanmerkelyke ontmoetingen in de zestien jaarige reize naa de Indiën. Haarlem, Jan Bosch, 1744. B595
  An account of travels to the East Indies by way of the Cape of Good Hope to Goa, overland to Cochin, and thence to Java.

Bucquoi, Jakob de. Sechzehnjährige Reise nach Indien. Aus dem Holländischen nach der zweyten Ausgabe übersetzt. Nebst einem Auszuge aus Jacob Frankens unglücklichen Reise in den Jahren 1756-1760. Leipzig, Christian Gottlob Hilscher, 1771. B596
  The author traveled in the East from 1719 to 1735, and his account includes observations on Eastern trade and piracy. Appended is Jacob Fancken's description of Bengal and southern Africa.

[Budgell, Eustace.] A letter to Mr. Law, upon his arrival in Great Britain. London, J. Roberts [1721]. B597
  A history of John Law's Mississippi Company, and a favorable comparison of it with England's South Sea Company.

Büsch, Johann Georg. Kleine Schriften von der Handlung und anderen gemeinnützigen Inhalte. Leipzig, Weidmanns Erben und Reich, 1772. B598
  A work in commercial theory, including banking and overseas commerce, with a considerable interest in colonial trade.

Büsch, Johann Georg. Über das Bestreben der Völker neuerer Zeit einander in ihrem Seehandel recht wehe zu thun. Hamburg, B. G. Hoffmann, 1800. B599
  A treatise on merchants' rights at sea during war, with information on Hanseatic and other European commerce.

Büsching, Anton Friedrich. Totius imperii Russici tabula generalis ... Berlin, 1769. B600
  A large map based on De l'Isle's Russian atlas of 1745, edited by an important commentator on Russian geography and exploration.

Bugnon, Didier. Relation exacte concernant les caravanes ou corteges des marchands d'Asie. Nancy, R. Charlot & P. Deschamps [1707]. B601
  A description of the organization and administration of a typical Asian overland merchant caravan.

Bulam Association. Report of the institution, proceedings, present state, and future purposes, of the Bulam Association. London, For the association, 1792. B602
  This report describes the origins and early colonizing activities of the Bulam Association which attempted to establish settlements at the mouth of the Rio Grande River in Africa.

Bulkeley, John. A voyage to the South-Seas in the years 1740-41. London, For Jacob Robinson, 1743. B603
  An account of the wreck of the *Wager* off the coast of South America and the survival of a portion of her crew.

Buonnani, Filippo. Trattato sopra la vernice detta comunemente cinese. Rome, Antonio de'Rossi, 1731. B604
  A description of the art of lacquering as it was practiced in China, with a brief treatment of Japanese methods also.

Burchardus de Monte Sion. Veridica Terre Sancte: regionūqz finitimarum: ac in eis mirabilium descriptio. Venice, Giovanni Tacuini de Tridino, 1519. B605
  The first separate edition of one of the more valuable accounts of the Holy Land, written by a German Dominican in the late thirteenth century.

Burchett, Josiah. Reasons for reducing the pyrates at Madagascar and proposals ... for effecting the same. [London, ca. 1704.] B606
  Proposes that the only way to get rid of the pirates in Madagascar is to invite them to return to England with full pardon, which would also bring to England a contingent of able seamen.

Burckhard, Christian. Ost-Indianische Reise-Beschreibung. Halle & Leipzig, Joh. Friedrich Zeitlers, 1693. B607
  An account of military service in the East Indies with the Dutch East India Company, containing observations on cities and islands and commentary on social conditions, products, and commercial rivalries.

Burg, Pieter van der. Curieuse beschrijving van ... verscheyden Oost-Indische gewesten en machtige landschappen. Rotterdam, I. Naeranus, 1677. B608
  A description of East Indian trade by one who lived in the East Indies from 1653 to 1677.

Burges, Bartholomew. A series of Indostan letters. New York, For the author by W. Ross [1790]. B609
  An unusual account of social life in India, informative and gossipy, with a list of commercially saleable items in the Calcutta area.

Burges, Sir James Bland. Letters lately published in *The Diary*, on the subject of the present disputes with Spain. London, G. Kearsley, 1790. B610
  A discussion of Spanish and English rights in Nootka Sound and the Falkland Islands.

Burgundy (France). Bureau des Finances. Jugement ... qui condamne Nicolas Vivien, du village de Pomoy ... à la peine des galéres pendant neuf ans ... pour prévarications dans son emploi. [Besançon, 1776.] B611
  A document relating to the punishment of Nicolas Vivien, who violated the tobacco trade laws.

Burgundy (France). Chambre et Cour des Comptes. Extrait des registres de la Chambre & cour des comptes, aides, domaine, & finances du comté de Bourgogne. [Dole, Pierre-Fr. Tonnet, 1771.] B612
  Relates to the regulation of the tobacco trade.

[Burke, Edmund.] An account of the European settlements in America. London, For R. and J. Dodsley, 1757. B613
  First edition of a highly popular account of the discovery and colonization of the New World, which includes extensive descriptions of the commerce of various colonies.

[Burke, Edmund.] An account of the European settlements in America. London, For R. and J. Dodsley, 1758. B614
  The second edition.

[Burke, Edmund.] An account of the European settlements in America. Dublin, For Peter Wilson, 1762. B615
  An Irish edition, the fourth in English.

[Burke, Edmund.] Histoire des colonies Européennes dans l'Amérique. Paris, Merlin, 1767. B616
  The first French edition.

Burke, Edmund. Mr. Burke's speech, in Westminster-Hall, on the 18th and 19th of February, 1788, with explanatory notes. London, For J. Debrett, 1792. B617
  The editor's purpose is to refute Burke's charges in the explanatory notes. A long preface contains further indictments of Burke for his alleged arrogance toward the East India Company and Parliament.

Burke, Edmund. Mr. Burke's speech, on the 1st December 1783, upon the question for the speaker's leaving the chair ... on Mr. Fox's East India bill. London, J. Dodsley, 1784. B618
  An eloquent speech in support of Fox's bill for reforming the administration of the East India Company, noting the dismal record of the Company's relationships with Indian governments.

Burke, Edmund. Mr. Burke's speech, on the motion made for papers relative to the directions for charging the Nabob of Arcot's private debts to Europeans, on the revenues of the Carnatic. February 28th, 1785. London, for J. Dodsley, 1785. B619
  An indictment of Paul Benfield and others to whom the Nabob of Arcot was indebted, citing their collusion with him in contracting this debt, to the detriment of his subjects and the dishonor of Great Britain.

Burke, Edmund. Mr. Edmund Burke's speeches at his arrival at Bristol and at the conclusion of the poll. London, For J. Dodsley, 1775. B620
  The first of these speeches relates almost entirely to the growing hostilities between Great Britain and her North American colonies.

[Burke, Edmund.] Observations on a late state of the nation. London, For J. Dodsley, 1769.
B621
A rebuttal to William Knox's *The Present State of the Nation*, which had questioned the advantages gained by Great Britain in its recent victorious wars with France.

Burke, Edmund. A representation to His Majesty, moved in the House of Commons. Dublin, For Luke White and Patt. Byrne, 1784.
B622
A rebuttal to the "Speech from the Throne" which opened Parliament in 1784. Burke contends for parliamentary supremacy in the regulation of the East India Company.

[Burke, William.] Remarks on the Letter address'd to two great men. In a letter to the author of that piece. London, For R. and J. Dodsley [1760].
B623
A rebuttal to John Douglas's pamphlet, urging a less punitive attitude toward France at the peace table, and favoring West Indian and African acquisitions rather than Canada.

Burnaby, Andrew. Travels through the middle settlements in North-America, in the years 1759 and 1760. London, For T. Payne, 1775. B624
The first edition of a popular travel account by a clergyman of the Church of England whose travels took him from Virginia to New England, providing opportunity for extensive observations on the social and cultural life of the colonies.

Burnaby, Andrew. Travels through the middle settlements in North America. London, For T. Payne, 1798.
B625
The third edition, revised, with extensive appendixes concerning the natural history and commerce of the American states, and notes on the Indians and on the Fairfax family of Virginia.

Burnaby, Andrew. Reisen durch die mittlern Kolonien der Engländer in Nord-Amerika, nebst Anmerkungen über den Zustand der Kolonien ... Hamburg und Kiel, Carl Ernst Bohn, 1776.
B626
This first German edition adds numerous footnotes by the translator-editor Christoph Daniel Ebeling, and a preface placing this work among others esteemed by Ebeling.

Burnaby, Andrew. Voyages dans les colonies du milieu de l'Amérique Septentrionale, faits en 1759 & 1760. Avec des observations sur l'état des colonies ... Traduit d'après la seconde édition, par M. Willd. Lausanne, Société Typographique, 1778.
B627
The only French edition, with a preface by the translator.

Burney, James. A chronological history of discoveries in the South Sea. London, L. Hansard, 1803-17.
B628
A history of the exploration of the Pacific Ocean by one who sailed with Captain Cook.

Burrish, Onslow. Batavia illustrata: or, A view of the policy and commerce of the United Provinces. London, For W. Innys [etc.] 1731.
B629
Contains a history of the development of Dutch commerce and descriptions of the contemporary trade of the major cities of the Netherlands.

Burroughs, William, Esq. A true and exact particular and inventory of all and singular the lands, tenements and hereditaments, goods, chattels, debts and personal estate whatsoever, of William Burroughs, esq.; ... London, S. Buckley, 1732.
B630
Burroughs was involved in a scandal concerning the management of the Charitable Corporation for the Relief of the Industrious Poor. See also the entry pertaining to this subject under Sir Robert Sutton.

Burton, John. The duty and reward of propagating principles of religion and virtue ... A sermon preach'd before the Trustees for establishing the colony of Georgia in America. London, J. March for Mount and Page, 1733.
B631
The sermon is followed by a statement of the finances of the colony, naming investors, and indicating purposes for which money was spent.

Busbecq, Ogier Ghislain de. Itinera Constantinopolitanum et Amasianum ... ad Solimannum Turcarum imperatorem. Antwerp, Christophori Plantini, 1581.
B632
This first edition contains only the first letter written by Busbecq to his friend Nicholas Michault, describing his travels to Turkey in 1554-55.

Busbecq, Ogier Ghislain de. Legationis turcicae epistolae quatuor ... Eiusdem de re militari contra Turcam instituenda consilium. Paris, Ex officina Plantiniana, apud Aegidium Beys, 1595.
B633
Busbecq's letters describing his diplomatic mission to Turkey were written in 1555, 1556, 1560, and 1562. This is the second collected edition of them.

Bussy-Castelnau, Charles-Joseph Patissier, marquis de. Mémoire à consulter et consultation ... au sujet de Mémoire que le Sieur de Lally ... vient de répandre dans le public. Paris, Michel Lambert, 1766.
B634
A reply to the comte de Lally's *Tableau historique de l'expédition de l'Inde* and *Vraies causes de la perte de l'Inde* including numerous letters between French officers serving in India in 1758-59.

[Butel-Dumont, Georges-Marie.] Histoire et commerce des colonies angloises, dans l'Amerique Septentrionale. London, et se vend à Paris, Le Breton [etc.] 1755. B635
A survey of the English colonies in North America from Hudson Bay to Georgia, noting the government, natural products, and commerce of each.

[Butel-Dumont, Georges-Marie.] Histoire et commerce des colonies angloises, dans l'Amerique Septentrionale. London, et se vend à Paris, Le Breton [etc.] 1755. B636
Another printing of the previous work.

Butel-Dumont, Georges-Marie. Der engländischen Pflanzstädte in Nord-America Geschichte und Handlung nebst einer zuverlässigen Nachricht von der gegenwärtigen Anzahl der dasigen Einwohner ... Stuttgart, Johann Benedict Metzlers, 1755. B637
A systematic and detailed description of each of the British mainland North American colonies. This is one of two German editions published in 1755, based on a French edition of the same year.

[Butel-Dumont, Georges-Marie]. Die Geschichte der Errichtung und des Handels der englischen Colonien im mitternächtlichen Amerika. Rostock und Wismar, Berger und Boedner, 1756. B638
A translation from the French edition of the previous year, with a few notes by the anonymous translator.

[Butel-Dumont, Georges-Marie.] Geographische und historisch-politische Nachrichten von demjenigen Theil des Nördlichen Amerika ... und mit der nordamerikanischen Kriegs-Geschichte, von englischer Seite herausgegeben, begleitet. Frankfurt & Leipzig, 1756. B639
This work is in two parts, the first being a translation of *Histoire et commerce des colonies angloises*; the second is a history of conflicting French and English claims in North America from an unidentified English source.

Butel-Dumont, Georges-Marie. Histoire et commerce des Antilles angloises. [Paris] 1758. B640
A survey of the history and commerce of England's possessions in the West Indies, with special emphasis on the sugar trade.

Butler, Joseph. A Sermon preached before the Incorporated Society for the Propagation of the Gospel in Foreign Parts; at their Anniversary Meeting in the Parish-Church of St. Mary-le-Bow, on Friday, February 16, 1738-9. London, J. and P. Knapton, 1739 B641
This sermon shows concern for slaves who are viewed as inferior, but members of the same human family, and therefore their owners should see to their religious education.

Byron, John. The narrative ... containing an account of the great distresses suffered by himself and his companions on the coast of Patagonia ... London, S. Barker, G. Leigh, and T. Davies, 1768. B642
This account of a circumnavigation of 1740-1746 contains information on the navigation and trade of the southwest coast of South America.

Byron, John. A narrative of the Honourable John Byron ... containing an account of the great distresses suffered by himself and his companions on the coasts of Patagonia from the year 1740, till their arrival in England, 1746 ... Wigan, W. Bancks, 1784. B643
A reprint of the London, 1768 edition. Wigan is a small city near Manchester.

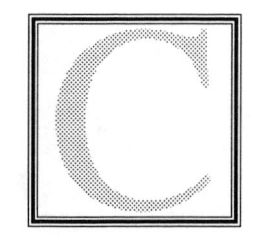

Cà da Mosto, Alvise. Nuouo portolano non piu stampato molto particolare de'l Levante e de'l Ponente ... Venice, Paulo Gerardo, 1544.　C1
　A guide to navigation of the Mediterranean Sea with particular emphasis on the eastern part of it.

Cabral, Pedro Alvares. Twee bysondere scheeps-togten na Oost-Indien, van Pedralverez Cabral, in het jaar 1501, en Joan de Nova, in het jaar 1501. Leiden, Pieter van der Aa, 1706.　C2
　Brief accounts of the first two commercial voyages to India from Portugal.

Cabreira, José. Navfragio da nao N. Senhora de Belem feyto na terra do Natal no cabo de Boa Esperança & varios sucessos que teve o Capitaõ Joseph de Cabreyra, que nella passou à India no anno de 1633. Lisbon, L. Craesbeeck, 1636 [repr. 1737].　C3

Cacegas, Luís de. Primeira, [-quarta] parte da Historia de S. Domingos, particular do reino, e conquistas de Portugal. Lisbon, Antonio Rodrigues Galhardo, 1767.　C4
　Among the biographies and histories of Dominican institutions in Portugal and its empire are accounts of missions in India, Malacca, the Moluccas, Cambodia, and other places in the East.

Cadena de Vilhasanti, Pedro. Beschreibung des portugiesischen Amerika vom Cudena. Ein spanisches Manuscript zu wolfenbüttelschen Bibliothek, herausgegeben vom Herrn Hofrath Lessing. Braunschweig, Fürstl. Waysenhauses, 1780.　C5
　A seventeenth century Spanish manuscript in German translation by Gotthold Ephraim Lessing with commentary by Christian Leiste providing a geographical description of Brazil.

Cádiz (Spain). Señor. Cadiz siempre reconocida à la clemencia de Vuestra Magestad ... [Cadiz, ca. 1725.]　C6
　Cadiz protests against a royal decree which gave Seville a favored position with respect to American commerce.

Cádiz (Spain). Señor ... Cadiz, puesta à los piés de V. Magdice ... [Cadiz, ca. 1726.]　C7
　A further protest by Cadiz at loss of her predominance in the West Indian trade, due to the transfer of the colonial office to Seville.

Cádiz (Spain). Consulado de Comercio. Señor. Don Andrès del Alcazar y Zuniga ... [Seville, 1697.]　C8
　A protest from officials of Cadiz against the taxes and privileges granted by the king to certain merchants, with reference to the administration of Spanish colonies.

Caffarus. Liber annalium Genuensis Reipublicae inceptus ab anno de 1100 usque ad annum 1293. Manuscript. 16th century.　C9
　The Genoese annuals by Caffarus or Caffaro depict the secular spirit of the rising Italian communes.

Cahier, contenant les plaintes, doléances & réclamations des citoyens-libres & propriétaires de couleur, des isles & colonies françoises. [n.p., ca. 1789]　C10
　An attempt to re-define the legal positions of whites, free persons of color, and slaves according to the Declaration of the Rights of Man.

Cahier de doléances de messieurs les députés, négocians & armateurs de la ville de Marseille. Marseilles, Veuve Sibié, 1789.　C11
　A series of recommendations intended particularly to improve French trade.

Cairu, José da Silva Lisboa, Visconde de. Principios de direito mercantil e leis de marinha para uso da mocidade de Portugueza, destinado ao commercio. Lisbon, Regia Officina, 1798.　C12
　A treatise on maritime commercial insurance by Brazil's leading economist.

Caldera e Campoz, João, marques. Autograph letter signed. Manuscript in Portuguese. [Funchal, Madeira] 25 September 1779. C13
A letter to Charles Murray, British Consul General in Madeira, concerning a British pirate ship.

Caledonia; or, the pedlar turn'd merchant. A tragi-comedy, as it was acted by his majesty's subjects of Scotland, in the king of Spain's province of Darien. London, 1700. C14
A long poem, of 127 four-line verses, recounting the history and failure of the Scots' settlement at Darien and poking fun at Scottish efforts in international trade.

Calisto de San Joseph, fray. Representacion verdadera, y exclamacion rendida y lamentable, que toda la nacion Indiana haze ã la Magestad del Señor Rey de las Españas, y Emperador de las Indias, el D^n Fernando el Sexto ... que se presento por el alho en 23 de Agosto de 1750. Manuscript in Spanish. Peru, 1750. C15
A protest to the King of Spain against harsh treatment of Indians in Peru by Spaniards, supported by citations of Spanish laws and papal edicts.

Cambridge, Richard Owen. Memoires du Colonel Lawrence, contenant l'histoire de la guerre dans l'Inde, entre les Anglois & les François, sur la côte de Coromandel, depuis 1750, jusque'en 1761. Amsterdam, Boudet, 1766. C16
An account of the Anglo-French wars in India collected from several sources, but most notably from Colonel Stringer Lawrence, a participant in the events.

Camocio, Giovanni Francesco, publisher. [Collection of engraved maps on thirty-four sheets.] Venice, 1560-75. C17
The sheets comprise maps of the world, Asia, Africa, and America, most of which are attributed to Giacomo Gastaldi.

Camões, Luis de. Os Lusiadas de Luis de Camoẽs principe da poesia heroica. Lisbon, Pedro Crasbeeck, 1609. C18
The fifth Portuguese edition of the epic poem celebrating the opening of the sea route to India by the Portuguese.

Camões, Luís de. Lusiadum libri decem. Lisbon, Gerardi de Vinea, 1622. C19
The only Latin edition, with an extensive set of notations.

Camões, Luís de. The Lusiad, or, Portugals historicall poem. London, H. Moseley, 1655. C20
The first English edition.

Camões, Luís de. Lusiada Italiana. Lisbon, Henrico Valente de Oliveira, 1659. C21
The second Italian edition, translated by Carlo Antonio Paggi.

Camões, Luís de. La Lusiade du Camoens, poeme heroique, sur la decouverte des Indes Orientales. Paris, Huart [etc.], 1735. C22
This first French edition of the *Lusiads*, a prose translation by Duperron de Castera, includes a brief life of Camões, some notes to the text and illustrations.

Campana, Cesare. Delle historie del mondo. Venice, G. Angelieri, 1596. C23
The first edition of Campana's world history, mainly covering the years 1580-1590. It includes sections on Africa, Persia, China and Japan, as well as an account of Drake's 1586 and 1595 expeditions.

Campanella, Tommaso. Thomas Campanella, von der spannischen Monarchy, erst unnd ander Theyl ... n.p., 1623. C24
A wide-ranging essay on the art of government, a basic political economy text for the seventeenth century, including a chapter on governing the American colonies and one on navigation.

Campanella, Tommaso. Thomas Campanella, an Italian friar and second Machiavel—his advice to the King of Spain for attaining the universal monarchy of the world ... London, Philemon Stephens, [1659 or 1660.] C25
The first English edition.

Campbell, Alexander. The sequel to Bulkeley and Cummins's voyage to the South-Seas. London, For the author, 1747. C26
An account of shipwreck and suffering which includes descriptions of the commercial potentialities of Chiloe Island and Chile.

Campbell, Donald. A journey over land to India, partly by a route never gone before by any European. London, For Cullen and Company, 1795. C27
An account of travels between 1781 and 1783, with extensive descriptions of Turkey and India, and a good account of caravan travel.

Campbell, George. The nature, extent, and importance of the duty of allegiance: a sermon preached at Aberdeen, December 12, 1776 ... on account of the rebellion in America. Aberdeen, J. Chalmers, 1778. C28
Self-serving leaders with ignorant followers persuaded by misrepresentation of facts is the picture of the American rebellion presented by this Scottish preacher.

[Campbell, John.] Algemeine Geschichte der ost-und westindischen Handlungsgesellschaften in Europa. Halle, J. J. Gebauer, 1764. C29
A history of major European trading companies, including an excellent history of the Ostend Company, translated and edited by Johann Salomon Samler, from the *Universal history*.

Campbell, John. Candid and impartial considerations on the nature of the sugar trade. London, R. Baldwin, 1763. C30
An evaluation of Grenada and St. Lucia in the West Indies, with respect to the sugar trade.

[Campbell, John.] Conciderações candidas e imparciaes sobre a natureza do commercio do assucar; e importancia comparativa das ilhas Britannicas, e Francezas das Indias Occidentaes. Lisbon, Casa Litteraria do Arco do Cego, 1800. C31
The purpose of this translation of the preceding tract was to increase sugar production in Brazil, specifically in the northern provinces.

[Campbell, John.] A concise history of the Spanish America. London, For John Stagg and Daniel Browne, 1741. C32
A survey of Spanish discovery, conquest, settlement, and trade in America.

Campbell, John. The conduct of His Grace the D-ke of Ar--le for the four last years review'd. London, For Mr. Webb, 1740. C33
A defense of the Duke of Argyle's conduct, relating primarily to relations with Spain in the West Indies.

[Campbell, John.] An exact and authentic account of the greatest white-herring-fishery in Scotland. London, For J. Davidson, 1750. C34
A description of the Dutch fishing trade in the Shetland Island region, with a plea for improvement of English fishing there.

Campbell, John. A political survey of Britain. London, For the author, 1774. C35
An extensive survey of the historical development of British commerce, with a discussion of those areas which could be further improved and commentary on the country's ability to maintain a large commercial empire.

Campbell, John. A political survey of Britain. Dublin, T. Ewing, 1775. C36
The first Irish edition.

[Campbell, John.] The travels and adventures of Edward Brown, Esq. London, J. Applebee for A. Bettesworth [etc.], 1739. C37
A fictional travel, with interesting descriptions of Egypt and Ethiopia, as well as accounts of France, Italy and Switzerland.

Campbell, John. A view of the dangers to which the trade of Great-Britain to Turkey and Italy will be exposed ... London, W. Mears and O. Payne, 1734. C38
A plea for an active policy to protect English commerce to the Levant against the Spanish-French dominance of the Mediterranean.

Campillo y Cosío, José del. Nuevo sistema de govierno económico para la América. Manuscript. Madrid, 1767. C39
This work, first written in 1743, circulated in manuscript until it was published in 1789. The author was concerned with improving Spanish colonial commerce, and he compares it to the commerce of the French and British colonies.

Campillo y Cosío, José del. Nuevo sistema de govierno económico para la América: con los males y daños que el causa el que hoy tiene, do los que participa copiosamente España ... Madrid, Benito Cano, 1789. C40
The first printed edition.

[Campomanes, Pedro Rodríguez, conde de.] Discurso sobre el fomento de la industria popular. Madrid, Antonio de Sancha, 1774. C41
Proposals for changes in many aspects of Spain's economy.

Campomanes, Pedro Rodríguez, conde de. Discurso acerca do modo de fomentar a industria do povo ... Lisbon, Typografia Rollandiana, 1778. C42
This Portuguese edition contains a preface applying some of the principles of Campomanes to the Portuguese economy.

Campomanes, Pedro Rodríguez, conde de. Discurso sopra il fomento dell' industria popolare del conte di Campomanes tradotto dallo Spagnuolo da Don Antonio Conca ... Venice, Carlo Palese, 1787. C43
The first Italian edition, with an extensive note by the translator, Antonio Conca.

Campomanes, Pedro Rodríguez, conde de. Discurso sobre el fomento de la industria popular. Sampaloc, Hermano B.M.D. Franciscano, 1793. C44
This is a Philippine edition of *Discurso sobre el fomento de la industria popular*, first published in 1774. In his work Campomanes calls for the formation of local economic societies and this edition was printed with the help of one such society in Manila, the Real Sociedad Económica de la Ciudad de Manila.

Canada. Governor General. Extract of so much of the royal commission of the governor-general of Canada as defines the boundaries of that province. [London, 1857.] C45
Commissions of 1763, 1846, and 1854 are cited, showing the extension of the governor general's jurisdiction.

Canepa, Albino de. Portolan chart. [Genoa] 1489. C46
This chart includes all of Europe, extending to the Black and Red seas in the east, and shows Antilia at the western extreme. The cartographer was Genoese, and he indicates the Genoese trading stations in the Black Sea area.

[Canning, George.] A letter to the Right Honourable Wills, Earl of Hillsborough, on the connection between Great Britain and her American colonies. London, For T. Becket, 1768. C47
A discussion of the taxation problem, in its second issue, with a postscript more clearly stating the author's position.

Cano, Tomás. Arte para fabricar, fortificar, y apareiar naos de guerra, y merchante ... Seville, Luys Estupiñan, 1611. C48
This work concerns the construction and equipping of ships of war and of commerce, measuring their capacities, and some elements of navigation. It includes a glossary of marine terms.

Canovai, Stanislao. Viaggi d' Amerigo Vespucci. Florence, G. Pagani, 1817. C49
A detailed treatment of the question of Vespucci's disputed voyage of 1497.

Cantillon, Philip. The analysis of trade, commerce ... and foreign exchange. London, For the author, 1759. C50
Trade is considered from the national and international point of view. "Commerce makes those we negotiate with our friends, conquest, those we conquer our enemies." This text is based on Richard Cantillon's *Essai sur la nature du commerce en général*, but is so altered as to be considered a new work.

Cantillon, Richard. Essai sur la nature du commerce en général. London, Fletcher Gyles, 1755. C51
A theoretical work on economics and commerce believed to have influenced Adam Smith and other eighteenth-century economists.

Cantofer, Louis. Memoire relatif au commerce des Espagnols aux Indes Orientales et en Afrique. Manuscript. [France, ca. 1760]. C52
A survey of Spanish commerce in the East and in Africa, reflecting French interest in the scope and content of Spanish trade.

Capell, Rudolph. Vorstellungen des Norden, oder Bericht von einigen nordländern ... Hamburg, J. Naumann & G. Wolff, 1675. C53
Deals with the possibility of finding a Northeast Passage, and also contains descriptions of northern North America.

Capellen, R. J. (Robbert Lieve Jasper), baron van der. Origineel advys van Jonkheer R.J. Baron van der Capellen tot de Marschen Lathmer. [n.p., ca. 1782.] C54
Advice against the Netherlands making a separate peace with England.

Capitan de Fragata D. Fernando Quintano. Navegacion de China à Cadiz en tiempo de la monzon del S.O. por el Cabo de Buena Esperanza ò por el de Hornos: dada por el Capitan de Fragata D. Fernando Quintano. Manuscript in Spanish. [n.p., ca. 1790]. C55
A navigator's guide for sailing back to Cadiz from China by way of the East Indies archipelago and Cape Horn.

Capmany y de Montpalau, Antonio de. Memorias historicas sobre la marina, comercio y artes de la antigua ciudad de Barcelona. Madrid, A. de Sancha, 1779-92. C56
A history of the development of Barcelona's commerce from the earliest times.

Capper, James. Observations on the passage to India, through Egypt and across the great dessert. London, For W. Faden, J. Robson, and R. Sewell, 1784. C57
The author pleads for negotiations that will make possible the use of a Red Sea route to India, and describes his travels to India via the overland route through Mesopotamia.

Capper, James. Observations on the winds and monsoons. London, J. Debrett [etc.], 1801. C58
An extensive study of the winds and monsoons of the Indian Ocean, based on the author's observations and on the journals of navigators and others. A preface discusses the subject of winds in general, and of related meteorological subjects.

Captain Cook's voyages round the world. Newcastle, M. Brown, 1790. C59
This set contains fifty-one illustrations, more than half of them by Thomas Bewick and his partner Beilby.

Caradoc of Llancarvan. The historie of Cambria, now called Wales. London, R. Newberie and H. Denham, 1584. C60
Contains an account of the supposed discovery of America by the Welsh in 1170.

Carafa, Vincentio. Fondation faite par Mrs. De St-Gilles d'une maison de Jesuittes a la Nouvelle France. Manuscript. Rome, 1 Julliet 1647. C61
An autograph letter announcing the foundation of a Jesuit mission to the Hurons in New France, 1646-47.

[Cardenas, Alonso de.] A speech or complaint, lately made by the Spanish embassadour to His Majestie at Oxford, upon occasion of the taking of a ship called Sancta Clara in the port of Sancto Domingo. London, N. Butter, 1643. C62
Includes also the reply to the complaint and proclamation prohibiting purchase of goods from the ship.

Cardim, Antonio Francisco. Catalogus regularium, et secularium, qui in Japponiae regnis usque à fundata ibi a S. Francisco Xaverio gentis apos-

tolo ecclesia ab ethnicis in odium Christianae fidei sub quatuor tyrannis violenta morte sublati sunt ... Rome, Heredum Corbelletti, 1646.
C63

A listing of Christians executed in Japan from 1557 to 1640, with time and place indicated, and usually nationality of the victims as well as the manner of execution.

Cardim, Antonio Francisco. Fasciculus e Japponicis floribus, suo adhuc madentibus sanguine ... Rome, Heredum Corbelletti, 1646.
C64

Brief biographies of Jesuits who suffered death for their faith in Japan to 1637, including illustrations depicting the manner of their death.

Cardim, Antonio Francisco. Relaçam da viagem do galeam Saõ Lovrenço e sua perdicaõ nos bayxos de Moxincale em 3. de Setembro de 1649. Lisbon, Domingos Lopes Roza, 1651 [repr. 1737].
C65

Cardim, Antonio Francisco. Relaçaõ da gloriosa morte de quatro embaixadores Portuguezes, da cidade de Macao, com sincoenta, & sete Christaõs de sua companhia ... em Nangassaqui ... a tres de Agosto de 1640. Lisbon, Lorenço de Anueres, 1643.
C66

An account of the execution of members of an embassy from Macao which sought to restore commercial relations with Nagasaki after a decree of 1639 had prohibited it.

Cardim, Antonio Francisco. Cort verhael vande glorieuse doodt, van vier Portugiesche ambassadeurs vande stadt Macao met seven en vijftich Christenen van hun gheselschap, onthalst voor het Christen gheloof binnen Nangassaqui een stadt in Japonien den 3. Augusti 1640 ... Antwerp, Hendrick Aertssens, 1644.
C67

The first Dutch edition.

Cardim, Antonio Francisco. Mors felicissima quatuor legatorum Lusitanorum et sociorum quos Japponiae imperator occidit in odium Christianae religionis ... Rome, Heredum Corbelletti, 1646.
C68

The earlier Latin edition was published in Ingolstadt, 1644. The second Latin translation.

Cardoso, Fernando. Por el commercio de la ciudad de Sevilla ... n.p. [1647?].
C69

The record of a dispute between a merchant and Seville authorities concerning restrictions on imports.

Cardoso, Jorge. Agiologio Lusitano dos sanctos, e varoens illustres em virtude do reino de Portugal, e suas conquistas ... Lisbon, Officina Craesbeekiana, 1652-1744.
C70

A massive calendar of saints' days, with biographies of many saints whose work involved participation in Portuguese missions abroad.

Carle, Henri. Discours sur la question proposée par M. l'abbé Raynal: La découverte de l'Amérique a-t-elle été utile ou nuisible au genre humain? Paris, Moutard, 1790.
C71

An attempt to evaluate the total influence of America, considering its economic benefits and also the maltreatment of its natives, the impetus it gave to the slave trade, and other unfortunate factors.

Carletti, Francesco. Ragionamenti di Francesco Carletti Fiorentino sopra le cose da lui vedute ne' suoi viaggi. Florence, G. Manni, 1701.
C72

An account of the travels of a Florentine merchant to Mexico, Persia, India, China, the Philippines, and St. Helena.

Carli, Dionigi de. Il moro transportato nell' inclita città di Venetia, overo Curioso racconto de costumi, riti, e religione de popoli dell' Africa, America, Asia & Europa. Bassano, Gio. Antonio Remondini, 1687.
C73

An account of a Capuchin missionary's travels in Brazil, Africa, the Mediterranean, the Levant and Middle East.

Carli, Gian Rinaldo, conte. Delle lettere Americane. [Florence] 1780.
C74

A discussion of the origins of the American Indians, including a substantial bibiography of the literature of New World exploration.

[Carli, Gian Rinaldo, conte.] Le lettere americana. Cremona, Lorenzo Manini, 1781-83.
C75

The first volume concerns the old Central and South American civilizations; volumes two and three attempt to prove that the American aboriginals descended from the Atlantides.

Carli, Gian Rinaldo, conte. Lettres américaines, dans lesquelles on examine l'origine, l'etat civil, politique, militaire, & religieux, les arts, l'industrie, les sciences, les moeurs, les usages des anciens habitans de l'Amérique. Boston; Paris, Buisson, 1788.
C76

The translator, Jean Baptiste Lefebvre de Villebrune, adds extensive notes and a preface while reducing the number of letters to forty-nine from fifty-five in the 1780 edition.

[Carlier, Claude.] Dissertation ... du commerce de France. Paris, Thiboust, 1753.
C77

A discussion of the commerce of France from the fifth to the ninth centuries.

Caron, François. Beschrijvinghe van het machtigh coninckrijcke Japan. Amsterdam, Joost Hartgers, 1648.
C78

Includes a wide range of information on Japanese commerce, gathered by the governor of the Dutch East India Company there.

Caron, François. Fr. Carons und Jod. Schouten wahrhaftige Beschreibung en zweyer mächtigen Königreiche, Jappan und Siam. Nuremberg, M. and J. F. Endters, 1663.   C79
    A collection of East Indian travels containing the first edition of Jacob Merklein's account based on nine years in the East Indies, and also a description of Siam written by Joost Schouten.

Caron, François. A true description of the mighty kingdoms of Japan and Siam. London, Samuel Broun and John de l'Ecluse, 1663.   C80
    The first separate publication in English.

Caron, François. A true description of the mighty kingdoms of Japan and Siam. London, For Robert Boulter, 1671.   C81
    The second English edition.

Caron, Noel de. Nieus uyt Engelant gheschreven door den Heer Ambassadeur Noel de Caron aen de ... Staten Generael ... n.p., 1621.   C82
    The ambassador fears a decline in relations with the English, due primarily to the rivalry of the two countries in the East Indies.

Carpani, Melchiorre. Memorie sopra la vita di Hyder Aly Kan. Lodi, Antonio Pallavicini, 1782.   C83
    A biography of an important political figure in southern India, written by a Barnabite priest.

Carpeau de Saussay. Voyage de Madagascar. Paris, J.L. Nyon, 1722.   C84
    Describes a voyage to Madagascar undertaken in 1663, with observations on the economic opportunities there and on adjacent islands.

Carranza, Alonso. El aiustamiento i proporcion de las monedas de oro, plata i cobre. Madrid, F. Martinez, 1629.   C85
    A discussion of the relationship of gold and silver to commerce.

Carrasco del Saz, Francisco. Opera ominibus iurium scientiae stusiosis utillissima pristino nitori restituta, ab auctoris filio ... Madrid, Julianum de Paredes, 1648.   C86
    A compilation of laws for governing Spanish America compiled by a judge and senator in the royal audiencia of Panama.

Carrasco, Mem. Lopo. Copey eines Sendbriefs, der des nechstuerschinen 1571 Jars, dem durchleuchtigisten Künig zů Portugal auss India. [Dillingen, Sebaldum Mayer] 1572.   C87
    An account of the survival of a Portuguese ship that was set upon by a fleet from Achin as it sailed from Cochin to Sunda in 1569.

Carré. Voyage des Indes Orientales, mêlé de plusieurs histoires curieuses. Paris, Veuve de Claude Barbin, 1699.   C88
    A collection of geographical and historical information on India, Persia, and Asia Minor by an author who claimed to have traveled there at the instance of Colbert.

Carta en que se vindica la iusticia, y equidad de las reales sentencias pronunciadas sobre la pertenencia del dinero salvado de la perdida de Cobadonga ... contra la Real Audiencia de estas islas ... Manila, Nicolas de la Cruz Bagay, 1747.   C89
    A legal argument resulting from the loss of the Manila galleon *Covandonga* to the English Commodore George Anson in 1743 off the Philippine Islands.

Carter, George. A narrative of the loss of the Grosvenor East Indiaman. London, For J. Murray and William Lane, 1791.   C90
    An account of the loss of an English East Indiaman on the coast of Africa, with a description of the tragic overland march to Dutch settlements.

[Carter, William.] England's interest asserted, in the improvement of its native commodities; and more especially the manufacture of wool ... London, For Francis Smith, 1669.   C91
    Stressing the importance of wool and woolen manufactures to England's economy, the author advocates restrictions upon the export of raw wool so as to increase the cloth manufacture of England.

Carter, William. Englands interest by trade asserted, shewing the necessity and excellency thereof. London, For the author, 1671.   C92
    The second edition.

Cartier, Jacques. A shorte and briefe narration of the two navigations and discoveries to the north-weast partes called Newe Fraunce. London, H. Bynneman, 1580.   C93
    The first English edition, translated by John Florio, recounting the events of Cartier's voyages of 1534 and 1535, published at the prompting of Richard Hakluyt whose interests in English colonization are apparent in the introduction.

Cartwright, George. A journal of transactions and events during a residence of nearly sixteen years on the coast of Labrador. Newark [England] Allin and Ridge, 1792.   C94
    An intimate and detailed description of the life of an English fur trader in Labrador.

Cartwright, John. The preachers travels. London, For T. Thorppe, 1611.   C95
    An account of travels in the Middle East in 1602-03, noting the products, routes in use, and potential opportunities for English commerce.

[Carvalho, Jorge de.] Relação verdadeira dos sucessos do conde de Castel Melhor, preso na cidade de Cartagena de Indias ... Lisbon, D. Lopes Rosa, 1642. C96
Concerns the activities of João Rodrigues de Sousa against the Dutch in South America, primarily in Cartagena. He later fought the Dutch around Pernambuco.

Carvalho, Valentin. Lettera della Cina dell' anno 1601. Rome, Luigi Zannetti, 1603. C97
This letter reports on the Jesuit College at Macao, and also on the Society's efforts in China, particularly Peking, Nanking, and Chang-chow.

Carver, Jonathan. Travels through the interior parts of North-America, in the years 1766, 1767 and 1768. London, For the author, 1778. C98
The first edition of a classic in the history of the exploration of the Great Lakes and upper Mississippi regions.

Carver, Jonathan. Travels through the interior parts of North America, in the years 1766, 1767, and 1768. London, For the author by William Richardson, 1779. C99
The second edition, with an illustration of the tobacco plant not found in the first edition.

Carver, Jonathan. Travels through the interior parts of North-America, in the years 1766, 1767, and 1768. Dublin, For S. Price [etc.] 1779. C100
The only map in this Dublin edition varies from maps in the other editions.

Carver, Jonathan. Travels through the interior parts of North America, in the years 1766, 1767, and 1768. London, C. Dilly, H. Payne, and J. Phillips, 1781. C101
The text is a reissue of the 1779 London edition, with introductory material and index added, and with the maps and three of the illustrations colored.

Carver, Jonathan. Three years travels, through the interior parts of North-America. Philadelphia, Joseph Crukshank and Robert Bell, 1784. C102
The first American edition.

Carver, Jonathan. Three years travels through the interior parts of North-America. Philadelphia, Printed by J. Crukshank, 1789. C103
Dedicated to Sir Joseph Banks. Includes vocabularies of Dakota and Ojibwa languages.

Carver, Jonathan. Three years travels throughout the interior parts of North-America. Portsmouth, New Hampshire, C. Peirce for D. West, 1794. C104
As above, dedicated to Sir Joseph Banks, and including the vocabularies of the Dakota and Ojibwa languages.

Carver, Jonathan. Three years travels through the interior parts of North-America, for more than five thousand miles. Philadelphia, Key & Simpson, 1796. C105
This edition includes a list of subscribers.

Carver, Jonathan. Reisen durch die innern Gegenden von Nord-Amerika in den Jahren 1766, 1767 und 1768. Hamburg, Carl Ernst Bohn, 1780. C106
The first German edition.

Carver, Jonathan. Voyage dans les parties intérieures de l'Amérique Septentrionale. Paris, Pissot, 1784. C107
The unknown translator of this first French edition adds to Carver's text numerous notes and two supplementary chapters on western exploration.

Carver, Jonathan. Voyage dans les parties interiéures de l'Amérique Septentrionale. Yverdon, 1784. C108
The second French edition, differing from the first of the same year by notes added by the translator, Jean-Etienne Montucla.

Carver, Jonathan. Reize door de binnenlanden van Noord-Amerika. Leiden, A. en J. Honkoop, 1796. C109
This Dutch translation by Jean David Pasteur is based on the 1781 English edition. Occasional notes are added by the translator.

Carver, Jonathan. A treatise on the culture of the tobacco plant. London, For the author, 1779. C110
A book of instruction for tobacco planting in Great Britain, intending to supplant the losses due to the interruption of American trade during the American Revolution.

[Carver Land Grant Papers.] A collection of twenty-three items, including deeds and correspondence, dated 1802-1816. C111
The Carver Land Grant was a claim upon land along the Mississippi River in Minnesota and Wisconsin based upon deeds allegedly made to Jonathan Carver in 1767 by Indian chiefs of that region.

Cary, John. A discourse concerning the East-India trade. London, 1696. C112
"One thing I aim at in this discourse, is to persuade the gentry of England to be more in love with our own manufactures ..."

Cary, John. A discourse concerning the East-India trade ... London, For E. Baldwin, 1699. C113
The author adds to his text of 1696 observations by Sir Josiah Child and Charles Davenant as well as a French decree prohibiting importing of calicoes, all intending to

support his contention of the need to adjust trade policy to domestic manufacturers' interests.

Cary, John. A discourse concerning the trade of Ireland and Scotland. London, 1696. C114
Taken from the author's *Essay on the state of England*, this tract advocates restriction of Irish woolen manufacturing and encouragement of her agriculture, and predicts failure for Scottish attempts to establish plantations abroad.

Cary, John. A discourse of the advantage of the African trade to this nation. n.p. [ca. 1712]. C115
"I take the African trade ... to be very beneficial to this kingdom, and would be made much more so ... were it laid open by being formed into a Regulated Company."

Cary, John. A discourse on trade. London, For T. Osbourne, 1745. C116
A consideration of the commerce of all countries with which England traded in the mid-eighteenth century.

Cary, John. Essai sur l'etat du commerce d'Angleterre. Paris, Guillyn, 1755. C117
The translator states that he used the editions of 1715 and 1745 as well as the original edition of 1695 in making this translation.

Cary, John. An essay on the state of England in relation to its trade ... Bristol, W. Bonny, for the author, 1695. C118
A Bristol merchant advances ideas to improve England's trade, dealing with both inland and overseas commerce.

Cary, John. A reply to a paper ... entituled *The linnen-drapers answer to that part of Mr. Cary's essay on trade that concerns the East-India trade*. [London, 1700.] C119
A reaffirmation of Mr. Cary's principle that the textile industry of Great Britain would flourish best if raw materials rather than textiles were imported.

Casas, Bartolomé de las. Aqui se contiene una disputa; o controversia: entre ... Bartholome de las Casas ... y el doctor Gines de Sepulveda. Seville, Sebastian Trugillo, 1552. C120
The first in a series of tracts written to declare the right of Indians in Spanish America to humane treatment. The following eight items were issued in support of the same cause.

Casas, Bartolomé de las. Aqui se contiene treynta proposiciones muy juridicas. Seville, Sebastiã Trugillo, 1552. C121

Casas, Bartolomé de las. Aqui se contiene unos avisos y reglas para los confessores. Seville, Sebastian Trugillo, 1552. C122

Casas, Bartolomé de las. Brevissima relacion de la destruycion de las Indias. Seville, Sebastian Trugillo, 1552. C123

Casas, Bartolomé de las. Entre los remedios que don Fray Bartolome de las Casas ... para reformacion de las Indias. [Seville, Sebastian Trugillo] 1552. C124

Casas, Bartolomé de las. Este es un tratado ... sobre la materia de los Yndios que se han hecho en ... esclavos. Seville, Sebastian Trugillo, 1552. C125

Casas, Bartolomé de las. Lo que se sigue es un pedaço de una carta y relacion que escrivio cierto hombre. [Seville, Sebastian Trugillo] 1552. C126

Casas, Bartolomé de las. Principia quedã ex quibus procedendum est disputatione ad manifestandam defendendam iusticiam Yndorum. Seville, Sebastiani Trugilli, 1552. C127

Casas, Bartolomé de las. Tratado comprobatorio del imperio soberano ... que los reyes de Castilla y Leon tienen sobre las Indias. Seville, Sebastiã Trugillo, 1552. C128

Casas, Bartolomé de las. Tyrannies et cruautez des Espagnols, perpetrees e's Indes Occidentale, qu' on dit le Nouveau monde ... traduictes par Jaques de Miggrode ... Antwerp, François Ravelenghien, 1579. C129
The first French edition of the *Destruction of the Indies*.

Casas, Bartolomé de las. The Spanish colonie, or briefe chronicle of the acts and gestes of the Spaniardes in the West Indies. London, For William Brome, 1583. C130
This is the first English edition of *The destruction of the Indies* first published in 1552. It was translated from the French edition of 1579.

Casas, Bartolomé de las. Narratio regionum Indicarum per Hispanos quosdam deuastarum verissima ... Anno veró hoc 1598 Latiné excusa. Frankfurt, Theodori de Bry & Ioanis Saurii, 1598. C131
The first Latin edition, translated from a French edition of 1579.

Casas, Bartolomé de las. Spieghel der Spaenscher tyrannye in West-Indien. ... Amsterdam, Cornelis Claesz, 1607. C132
This is the fourth Dutch edition, following closely the text of the first Dutch edition of 1578.

Casas, Bartolomé de las. Istoria ò brevissima relatione della distruttione dell' Indie

Occidentali ... Venice, Marco Ginammi, 1626. C133

The first Italian edition, with Spanish text in parallel columns.

Casas, Bartolomé de las. La libertà pretesa dal supplice schiavo Indiano di Monsignor Reverendiss. D. Bartolomeo dalle Case, ò Casaus, Sivigliano, dell' Ordine de' Predicatori, & Vescovo di Chiapa ... Venice, Marco Ginammi, 1640. C134

Translation of one of the tracts from 1552, with Spanish and Italian text in parallel columns.

Casas, Bartolomé de las. Istoria, ò brevissima relatione della distruttione dell' Indie Occidentali ... Venice, Marco Ginammi, 1643. C135

This is the third edition of the Spanish and Italian texts, differing from the first only in the dedicatory statement.

Casas, Bartolomé de las. Conquista dell' Indie Occidentali di Monsignor fra Bartolomeo dalle Case, ò Casaus, Sivigliano, Vescovo di Chiapa ... Venice, Marco Ginammi, 1645. C136

Spanish and Italian texts of Las Casas' tract *Acqui se contiene una disputa* ... with the *Principia quaedam ex quibus procedendum est in disputatione* ... placed between the *argomento* and the text.

Casas, Bartolomé de las. Il supplice schiavo Indiano di Monsig. reverendiss. D. Bartolomeo dalle Case, ò Casaus, Sivigliano, dell' Ordine de' predicatori, & vescovo di Chiapa ... Venice, Per li Ginammi, 1657. C137

The third edition of the Spanish and Italian texts, with new dedicatory material.

Casas, Bartolomé de las. Den vermeerderden spieghel der Spaensche tierannije geschiet in Westindien ... Amsterdam, Gillis Joosten Saeghman, 1664. C138

A late Dutch edition, much altered from earlier editions as each of the seventeen engravings is accompanied by a verse with anti-Spanish commentary.

Casas, Bartolomé de las. La decouverte des Indes Occidentales, par les Espagnols. Paris, André Pralard, 1697. C139

A highly edited translation of Las Casas' *Brevissima relacion*, including material from other Las Casas tracts as well as an account of his controversy with Sepulveda over the rights of American Indians.

Casas, Bartolomé de las. Relation des voyages et des découvertes que les Espagnols ont fait dans les Indes Occidentales: ecrite par Dom B. Las-Casas, evêque de Chiapa. Amsterdam, J. Louis de Lorme, 1698. C140

The second French edition, based on seven of the Las Casas tracts. Appended to it is an account of a voyage along the African coast by the pirate Montauban.

Casas, Bartolomé de las. An account of the first voyages and discoveries made by the Spaniards in America. London, J. Darby for D. Brown, 1699. C141

A translation from the French, containing abridgements of seven Las Casas tracts. *The art of traveling to advantage* is appended.

Casas, Bartolomé de las. A relation of the first voyages and discoveries made by the Spaniards in America. London, D. Brown and A. Bell, 1699. C142

This English translation contains six tracts. It is based upon the French translation of Amsterdam, 1698.

The case of Mainwaring, Hawes, Payne, and others, concerning a depredation made by the Spanish-West-India fleete. [London] 1646. C143

Concerns the seizure of English ships by Spanish and others in the West Indies.

The case of opposition stated, between the craftsman and the people. London, For J. Roberts, 1731. C144

A hostile reaction to *The Craftsman* for opposition to the government's conclusion of the Treaty of Seville.

The case of the bank contract. In answer to the infamous scurrilities of several libels lately printed in The Craftsman ... London, For T. Cooper, 1735. C145

A defense of Sir Robert Walpole for assisting in making a contract between the Bank of England and the South Sea Company in 1720 and for subsequently extricating the Bank from the agreement.

The case of the booksellers trading beyond the sea ... n.p. [ca. 1700]. C146

Concerns duties on books imported into England.

The case of the British northern colonies. n.p., [ca. 1750]. C147

A protest against proposed taxes on sugar and molasses from the French West Indies, pointing out how the northern colonies' fishing, lumbering, and other trades are tied to this commerce.

The case of the British sugar-colonies. [London, ca. 1731.] C148

A leaflet advancing the argument that New England merchants trading with the French West Indies in sugar and other commodities were in effect weakening the British presence in the West Indies and reducing its sugar trade to other parts of the world.

The case of the creditors of the Royal African-Company. n.p. [1711]. C149

The creditors note the efforts they had made to support the company's trade.

The case of the fann-makers; who have petitioned the honorable House of Commons. [London, ca. 1695.] C150
A request that the importing of fans from the East Indies be prohibited.

The case of the Hudson's-Bay Company. [London, ca. 1748.] C151
The company's response to critics who sought to deprive it of its monopoly.

The case of the Italian merchants. [London, ca. 1719.] C152
A defense of the Italian trade as one taking large amounts of English woolens and returning raw silk, the foundation of another English industry.

The case of the Italian merchants, importing goods of the growth of Asia, by way of Italy. [London, ca. 1719.] C153
The merchants trading to Italy contend that if Turkish silk comes to England by way of Leghorn it is because of the high prices charged by the Levant Company for its silk.

The case of the manufactures, and others, concerned in the making and vending of beaver hats. [London, 1752.] C154
The hatters request assistance and especially that the export of unmanufactured beaver be stopped, claiming that their trade had declined because of competition from abroad and the beaver trade monopoly of the Hudson's Bay Company.

The case of the merchants trading to and from America. [London, 1730]. C155
A plea from merchants of Bristol for more protection of their trade to the West Indies, noting losses to Spanish ships including crew, cargo and other details.

The case of the planters of tobacco in Virginia as represented by themselves. London, For J. Roberts, 1733. C156
Traces the progress of Virginia's tobacco trade through forty years from the planters' point of view.

The case of the present possessors of the French lands in the island of St. Christopher. London, For the author, 1721. C157
The author opposes giving some lands on St. Christopher to the South Sea Company because it would upset the sugar trade there.

Case of the proprietors of India annuities, on the notice given by the right honourable the speaker of the House of Commons, March 25, 1791; and the renewal of the charter of the East India Company now under discussion ... London, Printed for John Stockdale, 1793. C158
A discussion of the financial arrangements between the East India Company and the British government, involving a loan and sale of annuities, as they relate to the company's continued monopoly on East Indian commerce.

The case of the rope-makers of London. [London, ca. 1700.] C159
A broadside calling attention to the fact that English export duties on cordage make it impossible for English cordage to compete with that from other countries.

The case of the separate traders to Africa. With remarks on the African company's memorial. n.p. [ca. 1709]. C160
An argument against restoring the monopoly of the Royal African Company, and against the ten per cent duty paid by independent traders.

Casos notables, sucedidos en las costas de la ciudad de Lima, en las Indias, y como el armada Olandesa procurava coger el armadilla nuestra ... Desde el mes de Junio deste año passado de 1624. Madrid, Juan Gonçalez, 1625. C161
A newsletter account of an unsuccessful attempt by a Dutch fleet to capture a Spanish silver fleet off Callao. Much of the narrative is supplied by a Greek sailor from the Dutch fleet who was captured.

Cassani, José. Historia de la provincia de la Compañia de Jesus del Nuevo Reyno de Granada. Madrid, Manuel Fernandez, 1741. C162
This history of the Jesuit missions in New Granada also includes a map showing the location of the Jesuit establishments, and biographies of the leading figures in the mission from its beginnings in 1603 to 1686.

Cassel, Johann Philipp. Dissertatio philologico historica de navigationibus fortuitis in Americam. Magdeburg, Joan Christ Siegeler, 1742. C163
A collection from classical and Norse sources of writings that pertain to the possibility of a pre-Columbian discovery of America.

Castaneda, Balthasar de. Señor ... Castaneda ... dize: Que haviendo passado ... a las referidas Islas ... [Manila? ca. 1725.] C164
A memoir written by a friend of a former governor of the Philippines, giving information on the economy of the islands, and their relations with Spain, America, and Asia.

Castanheda, Fernão Lopes de. Le premier livre de l'histoire de l'Inde ... Paris, M. de Vascosan, 1553. C165
The first translation of volume one of Castanheda's great chronicle, from the 1551 Portuguese edition of which only one volume was published.

Castanheda, Fernão Lopes de. Historia del descubrimiento y conquista dela India por los Portugueses. Antwerp, Martin Nucio, 1554. C166

The first Spanish edition of the separately published first volume.

Castanheda, Fernão Lopes de. The first booke of the historie of the discoverie and conquest of the East Indias. London, Thomas East, 1582.
C167
The first English edition of the first volume.

Castanheda, Fernão Lopes de. Warhafftige und volkomene Historia von erfindung Calecut und anderer Königreich, Landen und Inseln in Indien ... [Augsburg?] 1565.
C168
The first German edition of the first volume, the original of which was issued in 1551 apart from the later eight-volume edition.

Castanheda, Fernão Lopes de. Historia do descobrimento e conquista da India pelos Portugueses. Coimbra, J. Barreira and J. Alvarez, 1552-61.
C169
This eight-volume set is one of the great chronicles of early Portuguese activities in India. The author lived for many years in India, and traveled widely in the East during the first half of the sixteenth century.

Castanheda, Fernão Lopes de. Historia dell' Indie Orientali. Venice, Francesco Ziletti, 1578.
C170
The first Italian edition.

Castell, William. A short discoverie of the coasts and continent of America. London, 1644.
C171
A description of areas for potential settlement by English colonists. Although the author was a clergyman, he is at least as concerned with commercial opportunities as with missionary work.

Castiglion Fiorentino. Laws, etc. Communitatis terre Castilionis Statuta ad publicam utilitatem impressa. [Perugia, Hieronymū Francisci Baldasarris de Cartholarijs, 1535.]
C172
Laws governing a commune in Arezzo, under Florentine rule from 1384.

Castiglioni, Luigi. Viaggio negli Stati Uniti dell' America Settentrionale fatto negli anni 1785, 1786, e 1787. Milan, Giuseppe Marelli, 1790.
C173
Travel account describing all of the states and Canada, noting commercial, social, political aspects of life, and containing an extensive survey of the natural history of North America.

Castilho, Antonio de. Commentario do cerco de Goa, e Chaul, no anno de 1570. Lisbon, Joaquiniana da Musica, 1736.
C174
The sieges of Goa and Chaul were important to the subsequent decline of Portuguese interests in India.

[Castilhon, Jean.] Anecdotes chinoises, japonoises, siamoises, tonquinoises, &c ... Paris, Vincent, 1774.
C175
A survey of the Far East with respect to the economies, peoples, cultures, and histories of the individual countries.

Castillo, Luis del. Compendio cronológico de la historia y del estado actual del imperio Ruso. Madrid, Aznar, 1796.
C176
A history and description of Russia, noting its political, religious, and military institutions as well as its social classes and its economy. A statistical table of the commerce of St. Petersburg for the period 1788-1791 is included.

Castleyn, Johannes. De victoorieuse voyagie van den Heer ... Adm. De Ruyter ... Haarlem, Johannes Castluyn [1665].
C177
A little known account of de Ruyter's sea engagements with the English.

Castro, Francisco de. La octava maravilla, y sin segundo milagro de Mexico, perpetuado en las rosas de Guadalupe ... Mexico, Viuda de Miguel de Rivera Calderō, 1729.
C178
Also included is the *Metrica passion de el humando dios* by the same author, a Jesuit. Both works are poetic in form and deal with the benefits of Christianity to the people of Mexico.

Castro, João de. Roteiro que fez dom João de Castro de viajem que fezeram os Portugueses desda India atee Soez. Manuscript. [Portugal, ca. 1543-45.]
C179
This roteiro from Goa to Suez was made following the voyage through the Red Sea by Estevão da Gama. In addition to text describing the coastal areas it contains sixteen colored maps of various harbors.

Castro, Pedro de, Captain. Causas eficientes, y accidentales del fluxo y refluxo del mar ... con la diversidad de corrientes en todo el ambito del orbe aquatil ... Madrid, Manuel Ruiz de Murga, 1694.
C180
This discussion of tides is largely a response to problems raised by Francisco de Seixas y Lovera in his *Theatro naval hydro-graphico*.

Catalogue des marchandises formant les cargaisons des navires Américains. [Antwerp], L.P. Delacroix, 1810.
C181
An auction catalog of the cargo of eighteen ships, impounded on the orders of Napoleon, to be sold on October 15, 1810 and the following days in Antwerp. The catalog lists tobacco, sugar, cotton, coffee, pepper and ivory from sixteen of the eighteen ships. A notice on the catalog explains that the remainder of the catalog will be printed prior to the sale.

A catalogue of the damages for which the English demand reparation from the United-Netherlands. London, H. Brome, 1664.
C182

A summary of complaints made against the Dutch in connection with commercial rivalries in the East Indies.

A catalogue of the different specimens of cloth collected in the three voyages of Captain Cook ... London, For A. Shaw, 1787.   C183
Contains samples of more than fifty varieties of bark cloth brought back to England from the South Sea, with information as to the methods of manufacture.

Catholic Church. Bishopric of Guadalajara (Spain). [Spanish manuscript collection.] ca. 900 documents. Orche, Guadalajara, Madrid, and other places, ca. 1663-1890.   C184
The documents included in the collection are wills and statements of wills, inventories of possessions at time of death, donations of real estate, baptismal certificates, receipts, letters, and accounts of expenses and income.

Catholic Church. Congregatio de Propaganda Fide. Demandes faites par les missionaires de la Chine, a la sacree Congregation de Propaganda Fide. Paris, Congregation de Propaganda Fide, 1645.   C185
Seventeen questions propounded to the Congregation by the Jesuits regarding the acceptance of Chinese customs within the community of Chinese Christians, with the Congregation's replies.

Catholic Church. Congregatio Sacrorum Rituum. Sacra rituum congregation ... Card. Paulutio Limana beatificationis, & Canonazionis ven. servi Dei Francisci Camacho ... Rome, Reverendae Camerae Apostolicae, 1753.   C186
Proceedings for the beatification of Francisco Camacho who served thirty-five years as a missionary in Peru.

Catholic Church. Congregation Sacrorum Rituum. Congregatione sacrorum rituum sive eminentissimo, ac reverendissimo D. Card. Azzolino Japponen. Canonizationis, seu declarationis martyrii ... Alphonsi Navarette ... Petri de Avila ... Petri de Zunica ... Caroli Spinulae ... pro fide catholica in Japponia interemptorum. Rome, Typographia Rever. Cam. Apostolicae, 1675.   C187
A collection of documentation relating to the canonization of missionaries in Japan who died in the "Great Martyrdom" of 1622.

Catholic Church. Pope. Bullarum collectio quibus serenissimis Lusitaniae, Algarbiorumque regibus terrarum omnium, atque insularum ultra mare transcurrentium. Lisbon, Valentini A'Costa Deslandes, 1707.   C188
This is a collection of more than forty bulls and other papal pronouncements with reference to Portuguese discoveries, exploration, and commerce in the East and West Indies from 1514 to 1668.

Catholic Church. Pope (1572-1585: Gregory XIII). Acta consistorii publice exhibiti a S.D.N. Gregorio Papa XIII. Regum Japoniorum legatis Romae, die XXIII Martii. M.D.L.XXXV. Rome, apud Franciscum Zannettum, 1585.   C189
The first edition of the first account of Pope Gregory's public reception of the first Japanese embassy to Europe.

Catholic Church. Pope (1623-1644: Urban VIII). Indultum S.D.N. Urbani VIII. celebrandi Missam, & recitandi officium, de tribus martyribus Paulo Michi, Ioanne de Goto, & Didaco Quizai e Societate Iesu. Rome, Ex Typographia Reu. Camerae Apostolicae, 1627.   C190
An indulgence granted on the canonization of three Japanese Jesuits who had been crucified in 1597.

Catholic Church. Pope (1644-1655: Innocent X). Bref de nostre saint pere le pape Innocent X. Sur le differend d'entre l'Evesque d'Angelopolis ... en la Nouvelle Espagne dans les Indes Occidentales, & les PP. Iesuites ... Rome, Typographia Reverendae Camerae Apostolicae, 1659.   C191
An adjudication of a dispute between the bishop of Angelopolis, Juan Palafox y Mendoza, and the Jesuits in Mexico over the rights of the latter.

Catholic Church. Pope (1740-1758: Benedict XIV). Lettres en forme de bref, de N.S.P. le Pape Benoist XIV, par lesquelles, ... il établit & constitute l'Eminentissime et Reverendissime François de Saldanha ... visiteur & reformateur des clercs réguliers de la Compagnie de Jesus, dans les royaumes de Portugal & des Algarves ... Lisbon, Michel Rodrigues, 1758.   C192
A decree of 1 April 1758 with instructions to Cardinal Saldanha to relieve the Jesuits in Portugal and its colonies of all properties and possessions.

Catholic Church. Pope (1758-1769: Clement XIII). Lettre ... sur l'observance des loix canoniques, contre les clercs qui sont le négoce, & qui s'ingérent dans les affaires séculieres. Rome, Imprimerie de la Chambre Apostolique, 1759.   C193
A papal letter which clarifies church regulations on the participation of Jesuits in mercantile affairs.

Catholic Church. Province of Mexico City (Mexico). Concilio provincial (1st: 1555; 2nd: 1565; 3rd: 1585). Concilios provinciales primero, y segundo [y tercero] celebrados en la muy noble, y muy leal ciudad de México. Mexico, Joseph Antonio de Hogal, 1769.   C194
Texts of three councils of the Catholic Church held in Mexico City in 1555, 1565, and 1585 to review and establish church policy there. The editor, Cardinal Francisco Antonio Lorenzana y Butrón, has added considerable biographical material on prominent churchmen in Mexico.

Catholic Church. Province of Mexico City (Mexico). Concilio Provincial (3rd: 1585). Concilium Mexicanum provinciale, celebratum Mexici anno MDLXXXV ... Et postea iussu regio editum Mexici anno MDCXXII. Paris, 1725. C195

This third provincial council was the most important held during the viceregal period in North America and greatly affected the religious, social and political life of New Spain.

Catholic Church. Province of Peru. Concilio Provincial (3rd : 1583) Concilium Limense. Celebraium anno 1583 sub Gregorio XIII. Sum. Pont. auctoritate Sixti Quinti Pont. Max. approbatum. Madrid, J. Sanchez, 1614. C196

The second edition of an account of the ecclesiastical council in Peru first published in 1591. Authorship has been attributed to José de Acosta. Contains information on the Church's relationship with the Peruvian Indians.

Catholic Church. Rota Romana. Laws, etc. Aegidiane constitutiones recognitae, ac novissime impressae. [Rome, Francisci Priscianensis, 1543.] C197

Constitutions governing the Marches, under papal jurisdiction, including the major city of Ancona.

Catholic Church. [Treaties, etc. France, 1734 Mar. 11] Concordat sur le tabac, les Indiennes, et le commerce, fait entre les commissaires da Sa Sainteté & de Sa Majesté tres-Chrétienne le 11 mars 1734. Avignon, Joseph Mouries, 1759. C198

The publication of an earlier agreement between the French king and papal authorities concerning the trade in tobacco and certain types of cloth.

Caulín, Antonio. Historia coro-graphica natural y evangelica de la Nueva Andalucia provincias de Cumaná, Guayana, y vertientes del Rio Orinoco. Madrid, Juan de San Martin, 1779. C199

An account of the geography, natural history, discovery and conquest, and missionary activities of Spaniards in Venezuela by one who had been a missionary there.

Causa Jesuitica de Portugal, o documentos autenticos, bulas, leyes reales, despachos de la secretaria de estado, y otras piezas originales, que precedieron á la reforma, y motivaron despues la expulsion de las Jesuitas de los dominios de Portugal. Madrid, Imprenta Real de la Gazeta, 1768. C200

Documents from the period 1754-1758 relative to the Jesuits in South America and their expulsion.

The causes of Scotland's miseries. A poem in imitation of the vi ode of the third book of Horace. Edinburgh, James Watson, 1700. C201

Scotland's failure in its effort at colonization in America is attributed to moral decline at home.

Cavallotto, Giandomenico. Saggio di osservazioni particolari sopra lo stato in cui attrovasi presentemente la naval costruzione in Venezia. Venice, Modesto Fenzo, 1766. C202

An essay on problems of constructing ships for commercial use that also contains some history of the building of commercial ships.

Cavazzi, Giovanni Antonio. Istorica descrizione de' tre' regni Congo, Matamba, et Angola. Bologna, Giacomo Monti, 1687. C203

A description of western Africa, with material on the competition between the Dutch and Portuguese for bases on the coast.

Cavazzi, Giovanni Antonio. Historische Beschreibung der ... drey Königreichen, Congo, Matamba und Angola. Munich, Johann Jäcklin, 1694. C204

The first German edition.

Cavazzi, Giovanni Antonio. Relation historique de l'Ethiopie occidentale. Paris, Charles-Jean-Baptiste Delespine, 1732. C205

This edition by Jean Baptiste Labat is augmented by several Portuguese accounts of West Africa. It also includes illustrative material not in earlier editions.

Cavendish, Thomas. Copye, overgeset wt de Engelsche taele in onse Nederlandtsche spraecke gheschreven aen Milore Tresorier. Van Mr. Thomas Candische ... Amsterdam, Cornelis Claesz [1588?]. C206

A Dutch translation of Cavendish's letter to Lord Hunsdon describing his circumnavigation, the first account of it to be written, dated September 9, 1588.

Cawood, Francis. Navigation compleated: being a new method never before attain'd to by any. Whereby the true longitude of any place in the world may be found ... London, For the author, 1710. C207

A rejoinder against critics of the author's theories which appear to be abstract and inconsequential to the development of navigation.

Cedillo, Pedro Manuel. Tratado de la cosmographia, y nautica. Cadiz, Dom Manuèl Espinosa de los Monteros [1745]. C208

A handbook on cosmography and navigation which contains considerable geographical information, including speculations about the northwest passage and evidence of Spanish awareness of Russian discoveries on the North American coast.

Cellarius, Christoph. Geographia antiqua iuxta & nova, recognita denuo & ad veterum nouorumque scriptorum sidem, historicorum maxime, idemtidem castigata, & nova editione plurimis locis aucta ac immutata. Jena, Jo. Bielkii, 1706. C209

Cellarius was professor of history and rhetoric at the University of Halle. This is the last edition of this popular world geography published during the author's lifetime. It has been revised throughout and includes the latest information on North and South America, Africa and Asia.

Cellarius, Christoph. Nucleus geographiae antiquae et novae. Jena, Bielckianis, 1676. C210
The first edition of this world geography by Cellarius. The work was considerably augmented by others after the author's death in 1707. This pocket-sized edition was designed for school use.

Censure de quelques propositions des pp. Le Comte et Le Gobien, Jesuites, publiée sous le nom de la Faculté de Théologie de Paris, refutée par les ecrits des Dominiquains & des Franciscains missionaires de la Chine les plus opposez aux Jesuites. n.p., 1700. C211
An attempt to refute the censure of Le Gobien's *Memoires de la Chine* by comparing sections of it to Domingo Fernández Navarrete's *Tratados historicos ... de la monarchie de China*, Madrid, 1676, together with a reply to the Jesuit position.

Centellas, Joachim de. Les voyages et conquestes des roys de Portugal es Indes d'Orient. Paris, Jean d'Ongoys, 1578. C212
Chiefly concerned with the Portuguese in Africa. No Portuguese edition is known, despite the fact that the author was Portuguese.

Centeno, Amaro. Historia de cosas del Oriente. Cordova, D. Galvan, 1595. C213
A description of various countries of Asia, including accounts of major products and leading commercial centers.

[Central American notarial documents, 1569-1758.] A collection of 200 notarial documents. Manuscripts in Spanish, and printed forms. Various places, 1569-1758. C214
The documents cover a broad range of topics including transfer of property, sale of slaves, acknowledgement of debts, powers of attorney, and collection of taxes. The documents relate primarily to Guatemala.

Cepeda, Fernando de. Relacion que embiò à su Magestad el Marquès de Cadereyta, virrey de la Nueva España ... en la detencion de la flota, por el gran peligro que tenia de los enemigos en el camino ... Madrid, Diego Diaz, 1639. C215
A report to the King of Spain announcing the good fortune resulting from the treasure fleet's delay in sailing, thereby avoiding capture by Dutch pirates lying in wait for it.

[Cerisier, Antoine-Marie.] Le destin de l'Amerique ou Dialogues pittoresques dans lesquels on developpe la cause des evenemens actuels, la politique et les interests des puissances de l'Europe relativement a cette guerre. London, For J. Bew [1780]. C216
An imaginary series of conversations between the British king, varous officials, and representatives from other countries in which British colonial policy, and all colonial policy is criticized.

[Cerisier, Antoine-Marie.] Het oor in het kabinet ... Uit het Engelsch vertaald. London, J. Bew [ca. 1780]. C217
An imaginary series of conversations among prominent Englishmen and others presenting a negative view of the British position in the American Revolution.

Cerqueira, Luis de, Bishop of Japan. Relatione della gloriosa morte, patita da sei Christiani Giaponesi per la fede di Christo alli 25 de Gennaro 1604. Rome, Bartolomeo Zannetti, 1607. C218
An account of the crucifixion of six Japanese Christians of noble families in the province of Fingo.

Cerri, Urbano. An account of the state of the Roman-Catholick religion throughout the world. London, For J. Roberts, 1715. C219
This survey of the state of Catholicism in all parts of the world is preceded by a long essay on religious establishments by Sir Richard Steele, the famous English essayist and journalist.

Certain considerations relating to the Royal African Company of England. [London] 1680. C220
A description of the trade of the Royal African Company, and an argument in behalf of continuing its dominance of England's West African trade.

Céspedes y Meneses, Gonzalo de. Historia de Don Felipe IIII, rey de las Españas. Barcelona, Sebastian de Cormellas, 1634. C221
During much of the reign of Philip IV the crowns of Spain and Portugal were united, so this chronicle includes matters relating to affairs of the Portuguese in Asia and Africa as well as Spanish interests in the western hemisphere.

[Ceva, Tommaso.] Risposta ad un libro contro le dodici reflessioni intitolato Defesa del giudizio, formato dalla S. Sede Apostolica nel di 20. Novembre del 1704. n.p. [ca. 1710]. C222
Arguments in support of Jesuit actions in China, concerning the Chinese rites.

Chabert de Cogolin, Joseph Bernard, marquis de. Voyage fait par ordre du roi en 1750 et 1751, dans l'Amérique Septentrionale. Paris, Imprimerie Royale, 1753. C223
A description, with maps, of places in Acadia, Isle Royale, and Newfoundland, based on astronomical observations made during the voyage.

Chabert de la Cheriére, Hillaire-François. Plan de constitution pour la colonie de Saint-Domingue, suivi d'une dissertation sur le commerce des colonies, relative à ce plan; et de considérations générales sur la navigation et le commerce de France. Paris, J.B. Crapart, 1791. C224

This author introduces important commercial issues into the debate over the colonial government of St. Domingue.

[Chalderia, Franciscus.] Rerum & regionum Indicarum: per Serenissimum Emanuelem Portugallie Regem ... [Rome, Jacobus Mazochius or M. Silber, after June 20, 1514.] C225

A newsletter relating particularly to the capture of Malacca by the Portuguese.

Chalkokondyles, Laonikos. Laonici Chalcondylae Atheniensis, de origine et rebus gestis Turcorum libri decem, nuper è Graeco in Latinum conversi: Conrado Clausero Tigurino interprete ... Basel, Ioannem Oporinum [1556]. C226

This history of Turkey is compiled from many sources, and in this edition includes material added after the author's death.

Chalmers, George. An estimate of the comparative strength of Britain ... and of the losses of her trade from every war since the revolution. London, C. Dilly and J. Bowen, 1782. C227

The author describes his book as "a chronological account of commerce from the Restoration to the year 1780."

Chalmers, George. An estimate of the comparative strength of Great-Britain, during the present and four preceding reigns, and of the losses of her trade from every war since the revolution. London, For John Stockdale, 1786. C228

An attempt to counter the fears that Great Britain was in a state of decline. Historical analysis and statistics tend to prove the vigor of the economy.

Chalmers, George. An estimate of the comparative strength of Great-Britain and of the losses of her trade from every war since the revolution. London, John Stockdale, 1794. C229

This third edition has as its major objective the rebuttal of arguments of James Currie the author of "Jaspar Wilson's Letter" which took exception to Chalmers' contention that wars were of benefit to the national economy of Great Britain.

Chalmers, Lionel. Nachrichten über die Witterung und Krankheiten in Südcarolina. Stendal, Franz-und Grossischen Buchhandlung, 1796. C230

A scientific work on weather and disease in South Carolina by a Charleston physician whose research concerned the effect of weather on health.

[Chamberlayne, Edward.] Englands wants: or, Several proposals probably beneficial for England, humbly offered to the consideration of all good patriots in both houses of Parliament. London, Randal Taylor, 1685. C231

A collection of seventy-four proposals for improving the economic, social and religious life of England through a series of taxes and regulations, with reference to increased missionary activity in the American colonies.

[Chamberlayne, John.] The natural history of coffee, thee, chocolate, tobacco. London, For Christopher Wilkinson, 1682. C232

Contains also a section describing the use of juniper berries and elderberries in drinks, as well as a commentary on making rum.

Chamberlayne, Peregrine Clifford. Compendium geographicum: or, A more exact, plain, and easie introduction into all geography ... 2d ed. London, Printed for William Crook, 1685. C233

A handbook of geographical instruction for the use of young noblemen and gentry, with a brief description of the uses of maps and globes.

Chambon. Le commerce de l'Amérique par Marseille. Avignon, 1764. C234

Contains numerous documents with explanations pertaining to commerce between the port of Marseilles and North America, the West Indies, and parts of Africa. The second volume is devoted exclusively to the slave trade.

[Chambon.] Traité général du commerce de l'Amérique ... Amsterdam, M.M. Rey, et se trouve ci Marseille chez J. Mossy, 1783. C235

A new edition of the preceding work.

Chambre de Commerce de Dunkerque. A collection of memoires and correspondence relative to securing the right to trade with the French possessions in America through the Compagnie des Indes. Manuscript in French. [Dunkirk] August-September, 1719. C236

The papers reflect conflict between merchants of Dunkirk and the Compagnie des Indes over trading rights in America.

Champigny, Jean Bochart, chevalier de. La Louisiane ensanglantée, avec toutes les particularités de cette horrible catastrophe, redigées sur le serment de temoins dignes de foi. Londres, Aux dépens de l'editeur: chez Fleury Mesplet, 1773. C237

An account of the rebellion of Louisiana colonists against Spanish authority in 1768-69 and the suppression of their rebellion by Alejandro O'Reilly.

[Champion, Pierre.] Vie du vénérable dom Jean de Palafox. Cologne, Paris; Nyon, 1767. C238

This life of Palafox was based upon a manuscript written in 1688. The editor, Joseph Antoine Toussaint

Dinouart, notes that he remedied the faults in the original manuscript, and consulted other sources also.

Champion, Richard. Comparative reflections on the past and present political, commercial, and civil state of Great Britain: with some thoughts concerning emigration. London, Printed for J. Debrett, 1787. C239

A review of the political, economic, and social situation in Great Britain by one who subsequently emigrated to South Carolina. The author measures Britain's situation in terms of pre-Revolution and later opportunities.

Champion, Richard. Considerations on the present situation of Great Britain and the United States ... with a view to their future commercial connections. London, For J. Stockdale, 1784. C240

A confident view on the early restoration of trade between England and her former American colonies, for "however great their obligations to France, manners, customs, and ancient habits will be too powerful to overcome."

Champlain, Samuel de. Des sauvages, ou, Voyage de Samuel Champlain de Brouage, fait en la France nouvelle. Paris, Claude de Monstr'oeil [1603]. C241

An account of Champlain's first voyage to Canada in which he explored the St. Lawrence River as far as Montreal, and the lower Tadoussac River as well.

Champlain, Samuel de. Les voyages. Paris, Jean Berjon, 1613. C242

An account of the exploration and early development of the fur trade in Canada from 1604-1613.

Champlain, Samuel de. Voyages et descouvertures faites en la Nouvelle France, depuis l'année 1615 jusques à la fin de l'année 1618. Paris, Claude Collet, 1619. C243

Champlain's account of this period in New France includes his winter among the Hurons and a detailed description of them, other western exploration, and the introduction of Recollet missionaries into Canada. Contains Brûlé's narrative of his life among the Indians.

Champlain, Samuel de. Voyages et descouvertures faites en la Nouvelle France ... Paris, C. Collet, 1620. C244

A reissue of the 1619 edition with a new imprint date and some very minor changes in text.

Champlain, Samuel de. Voyages et descouvertures faites en la Nouvelle France, depuis l'année 1615 jusques à la fin de l'année 1618. Paris, Claude Collet, 1627. C245

The second edition.

Champlain, Samuel de. Les voyages de la Nouvelle France occidentale, dicte Canada. Paris, Pierre Le-Mur, 1632. C246

The last work of Champlain published during his lifetime, this is a collected account of his various expeditions, the accompanying map showing awareness of the eastern end of Lake Superior.

Champlain, Samuel de. Les voyages de la Nouvelle France. Paris, C. Collet, 1640. C247

This edition is a reissue of the 1632 edition, but with a new title page.

[Chandler, Thomas Bradbury.] What think ye of the Congress now? Or, An enquiry, how far the Americans are bound to abide by, and execute the decisions of, the late Congress? New York, James Rivington, 1775. C248

Chandler contends that the Continental Congress was not representative of any considerable element of the population of the colonies, that it was being managed by radicals, that its purposes had been exceeded, and therefore no allegiance was due its pronouncements.

[Chanvalon, Jean-Baptiste Thibault de.] Voyage à la Martinique ... 1715. Paris, J.B. Bauche, 1763. C249

A description of Martinique, its people, products, industry, and trade.

Chapin, Walter. The missionary gazetteer, comprising a view of the inhabitants and a geographical description of the countries and places, where Protestant missionaries have labored ... Woodstock, David Watson, 1825. C250

The descriptions of places contain basic geographic and population information, brief notes on the origins and progress of the missions, and in some instances relations with local governments.

Chappe d'Auteroche, abbé. Voyage en Sibérie. Paris, Debure, 1768. C251

An extensive description of Siberia, including maps.

Chappe d'Auteroche, abbé. A journey into Siberia. London, For T. Jefferys, 1770. C252

The first English edition, much abridged from the French.

Chappe d'Auteroche, abbé. Voyage en Californie pour l'observation du passage de Vénus sur le disque du soleil, le 3 juin 1769. Paris, Charles-Antoine Jombert, 1772. C253

In addition to astronomical observations the expedition reported on natural history and other aspects of Mexico en route to the point of observation at Cape San Lucas.

Chappell, Edward. Narrative of a voyage to Hudson's Bay. London, For J. Mawman, 1817. C254

An officer's account of a voyage made to Hudson Bay in 1814, with his comments on the activities of the Hudson's Bay Company there.

Chappuzeau, Samuel. Histoire des joyaux, et des principales richesses de l'Orient & de l'Occident ... Geneva, I.H. Widerhold, 1665. C255
  A brief worldwide survey of jewels and the jewel trade, including indications of location, quality, value, and standards for measurement.

The character, and necessary qualifications of a British minister of state. London, For M. Cooper, 1759. C256
  A merchant's view of British commercial policy, calling for lower export and import taxes as well as a more commercially oriented ministry.

[Charant, Antoine.] A letter, in answer to divers ... questions concerning the religion, manners, and customs ... of Tafiletta. London, B.G., 1671. C257
  Describes the gold trade of Timbuktu.

Chardin, Sir John. Journal du voyage ... en Perse & aux Indes Orientales. London, Moses Pitt, 1686. C258
  The author's observations show a persistent concern for mercantile affairs in the countries he visited.

Chardin, Sir John. The travels of Sir John Chardin into Persia and the East Indies. London, For Moses Pitt, 1686. C259
  The first English edition.

Chardin, Sir John. Curieuse Persian-und Ost-Indische Reise-Beschreibung. Leipzig, Johann Friedrich Gleditsch, 1687. C260
  The first German edition.

Chardin, Sir John. Voyages ... en Perse, et autres lieux de l'Orient. Amsterdam, Jean Louis de Lorme, 1711. C261
  The first edition to contain all three volumes of Chardin's observations of the life, culture, and economy of Persia.

[Chardon, Daniel-Marc-Antoine.] Essai sur la colonie de Sainte-Lucie. Neuchâtel, Société Typograpique, 1779. C262
  A description of the island of St. Lucia, with a history of French settlements there, and consideration of commercial opportunities on the island. Includes two "Memoires concernant les Jesuites" by Louis Nicolas Prétrel.

Charles (Ship). [Accounts of the ship *Charles* of Leith, John Angus, Master.] Manuscript. Scotland, 1668-1669. C263
  These accounts record shipping between Spain, Ireland and Scotland, noting cargoes and charges for various services connected with shipping.

Charlevoix, Pierre-François-Xavier de. Histoire du Paraguay. Paris, Didot, Giffart, Nyon, 1756. C264
  This general history of Paraguay places considerable emphasis on Jesuit missionary activity there. It also includes fifty-seven documents important in Paraguay's history.

Charlevoix, Pierre-François-Xavier de. Geschichte von Paraguay und dem Mission-swerke der Jesuiten in diesem Lande aus dem Französischen ... Nuremberg, Gabriel Nicolaus Raspe, 1768. C265
  This German translation, from the French edition of 1756, includes portions of the account of travels in Paraguay by a German Jesuit, Anton Sepp von Reinegg.

Charlevoix, Pierre-François-Xavier de. Histoire de l'établissement, des progrés et la décadence du Christianisme dans l'empire du Japon. Rouen, Jacques Joseph Le Boullenger, 1715. C266
  The rise and fall of Christian missions in Japan is traced from beginnings in 1542 to about 1650, with only a few summary pages on the subsequent period.

Charlevoix, Pierre-François-Xavier de. La vie de la Mere Marie de l'Incarnation. Paris, P.G. Le Mercier, 1735. C267
  Biography of the founder and first Superior of the Ursuline convent at Quebec in the mid-seventeenth century.

Charlevoix, Pierre-François-Xavier de. Histoire de l'isle Espagnole ou de S. Domingue. Paris, François Barois, 1730-31. C268
  A history of both Spanish and French occupation of Santo Domingo, with reference also to English interests in that area.

Charlevoix, Pierre-François-Xavier de. Histoire et description generale de la Nouvelle France. Paris, Nyon, 1744. C269
  A history and general description of Canada based on a survey made in 1721-22, and richly illustrated with maps by Jacques Nicolas Bellin.

Charlevoix, Pierre-François-Xavier de. Histoire et description generale de la Nouvelle France, avec le Journal historique d'un voyage fait par ordre du roi dans l'Amérique Septentrionale. Paris, Didot, 1744. C270
  A six-volume set in 12mo with a preface to the maps.

Charlevoix, Pierre-François-Xavier de. Journal of a voyage to North-America. London, R. and J. Dodsley, 1761. C271
  Charlevoix's journal of his travels through North America is presented in the form of a series of letters to the Duchess de Lesdiguières.

Charlevoix, Pierre-François-Xavier de. A voyage to North-America: undertaken by command of the present King of France. Dublin, John Exshaw and James Potts, 1766. C272

This edition varies from the London editions of 1761 and 1763, both in text and in the inclusion of several additional maps.

Charlevoix, Pierre-François-Xavier de. Letters to the Dutchess of Lesdiguières. London, For R. Goadby, 1763. C273

A different translation from the 1761 edition of the same journal.

Charlevoix, Pierre-François-Xavier de. [Autograph petition, signed in the text, relative to expenses incurred during travels in North America.] n.p., 1723. C274

The expenses total 1230 livres which Charlevoix requests be refunded to him from funds at the disposal of the Comte de Toulouse.

[Charpentier, M. (François).] Discours d'un fidele sujet du roy touchant l'establissement d'une compagnie françoise pour le commerce des Indes Orientales. Paris, 1664. C275

A review of East Indian commerce, with the recommendation that the French participate in it through the formation of a French East India Company.

Charpentier, M. (François). Relation de l'establissement de la Compagnie françoise pour le commerce des Indes Orientales. Paris, S. Cramoisy & S.B. Mabre-Cramoisy, 1665. C276

The author advocates the establishment of a French East India Company, noting the advantages that it would bring to France.

Charpentier, M. (François). Relation de l'establissement de la Compagnie françoise, pour le commerce des Indes Orientales. Paris, S. & S.B. Cramoisy, 1666. C277

The second edition contains additional documentary material.

[Charpentier, M. (François).] A treatise touching the East-Indian trade. London, For H.B. and sold by R. Boulter, 1676. C278

The first English edition.

[Charpentier de Cossigny, Joseph François.] Mémoire pour la colonie de l'Isle de France, en réponse au précis et au Mémoire des actionnaires de la Compagnie des Indes. Paris, P. Fr. Didot le Jeune, 1790. C279

An argument against the monopoly of the Compagnie Nouvelle des Indes as an infringement upon the liberty of commerce and an ineffective means of carrying on the East Indian trade.

[Charpentier de Cossigny, Joseph François.] Notes sommaires en réponse aux Observations sommaires, sur le Mémoire publié pour la colonie de l'Isle de France. Paris, P. Fr. Didot le Jeune, 1790. C280

A response to a defense of its monopoly position in the East Indian trade by the Compagnie Nouvelle des Indes.

Charpentier de Cossigny, Joseph François. Resa til China. Stockholm, Carl Schiöström, 1803. C281

An abridged translation from the original French account published in 1799, with notes added by the translator, Pehr Olof Gravander.

The Charters of the British colonies in America. Dublin, For John Beatty, 1776. C282

Includes charters of Massachusetts Bay, Connecticut, Rhode Island, Virginia, Pennsylvania, Maryland, and Georgia.

[Chastellux, François Jean, marquis de.] Discours sur les avantages ou les désavantages qui résultent, pour l'Europe, de la découverte de l'Amérique. Objet du prix proposé par M. L'abbé Raynal. Londres, et se trouve à Paris, Prault, 1787. C283

The author answers the question in the affirmative, noting the new sources of goods, increase in wealth, and haven for persecuted peoples, despite attention to the negative aspects, chiefly the growth of slavery.

Chastellux, François Jean, marquis de. Voyages ... dans l'Amérique Septentrionale, dans les années 1780, 1781, & 1782. Paris, Prault, 1788-1791. C284

The author's observations cover a wide range of topics concerning the geography, society, and history of the emerging United States, and include many references to events of the American Revolution.

Chastellux, François Jean, marquis de. Voyage de Mr. le chevalier de Chastellux en Amérique. [Cassel] 1785. C285

This edition is made up of excerpts from the author's journal issued in a periodical in Gotha, 1785.

Chastellux, François Jean, marquis de. Reise durch Amerika. Aus dem Französischen. Frankfurt und Leipzig, 1786. C286

This German edition is a translation of the Cassel edition in French.

Chastenet-Desterre, Gabriel. Considérations sur l'état présent de la colonie française de Saint-Domingue, ouvrage politique et législatif ... n.p., 1796. C287

This author favors changes in the French administration of the island, but is against a complete independence from the mother country.

Chateauveron, De. Le matelot politique. Manuscript. [France, ca. 1765.] C288

The manuscript version of a book published at The Hague, ca. 1765. It is extemely critical of French naval administration and policy and of the failure to integrate more closely the navy and the merchant marine.

Chatelain, Henri Abraham. Carte generale des etats du Czar Empereur de Moscovie ... [Amsterdam, L'Honore et Châtelain, 171-?] C289

The cartography on this map is quite obsolete, but it contains interesting textual and tabular information in the borders.

[Chatelain, Henri Abraham.] Carte particuliere du fleuve Saint Louis. [Amsterdam, 1732.] C290

From the *Atlas historique*, this map describes the commerce of the Great Lakes, St. Lawrence, and Mississippi areas.

Chaumette, Pierre-Gaspard. Discours prononcé par le citoyen Chaumette, au nom de la Commune de Paris. [Paris, Imprimerie Nationale, 1794.] C291

A speech celebrating the abolition of slavery.

Chaumont, Alexandre, chevalier de. Relation de l'ambassade de M. le chevalier de Chaumont à la cour du roy de Siam. Amsterdam, P. Mortier, 1686. C292

An account of a voyage to Siam in 1685.

Chavarri, Francisco Justiniano. Por D. Francisco Justiniano Chavarri ... Alguazil Mayor del Consejo Real de las Indias ... con Juan Baptista Berardo, receptor del mesmo consejo ... sobre la precedencia del lugar, y assiento. [n.p., ca. 1650.] C293

A legal treatise apparently designed to establish the position of alguazil mayor as dominant in the Council of the Indies and within localities in the Spanish empire.

Chénier, Louis de. Commerce des François dans les états du Grand-Seigneur. n.p., 1789. C294

A review of French trade in the Levant, including its history, importance to the French economy, and the best means of maintaining and developing it further.

Chénier, Louis de. Recherches historiques sur les Maures. Paris, l'Auteur [etc.] 1787. C295

Includes material on Moroccan commerce with France and with other European countries.

Chéreau, Jacques. [Collection of three hand-colored prints depicting events in New York during 1776.] Paris, J. Chereau [1776]. C296

Based on the engravings of Franz Xavier Habermann of Augsburg, these prints show the distruction of the statue of George III, the British capture of New York, and the subsequent fire.

Cheyne, James. De geographia ... accessit Gemmae Phrysii ... De orbis divisione. Douai, Lodovici de Winde, 1576. C297

A textbook in geography, given largely to theory rather than description. Gemma Frisius' *De orbis divisione* is from his *De principiis astronomiae & cosmographiae*, 1530.

Chiarini, Giorgio. Questo e el libbro che tracta di mercatantie et usanze de paesi. [Florence, Bartolommeo de Libri for Piero de Pescia, ca. 1497.] C298

A commercial handbook chiefly concerned with the relationship between Florence and other European cities.

[Child, Sir Josiah.] A discourse concerning trade, and that in particular of the East Indies. London, Andrew Sowle, 1689. C299

An abstract of the author's *Treatise* of 1681, work with additional commentary on the East India Company by the abstractor.

[Child, Sir Josiah.] A supplement, 1689, to a former treatise concerning the East-India trade. [London, 1689.] C300

A résumé of the counter actions taken by the East India Company in the face of increased Dutch competition.

Child, Sir Josiah. A new discourse of trade. London, John Everingham, 1693. C301

This answer to Culpepper's *Interest of money mistaken* is a general discussion of the English economy, including a discussion of high interest rates as a cause for England's decline in international trade.

Child, Sir Josiah. A new discourse of trade. London, Samuel Crouch [etc.] 1694. C302

The second edition.

Child, Sir Josiah. A new discourse of trade. London, T. Sowle, 1698. C303

A close reprint of the 1693 edition.

Child, Sir Josiah. Traités sur le commerce. Amsterdam et Berlin, Jean Neaulme, 1754. C304

The first French edition of Child's *A new discourse of trade*.

[Child, Sir Josiah.] A discourse of the nature, use and advantages of trade. London, Randal Taylor, 1694. C305

An essay on the advantages of commerce to a nation, with suggestions for the improvement of England's overseas trade.

[Child, Sir Josiah.] A treatise wherein is demonstrated, I. That the East-India trade is most national of all foreign trades ... London, T. F. for R. Boulter, 1681. C306

A five-point defense of the East India Company, calling opposition to it "Sinister, Selfish, or Groundless."

Chiquet, Jacques. Le nouveau et curieux atlas geographique et historique, ou Le divertissement des empereurs, roys, et princes ... Paris, Chereanau Grand St. Remy [1719]. C307

A rather elementary atlas with twenty-four maps and other plates illustrative of armillary spheres, etc. The text accompanying each map is engraved. Asia, Africa, North and South America are included.

Chirino, Pedro. Relacion de las Islas Filipinas i de lo que en ellas an trabaiado los padres dae la Compañia de Jesus. Rome, Estevan Paulino, 1604. C308
A history of the Jesuit mission in the Philippines, with extensive description of the islands and the culture of their inhabitants.

[Choiseul, Etienne-François, duc de.] Mémoire historique sur la négociation de la France & de l'Angleterre ... avec les pièces justificatives. Paris, Imprimerie Royal, 1761. C309
A collection of thirty-one items of correspondence, memorials, etc., concerning Anglo-French negotiations, frequently involving matters of overseas trade. The introductory commentary suggests that Great Britain had impeded progress toward peace.

[Choiseul, Etienne-François, duc de.] An historical memorial of the negotiation of France and England, from the 26th of March, 1761, to the 20th of September of the same year, with the vouchers. London, For D. Wilson [etc.] 1761. C310
The first English edition.

[Choiseul, Etienne-François, duc de.] Mémoire historique sur la négociation de la France & de l'Angleterre, depuis le 26 mars 1761, jusqu'au 20 septembre de la même annee. London, D. Wilson, T. Becket & P.A. De Hondt, 1761. C311
This French edition from London was issued by the same publishers as the English edition of 1761.

[Choisy, abbé de.] Journal du voyage de Siam. Paris, S. Mabre-Cramoisy, 1687. C312
An account of an embassy to Siam and the negotiation of an alliance between the two countries, including observations on the government, people and products of Siam.

Choisy, abbé de. Journal ou suite du voyage de Siam, en forme des lettres familieres. Amsterdam, Pierre Mortier, 1687. C313
This edition includes the list of gifts sent to Louis XIV by the king of Siam.

Cholmley, Hugh. A discours of Tangir. Manuscript. [Tangier or England, ca. 1680.] C314
The author appears to have lived in Tangier during part of the time it was under English government, 1662-84. He comments on its value to England and makes recommendations for its government.

Cholmley, Hugh. An account of Tangier. n.p., 1787. C315
A description of Tangier and an account of events there from 1662 to about 1680, published from the preceding manuscript.

Christy, Miller. The silver map of the world. London, H. Stevens, Son, and Stiles, 1900. C316
An essay on a medallion containing a map of the world, commemorative of Drake's circumnavigation.

Chronander, Gustavus. Utilitates, quae ex commerciis & coloniis in calidioribus mundi partibus patriae adfluerent. Abo, Jacob Merckell [1757]. C317
A consideration of the value of tropical goods including products from South America, Africa, and the East Indies.

Chronicorum Turcicorum; in quibus Turcorvm origo, principes, imperatores, bella, praelia, caedes, victoriae, reiqvi militaris ratio ... Frankfurt, Joan Wechelus, 1584. C318
A compilation of information on Turkey, it rulers, history, islands under its control, systems of government, etc.

Chrusanthos, Notaras, Patriarch of Jerusalem. Introductio ad geographiam, et sphaeram ... Paris, 1716. C319
A basic geography text, well illustrated with diagrams and including a double hemisphere world map. The text is in Greek.

[Churchill, Awnsham.] A collection of voyages and travels ... London, Printed by assignment from Messrs. Churchill, for H. Lintot and John Osborn, 1744-46. C320
The third edition of this valuable compilation of travel accounts, containing a number of items printed from original manuscripts, translated into English for the first time, or reprinted because of scarcity.

Chytraeus, Nathan. Variorum in Europa itinerum deliciae ... Herborn, 1594. C321
This book contains the inscriptions from a map drawn by Sebastian Cabot in 1549. The map is not known to exist at present, and is not described in any other source.

Cicé, Louis de. Lettre ... aux RR. PP. Jesuites sur les idolatries et sur les superstitions de la Chine. [Paris?, 1700.] C322
An argument against the Jesuit position with respect to Chinese Christians. The author was vicar apostolic for Japan and Siam and a French missionary who had been in the East since 1682.

Cicé, Louis de. Lettre ... aux RR. PP. Jesuites sur les idolatries et sur les superstition de la Chine. n.p. [ca. 1700]. C323
This edition contains a four-page *Avis*, which is a brief commentary on recent Jesuit publications from an anti-Jesuit point of view.

Cicé, Louis de. Lettre de M. Louis de Cicé ... aux RR. PP. Jesuites sur les idolatries & sur les superstitions de la Chine. Cologne, Heritiers de Corneille d'Egmond, 1700. C324

Cieza de León, Pedro de. La chronica del Peru. Antwerp, Martin Nucio, 1554. C325
One of the more important sources for the early history of Peru. The author describes Peru's resources, vegetation, and Indian tribes from personal experience, and also comments on Spanish administration of the region.

Cieza de León, Pedro de. Historia, over cronica del gran regno del Peru. Venice, Giovanni Bonadio, 1564. C326
A translation by Agostino de Cravaliz, it is the sixth Italian edition of a projected three-part work on the history and civilization of the Incas.

Cieza de León, Pedro de. Cronica del gran regno del Peru. Venice, Camillo Franceschini, 1576. C327
The text follows closely the 1564 edition above.

Cieza de León, Pedro de. La Prima parte dell' istorie del Perù. Venice, Andrea Arivabene, 1556. C328
This text differs from the translation of Cravaliz which was published in Rome the previous year and in subsequent editions.

Cieza de León, Pedro de. The seventeen years travels of Peter de Cieza, through the mighty kingdom of Peru ... London, 1709. C329
The first English edition.

Cinamo, Leonardo. Vita, e morte del padre Marcello Francesco Mastrilli della Compagnia di Giesù. Viterbo, Diotallevi, 1645. C330
This life of Mastrilli includes his account of his voyage to the East which included reports of his visits to Goa and the Philippines.

The circumstances of Scotland consider'd, with respect to the present scarcity of money: together with some proposals for supplying the defect thereof, and rectifying the ballance of trade. Edinburgh, James Watson, 1705. C331
An analysis of Scotland's troubled financial state, attributing it to the failure of the Darien colony, poor quality of goods exported, policies of the Bank of Scotland, and conversion of coinage into plate.

Cisneros, Hieronymo. La mas verdadera relacion que à venido ... de los prodigiosos y vetruosos os sucessos del valeroso cavallero Juan Baptista Suarez Gallinato ... de las provinsias reyno de Camboja, cercano a la gran China. [Seville, Alonso Rodriguez, 1604.] C332
An account of an abortive attempt by Juan Baptista Suarez Gallinato to extend Spanish influence into Cambodia by supporting a recently deposed king. The three ships of the expedition were separated by a storm and Gallinato returned to his base in the Philippines.

The citizen's procession, or, The smuggler's success and the patriots disappointment. Being an excellent new ballad on the Excise-bill. London, For A. Dodd, 1733. C333
The ballad deplores the defeat of the Excise Bill designed to tax tobacco and wine, and attributes the defeat to the influence of smugglers.

Cittadella, Baldassar. Copia di una lettera di ragguaglio del viaggio, in una missione per il Giappone, scrita di Goa i 15 Feb. 1636. Manuscript in Italian. Goa, 15 Feb. 1636. C334
A copy of an unrecorded original, describing a Jesuit missionary's voyage to the East, noting both missionary and mercantile matters en route.

Clagett, Nicholas. A sermon preached before the Incorporated Society for the Propagation of the Gospel in Foreign Parts; at their Anniversary Meeting in the Parish-Church of St. Mary-le-Bow, on Friday, February 18, 1736. London, J. and J. Pemberton, 1737. C335
The "proceedings" appended to this sermon note a considerable number of Negroes being accepted into the church through baptism.

Clark, William. Invoice of sundries shiped [sic] aboard the Ship Sussanah, Samuel Cary master ... Manuscript. Boston, 7 August 1734. C336
The cargo consisted primarily of furs which are identified as to type and price.

Clarke, Samuel. A geographical description of all the countries of the known world. London, Tho. Milbourn for Robert Clavel [etc.] 1671. C337
This general geography gives considerable emphasis to the economies of the regions described. It includes *A true and faithful account of the four chiefest plantations of the English in America.*

Clarke, Samuel. A new description of the world. London, H. Rhodes, 1689. C338
Descriptions of many countries, with information on their trade.

[Clarke, William.] Observations on the late and present conduct of the French, with regard to their encroachment upon the British colonies in North America. Boston, S. Kneeland, 1755. C339
In describing the French threat to British supremacy in America the author gives a survey of the commerce of the interior, and indicates the importance of various branches of American commerce to Britain.

Clarkson, Thomas. An essay on the slavery and commerce of the human species, particularly the

African, translated from a Latin dissertation ... Philadelphia, Joseph Crukshank, 1786. C340
The first American edition of Clarkson's influential essay.

Clarkson, Thomas. An essay on the slavery and commerce of the human species, particularly the African. Dublin, W. Porter, 1786. C341
While this is primarily a moral treatise, it also contains details on the African-West Indian slave trade and its history.

Clarkson, Thomas. Afhandling om slafvariet och slafhandeln, särdeles rörande negrerne, så väl i Africa, som West-Indien ... Öfversatt från Engelskan. Stockholm, A. Jacobson Nordström, 1796. C342
The first Swedish edition.

Clarkson, Thomas. An essay on the impolicy of the African slave trade. London, J. Phillips, 1788. C343
An attempt to interest merchants in African products other than slaves.

Clarkson, Thomas. Essai sur les désavantages politiques de la traite des negres. Neufchatel, 1789. C344
In addition to the translation of *An essay on the impolicy of the African slave trade*, this work includes translated excerpts from Clarkson's *An essay on the slavery and commerce of the human species* as well as an introduction on the application of these ideas to the French West Indian colonies.

Clarkson, Thomas. An essay on the comparative efficiency of regulation or abolition, as applied to the slave trade ... London, James Phillips, 1789. C345
Clarkson enumerates the arguments of the opponents for the anti-slavery movement, and urges along with prohibition of slavery the development of an economy in west Africa which does not rely on the slave trade.

Clarkson, Thomas. Letters on the slave-trade, and the state of the natives in those parts of Africa, which are contiguous to Fort St. Louis and Goree ... London, James Phillips, 1791. C346
A response to queries about the slave trade by anti-slave trade people in France in which Clarkson describes the African society from which most slaves were taken for use in French plantations.

Clarkson, Thomas. The history of the rise, progress, and accomplishment of the abolition of the African slave-trade by the British Parliament. London, R. Taylor, 1808. C347
A detailed account of the debates and legislation that led to the abolition of the slave trade in Great Britain, by one of the leaders of the anti-slave trade movement.

Classon, Johan. Tal, om Sveriges handels omskriften. Stockholm, Lars Salvius [1751]. C348
A survey history of Swedish commerce from the twelfth to the middle of the eighteenth century.

Claude, d'Abbeville, père. L'arrivee des peres capucins & la conversion des sauvages à nostre saincte foy. Paris, Jean Nigaut, 1613. C349
An account of the 1612 attempt by the French to settle a colony at Maranhão written by a priest who accompanied the colonists. He reports on the products known or rumored to be in the area.

Claude, d'Abbeville, père. Discours et congratulation a la France sur l'arrivée des peres capucins en l'Inde nouvelle ... en la terre du Brasil. Paris, Denis Langloys, 1613. C350
Includes extracts of letters written by Father Arsène of Paris about Maranhão, as well as other reports about the colony.

Claude, d'Abbeville, père. Histoire de la mission des péres capucins en l'isle de Maragnan ... Paris, F. Huby, 1614. C351
A report by a Capuchin priest who accompanied a French colonial expedition to the island of Maranhão. He describes the natives, their customs, and the products of northern South America.

Claude, d'Abbeville, père. Lettre d'un pere capucin ... en l'Inde Occidentale. Paris, Gilles Blaisot, 1612. C352
One of two editions published in 1612 which describe the beginnings of French settlement on Maranhão Island, off the coast of Brazil.

Clausson, Neils Christian. Undersøgelse, om Amerikas opdagelse har mere skadet end gavnet det menneskelige kiøn? Copenhagen, Lauritz Christian Simmelkiaer, 1785. C353
A Danish churchman considers the impact of the discovery of America on the world and reaches negative conclusions.

Claustre, André de. Historia de Thamas Kovli-Kan, Sophi de Persia. Madrid, J. de Ariztia, 1742. C354
The book was originally published in French in 1740 and was translated into English the same year. This Spanish translation does not appear in the standard sources. The translator is Don Jacinto de Lisasueta.

[Claustre, André de.] Histoire de Thamas Koulikan nouveau roi de Perse, ou Histoire de la derniére révolution de Perse, arrivée en 1732. Paris, Briasson, 1742. C355
Primarily an account of the political and military activities of Nadir Shah who drove the Turks out of Persia and extended his conquests into India.

[Clavell, Robert.] His Majesties propriety, and dominion on the Brittish seas asserted. London, T. Mabb for Andrew Kembel [etc.] 1665.   C356

An argument in behalf of England's rights to the fishing grounds off her coast which were dominated by the Dutch.

Clavigero, Francesco Saverio. Storia antica del Messico, cavata da' migliori storici Spagnuoli, e da' manoscritti, e dalle pitture antiche degl' Indiani ... Cesena, Gregorio Biasini, 1780-81.   C357

A general history of Mexico to about 1540, with heavy emphasis on the pre-conquest period. Also included are nine dissertations on special topics.

Clavigero, Francesco Saverio. The history of Mexico. Collected from Spanish and Mexican historians, from manuscripts, and ancient paintings of the Indians. London, For G.G.J. and J. Robinson, 1787.   C358

The first English edition.

Clavigero, Francesco Saverio. Storia della California ... Venice, M. Fenzo, 1789.   C359

A history of the Jesuit mission in Lower California, preceded by a natural history of the region, and including some history of early Spanish contact there.

Clavius, Christoph. In Sphaeram Joannis de Sacro Bosco commentarius. Rome, Victorium Helianum, 1570.   C360

The first edition of this commentary on the *Sphaera mundi* of Sacroboso, which was to go through at least fourteen editions by 1618, with additions made to the commentary in subsequent editions.

Clavius, Christoph. Astrolabium. Rome, Bartholomaei Grassi, 1593.   C361

An extensive compendium of information on the use and theory of the astrolabe, with numerous woodcut illustrations.

Clavius, Christoph. Christophori Clavii ... In Sphaeram Joannis de Sacro Bosco commentarius: nunc iterum ab ipso auctore recognitus, & multis ac variis locis locupletatus. Rome, Dominici Basae, 1581.   C362

This edition of the commentary on the *Sphere* of Sacro Bosco adds material critical of Copernicus but supportive of Galileo in the controversy over the place of the earth in the solar system.

Clavus, Claudius. [1427 map of Scandinavia. Facsimile. Sweden, ca. 1910.]   C363

A facsimile, with accompanying text, of a map added to Ptolemy's *Geographia* in 1427.

Cleeve, Bourchier. A scheme for preventing a further increase of the national debt, and for reducing the same ... London, R. and J. Dodsley, 1756.   C364

A pamphlet in support of a proposal by Sir Matthew Decker for replacing all import duties with a single tax on houses, the effect of which was to make all of Great Britain a free port and emporium of goods.

[Cleirac, Estienne.] Les us, et coutumes de la mer. Rouen, Eustache Viret, 1671.   C365

A compilation of medieval and modern maritime law for the regulation of maritime commerce.

[Cleland, William.] The present state of the sugar plantations consider'd ... London, Printed and sold by John Morphew, 1713.   C366

The author discusses the trade, agricultural products, and government of Barbados and British colonies in general and offers regulations for their improvement.

Clement, Simon. The interest of England, as it stands with relation to the trade of Ireland. London, J. Astwood, 1698.   C367

The author, a London merchant, seeks to restrain all manufactures in Ireland and the American colonies which would compete with England's manufactures.

[Clement, Simon.] Remarks upon a late ingenious pamphlet, entituled, A short but thorough search into what may be the real cause of the present scarcity of our silver coin, &c. London, For S. Baker, 1718.   C368

A reply to David Clayton's pamphlet of 1717, in which Clement rejects the idea of coining all the silver in England, advocating instead less export of it through the East India trade.

Clerc, Nicolas-Gabriel. Histoire physique, morale, civile et politique de la Russie ancienne. Paris, Froullé; Versailles, Blaizot, 1783-84.   C369

Part of the following large work describing and discussing Russia. This portion of the set is concerned primarily with Russian rulers and their accomplishments.

Clerc, Nicolas-Gabriel. Histoire physique, morale, civile et politique de la Russie moderne. Paris, Froullé et Maradan; Versailles, Blaizot, 1783-85.   C370

An interesting compilation of information about eighteenth-century Russia and its people. A fine volume of plates accompanies the set. Charts on Russian economic matters and a large map of the country are included.

Clercq, P. le (Pieter). Algemeene verhandeling van de heerschappy der zee: en een compleet lichaam van de zee-rechten ... Amsterdam, D. Onder de Linden, 1757.   C371

A large collection of translated documents on sea laws from various European nations. Includes the laws of Rhodes, orders of Charles V and Philip II of Spain, laws of the Hanseatic League, the maritime customs of European nations, etc.

[Clerk, Sir John.] An essay upon the XV. article of the Treaty of Union. [Edinburgh] 1706.   C372

The author critically examines the impact on Scotland of the tariff union with England proposed in Article XV of the Treaty of Union.

[Clerke, Charles.] A voyage round the world, in His Majesty's ship the *Dolphin*. London, For Newbery and Carnan, 1768.   C373

The narrative places particular emphasis on the South Sea and Patagonia.

[Clicquot de Blervache, Simon.] Considerations sur le commerce. Amsterdam, 1758.   C374

A general discussion of commerce, with particular attention to trading companies and societies.

[Clicquot de Blervache, Simon.] Considérations sur le traité de commerce entre la France et la Grande-Bretagne, du 26 Septembre 1786. Paris, Prault, 1789.   C375

The author criticizes the French government for entering an unfavorable commercial treaty with Great Britain without consulting the mercantile element in France, and notes the ways in which the treaty will aid England's commerce at the expense of France.

Clicquot de Blervache, Simon. Mémoire sur l'état du commerce intérieur et extérieur de la France depuis la première croisade, jusqu'au règne de Louis XII. Paris, Prault, 1790.   C376

A history of French commerce to the beginning of the sixteenth century, emphasizing information on privileges obtained by various cities, and the countries with which they traded.

Clifford, Jeronimy. The case of Jeronimy Clifford, merchant and planter of Surinam. [London, 1711.]   C377

An English merchant's legal problems in carrying on his sugar trade in Dutch Surinam, with an interesting description of the Dutch colony.

Clifford, Jeronimy. The case and replication of the legal representatives of Jeronimy Clifford. London, C. Say, 1763.   C378

A much-expanded treatment of the preceding case.

Clive, Robert Clive, Baron. Lord Clive's speech, in the House of Commons, 30th March, 1772. London, J. Walter [1772].   C379

In his defense against charges of mismanagement and monopolization of certain commodities, Clive gives information on the management of Indian commerce by the East India Company.

[Clodoré, Jean.] Relation de ce qui s'est passé dans les isles & Terre-Ferme de l'Amérique, pendant la dernière guerre avec l'Angleterre. Paris, Clouzier, 1671.   C380

An account of French settlements in the Caribbean and in Guiana, and of the rivalry with the English there.

Clüver, Philipp. Introductionis in universam geographiam, tam veterem quàm novam, libri VI ... Leiden, Elzeviriana, 1624.   C381

The first edition of one of the most popular geography texts in the seventeenth century.

Clüver, Philipp. Introductionis in universam geographiam, tam veterem quàm novam. Amsterdam, Hondius [ca. 1630].   C382

This edition includes the *Breviarium totius orbis terrarum* by Petrus Bertius.

Clüver, Philipp. Introductionis in universam geographiam tam veterem quam novam libri VI. Amsterdam, Ludovicum Elzevirium, 1651.   C383

This edition also contains the geographical treatise by Petrus Bertius.

Clüver, Philipp. Introductionis in universam geographiam. Cadomi, I. Cavelier, 1669.   C384

This edition is a pocket-size volume and as such does not contain the many maps and illustrations found in the other larger editions, save for one folded illustration.

Clüver, Philipp. Introductio in universam geographicam. London, J. Nicholson, 1711.   C385

A general geography with numerous maps.

Clüver, Philipp. Introductionis in universam geographiam. Amsterdam, Joannem Pauli, 1729.   C386

This late edition includes comments by Bruzen de la Martiniere, Johann Bruno, Johann Friedrich Heckel, and John Reiske who had been earlier editors of this popular geography text.

Clúny, Alexander. The American traveller: or, Observations on the present state, culture and commerce of the British colonies in America. London, For E. and C. Dilly, 1769.   C387

The author describes economic conditions and the importance of the British colonies in America to Britain.

[Clúny, Alexander.] Reisen durch Amerika ... in Briefen an den Grafen von Chatam gerichtet. Leipzig, Carl Friederich Schneider, 1783.   C388

A German translation from the English edition of 1769.

Clusius, Carolus. Aliquot notae in Garciae Aromatum Historiam ... que à generoso viro Francisco Drake equite Anglo, & his observatae sunt. Antwerp, Christopher Plantin, 1582.   C389

A botany of Drake's circumnavigation, based upon Garcia de Orta's *Aromatum, et simplicium aliquot medicamentorum ... historia* which l'Écluse had edited the previous year, and on his own acquaintance with Drake.

Clusius, Carolus. Caroli Clusi Atrebatis ... Rariorum plantarum historia. Antwerp, ex officina Plantiniana apud Ioannem Moretum, 1601.
C390

A botanical compilation that is world-wide in scope, citing the plants recently discovered in America along with those known to ancient science.

Clusius, Carolus. Caroli Clusii Atrebatis curae posteriores, seu plurimarum non ante cognitarum, aut descriptatum stirpium, peregrinorumque aliquot animalum novae descriptiones ... [Antwerp] Plantiniana Raphelengii, 1611.
C391

Compiled after the author's death, this is a list of addenda, including also some examples of animal life. It also contains a funeral oration honoring l'Écluse by Aelius Everhardus Vorstius.

Coade, G. (George). A letter to the honourable the Lords Commissioners of Trade and Plantations. Wherein the grand concern of trade is asserted and maintained ... London, Jacob Robinson, 1747.
C392

A review of British commercial policy from a protectionist point of view, advocating more representation of merchants in Parliament, a steady alliance with the Dutch, control of smuggling, and various laws which the author feels would promote national commercial interests.

Cocherel, Nicholas-Robert, marquis de. Dernière réponse de M. de Cocherel ... à messieurs les députés du commerce. Versailles, Baudouin [ca. 1789].
C393

A plea for the import of flour from the United States into Saint Domingue, which was opposed to the interests of French exporters.

Cocherel, Nicolas-Robert, marquis de. Aperçu sur la constitution de Saint-Domingue. [n.p., 1790]
C394

A deputy from Saint-Domingue argues that his constituency cannot be perceived of as a colony, or as a part of France, preferring to have it called a Franco-American province.

Cocherel, Nicolas-Robert, marquis de. Observations de M. de Cocherel, Député de Saint-Domingue, à l'Assemblée nationale, sur la demande des mulâtres. Paris, Clousier, [1789?]
C395

An argument on behalf of the mulattoes of Saint-Domingue, urging their fair representation in the National Assembly in Paris.

Cochrane, John. Examination of the plans proposed for the East India Company's shipping. London, For John Stockdale, 1795.
C396

An argument written in 1786 in favor of larger ships for most of the East India trade, since such ships would be useful for both commercial and war purposes.

Cockburn, John. A journey over land, from the Gulf of Honduras to the great South-Sea. London, C. Rivington, 1735.
C397

A narrative of a journey across Central America; also an account of travels in India by Nicholas Withington, a factor for the East India Company.

Code des loix des gentoux, ou réglemens des brames ... Paris, Imprimerie de Stoupe, 1778.
C398

A translation from the English of a code of laws which formed the basis for Hindu jurisprudence, with preface and notes by the French translator, Jean Baptiste René Robinet.

A code of Gentoo laws, or, Ordinations of the pundits, from a Persian translation, made from the original, written in the Shanskrit language. London, 1776.
C399

The first English version of the system of Indian law, designed to aid in formulation of East India Company administrative policy which would be as compatible as possible with local legal traditions.

Codogno, Ottavio. Nuovo itinerario delle poste per tutto il mondo. Venice, Lucio Spineda, 1620.
C400

A guide to the postal service of Europe, with connections for service to the East and West Indies.

Coelho de Barbuda, Luiz. Empresas militares de Lusitanos ... Lisbon, Pedro Craesbeeck, 1624.
C401

The major portion of this work is given to accounts of Portuguese military and naval enterprises in the East Indies and in Africa, concluding with the earliest conflicts with the Dutch in the East.

Coignet de la Tuillerie, Gaspard. Propositie gedaen door den Heere De la Thuillerye, ambassadeur van Vranckrijck ... n.p., 1646.
C402

The French ambassador to the Hague protests against Dutch negotiations with the Spanish.

Coignet de la Tuillerie, Gaspard. Twee propositien gedaen door den heer de la Thullerie. Utrecht, Frans Levyn, 1648.
C403

Proposals by the French ambassador for the continuation of the war against Spain, with observations on those proposals.

Coke, Roger. A discourse of trade. London, H. Brome and R. Horne, 1670.
C404

The author views the establishment of English colonies as a threat to trade, drawing off the most competent persons.

[Coke, Roger.] A treatise concerning the regulation of the coyn ... London, For R. Clavel, 1696.
C405

The regulation of currency is related to the East India trade.

Colden, Cadwallader. The history of the five Indian nations of Canada, which are dependent on the province of New-York in America. London, For T. Osborne, 1747. C406
A chronicle of Indian affairs in the eastern Great Lakes area, relating largely to the fur trade and resulting competition and wars between the French and British. This edition includes numerous documents.

Cole, Captain Thomas. A short narrative of the proceedings, of the society appointed to manage the British white herring fishery. London, 1750. C407
Deals with competition in fishing between the Dutch and the English, with proposals to improve English fishing.

[Colebrooke, H. T. (Henry Thomas).] Remarks on the present state of the husbandry and commerce of Bengal. Calcutta, 1795. C408
A survey of the economy of Bengal, urging changes in policy to increase both the agricultural production and the commerce of that province.

Colección de las aplicaciones que se van haciendo de los bienes, casas, y colegios que fueron de los regulares de la Compañia de Jesús, expatriados de estos reales dominios : siguiendo en todo lo adaptable las reglas que prescribe la Real Cèdula dada en Madrid à 9. de Julio de 1769 : primera[-segunda] parte ... Lima, En la Oficina de la Calle de S. Jacinto, 1772-1773. C409
This edition incorporates additions in manuscript from a previous edition.

Coleccion general de las providencias hasta aqui tomadas por el gobierno sobre el estrañamiento y ocupacion de temporalidades de los regulares de la Compañia que existian en los Dominios de S.M. de España, Indias, e islas Filipinas á consequência del real decreto de 27 de febrero, y pragmatica-sanction de 2 de abril de este año. Madrid, Imprenta Real de la Gazeta, 1767-1769. C410
A collection of decrees relating to the expulsion of the Jesuits from Spain and its overseas possessions, identifying specific Jesuit establishments in the colonies and providing for their confiscation.

Coleti, Giovanni Domenico. Dizionario storico-geografico dell' America Meridionale. Venice, Coleti, 1771. C411
A geographical dictionary of South America, including a map, compiled by a Jesuit who had long resided there.

Colin, Francisco. Labor evangelica, ministerios, apostolicos de los obreros de la Compañia de Iesus, fundacion, y progressos de su provincia en las Islas Filipinas ... Madrid, Ioseph Fernandez de Buendia, 1663. C412
In addition to being a history of the Jesuit mission in the Philippines, this work includes an extensive description of the islands and their peoples as well as a history of Spanish conquest there.

Coljer, Justinus. Dagh-register ... op de reyse van Constantinopolen tot Adrianopolen. The Hague, 1668. C413
An account of an embassy sent to Turkey to improve Dutch-Turkish commerce.

Collecçaõ dos breves pontificos, e leys regias, que foraõ expedidos, e publicadas desde o anno de 1741, sobre a liberdade das pessoas, bens, e commercio dos Indios do Brasil ... [Lisbon] Secretaria de Estado [1759]. C414
This collection of documents relates to the expulsion of the Jesuits from Brazil in 1759.

Coleccion legal de cartas, dictamentes, y otros papeles en derecho ... Lima, Officina de los Huérfanos, 1761. C415
A collection of legal arguments on various subjects pertaining to the governing of Peru, including some apparent conflicts between the church and colonial government.

Collectio peregrinationum in terras orientales. Manuscript. Germany [ca. 1424-27]. C416
Two volumes of manuscript accounts of travels to the eastern Mediterranean and Asia by several medieval authors, mostly of the fourteenth century. The *Itinerarium* of Mandeville is included.

Collection complette de tous les ouvrages pour et contre M. Necker. Utrecht, 1782. C417
A collection of twenty tracts with notes and comments by the anonymous editor, all relating to the *Compte rendu au roi* issued by Jacques Necker the previous year.

[Collection of documents relating to the activities of the English East India Company, n.p., ca. 1766.] C418
Includes copies of contracts and licenses between the East India Company and its various factories and local Indian rulers from 1756 to 1766 as well as charters of the company from 1661 to 1758.

[A collection of Dutch political caricatures relating to relations with Great Britain. n.p., 1760-90.] C419
The cartoons reflect Dutch interpretations of the plight of the British during their troubles with the American colonies and related diplomatic problems in Europe.

[Collection of German newspapers.] Leipzig, 1657-68. C420
Fifty-six numbers of three Leipzig newspapers reporting a variety of events, many concerning commercial affairs.

A collection of letters relating to the East India Company, and to a free trade. London, For W. Owen, 1754. C421

These letters deal with various aspects of the company's activities. Several of them urge the extension of company, or independent, trade in the East.

A collection of papers relating to the East India trade. London, For J. Walthoe, 1730.   C422
A series of arguments supporting the view that the East India Company, and monopolies in general, are not the most beneficial way of carrying on overseas trade.

A collection of papers relating to the trade to Africa. n.p. [1709?].   C423
Documents, letters, and reports offering proof that private traders or a regulated company could operate the African trade more profitably than the joint-stock company.

[Collection of reports concerning French colonies.] Paris, 1789-91.   C424
Thirty-one reports made to the National Assembly relative to the commerce of France with her colonies in Africa and America.

[Collection of three charts of the Arctic regions.] Manuscript. [England, ca. 1765.]   C425
These manuscript charts depict the north-western area of North America and eastern Siberia, the area adjacent to Hudson Bay, and the coasts of Greenland. They include brief comments on some of the geographical features portrayed.

College, Academy, and Charitable Schools of Philadelphia. Four dissertations, on the reciprocal advantages of a perpetual union between Great-Britain and her American colonies. Philadelphia, William and Thomas Bradford, 1766.   C426
The essays are by John Morgan, Stephen Watts, Joseph Reed, and Francis Hopkinson, with an introduction by William Smith, Provost of the College of Philadelphia, to which the essays were submitted in competition for a prize offered by John Sargent.

Colliber, Samuel. Columna rostrata: or, A critical history of the English sea-affairs. London, For R. Robinson, 1727.   C427
A critical account of British maritime history, with particular emphasis on the Dutch wars of the seventeenth century.

Colling, Lars Johan. Dissertatio juridica de mercatura nobili quam praeside D. Lars Joh. Colling. Lund, Caroli Gustavi Berlig [1761].   C428
An academic dissertation submitted by Jöns M. Båt on the subject of participation in commerce by the nobility, relating it to Sweden's experience.

Collins, David. An account of the English colony in New South Wales. London, For T. Cadell, Jun. and W. Davies, 1798-1802.   C429

This marine veteran of Bunker Hill was named judge-advocate of Australia, and his book is a detailed chronicle of English settlement there.

Collins, John. A plea for the bringing in of Irish cattel, and keeping out of fish caught by foreigners. London, A. Godbid & J. Playford, 1680.   C430
A general review of England's commercial situation with recommendations designed to improve England's position with respect to Holland.

Collins, John. Salt and fishery, a discourse thereof. London, A. Godbid [etc.] 1682.   C431
Beginning with a discussion about the English salt trade, with particular reference to the curing of fish, the author wanders into other interesting subjects including the commerce of Iceland, the fishing trade of Newfoundland, methods of preserving meat, and the English tin trade.

[Collins, Samuel.] The present state of Russia. London, J. Winter, for D. Newman, 1671.   C432
A description of the government, commerce, population, etc., of Russia, by a nine-year resident of Moscow.

Collo, Francesco da. Trattamento di pace tra il serenissimo Sigismondo Re di Polonia et Gran Basilio prencipe di Moscovia. Padua, Lorenzo Pasquati, 1603.   C433
An account of a mission from the Holy Roman Emperor Maximilian I to Muscovy in 1518, an attempt to mediate peace between Poland and Muscovy.

Colnett, James. A voyage to the South Atlantic and round Cape Horn. London, W. Bennet, 1798.   C434
The purpose of the voyage was to search for suitable bases for the refitting of whaling vessels in islands lying to the west of South America.

Colón, Fernando. Historie del Sig. Don Fernando Colombo ... & vera relatione della vita & de' fatti dell' Ammiraglio Don Christophoro Colombo su padre ... Milan, Girolamo Bordoni [1614].   C435
The third edition, incorporating letters and the testament of Columbus which were not included in previous editions.

Colón, Fernando. Historie ... nelle quali s'ha particolare, & vera relatione della vita, & de fatti dell' ammiraglio d. Christoforo Colombo. Venice, Francesco de Franceschi Sanese, 1571.   C436
The biography of Columbus by his son is especially valuable as a major source of information on the first and fourth voyages.

Colonies Amerique et Afrique, 1775 - ca. 1776 [de] St. Malo: etat qui fait connoitre ce qu'a couté sur chaque batiment ... qui sont aller dans les colonies ... Manuscript. St. Malo, 18 May 1785. C437

This manuscript pertains to the years 1775 and 1776, concerning the cost of carrying passengers to the French colonies in America and Africa.

Columbus, Christopher. Epistola Christofori Colom ... [Rome, Stephanus Planck, 1493.] C438

The first issue of the first Latin edition of Columbus's letter to Ferdinand and Isabella upon his return from his first voyage.

Com permissaõ de Sua Magestade Fidelissima tem determinado Manoel Eleuterio de Castro, Joaõ Rodrigues Caldas, Manoel Ferreira da Costa, Joaquim Pedro Bello mandar huma nau para a Cidade de Nome de Deos de Macau na proxima monçaõ com as condiçoens seguintes. Lisbon, Antonio Rodrigues Galhardo, 1772. C439

A statement of conditions governing the licensing of a ship for trade to China under the management of four Portuguese investors.

Combés, Francisco. Historia de las islas de Mindanao, Iolo, y sus adyacentes. Progressos de la religion, y armas catolicas. Madrid, Heredos de Pablo de Val, 1667. C440

This work is an account of the progress of the Jesuits in the Philippines and ethnography of many of the islands in the southern Philippines, noting social and political institutions.

[Combrune, Michael.] An enquiry into the prices of wheat, malt, and occasionally of other provisions ... as sold in England, from the year 1000 to the year 1765 ... London, T. Longman, 1768. C441

In addition to prices of grains, prices of many other consumer commodities are given, and also wages of various types of workers. The impact of periods of war and peace on the economy are also noted.

Comeiras, Victor Delpuech de. Considérations sur la possiblité, l'intérêt et les moyens qu'auroit la France de r'ouvrir l'ancienne route du commerce de l'Inde. Paris, Debray & Laran, 1798. C442

A proposal to build a canal through the Isthmus of Suez.

Commelin, Isaac. Begin ende voortgangh van de Vereenighde Nederlantsche geoctroyeerde Oost-Indische Compagnie. [Amsterdam] 1646. C443

A collection of twenty-one narratives of Dutch voyages to the East Indies from 1594 to 1631, constituting a history of the "beginning and progress of the Dutch East India Company."

Commerce de la Côte d'Afrique. Manuscript. [France, ca. 1785.] C444

This survey of the west coast of Africa pays particular attention to the slave trade, including discussions of the French, European, and American interest in it.

Commerce maritime: etat pour etablir la mise dehors d'un navire ... désignée pour un voyage aux isles françaises de l'Amérique ... Manuscript. St. Malo, 11 July 1783. C445

A broadside containing statement of costs incurred in shipping goods from France to St. Domingue.

[Commercial handbook: tables and text on European currencies and exchange.] Manuscript in German. [between 1790 and 1800.] C446

A collection of five treatises dealing with aspects of international monetary exchange and management.

Commercie Compagnie van Middelburg. Reglement van de Commercie Compagnie der stad Middelburg in Zeeland. [Middelburg, ca. 1729.] C447

This trading company of Middelburg was established in 1721. Its charter contains twenty-seven provisions for the administration of the company.

Commissioners for Adjusting the Boundaries of the British and French Possessions in North America. Mémoires des Commissaires du Roi et de ceux de Sa Majesté Britannique sur les possessions ... en Amerique. Paris, Impr. Royale, 1755-57. C448

These four volumes contain the deliberations of an Anglo-French committee to determine the boundaries of Acadia, and include numerous documents dating back to the earliest contacts these two countries had with America.

Compagnie de l'Assiente. Je soussigné caissier de la Compagnie Royale de l'Assiente ... [Paris, 1701.] C449

Subscription sheet for subscribers to a company which grew out of an agreement between the Spanish and French kings.

Compagnie de la Nouvelle France. Articles accordez entre les directeurs et associez en la Compagnie de la Nouvelle France; et les deputez des habitans dudit pays: agreez et confirmez par le roy. Paris, S. Cramoisy, 1645. C450

The statement of accord between the company and the inhabitants of Canada, in which the company ceded its monopoly of the fur trade to the Canadians in obedience to a royal decree.

Compagnie de la Nouvelle France. Extraict des registres du Conseil d'estat. Paris, 1643. C451

Decree regulating the acquittance of the debts of the company.

Compagnie des Indes. Au Roy. [Presenté le 3. avril 1721.] Paris, Jean-François Knapen, 1721. C452

The directors of the Compagnie des Indes seek to prove that the company is not related to the bank established by John Law.

Compagnie des Indes. Avis aux actionnaires. Paris, Imprimerie Royale, 1734.　C453
An announcement of the renewing of the stock of the company, and the payment of dividends.

Compagnie des Indes. Café de Moka. [Lille, 1764.]　C454
A complaint against fraudulent import of coffee.

Compagnie des Indes. [Cargo descriptions.] n.p. [1772-74].　C455
Two volumes of separately paged leaflets announcing cargo offered for sale upon return of ships from the East Indies.

Compagnie des Indes. Copie de la lettre de la Compagnie, écrite à M. Morel, directeur. [Paris, 1774.]　C456
Concerns duties on foreign imports of salted cod.

Compagnie des Indes. Copie d'une lettre de la Compagnie écrite à M. Morel. Lille, 1775.　C457
An attempt to simplify the handling of contraband seized by customs officials.

Compagnie des Indes. Copie de la lettre de la Compagnie, écrite à M. Morel, directeur des fermes à Lille. [Lille, 1777.]　C458
A request that certain misunderstandings of import duties dating from 1745 and 1767 be cleared up.

Compagnie des Indes. Copie de la lettre de la Compagnie, écrite à M. Morel, directeur des fermes à Lille. [Lille, 1778.]　C459
Concerns the setting of duty on stockfish in relation to duties on cod.

Compagnie des Indes. Copie de la lettre de la Compagnie, écrite à M. Morel, directeur général des fermes du roi, à Lille. [Lille, 1778.]　C460
Concerns duties on the importation of cod.

Compagnie des Indes. Copie de la lettre de la Compagnie, écrite à M. Morel, directeur des fermes du roi à Lille. [Lille, 1780.]　C461
The company reminds the director of revenues at Lille of the approaching expiration of duties on cod.

Compagnie des Indes. Copie de la lettre de la Compagnie, écrite à M. Morel, directeur des fermes du roi à Lille. 7 Juillet 1783. [Lille, 1783.]　C462
Contains instructions regarding duties on imported fish.

Compagnie des Indes. Copie de la lettre de la Compagnie, écrite à M. Morel, directeur des fermes du roi à Lille. 31 Juillet 1783. [Lille, 1783.]　C463
The company gives notice that it will shortly represent the Crown on the board of revenue.

Compagnie des Indes. Deliberation, par laquelle la Compagnie ne se reserve que le dixiéme seulement du produit des saises ... [Lille, 1740.]　C464
Only one-tenth of contraband goods was to be retained by the Compagnie des Indes, the balance went to the agent in charge of seizures.

Compagnie des Indes. Extrait du jugement du tableau des dettes du roy, et des actions interessées de la Compagnie des Indes. n.p. [ca. 1770].　C465
A table showing how the debts of the company are to be liquidated.

Compagnie des Indes. [Five coupons indicating investment in the Compagnie des Indes covering the period 1770 to 1772.] [n.p., 1770.]　C466
Shares issued near the end of the company's existence. It was dissolved in 1770.

Compagnie des Indes. [License printed on vellum. Paris, 1749.]　C467
The company's rights to the tobacco tax are granted to Jean Baptiste François Torchet de Boismelé.

Compagnie des Indes. Ordre générale de la Compagnie des Indes pour le tenue des journeaux. Paris [1730].　C468
Regulations for the bookeeping of the Compagnie des Indes.

Compagnie des Indes. Peaux du Canada venant d'Angleterre. [Lille, 1763.]　C469
Concerns Canadian furs reaching France by way of England.

Compagnie des Indes. Pelletries du Canada. [Lille, 1763.]　C470
A request that regular import duty be imposed on furs from Canada, because of England's dominance there.

Compagnie des Indes. Vous connoissez, Monsieur, la loi invariable suivant laquelle des marchandises expédiées ... [Lille, 1767.]　C471
A letter complaining against the administration of import duties.

Compagnie des Indes Orientales. Articles et conditions convenus entre des directeurs de la Compagnie Royale des Indes Orientalles & Messieurs Jourdan, Decoulange & Compagnie de la Chine. [n.p., 1700.]　C472
An agreement for opening trade to China through the ports of Canton and Nimpo.

Compagnie des Indes Orientales. Articles et conditions sur lesquelles les marchands ... suppleint ... le Roy de leur accorder sa declaration & les graces y contenuës pour l'établissement d'une compagnie ... Paris, 1664. C473
Proposed conditions for the establishment of the French East India Company, with the royal comments on each paragraph.

Compagnie des Indes Orientales. Liste des interessez en la Compagnie des Indes Orientales, qui ont voix active et passive pour la nomination des directeurs, cassier, & secretaire de la Compagnie. Paris, Sebastien Mabre-Cramoisy, 1675. C474
List of shareholders, with amounts of shares indicated.

Compagnie du Nord. Mémoire servant de remonstrance a nosseigneurs du Parlement, pour la Compagnie du Nort, establie ... pour la pesche des ballaines. n.p. [ca. 1645]. C475
A refutation of demands apparently made by a group of Paris merchants for the ending of a monopoly on northern whaling by an obscure group referred to as the Compagnie du Nord.

Companhia de Macao. Condições, com que os directores da Companhia de Macáo haõ de arrematar o resto da carga, que trouxe a fragata S. Pedro, e S. Joaõ entrada nesta porto em 12 de setembro de 1743. [n.p., 1743.] C476
A listing of the cargo of two ships from Macao, noting the quantity and price of the items, the numbers on the packing cases, and some description as to quality.

Companhia Geral de Pernambuco e Paraíba. Instituiçaõ da Companhia geral de Pernambuco, e Paraíba. Lisbon, Miguel Rodrigues, 1759. C477
Announces the establishment of the Company of Pernambuco and Paraíba, with information on the commerce of Brazil before the company's existence.

Companhia Geral do Graõ Pará e Maranhaõ. Directorio, que se deve observar nas povoaçoens dos Indios do Pará ... Lisbon, Miguel Rodrigues, 1758. C478
A Portuguese trading company sets forth regulations for merchants engaged in trading in Brazil.

Companhia Geral do Graõ Pará e Maranhaõ. Instituiçaõ da Companhia ... Lisbon, M. Rodrigues, 1755. C479
An appeal by Lisbon merchants for establishment of a trading company in northern Brazil.

Companhia Geral do Graõ Pará e Maranhaõ. A junta da administraçaõ da Companhia ... [Lisbon? ca. 1755.] C480
A broadside stating regulations set forth by the administration of a trading company established to carry on commerce in the northern part of Brazil.

Companhia Geral para o Estado do Brazil. Instituiçam da Companhia ... [Lisbon, Antonio Alvarez, 1649.] C481
A statement of the powers and rights sought by a Portuguese trading company to organize the trade of all Brazil.

Compañia de comercio de Manila. Ordenanzas de la Compañia de comercio, que se ha formado en esta ciudad de Manila. Manila, Collegio y Universidad del Señor Santo Thomas, por Thomas Adriano, 1755. C482
The statutes of a new commercial company formed by a group of merchants in Manila and approved by a royal decree.

Companies in joynt-stock unnecessary and inconvenient. [London, 1691.] C483
A proposal for a regulated East India Company to replace the joint-stock structure, with answers to arguments made by defenders of the status quo.

Company of Merchants of England Trading to the Levant. The allegations of the Turky Company and others against the East-India-Company. [London, 1681.] C484
This defense of the East India Company reveals many details of the company's trade and methods.

Company of Merchants of England Trading to the Levant. The case of the governor and Company of merchants of England, trading to the Levant seas. n.p. [1744]. C485
Cites the competition of the French as the cause of the decline of British trade to Turkey.

Company of Merchants of England Trading to the Levant. Considerations humbly offered to the Honourable the House of Commons. [London, ca. 1700.] C486
Warns of the adverse effects upon English trade if the wearing of silks is restricted.

Company of Merchants of England Trading to the Levant. Reasons for the bill now depending ... to repeal a clause in ... An Act for the Encouraging and Encreasing of Shipping and Navigation. [London, ca. 1719.] C487
The Levant merchants contend that their monopoly on the silk trade is being infringed upon by merchants bringing Turkish goods from Leghorn.

Company of Scotland Trading to Africa and the Indies. Copy of an act presented to the Parliament by the merchants. [Edinburgh, 1695.] C488
The draft of an act which was passed in May 1695. It called for the formation of a joint stock company to trade with Africa and the Indies.

Company of Scotland Trading to Africa and the Indies. The Company ... do hereby give notice. Edinburgh, 1696. C489

A document announcing the date and place where subscriptions to the company will be taken. Includes subscription form, receipt form, and form of the bond for those not paying in full.

Company of Scotland Trading to Africa and the Indies. Constitution agreed upon by the committee of the Company of Scotland trading to Africa and the Indies. [Edinburgh, 1696.] C490

The constitution of the company provides for directors, councils, and other administrative machinery for its management.

Company of Scotland Trading to Africa and the Indies. Edinburgh the 12 of May 1696. At a general meeting of the Company of Scotland Trading to Africa and the Indies. The Viscount of Tarbot chosen praeses. [Edinburgh? 1696?] C491

The meeting named the board of directors for the company.

Company of Scotland Trading to Africa and the Indies. A list of subscribers to the Company ... taken in Edinburgh &c. until the 21 of April inclusive 1696. [Edinburgh, 1696.] C492

A list of 1164 subscribers, their subscriptions ranging from 100 to 3000 pounds.

Company of Scotland Trading to Africa and the Indies. To His Grace His Majesties High Commissioner ... the humble petition of ... the Company of Scotland. [Edinburgh? 1698.] C493

A recitation of the obstructions placed in the way of the company by the English Parliament, and a plea for an end to such opposition.

Company of Scotland Trading to Africa and the Indies. The council-general of the Indian and African Company's petition to His Majesty. [n.p., 1699.] C494

A plea for the removal of restrictions decreed against English trade and communication with the Scottish colony at Darien.

Company of Scotland Trading to Africa and the Indies. An exact list of all the men, women and boys that died on board the Indian and African Company's fleet ... and since their landing in Caledonia. Edinburgh, 1699. C495

A listing of seventy-six persons among the 1,200 who were sent out by the company, noting the cause of death in each instance and the position of the deceased in the colony.

Company of Scotland Trading to Africa and the Indies. Certain propositions relating to the Scots plantation of Caledonia. Glasgow, 1700. C496

A series of fourteen arguments on behalf of the Scots colony on Darien, noting the inevitability of its failure if restrictions against English trade there are not removed.

Company of Scotland Trading to Africa and the Indies. The original papers and letters relating to the Scots Company. Faithfully extracted from the Companies books. [Edinburgh?] 1700. C497

A collection of papers and letters published to alleviate criticism of the Scottish colony at Darien.

Company of Scotland Trading to Africa and the Indies. The representations and petitions of the council-general of the Indian and African Company to the Parliament. Edinburgh, 1700. C498

A formal petition to Parliament for assistance to the company.

Company of Scotland Trading to Africa and the Indies. Scotland's right to Caledonia (formerly called Darien) and the legality of its settlement, asserted in three several memorials. [Edinburgh?] 1700. C499

The three memorials attempt to dispose of the argument that the Scots were encroaching on Spanish territory and that the company would be a competitor to English plantations in America.

Company of Scotland Trading to Africa and the Indies. To His Grace His Majesty's High Comissioner, and the right honourable the Estates of Parliament. The humble representation and petition of the council-general of the Company ... [Edinburgh, 1700.] C500

A review of the company's misfortunes and a plea for royal assistance.

Company of the Royal Fishery of England. A collection of advertisements, advices, and directions relating to the royal fishery. London, For H. M., 1695. C501

A detailed review of the policies and practices followed to encourage English fishing, with comments about how English general commerce might be improved by a better fishing trade. The Dutch are repeatedly referred to as an example.

Company of the Royal Fishery of England. A discourse concerning the fishery within the British seas and other His Majesties dominions. London, For the Company of the Royal Fishery, 1695. C502

A description of the recently formed company, and an argument on behalf of improving England's fishing trade as a means of stimulating the general economy.

Company of the Royal Fishery of England. A discourse concerning the fishery within the

British seas and other His Majesties dominions. London, For the Company of the Royal Fishery, 1695. C503

Similar to the above, with an advertisement, designed to encourage people to invest in the company. The company expects good profits: "according to the best Estimate and Computation ... by the Blessing of God upon Mens Prudence, Faithfulness and Diligence, Produce about *Cent. per Cent. per Annum* ..."

A comparison between the British sugar colonies and New England, as they relate to the interest of Great Britain. London, For James Roberts, 1732. C504

The author maintains that the sugar colonies should be encouraged and promoted over the North American colonies, which are likely to become independent of Britain.

Compendio de los sucesos, que con grande gloria de Dios ... en defensa de estas Christiandades, e islas de Bisayas, se consiguieron contra los Mahometanos enemigos ... Manila, Compañia de Jesus, 1755. C505

A newsletter published by Jesuits in Manila reporting military actions between Moslem invaders and local people of Bisaya.

Compendio general de las contribuciones, y gastos que ocasionan todos los efectos ... se trafican entre los reynos de Castilla, y America. Cadiz, Don Manuel Espinosa de los Monteros, 1762. C506

A handbook of instructions for merchants and seamen engaged in commerce between Spain and Spanish America.

A compendious geographical and historical grammar: exhibiting a brief survey of the terraqueous globe ... London, W. Peacock, 1795. C507

A brief geography text, including thirteen maps.

A compendious geographical dictionary, containing a concise description of the most remarkable places, ancient and modern, in Europe, Asia, Africa, & America ... The 2d ed. London, W. Peacock, 1795. C508

A geographical dictionary, including a list of all the fairs in Great Britain and a table of currencies.

A complaint to the ____ of ____ against a pamphlet intitled, A speech intended to have been spoken on the bill for altering the charters of the Colony of Massachuset's Bay. London, For Benjamin White, 1775. C509

A sharp criticism of a publication in which the rights of the American colonies were asserted against the claims of Parliamentary supremacy.

Conceição, Nuno da. Relaçam da viagem, e svcesso que teve a nao capitania Nossa Senhora do Bom Despacho: de que era Capitaõ Francisco de Mello, vindo da India no anno de 1630. Lisbon, Pedro Crasbeeck, 1631 [repr. 1737] C510

Concept ofte seker middel, machtig op te brengen de kosten, noodig tot het uitrusten ende onderhouden van noch wel 70 of 80 capitale oorlog-scheepen. Leiden, I. Abrahamsz., 1653. C511

A plan for raising money to provide more naval vessels to protect Dutch shipping.

A concise historical account of all the British colonies in North America, comprehending their rise, progress, and modern state ... London, For J. Bew, 1775. C512

This brief work is dominated by the description and history of New England. Authorship is frequently attributed to Paul Wein.

Concolorcorvo. El Lazarillo de Ciegos Caminantes desde Buenos-Ayres, hasta Lima con sus itinerarios segun las mas puntual observacion ... Gijon [Peru] Imprenta de la Rovada, 1773. C513

A guidebook for merchants and others travelling between Montevideo and Lima.

Condiçoens com que o doutor Luiz Maxado Teixeira ... Lisbon, Antonio Rodrigues Galhardo, 1787. C514

Copy of the catalog of goods at auction from two ships recently arrived from Macao. The goods were auctioned off at the Casa de India and include tea, silk, copper, Japanese lacquer, china and fans.

Condillac, Etienne Bonnot de. Le commerce et le gouvernement, considérés rélativement l'un à l'autre. Amsterdam, 1776. C515

An argument for greater freedom in economic life.

Condorcet, Jean-Antoine-Nicolas de Caritat, marquis de. Reflexions sur l'esclavage des Negres. Neufchatel, Société Typographique, 1781. C516

A review of all of the arguments against slavery as well as the contentions for its necessity by its defenders, all from an abolitionist point of view.

[Condorcet, Marie Antoine Nicolas Caritat, marquis de.] Du commerce des bleds. Paris, Grangé, 1775. C517

A reply to a previously published work, *Sur la législation & le commerce des grains*, which had advocated restrictions upon the grain trade.

The conduct of the Dutch, relating to their breach of treaties with England. London, C. Say, 1760. C518

A review of Anglo-Dutch rivalry, primarily with regard to Surinam from 1665 to 1760. Contains a detailed discussion of the case of Jerominy Clifford, an English planter who was deprived of his plantation in Surinam.

The conduct of the East-India Company, with respect to their wars, &c. London, 1767. C519
A brief history of the East India Company's military activity in India.

Conestaggio, Girolamo Franchi di. Dell'unione del regno di Portogallo alla corona di Castiglia ... Genoa, Girolamo Bartoli, 1589. C520
This account of the union of the crowns of Spain and Portugal takes account of the overseas interests of both nations.

Confucius. Satyre nouvelle. n.p. [ca. 1700]. C521
A six-page satirical commentary on the Chinese rites controversy, lamenting the division among Christians and their close relation to commercial interests.

Consejo de Indias (Spain). Extracto historial del expediente que pende ... a instancia de la ciudad de Manila, y demàs de las islas Philipinas ... Madrid, J. de Ariztia, 1736. C522
Concerns chiefly the Spanish textile trade between China, the Philippines, and America.

Consejo de Indias (Spain). Ordenanzas del Consejo Real de las Indias. Madrid, Antonio Marin, 1747. C523
A collection of ordinances, decrees, resolutions, and edicts dated from 1524 to 1658, relating to the governing of Spanish America.

The consequences of the bill now depending in favour of the sugar colonies impartially considered: in a letter to a worthy member of the honourable House of Commons. [n.p., ca. 1731.] C524
A critical view of the West Indian sugar planters' pleas for higher prices for their product and for restraint upon trade between the northern colonies and the French West Indies planters.

The considerable advantages of a South-Sea trade to our English nation. London, For S. Popping [1711]. C525
A pamphlet proposing the colonization of Terra del Fuego to give England a base for active participation in the South Sea trade.

Consideratie of kort vertoog van Nederlandts, waar belang by dese Fransen oorlog. Amsterdam, P. Rotterdam, 1691. C526
An argument delivered to the States General, urging a quick victory over France, since the restrictions a long war would put upon Dutch trade would be ruinous.

Consideratien op de cautie van Portugael. n.p., 1647. C527
In view of an impending treaty with Portugal, this tract advocates that the Dutch seek to improve the position of the West India Company in Brazil.

Consideratien op de deductie en declaratie van oorlogh van den koningh van Groot Britanjen, tegens den koningh van Denemarcken. Rotterdam, D. Jansz., 1666. C528
Condemns the English for attacks upon Danish merchant shipping.

Consideratien op eenige resolutien genomen by de ... Staten van Holland ende West-Vriesland, tegens eenige predikanten in den Hage. Amsterdam, Pieter de Traister, 1652. C529
Critical observations on restraints imposed upon certain preachers for their remarks concerning the Dutch West India Company.

Consideratien over den tegenwoordigen toestand van het Vereenigde Nederland. [Amsterdam] 1672. C530
A consideration of Dutch affairs, chiefly rivalries with England in the East Indies and Surinam.

Consideratien van een hoofdparticipant der generale Nederlandsche Oostindische Compagnie, bevattende den staat derzelve zoo hier te lande als in de colonien ... n.p., 1791. C531
An argument in favor of free trade in the East Indies replacing the monopoly of the Dutch East India Company.

Considerations de religion et d'estat, sur la guerre angloise, & autres affaires du temps. n.p. [1653]. C532
A general discussion of Dutch commercial and political affairs, citing the cause of Dutch decline as the lack of protection for its commerce against the English.

Considerations occasioned by the bill for enabling the South-Sea Company to increase their capital stock. London, J. Roberts, 1720. C533
A prediction of the ruin of England's commerce due to the close relationship between the company and the national debt.

Considerations occasioned by The Craftsman upon excises. London, J. Roberts, 1733. C534
This tract favors the excise on wine and tobacco, but also suggests bounties on sugar manufacture to encourage the sugar trade.

Considerations offered to all the corporations of England. London, For T. Payne, 1722. C535
This writer contends that English trade can be restored only by a Parliament strongly representative of England's merchant class.

Considerations on the advantages of yielding up to Spain the un-expired term of the Assiento

contract for an equivalent. London, For M. Cooper and G. Woodfall [1748]. C536
The Assiento contract is seen as a reason for loss of trade to Britain's rivals and for the continued hostility of Spain, to the disadvantage of British trade abroad.

Considerations on the American trade, before and since the establishment of the South-Sea Company. London, For J. Roberts, 1739. C537
A criticism of the South Sea trade as managed by the South Sea Company.

Considerations on the attempt of the East India Company to become manufacturers in Great Britain. London, 1796. C538
An attack upon plans of the East India Company to manufacture silk in England.

Considerations on the expediency of a Spanish war: containing reflections on the late demands of Spain: and on the negociations of Mons. Bussy. London, For R. Griffiths, 1761. C539
A survey of the balance of power in Europe, giving evidence that Spain has neither the motives nor the means to open a war against Great Britain.

Considerations on the management of the late secret expeditions, and the conduct of the court of France. In a letter to - - -. London, For W. Webb, 1740. C540
The expeditions in question are Admiral Vernon's to the West Indies and Lord Anson's to the Pacific Ocean, both cited as examples of improper prosecution of the war against Spain by the Walpole ministry.

Considerations on the present dangerous state of the sugar colonies. n.p. [ca. 1750]. C541
Also includes tracts titled: *A memorial, and observations, concerning the islands of St. Lucia, Dominico, St. Vincents, and Tobago* and *Queries and answers relating to the African trade.*

Considerations on the present peace, as far as it is relative to the colonies, and the African trade. London, For W. Bristow, 1763. C542
This defense of the treaty of 1763 analyzes Britain's colonial position in America relative to the slave trade and sugar trade.

Considerations on the present state of the East-India Company's affairs. London, For W. Nicoll and W. Richardson [1764]. C543
A criticism of the return of Clive to India with political and military power, noting the danger to both the East India Company and the future of India.

Considerations on the war. London, For J. Roberts, 1742. C544
Cites the commercial advantages to be gained by England through her war with Spain.

Considérations politiques sur le commerce du royaume. n.p., 1789. C545
Contains a discourse on the commerce of Picardy and a survey of French commerce.

Considérations politiques sur les esclaves des colonies françoises de l'Amérique, et sur leurs gens de couleur libres. Paris, Moutard, 1791. C546
A defense of slavery and the slave trade as the only means to maintaining a plantation economy in the French West Indies.

Considerations requiring greater care for trade in England, and some expedients proposed. London, For S. Crouch, 1695. C547
A proposal for the establishment of a council of merchants to assist the government in matters relating to commerce.

Considérations sur le commerce des États-Unis avec St. Domingue et autres isles françaises. Manuscript. France [1788]. C548
Discusses the reciprocal advantages that will come to the United States and the French West Indies from an active trade in indigo, cotton, leather, mahogany, sugar, and other goods.

Considérations sur le tabac, par un député suppléant. Paris, 1790. C549
Presentation of a plan for continuing the national monopoly on tobacco in France.

Considérations sur les manufactures de mousseline et de callico, dans le Grande Bretagne. Manuscript. France [1785]. C550
Describes new textile machines, new methods of growing cotton in the West Indies, and the distress caused to English textile manufactures by the Compagnie des Indes.

Considerations upon the rights of the colonists to the privileges of British subjects. New York, John Holt, 1766. C551
An argument on behalf of the colonists' right to representation in Parliament based upon the history of the English constitution.

Considerations upon the trade to Guinea. London, 1708. C552
Deals with the advantages to Great Britain of open trade compared to monopolistic joint-stock companies, especially in Guinea.

Considerazioni sù la scrittura intitolata riflessioni sopra la causa della Cina dopò venuto in Europa in decreto dell'Em̃[inentissim]o di Tournon. [Rome, 1709.] C553
This work is a part of the Chinese Rites controversy, a response to a Jesuit publication titled *Alcune riflessioni intorno alle cose presenti della Cina*, 1709.

Consolat de mar. Libre appellat Consolat de mar. Barcelona, Johan Rosembach, 1518.   C554

The third known edition, with considerable extension of text, of a code of sea law which grew up at Barcelona out of decisions of magistrates who were called upon to exercise jurisdiction over Catalan merchants.

Consolat de mar. Capituli et ordinatione di mare & di mercantie. [Rome, Antonio de Bladi de Asola, 1519.]   C555

The first Italian edition.

Consolat de mar. Libro di Consolato. Venice, Giovanni Padoanno, 1539.   C556

The second Italian edition.

Consolat de mar. Libre apellat Cõsolat de mar: ara novament estampat y corregit. [Barcelona, Carles Amoros] 1540.   C557

The fourth Barcelona edition.

Consolat de mar. Libro del consolato de' marinari ... con l'aggiunta delle ordinationi sopra l'armate di mare, sicurtà, entrate, & uscite. Venice, Andrea Ravenoldo, 1566.   C558

This edition adds material dealing with ships sailing in convoy, maritime insurance, and trade in Sicily.

Consolat de mar. Llibre de consolat dels fets maritims. Barcelona, Honoffre Guari, 1592.   C559

In addition to extensions within the code, this augmented edition contains sections on maritime insurance, commercial privileges, and regulations for departure and entry at Barcelona.

Consolat de mar. Il consolato del mare; nel quale si comprendono tutti gli statuti, & ordini: disposti da gli antichi, per ogni caso di mercantia & di navigare ... Venetia, Lucio Spineda, 1599.   C560

This appears to be the earliest edition to include a portolan for the Mediterranean Sea. It also includes a collection of maritime laws not a part of the code.

Consolat de mar. Il consolato del mare ... con il portolano del mare ... & ampliato delle leggi della sereniss. repub. di Venetia. Venice, Marco Ginammi, 1637.   C561

This edition adds a portolan for the Mediterranean, attributed to Alvìse da Cà da Mosto, a navigational handbook, and a collection of Venetian mercantile laws from the years 1428-1632.

Consolat de mar. Il consolato del mare, nel quale non solo si comprendono tutti gli ordini, e statuti per ogni caso di mercantia, e di naviganti ... Venice, Francesco Brogiollo, 1668.   C562

This edition includes the portolan of the Mediterranean Sea.

Consolat de mar. Il consolato del mare, nel quale non solo si comprendono tutti gli statuti, & ordini, disposti da gli antichi per ogni cosa de mercantia, & di navigare ... Nieulyks uyt het Italiaans in het Nederduyts vertaalt. Leiden, Joannes du Vivié, and Isaak Severinus, 1704.   C563

The first and apparently only Dutch edition, with the text in Italian also. The edition was prepared by Abraham Westerveen.

Consolat de mar. Consulado del mar de Barcelona, nuevamente traducido de Cathalan en Castellano por Don Cayetano de Pallejá ... Barcelona, Juan Piferrer, 1732.   C564

A new translation from Catalan, the original language of the code, into Spanish, with references to commentary on the separate chapters in other works on maritime law.

Consolat de mar. Il consolato del mare. Venice, F. Piacentini, 1737.   C565

This edition contains the portolan describing various Mediterranean trade routes.

Consolat de mar. Codigo de las costumbres maritimas de Barcelona. Madrid, A. de Sancha, 1791.   C566

A history of the development of sea law governing mercantile activity at Barcelona, translated by Antonio de Capmany y Montpalau.

Constitutional considerations on the power of Parliament to levy taxes on the North American colonies. London, For J. Wilkie, 1766.   C567

An argument contending that representation of the colonies in Parliament is neither guaranteed or possible, and that taxing them is essential to national security.

Contarini, Ambrogio. El viazo ... al Signor. Uxuncassam Re de Persia. Venice, Hannibal Foxius, 1487.   C568

The first edition of this account of an early commercial and diplomatic mission from Venice to Persia, including descriptions of southern Russia and Muscovy.

Contarini, Ambrogio. Itinerario ... mãdado nel anno 1472 ad Usuncassan Re de Persia. Venice, Francesco Bindoni and Mapheo Pasini, 1524.   C569

The second edition.

Contarini, Ambrogio. Il Viazo ... al Signor Uxuncassan Re de Persia. Venice, 1543.   C570

One of two editions of this year, differing considerably from the 1487 printing.

Continuatio Historiae cultus Sinensium, seu Varia scripta de cultibus Sinarum, inter vicarios apostolicos Gallos aliosque missionarios, & patres Societatis Jesu controversis. Cologne, 1700.   C571

This continuation adds six items to the twenty-five found in the earlier work published in Cologne the same year.

Contreras, Francisco de. Informacion sobre que los electos para Obispos no pueden consagrarse, ni tomar la possession de sus Obispados ... [Madrid?] 1647. C572

Contreras, writing from Lima, challenges the authority of Bishop Bernardino de Cárdenas of Paraguay. The text is preceded by sixteen leaves of "Aprobaciones," followed by twenty-three leaves in contemporary handwriting titled "Dudas" (Doubts).

Contzen, Adam. Methodus doctrinae civilis, seu Abissini regis historia. Cologne, Joannem Kinckium, 1628. C573

This work purports to be a history of Ethiopia, but is actually a political novel. The author was a Jesuit and a political economist.

Conveniencias q faz el Rey N.S. que Deos g. De convindo, e formando a Comp. a de cacheu que se lhe offerce ... Manuscript. [Portugal, ca. 1750.] C574

An anonymous memorandum concerning Portuguese trade in West Africa, and related commerce in Brazil, with reference to English presence there and the intended formation of the Company of Cacheu to control this trade.

Cook, James. Captain Cook's voyages round the world. Newcastle, M. Brown, 1790. C575

This edition includes all three voyages and is illustrated by forty-seven maps and plates. Also included are the journal of Baron Mulgrave's arctic voyage and that of Arthur Phillip to Australia.

Cook, James. Reis naar de Zuidpool en rondom de weereld ... met de schepen de Resolutien en de Adventure, in de jaren 1772, 1773, 1774, en 1775 ... Rotterdam, A. Bothall, D. Vis en P. Holsteyn, 1778. C576

The first Dutch edition of Cook's account of his second voyage. The illustrations from the English edition are not included.

Cook, James. Reis naar den Stillen Oceaan. Rotterdam, A. Bothall en D. Vis, 1787. C577

The first Dutch edition of Cook's third voyage to the Pacific in which Cook was killed in Hawaii. The single illustration is a depiction of his death.

Cook, James. Reize rondom de waereld, door James Cook. Leiden, Amsterdam, and the Hague, Honkoop, Allart, en van Cleef, 1795-1803. Amsterdam, J. Allart, 1809. C578

This Dutch edition has commentary by the translator-editor, J.D. Pasteur, and extensive observations on the second and third voyages by Georg Forster. It also includes an index volume by W. Chevallerau.

Cook, James. Sammandrag af Capitain Jacob Cooks åren 1772, 73, 74 och 1775 omkring Södra Polen förrättade resa, hwarwid Herrar Forsters och Furneaux journaler blifwit jämnförde och nyttjade ... Upsala, Johan Edman, 1783. C579

This Swedish abridgement includes material from Cook's *Voyage toward the South Pole*, and from the *Voyage* of Georg Forster both of which were published in 1777.

Cook, James. Sammandrag af Capitain Jacob Cooks tredje resa, i söderhafwet och emot Norra Polen. Upsala, Johan Edman, 1787. C580

This translation was probably made by Samuel Ödmann. Numerous notes are added to the text, and a curious map of the Pacific Ocean is included.

Cook, James. Troisième voyage de Cook, ou Voyage a l'Ocean Pacifique ... pour faire des découvertes dans l'hémisphere nord. Paris, Hôtel de Thou, 1785. C581

The portion of the voyage following Cook's death is by James King. This four-volume translation is by Jean Nicolas Demeunier.

Cook, James. Voyage dans l'hémisphère austral, et autour du monde ... en 1772, 1773, 1774, & 1775. Paris, Hôtel de Thou, 1778. C582

J.B.A. Suard's translation in five volumes of Cook's account of his second circumnavigation, incorporating extensive additions from Georg Forster's narrative of the voyage.

Cook, James. A voyage to the Pacific Ocean. London, H. Hughes for G. Nicol and T. Cadell, 1785. C583

The third edition of the official account of Cook's third voyage in which he explored the northern Pacific Ocean and the northwest coast of North America.

Cook, James. A voyage to the Pacific Ocean undertaken by command of His Majesty for making discoveries in the northern hemisphere. 2nd ed. Perth, R. Morison, 1785-1787. C584

This four volume set contains several illustrations but none of the maps found in the larger edition. The text is a condensed version.

Cook, James. A voyage towards the South Pole, and round the world. London, For W. Strahan and T. Cadell, 1777. C585

The official account of Cook's second voyage, which included observations of the 1769 transit of Venus and a search for the elusive "Great Southern Continent."

Cooke, Captain Edward. A voyage to the South Sea. London, H.M. for B. Lintot and R. Gosling, 1712. C586

An account of the voyage of Woodes Rogers, containing many maps and excellent descriptive material on western South America and the Pacific Ocean.

Coope, Richard. A letter to the proprietors of the South-Sea Company. With a dedication to George Heathcote, Esq. ... London, A. Dodd, 1739. **C587**
A former director of the South Sea Company defends his own policies and warns against a continuation of troubles for the company because inadequate prosecution of wrongdoing in the company has allowed evils to continue.

[Cooper, Samuel.] The crisis. Or, a full defence of the colonies. London, For W. Griffin, 1766. **C588**
This argument is primarily on behalf of a proper representation for the British Colonies so that their concerns can be brought before Parliament.

Cooper, Thomas. Some information respecting America. London, For J. Johnson, 1794. **C589**
Five letters describing many aspcts of life in America, particularly in Pennsylvania.

Cooper, Thomas. Some information respecting America. Dublin, For P. Wogan [etc.] 1794. **C590**
A close reprint of the London edition.

Cooper, Thomas. Renseignemens sur l'Amérique. Hamburg, Pierre François Fauche, 1795. **C591**
This French edition adds a translator's note appealing to the various types of Europeans who might wish to emigrate to America.

Coote, Sir Eyre, et al. A letter from certain gentlemen of the council at Bengal ... containing reasons against the revolution in favor of Meir Cossim Aly Chan. London, For T. Becket and P.A. De Hondt, 1764. **C592**
A criticism of the actions of Henry Vansittart, successor to Robert Clive in Bengal, whereby the East India Company renounced its relationship with Mir Jaffer Aly Chan in favor of Mir Mohammed Cossim Aly Chan.

Copia da reposta de hua carta, que monsieur de Belf, morador em Lisboa, mandou à hum seu natural, assistente na Corte de Paris, em reposta de outra, na qual lhe mandava pedir noticia do estado da nova Companhia de Macaõ. n.p. [1748]. **C593**
An account of the organization and operations of a Portuguese trading company engaged in the Macao trade, with major emphasis on merchandising of tea.

Copia de un papel ... En el qual no se nombra el autor, no tampoco la parte adonde fue impresso. [Augsburg?] 1626. **C594**
A translation of a Dutch tract critical of many Dutch policies, including those relating to the East and West India companies.

Copia de una carta, escrita al Padre Fray Alonso Sandin ... procurador general de la provincia del Santo Rosario de Philipinas en esta corte; en que dà noticia de el estado de aquillas islas. [Madrid? 1684?] **C595**
A letter to the procurator general of the Dominicans in the Far East noting the deplorable condition of the missions in the Philippines, and alleging a conspiracy against the Dominicans to discredit them with the Spanish government.

Copia de una littera del Re de Portagallo mandata al Re de Castella del viaggio & successo de India. Rome, J. de Besicken, 1505. **C596**
An account of the first four commercial voyages from Portugal to India. Included are descriptions of African and Indian peoples, cities, and products. It contains the first printed account of Brazil.

Copia de una littera del Re de Portagallo mandata al Re de Castella del viaggio & sucesso de India. Milan, P.M. di Mantegazzi, 1505. **C597**
A reprint of the preceding item.

Copia der newen Zeytung auss Presillg Landt. Augsburg [ca. 1514]. **C598**
A German newsletter describing a voyage made to South America, presumably to the Plate River. The land, people, and products acquired are described.

Copia di due lettere annue scritte dal Giapone del 1589 & 1590, l'una dal P. viceprovinciale al P. Alesandro Valignano l'altra dal P. Luigi Frois al P. Generale della Compagnia di Giesu. Brescia, Policreto Turlini, 1593. **C599**
The letters are dated Cansuca, 7 October 1589, and Nagasaki, 12 October 1590. They report events from the various mission stations and include hostilities to some of the missions by government officials.

Copia di scrittura informativa concernente le presenti vertenze di Portogallo con li pp. Gesuiti, secondo le notizie trasmesse in Roma da Monsignor Nunzio alla segretaria di stato ... [n.p., 1758?] **C600**
An Italian translation of the formal charges made against the Jesuits in Paraguay to the Holy Office in Rome.

Copie. Brief van een Hollander in London, betreffende zekere propositien van Zyn Doorl. H:H: voorkomende in het extract uit de resolutien van H:H: Moogenden de Heeren Staaten van Holland en Westfriesland, enz. [n.p., 1779]. **C601**
The letter is dated March 3, 1779 and deals with diplomatic and mercantile affairs. It contains a list of thirty-seven pamphlets concerned with similar matters.

Copie de l'instruction donne par leur Altesses au Marquis Ambrosio Spinola ... n.p., 1608. **C602**
Instructions to Hapsburg negotiators for peace with the Dutch. Trade was to be permitted with Spain, but not with the East and West Indies.

Copie van requesten van de goede gehoorsame burgeren ende gemeente deser stedet Amstelredamme ... n.p., 1628. C603
   The West India Company here attempts to use its influence to prevent the growth of the Arminian sect which had opposed the company earlier.

Copie van seeckere missive, geschreven uyt 's Graven-Hague aen een vrient in Zeelandt. Middelburg, Jan Woutersz, 1653. C604
   Contains orders from the States General for the requisitioning of merchant ships for defense against the English.

Coppie dunes lettres missives envoyees a Romme a Monseigneur le reverēdissime Cardinal de Cueua, cõtenant la prinse nouvellemēt faicte sur les Turcqs, d'une ville nommee Afrique ... Paris, Jehã Dallier [1550]. C605
   A newsletter reporting the capture of Mahedia in Tunisia by a fleet of emperor Charles V under the command of Andrea Doria.

Coppier, Guillaume. Histoire et voyage des Indes Occidentales. Lyons, I. Huguetan, 1645. C606
   An account of peoples, places, and products noted during a voyage to America.

Coppino, Aquilino. De Hispanicae monaechiae amplitudine ... oratio. Milan, Malatestas Typographos Regios [1612]. C607
   An oration presented before the senate of Milan, celebrating the greatness of Phillip II of Spain, noting Spanish possessions in the West and East Indies.

A copy of a letter from a gentleman in Virginia to a merchant in Philadelphia. n.p. [1768]. C608
   A criticism of Philadelphia's merchants for not taking a firm stand against taxes imposed by Parliament on colonial commerce following repeal of the Stamp Act.

A copy of a letter from Quebeck in Canada to a Pr_____ M____r in France. n.p. [ca. 1747]. C609
   A Scotsman proposes that Parliament declare the paper currency of the colonies illegal.

A copy of a letter [proposing the establishment of a new trading company to be called the China Company]. n.p., 1695. C610
   Notes the advantage of Far Eastern trade via the Strait of Magellan.

A copy of some reasons formerly offered by the Gloucestershire clothiers, to shew the true cause of the decay of the Worcester trade. n.p. [ca. 1735]. C611
   This handbill rejects the plea from Worcester that the woolen trade in Gloucester, Somerset, and Wiltshire be removed to Worcester because its clothiers had fallen on hard times.

Copy papers concerning the payment of certain law expences incurred by Warren Hastings, esq. [London? 1795?] C612
   A collection of legal opinions justifying disbursement of funds by the East India Company for payment of Warren Hastings' expenses incurred in his impeachment trial.

Copye translaet uyt het Francois ... De memorie ende gheschrift inhouden de 19 artijckelen, hier onder verhaelt. n.p. [1647]. C613
   Nineteen proposals by the French ambassador with respect to Spanish-Dutch relations, including commerce, with unfavorable comments by the editor.

Copye van een brief die een burgher van Sevilien geschreven heeft aen zijn vrient ... Amsterdam, C. Menlemand, 1626. C614
   Announces a flood in Seville which destroyed large quantities of goods recently arrived from the West Indies.

Copye van een brief van d'een vrundt aen d'ander gheschriven waer in de saken ter zee ... n.p., 1636. C615
   This tract is concerned with maritime affairs, particularly the regulation of trading companies and the manning of convoys for merchant ships.

Copye van seeckeren brief geschreven by een van qualiteyt ... n.p., 1599. C616
   A commentary criticizing Spanish proposals that they be allowed to supervise Dutch overseas trade.

Copyen van drie missiven. Amsterdam, Jan van Hilten, 1641. C617
   Three letters from Brazil reporting activities there, including relations with the Portuguese, progress of Dutch settlements, sailings of ships for Holland, and prospects for the sugar crop.

[Coquereau, Jean-Baptiste-Louis.] Mémoires de l'abbé Terrai, controlleur-général des finances ... Londres, 1776. C618
   Abbé Terray was general controller of finance under Louis XV, and this work relates to some of his commercial policies.

Cordeyro, Antonio. Historia insulana das ilhas a Portugal sugeytas no Oceano Occidental. Lisbon, Antonio Pedrozo Galram, 1717. C619
   A history of Portuguese exploration, colonization, and colonial administration in the islands of the Canary, Madeira, Azores, and Cape Verde groups.

Córdova Salinas, Diego de. Vida virtudes, y milagros del apostol del Peru el B.P. Fr. Francisco Solano, de la serafica orden de los menores de la regular observancia, patron de la ciudad de Lima ... Madrid, Imprenta Real, 1676. C620
   A biography of a prominent Franciscan missionary who served in Peru, Paraguay, and Argentina.

Coreal, Francisco. Voyages ... aux Indes Occidentales. Amsterdam, J. Frederic Bernard, 1722.   C621

In addition to the author's own account of the Caribbean area, this work contains translations of Raleigh's description of Guiana, Narborough's *Voyages*, and the narrative of Tasman's circumnavigation of Australia.

[Cormatin.] Voyage du ci-devant duc du Chatelet, en Portugal. Paris, F. Buisson, 1798.   C622

A general survey of the political and economic situation in Portugal, with extensive information on overseas trade.

Cornut, Jacques Philippe. Iac Cornuti ... Canadensium plantarum ... historia. Paris, Simon Le Moyne, 1635.   C623

The first treatise on Canadian plants.

Coronelli, Vincenzo. Atlante Veneto. Venice, Domenico Padovani, 1690.   C624

A collection of 143 maps without text, published and bound under the same title as a work, also issued in 1690, that consisted of 72 maps and 154 pages of text.

Coronelli, Vincenzo. Epitome cosmografica. Venice, Andrea Poletti, 1693.   C625

The section on geography contains two excellent hemispheric maps, and the bibliography of works consulted is very revealing of seventeenth-century scholarship.

Coronelli, Vincenzo. Partie occidentale du Canada ou de la Nouvelle France. Paris, J.B. Nolin, 1688.   C626

This map depicts the region from Hudson Bay to the Wabash River, and from Montreal to the Mississippi, and includes numerous forts and Jesuit mission stations.

Corporation of London. Court of Common Council. The petition of the Lord Maior, Aldermen, and Common-Council-men of the City of London ... to the Parliament. London, T.J. for Ralph Smith, 1662.   C627

The petition calls for well-organized trading associations to regulate the trade to France, Italy, Spain, and Portugal.

Corrêa, Francisco. Relaçam do successo, que teve o patacho chamada N. Sra. da Candelaria da ilha da Madeira, o qual vindo da costa de Guinè no anno de 1693 huma rigorosa tempestade o fez varar na ilha incognita. Lisbon, Bernardo da Costa de Carvalho, 1734.   C628

A tale of storm and shipwreck in the South Atlantic. Precise locations are not given, and it is possibly an imaginary account.

[Correa, João de Medeiros.] Relaçam verdadeira de tudo o succedido na restauração da Bahia. Oporto, João Rodriguez, 1625.   C629

One of three 1625 editions of the account of the recapture of Bahia from the Dutch by a Spanish fleet.

Corsali, Andrea. Lettera di Andrea Corsali allo ill. principe et signore Laurentio de Medici duca d'Urbino. ex India. [Florence, after Sept. 18, 1517.]   C630

The second letter of Corsali, a Florentine in Portuguese service. He describes his voyage with the Portuguese from Cochin to Ethiopia and the Persian Gulf area.

Cort begrijp vanden staet van het groot rijck van China ende van het Christendom aldaer van het iaer 1637 tot 1649. Overgheset uyt het Spaensch ghedruckt tot Mexico. Antwerp, Guilliam Verdussen, 1651.   C631

A brief account of the progress of the Jesuit missions in China, together with a report on the Manchu invasion from the north and other political developments.

Een cort ende warachtich verhael vande ghedenckweerdige gheschiedenisse in Barbaryen, ende vanden grooten slagh ontrent Maroques, gheschiet den 25 Aprilis, 1607. The Hague, Hillebrant Jacobsz, 1607.   C632

An account of a conflict in North Africa in which a number of European participants, presumably merchants, were killed.

Cort verhael van den staet en gelegentheyt van de saecken, tusschen d'Engelsche en Nederlantsche Oost-Indische compagnie. Amsterdam, Pieter Guldemont, 1664.   C633

An account of Anglo-Dutch rivalry in the East Indies.

Cortés, Hernán. De insulis nuper inventis. Cologne, Arnold Birckman, 1532.   C634

The second Latin editions of the second and third letters from Cortés to Charles V, reporting activities in the New World. Additional material from Peter Martyr, Martin de Valencia, and Bishop Zumarraga is included.

Cortés, Hernán. Historia de Nueva-España ... aumentada con otros documentos, y notas, por Don Francisco Antonio Lorenzana. Mexico, Joseph Antonio de Hogal, 1770.   C635

Contains the second, third, and fourth letters from Cortés to the Emperor Charles V, and commentary by the editor, Francisco Antonio Lorenzana y Buitron, dealing with the history of Mexico both before and after Cortés' expeditions.

Cortés, Hernán. Tertia Ferdinandi Cortesii ... narratio. Nuremberg, Foedericum Arthemesium, 1524.   C636

The first Latin edition of the third letter written by Cortés to Charles V, reporting activities in the New World from October 30, 1520, to May 22, 1522.

Cortés, Hernán. Von dem Newen Hispanien ... zwo gantz lustige unnd fruchtreiche Historien. Augsburg, Philipp Ulhart, 1550.   C637

The first German edition of the second and third Cortés letters, with additional material relating to German exploration in Venezuela.

[Cortés Ossorio, Juan.] Reparos historiales apologeticos ... propuestos de parte de los missioneros apostolicos del imperio de la China. Pamplona, Tomás Baztan [ca. 1677?]. C638

A refutation of Fernández Navarrete's *Tratados historicos* which was critical of the Jesuit mission in China.

Costa, Christovam da. Tractado de las drogas, y medicinas de las Indias Orientales. Burgos, Martin de Victoria, 1578. C639

An illustrated treatise on East Indian spices and drugs, with indications of the chief markets for them.

Costa, Christovam da. Trattato della historia, natura, et virtu delle droghe medicinali ... Venice, Francesco Ziletti, 1585. C640

The first Italian edition of this early herbal which contains forty-five full-page woodcuts of commercially valuable plants.

Costa, Diogo da. Relaçam das guerras da India desde o anno de 1736 até o de 1740. Lisbon, Antonio Isidoro da Fonseca, 1741. C641

A newsletter account of Portuguese military engagements with Marattas in northwestern India, noting success by the Portuguese particularly at Baçaim, but at other fortresses also.

[Costa, José da.] Relação da prizão, e morte dos quatro veneraveis padres da Companhia, Bartholomeo Àlvarez, Manoel de Abreu, Vicente de Cunha (Portuguezes) e João Gaspar Cratz (Alemão) mortos em odio da fè na corte de Tunkim aos 12 de Janeiro de 1737 ... Lisbon, Antonio Isidoro da Fonseca, 1738. C642

An account of the capture and death of a group of Jesuit missionaries in Tonking, together with events leading up to it.

Costa, Manuel da. Kurtze Verzeichnuss und historische Beschreibung deren Dingen so von der Societet Jesu in Orient von dem Jar nach Christi Geburt 1542. biss auff das 1568. gehandlet worden ... Ingolstadt, David Sartorium, 1586. C643

Based upon earlier Latin editions translated by Giovanni Pietro Maffei, this first German edition contains letters from eastern Jesuit missions from 1544 to 1554.

Costantini, Giuseppe Antonio. Elementi di commerzio o siano regole generali per coltivarlo ... Genoa; Venice, Giambatista Novelli, 1672. C644

The second edition of a treatise by an Italian mercantilist, a follower of Jean François Melon.

Cotejo de la conducta de S.M. con la de el rey Britanico, assi en lo acaecido antes de la convention de 14 de Enero de este año de 1739 como en lo obrado despues, Hasta la publicacion de represalias, y declaracion de guerra. Madrid, Antonio Marin [1739]. C645

A statement of causes for the outbreak of war between Spain and Great Britain from the Spanish point of view. This Madrid edition does not include the English text, as does the following edition.

Cotejo de la conducta de S.M. con la de el rey Britanico ... His Catholic Majesty's conduct compared with that of His Britannick Majesty. London, For T. Cooper, 1739. C646

In Spanish and English. Describes diplomacy in the period of commercial rivalry leading to the War of Jenkins' Ear.

Cotterel. Mémoire pour le Sieur Cotterel, capitaine ... de la Compagnie des Indes. [Paris, 1757.] C647

An account of services rendered the French East India Company by Captain Cotterel from 1735 to 1749.

Coup-d'oeil sur la question de la traite et de l'esclavage des noirs, considérée dans son rapport avec le droit naturel. [Paris] Momoro [ca. 1790]. C648

A sympathetic view toward the amelioration of the condition of slaves, but a warning against extreme views that could harm the French nation.

Couplet, Philippe. Historia de una gran señora Christiana de la China, llamada Doña Candida Hiù. Donde, con la ocasion que se ofrece, se explican los usos destos pueblos, el establecimiento de la religion ... y otras curiosidades, dignas de saberse. Madrid, Antonio Roman, 1691. C649

The conversion and pious life of the daughter of a Chinese official is the occasion for a generally favorable report on the progress of Christian missions in China.

[Courmenin, Louis Deshayes, Baron de.] Voyage de Levant, fait par le commandement du roy en l'annee 1621. Paris, A. Taupinart, 1629. C650

A detailed description of the people, cities, and islands of the eastern Mediterranean region.

Courmenin, Louis Deshayes, Baron de. Les voyages ... en Dannemarc. Paris, Pierre Promé, 1664. C651

Includes a description of the inland trade route from Turkey to Archangel.

Cournand, M. l'abbé de (Antoine). Réponse aux observations d'un habitant des colonies. n.p. [1789?]. C652

A vigorous defense of a speech by Father Gregory which was attacked by an anonymous opponent of rights for Negroes and Mulattoes in the French colonies.

Cournand, M. l'abbé de (Antoine). Requête présentée a nosseigneurs de l'Assemblée nationale, en faveur des gens de couleur de l'île de Saint-Domingue. n.p. [ca. 1790]. C653

An argument in favor of full civil rights for all Mulattoes in Saint Domingue.

Courrejolles, François-Gabriel. Mémoire en replique a la Justification publieé par M. de La Luzerne, sur le cinquième chef d'accusation. [n.p., ca. 1790]   C654
A deputy for Saint-Domingue responds to statements of the governor of a French colonial governor in an apparent vendetta between them. He includes several documents from 1786-1787.

The course of exchange between London and Paris before the revolution: or, a demonstration that our bullion was then exported upon the ballance of our trade with France. n.p. [ca. 1713].   C655
An argument to the effect that the French trade has been almost constantly unfavorable to England.

Court, Pieter de la. Historie der gravelike regering in Holland. n.p. [ca. 1662].   C656
A history of Holland from the ninth to the end of the sixteenth centuries.

Court, Pieter de la. Interest van Holland, ofte gronden van Hollands-welvaren. Amsterdam, Joan. Cyprianus vander Gracht, 1662.   C657
An appraisal of Holland's economic and political situation, and an affirmation of republican government closely tuned to mercantile interests as the surest way for Holland to continue its commercial importance in Europe.

[Court, Pieter de la]. Memoires de Jean de Wit, grand pensionnaire de Hollande. Ratisbon, Erasme Kinius, 1709.   C658
The first of three French editions published in 1709.

Court, Pieter de la. The true interest and political maxims of the republick of Holland and West-Friesland ... London, 1702.   C659
The first English edition of a work first published in the Netherlands, relating primarily to the overseas trade of the Dutch and domestic conditions which led to its encouragement.

[Courte de La Blanchardière, René.] A voyage to Peru; performed by the Conde of St. Malo, in the years 1745, 1746, 1747, 1748, and 1749. London, For R. Griffiths, 1753.   C660
An account of a voyage along the western coast of South America, with excellent description of natural history and colonial life there. The English editor adds an appendix on the mines and trade of Spanish America.

Coutinho, Francisco de Sousa. Propositie ghedaen ter vergaderinge van hare Hoogh Mog. d'Heeren Staten Generael der Vereenigde Nederlanden, in 'sGraven-Hage den 16 Augusti, 1647. [The Hague] 1647.   C661
The Dutch edition of *Propositio facta ... 16. Augusti 1647* written by the Portuguese ambassador to the States General. Coutinho protests Dutch involvement in Brazil.

Coutinho, Gonçalo. Discurso da jornada ... à villa de Mazagam ... Lisbon, P. Craesbeeck, 1629.   C662
An account of the Portuguese trade at Magasanu and its development. It was especially related to Brazil through the slave trade.

Couto, Diogo do. Decada ... da Asia. Lisbon, P. Crasbeeck, 1602, 1612, 1616; J. de Costa & D. Soarez, 1673; Paris, 1645.   C663
Decades four, five, six, seven, eight, and twelve by Couto constitute a supplement to the *Asia* of Barros, continuing the chronicle of the Portuguese in India to the beginning of the decline of their empire.

Couto, Diogo do. Decada decima da Historia da India. Manuscript. [Portugal, ca. 1670.]   C664
This tenth decade was not published with the original work, and did not appear in print until 1790. It describes the period from 1580 to 1588, during which time Durate de Meneses was viceroy of India.

Couto, Diogo do. Decadas da Asia. Lisbon, Domingos Gonsalves, 1736.   C665
This edition contains the first printing of a portion of decade nine of this important chronicle of Portuguese activities in India.

Couto, Diogo do. Observaçoes sobre as principaes causas da decadencia dos Portuguezes na Asia. Lisbon, Acad. Real das Sciencias, 1790.   C666
First publication of the analysis of the decline of Portuguese strength in India, forming the tenth decade of the chronicle.

Couto, Diogo do. Relaçaõ do naufragio da nao S. Thomè na Terra dos Fumos, no anno de 1589: e dos grandes trabalhos que passou D. Paulo de Lima nas terras da Cafraria anthè sua morte. Lisbon [s.n.] 1736.   C667

Cóvens, Jean. Carte generale de l'empire de Russie. Amsterdam, Covens and Mortier, 1748.   C668
An excellent portrayal of the arctic coast, reflecting information from the second Bering expedition.

Cóvens, Jean, and Mortier, Cornelius. L'Amerique dressée sur les observations de M:rs de l'Academie royal des sciences et sur les memoires les plus recens et mis au jour. Amsterdam, 1756.   C669
A wall map indicating the most recent discoveries in North America, with considerable historical information on the various islands in the Atlantic and Pacific oceans.

[Coventry, Sir William.] Appendix van Engelands apél en beroep. n.p., 1673. C670
A translation of an English pamphlet which considered the possible damages to English commerce if England engaged in war with Spain while still at war with the Dutch.

Coventry, Sir William. Engelandts apel en beroep ... Amsterdam, J. Bruyninck, 1673. C671
This work has been attributed to two other authors besides Coventry, Pierre Du Moulin and Baron de Lisola. Coventry was a member of the House of Commons and was very supportive of the war against the Dutch. Mention is made of the commerce between Europe and the Americas.

Coverte, Robert. A true and almost incredible report of an Englishman, that ... travelled by land through many unknowne kingdomes, and great cities. London, William Hall, for Thomas Archer and Richard Redmer, 1612. C672
An account of a voyage to the Indian Ocean, with several stops in Africa en route, of shipwreck and survival in the Indian Ocean, and of the return trip overland from India through Persia to the Mediterranean.

A covrante of newes from the East India. [London] 1622. C673
A newsletter reporting the capture of the islands of Lantore and Polaroon in the Banda Islands by the Dutch East India Company.

Cowley, John. A view of the British trade to the Mediterranean. London, For M. Cooper, 1744. C674
An argument for holding and improving British positions of strength in the Mediterranean, which is seen as the center of distribution to all parts of the world for British goods.

Coxe, Daniel. A description of the English province of Carolana. London, Edward Symon, 1727. C675
A description of the Mississippi Valley, with optimistic appraisals of the land, rivers, plants, and animals. This is the second edition of this attempt to arouse English interest in the interior of North America.

[Coxe, Tench.] A brief examination of Lord Sheffield's Observations on the commerce of the United States. Philadelphia, M. Carey, 1791. C676
A refutation of Lord Sheffield's belief that the newly established United States would continue to depend upon trade with Great Britain.

Coxe, Tench. A view of the United States of America. Dublin, For P. Wogan [etc.] 1795. C677
A survey of the U.S. economy and its potential for growth, by the commissioner of revenue. Contains tables of statistics on imports, exports, and production.

Coxe, William. Account of the Russian discoveries between Asia and America. London, J. Nichols for T. Cadell, 1780. C678
A history of Russian exploratory and commercial activity along the northwestern coast of North America and an account of their fur trade with the Chinese.

Coxe, William. Account of the Russian discoveries between Asia and America. London, J. Nichols for T. Cadell, 1787. C679
The third English edition, containing additions, particularly with regard to Cook's northern voyage.

Coxe, William. Die neuen Entdeckungen der Russen zwischen Asien und America. Frankfurt; Leipzig, Johann Georg Fleischer, 1783. C680
The first German edition. Four maps of voyages and a plate showing the town of Kiatka are included.

Coxe, William. Nouvelles découvertes des Russes entre l'Asie et l'Amérique. Paris, Hôtel de Thou, 1781. C681
The first French edition.

Coxe, William. Nouvelles découvertes des Russes entre l'Asie et l'Amerique. Neuchatel, Société Typographique, 1781. C682
The text follows the Paris edition of the same year, but this edition does not include the maps and illustrations.

Coxe, William. Reise durch Polen, Russland, Schweden, und Dänemark. Mit historischen Nachrichten, und politischen Bemerkungen begleitet. Zürich, Orell, Gessner, Füsslin und Kompagnie, 1785-1786. C683
The only German edition, two volumes only. A third volume may have been published after 1790.

Coxe, William. Travels into Poland, Russia, Sweden, and Denmark. London, For T. Cadell, 1785-90. C684
A traveling scholar's account of journeys in northern Europe, with particular emphasis on the social, cultural, and economic aspects of the areas visited.

Coxe, William. Travels into Poland, Russia, Sweden, and Denmark. London, For T. Cadell, 1792. C685
A reorganized five-volume edition with some additions to the text.

Coxe, William. Voyage en Pologne, Russie, Suède, Dannemarc, &c. Geneva, Barde, Manget & Comp.; Paris, Buisson, 1786. C686
Paul H. Mallet, the translator, adds an account of his own travels in Norway and many notes to the text.

Coyer, abbé (Gabriel François). La noblesse commerçant. Londres, et se trouve a Paris, Duchesne, 1756. C687

The author urges the French nobility, particularly the poorer elements, to participate in commerce to their own and their country's advantage.

Coyer, abbé (Gabriel François). La noblesse commerçant. Nouvelle edition. Londres, et se trouve a Paris, Duchesne, 1756. C688
Reprinting of the previous work.

Coyer, abbé (Gabriel François). La noblesse militaire et commerçante. Amsterdam, Paris, Duchesne, 1756. C689
This copy is bound with *La noblesse militaire* by P.A. Arcq.

Coyer, abbé (Gabriel François). Développement et défense du systême de la noblesse commerçante ... Amsterdam; Paris, Duchesne, 1757. C690
A further development of the author's *La noblesse commercante*, 1756, in which he responds to critics and advances further justification for the nobility participating in the commercial life of France.

Coyer, abbé (Gabriel François). La nobiltà commerciante. Florence, Allegrini & Pisoni, 1773. C691
The first Italian edition.

Craesbeck, Paulo. Commentarios do grande capitam Ruy Freyre de Andrada. Lisbon, Paulo Craesbeeck, 1647. C692
An account of military and naval actions in the Persian Gulf area through which the English East India Company displaced the Portuguese as the major commercial power there.

[Crafton, William Bell.] A short sketch of the evidence ... for the abolition of the slave trade. Tewkesbury, Dyde and Son [1791]. C693
An abstract of the parliamentary arguments against slavery.

Cramer, Matthijs. Borts voyagie, naer de kuste van China en Formosa ... Amsterdam, Pieter Dircksz. Boeteman, 1670. C694
An account, in poetry, of Balthasar Bort's attempt to reestablish Dutch presence on Formosa and his raids on the islands off the China coast.

Cramond, Robert. [Letter to Lord Shelburne.] Manuscript. Paris, 28 August 1766. C695
Cramond writes to Shelburne representing British commercial interests in France. He informs Shelburne of the differing views held by French officials regarding trade between Britain and the North American colonies with the French West Indies. He also requests Lord Shelburne's help in being appointed consul general to France.

Cranz, David. Alte und neue Brüder-Historie, oder, Kurz gefasste Geschichte der evangelischen Brüder-Unität. Barby, Heinrich Detlef Ebers; Leipzig, Weidmans Erben und Reich, 1771. C696
A history of the Moravian Church, with extensive accounts of its widespread missionary work in many parts of the world.

Cranz, David. Den gamle og nye brødre-historie eller: Det Evangeliske Brødre-Unitets korte historie i de aeldre tider og i saerdelesheid udi naervaerende aarhundrede. Copenhagen, Morten Hallager, 1772. C697
First Danish edition, translated from the German edition of the previous year.

Cranz, David. Historie von Grönland. Barby, Heinrich Detlef Ebers; Leipzig, In Commission bey Weidmanns Erben und Reich, 1765. C698
A chronicle of the settlement of the United Brethern in Greenland, together with a description of Greenland and a history of the ancient Norse settlements there.

Cranz, David. Historie van Groenland ... en in 't bijzonder de verrichtingen der missionarissen van de Broeder-Kerk, door welken twee gemeenten van bekeerde heidenen aldaar gesticht zijn ... Haarlem, C.H. Bohn; Amsterdam, H. De Wit, 1767. C699
The first Dutch edition, in general following the 1765 German edition in text and illustrations.

Cranz, David. Historia om Grönland, deruti landet och dess inbyggare &c. i synnerhet Evangeliska Brödra-Församlingens där warande mission, och dess förrättningar i Ny-Herrnhut och Lichtenfels. Stockholm, Johan Georg Lange, 1769. C700
The first Swedish edition of this narrative of missionary activity in Greenland, with the continuation from 1763 to 1768 of an earlier version.

Cranz, David. Fortsetzung der Historie von Grönland, insonderheit der Missions-Geschichte der evangelischen Brüder zu Neu-Herrnhut und Lichtenfels von 1763 bis 1768. Barby, Heinrich Detlef Ebers; Leipzig, Weidmanns Erben und Reich, 1770. C701
A continuation of the author's *Historie von Grönland*, 1765, including the narrative of Matthaeus Stach's travels in the south of Greenland and extensive observations on the natural history, climate, and people of Greenland.

Cranz, David. Kørt beskrivelse over Grønland. Viborg, C.H. Mangor, 1775. C702
In editing this work, Jorgen Stauning drew upon the writings of Hans Egede as well as Cranz in presenting a history and description of Greenland, including its economic resources and population.

[Crasset, Jean]. The history of the church of Japan. London, 1705. C703

A history of the rise and decline of the Jesuit mission in Japan, with particular emphasis on the relationship between the missions and local Japanese authorities.

Crasset, Jean. Ausführliche Geschicht der in dem äussersten Welt-Theil gelegenen japonisischen Kirch ... Augsburg, Frantz Antoni Ilger, 1738. C704

The first German edition, with illustrations depicting Japanese customs and incidents in the history of the mission.

Crasset, Jean. Histoire de l'eglise du Japon, 2d ed. Paris, Montalant, 1715. C705

The third French edition.

Crema (Italy). Laws, etc. Municipalia Cremae. Venice, Aurelius Pincius, 1536. C706

These statutes of Crema contain material on the commercial life of the city.

Crema (Italy). Laws, etc. [Statuta Cremae.] Brescia, Miniatus Delsera, 1484. C707

The laws of Crema, containing examples of commercial regulation in that city.

Crema (Italy). Laws, etc. Statuta mercantiae mercatorum. Bergamo, typis Comini Venturae, 1596. C708

Includes 107 statutes pertaining to the commercial life of the city of Crema.

Cremona (Italy). Laws, etc. Provisiones et ordines navigii ... cum additionibus diversis ad officium navigii praedicti pertinen. Cremona, Christophorum Draconium, 1589. C709

The earliest set of regulations for the management and commercial development of a canal meant to join the Po and Oglio rivers at the city of Cremona.

Crescentio Romano, Bartholomeo. Nautica Mediterranea. Rome, Bartolomeo Bonfadino, 1602. C710

In addition to information of interest regarding Mediterranean commerce, this work contains an outstanding engraved portolan chart of the Mediterranean.

Crespel, Emmanuel. Voiages ... dans le Canada et son naufrage en revenant en France. Frankfurt am Main, 1742. C711

Contains eight letters from Crespel, a Recollet missionary, written during a residence in Canada from 1724 to 1738.

Crespel, Emmanuel. Voyage au Nouveau-Monde, et histoire interessante du naufrage du R.P. Crespel. Avec des notes historiques & geographiques. Amsterdam, 1757. C712

The third edition, in which the epistolary format of the earlier editions is not used. The historical and geographical notes are extensive in the earlier part of the text.

Crespo, Sebastian. Memorial del Capitan Sebastian Crespo, vezino, y natural de la ciudad de Cartagena de las Indias, en que representa á su Magestad el agravio que le hizo la nacion Inglesa en apresarle un navio cargado de mercaderias ... y las hostilidades que usan los Ingleses con los Españoles en las Indias. [Madrid, ca. 1669]. C713

A collection of documents relating to Anglo-Spanish conflict in the West Indies during a time of nominal peace. The primary issue is English piracy against Spanish shipping in the Caribbean.

Cressett, Edward. A sermon preach'd before the Incorporated Society for the Propagation of the Gospel in Foreign Parts; at their Anniversary Meeting in the Parish-Church of St. Mary-le-Bow, on Friday, February 16, 1753. London, Edward Owen, 1753. C714

The report of the Society's progress lists eighty-one missionaries, one of whom was in Africa.

Creuzé, Michel Pascal. Lettre ... à Jean-Philippe Garan ... sur son rapport des troubles de St. Domingue. Paris, Maret [et] Desenne, 1797. C715

A sharp criticism of slavery and the slave trade in Saint Domingue, and a condemnation of the actions of French officials there, especially those of Sonthonax.

Croftes, Richard. [Indenture for transferring shares held by the late Mary Croftes in the Company for Making Iron in North America to Richard Harris, agent for the Company] Manuscript in English. London, 14 January 1774. C716

Signed by Richard Croftes and Michael Harris.

[Cromarty, George Mackenzie, Earl of.] Parainesis pacifica; or, A perswasive to the union of Britain. Edinburgh, A. Symson, 1702. C717

Designed to show the beneficial effect the union of England and Scotland would have on the commerce of both countries.

Crosfeild, Robert. England's glory reviv'd. London, 1693. C718

Charges that England's lack of strength at sea is due to bad treatment of sailors. Also deals with trade in wartime.

Crosse, William. The nature and office of good angels, set forth in a sermon, preach'd before the honourable Company of Merchants Trading to the Levant-Seas, as St. Bennet-Fink, on Sunday Dec. 14, 1712. London, For Daniel Brown, 1713. C719

A general treatment of ethics by a newly appointed chaplain to the Levant Company.

[Crouch, Nathaniel.] The English acquisitions in Guinea and East-India. London, For N. Crouch, 1700. C720
The second edition.

[Crouch, Nathaniel.] A view of the English acquisitions in Guinea, and the East Indies. London, For N. Crouch, 1686. C721
Describes major strongholds and commercial stations of the Royal African and East India companies, and also includes a history of Portuguese and Dutch commercial development of these areas.

[Crowley, Thomas.] Letters and dissertations on various subjects ... on the disputes between Great Britain and America. London, For the Author [1776?]. C722
A collection of 123 items previously published as pamphlets or in newspapers between January 1765 and March 1776, many of them dealing with matters of political interest in North America and India.

Croze-Magnan, Jean-Baptiste. Memoire pour les negocians françois établis en Syrie; présenté à l'Assemblée national de France. [Paris] Demonville [ca. 1791]. C723
A protest against the treatment of French merchants in Acre and Sidon through the arbitrary actions of local rulers there.

Crozet. Neue Reise durch die Südsee, im Jahr 1771 und 1772, angefangen von dem Herrn von Marion, und geendiget durch den Ritter Duclesmeur, aus den Tagebüchern der Schiffe zusammengetragen von Herrn Crozet. Leipzig, Caspar Fritsch, 1783. C724
Published the same year as the French original, this German edition adds prefatory matter and several notes by the translator. It includes an account of Surville's voyage in the Pacific.

Crozet. Nouveau voyage a la Mer du Sud. Paris, Barrois, 1783. C725
An account of a voyage from Isle de France, near Madagascar, into the South Pacific in 1771.

Crull, J. (Jodocus). The antient and present state of Muscovy ... London, A. Roper and A. Bosvile, 1698. C726
Describes the whaling and fishing trades of northern waters, and the commerce of Russia with China and other Asiatic countries.

Cruys, Cornelis. Nieuw pas-kaart boek, behelsende de groote rivier Don of Tanais. Amsterdam, H. Doncker [1704]. C727
An atlas of the Don and Volga river systems made as a part of Peter the Great's plan for linking the two rivers with a canal which was to follow a historic trade route.

Cruz, Gaspar da. Tractado em que se cõtam muito por estêso as cousas da China. Evora, Andre de Burgos, 1569. C728
An account of the coastal region of China, with observations on the trade there by a Dominican priest from Portugal.

Cruz, Ramón de la. Mapa geográfico de America meridional. London, G. Faden, 1779. C729
The three-sheet edition, giving detailed information on the geography of South America, including locations of roads, Indian tribes, mines, and postal routes, in addition to political divisions.

Ctesias. Ex Ctesia, Agatharchide, Memmone excerptae historiae. [Geneva] Henrici Estienne, 1557. C730
A collection of excerpts from leading classical geographers and historians. The text is in Greek, with introductory material and notes in Latin.

Cubero, Pedro Sebastian. Breve relacion, de la peregrinacion que ha hecho de la mayor parte del mundo ... Madrid, Juan Garcia Infançon, 1680. C731
An account of a missionary's circumnavigation, traveling from across the Pacific to America and to Europe.

Cubero, Pedro Sebastian. Peregrinazione del mondo ... tradotta dalla lingue Spagnola nell' Italiana. Napoli, Carlo Porsile, 1683. C732
An account of a circumnavigation from east to west.

Cubero y Sebastian, Antonio. Illustrissimo señor. Antonio Cubero y Sebastian ... ha navegado por diferentes provincias, y portas de mar ... [Calatayud? ca. 1673.] C733
The author compares naval and commercial policies and activities of France, England, and the Netherlands with those of Spain, and recommends changes in Spain's policies.

Le cueur de philosophie. Paris, François Regnault, 1529. C734
This work incorporates three separate parts: *Secrets au philosophes*, *l'Espere du ciel et du monde* by Sacro Bosco, and *Traicté du compost et kalendrier*.

Cunha, Francisco da. Relaçam da prodigioza navegaçam da nao chamada S. Pedro, e S. Joam da Companhia de Macao, por merce da milagrozissima imagem N.S. de Penha de França venerada proctetoria das naos de comercio deste reino ... Lisbon, Jozé da Silva da Navidade, 1743. C735
An unusual publication in which a voyage of a Macao Company ship is the background for a discourse on serpents and related creatures.

Cunha, Simão da. Serman que pregou ... dia de Nossa Senhora da Assumpçao em acçao de

graças da felice acclamaçao del Rey nosso Senhor Dom João o Quarto. Na cidade da Madre de Deos de Macau. Lisbon, 1644. C736
A sermon delivered in Macao celebrating the accession of João IV to the Portuguese throne.

Cunha de Azaredo Coutinho, José Joaquim da. Analyse sur la justice du commerce du Rachat des esclaves de la côte d'Afrique. Londres, Baylis, 1798. C737
A defense of the slave trade as a necessity and an institution within the laws of nations, and an attack upon the doctrine of natural rights.

Cunha de Azaredo Coutinho, José Joaquim da. Ensaio economico sobre o comercio de Portugal e suas colonias oferecido ao serenisimo princepe do Brazil ... Lisbon, Oficina da Mesma Academia, 1794. C738
While concerned with Portuguese overseas trade in general, more than half of this work is devoted to Brazil, and it includes a reprint of the author's earlier work on the price of sugar.

Cunningham, William. The cosmographical glasse, conteinyng the pleasant principles of cosmographie, geographie, hydrographie, or navigation. London, John Day, 1559. C739
The first substantial treatise on geography published in the reign of Elizabeth I, showing some familiarity with recent explorations and geographical literature.

Curieuse Anmerckungen über den Staat von Franck-reich. [Leipzig] Missisippische Staatsdruckerey, 1720. C740
Relates to John Law's financial and commercial plans.

Curious enquiries being six brief discourses ... London, R. Taylor, 1688. C741
The six *Curious enquiries* are essays on longitude, astrological quacks, the depth of the sea, tobacco, etc.

Custine, Adam Philippe, comte de. Observations sur l'administration & le commerce des colonies françoises. Paris, Baudouin, 1790. C742
A discourse on the best ways to administer the French colonies so as to foster their trade and value to France.

Custos, Dominicus. Fuggerorum et Fuggerarum. [Augsburg] Andrea Asperger, 1618. C743
A series of brief biographies of members of the Fugger family, with 127 full-page engravings.

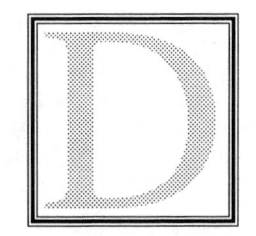

Dablon, Claude. Relation de ce qui s'est passé de plus remarquable aux missions des peres de la Compagnie de Jesus en la Nouvelle France, les années 1670 & 1671. Paris, Sebastien Mabre-Cramoisy, 1672.   D1

    This account of the extension of the Canadian missions to the west includes an excellent map of Lake Superior.

Dablon, Claude. Relation de ce qui s'est passé de plus remarquable aux missions de peres de la Compagnie de Jesus en la Nouvelle France, les années 1670 & 1671. Paris, Sebastien Mabre-Cramoisy, 1672.   D2

    A variant of the previous item.

Dablon, Claude. Relation de ce qui s'est passé de plus remarquable aux missions de peres de la Compagnie de Jesus en la Nouvelle France, les années 1671 & 1672. Paris, Sebastien Mabre-Cramoisy, 1673.   D3

    The last of the Jesuit Relations of New France. It announces the discovery of a land route to Hudson Bay, the departure of Marquette for the Mississippi, and the discovery of copper near Lake Superior.

Dablon, Claude. Relation de ce qui s'est passé de plus remarquable aux missions de peres de la Compagnie de Jesus en la Nouvelle France, les années 1671 & 1672. Paris, Sebastien Mabre-Cramoisy, 1673.   D4

    A variant of the previous item.

Dahlman, Sven. Beskrifning om S. Barthelemy, Swensk ö uti Westindien. Stockholm, Anders Jacobsson Nordström, 1786.   D5

    A description of the Swedish colony of St. Barthelemy in the West Indies, including a large folding map of the island.

Dalager, Lars. Grønlandske relationer: indeholdende Grønlaendernes liv og levnet. Copenhagen, Ludolph Henrich Lillies Enke [1758].   D6

    An account of Greenland by the factor at Frederikshaab with extensive comments on the Greenlanders.

[Dalrymple, Alexander.] An account of the discoveries made in the South Pacifick Ocean, previous to 1764. London, 1767.   D7

    The last strong plea by an Englishman for the existence of a great southern continent, generally named Terra Australis Incognita. Dalrymple was an official of the East India Company and urged English establishment on the supposed continent before the French would find it.

Dalrymple, Alexander. An account of the loss of the Grosvenor Indiaman, commanded by Capt. John Coxon. London, Sold by P. Elmsly [etc.] 1783.   D8

    Based on the accounts of four survivors, this report tells of a shipwreck in South Africa and of the adventures experienced as the survivors made their way overland to Dutch settlements.

Dalrymple, Alexander. An account of what has passed between the India directors and Alexander Dalrymple. London, For the author, 1769.   D9

    A statement of the obstructions placed in the way of the author's plan to establish a trading station on Balambangan, off the north coast of Borneo, by the East India Company.

Dalrymple, Alexander. [A collection of eight charts.] London, 1769-72.   D10

    All of these maps pertain to southern Asia and the Indonesian archipelago.

Dalrymple, Alexander. [A collection of twenty maps of the Persian Gulf.] [London] A. Dalrymple, 1774-93.   D11

    These maps are based on a variety of sources, including earlier published maps and manuscripts given to Dalrymple by persons in the East India Company.

Dalrymple, Alexander. A collection of views of land in the Indian navigation. London, G. Bigg, 1783. D12

This description of views in one of Dalrymple's published collections also indicates the sources of his engravings.

Dalrymple, Alexander. A collection of voyages chiefly in the Southern Atlantick Ocean. London, For the author, 1775. D13

These accounts of southern navigation include material from French and Spanish sources as well as descriptions of two voyages by Edmund Halley and a set of weather observations from the Falkland Islands made by John McBride.

[Dalrymple, Alexander.] Considerations on a pamphlet, entitled "Thoughts on our acquisitions in the East-Indies, particularly respecting Bengal." London, Sold by J. Nourse [etc.] 1772. D14

This reply to a pamphlet by George Johnstone calling for a reorganization of the East India Company discusses various means of improving the company's administration.

Dalrymple, Alexander. Explanation of the map of the East-India Company's lands on the coast of Choromandel. [London] Alexander Dalrymple, 1778. D15

A guide to a map of the area around Fort St. George which identifies places listed on the map only by letter symbols.

Dalrymple, Alexander. A full and clear proof, that the Spaniards can have no claim to Balambangan. London, For the author, 1774. D16

A pamphlet disputing Spain's rights in Balambangan, where Dalrymple hoped to establish a base for the East India Company, and challenging Spain's claim to Jolo (Sulu) also.

Dalrymple, Alexander. General collection of nautical publications. London, G. Bigg, 1783. D17

A review of three map collections, arranged according to the manner of their origin, which incorporates Dalrymple's comments on the problems of charting East Indian waters.

Dalrymple, Alexander. General introduction to a collection of plans of ports, &c. in the Indian navigation. [London, G. Bigg, ca. 1783.] D18

An account of Dalrymple's engagement as hydrographer for the East India Company and a detailed description of five map collections issued by him.

Dalrymple, Alexander. General introduction to the charts and memoirs. London, 1772. D19

An introduction describing six of the author's essays. Five relate to charts of the China coast and adjacent islands and one is an essay on marine surveying.

Dalrymple, Alexander. An historical collection of the several voyages and discoveries in the South Pacific Ocean. London, For the author, 1770-71. D20

Contains a chronological table of discoveries in the southern hemisphere with a reference to the original accounts of them.

[Dalrymple, Alexander.] The measures to be pursued in India. London, For J. Nourse, 1772. D21

A plan calculated to produce order in the then corrupt government in India. With his plan Dalrymple includes a review of Indian commerce.

Dalrymple, Alexander. Memoir of a chart from St. John's on the coast of India to Cape Arubah on the coast of Persia. London, G. Bigg, 1784. D22

A description of a chart which identifies fifteen source charts used in its construction.

Dalrymple, Alexander. Memoir of a map of the lands around the North-Pole. London, George Bigg, 1789. D23

Dalrymple makes observations on a map based upon various sources, including materials supplied by the Hudson's Bay Company, and compares the information from other sources.

[Dalrymple, Alexander.] Observations on the present state of the East India Company. London, For J. Nourse, 1771. D24

A review of East Indian affairs with the recommendation that parliamentary action be taken to support military requirements and to curb injustices practiced by the company.

Dalrymple, Alexander. A plan for extending the commerce of this kingdom, and of the East-India-Company. London, For the author, 1769. D25

A detailed description of the Balambangan area of Borneo. Dalrymple proposes the establishment there of an emporium to increase the commerce of the East India Company with China and the East Indies.

Dalrymple, Alexander. A plan for extending the commerce of this kingdom, and of the East-India Company. London, For the author, 1769. D26

The second edition, with numerous alterations in the text and the addition of a map.

Dalrymple, Alexander. Plan for promoting the fur-trade, and securing it to this country by uniting the operations of the East-India and Hudson's-Bay Companys. London, George Bigg, 1789. D27

A plan to use interior waterways of Canada to transport furs from Hudson Bay to the Pacific coast where they could be carried to China by ships of the East India Company.

[Dalrymple, Alexander.] State of the East India Company, with an examination of the propositions now before the proprietors. London, For J. Sewell, 1780.   D28

A critique of the British government's proposal that, along with certain other conditions, the East India Company loan it one million pounds without interest in exchange for a ten-year extension of exclusive trading privileges in India.

Dalrymple, Alexander. Voyages dans la Mer du Sud, par les Espagnols et le Hollandois. Paris, Saillant & Nyon; Pissot, 1774.   D29

An abridged translation from Dalrymple's 1770 edition, adding notes and a commentary on the maps in a preface.

[Dalrymple, Sir John.] The address of the people of Great-Britain to the inhabitants of America. London, For T. Cadell, 1775.   D30

A warning to the colonists that rebellion and commercial isolation would ruin them, and an appeal for calm consideration of the divisive issues between Britain and America.

Dalrymple, Sir John. Queries concerning the conduct which England should follow in foreign politics in the present state of Europe. London, J. Debrett, 1789.   D31

The author urges a foreign policy based on Britain's natural commercial relationship with Russia.

Dalzel, Archibald. The history of Dahomy, an inland kingdom of Africa; compiled from authentic memoirs. London, For the author by T. Spilsbury & son [etc.], 1793.   D32

This is primarily an account of warfare between Dahomy and its neighbors, but includes also descriptions of the land, peoples, customs, and products of this inland part of West Africa.

[Damius, Matthias.] Treves-krack. Door een gespreck van twee slechte gesellen. n.p., 1630.   D33

A discussion between two men who show that peace with Spain would be a blunder, religiously, economically, and ethically.

Dampier, Thomas. A sermon preached before the Incorporated Society for the Propagation of the Gospel in Foreign Parts; at their anniversary meeting in the parish church of St. Laurence Jewry, on Friday February 21, 1806. London, S. Brooke, 1806.   D34

Less a sermon than a report, this message comments on the progress of the missions in North America over a century, noting the difficulties overcome and successes achieved.

Dampier, William. A new voyage round the world. London, For James Knapton, 1697.   D35

The account of Dampier's first circumnavigation, a voyage of piracy, which contains numerous observations on commerce of various places.

Dampier, William. Voyages and descriptions ... a supplement to the voyage round the world. London, For James Knapton, 1699.   D36

Supplementary to his *A new voyage round the world*, this work gives detailed information on the East Indies and Yucatan.

Dampier, William. A voyage to New Holland. London, For James Knapton, 1703.   D37

Tells of Dampier's voyage to Australia, New Guinea, and New Britain in 1699.

Dampier, William. A continuation of a voyage to New-Holland, &c. London, W. Botham for James Knapton, 1709.   D38

This supplement to the author's previous work gives additional material on the East-Indies.

Dampier, William. Nouveau voyage autour du monde ... Amsterdam, Paul Marret, 1701.   D39

This second French edition includes the additions made in the 1699 London edition.

Dan, Pierre. Histoire de Barbarie, et de ses Corsaires. Paris, Pierre Rocolet, 1649.   D40

The second edition of Dan's work, first published in Paris, 1637. This augmented edition contains much on Algers, Tripoli and the Arabs.

Dan, Pierre. Historie van Barbaryen, en des zelfs zee-roovers. Behelzende een beschrijving van de koningrijken en steden Algiers, Tunis, Salé, en Tripoli ... Vervolgd met een tweede deel ... van de zee-roovers in Barbaryen, van 't jaar 1590 tot op 't jaar 1684 ... door S. de Vries. Amsterdam, Jan ten Hoorn, 1684.   D41

A history of the Barbary pirates to which is added an account of Dutch relations with the Barbary States.

Danckaert, Jan. Beschrijving van Moscovien ofte Ruslandt. Amsterdam, G. J. Saeghman [1660].   D42

This edition contains woodcuts showing various aspects of Russian life.

Dandini, Girolamo. A voyage to Mount Libanus, wherein is an account of the customs, manners, &c., of the Turks ... [London] J. Orme [etc.] 1698.   D43

An account of sixteenth-century travels in the Levant by a papal representative. This English edition includes extensive notes by Richard Simon from the French edition of 1675.

Danforth, Salome. Journal of a voyage from Boston, Massachusetts to Smyrna, 9 June to 2 August, [1836?] Manuscript in English. 9 June to 2 August, [1836?]   D44

An account of a voyage in a cargo ship carrying passengers also. It is very informative as to life aboard ship for both passengers and crew, and also descriptive of Malta and Smyrna.

The danger of Great Britain and Ireland becoming provinces to France. London, 1745-46.
D45

A protest against the smuggling of wool out of Britain, depriving workers of opportunities and giving France the advantage of selling woolen cloth throughout Europe.

The danger of the political balance of Europe. Translated from the French of the King of Sweden, with a preliminary discourse, and additional notes, by the Right Hon. Lord Mountmorres. London, T. Becket, 1791. D46

Apparently translated from a French manuscript by Hervey Redmond Morres, viscount Montmorres, with a view to calling attention to the increasing influence of Russia in European politics and to note Great Britain's commercial relationships with that country.

Dangers. [An essay, on the need for erecting a new African company]. Manuscript. [England, ca. 1760.] D47

A discussion of the slave trade as carried on by the Royal African Company, with suggestions for its improvement through the establishment of a new company with permanent bases in Africa.

Daniel, Charles. La prise d'un seigneur escossais. Rouen, J. Le Boullenger, 1630. D48

An account of an attack upon French fishermen off Cape Breton by a Scottish seaman and his subsequent defeat and capture by Captain Daniel of the Company of New France.

[Daniel, Gabriel]. Histoire apologetique de la conduite des Jesuites de la Chine, adressée a Messieurs des Missions étrangeres. n.p., 1700.
D49

A broad general defense of the Jesuit's position with respect to the Chinese Rites controversy, aimed particularly at the Seminaire des missions étrangeres.

Daniel, Thomas. The present state of the British customs ... being the only complete system of duties extant. London, E. Cave, 1752. D50

An exhaustive list of import duties for Great Britain together with instructions for customs procedures.

Danmarks og Norges oeconomiske magazin, befattende en blanding af adskillige velsindede patrioters indesendte smaae skrifter, angaaende den muelige forbedring i ager-og have-dyrkning, skov-plantning, mineral-brug, huus-bygning, fae-avling, fiskerie, fabrik-vaesen og deslige. Copenhagen, Andreas Hartvig Godiche, 1757-1764. D51

A journal devoted to economic development in Denmark and Norway, with particular emphasis on basic industries such as agriculture and fishing.

Danske Asiatiske Kompagni. Allerunderdanigst rapport fra commissionen til cassamangelens undersøgelse ved det Asiatiske-Compagnie af 26 Junii 1784; og revisions-commissionens forretning ved samme Compagnie af 18 Junii 1784. Copenhagen, N. Møller, 1784. D52

A review of the financial condition of the Danish Asiatic Company, covering the years 1779-1783.

Danske Asiatiske Kompagni. Besvarelse af directeurene for det Kongelige Danske Asiatiske Compagnie paa revisorernes udsatte erindringer fra 12 April 1774 til Martii maaneds udgang 1775. Copenhagen, N. Møller [1775]. D53

Statements made concerning the company's finances by auditors and the company's responses to them.

Danske Asiatiske Kompagni. Commissariennes betaenkninger over den opkastede quaestion: om factoriernes vedblivelse eller ophaevelse, foranledigede af interessenternes beslutning i generalforsamlingen, holden den 18 Januarii 1796. Copenhagen, Sebastian Popp [1796]. D54

Memoranda from several Danish East India Company officials relative to their factories in Bengal and Tranquebar.

Danske Asiatiske Kompagni. Forskjaellige betaenkninger, betraeffende factoriernes afskaffelse eller vedblivelse, foranledigede ved udarbeidelsen af det Asiatiske Compagnies conventions ... holden den 18 Februarii 1796. Copenhagen, 1796. D55

A collection of memorials on affairs of the Danish East India Company by several people, with numerous statistical tables.

Danske Asiatiske Kompagni. Forskjaellige grunde for og mod befragtnings-systemets atagelse ved det Danske Asiatiske-Compagnie, trykte efter de herrer interessenteres beslutning i general-forsamlingen den 19 Sept. 1796. Copenhagen, N. Möller og sön [1796]. D56

A collection of memorials dealing with freighting problems of the Danish Asiatic Company, including folding tables naming ships involved in the Asiatic trade.

Danske Asiatiske Kompagni. Til publicum i anledning af Herr Etatsraad De Conincks forerindring af 18 Juli 1791, pagina III til V. Copenhagen, Johan Fredrik Schultz [1791].
D57

Concerns a lawsuit brought by the Danish Asiatic Company.

Danzig (Germany). Deductie ende verklaringe vande getrouwe stadt Dantzick. [n.p.] Jan Jansz, 1656. D58
Danzig declares it does not want to be involved in any agreement between the Dutch and Swedes which would leave it without absolutely free trade.

Danzig (Germany). Citizens. Antwoort van burgemeesters; raedt, schepenen, ende ganscher gemeente der stadt Dantzick ... The Hague, Christianus Calaminus, 1656. D59
The people of Danzig reproach the King of Sweden for destroying the peace and commerce of their city.

Dapper, Olfert. Asia. Amsterdam, Jakob van Meurs, 1672. D60
A massive compilation of historical, geographical, and commercial information, abundantly illustrated, describing India, Persia, and adjacent regions.

Dapper, Olfert. Naukeurige beschryving van Asie; behelsende de gewesten van Mesopotamie, Babylonie, Assyrie, Anatolie, of Klein Asie; beneffens eene volkome beschrijving van gansch ... Arabie ... Amsterdam, Jacob van Meurs, 1680. D61
Copiously illustrated account of the Middle East, with text gathered from both ancient and modern sources.

Dapper, Olfert. Asia, oder genaue und gründliche Beschreibung des gantzen Syrien und Palestins, oder Gelobten Landes ... Amsterdam, Jacob von Meursen, 1681. D62
The first German edition of an extensive description of Syria and Palestine, with numerous illustrations and maps.

Dapper, Olfert. Naukeurige beschrijvinge der Afrikaensche gewesten. Amsterdam, Jacob van Meurs, 1668. D63
The first edition of a highly descriptive and well-illustrated account of the various regions of Africa.

Dapper, Olfert. Umbständliche und eigentliche Beschreibung von Africa. Amsterdam, Jacob von Meurs, 1670. D64
The first German edition.

Dapper, Olfert. Description de l'Afrique. Amsterdam, Wolfgang, Waesberge, Boom & van Someren, 1686. D65
The first French edition of a broad survey of African geography, peoples, products, and natural history.

Dapper, Olfert. Naukeurige beschrijvinge der Afrikaensche eylanden. Amsterdam, Jacob van Meurs, 1668. D66
Contains descriptions, with numerous maps, charts, and illustrations, of the islands and island groups off the coast of Africa.

Dapper, Olfert. Naukeurige beschriving van gantsch Syrie, en Palestyn of Heilige Lant ... Amsterdam, Jacob van Meurs, 1677. D67
Like Dapper's other geographical works this one contains numerous illustrations and maps. It is of particular significance for the geography of places of religious importance in Palestine.

Dapper, Olfert. Description exacte des isles de l'archipel. Amsterdam, G. Gallet, 1703. D68
Describes islands of the eastern Mediterranean, and the commerce of some of them. The first French edition.

Darell, John. Strange news from th' Indies. Or, East-India passages further discovered. London, For Stephen Bowtel, 1652. D69
A plea on behalf of William Courten who lost two ships to the Dutch in the East Indies in 1641, and who had been opposed in his eastern trade by the East India Company.

Darell, John. A true and compendious narration ... of ... acts of hostility which the Hollanders have exercised from time to time against the English nation in the East Indies. London, Thomas Mabb for Nathaniel Brooke, 1665. D70
A collection of indictments of the Dutch for their alleged infringements on English commercial rights in the East Indies.

Dassié, F. Description generale des costes de l'Amérique. Rouen, B. Le Brun, 1677. D71
A guide for navigators with notes on the commerce of various coastal regions.

Dassié, F. Le routier des Indes Orientales et Occidentales. Paris, J. de la Caille, 1677. D72
A description of the major trade routes to the East and West Indies; with this copy is bound the author's *l'Architecture navale*, 1677.

Daudibert-Caille, E. Note par laquelle on propose un moyen pour punir l'Angleterre d'une multitude de pirateries qu'elle a commises au préjudice de plusiers français. Manuscript. France, 1795. D73
The author proposes that the nations of Europe act jointly in refusing to admit British ships into their ports.

[Daulier Deslandes, André.] Les beautez de la Perse. Paris, Gervais Clouzier, 1673. D74
Describes the author's travels through Anatolia and Persia, giving particular attention to the cities of Tauris, Ispahan, and Shiras. A map of the author's route and several other illustrations are included.

Davenant, Charles. Discourses on the publick revenues, and on the trade of England. London, For J. Knapton, 1698. D75
Discusses taxation, foreign trade, colonies, and other matters of commercial interest.

118   Davenant, Charles

Davenant, Charles. An essay upon the probable methods of making people gainers in the ballance of trade. London, For James Knapton, 1699.   D76
   A general review of England's economy, with advice for its proper administration.

Davenant, Charles. Davenants afhandling, angående sätt och utvägar, hvarigenom et folk kan winna uti handels-wågen. Öfversatt ifrån Engelskan. Stockholm, Lor. Ludv. Grefing, 1756.   D77
   The first Swedish edition.

Davenant, Charles. The memorial ... relating to trade. Manuscript. [London] 20 August 1713.   D78
   A report to the Lord High Treasurer calling for a thorough examination of commercial statistics as a basis for discussion of the wisdom of a treaty with France.

Davenant, Charles. The political and commercial works of Charles D'Avenant. London, For R. Horsfield [etc.] 1771.   D79
   This collection includes eleven works by Davenant published between 1695 and 1712 and edited by Sir Charles Whitworth. Most of these writings concern British overseas colonies and commerce.

[Davenant, Charles.] Reflections upon the constitution and management of the trade to Africa. London, John Morphew, 1709.   D80
   After reviewing the historical background and examining the peculiar nature of the West African trade, the author concludes that it can best be managed by the Royal African Company.

[David, M. (Jean-Pierre).] Dissertation sur la figure de la terre. Paris, Desaint, 1769.   D81
   The theory that the earth is slightly flattened at the poles is attacked here in favor of the view that it is elongated at the poles.

[David, M. (Jean-Pierre).] Replique a la lettre de M. de La Condamine. The Hague, 1769.   D82
   A rejoinder to La Condamine's criticism of the author's *Dissertation sur la figure de la terre*, including La Condamine's comments which had been published in *Mercure de France*.

Davies, Joseph. An humble proposal ... that may be a better security for all our shipping that trades in the streights. Southwark, For the author by George Lee, 1732.   D83
   A proposal to make the English Mediterranean trade less hazardous by having ships towed past Gibraltar out of range of Spanish guns by galleys manned by prisoners.

Dávila Padilla, Agustín. Historia de la fundacion y discurso de la provincia, de Santiago de Mexico, de la orden de Predicadores por las vidas de sus varones insignes y casos notables de Nueva España. Brussels, Ivan de Meerbeque, 1625.   D84
   An account of the Domincan order's activities in Mexico, with many biographies of Domincan missionaries who served there.

De contractibus et vitalitiis. [Strassburg, Printer of Henricus Ariminensis, ca. 1476.]   D85
   A treatise on business ethics with particular concern for the taking of interest. It is largely based on the writings of Johannes Nider, Nicolaus von Dinkensbühl, Heinrich von Oyta, and Heinrich von Langenstein.

De jure et facto wel-gegronde remonstrantie aengaende de huldigingh door Sijn Konincklijcke Majesteyt van Denemarken, Noorwegen, &c. n.p., 1686.   D86
   Concerns the trade between Hamburg and the Scandinavian countries.

De l'état des negres rélativement à la prospérité des colonies françaises et de leur métropole; discours aux réprésentans de la nation. n.p., 1789.   D87
   The anonymous author reviews the importance of the colonial economies to that of France and sees slavery as essential to their continuance. The agitation of the Amis des noirs is seen as a British influence designed to weaken France.

De mercatura decisiones, et tractatus varii, et de rebus ad eam pertinentibus; in quibus omnium authorum, praecipue Benvenuti Stracchae ... Cologne, Cornelium ab Egmont de Grassis, 1622.   D88
   A collection of treatises on various aspects of commercial law, including decisions of the Rota of Genoa and Benvenuto Stracca's *Tractatus de mercatura*.

Debates in the Asiatic Assembly. London, W. Nicoll, 1767.   D89
   A burlesque on the proceedings of the council of the East India Company.

De Britaine, William. The Dutch usurpation. London, For Jonathan Edwin, 1672.   D90
   A history of Anglo-Dutch commercial relations and rivalries, concluding that "it is time to reduce these men to justice and reason."

[De Britaine, William.] The interest of England in the present war with Holland. London, For Jonathan Edwin, 1672.   D91
   The war with Holland is justified as the means of saving England's commerce.

The debts of the nation stated and consider'd in four papers. London, For J. Baker, 1712.   D92
   Includes papers on the relationship between the South Sea Company and the national debt.

Dechales, Claude-François Milliet. L'art de naviger demontré par principes confirmé par plusieurs observations tirées de l'experience. Paris, Estienne Michallet, 1677. D93
An elementary navigation text with an introductory chronological bibliography on the subject.

[Decker, Sir Matthew.] An essay on the causes of the decline of the foreign trade, consequently of the value of the lands of Britain, and on the means to restore both. London, For John Brotherton, 1744. D94
Taxes, monopolies, bad laws, and the national debt are seen as the enemies of trade. The author advances eleven proposals for its improvement.

[Decker, Sir Matthew.] An essay on the causes of the decline of the foreign trade. Edinburgh, 1756. D95
The second edition.

[Decker, Sir Matthew.] Essai sur les causes du déclin du commerce étranger de la Grande Bretagne. n.p., 1757. D96
This translation by the Abbé de Gua de Malves contains extensive comments by the translator.

[Decker, Sir Matthew.] Serious considerations on the several high duties which that nation in general ... labours under: with a proposal for preventing the running of goods. London, John Palairet [etc.] 1744. D97
A proposal for a tax upon families that use tea and upon public houses that serve it, replacing the import duty on that item. The author also proposes a tax on houses to supplant other import duties.

Declaratie van de causen, moverende hare Coninckljjcke Majesteyt van Enghelandt ... Delft, Jan. Andriesz [1596?]. D98
Queen Elizabeth had this tract printed in a number of European languages. She warns all merchants to keep their ships out of Spanish harbors.

A declaration of the demeanor and carriage of Sir Walter Raleigh. London, B. Norton and J. Bill, 1618. D99
A defense of Raleigh after his conviction for treason resulting from Spanish hostility to his Guiana undertakings.

Deducção chronologica, e analytica ... Na qual se manifestão pela successiva serie de cada hum dos reynados da monarquia portugueza ... Que a companhia denominada de Jesus fez em Portugal. Lisbon, Miguel Manescal da Costa, 1768. D100
Five volumes of documents exhibiting the influence of the Jesuits in Portuguese affairs both at home and abroad, tending to justify their expulsion in 1759.

Deductie, gedaan maken by ofte van wegen Hendrik van Dam, Fiscaal Auditeur, ende Secretaris van de Eylanden St. Eustasius ende Zaba. [n.p., 1703]. D101
A memorial concerning events in the Dutch West Indies, noting mismanagement of the governor, I. Lamont.

Deductie ingestelt tot onderrichtinge van den Koningh van Groot Britannien. The Hague, 1664. D102
A series of dispatches and resolutions sent back and forth between England and the Netherlands concerning interference in each other's trade in Africa, India, and South America.

A defence of Mr. Sulivan's propositions, with an answer to the objections against them; in a letter to the proprietors of East India stock. London, For W. Nicoll, 1767. D103
Sulivan's proposal was to re-charter the company for fifty years, raise capital to four million pounds, and pay the government 800,000 pounds plus income from Indian revenues beyond fourteen percent of total capitalization.

A defence of Mr. Vansittart's conduct, in concluding the treaty of commerce with Mhir Cossim Aly Chawn. London, For T. Becket and P.A. De Hondt, 1764. D104
This defense of Vansittart contains excellent documentation of the way in which servants of the East India Company engaged in private trade.

A defence of the African Company's creditors. [n.p., 1711.] D105
A plea that the trade to West Africa not be opened to non-company merchants as it would reduce the company to inability to pay its debts.

A defence of the Dutch, against the imputations of fraud, cruelty, and perfidiousness ... To which is added, a supplement, relative to the settlement of Nova Scotia. London, For R. Spavan, 1749. D106
The anonymous author favors policies that will induce Dutch merchants to settle in Scotland to the benefit of the British fishing industry, and urges settlement of Nova Scotia in small tracts of land to encourage the rapid growth of population and industry there.

A defence of the observations on the assiento trade. London, H. Whitridge, 1728. D107
A discussion of the Jamaica slave trade and the monopoly of the South Sea Company, noting the adverse effect of the monopoly upon English trade.

Defoe, Daniel. Les avantages visibles de la prochaine guerre pour la Grande Bretagne & ses alliez, particulièrement par rapport au commerce. The Hague, J. van Duren, 1727. D108
A description of Spanish commerce in America and the means by which it could be taken over by other countries.

It is a translation of Defoe's *Evident advantages to Great Britain and its allies from the approaching war.*

[Defoe, Daniel.] A brief deduction of the original, progress, and immense greatness of the British woollen manufacture. London, J. Roberts and A. Dodd, 1727. D109

A survey of the English wool trade, noting its importance in the development of English overseas commerce and colonies.

[Defoe, Daniel.] A brief state of the question between the printed and painted callicoes, and the woolen and silk manufacture. London, For W. Boreham, 1719. D110

A proposal for prohibiting the wearing of calicoes in England as a means of protecting the silk and woolen industries there.

[Defoe, Daniel.] The case fairly stated between the Turky Company and the Italian merchants. London, 1720. D111

Concerns the silk trade of the Levant, and the various competitors for it.

[Defoe, Daniel.] The chimera: or, the French way of paying national debts, laid open. London, For T. Warner, 1720. D112

A critical view of John Law's Mississippi Company with the prediction that it would fail shortly.

[Defoe, Daniel.] An essay on the South-Sea trade. London, For J. Baker, 1712. D113

Criticizes the close relationship between the South Sea Company and the national treasury.

[Defoe, Daniel.] An essay upon the trade to Africa, in order to set the merits of that cause in a true light. [London] 1711. D114

Defoe argues for continued domination of the African trade by the Royal African Company because of the need for continuity in that trade through good years and bad which could not be assured by independent traders.

Defoe, Daniel. Histoire des pirates anglois depuis leur etablissement dans l'Isle de la Providence, jusque'a present. Paris, Etienne Ganeau et Guillaume Cavelier fils, 1726. D115

[Defoe, Daniel.] The history of the principal discoveries and improvements, in the several arts and sciences: particularly the great branches of commerce, navigation, and plantation, in all parts of the known world. London, For W. Mears [etc.] 1727. D116

A collected edition of four essays published in 1725 and 1726 using ancient history primarily to demonstrate the need for continued discoveries and improvements for the betterment of the modern world.

[Defoe, Daniel.] A letter concerning trade, from several Scots-gentlemen that are merchants in England. [Edinburgh, 1706.] D117

A series of contentions that show the advantages Scottish commerce would gain through union with England.

Defoe, Daniel. A letter to the independent Whig, occasioned by his considerations of the importance of Gibraltar to the British Empire. London, For A. Moore, 1720. D118

Concerns the efforts of France to have Gibraltar returned to Spain in order to remove it from British control.

[Defoe, Daniel.] Madagascar: or, Robert Drury's journal during fifteen years captivity on that island. London, W. Meadows [etc.] 1729. D119

Defoe apparently transcribed Robert Drury's manuscript into a more agreeable style. The narrative contains many strange adventures and also considerable information on Madagascar and its people.

[Defoe, Daniel.] A plan of the English commerce. London, For Charles Rivington, 1728. D120

A thorough survey of English agriculture, manufacturing, and overseas commerce, with suggestions for improving the latter.

[Defoe, Daniel.] Reasons for a war, in order to establish the tranquility and commerce of Europe. London, For A. Dodd, etc., 1729. D121

War with Spain is advocated as a proof to the Spaniards that England values its West India trade highly.

[Defoe, Daniel.] Some further observations on the treaty of navigation and commerce, between Great Britain and France; and on the scheme of the French trade, from 1668 to 1669. [n.p., 1713]. D122

The author favors higher duties on French goods, and greater freedom of trade in the French colonies for English shippers.

[Defoe, Daniel.] The trade with France, Italy, Spain, and Portugal, considered. London, J. Baker, 1713. D123

Considers the volume, products, and value to England of the trade with these countries.

Defoe, Daniel. A true account of the design and advantages of the South Sea trade ... London, J. Morphew, 1711. D124

A statement of the advantages to England of the South Sea trade, with reference to possible imports and exports.

Delacroix. [Letters to Jean Baptiste and Pierre Honore Roux. Manuscript. Paris, 25 Oct. 1737, and Martinique, 21 July 1739.] D125

Letters to business associates concerning matters in Martinique, with indications of some expenses.

De la Forest, Gabriel. Factum for Gabriel De la Forest. [London, ca. 1697.]   D126
Concerns the mistreatment of this French governor of Fort Bourbon on Hudson Bay, following its capture by the English.

Delattre, François-Pascal. Rapport ... sur les colonies. [Paris, Imprimerie Nationale, 1791.]   D127
A general review of the problems facing the French government in the administration of French colonies.

Delattre, François-Pascal. Rapport fait à l'Assemblée nationale ... sur la pétition des pêcheurs françois, de pouvoir s'approvisionner de sel étranger. Paris, Imprimerie Nationale, 1790.   D128
The presentation of an argument for allowing the import of foreign salt to encourage the French fishing industry.

Delattre, François-Pascal. Rapport sur la recherche à faire de M. de la Perouse, fait à l'Assemblée Nationale. Paris, Imprimerie Nationale, 1791.   D129
Two speeches praising Lapérouse and his companions and recommending that search parties be sent out after them.

Delfini, Eustachio. Memorie storiche intorno all' Indie Orientali ed al ritorno dalle medesime in Europa. Turin, Giammichele Briolo, 1786.   D130
A survey of the geography of the Indian Ocean region, with particular interest in the missionary establishments in southern and southeast Asia.

Delisle de La Drevetière, Louis-François. La decouverte des longitudes. Paris, A. Cailleau, 1740.   D131
This work on determining longitude argues the lunar position method—observing the moon's orbit and relating it to the sun and the zodiac. The illustration gives the position of the moon's orbit for each month.

Dell' influenza del commercio sopra i talenti e sui costumi. Cremona, Lorenzo Manini, 1782.   D132
A response to a question proposed by the Royal Academy of Marseille in 1777: What has been the effect of commerce on the spirit and manners of people throughout history?

Della Valle, Pietro. Viaggi di Pietro della Valle il pellegrino ... divisi in tre parti, cioè la Turchia, la Persia, e l'India. Rome, Vitale Mascardi, 1650.   D133
The first edition of the accounts of Turkey and the Euphrates Valley, written by the author in the form of letters to Dr. Mario Schipano.

Della Valle, Pietro. Viaggi ... descritti ... in lettere familiari all' erudito ... Mario Schipano. Rome, Deversin, 1658.   D134
The first edition of this author's letters describing Persia.

Della Valle, Pietro. Les fameux voyages de Pietro della Valle. Paris, Gervais Clouzier, 1663-65.   D135
The first French edition, including all of the letters of the author.

Della Valle, Pietro. De voortreffelyke reizen van de deurluchtige reiziger Pietro della Valle ... in veel voorname gewesten des werrelts, sedert het jaar 1615, gedaan ... Amsterdam, Voor de weduw van Jan Hendriksz Boom [etc.] 1664.   D136
The first Dutch edition of all of the letters.

Della Valle, Pietro. The travels of Sig. Pietro della Valle ... into East-India and Arabia Deserta. London, J. Macock, 1665.   D137
The first English edition adds Sir Thomas Roe's *A voyage to East India* which notes products to be had in the Indies.

Della Valle, Pietro. Reisz-Beschreibung in unterschiedliche Theile der Welt. Geneva, Johann-Herman Widerhold, 1674.   D138
The first German edition, containing numerous illustrations, and including all of the letters written by the author.

Dellon, Gabriel. Naauwkeurig verhaal van een reyse door Indien. Utrecht, Johannes Ribbius, 1687.   D139
Dutch translation by Willem Calebius, the only edition in Dutch of a book by a French physician who spent ten years in the East Indies.

Dellon, Gabriel. A voyage to the East Indies. London, For D. Browne [etc.] 1698.   D140
This translation gives English merchants information useful for their expanding trade in the East Indies.

Dellon, Gabriel. Neue Reise-Beschreibung nach Ost-Indien. Dresden, Johann Jacob Wincklern, 1700.   D141
The first German edition.

[Dellon, Gabriel]. Relation de l'inquisition de Goa. Amsterdam, d'Etienne Roger, 1719.   D142
This vivid account of the Inquisition in Goa went through a number of different editions, this being a later one. Includes a brief description of Brazil, which Dellon visited after leaving Goa.

Del Pico, Daniele. Raccolta d'alcune decisioni ed'istruzioni colle quali se dimostra qual sia stata la pratica della chiesa nel propagare la fede,

e nel decidere controversie inforte tra missionarij. Augusta, 1702. D143
The author was probably Baldassare Francolini who is attempting to reconcile differences between Jesuits and others in the Chinese Rites controversy.

Demanet, M. l'abbé. Nouvelle histoire de l'Afrique françois ... Paris, Veuve Duchesne; Lacombe, 1767. D144
An account of French possessions in west Africa.

De Mey van Streefkerk family. Papers. 1725-1830. D145
A collection of 336 items including letter-books, records, etc., relating to the management of Dutch plantations in Surinam.

Dempster, George. A discourse containing a summary of the proceedings of the Society for Extending the Fisheries and Improving the Sea Coasts of Great Britain since the 25th March, 1788. London, G. and T. Wilkie and J. Debrett, 1789. D146
This pamphlet describes plans undertaken for improving the economy of Scotland and thereby slowing emigration to America by encouraging the fishing industry and other aspects of the Scottish economy.

Denmark. Admiraliteter. Reglemente om segelstykande i sundet. [n.p., 1729.] D147
A regulation on the manner in which sails are to be struck on ships passing through Oresund.

Denmark. Directoratet for den kongelige Grønlandse handel. Instrux, hvorefter kiøbmaendene eller de som enten bestyre handelen eller forestaae hvalfangeranlaeggene i Grønland. [n.p., ca. 1782]. D148
Instructions to traders in Greenland with particular reference to the whaling industry.

Denmark. Laws, etc. [A collection of Danish official government documents covering the period 1643-1803.] Copenhagen, 1667-1803. D149
Among the laws included here are many relating to overseas commercial topics, including Iceland, Greenland, the Danish East India Company, the Danish West Indies, Mediterranean trade, etc.

Denmark. Laws, etc. Kongelige Maiestatus obne breff, lydendis om hues almindelige mandater oc forordning, Hans Maiestat paabiuder oc dog icke effterkommis som det sig bør ... Copenhagen, Matz Vingaard, 1590. D150
A collection of laws passed between 1582 and 1590.

Denmark. Laws, etc. Placat, angaaende høkkerne udi Kiøbenhavn. Copenhagen [1741]. D151
Regulations upon provisioners and other merchants of Copenhagen.

Denmark. Laws, etc. Placat og forbud, paa fremmed trans indførsel udi Danmark. Copenhagen, Johann Jorgen Hopffner [1745]. D152
Prohibits the import of whale oil into Denmark.

Denmark. Laws, etc. Stadsretten. Manuscript. Denmark, 1584. D153
Laws of Danish and Norwegian cities.

Denmark. Sovereign (1559-1588 : Frederick II). Den Danske Søraet, som stormectigste høyborne første oc Herre, Her Frederich den Anden ... Huor effter huer skipper, skibsfolck, oc andre som bruge deris handel til søes, skulle skicke dennen inden skibs borde oc uden. Copenhagen, Matz Vingaard, 1590. D154
A code of sea law fist issued in 1561.

Denmark. Sovereign (1588-1648 : Christian IV). [A collection of 156 laws, decrees, proclamations, etc., bound together.] Copenhagen, 1613-41. D155
Many of the topics dealt with in these documents relate to the Danish economy and overseas trade, including duties on imports, trade in oil, precious stones, gold, silver, wine, tobacco, saltpeter, and silk.

Denmark. Sovereign (1588-1648 : Christian IV). Copia eines Schreibens ... an ... Herrn Vladisslavo dem Vierden, Könige in Pohlen ... [n.p., ca. 1635]. D156
An appeal to the King of Poland for advantageous commercial relations in the eastern Baltic, particularly with respect to Danzig.

Denmark. Sovereign (1588-1648 : Christian IV). Copie van een schriftelijck antwoordt ... Amsterdam, Michiel Colijn, 1613. D157
The Danish King announces that his country will not trade with Lubeck, but will permit ships of Lubeck to pass through the Sound and other Danish waters upon payment of a toll.

Denmark. Sovereign (1588-1648 : Christian IV). Copien van twee messiven van sijn Majesteyt van Dennemarcken. n.p., 1644. D158
The first letter, to the States General, asks for sympathy for the Danish cause in the Baltic. The other letter explains Danish conduct in stopping certain Swedish ships.

Denmark. Sovereign (1588-1648 : Christian IV). Forbud paa de fremmede varis indførsel som her i riget giøris. [Copenhagen, 1622.] D159
Prohibits the import of manufactured goods into Denmark.

Denmark. Sovereign (1588-1648 : Christian IV). Forordning huor effter de sig haffuer at

rette, som paa Kongen aff Spaniens tilhørige lande handler. [Copenhagen, 1625.] D160
Shipping regulations concerning Danish trade with Spain and the Netherlands.

Denmark. Sovereign (1588-1648 : Christian IV). Forordning om confoye paa Hispanian. [Copenhagen, 1622.] D161
Concerns the convoying of ships engaged in trade with Spain.

Denmark. Sovereign (1588-1648 : Christian IV). Forordning om den Spanske handel oc Kiøbmandskab. [Copenhagen, 1622.] D162
Regulations upon trade with Spain.

Denmark. Sovereign (1588-1648 : Christian IV). Forordning om marckeder. [Copenhagen, 1622.] D163
Regulations upon fairs in Denmark and Norway.

Denmark. Sovereign (1588-1648 : Christian IV). Verklaringe van Sijne Koincklijcke Majesteyt van Denemarken ... aengaende den Sweedischen herault. n.p., 1644. D164
Complaints against extension of Swedish control in the Baltic.

Denmark. Sovereign (1648-1670 : Frederick III). Declaratie ... behelsende de redenen ende motiven ... de wapenen tegens den Coningh van Sweeden aen te neemen. The Hague, Casparus Dol, 1657. D165
The King of Denmark cites fraudulent practices by the Swedes, to escape paying Oresund tolls, and the blockade of Danzig as causes for war aginst Sweden.

Denmark. Sovereign (1648-1670 : Frederick III). Declaratien van den Koningh van Denemarcken, nopende de Englesche koop-vaerdy-schepen leggende in Coppenhagen. Amsterdam, I. Thijsz, 1653. D166
Relates to the confinement of eighteen English merchant ships in Copenhagen during the English war with the Dutch.

Denmark. Sovereign (1730-1746 : Christian VI). Forordning og told-rulle ... Copenhagen, J.J. Hopffner, 1732. D167
Regulations for Danish and Norwegian commerce with other European countries and their colonies. Includes thirty-six pages of tariff schedules.

Denmark. Sovereign (1730-1746 : Christian VI). Kongelig allernaadigste octroye for det Islandske Societet eller interessentskab. Copenhagen, Hans Kongel. Majestets privilegerede bogtrykkerie, 1747. D168
A license granted to a group of merchants to fish and trade in and about Iceland for a period of ten years from January 1, 1743.

Denmark. Sovereign (1730-1746 : Christian VI). Kongelig allernaadigste octroye hvorefter Findmarkens handel til det Islandske Compagnie. Copenhagen, Hans Kongel. Majestets privilegerede bogtrykkerie, 1747. D169
A license for the Iceland Company to trade in Finnmark, specifying places, goods, and taxes to be paid on them.

Denmark. Sovereign (1746-1766 : Frederick V). Forordning, angaaende det oprettede Westindiske og Guinaeiske rente-samt general-told-cammer. Copenhagen, N.C. Høpffner [1760]. D170
An ordinance concerning customs duties in the Danish West Indian and Guinea Company.

Denmark. Sovereign (1746-1766 : Frederick V). Octroy for det Africanske Compagnie. Copenhagen, Universitaets bogtrykkerie [1755]. D171
The charter of a new Danish African Company, established upon the termination of its predecessor in 1754.

Denmark. Sovereign (1766-1808 : Christian VII). Kongelig allernaadigst bevilget octroy for det Danske Asiatiske Compagnie udi 20 aar fra 12 April 1792. Copenhagen, N. Möller og sön, 1792. D172
A renewal for twenty years of the Danish Asiatic Company's charter granting it a monopoly on the trade to China and the East Indies.

Denmark. Sovereign (1766-1808 : Christian VII). Octroy for det Kongelige Danske, Norske, Slesvigske og Holsteenske foreendede handels- og canal-compagnie paa 40 aar. Christianborg Slot den 10 May 1782. Copenhagen, N.C. Hopffner [1782]. D173
A charter for an all-purpose Danish company for building canals, improving the economy of Denmark, and carrying on overseas trade.

Denmark. Sovereign (1766-1808 : Christian VII). Placat angaaende bedblivelsen af de beveligede understøttelser for skibes udrustning til robbe-og hvalfiskfangsten i Strat-Davis og ved Spitsbergen. Copenhagen, Johan Frederik Schultz [1800]. D174
Document relating to whaling.

Denmark. Sovereign (1766-1808 : Christian VII). Skibs-articler; saavel for ober- og under-officerer, som for alle og enhver, gemeene og andre, der fare paa de coffardie-skibe, som seyle til Vest-Indien, Guinea, samt middel-havet, eller paa lange reyser om de west. Copenhagen, August Friderich Stein, 1785. D175
A collection of regulations for the management of commercial voyages to the West Indies, Guinea and the Mediterranean previously issued in 1758. A manuscript note added relates these regulations to an East India voyage in 1788.

Denmark. Sovereign (1766-1808 : Christian VII). Verordnung, betreffend den ostindischen Handel, für die dänisch-europaischen Staten und für die dänischen Etabillemente in Ostindien. Copenhagen, Johann Friederich Schultz [1797]. D176

Sixty-one articles of regulation on Danish commerce with the East Indies.

Denmark. Treaties, etc. Conventie tusschen ... Denemarcken ... Groot Brittannien, ende ... der Vereenighde Nederlanden. The Hague, J. Scheltus, 1692. D177

An amplification of earlier agreements concerning shipping.

Denmark. Treaties, etc. Tractaet, noopende de tollen in den Orisont ende Noorwegen tusschen Sijne Koninghlijcke Majesteyt van Denemarcken en Noorwegen ... en de Hoogh Mog. Heeren Staten Generael der Vereenighde Nederlanden ... The Hague, Paulus Scheltus, 1701. D178

Commercial treaty between Denmark and the Netherlands.

Denmark. Treaties, etc. Tractaet van bestendinge vrundt-ende nabuyrschap, midtsgaders verdragh noopende de commercien ende thollen ... The Hague, Wedue ende erfgenamen van wylen H.J. van Wouw, 1645. D179

Dutch printing of a treaty with the Netherlands, regulating Baltic commerce.

Denmark. Treaties, etc. Tractaet van guarantie ghemaeckt tusschen ... Denemarcken ende de ... Staten Generael. [n.p.] 1656. D180

The Netherlands and Denmark agree to assist Danzig, and that city agrees to admit Danish and Dutch ships duty free.

Denmark. Treaties, etc. Traite de commerce entre Sa Majeste le Roi de Dannemarc Norvegue, et Sa Majeste tres Chretienne, le Roi de France et de Navarre, conclû à Copenhague le 23 d'aout. 1742. Copenhagen, Joh. Georg Höpffner, 1743. D181

The treaty covers all aspects of maritime commerce between the two nations including French ships passing through the Sund.

Denmark. Treaties, etc. Traité perpétuel d'amitié et de commerce ... entre S. M. le Roi de Dannemarc ... et la ... république de Gènes. Copenhagen, Jean Frederic Schultz, 1791. D182

Signed in 1756 and revised in 1789, this treaty deals with commercial activities conducted under conditions of war. The text is in French, German, and Danish.

Denys, Nicolas. Description geographique et historique des costes de l'Amerique Septentrionale. Paris, Loüis Billaine, 1672. D183

A résumé of forty years' residence in New France, containing information on Nova Scotia, New Brunswick, Prince Edward Island, and parts of Quebec and Maine.

Deperthes, Jean Louis Hubert Simon. Histoire des naufrages. Paris, Née de la Rochelle, 1788-1789. D184

A collection of travel narratives, with particular emphasis on shipwrecks at sea.

Derde deel vervolgh-troef grooten troef ... [n.p.] 1665. D185

Part three of a discussion of the commercial rivalries of the Dutch and English, presented as a card game with representatives of other European countries looking on.

Derde discours. By forma van missive, daer in kortelijck ende grondich vertoont wort de nootwendicheyt des Oost ende West-Indische navigatie ... [n.p.] Liefhebbers der Nederlandtsche vryheyt, 1622. D186

A pamphlet which demonstrates "the necessity of East and West-India commerce; and also ... by good and fundamental reasons, that by no other means can a sure and solid peace be hoped for or expected."

Dernieres decouvertes dans l'Amerique Septentrionale de M. de La Sale. Paris, Au palais, J. Guignard, 1697. D187

An account of La Salle's undertakings in North America probably based on writings of his assistant, Henri de Tonti.

Dernis. Recueil ou collection des titres, édits ... & autres pieces concernant la Compagnie des Indes Orientales ... Paris, A. Boudet, 1755-56. D188

A documentary history of French overseas commerce and trading companies compiled by the head of the Bureau of Archives of the Compagnie des Indes, including more than a thousand documents as well as narrative history.

Desaint, Pierre Louis. Table chronologique et analytique des lois ... concernant la marine et les colonies. Paris, Imprimerie Nationale, 1799. D189

A list of laws passed between 1789 and 1799 pertaining to French maritime and colonial affairs, many dealing with colonial trade.

Des Barres, Joseph F. W. (Joseph Frederick Wallet). The Atlantic Neptune. London, 1780-81. D190

This great sea atlas was made at the command of the British Admiralty. It depicts the coasts of North America from Newfoundland to the Gulf of Mexico, and contains more than 200 maps, charts, and views.

Deschateles Esnoul. Replique du maire de l'Orient, à un mémoire des directeurs du com-

merce de la province de Guyenne. [Paris, J.P.B. Durand, 1775.] **D191**
  A reply to the proclamation of 1769 which threw open the trade of the Compagnie des Indes to all French citizens.

[Descourtilz, M. E. (Michel Etienne).] Histoire des désastres de Saint-Domingue, précédée d'un tableau du régime et des progrès de cette colonie, depuis sa fondation, jusqu' à l'époque de la Révolution française. Paris, Garnery, 1795. **D192**
  A history of events of 1790-93 in Saint Domingue, preceded by a description of the French colony in the previous years as a peaceful and profitable asset to the French nation.

Descriptio hydrographica accommodata ad Battavorum navigationem in Javam insulam Indiae Orientalis. [Germany, ca. 1597.] **D193**
  A map of Africa, the Indian Ocean, and the East Indies, including part of Australia. The map was made to portray the voyage of Cornelis Houtman, which was the first Dutch expedition to that area.

Description du royaume de Siam. Paris, J. Besson, 1686. **D194**
  An account of the geography, economy, politics, and religion of Siam in broadside format.

Description exacte de tout qui s'est passé dans les guerres ... Amsterdam, J. Benjamin, 1668. **D195**
  A translation of the *Kort en bondigh verhael* published the previous year.

A description of the port and island of Bombay. [n.p.] 1724. **D196**
  A statement tracing the history of the conflict between England and Portugal over the possession of Bombay. The port, of which a map is included, was granted to England in 1662, but was not willingly relinquished by the resident Portuguese authorities.

A description of the Windward passage and gulf of Florida, with the course of the British trading-ships to and from the island of Jamaica. London, J. Applebee [etc.] 1739. **D197**
  Because of dangers in West Indian navigation the author cites a need to take a base from Spain, to be administered by the West India or South Sea Company.

Descrizione geografica, politica, istorica del regno del Paraguay formatosi dai PP. Gesuiti. Venice, 1767. **D198**
  A description of Paraguay and of the Jesuit colony there from an anti-Jesuit point of view.

Des Glanières, Richard. Plan d'imposition économique et d'administration des finances, présenté a Monseigneur Turgot. Paris, Pierre-Guillaume Simon, 1774. **D199**
  A proposed tax system for France in which the population is divided into eight main categories with subdivisions. Each person is taxed according to his position within this structure.

[Deslandes, M. (André François).] Essai sur la marine et sur le commerce. Amsterdam, François Changuion, 1743. **D200**
  Advocates a strong navy as a guarantee of commercial dominance and national power.

[Desmarquets, Jean-Antoine-Sanson.] Mémoires chronologiques pour servir a l'histoire de Dieppe. Paris, Desauges, 1785. **D201**
  Contains material relative to the commerce of Dieppe from earliest times.

Desnos, L.C. Catalogue des ouvrages, tant anciens que modernes, du fonds du Sr Desnos, ingénieur-géographe pour les globes & spheres. Paris, 1765. **D202**
  A catalog of globes, atlases, maps, and instruments comprising the inventory of one of the foremost producers of these items in mid-eighteenth century France.

Despecher Guillemant, fils. [Contract agreement to employ and equip the ship *Le Triton*, commanded by Capt. Christophe Cochard to fish off Newfoundland. St. Malo, 21 March 1771.] Manuscript in French. [Malo, 21 March 1771.] **D203**
  The contract contains signatures of the officers and crew and is notarized by two royal notaries.

Destructie van de Spaensche vloot anno 1639. Leiden, Willem Christiaens voor Jacob Roels, 1640. **D204**
  An account of the Dutch victory over the Spanish armada of 1639.

The detector detected: or, State of affairs on the Gold Coast. London, For the author, sold by W. Owen, 1753. **D205**
  A severe criticism of the management of the West African trade by independent merchants following the loss of monopoly by the Royal African Company.

[Deutz, J.] Proeve over de middelen die tot bescherming van de zeevaart en koophandel, en tot verdediging van de binnen-en buitenlandsche bezittingen der republicq in de Oost-Indien en op 't vaste land van America zouden kunnen aangewend worden. Amsterdam, By d'erven E. van Harrevelt, 1783. **D206**
  A survey of Dutch commerce world-wide, with consideration of the means to improve it. The author shows a wide reading of travel and geographical literature.

Devis, Ellin. An introduction to geography: for the use of Mrs. Devis's little society. [London? ca. 1790.] **D207**
  An elementary text in geography for British students.

A dialogue between a director of the new East-India Company, and one of the committee for preparing by-laws for the said Company. London, For Andrew Bell, 1699. D208
 The dialogue concerns proposed bylaws which would rotate one third of the company's directors off the board each year and would eliminate the acceptance of presents by directors.

A dialogue between an English-man and a Dutch-man, on the subject of trade. London, For J. Roberts, 1737. D209
 The dialogue leads to the author's proposal for a joint-stock company to improve the fishing industry of Great Britain.

A dialogue between Jest, an East-India stock-jobber, and Earnest, an honest merchant. London, 1708. D210
 A discussion about the chartering of the South Sea Company, and the opposition of the East India Company to it.

A dialogue between Sir Andrew Freeport and Timothy Squat, esquire, on the subject of excises. London, For J. Roberts, 1733. D211
 The pros and cons of the proposed excise tax on tobacco and wine are discussed, with the arguments in favor of it winning out.

Dialogus ofte t'samenspreeckinge tusschen Ian Andersorgh ende Govert Eygen-sin. [n.p.] 1630. D212
 Advocates a continuation of the war with Spain in the interest of the Dutch West Indian commerce.

Diario de la guerra de los Guaranies año de 1754. Manuscript. [Paraguay or Uruguay, 1757.] D213
 The manuscript reflects the conflict in Paraguay between Jesuits and their Guarani missions and the forces of Spain and Portugal over disputed territory.

Diario de todo lo ocurrido en la expugnacion de los fuertes de Bocachica, y sitio de la ciudad de Cartagena de las Indias. [Madrid] De orden de Su Magestad, 1741. D214
 An account of the siege of Cartagena, 1741, in which an English landing force was defeated.

Dias, Henrique. Relaçaõ da viagem, e naufragio da nao S. Paulo que foy para a India no anno de 1560: De que era capitaõ Ruy de Mello da Camera, mestre Joao Luis, e piloto Antonio Dias. Lisbon [s.n.] 1735. D215

[Diaz, Pierre.] Nouveaux advertissemens tres certains. Venus du pays des Indes Meridionales: contenans la conversion de trois grands rois infideles. Rouen, Richard l'Allemand, 1571. D216
 A missionary letter written from Madeira concerning important conversions made in India.

Díaz del Castillo, Bernal. Historia verdadera de la conquista de la Nueva España. Madrid, Emprenta del Reyno [1632]. D217
 One of the most informative and colorful accounts of the Spanish conquest of Mexico, written by one who participated as a soldier from 1518-1539.

Díaz del Castillo, Bernal. The true history of the conquest of Mexico. London, For J. Wright, 1800. D218
 The first English edition.

Diccionario universal das moedas assim metallicas, como ficticias, imaginarias, ou de conta ... que se conhecem na Europa, Asia, Africa, e America. Lisbon, Simão Thaddeo Ferreira, 1793. D219
 A worldwide guide to currencies.

[Dickinson, John.] An address to the Committee of Correspondence in Barbados. Philadelphia, William Bradford, 1766. D220
 Dickinson scolds the Barbados committee for its aspersions upon the "rebellious" northern colonies and for their own timidity in responding to the Stamp Act.

[Dickinson, John.] An essay on the constitutional power of Great-Britain over the colonies in America; with the resolves of the committee for the province of Pennsylvania. Philadelphia, William and Thomas Bradford, 1774. D221
 An essentially conservative statement of colonial rights, noting precedent for equality with other British subjects, and the expediency that brought about suggestions for their "dependent" position.

[Dickinson, John.] The late regulations respecting the British colonies on the continent of America considered. Philadelphia, William Bradford, 1765. D222
 A commentary on the restraints upon colonial commerce and manufacture, to which the Stamp Act was considered an unbearable addition.

[Dickinson, John.] A new essay by the Pennsylvania Farmer on the constitutional power of Great-Britain over the colonies in America; with the resolves of the committee for the province of Pennsylvania. London, For J. Almon, 1774. D223
 A forceful statement of the colonial position that Parliament had no right to legislate in internal colonial matters, particularly affairs concerned with property and commerce.

Dickinson, John. A reply to a piece called The Speech of Joseph Galloway, Esquire. Philadelphia, William Bradford, 1764. D224
 Galloway's speech had been published August 11; this one was issued September 4. The issue between the two Pennsylvanians was the proposed change in the colony's form of government due to tension with London.

Dictionnaire portatif du commerce. Paris, Jean-François Bastien, 1777. D225
   This commercial handbook gives a brief history of French commerce and supplies information on the commerce of leading European cities, particularly noting problems of exchange rates.

Diéreville. Relation du voyage du Port Royal de l'Acadie ... Rouen, J. Besongne, 1708. D226
   A description of Acadia, the French settlements there, and the state of the beaver trade.

Díez de la Calle, Juan. Memorial, y noticias sacras, y reales del imperio de las Indias Occidentales. [Madrid] 1646. D227
   A survey of Spanish possessions in the New World and in the Philippines which describes the origin and appearance of various cities there and notes also the number and types of officials who served them.

Difesa della riforma ultimamente progettata per l'arte della seta. Florence, Sant' Apollinare, 1736. D228
   A discussion primarily about regulations upon the silk trade of Florence and Lucca, with references to the earlier history of the trade.

[Digges, Sir Dudley.] The defence of trade. London, W. Stansby, 1615. D229
   A defense of the East India Company against an unnamed critic who published *The trades increase*.

Diodorus, Siculus. Bibliothecae historicae libre VI. Venice, Andreas de Paltasichis, 1476. D230
   A second edition of this summary of classical geographical knowledge, gathered in the first century B.C. and first published in 1472. It was translated from the Greek by Poggio Bracciolini.

Diodorus, Siculus. [Bibliotheca historica.] Venice, Joannem de Cereto de Tridino, 1496. D231
   This edition was edited by Bartholomeus Merula.

Diodorus, Siculus. Bibliothecae historicae libri XV ... Sebastiano Castalione totius operis correctore, partim interprete ... Basel [Henricum Petri, 1559]. D232
   This edition includes extensive additions not found in the early editions of Diodorus. The editor was Sebastien Châteillon.

Diodorus, Siculus. Delle antiche historie favolose. Novamenee con somma diligenza stampato. Con la tavola. Venice, Gabriel Giolito de Ferrari, 1547. D233
   The third Italian edition.

Diogo de Santa Anna, father. Relação verdadeira do milagroso portento, & portentoso milagre, q̃ acõteceo na India no santo crucifixo, que està no coro do observantissimo mosteiro das freiras de S. Monica da cidade de Goa ... [Lisbon, Antonio Alvarez, 1640.] D234
   An account of a portent in the form of a crucifix, seen as a favorable omen to the efforts of the Augustinian missionaries at Goa.

Diogo del Sacramento, fray. Copia de una carta de los padres Carmelitas descalços del Convento de Nuestra Señora de la Concepcion de Congo ... Fecha a 14 de deziembre de M.D. LXXXIIII. [Lisbon, ca. 1585.] D235
   A report from the Carmelite mission in the Congo, including an account of the outward voyage and of relations with the local ruler.

Dionysius *Periegetes*. De situ orbis. Venice. Bernardum Pictorem, Erhardum Ratdolt, Petro Loslein, 1477. D236
   The first edition of this first-century world geography originally written in Greek verse, translated by Antonius Beccaria.

Dionysius *Periegetes*. De situ orbis. Venice, Franciscus Renner de Heilbronn, 1478. D237
   The second Venice edition.

Dionysius *Periegetes*. De situ orbis. Venice, Christophorus de Pensis, 1498. D238
   The fourth edition of the translation by Antonius Beccaria.

Dionysius *Periegetes*. De situ orbis. Ferrara, Joannes Maciochus Bondenus, 1512. D239
   This first Greek edition also includes the Latin text with commentary by Celio Calcignini.

Dionysius *Periegetes*. De totius orbis situ. Basel, Henric Petri, 1534. D240
   Includes also the *Rudimentorum cosmographiae* of Johannes Honter.

Dionysius *Periegetes*. De situ habitabilis orbis. Venice, Bartholomeus Imperator, 1543. D241
   The present edition of this well-known classical geography contains a long poem by the German editor, Simon Lemnius, in which he comments on the mistakes and oversights of the ancient author and calls attention to the discoveries and voyages made in recent years.

Discours, aengaende treves of vrede, met de infante ofte koning van Hispanien. Haarlem, Adrian Rooman, 1629. D242
   An attack upon the arguments of proponents of peace with Spain, with new arguments on why peace should be avoided.

A discours consisting of motives for the enlargement and freedome of trade, especially that of cloth, and other woolen manufactures. London, Richard Bishop for Stephen Bowtell, 1645.
D243

An argument against renewing the patent of the Merchant Adventures, claiming that their restrictive practices have harmed the woolen industry and trade of England.

Discours, daer in kortelijck ende grondigh werdt vertoont, hoe veel de Vereenighde Nederlanden ghelegen is aen de Oost ende West Indische navigatie ... Arnhem, Ian Iansz, 1621. D244

Advocates vigorous Dutch activity in the West Indies to increase their trade, and also to plant colonies there and damage Spain as much as possible.

Discours in ghevolgh vande vrede. Rotterdam, Isaac de Wilde, 1648. D245

Concerns the Peace of Westphalia.

Discours op den swermenden treves. Middelburg, Symon Janszoon, 1609. D246

Another argument against the peace with Spain which limited Dutch trade.

Discours op ende teghen de Conscientieuse bedenckinghen, ofmen in goede conscientie trefves met Spaengien maken mach. Haarlem, Jacob de Wit, 1630. D247

A critical examination of an earlier pamphlet discussing whether the Dutch could make peace with the Spaniards in good conscience.

Discours op verscheyde voorslaghen rakende d'Oost-en West-Indische trafyken. [n.p.] 1645. D248

"Discourse on different proposals regarding the East and West India traffic."

Discours over den Nederlandtschen vrede-handel ... Leeuwarden, D. Albertsz., 1629. D249

A warning against peace with the Spanish which would not give peace to Dutch sea trade.

Discours rakende de vergaderingh der generale vrede-handelingh tot Ceulen, ghesteldt by een secretaris vande Pausselijcke legaet aldaer. [n.p.] 1639. D250

Negotiations involving the Netherlands, Sweden, and France.

Discours tusschen twee wel-meenende patriotten wegens dese tegenwoordige verschillen. [n.p.] 1684. D251

Among other things, the two patriots discuss the commercial rivalry of Antwerp and Amsterdam.

A discourse of the duties on merchandize, more particularly of that on sugars. London, 1695. D252

An attempt to show how the duties on sugar might be applied to the benefit of both England and the plantations.

A discourse on trade: more particularly on sugar and tobacco. London, For J. Roberts, 1733. D253

Using the sugar trade as an example, the author warns the tobacco planters of Virginia against practices which raise the price of their product beyond the point where it can compete with tobacco grown elsewhere.

A discourse touching Tanger: in a letter to a person of quality. London, For the author, 1680. D254

An evaluation of Tangier as a stronghold for the protection of England's Mediterranean commerce.

A discovery of some gross abuses and disorders in the retail of strong waters. London, 1720. D255

The author is trying to convince Parliament of the need for legislation to control excessive drinking and illegal traffic in liquors.

Disertaciones sobre la navegacion a las Indias Orientales por el norte de la Europe. Isla de Leon, T.D.C.G.M., 1798. D256

Dissertations on the practicability of a northwest passage into the South Sea.

The dispute between the northern colonies and the sugar islands, set in a clear view. [London, ca. 1731.] D257

An argument favoring the New England merchants as more beneficial to the empire than the sugar planters.

A dissertation on the present conjuncture; particularly with regard to trade. London, For John Clarke, 1739. D258

An advocate of war with both France and Spain, the anonymous author points out the commercial advantages to be obtained from such a war, including advancement of British colonial interests.

Ditzel, Hieronymus. Paedia geographiae generalis sive mathemathicae methodo accurata in usum studiosae juventutis, praeprimis auditorum suorum conscripta, cui Carmen Wendelini Helbachii. Leipzig, M. Theodore Heybey, 1716. D259

The only edition of this geographical textbook, which includes an introduction to astronomy, a section on the principles of geography, and a series of problems and their solutions.

Dixon, George. Remarks on the voyages of John Meares ... London, For the author, 1790. D260

Dixon and Meares had met on the northwest coast of North America, where both were trading in furs. In Meares's account of his voyage he complained of bad treatment at the hands of Dixon. Dixon here defends his conduct and calls into question the conduct of Meares.

Dizionario del filugello o sia baco da seta. Torino, F.A. Mairesse, 1771. D261

Includes a history of the silk-worm, citing its origin in China and its introduction into Europe. Especially useful is the section on the market value of silk, and the bibliography of earlier Italian works on the silk-worm.

Dobbs, Arthur. An account of the countries adjoining to Hudson's Bay, in the north-west part of America. London, For J. Robinson, 1744. D262

An account of the Hudson Bay region by England's most ardent proponent of the search for a northwest passage in that area.

Dobbs, Arthur. Remarks upon Captain Middleton's defence. London, For the author, 1744. D263

An attempt to prove that Captain Middleton did not try to find a northwest passage.

Dobbs, Arthur. A reply to Captain Middleton's answer. London, J. Robinson, 1745. D264

Further attacks upon Middleton's conduct of his expedition.

Dobrizhoffer, Martin. Geschichte der Abiponer, einer berittenen und kriegerischen Nation in Paraguay. Vienna, Joseph Edlen von Kurzbek, 1783-1784. D265

In addition to its discussion of the Abipone Indians of Paraguay, this work also contains commentary on the political events relating to Spanish and Portuguese claims there and to the controversy involving the Jesuits in Paraguay.

Does, George van der. De itinere suo Constantinopolitano, epistola. Accesserunt veteres inscriptiones Byzantio & ex reliqua Graecia nunc primum in lucem editae, cum quibusdam doctorum virorum epistolis. [Antwerp] ex officina Plantiniana, apud Christophorum Raphelengium, 1599. D266

An account of travels by a Dutch scholar who visited Constantinople to study Greek, Latin and Arabic inscriptions and other antiquarian objects.

Domenico, da Fano, padre. Relation du royaume de Lassa au Thibet ou pays de Boutant, par le p. Dominique de Fano, Cap. [n.p., between 1708 and 1725]. D267

A general description of Tibet, based on a narrative which has not survived. Domenico de Fano went to Tibet in 1706 as a member of a Capuchin mission.

Domingos do Espirito Sancto. Breve relaçam das Christandades que os religiosos de n. padre Sancto Agostinho tem a sua conta nas partes do Oriente ... Lisbon, Antonio Alvarez, 1630. D268

A collection of information about the progress of Christian missions in Asia and East Africa with particular emphasis on the Augustinians.

Dominica. Committee of Correspondence. Extract of a letter from the Committee of Correspondence in Dominica, to the agent, W. Knox, Esq. Dated February 15, 1791. [n.p., 1791]. D269

An account of an abortive slave rebellion on Dominica, including testimony by a free Mulatto apparently privy to the plans of its leaders.

Dominicans. Constitutiones declarationes et ordinationes capitulorum generalium S. Ordinis Praedic, ab anno MCCXX usque ad MDCL emanatae ... a patre F. Vincentio Maria Fontana ... Rome, Francisci Caballi, 1655-1656. D270

A collection of the governing regulations for the order of friars preachers (Dominicans) from 1220 to 1650.

Don John further display'd: being a supplement to consideration on the American trade. London, For J. Roberts, 1740. D271

Charges an official of the South Sea Company with smuggling.

Donck, Adriaen van der. Beschryvinge van Nieuw-Nederlant. Amsterdam, Evert Nieuwenhof, 1655. D272

One of the earliest accounts of the Dutch settlements in New Netherland, describing the various products of that region and including an engraving depicting New Amsterdam.

Doncker, Hendrick. De zee-atlas ofte waterwaereld, vertoonende alle de zee-kusten. Amsterdam, Hendrick Doncker, 1661. D273

A sea atlas including twenty-six charts, and an introductory text.

Dordrecht (Netherlands). Sententie, by Mijne ed: heeren van den gerechte der stadt dordrecht, op den xxvi. September, anno 1663. Dordrecht, By Matheus van Nispen [1663]. D274

Account of sentencing of Laurenz Davidsz to 33 years imprisonment for acts of piracy in the Red Sea, Martinique, St. Helena and St. Christopher.

Dos missionarios do estado do Maranhão: 1741 Mar. 23. Manuscript. D275

An anonymous document reflecting conflict between church and state in the province of Maranhão, dealing largely with the problem of slavery.

[Doubleth, George Rataller.] De zee is de Helena waerom de Enghelse den onrechtveerdighen oorloch de Vereenichde Nederlantse Provintien aendoen. The Hague, Adriaen Vlack, 1552 [i.e. 1652]. D276

Anglo-Dutch rivalries at sea are reviewed in terms of fifteenth and sixteenth century agreements and seventeenth century violations of them by the English. The author was a lawyer in The Hague.

[Douglas, John.] A letter addressed to two great men, on the prospect of peace; and on the terms necessary to be insisted upon in the negotiation. London, For A. Millar, 1760. **D277**

A plea for firmness in making the forthcoming treaty with France, citing numerous instances of France's breach of treaties in the past. The author is particularly concerned that all of Canada be ceded to Great Britain.

Douglas, John. Seasonable hints from an honest man on the present important crisis of a new reign and a new Parliament. London, A. Millar, 1761. **D278**

An articulate set of arguments for the return of landed interests to the position of leadership in British politics. The war in North America figures in the author's arguments.

[Douglas, Neil.] The African slave trade: or A short view of the evidence, relative to that subject, produced before the House of Commons, interspersed with such remarks as naturally flowed from it ... Edinburgh, J. Guthrie, 1792. **D279**

An anti-slave trade argument, based largely on a religious point of view. It contains detailed accounts of all aspects of the trade and on slavery in the American colonies as well. The author was a Scottish preacher and poet, a prolific author.

[Douglass, William]. A discourse concerning the currencies of the British plantations in America ... London, 1751. **D280**

In presenting an anti-paper currency argument the author gives a history of the issuing of currency in each of the British American colonies.

Douglass, William. A summary, historical and political, of the first planting ... and present state of the British settlements in North America. Boston, Rogers and Fowle, 1749-1751. **D281**

A massive collection of information on the discovery and colonization of North America by various European nations.

Douglass, William. A summary, historical and political, of the first planting, progressive improvements, and present state of the British settlements in North-America. London, For R. Baldwin, 1755. **D282**

In five parts, the first of which deals with European colonization in North America in general, followed by histories of British settlement in Hudson Bay, Newfoundland, Nova Scotia, and New England.

Douglass, William. A summary, historical and political, of the first planting, progressive improvements, and present state of the British settlements in North-America. London, R. and J. Dodsley, 1760. **D283**

A reprinting, with some corrections, of the previous item, with the addition of a map to accompany the text.

Dove, Sir Robert. [Petition addressed to Sir Julius Caesar.] Manuscript. England, 7 February, 1604. **D284**

A petition to initiate legal action against Sir Francis Cherry for private trading while a member of the Muscovy Company.

Dover, Joseph Yorke, Baron. Mémoire présenté ... à leurs hautes puissances les Etats Généraux des Provinces Unies des Païs-Bas, le 9 avril 1779. [n.p., 1779.] **D285**

Great Britain's protest to the Netherlands for Dutch support of the American Revolution through continued trade with France. Text in French and Dutch.

Downing, Sir George. A discourse ... vindicating his Royal Master from the insolencies of a scandalous libel. London, J.M., 1664. **D286**

The English ambassador contends that in spite of English efforts to establish peace with the Netherlands, the Dutch are persistent in their preparations for war and are constantly attacking English ships.

Downing, Sir George. A discourse ... vindicating his royal master from the insolencies of a scandalous libel ... Whereunto is added a relation of some former and later proceedings of the Hollanders: by a meaner hand. London, Dorman Newman and John Luttone, 1672. **D287**

An anti-Dutch tract, enlarging upon the *Discourse* of 1664, citing the Amboyna massacre of 1623 and Dutch fishing off the British coast as part of the propaganda to sustain public interest in the Anglo-Dutch naval war.

Downing, Sir George. Memorie ... afgesante van Syne Majesteyt van Groot Britannien. [n.p., 1665]. **D288**

The English ambassador places blame upon the Netherlands for the outbreak of hostilities between the two countries.

Downing, Sir George. Replicatie ... overgegeven den 13. Julij, 1662 op de antwoorde van de Staten Generael ... aengaende de schepen Bonne Esperance ende Henry Bonne Advanture. [n.p., 1662]. **D289**

Complaints from the English ambassador about Dutch seizure of two English ships, failure by the Dutch to pay debts to the English, and accusations about Dutch designs on trade to China.

Downing, Sir George. A reply ... to the remarks of the deputies of the Estates-General upon his memorial of December 20, 1664. London, 1665. **D290**

A detailed statement of English grievances against the Dutch, citing misdeeds in the East Indies, Africa, Guiana, and North America.

Doyle, William. Two letters wherein the sovereignty of the British seas ... is demonstratively

maintain'd and asserted. London, J. Brett, 1738.
D291
A reaction to the proposed establishment of a fishing company in the Austrian Netherlands.

[Drake, Sir Francis.] The world encompassed. London, Nicholas Bourne, 1628. D292
This first separately printed account of Drake's circumnavigation of the earth was published by his nephew from the notes of Francis Fletcher, the Edward Cliffe narrative, and other sources.

Dralsé de Grandpierre. Relation de divers voyages faits dans l'Afrique, dans l'Amerique, & aux Indes Occidentales. Paris, Claude Jombert, 1718. D293
An account of travels to Buenos Aires, Cuba, Vera Cruz, Mexico City, West Africa, and Martinique, together with a missionary's description of islands in the Strait of Malacca.

[Draper, Sir William.] A plain narrative of the reduction of Manilla and the Phillippine Islands. [London, 1764.] D294
Draper was commander of troops at the capture of Manila in 1762. Here he sets forth terms of the surrender which involved payment of four million dollars by the Spaniards and the devices they had used to avoid making payment.

Dresser, Matthaeus. Historien und Bericht von dem newlicher Zeit erfundenen Königreigh China ... Halle, P. Grebern, 1598. D295
A description of various parts of the earth, including China, Africa, the East Indies, and Virginia, noting the products of each.

Drey merckliche Relationes. Erste von der Victori Sigismundi III ... uber der Moscowiter ... Andere von beköruhg und Tauff dreyer junger Herren und Vettern dess mächtigen Königs Mogor in Indien ... Dritte, wie de Insul und Königreich Ternate ... Den Moren und Holländern widerumb sighafft abgetrungen. Augsburg, Chrysostomo Dabertzhoffer, 1611.
D296
A newsletter combining events in Russia with accounts of missionary and naval activities in the East Indies.

Drie voyagien gedaen na Groenlandt, om te ondersoecken of men door de Naeuwte Hudsons soude konnen Seylen. Amsterdam, Gillis Joosten Saeghman [1663]. D297
An account of three Danish expeditions to Greenland in 1605, 1606, and 1607; Jens Munk's voyage to Hudson Bay in 1619; and Martin Frobisher's voyage in 1577.

Du Bengale, et les autres possessions anglaises, dans l'Inde. Paris, H.J. Jansen [1800]. D298
An account of British India taken from an English source, giving a history, description of administration, and commercial statistics of both Bengal and Malabar.

Dubois, J.P.I. Vies des gouveneurs généraux. The Hague, P. de Hondt, 1763. D299
A history of the Dutch in the East Indies.

Dubos, abbé, (Jean-Baptiste). Interesses de Inglaterra mal entendidos en la guerra presente con España. Mexico, Joseph Bernardo de Hogal, 1728. D300
A discussion of advantages and disadvantages to England of the War of the Spanish Succession in terms of commerce, with a preface pointing out the advantages to Spain of free trade in her colonies.

Dubreil de Fonraux. Correspondence. Manuscript. n.p., 1765-1780. D301
Thirty-eight letters addressed to a minor administrative official in Saint Domingue, relating in large part to his functions as census-taker, tax administrator and commander of militia.

Dubu de Longchamp, Jean-François. Point de la question sur les colonies. Paris, Seguy-Thiboust, 1790. D302
The author argues against trade policies initiated in a law of 30 August 1784 which permitted importing of English and American goods into the French West Indies, but did not permit free export of goods from them.

[Dubuisson, Pierre Ulric.] Lettres critiques et politiques sur les colonies ... Geneva, 1785.
D303
Essays on the commerce of the French American colonies, with suggestions for its improvement.

Ducastel, Jean-Baptiste Louis. Opinion de M. Ducastel ... dans l'affaire des colonies, prononcée à la séance du 7 décembre 1791. [Paris, Imprimerie Nationale, 1791.] D304
Concerns the dispatching of troops to maintain order in Saint Domingue.

Du Chilleau, Marie Charles, marquis. Correspondance de M. le marquis du Chilleau, Gouverneur-Général de St-Domingue, avec M. le comte de la Luzerne, Ministre de la Marine, & M. de Marbois, Intendant de Saint-Domingue, relativement à l'introduction des farines étrangères dans cette colonie ... [Port-au-Prince, 1789.] D305
The correspondence concerns the restrictions on the importing of foreign flour into Saint Domingue and the desire of colonists to have the restriction removed.

Ducos, Jean François. Opinion de Jean-François Ducos, sur l'exécution provisoire du concordat, & des arrêtés de l'Assemblée coloniale confirmatifs de cet accord. Paris, Imprimerie Nationale, 1791. D306
Concerns the position of the Mulattoes in the rebellion under way in Saint Domingue.

Du Creux, François. Historiae Canadensis, seu Novae-Franciae. Paris, Sebastian Cramoisy & Sebastian Mabre-Cramoisy, 1664.   D307
   This history was compiled from the annual Jesuit Relations. It is richly illustrated and includes a map which is quite detailed for the St. Lawrence-Great Lakes region.

Dufour, Philippe Sylvestre. Traitez nouveaux & curieux du café, du thé, et du chocolate ... 2d ed. Lyon, Jean Baptiste Deville, 1688.   D308
   A systematic discourse on coffee, tea, and chocolate, noting historical locations and uses, reference to early sources, medicinal uses and trade in these products.

Du Guay-Trouin, René. Memoires de Monsieur du Guay-Trouin, lieutenant general des armées navales ... Amsterdam, Pierre Mortier, 1740.   D309
   A popular autobiographical account of one of the most prominent naval figures of the Louis XIV period.

Du Halde, J.-B. (Jean-Baptiste). Description geographique, historique ... de l'empire de la Chine et de la Tartarie chinoise. Paris, P. G. Mercier, 1735.   D310
   A study of China based upon missionary sources, with maps showing the trade routes of the interior.

Du Halde, J.-B. (Jean-Baptiste). The general history of China. London, John Watts, 1736.   D311
   The first English edition.

Du Halde, J.-B. (Jean-Baptiste). Description of the empire of China and Chinese Tartary, together with the kingdoms of Korea and Tibet. London, T. Gardner for Edward Cave, 1738-1741.   D312
   The second English issue, including a preface indicating the problems of dealing with Chinese terms coming through the French idiom, and also a dedication to the Prince of Wales noting European impressions of the Chinese monarchy.

Du Halde, J.-B. (Jean-Baptiste). The general history of China ... London, J. Watts, sold by B. Dod, 1741.   D313
   This purports to be a third English printing, but appears to be a re-issue of the 1736 sheets.

Du Halde, J.-B. (Jean-Baptiste). Ausfürliche Beschreibung des chinesischen Reichs und der grossen Tartarey. Rostock, Johann Christian Koppe, 1747-1749.   D314
   This German edition contains significant additions by the translator, Johann Lorenz Mosheim, and it includes Kaempfer's *History of Japan* as well as Mailla's account of the Manchus.

Du Halde, J.-B. (Jean-Baptiste). Gründlicher Unterricht von Seidenbau. Wolfenbüttel, Johann Christoph Meissner, 1753.   D315
   An account of Chinese silk and mulberry culture.

Duhamel du Monceau, M. Du transport, de la conservation et de la force des bois; ou l'on trouvera des moyens d'attendrir les bois, de leur donner diverses courbures, surtout pour la construction des vaisseaux ... Paris, L.F. Delatour, 1767.   D316
   A study of harvesting, curing, storing and transporting timber, with particular reference to its use in shipbuilding.

Duhamel du Monceau, M. Grondbeginselen van den scheepsbouw, of werkdadige verhandeling der scheepstimmerkunst. The Hague & Amsterdam, Ottho van Thol & Gerrit de Groot, 1759.   D317
   A copiously illustrated textbook on shipbuilding.

Duhamel du Monceau, M. Traité de la fabrique des manoeuvres pour les vaisseaux; ou l'Art de la corderie perfectionné. Paris, Imprimerie Royale, 1747.   D318
   A definitive treatise on rope-making by France's inspector of ports and harbors.

Duhamel du Monceau, M. Traité général des pesches, et histoire des poissons qu'elles fournissent, tant pour la subsistance des hommes, que pour plusieurs autres usages qui ont rapport aux arts et au commerce. Paris, Saillant & Nyon [etc.] 1769.   D319
   An extensive discourse on commercial fishing by one of France's leading natural historians. The work is enhanced by ninety-two plates.

Du Jarric, Pierre. Histoire des choses plus memorables advenues tant ez Indes Orientales. Bordeaux, S. Millanges, 1608-14.   D320
   Compiled from many sources, this work is a descriptive chronicle of Jesuit missionary activities in the Portuguese empire.

[Duke, William.] Memoirs of the first settlement of the island of Barbados, and other the Carribbee Islands ... London, For E. Owen and W. Meadows, 1743.   D321
   A history of the British colony on Barbados, with emphasis on the numerous instances of conflict in its governance.

[Dulany, Daniel.] Considerations on the propriety of imposing taxes in the British colonies. London, For J. Almon, 1766.   D322
   An attempt to prove discrimination against Americans in representation in Parliament, and a condemnation of tax policy based upon this unfair representation.

Dumas, Mathieu, comte. Opinion de M. Dumas ... sur les troubles de St.-Domingue, & les secours à y apporter; prononcée dans la séance du jeudi 22 mars 1792. [Paris, Imprimerie Nationale, 1792.]   D323
   The author attributes the rebellion in St. Domingue to the institution of slavery.

Du Mas le Fores, Isaac. La clef de la geographie generale. Paris, Jean Boisseau & Louys Vendosme, 1645.   D324

A pocket atlas with interesting concepts of the northeast and northwest passages and the St. Lawrence River.

Dummer, Jeremiah. A defence of the New-England charters. London, For J. Almon [1765].   D325

This response to parliamentary discussion concerning the possible revocation of colonial charters notes the commercial value the colonies had for the mother country since their establishment.

Dumont de Montigny. Mémoires historiques sur la Louisiane. Paris, C. J. B. Bauche, 1753.   D326

A history of early French activities on the Mississippi by an officer who spent twenty-two years there.

Du Morier, Joseph-Pierre. A l'Assemblée nationale, contra la motion faite par M. Gaudet, relative à l'état politique des gens de couleur, et contre toute autre motion tendante à faire révoquer ou altérer le décret du 24 septembre 1791. Paris, Didot le Jeune, 1791.   D327

A plea for recognition of the French colonies as a part of France and for sustaining a decree of 24 September 1791 which the author felt would accomplish that.

Du Morier, Joseph-Pierre. Sur les troubles des colonies, et l'unique moyen d'assurer la tranquillité, la prospérité et la fidélité de ces dépendances de l'empire. Paris, Didot, 1791.   D328

The author ties the troubles in Saint Domingue to the revolutionary spirit of France.

Du Morier, Joseph-Pierre. Extrait de l'Ami des Patriotes, (numéro XVI). Sur les troubles des colonies ... [Paris, Demonville, 1792.]   D329

An excerpt from the previous item.

[Dumouriez, Charles François Du Périer.] État présent du royaume de Portugal, en l'année MDCCLXVI. Lausanne, François Grasset, 1775.   D330

This Frenchman's general discussion of Portugal contains considerable information on the commerce of Portugal and her colonies.

Duncan, Charles. Sketch of the entrance of the Strait of Juan de Fuca ... 15th August 1788. [London] A. Dalrymple, 1790.   D331

This appears to be the earliest published map to show details of Puget Sound. Duncan was master of the *Princess Royal* in the employ of the King George's Sound Company.

Dunn, Samuel. An introduction to latitude, without meridian altitudes, and longitude at sea ... London, Printed for the author, 1782.   D332

An elucidation of new methods for determining longitude and latitude, providing more flexibility in the time used for observations.

Dunn, Samuel. The linear tables described, and their utility verified; with precepts and examples for shortening calculations and preserving accuracy, in the lunar method of finding longitude at sea. London, For the author, 1783.   D333

A contribution by one of England's foremost mathematicians to the problem of determining longitude at sea.

Dunn, Samuel. The navigator's guide, to the Oriental or Indian seas, or, The decsription [sic] and use of a variation chart of the magnetic needle, designed for shewing the longitude ... London, Printed for the author [etc.] [1775].   D334

A basic brief text on the principles of navigation with particular reference to determining latitude and longitude, and the variation of the compass.

Dunn, Samuel. A new atlas of the mundane system; or of geography and cosmography ... 2d ed. London, For Robert Sayer, 1788.   D335

In addition to maps, this work includes a text on cosmography, elaboration on some of the maps, and general principles of geography and cartography.

Du Noyer de Saint-Martin, François. Ce sont icy partie des moyens et raisons que François du Noyer ... propose à leurs Majestez & à messieurs de son Conseil. Paris, Jean Regnoul, 1614.   D336

Plans and proposals for the establishment of a large general trading company in France.

Du Noyer de Saint-Martin, François. Offres, articles, et privileges; accordez au Conseil du Roy, pour l'establissement de la Royale Compagnie de la Navigation & Commerce ... Rennes, Jean Durand, 1623.   D337

Collection of documents relating to the proposed company.

Du Noyer de Saint-Martin, François. Propositions, advis et moyens ... approuvez & jugez suffisans & capables ed remettre la France en son premier lustre & splendeur. Paris, Jean Regnoul, 1614.   D338

A further elaboration of plans for a general trading company.

Du Pin, Louis Ellies. Defense de la censure de la Faculté de theologie de Paris, du 18. octobre 1700 ... Paris, André Pralard, 1701.   D339

This work supports the Faculty of Theology at the University of Paris for its condemnation of books by Louis Daniel Le Comte and Charles Le Gobien which were major issues in the Chinese Rites controversy.

Dupleix, Claude Thérèse de Chatenay de Lanty. Lettre de madame Dupleix au chevalier Law. Paris, Louis Cellot, 1764. D340
A retraction of statements unfavorable to Jean Law, who held military command under Dupleix in India, by the widow of the former French commander there.

Dupleix, Joseph-François, marquis. Mémoire pour le sieur Dupleix. Contre la Compagnie des Indes ... Paris, P. Al. le Prieur, 1759. D341
A defense of Dupleix and his administration of the French interests in India, including a fairly extensive history of the French East India Company.

Dupleix, Joseph-François, marquis. Précis ... servant de réponse préparatoire au Mémoire de la Compagnie des Indes. [Paris] Louis Cellot, 1763. D342
A rebuttal by the former director-general of the Compagnie des Indes to unfavorable comments made in a *Memoire* published by the company.

Du Pont de Nemours, Pierre Samuel. Considérations sur la position politique de la France, de l'Angleterre et de l'Espagne. [Paris, 1790.] D343
An expression of concern for the conflict between Spain and Great Britain and its implications for French trade with Spain. The Nootka Sound controversy is discussed in this context.

Du Pont de Nemours, Pierre Samuel. De l'exportation et de l'importation des grains. Soissons, Paris, P.G. Simon, 1764. D344
In addition to his own arguments in favor of free trade in grain, the author includes arguments published against it.

[Du Pont de Nemours, Pierre Samuel.] Lettre a la Chambre du Commerce de Normandie ... relativement au traité de commerce avec l'Angleterre. Rouen; Paris, Moutard [etc.] 1788. D345
Cites the advantages of the Anglo-French commercial treaty, especially for agriculture, and suggests improvements for industries in close competition with those of Britain, especially the cloth industry.

Dupré, Joseph. Memoire sur la traite des noirs. [Paris, Devaux, 1790.] D346
An argument in favor of continuing the slave trade, contending the importance of the West Indian colonies to France and the necessity of slavery there.

Dupré, Joseph. Mémoire sur le commerce en général, et celui du Languedoc. Paris, Imprimerie Nationale, 1790. D347
A survey of the depressed state of French commerce, with particular reference to Languedoc. Contains suggestions for improving the entire French economy.

Dupré de Saint-Maur, Nicolas-François. Mémoire sur la décadence du commerce de Bayonne et Saint-Jean-de-Luz, et sur les moyens de le rétablir. Bordeaux, Michel Racle, 1783. D348
The decline in the commerce of Bayonne and its surrounding area is attributed to both natural and political causes, and the means of recovery suggested include a new constitution for Bayonne, encouragement of commerce with America, and navigational improvements.

Dupuch, Élie-Louis. Observations présentées a l'Assemblée nationale, par les membres de municipalité de la Basse-Terre-Guadeloupe, et par les citoyens de la même ville. Paris, Imprimerie Nationale, 1792. D349
A series of complaints against legislation of the colonial assembly of Guadeloupe by representatives and citizens of Basse-Terre.

Du Puis, Mathias. Relation de l'establissement d'une colonie françoise dans la Gardeloupe ... Caen, Marin Yvon, 1652. D350
A description of the earliest French settlements on Guadeloupe, and the history of their development from 1635 to 1646 as an enterprise of the Compagnie des Isles de l'Amerique.

Durão, José de Santa Rita. Caramurú. Poema epico do descubrimento da Bahia. Lisbon, Regia officina typografica, 1781. D351
The first edition of the classic Brazilian epic poem, celebrating the early Portuguese presence at Bahia as well as the emerging Brazilian national spirit.

Duret, Claude. Thresor de l'histoire des langues de cest univers. Yverdon, Societé Helvetiale Caldoresque, 1619. D352
This description and commentary on languages is accompanied by extensive geographical and historical material, showing the author's familiarity with ancient and modern sources.

Durnford, Andrew. Observations & remarks upon the island Bermuda. Manuscript. St. George's, Bermuda, October 20, 1783. D353
A description of Bermuda's defenses, with recommendations for fortifications and for lighthouses to benefit ships trading to the West Indies.

Durret. Voyage de Marseille à Lima. Paris, J.B. Coignard, 1720. D354
Contains useful information on the products of the South American coast.

Du Tertre, Jean Baptiste. Histoire generale des Antilles habitées par les François. Paris, T. Jolly, 1667-71. D355
A four-volume work devoted to the earliest history of French activities in the Antilles. The people, flora, and fauna are also described.

Du Tertre, Jean Baptiste. Histoire generale des isles de S. Christophe ... et autres dans l'Amérique. Paris, J. Langlois et E. Langlois, 1654.　　　　　　　　　　　　　　　D356
   A history of the early years of the Company of St. Christopher, with descriptions of the commercial opportunities of several islands in the Caribbean area.

[Dutot.] Reflexions politiques sur les finances et le commerce. The Hague, Vaillant & Nicolas Prevost, 1738.　　　　　　　　　　　　　　　D357
   The first edition of an analysis of France's commercial situation, noting the state of her foreign exchange and the reasons for the failure of John Law's financial system.

[Dutot.] Political reflections upon the finances and commerce of France. London, A. Millar, 1739.　　　　　　　　　　　　　　　D358
   Translation of the previous item.

Duval, P. (Pierre). A geographical dictionary, in which are described the most eminent countreys, towns, ports, seas, streights, and rivers in the whole world. London, M. C. for Henry Brome, 1678.　　　　　　　　　　　　　　　D359
   This pocket-type geographical dictionary is characterized by brief information for each of the items, all arranged in one alphabet.

Duval-Pyrau, abbé. Eloge de Nicolas Sahlgren, commandeur de l'ordre de Wasa et directeur de la Compagnie des Indes &c. [Frankfurt] Aux depens de l'auteur [1777].　　　　　　　D360
   This is an oration commemorating the life of Nicolas Sahlgren, a Swedish merchant who was a director of the Swedish East India Company.

[Duval-Sanadon, David.] Réclamations et observations des colons, sur l'idée de l'abolition de la traite et de l'affranchissement des Négres. [Paris?] 1789.　　　　　　　　　　　　　D361
   An argument against ending the slave trade and liberating slaves. The author admits the evils of slavery, but sees worse evils resulting from its termination in the West Indies.

[Duval-Sanadon, David.] Tableau de la situation actuelle des colonies, présenté a l'Assemblée nationale. [n.p., 1789.]　　　　　　　　　D362
   A proposal for the independence of the French colonies in the West Indies and the liberation of slaves there.

E

Early commercial newspapers. London, 1687-1705.   E1

A collection of eight numbers of three different newspapers, all reporting goods for sale which were brought from the East Indies. The titles are *Vente faite a Londres*, *Whiston's Merchants Weekly Advertiser*, and *Sold by the English East-India Company, London*.

East India Company. [Account book of an East India merchant at Fort St. George.] Manuscript. Fort St. George, 1725-30.   E2

A record of commercial activities including many types of merchandise handled, dealings with local suppliers, voyages to China, etc.

East India Company. Accounts of expenses and investments of an unidentified English business. Manuscript. [n.p.] 1623-25.   E3

Three pages of miscellaneous accounts, giving prices for a variety of East Indian goods.

East India Company. At a court of committees for the honourable East India Company, holden the 25th. day of August, 1680. [London, 1680.]   E4

This broadside clarifies the rights of persons going to India in the company's service to engage in private trade in specified commodities.

East India Company. The case of the East India Company. London, 1784.   E5

Arguments for and against a bill "for the better management of the territories, revenues and commerce of this kingdom in the East Indies."

East India Company. The case of the Governour and Company of Merchants of London trading to the East-Indies. [London, 1698.]   E6

An account of the company's history, urging its continuance as a monopoly.

East India Company. Charters granted to the East-India Company, from 1601; also the treaties and grants, made with, or obtained from, the princes and powers in India from the year 1756-1772. [London, 1773.]   E7

Contains many charters, letters patent, and other grants from the English sovereigns to the East India Company.

East India Company. [Collection of twenty-two manuscript maps and plans relating to the administration and military campaigns in India.] Manuscript. [India, 1773-85.]   E8

The designers of the maps are identified in some instances. In addition to routes of various campaigns, plans of particular forts and other buildings are included. The collection is associated with the administration of Warren Hastings.

East India Company. A continuation of the series of the several debates that have taken place at the India-House, on the following important subjects: The general principles of the Company's new charter ... and also, the debates upon the important services of Marquis Cornwallis ... London, B and J. White [etc.] 1793.   E9

A review of Lord Cornwallis's administration in India and a reporting of the debate about renewing the charter of the East India Company.

East India Company. Copy of the treaty between Shuja-ud-Daula and the East India Company of July 10th, 1763. [n.p., ca. 1857.]   E10

A commercial treaty between the Nawab and the East India Company. The document is not the original of 1763 but a photostat made in 1857. The original is presumed destroyed.

East India Company. A defence of the United Company of Merchants of England. London, J. Brotherton, 1762.   E11

An answer to Dutch criticisms of the company's activities in Bengal.

East India Company. Defense de la Compagnie Unie, de Marchands d'Angleterre Commerçans aux Indes Orientales. The Hague, Pierre de Hondt, 1762.   E12

A defense of English actions against the Dutch in 1759, including documents relating to hostilities in Bengal between the English and Dutch East India companies.

East India Company. First, second, and third reports of the select committee, appointed by the court of directors of the East India Company, to take into consideration the export trade from Great Britain to the East Indies. [London] 1793. E13

These reports include statistical tables on the Indian trade, and letters from company officials discussing various commercial problems. Bound with this volume is *At a Committee of accounts, 15th February, 1793*, which describes the company's affairs in India and Europe.

East India Company. For sale at the East-India-House, 21 September 1675. [London, 1675.] E14

A leaflet listing the goods for sale from eighteen ships of the East India Company.

East India Company. A list of names of all the members of the English company trading to the East Indies. [London? 1700?] E15

Notes voters, non-voters, and those eligible to be chosen directors.

East India Company. A list of the names of all the proprietors of East India stock; distinguishing the principal stock each proprietor now holds, and the time when such proprietors became possessed thereof. [n.p.] 1773. E16

A listing of over three thousand stockholders and the value of their shares.

East India Company. A memento to the East-India companies. Or, An abstract of a remonstrance, presented to the House of Commons by the East-India Company, in ... 1628. London, 1700. E17

Based on a document of 1628, this tract adds commentary to advance the arguments of the company against those who opposed rechartering it.

East India Company. [Memoranda on the cloth trade of Oude ...] Manuscript. [n.p.] 1788, 1807. E18

This manuscript also describes the salt trade of the Carnatic, and describes the services of John Pindred Scott to the East India Company.

East India Company. Papers respecting illicit trade. [London? 1799.] E19

A collection of documents concerning illicit trade between various countries and regions to which the East India Company had exclusive rights.

East India Company. Papers respecting the negotiations for a renewal of the East-India Company's exclusive trade. Printed by the court of directors. [n.p., 1793]. E20

A group of letters dealing with the impending renewal of the company's exclusive trading rights.

East India Company. The petition and remonstrance of the Governor and Company of Merchants, trading to the East Indies, exhibited to the Honorable the House of Commons assembled in Parliament. London, N. Bourne, 1628. E21

A pamphlet demonstrating how the East India Company has improved England's naval power and increased the national wealth.

East India Company. The petition and remonstrance of the Governour and Company of Merchants of London trading to the East-Indies. London, 1641. E22

"As the publick profit by foreign trade is the only means whereby we gain our treasure: So this trade to the East Indies ... doth far excell all others."

East India Company. [A petition to Parliament regarding the East India trade and a list of regulations for forming a new East India Company.] Manuscript. [London, ca. 1695.] E23

This manuscript includes answers to those who sought to prohibit importing goods from India because of the alleged damage these imports did to English industry.

East India Company. Proceedings at a general court of proprietors of East India stock. London, J. Debrett, 1783. E24

The court decided against censure of Warren Hastings, and voted to congratulate Hastings for his actions in the War of the Carnatic.

East India Company. Proceedings relative to ships tendered for the service of the United East-India Company, from the first of January, 1780, to the twenty-first of March, 1791; with an appendix. [n.p., 1791]. E25

A collection of minutes of the Court of Directors and the Committee on Shipping, recording all deliberations and actions with respect to procuring ships for the company's use.

East India Company. A remonstrance of the directors of the Netherlands East India Company ... and a reply of the English East India Company ... London, I. Dawson for the East India Company, 1632. E26

A statement of charges by the Dutch concerning the Amboyna massacre of 1623, and a defense by the English.

East India Company. A reply ... to a paper of complaints, commonly called the thirteen articles. [London, 1691.] E27

A defense of the company against each of the thirteen criticisms of it.

East India Company. A report from the Committee of Warehouses of the United East-

India Company, relative to the culture of sugar. London, 1792. E28

A presentation on behalf of the company's hope to become a major supplier of sugar in the British market.

East India Company. Report of the committee of warehouses. [London, 1793?] E29

Deals with the importing of saltpeter and the exporting of gunpowder by the East India Company.

East India Company. Report of the select committee of the Court of Directors of the East-India Company, upon the subject of the cotton manufacture in this country. [London] 1793. E30

Detailed information on cotton exports to India.

East India Company. A sketch of the debate that took place at the India-House in Leadenhall Street on Wednesday, the 19th of October Inst. on the following motion of William Lushington esq. London, Printed by the Reporter, 1794. E31

The debate concerned the motion of the East India Company to supply three regiments for military service against Napoleon as a demonstration of the company's support of the crown in the war.

East India Company. Treaties and grants from the country powers. [n.p.] 1774. E32

Treaties and grants from 1756 to 1772 defining English authority in Fort St. George, Fort William and Bombay.

East India Company. Treaty of commerce between Charles Earl Cornwallis ... on the part of the ... United Company and His Excellency the Vizier ... Calcutta, At the Honorable Company's Press, 1788. E33

English, Arabic, and Sanskrit texts of an agreement between the East India Company and an Indian ruler, relative to the levying of duties on goods passing between territory controlled by the company and that of the ruler.

East India Company. A true relation of the unjust, cruell, and barbarous proceedings against the English at Amboyna. London, H. Lownes for N. Newberry, 1624. E34

The first edition of materials pertaining to the Amboyna massacre.

East India Company. A true relation of the unjust, cruell, and barbarous proceedings against the English at Amboyna. London, G. Purslowe for Nathaniel Newberry, 1632. E35

This third edition, published eight years after the first edition, testified to the continued English-Dutch hostility in the East Indies.

East India Company. A true relation of the unjust, cruell, and barbarous proceedings against the English at Amboyna. London, Thomas Mabb for William Hope, 1665. E36

This late edition was published in the interest of maintaining English hostility against the Dutch in the East Indies.

East-India-Company's case, with relation to the separate traders to the East-Indies. [n.p., 1713.] E37

This document notes the intention of the company to pay John Powell from annuities authorized by legislation as a part of the reorganization of the East India Company in 1698.

The East India Examiner. Reprinted from the original papers of the periodical publication. London, For W. Nicoll, 1766. E38

The directors of the East India Company are criticized for their mismanagement of the company in this reprint of a periodical originally issued between September 6 and November 19, 1766.

The East-India trade. A true narration of divers ports in East-India; of the commodities, and trade one kingdome holdeth with another; whereby it appeareth, how much profit this nation is deprived by restraint of trade to those parts, which is farre greater then all the trade of Europe. [n.p., ca. 1641]. E39

A survey of the commercial possibilities of the East Indies, giving the commodities of all major places east of the Cape of Good Hope, and urging a wider participation in that trade by English merchants.

Eastland Company. Reasons humbly offered by the governour, assistants, and fellowship of Eastland-merchants, against the giving a general liberty to all persons whatsoever to export the English woollen-manufacture whither they please. London, 1689. E40

A defense of the monoply the Eastland company enjoyed on Baltic trade, contending that opening it to all merchants would reduce the quality of merchandise, threaten other monopolistic companies, and reduce the total volume of trade.

Eaton, Richard, of the Custom-House, Dublin. A book of rates, inwards and outwards: with the neat-duties and drawbacks payable on importation and exportation of all sorts of merchandize. Dublin, Boulter Grierson, 1767. E41

The tables of rates are introduced by a series of definitions of the various types of duties included and a statement of penalties for violations of customs regulations.

Ebeling, Christopher, editor. Neue Sammlung von Reisebeschreibungen. Hamburg, Carl Ernst Bohn, 1780-90. E42

A ten-volume collection of voyages and travels, including twenty-four individual narratives.

Ebülgâzî Bahadir Han, Khan of Khorezm. Historei généalogique des Tatars traduite du manuscript tartare ... & enrichie d'un grand nombre de remarques ... Leyden, Abraham Kallewier, 1726. E43

A heavily annotated edition of a history of central Asia written by one of its rulers. The notes comprise a substantial geography of northern and central Asia.

Echard, Laurence. The gazetteer's, or newsman's interpreter; being a geographical index. London, For John Nicholson and Samuel Ballard, 1703. E44

The first part covers Europe, and the second part, first printed in 1704, is devoted to non-European areas.

Echard, Laurence. The gazetteer's or newsman's interpreter. Being a geographical index of all the considerable cities ... in Europe ... London: Printed by James Orme for John Nicholson, 1707. E45

The ninth edition of a geographical dictionary first published in 1692, pertaining to Europe only.

Echevelar, Manuel de. Instruccion exacta, y util de la derrotas, y navigaciones ... en la America Septentrional. Cadiz, Real Imprenta de Marina [1753]. E46

A sailing guide for the West Indies, with fifteen routes to various islands and ports included.

Economia politica, feita em 1795, por M.J.R. negociante de praca de Lisboa por J.L. dos S.L. Lisbon, Alcobia [1821]. E47

A general treatise on political economy with some specific application to Portuguese domestic and colonial situations.

Eden, Richard. The decades of the newe worlde, or West India. London, G. Powell, 1555. E48

This earliest collection of voyages in English contains in addition to Anghiera's first three *Decades*, sections describing Russia and Cathay, the spice trade of the East Indies, and narratives of discovery and exploration.

Eden, Richard. The history of travayle in the West and East Indies, and other countreys lying eyther way, towardes the fruitfull and ryche Moluccaes. London, R. Jugge, 1577. E49

This edition, edited by Richard Willes, omits some material found in the edition of 1555, but it also contains some significant additions, including an account of Frobisher's voyage and an abridgment of Anghiera's fifth, sixth, seventh, and eight *Decades*.

Eder, Francisco Javier. Descriptio provinciae Moxitarum in regno Peruano. Buda, Typis universitatis, 1791. E50

The first edition of a Jesuit's description of Bolivia and the Mojo Indians. Included is a fine map of "Upper Peru" and seven engraved plates.

Edgar, William, Inspector General of the Ports in North-Britain. Vectigalium systema: or, A complete view of that part of the revenue ... commonly called customs. London, John Baskett [etc.] 1714. E51

A survey of customs duties, shipping regulations, and other matters of interest to British maritime trade.

Edinburgh Whale-Fishing Company. Contract of copartnery of the Edinburgh Whale-Fishing Company. [Edinburgh, 1749.] E52

The contract of a whaling company organized to hunt in the Arctic. The document names officers and their duties, specifies conditions for the purchase of company shares, and lists stockholders.

Edwards, Bryan. An historical survey of the French colony in the island of St. Domingo. London, For John Stockdale, 1797. E53

Although largely concerned with British military intervention in the island in the 1790s, this work also includes statistical information on the commercial value of the colony.

Edwards, Bryan. Storia dell'isola di S. Domingo ricavata dalla storia civile e del commercio delle Antille ... tradotta dall'Inglese da J. B. Breton ... e transportata dal Francese in Italiano da Giammichele Brolio. Torino, Stamperia Soffietti, 1803. E54

This Italian translation was based on the French edition of the abridged Edinburgh edition.

Edwards, Bryan. The history, civil and commercial, of the British colonies in the West Indies. London, John Stockdale, 1794. E55

An excellent and full general survey of the peoples, products, government, and history of the islands in the West Indies under British control, in its second edition.

Edwards, Bryan. A speech delivered at a free conference between the honourable the Council and Assembly of Jamaica, held the 19th of November 1789 ... concerning the slave trade. Kingston, Jamaica, printed. London, Reprinted for J. Debrett, 1790. E56

A response to the threat of Parliamentary legislation to end the slave trade in British possessions, predicting a complete disruption of the West Indian economy.

Edwards, Bryan. Thoughts on the late proceedings of government. London, For T. Cadell, 1784. E57

An argument against the policy of restricting the commerce of the British West Indies with the United States to British ships.

Eeg, Erich. Til publicum og S.T. Hr. kammeradvocat Schønheyder, af Erich Eeg. Copenhagen, Svares Enke, 1787. E58

A legal proceeding concerning a ship's captain and his assistant in the service of the Danish Asiatic Company.

Eenighe advijsen ende verklaringhen uyt Brasilien. Amsterdam, Philips van Macedonien, 1648.　　　　　　　　　　　　　　　E59
Reports on the West India Company's critical situation in Recife and Olinda.

Eerstelinck der vrede of ophoudinghe van vyandtschap ter zee. Van wegen Spangien. [n.p.] 1647.　　　　　　　　　　　　　　　E60
Concerns Dutch relations with both France and Spain.

Egede, Hans. Des alten Grönlands neue Perlustration, oder Eine kurtze Beschreibung derer alten nordischen Colonien ... in Grönland. Frankfurt, Stocks Erben und Schilung, 1730.　　　E61
The first description of Greenland, based on the author's diaries. He was the founder of the Danish mission in Greenland and resided there from 1721 to 1736.

Egede, Hans. Det gamle Grønlands nye perlustration, eller Naturel-historie. Copenhagen, Johan Christoph Groth, 1741.　　　　　　　E62
A much-enlarged edition of the previous work.

Egede, Hans. Ausführliche und warhafte Nachricht vom Anfange und Fortgange der gronländischen Mission. Hamburg, Christian Wilhelm Brandt, 1740.　　　　　　　E63
The first German edition.

Egede, Hans. Beschryving van oud-Groenland, of eigentlyk van de zoogenaamde Straat Davis. Delft, Reinier Boitet, 1746.　　　　　　E64
The first Dutch edition.

Egede, Hans. Description et historie naturelle du Groenland. Copenhagen & Geneva, C. & A. Philibert, 1763.　　　　　　　　　　　E65
The first French edition.

Egede, Hans. A description of Greenland. London, For C. Hitch, S. Austen, J. Jackson, 1745.　　　　　　　　　　　　　　　E66
The first English edition.

Egede, Niels Rasch. Tredie continuation af relationerne betreffende den Grønlandske missions tilstand og beskaffenhed. Copenhagen, Johann Christoph Groth [1744].　　　　　　　E67
A diary of a merchant-missionary in Greenland, covering the years 1738-1742.

Egede, Poul Hansen. Efterretninger om Grønland, uddragne af en journal holden fra 1721 til 1783. Copenhagen, Hans Christopher Schrøder [1789].　　　　　　　　　　E68
A history of Danish Greenland by a missionary who served there and whose father was one of the earliest Danish settlers of that area.

Egmont, John Perceval, Earl of. To the King's most excellent Majesty, the memorial of John Earl of Egmont. [London, 1764.]　　　　E69
A proposal for the settlement of Prince Edward Island.

Ehrenström, Olof. Anmärkningar öfver det Gensvar som en obekant autor utgifvit emot det som uppå Herr ammiralen och landshöfdingens Theodor Ankarcronas, den 12 Julii 1744 hollne tal är gifvit af Herr inspectoren Jacob Faggot, författade af Olof Ehrenström. Stockholm, Lorentz Ludewig Grefing [1744].　　　E70
A commentary on the following work.

[Ehrenström, Olof.] Genswar emot det, som uppå Herr ammiralens och landshöfdingens Theodor Ankarcronas, den 12 Julii 1744 hållne tal, är gifwit af Herr inspect. Jacob Fagot. Stockholm, Lorentz Ludewig Grefing [1744].　　　E71
A negative commentary by Jacob Fagot on Theodor Ankarcronas, *Tal om förbindelsen emellan landtbruk, manufacturer, handel ock siöfart*.

Eigentlicher und warhafftiger Bericht und politische Betrachung ... so in America zwischendenen Spaniern und Engellämdern entstanden. [Frankfurt, 1674.]　　　　　　　　　E72
A report on the diplomatic conflict between Spain and England over the molesting of Spanish trade in the West Indies by English pirates. It is an excerpt from the *Diarium Europaeum*.

Ekeberg, Carl Gustav. Ostindiska resa åren 1770 och 1771. Stockholm, Henr. Fougt, 1773.　E73
An account of travels to China, with observations on the cities, rivers, and commerce there and about places along the route via the Cape of Good Hope.

Ekeberg, Carl Gustav. Précis historique de l'économie rurale des Chinois. Milan, Freres Reycends, 1771.　　　　　　　　　　E74
The first French edition of a paper presented to the Royal Academy of Sciences of Sweden.

[Elking, Henry.] The interest of England consider'd, with respect to its manufactures. London, For T. Bickerton and A. Dodd, 1720.　　E75
A commentary on the decline of England's commerce, with particular interest in the wool trade.

Elking, Henry. A view of the Greenland trade and whale-fishery. London, For J. Roberts, 1722.
　　　　　　　　　　　　　　　　　E76
A review of commercial opportunities in Greenland submitted to the directors of the South Sea Company.

[Ellice, Edward.] Les communications de Mercator, sur la conteste entre le comte de Selkirk ... et la Compagnie du Nord-Ouest ... Montreal, C.B. Pasteur & H. Meziere, 1817.
　　　　　　　　　　　　　　　　　E77

A series of letters which first appeared in the *Montreal Herald*, presenting the case against Selkirk.

Ellis, Henry. A voyage to Hudson's-Bay, by the *Dobbs Galley* and *California*, in the years 1746 and 1747, for discovering a north west passage. London, For H. Whitridge, 1748. E78
The author was hydrographer, mineralogist, and surveyor in the expedition sponsored by Arthur Dobbs, and this book contains his observations on the coastal regions it explored.

Ellis, Henry. Voyage de la baye de Hudson fait en 1746 & 1747 ... Paris, Ballard, 1749. E79
The first French translation.

Ellis, Henry. Reise nach Hudsons Meerbusen. Goettingen, Abram Vandenhoeck, 1750. E80
The first German translation.

Ellis, Henry. Reize naar de Baai van Hudson, ter ontdekking van eenen noord-wester doortogt, gedaan in de Jaaren 1746 en 1747. Leiden, Elias Luzac, jun., 1750. E81
Translated from the English, this Dutch edition contains a few editorial notes.

Ellis, William. An authentic narrative of a voyage performed by Captain Cook and Captain Clerke. London, For G. Robinson, J. Sewell, and J. Debrett, 1782. E82
An unauthorized account of Cook's last voyage, written by a surgeon's mate.

Ellys, Anthony. A sermon preached before the Incorporated Society for the Propagation of the Gospel in Foreign Parts; at their anniversary meeting in the parish church of St. Mary-le-Bow, on Friday February 23, 1759. London, E. Owen and T. Harrison, 1759. E83
This preacher sees religious care of the colonists as the primary concern, being a defense against the spread of Roman Catholicism in America.

Elzevier, Racquette. [Printed commercial announcement with manuscript date and signatures / signed by] Racquette Elzevier, [second name illegible]. Rotterdam, [Elzevier and ... ?], 1795. E84
Announces the reorganization of government along revolutionary lines, and advertises demand for a variety of products. Printed in English, the appeal appears to be to American merchants.

[Emerson, William.] The mathematical principles of geography. [and] Dialling, or the art of drawing dials, on all sorts of planes whatsoever. London, J. Nourse, 1770. E85
This mathematical manual for young students includes a chapter on navigation. The book is well illustrated and contains a table of longitude and latitude of place names.

Enciso, Martin Fernández de. Suma de geographia. Seville, Jacob Cromberger, 1519. E86
A Spanish navigation and geography book describing both the East and West Indies, and laying strong claim to eastern regions for Spain.

Engel, Samuel. Extraits raisonnés des voyages faits dans les parties septentrionales de l'Asie et de l'Amerique, ou Nouvelles preuves de la possibilité d'un passage aux Indes par le nord ... Lausanne, Jules Henri Pott, 1779. E87
A reissue of the sheets published under the title *Memoires et observations geographiques ...* Lausanne, 1765, with additions only to the section "Nouvelles corrections et additions."

Engel, Samuel. Geographische und kritische Nachrichten und Anmerkungen über die Lage der nördlichen Gegenden von Asien und Amerika. Mitau [etc.] Jacob Friedrich Hinz; Basel, Carl August Gerini, 1772-77. E88
The first volume is a translation from the French, with additions and corrections, of the previous work. The second volume contains arguments for a northwest passage.

[Engel, Samuel.] Memoires et observations geographiques. Lausanne, A. Chapuis, 1765. E89
A study of northern Asia and America with an essay on the northeast passage and the South Sea trade.

Engelland beweinestu deinen König nicht? Frankfurt & Leipzig, Christian Weidmannen, 1685. E90
A warning by a German citizen to England, advising her to be careful lest France come to dominate her trade while the English are concerned with problems of succession.

Engelsch praetjen, tusschen een Parlementarische, Koningsche, Nederlandsch Koopman, en een Bootsgesel ... Middelburg, 1652. E91
Reflects the English political situation and the Dutch relationship to it.

Engelsche-duymdrayery, ofte 't geen de Oost-Indische Compagnie in Nederland ... Amsterdam, H. Stam, 1652. E92
The Amboyna massacre is revived, as this tract continues to contend that an English conspiracy caused it.

Engelschen alarm: of Oorlogs-teyken. Amsterdam, H. vander Stefen, 1652. E93
Concerns naval warfare between the Dutch and English.

Engelschen oorlog, ontsteken door haar brandende gierigheyd de Rooverye ter zee ... Amsterdam, J. van Noorden, 1652. E94
"The English war, touched off by their burning avarice and piracy at sea and the humility of the seven United Provinces."

Den Engelsen blixem ... waer door Engelant den onrechtveerdigen oorlooch desen staet soeckt aen te doen. [n.p.] 1665. E95
    Reviews the causes of the second Anglo-Dutch War, including trade rivalries in America and Africa.

England and Wales. An act for the promoting and propagating the gospel of Jesus Christ in New England. London: Printed for Edward Husband, 1649. E96
    The organization established was to have sixteen directors, and clergy were to urge contributions. In addition to religious work the organization was to establish "universities, schools, and nurseries of literature" among the Indians.

England and Wales. An act to prevent frauds and concealments of His Majesties customs and subsidies. [London, 1660]. E97
    The act allowed for seizure of goods within one month after their landing, and for penalties against erroneous informers.

England and Wales. [Charter granted to the Society for the Promotion of the Gospel in Foreign Parts, the 16th of June, 1701.] London, J. Downing, ca. 1702. E98
    An early printing of the charter, noting the founding members, principles for the Society's governance, and names of members elected since the founding.

England and Wales. Sovereign (1660-1685: Charles II). A proclamation declaring His Majesties pleasure to settle and establish a free port at his city of Tanger in Africa: by the King. London, John, Bill, and Christopher Barker, 1662. E99
    The intention suggested in this proclamation is to create an emporium for goods at the entrance of the Mediterranean, to enhance English trade to that area.

England and Wales. Treaties, etc. Spain, 1667 May 23. Articles of peace, commerce, & alliance, between the crowns of Great Britain and Spain. Savoy [London], J. Bill and C. Barker, 1667. E100
    The commercial treaty included their respective colonial possessions as well, followed by "The form of letters which ought to be given by the towns and sea-ports, to the ships and vessels setting sail from thence."

England's advocate, Europe's monitor: being an intreaty for help, in behalf of the English silk-weavers and silk-throsters. London, George Larkin to be sold by J. Nut, 1699. E101
    The East India Company is indicted here for ruining the silk industry by importing large quantities of very popular Indian cloth.

The English pilot, the second part. Describing the sea-coasts, capes, head-lands, soundings, sands, shoals, rocks and dangers ... In the whole northern navigation ... London, For Richard Mount, 1708. E102
    The "Northern Navigation" covers the coast of Europe from the Zuider Zee northward and eastward to the White Sea and the Baltic.

The English pilot. The third book. London, For William Mount and Thomas Page, 1734. E103
    This pilot guide for navigation to the East Indies contains a map of the world and forty-two double-page charts with text giving navigation instructions.

The English pilot for the southern navigation. London, For J. Mount, T. Page, W. Mount, and T. Page, 1779. E104
    Presents geographical and navigational information in both maps and text for the British Isles, Western Europe, the Canary, Cape Verde, and Madeira Islands.

The English pilot. Describing the West-India navigation, from Hudson's Bay to the river Amazones. London, For Mount and Davidson, 1789. E105
    The "Fourth Book" of the English pilot, containing maps and sailing instructions for the American coasts and islands.

The Englishman deceived: a political piece, wherein some very important secrets of state are briefly recited. London, G. Kearsly, 1768. E106
    A bitter denunciation of policies restricting the trade of the American colonies.

An enquiry into the causes of the miscarriage of the Scots colony at Darien. Glasgow, 1700. E107
    An attack on hostility to the Darien colony, and on the defenders of that attitude.

An enquiry into the melancholy circumstances of Great Britain. London, For W. Bickerton [1743?] E108
    Advocates efficiency in government, more work from the populace, and lower interest rates as the means to restore England's commerce.

An enquiry into the misconduct and frauds committed by several of the factors, super-cargoes, and others ... of the S--- S--- company. London, R. Walker, 1736. E109
    A catalog of the misdeeds of certain officials and factors of the company, with reference to English trade in the Caribbean area.

An enquiry into the rights of the East-India company of making war and peace. London, For W. Shropshire and S. Bladon, 1772. E110
    A criticism of the extensive powers of the East India Company.

Ens, Gaspar. Newer unpartheyischer teutscher Mercurius. Cologne, Peter von Brachel, 1629. E111
A news publication with information on the Dutch victory over the Spanish silver fleet in 1628, listing the cargoes which were captured, bringing the West India Company a profit of seven million florins.

Ens, Gaspar. West-unnd ost-indischer Lustgart. Cologne, Wm. Lützenkirchen, 1618. E112
Descriptions of the East and West Indies, with particular reference to their products.

Entick, John. The present state of the British Empire. London, B. Law [etc.] 1774. E113
A four volume work, the first three describing England, the fourth comprising Scotland, Ireland, the North American colonies, and the East Indies.

Enumeratio urbium in usum itineris ab Egypto usque ad Constantionipolem saec. IV-V. Papyrus leaf. 4th-5th cent. E114
A list of sixty-two towns indicating an itinerary from Egypt to Constantinople.

Eon de Beaumont, Charles Geneviève Louis Auguste André Timothée d'. Les loisirs du chevalier d'Eon de Beaumont. Amsterdam, 1775. E115
A thirteen-volume set compiled by a French ambassador to Great Britain. Some of the volumes deal with the commerce of France, Russia, Great Britain, and various cities in Italy. Import and export statistics are included.

An epistle to the Hon. Arthur Dobbs. London, For the author, 1752. E116
A commendatory poem to Arthur Dobbs, explorer of the Hudson Bay region.

[Eprémesnil, Jacques Du Val d'.] Lettre à M. *** sur l'imputation faite a M. Colbert d'avoir interdit la liberté du commerce des grains. Paris, Panckoukcke, 1763. E117
A defense of Colbert's restrictions upon the grain trade.

Eprémesnil, M. d' (Jean-Jacques). Lettre circulaire de M. d'Eprémesnil a tous les membres du Conseil du roi ... [Paris, 1785.] E118
Gives several pages of evidence justifying General Lally's death as a traitor for his actions in India.

Eprémesnil, M. d' (Jean-Jacques). Lettre et mémoires adresses à M. le garde-des sceaux ... [Paris, 1786.] E119
The author declares that General Lally was guilty not only of treason, but also of various other crimes in India.

Eprémesnil, M. d' (Jean-Jacques). Seconde lettre circulaire de m. d'Eprémesnil a tous les membres du Conseil du roi, jointe a cele du 21 février 1785. [Paris, 1786.] E120

Equiano, Olaudah. Olaudah Equiano's oder Gustav Wasa's, des Afrikaners merkwürdige Lebensgeschichte von ihm selbst geschrieben. Göttingen, Johann Christian Dieterich, 1792. E121
The author recounts his early life in Africa, subsequent enslavement in Virginia, and later travels in Europe and the West Indies. Translated from the English edition first published in 1789.

Ercilla y Zúñiga, Alonso de. Primera, segunda, y tercera partes de la Araucana. Madrid, Pedro Madrigal, 1590. E122
The first complete edition of the classic epic poem describing the Spanish conquest of the Araucana region of Chile.

Ericeira, Francisco Xavier de Menezes, conde da. Relaçam da vitoria que os Portuguezes alcánçaraõ no Rio de Janeyro contra os Francezes, em 19 de Septembro de 1710. Publicada em 21 de Fevereyro. Lisbon, Pedrozo Galraõ, 1711. E123
A newsletter account of the defeat of a French expedition against Brazil.

Ernstig gesprek, voor-gevallen tusschen drie personen, nopende onse en der Engelsche gelegentheyd ... Louvesteyn, Hollandsche Patriotten, 1652. E124
A Dutch political discussion centering largely on the need for protection of Dutch merchant ships against the English.

Erzelung der Künigreych in Hispanien auch der selben järlich Nutzung und Einkomens mit sampt dë Herschafften dem selben Künigreych zügehörig. Mer ein alte Prophecey Kay. Carl Betreffend. [Augsburg, H. Steiner] 1532. E125
A statement of the income of Charles I from his many dominions, including an entry for "the island from which the gold comes."

Esame teologico contro un libro ingiurioso intitolato Difesa del giudizio, formato dalla S. Sede Apostolica nel di 20. Novembre 1704. [n.p., 1709]. E126
Includes several Latin texts of documents important to the Chinese rites dispute.

Escalante, Bernardino de. Discurso de la navegacion que los Portugueses hazen à los reinos y provincias del Oriente. Seville, Alonso Escrivano, 1577. E127
An account of Portuguese navigation, commerce, and colonization in Asia, with descriptions of the major centers of trade in China, India, and adjacent areas.

Escalante, Bernardino de. A discourse of the navigation which the Portugales doe make to the realmes and provinces of the east partes of the world. London, Thomas Dawson, 1579. E128

The first English edition, translated by John Frampton.

Escalona y Agüero, Gaspar de. Gazophilatium regium Perubicum. Madrid, Antonio Gonzales Reyes, 1675. E129

A compendium of information for Spanish officers and administrators serving in South America, including many provisions relating to the conduct of trade, the administration of mines, and the buying and selling of slaves.

Eschelskroon, Adolph. Allerunterthänigster Bericht an seiner königlichen Hoheit, den Prinzen Friderich ... wegen die königliche dänische Insuln, die Nicobaren. Copenhagen, Johann Rudolph Thiele [1785]. E130

An account of the Nicobar Islands, with recommendations that they be developed by the Danish government as a commercial emporium of the East Indies.

Eschelskroon, Adolph. Beschreibung der Insel Sumatra. Hamburg, Carl Ernst Bohn, 1781. E131

A description of Sumatra from a commercial point of view, noting Dutch and English commerce there. A large map of Sumatra is included, and an introduction considers other recent publications relating to Sumatra.

Eschelskroon, Adolph. Beschryving van het eiland Sumatra. Haarlem, C.H. Bohn en Zoon, 1783. E132

Dutch edition of the previous item.

Eschinardi, Francesco. Lettera del padre Francesco Eschinardi ... al Signor Francesco Redi. Rome, Nicol' Angelo Tinassi, 1681. E133

Contains a treatise exploring the idea of a canal between the Mediterranean and Red seas.

Eschuid, Joannes. Summa astrologiae judicialis de accidentibus mundi ... Venice, Johannis Lucilii Sanctiter for Francisci Bolani, 1489. E134

The first part of this work deals with astronomy, with discussions of the zodiac, planets and fixed stars. A world map is based on the model found in Macrobius, *In somnium Scipionis*.

Espinosa, Isidro Félix de. El peregrino septentrionale Atlante: delineado en la exemplarissima vida del venerable padre F. Antonio Margil de Jesus ... Mexico City, Joseph Bernardo de Hogal, 1737. E135

A biography of Father Antonio Margil, founder of Franciscan missions in east Texas which were part of the Spanish response to French establishments in the lower Mississippi valley.

[Espinosa y Tello, Josef.] Relacion del viage hecho por las goletas *Sutil* y *Mexicana* en el año de 1792, para reconocer el estrecho de Fuca. Madrid, Imprenta Real, 1802. E136

An account of a Spanish exploring expedition to the northwest coast of North America led by Dionisio Galiano and Cayetano Valdés. The narrative is accompanied by an atlas, and is preceded by an essay on the history of exploration of that region.

Essais sur l'administration. [n.p.] 1786. E137

Includes a chapter on the importance and function of commerce in the state.

An essay for promoting of trade, and increasing the coin of the nation. [Edinburgh, ca. 1700.] E138

Contains proposals for stimulating the fishing trade and for the formation of a national committee for the improvement of trade.

An essay on the management of the present war with Spain. London, For T. Cooper, 1740. E139

Before his discussion of the war the author reviews the commercial rivalry which was its major cause.

An essay on the trade of the northern colonies of Great Britain in North America. London, For T. Becket and P.A. De Hondt, 1764. E140

A review of the commerce of the American colonies, expressing a view in favor of their freedom to trade.

An essay to demonstrate an easie acquisition of the Spanish West-Indian trade, to the English government. London, For J. Nutt, 1703. E141

A broadside intended to interest Englishmen in a colonial project on the Isthmus of Panama at a point near New Caledonia. "This is the best scituated Port for a General Emporium."

An essay towards restoring of publick credit. London, For J. Roberts, 1721. E142

Proposes a new national debt, a new interest rate, and new currency to revive England's commerce.

An essay upon the government of the English plantations on the continent of America. London, For Richard Parker, 1701. E143

A statement of the problems in governing the colonies with respect to religious freedom, clarity of laws, court procedures, and commercial regulations, encouragement of immigration, harmony in separate colonial governments and communication between crown and colonies.

An essay upon trade, and publick credit. London, John Morphew, 1714. E144

A rather vicious tract attacking Whig principles and politicians and noting the damage they had done through the mismanagement of the nation's economic policies to the advantage of a few undeserving people.

Estacio do Amaral, Melchior. Tratado das batalhas, e sucessos do galeao Sanctiago com os Olandeses na ilha Sancta Elena. Lisbon, Antonio Alvarez, 1604. E145
  A description of the decline of Portuguese dominance of the East Indian trade, noting the rising powers of the Dutch and the English.

Estacio do Amaral, Melchior. Tratado das batalhas: e successos do galeavo Santiago com os Olandezes na ilha de Santa Elena: e da nao Chagas com os Inglezes entre as ilhas dos Açores: ambas capitanias de Carreira da India; e da causa, e desastres, porque em vinte annos se perdérão trinta e oito naos della. Lisbon, [s.n.], 1736. E146

Estacio do Amaral, Melchior. Tratado das batalhas, e sucessos do galeam Santiago com os Olandezes na ilha de Santa Elena : e da nao Chagas com os Inglezes entre as ilhas dos Açores : ambas capitanias de Carreyra da India, & da causa, & desastres, porque em vinte annos se perdérão trinta, & oyto naos della : escrita por Melchior Estacio do Amaral. [Lisbon?] : Na Officina de Antonio Alvares, 1604, [reprinted 1737?] E147

Estat general de toutes les marchandises d'ont on fait commerce a Marseille avec l'explication de leur qualité ... en la presente année 1688 ... Manuscript in French. [Marseille, 1688.] E148
  A catalog of the commerce of Marseilles for 1688, noting 360 different products.

Estbergen, Mathias. Journal, på Hållåndske West-Indiske Compagniets skepp Johanna ... Stockholm, Kongl. Trykeriet [ca. 1736]. E149
  The journal of a Dutch West India Company ship to which the editor has added extensive notes relating to the Dutch and Swedish West India companies.

Estourmel, Louis-Marie, marquis d'. Opinion sur le projet de décret, concernant le revenu public provenant de la vente exclusive du tabac. Paris, Imprimerie Nationale, 1790. E150
  Gives a history of the tobacco trade in France, and urges closer restrictions on it.

Estrades, comte d' (Godefroy). Letters and negotiations of Count d'Estrades, in England, Holland, and Italy; from MDCXXXVII to MDCLXII. Containing ... the dispute about the honour of the flag, and that about the cession of Acadie or Nova-Scotia ... London, R. Willock, 1755. E151
  This diplomatic correspondence deals largely with France's relations with England and the Netherlands. It includes a letter of March 13, 1662 concerning French claims to Nova Scotia.

Estwick, Samuel. A letter to the Reverend Josiah Tucker ... in answer to his Humble address and earnest appeal. London, For J. Almon, 1776. E152
  A reply to Tucker's argument that Britain would be better off without American colonies, ascribing the major cause of the conflict in America to landed interests as opposed to merchant rights.

Etablissements des Europeans à la Chine. Manuscript. [France, ca. 1732.] E153
  From the papers of the Comte de Maurepas, this memorandum sets forth the points at which various European trading companies are established in China, and comments particularly on the situation at Canton from which the French and other traders had been expelled in 1731.

État actuel de l'Inde, en considérations sur les établissemens & le commerce de la France dans cette partie du monde. London, 1787. E154
  A consideration of the areas in which the newly formed Compagnie des Indes would operate.

État des droits qui se perçoivent aux bureaux d'entrée et de sortie à Bordeaux. [Bordeaux, 1734.] E155
  An extensive survey of the import duties on goods coming into Bordeaux.

État présent de la Pensilvanie. n.p., 1756. E156
  A French edition, abridged and translated by Jean Ignace de La Ville, containing a map of Pennsylvania not included in the English edition of William Smith's *A brief view of the conduct of Pensilvanie* which is incorporated in this text.

Etches, John. An authentic statement of all the facts relative to Nootka Sound: its discovery, history, settlement, trade, and the probable advantages to be derived from it; in an address to the king. London, J. Debrett, 1790. E157
  A petition to recover damages from losses incurred by merchants undertaking trade between Nootka Sound and China, with a history of Anglo-Spanish conflict leading to such losses.

Eton, William. A survey of the Turkish empire. London, T. Cadell and W. Davies, 1798. E158
  Contains a chapter on Anglo-Turkish trade, noting its gradual decline which the author attributes to the monopoly of the Levant Company.

Etrobius, Johannes. Comentarium seu potius diarium expeditionis Tuniceae, a Carolo V, imperator. Louvain, Jacobus Batius, 1547. E159
  An account of an expedition ordered by Charles V and commanded by Andrea Doria which conquered Tunis in 1535.

Eumenes. A plan for the government of Bengal, and for the protection of the other British settlements in the East Indies. London, For J. Almon, 1772. E160

Euphrasén, Bengt Anders

A proposal directed to Lord North for a royally-appointed governor and a council made up equally of government and East India Company representatives to rule Bengal, with no pretense of ruling through Indian rulers.

Euphrasén, Bengt Anders. Beskrifning öfver Svenska Westindiska ön St. Barthelemi, samt öarne St. Eustache och St. Christopher. Stockholm, Anders Zetterberg, 1795. E161

An account of travels in the Swedish West Indian island of Saint Bartholomew, with particular attention given to the classification of plant and animal life there. Brief accounts are also given of St. Christopher and St. Eustatius.

Euphrasén, Bengt Anders. Reise nach der schwedisch-westindischen Insel St. Barthelemi, und den Inseln St. Eustache und St. Christoph. Göttingen, Johann Christian Dietrich, 1798. E162

The first German edition.

Eusebius, of Caesarea, Bishop of Caesarea. Chronicon. Paris, H. Estienne, 1512. E163

A general chronological history, containing as an entry for 1509 an account of the arrival at Rouen of some aborigines from the New World.

Eusebius, of Caesarea, Bishop of Caesarea. Chronicon. Paris, H. Estienne, 1518. E164

The second Estienne edition. A reprint of the preceding work.

[Evans, Caleb.] A letter to the Rev. Mr. John Wesley, occasioned by his Calm address to the American colonies. London, For Edward and Charles Dilly, 1775. E165

Wesley's book was based on Samuel Johnson's *Taxation no tyranny*, and this attack upon it is a vigorous defense of the colonists' position against taxation without representation.

Evans, Lewis. Geographical, historical, political, philosophical and mechanical essays. Philadelphia, B. Franklin and D. Hall, 1755. E166

Contains an excellent colored map of the Middle Atlantic colonies and the Ohio River region.

Evans, Lewis. Geographical, historical, political, philosophical and mechanical essays number II. London, R. and J. Dodsley, 1756. E167

This second essay contains observations on the war in America between the French and English, with statements on England's right to inland navigation.

Evans, Rowland. [Autograph letter signed, to Thomas Crosse.] Philadelphia, 16 April, 1755. E168

Evans writes to a friend in London, commenting on legislative attempts to raise funds for war against the French, and a meeting of three colonial governors with General Braddock to plan the summer's campaign.

Evelyn, John. Navigation and commerce, their original and progress. London, T. R. for B. Tooke, 1674. E169

A history of commerce, with particular emphasis on the development of England's trade.

Everett, George, shipwright. Encouragement for seamen & mariners. London, 1695. E170

Proposals for improvement of the navy and fishery by providing better conditions for seamen.

Every one's interest in the South-Sea examined; and by rules of justice and equity settled. London, For T. Bickerson, 1721. E171

This tract calls for the relief of the subscriber at the expense of the South Sea Company.

Ewer, John. A sermon preached before the Incorporated Society for the Propagation of the Gospel in Foreign Parts; at their anniversary meeting in the parish church of St. Mary-le-Bow, on Friday February 20, 1767. London, E. Owen and T. Harrison, 1767. E172

This sermon emphasizes the necessity of teaching if morality is to be sustained. The American mission lists 104 persons serving in various capacities.

The exact dealer's daily companion: instructing him ... in the ... mystery of trade. London, T. Norris, 1721. E173

A handbook for English merchants, with information on companies, customs, commodities, fairs, etc.

Examen vande valsche resolutie vande heeren burgemeesters ende raden tot Amsterdam. Op't stuck vande West-Indische Compagnie. Amsterdam, A. de Bruyn, 1649. E174

"Examination of the false resolutions of the Burgomasters and Common Council of Amsterdam on the question of the West India Company.

An examination and explanation of the South-Sea Company's scheme, for taking in the publick debts. London, J. Roberts, 1720. E175

A pessimistic view of the company's ability to pay dividends of ten per cent as promised.

An examination of a pamphlet entitled His Catholic Majesty's manifesto. London, T. Gardner, 1739. E176

A discussion of Spanish refusal to pay damages to the South Sea Company.

An examination of the commercial principles of the late negotiations ... London, For R. and J. Dodsley, 1762. E177

The author feels that England gave up too much and received too little territory of commercial potential in the treaty with France.

An examination of the rights of the colonies, upon principles of law. By a gentleman at the bar. London, For R. Dymott and J. Almon, 1766. E178

A response to colonial objections to the Stamp Act, noting the objections which were based on Magna Carta which the author claims has no relevance to the colonial claims.

Excerpta De legationibus, ex Dexippo Atheniense, Eunapio Sardiano, Petro Patricio et Magistro, Prisco Sophista, Malcho Philadelphense, Menandro Protectore, haec Carolus Canto clarus ... Paris, Petrum Chevalerium, 1609. E179

Among the fragments of Greek and Byzantine histories found in this work are excerpts from Menander the Protector's account of conquests among the peoples of western Asia and India which brought that region within the Greek commercial orbit.

The excise-bill versify'd. London, W. James, 1733. E180

While reviewing the provisions of the excise bill optimistically in verse form, the author sarcastically points out its flaws and inconsistencies in footnotes.

Experience preferable to theory. An answer to Dr. Price's Observations on the nature of civil liberty and the justice and policy of the war with America. London, For T. Payne, 1776. E181

This reply to Richard Price's book takes issue with the notion that democracy is a guarantee of liberty and attributes the American Revolution to "a departure from fundamental principles of government."

Expilly, M. l'abbé (Jean-Joseph). Le géographe manuel. Paris, Le Jay, 1777. E182

A pocket-sized geography of the world, with tables of weights and measures, and money valuations of the various countries.

Exposé des motifs de la conduite du roi, relativement à l'Angleterre. Paris, Imprimerie Royale, 1779. E183

A recitation of events leading to Anglo-French hostilities as a result of the American Revolution.

Exquemelin, A. O. (Alexandre Olivier). De Americaensche zee-roovers. Amsterdam, Jan ten Hoorn, 1678. E184

The first edition of the first work to popularize pirate stories, written by a West Indian buccaneer.

Exquemelin, A. O. (Alexandre Olivier). Piratas de la America. Cologne, Lorenzo Struickman, 1681. E185

The first Spanish edition.

Exquemelin, A. O. (Alexandre Olivier). Bucaniers of America: or, A true account of the most remarkable assaults committed of late years upon the coasts of the West-Indies ... London, For William Crooke, 1684-85. E186

The first English edition, including the second volume by Basil Ringrose.

Exquemelin, A. O. (Alexandre Olivier). Bucaniers of America: or, A true account of the most remarkable assaults committed of late years upon the coasts of the West-Indies ... London, For William Crooke, 1684-85. E187

The second English edition.

Exquemelin, A. O. (Alexandre Olivier). Histoire des avanturiers qui se sont signalez dans les Indes. Paris, Jacques Le Febvre, 1686. E188

This first French edition includes much descriptive material not in earlier editions and adds an appendix, "Establissement d'une chambre des comptes dans les Indes."

[Exquemelin, A. O. (Alexandre Olivier).] Historie der boecaniers, of vrybuyters van America. Amsterdam, Nicolaas ten Hoorn, 1700. E189

The second Dutch edition with additional material, making it more than twice as large as the first Dutch edition.

Extract uut sekere brieven den 24 Meert 1588 ... gheschreven ende ghesonden aen een Edelman tot Bremen. [n.p.] 1588. E190

These extracts from letters sent to a gentleman in Bremen express the fear that too strong an English influence in the Netherlands might not be beneficial to trade relations between the Dutch and the Danish and Baltic ports.

Extract uyt een missive van het Recif van den 25 Meert 1651. Amsterdam, J. van Hilten, 1651. E191

Condensation of three letters from Brazil reporting favorable conditions there by representatives of the Dutch West India Company.

Extract van een brief, geschreeven uit Parys ... Over de geruchten van oorlog die 'er tegenwoordig loopen. [n.p.] 1688. E192

Contains comments on various aspects of Dutch trade, including the profits of the East and West India Companies.

Extracts of letters from Livorno ... Relating to Turkey raw silk. [London, ca. 1719.] E193

A statistical statement of the amount of silk sent from Marseilles to Leghorn in 1715.

Extrait analytique d'un mémoire, ou observations sur les rapports commerciaux entre la France et l'Angleterre. Manuscript. France, 1796. E194

The memorandum points out the danger of too much free trade with England for the danger it could cause to French manufacturers.

Extrait de plusieures lettres ecrites au S. Hubert. Manuscript. Louisiana [ca. 1738]. E195

Excerpts from thirty-three letters written to Sieur Hubert primarily in the period 1718-23 when he was the leader of the opposition to Bienville's government in Louisiana.

Extrait des douze matieres contenans dans douze mémoires particuliers pour l'établissement de la Louisianne. Manuscript. [France, ca. 1720.] E196

A statement of intended plans for the establishment of a colony on the lower Mississippi.

Extrait du journal d'un officier de la Marine de l'escadre de M. Le comte d'Estaing. [n.p.] 1782. E197

An account of the meeting of the French and English fleets at Delaware Bay in 1778 which is critical of the Comte d'Estaing's management of the French fleet.

Eyndelijcke justificatie der misnoechde participanten tegens de onware calumnien by sommige haer t'onrecht opgetichtet. [n.p., 1625.] E198

Concerns the management of the Dutch East India Company.

[Eyndhoven, Jan van.] Journael, ofte dagh-register, over de reyse, gedaen door ... M.A. de Ruyter. Amsterdam, Jacob Venckel, 1665. E199

An account of the exploits of Admiral de Ruyter against the English in Africa and the West Indies.

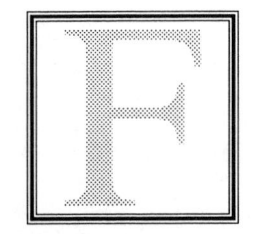

F.A. Brockhaus / Leipzig (Firm). Bibliothèque américaine : catalogue raisonné d'une collection de livres précieux sur l'Amérique parus depuis sa découverte jusqu'a l'an 1700. Leipzig, F.A. Brockhaus, 1861. F1

A major bibliographic catalog for the discovery, exploration, conquest, and settlement of the New World.

Fabbroni, Adamo. Della economia agraria dei Chinesi. Venezia, Graziosi, 1802. F2

An academic dissertation on Chinese agriculture based largely, it seems, on reports of the Macartney embassy.

Fabre, B. Mémoire au roi, sur les moyens à employer pour ramener la colonie de Saint Domingue souci la domination de Sa Majesté. Manuscript. Marseilles, 25 November 1814. F3

A proposal for the recovery of the French colony of Saint Domingue through a more moderate treatment of slaves there.

Fabre, Jacques. A nosseigneurs de la Cour des aydes ... Les poursuites du suppliant ont pour objet la restitution d'une caisse ... contenant cent livres net de dentelles de fil destinées pour les isles françoises ... [n.p.] Veuve Lamesle [1762]. F4

A legal action involving customs procedures.

Fabri, Felix. Eigentliche Beschreibung der hin unnd wider Farth zu dem Heyligen Landt gen Jerusalem. [Frankfurt?] 1556. F5

The author accompanied Bernhard Breydenbach on his trip to the Holy Land in 1483. This is the first edition of this account of the journey.

Fabricius, Christian Albrecht. Befvarelser foranledige ved den allerunderdanigste rapport fra commissionen til cassamangelens undersøgelse af 26 de Junii 1784, og revisions-commissionens forretning ved det Asiatiske Compagnie af 18 de Junii 1784. Copenhagen, Johan Frederik Schultz, 1785. F6

An examination of the financial records of the company, including commercial shipping in the East Indies and China. The text is signed by N. Ryberg and P. V. Hemmert.

Fabricius, Johann Albert. Salutaris lux evangelii toti orbi per divinam gratiam exoriens, sive Notitia historico chronologica literaria et geographica propogatorum per orbem totum Christianorum sacrorum delineata. Hamburg, Viduae Felgineriae, 1731. F7

A history and bibliography of the beginnings and growth of Christianity in all parts of the world by a learned philologist.

Fabronius, Herman. Newe summarische Welt-Historia. Schmalkalden, Wolffgang Ketzel, 1614. F8

A general description of the world, divided according to continents, with both history and geography included in the accounts of the various countries.

Facts relating to the treaty of commerce, lately concluded by Governor Vansittart ... with the Nabob of Bengal: together with copies of some original papers. London, For T. Becket and P.A. DeHondt, 1764. F9

"This treaty was so far from tending to prevent future violences, that from the moment it was published ... the whole country became a scene of disorder and confusion, and the trade of the English was everywhere obstructed."

A fair representation of His Majesty's right to Nova-Scotia or Acadie. London, E. Owens, 1756. F10

A statement of England's legal right to Nova Scotia and its importance to the trade and security of her other American colonies.

Fair trade, besides the heavy duties it lies under, suffers yet more from frauds of smuglers and the

exactions of officers ... [London, ca. 1680.] F11
This leaflet discusses the provisions of a bill intended to regulate customs inspection more carefully.

Faits et idées sur Saint-Domingue, relativement a la révolution actuelle. Paris, Siguy-Thiboust, 1789. F12
An advisory letter to French colonials in Saint Domingue, reporting developments in Paris relative to proposals for colonial representation in the Estates General.

Falconbridge, A.M. (Anna Maria). Narrative of two voyages to the river Sierra Leone. London, L.I. Higham, 1802. F13
A series of letters from the wife of an employee of the St. George's Company, an organization related to the Sierra Leone Company, giving her view of the slave trade.

Falconbridge, Alexander. An account of the slave trade on the coast of Africa. London, J. Phillips, 1788. F14
A concise and excellent account of all aspects of the slave trade from procuring slaves in the interior by African traders to their eventual sale in the West Indies.

Falconi, Alessandro. Breve instruzione appartenente al capitano de vasselli quadri. Florence, Cosimo Giunti, 1612. F15
A textbook in seamanship, covering navigation, astronomy, instruments, etc.

Falkner, Thomas. A description of Patagonia, and the adjoining parts of South America. Hereford, C. Pugh, 1774. F16
The earliest detailed description of the region south of the Plate River, including a map of the area, by a medical missionary who lived there for thirty-six years.

Falkner, Thomas. Beschreibung von Patagonien. Gotha, C. W. Ettinger, 1775. F17
The first German translation.

Fall, Robert. Observations on the report of the committee of the House of Commons appointed to enquire into the state of the British fishery. London, For J. Debrett, 1786. F18
The arguments of a Scotsman for encouraging the expansion of the northern sea fisheries as a means of slowing emigration to America.

Farcot, Joseph-Jean-Chrysostome. Questions constitutionelles sur le commerce et l'industrie. Paris, Le Clere, 1790. F19
Points out numerous advantages of a policy of free trade over one of restrictiveness.

Faria, Manoel Severim de. Noticias de Portugal ... Lisbon, Craesbeeck, 1655. F20
A commentary on the decline of Portuguese population and trade.

Faria e Sousa, Manuel de. Epitome de las historias Portuguesas. Madrid, Francisco Martinez, 1628. F21
The first edition of a general history of Portugal from the earliest times to 1628, noting the voyages of discovery and establishment of overseas commerce.

Faria e Sousa, Manuel de. Epitome de las historias Portuguesas, dividido en quatro partes: por Manuel de Faria y Sousa. Brussels, Francisco Foppens, 1677. F22
This edition contains portraits of the Portuguese kings.

Faria e Sousa, Manuel de. The history of Portugal, from the first ages of the world, to the late great revolution, under King John IV in the year MDCXL. London, W. Rogers and Abel Roper [etc.] 1698. F23
In this English edition Captain Stevens has added a chronicle for the period 1640-1697, dealing extensively with conflicts between the Dutch and Portuguese in Brazil.

Faria e Sousa, Manuel de. Asia Portuguesa. Lisbon, H. Valente de Oliveira, 1666-75. F24
A retelling, based on manuscripts and printed works, of the story of Portuguese discoveries in Africa, India, China, Japan, and other eastern countries up to about 1600.

Faria e Sousa, Manuel de. The Portugues Asia: or, The history of the discovery and conquest of India by the Portugues. London, For C. Brome, 1695. F25
An abridged translation by Captain John Stevens. The original was published in Spanish from 1666 to 1675.

Farissol, Abraham ben Mordecai. Itinera mundi, sic dicta nempe cosmographia ... Oxford, Seldoniano, 1691. F26
The text is in Latin and Hebrew, edited with extensive notes by Thomas Hyde. Originally written in 1524-25 it includes accounts of Portuguese overseas expansion and a description of the New World.

Faro, Francisco de Azevedo Couttinho e. Oração funebre em a morte do Senhor Francisco Xavier de Assis Pacheco e Sampayo, do conselho de S. Magestade Fidelissima, e do ultramar, e antes embaixador extraordinario á Corte de Pekin ... Lisbon, Miguel Manescal da Costa, 1767. F27
A funeral oration celebrating the life of one of the members of the Portuguese overseas council who finished his diplomatic career as ambassador extraordinary to Peking.

A farther examination and explanation of the South Sea Company's scheme. London, J. Roberts, 1720. F28
The question is raised as to the value to England of having one company replace several.

Faulconnier, Pierre. Description historique de Dunkerque. Brugge, Pierre vande Cappelle et André Wydts, 1730. F29
  A history of Dunkirk, written by the president of its Chamber of Commerce, tracing the development of the city from the seventh century to 1718.

Fauquier, Francis. An essay on ways and means for raising money for the support of the present war, without increasing the public debts. London, For M. Cooper [etc.] 1756. F30
  In this second edition the author responds to criticism of his house tax proposal, suggesting instead a graduated capitation tax as a means of supporting Britain's war against France.

Favolius, Hugo. Theatri orbis terrarum enchiridion. Antwerp, Christophe Plantin, 1585. F31
  An atlas including eighty-three maps engraved by Philippe Galle, with the text in Latin poetic form.

Favre, Pierre François. Lettres edifiantes et curieuses sur la visite apostolique de M. de La-Baume, evêque d'Halicarnasse, a la Cochinchine en l'année 1740 ... Venice, Barzotti, 1746. F32
  A review of the Christian mission situation in Vietnam from an anti-Jesuit point of view.

Fea, James. Considerations on the fisheries in the Scotch islands. London, Printed for the Author, 1787. F33
  A detailed description of the Orkney and Shetland Islands with a view to promoting the establishment of a fishery there.

Federici, Cesare. Viaggio ... nell' India Orientale et oltra l'India. Venice, Andrea Muschio, 1587. F34
  The first edition of one of the most comprehensive commercial reports on the Levant and India. The author was a Venetian merchant whose narrative is based on eighteen years of eastern travels.

Federici, Cesare. The voyage and travaile of M. Caesar Frederick, merchant of Venice, into the East India ... London, Richard Jones and Edward White, 1588. F35
  This English edition was translated by Thomas Hickock.

Felden, Johann von. Annotata ad H. Grotium De jure pacis et belli, quibus immixtae sunt responsiones ad stricturas Graswinckelii. Jenae, Matthaei Birckneri, 1663. F36
  A commentary on Grotius's *The law of war and peace*, taking into account the observations on it of Dirk Graswinckel in his *Stricturae ad censuram*.

Feliz vitoria que ha tenido Don Fadrique de Toledo, General de la Real Armada de su Magestad de quarenta naos Olandesas, las seis que encontro en ... la Islas de las Canarias, y las treinta y quatro, que estauan en la isla de S. Lorenço en las Indias ... Seville, Francisco de Lira, 1630. F37
  An account of a victory by a Spanish armada over a Dutch fleet off the Canary Islands.

[Fenning, Daniel.] Neue Erdbeschreibung von ganz Amerika ... Göttingen & Leipzig, Weygandschen Buchandlung, 1777. F38
  This translation was based on the fourth edition of Fenning and Joseph Collyer's *A new system of geography*, London, 1772, and was edited by August Ludwig von Schlözer.

Fer, Nicolas de. La Nouvelle France ou la France Occidentale et le cours des grandes rivieres des St. Laurens et de Mississippi ... Paris, 1718. F39
  A wall map measuring 112 x 104 cm. in four sheets, based on French sources from 1681 to 1717, and published for promotion of the Compagnie d'Occident.

Ferguson, Adam. Remarks on Dr. Price's Observations on the nature of civil liberty, &c. London, G. Kearsley, 1776. F40
  A rebuttal to Price's popular work on civil liberty, contending that the colonists are no more oppressed than other British citizens.

Ferguson, C. A letter address'd to every honest man in Britain: and most respectfully submitted to the serious and patriot[ic]al perusal of the Ministry ... London, John Cooper, 1738. F41
  An argument in favor of war with Spain as a means of protecting British West Indian commerce.

[Ferguson, Robert.] A brief account of some late incroachements and depredations of the Dutch upon the English ... [London? 1695.] F42
  A discussion of the decay of English trade through the encroachments by the Dutch upon the territories of the East India and Royal African companies.

Ferguson, Robert. A just and modest vindication of the Scots design. [Edinburgh?] 1699. F43
  An attack upon those who favored abdicating Darien, and a defense of Scottish commercial interests there.

Fermanel de Favery, Luc. Relatione delle missioni de vescovi vicarii apostolici, mandati dalla s. sede apostolica alli regni di Siam, Cocincina, Camboia, e Tunkino. Rome, Sac. Cong. de Prop. Fide, 1677. F44
  An account of missionary activity in Thailand, Cochin, Cambodia, and Tunkin.

Fermiers généraux des fermes royales unies. Ordre de la direction, a observer dans les expéditions qui doivent être délivrées dans les bureaux, pour les merceries ... qui se transporteront vers le Luxembourg, Namur & Pays de Liege. [Paris, 1755] F45

A regulation requiring bonding of certain shipments of foreign goods across France.

Fermin, Philippe. Déscription générale, historique, géographique et physique de la colonie de Surinam. Amsterdam, E. van Harrevelt, 1769. F46
A description of the economy and society of the Dutch colony of Surinam.

Fermin, Philippe. Nieuwe algemeende beschryving van de colonie van Suriname. Harlingen, V. van der Plaats, 1770. F47
The first Dutch edition.

Fermin, Philippe. Ausführliche historisch-physikalische Beschreibung der Kolonie Surinam. Berlin, Joachim Pauli, 1775. F48
The first German edition.

Fermin, Philippe. Tableau historique et politique de l'état ancien et actuel de la colonie de Surinam. Maestricht, Jean-Edme Dufour & Philippe Roux, 1778. F49
A survey of the history and current situation in the Dutch colony of Surinam, with errors of earlier administrations pointed out and suggestions made for improving the government and economy of the colony.

Fermin, Philippe. Reise durch Surinam. Potsdam, Carl Christian Horvath, 1782. F50
A re-issue of the 1775 Berlin edition, with two additional illustrations.

Fernandez, Antonio. Copia eines Schreibens P. Antonii Fernandez, Obristen der Residentien der Societet Jesu, in Keyserthumb Aethiopien ... den 11 Junii, 1626. Munich, Melchoir Segen, 1628. F51
An announcement that the Christian church of Ethiopia had accepted allegiance to Rome.

Fernández, Diego. Primera, y segunda parte, de la historia del Peru. Seville, Hernando Diaz, 1571. F52
A history of events, particularly in the 1540s and 1550s, centering around the administration of Pedro de la Gasca and the rebellion of Francisco Hernández Girón.

Fernández, Juan Patricio. Historica relatio, de apostolicis missionibus ... apud Chiquitos, Paraquariae populos. Augsburg, Mathiae Wolff, 1733. F53
An account of missionary work in the Paraná and Plate River area of South America.

Fernandez de Castro, Alonso. Puntos principales de la materia de la contratacion de las Filipinas. [n.p., ca. 1603.] F54
A summary of existing commercial legislation concerning trade to the Philippine Islands prepared by the secretary of the Council of the Indies.

Fernández de Medrano, Sebastian. Geographia; o Moderna descripcion del mundo, y sus partes, dividida en dos tomos ... Antwerp, Henrico y Cornelio Verdussen, 1709. F55
A general world geography including also narratives of exploration and travel, among them narratives of Adam Brand and Father Hennepin.

Fernández de Oviedo y Valdés, Gonzalo. La historia general de las Indies. Seville, Juan Cromberger, 1535. F56
The first edition of one of the great histories of Spanish America. The author takes note of the opportunities for trade existing in South America and urges that Spaniards take less interest in gold and more in trade.

Fernández de Oviedo y Valdés, Gonzalo. Libro XX. De la segunda parte de la general historia de las Indias. Valladolid, Francisco Fernandez de Cordova, 1557. F57
The first book of a projected second part to the author's history of Spanish America. His death prevented its continuation.

[Fernández de Oviedo y Valdés, Gonzalo.] l'Histoire naturelle et generalle des Indes, isles, et terre ferme de la grand mer oceane. Paris, Michel de Vascosan, 1556. F58
The first French edition.

Fernández de Piedrahita, Lucas. Historia general de las conquistas del nuevo reyno de Granada. Antwerp, Juan Baptista Verdussen, 1688. F59
This history covers the period up to 1563 and describes the Spanish conquest and settlement of New Granada. It was compiled chiefly from the manuscripts of the conqueror Gonzalo Ximines Quesada.

Fernández Navarrete, Domingo. Tratados historicos, politicos, ethicos, y religiosos de la monarchia de China. Madrid, En la Imprenta Real, Por Juan Garcia Infançon, 1676. F60
A relation of the author's voyages and travels through Mexico, the Philippine Islands, China, and other parts of southern Asia. A detailed history and description of China is included.

Fernando de Santa Maria, frei. Exemplar literarum ex Indiis Orientalibus ad Reuerendissimum P. Magistrum Ordinis, quarum hec superscriptio ... [Rome, Haeredes Antonii Bladii, 1571.] F61
A newsletter reporting an unsuccessful attempt by Dominican missionaries to establish themselves in Thailand in 1567 in the company of Portuguese merchants.

Fernel, Jean. Cosmotheria, libros duos complexa. Paris, Simon Colines, 1528. F62
A treatise on mathematics and navigation which contains what is believed to be the first printed mention of the St. Lawrence River.

Ferrara (Italy). Ordinances. Statuta urbis Ferrariae. Ferrara, Franciscus Rubeus de Valentia, 1567. F63
These statutes of Ferrara constitute an important source for information about the economic life of the city.

Ferrarius, Philippus. Lexicon geographicum in quo universi orbis urbes provinciae, regna, maria, & flumina recensentur. Paris, Franciscum Muguet, 1670. F64
This important geographical dictionary was first published in Milan in 1627. This edition includes material by Michel-Antoine Baudrand that more than doubles the text. Includes tables giving the longitude and latitude of over 2500 cities and towns.

[Ferreira, Christovão]. Relatione delle persecutioni mosse contro la Fede di Christo in varii regni del Giappone, ne gl'anni MDCXXVIII, MDCXXIX, e MDCXXX. Rome, Francesco Corbelletti, 1635. F65
An account of difficult times for the Jesuit mission in Japan compiled by Christavão Ferreira.

[Ferreira, Manuel.] Noticias summarias das perseguições da missam de Cochinchina, principada, & continuada pelos padres de Companhia de Jesu ... Lisbon, Miguel Manescal, 1700. F66
A history of the Jesuit mission in Vietnam, noting numerous martyrdoms of new converts as well as substantial progress of the mission.

Ferreira da Sylva, Silvestre. Relação do sitio ... da nova Colonia do Sacramento. Lisbon, Francisco Luiz Ameno, 1748. F67
A history of the conflict resulting from the attempt by the Portuguese to establish a colony at Colonia do Sacramento on the north side of the Plate River estuary.

Ferrer Maldonado, Lorenzo. Imagen del mundo, sobre la esfera, cosmografia, y geografia, teorica de planetas, y arte de navegar. Alcala, Juan Garcia y Antonio Duplastre, 1626. F68
A textbook of navigation, cosmography, and astronomy, including descriptions of the four known continents.

Ferrer Maldonado, Lorenzo. Voyage de la mer Atlantique a l'Ocean Pacifique ... Plaisance, Del Majno, 1812. F69
An account of a pretended voyage by a Spanish navigator, author of the previous work, from the Atlantic Ocean to the Pacific through a northwest passage in 1588.

[Ferrero, Carlo Giacinto.] La voce della verita risvegliata dallo strepito delle calunnie a favore dell' innocenza risposte ad un libro intitolato Difesa del giudicio formato dalla Santa Sede Apostolica nel di 20. Novembre 1704. [n.p., 1709.] F70
This edition includes only the first three letters previously published as *Lettere d'auviso d'un buon' amico al dottore di Sorbonna*.

Ferrières-Sauvebouf, Louis François, comte de. Mémoires historiques, politiques et géographiques des voyages du comte de Ferrières-Sauveboeuf, faits en Turquie, en Perse, et en Arabie ... Paris, Buisson, 1790. F71
The author's observations include commercial relations of the Near and Middle East with western and central Asia.

Ferro Machado, Juan. Señor—El doctor don Juan Ferro Machado ... dize, que con ocasion de no averse visitado aquellas provincias de la Florida por su propio obispo desde el año de 1595 ... [Madrid, 1701.] F72
A series of recommendations for strengthening the Spanish colony of Florida, including the creation of a subbishopric there and the settling of fifty families north of St. Augustine.

Feuillée, Louis. Journal des observations physiques, mathematiques et botaniques, faites ... sur les côtes orientales de l'Amerique meridionale, & dans les Indes Occidentales. Paris, Pierre Giffart, 1714; Jean Mariette, 1725. F73
Three volumes of observations based on an expedition sent out in 1707, returning in 1711, to determine exact locations of places on the west coast of South America. Volume three has a strong botanical interest.

A few words on the Hudson's Bay Company. London, C. Gilpin, 1846. F74
An attack upon the legality of the Hudson's Bay Company.

Feyerabend, Sigmund. Reyszbuch desz Heyligen Lands. Frankfurt, 1584. F75
The accounts of seventeen travelers to the Near East, most of them German, whose travels spanned the period from the eleventh to the sixteenth century.

[Feynes, Henri de.] An exact and curious survey of all the East Indies, even to Canton, the chiefe cittie of China. London, Thomas Dawson for William Arondell, 1615. F76
An account of the travels of a French gentleman through the Near East, Mesopotamia, Persia, India, China and Indo-China, returning by way of South Africa. He comments on the commerce, political situation, and fortifications of places he visited.

Figueiredo, Manuel de. Roteiro e navegação das Indias Occidentais. Lisbon, Pedro Crasbeeck, 1609. F77
A practical navigation guide for pilots sailing in the Caribbean area and to the mainland of South America. Instructions for sailing to and from the Canary Islands are also included.

Filson, John. Histoire de Kentucke, nouvelle colonie à l'ouest de la Virginie. Paris, Buisson, 1785. F78
   This French edition includes Filson's map, and numerous additions and comments by the tranlator, J.P. Parraud.

Fin de la guerre. Dialogus, of t'samensprekinge, p. Scipio Aficanus raedt den Romeynen datmen naer Africam most trecken om Carthago. Amsterdam, P. Aertz. van Ravesteyn [1624]. F79
   Asserts that the West India Company is the best means to drive the Spanish out of the area.

Fine, Oronce. Nova et integra universi orbis descriptio. Paris, A. Augerellum, 1531. F80
   This map introduced Fine's double cordiform projection which was copied by Mercator and others in the sixteenth century.

Fine, Oronce. Protomathesis: opus varium, ac scitu non minus utile quàm iucundum, nunc primùm in lucem foeliciter emissum ... Paris [impensis Gerardi Morrhii & Ioannis Petri, 1532.] F81
   A collection of four works by Fine: *De Arithmetica, De Geometria, De Cosmographia,* and *De solaribus horologis,* all published here for the first time.

Fine, Oronce. De mundi sphaera, sive cosmographia, primáve Astronomia parte, Lib. V: inaudita methodo ab authore renovati, propriisque tum commentariis & figuris ... Paris, Simonis Colinaei, 1542. F82
   The first separately published edition, a revised version of the 1532 edition, with two other mathematical works appended.

Fiott, John. To the independent gentlemen of East-India stock. [n.p., 1791]. F83
   The author led a movement to investigate freight rates being paid to ship owners who were in some instances proprietors of the East India Company.

Fiott, John. A second address to the proprietors of the East-India stock. London, W. Richardson [etc.] 1792. F84
   Opposes the East India Company's exclusion of all but their own ships from the company's service.

Fischer, Johann Eberhard. Recherches historiques sur les principales nations établies en Sibirie et dans les pays adjacens, lors de la conquête des Russes. Paris, Laran [1801]. F85
   A brief commentary on ninety-five topics, with notes from the original edition of 1774 and from the translator as well.

The fisheries revived: or, Britain's hidden treasure discovered. London, For J. Robinson and J. Millan, 1750. F86
   The author's plan for improving the British fishing industry includes recalling of British fishermen serving abroad, training more fishermen, and increasing British consumption of fish.

[Fitch, Thomas.] Reasons why the British colonies, in America, should not be charged with internal taxes. New Haven, B. Mecom, 1764. F87
   As governor of Connecticut, this writer gives strong arguments against the enactment of the Stamp Act, basing his objections to it on social, economic, and constitutional arguments.

Fitzgerald, Gerald. The injured islanders, or, The influence of art upon the happiness of nature. London, J. Murray, 1779. F88
   A poem purporting to be an address from Berea, the deposed queen of Tahiti, to Samuel Wallis, the English explorer, deploring the effect of his visit to the island.

Fitzpatrick, Sir Jeremiah. Suggestions on the slave trade, for the consideration of the legislature of Great Britain. London, For John Stockdale, 1797. F89
   Proposals are advanced for strict inspection of slave ships to assure healthful conditions, treatment of slaves in the West Indian colonies as indentured servants with freedom for them after seven years, and conditions conducive to health and dignity for slaves in the plantations.

Fix, Johan Leonhard. Proceduren for høiesteret, tilligemed denne rets og de foregaaende ho-fog stadsrets-domme, udi sagerne imellem agent Duntzfelt & Compagnie, og det Asiatiske Compagnie, samt Directeur Fix. Copenhagen, N. Møller og søn, 1800. F90
   Documentation relating to the two companies' trade in the East Indies and in China.

Flachat, Jean-Claude. Observations sur le commerce et sur les arts d'une partie de l'Europe, de l'Asie, de l'Afrique, et même des Indes Orientales. Lyon, Jacquenod & Rusand, 1766. F91
   A wide-ranging text emphasizing particularly manufacturing techniques and machines, including material on the cloth trade and Mediterranean commerce.

Flacourt, Etienne de. Dictionnaire de la langue de Madagascar. Paris, Georges Josse, 1658. F92
   The author was for seven years French commander on Madagascar. The dictionary includes some words from South African languages, and its introduction describes missionary efforts in Madagascar. The *Petit catechisme* first published in 1657 is also included.

Flacourt, Etienne de. Histoire de la grand isle Madagascar. Paris, P. L'Amy, 1658. F93

The first account of the French activities on Madagascar, written by one who had been governor of the French colony there.

Flacourt, Etienne de. Histoire de la grande isle Madagascar. Avec une relation de ce qui s'est passé és années 1655, 1656, & 1657. Paris, Gervais Clouzier, 1661. F94
This second edition adds seventy pages describing events of 1655-57, following the departure of Flacourt from Madagascar.

Flecknoe, Richard. A relation of ten years travells in Europe, Asia, Affrique and America. London, For the author [1656]. F95
The author's travels took him to Brazil, and this is the first published narrative of an Englishman's travels in that country. It is chiefly concerned with the area around Rio de Janeiro.

Fletcher, Giles. Of the Russe common-wealth. Manuscript. England [ca. 1589]. F96
An account of Russia by Queen Elizabeth's ambassador. This manuscript stands between earlier known manuscripts and the published version of 1591.

[Fletcher, Giles.] Of the Russe commonwealth. London, T.D. for Thomas Charde, 1591. F97
The first edition of the first extensive account of Russia in English.

Fletcher, Giles. The history of Russia. [London] W.M., 1643. F98
The second edition.

Fletcher, John. American patriotism farther confronted with reason, scripture, and the constitution: being observations on the dangerous politicks taught by the Rev. Mr. Evans, M.A., and the Rev. Dr. Price. Shrewsbury, J. Eddowes and J. Buckland, 1776. F99
A response to Evans, *A reply to the Rev. Mr. Fletcher's Vindication of Mr. Wesley's Calm address* and to Price, *Observations on the nature of civil liberty.*

Fletcher, John. A vindication of the Rev. Mr. Wesley's "Calm address to our American colonies": in some letters to Mr. Caleb Evans. London, R. Hawes, 1776. F100
Fletcher asserts the right of a government to tax as an expression of the power to govern, and sees in the British government a nice balance between "lawless kings" and "lawless mobs".

Fleuriau, Bertrand Gabriel. La vie du vénérable pere Pierre Claver, de la Compagnie de Jesus, apôtre de Cartagene et des Indes Occidentales ... Paris, Bordelet, 1751. F101
A biography of Peter Claver, "the saint of the slaves", a Jesuit missionary whose work among the slaves of Cartagena earned him canonization in 1888.

Fleurieu, C. P. Voyage fait par ordre du roi en 1768 et 1769, à différentes parties du monde. Paris, Imprimerie Royale, 1773. F102
A report on a voyage undertaken to test the marine clocks of Ferdinand Berthoud. Included are sea charts of the Atlantic and of specific islands in it.

[Fleurieu, C. P.] Découvertes des François, en 1768 & 1769, dans le sud-est de la Nouvelle Guinée. Paris, Imprimerie Royale, 1790. F103
Presents French claims to discovery of several islands to the southeast of New Guinea and includes maps of that area.

[Fleurieu, C. P.] Discoveries of the French in 1768 and 1769, to the south-east of New Guinea. London, For John Stockdale, 1791. F104
This English edition concedes prior French discovery of the Solomon Islands, and notes the importance that route will have for the commerce between Australia and China.

Fleurieu, C. P. Voyage autour du monde pendant les années 1790-92. Paris, l'Impr. de la République [1797-1800]. F105
Includes also comments on the circumnavigations of Drake and Roggeveen.

Fleurieu, C. P. A voyage round the world, performed during the years 1790, 1791, and 1792. London, For T. N. Longman and O. Rees [etc.] 1801. F106
The first English edition, a translation of volumes one and two of the above Paris edition.

Flintberg, Jacob Albrecht. Anmärkningar till Sweriges rikes sio-lag, jämte föfattningarne om hwarje, å utrikes ort wistande Swensk agents, handels-agents eller general handels-agents ... Stockholm, Anders Zetterberg, 1802. F107
A collection of Swedish maritime law, together with information on Swedish consular establishments in the major commercial cities of Europe and in America.

Florence (Italy). Stratto delle gabelle di Fiorenza, ridotte à moneta Fiorentina di buon conio, et giusto peso ... per ordine di legge dell' anno 1544 et di nuovo 1. 1579. Manuscript. [Florence, 1603.] F108
A schedule of tolls on thirteen broad categories of goods entering Florence with a subsequent section for similar duties in Pisa, and a third for Passo.

Florence (Italy). Tariffa delle gabelle per Firenze. Florence, Gaetano Cambiagi, 1791. F109
Schedule of duties on a large number of imports.

Florence (Italy). Laws, etc. Bando delle Compagnie delli Speziali, et d'altri artieri sottoposti all' arte de' medici, e speziali, di Fiorenza, e suo dominio. Florence, Zanobi Pignoni, 1618. F110

A reaffirmation of a law of 1586 regulating pharmacists and others using drugs in the practice of medicine.

Florence (Italy). Laws, etc. Statuti della mercanzia di Firenze. Manuscript. Florence, 1577. F111

The statutes of a merchant court of Florence established in 1308 for regulating trade practices in the city.

Flórez, F. Jerónimo. Provincia peruana de Predicadores, referida por el Padre Maestro F. Geronimo Florez hijo suyo. [n.p., ca. 1640.] F112

A collection of biographies of twenty-two Dominicans who had served in the mission of San Juan Bautista since its founding in 1540.

[Foache, Stanislas.] Reflexions sur le commerce, la navigation et les colonies. [n.p., 1787.] F113

A criticism of French commercial policy, with particular regard to the admission of foreign commerce into French colonies.

Focard, Jacques. Paraphrase de l'astrolabe. Lyon, J. de Tournes, 1546. F114

Focard's book contains thirty woodcut illustrations showing the astrolabe and its uses. The New World is mentioned with references to cannibals and the giants of Patagonia.

Foglietta, Uberto. Genvensis, Historiae Genuensium libri XII. Genoa, H. Bartolum, 1585. F115

A history of Genoa to 1528 covering the previous four centuries during which the city became established as a major commercial center.

Fogström, Johannes. De navigatione in Indiam per septentrionem. Upsala, Wernerianis [1704]. F116

A history of the attempts by various European navigators to reach the East Indies by northern routes, particularly the northeast passage.

Fonseca, Félix Feliciano da. Relaçaõ dos felicissimos successos obrados na India Oriental em o vicereinado ... Marquez de Tavora ... Lisbon, Domingos Rodrigues, 1753. F117

A newsletter chronicling the events of the viceroyalty of the Marquez de Tavora, a period of minor military engagements against the Mahrattas and the others.

[Fontana, Giovanni da.] Liber Pompilii Azali Placentini De omnibus rebus naturalibus quae continentur in mundo videlicet. Venice, Octavium Scotum D. Amadei, 1544. F118

A cosmography by an obscure author, who used Marco Polo, Odoric of Pordenone, Sir John Mandeville, and other late medieval travelers as his sources for geography.

Fontano, Francisco. Introductio ad cosmographiam ex variis autoribus. Salamanca, Joannes à Canova, 1557. F119

A small cosmography, dealing with the usual problems of the sphere, the zodiac, longitude, latitude, etc., with several references to Vespucci's navigations.

Fontenay, Henri, Comte de. Rapport ... sur le commerce au-delà du Cap de Bonne-Espérance. [Paris, Imprimerie Nationale, ca. 1790.] F120

A discussion of the French East Indian commerce and the part the Compagnie des Indes was to play in it.

[Forbes, Duncan.] Some considerations on the present state of Scotland. Edinburgh, W. Sands, A. Murray and J. Cochran, 1744. F121

An appeal to Scottish landlords in coastal areas to help restrict smuggling of tea which was replacing malt liquor as the standard beverage and thus threatened the welfare of the grain farmer of Scotland.

Forbes, Thomas. [Letter] 1784 May 3, London [to] Robert Edmeston, Berwick: Thos. Forbes. London, 1784. F122

The author of this letter was seeking some means to recover property in Florida which had been ceded to Spain by Great Britain. He had been an active trader with the Indians of the Gulf of Mexico area.

[Forbonnais, François Véron Duverger de.] Considerations sur les finances d'Espagne ... Augmentée de Réflexions sur la nécessité de comprendre l'étude du commerce & des finances dans la celle politique. Paris, 1755. F123

A critique of Spain's economic and financial policies, attributing the country's decline to depopulation through colonial expansion.

[Forbonnais, François Véron Duverger de.] Elemens du commerce. Amsterdam, Chez F. Changuion, 1755. F124

A general discussion of the history and nature of commerce.

Forbonnais, François Véron Duverger de. Lettre à m. F., ou Examen politique des prétendus inconvéniens de la faculté de commercer en gros, sans déroger à sa noblesse. [n.p.] 1756. F125

A denunciation of the idea of the nobility participating in commerce.

[Forbonnais, François Véron Duverger de.] Lettre d'un banquier a son correspondent de province. [n.p.] 1759. F126

An examination of plans to review pensions being paid by the French government and to cancel exemptions to the taille as a means of helping to pay for France's involvement in the Seven Years War.

Forbonnais, François Véron Duverger de. Mémoires et considérations sur le commerce et

les finances d'Espagne. Amsterdam, François Changuion, 1761. F127
    A rather detailed history of Spain, concentrating of course on Spain's commerce and trade.

[Forbonnais, François Véron Duverger de.] Questions sur le commerce des François au Levant. Marseilles, Carapatria, 1755. F128
    Concerns prices, shipping costs, duties, trade via Italy, etc.

Formaleoni, V.A. (Vincenzio Antonio). Saggio sulla nautica antica de' Veneziani. Venice, Presso l'autore, 1783. F129
    A history of Venetian navigation with emphasis on the discoveries made by the Venetians. Includes reproductions of two maps of Andrea Bianco.

Formaleoni, V.A. (Vincenzio Antonio). Storia filosofica, e politica della navigazione, del commercio ... nel mar Nero. Venice, Tipografia dell' autore, 1788-89. F130
    A history of Black Sea commerce from the ancient Greek voyages to the end of the fifteenth century.

Forman, Charles. A letter to the right honourable Sir Robert Walpole, for re-establishing the woolen manufactures of Great Britain upon their ancient footing ... London, For T. Warner, 1732. F131
    Includes concern for many aspects of British trade in addition to woolens, among them the international book trade.

Forman, Charles. Mr. Forman's letter to the Right Honourable William Pulteney, Esq.; shewing how pernicious, the imperial company of commerce and navigation, lately established in the Austrian Netherlands, is likely to prove to Great Britain, as well as to Holland. London, For S. Bussey, 1725. F132
    The author offers his ideas on the origins of the Ostend Company and urges a strong resistance in England to its pretensions.

The forreign excise considered. London, John Macock, 1663. F133
    An argument in favor of a consumer's tax upon imports as a means of stimulating reexport of most of the goods coming into England from abroad.

Forrest, Thomas. A voyage to New Guinea and the Moluccas from Balambangan. London, J. Robson [etc.] 1780. F134
    An account of a voyage undertaken in 1774-76.

Forrest, Thomas. Voyage aux Moluques et a la Nouvelle Guinée, fait sur la galere La Tartare en 1774, 1775, & 1776. Paris, Hôtel de Thou, 1780. F135
    The first French edition.

Forrest, Thomas. A voyage from Calcutta to the Mergui archipelago, lying on the east side of the Bay of Bengal. London, J. Robson and I. Owen; Edingburgh, Balfour, 1792. F136
    This work encompasses several subjects, including navigation to and commerce on the Malay coast, Sumatra, Celebes, and adjacent islands; the eastern monsoons; and methods of provisioning ships for the East Indian trade.

Forster, Georg. A voyage round the world. London, B. White [etc.] 1777. F137
    An account of Cook's second voyage, based upon the journals of Johann Reinhold Forster, the naturalist who accompanied the expedition.

Forster, Georg. Johann Reinhold Forster's Reise um die Welt während den Jahren 1772 bis 1775. Berlin, Haude & Spener, 1778. F138
    This German edition of the naturalists' account of Cook's second expedition contains illustrative material not found in the 1777 English edition.

Forster, Georg. Professor Georg Forsters Strödde underrättelser om Capitaine Cooks sista resa och olyckeliga död i Söderhafwet. Stockholm, Tryckt hos P.A. Brodin, 1781. F139
    A translation of an article, based on information the author received from Heinrich Zimmerman and Barthold Lohmann, first published in the *Göttingisches Magazin* for 1780.

Forster, Georg. Kleine Schriften, ein Beytrag zur Völker- und Länderkunde, Naturgeschichte und Philosophie des Lebens. 6 vols. Berlin, 1794-1803. F140
    This collection includes many of Forster's narratives of Cook's exploration of the Pacific Ocean.

Forster, George. A journey from Bengal to England. London, For R. Faulder, 1798. F141
    An account of overland travel from Bengal to St. Petersburg by way of northern India, with comments on many aspects of the commercial activities of the cities visited by the author.

Forster, George. Voyage du Bengale a Pétersbourg. Paris, Delance, 1802. F142
    This edition was translated and edited by Louis Mathieu Langlès, and contains extensive additions by him, including a history of the Sikhs and the Rohillas, and a chronology of the khans of Crimea.

Forster, Johann Reinhold. Geschichte der Entdeckungen und Schiffahrten in Norden. Frankfurt an der Oder, C.G. Strauss, 1784. F143
    The first edition of a history of northern seafaring in ancient, medieval and modern times.

Forster, Johann Reinhold. History of the voyages and discoveries made in the north. London, For G.G.J. and J. Robinson, 1786. F144

The translator states that he has corrected Forster's errors, eliminated some of his invective, and supplied new maps.

Forster, Johann Reinhold. History of the voyages and discoveries made in the North. Dublin, Luke White and Pat. Byrne, 1786. F145
The first Irish edition.

Forster, Johann Reinhold. Histoire des découvertes et des voyages faits dans le Nord. Paris, Cuchet, 1788. F146
The first French edition.

Forsvar for Gouverneur Abbestee, og Harrop og Stevenson, udi sagerne nummerne 58 og 59 paa dette aars Høiesterets orden: Etatsraaderne de Coninck og Reiersen, contra C.S. Blachs Enke og Comp., Og Banco Commissair L.J. Cramer, paadømte i Høiesteret den 27 Junii 1789 ... Copenhagen, Johan Frederik Schultz, 1789. F147
Concerns a lawsuit brought by the Danish Asiatic Company in attempting to protect its monopoly on Danish trade to the East Indies.

Fortrey, Samuel. Englands interest and improvement. Consisting in the increase of the store, and trade of this kingdom. Cambridge, John Field, 1663. F148
A series of observations and recommendations in the mercantilist vein for improving the commerce and prosperity of England.

Fortrey, Samuel. England's interest and improvement, consider'd in the increase of the trade of this kingdom. London, W. Bickerton, 1744. F149
The fourth edition.

Fortunato, Nicola. Riflessioni ... intorno al commercio antico, e moderno del regno di Napoli ... Naples, Stamperia Simoniama, 1760. F150
A history of the commerce of Naples and commentary on commercial policy with respect to maritime trade.

Foulgat, John. [Certificate indicating five year enlistment in the service of the East India Company as a seaman.] [n.p.] 1769. F151
The document is printed, with manuscript insertions of the names and dates, and with the printed word "soldier" crossed out and "seaman" written in.

Four and twenty queries relating to the East-India trade. London, A. Baldwin, 1699. F152
A satirical broadside criticizing the champions of the Indian trade.

[Fournier, Georges.] Asiae nova descriptio. Paris, Sebastian Cramoisy, 1656. F153
A general description of Asia compiled by a Jesuit.

Fournier-l'Héritier, Claude. Dénonciation aux états généraux, des vexations, abus d'autorité, et déni de justice, commis envers le sieur Claude Fournier, habitant de l'île Saint-Domingue. [Paris] 1789. F154
A complaint against the system of justice in both Saint Domingue and Paris which had deprived the author of satisfaction in the matter of his attempt to establish a rum distillery in Saint Domingue.

Fowke, Joseph. The trial of Joseph Fowke, Francis Fowke, Maha Rajah Nundocomar, and Roy Rada Churn, for a conspiracy against Warren Hastings, esq., and that of Joseph Fowke, Maha Rajah Nundocomar, and Roy Rada Churn, for a conspiracy against Richard Barwell, esq. ... London, T. Cadell, 1776. F155
An extensive legal proceeding in which the charges of conspiracy against Hastings were not sustained, but Fowke and Nundocomar were found guilty in the Barwell case.

Fox, George. The line of righteousness and justice stretched forth over all merchants. London, For Robert Wilson, 1661. F156
The founder of the Society of Friends exhorts businessmen to deal honestly with all men.

[Fox, William.] An address to the people of Great Britain, on the propriety of abstaining from West India sugar and rum. London, M. Gurney, 1791. F157
A popular pamphlet designed to mobilize opinion in the anti slave-trade movement.

Fox, William. A summary view of the evidence delivered before a committee of the House of Commons, relating to the slave trade. London, M. Gurney, 1792. F158
An abridgment of the author's *An address to the people of Great Britain* describing the procuring, shipping, and marketing of slaves within the British Empire, noting also alternatives to the slave trade in economic relations with west Africa.

Foxe, Luke. North West Fox, or, Fox from the northwest passage ... London, Alsop & Fawcet, 1635. F159
Accounts of earlier voyages in search of a northwest passage, as well as the author's own narrative of his expedition in 1631.

[Foy de la Neuville.] Relation curieuse et nouvelle de Moscovie. The Hague, M. Uytwerf, 1699. F160
Contains an account of the fur trade between Russia and China.

[Foyer, Archibald.] A defence of the Scots settlement at Darien, with an answer to the Spanish memorial against it. Edinburgh, 1699. F161

A rejection of Spain's claim that the Scots settlement at Darien was an intrusion on Spanish territory, and an appeal for assistance from England in making the colony a success. Authorship has been ascribed to Andrew Fletcher.

[Foyer, Archibald.] A defence of the Scots settlement at Darien. Edinburgh, 1699. F162
A differnt printing of the preceding.

[Foyer, Archibald.] Overtures offered to the Parliament ... for reforming our standard. Edinburgh, John Reid, 1700. F163
A proposal to devalue Scottish currency to bring it into line with that of England, and therefore end the disadvantage which was harmful to Scottish trade abroad. Has been attributed to Andrew Fletcher.

[Foyer, Archibald.] Scotland's grievances relating to Darien ... [Edinburgh?] 1700. F164
A plea to the Scottish Parliament to come to the assistance of the Company of Scotland trading to Africa and the Indies.

[Foyer, Archibald.] Scotland's present duty: or, A call to the nobility, gentry, ministry ... vigorously to act for, our common concern in Caledonia. [Edinburgh?] 1700. F165
The author calls upon the people of Scotland to support the Darien colony. Has been attributed to Andrew Fletcher.

[Foyer, Archibald.] A short and impartial view of the manner and occasion of the Scots colony's coming away from Darien. [Edinburgh] 1699. F166
The failure of the Darien colony is here attributed to no fault of the directors or colonists, but to English actions in banning trade between it and their American plantations. Has been attributed to Andrew Fletcher.

Fracanzano da Montalboddo. Paesi novamente retrovati. Venice, V. Vicento, 1507. F167
One of the earliest printed collections of voyages, containing accounts of the voyages of da Gama, Columbus, Vespucci, Pinzon, Cabral, and others. It may be regarded as foremost among the books to spread news of the discoveries in Asia and America to readers in Europe.

[Fracanzano da Montalboddo.] Paesi novamente ritrovati. Venice, Zorzo de Rusconi, 1521. F168
The last of the early Italian editions. It follows the contents of the first edition very closely.

Fracanzano da Montalboddo. Itinerarium Portugallensium e Lusitania in Indiam. Milan, 1508. F169
The first Latin edition.

Fracanzano da Montalboddo. Newe unbekanthe Landte und ein newe Weldte in kurtz verganger Zeythe erfunden. Nuremberg, G. Stuchs, 1508. F170
The first German edition.

Fracanzano da Montalboddo. Le nouveau monde et navigaciones faictes par Emeric de Vespuce ... Paris, G. du Pre, 1516. F171
The first French edition.

France. Deliberation de la Compagnie des Indes, relativement au Titre VIIme du Reglement touchant sa marine, du 24. novembre 1735. Paris, Imprimerie Royale, 1740. F172
Recommendations for amending one part of the *Reglement touchant marine*.

France. Reglement touchant la marine de la Compagnie des Indes, arresté en l'assemblée d'administration du 16. septembre 1733. Paris, Imprimerie Royale, 1734. F173
A comprehensive collection of regulations concerning the manning of ships, payment of officers, lading, arming and equipping of ships as well as smuggling, slave trade, keeping of journals, etc.

France. Table des edits, declarations, arrests et reglemens concernant les fermes royales unies ... Paris, Veuve Saugrain & Pierre Prault, 1725-1749. F174
A collection of indexes to the laws of France which relate primarily to economic matters between 1723 and 1744.

France. Assemblée des notables (1786-1787). [Collection of documents.] Versailles, Ph.-D. Pierres, 1787-1788. F175
These twenty-five related publications, bound together, deal with various royal plans to improve economic conditions in France on the eve of the Revolution.

France. Assemblée des notables (1786-1787). Procès-verbal de l'Assemblée de notables, tenue à Versailles, en l' année M.DCCLXXXVIII. Paris, Imprimerie Royale, 1789. F176
The 1788 session of the Assembly concerned itself primarily with procedures relative to the forthcoming meeting of the Estates General.

France. Assemblée des notables (1786-1787). Procès-verbal de l'Assemblée de notables tenue à Versailles, en l' année M.DCCLXXXVII. Paris, Imprimerie Royale, 1788. F177
The Assembly of Notables was gathered to consider new tax proposals advanced by Calonne, the controller general.

France. Assemblée nationale constituante (1789-1791). Assemblée nationale. Séances très-remarquables, du mardi premier décembre 1789, soir, & du mercredi 2 matin. [n.p., 1789.] F178

A brief summary of debate over the issue of a self-governing body for Saint Domingue, Martinique, and Guadeloupe.

France. Assemblée nationale constituante (1789-1791). Decret ... sur les colonies & le commerce, du 8 mars 1790. [Marseille, Jean Mossy, pere & fils, 1790.] F179
Decrees aimed at improving colonial relations by better means of making colonial grievances known.

France. Assemblée nationale constituante (1789-1791). Décrets de l'Assemblée nationale concernant les colonies, suivis d'une instruction pour les isles de Saint-Domingue, la Tortue, la Gonave et l'Isle-à-Vaches. Paris, Imprimerie Nationale, 1790. F180
Six articles covering administration of the French colonies followed by twenty-six pages of instructions to the colonies from the National Assembly.

France. Assemblée nationale constituante (1789-1791). Instruction pour les colonies françoises contenant un projet de constitution. Paris, Imprimerie Nationale, 1791. F181
Many articles outlining the political and military organization of the colony of Saint Domingue with duties and responsibilities of various officials indicated.

France. Assemblée nationale constituante (1789-1791). Nouvelles officielles extrêmement importantes, arrivées hier a Paris. Paris, Imprimerie nationale, [1790]. F182
A communication from the Députés of the Assemblée générale of Saint-Domingue in support of the denunciation of C.H. de la Luzerne made by L.M. de Gouy d'Arsy in the French National Assembly.

France. Assemblée nationale constituante (1789-1791). Rapport fait a l'Assemblée nationale, sur les colonies, au nom des comités de constitution, de marine, d'agriculture, de commerce & des colonies. Paris, Imprimerie Nationale, 1791. F183
Antoine Pierre Joseph Marie Barnave reports on proposed means whereby the colonial governments, Saint Domingue primarily, may have some initiative in local government without weakening ties to Paris.

France. Assemblée nationale constituante (1789-1791). Comité d'agriculture et de commerce. Franchise de Bayonne; rapport fait a l'Assemblée nationale, au nom du Comité d'agriculture et de commerce, par M. Delatre ... [Paris, Imprimerie Nationale, 1791.] F184
A statement against continuing the exemption of import duties for Bayonne in the interest of greater unity in French commercial policy.

France. Assemblée nationale constituante (1789-1791). Comité d'agriculture et de commerce. Rapport fait à l'Assemblée nationale, au nom du comité d'agriculture et de commerce, sur les encouragemens pécuniaires à accorder à l'agriculture, aux manufactures, à la navigation et au commerce; par M. Roussillou, député de Toulouse. [Paris] Imprimerie Nationale [1791]. F185
The committee is primarily concerned with means of assisting the fishing industry of France.

France. Assemblée nationale constituante (1789-1791). Comité d'agriculture et de commerce. Rapport sur la nécessité d'étendre à tous les armateurs la prime de 50 livres par tonneau, accordée sur les navires baleiniers expédiés par les Nantuckois établis à Dunkerque & l'Orient. [Paris, Imprimerie Nationale, 1791.] F186
A recommendation that French whalers receive the same subsidy as those from Nantucket who had been relied upon to meet French needs for whale oil.

France. Assemblée nationale constituante (1789-1791). Comité de l'imposition. Rapport fait au nom du comité de l'imposition. Paris, Imprimerie Nationale [1790]. F187
An address consisting of six questions and their answers concerning the money received by the state in the tobacco trade.

France. Assemblée nationale constituante (1789-1791). Comité des finances. Depenses générales de la Marine. [n.p., 1791?] F188
Statistics of expenses of the navy.

France. Assemblée nationale constituante (1789-1791). Comité des finances. Rapport de la dépense des colonies, fait a l'Assemblée nationale par le Comité des finances. Paris, Baudouin [1789]. F189
A colony by colony account of expenditures, including French possessions in the West Indies, in Africa, and east of the Cape of Good Hope.

France. Assemblée nationale legislative (1791-1792). Loi relative aux droits d'entrée dus sur les sucres bruts, et autres denrées coloniales. Du 27 août 1792 ... [Grenoble, J.M. Cuchet, 1792.] F190
Specifies rates and entry regulations for sugar imported from the French West Indies.

France. Assemblée nationale legislative (1791-1792). Comité colonial. Rapport fait a l'Assemblée nationale, au nom du Comité des colonies, concernant les troubles arrivés à la Guadeloupe. Paris, Imprimerie Nationale, 1792. F191
A chronicle of events, including documents, leading to the outbreak of revolution in Guadeloupe.

France. Assemblée nationale legislative (1791-1792). Comité colonial. Rapport sur l'isle de

Cayenne & la Guiane-française. [Paris, l'Imprimerie Nationale, 1792.]   F192
A review of the problems and prospects of French Guiana, with recommendations for the future administration of the colony, written by Pierre Levavasseur.

France. Assemblée nationale législative (1791-1792). Comité colonial. Troisième rapport, fait au nom du Comité des colonies, sur les secours à accorder à Saint-Domingue ... Paris, Imprimerie Nationale, 1792.   F193
Relates to the slave rebellion in Saint Domingue.

France. Assemblée nationale legislative (1791-1792). Comité de marine. Rapport et projet de décret, concernant M. Poissonnier, inspecteur & directeur général des hôpitaux de la marine & des colonies. Paris, Imprimerie Nationale [1792]   F194
A proposal by Henri Gregoire to continue the incumbent in the position of inspector general of hospitals for the navy and colonies despite a decree dismissing all officers in that administration.

France. Bailliage (Caen). Jugement souverain, rendu en la commission établie à Caen, qui condamne le nommé Jean Lasseur ... pour avoir, en récidive, vendu & debité au public de la poudre de tourbe & tan, pour du tabac. [Paris, Imprimerie Royale, 1773.]   F195
Prescribes punishment for illegal trading in tobacco.

France. Bailliage (Lille). Jugement souverain en dernier ressort, du 30 octobre 1777, rendu contre une bande d'environ trente fraudeurs ... Lille, N.J.B. Peterinck-Cramé, 1777.   F196
A judgment against a group of some thirty smugglers.

France. Bailliage (Lille). Procès-verbal de la publication de la paix, à Lille. Extrait des registres ... [Lille, N.J.B. Peterinck-Crame, 1783.]   F197
Provides for the public celebration of the Peace of Paris.

France. Bureau de commerce. Sommaire de l'instance pour Pierre Vallet ... contre Pierre Chaloineau de la Chauverie ... & Claude-Pierre Testu. Paris, Veuve d'André Knapen, 1736.   F198
Summary of a case at law relative to the trade in naval stores from the Baltic area by the "Societé pour le Commerce du Nord."

France. Bureau général de la balance du commerce. Mémoire sur l'origine d'un Bureau de la balance du commerce en France; sur la nouvelle consistance en 1782, & sur lere progrès & la situation actuelle de cet etablissement. [Paris] Lamesle [1786].   F199
A description of the functioning of the Office of the Balance of Commerce, designed to provide up to date information on French trade with all major commercial connections.

France. Commissaires du conseil pour la regie de la Compagnie des Indes. Ordonnance de nosseigneurs les commissaires du conseil ... en faveur des habitans de la colonie de la Louisianne. Paris, Veuve Saugrain & P. Prault, 1721.   F200
A series of regulations upon the administration and commerce of Louisiana.

France. Commission nationale civile aux Iles sous le vent. [Proclamation reaffirming the freedom from slavery of Africans and their descendants in Saint-Domingue]. [Saint Marc] François Lamothe [1793].   F201
The proclamation was a response to an unauthorized and contradictory proclamation issued by Adrien-Nicolas Lasalle.

France. Conseil d'État. Arrest du conseil privé du roy, ... [etc.] Orleans, G. Hotot, 1626-1643.   F202
A collection of twenty-three documents bound together, dealing with regulation of commercial traffic on the Loire River.

France. Conseil d'État. Arrest ... portant reglement en execution des ordonnances, sur le jugement des prises. Le 2 iour de decembre 1656. [n.p., 1656.]   F203

France. Conseil d'État. Arrest ... portant deffences à tous les maistres chapeliers du royaume, méme à ceux qui sont dans des lieux privilegiez, de fabriquer ny faire fabriquer aucuns chapeaux de castor, sinon de pur castor ... Paris, Imprimeurs ordinaires du Roy, 1666.   F204
A prohibition against mixing inferior beaver with that of high quality from Canada or Russia in the making of hats.

France. Conseil d'État. Arrest ... qui ordonne que toutes les marchandises qui seront chargées dans les vaisseaux de la Compagnie des Indes Occidentales ... pour estre portées és costes de Guinée, jouiront de l'exemption des droits de sortie, &c. [n.p., 1671.]   F205

France. Conseil d'État. Arrest ... portant que les manufactures de quincailleries, & rubanteries des villes de Saint Estienne & S. Chamond, & les marchandises qui viennent du côte de Ponant ... pourront estre conduites à droicture, sans passer par la ville de Lyon, à l'exception des drogueries & espiceries. Lyons, Antoine Jullieron, 1672.   F206

France. Conseil d'État. Arrest ... qui regle les droits d'entrée & sortie du Royaume, des marchandises venans pour la Compagnie des Indes Orientales ... [Paris? 1672.]   F207
This document is chiefly concerned with cloth imports.

France. Conseil d'État. Arrest ... portant que faute par les marchands negocians, qui feront porter des marchandises ès isles de l'Amérique & de Canada ... [n.p.] 1682. F208

Exporters taking advantage of the free export of goods to America are required to give evidence of the discharge of their goods in America within eight months after sailing.

France. Conseil d'État. Arrest ... qui maintient la Compagnie du Sénégal en la faculté de faire seule le commerce és costes d'Afrique depuis le Cap Blanc jusques à la riviere de Serre-Lionne. Paris, Sebastien Mabre-Cramoisy, 1684. F209

France. Conseil d'État. Arrest ... par lequel Sa Majesté ordonne qu'il sera levé ... un escu pour chacun livre pesant de peaux de castors ... [Paris, 1685.] F210

France. Conseil d'État. Arrest ... concernant les toiles de cotton peintes aux Indes ou contrefaites dans le Royaume ... étoffes de soye à fleurs d'or & d'argent de la Chine ... Paris, Veuve Saugrain & P. Prault, 1686. F211

A decree designed to protect the domestic industry by curbing the importing of Oriental textiles.

France. Conseil d'État. Arrest ... que celuy du 30 avril dernier concernant les toiles & ouvrages de coton ... & regle la levée des droits sur lesdites toiles de coton. Paris, Sebastien Mabre-Cramoisy, 1686. F212

Duties are levied on all imported cotton and linen goods.

France. Conseil d'État. Arrest ... qui confirme les traitez des 24 & 30 aoust 1685. Paris, Veuve Saugrain & P. Prault [1686]. F213

Renews peace between France and Tunis, and gives permission for the establishment of a French company at Cap Negre to trade in fish, coral, and other products.

France. Conseil d'État. Arrest ... qui confirm les privileges accordez par Sa Majesté à la Compagnie des Indes Orientales. [n.p., 1687.] F214

A reconfirmation of earlier edicts, plus additional regulations on the sale of East Indian cloth in France.

France. Conseil d'État. Arrest ... servans de reglemens entre les marchands drapiers & les marchands merciers. Paris, Denys Thierry, 1687. F215

Regulations upon domestic and foreign trade in woolen goods.

France. Conseil d'État. Arrest ... portant confiscation ... des vaisseaux & marchandises ... appartenans aux Hollandois. Paris, Estienne Michallet, 1688. F216

This document records that it was the interruption of French commerce by the Dutch which brought about the confiscation of their ships and merchandise.

France. Conseil d'État. Arrest ... qui confirme les privileges accordez par Sa Majesté à la Compagnie des Indes Orientales. Paris, François Muguet, 1688. F217

France. Conseil d'État. Arrest ... pour la vente des toiles blanches & marchandises arrivées dans le vaisseau de la Compagnie des Indes Orientales, en la ville de Nantes. [Paris] F. Léonard, 1691. F218

France. Conseil d'État. Arrest ... qui ordonne que les draps des manufactures du Languedoc, qui passeront par la ville de Bordeaux, pour le compte & le commerce de la Compagnie des Indes Orientales, seront exempts de la moitié des droits. Paris, Veuve Saugrain [1691]. F219

France. Conseil d'État. Arrest ... qui ordonne que les marchandises que la Compagnie des Indes Orientales sera venir des païs de sa concession ... payeront pour tous droits d'entrées dans le royaume, trois pour cent. [Paris, Veuve Saugrain, 1692.] F220

France. Conseil d'État. Arrest contradictoire ... du vingt-deux novembre 1692. Qui ordonne, que l'arrest du vingt-neuf avril dernier sera executé; ce faisant que les armousins ... ensemble cells meslées de soye, or, ou argent ... sur les vaisseaux de la Compagnie des Indes ... Paris, 1692. F221

France. Conseil d'État. Arrest ... qui ordonne que le nommé Amyeux ... payera les droits de comptablie de Bordeaux, pour les marchandises par luy achetées à Nantes de la Compagnie des Indes, & déclarées pour Toulouse. [Paris? 1693.] F222

France. Conseil d'État. Arrest ... qui ordonne ... castors seront receus au Bureau de fermes à Quebec sur trois sortes & qualitez ... [n.p., 1695.] F223

An influx of inferior beaver from the south brought forth this order that only the three highest grades of beaver be purchased.

France. Conseil d'État. Arrest ... qui ordonne que les directeurs de la Compagnie des Indes Orientales pourront faire apporter dans leurs vaisseaux pendant trois années, des toiles peintes des jusqu' à la valeur de cent cinquante mille livres, par chacun an. Paris, Veuve Saugrain & Pierre Prault [1695]. F224

France. Conseil d'État. Arrest ... qui approuve les articles de societé faits entre les directeurs de la Compagnie des Indes Orientales ... [Paris, Veuve Saugrain & P. Prault, 1696.]   F225
    Concerns goods from India stored at Brest by the Marquis de Nesmond.

France. Conseil d'État. Arrest ... qui décharge les marchandises venduës par la Compagnie des Indes Orientales, des droits de la pancarte de la ville de Nantes. [Paris, Veuve Saugrain & Pierre Prault, 1696.]   F226

France. Conseil d'État. Arrest ... qui ordonne que l'edit du mois d'aoust 1664 ... seront executez ... & en consequence a dechargé les directeurs de la Compagnie des Indes Orientales des droits de lots & ventes. [n.p., 1696.]   F227

France. Conseil d'État. Arrest ... qui ordonne que les marchandises prises par les vaisseaux de Sa Majesté ... seront venduë à Nantes ... par les directeurs de la Compagnie des Indes Orientales. [n.p., 1696.]   F228

France. Conseil d'État. Arrest ... concernant la marque des toiles & moussellines apportées sur les vaisseaux de la Compagnie des Indes Orientales. [Paris, Veuve Saugrain & P. Prault, 1698.]   F229
    A decree making it obligatory to mark the imported textiles.

France. Conseil d'État. Arrest ... qui augmente dans tout le royaume, les especes de la premiere reforme ... [n.p., 1699.]   F230
    Concerns the issue of new currency and its relation to coins then in circulation.

France. Conseil d'État. Arrest ... portant que ceux des habitans de Dunkerque qui voudront aller à la pesche des moruës ... Paris, La veuve & M.G. Jouvenel [1700].   F231
    Requires Dunkirk fishermen to mark their casks in a special manner to keep Dutch fishermen from taking advantage of Dunkirk rates.

France. Conseil d'État. Arrest ... qui ordonne que les droits d'entrée des cotons filez ... feront levez à l'entrée des cinq grosses fermes ... Lyons, A. Jullieron, 1700.   F232
    Import duties on cottons from the Levant and America are to be levied at Lyons.

France. Conseil d'État. Arrest ... qui regle la quantité desétoffes de soye, d'or & d'argent, que la Compagnie des Indes Orientales peut faire venir des Indes & vendre en France ... Paris, F. Léonard, 1700.   F233

France. Conseil d'État. Arrest ... qui ordonne que ... il sera fait inventaire des toiles de coton ... & autres marchandises sujettes à la marque. Paris, Veuve Saugrain & P. Prault, 1701.   F234
    A decree ordering a certain government official in Brittany to take an inventory of goods that arrived on a ship from India.

France. Conseil d'État. Arrest ... qui permet aux directeurs de la Compagnie Royale des Indes Orientales, de vendre des étoffes de soye, or & argent, & d'écorces d'arbres qu'elle a récûës des Indes. Paris, Veuve Saugrain & P. Prault, 1701.   F235

France. Conseil d'État. Arrest ... qui ordonne ... les directeurs de la Compagnie des Indes Orientales remettront ... les noms des marchands & autres ... qui acheté les 7164 pieces de toiles peintes ... [Paris, Frederic Léonard, 1702.]   F236

France. Conseil d'État. Arrest ... qui ordonne que la déclaration du 9 may 1702 sera executée selon sa forme & teneur; & fait défenses aux directeurs de la Compagnie des Indes ... [Paris, Frederic Léonard, 1702.]   F237

France. Conseil d'État. Arrest ... portant qu'il sera fait inventaire des toiles de cotton ... venuës par le vaisseau le S. Loüis, pour la Compagnie des Indes. [Paris, Veuve Saugrain & Pierre Prault, 1703.]   F238

France. Conseil d'État. Arrest ... portant revocation du transit de Marseilles à Geneve. Paris, Imprimerie Royale, 1704.   F239
    The right to trade in cloth without paying duty between Marseilles and Geneva was revoked because of protests from the Lyons merchants, whose trade was declining.

France. Conseil d'État. Arrest ... qui ordonne ... les vaisseaux appartenans aux habitans des Païs-Bas Espagnols qui viendront dans les ports du royaume pendant la presente guerre. [n.p., F. Léonard, 1704.]   F240
    Grants exemption from duties to ships from the Spanish Netherlands coming to French ports during the war then in progress.

France. Conseil d'État. Arrest ... Du douze decembre 1705, qui déclare l'Article XXVIII du titre premier de l'ordonnance du mois de juillet 1681 concernant le commerce du tabac, commun pour ce qui regarde la gabelle ... [n.p., 1705.]   F241
    An attempt to stop the smuggling of salt and tobacco by soldiers and sailors operating between France and Spain.

France. Conseil d'État. Arrest ... qui ordonne que ceux des marchands de Paris qui ont chez eux des etoffes des Indes ... remettre au Sieur d'Argenson ... un etat certifié & signé d'eux de toutes les pieces desdites etoffes. [n.p., 1705.] F242

France. Conseil d'État. Arrest ... concernant le commerce des castors de Canada. Paris, V. Saugrain, 1707. F243
Outlines plans for the insuring of beaver shipments to France.

France. Conseil d'État. Arrest ... concernant les creanciers de la Compagnie du Senegal. [n.p., 1709.] F244
An excerpt from documents relating to payment to the creditors of the Company of Senegal.

France. Conseil d'État. Arrest ... qui fait défenses à tous negocians, marchands, & autres personnes de quelque qualité & condition qu'elles soient, de faire commerce ... aucunes étoffes des Indes, de la Chine, ou du Levant. Paris, La veuve & M.G. Jouvenal, 1709. F245

France. Conseil d'État. Arrest ... qui ordonne que les interessez aux vaisseaux arrivez & qui arriveront de la Mer du Sud ... payer l'indult de six pour cent. Paris, F. Léonard, 1709. F246
A decree placing a tax upon grains coming into France from Peru.

France. Conseil d'État. Arrest ... qui regle moderément les droits d'entrée en faveur des marchandises qui auront été prises en mer. [n.p., 1709.] F247
Lists numerous types of cloths to which the new rates will apply.

France. Conseil d'État. Arrest ... qui fait très-expresses inhibition & défenses à tous fabriquans de fabriquer ... aucune étoffe à l'imitation des celles des Indes, de la Chine & du Levant ... Paris, F. Léonard, 1710. F248

France. Conseil d'État. Arrest ... qui fait défenses à la veuve Petit ... de faire pour-suite ailleurs que pardevant ... Compagnie du Senegal. [n.p., 1711.] F249
Concerns the inheritance of interests in the Company of Senegal.

France. Conseil d'État. Arrest ... qui ordonne que tous ceux qui auront des tableaux, billets de la Compagnie de Senegal ... seront tenus de les rapporter ... [n.p., 1711.] F250
Refers to the heirs and creditors of M. de Montarsy and his interests in the Company of Senegal.

France. Conseil d'État. Arrest ... en interpretation des arrests de 28. avril 1711. & 29. mars 1712. [n.p., F. Léonard, 1712.] F251
A regulation concerning the proper marking of imported cotton cloth.

France. Conseil d'État. Arrest ... portant établissement de la Compagnie de la Chine. Paris, Veuve Saugrain & Pierre Prault [1712]. F252
The failure of earlier companies to get any significant trade started with China resulted in the formation of this third China Company of France.

France. Conseil d'État. Arrest ... qui ordonne que les marchandises apportées des Indes ... seront marquées de la marque que sera choisie par le sieur Ferrand ... & venduës en la manniere accoutemée en la ville de Nantes. [Paris] Frederic Leonard [1712]. F253

France. Conseil d'État. Arrest ... du 9. septembre 1713. Qui décharge les morües & les huiles ... de tous droits ... [n.p., 1713.] F254
Removes duties on cod and fish oils brought from Isle Royale, Cape Breton.

France. Conseil d'État. Arrest ... qui décharge Ysembert de la demande en restitution ... [n.p., 1713.] F255
Clarifies the laws regarding re-exporting of goods from France to her American colonies.

France. Conseil d'État. Arrest ... qui ordonne la vente des marchandises arrivées sur la fregate l'Adelaide, & la marque des marchandises sujettes à icelle. Paris, Veuve Saugrain & Pierre Prault [1713]. F256
Concerns the sale of goods taken from an English ship.

France. Conseil d'État. Arrest ... qui permet à la Compagnie des Indes Orientales de vendre les etoffes venues pour son compte, défend à tous marchands de vendre aucunes marchandises sujetes à la marque, qu'elles ne soient marquées. Paris, Veuve Saugrain & Pierre Prault [1713]. F257

France. Conseil d'État. Arrest ... concernant les soyes étrangères, & celles qui viennent des Indes & de la Chine. Paris, Veuve Saugrain & P. Prault, 1714. F258
In answer to complaints by the city of Marseilles the King decrees that the imports of silk that do not come from the Orient should pass through Marseilles.

France. Conseil d'État. Arrest ... portant reglement sur les toiles de coton peintes ou blanches, mousselines & étoffes des Indes, de la Chine & du Levant ... Paris, Imprimerie Royale, 1714. F259
Reaffirms the intent of a law of 1709, to limit the importing of cloth to certain varieties licensed to the Compagnie des Indes Orientales.

France. Conseil d'État. Arrest ... pour deffendre le commerce, port & usage des étoffes des Indes, de la Chine & du Levant dans les villes de Flandre & d'Artois. [n.p., 1714.] F260

Applies the restriction against importing cloth to Flanders and Artois, which had just been reunited with France and in which many of these imports were to be found.

France. Conseil d'État. Arrest ... qui décharge les directeurs de la Compagnie des Indes Orientales ... & en consequence les condamne à payer ausdits directeurs les sommes dont ils sont debiteurs pour vente de marchandises des Indes. Paris, Veuve Saugrain & Pierre Prault [1714]. F261

France. Conseil d'État. Arrest ... qui ordonne, pour faciliter l'execution de l'arrest du 27. aoust 1709, concernant les toiles peintes. Paris, Imprimerie Royale, 1714. F262

Announces an impending investigation of persons holding or offering for sale cloth from the East Indies, China, or the Levant.

France. Conseil d'État. Arrest ... qui ordonne que les chairs salées venant des païs de Bordeaux, seront déchargées du droit de cinq livres par cent pesant ... [n.p., 1714.] F263

Contains information on earlier regulations upon the importing of meat into France.

France. Conseil d'État. Arrest ... qui permet aux négocians qui font commerce de sel dans les provinces de la Haute Xaintonge, Angoumois ... d'aller prende les sels dont ils auront besoin en Espagne, ou en Portugal, 1714. [n.p., 1714.] F264

France. Conseil d'État. Arrest ... concernant les mousselines, toiles de coton des Indes, de la Chine ou du Levant. Paris, Imprimerie Royale, 1715. F265

Announces the forthcoming investigation and reporting of merchants holding undeclared cloth from the Levant, China, or the East Indies.

France. Conseil d'État. Arrest ... qui casse celuy de la Cour des Aydes du 29. août 1714. Paris, Veuve Saugrain & P. Prault, 1715. F266

Confirmation of old laws regulating the dues on Levantine goods brought to Marseilles.

France. Conseil d'État. Arrest ... qui décharge de tous droits d'entrée pendant dix années le charbon de terre provenant des mines de l'Isle Royale. Paris, Imprimerie Royale, 1715. F267

France. Conseil d'État. Arrest ... qui fixe jusqu'au premier may prochain le delay pour declarer les meubles composez de toiles peintes & etoffes des Indes. Paris, Imprimerie Royale, 1715. F268

The types of goods which must be declared are enumerated.

France. Conseil d'État. Arrest ... qui ordonne que les drogueries & epiceries provenant du commerce de la Compagnie des Indes, qui seront achetées par les marchands & habitans de Lyon ... ne payeront que le quart des droits du tarif de 1664. [Paris] Georges Jouvenel [1715]. F269

France. Conseil d'État. Arrest ... qui proroge pour deux mois le delay accordé pour la marque des toiles peintes. Paris, Imprimerie Royale, 1715. F270

France. Conseil d'État. Arrest ... concernant la vente des marchandises apportées par la Compagnie des Indes Orientales. Paris, Veuve Saugrain [1716]. F271

Concerns the sale of goods from mixed cargoes brought to Brest and Nantes.

France. Conseil d'État. Arrest ... concernant les etoffes des Indes, de la Chine, & du Levant ... Paris, J. de la Caille, 1716. F272

Requires the marking of certain cloths from China and the East Indies on pain of confiscation.

France. Conseil d'État. Arrest ... concernant les mousselines & etoffes des Indes. Paris, Veuve Saugrain, 1716. F273

Concerns a case of illegal importing of muslin from India.

France. Conseil d'État. Arrest ... contenant quelques nouveaux articles ... faits pour la fabrique des toiles appellées fleurets & blancards. Paris, Imprimerie Royale, 1716. F274

Additions to the regulations upon the cloth trade, taking into account special requests of the Chamber of Commerce of Rouen.

France. Conseil d'État. Arrest ... pour l'observation des reglemens generaux des manufactures dans les trois eveschez de Metz, Toul & Verdun. Paris, Imprimerie Royale, 1716. F275

Enforces regulations on imports, but provides exceptions in export duties.

France. Conseil d'État. Arrest ... que décharge des droits de foraine & doüanne de Valence les moruës seches, & les huiles qui proviendront de la pesche des sujets de Sa Majesté à l'Isle Royale. Paris, Imprimerie Royale, 1716. F276

A ten-year moratorium on import duties and customs on dried codfish and oil coming from Cape Breton in Canada.

France. Conseil d'État. Arrest ... que la caution d'Olanier & Audifred ... Paris, Veuve Saugrain, 1716.   F277
   Concerns a case involving import duties levied on a cargo of cotton and pepper brought to Nantes in 1693.

France. Conseil d'État. Arrest ... qui modere les droits d'entrées dans le royaume, des huiles & graisses de baleine, et d'autres poissons. Paris, Imprimerie Royale, 1716.   F278
   Alters the duties on whale and fish oil at the request of merchants of Dunkirk.

France. Conseil d'État. Arrest ... qui ordonne les negocians qui ont envoyé des navires en Guinée ... joüiront de l'exemption de la moitié des droits. Paris, Imprimerie Royale, 1716.   F279
   Merchants who had departed for Africa since November 1713 were to enjoy the same duty rates as those decreed in new letters patent in January 1716.

France. Conseil d'État. Arrest ... qui ordonne que huiles provenant des baleines, des moruës & autres poissons seront déchargées du nouveau droit imposé au profit du Roy ... Paris, Imprimerie Royale, 1716.   F280

France. Conseil d'État. Arrest ... qui ordonne que les negocians qui ont envoyé des navires en Guinée depuis le mois de novembre 1713 joüiront de l'exemption de la moitié des droits. Paris, Imprimerie Royale, 1716.   F281
   Pertains chiefly to shippers engaged in the slave trade.

France. Conseil d'État. Arrest ... qui ordonne que toutes les toiles peintes, etoffes de la Chine & du Levant, mousselines, &c seront brûlées, même la moitié qui devoit être envoyée à l'etranger, & les dénonciateurs payez de la totalité aux dépens du Roi. [n.p., 1716.]   F282

France. Conseil d'État. Arrest ... qui permet ... de transporter hors du Royaume par tous les ports, bureaux & passages les orges, baillarges & bleds d'Espagne ou d'Inde, sans payer aucuns droits de sortie. Paris, Imprimerie Royale, 1716.
F283

France. Conseil d'État. Arrest ... concernant les maîtres-ouvriers & faiseurs de bas au métier; et autres ouvrages tant de soye, que de fil, laine, poil & castor. Paris, Imprimerie Royale, 1717.
F284
   Confirmation of an earlier decree ordering the marking with the government's seals of hosiery and other products of the textile industry.

France. Conseil d'État. Arrest ... qui fait deffenses aux Commis des fermes & à tous autres qui feront des saisies de mousselines & autres marchandises des Indes. Paris, Veuve Saugrain [1717].   F285

France. Conseil d'État. Arrest ... qui ordonne que les lettres patentes du mois d'avril dernier seront communes pour le commerce de Canada. Paris, Imprimerie Royale, 1717.   F286
   This document makes applicable to the trade of Canada a set of regulations made in April 1717 for application to other French American colonies.

France. Conseil d'État. Arrest ... concernant les retrouves des tabacs. [Paris, Imprimerie Royale, 1718.]   F287
   Concerns the transfer of the right of sale of certain tobacco from Guillaume fils to Jean Ladmiral.

France. Conseil d'État. Arrest ... concernant les soldats, ouvriers, et autres gens engagez au service de la Compagnie d'Occident ... Paris, Veuve Saugrain & P. Prault, 1718.   F288
   Urges those who have signed indenture contracts with companies or individuals in Louisiana to resettle immediately.

France. Conseil d'État. Arrest ... portant diminution de droits sur le thé. Paris, Veuve Saugrain, 1718.   F289

France. Conseil d'État. Arrest ... qui attribue jurisdication à Mrs. les intendans des provinces & generalitez du royaume, des contestations meües & à mouvoir, en execution de l'arrest du Conseil du 28 novembre 1718. concernant les retrouves des tabacs. [Paris, Imprimerie Royale, 1718.]   F290
   Provides for the adjudication of cases arising from results of the previous document.

France. Conseil d'État. Arrest ... concernant la réünion des Compagnies des Indes Orientales & de la Chine, à la Compagnie d'Occident. Paris, Veuve Saugrain & Pierre Prault [1719].   F291

France. Conseil d'État. Arrest ... concernant les billets de banque. Du premier decembre 1719. Paris, Imprimerie Royale, 1719.   F292

France. Conseil d'État. Arrest ... par lequel Sa Majesté casse & annule ... le bail des fermes generales fait à la Compagnie des Indes. Paris, Veuve Saugrain & P. Prault, 1719.   F293
   The Compagnie des Indes is made the sole collector of royal revenues.

France. Conseil d'État. Arrest ... pour la prise de possession de la Ferme des Domaines d'Occident, sous le nom d'Aymard Lambert, pour six années qui commenceront le premier janvier 1719. Paris, Imprimerie Royale, 1719.
F294

France. Conseil d'État. Arrest ... pour la prise de possession de bail des fermes generales unies, par la Compagnie des Indes, sous le nom d'Armand Pillavoine ... Paris, Veuve Saugrain & P. Prault, 1719. F295
  Another regulation concerning the lease of all state revenues by the Compagnie des Indes.

France. Conseil d'État. Arrest ... qui commet les srs. Robineau & Cochois, pour signer au lieu & place des directeurs de la Compagnie des Indes les marques en parchemin ... provenant du commerce de ladite compagnie. Paris, Imprimerie Royale, 1719. F296

France. Conseil d'État. Arrest ... qui ordonne le remboursement de toutes les rentes perpetuelles sur l'Hôtel de Ville de Paris. Paris, Imprimerie Royale, 1719. F297
  A decree in connection with John Law's scheme to liquidate the French national debt.

France. Conseil d'État. Arrest ... qui ordonne qu' à commencer du premier janvier 1720 toutes les rentes assignées sur la ferme des greffes & autres fonds & revenus de l'estat; les augmentations de gages ... Paris, Imprimerie Royale, 1719. F298

France. Conseil d'État. Arrest ... qui ordonne que les commis & employes dans les sous-fermes, continuëront leurs exercices sans estre tenus de prêter de nouveaux sermens. Paris, V. Saugrain [1719]. F299

France. Conseil d'État. Arrest ... qui ordonne que tous commis, capitaines, gardes, & autres employez par la Compagnie des Indes, pour les gabelles, cinq grosses fermes, tabac, aydes, papier & parchemin timbrez, controlle des actes, greffes, domaines, amortissemens & francs-fiefs ... Paris, Veuve Saugrain & Pierre Prault [1719]. F300

France. Conseil d'État. Arrest ... qui ordonne une diminution sur les nouvelles especes & les matieres d'or & d'argent. Toulouse, Claude-Gilles Le Camus [1719]. F301

France. Conseil d'État. Arrest ... qui permet la vente à Nantes des marchandises venües des Indes par les vaisseaux de la Compagnie de France. Paris, Imprimerie Royale, 1719. F302

France. Conseil d'État. Arrest ... concernant les actions de la Compagnie des Indes. Du 24 octobre 1720. Paris, Imprimerie Royale, 1720. F303

France. Conseil d'État. Arrest ... concernant les actions de la Compagnie des Indes. Du 3 juin 1720. Paris, Imprimerie Royale, 1720. F304

France. Conseil d'État. Arrest ... concernant les actions interessées non remplies de la Compagnie des Indes. Paris, Imprimerie Royale, 1720. F305

France. Conseil d'État. Arrest ... du vingt-septiéme may 1720 ... concernant les actions de la Compagnie des Indes & les billets de banque. Grenoble, G. Giroud [1720]. F306
  Annulment of an earlier decree concerning the shares of the Compagnie des Indes and the bank notes.

France. Conseil d'État. Arrest ... en faveur de la Compagnie des Indes: Ordonne que les toiles peintes & etoffes des Indes ne seront plus brûlées, qu'elles seront remises à la Compagnie ... Paris, La Veuve & M.G. Jouvenel [1720]. F307

France. Conseil d'État. Arrest ... en faveur de la Compagnie des Indes. Paris, Imprimerie Royale, 1720. F308
  Reaffirms the company's rights in the tobacco trade, coinage, and taxation.

France. Conseil d'État. Arrest ... en faveur de tous les commis employez par la Compagnie des Indes, au sujet des privilèges ... Paris, Veuve Saugrain & P. Prault, 1720. F309
  Employees of the Compagnie des Indes are entitled to privileges and exemptions, such as billeting of soldiers.

France. Conseil d'État. Arrest ... ordonne l'execution de l'édit du présant mois, qui accorde à la Compagnie des Indes ... tous les droites & privilèges concernant son commerce. Paris, Imprimerie Royale, 1720. F310
  The Compagnie des Indes is given perpetual commercial privileges in return for assuming the obligation of redeeming 600 million livres in bank notes formerly held by the government.

France. Conseil d'État. Arrest ... par lequel Sa Majesté nomme les Srs. Le Pelletier Desforts, d'Ormesson & de Landivisiau commissaires généraux, tant de la banque, que de la Compagnie des Indes. Paris, Imprimerie Royale, 1720. F311

France. Conseil d'État. Arrest ... portant défenses ... d'introduire dans le royaume aucunes étoffes ou toiles des Indes ... [Lille? 1720.] F312

France. Conseil d'État. Arrest ... portant que les arrêts rendus pour la confirmation des privilèges accordez à la Compagnie des Indes Orientales

seront executez. Paris, Veuve Saugrain & Pierre Prault, 1720. F313
   A reprint of a decree of November 30, 1688.

France. Conseil d'État. Arrest ... portant règlement entre la Compagnie des Indes, & les marchands et habitants de la ville de Dieppe. Paris, J.F. Knapen, 1720. F314
   Relates to fishing and salting of fish by Dieppe merchants.

France. Conseil d'État. Arrest ... portant règlement por la vente des marchandises arrivées par les vaisseaux La Paix, Le Comte de Toulouse & Les deux Couronnes. Paris, Imprimerie Royale, 1720. F315
   The three ships belonged to the Compagnie des Indes.

France. Conseil d'État. Arrest ... portant règlement pour l'entrepost des marchandises prohibées, et qui renouvelle les deffenses du port et de l'usage des etoffes des Indes et de la Chine. Paris, Imprimerie Royale, 1720. F316

France. Conseil d'État. Arrest ... portant règlement pour les billets de banque, et les actions de la Compagnie des Indes. Paris, Imprimerie Royale, 1720. F317

France. Conseil d'État. Arrest ... qui accorde a réunit à perpétuité à la Compagnie des Indes le privilege exclusif pour le commerce de la côte de Guinée. Paris, Imprimerie Royale, 1720. F318

France. Conseil d'État. Arrest ... qui décharge les directeurs generaux de la Compagnie du Commerce des Indes Orientales, du payement du droit d'un pour cent, accordé par Sa Majesté aux habitans de la Rochelle. Paris, Veuve Saugrain & Pierre Prault, 1720. F319
   A reprint of a decree of August 4, 1674.

France. Conseil d'État. Arrest ... qui exempte des quatre sols pour livre, ceux qui payeront les droits des fermes generales de Sa Majesté en billets de banque. Paris, Veuve Saugrain & Pierre Prault, 1720. F320
   This decree encourages payment of taxes in bank notes issued by the bank of John Law.

France. Conseil d'État. Arrest ... qui maintient la Compagnie des Indes dans les privileges & exemptions. Paris, Veuve Saugrain & Pierre Prault, 1720. F321
   A reprint of a decree of February 15, 1676.

France. Conseil d'État. Arrest ... qui nomme des commis pour signer & viser les actions rentieres de la Compagnie des Indes. Paris, Imprimerie Royale, 1720. F322

France. Conseil d'État. Arrest ... qui nomme les directeurs de la Compagnie d'Occident. Paris, Veuve Saugrain & P. Prault, 1720. F323
   Six directors are named to conduct the company's affairs.

France. Conseil d'État. Arrest ... qui ordonne l'establissement d'un conseil pour la régie & administration générale de la Compagnie des Indes ... Paris, Imprimerie Royale, 1720. F324
   This document establishes a simplified structure of governance for the Compagnie des Indes, dividing it into fourteen departments and naming the persons in charge of each.

France. Conseil d'État. Arrest ... qui ordonne l'etablissement d'un conseil pour la régie & administration générale de la Compagnie des Indes. Paris, Imprimerie Royale, 1720. F325
   A reprinting of the previous document.

France. Conseil d'État. Arrest ... qui ordonne l'inféodation de l'isle, terre & marquisat de Belle-Isle ... Paris, Veuve Saugrain & P. Prault, 1720. F326
   The Compagnie des Indes is given extensive commercial and cultivation rights in Belle-Isle.

France. Conseil d'État. Arrest ... qui ordonne qu'il ne sera plus envoye de vagabons, gens sans aveû, fraudeurs et criminels à Louisianne. Paris, Veuve Saugrain & P. Prault, 1720. F327
   Prohibits the further deportation of criminals and vagrants to Louisiana.

France. Conseil d'État. Arrest ... qui ordonne qu'il sera fait inventaire des toiles de cotton, etc. ... écorces d'arbes qui se trouveront dans les vaisseaux de la Compagnie des Indes Orientales. Paris, Veuve Saugrain & P. Prault, 1720. F328

France. Conseil d'État. Arrest ... qui ordonne que le commerce du chanvre dans l'interieur du royaume sera libre ... Du 29 decembre 1719. Paris, Imprimerie Royale, 1720. F329
   The Compagnie des Indes is granted permission to establish warehouses and to fix prices for locally produced hemp.

France. Conseil d'État. Arrest ... qui ordonne que le commerce du castor demeurera libre, et convertit le privilege exclusif de la Compagnie des Indes. Paris, Imprimerie Royale, 1720. F330

France. Conseil d'État. Arrest ... qui ordonne que les propriétaires des offices & droits supprimez ... seront remboursez ... Paris, Imprimerie Royale, 1720. F331
   Refers to payment of taxation officials from money loaned to the King by the Compagnie des Indes.

France. Conseil d'État. Arrest ... qui ordonne que les tabacs pourront entrer dans le royaume par le port de l'Orient, & que la manufacture establie dans la ville de l'Orient, y restera nonobstant les dispositions portées par la déclaration du dix-sept octobre dernier. Paris, Veuve Saugrain & Pierre Prault, 1720. F332

    Concerns the rights of l'Orient to continue to engage in the tobacco trade with respect to shipments of that product from Louisiana.

France. Conseil d'État. Arrest ... qui ordonne que toutes les toiles peintes aux Indes seront envoyées hors de royaume aprés le dernier décembre 1688, & le remboursement de celles provenant des ventes de la Compagnie des Indes Orientales. Paris, Veuve Saugrain & P. Prault, 1720. F333

France. Conseil d'État. Arrest ... qui permet ... d'établir une pêche le long de la Cote de l'Acadie & de la Riviere Saint-Jean. Paris, Veuve Saugrain & P. Prault, 1720. F334

France. Conseil d'État. Arrest ... qui permet à la Compagnie des Indes de continüer la conversion en actions de ladite Compagnie non remplies, pendant le cours de present mois de septembre seulement, des actions d'Occident, souscriptions, primes & promesses. Paris, Imprimerie Royale, 1720. F335

France. Conseil d'État. Arrest ... qui permet à tous les sujets de Sa Majesté, de faire venir des tabacs en feüilles de la Havanne & du Levant, en payant les droits d'entrée au brut ... Paris, Imprimerie Royale, 1720. F336

    Import duties are levied on tobacco from Cuba and from the Levant.

France. Conseil d'État. Arrest ... qui permet aux directeurs interessez en l'armément du vaisseau nommé la Paix, de vendre ... les quinze cens balles de caffé dont il est chargé. Paris, Imprimerie Royale, 1720. F337

France. Conseil d'État. Arrest ... qui permettent au sujets du Roy & aux etrangers de faire commerce dans les Indes Orientales, à condition de se servir des vaisseaux de la Compagnie des Indes. Paris, Veuve Saugrain & Pierre Prault, 1720. F338

    A reprint of decrees of January 6 and 20, 1682.

France. Conseil d'État. Arrest ... qui revoque, à compter du jour de la publication du present arrest, le privilege exclusif de la vente du tabac accordé à Jean Ladmiral ... et permet à tous les sujets de Sa Majesté d'en faire commerce en gros & en detail, même de la faire fabriquer ... Paris, Imprimerie Royale, 1720. F339

    While the trade and manufacture of tobacco is made free it is forbidden to plant or cultivate it in France.

France. Conseil d'État. Arrest ... qui revoque tous les affranchissemens des tailles & autres impositions ... et ordonne que les acquereurs ... seront remboursez de la finance par eux payée, sur le caissier de la Compagnie des Indes. Paris, Imprimerie Royale, 1720. F340

France. Conseil d'État. Arrest ... qui supprime tous les droits, de quelque nature ils soient, qui se percevoient dans les echelles de Levant & de Barbarie par les consuls de France. [Paris, Imprimerie Royale, 1720.] F341

France. Conseil d'État. Arrest ... en interpretation de celuy de 10 juin 1721 qui renouvelle les défenses ... des etoffes des Indes, de la Chine & du Levant. [Lille, 1721.] F342

    A reprinting of the previous document.

France. Conseil d'État. Arrest ... en interpretation de celuy du 10. juin 1721 qui renouvelle les deffenses de l'introduction dans le royaume, et du commerce, port, & usage des étoffes des Indes, de la Chine & du Levant ... Paris, Veuve Saugrain & P. Prault, 1721. F343

France. Conseil d'État. Arrest ... portant restablissement du privilege exclusif de la vente du castor, en faveur de la Compagnie des Indes. Paris, Imprimerie Royale, 1721. F344

France. Conseil d'État. Arrest ... qui commet Jean Camialle pour signer au lieu & place du nommé Cochois, les marques en parchemin ... provenant du commerce de la Compagnie des Indes. Paris, Imprimerie Royale, 1721. F345

France. Conseil d'État. Arrest ... qui ordonne que les traitez faits avec la Compagnie des Indes pour raison du benefice des monnoyes ... demeureront nuls & resolus. Paris, Veuve Saugrain & P. Prault, 1721. F346

    Discharges the Compagnie des Indes from collecting taxes, except on tobacco.

France. Conseil d'État. Arrest ... qui permet à tous negocians de faire le commerce du Levant par le port de Cette. [n.p., 1721.] F347

    Cette is to be used as the port of departure for ships engaged in the Levant trade until the province of Languedoc is able to control a contagious disease which has seriously disrupted the Levant trade normally proceeding from that area.

France. Conseil d'État. Arrest ... qui permet l'usage des etoffes des Indes dans la ville & territoire de Marseille. [Paris] Veuve & G. Jouvenel [1721]. F348

France. Conseil d'État. Arrest ... qui renouvelle les défenses, cy-devant faites, de l'introduction dans le royaume, & du commerce, port & usage de étoffes des Indes, de la Chine & du Levant; & des toiles peintes, et autres venant desdits pays. Paris, La veuve & G. Jouvenel, 1721. F349

France. Conseil d'État. Arrest ... qui renouvelle les deffenses d'introduire dans le royaume ou faire aucun commerce ni usage de toiles peintes ou étoffes des Indes, de la Chine ou du Levant ... provenant des ventes faites par les directeurs de la Compagnie des Indes. Paris, G. Jouvenel, 1721. F350

France. Conseil d'État. Arrest ... qui resilie & annulle, à commencer du premier septembre 1721 le bail de la ferme generale de la vente exclusive des tabacs ... fait à la Compagnie d'Occident ... & revoque ... le privilege de l'entrée & vente en gros des tabacs, qui avoit été accordé ladite Compagnie des Indes par la declaration du 17 octobre 1720. Paris, Veuve Saugrain, & Pierre Prault, 1721. F351

France. Conseil d'État. Arrest ... qui surseoit l'execution de celuy du 30. may 1721 qui rêtablit, en faveur de la Compagnie des Indes, le privilege exclusif de la vente du castor. Paris, Imprimerie Royale, 1721. F352
Reaffirms the monopoly of the Compagnie des Indes on the beaver trade.

France. Conseil d'État. Arrest ... concernant les marchandises de fabrique estrangere, qui seront saisies en Canada. [Paris, Imprimerie Royale, 1722.] F353
Foreign goods seized in Canada were to be returned to France as the property of the Compagnie des Indes.

France. Conseil d'État. Arrest ... par lequel Sa Majesté fait don à la Compagnie des Indes, à perpetuité, des munitions ... Paris, Imprimerie Royale, 1722. F354
Confirms the right of the Compagnie des Indes to movables found in forts and warehouses in Guinea.

France. Conseil d'État. Arrest ... portant reglement pour la ferme generale du tabac, en interpretation de l'article xi de la declaration du Roy du premier aoust 1721. Et lettres pattentes sur iceluy. Paris, V. Saugrain, & Pierre Prault, 1722. F355

France. Conseil d'État. Arrest ... qui décharge de tous les droits des fermes de Sa Majesté, & de ceux des seigneurs particuliers, villes & communautés, péages, octrois, & autres generalement quelsconques, tant les tabacs fabriquez, que les matieres & ustancils servant à leur fabrication ... Paris, Veuve Saugrain & Pierre Prault, 1722. F356

France. Conseil d'État. Arrest ... qui ordonne l'execution de celuy du 30 may 1721, portant establissement du privilege exclusif de la vente de castor, en faveur de la Compagnie des Indes. Paris, Imprimerie Royale, 1722. F357
Rejects a request for revocation of the order granting monopoly in the beaver trade to the Compagnie des Indes.

France. Conseil d'État. Arrest ... qui permet à la Compagnie des Indes de faire entrer par les ports de l'Orient & de Nantes, les soyes cruës ... Paris, Georges Jouvenel [1722]. F358

France. Conseil d'État. Arrest ... concernant le droit de marque de tabac, establi par la déclaration du premier aoust 1721. Paris, Veuve Saugrain & P. Prault, 1723. F359
Regulations concerning taxes on tobacco.

France. Conseil d'État. Arrest ... concernant le droit de marque du tabac, établi par la declaration du premier août 1721. [n.p.] C.M. Cramé [1723]. F360

France. Conseil d'État. Arrest ... pour faire remettre à la Compagnie des Indes les etoffes des Indes & autres qui seront saisies par les employez de fermes. Paris, Imprimerie Royale, 1723. F361

France. Conseil d'État. Arrest ... pour faire remettre dans les magasins de la Compagnie des Indes, sous deux clefs, les cafez ... Paris, Imprimerie Royale, 1723. F362
Requires all merchants dealing in coffee to declare their stocks as of November 1, 1723, the date the monopoly of the Compagnie des Indes became effective.

France. Conseil d'État. Arrest ... pour indiquer une assemblée de la Compagnie des Indes, à l'effet de procéder à l'election de huit syndics. Paris, Imprimerie Royale, 1723. F363

France. Conseil d'État. Arrest ... pour la marque du tabac. Du 4. septembre 1723. [Paris, Imprimerie Royale, 1723.] F364
Regulations concerning the marking of various qualities of tobacco for purposes of taxation.

France. Conseil d'État. Arrest ... pour la prise de possession par la Compagnie des Indes du privilège de la vente exclusive du caffé, sous le nom de Pierre le Sueur ... [Paris, 1723.] F365

France. Conseil d'État. Arrest ... qui accorde à la Compagnie des Indes le privilège exclusif de la vente du caffé. Paris, Imprimerie Royale, 1723.
F366

France. Conseil d'État. Arrest ... qui décharge du Parisis du droit de la prevosté d'Angers à l'entrée du royaume, les sucres mascouades & autres marchandises ... Paris, Imprimerie Royale, 1723.
F367
A reprint of a privilege consisting of exemptions from import taxes originally granted in 1685.

France. Conseil d'État. Arrest ... qui forme le conseil de la Compagnie des Indes, et fixe le dividende des actions. Paris, Veuve Saugrain & Pierre Prault, 1723.
F368

France. Conseil d'État. Arrest ... qui ordonne que ... il sera passé contract d'alienation à la Compagnie des Indes du privilege exclusif de la vente du tabac. Paris, Imprimerie Royale, 1723.
F369

France. Conseil d'État. Arrest ... qui ordonne que les commis & employez de la Compagnie des Indes pour l'exploitation des privileges du tabac & du café, procederont aux visites & execution au sujet des toiles peintes & etoffes des Indes, de la Chine & du Levant. [n.p., 1723].
F370

France. Conseil d'État. Arrest ... qui ordonne que les proprietaires & porteurs des billets d'emprunt de la Compagnie des Indes ... seront tenus de les remettre dans le premier octobre prochain pour tout delay, au Garde du Tresor Royale ... [n.p.] C.M. Cramé [1723].
F371

France. Conseil d'État. Arrest ... qui ordonne que par les commissaires du conseil qui seront nommez à cet effet, il sera passé contrat d'alienation à la Compagnie des Indes, du privilege exclusif de la vente du tabac. Toulouse, D. G. Lecamus, 1723.
F372

France. Conseil d'État. Arrest ... qui ordonne que par les commissaires du conseil qui seront nommez à cet effet, il sera passé contract d'alienation à la Compagnie des Indes du privilege exclusif de la vente du tabac. Paris, Imprimerie Royale, 1723.
F373

France. Conseil d'État. Arrest ... qui ordonne que par les commissaires du conseil qui seront nommez à cet effet, il sera passé contract d'alienation à la Compagnie des Indes du privilege exclusif de la vente du tabac. [n.p.] C.M. Cramé [1723].
F374

France. Conseil d'État. Arrest ... qui proroge jusqu'au premier octobre 1724 la moderation des droits d'entrée sur le charbon de terre ... [Lyons, P. Valfray, 1723.]
F375
Specifies duties on coals coming from Scotland, England, and Ireland.

France. Conseil d'État. Arrest ... qui règle la forme de l'administration de la Compagnie des Indes. Paris, Imprimerie Royale, 1723. F376
The company will henceforth be administered by twelve directors.

France. Conseil d'État. Arrest ... qui renouvelles des défenses ... de l'introduction dans le royaume, & du commerce, port, & usage des étoffes des Indes ... Lille, 1723.
F377
Lists in detail cloths that are not to be imported.

France. Conseil d'État. Arrest ... qui resilie, à commencer au premier octobre prochain 1723 le bail fait à Edoüard Duverdier le 19 août 1721 de la ferme de tabac. [n.p., 1723].
F378

France. Conseil d'État. Arrest ... servant de reglement pour la forme & maniere en laquelle seront faites les déclarations des marchands negocians, pour les marchandises ... Paris, Veuve & M.G. Jouvenel, 1723.
F379

France. Conseil d'État. Arrest ... concernant le privilege éxclusif des loteries ... Paris, Imprimerie Royale, 1724.
F380
The privilege of lotteries is granted to the Compagnie des Indes.

France. Conseil d'État. Arrest ... portant nouveau règlement, pour empêcher l'entree, l'usage & le port, des etoffes des Indes, de la Chine & du Levant ... Paris, Veuve & G. Jouvenel, 1724.
F381
A decree providing measures to stop the importation of the Oriental textiles and to reward the custom officials.

France. Conseil d'État. Arrest ... portant reglement pour ... offices de vendeurs de poisson de mer ... Paris, Veuve Saugrain & P. Prault, 1724.
F382
Regulations upon the fishing trade along the coasts of Normandy and Piccardy, originally issued in 1680.

France. Conseil d'État. Arrest ... portant reglement sur les fonds en argent ou en marchandises, qui seront furtivement chargez sur les vaisseaux de la Compagnie des Indes. Paris, Imprimerie Royale, 1724.
F383

France. Conseil d'État. Arrest ... qui accorde à la Compagnie des Indes l'exemption des droits d'octrois ... sur tous les cafez qu'elle fera entrer ... Paris, Imprimerie Royale, 1724.
F384

Exempts the Compagnie des Indes from coffee duties in Toulouse and Nantes.

France. Conseil d'État. Arrest ... qui fait deffenses aux habitans des parroisses situées dans les trois lieuës des limites des provinces de Champagne, Bourgogne & Bresse, dénommées au present arrest, de faire aucune plantation & culture de tabac, d'en tenir des magasins & entrepostz, soit en feüilles, en corde en poudre ou autrement fabriquez. Paris, Imprimerie Royale, 1724. F385
This decree gives a concise statement of the nature of the tobacco monopoly in the provinces indicated.

France. Conseil d'État. Arrest ... qui permet qux capitaines generaux préposez pour la regie du privilege des ventes exclusives du tabac & du café ... Paris, Imprimerie Royale, 1724. F386
Permits the search of premises suspected of holding coffee and tobacco in violation of the monopoly of the Compagnie des Indes.

France. Conseil d'État. Arrest ... concernant la signature des marques en parchemin à attacher au chef ... provenant du commerce de la Compagnie des Indes. Paris, Imprimerie Royale, 1725. F387

France. Conseil d'État. Arrest ... qui ordonne que les sucres & autres marchandises qui seront declarées provenir de la traitte des nègres, pour le compte des négocians qui ont fait le commerce en Guinée ... païeront dans les ports designez ... la totalité des droits portez par les lettres patentes ... [Paris] Veuve & M.-G. Jouvenel [1725]. F388

France. Conseil d'État. Arrest ... qui ordonne que les sucres de Cayenne provenans de la traite des noirs, que la Compagnie des Indes fera entrer dans le royaume par les ports de Bretagne, ne payeront à leur arrivée que la moitié des droits de la Prevôte de Nantes ... [Paris] Veuve & M.-G. Jouvenel [1725]. F389

France. Conseil d'État. Arrest ... qui ordonne que toutes les toilles peintes, étoffes de la Chine & du Levant, mousselines, etc. seront brûlées ... Paris, Veuve & G. Jouvenel, 1725. F390

France. Conseil d'État. Arrêt ... concernant les défenses faites ... dans les pays de la concession de la Compagnie des Indes. Paris, A. Boudet, 1726. F391
Independent merchants who encroach on the concessions of the Compagnie des Indes will be punished and their vessels confiscated.

France. Conseil d'État. Arrest ... portant confirmation des privileges accordez à la Compagnie des Indes, & exemption de droits en faveur de ladite Compagnie. Paris, Veuve Saugrain & Pierre Prault, 1726. F392

France. Conseil d'État. Arrest ... pour la prise de possession du bail de la ferme generale des domaines d'occident ... Pierre Carlier ... Paris, Imprimerie Royale, 1726. F393

France. Conseil d'État. Arrest ... qui modere les droits d'entrée sur le thé à dix sols la livre pesant poids de marc. Paris, Imprimerie Royale, 1726. F394

France. Conseil d'État. Arrest ... qui ordonne conformément à l'arrest ... que la caution d'Olanier & Audifred sera tenuë de payer à Nerville les droits de la foraine de Languedoc pour trente-deux balles de toilles de coton achetées ... à Nantes & declarées pour Avignon. Paris, Veuve Saugrain & Pierre Prault, 1726. F395

France. Conseil d'État. Arrest ... qui réitere les défenses de faire commerce, port, & usage des étoffes & toiles peintes des Indes ... Lille, C. M. Cramé, 1726. F396

France. Conseil d'État. Arrest ... au sujet du dépost des marchandises des Indes, de la Chine & du Levant qui auront esté saisies. Paris, Imprimerie Royale, 1727. F397

France. Conseil d'État. Arrest ... portant reglement general pour le commerce du tabac au Comté de Bourgogne. Paris, Imprimerie Royale, 1727. F398
Burgundy is identified as the source of a very large amount of contraband tobacco, and this set of twenty-six regulations is designed to remedy that situation.

France. Conseil d'État. Arrest ... portant reglement au sujet des contestations entre l'Amirauté de France & les fermiers généraux. Paris, Imprimerie Royale, 1728. F399
Concerns smuggling and contraband.

France. Conseil d'État. Arrest ... qui casse & annule les procédures & sentence diffinitive faites & rendue par les officers de police de la ville de Nuits, contre les employez du tabac ... Paris, P. Prault, 1728. F400
Suspension of a court sentence in a case involving the tobacco trade.

France. Conseil d'État. Arrest ... qui donne l'attribution aux sieurs intendans & commissaires départis dans les provinces de Flandres ... pour connoître des contestations ... Lille, 1728. F401

Gives authorities in certain provinces jurisdiction over cases involving the importation of cloth.

France. Conseil d'État. Arrest ... qui ordonne que les habitans de la ville de Marseille ... joüiront ... des exemptions ... en faveur du commerce. Paris, Veuve Saugrin & P. Prault, 1728. F402
Declares the port of Marseilles free for all kinds of commodities.

France. Conseil d'État. Arrest ... concernant le commerce de Guinée. Paris, Imprimerie Royale, 1729. F403
Requires that merchants trading from West Africa to Holland and northern Europe must register with the admirality.

France. Conseil d'État. Arrest ... qui fixe à quatre sols la livre pesant, les droits d'entrée du cacao. Paris, Imprimerie Royale, 1729. F404
Reduces the duty on cacao from the island of Carak in the Caribbean from earlier levels decreed in 1693 and 1717.

France. Conseil d'État. Arrest ... qui ordonne l'execution dans les port & ville de Dunquerque, des édits, déclarations, arrests, & reglemens concernat le commerce de la Compagnie des Indes. Paris, Imprimerie Royale, 1729. F405
Notes the manner in which the Chamber of Commerce of Dunkirk has flouted regulatory laws, particularly in the coffee trade.

France. Conseil d'État. Arrest ... concernant les formalitez à observer, pour le transit des sucres rafinez dans le roïaume. Rouen, J.B. Besongne, 1730. F406
Regulations conerning the distribution of refined sugar within France.

France. Conseil d'État. Arrest ... por faire retirer les actions de la Compagnie des Indes. Paris, Imprimerie Royale, 1730. F407

France. Conseil d'État. Arrest ... portant exemption de logemens de gens de guerre, pour tous les commis qui seront employés dans les bureaux & magasins de maître Jean Breton, Fermier du Tabac. [Paris, Veuve Saugrain & Pierre Prault, 1730.] F408
A prohibition upon lodging troops in any warehouses or other places designated to the Fermier du Tabac. Reprint of a law of 1675.

France. Conseil d'État. Arrest ... portant permission aux fermiers du tabac, de faire visite dans les places, châteaux, maisons royales, celle des princes & seigneurs, convents & communautes. [Paris, Veuve Saugrain & Pierre Prault, 1730.] F409

France. Conseil d'État. Arrest ... portant qu'il sera ouvert une loterie ... pour le remboursement de ... actions de la Compagnie des Indes. Paris, Imprimerie Royale, 1730. F410

France. Conseil d'État. Arrest ... qui déclare les caffées venans pour le compte de la Compagnie des Indes, exempte de tous droits de péages. Paris, Veuve Saugrain & P. Prault, 1730. F411

France. Conseil d'État. Arrest ... qui déclare les tabacs destinez pour la provision de la Ferme generale du Tabac, exempts de tous droits d'octroys, d'admodiations, ou autres de la ville de Mezieres ... [Paris, Veuve Saugrain & Pierre Prault, 1730.] F412
Republication of a decree of 1712 incorporating provisions of several decrees of the previous five years.

France. Conseil d'État. Arrest ... qui défend au lieutenant criminel & officiers du bailliage de Gray, de connoître à l'avenir sous quelque prétexte que ce soit, des affaires concernant la regie du tabac, tant en matiere civile que criminelle ... [Paris, Veuve Saugrain & Pierre Prault, 1730.] F413
Concerns the prosecution of persons arrested for tobacco fraud in Franche-Comté.

France. Conseil d'État. Arrest ... qui défend aux juges des traites foraines de Dijon, & à tous autres juges, d'admettre la preuve testimoniale contre les procés-verbaux des Commis du Tabac ... [Paris, Veuve Saugrain & Pierre Prault, 1730.] F414
Decree covering admission of testimony in tobacco fraud cases.

France. Conseil d'État. Arrest ... qui dénomme les paroisses de l'Artois, qui sont dans la distance des trois lieuës de Picardie, & des paroisses de l'Artois, qui sont dans la distance de trois lieuës du pays de Boulonnois, au sujet des magasins, plantations, fabrique & vente du tabac, &c. [Paris, Veuve Saugrain & Pierre Prault, 1730.] F415
Re-issue of a decree of 1690 concerning jurisdiction of the Ferme du Tabac in Artois, Picardie and Boulonnois.

France. Conseil d'État. Arrest ... qui fait main levée des saisies de tabac, faites sur deux débitans de la ville d'Avranches ... sous pretexte qu'ils n'avoient pas payé lesdits droits; & qui ordonne que le tabac sera exempt desdits droits. Paris, Veuve Saugrain & Pierre Prault, 1730. F416
A dispute over seizure of tobacco leads to a regulation that tobacco destined for the provisioning of the Ferme and to be consumed there should not be subject to duty.

France. Conseil d'État. Arrest ... qui ordonne l'execution de la sentence du Viguier de Toulouse, du 13 juin 1690, qui condamne les nommés Pierre Verdier, Jean Becq, & Pierre Baissiere, pour fraude de tabac, en cinq cens livres chacun d'amende ... [Paris, Veuve Saugrain & Pierre Prault, 1730.] F417
Reprint of a case from 1690 which was based upon violation of an ordinance of 1681.

France. Conseil d'État. Arrest ... qui ordonne la confiscation de quatorze ballots de tabac saisis sur le vaisseau le Saint Jean-Baptiste ... & condamne le capitaine en l'amende de mille livres pour n'avoir pas fait sa déclaration des tabacs au port de Marseille ... [Paris, Veuve Saugrain et Pierre Prault, 1730.] F418
The *Saint Jean-Baptiste*, Captain Joseph Bocry, carried tobacco among other things from Amsterdam, and failed to declare it at Marseilles.

France. Conseil d'État. Arrest ... qui ordonne qu'en interpretant l'Article XXI de l'ordonnance du mois de juillet 1681. le Fermier du Tabac, & ses sous-fermiers auront sur les tabacs en feüilles la mesme preference qu'ils ont sur les tabacs fabriquez, en payant le prix qui aura esté convenu entre le vendeur & l'acheteur ... [Paris, Veuve Saugrain et Pierre Prault, 1730.] F419
Re-issue of a decree of 1712 regarding the sale of manufactured and unmanufactured tobacco.

France. Conseil d'État. Arrest ... qui ordonne que les Commis du Tabac, mis ès prisons d'Arras par de prétendus archers & une troupe de paysans, seront élargis. Paris, Veuve Saugrain et Pierre Prault, 1730. F420
Calls for the restitution of tobacco illegally confiscated.

France. Conseil d'État. Arrest ... qui ordonne que les tabacs du crû du royaume, & autres tabacs destines pour les pays etrangers, ne pourront sortir que par les ports y denommés à peine de confiscation, & de trois mille livres d'amende. [Paris, Veuve Saugrain & Pierre Prault, 1730.] F421
Fourteen ports are named as points from which tobacco may be shipped. Reprint of a law of 1676.

France. Conseil d'État. Arrest ... qui permet à la Compagnie des Indes, de vendre & faire vendre les tabacs superieurs, composés de feüilles des crûs de Guyenne & Languedoc, où les plantations avoient lieu avant la suppression qui en a esté ordonnée par l'arrest du conseil du 29 decembre 1719 ... [Paris, Veuve Saugrain & Pierre Prault, 1730.] F422
Tobacco remaining from Guienne and Languedoc after the suppression of production there by decree of 29 December 1719 would be available to the Compagnie des Indes.

France. Conseil d'État. Arrest ... qui permet aux habitans des generalités de Bordeaux & Montauban, & des environs de Montdragon, Saint Maixant, Lery & Metz, de continuer la recolte des tabacs ... [Paris, Veuve Saugrain & Pierre Prault, 1730.] F423
Reprint of a law of 1676 restricting the cultivation of tobacco to designated areas.

France. Conseil d'État. Arrest ... qui renouvelle les deffenses de l'introduction, port, & usage des toiles peintes ou teintes ... de la Chine, des Indes & du Levant ... Paris, Imprimerie Royale, 1730. F424

France. Conseil d'État. Arrest ... rendu sur l'avis de Monsieur Feideau de Brou, qui reduit la plantation du tabac dans les paroisses de Lery, Lesdamps, & Vaudreuil & leurs dépendances, à cent acres de terre; & en fixe le prix à dix livres du cent pesant. [Paris, Veuve Saugrain & Pierre Prault, 1730.] F425
Both fraud in the production of tobacco and the poor quality of it are reasons for reducing the acreage designated for production.

France. Conseil d'État. Arrest ... concernant les declarations à fournir pour le café qui entre & sort de la ville de Marseille. Paris, Imprimerie Royale, 1731. F426

France. Conseil d'État. Arrest ... par lequel il est permis aux Commis de la Ferme du Tabac ... de faire vendre sur la permission des juges royaux ou leurs lieutenans ... tous les effets saisis sur les fraudeurs, ou par eux abandonnez. Du 25 juillet 1713. [Paris, Veuve de Georges Jouvenel, 1731.] F427
Re-issue of a decree of 1713 authorizing sale of equipment seized from persons violating the tobacco sale regulations.

France. Conseil d'État. Arrest ... par lequel le Roy accepte la retrocession faite à Sa Majesté, par les syndics & directeurs de la Compagnie des Indes ... du privilege du commerce de la coste de Barbarie. Paris, Imprimerie Royale, 1731. F428

France. Conseil d'État. Arrests ... qui déclarent des caffés saisis pour fausse déclaration ... au profit de la Compagnie des Indes ... Paris, Veuve Saugrain & P. Prault, 1731. F429

France. Conseil d'État. Arrest ... qui ordonne que le Sieur Jacques Auriol & ses associez joüiront pendant dix années, à commencer au premier janvier 1731 au lieu & place de la Compagnie des Indes, du commerce de la coste de Barbarie, pour en joüir & y faire le commerce exclusif, sous le nom de Compagnie d'Afrique. Paris, Veuve Saugrain & Pierre Prault, 1731. F430

France. Conseil d'État. Arrest ... qui permet l'entrée sur le port de Marseille des caffez venant des echelles du Levant ... Paris, Veuve Saugrain & P. Prault, 1731. F431

France. Conseil d'État. Arrest ... concernant la vente & distribution du tabac dans les villes de Dole, Gray & Lons-le-Saunier: et reglement pour empêcher la fraude dans la province de Franche-Comté. Du 14 octobre 1732. [n.p., ca. 1732.] F432
Strict regulations for the sale of tobacco in the towns named in response to violations of earlier regulatory legislation.

France. Conseil d'État. Arrest ... concernant les sucres rafinez à Sette. Paris, Imprimerie Royale, 1732. F433

France. Conseil d'État. Arrest ... portant reglement sur l'entrée des marchandises du crû & fabrique d'Angleterre, Ecosse, Irelande & pays en dépendans. Paris, Veuve G. Jouvenel, 1732. F434

France. Conseil d'État. Arrest ... qui déboute les habitans des paroisses & communautez de Comtes, Cauron & St. Vast en Artois, à eux joints les estats de ladite province, de leurs demandes ... Paris, Imprimerie Royale, 1732. F435
The inhabitants of the towns mentioned are acquitted of a recent legal action against them, but are to conform to earlier legislation with respect to the tobacco trade.

France. Conseil d'État. Arrest ... qui fait défenses d'aller ni d'envoyer à la pêche du haran ... Paris, Veuve Saugrain & P. Prault, 1732. F436
A restriction against fishing for herring after the end of December, the fish taken after that date being of poor quality.

France. Conseil d'État. Arrest ... qui fixe à six livres du cent pesant, les droits d'entrée sur les thez provenant des ventes faites par la Compagnie des Indes à Nantes ... Paris, Imprimerie Royale, 1732. F437

France. Conseil d'État. Arrest ... qui ordonne la suppression des secondes marques en parchemin & en plomb sur les toiles de coton blanches, mousselines & mouchoirs, provenant des pays de la concession de la Compagnie des Indes. Paris, Imprimerie Royale, 1732. F438

France. Conseil d'État. Arrest ... concernant les marques qui doivent estre apposées sur les toiles de coton blanches, mousselines & mouchoirs, provenant des ventes de la Compagnie des Indes. Paris, Imprimerie Royale, 1733. F439

France. Conseil d'État. Arrest ... portant reglement pour empescher les fraudes & abus qui se commettent à l'occasion de la vente des tabacs à diminution de prix sur les frontieres des provinces privilegiées. Paris, Imprimerie Royale, 1733. F440
An attempt at prevention of tobacco sales below the official price.

France. Conseil d'État. Arrest ... qui fixe ... les droits d'entrée des cinq grosses fermes sur les toiles de coton, mousselines ... provenant des ventes de la Compagnie des Indes. Paris, Imprimerie Royale, 1733. F441

France. Conseil d'État. Arrest ... qui ordonne ... les actionnaires de l'ancienne Compagnie des Indes Orientales ... à la nomination de syndics ... Paris, Guillaume Saugrain, 1733. F442
Requires the naming of spokesmen to present the company's case to the Compagnie d'Occident.

France. Conseil d'État. Arrest ... qui ordonne que ... il sera procédé par les actionnaires de l'ancienne Compagnie des Indes Orientales ... de deffendre à celles des directeurs de la nouvelle Compagnie d'Occident. Paris, Guillaume Saugrain, 1733. F443
The Compagnie des Indes Orientales is required to appoint spokesmen to settle affairs with the Compagnie d'Occident, which had acquired most of the rights and privileges held by the former company.

France. Conseil d'État. Arrest ... portant nouveau règlement pour empêcher l'entrée, le port & usage des toiles peintes ou teintes ... de la Chine ... Lille, C.M. Cramé, 1736. F444

France. Conseil d'État. Arrest ... portant reglement pour empescher dans l'interieur des provinces de la Ferme, les versemens de tabacs qui sortent de celle d'Alsace. Du 11 decembre 1736. [Paris, Imprimerie Royale, 1736.] F445
An attempt to tighten up the regulations on the transport of tobacco and other commodities from Alsace to other provinces.

France. Conseil d'État. Arrest ... qui permet l'entrée des drogueries & espiceries, par le port du Havre de Grace. Paris, Imprimerie Royale, 1736. F446
Also includes provisions concerning codfish and sugar from the American colonies.

France. Conseil d'État. Arrest ... concernant le produit des confiscations & amendes, provenant des saisies de tabacs de contrabande dans l'es-

tenduë du coustumat de Bayonne. [Paris, Imprimerie Royale, 1737.] F447
 Concerns the disposition of income from confiscated contraband tobacco in a case then pending.

France. Conseil d'État. Arrest ... portant reglement general pour le commerce du tabac au Comté de Bourgogne. Paris, Imprimerie Royale, 1737. F448

France. Conseil d'État. Arrest ... servant de reglement pour la vente & distribution du tabac dans l'estenduë des trois paroisses qui composent la Baronnie d'Estraong en Haynault. Du 30 juillet 1737. [Paris, Imprimerie Royale, 1737.] F449
 An attempt to restore close regulation of the tobacco business in the Barony of Estroang in Haynault where an administrator apparently had been lax, allowing the tobacco trade to develop where it was to have been restricted.

France. Conseil d'État. Arrest ... concernant les actionnaires de l'ancienne Compagnie des Indes Orientales. [Paris] Imprimerie de P.J. Mariette [1738]. F450

France. Conseil d'État. Arrest ... concernant les directeurs de l'ancienne Compagnie des Indes Orientales. [Paris] P. J. Mariette [1738]. F451
 An attempt to clarify the position of the directors of the Compagnie des Indes after it had been merged with the Compagnie d'Occident, and subsequently reorganized.

France. Conseil d'État. Arrest ... qui authorise les cautions de Jacques Forceville adjudicataire de la Ferme du Tabac, à traiter pour se faire subroger aux adjudicataires des Fermes du Tabac de Valenciennes, Saint-Amand, & des autres villes, bourgs & communautez qui ne sont point compris dans l'estenduë de la Ferme generale du Tabac. Paris, Imprimerie Royale, 1738. F452
 Jacques Forceville is deputized to act in the name of the Ferme du Tabac in an area not covered by the Ferme's general jurisdiction.

France. Conseil d'État. Arrest ... qui ordonne le payement ... à la Compagnie royale de la Mer du Sud. Paris, Imprimerie de la veuve Knapen, 1738. F453
 Authorizes an indemnity to the French South Sea Company. Much of the payment is interest, for the case had been pending for forty years.

France. Conseil d'État. Arrest ... qui ordonne qu'à commencer du premier avril 1739 le droit d'avarie d'entrée, dont la levée a esté ordonnée ... dans toutes les eschelles du Levant. Paris, Imprimerie Royale, 1738. F454

France. Conseil d'État. Arrest ... qui ordonne que par l'adjudicataire général des fermes, il sera expédié des acquits à caution pour les marchandises ... Paris, Imprimerie Royale, 1738. F455
 Concerns goods entering France and destined for other countries.

France. Conseil d'État. Arrest ... portant reglement pour le commerce & l'interdiction des plantations, cultures, magasins & entrepots de tabac, dans les trois lieuës de la frontiere de Franche-comté, limitrophes de duchez de Lorraine & de Bar. Paris, Imprimerie Royale, 1739. F456
 The unworkability of earlier legislation makes necessary this new restriction upon the tobacco trade in the area indicated.

France. Conseil d'État. Arrest ... qui maintient les chapitres de l'eglise cathedrale de Saint Estienne, & de l'eglise collegiale de Saint Caprary de la ville d'Agen, dans la possession & jouissance des droits de peage ou leude, sur le sel & poisson salé passant sur la riviere de Garonne. Paris, Imprimerie Royale, 1740. F457

France. Conseil d'État. Arrest ... portant homologation du traité fait par la Compagnie de Senegal. Paris, Imprimerie Royale, 1741. F458
 Confirms an agreement between M. Le Tessier de Montarry and the directors and associates of the Company of Senegal.

France. Conseil d'État. Arrest ... qui fait défenses de modérer les amendes qui seront prononcées contre ceux qui auront contrevenu ... usage des toiles peintes. Lille, C.M. Cramé, 1741. F459

France. Conseil d'État. Arrest ... qui permet aux négocians & armateurs des ports authorisés à faire le commerce des colonies de l'Amérique, d'armer & équiper leurs vaisseaux pour la côte de Guinée ... Du 30. septembre 1741. Lille, Veuve C.M. Cramé, 1741. F460
 This combining of American and African commerce relates to letters patent and legislation from 1716 to 1720.

France. Conseil d'État. Arrest ... et lettres patentes, qui autorisent les capitaines généraux des fermes, à faire des visites dans les maisons privilégiées. Rouen, J.B. Besongne, 1743. F461

France. Conseil d'État. Arrest ... et lettres patentes sur icelui, qui fixent à deux livres par mois la consommation du tabac pour chaque chef de famille du village de Dianne-Capel ... Paris, Imprimerie Royale, 1743. F462
 Limits the amout of tobacco that each head of a family in Dianne-Capel may purchase.

France. Conseil d'État. Arrest ... qui révoque la permission accordée ... aux négocians de Marseille, d'introduire ... des caffés des isles françoise de l'Amérique. Paris, Imprimerie Royale, 1746. F463

The privilege of the Marseilles merchants was revoked because they were smuggling coffee in from the Levant under false label.

France. Conseil d'État. Arrest ... qui permet à la Compagnie des Indes de créer douze cens mille livres de rentes viagères, à prendre sur les neuf millions de rente à elle constituée par Sa Majesté en execution de l'édit du mois de juin dernier. Paris, Imprimerie Royale, 1748. F464

The funds are being raised by the Compagnie des Indes "to satisfy the expenses of the expeditions projected by them."

France. Conseil d'État. Arrest du Conseil d'Etat du roy, portant que les e'quipages des navires revenus des isles de l'Amérique sous l'escorte des vaisseaux de Sa Majesté ... Paris, l'imprimerie Royale, 1748. F465

Law requiring the payment in full of officers and seamen's salaries of fleets returning from American shores.

France. Conseil d'État. Arrest ... portant réglement pour le renouvellement des actions. Paris, Imprimerie Royale, 1749. F466

Regulations concerning the increased number of shares of the Compagnie des Indes.

France. Conseil d'État. Arrest ... qui, en révoquant l'arrêt du Conseil du 4 may 1745, ordonne que, conformément à celuy du 3 may 1723, les marchandises destinées pour les isles & colonies françoises, ne jouiront plus à l'avenir que d'une année d'entrepôt. Pau, Jean Dupoux, 1749. F467

France. Conseil d'État. Arrest ... qui, en révoquant les arrêts du Conseil des 20 avril 1744 & 19 juin 1745 ordonne l'exécution de l'article II des lettres patentes de 1717 pour le retour des navires destinez pour les isles & colonies françoises de l'Amérique, dans le port d'où ils seront parties. Lille, C.M. Cramé, 1749. F468

The decrees of 1744 and 1745, invoked during wartime are hereby revoked, and the regulation requiring ships to return to the ports from which they had embarked for America is reaffirmed.

France. Conseil d'État. Arrest ... qui ordonne qu'il sera incessamment procédé à l'apposition gratuite des nouveaux plombs ... sur toutes les pièces de mousselines ... Lille, C.M. Cramé, 1749. F469

Concerns the marking of imported fabrics.

France. Conseil d'État. Arrest ... qui fixe le prix des tabacs du crû de la Louisiane à trente livres le quintal, dont vingt-sept livres dix sols seront payées par le fermier, & deux livres dix sols par le Roy. Paris, l'Imprimerie Royale, 1750. F470

In addition to fixing prices and taxes upon tobacco from Louisiana, this regulation specifies the manner in which it is to be shipped, ports of entry, and other conditions of importation.

France. Conseil d'État. Arrest ... qui indique les bureaux pour l'entrée des tabacs étrangers, dans la province d'Alsace. Paris, Imprimerie Royale, 1750. F471

France. Conseil d'État. Arrest ... portant interdiction du commerce direct, des ports du royaume sur l'océan, avec ceux des états de Barbarie & de Maroc. Paris, Imprimerie Royale, 1751. F472

France. Conseil d'État. Arrest ... qui ordonne que les droits d'entrée, perçûs sur les cires jaunes venues de l'étranger, seront réstitués ... Aix, Veuve J. David & E. David, 1751. F473

France. Conseil d'État. Arrest ... qui permet l'entrée dans le royaume ... des beurres venant d'Angleterre ... Aix, Veuve J. David & E. David, 1751. F474

France. Conseil d'État. Arrest ... qui homologue les deux délibérations de la Compagnie des Indes, des 24 & 29 décembre 1751; en consequence, autorise ladite compagnie d'emprunter à constitution de rentes la somme de dix-huit millions. Paris, Imprimerie Royale, 1752. F475

Confirmation of two resolutions passed by the Compagnie des Indes authorizing it to raise a sum of eighteen million livres.

France. Conseil d'État. Arrest ... qui ordonne que celui du 5 juin 1725, sera exécuté selon sa forme & teneur, & en conséquence, que faute par le nommé Laurent ... d'avoir payé dans le mois la somme de mille liv. d'amende, en laquelle il a été condamné par ledit arrêt. Paris, P. Prault, 1754. F476

A decree concerning the conviction of Antoine Laurent who had been arrested in 1725 on a charge of smuggling contraband goods.

France. Conseil d'État. Arrest ... qui hómologue la délibération de la Compagnie des Indes, du 18 septembre 1755 en consequense, autorise ladite compagnie d'emprunter à constitution de rentes, la somme de douze millions. Paris, Imprimerie Royale, 1755. F477

France. Conseil d'État. Arrest ... qui ordonne qu'à compter du jour de la publication d'icelui, les armes blanches venant des pays étrangers,

France. Conseil d'État. payeront ... trente pour cent de leur valeur. Paris, Imprimerie Royale, 1755. F478

France. Conseil d'État. Arrest ... qui ordonne que ... tous les savons qui seront fabriqués dans le royaume ... seront déchargés de tous droits de sortie. Paris, Imprimerie Royale, 1757. F479

France. Conseil d'État. Arrest ... qui ordonne qu'il sera de nouveau sursis à l'exécution des lettres patentes du 5 septembre dernier, concernant l'entrée des toiles de coton blanches & les toiles peintes venant de l'étranger. Paris, Imprimerie Royale, 1759. F480

France. Conseil d'État. Arrest ... qui évalue les droits que les toiles, peintes ... venant de l'étranger, payeront a l'entrée ... Lille, C.M. Cramé, 1760. F481

France. Conseil d'État. Arrest ... qui ordonne que ... les huiles de baleines .. jouiront ... l'exemption de droits ... Paris, Imprimerie Royale, 1760. F482

France. Conseil d'État. Arrest ... qui ordonne que, jusqu'à ce qu'il en soit autrement ordonne, les peaux & poils de castor entreront librement dans le royaume. Paris, P. Prault, 1760. F483

France. Conseil d'État. Arrest ... qui juge que tous marchands & negocians, de quelque qualité & condition qu'ils soient, doivent accepter & remplir les places de juge & de consuls auxquelles ils sont élus. Paris, L. Cellot, 1762. F484

Provision for election of judges and consuls in Bordeaux, revoking a law of 1762.

France. Conseil d'État. Arrest ... qui admet le port de Fécamp ... faire directement le commerce des isles & colonies françoises de l'Amérique. Paris, Imprimerie Royale, 1763. F485

France. Conseil d'État. Arrest ... qui admet le port de Grandville au nombre de ceux par lesquels il est permis de faire directement le commerce des isles & colonies françoises de l'Amérique. Lille, N.J.B. Peterinck-Cramé, 1763. F486

France. Conseil d'État. Arrest ... qui fixe des epoques pour le payement des dettes des colonies, contractées en France. [n.p.] Veuve C.M. Cramé, 1763. F487

France. Conseil d'État. Arrest ... qui ordonne qu'à l'avenir les farines de minot venant de l'étranger, payeront ... six sols par quintal. Paris, Imprimerie Royale, 1763. F488

France. Conseil d'État. Arrest ... qui ordonne qu'à l'avenir toutes les dentelles indistinctement, ne payeront que dix sous par livre ... Paris, Imprimerie Royale, 1763. F489

Establishes a low export duty on lace to encourage its manufacture.

France. Conseil d'État. Arrest ... qui ordonne que les lettres de change tirées de l'Isle-Royale, la Louisiane, la Martinique & St. Domingue, sur les exercises 1755. 1756. 1757. & 1758. seront acquittées en 1764. aux époques qui y sont fixées. [n.p.] Veuve C.M. Cramé, 1763. F490

France. Conseil d'État. Arrest ... qui règle les droits à percevoir à toutes les entrées du royaume, sur les sucres vergeois venant de l'étranger. [n.p.] Veuve C.M. Cramé, 1763. F491

France. Conseil d'État. Arrest ... qui règle les droits à percevoir à toutes les entrées du royaume, sur les sucres vergeois de l'étranger. Paris, Imprimerie Royale, 1763. F492

Exempts raw sugar from duties, and explains what sugars are to be termed "raw."

France. Conseil d'État. Arrest ... qui rétablit les droits sur les poissons de pêche etrangère, suivant les anciens réglemens. [n.p.] Veuve C.M. Cramé, 1763. F493

France. Conseil d'État. Arrest ... concernant les reconnoissances qui se seront données en payement des papiers du Canada. Lille, N.J.B. Peterinck-Cramé, 1764. F494

A decree regulating the redemption of Canadian bills of exchange.

France. Conseil d'État. Arrest ... portant réglement pour le dépôt à faire par les dépositaires volontaires ou judiciaires des effets appartenans aux nommés Bigot, Varin & autres ... dans l'affaire du Canada. Lille, N.J.B. Peterinck-Cramé, 1764. F495

France. Conseil d'État. Arrest ... portant réglement pour les déclarations à faire les dépositaires volontaires ou judiciaires des biens des nommés Bigot, Varin & autres condamnés dans l'affair du Canada. Lille, N.J.B. Peterinck-Cramé, 1764. F496

France. Conseil d'État. Arrest ... qui admet le port de Grandville au nombre de ceux par lesquels il est permis de faire directement le commerce des isles & colonies françoises de l'Amérique. Paris, Imprimerie Royale, 1764. F497

France. Conseil d'État. Arrest ... qui ordonne la liquidation des lettres de change & billets de monnoye du Canada. Lille, N.J.B. Peterinck-Cramé 1764. F498
   Settlement regarding the Canadian bills of exchange and paper money.

France. Conseil d'État. Arrest ... qui proroge ... le délai des déclarations à faire concernant les papiers de Canada. Lille, N.J.B. Peterinck-Cramé, 1764. F499
   A decree extending the settlement of claims connected with the loss of Canada.

France. Conseil d'État. Arrest ... qui proroge ... le délai porté par l'arrêt du conseil du 13. mars 1762. pour la représentation des titres de créances en Canada. Lille, N.J.B. Peterinck-Cramé, 1764. F500
   Another decree extending the settlement of claims connected with the loss of Canada.

France. Conseil d'État. Arrest ... qui règle les droits de la douane de Lyon & de la table de mer, sur les cuirs étrangers y dénommés, leur entrées en Provence & en Languedoc. Lille, N.J.B. Peterinck-Cramé, 1764. F501
   Custom regulations of Lyons concerning hides which were imported to Provence and Languedoc.

France. Conseil d'État. Arrest ... qui admet le port des Sables-d'Olonne ... de faire directement le commerce des isles & colonies françoises de l'Amérique. Paris, Imprimerie Royale, 1765. F502
   The document calls attention to the former commercial greatness of the port and its recent decline. It is hoped that the situation will be remedied by this permission to trade directly with America.

France. Conseil d'État. Arrest ... qui fixe ... des droits d'entrée sur les marchandises en batterie de fer. Paris, Imprimerie Royale, 1765. F503

France. Conseil d'État. Arrest ... qui fixe ... les droits d'entrée de l'amidon. Paris, Imprimerie Royale, 1765. F504

France. Conseil d'État. Arrest ... qui ordonne la liquidation des differentes dettes du Canada. Lille, N.J.B. Peterinck-Cramé, 1765. F505

France. Conseil d'État. Arrest ... qui ordonne le payement des dettes du Canada, liquidées en conséquence de l'arrêt du conseil du 15. février 1765. Lille, N.J.B. Peterinck-Cramé, 1765. F506

France. Conseil d'État. Arrest ... qui permet l'entrée de toutes les drogues & drogueries servant aux teintures. Paris, Imprimerie Royale, 1765. F507
   Duties on dye chemicals from England are equated with those on similar goods from other countries.

France. Conseil d'État. Arrest ... qui permet l'entrée des soies blanches de la Chine ... par le port de Rouen. Paris, Imprimerie Royale, 1765. F508
   Permits the importation of white silk at the port of Rouen, with the provision that it is to be sent directly to Paris or Lyons for taxing.

France. Conseil d'État. Arrest ... qui régle les quantités de vin, cidre ou poiré, & eau-devie qui pourront être à l'avenir embarquées en exemption de droits pour l'avitaillement des naivires destinés à la pêche de la morue. Lille, N.J.B. Peterinck-Cramé, 1765. F509

France. Conseil d'État. Arrest ... concernant les intérêts des reconnoissances données en échange des papiers du Canada; & qui fixe les délais pour achever la liquidation desdits papiers. Lille, N.J.B. Peterinck-Cramé, 1766. F510

France. Conseil d'État. Arrest ... qui ordonne que les bois de teinture venant de l'étranger, payeront à toutes les entrées du royaume, quarante sous par quintal. Paris, Imprimerie Royale, 1766. F511

France. Conseil d'État. Arrest ... qui ordonne que toutes les étoffes de coton ... seront regardées comme contonnades & jouiront des exemptions. Paris, Imprimerie Royale, 1766. F512
   A clarification of the status of velveteen with respect to import duties upon it.

France. Conseil d'État. Arrest ... portant règlement sur les pacotilles en Levant. Paris, P.G. Simon, 1767. F513
   Seamen engaging in private trade are subjected to the same regulations as other merchants.

France. Conseil d'État. Arrest ... qui ... defenses, sous peine de confiscation ... d'introduire dans la ville, port & territoire de Marseille, aucuns draps, ouvrages de bonneterie, & tous ouvrages & étoffes de laine ou mêlés de laine, de fabrique étrangère. Paris, P.G. Simon, 1767. F514

France. Conseil d'État. Arrest ... qui autorise le sieur de la Rochette, préposé à la liquidation de papiers du Canada, à payer aux particuliers dénommés dans l'état annexé à la minute du présent arrêt, les sommes pour lesquelles chacun d'eux y est compris. Lille, N.J.B. Peterinck-Cramé, 1767. F515

France. Conseil d'État. Arrest ... qui autorise le sieur Guillot à signer, au lieu & place du sieur Oblet, le cinquième coupon des reconnoissances ordonnées par l'arrêt du 20 juin 1764 & autres arrêts subséquens, pour le payement de la liquidation des papiers du Canada. Lille, N.J.B. Peterinck-Cramé, 1767. F516

France. Conseil d'État. Arrest ... qui fixe les droits d'entrée à percevoir à l'avenir sur les coquilles de nacre de perle, & sur nacres ouvragées, provenant, soit du commerce de la Compagnie des Indes, soit de l'etranger. Lille, N.J.B. Peterinck-Cramé, 1767. F517

France. Conseil d'État. Arrest ... qui ordonne, entr'autres dispositions, que les toiles peintes & blanches étrangeres, acquitteront, à l'entrée du port de Marseille, les droits établis ... Paris, P.G. Simon, 1767. F518

France. Conseil d'État. Arrest ... qui ordonne qu'à l'avenir les martres, autres que zibelines, qui seront apportées d'Angleterre, payeront a toutes les entrées du royaume, tant des cinq grosses fermes, que des provinces reputées étrangères ... [Lille? 1767.] F519

France. Conseil d'État. Arrest ... qui ordonne que les sucres étrangers de toute espéce, acquitteront à toutes les entrées du royaume, même en tems de foire, les droits ausquels ils ont été imposés. Lille, N.J.B. Peterinck-Cramé, 1767. F520

France. Conseil d'État. Arrest ... qui prescrit les nouvelles formalités à observer par les négocians qui expédieront des bonnets façon de Tunis, à destination du Levant. Paris, Imprimerie Royale, 1767. F521

France. Conseil d'État. Arrest du Conseil d'état du roi, du 26 décembre 1767. Paris, Imprimerie Royale, 1767. F522
A document concerning testimony of one Sieur Chardon with respect to the government of Cayenne in French Guiana.

France. Conseil d'État. Arrêt ... du 15 mars 1768 ... que les rapes, moulin, tamis, & autres utensiles propres à réduire le tabac en poudre, saisis par procès-verbal, au domicile du nommé Bridel ... demeureront acquis & confisqués au profit du fermier ... [Paris? G. Lamesle, 1768.] F523
Concerns a case of illegal processing of tobacco.

France. Conseil d'État. Arrest ... qui casse une sentence rendue le 3 avril 1767, au siége de la table de marbre à Paris, portant homologation d'un prétendu règlement, concernant une enterprise annoncée sous le titre d'Association de commerce maritime. Paris, Imprimerie Royale, 1768. F524
The Association is hereby declared to have not been authorized and therefore is of no validity.

France. Conseil d'État. Arrest ... qui permet d'entreposer dans les ports du royaume, pour être transportés à l'étranger ... en exemption de tous droits ... les sirops & tafias ... des morues sèches de la pêche nationale. Paris, Imprimerie Royale, 1768. F525

France. Conseil d'État. Arrest ... qui supprime le Bureau de législation des colonies. Paris, Imprimerie Royale, 1768. F526
A legislative commission established in 1761 is abolished, with the power to legislate for the colonies reverting to the king.

France. Conseil d'État. Arrest ... concernant le commerce de l'Inde. Paris, P.G. Simon, 1769. F527
Failure of the Compagnie des Indes to fulfill its eastern trade obligations opens the commerce east of the Cape of Good Hope to all French subjects.

France. Conseil d'État. Arrest ... concernant les reconnoissances non converties en billets de la loterie de la Compagnie des Indes. Paris, P.G. Simon, 1769. F528
Regulations on the handling of lottery chances by the Compagnie des Indes.

France. Conseil d'État. Arrest ... portant règlement pour le commerce de l'Inde. Paris, P.G. Simon, 1769. F529
Corrects faults in the edict of August 13, 1769, regarding the opening of trade to the East Indies to all French subjects.

France. Conseil d'État. Arrest du Conseil d'etat du roi, qui permet, aux conditions y énoncées, l'entrepôt dans le port de Roscoff, des tafias qui y sont apportés des autres ports faisant le commerce des isles, du 3 Septembre 1769. [n.p., 1769] F530
A broadside announcing a grant of permission to the port of Roscoff to participate in the rum trade of the French West Indies.

France. Conseil d'État. Arrest ... concernant les ouvrages d'orféverie destinés pour les pays étrangers & pour les colonies. Paris, Imprimerie Royale, 1770. F531
A supplement to a law of 6 April 1770.

France. Conseil d'État. Arrest ... qui homologue la déliberation prise dans l'assemblée générale des actionnaires de la Compagnie des Indes. Paris, Imprimerie Royale, 1770. F532

Confirms the transfer to be made of certain property of the company, and declares how its debts are to be liquidated.

France. Conseil d'État. Arrest ... qui ordonne, conformément à celui du 1er. août 1773, que la déclaration à laquelle sont assujettis les marchands & ouvriers qui destinent de la vaisselle ou d'autres ouvrages d'or & d'argent pour les pays étrangers & pour les colonies ... Paris, Imprimerie Royale, 1770. F533

France. Conseil d'État. Arrest ... qui permet, aux conditions y énoncées, l'entrepôt dans le port de Roscoff, des tafias qui y sont apportés des autres ports faisant le commerce des isles. Paris, P.G. Simon, 1770. F534
The port of Roscoff is opened to the trade in rum from the West Indies, a part of the fish and rum trade of France.

France. Conseil d'État. Arrêt du Conseil d'état du roi, qui proroge jusqu'au premier juillet prochain, la liquidation des billets de caisse de la colonie de la Louisiane ... Lyon, P. Valfriay, 1770. F535

France. Conseil d'État. Arrest ... et lettres patentes sur icelui ... qui fixent le prix auquel les matières d'or & d'argent, seront reçues au change des hôtels des monnoies. Paris, Imprimerie Royale, 1771. F536
Promulgation of new rates of exchange.

France. Conseil d'État. Arrest ... qui casse un arrêt de la Cour des Aides de Bordeaux du 3 mai 1769; confisque au profit de l'adjudicataire, six cents vingt-une livres de faux tabac saisies le 20 juin précédent ... Paris, P.G. Simon, 1771. F537

France. Conseil d'État. Arrest ... qui commet M. le lieutenant général de police, pour connoître par voie de police & administration ... de faux tabacs en poudre ou en bouts, ou de telle autre poudre factice ou mélangée avec du tabac, distribuée sous le dénomination de tabacs ... Paris, Imprimerie Royale, 1771. F538
The Lieutenant General of Police in Paris is given power to proceed against smugglers of tobacco and others dealing in such tobacco in Paris and suburbs, with no appeal available to those judged guilty.

France. Conseil d'État. Arrest ... qui ordonne qu'à l'avenir les pierres à arquebuses, à fusil & à briquet ... [n.p., 1771.] F539
This decree brings into line the export duties on various types of striking stones.

France. Conseil d'État. Arrest ... qui commet le sieur Risteau, ancien directeur de la Compagnie des Indes, pour faire le recouvrement de toutes les sommes dûes à la Compagnie dans les isles françoises de l'Amérique. Paris, P.G. Simon, 1772. F540

France. Conseil d'État. Arrest ... qui modere les droits d'entrées sur les toiles ... venant de l'etranger. Paris, P.G. Simon, 1773. F541

France. Conseil d'État. Arrest ... qui ordonne que le droit de consommation ne sera plus perçu sur les morues séches ... que sur le pied de dix sous du cent pesant, au lieu de vingt sous du cent, compte marchand. Lille, N.J.B. Peterinck-Cramé, 1773. F542

France. Conseil d'État. Arrest ... qui ordonne que les ancres destinées pour le service de la marine, venant de l'étranger, payeront désormais à toutes les entrées & dans tous les ports du royaume indistinctement, quarante sous par quintal. [n.p., 1773.] F543
Establishment of import duty on foreign-made anchors.

France. Conseil d'État. Arrest ... qui ordonne que les porteurs de reconnoissances du caissier de la Compagnie des Indes, portant promesse de fournir des billets ... Paris, P.G. Simon, 1773. F544
Regulations designed to stimulate the lottery organized by the Compagnie des Indes.

France. Conseil d'État. Arrest ... portant réglement pour la perception du droit d'indult sur les marchandises provenant du commerce de l'Inde. Paris, P.G. Simon, 1774. F545

France. Conseil d'État. Arrest ... pour la prise de possession du bail des fermes générales, sous le nom de Laurent David ... [Paris?] Guillaume Desprez, 1774. F546

France. Conseil d'État. Arrest ... qui homologue la délibération prise par les députés, syndics & directeurs de la Compagnie des Indes, le 7 avril 1770. Paris, P.G. Simon, 1774. F547

France. Conseil d'État. Arrest ... qui ordonne qu'à l'avenir les fers-blancs ... venant de l'étranger ... quatre livres par quintal. [Paris] C.J. Daclin [1774]. F548
Revises a tariff of 1692, giving more uniformity to duties on two types of tin plate.

France. Conseil d'État. Arrest ... qui ordonne que le transport des grains, farines & légumes, dans le port de Saint-Jean-de-Luz & Sibourre, sera libre de tous les ports. Lille, N.J.B. Peterinck-Cramé, 1774. F549

France. Conseil d'État. Arrest ... qui permet aux armateurs établis dans les ports de pêche de l'océan & de la Manche de faire venir d'Espagne & de Portugal, sur vaisseaux françois seulement, les sels dont ils auront besoin pour la salaison de leurs morues. Lille, N.J.B. Peterinck-Cramé, 1774.　　　　　　　　　　　　　　F550

France. Conseil d'État. Arrest ... concernant les ouvrages d'orfévrerie destinés pour les pays étrangers & pour les colonies. Paris, P.G. Simon, 1775.　　　　　　　　　　　　　　F551

France. Conseil d'État. Arrest ... dont le premier casse & annulle, tant une sentence des officiers de l'election de Saint-Lo ... Paris, P.G. Simon, 1775.　　　　　　　　　　　　　　F552
　A legal case arising from a seizure of illegally owned tobacco.

France. Conseil d'État. Arrest ... portant augmentation des droits sur les peaux & poils de lapins & lièvres, à la sortie du royaume. Paris, P.G. Simon, 1775.　　　　　　　　F553

France. Conseil d'État. Arrest ... qui accorde ... vingt-cinq sous par quintal de morues seches de pêche françoise qui seront transportées dans les isles françoises. [n.p.] G. Desprez, 1775.　F554
　The declaration of a special bonus for merchants who export codfish to the French West Indian islands.

France. Conseil d'État. Arrest ... qui commet le sieur Broutin pour faire le recouvrement de toutes les sommes dûes à la Compagnie des Indes, aux isles de France & de Bourbon. Paris, Guillaume Desprez [1775].　　　　F555

France. Conseil d'État. Arrest ... qui defend la sortie hors du royaume des sels des marias salans de Bretagne ... & côtes françoises de l'océan; & permet aux armateurs établis dans les ports de pêche de l'océan & ... de la Manche, de faire venir d'Espagne & de Portugal ... le sels dont ils auront besoin. Paris, P.G. Simon, 1775.　　　　　　　　　　　　　　F556

France. Conseil d'État. Arrest ... qui fixe l'étendue des trois lieues d'Alsace, limitrophes aux trois evêchés, à la Lorraine, à la Franche-Comté & au Montbéliard, & le nombre des marchands auxquels ils permet un approvisionnement de mille livres de tabac à la fois, pour la consommation des habitans de ces trois lieues. [n.p., ca. 1775.]　　　　　　　　　　　　　　F557
　The districts and towns covered in this decree are enumerated.

France. Conseil d'État. Arrest ... qui fixent le prix des piastres aux deux globes qui seront apportées aux hôtels des monnoies. Paris, P.G. Simon, 1775.　　　　　　　　　　　F558
　A decree fixing the price of the Spanish piastres from Peru.

France. Conseil d'État. Arrest ... qui ordone que les déclarations des marchandises dans le port de Marseille, seront faites dans la forme prescrite pour les autres ports du royaume. Paris, P.G. Simon, 1775.　　　　　　　　　　F559

France. Conseil d'État. Arrest ... qui ordone que les lettres de change tirées des isles de France & de Bourbon ... seront représentées au sieur de Mory caissier de la Compagnie des Indes ... [n.p., G. Desprez, 1775.]　　　　　　F560

France. Conseil d'État. Arrest ... qui ordonne ... les marchands & ouvriers qui destinent de la vaisselle ou d'autres ouvrages d'or & d'argent pour les colonies, contiendra le nom & la demeure des habitans lesdits pays ... Paris, P.G. Simon, 1775.　　　　　　　　F561

France. Conseil d'État. Arrest ... qui ordonne ... morues sèches de pêche françoise, seront exemptes de tous droits. Paris, Imprimerie Royale, 1775.　　　　　　　　　　　F562
　Import exemption on cod is extended to all French ports, whereas it had previously applied to Normandy only.

France. Conseil d'État. Arrest ... qui ordonne qu'à l'avenir les droits sur les fers-noirs en feuilles doubles ou simples ... [Paris, C.J. Daclin, 1775.]　　　　　　　　　　　　F563
　This decree attempts to define types of sheet iron and to set import duties on them.

France. Conseil d'État. Arrest ... qui ordonne qu'à l'avenir les sucres raffinés, en pains & en poudre ou candi, provenant du commerce des îles de France & de Bourbon, payeront comme ceux provenant des isles & colonies françoises de l'Amérique. Paris, Imprimerie Royale, 1775.　　　　　　　　　　　　F564

France. Conseil d'État. Arrest ... qui proroge ... la liquidation des billets de caisse de la colonie de la Louisiane ... Paris, P.G. Simon, 1775.　　　　　　　　　　　　　　F565

France. Conseil d'État. Arrest ... rendu en interprétation de celui du 29 juillet 1767, concernant l'établissement d'un entrepôt au port de Carénage, dans l'île de Saint-Lucie. Paris, Imprimerie Royale, 1775.　　　　　　F566

France. Conseil d'État. Arrest ... concernant la police des noirs. Du 8 septembre 1776. Paris, Imprimerie Royale, 1776.　　　　　　F567

Cases concerning slaves in the French colonies are to be returned to France for hearings.

France. Conseil d'État. Arrest ... portant réglement pour le paiement des rentes à quatre pour cent, dûes aux Indiens ou domiciliés dans l'Inde, à cause des contrats ou promesses de passer contrat, qui leur ont été donnés en paiement de leurs créances sur la Compagnie. Paris, P.G. Simon, 1776. F568

France. Conseil d'État. Arrest ... portant révocation de toutes les contestations nées & à naître aux isles françoises de l'Amérique, concernant la liquidation de la Compagnie des Indes. Paris, Imprimerie Royale, 1776. F569

France. Conseil d'État. Arrest ... que les verres & ouvrages de verreries venant de l'étranger dans le royaume ... [Paris] C.J. Daclin [1776]. F570
Port of entry and duties are specified for glass imported into France.

France. Conseil d'État. Arrest ... qui ... ordonne que les négocians des ports de Saint-Brieuc, Binic, & Porterieux, ne pourront à l'avenir faire directement le commerce des isles & colonies françoises de l'Amérique que par le port de Saint-Brieuc ... Paris, P.G. Simon, 1776. F571

France. Conseil d'État. Arrest ... qui commet le sieur Broutin pour faire le recouvrement de toutes les sommes dues à la Compagnie des Indes, aux isles de France & de Bourbon. Paris, P.G. Simon, 1776. F572

France. Conseil d'État. Arrest ... qui défend, à peine de 1000 livres d'amende, au sieur Rigaud, fermier des droits du tarif de la ville de Bressuire ... aucuns droits sur les tabacs de la ferme, qui entreront dans la ville de Bressuire ... [n.p., G. Lamesle, 1776.] F573
Decree requiring restitution of tobacco taxes illegally and unjustly received by the collector in Bressuire.

France. Conseil d'État. Arrest ... qui, en interprétant celui du 14 mars dernier, ordonne que les négocians des ports de Saint-Brieuc, Binic & Porterieux, ne pourront à l'avenir faire directement le commerce des isles & colonies françoises de l'Amérique ... Paris, Imprimerie Royale, 1776. F574

France. Conseil d'État. Arrest ... qui nomme des commissaires pour procéder à la liquidation des dettes de la succession de sieur Dupleix. Paris, P.G. Simon, 1776. F575
Commissioners are appointed to liquidate debts incurred on behalf of the Compagnie des Indes by Dupleix, governor general of Pondicherry from 1742 to 1754.

France. Conseil d'État. Arrest ... qui ordonne le renvoi en France, des originaux des titres de créance sur la Compagnie des Indes, déposés dans les greffes des conseils des Indes & des isles de France & de Bourbon. Paris, Imprimerie Royale, 1776. F576

France. Conseil d'État. Arrest ... qui ordonne qu'à compter du jour de sa publication les morues sèches de pêche françoise, seront exemptes de tous droits appartenans au Roi. Paris, P.G. Simon, 1776. F577

France. Conseil d'État. Arrest ... qui ordonne qu'à l'avenir les sucres raffinés, en pains & en poudre ou candi, provenant du commerce des isles de France & de Bourbon, payeront comme ceux provenant des isles & colonies françoises de l'Amérique ... Paris, P.G. Simon, 1776. F578

France. Conseil d'État. Arrest ... qui ordonne que les lettres de change tirées des isles de France & de Bourbon ... seront représentées au sieur de Mory, cassier de la Compagnie des Indes ... Paris, P.G. Simon, 1776. F579

France. Conseil d'État. Arrest ... qui permet aux négocians de Rochefort, de faire directement par le port de cette ville le commerce des isles & colonies françoises de l'Amérique, en se conformant aux dispositions des lettres patentes du mois d'avril 1717. Paris, Imprimerie Royale, 1776. F580
The decree recognizes Rochefort's natural advantages for trade with America and renews letters patent originally granted in 1717.

France. Conseil d'État. Arrest ... qui permet aux négocians des ports de Saint-Brieuc, Binic, & Portérieux, de faire directement le commerce des isles & colonies françoises de l'Amérique. Paris, Imprimerie Royale, 1776. F581

France. Conseil d'État. Arrêt ... concernant le retour des noirs, mulâtres ou autres gens de couleur aux colonies. Paris, Imprimerie Royale, 1777. F582
Concerns disposition of slaves of French colonials during delays in hearings.

France. Conseil d'État. Arrêt ... portant prorogation et amélioration des octrois et revenus de la ville de Bordeaux, enrégistrés au Parlement. Bordeaux, Michel Racle, 1777. F583
A decree improving the collection of revenues in the city of Bordeaux.

France. Conseil d'État. Arrêt ... portant suppression d'un ouvrage intitulé: *Considérations sur*

l'état présent de la colonie françoise de Saint-Domingue. Paris, Imprimerie Royale, 1777.
F584

The book in question was published in 1776 and is attributed to Michel-René Hilliard d'Auberteuil.

France. Conseil d'État. Arrest ... qui accorde ... aux syndics, administrateurs & intéressés dans la Compagnie de la Guyane françoise, le privilege exclusif de la traite des noirs & du commerce en l'isle de Gorée & sur les côtes d'Afrique, depuis le Cap-Verd jusqu'à rivière de Casamance. Paris, P.G. Simon, 1777. F585

France. Conseil d'État. Arrêt ... qui accorde pour le terme & espace de quinze ans, ... la Compagnie de la Guyane françoise, le privilége exclusif de la traite des Noirs ... du 14 août 1777. Paris, Imprimerie Royale, 1777. F586

The monopoly on the trade in American slaves extended from Cape Verde to the Casamance River.

France. Conseil d'État. Arrest ... qui défend de faire payer ... les avanies, les emprunts demandés à la nation dans les echelles du Levant & de Barbarie, etc., et qui défend également au négocians établis dans lesdites echelles. Paris, P.G. Simon, 1777. F587

France. Conseil d'État. Arrest ... qui défend toute espèce d'entrepôt & magasin au Pont-de-Beauvoisin: et ordonne que tout voiturier qui enlèvera des marchandises dudit lieu, sera tenu d'être porteur de l'acquit des droits. Paris, P.G. Simon, 1777. F588

France. Conseil d'État. Arrest ... qui ordonne à la Chambre du Commerce de Marseille, d'emprunter onze cens mille livres au denier vingt-cinq; & d'employer cette somme au payement des dettes des echelles du Levant & Barbarie. Paris, P.G. Simon, 1777. F589

France. Conseil d'État. Arrest ... qui ordonne la liquidation & le paiement de ce qui reste dû aux négocians de Morée, & des dettes des echelles du Levant & de Barbarie. Paris, P.G. Simon, 1777. F590

Payments will liquidate debts contracted by the military and will indemnify for losses suffered by merchants in 1770.

France. Conseil d'État. Arrêt ... qui ordonne qu'à l'avenir les toiles de Nankin, provenant tant de l'étranger, que du commerce de l'Inde, payeront les mêmes droits, & seront assujetties aux mêmes formalités que les toiles de coton blanches ... Paris, Imprimerie Royale, 1777. F591

France. Conseil d'État. Arrest ... qui ordonnent ... apres la publication desdites lettres patentes, il sera payé, au profit de l'Hôpital Général, un droit de vingt livres par quintal sur toute la melasse qui entrera dans la ville ... de Paris. Paris, P.G. Simon, 1777. F592

Establishment of an extraordinary tax on molasses brought to the city of Paris.

France. Conseil d'État. Arrest ... qui réduit toutes les impositions établies sur le commerce du Levant & de Barbarie, au droit unique de cinq pour cent, sous la dénomination de droit du consulat. Paris, P.G. Simon, 1777. F593

France. Conseil d'État. Arrest ... concernant le retour des noirs & gens de couleur aux colonies. Aix, E. David, 1778. F594

France. Conseil d'État. Arrest ... concernant le retour des noirs & gens de couleur aux colonies. [Paris?] Imprimerie Royale, 1778. F595

France. Conseil d'État. Arrest ... concernant les avances à faire par les armateurs aux équipages des corsaires. Paris, P.G. Simon, 1778. F596

Decree concerning the advance loans granted to privateers.

France. Conseil d'État. Arrest ... concernant les bâtimens anglois détenus dans les ports du royaume, en vertu des ordres de Sa Majesté; & les navires françois pris par les corsaires des isles de Jersey & de Guernesey. Paris, P.G. Simon, 1778. F597

France. Conseil d'État. Arrest ... portant nomination des commissaires pour tenir le conseil des prises près l'Amiral de France. Paris, P.G. Simon, 1778. F598

France. Conseil d'État. Arrest ... portant réglement pour les marchandises provenant des prises faites en mer sur les ennemis de l'etat. Lille, N.J.B. Peterinck-Cramé, 1778. F599

France. Conseil d'État. Arrest ... portant suppression d'un ouvrage intitulé: *Considérations sur l'état présent de la colonie françoise de Saint-Domingue.* Paris, P.G. Simon, 1778. F600

The offending book was critical of the administration in Saint Domingue.

France. Conseil d'État. Arrêt ... contenant le nouveau tarif des droits sur les denrées & marchandises de Hollande. Paris, Imprimerie Royale, 1779. F601

This document interprets provisions in the tariff relating to dyes, certain cloths, and various woods.

France. Conseil d'État. Arrest ... portant réglement pour l'election des députés du commerce. Paris, Imprimerie Royale, 1779. F602

France. Conseil d'État. Arrêt ... portant révocation de la permission accordée aux armateurs, de tirer de l'Espagne & du Portugal les sel nécessaires à la pêche de la morue. Paris, Imprimerie Royale, 1779. F603

France. Conseil d'État. Arrêt ... qui ... révoque, à l'égard des sujets de la république des Provinces-Unies des Pays Bas la ville d'Amsterdam exceptée, les avantages ... pour les navigations des neutres: ordonnes que pour celle des bâtimens hollandois ... Paris, Imprimerie Royale, 1779. F604

France. Conseil d'État. Arrest ... qui accorde aux créanciers & prétendans droits sur la succession du sieur Dupleix, un dernier délai de trois mois pour la production de leurs titres. Paris, P.G. Simon, 1779. F605

France. Conseil d'État. Arrest ... qui interdit & prohibe ... l'entrée des fromages de Nord-Hollande. Paris, P.G. Simon, 1779. F606

France. Conseil d'État. Arrêt ... qui ordonne qu'il sera sursis à la perception des droits de fret ... Paris, Imprimerie Royale, 1779. F607
The stay in collection of duties applies only to the ships of Holland.

France. Conseil d'État. Arrest ... concernant l'epizootie. Lille, N.J.B. Peterinck-Cramé, 1780. F608
In an effort to prevent the spreading of disease, all imports of products from cattle in Spanish America are prohibited.

France. Conseil d'État. Arrest ... concernant les avances à payer aux équipages des corsaires qui seront armés à Dunkerque. Paris, Imprimerie Royale, 1780. F609

France. Conseil d'État. Arrêt ... concernant les dettes des habitans de l'Isle de la Grenade. Paris, Imprimerie Royale, 1780. F610

France. Conseil d'État. Arrêt ... concernant les droits des officiers des amirautés pour les dépôts des actes de cautionnement des armateurs en course ... Paris, Imprimerie Royale, 1780. F611

France. Conseil d'État. Arrêt ... portant défenses à tous capitaines de corsaires de rançonner en mer les bâtimens ennemis. Paris, Imprimerie Royale, 1780. F612

France. Conseil d'État. Arrêt ... pour la prise de possession du bail des fermes générales, sous le nom de Nicolas Salzard. Paris, Imprimerie Royale, 1780. F613

France. Conseil d'État. Arrêt ... qui ordonne l'établissement d'une navigation réglée sur la Loire & rivières y affluentes. Paris, Imprimerie Royale, 1780. F614

France. Conseil d'État. Arrêt ... qui révoque ceux des 14 janvier, 27 avril, 15 juin & 18 septembre de l'année dernière, relatifs à la navigation & au commerce, dans les ports du royaume, des sujets des États-généraux des Provinces-Unies des Pays-bas ... Paris, Imprimerie Royale, 1780. F615

France. Conseil d'État. Arrest de réglement, concernat les fermes & les régies du Roi. Lille, N.J.B. Peterinck-Cramé, 1780. F616

France. Conseil d'État. Arrêt ... concernant le dépôt aux greffes des amirautés, des liquidations particulieres, & des comptes de dépenses des relâches & du désarmement des corsaires. Paris, Imprimerie Royale, 1781. F617
The privateers are enjoined to report their prizes properly.

France. Conseil d'État. Arrêt ... qui attribue aux régisseurs des diligences, messageries royales & du roulage ... le privilege exclusif du transport, tant par eau que par terre, des marchandises qui jouissent de la faveur du transit. Paris, Imprimerie Royale, 1781. F618

France. Conseil d'État. Arrêt ... qui confirme l'adjudicataire de la ferme générale du tabac, dans la préférence pour les tabacs provenans de prises amenées dans les ports du royaume. Paris, Imprimerie Royale, 1781. F619

France. Conseil d'État. Arrêt ... qui défend les ventes & marchés faits avec des gens de mer, pour des parts de prises. Paris, Imprimerie Royale, 1781. F620

France. Conseil d'État. Arrest ... qui fixe à dix pour cent les droits que doit payer à l'entrée du royaume la bonneterie étrangère. [Paris] Veuve Daclin [1781]. F621
A revision of a 1664 tariff on hosiery.

France. Conseil d'État. Arrest ... qui ordonne ... les fers en tôle venant de l'étranger. [Paris] Veuve Daclin [1781]. F622
The duty on sheet iron is set at thirty sous per quintal.

France. Conseil d'État. Arrest ... qui ordonne que ... les soies de Nankin venant de l'étranger ... ne seront assujetties qu'au paiement du droit de quatorze sous pour livre. Lille, N.J.B. Peterinck-Cramé, 1781. F623
  Specifies ports of entry and duty for Nanking silk.

France. Conseil d'État. Arrêt ... qui permet l'entrée dans le royaume ... des soies blanches dites Nanquin: et fixe le droit qu' elles acquitteront. Paris, Imprimerie Royale, 1781. F624

France. Conseil d'État. Arrest ... qui révoque celui du 25 juillet dernier ... [n.p., 1781.] F625
  The repeal of an earlier law which permitted free trade in remnants of certain types of cloth up to six ells in length.

France. Conseil d'État. Arrêt ... concernant les pièces a produire pour la réclamation des parts de prises appartenantes aux officiers-mariniers & matelots étrangers. Paris, Imprimerie Royale, 1782. F626

France. Conseil d'État. Arrêt ... qui ... ordonne que les ouvrages & matières d'or & d'argent qui se trouveront à bord des prises, seront portés aux hôtels des monnoies ou aux changes les plus prochains. Paris, Imprimerie Royale, 1782. F627

France. Conseil d'État. Arrêt ... qui déboute les sieurs Doekscheer, Steenbergen & autres négocians, de leurs appels des jugemens du conseil des prises ... Paris, Imprimerie Royale, 1782. F628
  A legal case arising from the seizure of several ships belonging to merchants of Amsterdam.

France. Conseil d'État. Arrest ... qui fixe les droits que doivent payer par douzaine les chapeaux à leur entrée & sortie des cinq grosses fermes. Lille, N.J.B. Peterinck-Cramé, 1782. F629

France. Conseil d'État. Arrêt ... qui fixe les droits que doivent payer par douzaine, les chapeaux à leur entrée & sortie des cinq grosses fermes. Paris, Imprimerie Royale, 1782. F630
  Includes rates for beaver hats.

France. Conseil d'État. Arrest ... qui fixe les droits sur les sucres raffinés venant de l'etranger. Lille, N.J.B. Peterinck-Cramé, 1782. F631

France. Conseil d'État. Arrest ... qui ordonne que le droit de demi pour cent accordé à la chambre du commerce de Marseille ... sera perçu à son profit dans les ports du ponant, sur les bâtimens armés à Marseille pour les isles françoises. Lille, N.J.B. Peterinck-Cramé, 1782. F632

France. Conseil d'État. Arrêt ... qui ordonne que le droit de demi pour cent accordé à la Chambre du commerce de Marseille ... sur le bâtimens armés à Marseille pour les isles françoises d'Afrique ou de l'Inde, lors de leur retour dans ces ports. Paris, Imprimerie Royale, 1782. F633
  Imposes a duty of one half per cent on the profits of a ship leaving Marseille for the French colonies and returning to another port.

France. Conseil d'État. Arrêt ... qui ordonne que les créanciers des sieurs Miran & Abeille seront tenus de remettre ... leurs titres, ès mains des directeurs de la Compagnie des Indes. Paris, Imprimerie Royale, 1782. F634

France. Conseil d'État. Arrêt ... qui prescrit les formalités à observer lors de la sortie des ports du royaume, des marchandises provenant des prises. Paris, Imprimerie Royale, 1782. F635

France. Conseil d'État. Arrest ... qui révoque celui du 9 août 1781, concernant le privilége exclusif du transport, tant par eau que par terre, des marchandises qui jouissent de la faveur du transit. Lille, N.J.B. Peterinck-Cramé, 1782. F636

France. Conseil d'État. Arrêt ... sur les armes blanches étrangères ... [n.p., 1782.] F637
  Specifies duties on imported side arms.

France. Conseil d'État. Arrêt ... au sujet des armateurs qui sont en retard de payer les parts appartenantes aux équipages des bâtimens armés en course, dans les prises qu'ils ont faites sur les ennemis de l'état. Paris, Imprimerie Royale, 1783. F638

France. Conseil d'État. Arrêt ... concernant l'expédition de commerce à faire à la Chine, de 1783 à 1784. Paris, Imprimerie Royale, 1783. F639

France. Conseil d'État. Arrest ... concernant le bail des fermes générales. Paris, P.G. Simon & N.H. Nyon, 1783. F640

France. Conseil d'État. Arrest ... concernant le commerce de la Chine. Paris, Imprimerie Royale, 1783. F641
  The king authorizes Grandclos-Meslé to undertake a commercial voyage to China on his behalf.

France. Conseil d'État. Arrêt ... concernant le payement des lettres de change de l'Inde & de

l'Amérique. Paris, Imprimerie Royale, 1783.
F642

France. Conseil d'État. Arrest ... portant défenses à tous capitaines ou commandans des bâtimens armés en course, de revendre en mer, à des ennemis de l'état, les prises qu'ils auront faites sur eux. Lille, N.J.B. Peterinck-Cramé, 1783. F643

France. Conseil d'État. Arrêt ... portant établissement de paquebots pour communiquer avec les États-unis de l'Amérique. Paris, Imprimerie Royale, 1783. F644
  This decree provides for regular sailings between Port-Louis and New York.

France. Conseil d'État. Arrêt ... qui fait mainlevée d'une opposition formée par le sieur Belle ... à la délivrance des deniers provenans de la vente des prises angloises le *Wrein* & le *Recovery*. Paris, Imprimerie Royale, 1783.
F645

France. Conseil d'État. Arrest ... qui fixe l'époque du paiement des lettres de change de l'Inde & de l'Amérique, non déjà enrégistrées ... Lille, N.J.B. Peterinck-Cramé, 1783. F646

France. Conseil d'État. Arrêt ... qui ordonne ... l'exécution des dispositions de l'arrêt du six juin 1763, concernant le poisson de pêche étrangère. Lille, N.J.B. Peterinck-Cramé, 1783. F647
  A decree renewing dues on all fish caught in foreign waters.

France. Conseil d'État. Arrêt ... qui ordonne l'exécution dans le port de Dunkerque, des arrêts & règlements qui accordent la préférence à la ferme générale, dans les adjudications de tabacs provenans de prise. Paris, Imprimerie Royale, 1783. F648

France. Conseil d'État. Arrest ... qui ordonne qu'il soit fait mention dans les affiches pour la vente & adjudication des tabacs provenant des prises qui pourroient être amenées dans le port de Dunkerque. Lille, N.J.B. Peterinck-Cramé, 1783. F649
  A decree ordering the announcement of a sale of tobacco that had been seized from the enemy and brought to the port of Dunkirk.

France. Conseil d'État. Arrest ... qui permet aux bâtimens étrangers, arrivant directement des côtes d'Afrique, avec des cargaisons de ... noirs ... d'aborder dans le port principal de chacune des isles de la Martinique, la Guadeloupe, Sainte-Lucie & Tabago ... Paris, P.G. Simon & N.H. Nyon, 1783. F650

France. Conseil d'État. Arrêt ... qui supprime un ouvrage intitulé: *Relation de deux voyages dans les mers Australes & des Indes, faits par M. de Kerguelen en 1771*. Paris, Imprimerie Royale, 1783. F651
  The book was suppressed because it contained criticisms of the government.

France. Conseil d'État. Arrêt ... concernant la vente & le débit du tabac. Paris, Imprimerie Royale, 1784. F652
  Attempts to regulate the quality of tobacco sold in all parts of France.

France. Conseil d'État. Arrêt ... concernant le commerce étranger dans les isles françoises de l'Amérique. Paris, Imprimerie Royale, 1784.
F653

France. Conseil d'État. Arrest ... concernant les armemens de commerce pour les isles & colonies françoises. Aix, A. David, 1784. F654

France. Conseil d'État. Arrêt ... concernant les armemens de commerce pour les isles & colonies françoises. Paris, Imprimerie Royale, 1784. F655
  Outfitters of ships destined for voyages to the French colonies are permitted to operate in all French ports.

France. Conseil d'État. Arrêt ... concernant les marchandises des manufactures ... destinées pour l'étranger. [n.p., 1784.] F656
  In order to enjoy the freedom to export without paying duties, the exporter must declare the quality of his goods, their destination, and the route by which they will be carried.

France. Conseil d'État. Arrêt ... portant confirmation & établissement de ports francs dans le royaume. Paris, Imprimerie Royale, 1784.
F657
  Granting of special privileges to the ports of Orient, Bayonne, and Saint-Jean-de-Luz.

France. Conseil d'État. Arrêt ... portant que les armateurs, qui sont débiteurs de parts de prises, seront tenus d'en fournir caution, ou d'en déposer le montant aux greffes des amirautés. Paris, Imprimerie Royale, 1784. F658

France. Conseil d'État. Arrêt ... portant règlement pour la franchise du port de l'Orient. Paris, Imprimerie Royale, 1784. F659

France. Conseil d'État. Arrêt ... portant règlement pour la perception du droit d'indult. Paris, Imprimerie Royale, 1784. F660
  Adjustments are made and exceptions provided for, upon a policy of payments on goods imported from the East Indies, China, and the Cape of Good Hope.

France. Conseil d'État. Arrêt ... portant règlement sur la franchise accordée au port & à la ville de l'Orient. Paris, Imprimerie Royale, 1784. F661

France. Conseil d'État. Arrêt ... portant règlement sur la manière dont le tabac fabriqué doit jouir de la franchise du port de l'Orient. Paris, Imprimerie Royale, 1784. F662
The original purpose of the franchise for tobacco at l'Orient was that of an emporium for foreign sales. This document allows domestic sales as well.

France. Conseil d'État. Arrêt ... qui, à compter du 10 novembre prochain, convertit en gratifications & primes l'exemption du demi-droit accordée aux denrées coloniales provenant de la traite des noirs. Paris, Imprimerie Royale, 1784. F663

France. Conseil d'État. Arrest ... qui accorde différentes faveurs au commerce du nord. Paris, P.G. Simon & N.H. Nyon, 1784. F664
Adjustments are to be made in export and import duties and in payments to captains and shipowners to encourage the Baltic and North Sea commerce.

France. Conseil d'État. Arrêt ... qui casse la sentence du juge de police de la ville de Rennes ... & l' arrêt de la chambre des vacations de Parlement de la même ville ... par lesquels la saisie conservatoire de différentes quantités de tabac avoit été confirmée. Paris, Imprimerie Royale, 1784. F665

France. Conseil d'État. Arrest ... qui fixe huit livres par quintal les droits d'entrée du royaume, sur le plomb fabriqué ... [n.p., 1784.] F666
A tariff on lead to give protection to the manufacturers of shot and plates.

France. Conseil d'État. Arrest ... qui ordonne que les créanciers de sieurs Miran & Abeille, seront tenus de remettre ... leurs titres ès mains des directeurs de la Compagnie des Indes ... Paris, P.G. Simon & N.H. Nyon, 1784. F667
Transactions connected with the liquidation of the Compagnie des Indes.

France. Conseil d'État. Arrêt ... qui prolonge ... l'effet de lettres patentes du 1.er mai 1768, qui accordoient à l'isle de Cayenne & à la Guyane françoise, la liberté de commerce avec toutes les nations. Paris, Imprimerie Royale, 1784. F668
Cayenne and French Guiana were to be free trade areas until July 1, 1792.

France. Conseil d'État. Arrêt ... qui règle le payement des récépissés de papier-monnoie des isles de France & de Bourbon, ordonne la vérification de tous papiers-monnoie existans dans les dites isles ... Paris, Imprimerie Royale, 1784. F669

France. Conseil d'État. Arrêt ... qui supprime le privilége exclusif de la traite des noirs ... Paris, Imprimerie Royale, 1784. F670
Abolishes the monopoly on slave trade in Goree held by the Compagnie de la Guyane françoise.

France. Conseil d'État. Arrêt ... concernant l'expédition d'un vaisseau pour la Chine. Paris, Imprimerie Royale, 1785. F671
Certain French merchants trading with China are directed to send a ship of six or seven hundred tons to China for the express purpose of bringing home a cargo of Nanking silks.

France. Conseil d'État. Arrest ... concernant la balance du commerce. Paris, P.G. Simon, 1785. F672
Provides for the establishment of a new office with the balance of commerce as its primary concern.

France. Conseil d'État. Arrêt ... concernant la nomination d'un Député por le Commerce, représentant les six corps de marchands de la ville de Paris. Paris, Imprimerie Royale, 1785. F673

France. Conseil d'État. Arrest ... concernant la régie & perception des droits de vente exclusive du sel & du tabac & autres droits acquis par Sa Majesté. Paris, P.G. Simon & N.H. Nyon, 1785. F674

France. Conseil d'État. Arrest ... concernant le commerce du tabac dans le pays limitrophe de l'Orient & de Bayonne. Paris, P.G. Simon & N.H. Nyon, 1785. F675

France. Conseil d'État. Arrest ... concernant les marchandises étrangères, prohibées dans le royaume. Paris, P.G. Simon & N.H. Nyon, 1785. F676
This decree is particularly directed against imports from Great Britain, but it lists goods which may still be imported.

France. Conseil d'État. Arrêt ... portant à cinq livres par quintal la taxe imposée sur la morue de pêche étrangere, qui sera importée aux isles de l'Amérique du Vent & Sous le Vent. Paris, P.G. Simon and N.H. Nyon, 1785. F677

France. Conseil d'État. Arrêt ... portant cession & transport à la nouvelle Compagnie des Indes ... du vaisseau le *Dauphin*, expédié en Chine pour le compte de Sa Majesté, le 27 février dernier. Paris, Imprimerie Royale, 1785. F678

France. Conseil d'État. Arrêt ... portant établissement d'une nouvelle Compagnie des Indes. Paris, Imprimerie Royale, 1785. F679

France. Conseil d'État. Arrêt ... portant homologation des statuts & règlemens de la Compagnie des Indes. Paris, Imprimerie Royale, 1785. F680

France. Conseil d'État. Arrêt ... pour la nomination des administrateurs de la nouvelle Compagnie des Indes. Paris, Imprimerie Royale, 1785. F681

France. Conseil d'État. Arrêt ... qui accorde des primes d'encouragement aux négocians françois qui transporteront des morues sèches de pêche nationale dans les Îles du Vent & Sous le Vent, ainsi que dans les ports de l'Europe. Paris, Imprimerie Royale, 1785. F682

France. Conseil d'État. Arrest ... qui, en supprimant le droit de deux pour cent, perçu à l'expédition de Marseille, des marchandises du royaume pour le Levant & la Barbarie, réduit à trois pour cent la totalité du droit, jusqu'à présent de cinq pour cent. Paris, P.G. Simon & N.H. Nyon, 1785. F683

France. Conseil d'État. Arrêt ... qui impose les couperoses vertes apportées de l'étranger ... [n.p., 1785.] F684
This document regulates the import of iron sulfates and traces briefly the history of regulation of that product.

France. Conseil d'État. Arrêt ... qui nomme le sieur de Boullongne ... pour être chargé ... de la suite des affaires concernant la Compagnie des Indes ... Paris, Imprimerie Royale, 1785. F685

France. Conseil d'État. Arrêt ... qui nomme les administrateurs & les employés de la Compagnie des Indes. Paris, Imprimerie Royale, 1785. F686

France. Conseil d'État. Arrêt ... qui ordonne que la gratification accordée au commerce pour la traite des nègres, sera restituée à l'adjudicataire des fermes, avec moitié en sus, par les armateurs qui l'auront reçue, & qui n'auront pas importé des noirs aux colonies. Paris, Imprimerie Royale, 1785. F687
Deals with encouragement and premiums allotted to merchants trading in slaves.

France. Conseil d'État. Arrest ... qui permet aux fabricans étrangers de s'établir dans le royaume. Paris, Imprimerie Royale, 1785. F688

France. Conseil d'État. Arrêt ... qui proroge ... le délai fixé à six semaines, à compter du 10 juillet dernier, pour l'entrée des toiles de coton blanches & peintes ... Paris, Imprimerie Royale, 1785. F689

France. Conseil d'État. Arrest ... qui renouvelle les anciennes défenses d'introduire dans le royaume, aucunes toiles ... Paris, P.G. Simon & N.H. Nyon, 1785. F690
Renews prohibition on importing calico except for the Compagnie des Indes.

France. Conseil d'État. Arrêt ... qui renouvelle les anciennes défenses d'introduire dans le royaume, aucunes toiles de coton & mousselines venant de l'étranger, autres que celles de l'Inde apportées par le commerce national. Paris, Imprimerie Royale, 1785. F691

France. Conseil d'État. Arrest ... qui supprime les délibérations prises par une partie des actionnaires de la Compagnie des Indes, en l'assemblée du 3 de ce mois; & ordonne une assemblée générale desdits actionnaires. Paris, P.G. Simon & N.H. Nyon, 1785. F692

France. Conseil d'État. Arrêt ... qui suspend l'exécution de ceux des 10 & 22 mai 1723 ... & ordonne que l'affranchissement ... aura lieu en faveur des provinces de la Loire. Paris, Imprimerie Royale, 1785. F693
Special provisions for the province of Loire regarding its export of wine abroad.

France. Conseil d'État. Arrêt du Conseil d'Etat du roi, concernant le commerce interlope des colonies, du 23 septembre 1785. Paris, Imprimerie Royale, 1785. F694
Decree concerning unauthorized or illegal trade in the colonies and specifying what constitutes permissible cargo.

France. Conseil d'État. Arrêt ... concernant le commerce interlope des colonies. Paris, P.G. Simon & N.H. Nyon, 1786. F695

France. Conseil d'État. Arrêt ... concernant le commerce interlope des colonies. Paris, Imprimerie Royale, 1786. F696
A review of recent cases of interloping in the West Indies, with reaffirmation of decrees of 1727, 1766, and 1784 to control it.

France. Conseil d'État. Arrêt ... concernant les raffineries des sucres. Paris, Imprimerie Royale, 1786. F697
The government promises to pay back to the refiner the duties collected on sugars imported from France's American plantations.

France. Conseil d'État. Arrêt ... portant règlement pour la marque & visite des toiles blanches & imprimées des manufactures d'Alsace. Paris, Imprimerie Royale, 1786. F698

France. Conseil d'État. Arrêt ... portant règlement pour la vente des marchandises provenant du commerce de l'Inde. Paris, P.G. Simon & N.H. Nyon, 1786. F699

France. Conseil d'État. Arrêt ... portant règlement pour la vente des marchandises provenant du commerce de l'Inde. Paris, Imprimerie Royale, 1786. F700

France. Conseil d'État. Arrêt ... portant suppression du droit local de cinquante sous par quintal, qui se perçoit sur les cires & les sucres, dans la ville de Rouen. Paris, P.G. Simon & N.H. Nyon, 1786. F701

France. Conseil d'État. Arrêt ... pour la prise de possession du bail des fermes générales, sous le nom de Jean-Baptiste Mager. Paris, Imprimerie Royale, 1786. F702

France. Conseil d'État. Arrêt ... qui annulle les passeports expédiés par la Compagnie des Indes ... Paris, P.G. Simon & N.H. Nyon, 1786. F703
Nullifies permits issued for importation of calico.

France. Conseil d'État. Arrêt ... qui annulle les passeports expédiés par la Compagnie des Indes ... pour l'introduction des toiles de coton blanches & peintes venant de l'étranger. Paris, Imprimerie Royale, 1786. F704

France. Conseil d'État. Arrest ... qui déclare de nul effet ... les passe-ports expédiés par la Compagnie des Indes. Lille, C.M. Peterinck-Cramé, 1786. F705
Voids passports for those importing prohibited goods.

France. Conseil d'État. Arrêt ... qui déclare de nul effet ... les passeports expédiés par la Compagnie des Indes pour l'entrée des toiles de coton blanches & peintes. Paris, P.G. Simon & N.H. Nyon, 1786. F706

France. Conseil d'État. Arrêt ... qui déclare nuls & de nul effet les passeports illimités, délivrés par l'ancienne Compagnie des Indes aux négocians & armateurs ... Paris, Imprimerie Royale, 1786. F707

France. Conseil d'État. Arrêt ... qui fixe les chargemens de morue ... pour obtenir les primes d'encouragemens. Paris, Imprimerie Royale, 1786. F708
A minimum of fifty hundredweight is set for cod shipments from America on which a premium will be paid.

France. Conseil d'État. Arrêt ... qui nomme les commissaires du Conseil pour juger les contestations dans lesquelles la Compagnie des Indes sera partie. Paris, Imprimerie Royale, 1786. F709
Appointment of commissioners to judge cases involving the Compagnie des Indes.

France. Conseil d'État. Arrêt ... qui nomme les commissaires du Conseil pour juger les contestations dans lesquelles la Compagnie des Indes sera partie. Paris, P.G. Simon & N.H. Nyon, 1786. F710

France. Conseil d'État. Arrêt ... qui ordonne aux officiers des amirautés, de tenir la main à l'exécution de l'arrêt du 14 avril 1785, portant etablissement d'une nouvelle Compagnie des Indes, relativement aux passeports & aux congés à délivrer aux amirautés. Paris, Imprimerie Royale, 1786. F711

France. Conseil d'État. Arrêt ... qui ordonne qu'il sera perçu un droit de six livres par quintal de salpêtre, & de quinze livres par quintal de podres qui entreront dans le royaume. Paris, P.G. Simon & N.H. Nyon, 1786. F712

France. Conseil d'État. Arrest ... qui ordonne que les cotons en laine qui sortiront du royaume pour la destination de l'étranger, de l'Alsace, de la Lorraine & des Trois-Évêchés, acquitteront à leur sortie un droit de douze pour cent. Lille, C.M. Peterinck-Cramé, 1786. F713
Changes in custom dues levied on raw wool that was exported from France.

France. Conseil d'État. Arrest ... qui ordonne que toutes estampes & images y désignées ... venant de l'étranger, acquitteront les droits. Paris, Imprimerie Royale, 1786. F714
Establishes duties on prints, pictures, and engraved papers.

France. Conseil d'État. Arrêt ... qui permet aux administrateurs de la Compagnie des Indes de faire les balanciers & planches nécessaires pour graver les nouveaux plombs & bulletins. Paris, Imprimerie Royale, 1786. F715
A decree concerning the new lead seals for marking the textiles to be sold by the Compagnie des Indes.

France. Conseil d'État. Arrêt ... qui permet l'entrée ... des toiles peintes en Alsace ... & qui ordonne à l'adjudicataire des fermes de continuer à percevoir le droit ... sur les toiles ... provenant de commerce de la Compagnie des Indes. Paris, Imprimerie Royale, 1786. F716

France. Conseil d'État. Arrest ... qui porta à quarante millions les fonds de la Compagnie des Indes. Aix, A. David, 1786. F717
  Authorizes an increase in funds of the Compagnie des Indes.

France. Conseil d'État. Arrêt ... qui porte à quarante millions les fonds de la Compagnie des Indes; & qui prolonge ... la durée de son privilége. Paris, Imprimerie Royale, 1786. F718

France. Conseil d'État. Arrêt ... qui renvoie pardevant les commissaires nommés par l'arrêt du 31 décembre 1785, la connoissance de toutes les contestations relatives à l'expédition de Chine. Paris, P.G. Simon & N.H. Nyon, 1786. F719

France. Conseil d'État. Arrêt ... concernant l'établissement des paquebots pour la correspondance avec les colonies françoises & les Etats-Unis de l'Amérique. Paris, N.H. Nyon, 1787. F720

France. Conseil d'État. Arrêt ... concernant les toiles peintes d'Alsace, & les toiles de coton blanches, provenant du commerce de la Compagnie des Indes. Paris, P.G. Simon & N.H. Nyon, 1787. F721

France. Conseil d'État. Arrêt ... portant établissement de vingt-quatre paquebots, pour communiquer avec les colonies françoises aux Isles du Vent & Sous les Vent, les isles de France & de Bourbon, & les États-Unis de l'Amérique. Paris, Imprimerie Royale, 1787. F722

France. Conseil d'État. Arrêt ... qui accorde une prime de cinq livres par quintal de morue sèche de pêche françois importée dans les échelles du Levant. Paris, Imprimerie Royale, 1787. F723
  Fixes premiums on the exportation of dried codfish to the commercial centers of the Levant and other areas of the Mediterranean.

France. Conseil d'État. Arrêt ... qui commet le sieur de Selle ... pour coter & parapher les livres & registres établis & à établir pour les affaires de la Compagnie des Indes créée par arrêt du conseil du 14 avril 1785. Paris, Imprimerie Royale, 1787. F724

France. Conseil d'État. Arrêt ... qui nomme M. de Boullonge de Nogent, commissaire du Roi pour suivre les opérations de l'ancienne Compagnie des Indes. Paris, Imprimerie Royale, 1787. F725

France. Conseil d'État. Arrêt ... qui ordonne la translation de l'entrepôt de la Pointe-à-Pître à la Basseterre-Guadeloupe. Paris, N.H. Nyon, 1787. F726

France. Conseil d'État. Arrêt ... qui ordonne que les sieurs François-Jacques Dutertre-Macé & Léonard Peyrand, signeront les bulletins à apposer aux marchandises de l'Inde, conjointement avec les sieurs Laurent-André-Olivier-Bonaventure Besné & Jacques-Louis-Codercq. Paris, Imprimerie Royale, 1787. F727
  A decree dealing with the prominent merchants of the new Compagnie des Indes.

France. Conseil d'État. Arrêt ... qui porte à huit livres le droit ... sur la morue sèche de pêche étrangere. Paris, Imprimerie Royale, 1787. F728
  A duty of eight francs per hundredweight is levied on dried cod brought by foreign ships from the Leeward and Windward Islands.

France. Conseil d'État. Arrêt ... qui proroge jusqu'au premier août 1789, la permission ... d'introduire aux Isles du Vent ... des noirs de traite étrangere. Paris, N.H. Nyon, 1787. F729

France. Conseil d'État. Arrêt du Conseil d'état du roi, qui ordonne la translation de l'entrepôt de la Pointe-à-Pître à la Basseterre-Guadeloupe, du 28 décembre 1786. [Paris, Imprimerie Royale, 1787.] F730
  The port of entry for commerce on Gualeoupe is moved from Point-A-Pître to Basseterre.

France. Conseil d'État. Arrêt ... concernant les mousselines & toiles de cotton. Paris, N.H. Nyon, 1788. F731

France. Conseil d'État. Arrêt ... portant nomination d'une commission pour prendre connoissance de l'établissement actuel de la Compagnie des Indes, & des effets de son privilége exclusif. Versailles, Imprimerie Royale, 1788. F732

France. Conseil d'État. Arrêt ... portant prohibition ... des huiles de baleine & de spermacéti, provenant de pêche étrangère. Paris, N.H. Nyon, 1788. F733

France. Conseil d'État. Arrêt ... portant suppression du conseil des prises, au premier avril 1788. Paris, N.H. Nyon, 1788. F734

France. Conseil d'État. Arrêt ... pour encourager, par des primes, l'importation en France des blés & des farines venant des États-Unis de l'Amérique. Paris, N.H. Nyon, 1788. F735

France. Conseil d'État. Arrêt ... pour l'encouragement du commerce de France avec les États-

Unis de l'Amérique. Paris, Imprimerie Royale, 1788.　F736

France. Conseil d'État. Arrêt ... qui accorde une prime d'encouragement aux armateurs françois, qui feront préparer & porter dans les ports du royaume les rogues provenant de leur pêche. Paris, Imprimerie Royale, 1788.　F737

France. Conseil d'État. Arrêt ... qui excepte de l'entrepôt accordé, par l'arrêt du conseil du 29 décembre 1787, aux productions & marchandises des États-Unis, les poissons, huiles & autres marchandises provenant de leurs pêches. Paris, Imprimerie Royale, 1788.　F738

France. Conseil d'État. Arrêt ... qui ordonne que le port de Gravelines sera ouvert au commerce privilégié des colonies & des pêches. Paris, Imprimerie Royale, 1788.　F739

France. Conseil d'État. Arrêt ... qui permet l'admission en franchise des bâtimens étrangers au Port-Louis en l'Isle-de-France. Paris, N.H. Nyon, 1788.　F740

France. Conseil d'État. Arrêt ... qui permet l'entrée des mousselines rayées & quadrillées provenant du commerce françois, qui sont actuellement à l'Orient ... Paris, N.H. Nyon, 1788.　F741

France. Conseil d'État. Arrêt ... qui proroge ... le délai accordé pour l'entrée & le débit dans le royaume des mousselines rayées, cadrillées & brochées, dites doréas, provenant du commerce françois dans l'Inde. Paris, N.H. Nyon, 1788.　F742

France. Conseil d'État. Arrêt ... portant règlement pour le paquage de la morue à Dunkerque. Lille, C.M. Peterinck-Cramé, 1789.　F743
　A decree regulating the packing of cod that was initiated by the salt merchants of Paris.

France. Conseil d'État. Arrêt ... pour encourager par des primes, l'importation en France des blés & des farines venant des différens ports de l'Europe. Lille, C. M. Peterinck-Cramé, 1789.　F744
　Yielding to popular demand the King permitted importing of wheat and flour from European markets.

France. Conseil d'État. Arrêt ... pour proroger ... les primes accordées à l'importation en France des blés & farines venant des États-Unis de l'Amérique. Lille, C.M. Peterinck-Cramé, 1789.　F745

France. Conseil d'État. Arrêt ... pour proroger jusqu'au premier septembre les primes accordées a l'importation en France des blés & farines venant des États-Unis de l'Amérique. Lille, C. M. Peterinck-Cramé, 1789.　F746

France. Conseil d'État. Arrêt ... qui excepte de la prohibition portée par l'arrêt du 28 septembre dernier, les huiles de baleine & d' autres poissons, ainsi que les fanons de baleine, provenant de la pêche des États-Unis de l'Amérique. Paris, Imprimerie Royale, 1789.　F747

France. Conseil d'État. Articles et conditions sur lesquelles la Compagnie des Indes adjugera au plus offrant & dernier encherisseur, les marchandises apportées des Indes Orientales ... Paris, Veuve Saugrain & Pierre Prault, 1721.　F748
　A series of seventeen regulations dealing largely with duties on goods.

France. Conseil d'État. Direction de Lille. Ordre concernant les défenses aux femmes, enfants & domestiques d'employer des fermes ... Lille, 1743.　F749
　A warning to families of customs officials against wearing prohibited cloths.

France. Conseil d'État. Direction de Lille. Ordre concernant les toiles peintes. Lille, C.M. Cramé, 1736.　F750
　Orders provincial administrations to take action against cloth smugglers.

France. Conseil d'État. Direction de Lille. Ordre concernant les toiles peintes. Lille, 1740.　F751
　Upon a seizure of prohibited Indian fabrics, samples should be sent to Paris.

France. Conseil d'État. Extraict des registres du Conseil d'Estat. Le Roy ayant par ses edicts des mois de mars & de decembre 1654 autre edict du mois mars 1655 & arrest en consequence, ordonné la levée & augmentation de cinq sols pour livre ou parisis sur toutes sortes de droicts de quelque nature qu'ils soient ... [n.p., 1657.]　F752

France. Conseil d'État. Extraict des registres du Conseil d'Estat. Sur ce qui a esté représenté ... par ... la Compagnie des Indes Orientales ... l'exemption de tous droits d'entrées & sorties sur les munitions de guerres, vivres & autres choses ... Paris, 1665.　F753
　Relates to provisions for ships of the Compagnie des Indes Orientales.

France. Conseil d'État. Extraict des registres du Conseil d'Estat. Sur ce qui a esté représenté ... par ... Compagnie des Indes Orientales, que du nombre des officiers, pilotes, matelots ... qui ont fait voile pour l'isle Dauphine & pour les Indes ... Paris, 1666. F754

Concerns the earliest voyages of the Compagnie des Indes Orientales.

France. Conseil d'État. Extraict des registres du Conseil d'Estat. Sur ce qui a esté representé ... par la Compagnie du Commerce des Indes Orientales, que pour l'establissement dudit commerce dans les Indes ... Paris, 1665. F755

Concerns the recruiting of sailors and others for the service of the Compagnie des Indes Orientales.

France. Conseil d'État. Extraict des registres du Conseil d'Estat. Sur ce qui a esté representé ... par ... la Compagnie du Commerce des Indes Orientales ... par l'edit ... luy accorder ... privileges & exemptions pour l'entrée ... & la sortie ... des toutes les marchandises & denrées ... Paris, 1665. F756

Concerns goods to be shipped by the newly-formed company.

France. Conseil d'État. Extrait des registres du Conseil d'Estat ... par la quel il aurois esté ... ordonné que ... il seroit tenu une assemblée generale des interessez en la Compagnie du Commerce des Indes Orientales ... Paris, 1668. F757

France. Conseil d'État. Extrait des registres du Conseil d'Estat ... s'estant fait representer les lettres, journaux & relations ... venuës de l'isle Dauphine ... contenant tout ce qui s'est passé pendant le voyage de deux flottes envoyées ... par ... la Compagnie du Commerce des Indes Orientales ... Paris, 1668. F758

France. Conseil d'État. Extrait des registres du Conseil d'Estat. Sur ce qui a esté representé ... par ... la Chambre generale du commerce des Indes Orientales, que nonobstant les privileges concedez à ladite Compagnie par la declaration ... Paris, 1665. F759

Relates to the victualling of ships for the newly-established Compagnie des Indes Orientales.

France. Conseil d'État. Extrait des registres du Conseil d'Estat. Sur ce qui a esté representé ... par ... la Compagnie du Commerce des Indes Orientales que ... permet à ladite Compagnie de naviguer & negotier seule ... dans toutes les Indes & Mers Orientales ... Paris, 1667. F760

France. Conseil d'État. Extrait des registres du Conseil d'Etat. Le Roy ayant esté informé que plusieurs particuliers ont offert aux sieurs directeurs generaux de la Compagnie des Indes Orientales ... [n.p., 1682.] F761

Provision is made for exceptions to the monopoly held by the Compagnie des Indes on eastern trade.

France. Conseil d'État. Extrait des registres du Conseil d'État. Lille, C.M. Cramé, 1752. F762

States that the edict of 1726 restricting importation of fabrics from India is still in effect.

France. Conseil d'État. Jugement contradictoire, entre l'adjudicataire de la ferme générale du tabac, & les sieurs Godefroy, Saugrain, Huissiers-priseurs-vendeurs, & la communauté desdits Huissiers ... Paris, Lamesle, 1785. F763

Concerns the disposition of tobaccos found in inventories at the time of death of the owner.

France. Conseil d'État. Jugement des commissaires ... qui annule des marchés faits à terme, d'actions de la nouvelle Compagnie des Indes. Paris, Imprimerie Royale, 1786. F764

France. Conseil d'État. Jugement rendu ... qui condamne, par corps, le nommé Jean Vandal, marchand vinaigrier à Paris ... & la confiscation des tabacs & utensiles propres à la fabrication & distribution ... du tabac dans sa boutique sans la permission expresse ... Paris, Lamesle, 1781. F765

France. Conseil d'État. Jugement rendu ... qui condamne, par corps, le nommé Batifol, limonnacier, à Paris ... pour avoir été trouvé pesant, vendant & livrant du tabac dans sa boutique, sans la permission expresse ... Paris, Lamesle, 1781. F766

A prosecution for illegal sale of tobacco.

France. Conseil d'État. Jugement rendu ... qui condamne solidairement & pars corps le nommé Lelievre & sa femme, debitans de tabac ... Paris, Lamesle, 1780. F767

The persons condemned had been found with a quantity of tobacco adulterated with ashes.

France. Conseil d'État. Jugement rendu ... qui déclare bonne & valable la saisie de quarante-huit pieds en plan de tabac, faite sur le sieur Méteyer, marchand tabletier à Paris. Paris, Imprimerie Royale, 1777. F768

France. Conseil d'État. Jugement rendu ... qui prononce la confiscation du faux tabac saisi sur Isaac Patallier, tailleur, lui fait défenses de récidiver; le condamne, outre les dépens, en l'amende de mille livres ... Paris, Imprimerie Royale, 1776. F769

France. Conseil d'État. Jugement rendu ... qui prononce la confiscation du faux tabac saisi sur Antoine Vaché, marchand chauderonnier. Paris, Imprimerie Royale, 1776. F770

France. Conseil d'État. Jugement rendu ... qui prononce la confiscation du faux tabac saisi sur Jean Coqueret ... Paris, Imprimerie Royale, 1776. F771
Affirming the legality of a seizure of tobacco held illegally by a wine merchant.

France. Conseil d'État. Jugement rendu ... qui prononce la confiscation du faux tabac saisi sur Jacques Giret ... Paris, Lamesle, 1781. F772
An action against an owner of smuggled tobacco.

France. Conseil d'État. Ordonnance de m. de Marville ... qui confisque des étoffes de soyerie des Indes ... Paris, Imprimerie Royale, 1742. F773
Mlle. Evrard, lingerie merchant, is deprived of goods and license for selling prohibited materials.

France. Conseil d'État. Ordres nouveaux concernant le port & usage d'habillemens de toiles peintes. Lille, 1737. F774
Prohibits wearing or using cloths imported from India.

France. Conseil d'État. Propositions presentées au Roy par les directeurs de la Compagnie des Indes, pour entrer ... du commerce cy-devant fait par la Compagnie d'Afrique. Paris, Veuve Saugrain & Pierre Prault [1719]. F775

France. Conseil d'État. Réglement pour la police & discipline des équipages des navires marchands ... Paris, Imprimerie Royale, 1759. F776
Policy regulation for disciplining the merchant fleets sent to France's American colonies and for crew replacements for both royal and merchant ships.

France. Conseil d'État. Réglement pour les paquebots; établis par arrêt ... du 14 décembre 1786, pour communiquer avec les colonies françoises, aux Isles le Vent & Sous le Vent, les isles de France & de Bourbon, & les États-Unis de l'Amérique. Paris, N.H. Nyon, 1787. F777
Regulations concerning the mail ships sailing to the French colonies.

France. Conseil d'État. Resultat du Conseil pour la fourniture du tabac de cantine aux troupes. Paris, Veuve Saugrain & Pierre Prault, 1720. F778
The contract for providing tobacco to French soldiers and sailors is granted to a private company.

France. Conseil d'État. Tarif des droits d'entrée et de sortie des cinq grosses fermes ... sur toutes les marchandises. Rouen, Richard Lallement, 1758. F779
A history of French import and export taxes from 1664 to 1758.

France. Conseil de commerce. Memorials presented by the deputies of the Council of Trade in France to the Royal Council in 1701 ... London, J. and P. Knapton [etc.] 1737. F780
A collection of twenty memorials on various aspects of French trade, with text in both French and English.

France. Conseil du Roy. Arrests, commissions et privileges ... pour l'establissement de la Royale & General Compagnie du Commerce. Paris, Bertr. Martin, 1621. F781
This document authorized the establishment of a company directed by François du Noyer. It was unrestricted as to the type of products it was to trade in and also as to the locality of its activities.

France. Conseil du Roy. Tariffe de la taxe faite par le Roy, des marchandises et denrées. [n.p., ca. 1632.] F782
An alphabetical list of goods and the duties payable on them upon entry into France as of 1632.

France. Conseiller du Roy. Reglement faict par ... le conservateur des privileges royaux des foires de Lyon ... Lyons, L. Savine, 1608. F783
Pertains to bankruptcy of merchants at the Lyons fair.

France. Convention nationale. Decret de la Convention nationale du 16e jour de Pluviose, an second de la République Française ..., qui abolit l'esclavage des nègres dans les colonies. Marseille, Sans-Culotte Rochebrun [1794?] F784
Slaves are declared free and are given full French citizenship.

France. Convention nationale. Decret de la Convention nationale, du quatrieme jour de germinal, l'an second ... [i.e. 24 mars 1794], qui prescrit les formalités à observer de la part des militaires qui réclament une indemnité pour leurs équipages de guerre pris par l'ennemi. Dijon, P. Causse [1794?] F785
This document also includes the decrees of the same year liberating slaves in the French colonies.

France. Convention nationale. Décret no. 854 de la Convention nationale, du 9 mai 1793 ... relatif aux navires neutres chargés de comestibles ou de marchandises pour les puissances ennemies. Agen, Veuve Noubel & Fils, 1793. F786
Neutral ships bound for British ports are to be subject to seizure by French vessels in retaliation for British interference with French shipping.

France. Convention nationale. Décret de la Convention nationale ... concernant les relations de la République française avec les autres sociétés politiques. Paris, Imprimerie du Dépôt des Lois, 1793. F787

Statements of French policy toward her friends and enemies, with all assurances of true alliance with the United States.

France. Convention nationale. Décret de la Convention nationale ... portant que les tabacs fabriqués & les tafias en entrepôt dans les ports, seront admis dans circulation intérieure, en payant les droits d'entrée. Paris, Imprimerie Nationale exécutive du Louvre, 1793. F788

France. Convention nationale. Décret de la Convention nationale ... portant suppression des droits sur les denrées & productions des colonies françoises. Paris, Imprimerie Nationale executive du Louvre, 1793. F789

France. Convention nationale. Décret de la Convention nationale ... relatif aux mendians condamnés à la déportation. Paris, Imprimerie du Dépôt des Lois, 1793. F790
Rules concerning the handling of mendicants condemned to deportation.

France. Convention nationale. Décret de la Convention nationale, du 1.er juillet 1792 ... relatif au meurtre commis sur le navire Américain the *Little Cherub*. Paris, Imprimerie Nationale Exécutive du Louvre, 1793. F791
The murder of the clerk aboard the American schooner *Little Cherub* in Dunkirk prompted this decret from the National Convention.

France. Convention nationale. Décret de la Convention nationale, du 19 septembre 1793 ..., qui autorise le payement des primes et gratifications accordées au commerce, à l'exception de celle pour la trait des nègres. Marseille, Rochebrun et Mazet [1793?] F792
Subsidies for the French slave trade are terminated.

France. Convention nationale. Décret de la Convention nationale, du 21 juin 1793 ... relatif aux citoyens de Saint-Domingue ... Paris, Imprimerie nationale Exécutive du Louvre, 1793. F793
A decree by the French government offering aid and assistance to those citizens of Saint-Domingue, Guadeloupe and Martinique who were forced off or left their lands because of slave revolts, to return to their former homes.

France. Convention nationale. Décret de la Convention nationale, du 27 jour de pluviôse ... portant que les bibliothèques & instrumens relatifs à la marine ... Paris, Imprimerie nationale Exécutive du Louvre, [1793] F794
A law exempting libraries of works relating to the theory, practice and history of navigation, depositories of geographical and hydrographic maps, etc., used for the instruction of sailors and the production of nautical charts, from the law which requires all works relating to the arts and sciences be brought to the district county seats.

France. Convention nationale. Décret de la Convention nationale, du 5 mars 1793 ... qui déclare que toutes les colonies françoises sont en état de guerre. Paris, Imprimerie nationale Exécutive du Louvre, 1793. F795
Declaration stating that France along with her colonies is in a state of war and that all governor-generals and other civil administrators of the colonies are to cooperate with French officials and obey all instructions.

France. Convention nationale. Décret de la Convention nationale, du 6 mars 1793 ... qui approuve les mesures prises par les commissaires nationaux Polverel & Santhonax dans la colonie de Saint-Domingue. Paris, Imprimerie nationale Exécutive du Louvre, 1793. F796
Decree by the National Assembly approving of the measures taken by its commissaries, Polverel and Santhouax, in the colony of Saint-Domingue. The decree also authorizes them to take any measures they deem necessary to ensure the defense of the colony from enemies both from within and without.

France. Convention nationale. Décrets de la Convention nationale ... relatifs aux relations commerciales des États-Unis, avec les colonies françoises. Paris, Imprimerie Nationale exécutive du Louvre, 1793. F797
The decrees authorize favorable treatment to commerce of the United States.

France. Convention nationale. Décrets no. 950 de la Convention nationale, des 23 & 28 mai 1793 ... relatifs aux bâtimens des États-Unis. Agen, Veuve Noubel & Fils, 1793. F798
Ships of the United States bound for British ports will be exempt from seizure.

France. Convention nationale. Décrets relatifs aux prises et à l'armement en course. Paris, Imprimerie du Dépôt des Lois, 1793. F799
Four decrees concerning the shipping industry.

France. Convention nationale. Loi qui accorde des secours aux citoyens réfugiés des départmens et possessions françaises dans les colonies et en Corse. Paris, Imprimerie du Dépôt des Lois, 1794. F800
Monetary assistance is provided for those colonists who have been made refugees by the recent colonial wars.

France. Convention nationale. Loi qui applique aux habitans de Saint Domingue ou d'autres colonies françaises. Paris, Imprimerie du Dépôt des Lois, 1794. F801
Colonists who happend to be in the mother country at the time of the outbreak of colonial troubles, and suffered by them, are to be assisted as well as those still in the colonies.

France. Convention nationale. Relation détaillée des événemens malheureux qui se sont passés au Cap depuis l'arrivée du ci-devant général Galbaud, jusqu'au moment où il a fait brûler cette ville et a pris la fuite. Paris, Imprimerie Nationale, 1793. F802

An account of conflict between General Galbaud, the Commissioners of Saint Domingue, and 15,000 rebelling slaves who were declared free during the conflict.

France. Cour des Aides. Arrest ... contenant réglement sur le commerce au pecq, des cendres, soudes & gravelées, & les formalités requises à ce sujet. Paris, P.G. Simon, 1776. F803

France. Cour des Aides. Arrest ... Qui déboute Nicolas Tirard ... & Marie-Anne Lefebvre sa femme ... Paris, G. Lamesle, 1748. F804

Details of a legal case involving the sale of illegally owned tobacco.

France. Cour des Aides. Arrest ... qui fait défenses aux officiers des elections, de faire apporter les tabacs de saisies à leurs greffes, & de descendre dans les bureaux, à moins qu'ils n'en soient requis par le Fermier ou ses commis. Paris, Veuve Saugrain & Pierre Prault, 1730. F805

France. Cour des Aides. Arrest contradictoire ... Qui ... prononce la confiscation de cinq cents vingt-cinq livres de sucre, saisies sur Pierre Dromeau ... Paris, P.G. Simon, 1776. F806

France. Cour des Aides. Arrêt ... concernant l'arrivée des sucres, venant des provinces reputées étrangères. Paris, P.G. Simon & N.H. Nyon, 1786. F807

France. Cour des Aides. Arrêt ... qui fait défenses aux officiers des élections de faire mettre en leur greffe, des échantillons des tabacs saisies, & d'en faire laisser aux parties saisies, & de descendre dans les bureaux, s'ils n'en sont requis par le Fermier. Paris, G. Lamesle, 1775. F808

Re-publication of a law of 1708 regarding disposal of tobacco seized in illegal trade.

France. Cour des Aides. Lettres-patentes, portant établissement d'une commission à l'effet de connoître par voie de police & administration & juger en dernier ressort, de l'introduction & vente du tabac dans les villes de Paris & de Versailles, & dans l'étendue des prévôtés & vicomtés en dépendantes. Paris, Knapen, 1775. F809

France. Cour des comptes, aides et finances (Languedoc). Arrest ... portant condamnation aux galeres, banissement & abstention contre divers recolets du convent du Bourg Saint Andeol, pour crime de contrebande, rebellion à l'execution des ordonnances du Roy, concernant la Ferme du Tabac, & emotion populaire ... Paris, Veuve Saugrain et Pierre Prault, 1730. F810

An action against members of a religious house for illegal trading in tobacco and related offenses.

France. Cour des comptes, aides et finances (Montpellier). Arrêt ... qui ordonne aux entreposeurs du tabac, de détailler du tabac aux particuliers, jusques & à concurrence de demi-once, au prix de l'entrepôt, sans qu'ils puissent le vendre à un plus haut prix, à peine de concussion. Paris, Lamesle, 1786. F811

Prescribes manner and price of sale of tobacco by wholesalers.

France. Cour des comptes, aides et finances (Provence). Arrêt ... qui infirme une sentence du préfet de la Vallée de Barcelonette, du 27 février 1784, ordonne la confiscation de seize livres une once de faux tabac saisi ... Paris, Lamesle, 1786. F812

Reversal of a sentence in a case involving illegal sale of tobacco.

France. Dépôt des cartes et plans de la marine. Neptune Americo-septentrionale ... [Paris, 1778-80.] F813

A nautical atlas of high quality containing twenty-five maps, including general maps of the eastern coast of North America as well as detailed maps of harbors, ports, etc.

France. Députés des Manufactures et du Commerce. Avis des députés du commerce sur l'objet de désavantage que le commerce et les fabriques du royaume éprouvent de la part du traité conclu entre la France et l'Angleterre, et sur moyens propres à y remédier. Manuscript. [n.p.] 9 September, 1788. F814

A review of the commercial treaty between France and Great Britain, presumably that of 1787, which it is alleged gives the British a great advantage in exporting goods to France, to the ruin of the latter's manufactures.

France. Direction générale des douanes. Commerce des isles par le port de Granville. [Valence, 1764.] F815

A broadside calling for greater clarity in the rights of merchants of Granville to participate in the American trade.

France. Direction générale des douanes. Cotons filés sujets au droit de 20 livres par quintal aux entrées du royaume. [Valence. 1761.] F816

A broadside announcing a protective tariff levied on cottons imported from foreign countries and French colonies.

France. Direction générale des douanes. Direction de Lille. [Lille, 1767.]   F817
The administration at Lille is accused of improper handling of cases involving violation of the monopoly of the Compagnie des Indes.

France. Direction générale des douanes. Direction de Lille. [Lille, 1777.]   F818
It is ordered that cargoes of sugar seized by French ships be sent to a storehouse in Paris.

France. Direction générale des douanes. [Lettre] 10 déc. 1754. La Compagnie, Monsieur ... Les cotons destinez pour l'Alsace & les Trois Evêchés, doivant être traittez comme s'ils passoient à l'etranger. [Valence, 1754.]   F819
A broadside announcing a taxation policy with respect to the export of cotton.

France. Direction générale des douanes. Marchandises entreposées dans les villes & ports de Cherbourg & de Libourne, à la destination des isles & colonies françoises de l'Amérique, jouiront des privilèges & exemtions accordées aux négotians des ports de Bordeaux & autres admis au commerce desdites isles & colonies françoises de l'Amérique. [Valence, 1756.]   F820

France. Directoire exécutif. Arrêté ... concernant l'exécution des lois sur la conscription militaire relativement aux habitans des colonies. Paris, Imprimerie Impériale [1799].   F821
Colonisits meeting particular requirements are exempt from military conscription.

France. Laws, etc. Ordonnances royaulx de la ... prevoste des marchans & eschevinaige de la ville de Paris. Paris, Jaques Nyverd et Pierre le Prodeur [1528].   F822
The laws of Paris as they applied to merchants regulated the commerce in most goods that passed through the city. With the laws are sixty-three woodcuts portraying the various trades of Paris.

France. Laws, etc. Ordonnances du Roy, sur le fait de la marine & admirauté. Rouen, Martin le Mesgissier, 1612.   F823
A collection of regulations pertaining to the administration of the crew and the loading, arming and management of French ships.

France. Laws, etc. Ordonnances royaux, sur le faict de l'Admirauté. Rouen, Martin le Mesgissier, 1619.   F824
A reissue of the Admiralty Laws which were originally published in 1543.

France. Laws, etc. Les ordonnances royaux sur le faict et jurisdiction de la prevoste des marchands, & eschevinage de la ville de Paris. Paris, C. Morel, 1620.   F825
A collection of laws governing all aspects of the commercial life of Paris, including salt, cloth, wine and other trades, bridge care, fishing, shipping, etc.

France. Laws, etc. Tariffe generalle; des droicts de traites & impositions foraines, trépas de Loire, entrée de France, & nouvelles impositions d'Anjou, Duchez de Beaumont & de Thoüars, & autres droicts. Paris, Charles Chenault, 1660.   F826
A collection of French tariffs and tariff legislation.

France. Laws, etc. Édits, déclarations, réglemens et ordonnances du Roy sur le fait de la marine. Paris, Imprimerie Royale, 1677.   F827
Contains numerous documents on the trade with Canada and the West Indies.

France. Laws, etc. Ordonnance de Louis XIV Roy de France et de Navarre pour servir de reglement sur plusieurs droits de ses fermes. Montauban, Samuel Dubois [1681].   F828
Thirty provisions defining the ways in which tobacco was to be sold in France.

France. Laws, etc. Bail des gabelles; droits de sortie et d'entrée ... Paris, Frederic Léonard, 1691.   F829
Contains 447 clauses relating to the regulation of French commerce, noting the various import and export taxes as well as recent changes in the tax structure.

France. Laws, etc. Recueil d'edits, reglemens et arrests, concernant le droit de marque des chapeaux. Paris, Pierre Ribou, 1699.   F830
A collection of seven documents from the 1690s containing regulations upon the hat trade.

France. Laws, etc. Ordonnance du Roy, qui deffend tout commerce aux officiers sur les vaisseaux du Roy. Paris, Imprimerie Royale, 1717.   F831

France. Laws, etc. Ordonnance du Roy, servant de règlement pour le Conseil de marine. Paris, Imprimerie Royale, 1720.   F832
Includes a wide range of regulation upon French colonies and trade.

France. Laws, etc. Recueil des tarifs des droits d'entrées et sorties ... Rouen, J.B. Besongne le fils, 1725.   F833
Describes import and export duties from 1664 to 1725.

France. Laws, etc. Réglement pour les farines de Canada. Paris, Imprimerie Royale, 1732.   F834
Prescribes the sealing of barrels to prevent fraudulent declaration as to quality.

France. Laws, etc. Statuts, ordonnances et reglemens des marchands merciers-drapiers de la ville de Roüen. Rouen, Viret, 1732. F835
  A collection of regulations upon the manufacture of cloth in Rouen, including provisions concerning cloth merchants. The collection covers the period from 1545 to 1732.

France. Laws, etc. Le code noir, ou Recueil des reglemens ... concernant ... Negres dans les colonies françoises. Paris, Prault, 1742. F836
  Reprints of documents relating to slavery in the French colonies.

France. Laws, etc. Explication de l'ordonnance de Louis XIV concernant le commerce. Toulouse, G. Henault, 1743. F837
  Pertains chiefly to a law of 1673.

France. Laws, etc. Recueil de réglemens, concernant le commerce des isles & colonies françoises de l'Amérique. Paris, Libraries Associez, 1744. F838
  A collection relating to French commerce, particularly in America and Africa between 1664 and 1742, including material on the formation and development of various French African and West Indian companies.

France. Laws, etc. Statuts et reglemens pour la manufacture des draps de Carcassonne ... Carcassonne, J.B. Coignet, 1746. F839
  A collection of documents concerning the trade in woolen cloth between Carcassonne and the Levant.

France. Laws, etc. Réglemens pour la régie du tabac en Franche-Comté. Besançon, C.J. Daclin, 1757. F840
  A collection of documents on the tobacco trade in France, which traces its development from 1687 to 1755.

France. Laws, etc. Ordonnance de Louis XIV ... pour le commerce. Donnée à S. Germain en Laye, au mois de mars 1673. Paris, 1762. F841
  A series of laws and decrees issued between 1663 and 1739 known collectively as the "Code marchand."

France. Laws, etc. Le code noir, ou Recueil des reglemens rendus jusqu'à présent. Concernant le gouvernement, l'administration de la justice, la police, la discipline & le commerce des Negres dans les colonies françoises. Paris, Prault, 1767. F842
  The second to last edition, including regulations through 1762.

France. Laws, etc. Réglement pour les procédures dans les etablissemens françois de l'Inde. Paris, P.G. Simon, 1777. F843

France. Laws, etc. Réglement sur les places & rangs dans les églises, & dans les marches & cérémonies publiques, dans les établissemens françois de l'Inde. Paris, P.G. Simon, 1777. F844

France. Laws, etc. Ordonnance ... concernant les prises faites par les vaisseaux, frégates & autres bâtimens de Sa Majesté. Lille, N.J.B. Peterinck-Cramé, 1778. F845

France. Laws, etc. Réglement concernant la navigation des bâtimens neutres, en temps de guerre. Paris, Imprimerie de Prault [ca. 1778]. F846

France. Laws, etc. Règlement pour l'établissement du Conseil des prises, et la forme d'y procéder. Paris, Imprimerie Royale, 1778. F847

France. Laws, etc. Déclaration du Roi, en interprétation de l'ordonnance de 1681, concernant la Ferme du Tabac. Paris, Lamesle, 1779. F848
  A reprint of an earlier interpretation of the basic law governing the sale and production of tobacco in France.

France. Laws, etc. Ordonnance du Roi, pour porter le corps des volontaires d'Afrique à six compagnies de cent hommes, y compris une compagnie de canonniers-bombardiers. Paris, Imprimerie Royale, 1779. F849
  Provides for military forces to defend Senegal and other French West African establishments.

France. Laws, etc. Règlement concernant les prises que des corsaires françois conduiront dans les ports des États-Généraux des Provinces-Unies. Paris, Imprimerie Royale, 1781. F850
  The French privateers are permitted to unload and to sell their prizes in the Netherlands.

France. Laws, etc. Recueil de réglemens dépendans des droits confiés a l'administration de la régie générale. Paris, Prault, 1783. F851
  A collection of laws regulating many aspects of French economic life.

France. Laws, etc. Ordonnance du Roi, concernant la composition des équipages des navires marchands. Paris, P.G. Simon, 1784. F852

France. Laws, etc. Sentence de l'élection des Lannes, qui enjoint aux commis & préposés à la régie & perception des droits d'aides & autres impositions royales, de continuer de les lever & percevoir avec exactitude, conformément aux réglemens ... Dax, René Leclercq, 1789. F853
  A statement reaffirming the government's intention to enforce all laws concerning illegal sale of tobacco and giving assistance to those who participate in that trade.

France. Laws, etc. Loi relative à la fourniture du tabac au matelots. Paris, Imprimerie Royale, 1790. F854

Sailors in port are to be supplied with tobacco at the same rates as at sea and corresponding to prices charged to soldiers.

France. Laws, etc. Loi relative à la fourniture du tabac aux matelots. Dijon, Capel, 1790.　　F855
Another edition of the preceding item.

France. Laws, etc. Loi relative aux droits qui se percevaient sur les denrés venant des colonies ... Bourges, B. Cristo [1790].　　F856

France. Laws, etc. Loi concernant la pêche de la morue & du hareng, & le commerce de ces denrées. Gap, J. Allier, 1791.　　F857
A law regulating the inducements to increase importation of fish.

France. Laws, etc. Loi concernant les relations de commerce de Marseille dans l'intérieur du royaume dans les colonies & avec l'étranger. [n.p.] Imprimerie de Mallard, 1791.　　F858
Outlines the terms on which goods from French possessions and foreign countries may be received at Marseilles.

France. Laws, etc. Loi relative à l'importation du tabac. Donnée à Paris, le 27 mars 1791. Paris, Imprimerie Royale, 1791.　　F859
Laws for stricter regulation of the tobacco trade, including prohibitions on importing foreign manufactured tobacco.

France. Laws, etc. Loi relative à l'importation du tabac. Donnée à Paris, le 24 avril 1791. Toulon, Mallard, 1791.　　F860
Same as previous item, with endorsement making it applicable to the department of Var.

France. Laws, etc. Loi relative à l'importation du tabac. Donnée à Paris, le 24 avril 1791. Auxerre, L. Fournier, 1791.　　F861
Same as previous item, with endorsement applying it to the department of Yonne.

France. Laws, etc. Loi relative à l'importation du tabac. Donnée à Paris, le 24 avril 1791. Clermot-Ferrand, Antoine Delcros, 1791.　　F862
Same as above, with endorsement for application in the department of Pui-de-Dôme.

France. Laws, etc. Loi relative à l'importation du tabac. Donnée à Paris, le 24 avril 1791. Paris, Imprimerie Royale, 1791.　　F863
The U.S., Russia, Levant and the Spanish colonies are identified as sources of tobacco, and ports of entry for imports are identified.

France. Laws, etc. Loi relative à la décoration militaire pour les officiers des régimens coloniaux. [Paris, Imprimerie Royale, 1791.]　　F864
Special regulations for military advancement of officers serving in the colonies.

France. Laws, etc. Loi relative à la liberté de cultiver, fabriquer & débiter le tabac dans toute l'entendue du royaume. Clermont-Ferrand, Antoine Delcros, 1791.　　F865
Same text as previous items but with endorsement for provincial application.

France. Laws, etc. Loi relative à la liberté de cultiver, fabriquer & débiter le tabac dans toute l'éntendue du royaume. Paris, Imprimerie Royale, 1791.　　F866
The cultivation, manufacture and sale of tobacco is made free, but importation remains closely regulated.

France. Laws, etc. Loi relative à la situation de l'isle de la Martinique, & aux moyens de rétablir & assurer la tranquillité dans les colonies françoises des Antilles. [Toulon? Mallard, 1791.]　　F867

France. Laws, etc. Loi relative à la situation de l'isle de la Martinique, & aux moyens de rétablir & d'assurer la tranquillité dans les colonies françoises des Antilles. Lyon, d'Aime de la Roche, 1791.　　F868
Same text as the previous item, but with different endorsement information.

France. Laws, etc. Loi relative à la situation de l'isle de la Martinique, & aux moyens de rétablir & d'assurer la tranquillité dans les colonies françoises des Antilles. Paris, N.H. Nyon, 1791.　　F869
Action taken to restore order in Martinique, including dismissal of the Assembly.

France. Laws, etc. Loi relative à m. de la Peyrouse, & à l'impression des cartes par lui envoyées. Paris, Imprimerie Royale, 1791.　　F870
The journals and charts of Lapérouse are ordered to be published at government expense.

France. Laws, etc. Loi relative au commerce du Sénégal. Rouen, Louis Oursel, 1791.　　F871
Another edition of the previous item.

France. Laws, etc. Loi relative au prix du tabac manufacturé. Clermont-Ferrand, Antoine Delcros, 1791.　　F872

France. Laws, etc. Loi relative aux colonies. Paris, Imprimerie Nationale, 1791.　　F873
Gives areas of responsibility in lawmaking to the National Assembly and the Colonial Assembly.

France. Laws, etc. Loi relative aux droits d'entrée sur les denrées coloniales. Aix, Gibelin-David & Emeric-David, 1791.　　F874

France. Laws, etc. Concerns duties applied to imported sugar, indigo, coffee, beaver skins and other products of the French colonies.

France. Laws, etc. Loi relative aux indemnités accordées aux commandans des bâtimens de l'état, lorsqu'ils passeront à leur bord des personnes en vertu d'ordres du Roi. Orleans, L.P. Courlet, 1791. F875

France. Laws, etc. Loi relative aux membres de la ci-devant Assemblée générale de Saint-Domingue, à ceux du comité provincial de l'ouest de ladite colonie, & au sieur Santo-Domingo, commandant de vaisseau *le Leopard*. Paris, Imprimerie Royale, 1791. F876
A reversal of decrees of September 20 and October 12, 1790 against the parties identified in the title.

France. Laws, etc. Loi rélative au commerce audelà du Cap de Bonne-Espérance & aux colonies françoises. Paris, Imprimerie Royale, 1791. F877
A series of twenty-five regulations for carrying on trade between France and the west coast of Africa.

France. Laws, etc. Loi rélative au commerce du Sénégal. Paris, Imprimerie Royale, 1791. F878
Opens the Senegal trade to all Frenchmen.

France. Laws, etc. Loi rélative aux armemens des vaisseaux destinés pour le commerce des isles & colonies françoises. Paris, Imprimerie Royale, 1791. F879

France. Laws, etc. Loi qui accorde des secours aux enfans des habitans de Saint-Domingue, qui se trouvent en France. Paris, Imprimerie Royale, 1792. F880
A law giving assistance to sons and daughters of French colonists who had suffered because of colonial uprisings.

France. Laws, etc. Loi relative à différens objets de commerce. Paris, Imprimerie Royale, 1792. F881
Four laws, relating to trade in wool, gold, silver and tobacco.

France. Laws, etc. Loi relative à la police de la navigation, & des ports de commerce. Coutances, G. Joubert, 1792. F882

France. Laws, etc. Loi relative à la réduction des droits d'entrée sur le tabac ... [n.p.] Imprimerie de Besian, 1792. F883
Establishes rates for various types and qualities of tobacco imported.

France. Laws, etc. Loi relative à la réduction des droits d'entrée sur le tabac ... Auxerre, L. Fournier, 1792. F884
Same as previous item but with additional material applying the law to the department of Yonne.

France. Laws, etc. Loi relative à la réduction des droits d'entrée sur le tabac ... Amiens, J.B. Caron, 1792. F885
Same as previous item, but in this edition an incomplete endorsement statement indicates it could be applied to any locality.

France. Laws, etc. Loi relative aux Acadiens & Canadiens. Paris, Imprimerie Royale, 1792. F886
Gives certain Canadians special status with regard to colonial laws.

France. Laws, etc. Loi relative aux colonies, & aux moyens d'y appaiser les troubles. Lyons, d'Aimé Vater-Delaroche, 1792. F887
An attempt to reestablish orderly government in the West Indian colonies, allowing political rights to freed slaves and Mulattoes.

France. Laws, etc. Loi relative aux colonies, & particulièrement à celle de l'Isle de Cayenne & de la Guyane françoise. Lyons, d'Aime Vater-Delaroche, 1792. F888
Plans for reorganizing the government of French Guiana and Cayenne along principles of the French revolution.

France. Laws, etc. Loi relative aux commissaires civils nommés pour la pacification de colonies. Paris, Imprimerie Royale, 1792. F889
The civil commissioners were authorized to suspend local governments in the colonies in the interest of restoring peace.

France. Laws, etc. Loi rélative à l'envoi de commissaires civils dans les établissemens françois de Coromandel & du Bengale. Nevers, Veuve de la Febure, 1792. F890
The king states that commissioners will be sent out to France's eastern colonies in the hope of settling disputes there.

France. Laws, etc. Arrêté relatif aux bâtimens admis à faire le commerce dans la colonie française du Sénégal. Paris, Imprimerie du Dépôt des Lois [1801]. F891
Only French ships will be allowed to handle the trade to and from Senegal.

France. Ministère de la marine et des colonies. Le Duc de Vandosme, pair, Grand-Maistre, Chef & Sur-Intendant General de la navigation & commerce de France. Le trop grand nombre de commissaires ordinaires cy-devant establis en la marine, y ayant causé de la confusion & du desordre, en ce qu'il est souvent arrivé que dans un mesme port. [n.p., 1661.] F892

France. Ministère de la marine et des colonies. Instructions nautiques, relatives aux cartes & plans du pilote de Terre-Neuve publié au Dépôt général des Cartes. Paris, Imprimerie Royale, 1784.   F893
  Instructions for the navigation of American coastal waters.

France. Ministère de la marine et des colonies. Lettre du Ministre de la marine à la Convention nationale, du 11 mars 1793, l'an IIe de la République française: suivie d'autres pièces relatives à la réunion des Isles-du-Vent à la mère patrie. Paris, Imprimerie Nationale, 1793.   F894
  An announcement by the minister of the navy of the reunion of the Windward Islands, with several articles concerning the settlement of colonial problems.

France. Ministère de la marine et des colonies. Ordre portant defenses a tous capitaines & maistres de navires françois & estrangers, de descharger le lest de leurs vaisseaux, qu'auparavant ils n'ayent fair leur declaration pardevant les officiers de l'Admirauté des ports & havres où ils aborderont ... [n.p., 1660.]   F895

France. Ministère des finances. Compte rendu au Roi, par M. Necker. Paris, Imprimerie Royale, 1781.   F896
  Jacques Necker, the French director general of finances, gives the first public statement of the treasury's income and expenditures, causing great discussion of taxation and economic affairs in France.

France. Ministère du commerce. Armand Cardinal Duc de Richelieu & de Fronsac, pair, Grand Maistre, Chef, & Surintendant General de la navigation & commerce de France ... fait pour raison d'un bris arrivé en la coste de Treguenec en basse Bretagne, d'un vaisseau chargé de vin, le 14. janvier dernier ... [n.p., 1642.]   F897

France. Ministère du commerce. Reglement donné ... sur le faict des congez donnez aux maistres de navires. Rouen, Martin le Mesgissier, 1629.   F898
  A regulation requiring passes for ships engaged in foreign trade, with specifications for different fees required of ships trading with various countries, including Canada.

France. Parlement (Besançon). Extrait des registres du parlement. [Besançon, 1770.]   F899
  Dated May 12, this document concerns a recent edict relating to regulation of the tobacco trade in Burgundy.

France. Parlement (Besançon). Extrait des registres du parlement. [Besançon, 1770.]   F900
  Dated August 28, this document elaborates upon the preceding item.

France. Parlement (Bordeaux). Arrêt ... qui ordonne que les Lettres-Patentes & le tarif du 8 juillet 1759, enregistrês au Parlement, concernant la taxe des ports des lettres, seront exécutés selon leur forme & teneur. Bordeaux, P. Phillippot, 1787.   F901

France. Parlement (Bordeaux). Lettre du Parlement de Bordeaux au Roi ... Paris, 1785.   F902
  Proposes changes in the administration of commerce in the French island colonies in America.

France. Parlement (Bordeaux). Trés-humbles représentations qu'adressent au roi ... les gens tenant sa cour de parlement séant a Bordeaux. [n.p.] 1764.   F903
  A commentary on the depressed state of the economy of Bordeaux following the Seven Years War, with suggestions to bring about an improvement.

France. Parlement (Brittany). Arrest ... qui confirme les saisies des tabacs en poudre qui ont été faites par les différens juges de la province de Bretagne ... Rennes, Veuve de François Vatar, 1784.   F904
  A decree prohibiting the distribution of seized tobacco by one Nicolas Salzard or his agent.

France. Parlement (Brittany). Arrest ... rendu sur les conclusions de M. le Procureur general du Roy, qui fixe le temps aux fraudeurs de tabac, pour s'inscrire en faux contre les procès verbaux des employez, & nommer les témoins desquels ils entendent se servir ... Paris, Veuve Saugrain & Pierre Prault, 1730.   F905
  Re-issue of a decree of 1701 concerning submission of evidence by persons accused of frauds in the tobacco trade.

France. Parlement (Brittany). Arrest ... rendu sur les conclusions de Monsieur le Procureur general, qui fait défenses à toutes personnes de troubler les employez de la Ferme du tabac dans leurs fonctions ... Paris, Veuve Saugrain & Pierre Prault, 1731.   F906
  All persons, including judges, are urged to work with employees rather than against them in controlling those who would defraud the government in the tobacco trade.

France. Parlement (Brittany). Arrest ... rendu sur les conclusions de Monsieur le Procureur General du Roy, qui fait défenses à toutes personnes de donner retraite, à boire & à manger aux fraudeurs de tabac ... Paris, Veuve Saugrain et Pierre Prault, 1731.   F907
  Not only are all persons to deny food and shelter to defrauders in the tobacco business, but all are enjoined to seize them and bring them to justice.

France. Parlement (Brittany). Arrest ... rendu sur les conclusions de Monsieur le Procureur general du Roy, qui défend aux procureurs de la Cour, de lever aucuns défauts contre le procureur de Messieurs les fermiers generaux des cinq grosses Fermes du Roy & du tabac ... Paris, Veuve Saugrain & Pierre Prault, 1707. F908
  Concerns laws of 1677, 1687, 1691 relating to regulation of the tobacco trade.

France. Parlement (Flanders). Extrait des registres de la Cour de Parlement. [Lille, N.J.B. Peterinck-Cramé, 1766.] F909

France. Parlement (Grenoble). Arrest de la Cour de Parlement, Aides et Finances de Dauphiné. Du 9 janvier 1759. Sur l'augmentation du tabac. [Grenoble, André Giroud, 1759.] F910

France. Parlement (Normandy). Extrait des registres du Parlement séant a Rouen. [Rouen, Jac. Jos. Le Boullanger, 1762]. F911
  A response to an account of the execution of the Jesuit Gabriel de Malagrida for complicity in a plot on the life of the Portuguese king, countering the favorable view of Malagrida which had been given.

France. Parlement (Paris). Arrest de la Cour de Parlement, qui condamne un imprimé, en dix vol. in 8°, ayant pour titre; *Histoire philosophique & politique des etablissemens & du commerce des Européens dans les deux Indies*, par Guillaume-Thomas Raynal ... Paris, P.G. Simon, 1781. F912

France. Parlement (Paris). Arrest de la Cour de Parlement. Qui juge qu'un associé ne peut engager les autres associez par des pactions & autres acts faits peu de temps avant le banqueroute ouverte. Paris, L. Vaugon, 1713. F913
  Concerns private trade by a merchant at Quebec who was a member of a trading company.

France. Parlement (Paris). Procés verbal de ce qui s'est passé au lit de justice tenu par le roy au parlement, le Vendredy 88ᵉ jour de juin 1725. Paris, Imprimerie Royale, 1725. F914
  A description of a session of the Parlement at which new taxes were ratified.

France. Sovereigns. Publications under this heading are listed chronologically by individual sovereigns regardless of title, and alphabetically within the year of publication.

France. Sovereign (1547-1559 : Henry II). Edict ... par lequel il a declaré, statué, & ordonné ... aux estats & offices des Admiralitez. Rouen, Martin le Mesgissier, 1628. F915
  A republication of a decree of 1554 describing the organization of the Admiralty with particular reference to the ports of Normandy.

France. Sovereign (1559-1560 : Francis II). Lettres du Roy François deuxiéme du nom, confirmatives des privileges, & franchises des quatre foires de Lyon. Lyons, P. Fradin, 1560. F916

France. Sovereign (1559-1560 : Francis II). Ordonnances et privileges des foires de Lyon. Lyons, P. Fradin, 1560. F917
  A history of the Lyons fair, with accompanying documents, from the earliest times.

France. Sovereign (1560-1574 : Charles IX). Edict ... sur la creation et establissement en la ville de Rouen, d'une place commune pour les marchans. Rouen, Martin le Mesgissier, 1563. F918

France. Sovereign (1560-1574 : Charles IX). Lettres de revocation du Roy, des traictes, entrée & issue des draps d'or ... Lyons, B. Rigaud, 1563. F919
  Requires that cloth of Italian manufacture be imported through the Lyons customs house.

France. Sovereign (1560-1574 : Charles IX). Ordonnance ... sur le reiglement des usages de draps, toilles, passements & broderies d'or, d'argent & soye. Paris, Robert Estienne, 1563. F920
  A restriction upon the use of luxury cloths in dress as a means of preventing large expenditures for foreign goods.

France. Sovereign (1560-1574 : Charles IX). Ordonnance ... sur le taux et impositions des soyes, florets & fillozelles entrants dans son royaume. Paris, Robert Estienne, 1563. F921
  Duties are levied on imported silks in the interest of stimulating the French cloth trade.

France. Sovereign (1560-1574 : Charles IX). Edict ... sur l'election d'un juge et quatre consuls des marchans en la ville de Paris lesquels cognoistront de tous proces & differēds qui seront cy apres meuz entre lesdicts marchās pour faict de marchandise. Paris, Robert Estienne, 1564. F922
  A special court of five merchants is hereby established to settle merchants' cases in Paris when the amount involved is less than one hundred livres.

France. Sovereign (1560-1574 : Charles IX). Ordonnance ... le faict des entrées de tous draps d'or, d'argēt & de soye ... venans du pays d'Italie. Paris, Jean Dallier, 1564. F923
  A restriction upon the entry into France of a wide variety of cloths from Italy.

France. Sovereign (1560-1574 : Charles IX).
Permission du Roy a tous marchans d'envoyer resider leurs enfans & facteurs en la ville de Calais. Paris, Robert Estienne, 1564.   F924
  Permission for all French fishermen and merchants to use the port of Calais, because of the government's desire to improve the cod fishing industry.

France. Sovereign (1560-1574 : Charles IX).
Declaration & interpretation du Roy sur l'edict de l'eslection d'un juge & quatre consuls en sa ville de Paris. Paris, Robert Estienne, 1565.
F925
  Clarification of an edict of the previous year establishing a court for mercantile cases in Paris.

France. Sovereign (1560-1574 : Charles IX).
Lettres patentes ... sur la defense et prohibition des traictes & transports des bleds & grains hors son royaume. Paris, Robert Estienne, 1565.
F926
  Bad weather conditions and anticipated shortages of grain led to this restriction upon its export from France.

France. Sovereign (1560-1574 : Charles IX).
Ordonnance ... sur le faict des draps et fils d'or, d'argēt & de soye & autres marchandises ... entrans en son royaume. Paris, Robert Estienne, 1566.   F927
  Primarily concerns the import of cloth from the Levant.

France. Sovereign (1560-1574 : Charles IX).
Lettres patentes ... contenant prohibition & deffenses, de toutes traictes tant generales que particulieres, transportz & sorties de bledz ... hors le royaume de France. Lyons, Benoist Riguad, 1567.   F928

France. Sovereign (1560-1574 : Charles IX).
Lettres patentes ... touchant les estrangier ... Paris, Benoist Riguad, 1567.   F929
  Regulation limiting foreign residents in Paris to those useful to the city's business.

France. Sovereign (1574-1589 : Henry III).
Edict ... contenant le reiglement estably ... entre les marchans, bourgois & habitans des villes ... & les marchans foreins ... Paris, Nicolas Roffet, 1586.   F930
  A regulation on the sale of foreign goods in France that is also meant to curb abuses by French merchants themselves.

France. Sovereign (1589-1610 : Henry IV).
Lettres de declaration sur le restablissement des clercs & commissaires des fermes ... Paris, Claude de Monstr'oeil & Jean Richer, 1598.
F931
  Provides for the reestablishment of an earlier form of taxation on cloth, fish, wood, and other products.

France. Sovereign (1589-1610 : Henry IV).
[Grant to Master Captain Chauvin, of the Island of Bourbon, of Cape Breton, and other parts of the eastern portion of New France.] Manuscript. Paris, 15 January 1600.   F932

France. Sovereign (1610-1643 : Louis XIII).
Edict ... contenant les ordonnances et reiglement de la jurisdiction de l'Admirauté de France. Rouen, Martin le Mesgissier, 1620.   F933
  A series of one hundred regulations governing French maritime activity.

France. Sovereign (1610-1643 : Louis XIII).
Lettres patentes ... pour la revocation et suppression des charges de Connestable & Admiral de France. Rouen, Martin le Mesgissier, 1627.
F934
  This decree abolished the office of Admiral of France, which had exercised jurisdiction over French maritime commerce.

France. Sovereign (1610-1643 : Louis XIII). De par le Roy ... [Rouen, 1635.]   F935
  The king of France hereby prohibits French ships from going into Spanish ports or ports in Spanish possessions, because of the bad treatment received by French seamen at the hands of the Spaniards.

France. Sovereign (1610-1643 : Louis XIII).
Declaration ... pour faire levée sur le petun & tabac, de trente sols pour livre de droit d'entrée. Paris, Veuve Saugrain & Pierre Prault, 1727.
F936
  Tobacco coming from St. Christopher, Barbados and other West Indian islands is exempted from this tax. This is a reprint of a law of 1629.

France. Sovereign (1643-1715 : Louis XIV). [A proclamation forbidding the use of printed permits for ships sailing from French ports.] Paris, 1646.   F937
  Proclamation requiring handwritten sailing permits for ships departing for distant places as a means of being assured that ill-equipped ships would not sail.

France. Sovereign (1643-1715 : Louis XIV).
Declaration ... portant reglement sur le faict de la navigation ... [n.p.] 1650.   F938
  Regulations for French shipping, forbidding the capture of other ships, dealing in goods from captured ships, and loading cargo without proper permission.

France. Sovereign (1643-1715 : Louis XIV). De par le Roy. Sa Majesté voulant prevenir & empescher le prejudice que arriveroit au bien de son service, & à celuy de ses sujets, particulierement à ceux qui trafiquent sur mer si les vaisseaux des marchands qui vont & viennent de Bordeaux dans les ports de ce royaume ... [n.p., 1651.]   F939

France. Sovereign (1643-1715 : Louis XIV). De par le Roy. Les seigneurs de l'Isle de Grenade ... [n.p., ca. 1655.]   F940

    A broadside announcing that the proprietors of the Island of Grenada are about to settle a colony there, and they invite persons of all qualities to enlist in the venture.

France. Sovereign (1643-1715 : Louis XIV). De par le Roy. Sa Majesté ayant esté advertie que les Sieurs les Estats Generaux des Provinces Unies des pays-bas avoient ordonné la main-levée des saisies faictes par leur ordre des vaisseaux, marchandises, & effects appartenans aux subjets de Sa Majesté ... [n.p., 1657.]   F941

France. Sovereign (1643-1715 : Louis XIV). De par le Roy. Sa Majesté ayant esté advertie de ce qu'au prejudice des ordonnances generales de la Marine, & de celle particuliere du mois de septembre 1649 & autres faites en consequence ... qui est une contravention manifeste ausdites ordonnances, & dont les amis & alliez de Sa Majesté pourroient se plaindre avec raison & justice si elle ne l'empeschoit ... [n.p., 1658.]   F942

France. Sovereign (1643-1715 : Louis XIV). De par le Roy. Extrait des registres du Conseil d'Estat. Le Roy estant en son Conseil Royal des Finances, s'estant fait representer les diverses requestes, qui luy ont esté presentées depuis plus de dixhuit mois par ses sujets habitans des villes maritimes des provinces de Guiene, Xaintonge, Poitou, Bretagne, & Normandie ... [n.p., 1662.]   F943

France. Sovereign (1643-1715 : Louis XIV). De par le Roy. Extrait des registres du Conseil d'Estat. Le Roy estant en son Conseil Royal des Finances, s'estant fait representer les diverses requestes, qui luy ont esté presentées depuis plus de dixhuit mois par ses sujets habitans des villes maritimes des provinces de Guiene, Xaintonge, Poitou, Bretagne, & Normandie ... [n.p., 1662.]   F944

    This version dated sixteen days after the above item has additional text.

France. Sovereign (1643-1715 : Louis XIV). Extrait des registres du Conseil d'Estat. Le Roy ayant par un article separé du traité fait entre Sa Majesté & les Estats des Provinces Unies le 27 avril 1662 accordé que doresnavant l'imposition des cinquante sols pour tonneau des vaisseaux étrangers ne sera exigée des navires des ... Provinces Unies qu'une fois pour chaque voyage ... [n.p., 1663.]   F945

France. Sovereign (1643-1715 : Louis XIV). De par le Roy. Le Roy estant en son Conseil Royal des Finances, s'estant fait representer les estats & fonds extraordinaires qui ont esté employez par ses ordres pour le restablissement de la Marine, & l'entretien ses vaisseaux à la mer & dans ses ports ... [n.p., 1664.]   F946

France. Sovereign (1643-1715 : Louis XIV). Déclarations ... portant l'établissement d'une Compagnie pour le commerce des Indes Orientales. Lyons, A. Jullieron, 1664.   F947

France. Sovereign (1643-1715 : Louis XIV). Édit ... pour l'establissement de la Compagnie des Indes Occidentales. Paris, René Baudry, 1664.   F948

    A proclamation announcing the formation of the French West India Company to monopolize the commerce of North America and the west coast of Africa for forty years.

France. Sovereign (1643-1715 : Louis XIV). De par le Roy. Sa Majesté ayant receu diverses remonstrances de la part des marchands negocians par mer és provinces de Languedoc & Provence sur le sujet des deffenses ... de sortir des ports sans sa permission expresse ... [n.p., 1665.]   F949

France. Sovereign (1643-1715 : Louis XIV). De par le roy. On fait à sçavoir à tous, qu'une bonne, ferme, stable & solide paix, avec une amitié & reconciliation entiere & sincere a esté faite & accordée entre ... Prince Louis ... & tres-puissant Prince Philippes par les mesme grace Roy catholique des Espagnes ... [n.p., 1668.]   F950

France. Sovereign (1643-1715 : Louis XIV). Ce jour la cour ayant deliberé sur les avis donnez par le Lieutenant de Police ... en execution de l'arrest du 22 decembre derniere sur la tenue de la foire de S. Germain pour la presente année 1669 ... [n.p., 1669.]   F951

France. Sovereign (1643-1715 : Louis XIV). Déclaration ... portant establissement d'une Compagnie du Nord. Paris, Frederic Léonard, 1669.   F952

    Announces the formation of a French trading company, chartered for ten years, to carry on trade with northern Europe and Muscovy.

France. Sovereign (1643-1715 : Louis XIV). Édit ... portant creation des offices de vendeurs de poisson de mer. Paris, T. Charpentier, 1675.   F953

    Reissue of a law of 1583 regulating the sale of fish.

France. Sovereign (1643-1715 : Louis XIV). Édit ... portant revocation de la Compagnie des

Indes Occidentales. Paris, Veuve Saugrain, 1675. F954

Despite the fact that the Compagnie des Indes Occidentales was chartered for forty years, its patent was revoked because of the high cost incidental to the company's plans for the development of Canada.

France. Sovereign (1643-1715 : Louis XIV). De par le Roy ... Fait à Conde le 17 jour de may 1677. The Hague, J. Scheltus, 1677. F955

A decree by the French King outlining areas available for fishing along the coast of Europe, England, Greenland, and North America.

France. Sovereign (1643-1715 : Louis XIV). Declaration ... portant reglement pour le commerce du tabac dans le royaume, & des droits de marque sur l'or & l'argent, avec celuy des droits sur l'étain. Clermont, Michel & André Jacquard, 1681. F956

France. Sovereign (1643-1715 : Louis XIV). Ordonnance ... pour servir de reglement sur plusieurs droits de ses fermes. Paris, François Muguet, 1681. F957

Relates to trade in tobacco, hides, tin, wine, fish, and numerous other products.

France. Sovereign (1643-1715 : Louis XIV). Déclaration ... pour l'établissement d'une compagnie sous le titre de la Compagnie de Guinée. Paris, S. Mabre-Cramoisy, 1685. F958

Establishes the Guinea Company to monopolize the trade in Slaves and gold dust between the Sierra Leone River and the Cape of Good Hope.

France. Sovereign (1643-1715 : Louis XIV). Ordonnance ... portant declaration de guerre ... contre les Hollandois. Paris, Jacques Langlois, 1688. F959

The declaration of war includes express prohibition against any trade or communication with the Netherlands.

France. Sovereign (1643-1715 : Louis XIV). Ordonnance ... portant declaration de guerre par mer & par terre contre les Espagnols ... donné à Versailles le 15 avril 1689. Paris, Estienne Michallet, 1689. F960

The declaration of war stressed interdiction of all trade between the two countries.

France. Sovereign (1643-1715 : Louis XIV). Lettres patents du Roy, portant établissement d'une nouvelle Compagnie Royale du Sénégal. [n.p., 1696.] F961

The Senegal Company had the exclusive right of supplying slaves to the French colonies in America.

France. Sovereign (1643-1715 : Louis XIV). Ordonnance ... portant défenses de transporter des especes d'or & d'argent dans l'Amérique. Paris, Imprimerie Royale, 1699. F962

France. Sovereign (1643-1715 : Louis XIV). Déclaration ... portant revocation des prohibition & défenses contenuës dans la Déclaration du prémier octobre 1699. Et permission à toutes sortes de personnes, de faire, vendre, & distribuer du plomb en dragées & en balles. Grenoble, Alexandre Giroud, 1702. F963

France. Sovereign (1643-1715 : Louis XIV). Déclaration ... qui permet à la Compagnie des Indes Orientales de vendre les étoffes des Indes qu'elle a réçû par ses vaisseaux, tant celles de soye pure, que celle de soye meslée d'or & d'argent; & aux marchands qui en achéteront, de les débiter jusqu'au dernier décembre 1703. Paris, F. Léonard, 1702. F964

France. Sovereign (1643-1715 : Louis XIV). Declaration ... portant défenses à toutes personnes de debiter du tabac, sans qu'il aye été marqué & plombé du cachet de la Ferme du tabac. Grenoble, Alexandre Giroud, 1704. F965

France. Sovereign (1643-1715 : Louis XIV). Reglement angående siö-prijserne. [n.p., 1704?] F966

A proclamation by the King of France about the sea prizes taken during the war; also, how neutral and allied states and companies may achieve security for their shipping.

France. Sovereign (1643-1715 : Louis XIV). Declaration ... qui ordonne que la conversion des peines établies contre les fraudeurs & contrevenans à ce qui concerne la Ferme du tabac, ne pourra estre prononcée que du consentement du Fermier. Paris, Veuve François Muguet & Hubert Muguet, 1705. F967

Concerns punishment prescribed by a law of 1681 for illegal dealing in tobacco and its enforcement.

France. Sovereign (1643-1715 : Louis XIV). Lettres patentes ... portant établissement d'une compagnie royale pour le commerce de la Chine. [Paris, Veuve Saugrain & Pierre Prault, 1706.] F968

Grants a monopoly on the trade to Canton and Ningpo to a small group of merchants.

France. Sovereign (1643-1715 : Louis XIV). Declaration ... donnée à Versailles le 6 decembre 1707. Contre ceux qui seront trouvez saisis ou vendans du tabac en fraude. [Grenoble, Alexandre Giroud, 1708.] F969

France. Sovereign (1643-1715 : Louis XIV). Declaration ... qui dispense la communauté des inspecteurs sur le placement & arrangement des batteaux, de faire parapher leurs registres. Paris, Veuve François Muguet & Hubert Muguet, 1710. F970

France. Sovereign (1643-1715 : Louis XIV).
Declaration ... portant que la Compagnie des Indes jouira ... du dixième des prises dans les pays de sa concession. [Paris, F. Léonard, 1712.]
F971
This privilege is at the expense of the admiral of France.

France. Sovereign (1643-1715 : Louis XIV).
Lettres patentes ... qui permet au sieur Crozat ... de faire seul le commerce dans ... la Louisiane. Paris, Veuve Saugrain & P. Prault, 1712. F972
The letters patent granting a monopoly on the trade of the Mississippi Valley to Antoine Crozat.

France. Sovereign (1643-1715 : Louis XIV).
Déclaration ... donnée à Marly le 11 juin 1714. Portant défenses d'introduire dans le royaume, aucunes soyes ni marchandises de soyerie provenant des Indes Orientales, & de la Chine, à peine de confiscation. Paris, Veuve & G. Jouvenel, 1714. F973

France. Sovereign (1643-1715 : Louis XIV).
Declaration ... qui proroge pendant dix ans le privilege du commerce des Indes Orientales, en faveur de l'ancienne Compagnie. Paris, Veuve François Muguet & Hubert Muguet, 1714.
F974

France. Sovereign (1643-1715 : Louis XIV).
Déclaration ... qui renouvelle les défenses d'introduire dans le royaume, aucunes soyes ny marchandises de soyerie provenant des Indes Orientales & de la Chine. Paris, Veuve F. Muguet & H. Muguet, 1714. F975

France. Sovereign (1643-1715 : Louis XIV).
Déclaration du Roy, qui défend à tous ses sujets le commerce & la navigation de la Mer du Sud. Paris, Veuve F. Muguet, 1716. F976

France. Sovereign (1643-1715 : Louis XIV).
Déclaration ... concernant la Compagnie des Indes Orientales. Paris, Veuve Saugrain & P. Prault, 1719. F977
A reprint of a decree originally published in 1685 calling for a reorganization of the management of the French East India Company.

France. Sovereign (1643-1715 : Louis XIV).
Déclaration ... donnée à S. Germain en Laye le 20 fevrier 1677. Portant deffenses de moderer les amendes de contraventions faites au papier, & parchemin timbrez, & à la Ferme du tabac, à moins de cent livres, & trois cens livres, sauf à les augmenter suivant l'exigence des cas. Paris, Veuve Saugrain & Pierre Prault, 1723. F978
Republication of a law ameliorating penalties for violation of certain tax laws, including that dealing with taxes on tobacco.

France. Sovereign (1643-1715 : Louis XIV).
Declaration ... portant défenses de moderer les amendes des contraventions faites à la Ferme générale du tabac ... Paris, Veuve Saugrain et Pierre Prault, 1730. F979
A re-issue of a decree of 27 September 1678 reducing certain fines for offenses committed with respect to the laws governing the manufacture and sale of tobacco.

France. Sovereign (1643-1715 : Louis XIV).
Déclaration ... portant réglement pour la Ferme générale du tabac. [n.p., G. Lamesle, 1761.]
F980
A set of fifteen regulations dealing with persons defrauding the government in the tobacco trade; a reprinting of a 1707 decree.

France. Sovereign (1715-1774 : Louis XV). Édit ... concernant les monnoyes. Paris, Imprimerie Royale, 1715. F981
Announces a change in the coinage due to the pressures of Parisian merchants.

France. Sovereign (1715-1774 : Louis XV). Édit ... qui décharge les negocians de l'obligation de prendre des passeports. Paris, Veuve F. Muguet [etc.] 1716. F982
Releases merchants from the necessity of having passports to send ships to areas where trade is not prohibited.

France. Sovereign (1715-1774 : Louis XV) Edit du roy, donné à Paris au mois d'octobre 1716. Concernat les esclaves negres des colonies. Grenoble, G. Giroud, 1716. F983
Edict by Louis XV regulating slavery in the French American colonies. It consists of fifteen articles concerning the treatment of slaves.

France. Sovereign (1715-1774 : Louis XV).
Lettres patentes du Roi, pour la liberté du commerce de la côte de Guinée. [n.p.] 1716. F984
Free trade to the west coast of Africa from the Sierra Leone River to the Cape of Good Hope is given to the cities of Rouen, La Rochelle, Bordeaux, and Nantes.

France. Sovereign (1715-1774 : Louis XV).
Ordonnance ... servant de reglement pour le Conseil de Commerce. Paris, Imprimerie Royale, 1716. F985
Louis XV appoints seven members to a Council of Commerce and specifies the aspects of manufacture and trade which are to be the special concern of each member.

France. Sovereign (1715-1774 : Louis XV).
Reglement au sujet des engagez et fusils. Paris, Imprimerie Royale, 1716. F986
Sea captains are obliged to transport indentured servants and firearms to the American colonies.

France. Sovereign (1715-1774 : Louis XV).
Déclaration ... concernant la Guinnée. Qui ordonne que trois negrillons ne seront payez que

sur le pied de deux negres, et deux negrittes pour un negre. Paris, Imprimerie Royale, 1717. F987

Introduction of new tax rates payable by the merchants who were importing slaves to the Americas: three boys were to be counted as two men, two women as one man.

France. Sovereign (1715-1774 : Louis XV). Déclaration ... qui attribue la connoissance des affaires de la Compagnie de Saint Dominique ... Paris, Veuve F. Muguet [etc.] 1717. F988

The King assumes that the officers of the general board of the Admiralty have knowledge of the affairs of the Compagnie de Saint Domingue.

France. Sovereign (1715-1774 : Louis XV). Édit ... concernant le commerce des colonies françoises. Dijon, J. Ressayre, 1717. F989

In an effort to clarify the commercial policies of France, this document specifies ports for trade with colonies as well as import and export taxes.

France. Sovereign (1715-1774 : Louis XV). Édit ... portant reglement pour le commerce dans les isles & colonies françoises. [n.p] 1717. F990

Thirty-one articles regulating the French commerce to America, specifying which French ports may be used, points of lading and disembarkation in America, the manner of chartering ships, etc.

France. Sovereign (1715-1774 : Louis XV). Édit ... qui pronnonce des peines contre ceux qui introduiront dans le royaume des toilles ... de la Chine, des Indes & du Levant. Paris, G. Jouvenel, 1717. F991

France. Sovereign (1715-1774 : Louis XV). Lettres patentes du Roy, portant reglement pour le commerce des colonies françoises. Paris, Imprimerie Royale, 1717. F992

Names the ports which are to engage in colonial commerce, sets import duties, and eliminates duties on exports to the colonies.

France. Sovereign (1715-1774 : Louis XV). Lettres patentes en forme d'édit, portant établissement d'une ... Compagnie d'Occident. [Paris, 1717.] F993

A broadside announcing the formation of the Company of the West. Fifty-six articles outline the scope of the company's activities.

France. Sovereign (1715-1774 : Louis XV). Lettres patentes sur le règlement concernant les sieges d'Admirauté. Paris, Veuve F. Muguet [etc.] 1717. F994

Concerns locations of admiralty stations in French colonies, and cargo regulation.

France. Sovereign (1715-1774 : Louis XV). Edit ... concernant la Ferme generale du tabac. Paris, Veuve Saugrain & Pierre Prault, 1718. F995

The tobacco monopoly is granted to the Compagnie d'Occident for nine years along with other commercial and taxation rights.

France. Sovereign (1715-1774 : Louis XV). Ordonnance ... portant amnistie pour les forbans. Paris, Imprimerie Royale, 1718. F996

A proclamation of amnesty to the French West Indian pirates who will serve as soldiers for one year.

France. Sovereign (1715-1774 : Louis XV). Déclaration ... concernant les condamnez aux galeres, bannis, & vagabonds. Paris, Veuve F. Muguet, H. Muguet, & L.D. de la Tour, 1719. F997

This regulation permits the judges to send vagrants to the colonies and it forbids former galley slaves and deportees to settle in Paris.

France. Sovereign (1715-1774 : Louis XV). Édit ... portant réünion des Compagnie des Indes Orientales & de la Chine, à la Compagnie d'Occident. Paris, Veuve Saugrain & P. Prault, 1719. F998

Transfers privileges from the old company.

France. Sovereign (1715-1774 : Louis XV). Lettres patentes ... portant règlement pour le commerce ... aux isles françoises de l'Amérique. Paris, Imprimerie Royale, 1719. F999

France. Sovereign (1715-1774 : Louis XV). Lettres patentes ... portant règlement pour le commerce qui se fait de Marseille ... Paris, Imprimerie Royale, 1719. F1000

Prescribes certain goods that could be shipped to America from Marseilles only.

France. Sovereign (1715-1774 : Louis XV). Ordonnance ... portant amnistie pour les forbans. Paris, Imprimerie Royale, 1719. F1001

Repeat of the previous year's proclamation of amnesty to French West Indian pirates who will serve one year as soldiers.

France. Sovereign (1715-1774 : Louis XV). Déclaration ... concernant la Ferme du tabac. Paris, Veuve Saugrain & P. Prault, 1720. F1002

France. Sovereign (1715-1774 : Louis XV). Declaration ... pour abolir l'usage des especes d'or ... & pour indiquer les diminutions sur lesdites especes ... pour abolir pareillement ... l'usage de toutes les especes d'argent, à l'exception des sixiémes & douziémes d'ecus, & livres d'argent ... [n.p., 1720.] F1003

France. Sovereign (1715-1774 : Louis XV). Edit ... portant qu'il sera fabriqué de nouvelles

208   **France. Sovereign 1715-1774**

especes d'or & d'argent. Paris, Imprimerie Royale, 1720. F1004

France. Sovereign (1715-1774 : Louis XV). Lettres patentes du Roy, pour permettre aux négocians de Languedoc de faire le commerce de Guinée. Paris, Veuve Saugrain & P. Prault, 1720. F1005

France. Sovereign (1715-1774 : Louis XV). Declaration ... portant reglement general pour le tabac. Paris, Louis-Denis Delatour & Pierre Simon, 1721. F1006
   After brief experience with free trade in tobacco, the privilege is reestablished, and regulations revert largely to those of 1681.

France. Sovereign (1715-1774 : Louis XV). Lettres patentes du Roy, portant reglement pour le commerce des colonies françoises. Paris, Georges Jouvenel, 1721. F1007

France. Sovereign (1715-1774 : Louis XV). Lettres patentes sur le resultat. Données à Paris le 4e May 1721. Pour la regie des Fermes Générales, sous le nom de Cordier. Grenoble, Gaspard Giroud [1721]. F1008
   Following the collapse of the Compagnie des Indes, the Fermes generales is being re-organized under Charles Cordier.

France. Sovereign (1715-1774 : Louis XV). Reglement que le Roy veut & entend estre observé pour les recensemens qui se sont dans la colonie de Saint Domingue. Paris, Imprimerie Royale, 1721. F1009
   Requires landholders in Saint Domingue to declare to census officials all their productive facilities.

France. Sovereign (1715-1774 : Louis XV). Tarif des marchandises et denrées. Paris, Georges Jouvenel, 1721. F1010
   A list of import duties on goods coming into France.

France. Sovereign (1715-1774 : Louis XV). Bail general du tabac passé a Edouard du Verdier pour neuf ans un mois, à commencer au prémier septembre 1721 & finir à la fin de septembre 1730. [Grenoble, 1722.] F1011

France. Sovereign (1715-1774 : Louis XV). Ordonnance ... portant amnistie pour les forbans. Paris, Imprimerie Royale, 1722. F1012

France. Sovereign (1715-1774 : Louis XV). Declaration ... au sujet des fraudes qui se font aux entrées de Paris, avec violences attroupemens & ports d'armes. Paris, Louis-Denis Delatour & Pierre Simon, 1723. F1013

France. Sovereign (1715-1774 : Louis XV). Déclaration ... contres les fraudeurs des droits de la Ferme du tabac. [Paris?] J. Besongne & J.B. Besongne, 1723. F1014

France. Sovereign (1715-1774 : Louis XV). Declaration ... portant deffenses à tous sujets du Roy, de s'interesser dans la Compagnie de Commerce nouvellement établie à Ostende. Grenoble, Gaspard Giroud [1723]. F1015

France. Sovereign (1715-1774 : Louis XV). Déclaration ... qui fixe à un an le tems des entreposts des marchandises destinées pour les isles de l'Amérique. [n.p, Veuve & M.G. Jouvenel, 1723.] F1016

France. Sovereign (1715-1774 : Louis XV). Déclaration ... qui regle la maniere dont la Compagnie des Indes fera l'exploitation de la vente exclusive du café. Paris, Imprimerie Royale, 1723. F1017
   Thirty-seven articles of regulation on the importing and sale of coffee by the Compagnie des Indes.

France. Sovereign (1715-1774 : Louis XV). Déclaration ... qui regle la maniere dont la Compagnie des Indes fera l'exploitation de la vente exclusive du café. Grenoble, G. Giroud, 1723. F1018

France. Sovereign (1715-1774 : Louis XV). Declaration du Roy ... portant nouveau reglement sur le fait du commerce. [n.p, 1723.] F1019
   A declaration of general tightening up of shipping regulations at Rouen, because of difficulties there between merchants and tax authorities.

France. Sovereign (1715-1774 : Louis XV). Ordonnance ... portant que le produit du dixiéme des prises qui seront faites à l'avenir en commerce étranger dans les colonies continüera d'estre déposé entre les mains du Commis du tresorier de la marine. Paris, Imprimerie Royale, 1724. F1020

France. Sovereign (1715-1774 : Louis XV). Ordonnance ... qui declare ... Gilles Robon ... incapable de monter à l'avenir aucun bastiment ... Paris, Imprimerie Royale, 1724. F1021
   A French captain is penalized for contraband trade with the English.

France. Sovereign (1715-1774 : Louis XV). Édit ... portant confirmation des privileges accordez, concessions & alienations faites à la Compagnie des Indes. Paris, Imprimerie Royale, 1725. F1022
   Outlines privileges and commercial jurisdictions of the Compagnie des Indes.

France. Sovereign (1715-1774 : Louis XV). Édit ... portant des privileges accordez, concessions & alienations faites à la Compagnie des Indes. Aix, J. David, 1725. F1023

France. Sovereign (1715-1774 : Louis XV). Édit ... pour la décharge & liberation de la Compagnie des Indes. Toulouse, C.G. Lecamus, 1725. F1024

France. Sovereign (1715-1774 : Louis XV). Édit ... pour la décharge & libération de la Compagnie des Indes. Paris, Imprimerie Royale, 1725. F1025
Relieves the Compagnie des Indes of its control of the Royal Bank and other privileges following the collapse of John Law's financial program.

France. Sovereign (1715-1774 : Louis XV). Bail général du tabac passé a la Compagnie des Indes, sous le nom de Pierre le Sueur. [Grenoble, 1726.] F1026

France. Sovereign (1715-1774 : Louis XV). Edit ... qui ordonne une fabrication de nouvelles especes d'or & d'argent. Paris, Imprimerie Royale, 1726. F1027

France. Sovereign (1715-1774 : Louis XV). Édit ... qui prononce des peines contre ceux qui introduiront dans le royaume des toiles peintes ... Lille, 1726. F1028

France. Sovereign (1715-1774 : Louis XV). Ordonnance ... portant deffenses a tous chefs, officiers, gardes, gendarmes ... de se charger de faux sel & faux tabac, pour quelque cause que ce soit, sous les peines y contenuës. Paris, Veuve Saugrain & P. Prault, 1726. F1029
An ordinance enjoining all government officials and members of the armed forces to abstain from buying illegal salt and tobacco.

France. Sovereign (1715-1774 : Louis XV). Ordonnance ... servant de reglement pour le consulat de la nation françoise à Cadiz. Paris, Imprimerie Royale, 1728. F1030
A series of regulations upon French merchants trading in Cadiz.

France. Sovereign (1715-1774 : Louis XV). Déclaration ... qui établit des peines contre les contrebandiers. Metz, Veuve B. Antoine, 1729. F1031
A royal decree against smuggling of tobacco and cloth.

France. Sovereign (1715-1774 : Louis XV). Lettres patentes ... concernant la pêche de la moruë ... Paris, Pierre Simon, 1729. F1032

France. Sovereign (1715-1774 : Louis XV). Declaration ... portant defenses de moderer les amendes des contraventions faites à la Ferme général du tabac ... Paris, Veuve Saugrain & P. Prault, 1730. F1033

France. Sovereign (1715-1774 : Louis XV). Lettres patentes sur arrest ... concernant le transit des sucres raffines dans le royaume. Grenoble, Gaspard Giroud [1730]. F1034
A series of regulations upon refiners of imported sugar who transport their product overland.

France. Sovereign (1715-1774 : Louis XV). Ordonnance ... portant que ... tous cavaliers, dragons & soldats prévenus du crime de faux sel, ou de faux tabac, qui seront arrestés ... Paris, Veuve Saugrain & P. Prault, 1730. F1035
Soldiers apprehended in handling illegal tobacco are to come before a military tribunal.

France. Sovereign (1715-1774 : Louis XV). Ordonnance ... portant que toutes les marchandises des estrangers, qui seront embarquées en Levant sur des bastimens françois, seront declarées au juste aux chancelleries, à peine de confiscation. Paris, Imprimerie Royale, 1730. F1036

France. Sovereign (1715-1774 : Louis XV). De par le Roy. Ceberet, maréchal des camps & armées du Roy, commandant au gouvernement de Lille ... Lille, C.M. Cramé, 1731. F1037
An attempt to prevent fradulent dealing in tobacco, particularly among soldiers in the Lille vicinity.

France. Sovereign (1715-1774 : Louis XV). De par le Roy. Ceberet, maréchal des camps & armées du Roy, commandant au gouvernement de Lille ... [n.p., 1731.] F1038

France. Sovereign (1715-1774 : Louis XV). Ordonnance ... qui dispense les vaisseaux marchands ... d'y porter engagez & fusils. Paris, Imprimerie Royale, 1731. F1039
An order releasing merchant vessels from the necessity of transporting guns to Louisiana.

France. Sovereign (1715-1774 : Louis XV). Declaration ... concernant les cafez provenant des plantations & cultures de la Martinique, & autres isles françoises de l'Amerique y denommées. [n.p., 1733.] F1040

France. Sovereign (1715-1774 : Louis XV). Ordonnance ... portant nouvelles deffenses à tous gens de guerre, sur le commerce du faux sel, du faux tabac & des marchandises de contrebande. Paris, Imprimerie Royale, 1734. F1041
A royal ordinance prohibiting the members of the armed forces from patronizing the sale of contraband salt and tobacco.

France. Sovereign (1715-1774 : Louis XV). Lettres patentes sur arrest concernant l'entrepôt tant des marchandises destinées pour les isles & colonies françoises, que de celles qui en viennent. [n.p., 1738.]　　　　　F1042

France. Sovereign (1715-1774 : Louis XV). Bail des fermes royales-unies, fait a M. Jacques Forceville le 16. septembre 1738. Paris, Imprimerie Royale, 1739.　　　　　F1043
　　A statement of tax-farming procedures, indicating types of taxes to be paid, and including taxes upon specific imports and exports in various cities and provinces.

France. Sovereign (1715-1774 : Louis XV). Declaration ... qui exemte de tous droits les bleds, grains & légumes, qui entreront dans le royaume. Rouen, Jacques-Joseph Le Boullenger, 1740.　　　　　F1044

France. Sovereign (1715-1774 : Louis XV). Lettres patentes sur arrest données à Versailles le 28 may 1723. Qui deffendent de vendre & débiter du tabac rapé, sans permission du fermier. Grenoble, Veuve Giroud [1743].　　　　　F1045

France. Sovereign (1715-1774 : Louis XV). Lettres patentes ... concernant le commerce des isles françoises. Metz, François Antoine, 1744.　　　　　F1046
　　Regulations on the American trade are spelled out because of the persistence of abuses in that trade by the cities of La Rochelle, Rouen, Dieppe, and Sète.

France. Sovereign (1715-1774 : Louis XV). Déclaration ... qui ordonne la perception d'un droit de trente sols par chacune livre de seize onces sur tous les tabacs étrangers qui entront dans le royaume. Paris, P.G. Simon, 1749.　　　　　F1047

France. Sovereign (1715-1774 : Louis XV). Ordonnance ... portant déclaration de guerre contre le Roi d'Angleterre. Paris, Imprimerie Royale, 1756.　　　　　F1048

France. Sovereign (1715-1774 : Louis XV). Déclaration ... qui ordonne la perception des quatres sols pour livre sur les différentes especes de tabac, & suppression du droit de deux sols par livre pesant, sur les tabacs ficelés. Paris, Veuve Delatour, 1758.　　　　　F1049

France. Sovereign (1715-1774 : Louis XV). Lettres patentes ... concernant les toiles de coton blanches, & les toiles peintes, teintes & imprimées. Paris, P.G. Simon, 1759.　　F1050
　　A series of twenty-six regulations upon the importing of colored and uncolored cloth into France, specifying duties and ports of entry.

France. Sovereign (1715-1774 : Louis XV). Lettres patentes sur arrest, données à Versailles le 13 février 1759. Concernant le deux sols par livre pesant de tabac ficelé. Grenoble, André Giroud, 1759.　　　　　F1051

France. Sovereign (1715-1774 : Louis XV). Lettres patentes ... concernant les toiles de coton blanches, & les toiles peintes & imprimées. Paris, P.G. Simon, 1760.　　F1052

France. Sovereign (1715-1774 : Louis XV). Lettres-patentes ... concernant les toiles de coton blanches, & les toiles peintes & imprimées. Grenoble, André Giroud, 1760.　　F1053
　　A series of regulations upon imported cotton cloth.

France. Sovereign (1715-1774 : Louis XV). An historical memorial of the negotiation of France and England, from the 26th of March, 1761, to the 20th of September of the same year. London, For D. Wilson and T. Becket and P.A. Dehondt, 1761.　　　　　F1054
　　Translated from the French, this is a collection of diplomatic communications between French and British officials, tending to show Britain's culpability in the suspension of negotiations which involved the overseas possessions of both countries.

France. Sovereign (1715-1774 : Louis XV). Déclaration ... pour l'exécution des deux articles du traité conclu entre le Roi, & le Roi d'Espagne, qui regardent l'intérêt particulier de leurs sujets. Toulouse, Veuve de B. Pijon, 1762.　　　　　F1055

France. Sovereign (1715-1774 : Louis XV). Lettres patentes du Roi, qui autorisent les prevôt des marchands & êchevins de la ville de Paris, à emprunter à constitution de rente viagére ... Paris, Imprimerie Royale, 1762.　　F1056

France. Sovereign (1715-1774 : Louis XV). Lettres patentes du roi qui permettent au Corps de la Pelleterie d'emprunter 3000 livres ... données à Versailles le 21 mars 1762. Paris, P.G. Simon, 1762.　　　　　F1057
　　Paris furriers are authorized to borrow 3,000 livres for the construction of a ship.

France. Sovereign (1715-1774 : Louis XV). Ordonnance ... concernant le commerce de tabac qui se fait dans les maisons royales, hôtels des princes du sang, & des seigneurs ... & dans tous autres lieux prétendus privilégiés sans en excepter aucuns ... Isle Saint-Louis, G. Lamesle, 1762.　　　　　F1058
　　Persons attached to royal houses or other places supposedly exempt from tobacco regulations are prohibited from engaging in the tobacco trade.

France. Sovereign (1715-1774 : Louis XV). Déclaration du Roi ... concernant les privileges en fait de commerce. Toulouse, Veuve de Bernard Pijon, 1763. F1059

France. Sovereign (1715-1774 : Louis XV). Edit ... qui ordonne la réformation dans la monnoye de Paris ... [n.p., Veûve de C.M. Cramé, 1763.] F1060

France. Sovereign (1715-1774 : Louis XV). Lettres patentes du Roi, concernant la pour-suite des biens de la Société & Compagnie des Jésuites qui sont dans les colonies françoises. Paris, P.G. Simon, 1763. F1061
  Detailed provisions for the disposal of Jesuit goods and properties in the New World, due to their extreme indebtedness.

France. Sovereign (1715-1774 : Louis XV). Ordonnance ... concernant la distribution du tabac de cantine aux troupes. [n.p., G. Lamesle, 1763.] F1062
  In order to reduce the black market trade in tobacco by the soldiers, they are to be supplied with smaller amounts at more frequent intervals.

France. Sovereign (1715-1774 : Louis XV). Déclaration du Roi, concernant la Ferme du tabac. [n.p., G. Lamesle, 1764.] F1063
  Following price rises after the revocation of the tobacco monopoly on December 29, 1719, a new set of twenty-seven regulations is installed. Reprint of an earlier declaration.

France. Sovereign (1715-1774 : Louis XV). Édit ... concernant la liberté de la sortie & de l'entrée des grains dans le royaume. [Toulouse, Veuve de Me. Bernard Pijon, 1764.] F1064
  Provides for free trade in grain, both import and export.

France. Sovereign (1715-1774 : Louis XV). Édit ... portant confirmation de l'établissement de la Compagnie des Indes, sous le titre de Compagnie commerçante. Paris, P.G. Simon, 1764. F1065
  A decree authorizing the Compagnie des Indes to issue new shares to restore it to financial soundness.

France. Sovereign (1715-1774 : Louis XV). Lettres patentes ... concernant la liquidation des dettes de la Compagnie des Indes. Paris, P.G. Simon, 1764. F1066
  The government proposes a plan to help the Compagnie des Indes liquidate its debts.

France. Sovereign (1715-1774 : Louis XV). Lettres patentes ... concernant la vente & la discussion des biens ... de la Compagnie & Société des Jésuites, en la colonie de la Louisiane. Paris, P.G. Simon, 1764. F1067
  Relates to the remission of funds obtained in the sale of property of the Jesuits in Louisiana.

France. Sovereign (1715-1774 : Louis XV). Lettres patentes ... qui fixent les droits de sortie & d'entrée sur les grains. Paris, P.G. Simon, 1764. F1068
  Duties on grain, flour, and vegetables are set in accordance with the market value of the commodity.

France. Sovereign (1715-1774 : Louis XV). Déclaration ... concernant le droit de frêt sur les vaisseaux étrangers. Paris, Imprimerie Royale, 1765. F1069
  Increases freight charges for goods from French ports to Mediterranean destinations.

France. Sovereign (1715-1774 : Louis XV). Édit ... concernant la liberté de la sortie & de l'entrée des grains dans la royaume. Rouen, Jacq. Jos. Le Boullenger, 1765. F1070
  Provides for a large measure of freedom in the exporting and importing of grain and grain products.

France. Sovereign (1715-1774 : Louis XV). Lettres patentes qui fixent les droits de sortie & d'entrée sur les grains, qui pérmettent la circulation & sortie de toutes especes de grains. [Paris, Richard Lallemant, 1765.] F1071

France. Sovereign (1715-1774 : Louis XV). Recueil de lettres patentes, et autres pieces, en faveur des Juifs Portugais, contenant leurs privilèges en France. Paris, Moreau, 1765. F1072
  A collection of documents from 1550 to 1728 specifying the rights of Portuguese Jews to participate in commerce in several French provinces and in France as a whole.

France. Sovereign (1715-1774 : Louis XV). Déclaration ... portant condamnation contre les fraudeurs des droits de la Ferme du tabac. [n.p., G. Lamesle, 1766.] F1073
  Persons defrauding the government in the tobacco trade are to be fined 1000 livres and are to have all goods relating to the fraud confiscated. Reissue of a declaration of 1723.

France. Sovereign (1715-1774 : Louis XV). Déclaration ... concernant les remboursemens à faire par la caisse des amortissemens. Lille, N.J.B. Peterinck-Cramé, 1767. F1074

France. Sovereign (1715-1774 : Louis XV). Déclaration ... donnée à Marly le 17 mars 1767. Portant prorogation jusqu'au dernier septembre 1774, des quatre sols pour livre sur le tabac, établis par celle du 24 août 1758. [Grenoble, André Giroud, 1767.] F1075

France. Sovereign (1715-1774 : Louis XV). Edit ... qui ordonne la conversion de différens effets au porteur, en contrats. Lille, N.J.B. Peterinck-Cramé, 1767.   F1076

France. Sovereign (1715-1774 : Louis XV). Lettres patentes ... qui autorisent la Compagnie des Indes à faire un emprunt de douze millions par voie de loterie. Paris, P.G. Simon, 1767.   F1077
Authorizes a loan of twelve million livres in order that the Compagnie des Indes may conduct a lottery to raise money for a new expedition.

France. Sovereign (1715-1774 : Louis XV). Lettres patentes du Roi, concernant les billets de caisse, ordonnances, récépissés, & autres effets de la Compagnie des Indes. Paris, P.G. Simon, 1767.   F1078
Declares that the notes of the Compagnie des Indes will no longer be valid for trade or payments.

France. Sovereign (1715-1774 : Louis XV). Lettres patentes ... concernant la vente & discussion des biens de la Compagnie & Société des Jésuites dans les colonies. Paris, P.G. Simon, 1768.   F1079
An attempt to expedite the sale of Jesuit goods and properties in America through simplified judicial procedures.

France. Sovereign (1715-1774 : Louis XV). Lettres patentes ... contenant réglement général pour l'administration de la Compagnie des Indes. Paris, P.G. Simon, 1768.   F1080
Forty-five provisions pertaining to the management of the Compagnie des Indes.

France. Sovereign (1715-1774 : Louis XV). Lettres patentes ... qui accordent à l'isle de Cayenne & la Guyane françoise, la liberté de commerce avec toutes les nations, pendant douze ans. Paris, Imprimerie Royale, 1768.   F1081
Recognizing the lack of development in French Guiana, it is decreed that free trade with all nations would prevail there for a limited time in hopes that this would have a beneficial effect on the economy.

France. Sovereign (1715-1774 : Louis XV). Ordonnance ... qui défend à tous suisses, portiers, domestiques, & à toutes autres personnes logeant dans les maisons royales ou dans des lieux privilégiés, de vendre & débiter tabac, sans la permission par écrit de l'adjudicataire des fermes. Paris, Imprimerie Royale, 1768.   F1082

France. Sovereign (1715-1774 : Louis XV). Déclaration ... qui ordonne la perception d'un droit de trente sous par chacune livre de seize onces, sur tous les tabacs étrangers qui enteront dans le royaume pour autre destination que pour celle de la Ferme générale. Paris, Imprimerie Royale, 1769.   F1083
An attempt to keep local growers from importing tobacco of inferior quality and selling it as their own product.

France. Sovereign (1715-1774 : Louis XV). Extrait de la declaration du Roi, du premier août 1721, portant réglement général de tabac. Lille, N.J.B. Peterinck-Cramé, Imprimeur ordinaire du Roi, 1769.   F1084
A restatement of the earlier regulation, with reference also to decrees of 1686 and 1687.

France. Sovereign (1715-1774 : Louis XV). Édit ... portant création d'un contrat d'un million deux cens mille livres de rente, au principal de trente millions, au profit de la Compagnie des Indes. Paris, P.G. Simon, 1770.   F1085
Several financial settlements between the Compagnie des Indes and the state.

France. Sovereign (1715-1774 : Louis XV). Lettres patentes ... qui accordent a l'Isle de Cayenne & la Guyane françoise ... la liberté de commerce. Paris, P.G. Simon, 1770.   F1086
Grants free trade to Cayenne and French Guiana for twelve years.

France. Sovereign (1715-1774 : Louis XV). Édit portant création & établissement de jurisdiction dans le Comté de Bourgogne pour connoître & juger les contraventions aux droits d'entrée & de sortie, & aux réglemens faits pour la régie du tabac dans ladite province. [Besançon, 1771.]   F1087

France. Sovereign (1715-1774 : Louis XV). Lettres patentes ... qui autorisent les syndics & directeurs de la Compagnie des Indes à ouvrir une loterie, dont le fonds sera de douze millions. Paris, P.G. Simon, 1772.   F1088

France. Sovereign (1774-1792 : Louis XVI). Lettres patentes ... en faveur de la ville impériale de Reutlingen, pour l'exemption du droit d'aubaine, & la liberté du commerce. Paris, P.G. Simon, 1775.   F1089

France. Sovereign (1774-1792 : Louis XVI). Lettres patentes ... en faveur des vingt-trois villes impériales y dénommées, pour l'exemption du droit d'aubaine & la liberté du commerce. Paris, P.G. Simon, 1775.   F1090

France. Sovereign (1774-1792 : Louis XVI). Lettres patentes ... portant établissement d'une commission à l'effet de connoître ... de l'introduction & vente du tabac dans les villes de Paris & de Versailles. Paris, Imprimerie Royale, 1775.   F1091

France. Sovereign (1774-1792 : Louis XVI).
Lettres patentes ... qui ... ordonnent que l'amende de mille livres sera prononcée solidairement, tant contre chacun des auteurs & propriétaires de la fraude en tabac ... Paris, Imprimerie Royale, 1775. F1092
　Failure to enforce the laws of 1707 and 1721 in some jurisdictions brought forth this stronger statement of punishment for those in any way accomplices to tobacco fraud.

France. Sovereign (1774-1792 : Louis XVI).
Lettres-patentes, portant établissement d'un commission à l'effet de connoître par voie de police & d'administration & juger en dernier ressort, de l'introduction & vente du tabac dans les villes de Paris & de Versailles ... Paris, Knapen, 1775. F1093
　The members of the commission are named, and the manner of their proceedings are set forth.

France. Sovereign (1774-1792 : Louis XVI).
Memoire pour servir d'instruction au sieur Marquis de Vevac, allant a Copenhague pour y resider en qualité de Ministre Plénipotentiare du Roi auprés du Roi de Dannemarck. Manuscript signed. [Versailles, 3 septembre 1775.] F1094
　A review of Denmark's diplomatic situation, particularly with relation to England and Russia, but also including larger commercial and international problems.

France. Sovereign (1774-1792 : Louis XVI).
Édit ... portant suppression des jurandes & communautés de commerce, arts, & métiers. Paris, Imprimerie Royale, 1776. F1095
　A decree dissolving certain guilds in the interest of stimulating the nation's commerce.

France. Sovereign (1774-1792 : Louis XVI).
Édit ... portant suppression des offices d'intendans du commerce, vacance arrivant d'iceux. Paris, Imprimerie Royale, 1776. F1096

France. Sovereign (1774-1792 : Louis XVI).
Lettres patentes ... portant rétablissement de la commission établie à Caen par lettres patentes du 9 octobre 1768, pour juger les contrebandiers. Paris, P.G. Simon, 1776. F1097

France. Sovereign (1774-1792 : Louis XVI).
Lettres patentes ... qui ordonnent qu'il sera sursis au jugement des contestations concernant les noirs de l'un & de l'autre sexe ... Paris, P.G. Simon, 1776. F1098

France. Sovereign (1774-1792 : Louis XVI).
Lettres patentes ... qui subrogent M. le Noir, conseiller d'état, lieutenant général de police ... pour connoître, au lieu & place du sieur Albert, conformément aux lettres patentes du 29 août 1775, de l'introduction, vente, débit & colportage des tabacs de toute espece, dans l'étendue des villes de Paris, Versailles ... Paris, Imprimerie Royale, 1776. F1099
　An appointment to replace an earlier one for policing the tobacco trade in Paris and Versailles.

France. Sovereign (1774-1792 : Louis XVI)
Ordonnance du roi, pour la formation nouvelle du dépôt des recrues des colonies, établi à l'Isle de Ré. Du 12 septembre 1776. Paris, Imprimerie Royale, 1776. F1100
　A plan for reorganizing aspects of the French military establishment in the West Indies.

France. Sovereign (1774-1792 : Louis XVI).
Déclaration ... par laquelle Sa Majesté renouvelle les dispositions des anciennes ordonnances rendues pour empêcher la contrebande. Paris, P.G. Simon, 1777. F1101

France. Sovereign (1774-1792 : Louis XVI).
Déclaration ... pour la police des noirs. Paris, P.G. Simon, 1777. F1102
　Restrictions are placed upon bringing slaves into France from the American colonies.

France. Sovereign (1774-1792 : Louis XVI).
Déclaration ... qui ordonne que les comptoirs des marchands de vins, revêtus en plomb, ainsi que les vaisseaux de cuivre dont se servant les laitieres, & les balances de même métal qu'employent les regratiers de sel & les débitans de tabac, seront supprimés. Paris, P.G. Simon, 1777. F1103

France. Sovereign (1774-1792 : Louis XVI).
Déclaration ... qui permet l'entrée & l'entrepôt, dans les différens ports du royaume, des taffias venans des colonies françoises de l'Amérique. Paris, P.G. Simon, 1777. F1104

France. Sovereign (1774-1792 : Louis XVI).
Déclaration ... sur la contribution en cas de déconfiture, dans les établissemens françois de l'Inde. Paris, P.G. Simon, 1777. F1105

France. Sovereign (1774-1792 : Louis XVI).
Déclaration ... sur la discipline du Conseil supérieur de Pondichéry. Paris, P.G. Simon, 1777. F1106

France. Sovereign (1774-1792 : Louis XVI).
Déclaration ... sur l'administration des biens des mineurs dans les etablissemens françois de l'Inde. Paris, P.G. Simon, 1777. F1107

France. Sovereign (1774-1792 : Louis XVI).
Édit ... portant établissement à Versailles, d'un dépôt des papiers publics des colonies. [Paris, P.G. Simon, 1777.] F1108

France. Sovereign (1774-1792 : Louis XVI).
Edit ... portant suppression des quatre offices d'intendans du commerce, créés par edit du mois de juin 1724, & création de quatre commissions d'intendans du commerce. Paris, P.G. Simon, 1777. F1109

France. Sovereign (1774-1792 : Louis XVI).
Edit ... portant suppression du Conseil supérieur de Pondichéry; & creation d'un nouveau Conseil supérieur. Paris, P.G. Simon, 1777. F1110

France. Sovereign (1774-1792 : Louis XVI).
Lettres patentes ... pour régler les matières ... des établissemens françoise dans l'Inde ... Paris, P.G. Simon, 1777. F1111
  An authorization to officers in Pondicherry to conduct certain trials, thereby promising more local control over some aspects of Indian trade.

France. Sovereign (1774-1792 : Louis XVI).
Ordonnance ... concernant les consuls & autres officiers de Sa Majesté, dans les echelles du Levant & de Barbarie. Paris, P.G. Simon, 1777. F1112
  Defines the administrative structure of the consular service.

France. Sovereign (1774-1792 : Louis XVI).
Déclaration ... concernant la course sur les ennemis de l'etat. Aix, E. David, 1778. F1113
  A royal ordinance conerning privateering.

France. Sovereign (1774-1792 : Louis XVI).
Déclaration ... concernant l'abolition du droit d'aubaine, convenue entre la France & les Etats-Unis de l'Amérique Septentrionale. Paris, P.G. Simon, 1778. F1114

France. Sovereign (1774-1792 : Louis XVI).
Declaration ... qui ordonne que les comptoirs des marchands de vins, revêtus en plomb, ainsi que les vaisseaux de cuivre dont le servent les laitieres ... seront supprimés. Aix, Esprit David, 1778. F1115
  Prohibits the marketing of consumables from lead and copper containers.

France. Sovereign (1774-1792 : Louis XVI).
Instruction que le Roi veut être observée, par les officiers de ses vaisseaux, pour les prises qu'ils seront sur ses ennemis. Paris, P.G. Simon, 1778. F1116

France. Sovereign (1774-1792 : Louis XVI).
Lettre ... à m. l'Admiral, pour faire délivrer des commissions en course. [n.p., ca. 1778]. F1117
  A royal authorization to grant commissions to privateers.

France. Sovereign (1774-1792 : Louis XVI).
Lettres patentes ... par lesquelles le Roi approuve, ratifie & confirme la convention du traité de commerce & d'amitié conclu entre le Roi & les Etats-Unis de l'Amérique Septentrionale. Toulouse, J.A.H.M.B. Pijon [1778]. F1118

France. Sovereign (1774-1792 : Louis XVI).
Lettres patentes sur Arrest du Conseil, qui renouvellent les dispositions des anciennes ordonnances, & font défenses de planter & cultiver du tabac dans les forêts du Roi, dans les bois ... qui sont situes dans l'étendue de la vente exclusive, ou dans les trois lieues de ses limites. Rouen, J.J. Le Boullenger, 1778. F1119

France. Sovereign (1774-1792 : Louis XVI).
Ordonnance ... concernant les formalités qui doivent être observées par les officiers de ses vaisseaux, pour les prises qu'ils feront sur les ennemis de Sa Majesté. Paris, P.G. Simon, 1778. F1120
  A royal ordinance regulating the formalities to be observed by the naval officers while taking prizes.

France. Sovereign (1774-1792 : Louis XVI).
Ordonnance ... portant défenses aux capitaines de navires des laisser débarquer aucun noir, mulâtre ou autres gens de couleur, avant d'avoir fait leur rapport à l'amirauté. Paris, P.G. Simon, 1778. F1121

France. Sovereign (1774-1792 : Louis XVI).
Edit ... qui ordonne une fabrication dans la monnoie de Paris ... Paris, Imprimerie Royale, 1779. F1122

France. Sovereign (1774-1792 : Louis XVI).
Lettre ... a m. l'Amiral. Du 10 juillet 1778. Paris, P.G. Simon, 1779. F1123

France. Sovereign (1774-1792 : Louis XVI).
Lettre ... a son altesse sérénissime monseigneur l'Amiral. Du 5 juin 1779. [n.p., 1779.] F1124

France. Sovereign (1774-1792 : Louis XVI).
Lettres patentes ... concernant l'étendue & l'application des priviléges des ville & principautés de Sédan, Raucourt & Saint-Manges. Paris, P.G. Simon, 1779. F1125

France. Sovereign (1774-1792 : Louis XVI).
Ordonnance ... concernant les reprises faites par les vaisseaux, frégates & autres bâtimens de Sa Majesté. Paris, P.G. Simon, 1779. F1126

France. Sovereign (1774-1792 : Louis XVI).
Ordonnance du roi, pour régler un uniforme aux officiers réformés des troupes des colonies. Du

28 novembre 1779. Paris, Imprimerie royale, 1779. F1127
Regulation concerning the uniforms of the French colonial troops.

France. Sovereign (1774-1792 : Louis XVI).
Ordonnance du roi, qui défend le port d'armes & les épaulettes, à tous domestiques, & nommémemt à ceux appelés chasseurs, heiduques, & aux négres. Du 13 juin 1779. Paris, Imprimerie Royale, 1779. F1128
A prohibition against carrying arms by servant classes in France, presumably applicable to French colonies as well.

France. Sovereign (1774-1792 : Louis XVI).
Lettre ... à m. l'Amiral, concernant la navigation des bâtimens appartenans aux sujets des puissances neutres. Paris, Imprimerie Royale, 1780. F1129

France. Sovereign (1774-1792 : Louis XVI)
Mémoire sur les modifications nécessaires dans la jouissance des priviléges qui sont accordés à quelques provinces, relativement à l'impôt sur le tabac. [n.p., 1780?] F1130
A collection of three French documents regulating the cultivation, manufacture and use of tobacco. The *Mémoire* gives seven different proposals for regulations. The others are titled *Tabac circulaire*, one giving prices and the other a table for powdered and prepared tobacco.

France. Sovereign (1774-1792 : Louis XVI).
Ordonnance ... concernant la course & les armemens des corsaires. Paris, J.L.R. Mallard, 1780. F1131

France. Sovereign (1774-1792 : Louis XVI).
Ordonnance ... concernant le service des bureaux de la poste maritime. Paris, Imprimerie Royale, 1780. F1132
Establishes procedures for handling mail between France and her colonies.

France. Sovereign (1774-1792 : Louis XVI).
Edit ... portant augmentation de deux sols pour livre en sus des droits; établissement, suppression & modération de différens droits. [Paris, P.G. Simon, 1781.] F1133

France. Sovereign (1774-1792 : Louis XVI).
Edit ... portant augmentation de deux sous pour livre en sus des droits, établissement, suppression & modération des différens droits. Besançon, Veuve Daclin, 1781. F1134
An omnibus tax bill covering a wide variety of consumer goods.

France. Sovereign (1774-1792 : Louis XVI).
Edit ... qui ordonne une réformation dans la monnoie de Paris, de soixante mille marcs d'espèces de billon, pour être transportées aux Isles-de-France & de Bourbon, & aux colonies de l'Amérique où elles auront cours seulement. Paris, Imprimerie Royale, 1781. F1135

France. Sovereign (1774-1792 : Louis XVI).
Lettres patentes du Roi, concernant la Chambre du commerce de Marseille. Paris, Imprimerie Royale, 1781. F1136
Defines membership and functions of the Chambre du Commerce.

France. Sovereign (1774-1792 : Louis XVI).
Ordonnance ... portant attribution aux intendans & ordonnanteurs de la Marine, des ventes & autres opérations relatives aux prises faites par les vaisseaux de Sa Majesté. Paris, Imprimerie Royale, 1781. F1137

France. Sovereign (1774-1792 : Louis XVI).
Edit ... portant établissement d'un troisieme vingtieme sur tous les objets assujettis aux deux premiers vingtiemes, à l'exception de l'industrie, des offices & des droits. Paris, P.G. Simon, 1782. F1138

France. Sovereign (1774-1792 : Louis XVI).
Edit ... qui autorise les six corps des marchands, & les autres communautés d'arts & métiers de Paris, à percevoir une augmentation de droits sur les réceptions. Paris, P.G. Simon, 1782. F1139

France. Sovereign (1774-1792 : Louis XVI).
Edit ... qui ordonne une réformation dans la monnoie de Paris ... pour être transportées en l'isle de Cayenne, où elles auront cours seulement. Paris, Imprimerie Royale, 1782. F1140
Royal edict transferring a certain kind of specie to the French colony of Cayenne.

France. Sovereign (1774-1792 : Louis XVI).
Lettres patentes ... portant défenses de nourrir & de vendre des chiens, mâtins, propres à servir à la fraude du sel & du tabac. Paris, P.G. Simon, 1782. F1141

France. Sovereign (1774-1792 : Louis XVI).
Lettres patentes ... qui autorisent les six corps des marchands, & les communautés d'arts & métiers, à emprunter une somme de 1,500,000 livres, qu'ils ont offerte au Roi pour la construction d'un vaisseau. Paris, P.G. Simon, 1782. F1142

France. Sovereign (1774-1792 : Louis XVI).
Lettres patentes ... qui ordonnent l'enregistrement de celles du 21 août 1771, portant défenses à toutes personnes de faire entrer, vendre & transporter aucuns tabacs en fraude ... Aix, Joseph David, 1782. F1143

Sets forth penalties for all persons engaged in contraband trade in tobacco.

France. Sovereign (1774-1792 : Louis XVI).
Lettres-patentes ... portant défenses de nourrir & de vendre des chiens mâtins, propres à servir à la fraude du sel & du tabac. Paris, Knapen, 1782. F1144
An attempt to enforce regulations against smuggling salt and tobacco to evade taxes on them.

France. Sovereign (1774-1792 : Louis XVI).
Ordonnance ... concernant les termes de la cessation des hostilités en mer. Lille, N.J.B. Peterinck-Cramé, 1783. F1145

France. Sovereign (1774-1792 : Louis XVI).
Ordonnance ... pour la publication de la paix. Paris, P.G. Simon, 1783. F1146

France. Sovereign (1774-1792 : Louis XVI).
Déclaration ... portant réduction d'un dixième dans l'évaluation des droits sur les sucre, café & cire. Paris, Knapen & fils, 1784. F1147

France. Sovereign (1774-1792 : Louis XVI).
Lettres-patentes ... en forme d'edit, portant ratification du contrat d'échange passé le 11 mars 1784, entre le Roi & m. le prince de Condé ... Paris, Knapen & fils, 1784. F1148

France. Sovereign (1774-1792 : Louis XVI).
Règlement pour les paquebots établis par arrêt du conseil du 28 juin 1783. Paris, Imprimerie Royale, 1784. F1149
Regulations and a schedule of rates for goods, passengers, and letters passing from France to the United States.

France. Sovereign (1774-1792 : Louis XVI).
Déclaration ... qui détermine la déduction qui sera faite sur les droite d'entrée à Paris, relatifs au café, au sucre & à la cire, pour la tarre des tonneaux & emballages. Paris, P.G. Simon & N.H. Nyon, 1785. F1150

France. Sovereign (1774-1792 : Louis XVI).
Lettres patentes ... portant confirmation & interprétation des privileges de la ville de Bayonne. Paris, P.G. Simon & N.H. Nyon, 1785. F1151
Bayonne and other nearby cities are here given new trading privileges, including the freedom to trade with the French colonies.

France. Sovereign (1774-1792 : Louis XVI).
Ordonnance ... concernant les procureurs & économes-gérans des habitations situées aux Isles Sous le Vent. Paris, P.G. Simon & N.H. Nyon, 1785. F1152
State regulations upon various aspects of the economic life of the French colony on the Leeward Islands.

France. Sovereign (1774-1792 : Louis XVI).
Ordonnance ... qui révoque les articles 12, 13, & 15, titre III de celle du 3 mars 1781, en vertu desquels les etrangers avoient été admis au commerce de ses sujets en Levant & en Barbarie. Paris, P.G. Simon & N.H. Nyon, 1785. F1153

France. Sovereign (1774-1792 : Louis XVI).
Ordonnance ... concernant les officiers de port dans les colonies orientales & occidentales ... Paris, Imprimerie Royale, 1786. F1154
Considers the number and rank of French port officials.

France. Sovereign (1774-1792 : Louis XVI).
Règlement fait ... pour la composition des commissions & bureaux dépendans du conseil royal des finances & du commerce ... Paris, Imprimerie Royale, 1787. F1155
Deals with the composition of various commissions in charge of financial affairs.

France. Sovereign (1774-1792 : Louis XVI).
Règlement fait ... pour l'administration de ses finances & du commerce. Paris, Imprimerie Royale, 1787. F1156

France. Sovereign (1774-1792 : Louis XVI).
Règlement sur les commerce des colonies françoises en Amérique. Paris, Imprimerie Royale, 1787. F1157

France. Sovereign (1774-1792 : Louis XVI).
Edit ... qui ordonne la réformation en la monnoie de Paris ... pour être transportées en l'île de Cayenne, où elles auront cours seulement. Paris, N.H. Nyon, 1788. F1158

France. Sovereign (1774-1792 : Louis XVI).
Edit ... qui ordonne une fabrication de quatre-vingt mille marcs d'espèces de billon pour l'usage des Îles du Vent & Sous-le-Vent. Paris, N.H. Nyon, 1788. F1159

France. Sovereign (1774-1792 : Louis XVI).
Règlement fait ... concernant les fonctions & la composition du bureau du commerce. Paris, N.H. Nyon, 1788. F1160

France. Sovereign (1774-1792 : Louis XVI).
Edit ... portant création de six millions de papier-monnoie pour les isles de France & de Bourbon. Paris, Imprimerie Royale, 1789. F1161
To serve the trade in the Indian Ocean the King has decreed that new paper money shall be issued for the islands of Reunion and Mauritius.

France. Sovereign (1774-1792 : Louis XVI).
Lettres patentes ... qui ordonnent l'enrégistrement de l'un des articles du traité de commerce & d'amitié, conclu entre le Roi & les

États-Unis de l'Amérique Septentrionale. Lille, N.J.B. Peterinck-Cramé, 1789. F1162

Promulgation of one article of the treaty of friendship concluded between France and the United States of America.

France. Sovereign (1774-1792 : Louis XVI). Lettres-patentes ... qui ordonnent l'enrégistrement de l'un des articles du traité de commerce & d'amitié, conclu entre le Roi & les Etats-Unis de l'Amérique Septentrionale. Lille, N.J.B. Peterinck-Cramé, 1789. F1163

France. Sovereign (1774-1792 : Louis XVI). Proclamation ... pour accorder des primes en faveur de l'importation des grains. Lille, C.M. Peterinck-Cramé, 1789. F1164

France. Sovereign (1774-1792 : Louis XVI). Lettre du Roi. A nos bons & amés colons des Îles Sous le Vent. Paris, Imprimerie Royale, 1790. F1165

An expression of concern for the political rights of the colonists in the West Indies.

France. Sovereign (1774-1792 : Louis XVI). Proclamation ... sur le décret de l'Assemblée nationale. Paris, Imprimerie Royale, 1790. F1166

A royal proclamation concerning the organization of the army in the colonies.

France. Sovereign (1774-1792 : Louis XVI). Proclamation ... sur le décret de l'Assemblée nationale, concernant les colonies. Paris, N.H. Nyon, 1790. F1167

Provisions for the participation by colonists in government, both locally and at Paris.

France. Sovereign (1774-1792 : Louis XVI). Proclamation ... sur le décret de l'Assemblée nationale, du 3 avril, pour la liberté du commerce de l'Inde, au-delà du Cap de Bonne-Espérance. Paris, Imprimerie Royale, 1790. F1168

The trade to India and the Cape of Good Hope is opened to all Frenchmen.

France. Sovereign (1774-1792 : Louis XVI). Proclamation ... sur un décret de l'Assemblée nationale, du 17 juin, relatif à la fédération générale des gardes nationales & des troupes du royaume. Paris, Imprimerie Royale, 1790. F1169

France. Treaties, etc. Traicte faite entre le roy de France et le roy d'Angleterre pendant le treve touchant le commerce et la liberté des marchans allans et venans ausdits royaumes et trafiquans de toutes sortes de marchandises. Manuscript copy in French. [n.p., ca. 1535] F1170

A copy of a portion of the treaty of peace concluded between Edward IV of England and Louis XI of France at Amiens in 1475 which had provisions for freedom of trade.

France. Treaties, etc. Artijckelen vanden treffues oft bestant voor ghestelt by de Heeren Ambassadeurs vande Coninghen van Vranckrijck ende Groot Britagnien, inde vergaderinghe vande heeren Staten Generael. [n.p.] 1608. F1171

In the arrangment of a truce between the Netherlands and Spain, England and France acted as mediators, and these are their suggestions for resolving the differences over the East Indian trade.

France. Treaties, etc. Articles accordez entre Henry IIII ... et Jacques Roy de la Grand' Bretagne. Rouen, Martin le Mesgissier, 1629. F1172

Contains terms of a treaty of commerce made in 1607, calling for freedom of trade between England and France.

France. Treaties, etc. Articles accordez entre Louis XIII ... et Charles Roy de la Grand Bretagne. Rouen, Martin le Mesgissier, 1629. F1173

This treaty was signed at Suze, April 24, 1629, and it called for the restoration of French territory taken by the English and the renewal of trade between them. It thus invalidated the later victory of David Kirke over Champlain in New France in July 1629.

France. Treaties, etc. Les articles accordez entre la France & l'Angleterre, par le traité fait Westminster, en datte du 3 novembre 1655. [n.p., ca. 1655.] F1174

Nearly all of the twenty-nine articles of this treaty refer to commercial arrangements between the two nations. Provisions are included providing for free trade between France and England and their colonies.

France. Treaties, etc. Tractaet van vrede tusschen de croonen van Vranck-ryck ende Spaengien. The Hague, Adriaen Vlack, 1660. F1175

A treaty of peace between France and Spain, with free trade being restored.

France. Treaties, etc. De gantsche, ende geheele authenticke tractaten, ende alliantie, van guarantie, commertie, navigatie ende marine, tusschen den alder-Christelicxsten Koninck van Vranckrijck, ende Navarre ... [n.p., 1662.] F1176

France. Treaties, etc. Traicte & alliance, entre ... Roy de France et ... Estats Generaux des Provinces Unies ... [n.p., ca. 1662.] F1177

A treaty assuring freedom of trade between France and the Netherlands.

France. Treaties, etc. Articles extraits du traitté d'amitié, confoederation, navigation, commerce & de marine, entre le Roy de France, & messieurs les Estats Generaux des Provinces Unies des Païs-Bas. The Hague, H. van Wouw, 1663. F1178
   A treaty between France and the Netherlands calling for free trade between them and their colonies, as well as for joint action against pirates.

France. Treaties, etc. Geextraheerde articulen uyt het tractaet van vriendtschap ... The Hague, H. van Wouw, 1663. F1179
   A Dutch edition of the preceding treaty.

France. Treaties, etc. Traitte' de paix fait entre le royaume de France, et Tunis. Marseilles, Jean Penot & Charles Bregion [1666]. F1180
   Many of the provisions of the treaty deal with maritime and commercial matters.

France. Treaties, etc. Traitte'de paix fait entre le royaume de France, et la ville et royaume d'Alger. Marseilles, Jean Penot & Charles Bregion [1666]. F1181
   Most of the provisions of this treaty also concern maritime and commercial matters.

France. Treaties, etc. Eyschen vande koningen van Vranckryck en Engeland; aen de Staten der Vereenigde Nederlanden. Amsterdam, Pieter Voskuyl, 1672. F1182
   A review of demands of the French and English as prerequisites to peace with the Dutch, including large monetary payments and revocation of Dutch commercial restrictions.

France. Treaties, etc. Traittez de paix, et de commerce, navigation et marine, entre la France et ... Provinces Unies. Paris, F. Léonard, 1678. F1183
   The same degree of free trade is restored as existed before hostilities.

France. Treaties, etc. Traité de neutralité, conclu a Londres le 16 novembre 1686. Entre les rois de France et d'Angleterre. Paris, S. Mabre-Cramoisy, 1686. F1184
   This Treaty of Whitehall was an attempt to stop hostilities between France and England in America, and to curb illicit commerce.

France. Treaties, etc. Traité entre le Roi Louis XIII & Charles I Roi d'Angleterre, por la restitution de la Nouvelle France. [Paris, Léonard, 1693.] F1185
   A reprint of the treaty of 1632 covering the return of New France to France, with provisions for the reestablishment of peaceful commercial relations between France and England in the New World.

France. Treaties, etc. Articles of peace between the most serene and mighty Prince William the Third ... and Lewis the Fourteenth, concluded in the royal palace at Ryswicke the 10/20 day of September, 1697. London, Charles Bill and the executrix of Thomas Newcomb, 1697. F1186
   The Treaty of Ryswick provided for the resumption of trade between France and England, and for the restoration of French rights to hold positions in Hudson Bay.

France. Treaties, etc. Traitté de la paix, fait, conclu & arresté a Rijswijk en Hollande ... The Hague, P. Scheltus, 1697. F1187
   The Treaty of Ryswick, re-establishing normal trade between France and the Netherlands.

France. Treaties, etc. Tractaat van vreede en vriendschap, tusschen Zyn Alderchristelykste Majesteyt van Vrankryk, en haar Majestesteyt [sic] van Groot Bretagne ... Utrecht, Willem vande Water en Jacob van Poolsum, 1713. F1188

France. Treaties, etc. Traité de paix entre la France et le Portugal conclu à Utrecht le II avril 1713. Paris, François Fournier, 1713. F1189
   A treaty between France and Portugal concerning their colonies in Cayenne and Brazil.

France. Treaties, etc. Traitez de paix et de commerce, navigation et marine, entre la France et l'Angleterre. Paris, F. Fournier, 1713. F1190
   Contains provisions for the renewing of normal commercial relations between France and England, and defines conditions for trade in their colonies.

France. Treaties, etc. The treaty of peace, union, friendship, and mutual defense, between the crowns of Great-Britain, France, and Spain, concluded at Seville on the 9th of November, N.S. 1729. London, S. Buckley, 1729. F1191

France. Treaties, etc. Traité de commerce, navigation et marine, entre le Roy et les Estats Generaux ... Paris, Imprimerie Royale, 1740. F1192
   This treaty was concluded at Versailles on December 21, 1739, and specified duties on Dutch goods imported into France.

France. Treaties, etc. Traité de commerce, navigation et marine, entre le Roy et le Roy de Dannemarck. Paris, Imprimerie Royale, 1743. F1193
   The treaty includes terms governing the commerce of the two nations in peace and in war, duties on French ships passing through the Sund, whaling in northern waters, trade to the Faeroe Islands and to Greenland.

France. Treaties, etc. Tratado definitivo de paz concluido entre Sus Magestades Christianissima, y Britanica, y los Estados Generales de las Provincias Unidas ... Madrid, Imprenta del Mercurio, 1749. F1194

France. Treaties, etc. Articles préliminaires de paix entre le Roi, le Roi d'Espagne et le Roi de la Grande Bretagne. Signés à Fontainbleau le 3 novembre 1762. Paris, Imprimerie Royale, 1762. F1195
Twenty-six articles preparatory to the Treaty of Paris signed the following year.

France. Treaties, etc. Traité de paix entre le Roi, le Roi d'Espagne et le Roi de la Grande-Bretagne, conclu à Paris le 10 février 1763. Avec l'accession du Roi de Portugal. Paris, Imprimerie Royale, 1763. F1196
The Treaty of Paris which brought an end to the French and Indian War and the Seven Years' War.

France. Treaties, etc. Traités de la paix général de l'Europe en M.DCC.LXIII. Paris, La Gazette de France [1763]. F1197
A little known edition of the Treaty of Paris.

France. Treaties, etc. Traité de commerce et de marine entre Sa Majesté et la ville de Hambourg. Bordeaux, Jean Chappuis [1769]. F1198
Contains articles relating to the trade between Hamburg and France, including arrangements to be made regarding duties, pilotage, merchant courts, shipwreck, and trade in time of war.

France. Treaties, etc. Convention signée entre la France & l'Espagne, qui, en expliquant celle du 2 janvier 1768, pourvoit aux moyens d'empêcher la contrebande entre les sujets respectifs des deux nations. [Paris, G. Lamesle, 1775.] F1199
Twenty-three articles agreed upon to prevent the smuggling of tobacco into France and salt into Spain, in elaboration of a secret agreement of 1768 which had proved insufficient.

France. Treaties, etc. Traité d'amitié et de commerce, conclu entre le Roi et les États-Unis de l'Amérique Septentrionale, le 6 fevrier 1778. Paris, P.G. Simon, 1778. F1200

France. Treaties, etc. Traite de paix entre le Roi & le Roi de la Grande-Bretagne, conclu à Versailles le 3 septembre 1783. Lille, N.J.B. Peterinck-Cramé [1783?]. F1201
The treaty set forth fishing and territorial rights in North America, Africa, and Asia.

France. Treaties, etc. Traité de paix entre le roi et le roi de la Grande-Bretagne, conclu à Versailles le 3 septembre 1783. Paris, Imprimerie royale, 1783. F1202
This treaty between France, Great Britain and Spain ended years of European war. In it Great Britain acknowledged the independence of the United States, but maintained its claim to Canada. France recovered some West Indian islands lost in 1763 and Spain recovered East Florida.

France. Treaties, etc. Convention provisoire, pour servir d'explication à la convention préliminaire de commerce & de navigation ... Paris, P.G. Simon & N.H. Nyon, 1784. F1203
Fourteen articles amplifying certain features of the treaty of commerce between France and Sweden originally concluded in 1741.

France. Treaties, etc. Convention additionnelle et explicative du Traité de commerce avec l'Angleterre. Paris, Imprimerie Royale, 1787. F1204

France. Treaties, etc. Convention between his Britannick Majesty and the most Christian king. Signed at Versailles, the 15th of January, 1787. London, T. Harrison and S. Brooke, 1787. F1205
A continuation of a treaty signed September 1786 relating to duties on specific goods and consulary functions between the two nations.

France. Treaties, etc. Traité de navigation et de commerce entre la France et la Russie. Paris, N.H. Nyon, 1787. F1206
This treaty sets forth in detail the commercial arrangements to prevail between France and Russia.

France. Treaties, etc. Convention entre la République française et les États-Unis d'Amérique. Paris, Imprimerie de la République, 1800. F1207
This convention was an expedient settling of issues between the United States and France over maritime affairs growing out of Anglo-French warfare.

France. Treaties, etc. Projet de tráité d'amítié, de commerce et de navigation entre la République française et celle des États-Unis de l'Amérique. Manuscript. [Paris, ca. April 1800.] F1208
A preliminary draft of a treaty between France and the United States, prepared for the meeting of negotiators which eventually produced the Convention of October 1800. Includes an extensive review of American productions with reference to their importance to French trade.

Francheville, Joseph du Fresne de. Histoire de la Compagnie de Indes. Paris, De Bure, 1746. F1209
Concerns France's overseas commerce from 1664-1737.

Francis, Sir Philip. Original minutes of the governor-general and council of Fort William on the settlement and collection of the revenues of Bengal: with a plan of settlement, recommended to the court of directors in January, 1776. London, Printed for J.Debrett, 1782. F1210

An examination and recommendation relative to the troubles of the East India Company in Bengal, reported here by a faction hostile to the administration of Warren Hastings.

[Francisco de Ajofrín.] Carta familiar de un sacerdote, respuesta a un colegial amigo suyo, en que le dà cuenta de la admirable conquista espiritual del vasto imperio del Gran Thibèt ... Mexico, Bibliotheca Mexicana, 1765. F1211
Francisco de Ajofrín was a Mexican monk and this is his description of the Capuchin order. Includes accounts of Capuchin missionary activity in various parts of the world, including Tibet.

Francisco Jesús María de San Juan del Puerto. Mission historial de Marruecos : en que se trata de los martirios, persecuciones, y trabajos, que han padecido los missionarios ... Seville, Francisco Garay, 1708. F1212
A history of Christian missions in Morocco, largely the work of Franciscans.

Franck, Sebastian. Weltbuch: Spiegel und Bildtnisz des gantzen Erdbodens. Tübingen, U. Morhart, 1534. F1213
An early German encyclopedic geography, with extensive descriptions of Africa, Europe, Asia, and America.

Franck, Sebastian. Weltbuch: Spiegel und Bildenis des gantzen Erdtbodens. [n.p.] 1542. F1214
The second edition.

Franck, Sebastian. Dat wereltboeck, spiegel ende beeltenisse des gheheelen aertbodems. [Amsterdam] 1562. F1215
This Dutch edition is close in content to the earlier German versions.

Franck, Sebastian. Warhafftige Beschreibunge aller und mancherley sorgefeltigen Schiffarten. Frankfurt, M. Lechler, 1567. F1216
Contains accounts of Portuguese East Indian navigations, Staden's description of Brazil, and the first account by Schmidel of the Plate River area.

Francklin, William. Observations made on a tour from Bengal to Persia, in the years 1786-7 ... London, For T. Cadell, 1790. F1217
Following his report on various cities visited between Bengal and Persia, the author comments on the city of Shiraz in Persia and its antiquities and on political events in Persia.

Francklin, William. Resa ifrån Bengalen til Persien åren 1786 och 1787. Götheborg, Samuel Norberg, 1798. F1218
This travel narrative was first published in Calcutta in 1788. The Swedish translation is by Johann Reinhold Forster, who adds notes to the text.

François de Neufchâteau, Nicolas Louis, comte. Mémoire en forme de discours sur la disette du numéraire a Saint-Domingue. Metz, Claude Lamort; Paris, Bailly, Lefere, 1788. F1219
A commentary on the shortage of money in Saint Domingue and its effect on the economy, with suggestions for improvement.

Francoville, Charles-Bruno. Considérations sur la franchise des ports, et en particulier de celui de Dunkerque, par M. Francoville, Député de Calais et Ardres a l'Assemblée nationale. Paris, Imprimerie Nationale, 1790. F1220
A review of Dunkirk's trade with regard to the effect changes in the taxes on imports and exports would have on it.

Franklin, Benjamin. Information for those who would remove to America. [London, Barrell and Servanté, 1796. F1221
This tract was first published in 1784. It was designed to discourage indiscriminate immigration to the United States.

[Franklin, Benjamin.] Remarks on a late protest against the appointment of Mr. Franklin an agent for this province. Philadelphia, B. Franklin and D. Hall, 1764. F1222
Franklin defends his appointment as agent for Pennsylvania's Assembly in London, both in terms of his acceptability and his loyalty to the people of Pennsylvania.

Fredericks-Stadt. Policy Gerichts-Ordeninghe ende Stadts-recht. [Fredericks-stadt] 1635. F1223
The laws, including many dealing with commercial affairs, of Fredericks-stadt, a city established by Dutch refugees in northern Germany.

Free and candid remarks on a late celebrated oration; with some few occasional thoughts on the late commotions in America. London, For B. Law, 1766. F1224
A very conservative point of view, holding that the colonies must be held to obedience regardless of charter provisions as there was no other way of preventing their complete independence.

Free Society of Traders in Pennsylvania. The articles, settlement and officers of the Free Society of Traders in Pennsilvania. London, For Benjamin Clark, 1682. F1225
William Penn gave land and rights in Pennsylvania to a group of merchants, and this is the first publication of plans for the commercial development of that area. The conditions under which the merchants were to operate are outlined.

Fregoso, Battista. De dictis factisque memorabilibus collectanea. Milan, J. Ferrarius, 1509. F1226

A collection of biographical notes including a brief account of the discoveries of Christopher Columbus.

Freire de Andrade, Jacinto. The life of Dom John de Castro, the fourth vice-roy of India. London, H. Herringman, 1664. F1227
The first English edition.

Freire de Andrade, Jacinto. Vida de Dom João de Castro. Lisbon, Crasbeeck, 1651. F1228
A biography of a Portuguese viceroy of India, who was also a cartographer of distinction. One of De Castro's *roteiros* is in the library.

Freire de Andrade, Jacinto. Vida de D. Joam de Castro, quarto viso-rey da India. Lisbon, Joam da Costa, 1671. F1229
The second Portuguese edition.

Freire de Andrade, Jacinto. Vida de D. João de Castro, IV viso-rey da India. Lisbon, Officina da Musica, 1722. F1230
The fourth edition.

Freire de Andrade, Jacinto. Vida de dom João de Castrõ, quarto viso-rey da India. Paris [F.A. Didot] 1769. F1231
This edition includes a brief biography of the author, noting his other books.

Fréjus, Roland de. The relation of a voyage made into Mauritania ... for the establishment of a commerce in all the kingdom of Fez. London, W. Goodbid, 1671. F1232
A description of the commerce of Morocco by a French captain in the service of the Company of Albouzema.

French, Jonathan. A practical discourse against extortion. Boston, T. and J. Fleet, 1777. F1233
Jonathan French of Andover, Mass. was one of many New England pastors involved in the American Revolution. He declares profiteering a violation of natural laws and the profiteer a foe of God.

[Frere, George.] A short history of Barbados. London, For J. Dodsley, 1768. F1234
A general history of the island from the beginnings of English settlement, including a section on the products and exports of the colony.

Fréville, Anne François Joachim. Histoire des nouvelles découvertes faites dans la Mer du Sud en 1767, 1768, 1769, & 1770. Paris, De Hansy, 1774. F1235
Primarily an account of Cook's first voyage but also includes accounts of other explorers of the South Pacific.

Fréville, Anne François Joachim. Berättelse om de nya uptäckter, som blifwit giorde i Söderhafwet, ären 1767, 1768, 1769 och 1770. Upsala, Johan Edman, 1776. F1236
The first Swedish edition.

Frey, Andreas. A true and authentic account of Andrew Frey. London, J. Robinson, 1753. F1237
First edition in English, this anonymous translation was made from the German edition published in 1749. It is an attack on the practices of the Moravian Church and on Count Zinzendorf in particular.

Frézier, Amédée François. Relation du voyage de la Mer du Sud. Paris, J.G. Nyon [etc.] 1716. F1238
A French engineer's journal of a voyage to Chile, Peru, and Brazil in 1711-14.

Frézier, Amédée François. Relation du voyage de la Mer du Sud aux cotes du Chili, du Perou, et du Bresil. Amsterdam, Pierre Humbert, 1717. F1239
This edition adds an account of the Jesuits in Paraguay.

Frézier, Amédée François. A voyage to the South-Sea, and along the coasts of Chili and Peru. London, J. Bowyer, 1717. F1240
This English edition reflects interest in the South Sea trade.

Frézier, Amédée François. Reis-beschryving door de Zuid-Zee, langs de kusten van Chili, Peru en Brazil. Amsterdam, R. en G. Wetstein, 1718. F1241
This Dutch edition adds material on the Jesuits in Paraguay, a lengthy account of Peru, and a letter written from Potosí in 1692.

Frick, Christoph. Ost-Indianische Räysen und Krieges-Dienste. Ulm, Matthew Wagnern, 1692. F1242
A narrative of voyages to Africa, Ceylon, Japan and the East Indies by a physician on a Dutch East India Company ship.

Frick, Christoph. A relation of two several voyages made into the East-Indies. London, For D. Brown [etc.] 1700. F1243
The first English edition.

Fries, Lorenz. Carta marina universalis. Munich, Ludwig Rosenthal's Antiquariat [1926]. F1244
A facsimile in twelve sheets of a world map published in 1525. The original is in the Bayerischen Staatsbibliothek in Munich.

Fries, Lorenz. Underweisung und uszlegunge der Cartha Marina ... Strassburg, Johannes Grieninger, 1530. F1245
Originally designed to accompany the preceding map, this gazetteer contains descriptions of many countries and cities, noting the major commercial products of many of them.

Friesland (Netherlands). Provinciale Staten. Copye van het octroy ... om met die van

Hollandt, Zeelandt, ende West-Frieslandt, in ghemeenschap te treden. Leeuwarden, Pieter van den Rade, 1642. F1246
A patent permitting merchants of Friesland to participate in the East India trade.

Frietas, Seraphino de. De justo imperio Lusitanorum Asiatico. Valladolid, H. Morillo, 1625. F1247
A treatise on maritime law, dealing with the East Indian commerce of several European nations.

[Fritz, Isak.] Sentiments öfwer den här i riket i gång brackta Ostindiske handelen. Stockholm, Peter J. Nyström, 1734. F1248
A criticism of the Swedish East India Company because of the damage its trade was doing to the Swedish silk industry.

Friuli (Italy). Constitutiones patrie Foriiulij. [Venice, Bernardus de Vitalibus, 1524.] F1249
Contains a wide range of regulations upon business, notarial, and commercial affairs.

Froger, François. A relation of a voyage made ... on the coasts of Africa, Streights of Magellan, Brasil, Cayenna, and the Antilles. London, For M. Gillyflower [etc.] 1698. F1250
The first English edition telling of a voyage made by a French naval squadron in 1695-97. It includes interesting comments about the trade of West Africa.

Froger, François. Relation d'un voyage fait en 1695, 1696 & 1697 aux côtes d'Afrique, Détroit de Magellan, Brezil, Cayenne & isles Antilles. Paris, N. le Gras, 1700. F1251
The second French edition.

Fróis, Luís. De rebus Japonicis historica relatio, eaque triplex. Mainz, Joannis Albini, 1599. F1252
Three letters from a Portuguese Jesuit concerning events centering around the crucifixion of twenty-six Christians early in 1597.

Fróis, Luís. Lettera annua del Giappone dell' anno M.D.XCVI. Rome, Luigi Zanetti, 1599. F1253
A report on Jesuit mission stations, residences, and colleges in Japan just prior to the beginnings of active persecution of Christians by the Japanese government.

Fróis, Luís. Lettera del Giapone de gli anni 1591. et 1592. Scritta al R. P. generale della Compagnie di Giesu ... Mantova, Francesco Osanna, 1595. F1254
One of three 1595 editions of these letters written from Nagasaki.

Fróis, Luís. Literae annuae Japonenses anni 1591 et 1592, quibus res memoratu dignae, quae nouis Christianis ibidem toto biennio acciderunt, recensentur. Cologne, Henricum Falckenburg, 1596. F1255
This annual letter brings the progress of the Jesuit missions in Japan up to the time of sudden decline with the beginnings of strong anti-Christian policies by the Japanese government.

Fróis, Luís. Nova relatio historica de statu rei Christianae in Japonia. Mainz, Joannis Albini, 1598. F1256
Two letters written by Froes in 1595, relating to Portuguese religious and commercial activity in Japan, China, and the Philippines.

Fróis, Luís. Relatione della gloriosa morte di xxvi. posti in croce per comandamento del Re di Giappone. Rome, Luigi Zanetti, 1599. F1257
An account of the crucifixion of twenty-six missionaries in Japan, reflecting the rivalry between the Jesuits supported by the Portuguese and the Spanish Franciscans.

Fróis, Luís. Trattato d'alcuni prodigii occorsi l'anno M.D.XCVI. nel Giappone. Milan, Pacifico Pontio, 1599. F1258
This letter was written from Nagasaki, December 28, 1596. It is largely a report on an embassy from China.

Fróis, Luís. Zwey newe Jahrschreiben auss Japonia. Mainz, Johannem Albinum, 1598. F1259
The letters report progress of missionary work and also describe political rivalry in Japan's ruling circles.

Frossard, Benjamin-Sigismond. La cause des esclaves nègres et habitans de la Guinée, portée au tribunal de la justice, de la religion, de la politique. Lyons, Aimé de la Roche, 1789. F1260
This is one of the most important publications in the French anti-slavery movement.

Fryer, John. A new account of East-India and Persia. London, R. Chiswell, 1698. F1261
Eight letters describing customs, peoples, products, etc., of Persia and the East Indies.

Fryer, John. Negenjaarige reyse door Oost Indien en Persien ... Begonnen met den jaare 1672 en geeyndigt met den jaare 1681 ... The Hague, Abraham de Hondt [etc.] 1700. F1262
The only non-English edition, with illustrations based on the English edition of 1698.

Fuentes, Diego de. Conquista de Africa. Antwerp, Philippo Nutio, 1570. F1263
The volume celebrates victories over the Turkish fleet in the Mediterranean by European forces in the period 1550-1555. "Africa" was a fortress between Tunis and Jerba.

A full account of the proceedings in relation to Capt. Kidd. In two letters. Written by a person of quality to a kinsman of the Earl of Bellomont in Ireland. London, 1701. F1264

A defense of Kidd, and more particularly of the Earl of Bellomont who had been governor of New York and one of those responsible for Kidd's commission to eradicate pirates from the Atlantic shores of North America.

A full and exact collection of all the considerable addresses, memorials, petitions ... And other publick papers, relating to the Company of Scotland Trading to Africa and the Indies. Edinburgh, 1700. F1265
A collection of some sixty reprinted documents by various agencies of the government and the Darien Company.

A full and impartial account of the Company of Mississippi. London, For R. Francklin [etc.] 1720. F1266
A major promotion tract for John Law's Mississippi Company, giving a description of the Mississippi region, and the way it was to be exploited by the company.

A full and true relation of the great and wonderful revolution that hapned lately in the kingdom of Siam in the East-Indies. London, For Randal Taylor, 1690. F1267
A history of the developments of 1688 whereby French attempts to dominate Siam were foiled by a rebellion.

Fullerton, John. A journal of the fatal occurrences at Judda, 1727. Manuscript. English, ca. 1728. F1268
An eyewitness account of a riot in the city of Jidda, in which six Englishmen were attacked in their lodgings and all except the author were killed.

Fullerton, John. A short memorial of affairs of ship Prince George at Judda, 1728. Manuscript. English, ca. 1728. F1269
In this manuscript Fullerton relates the difficulties he encountered in attempting to carry on trade at Jidda after the "massacre."

Funnell, William. A voyage round the world. London, W. Botham, 1707. F1270
Describes the commercial opportunities in Chile and au Peru as well as the trade to the East Indies.

Furent presens en leurs personnes ... Seigneur Armand, Cardinal de Richelieu ... et Guillaume de Caën. Paris, ca. 1632. F1271
The appointment of Guillaume de Caën to accompany an expedition to Canada and take possession of Quebec after it was restored to the French by Charles I of England.

La furieuse defaite des Espagnols, et la sanglante bataille donnee au Perou, tant par mer que par terre. Paris, Jean Martin, 1625. F1272
An account of a Dutch victory over the Spaniards in Peru. The Dutch fleet was commanded by Jacques l'Hermite.

Furtado, Francisco. Informatio antiquissima de praxi missionariorum Sinensium Societatis Jesu, circa ritus Sinensis, data in China iam ab annis 1636 & 1640. Paris, Nicolaum Pepié, 1700. F1273
A letter from Furtado written in 1636 and a response to Dominican questions about the Jesuit missionary methods in China, written in 1640, both published here as a defense of the Jesuits during the Chinese Rites controversy.

Further reasons offer'd and fresh occasions given for making void and annulling fradulent and usurious contracts ... by the South-Sea Company. London, 1721. F1274
An attempt to restore private credit after the South Sea Bubble.

G

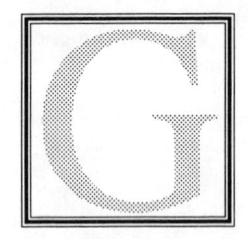

Gabrielle da Bologna. Lettera scritta dal Congo al M.R.P. Carlo Maria da Massa di Carrara stato colà missionario dal P. Gabrielle da Bologna, ambi Cappucini che da contezza di quello gl'è colà accaduto di Sogno, &c. [Venice, Girolamo Albrizzi, 1707.]   G1
   A letter dated Luanda, 30 December 1705, reporting Capuchin missionary work in that area. This is an excerpt from *La Galleria Minerva*, vol. IV.

Gaby, Jean Baptiste. Relation de la Nigritie. Paris, Edme Courterot, 1689.   G2
   A missionary's account of Senegambia with some emphasis on the products of the region and on European commerce there.

Gage, Thomas. The English-American, his travail by sea and land: or, A new survey of the West Indias. London, R. Cotes, 1648.   G3
   A detailed description of the Spanish West Indies by an Englishman who had gone there under Spanish authority as a priest.

Gage, Thomas. A new survey of the West-Indies. London, E. Cotes, 1655.   G4
   The second edition, with a new title, and the first to contain maps.

Gage, Thomas. A new survey of the West-Indies. London, A. Clark to be sold by John Martyn, 1677.   G5
   This third English edition omits one chapter in deference to the character of Archbishop Laud.

Gage, Thomas. Nouvelle relation, contenant les voyages de Thomas Gage dans la Nouvelle Espagne ... traduit de l'Anglois par le sieur de Beaulieu Huës O. Neil. Paris, Gervais Clouzier, 1676-77.   G6
   The first French edition, which includes a section on the Pogochi language used in Guatemala.

Gage, Thomas. Nouvelle relation, contenant les voyages de Thomas Gage dans la Nouvelle Espagne. Amsterdam, Paul Marret, 1695.   G7
   This edition contains a set of maps and plates not found in the English editions.

Gage, Thomas. Nieuwe ende seer naeuwkeurige reyse door de Spaensche West-Indien ... met seer curieuse soo land-kaerten als historische figueren verciert ... Overgeset door H.V.Q. Utrecht, Johannes Ribius, 1682.   G8
   The first Dutch edition, translated from the French, and with new introductory matter.

Gage, Thomas. Nieuwe ende seer naeuwkeurige reyse door de Spaensche West-Indien. Amsterdam, Willem de Coup [etc.] 1700.   G9
   The second Dutch edition, including maps and illustrations based on the French editions.

Gaignat de L'Aulnais, C.F. Guide du commerce. Paris, Despilly, Durand, et Valade [1764].   G10
   A commercial instruction book, with particular mention of trade to China, America, and the west coast of Africa.

Gaitan de Torres, Manuel. Reglas para el govierno destos reynos y delos delas Indias. [Jerez de la Frontera] 1625.   G11
   Concerns the administration and trade of Spanish possessions in America, with suggestions for their improvement.

[Galard-Terraube, Louis Antoine Marie Victor de, marquis.] Tableau de Cayenne ou de la Guiane française. Paris, Veuve Tilliard et fils, [1799].   G12
   An appraisal of French Guiana with particular concern for increasing cotton, coffee, and indigo exports.

Galard-Terraube, Louis Antoine Marie Victor de, marquis. Neue Reise nach Cayenne, oder, Zuverlässige Nachrichten von der französischen Guiana jetzigen Deportationsort der Franzosen ... aus dem Tagebuche eines französischen

Bürgers ; mit Anmerkungen von M. G**. Wien; Prag, Franz Haas, 1800. G13

The second German edition. The translator notes the considerable economic importance of the Cayenne colony beyond its function as a penal colony.

Galbaud-Dufort, François Thomas. A la Convention nationale ... [n.p., J.C. Laveaux, 1793?] G14

A former governor of Santo Domingo requests more freedom in order to prepare a defense of his actions in the colony.

[Galiani, Ferdinando.] Dialogues sur le commerce des bleds. [Paris, Merlin] 1770. G15

The grain trade controversy is used here by a Neapolitan temporarily resident in France to oppose generally the arguments of the Physiocrats and others who proposed to rely upon natural laws in the governing of economics.

[Galleani Napione, Gian Francesco.] Esáme critico del primo viaggio de Amerigo Vespucci ... Florence, Molini, Landi e compágno, 1811. G16

A critique of the literature of Amerigo Vespucci's disputed voyage of 1497.

Gallego y Valcarel, Manuel. [Manuscript collection of 159 autograph letters written to Gallego y Valcarel during his tenure as Secretary of the Vice-royalty of Buenos Aires, with an additional 20 documents relating to his slave holdings and government business.] 1791-1806. G17

Most of the archive, 213 items, is correspondence between Manuel and his business associates and family members, giving a view of Spanish administration in colonial Argentina.

Gallichon, Friderich, Christian de la Roche. Sendschreiben ... an den Herrn Verfasser des Politischen-Journals, betreffend die Wiederfindung des alten Grönlands, und der unzertrennlich damit sogenannten nordwestlichen-Durchfarth. Copenhagen, Chr. Frid. Holm, 1787. G18

A response to an article in the *Politisches-Journal nebst anzeige gelehrten und andern Sachen*, 1785, concerning the location of the lost Greenland colony. The author of this response relates the search for it to the continued hope for a northwest passage.

[Galloway, Joseph.] A candid examination of the mutual claims of Great-Britain, and the colonies: with a plan of accommodation, on constitutional principles. New York, James Rivington, 1775. G19

A rejection of the radical tendencies in colonial leadership leading toward independence, and a proposal for a colonial legislature and a royally appointed President General to preserve union with Great Britain.

[Galloway, Joseph.] Cool thoughts on the consequences to Great Britain of American independence. London, For J. Wilkie, 1780. G20

A Loyalist argument tending to prove that the continued subordination of the colonies was essential to the survival of Britain as a power of consequence in the world.

Gallucci, Giovanni Paolo. Theatro del mundo, y del tiempo ... Traduzido de Latin en Romance por Miguel Perez ... y añadido por el mismo muchas cosas al proposito desta ciencia que faltauan en el Latin. Granada, Sebastian Muñoz, 1612. G21

This 1612 issue is from the sheets of the 1606 edition, the first Spanish edition which is much altered and amended over the Latin edition of 1588.

Galvão, Antonio. The discoveries of the world from their first original unto the yeere of our Lord 1555. London, G. Bishop, 1601. G22

A translation by Richard Hakluyt of a chronicle of Portuguese discovery in Asia.

Galvão, Duarte. Chronica do muito alto, e muito esclarecido principe D. Affonso Henriques primeiro Rey de Portugal ... fielmente copiada do seu original, que se conserva no Archivo Real da Torre do Tombo. Lisbon, Officina Ferreyiana, 1727. G23

The author was royal chronicler for a time in the reign of Affonso V. This is the first edition of his chronicle, which records the beginnings of the Portuguese monarchy.

Gálvez, José de. Reglas que se propusieron para la formacion, y establecimiento de una compañia de navieros en esta ciudad de Malaga, para el commercio de Vera-Cruz ... Malaga, Impresor de la Dignidad Episcopal [1784]. G24

A series of proposals for the formation of a trading company to operate from Malaga, with government approval or commentary on the separate articles.

Gambara, Lorenzo. De navigatione Christophori Columbi libri quattuor ... Rome, Franciscum Zannettum, 1581. G25

A commendatory poem celebrating the 1492 voyage of Columbus.

García, Francisco. Vida, y martyrio de el venerable padre Diego Luis de Sanvitores, de la Compañia de Jesus ... Madrid, 1683. G26

A biography of the founder of the Jesuit mission in the Mariana Islands and a history of its progress in 1682.

García, Gregorio. Origen de los Indios de el Nuevo Mundo, e Indias Occidentales ... Valencia, Pedro Patricio Mey, 1607. G27

One of the earliest works to deal extensively with the origins of the American Indians, noting all of the theories advanced to that time.

Garcia de Céspedes, Andrés. Regimiento de navegacion. [Madrid, Juan de la Cuesta, 1606.]
G28
A navigation guide for both the East and West Indies, written by the Spanish royal cosmographer and mathematician.

García de Palacio, Diego. Vocabulario maritimo, y explicacion de los vocablos. Seville, H. Lopez de Haro [1722].
G29
Originally published in 1696, this maritime dictionary has been enlarged and corrected for this edition of 1722.

Garcia de Palacios, Alonso. Defensa legal, y de hecho, por Don Alonso Garcia de Palacios, y Don Joseph Antonio Gelabert, vecinos de la ciudad de la Habana ... [n.p., ca. 1750.]
G30
A legal brief concerning the sale of crown lands in Cuba by its governor.

Garcia y Gomez, Juan Joseph. Defensa militar y satisfaccion que expone Don Juan Joseph Garcia y Gomez ... Cadiz, D. Manuel Espinosa de los Monteros, 1780.
G31
A speech in defense of Francisco Javier Everardo Tilly y Paredes (the marqués de Casa-Tilly), who was court-martialed for his failure to fight the Portuguese while he was in command of a Spanish naval squadron off the coast of Brazil in 1776-1777.

Garderot, M. Pétition a l'Assemblée nationale, relative aux troubles de Saint-Domingue ... [Paris?] Imprimerie nationale [1791?].
G32
An appeal for honest administrators and troops to support order in the colony.

[Gardner.] Some reflections on a pamphlet, intituled, England and East-India inconsistent in their manufactures. London, 1696 [i.e. 1697].
G33
A reply to two pamphlets which had taken issue with Charles Davenant's *An Essay on the East-India Trade*, published in 1696.

Gardyner, George. A description of the world. London, Robert Leybourn, 1651.
G34
This work begins with a discourse on England's commerce, and its description of various parts of the New World is given largely to the economic opportunities they afford.

Gargiaria, Giovanni Camillo. Responsum pro Universitate drapperiorum, seu strazzarolorum cum Societate sutorum. Bologna, Clementis Ferronij, 1627.
G35
A discussion of regulations concerning working relationships between the drapers and the shoemakers.

Garnier, Blaise. Combats affreux, arrivés a l'isle St. Domingue ... Au Port de Paix, le 18 novembre 1790. Marseilles, J. Mossy [1791?].
G36
An account of events in October, 1790 when the revolutionary Ogé led an abortive uprising of mulattoes against the government of the French colony on Saint Domingue.

Gaspar de San Agustín, fray. Conquistas de las Islas Philipinas: la temporal, por las armas del Señor Don Phelipe Segundo el Prudente; y la espiritual, por los religiosos del orden de nuestro padre San Augustin. Madrid, Manuel Ruiz de Murga, 1698.
G37
A history of Spanish conquest in the Philippines and beyond into the Moluccas and the Marianas, with some account of Mexico as well.

Gaspar de São Bernardino. Itinerario da India por terra. Lisbon, Vincente Alvares, 1611. G38
A Portuguese Franciscan's account of travels in Madagascar, along the east coast of Africa, into the Persian Gulf, and overland to Palestine.

Gass, Patrick. A journal of the voyages and travels of a corps of discovery, under the command of Capt. Lewis and Capt. Clarke ... from the mouth of the river Missouri ... to the Pacific ocean. Pittsburgh, Zadok Cramer, 1807. G39
The first American edition of the first published account of the Lewis and Clark expedition.

Gass, Patrick. Journal of the voyages and travels of a corps of discovery, under the command of Capt. Lewis and Capt. Clarke ... from the mouth of the river Missouri ... to the Pacific Ocean. Philadelphia, Mathew Carey, 1812.
G40
The fourth American edition.

Gastaldi, Giacomo. La universale descrittione del mondo. Venice, Matthio Pagano, 1562. G41
A famous Italian geographer's tract to accompany a world map, now lost, which was similar to one published by Camocio. An important feature is its description of the eastern limit of Asia, where the author located the Strait of Anian.

Gaterau, M. Pétition présentée a l'Assemblée nationale, dans la séance du 11 décembre 1791. [Paris, Imprimerie Nationale, 1791.]
G42
Nearly identical to the petition of Garderot, above.

Gaudet. Opinion sur les colonies. [Paris, Imprimerie Nationale, 1792.]
G43
A strong indictment against the French government for mishandling colonial affairs in the West Indies.

Gautier de Tronchoy. Journal de la campagne des isles de l'Amérique. Troyes, J. le Febvre, 1709.
G44
Describes early French exploration, settlement, and trade in the islands of St. Christopher, Martinique, and Guadeloupe.

Gavy de Mendonça, Agostinho de. Historia do famoso cerco, que o xarife pos a fortaleza de

Mazagam deffendido pello valeroso Capitam Mòr della Alvaro de Carvalho. Lisbon, V. Alvarez, 1607. G45
A narrative of successful resistance by the Portuguese in the siege of Mazagan, one of their fortresses in Morocco, in 1562.

[Gayton, Edmund.] De burgerlycke oorlogen tot Bantam. [n.p., 1683.] G46
An account by an Englishman of an attempt to capture Bantam, the stronghold of the Dutch East India Company.

Gazeta extraordinaria de Londres, publicada por auctoridade. Quinta feira 30 de setembro de 1762 ... [Lisbon, Miguel Rodrigues, 1762.] G47
An account of the 1761 siege of Havana, including articles of capitulation, documents describing conditions within the city and abstracts from the diary of the chief engineer of Havana and Moro Castle.

Il gazzettiere americano. Leghorn, Marco Coltellini, 1763. G48
The first Italian edition, with numerous engravings of American harbors, plants, and animal life.

Het geamplieerde octroy de Oost-Indische Compagnie ... [n.p.] 1623. G49
The enlarged charter of the East India Company is followed by a plea for the support of the West India Company.

Gedanken über den Aufstand der englischen Colonien in dem nördlichen Amerika. Göttingen, Johann Christian Dieterich, 1776. G50
A brief account of the British colonies in North America with a review of events leading to the American Revolution.

Geddes, Michael. The history of the church of Malabar, from the time of its being first discover'd by the Portuguezes in the year 1501. London, Sam. Smith and Benj. Walford, 1694. G51
An account of the relations between Eastern and Western Christians in India, originally written by Aleixo de Menezes and published in Antonio de Gouveia's *Journada do Arcebispo de Goa*, 1601. Geddes provides commentary and additions to the text.

Gee, Joshua. The trade and navigation of Great-Britain considered. London, Samuel Buckley, 1729. G52
A review of England's commercial situation indicating trade carried on with many regions, and containing suggestions for England's greater prosperity through improvement of her commerce.

Gee, Joshua. The trade and navigation of Great-Britain considered: Shewing that the surest way for a nation to increase in riches, is to prevent the importation of such foreign commodities as may be rais'd at home ... Dublin, S. Powell [etc.] 1730. G53
The only Dublin edition of this popular mercantilist treatise.

Gee, Joshua. The trade and navigation of Great Britain considered. London, S. Buckley, 1731. G54
The third edition.

Gee, Joshua. The trade and navigation of Great-Britain considered. London, For J. Almon, 1767. G55
The last edition, containing notes not found in earlier editions.

Gee, Joshua. Considérations sur le commerce et la navigation de la Grande-Brétagne. London, A. Bettesworth [etc.] 1749. G56
The first French edition.

[Gee, Joshua.] Coup d'oeil rapide sur les progrés et la décadence du commerce & des forces de l'Angleterre. Amsterdam, Arkstée & Merkus; Paris, De Hansy, 1768. G57
A free and abridged translation of *Trade and navigation considered*, entirely different from the French translation of 1749.

[Gee, Joshua.] Aanmerkingen over den koophandel en de zeewart van Groot-Brittanje. Amsterdam, S. van Esveldi, 1750. G58
The first Dutch edition.

Gee, Joshua. Consideraciones sobre el comercio, y la navegacion de la Gran-Bretaña. Madrid, Juan de San Martin, 1753. G59
This Spanish edition contains two prefatory sections outlining the Spanish point of view regarding free trade and commercial cooperation among nations.

De geest van Dr. Dooreslaer wordt door de tijdt vertoont, en ontmomt 't aensicht der Hollanderen, en ontdeckt den leeuws klaew ... [n.p., 1652.] G60
A broadside using the symbolism of Dr. Isaac Doreslaer and the Amboyna Massacre in its treatment of events leading to war between the Dutch and English in 1652.

Gegenwärtiger zustand derer finantzen von Franckreich. Leipzig, J.F. Gleditschens Sohn, 1720. G61
Concerns John Law's financial program for France and its relation to the Compagnie d'Occident.

De gelukkige aanstaande gevolgen uit de unie en verbintenis tusschen ... Groot Britaine en de ... Vereenigde Nederlanden. The Hague, Johannes Albertz, 1689. G62
Shows concern for the enlargement of the French merchant fleet and for French pressure on the Dutch in the East Indies.

Gemelli Careri, Giovanni Francesco. Voyage du tour du monde, traduite de l'Italien ... par M.L.N. Paris, Froullé, 1776. G63
An account of an Italian's travels around the world by way of Turkey, Persia, India, China, the Philippines and South America.

Gemma, Frisius. Principiis astronomiae & cosmographie ... de orbis divisione, & insulis rebusq nuper inventis. Antwerp, Joannes Richard, 1544. G64
A navigational handbook with the novel suggestion that clocks could be used as a means of determining longitude.

Gemma, Frisius. De principiis astronomiae & cosmographie, deque usu globi ab eodem editi. Antwerp, Joannis Steelsii, 1553. G65
The fifth printing in Antwerp of this popular geographical treatise.

Genees-middelen voor Hollants-qualen. Vertoonende de quade regeringe de loevesteinse factie. Antwerp [1672]. G66
A pamphlet containing comments on numerous economic affairs, including the cost of protecting ships of the East India Company.

General chronicen das ist: Warhaffte eigentliche und kurtze Beschreibung ... Vieler ... Landtschafften ... Frankfurt, J. Schmidt, 1576. G67
Includes translations of the letters of Andrea Corsali, an account of Ethiopia based on Francisco Alvares, the history of Orosius, and a general geography of Europe, Asia, and Africa.

General Chronica, das ist: Warhaffte eigentliche und kurtze Beschreibung vieler namhaffter, und zum Theil biss daher unbekannter Landtschafften. Frankfurt [Sigmund Feyerabend] 1581. G68
Second edition

A general collection of voyages and discoveries, made by the Portuguese and the Spaniards, during the fifteenth and sixteenth centuries. London, W. Richardson, etc., 1789. G69
The Portuguese accounts are taken largely from Barros, but there are comparisons with other contemporary authors. The Spanish voyages relate only to the New World.

A general treatise of naval trade and commerce, as founded on the laws and statutes of this realm: in which those relating to letters of marque, reprisal and of restitution, privateers, and prizes, convoys, cruizers, and every other branch of trade, are particularly considered. London, E. and R. Nutt and R. Gosling, For E. Symon and J. Crokatt, 1739; For Edward Symon, 1740. G70
A review of all aspects of English maritime and commercial law, including hostility at sea, trading companies, international treaties, customs, admiralty jurisdiction, etc.

A general view of the dimensions of the most approved ship of each class in the British navy, with the exact dimensions ... according to the establishment in 1778. London, D. Steel, 1778. G71

Genius, Isaac. Neundte Schiffart, das ist: Gründliche Erklärung was sich mit den Holl- und Seeländer in Ost-Indien anno 1604 und 1605 unter dem Admiral Steffan von der Hagen zugetragen. Frankfurt am Mayn, Erasmo Kempffern, 1612. G72
This is the second edition of the ninth part of the Hulsius series of voyages. Van der Hagen's voyage was important in asserting Dutch dominance in the Spice Islands.

[Gennes, Pierre de.] Mémoire pour le sieur de la Bourdonnais. Paris, Delaguette, 1750. G73
A review of the conduct of Sieur de la Bourdonnais during his service in the East Indies, with the Compagnie des Indes.

[Gennes, Pierre de.] Supplement au Mémoire du sieur de la Bourdonnais. Paris, Delaguette, 1751. G74
A continuation of the previous work, containing testimony on the conduct of la Bourdonnais and Dupleix in India.

Genoa (Italy). Rota. Decisiones Rotae Genuae de mercatura et pertinentibus ad eam. Genoa, 1582. G75
A collection of 215 decisions arising out of Genoese commercial activities.

Genovesi, Antonio. Delle lezioni di commercio osia d'economia civile ... Milan, Federico Agnelli, 1768. G76
A series of lectures on population, free grain trade, the financing of commerce, and similar problems of economic interest.

Gensonné, Armand. Opinion sur les colonies ... prononcée à la séance du 22 mars 1792. Paris, Imprimerie Nationale, 1792. G77
The author attributes troubles in the French colony of St. Domingue to the deprivation of Mulattoes and free Negroes of political rights promised to them. He calls for new elections of provincial assemblies based on wider suffrage.

Gentleman, Tobias. Englands way to win wealth. London, For Nathaniel Butter, 1614. G78
A recommendation that England use her fishing grounds to greater advantage in international trade, citing the example of the Dutch.

A genuine account of Nova Scotia: containing, a description of its situation, air, climate, soil and its products ... To which is added, His Majesty's proposals, as an encouragement to those who are willing to settle there. Dublin, Philip Bowes, 1750. G79

An appeal for settlers to go to Nova Scotia, noting the geography, economic opportunity, government, and general conditions there, with a proposal to grant fifty acres to each settler and an additional ten to each member of his family.

Geographiae veteris scriptores graeci minores : cum interpretatione Latina, dissertationibus, ac annotationibus. Oxford, Sheldoniano, 1698-1712. G80

A collection of twenty-six classical and Arabic texts, edited with extensive commentary by Oxford scholar John Hudson.

Geographica et historica Herodoti, que Latine Mela exscripsit. Antwerp, Christophori Plantini, 1582. G81

A comparison of the texts of Herodotus and Pomponius Mela.

Geographische Beschreibung der Provinz Louisiana in Canada, von dem Fluss St. Lorenz bis an den Ausfluss des Flusses Missisipi. [n.p., ca. 1720.] G82

A broadside describing the St. Lawrence-Great Lakes-Mississippi River area designed to interest investors in John Law's Louisiana Company.

Geographische Beschreibung von Canada besonders der Hauptstadt Quebeck: nebst den Handlungen, Sitten, Gebräuchen und Lebensart der Einwohner überhaupt sowol Christen als Wilden, einer Nachricht von den dasigen deutschen Truppen, von einem Wilden Könige gehaltenen Rede ... [n.p., 1777]. G83

An account of Quebec and the surrounding area as well as relations between the British commander and the local Indians. The author appears to have been a preacher with the Braunschweig troop serving with the British.

Geographische tafel behelzende de graaden der breedte of poolshoogte en lengte of middagcirkel, van de meest bekende steeden, rivieren, caapen, baayen. En inzonderheid der voornaamste zeehavens des aardryks ... Amsterdam, Gerard Hulst van Keulen, 1790. G84

A listing and location of some 1600 places in all parts of the world, bound with and related to the *Schat-kamer* of Nicolaas de Vries.

Geographus Ravennas. Anonymi Ravennatis qui circa saeculum VII vixit de geographia. Paris, Simonem Langronne, 1688. G85

The earlist published edition of a seventh-century geography based on classical itineraries and other sources. It is edited by David Placide Porcheron, a Benedictine scholar.

Georgi, Johann Gottlieb. Bemerkungen einer Reise im russischen Reich ... St. Petersburg, Kayserl. Academie der Wissenschaften, 1775. G86

An account of travels in Siberia from 1772 to 1775, much of this time in the company of Peter Simon Pallas, the expedition being primarily of a scientific nature.

Georgi, Johann Gottlieb. Beschreibung aller Nationen des russischen Reichs, ihrer Lebensart, Religion, Gebräuche, Wohnungen, Kleidungen und übrigen Merkwürdigkeiten. St. Petersburg, Carl Wilhelm Müller, 1776-1780. G87

A detailed survey of the peoples of Siberia, with ninety-five hand-colored illustrations depicting costumes.

Georgi, Johann Gottlieb. Merkwürdigkeiten verschiedener unbekannten Völker des russischen Reichs. Frankfurt & Leipzig, 1777. G88

Excerpts on the peoples of Siberia from Georgi's *Bemerkungen einer Reise im russischen Reich*.

Georgi, Johann Gottlieb. Russia: or, A compleat historical account of all the nations which compose that empire. London, J. Nichols, T. Cadell, H. Payne, and N. Conant, 1780-1783. G89

This English translation by William Tooke contains an introduction of more than one hundred pages, and additional text not found in the German edition as well as notes to the text.

Georgi, Johann Gottlieb. Versuch einer Beschreibung der russisch keyserlichen Residenzstadt St. Petersburg und der Merkwürdigkeiten der Gegend. St. Petersburg, Carl Willhelm Müller, 1790. G90

A detailed description of St. Petersburg and its hinterland, noting commercial, religious, and cultural institutions. A plan of the city and a map of the region are included.

Georgia (Colony). Trustees for Establishing the Colony of Georgia in America. Copy of the minutes of the Trustees for Establishing the Colony of Georgia in America on Wednesday July 14th 1742. G91

The minutes call for an inquiry as to how the introduction of slaves could be brought about.

Georgijević, Bartolomej. Libellus vere Christiana lectione dignus diversas res Turcharum brevi. tradens. [Rome, Anthonium Bladum, 1552.] G92

A popular work on the manners and customs of the Turks by an author who had traveled widely in Turkey.

Geraldini, Alessandro. Itinerarium ad regiones sub aequinoctiali ... Rome, Facciotti, 1631. G93

The author was the first bishop of Hispaniola and an intimate friend of Columbus. This work, originally written in 1524, contains his impressions of the New World.

Gerbett, Gustav Friederich. Ost-Indische Natur-Geschichte, Sitten und Alterthümer, insonderheit bey den Malabaren. Halle, 1752. G94
Descriptions of India from reports of Danish missionaries stationed there.

[Gerbier, Sir Balthazar.] Advertissement for men inclyned to plantasions in America. Rotterdam, Herry Goddaeus, 1660. G95
The author explains a mutiny against his leadership of a Dutch colonial undertaking in Guiana, while continuing to advocate settlement of a colony there.

Gerbier, Sir Balthazar. Les effects pernicieux de meschants favoris et grands ministres d'estat ... et Des-abuzé d'erreurs populaires, sur le subject de Jacques & Charles Stuart, roys de la Grande-Bretagne. The Hague, Adrian Vlac, 1653. G96
Two essays on government administration relating in part to overseas matters. The author was to become a promoter of a colony in Guiana.

Gerbier, Sir Balthazar. A sommary description, manifesting that greater profits are to bee done in the hott then in the could parts off the coast off America. [Rotterdam, Herry Goddaeus] for Sir Balthazar Gerbier, 1660. G97
The author recommends Guiana as the ideal place for an American colony, identifies commercial products available there, and notes the types of people needed for a Guiana colony. A manuscript leaf bound in invites subscriptions to a Guiana settlement.

[Gerbier, Pierre-Jean-Baptiste.] Memoire pour le Marquis de Bussy, marechal des camps et armées du Roi contre les syndics et directeurs de la Compagnie des Indes. Paris, L. Cellot, 1767. G98
A collection of materials relating to a case of the Compagnie des Indes against a creditor; Gerbier was the lawyer for the Company.

[Gerbier, Pierre-Jean-Baptiste.] Precis pour le Marquis de Bussy, contre les syndics & directeurs de la Compagnie des Indes. Paris, L. Cellot, 1767. G99

[Gerbier, Pierre-Jean-Baptiste.] Second errata. Pour servir au supplement de Mémoire pour les syndics & directeurs de la Compagnie des Indes. Paris, L. Cellot, 1767. G100

[Gerritsz, Cornelis.] Diarium nauticum itineris Batavorum in Indiam Orientalem. Paris, Adrian Perier, 1598. G101
A Latin translation of the original journal of the first Dutch voyage to the East Indies under the command of Cornelis Houtman.

[Gerritsz, Hessel.] Descriptio ac delineatio geographica detectionis freti. Amsterdam, H. Gerardus, 1612. G102
This collection of voyages by a Dutch cartographer contains the earliest accounts of the discoveries of Henry Hudson in North America and the first map of the Hudson Bay region.

Gerritsz, Hessel. Histoire du pays nomme Spitsberghe. Amsterdam, 1613. G103
An attempt to prove that the Dutch had rights before any other nation did to the whaling industry in Spitzbergen. Also includes a description of the whaling trade there.

Gervaise, Nicholas. Description historique du royaume de Macaçar. Paris, Hilaire Foucault, 1688. G104
A French priest's account of Macassar, including observations on the natural resources, economy, commerce, religion, social life, and customs of the people there.

[Gervaise, Nicholas.] An historical description of the kingdom of Macasar in the East-Indies. London, Tho. Leigh and D. Midwinter, 1701. G105
The first English edition.

Gervaise, Nicholas. Histoire naturelle et politique du royaume de Siam ... Paris, Etienne Ducastin, 1689. G106
A survey of the geography, natural history, social customs, religious and intellectual life and politics of Siam at a time of intense interest in this subject in France.

Geschichte der englischen Kolonien in Nord-Amerika von den ersten Entdeckung dieser Länder durch Sebastian Cabot bis auf den Frieden 1763. Leipzig, Caspar Fritsch, 1775. G107
This is a translation by Anton Ernst Klausing of the anonymous *History of the British dominions in North America*, London, 1773.

Ghistele, Joos van. 'T voyage van Mher Joos van Ghistele. Ghent, Henrie van den Kerre, 1557. G108
The first printing of an account of travels to Palestine, Egypt, and Arabia in the fifteenth century.

Giannettasio, Niccolò Partenio. Piscatoria, et nautica. Naples, Typis regiis, 1685. G109
A didactic and descriptive poem on navigation and on fishing, including many references to early events in the age of discovery.

[Gibbon, Edward.] Memoire justificatif pour servir de réponse a l'Exposé, &c. de la cour de France. [London] 1779. G110
Writing at the instigation of the British government, Gibbon responds to a French publication, *Exposé des motifs de la conduite du Roi, relativement à l'Angleterre*, Paris, 1779, which had justified French assistance to the American colonies in their rebellion.

Gilbert, John. A sermon preached before the Incorporated Society for the Propagation of the Gospel in Foreign Parts; at their anniversary meeting in the parish-church of St. Mary-le-Bow, on Friday, February 17, 1743-4. London, J. and H. Pemberton, 1744. G111
Among instances of progress noted is a school established in Barbados.

Gilbert, Thomas. Voyage from New South Wales to Canton, in the year 1788. London, For J. Debrett, 1789. G112
This early commercial voyage from Australia to China revealed the Gilbert and Marshall islands and produced a good description of Tinian.

Gillet-Lajaqueminière, Louis-Charles. Rapport ... de la réclamation des députés de Saint-Domingue, relative à l'approvisionnement de l'isle. Paris, Baudouin, 1789. G113
A survey of the commerce of Saint Domingue with particular reference to the grain and flour trade.

Ginnaro, Bernardino. Saverio orientale ò vero istorie de Cristiani illustri dell' oriente. Naples, Francesco Savio, 1641. G114
A history of the Jesuit mission in Japan from 1542 to the end of the sixteenth century, citing more than a hundred authors on whom he relied.

Giorgini, Giovanni. Il mondo nuovo del Sig. Giovanni Giorgini da Iesi ... Iesi, Pietro Farri, 1596. G115
A poem in twenty-four cantos of ottava rima celebrating Spanish discovery and conquest in the New World from Columbus to Cortes.

[Giovanni, da Pian del Carpine, Archbishop of Antivari.] Opera ... si contiene doi itinerarii in Tartaria. [Venice, Giovan'Antonio de Nicolini da Sabio, 1537.] G116
The first printing of this narrative of travels to the East, undertaken in 1245-47.

Giovanni Francesco da Roma. Breve relatione del successo della missione de' Frati Minori Capuccini del serafico Padre San Francesco al regno del Congo e delle qualità, costumi, e maniere di vivere di quel regno, e suoi habitatori. Milan, Francesco Mognaga, 1649. G117
In addition to accounts of missionary progress, this report includes reference to Dutch activity in the Congo and also a description of the Congo region.

Giovio, Paolo. Commentario de la cose de Turchi. Venice, Giovanni Andrea Vovassore detto Guadagnino & Florio fratello. [ca. 1540]. G118
A collection of biographies of Turkish sultans going back nearly two centuries.

Giovio, Paolo. Von der türckischen Keyseren Härkommen, Aufgang, unnd Regiment mit sampt allen Historien unnd namhafftigen Geschichten. Basel, 1564. G119
In addition to the history of Turkey, particularly in the fifteenth century, this edition includes an account of the sack of Rome by Charles V in 1527, and the description of Russia based on the embassy of Demetrius to Pope Clement VII.

Giovio, Paolo. Libellus de legatione Basilii magni Principis Moscoviae ad Clementem VII. Rome, Franciscus Minitius Calvus, 1525. G120
A description of Russia based on information obtained from a member of a Russian embassy to Pope Clement VII.

Giovio, Paolo. Libellus de legatione Basilii magni Principis Moschoviae. Basel, J. Froben, 1527. G121
The second edition.

Giovio, Paolo. Moschovia, in qua situs regionis antiquis incognitus ... Basel [Henricum Petri et Petrum Pernam] 1561. G122
This is part 2 of the Author's *Descriptiones*, ed. by J.B. Herold.

Giovio, Paolo. Operetta dell' ambascieria de Moschoviti. Venice, 1545. G123
The first Italian edition.

Giradin, Alexandre Louis Robert, Comte de. [Autographed letter signed.] St. Domingue, 13 September 1792. G124
A letter of advice to an unnamed general with respect to landing troops in Saint Domingue.

Giraldi, Lilio Gregorio. De re nautica libellus, admiranda quadam & recondita eruditione refertus, nunc primum & natus & aeditus. Basel, Mich. Isingrinium, 1540. G125
A history of ancient seafaring including the voyage of the Argonauts, the Odyssey, the Indian campaign of Alexander the Great, and the voyage of Hanno.

Girão João Rodrigues. Relacion de la vitoria que los Portugueses alcançaron en la ciudad de Macao, en la China, contra los Olandeses, en 24 de Iunio de 1622. traduzida ... de aquellas partes, a los padres de su Colegio de Madrid. [Madrid, Antonio Noguera Barrocas, 1623.] G126
An account of an important military-naval engagement at Macao between Dutch and Portuguese forces, in which the Portuguese were victorious, thereby forcing the Dutch to alter their plans for seeking a position for trade in China.

Girava, Geronimo. Dos libros de cosmographia. Milan, Juan Antonio Castellon & Christoval Caron, 1556. G127
An early geography with particular value for the Spanish-occupied areas of the New World, but with good

descriptions also of Asia and Africa. Contains a map made from one of Caspar Vopell's projections.

[Girod-Chantrans, Justin.] Voyage d'un Suisse dans différentes colonies d'Amérique. Neuchatel, Société Typographique, 1785.   G128
Descriptions, chiefly of Haiti, in which the author gives keen observations on the problems of the European colonists and their slaves.

Giustiniani, Agostino. Castigatissimi annali con la loro copiosa tavola della eccelsa & illustrissima republi. de Genoa. Genoa [Antonio Bellono] 1537.   G129
A history of Genoa through the period of its major importance as a Mediterranean maritime power and commercial center.

Glanius, Mr. Relation du naufrage d'un vaisseau hollandois, nommé Ter Schelling, vers la côte de Bengala. Amsterdam, J. van Meurs, 1681.   G130
Describes an ill-fated Dutch voyage from Batavia in 1651, with much descriptive material on Bengal.

Glanius, Mr. A relation of an unfortunate voyage to the kingdom of Bengala. London, H. Bonwick, 1682.   G131
The first English edition.

Glanius, Mr. A new voyage to the East-Indies. London, H. Rodes, 1682.   G132
The second English edition.

Glantzby. Les voyages de Glantzby dans les mers orientales de la Tartarie. Paris, Theodore Le Gras, 1729.   G133
An account of travels in Tartary, China, and Japan.

Glareanus, Henricus. De geographia. Basel, Joannes Faber, 1527.   G134
The first half of this work is a geometric treatise on the earth as a sphere; the last contains brief descriptions of various parts of the earth.

Glareanus, Henricus. Geographia. Freiburg, J. Faber, 1536.   G135
Another edition of this popular sixteenth-century geography, containing descriptions of the continents, including the New World.

Glareanus, Henricus. Brevissima totius habitabilis terrae descriptio. Paris, Christian Wechel, 1542.   G136
This edition omits the chapters on the earth as a sphere.

[Glen, James.] A description of South Carolina. London, For R. and J. Dodsley, 1761.   G137
An excellent discourse on the colony and its trade, written by the governor of South Carolina.

Glogowezyk, Jan. Introductorium compendosium in Tractatum spere materialis magistri Joannis de Sacrobusto ... Cracow, J. Haller, 1506.   G138
This commentary on the *Sphere* of Sacro Bosco by one of the teachers of Copernicus contains references to the new discoveries in the Orient and in the New World.

Glover, Richard. The evidence delivered on the petition presented by the West-India planters and merchants. [London, 1775.]   G139
This edition differs from the one of the same year (below), by including testimony giving much detailed information on the commercial situation in the West Indies.

Glover, Richard. The substance of the evidence delivered ... by the merchants and traders of London. London, For J. Wilkie, 1774.   G140
Relates particularly to the linen trade of England and Scotland.

Glover, Richard. The substance of the evidence on the petition presented by the West-India planters and merchants. London, H.S. Woodfall for T. Cadell [1775].   G141
A plea to Parliament to alter its policies with respect to North American commerce, as the American colonies had announced their intention to discontinue purchase of major West Indian products.

Gmelin, Johann Georg. Reise durch Sibirien, von dem Jahr 1733. bis 1743. Göttingen, Abram Vandenhoecks seel. Wittwe, 1751-52.   G142
An account of nearly ten years of exploration in Siberia by a German botanist and chemist in the service of the Academy of Sciences in St. Petersburg.

Gmelin, Johann Georg. Reize door Siberiën naar Kamtschatka; van't jaar 1733 tot 1743. Haarlem, Izaak en Johannes Enschede, 1752-57   G143
A Dutch edition of Gmelin's travels in Siberia, in four volumes.

Gmelin, Johann Georg. Voyage en Siberie. Paris, Desaint, 1767.   G144
The first French edition, rewritten and much abridged.

Gmelin, Samuel Gottlieb. Puteshestvie po Rossii dlia izsliedovaniia trekh tsarstv. St. Petersburg, Imperatorsko Akademii nauk, 1771-1785.   G145
A translation from the German edition with numerous natural history illustrations and maps of local areas.

Godeheu. Journal maritime de Mr. le Commandeur Godeheu aux Indies Orientales, 1754 et 1755. Manuscript. [n.p.] 1754-1755.   G146
The author was sent to India to arrest and replace Dupleix. His journal records stops at Senegal, Goree, Ile de France, Bourbon, Karikal, Pondichéry and Gingy.

Godinho, Manuel. Relação do novo caminho que fez por terra, e mar, vindo da India para Portugal no anno 1663. Lisbon, Henrique Valiente de Oliveira, 1665. G147
An account of a Jesuit priest's travels from India to Portugal, noting commodities along the way as he passed through Persia, Syria, Arabia, and Egypt.

Godinho, Nicolao. De Abassinorum rebus, déque Aethiopiae patriarchis Joanne Nonio Barreto, & Andrea Oviedo. Leiden, Horatio Cardon, 1615. G148
A history of Portuguese and Jesuit penetration of Ethiopia in the period after 1557, including also a description of the country and peoples of eastern Africa.

Godinho Cardozo, Manoel. Relaçaõ do naufragio da nao Santiago no anno de 1585 : e itinerario da gente que delle se salvou : escrita por Manoel Godinho Cardozo, e agora novamente acrescentada com mais algumas noticias. Lisbon, Na Officina da Congregaçaõ do Oratorio, 1736. G149

Godinho Cardozo, Manoel. Relaçam do navfragio da nao Santiago, & itenerario da gente que delle se salvou : escrita por Manoel Godinho Cardozo. Lisbon, Impresso por Pedro Crasbeeck, 1602 [reprinted 1737?]. G150

[Goens, Rijklof Michaël van.] Politiek vertoog over het waar sistema van de stad van Amsterdam ... [n.p.] 1781. G151
A commercial history of Amsterdam, with particular emphasis on events of the 1770s relating to Dutch interest in the American Revolution.

[Goens, Rijklof van.] Javaense reyse, gadaen van Batavia over Samarangh ... Dordrecht, Vincent Caimax, 1666. G152
An account of a trip through Java, noting the roads, customs, economy, etc., of a little known part of the island.

Góis, Damião de. Aliquot opuscula. Louvain, Rutgeri Rescius, 1544. G153
A collected edition of the earlier writings of this important Portuguese humanist and historian, including accounts of early Portuguese relations with Ethiopia.

Góis, Damião de. Avisi de le cose fatte da Portuesi ne l'India. Venice, 1539. G154
This Italian translation omits some material on the general history of Portuguese expansion included in the Latin edition.

Góis, Damião de. Chronica do felicissimo Rei Dom Emanuel. Lisbon, F. Correa, 1566-67. G155
A history of the reign of Manuel the Fortunate, 1495-1521, which contains considerable information on the early Portuguese enterprises in India.

Góis, Damião de. Chronica do principe Dom Joam. Lisbon, F. Correa, 1567. G156
Actually a history of the events leading up to the reign of John II, in which an account of the voyages along the African coast in the fifteenth century is given.

Góis, Damião de. Commentarii rerum gestarum in India citra Gangem a Lusitanis anno 1538. Louvain, Rutgeri Rescius, 1539. G157
A letter to Pietro Bembo, in which the author relates the siege of Diu and a history of the Portuguese conquests in India.

Góis, Damião de. Glaubhafftige Zeyttung und Bericht des Kriegs so zwischen dem Künig auss Portugall und dem türckischen Kaiser in India ... [Augsburg, Philipp Ulhart] 1540. G158
A translation from the Latin edition of the previous year, this is an account of the siege of Diu, 1539, adding a general history of the growth of Portuguese power in India.

Góis, Damião de. De bello Cambaico ultimo commentarii tres. Louvain, Servatius Sassen, 1549. G159
Commentaries on the siege of Diu.

Góis, Damião de. Fides, religio, moresque Aethiopum sub imperio Preciosi Joannis (quem vulgò Presbyterum Joannem vocant) degentium. Paris, Christianum Wechelum, 1541. G160
The second edition of a basic collection of information on Ethiopia, including letters from Ethiopian rulers to the Kings of Portugal and the Pope, from 1509 to 1524.

Góis, Damião de. Hispania Damiani a Goes, equitis Lusitani. Louvain, Rutergus Rescius, 1542. G161
A description of Spain designed to correct errors made by other writers, noting among other things the products imported into Spain from her overseas dominions.

Góis, Damião de. Urbis Olisiponis descriptio. [Evora, A. Burgensem] 1554. G162
A history of Lisbon and its commerce from Phoenician times, including material on other commercial settlements in the Mediterranean region.

Goldson, William. Observations on the passage between the Atlantic and Pacific oceans, in two memoirs on the Straits of Anian, and the discoveries of De Fonte. Portsmouth, W. Mowbray, 1793. G163
The author urges that premiums be offered for further discoveries in northern North America.

Gonzaga, Francesco. Englischen liebbrinnendten S. Francisci Ordens Relations Continuation. Ingolstadt, Elisabeth Angermayrin, 1617. G164
An abridgement of *De originie seraphicae religionis Franciscanae*, Rome, 1587.

González Dávila, Gil. Teatro eclesiastico de la primitiva iglesia de las Indias Occidentales : vidas de sus arzobispos, obispos, y cosas memorables de sus sedes ... Madrid, Diego Diaz de la Carrera, 1649-1655. G165
A history of the Roman Catholic Church in Spanish America, being primarily a set of biographies of church officials.

González de Agüeros, Pedro. Descripcion historial de la provincia y archipielago de Chilóe en el reyno de Chile ... Madrid, Benito Cano, 1791. G166
This author gathered his data on Chiloé during his stay there as a missionary priest and while serving the Franciscan missionary college of Santa Rosa at Ocapa.

González de Clavijo, Ruy. Historia del gran Tamorlan e itinerario y enarracion del viage, y relacion de la embaxada que Ruy Gonçalez de Clavijo ... Seville, A. Pescioni, 1582. G167
The first edition of a travel narrative describing a mission to the court of Tamerlane at Samarkand undertaken by the Castilian ambassador in 1403.

González de Mendoza, Juan. Historia de las cosas mas notables ... del gran reyno de la China. Rome, B. Grassi, 1585. G168
The first edition of one of the most popular books on China in the sixteenth century, and it also includes material on Spanish America, Africa, and the East Indies.

González de Mendoza, Juan. Historia de las cosas mas notables, ritos y costumbres del gran reyno de la China. Madrid, Querino Gerardo Flamenco, 1586. G169
The first of three Spanish editions of the expanded text, which add the Espejo account of New Mexico.

González de Mendoza, Juan. Historia de las cosas mas notables, ritos y costumbres del grã reyno de la China. Medina del Campo, Heredeios de Benito Boyer, 1595. G170
This edition is similar to the Gerardo Flamenco edition of Madrid, 1586, but with some rearrangement of preliminary matter.

González de Mendoza, Juan. Historia de las cosas mas notables, ritos y costumbres del gran reyno de la China. Antwerp, Pedro Bellero, 1596. G171
This edition includes the *Itinerario* of Martin Ignacio.

González de Mendoza, Juan. Dell' historia della China. Rome, Bartolomeo Grassi, 1586. G172
One of six issues of the Rome edition of 1586.

González de Mendoza, Juan. Dell' historia della China. Rome, Giovanni Martinelli, 1586. G173
Another of the 1586 Rome editions sold by different booksellers, all of which contained the shorter form of the text.

González de Mendoza, Juan. Dell' historia della China. Rome, V. Pelagallo, 1586. G174
One of three Italian editions issued in 1586.

González de Mendoza, Juan. Dell' historia della China. Venice, Andrea Muschio, 1586. G175
The first Venice edition, containing the shorter form of the text.

González de Mendoza, Juan. Dell' historia della China. Genoa, Gieronimo Bartoli, 1586. G176
This, the only Genoa edition, is the shorter version of the author's text.

González de Mendoza, Juan. Dell' historia della China. Venice, Andrea Muschio, 1588. G177
Contains slight variations from the Venice edition of 1586.

González de Mendoza, Juan. Dell' historia della China. Venice, Andrea Muschio, 1590. G178
The fifth Italian edition.

González de Mendoza, Juan. Histoire du grand royaume de la Chine. Paris, Jeremie Perier, 1588. G179
The first French edition.

González de Mendoza, Juan. Histoire du grand royaume de la Chine. Paris, N. du Fosse, 1589. G180
One of two French editions of this year, following the first French edition of 1588.

[González de Mendoza, Juan.] Histoire du grand royaume de la Chine. [Geneva] Jean Arnaud, 1606. G181
The sixth French edition, adding a twenty-six page section from an unnamed Latin source descriptive of China.

González de Mendoza, Juan. Histoire du grand royaume de la Chine. Rouen, N. Angot, 1614. G182
A reprint of the 1588 edition.

González de Mendoza, Juan. The historie of the great and mightie kingdome of China ... London, J. Wolfe for Edward White, 1588. G183
The first English edition, translated from the Spanish by Robert Parke.

González de Mendoza, Juan. Nova et succincta vera tamen historia de ... regno China. Frankfurt [1589]. G184
The first Latin edition.

González de Mendoza, Juan. Rerum morumque in regno Chinensi. Antwerp, Vidua & haeredes, F. Fickaert, 1655. G185
This edition omits the *Itinerario*, with its description of the Philippine Islands.

González de Salcedo, Pedro. Tratado juridico politico del contra-bando. Madrid, Juan Muñoz, 1729. G186
Considers the problems of prohibited trade and smuggling within the Spanish empire.

González de Urueña, Juan. Delineacion de lo tocante al conocimiento del punto de longitud del globo de tierra, y agua, y de la causa de las crecientes, y menguantes del mar. Madrid, Diego Miguel de Peralta, 1740. G187
A navigation book with particular reference to the problem of ascertaining longitude, applicable primarily to the Gulf of Mexico and the Caribbean.

Goos, Pieter. Der nieuwe groote zee-spiegel, inhoudende de beschryvinge der zee-kusten van de noordsche en oostersche ship-vaert. Amsterdam, Pieter Goos, 1668. G188
A pilot guide for Europe, Greenland, the Canary Islands, northern Africa, and northeast to Novaya Zemlya, including sixty folding and double-page maps.

[Gordon, Thomas.] An appeal to the unprejudiced. London, For T. Cooper, 1739. G189
Describes public discontent in England after the signing of the treaty of El Pardo.

[Gordon, Thomas.] Considerations offered upon the approaching peace, and upon the importance of Gibraltar to the British Empire. London, For J. Roberts, 1720. G190
An argument against giving up Gibraltar in any forthcoming peace negotiations, noting its strategic and commercial value in dominating both Atlantic and Mediterranean shipping.

[Gordon, Thomas.] General remarks on the British fisheries. London, For J. Murray [etc.] 1784. G191
The author is concerned primarily with the economy of the Shetland Islands and the effects of proposed improvements in the techniques of curing fish there.

Gordon, William, Rector of St. James's, Barbadoes. A representation of the miserable state of Barbadoes, under the arbitrary and corrupt administration of His Excellency, Robert Lowther, esq; the present governor ... London, Bernard Lintot [1719]. G192
The governor of Barbados is accused of corruptly gaining control of the legislature, the courts and the militia, with a resulting restraint on citizens from their normal rights and activities.

Gottfried, Johann Ludwig. Newe Welt und americanische Historien. Frankfurt, Matthew Merian, 1631. G193
An abridgment of the *Great Voyages* of De Bry, compiled by one who worked for the famous Frankfurt publishers of voyages. Many plates from De Bry are used in it. At one time attributed to Johann Philipp Abelin.

Gottfried, Johann Ludwig. Newe Welt und americanische Historien. Frankfurt, Merian, 1655. G194
The second edition.

[Goudar, Ange.] Débats en Parlement d'Angleterre, au sujet des affaires générales de l'Europe. Londres [i.e. Paris] 1758. G195
Purports to be translations of an alleged series of debates in the British Parliament relative to the damage being done to commerce by the war in Europe.

[Goudar, Ange.] Les intérêts de la France mal entendus. Amsterdam, Jacques Coeur, 1756. G196
Strong criticism of French policy with respect to commerce, agriculture, and manufactures.

[Goudar, Ange.] Naples ce qu'il faut faire pour rendre ce royaume florissant. Amsterdam [i.e. Venice] 1771. G197
A wide range of proposals to make Naples a more productive and prosperous kingdom, most of which, being reformist in tone, were applicable to other states as well.

Goudard, Pierre-Louis. Rapport ... sur la situation du commerce extérieur de la France pendant la révolution, en 1789. Paris, Imprimerie Nationale, 1791. G198
A refutation of arguments that French foreign trade declined during 1788 and 1789.

Gouveia, António de. Jornado do arcebispo de Goa Dom Frey Aleixo de Menezes. Coimbra, Diogo Gomez Loureyro, 1606. G199
The account of visits in 1599 to the communities of the St. Thomas Christians in Malabar by Aleixo de Menezes, archbishop of Goa.

Gouvernement de la Compagnie des Indes Orientales tant en ces provinces que dans les Indes ... [Amsterdam? 1608.] G200
Describes the formation and administration of the Dutch East India Company.

Gouy, Louis-Marthe de. Premiere dénonciation solemnelle d'un ministre fait a l'Assemblée nationale, en la personne de comte de la Luzerne, Ministre d'État, de la Marine et des Colonies. Paris, Demonville, 1790. G201
The author was a deputy from Saint Domingue and represented the plantation owners there.

Gowinius, Swen. Enfaldiga tankar om nyttan som England kan hafva af sina nybyggen in Norra America. Åbo, Johan C. Frenckell, 1763. G202
An appraisal of the British colonies in North America with particular emphasis on the commodities of each.

[Goyon de La Plombanie, Henri de.] Vues politiques sur le commerce. Amsterdam, Paris, 1759. G203

A proposal for improving the agricultural economy of France through the creation of an agriculture company which would manage storage and marketing facilities for agricultural products.

Graaf, Abraham de. De seven boecken van de groote zeevaert, zijnde een volkomen klare, en konstige beschrijvinghe der navigatie. Amsterdam, Pieter Goos, 1658. G204
A compendium on many aspects of navigation, including astronomy, and ship building, lading, etc.

Graaf, Nikolaas de. Reysen ... na de vier gedeeltens des werelds, als Asia, Africa, America en Europa. Hoorn, Feyken Rijp, 1704. G205
A collection of accounts of the author's travels which lasted from 1639 to 1687.

Grammaticus, Nicasius. Problema geographicum de longitudine locorum terrae per acum nauticum indaganda ... Ingolstadt, Thomae Gras, 1723. G206
A treatise on the use of the magnetic needle to determine longitude.

Granados y Gálvez, José Joaquín. Tardes Americanas : gobierno gentil y catolico : breve y particular noticia de toda la historia Indiana ... Mexico, D. Philipe de Zuñiga y Ontiveros, 1778. G207
The first part of this book is a discussion of the history, culture, institutions and government of the Mexicans in the pre-conquest period. The second part describes the coming of Christianity to Mexico.

The grand concern of England explained. London, 1673. G208
Proposals offered to the British parliament to pay the public debt, encourage trade, and raise land rents.

Grandpré, L. de (Louis). Voyage a la côte occidentale d'Afrique, fait dans les années 1786 et 1787 ... Suivi d'un voyage fait au cap de Bonne-Espérance, contenant la description militaire de cette colonie ... Paris, Dentu, 1801. G209
An account of West African natural history, peoples, and commerce, with introductory matter on errors in recent publications describing Africa. Maps and illustrations are included.

Granger, sieur. Relation du voyage fait en Egypte par le sieur Granger en l'année 1730 ... Paris, Jacques Vincent, 1745. G210
The author's major concerns were the antiquities of Egypt and the Nile River, its rise and fall and lands along its course.

Grant, Sir Archibald. A true and exact particular and inventory of all and singular the lands, tenements and hereditaments, goods, chattels, debts and personal estate whatsoever, which I Sir Archibald Grant ... was seized or possessed of ... upon the first day of January ... one thousand seven hundred and thirty ... London, S. Buckley, 1732. G211
Related to a case involving the South Sea Company.

[Graswinckel, Theod. I.F.] Aen-spraeck aen den getrouwen Hollander, nopende de proceduren der Portugesen in Brasill. The Hague, I. Burghoorn, 1645. G212
"Advice to the faithful of Holland on the proceedings of the Portuguese in Brazil."

Graswinckel, Theod. I.F. Maris liberi vindiciae: adversus Gulielmum Welwodum Britannici maritimi domini assertorem. The Hague, Adrian Vlac, 1653. G213
A response to William Welwood's *De dominio maris*, a part of the continuing debate over maritime law.

Grau y Monfalcón, Juan. Justificacion de la conservacion, y comercio de las Islas Filipinas. [Madrid, 1640.] G214
A statement regarding the importance of the Philippine trade to Spain, and a description of its declining position due to restrictions upon commerce from the islands to the rest of the Spanish empire.

Graves, John. A memorial: or, A short account of the Bahama-Islands ... deliver'd to the lords, proprietors of the said islands, and the honourable commissioners of Her Majesty's customs. [n.p., ca. 1707.] G215
The author was collector of customs in the Bahamas, and he urges the development of New Providence as a commercial emporium for trade with Spanish America. He also calls attention to London's negligence in the governing of these islands.

[Gray, Jeffery.] A proposal fully to prevent the smugling of wool. London, For the author, 1732. G216
Suggests transportation as the penalty for wool smugling which results in great financial loss and hardship for England.

[Gray, John.] The right of the British legislature to tax the American colonies vindicated; and the means of asserting that right proposed. London, For T. Becket, 1774. G217
A highly legalistic argument defending Parliament's right to tax the American colonies, rejecting arguments based on Locke, on natural rights, and on the alleged inability of the colonists to pay.

Great Britain. Official papers relative to the dispute between ... Great Britain and Spain on the subject of the ships captured in Nootka Sound. London, J. Debrett, 1790. G218
Transcripts of parliamentary debates and other state papers regarding the Nootka controversy.

Great Britain. [Passport issued to Captain Thomas Clarke, commander of the Elizabeth, of London, for a commercial voyage to the Canary Islands and other ports of Spain.] Manuscript. London, 9 October 1719. G219

The passport requires that its bearer not be engaged in carrying arms or other contraband.

Great Britain. Admiralty. [Orders to all officials issuing letters of marque against Spain and France to observe terms of the treaty of 1674 with the Netherlands regarding the rights of Dutch ships.] Manuscript. London, 1744. G220

An order of restraint upon officials issuing letters of marque, enjoining them to caution all holders of such letters to observe strictly the 1674 treaty with the Netherlands exempting their ships from seizure.

Great Britain. Admiralty. Sailing and fighting instructions for His Majesty's fleet. [n.p., ca. 1720] G221

Detailed instructions for maneuvering ships in a fleet, of giving and receiving signals, of concerted action, both in situations of conflict and otherwise.

Great Britain. Admiralty. Since there have been made severall voyages to the north of Russia, to finde a passage through the frozen sea & so to make a shorter way to China ... Manuscript. [17—?] G222

Proposal addressed to the "Commissioners of the Admiralty & other Gentlemen of Quality."

Great Britain. Army. Rules and articles for the better government of the officers and soldiers in the service of the United Company of Merchants of England. London, Thomas Baskett and the assigns of Robert Baskett, 1754. G223

A law applying the "Articles of War" to officers and men in the service of the East India Company.

Great Britain. Army. Council. A declaration of His Excellency the Lord Fairfax, Lord General, and his Councel of war, concerning their resolution to preserve and protect the freedom of trade and commerce. London, John Partridge, 1648. G224

Public assurance that the trade and commerce of the kingdom will be protected.

Great Britain. Board of Trade. Copy of a representation of the Board of Trade to the House of Lords ... relating to the laws made, manufactures set up, and trade carried on, in His Majesty's plantations in America. London, 1749. G225

Reprint of a report originally published in 1734, containing a review of economic development in the American colonies, in response to complaints by London merchants.

Great Britain. Board of Trade. A list of copies of charters, from the Commissioners for Trade and Plantations, presented to the honourable the House of Commons ... London, 1741. G226

Includes the charters of Maryland, Connecticut, Rhode Island, Pennsylvania, Massachusetts, and Georgia.

Great Britain. Board of Trade. Minutes of the evidence taken before the committee of council appointed for the consideration of ... the stock of grain in this country ... and also, Minutes of the evidence taken before the lords of His Majesty's most honourable Privy Council ... [n.p.] 1795. G227

Great Britain. Board of Trade. Papers laid before the honourable House of Commons ... for the better securing, improving, and extending the trade to Africa. London, 1750. G228

A collection of papers concerning the slave trade presented by the Royal African Company, independent merchants, and the sugar planters of the British West Indian colonies.

Great Britain. Board of Trade. Report ... concerning the present state of the trade to Africa, and particularly the trade in slaves. London, 1789. G229

An extensive report giving a good picture of British commerce in the South Atlantic.

Great Britain. Board of Trade. Representation from the Commissioners for Trade and Plantations. London, J. Baskett, 1734. G230

A detailed account of the commerce of Jamaica, Barbados, the Leeward Islands, the Bahamas, and Bermuda.

Great Britain. Board of Trade. Return from the Commissioners for Trade and Plantations, to the honourable House of Commons, in consequence of the address of the said House to His Majesty, of the 29th day of January 1777; relating to the general state of the trade to Africa. [London] 1777. G231

The report accuses the governors and other officials at British stations on the Gold Coast of conniving to secure a monopoly on much of the trade there, frequently using funds appropriated for the building and maintenance of the forts.

Great Britain. Colonial Office. Hudson's Bay Company. Papers presented by command of Her Majesty to the House of Commons ... to ascertain the legality of the powers in respect to the territory, trade, taxation and government, ... claimed or exercised by the Hudson's Bay Company ... [London] 1850. G232

Great Britain. Colonial Office. Hudson's Bay Company. (Red River Settlement.) Return to an address by the honourable the House of

238   Great Britain. Colonial

Commons, dated 9 February 1849. [London] 1849.   G233

A petition against the Hudson's Bay Company because "discontent and misery prevail amongst the natives of Rupert's Land to an unparalleled extent ..." Supporting documents are included.

Great Britain. Colonial Office. Hudson's Bay Company. Return (in part) to an address of the House of Lords, dated 2d July, 1863. London, 1863.   G234

Correspondence relative to a proposed road and telegraph across Canada to British Columbia, and a transfer of the rights of the Hudson's Bay Company.

Great Britain. Colonial Office. Hudson's Bay Company. Return to an address of the honourable the House of Commons, dated 19 February 1857. [London] 1857.   G235

Notes the intention of the government to bring the affairs of Hudson's Bay Company under investigation by a committee of the House of Commons.

Great Britain. Colonial Office. Hudson's Bay Company. Return to an address of the honourable the House of Commons, dated 29 May 1857. [London, 1857.]   G236

An argument for defining the limits of jurisdiction of the Hudson's Bay Company.

Great Britain. Colonial Office. Hudson's Bay Company. Return to an address of the honourable the House of Commons, dated 26 May 1842. [London] 1842.   G237

Concerns renewal of the company's charter, reprinting the first charter, and noting the subsequent renewals.

Great Britain. Colonial Office. II. Hudson's Bay Company. Continuation of letters and despatches. London, 1868.   G238

Copies of five letters from British officials regarding the surrender of the company's rights to the Crown.

Great Britain. Colonial Office. Letter from the Colonial Office to the Governor of the Hudson's Bay Company. London, J. Causton and sons, 1869.   G239

A proposal of compromise between the Canadian government and the Hudson's Bay Company.

Great Britain. Colonial Office. Papers relating to the Red River Settlement. [London] 1819.   G240

A collection of forty-one documents from the period 1815-1819.

Great Britain. Colonial Office. Papers relative to the Hudson's Bay Company's charter ... London, G.E. Eyre & N. Spottiswoode, 1859.   G241

A series of twenty-nine letters and dispatches relative to the rights of the Hudson's Bay Company and the legality of its charter.

Great Britain. Colonial Office. Pending questions about Hudson's Bay territory. [London] 1868.   G242

A discussion of the problems involved in transferring the government of the Hudson's Bay territory to Canada.

Great Britain. Colonial Office. Précis on the Hudson's Bay Company. London, 1868.   G243

A review of the recent history of the company and the geography of its holdings in view of a proposal that they be taken over by the Crown.

Great Britain. Colonial Office. Vancouver's Island. Return to an address of the honourable the House of Commons, dated 7 August 1848. [London] 1848.   G244

Concerns the settlement of British territory west of the Rocky Mountains.

Great Britain. Colonial Office. Vancouver's Island. Returns to three addresses of the honourable the House of Commons, dated respectively 16 August, 1848, 6 February & 1 March 1849. [London] 1849.   G245

Concerns the grant of Vancouver Island to the Hudson's Bay Company.

Great Britain. Commissioners for adjusting the boundaries for the British and French possessions in America. All the memorials of the courts of Great Britain and France, since the peace of Aix la Chapelle, relative to the limits of the territories of both crowns in North America. The Hague, 1756.   G246

Great Britain. Commissioners for adjusting the boundaries for the British and French possessions in America. Memoires des Commissaires de Sa Majesté trés-chretienne et de ceux de Sa Majesté brittanique, sur les possessions ... en Amerique. Amsterdam & Leipzig, J. Schreuder & Pierre Mortier le Jeune, 1755.   G247

Based upon the Paris edition of 1755, this edition omits Latin and English text and rearranges some of the material.

Great Britain. Commissioners for adjusting the boundaries for the British and French possessions in America. Mémoires des Commissaires du Roi et de ceux de Sa Majesté britannique, sur les possessions & les droits respectifs des deux couronnes en Amérique; avec les actes publics & pièces justificatives. Paris, Imprimerie Royale, 1756.   G248

An extensive documentation of the English and French exploration and settlement of North America.

Great Britain. Commissioners for adjusting the boundaries for the British and French possessions in America. The memorials of the English and French Commissaries concerning the limits of Nova Scotia or Acadia. London, 1755. G249

This English version of the presentations made by the boundary commissioners includes material not in the Paris edition, omits some of the French observations from that edition, and presents much of the material in both languages. The second volume concerns St. Lucia.

Great Britain. Council for Virginia. A declaration of the state of the colony and affaires in Virginia. London, Thomas Snodham, 1620. G250

An official publication of the Council, which predicts a bright future for the colony and defends it against "false and malicious rumors."

Great Britain. Inspector General of Exports and Imports. An account of the foreign produce and manufactures, exported from Great Britain to France, between the 5th of January 1714 and the 5th of January 1787. [London] 1787. G251

Great Britain. Inspector General of Exports and Imports. An account of the number of ships and vessels, with their tonnage, cleared outwards from the different ports of Great Britain, for the coast of Africa, distinguishing each port, for the years 1772, 1773, 1774, 1775, 1776, 1777, 1778, 1779, 1780, 1781, 1782, 1783, 1784, 1785, 1786, and 1787. [London, 1789.] G252

Great Britain. Inspector General of Exports and Imports. An account of the quantity and value of the imports into Great Britain from France between the 5th of January 1714 and the 5th of January 1787. [London, 1787.] G253

Great Britain. Inspector General of Exports and Imports. An account of the value and amount of foreign goods entered for exportation to the coast of Africa, from the several ports of Great Britain, for the years 1772, 1773, 1774, 1775, 1776, and for the years 1783, 1784, 1785, 1786, and 1787; distinguishing each port, and also distinguishing what proportion of goods so exported were purchased from the East India Company. [London] 1789. G254

Great Britain. Inspector General of Exports and Imports. An account of the value and amount of foreign goods entered for exportation to the coast of Africa, from the several ports of Great Britain, for the years 1777, 1778, 1779, 1780, 1781, and 1782; distinguishing each port, and also distinguishing what proportion of goods so exported were purchased from the East India Company. [London, 1788.] G255

Great Britain. Inspector General of Exports and Imports. An account of the value and amount of goods entered for exportation to the coast of Africa from the several ports of Great Britain, for the years 1777, 1778, 1779, 1780, 1781, and 1782; distinguishing each port, and what proportion of goods so exported were British, foreign, or purchased from the East India Company. [London, 1789.] G256

Great Britain. Inspector General of Exports and Imports. An account of the value and amount of goods entered for exportation to the coast of Africa from the several ports of Great Britain, for the years 1772, 1773, 1774, 1775, and 1776, distinguishing what proportion of goods so exported were British, foreign, or purchased from the East India Company. [London, 1789.] G257

Great Britain. Inspector General of Exports and Imports. An account of the value and amount of goods, being British produce or manufacture entered for exportation for the coast of Africa, from the several ports of Great Britain, for the years 1772, 1773, 1774, 1775, and 1776, and for the years 1783, 1784, 1785, 1786, and 1787; distinguishing each port. [London, 1788.] G258

Great Britain. Inspector General of Exports and Imports. An account of the value and amount of goods being British produce or manufacture, entered for exportation to the coast of Africa, from the several ports of Great Britain, for the years 1777, 1778, 1779, 1780, 1781, and 1782; distinguishing each port. [London, 1788.] G259

Great Britain. Inspector General of Exports and Imports. An account of the value and amount of the production of Africa, imported into Great Britain, from the year 1771 to 1788; distinguishing the productions, and amount for each year, and the ports of importation; pursuant to an order of the honourable House of Commons, dated the 18th of March 1788. Ordered to be printed 24th March 1789. [London, 1789.] G260

Great Britain. Inspector General of Exports and Imports. An account of the value of all goods, wares, and merchandize, exported from, and imported into, Great Britain; distinguishing each place: from Christmas 1782 to Christmas 1785. [London, 1787.] G261

Great Britain. Inspector General of Exports and Imports. Navigation, revenues, and commerce of Great Britain for 1797: annual accounts 1798. Manuscript in English. [London, 1798.] G262

A massive tabulation of Great Britain's export and import trade for 1797.

Great Britain. Laws, etc. An ordinance ... declaring, that it shall and may be lawfull for all foreigners and strangers, in amity with this kingdome, to have free trade. London, For John Wright, 1644. G263

This ordinance provides for the interruption of trade to ports disloyal to the government and for seizure by foreign merchants of goods belonging to them in disloyal ports.

Great Britain. Laws, etc. The schedule. In this schedule is contained the excise, set and to be set upon severall commodities. Oxford, Leonard Litchfield, 1644. G264

A detailed schedule of duties to be paid on many commodities, both foreign and domestic, with instructions for the administration of excise taxes.

Great Britain. Laws, etc. An ordinance ... for freeing and discharging the vintners ... concerning the imposition ... on wines. [London] T.W. For Ed. Husband, 1645. G265

Relates to the attempt of the Company of Vinters to avoid the duties on wine by a payment of four thousand pounds to Parliament.

Great Britain. Laws, etc. An ordinance ... for the leavying of moneys, by way of excise, or, new-impost, as well for the better securing of trade, as for the maintenance of the army raised by the Parliament, and payment of the debts on the common-wealth. London, Richard Cotes and Ruth Raworth, 1643 [i.e. ca. 1646.] G266

Tax laws concerning imports and exports.

Great Britain. Laws, etc. An act for setled convoys, for securing the trade of this nation. London, E. Husband & J. Field, 1650. G267

An act for tightening customs regulations, and using customs receipts for maintaining convoys for merchant shipping.

Great Britain. Laws, etc. An act for the advancing and regulating of the trade. London, E. Husband & J. Field, 1650. G268

This act created a commission of trade to study the commercial policies and possibilities of the Commonwealth.

Great Britain. Laws, etc. An act prohibiting trade with the Barbada's, Virginia, Bermuda's and Antego. London, E. Husband and J. Field, 1650. G269

Trade with the American colonies was forbidden because of their friendliness to the Royalists in England.

Great Britain. Laws, etc. An act for increase of shipping, and encouragement of the navigation of this nation. London, John Field, 1651. G270

The Navigation Act of 1651 required that imports into England must be made in English ships, or ships of the country which produced the goods in the cargo.

Great Britain. Laws, etc. Een placcaet tot aenwas der schepen, ende moet-ghevinge aen de zeevaert van dese natie. The Hague, D. Pommerede, 1651. G271

A Dutch edition of England's Navigation Act of 1651.

Great Britain. Laws, etc. An act for the exportation of several commodities of the breed, growth, and manufacture of this commonwealth. London, Henry Hills and John Field, 1656. G272

An extensive list of goods which can be exported, with rates of duties for native Englishmen and for foreigners.

Great Britain. Laws, etc. An act for continuing ... the subsidie of tunnage and poundage. London, H. Hills and J. Field, 1657. G273

Also deals with duties on sugar, wine, fruit, and cloth.

Great Britain. Laws, etc. An act for the exportation of several commodities of the breed, growth, and manufacture of this commonwealth. London, Henry Hills and John Field, 1657. G274

Grants an increased measure of free trade between England and her colonies, particularly in agricultural goods.

Great Britain. Laws, etc. An act giving licence for transporting fish in forreign bottoms. London, Henry Hills and John Field, 1657. G275

Also specifies duties to be paid on various types of fish, and grants freedom to import fish from Newfoundland and New England without duty.

Great Britain. Laws, etc. An additional act for the better improvement and advancing the receipts of the excise and new-impost. London, Henry Hills and John Field, 1657. G276

Great Britain. Laws, etc. Een acte, tot encouragement en voorsettinghe der schip-vaert en navigatie. [n.p.] 1660. G277

A modification of the original Navigation Act of 1651.

Great Britain. Laws, etc. The act of tonnage and poundage, and Book of rates; with several statutes at large relating to the customs. London, Assigns of John Bill and Christopher Barker, 1675. G278

A collection of information useful to merchants engaged in overseas trade, including rates inward and outward, regulations, laws, fees, etc.

Great Britain. Laws, etc. The act of tonnage and poundage, and Book of rates; with several

statutes at large relating to the customs; carefully examined by the records ... London, Charles Bill and Thomas Newcomb, 1689. G279
   Enlarged edition.

Great Britain. Laws, etc. [An act for confirming to the governour and Company Trading to Hudsons-Bay their priviledges and trade.] London, Charles Bill and Thomas Newcomb, 1690. G280
   A confirmation of the Hudson's Bay Company charter for seven years, conditioned upon its holding at least two sales of coat-beaver annually.

Great Britain. Laws, etc. [An act for the regaining, encouraging and settling the Greenland trade.] London, Charles Bill and the executrix of Thomas Newcomb, 1692. G281
   This act creates the Company of Merchants of London Trading to Greenland, noting earlier attempts by English merchants to engage in Greenland whaling.

Great Britain. Laws, etc. [An act for preventing frauds ... in the plantation trade.] London, Charles Bill and the executrix of Thomas Newcomb, 1696. G282
   Prohibits the carrying on of trade with England or its colonies in foreign ships.

Great Britain. Laws, etc. [An act for the further encouragement of the manufacture of lustrings and alamodes.] London, Charles Bill, 1697. G283
   This act marks an attempt by England to compete with France in silk manufacture.

Great Britain. Laws, etc. A collection of all the statutes now in force relating to excises and duties upon salt, malt, and leather. London, Charles Bill and the executrix of Thomas Newcomb, 1697. G284
   The list of taxes goes back as far as 1672.

Great Britain. Laws, etc. [An act for enlarging the time for registring of ships, pursuant to the Act for preventing frauds, and regulating abuses in the plantation trade.] London, Charles Bill and the executrix of Thomas Newcomb, 1698. G285

Great Britain. Laws, etc. [An act for raising a sum not exceeding two millions ... and for settling the trade to the East Indies.] London, Charles Bill and the executrix of Thomas Newcomb, 1698. G286
   This act provided for the continuation of the monopoly on the East Indian trade by the new East India Company.

Great Britain. Laws, etc. The act of tonnage and poundage, and rates of merchandize. London, Chas. Bill, and the executrix of T. Newcomb, 1702. G287
   Includes numerous laws, regulations, and duties pertaining to English commerce from 1690 to 1702.

Great Britain. Laws, etc. An act for the encouragement of the trade to America. London, Charles Bill and the executrix of Thomas Newcomb, 1708. G288
   The purpose of this act was to encourage privateering as a means of developing sea power for use against Great Britain's enemies.

Great Britain. Laws, etc. An act for continuing several impositions and duties, to raise money by way of loan; and for exporting British copper and brass-wire duty-free ... London, Charles Bill and the executrix of Thomas Newcomb, 1709. G289
   The act provides for continuation of duties on wine, tobacco, East Indian products and whale-fins; and new duties on fish oils.

Great Britain. Laws, etc. [An act to prohibit the exportation of corn, malt, meal, flour, bread, biscuit, and starch, and low wines, spirits, worts, and wash drawn from malted corn.] London, Charles Bill and the executrix of Thomas Newcomb, 1709. G290

Great Britain. Laws, etc. [An act for continuing several impositions, additional impositions, and duties upon goods imported.] London, Assigns of Thomas Newcomb and Henry Hills, 1710. G291
   A comprehensive act covering duties on salt, coal, wine, naval stores, and other commodities.

Great Britain. Laws, etc. An act for the encouragement of trade to America. London, The assigns of Thomas Newcomb and Henry Hills, 1711. G292
   A refinement of a 1708 law stating that all goods brought to port as prizes must pay the normal customs duties.

Great Britain. Laws, etc. [An act for the preservation of white and other pine-trees growing in Her Majesties colonies.] London, Assigns of Thomas Newcomb and Henry Hills, 1711. G293
   Trees suitable for masts were not to be cut without royal permission. Surveyors were to mark and register such trees which were not on private property.

Great Britain. Laws, etc. [An act for continuing the trade to the South-Seas.] London, J. Baskett and the assigns of T. Newcomb, 1712. G294
   Provides that forts, factories, and privileges of the South Sea Company would continue after Parliament had withdrawn its active interest.

Great Britain. Laws, etc. [An act for explaining several clauses in an act ... for the relief of the sufferers in the islands of Nevis and Saint Christopher, by reason of the invasion of the French there.] London, John Baskett and the assigns of Thomas Newcomb and Henry Hills, 1712. G295

Great Britain. Laws, etc. An act for the relief of merchants importing prize-goods from America. London, John Baskett and the assigns of Thomas Newcomb and Henry Hills, 1712. G296

Duties on prize goods are set at the level of the same goods coming from the British colonies in America.

Great Britain. Laws, etc. An act for continuing an Act ... for encouraging the importation of naval stores from ... America and ... Scotland. [London, 1713.] G297

Great Britain. Laws, etc. An act for continuing an act made in the third and fourth years of the reign of Her present Majesty, intituled, An act for encouraging the importation of naval stores from Her Majesty's plantations in America ... London, John Baskett and the assigns of Thomas Newcomb and Henry Hills, 1713. G298

The act also provides encouragement for the trade in naval stores from Scotland.

Great Britain. Laws, etc. An act for making perpetual the act made ... intituled An act for the better relief of the poor of this kingdom ... an Act for the importation of cochineal ... and for reviving a clause in an act ... for settling the trade to Africa ... London, John Baskett and the assigns of Thomas Newcomb and Henry Hills, 1713. G299

Great Britain. Laws, etc. An act for the better encouragement of the making of sail-cloth in Great Britain. London, John Baskett and the assigns of Thomas Newcomb and Henry Hills, 1713. G300

The act provides for increased import duties on foreign sail cloth.

Great Britain. Laws, etc. A collection of the statutes now in force, relating to the stamp-duties. London, J. Baskett [etc.] 1716-1722. G301

Great Britain. Laws, etc. [An act for continuing the liberty of exporting Irish linen cloth to the British plantations in America duty-free.] London, John Baskett and the assigns of Thomas Newcomb and Henry Hills, 1717. G302

Great Britain. Laws, etc. [An act for continuing an act made in the twelfth year of the reign of Her late Majesty Queen Anne, intituled, An act for encouraging the tobacco trade.] London, John Baskett, and the assigns of Thomas Newcomb and Henry Hills, 1719. G303

An extension of the act of June 1, 1714 for an indefinite period. The terms of the act are not repeated, but it had proved "beneficial to the said trade, and of good use for the purposes thereby designed."

Great Britain. Laws, etc. [An act for the better securing the lawful trade of His Majesties subjects to and from the East-Indies; and for the more effectual preventing all His Majesties subjects trading thither under foreign commissions.] London, J. Baskett, 1719. G304

Great Britain. Laws, etc. [An act for the relief of such sufferers of the islands of Nevis and St. Christophers as have settled in either of those islands.] London, John Baskett and the assigns of Thomas Newcomb and Henry Hills, 1719. G305

The act provides encouragement for the resettlement of the islands following a French invasion which had displaced some settlers.

Great Britain. Laws, etc. [An act for prohibiting the importation of raw silk and mohair yarn of the product or manufacture of Asia, from any ports or places in the Streights or Levant seas, except from such ports and places as are within the dominions of the Grand Seignior. London, John Baskett, and the assigned of Thomas Newcomb and Henry Hills, 1720. G306

An attempt to prevent British merchants from buying Turkish silks and mohair in France where it was being imported in exchange for French woolens.

Great Britain. Laws, etc. [An act for making several provisions to restore the publick credit, which suffers by the frauds and mismanagements of the late directors of the South-Sea Company, and others.] London, J. Baskett, 1721. G307

Great Britain. Laws, etc. [An act for raising money upon the estates of the late sub-governor, deputy-governor, directors, cashire, deputy-cashire, and accountant of the South-Sea Company and of John Aislabie ... and likewise of James Craggs senior ...] London, John Baskett, and the assigns of Thomas Newcomb and Henry Hills, 1721. G308

The properties of the officers and directors of the company are placed in trust, with exceptions indicated for the maintenance of their families and themselves.

Great Britain. Laws, etc. [An act for restraining the sub-governor, deputy governor, directors, treasurer or cashire, deputy-cashire, and accountant of the South-Sea Company, from going out of this kingdom for the space of one year ...] London, John Baskett, and the assigns of Thomas Newcomb and Henry Hills, 1721. G309

The officers and directors being restrained are named, and the reason is their "many notorious, fradulent, and indirect practices ... to the great detriment of the public, in breach of their trust ..."

Great Britain. Laws, etc. [An act for the further preventing His Majesties subjects from trading to the East-Indies under foreign commissions.] London, John Baskett, and the assigns of Thomas Newcomb and Henry Hills, 1721. G310

Great Britain. Laws, etc. [An act to disable the present sub-governor, deputy-governor, and directors of the South-Sea Company ... to take, hold, or enjoy any office, place or employment in the said Company, or in the East-India Company, or Bank of England, and from voting upon elections in the said Company.] London, John Baskett, and the assigns of Thomas Newcomb and Henry Hills, 1721. G311

The officers and Directors "have been guilty of a notorious breach of trust in the execution of their said offices ..."

Great Britain. Laws, etc. [An act for encouragement of the silk manufactures of this kingdom; and for taking off several duties on merchandizes exported; and for reducing the duties upon beaver skins, pepper, mace, cloves, and nutmegs imported; and for importation of all furs of the product of the British plantations, into this kingdom only.] London, John Baskett, and the assigns of Thomas Newcomb and Henry Hills, 1722. G312

Great Britain. Laws, etc. [An act giving further encouragement for the importation of naval stores.] London, John Baskett, 1722. G313

Concerns timber and tar produced in the American plantations.

Great Britain. Laws, etc. [An act to prevent the clandestine running of goods, and the danger of infection thereby; and to prevent ships breaking their quarantine ...] London, John Baskett and the assigns of Thomas Newcomb and Henry Hills, 1722. G314

A law to regulate smuggling in general, with particular emphasis on spiritous liquors.

Great Britain. Laws, etc. [An act for encouraging the Greenland fishery.] London, John Baskett, and the assigns of Henry Hills, 1724. G315

Great Britain. Laws, etc. [An act for repealing certain duties ... payable upon coffee, tea, cocoa nuts, chocolate, and cocoa paste imported.] London, John Baskett, 1724. G316

The duties are repealed owing to the smuggling they caused. Other regulations upon the sale of these commodities are inaugurated.

Great Britain. Laws, etc. [An act for laying certain duties upon hides and skins ... for the term of thirty two years, for prosecuting the war, and other her Majesties most necessary occasions.] London, John Baskett and the assigns of Henry Hills, 1725. G317

A schedule of duties on a wide variety of hides and skins with provisions for administering the taxes.

Great Britain. Laws, etc. An act to continue several acts therein mentioned for preventing frauds committed by bankrupts; for encouraging the silk manufactures of this kingdom; for preventing the clandestine running of goods ... London, John Baskett and assigns of Henry Hills, 1725. G318

Includes numerous duties upon goods and commercial regulations.

Great Britain. Laws, etc. [An act for repealing the duty laid upon snuff ...] London, John Baskett and Thomas Norris, 1726. G319

Great Britain. Laws, etc. [An act for importing salt from Europe into the province of Pensilvania in America.] London, John Baskett and Tho. Norris, 1727. G320

An act to encourage the fishing industry in the Delaware Bay area. Salt was to be imported in British ships only.

Great Britain. Laws, etc. [An act for granting an aid to His Majesty ... and for further applying the procedure of the sinking fund, and for enlarging the time for exchanging Nevis and St. Christopher's debentures for annuities.] London, John Baskett and Tho. Norris, 1728. G321

Great Britain. Laws, etc. [An act for better preservation of His Majesty's woods in America.] London, Assigns of His Majesty's printer and Henry Hills, 1729. G322

Regulates cutting white pine trees in America, provides for premiums for naval stores, and encourages the harvesting of timbers in Scotland for naval use.

Great Britain. Laws, etc. [An act for importing salt from Europe into the colony of New York in America.] London, Assigns of His Majesty's printer and of Henry Hills, 1730. G323

Great Britain. Laws, etc. [An act for taking off certain duties on salt, and for making good any deficiencies in the funds, that may happen thereby ...] London, Assigns of His Majesty's printer, and of Henry Hills, 1730. G324

Adjustments in the taxes upon salt and salted products, replacing income due the East India Company.

Great Britain. Laws, etc. An act granting liberty to carry rice from his Majesty's province of Carolina in America directly to any part of Europe southward of Cape Finisterre ... London, Assigns of His Majesty's Printer and of Henry Hills, 1730. G325

Rice from Carolina is exempted from regulations applying to that product from other places.

Great Britain. Laws, etc. [An act for importing from His Majesty's plantations in America, directly into Ireland, goods not enumerated in any act of Parliament.] London, Assigns of His Majesty's printer and of Henry Hills, 1731. G326

Great Britain. Laws, etc. An act for the more easy recovery of debts in his Majesty's plantations in America. London, John Baskett, 1732. G327

Lands, houses, slaves and other properties may be claimed in settling debts.

Great Britain. Laws, etc. [An act to explain an act ... for importing from His Majesties plantations ... hops into Ireland.] London, John Baskett, 1732. G328

It is made clear that hops coming from America were to be excluded from Ireland.

Great Britain. Laws, etc. [An act to prevent the exportation of hats out of any of His Majesties colonies or plantations in America ... and for the better encouraging the making hats in Great Britain.] London, John Baskett, 1732. G329

Great Britain. Laws, etc. An act for enabling his Majesty to apply five hundred thousand pounds out of the Sinking Fund ... by paying off one million of South Sea annuities ... and ten thousand pounds to the trustees for establishing the colony of Georgia in America ... London, John Baskett, 1733. G330

Proceeds from land sales in St. Christopher would support the founding of a colony in Georgia.

Great Britain. Laws, etc. [An act for repealing an act for laying a duty on compound waters or spirits.] London, John Baskett, 1733. G331

The act altered duties on French brandy, tightened restrictions on the importation of liquor, and made the provisions for exporting British grain more lenient.

Great Britain. Laws, etc. A bill for repealing several subsidies and an impost now payable on tobacco of the British plantations. London, For W. Webb, 1733. G332

A bill calling for a reduced duty on tobacco and outlining new provisions for taxation and control of the colonial tobacco trade.

Great Britain. Laws, etc. An act to continue an act ... intituled An act for granting liberty to carry rice from his Majesty's province of Carolina in America, directly to any part of Europe southward of Cape Finisterre . . and to extend that liberty to his majesty's province of Georgia in America. London, John Baskett, 1735. G333

Great Britain. Laws, etc. [An act to continue two several acts therein mentioned; one for encouraging the growth of coffee in His Majesty's plantations in America, and the other for the better securing and encouraging the trade of His Majesty's sugar colonies in America.] London, John Baskett, 1738. G334

The coffee and sugar acts being continued by this legislation were passed in 1735 and 1733 respectively.

Great Britain. Laws, etc. [An act for granting a liberty to carry sugars, of the growth, produce, or manufacture of any of His Majesty's sugar colonies in America ... to foreign parts ...] London, John Baskett, 1739. G335

The freedom to export sugar directly to foreign ports is granted, with numerous restrictions, so that the British sugar colonies could more effectively compete with other West Indian sugar producers.

Great Britain. Laws, etc. An act for the more effectual securing and encouraging the trade of His Majesty's British subjects to America. London, John Baskett, 1739. G336

This law authorizes officers, seamen, and soldiers to make prizes of Spanish ships and to retain sole possession of them.

Great Britain. Laws, etc. An act for continuing an act ... to explain and amend a former act ... for the better regulating the manufacture of cloth in the West Riding of the county of York. London, John Baskett, 1741. G337

Great Britain. Laws, etc. [An act for opening a trade to and from Persia through Russia.] London, John Baskett, 1741. G338

The act provides for the importation of Persian silk bought with the sale of British woolens. The silk was not to be worn in Great Britain but exported.

Great Britain. Laws, etc. An act to continue an act for relief of debtors ... and also to continue an act for the free importation of cochineal and indigo. London, John Baskett, 1741. G339

Great Britain. Laws, etc. A collection of all the Irish and English statutes now in force and use,

relating to His Majesty's revenue of Ireland ... With A view of the rates of goods and merchandizes imported and exported ... by James Fleming. Dublin, For the author, 1741. G340
Commercial laws of Ireland including import and export duties.

Great Britain. Laws, etc. An act for further regulating the plantation trade; and for the relief of merchants importing prize goods from America ... London, Thomas Baskett and Robert Baskett, 1742. G341

Great Britain. Laws, etc. [An act to impower the importers or proprietors of rum or spirits of the British sugar plantations to land the same before payment of the duties.] London, Thomas Baskett and Robert Baskett, 1742. G342

Great Britain. Laws, etc. [An act to revive several acts for the punishment of persons destroying turnpikes ...] London, Thomas and Robert Baskett, 1742. G343
The act also includes regulations upon the sugar and rice trades of the British North American colonies.

Great Britain. Laws, etc. [An act for continuing several laws relating to the allowance upon exportation of British made gunpowder.] London, Thomas and Robert Baskett, 1743. G344
Also regulates the trade in naval stores in North America, and linen in Ireland.

Great Britain. Laws, etc. [An act for giving a publick reward to such person or persons, His Majesty's subjects, as shall discover a north west passage through Hudson's Streights, to the western and southern ocean of America.] London, Thomas Baskett and the assigns of Robert Baskett, 1745. G345

Great Britain. Laws, etc. [An act for the better encouragement of the trade of His Majesty's sugar colonies in America.] London, Thomas Baskett and the assigns of Robert Baskett, 1746. G346

Great Britain. Laws, etc. [An act for the more effectual securing of the duties now payable on foreign-made sail cloth imported into this kingdom.] London, Thomas Baskett and the assigns of Robert Baskett, 1746. G347

Great Britain. Laws, etc. [An act to continue two acts ... for encouraging the growth of coffee in His Majesty's plantations in America, and ... the better securing and encouraging the trade of His Majesty's sugar colonies in America.] London, Thomas Baskett, and the assigns of Robert Baskett, 1746. G348

Great Britain. Laws, etc. An act to continue several laws for prohibiting the importation of books reprinted abroad, and first composed or written and printed in Great Britain ... London, Thomas Baskett and the assigns of Robert Baskett, 1747. G349
The act also covers rates for East India goods, deals with frauds at customs, trade in rice, copper, cochineal, and indigo.

Great Britain. Laws, etc. [An act for encouraging the making of indico in the British plantations in America.] London, Thomas Baskett and the assigns of Robert Baskett, 1748. G350
The act provides for a premium of six pence per pound for indigo produced in any of the American colonies.

Great Britain. Laws, etc. [An act for permitting tea to be exported to Ireland, and His Majesty's plantations in America, without paying the inland duties.] London, Thomas Baskett and the assigns of Robert Baskett, 1748. G351

Great Britain. Laws, etc. [An act for encouraging the people known by the name of Unitas Fratrum or United Brethren, to settle in His Majesty's colonies in America,] London, Thomas Baskett and the assigns of Robert Baskett, 1749. G352
Members of the United Brethren in America are exempted from oaths and military service.

Great Britain. Laws, etc. [An act for the further encouragement and enlargement of the whale fishery, and for continuing such laws as are therein mentioned relating thereto ...] London, John Baskett, 1749. G353
The act provides a subsidy of twenty shillings per ton of shipping and for licensing and subsidizing ships built in America for the whaling trade.

Great Britain. Laws, etc. An act for enabling His Majesty to raise the several sums of money ... to pay off the old and new unsubscribed South Sea annuities. London, Thomas Baskett, 1750. G354

Great Britain. Laws, etc. An act for encouraging the growth and culture of raw silk in his Majesty's colonies or plantations in America. London, Thomas Baskett and the assigns of Robert Baskett, 1750. G355
The act provides for duty-free import of raw silk produced in the American colonies.

Great Britain. Laws, etc. [An act for extending and improving the trade of Africa.] London, Thomas Baskett, 1750. G356

Grants freedom to all British subjects to trade in any African port between Port Sally in south Barbary and the Cape of Good Hope.

Great Britain. Laws, etc. An act for giving further time to the proprietors of annuities ... and for impowering the East India Company to raise certain sums by transferable annuities. London, Thomas Baskett, 1750. G357

Great Britain. Laws, etc. An act for the encouragement of the British white herring fishery. London, Thomas Baskett, 1750. G358
This document lists the incorporators and includes the letters patent of the Society of the Free British Fishery.

Great Britain. Laws, etc. An act to encourage the importation of pig and bar iron from His Majesty's colonies in America; and to prevent the erection of any mill or other engine for slitting or rolling of iron; or any plateing forge to work with a tilt hammer; or any furnace for making steel in any of the said colonies. London, Thomas Baskett, assigns of Robert Baskett, 1750. G359

Great Britain. Laws, etc. A bill for extending and improving the trade to Africa. [London, 1750.] G360
This bill sets forth the structure of membership and management for the Company of Merchants Trading to Africa, which replaced the Royal African Company as Britain's major vehicle for the west African trade.

Great Britain. Laws, etc. An act for encouraging the making of pott ashes and pearl ashes in the British plantations in America. London, Thomas Baskett and the assigns of Robert Baskett, 1751. G361

Great Britain. Laws, etc. [An act for explaining, amending and enforcing ... An act for the better regulation of the linen and hempen manufactures in ... Scotland.] London, Thomas Baskett, 1751. G362

Great Britain. Laws, etc. [An act for reducing the interest upon the capital stock of the South Sea Company ... and for preventing of frauds committed by the officers and servants of the said company.] London, Thomas Baskett, 1751. G363

Great Britain. Laws, etc. [An act for the more effectual securing the duties upon tobacco.] London, Thomas Baskett and the assigns of Robert Baskett, 1751. G364
"Many great frauds and abuses are frequently contrived, committed, and carried on, by several ill-designing persons ..."

Great Britain. Laws, etc. An act to continue several laws therein mentioned; for preventing theft and rapine on the northern borders of England ... London, Thomas Baskett and the assigns of Robert Baskett, 1751. G365
Among the laws extended are one for duty-free importation of American sugar orginally passed in 1739 and a similar one for naval stores passed in 1722.

Great Britain. Laws, etc. An act to regulate and restrain paper bills of credit in His Majesty's colonies or plantations of Rhode Island, and Providence, Connecticut, the Massachusetts Bay, and New Hampshire in America ... London, Thomas Baskett and the assigns of Robert Baskett, 1751. G366
The colonies named in the act are cited for issuing large amounts of paper currency which has caused a disruption of normal trade.

Great Britain. Laws, etc. A collection of the acts of Parliament, now in force, relating to the linen manufacture. Edinburgh, Assigns of Robert Freebairn, 1751. G367
Excerpts from laws dating back to 1713 relating to many aspects of the linen trade, including exports, maintenance of quality, prohibition upon wearing competing foreign cloths, and restrictions against workers' organizations for improvement of conditions.

Great Britain. Laws, etc. An act for avoiding and putting an end to certain doubts and questions, relating to the attestation of wills and codicils ... in His Majesty's colonies and plantations in America. London, Thomas Baskett and the assigns of Robert Baskett, 1752. G368

Great Britain. Laws, etc. [An act for continuing the act for encouraging the growth of coffee in His Majesties plantations in America.] London, Thomas Baskett and assigns of Robert Baskett, 1752. G369
The act also provides for the conservation of American forests useful for shipbuilding by using more timber from Scotland.

Great Britain. Laws, etc. An act to restrain the making insurances on foreign ships bound to or from the East Indies. London, Thomas Baskett and the assigns of Robert Baskett, 1752. G370
One of several laws designed to prevent British participation of any kind in East India Companies based in other countries.

Great Britain. Laws, etc. [An act for continuing several laws relating to the punishment of persons going armed or disguised in defiance of the laws of customs and excise ...] London, Thomas Baskett, the assigns of Robert Baskett, 1753. G371

This act includes regulations on copper, sail cloth, silk, sugar, soap, candles, and on whaling and fishing in Greenland waters.

Great Britain. Laws, etc. [An act for reducing the number of directors of the corporation ... trading to the South Seas.] London, Thomas Baskett and assigns of Robert Baskett, 1753. G372

The number of directors is reduced from twenty-one to fifteen.

Great Britain. Laws, etc. An act for the more effectually preventing the fraudulent removal of tobacco by land or water ... London, Thomas Baskett and the assigns of Robert Baskett, 1753. G373

An attempt to make sure that tobacco imported after September 29, 1751 is not declared to be of an earlier date.

Great Britain. Laws, etc. [An act for punishing mutiny and desertion of officers and soldiers in the service of the United Company of Merchants trading to the East Indies.] London, Thomas Baskett and the assigns of Robert Baskett, 1754. G374

A law providing for courts-martial and sentences, including the death penalty, for soldiers engaging in mutiny when in the service of the East India Company.

Great Britain. Laws, etc. [An act to continue several laws for prohibiting the importation of books reprinted abroad, and first composed or written, and printed in Great Britain.] London, Thomas Baskett and the assigns of Robert Baskett, 1754. G375

The act also includes regulations upon importing of cochineal, indigo, rice, and copper.

Great Britain. Laws, etc. An act for continuing, explaining, and amending, the several acts of Parliament made for the further encouragement of the whale fishery carried on by His Majesty's subjects. London, Thomas Baskett and the assigns of Robert Baskett, 1755. G376

The act extends previous legislation relating to whaling in Greenland waters and is concerned with further provisions regarding bounties and insurance for whaling ships.

Great Britain. Laws, etc. An act for extending the act ... for amending, explaining, and reducing into one act of Parliament, the laws relating to the government of His Majesty's ships, vessels, and forces by sea ... employed upon the lakes, great waters, or rivers in North America. London, Thomas Baskett and the assigns of Robert Baskett, 1756. G377

This act extends a law of 1751 covering sailors and troops in North America who might commit crimes outside of any regular colonial jurisdiction.

Great Britain. Laws, etc. An act to enable His Majesty to grant commissions to a certain number of foreign Protestants who have served abroad as officers, or engineers ... in America ... London, Thomas Baskett and the assigns of Robert Baskett, 1756. G378

The act makes a grant of citizenship to military officers recruited abroad upon residence of seven years in the North American colonies.

Great Britain. Laws, etc. [An act to extend the liberty granted ... of importing bar iron from His Majesty's colonies in America.] London, Thomas Baskett and the assigns of Robert Baskett, 1757. G379

American-made bar iron is to be freely admitted, and regulations are prescribed for the internal and coastwise trade in iron.

Great Britain. Laws, etc. An act to prohibit for a limited time the exportation of corn ... and other victual ... from His Majesty's colonies and plantations in America ... London, Thomas Baskett and the assigns of Robert Baskett, 1757. G380

Great Britain. Laws, etc. An act for continuing certain laws therein mentioned relating to British sail cloth, and the duties to be paid on foreign sail cloth ... London, Thomas Baskett and the assigns of Robert Baskett, 1758. G381

In addition to sail cloth, the act concerns gunpowder, liquor imported from the West Indies, and calicoes from India.

Great Britain. Laws, etc. An act for repealing the duty ... on silver plate, made, wrought, touched, assayed, or marked in Great Britain ... London, Thomas Baskett and the assigns of Robert Baskett, 1758. G382

Duties on silver and gold items are replaced by a fee for licensing dealers in these products.

Great Britain. Laws, etc. [An act to continue several laws ... relating to the clandestine running of uncustomed goods, and preventing frauds relating to the customs.] London, Thomas Baskett and the assigns of Robert Baskett, 1760. G383

Great Britain. Laws, etc. [An act to continue an act intituled, An act for the better securing and encouraging the trade of His Majesty's sugar colonies in America.] London, Thomas Baskett, and the assigns of Robert Baskett, 1761. G384

Great Britain. Laws, etc. [An act to extend the provisions relating to the holding of courts-martial, and to the punishment of offences committed in the East Indies.] London, Thomas Baskett, and the assigns of Robert Baskett, 1761. G385

Great Britain. Laws, etc. An act for importing salt from Europe into the colony of Nova Scotia in America. London, Mark Baskett and the assigns of Robert Baskett, 1762. G386

Great Britain. Laws, etc. An act for naturalizing such foreign Protestants as have served ... as officers or soldiers in His Majesty's Royal American regiment, or as engineers in America. London, Mark Baskett and the assigns of Robert Baskett, 1762. G387

An enlistment for two years with British troops in America qualified foreign protestants for citizenship.

Great Britain. Laws, etc. An act for the further improvement of His Majesty's customs; and for the encouragement of officers making seizures ... London, Mark Baskett and the assigns fo Robert Baskett, 1763. G388

As an encouragement to customs officers to do their duty they are allowed half the proceeds of seized goods to be sold at auction.

Great Britain. Laws, etc. [An act to continue and amend two acts ... for encouraging the making of indico in the British plantations in America; and for extending the provisions of an act ... with respect to bringing prize goods into this kingdom, to Spanish prize goods taken since the late declaration of war with Spain.] London, Mark Baskett, and the assigns of Robert Baskett, 1763. G389

Great Britain. Laws, etc. [An act for continuing certain laws therein mentioned relating to British sail cloth, and to the duties payable on foreign sail cloth, and to the allowance upon ... British made gunpowder, and for giving encouragement for the importation of naval stores from the British colonies in America.] London, Mark Baskett and the assigns of Robert Baskett, 1764. G390

This act renews legislation for the encouragement of the manufacture of sail cloth originating in 1736, of gunpowder, 1731, and of naval stores, 1722.

Great Britain. Laws, etc. [An act for continuing several acts of Parliament made for the encouragement of the whale fishery carried on by His Majesty's subjects.] London, Mark Baskett, and the assigns of Robert Baskett, 1764. G391

Great Britain. Laws, etc. [An act for granting a bounty upon the importation of hemp, and rough and undressed flax from His Majesty's colonies in America.] London, Mark Baskett, and the assigns of Robert Baskett, 1764. G392

Great Britain. Laws, etc. [An act for granting certain duties in the British colonies and plantations in America; for continuing, amending, and making perpetual, an act passed in the sixth year of the reign of ... George the Second, (intituled, An act for the better securing and encouraging the trade of His Majesty's sugar colonies in America) ...] London, Mark Baskett and the assigns of Robert Baskett, 1764. G393

Great Britain. Laws, etc. [An act for granting, for a limited time, a liberty to carry rice from His Majesty's provinces of South Carolina and Georgia, directly to any part of America to the southward of the said provinces, subject to the like duty as is now paid on the exportation of rice from the said colonies, to places in Europe situate to the southward of Cape Finisterre.] London, Mark Baskett, and the assigns of Robert Baskett, 1764. G394

Great Britain. Laws, etc. [An act for importing salt from Europe into the province of Quebec in America, for a limited time.] London, Mark Baskett and the assigns of Robert Baskett, 1764. G395

The importation of salt is authorized for one year as an encouragement to the fishing industry of Quebec.

Great Britain. Laws, etc. [An act for raising a certain sum of money by loans or exchequer bills ...] London, Mark Baskett, and the assigns of Robert Baskett, 1764. G396

This appropriation measure identifies intended expenditures, including colonial administration and geographical surveys in America and the maintenance of forts and settlements in Africa.

Great Britain. Laws, etc. [An act for repealing the duties now payable upon bever skins imported, and for granting other duties in lieu thereof; and for granting certain duties upon the exportation of bever skins and bever wool; and for taking off the drawback allowed on the exportation of such skins.] London, Mark Baskett, and the assigns of Robert Baskett, 1764. G397

Great Britain. Laws, etc. [An act for the encouragement of the whale fishery in the gulph and river of Saint Lawrence, and on the coasts of His Majesty's colonies in America.] London, Mark Baskett, and the assigns of Robert Baskett, 1764. G398

Great Britain. Laws, etc. [An act for vesting the fort of Senegal, and its dependencies, in the Company of Merchants trading to Africa.] London, Mark Baskett, and the assigns of Robert Baskett, 1764. G399

Great Britain. Laws, etc. An act to continue several laws for the better regulating of pilots ... up the rivers of Thames and Medway; relating to the landing of rum or spirits of the British sugar plantations before duties of excise are paid. London, Mark Baskett and the assigns of Robert Baskett, 1764.   G400

Great Britain. Laws, etc. [An act to prevent paper bills of credit, hereafter to be issued in any of His Majesty's colonies or plantations in America, from being declared to be a legal tender in payments of money ...] London, Mark Baskett and the assigns of Robert Baskett, 1764.   G401

Colonial issues of paper money had meant that "debts have been discharged with a much less value than was contracted for, to the great discouragement and prejudice of the trade and commerce of His Majesty's subjects."

Great Britain. Laws, etc. [An act for granting and applying certain stamp duties, and other duties, in the British colonies and plantations in America, towards further defraying the expences of defending, protecting and securing the same ...] London, Mark Baskett and the assigns of Robert Baskett, 1765.   G402

Great Britain. Laws, etc. [An act for granting to His Majesty certain duties on the exportation of coals; and, of several East India goods; and upon policies of assurance for retaining, upon the exportation of white callicoes and muslins, a further part of the duties paid on the importation thereof; and for obviating a doubt with respect to stamp duties imposed upon deeds by two former acts.] London, Mark Baskett and the assigns of Robert Baskett, 1765.   G403

Great Britain. Laws, etc. [An act for laying certain duties upon gum senega and gum arabic imported into or exported from Great Britain, and for confining the exportation of gum senega from Africa to Great Britain only.] London, Mark Baskett and the assigns of Robert Baskett, 1765.   G404

Great Britain. Laws, etc. [An act for more effectually securing and encouraging the trade of His Majesty's American dominions; for repealing the inland duty on coffee ... and for granting an inland duty on all coffee imported (except coffee of the growth of the British dominions in America) ...] London, Mark Baskett and the assigns of Robert Baskett, 1765.   G405

Great Britain. Laws, etc. [An act for prohibiting the importation of foreign manufactured silk stockings, silk mitts, and silk gloves, into Great Britain and the British dominions ...] London, Mark Baskett and the assigns of Robert Baskett, 1765.   G406

Great Britain. Laws, etc. An act for rendering more effectual an act made in the twelfth year of the reign of Her late Majesty Queen Anne, intitled, An act for providing a publick reward for such person or persons as shall discover the longitude at sea ... London, Mark Baskett and the assigns of Robert Baskett, 1765.   G407

This act related to John Harrison's claim to the award for developing a workable chronometer to make possible determination of longitude at sea.

Great Britain. Laws, etc. An act for rendering more effectual two acts ... for providing a publick reward for such person or persons as shall discover the longitude at sea ... London, Mark Baskett and the assigns of Robert Baskett, 1765.   G408

This act related to John Harrison's claim to the award for developing a workable chronometer to make possible determination of longitude at sea.

Great Britain. Laws, etc. [An act for repealing the act made in the last session of Parliament, intituled, An act for vesting the fort of Senegal, and its dependencies, in the Company of Merchants trading to Africa ...] London, Mark Baskett and the assigns of Robert Baskett, 1765.   G409

Great Britain. Laws, etc. [An act for repealing the duties now payable upon raw silk imported, and for granting other duties in lieu thereof; for allowing a drawback on the exportation of raw or thrown silk to Ireland, and for prohibiting the exportation of raw silk from Ireland.] London, Mark Baskett and the assigns of Robert Baskett, 1765.   G410

Great Britain. Laws, etc. [An act for the further encouragement of the British white herring fishery.] London, Mark Baskett and the assigns of Robert Baskett, 1765.   G411

Great Britain. Laws, etc. An act to amend and render more effectual, in His Majesty's dominions in America, an act ... intituled, An act for punishing mutiny and desertion, and for the better payment of the Army and their quarters. London, Mark Baskett and the assigns of Robert Baskett, 1765.   G412

The second version of the Quartering Act, removing the provision for quartering troops in homes, but providing for locating them in public places such as inns and taverns.

Great Britain. Laws, etc. [An act to enable His Majesty ... to prohibit the exportation of wheat, wheaten meal, flour, bread, biscuit and starch, during the next recess of Parliament.] London, Mark Baskett and the assigns of Robert Baskett, 1765.   G413

Great Britain. Laws, etc. [An act for allowing the importation of corn and grain, from His Majesty's colonies in America, into this kingdom, for a limited time, free of duty.] London, Mark Baskett and the assigns of Robert Baskett, 1766. G414

Great Britain. Laws, etc. [An act for allowing the importation of wheat and wheat flour from His Majesty's colonies in America into this kingom, for a limited time, free of duty.] London, Mark Baskett and the assigns of Robert Baskett, 1766. G415

Great Britain. Laws, etc. An act for indemnifying persons who have incurred certain penalties inflicted by an act of the last session of Parliament, for granting certain stamp duties in the British colonies and plantations in America ... London, Mark Baskett and the assigns of Robert Baskett, 1766. G416

Great Britain. Laws, etc. [An act for repealing certain duties, in the British colonies and plantations, granted by several acts of Parliament; and also the duties imposed by an act made in the last session of Parliament upon certain East India goods exported from Great Britain ...] London, Mark Baskett and the assigns of Robert Baskett, 1766. G417

Great Britain. Laws, etc. [An act for the better securing the dependency of His Majesty's dominions in America upon the Crown and Parliament of Great Britain.] London, Mark Baskett and the assigns of Robert Baskett, 1766. G418

Great Britain. Laws, etc. An act to amend and render more effectual, in His Majesty's dominions in America, an act past in this present session of Parliament, intituled, An act for punishing mutiny and desertion, and for the better payment of the Army and their quarters. London, Mark Baskett and the assigns of Robert Baskett, 1766. G419

Extends the duration of the legislation from 24 March 1767 to 24 March 1768.

Great Britain. Laws, etc. [An act to amend so much of an act made in the last session of Parliament, intituled, An act for repealing certain duties in the British colonies and plantations, granted by several acts of Parliament; and also the duties imposed by an act made in the last session of Parliament upon certain East India goods exported from Great Britain ...] London, Mark Baskett and the assigns of Robert Baskett, 1766. G420

Great Britain. Laws, etc. [An act to continue an act ... for importing salt from Europe, into the province of Quebec in America, for a limited time.] London, Mark Baskett and the assigns of Robert Baskett, 1766. G421

Originally passed in 1764, this salt trade legislation is here extended to 1773.

Great Britain. Laws, etc. [An act to continue several laws ... relating to ... the exportation of copper bars imported; to the encouragement of the silk manufactures ... to the premium upon masts, yards, and bowsprits ... to the encouraging the growth of coffee in ... America ...] London, Mark Baskett and the assigns of Robert Baskett, 1766. G422

The law extends existing legislation covering duties on a variety of commodities, including beaver skins, other furs, various spices, and naval stores to 1774.

Great Britain. Laws, etc. An act to prohibit the importation of foreign wrought silks and velvets, for a limited time; and for preventing unlawful combinations of workmen employed in the silk manufacture. London, Mark Baskett and the assigns of Robert Baskett, 1766. G423

A law restricting the importing of silk goods, and providing for the death penalty for persons damaging woolen cloth or machines for making it.

Great Britain. Laws, etc. [An act to remove a doubt concerning such part of an act made in the last session of Parliament, as relates to the ascertaining of duties upon importation of certain linen cloth of the manufacture of Russia; and to obviate all doubts with respect to the importation of tea.] London, Mark Baskett and the assigns of Robert Baskett, 1766. G424

Great Britain. Laws, etc. [An act to repeal an act made in the last session of Parliament, intituled, An act for granting and applying certain stamp duties and other duties, in the British colonies and plantations in America, towards further defraying the expenses of defending, protecting, and securing the same ...] London, Mark Baskett and the assigns of Robert Baskett, 1766. G425

The repeal of the infamous Stamp Act because it "would be attended with many Inconveniencies and may be productive of Consequences greatly detrimental to the Commercial Interests of these Kingdoms."

Great Britain. Laws, etc. A bill for opening and establishing certain ports in the islands of Jamaica and Dominica. [London, 1766.] G426

Provides for more free trade in certain commodities at three ports in Dominica and two in Jamaica.

Great Britain. Laws, etc. [An act for allowing the free importation of rice, sago powder, and vermicelli, into this kingdom, from His Majesty's colonies in North America, for a limited time.] London, Mark Baskett and the assigns of Robert Baskett, 1767. G427

Great Britain. Laws, etc. [An act for establishing an agreement for the payment of the annual sum of four hundred thousand pounds, for a limited time, by the East India Company, in respect of the territorial acquisitions and revenues lately obtained in the East Indies.] London, Mark Baskett and the assigns of Robert Baskett, 1767. G428

Great Britain. Laws, etc. [An act for for taking off the inland duty of one shilling per pound weight upon all black and singlo teas consumed in Great Britain; and for granting a drawback upon the exportation of teas to Ireland, and the British dominions in America, for a limited time, upon such indemnification to be made in respect thereof by the East India Company ...] London, Mark Baskett and the assigns of Robert Baskett, 1767. G429

Great Britain. Laws, etc. [An act for further continuing an act of the last session of Parliament, intituled, An act to amend and render more effectual, in His Majesty's dominions in America, and act passed in this present session of Parliament, intituled, An act for punishing mutiny and desertion, and for the better payment of the Army and their quarters.] London, Mark Baskett and the assigns of Robert Baskett, 1767. G430

Great Britain. Laws, etc. [An act for granting certain duties in the British colonies and plantations in America.] London, Mark Baskett, 1767. G431

A law levying a tax upon the glass, lead, tea, paint, and paper in the American colonies.

Great Britain. Laws, etc. [An act for granting certain duties in the British colonies and plantations in America; for allowing a drawback of the duties of customs upon the exportation, from this kingdom, of coffee and cocoa nuts of the produce of the said colonies or plantations; for discontinuing the drawbacks payable on china earthen ware exported to America ...] London, Mark Baskett and the assigns of Robert Baskett, 1767. G432

Great Britain. Laws, etc. [An act for regulating certain proceedings of the general courts of the United Company of Merchants of England trading to the East Indies.] London, Mark Baskett and the assigns of Robert Baskett, 1767. G433

Great Britain. Laws, etc. [An act for restraining and prohibiting the Governor, Council and House of Representatives, of the province of New York, until provision shall have been made for furnishing the King's troops with all the necessaries required by law.] London, Mark Baskett and the assigns of Robert Baskett, 1767. G434

Great Britain. Laws, etc. [An act for the free importation of Indian corn, or maize, from any of His Majesty's colonies in America, for a time therein limited.] London, Mark Baskett and the assigns of Robert Baskett, 1767. G435

Great Britain. Laws, etc. [An act to continue and amend an act ... to prohibit for a limited time the exportation of corn grain, meal, malt, flour, bread, biscuit, and starch, and also for the extraction of low wines and spirits from wheat and wheat flour.] London, Mark Baskett and the assigns of Robert Baskett, 1767. G436

Great Britain. Laws, etc. [An act to continue several acts made in the last session of Parliament, for allowing the importation of wheat, wheat flour, barley, barley meal, pulse, oats, oatmeal, rye, and rye meal, duty free; and also so much of an act made in the same session as relates to the free importation of rice from His Majesty's colonies in North America ...] London, Mark Baskett and the assigns of Robert Baskett, 1767. G437

Great Britain. Laws, etc. [An act to continue several laws ... relating to the clandestine running of uncustomed goods, and preventing frauds relating to the customs.] London, Mark Baskett and the assigns of Robert Baskett, 1767. G438

Great Britain. Laws, etc. [An act to enable His Majesty to put the customs, and other duties, in the British dominions in America, and the execution of the laws relating to trade there, under the management of commissioners to be appointed for that purpose, and to be resident in the said dominions.] London, Mark Baskett and the assigns of Robert Baskett, 1767. G439

Great Britain. Laws, etc. [An act for further continuing an act of the sixth year of His present Majesty's reign, intituled, An act to amend and render more effectual, in His Majesty's dominions in America, an act passed in this present session of Parliament, intituled, An act for punishing mutiny and desertion, and for the better payment of the Army and their quarters.] London, Printed by Mark Baskett and the assigns of Robert Baskett, 1768. G440

Great Britain. Laws, etc. [An act for further regulating the proceedings of the United Company of Merchants of England trading to the East Indies, with respect to the making of dividends.] London, Printed by Mark Baskett and the assigns of Robert Baskett, 1768. G441

Great Britain. Laws, etc. [An act for reducing the duties on foul salt to be used for manure; for altering the stamp duties on certain policies of assurance ...] London, Mark Baskett and the assigns of Robert Baskett, 1768. G442

Great Britain. Laws, etc. [An act for the further continuing several acts of Parliament made for the encouragement of the whale fishery carried on by His Majesty's subjects.] London, Printed by Mark Baskett and the assigns of Robert Baskett, 1768. G443

Great Britain. Laws, etc. [An act for the more easy and effectual recovery of the penalties and forfeitures inflicted by the acts of Parliament relating to the trade or revenues of the British colonies and plantations in America.] London, Printed by Mark Baskett and the assigns of Robert Baskett, 1768. G444

Great Britain. Laws, etc. [An act to allow for a further time the free importation of rice into this kingdom, from His Majesty's colonies in North America.] London, Printed by Mark Baskett and the assigns of Robert Baskett, 1768. G445

Great Britain. Laws, etc. [An act to continue ... An act for importation of salted beef, pork, bacon, and butter from Ireland, for a limited time.] London, Mark Baskett and the assigns of Robert Baskett, 1768. G446

Great Britain. Laws, etc. [An act to continue and amend an act made in the fifth year of the reign of His present Majesty, intituled, An act for the importation of salted beef, pork, bacon, and butter, from Ireland, for a limited time; and for allowing the importation of salted beef, pork, bacon, and butter, from the British dominions in America, for a limited time.] London, Printed by Mark Baskett and the assigns of Robert Baskett, 1768. G447

Great Britain. Laws, etc. [An act for amending and further continuing an act ... intituled, An act to amend and render more effectual, in His Majesty's dominions in America, an act passed in this present session of Parliament, intituled, An act for punishing mutiny and desertion, and for the better payment of the Army and their quarters.] London, Mark Baskett and the assigns of Robert Baskett, 1769. G448

Great Britain. Laws, etc. [An act for carrying into execution certain proposals made by the East India Company for the payment of the annual sum of four hundred thousand pounds, for a limited time, in respect of the territorial acquisitions and revenues lately obtained in the East Indies.] London, Mark Baskett and the assigns of Robert Baskett, 1769. G449

Great Britain. Laws, etc. [An act for further encouraging the growth and culture of raw silk in His Majesty's colonies and plantations in America.] London, Mark Baskett and the assigns of Robert Baskett, 1769. G450

Great Britain. Laws, etc. [An act for granting to His Majesty a certain sum of money ... and for applying a certain sum therein mentioned ... and for further appropriating the supplies granted.] London, Mark Baskett and the assigns of Robert Baskett, 1769. G451

Allocation of expenditures include items for colonial government, geographical surveys, and maintenance of garrisons, forts and other aspects of empire.

Great Britain. Laws, etc. [An act to continue an act ... intituled, An act to continue and amend an act ... intituled, An act for importation of salted beef, pork, bacon, and butter, from Ireland, for a limited time; and for allowing the importation of salted beef, pork, bacon, and butter, from the British dominions in America for a limited time.] London, Mark Baskett and the assigns of Robert Baskett, 1769. G452

Great Britain. Laws, etc. [An act to continue certain laws therein mentioned, for granting, for a limited time, a liberty to carry rice from His Majesty's provinces of South and North Carolina and Georgia, directly to any part of America to the southward of the said provinces ...] London, Mark Baskett and the assigns of Robert Baskett, 1769. G453

Great Britain. Laws, etc. [An act to permit the free importation of certain raw hides and skins from Ireland and the British plantations in America, for a limited time; and for taking off the duties upon seal skins tanned or tawed in this kingdom, and for granting another duty in lieu thereof ...] London, Mark Baskett and the assigns of Robert Baskett, 1769. G454

Great Britain. Laws, etc. [An act to permit the inhabitants of Jersey and Guernsey to export directly from thence to Newfoundland, or the British colonies in America, goods necessary for the fishery, under certain restrictions; and to import from thence non-enumerated goods (except rum) and to land the same in the said islands.] London, Mark Baskett and the assigns of Robert Baskett, 1769. G455

Great Britain. Laws, etc. [An act for better regulating persons employed in the service of the East India Company, and for other purposes therein mentioned.] London, Charles Eyre and William Strahan, 1770. G456

Great Britain. Laws, etc. [An act for continuing so much of an act made in the third year of His present Majesty's reign, intituled, An act to continue and amend two acts made in the twenty-first and twenty-second years of His late Majesty's reign, for encouraging the making of indico in the British plantations in America.] London, Charles Eyre and William Strahan, 1770. G457

Great Britain. Laws, etc. [An act for extending like liberty, in the exportation of rice from East and West Florida to the southward of Cape Finisterre in Europe, as is granted, by former acts of Parliament, to Carolina and Georgia.] London, Charles Eyre and William Strahan, 1770. G458

Great Britain. Laws, etc. An act to continue an act made in the last session of Parliament, intituled ... an act for punishing mutiny and desertion, and for better payment of the army and their quarters. London, Charles Eyre and William Strahan, 1770. G459

Great Britain. Laws, etc. [An act to continue for a further time ... An act for importation of salted beef, pork, bacon, and butter, from Ireland, for a limited time; and for allowing the importation of salted beef, pork, bacon, and butter, from the British dominions in America, for a limited time.] London, Charles Eyre and William Strahan, 1770. G460

Great Britain. Laws, etc. [An act to enable the Governor, Council, and Assembly of His Majesty's colony of New York, to pass an act of Assembly for creating and issuing upon loan paper bills of credit to certain amount; and to make the same a legal tender in payments into the loan offices and treasury of the said colony.] London, Charles Eyre and William Strahan, 1770. G461

Great Britain. Laws, etc. [An act to repeal so much of an act made in the seventh year of His present Majesty's reign, intituled, An act for granting certain duties in the British colonies and plantations in America; for allowing a drawback of the duties of customs upon the exportation, from this kingdom, of coffee and cocoa nuts of the produce of the said colonies or plantations.] London, Charles Eyre and William Strahan, 1770. G462

Great Britain. Laws, etc. [An act for further continuing two acts made in the sixth and ninth years of His Majesty's reign, for punishing mutiny and desertion, and for the better payment of the army and their quarters, in His Majesty's dominions in America.] London, Charles Eyre and William Strahan, 1771. G463

Great Britain. Laws, etc. [An act for granting a bounty upon the importation of white oak staves, and heading, from the British colonies or plantations in America.] London, Charles Eyre and William Strahan, 1771. G464

Great Britain. Laws, etc. [An act for the better support and establishment of the Greenland and whale fishery.] London, Charles Eyre and William Strahan, 1771. G465

Great Britain. Laws, etc. [An act for the encouragement of the white herring fishery.] London, Charles Eyre and William Strahan, 1771. G466

Great Britain. Laws, etc. [An act to amend an act ... intituled, An act for extending like liberty in the exportation of rice from East and West Florida to the southward of Cape Finisterre in Europe, as is granted by former acts of Parliament to Carolina and Georgia.] London, Charles Eyre and William Strahan, 1771. G467
Permission is granted for the export of rice from East and West Florida "to any part of America southward of South Carolina and Georgia."

Great Britain. Laws, etc. An act to continue for a further time an Act for importation of salted beef, pork, bacon, and butter from Ireland, for a limited time; and ... from the Britsh dominions in America for a limited time. London, Charles Eyre and William Strahan, 1771. G468

Great Britain. Laws, etc. [An act to explain ... An act giving further encouragement for the importation of naval stores ... so far as relates to the importation of unmanufactured wood of the growth and product of Amerca.] London, Charles Eyre and William Strahan, 1771. G469

Great Britain. Laws, etc. [An act for allowing the free importation of rice into this kingdom, from any of His Majesty's colonies in America, for a limited time.] London, Charles Eyre and William Strahan, 1772. G470

Great Britain. Laws, etc. [An act for explaining and amending an act made in the seventh year of

His present Majesty, intituled, An act for taking off the inland duty of one shilling per pound weight upon all black and singlo teas consumed in Great Britain; and for granting a drawback upon the exportation of teas to Ireland, and the British dominions in America, for a limited time ...] London, Charles Eyre and William Strahan, 1772.   G471

Great Britain. Laws, etc. [An act for the further encouragement of the herring fishery on the coasts of the Isle of Man; and for obviating a doubt which has arisen with respect to the allowing the bounties upon the British white herring fishery.] London, Charles Eyre and William Strahan, 1772.   G472

Great Britain. Laws, etc. [An act to continue for a further time an act, made in the eighth year of His present Majesty's reign, intituled An act to continue and amend an act, made in the fifth year of His present Majesty, intituled, An act for importation of salted beef, pork, bacon, and butter, from Ireland, for a limited time, and for allowing the importation of salted beef, pork, bacon, and butter, from the British dominions in America, for a limited time.] London, Charles Eyre and William Strahan, 1772.   G473

Great Britain. Laws, etc. [An act to continue several laws relating to the allowance upon the exportation of British-made gunpowder; to the giving further encouragement for the importation of naval stores from the British colonies in America; to the further encouraging the manufacture of British sail cloth, and to the duties payable on foreign sail cloth ...] London, Printed by Charles Eyre and William Strahan, 1772.
G474

Great Britain. Laws, etc. A bill for regulating the election of committee men for managing the affairs of the African Company. [London, 1772.]
G475

It is required that proof of financial interest be supplied before membership in the Company of Merchants Trading to Africa could be granted to persons paying the dues of forty shillings.

Great Britain. Laws, etc. [An act for allowing the free importation of rice into this kingdom, from any of His Majesty's colonies in America, for a limited time; and for encouraging the making of starch from rice.] London, Charles Eyre and William Strahan, 1773.   G476

Great Britain. Laws, etc. [An act for allowing the importation of wheat, wheat-flour, Indian corn, Indian meal, biscuit pease, beans, tares, callivancies, and all other sorts of pulse, from His Majesty's colonies in America, into this kingdom, for a limited time, free of duty.] London, Charles Eyre and William Strahan, 1773.   G477

Great Britain. Laws, etc. [An act for allowing the importation of wheat, wheat-flour, rye, ryemeal, barley, barley-meal, oats, oat-meal, pease, beans, tares, callivancies, and all other sorts of pulse from any part of Europe or Africa, into this kingdom, for a limited time, free of duty.] London, Charles Eyre and William Strahan, 1773.   G478

Great Britain. Laws, etc. [An act for establishing certain regulations for the better management of the affairs of the East India Company, as well in India as in Europe.] London, Charles Eyre and William Strahan, 1773.   G479

Great Britain. Laws, etc. [An act for further continuing an act ... for importing salt from Europe in the province of Quebec in America, for a limited time.] London, Charles Eyre and William Strahan, 1773.   G480

Permission to import salt from Europe to Quebec is continued to 1780.

Great Britain. Laws, etc. An act for further continuing two acts, made in the sixth and ninth years of His Majesty's reign for punishing mutiny and desertion, and for the better payment of the Army of their quarters, in His Majesty's dominions in America. London, Charles Eyre and William Strahan, 1773.   G481

Great Britain. Laws, etc. [An act for granting to His Majesty a sum of money to be raised by exchequer bills; and to be advanced and applied in the manner, and upon the terms therein mentioned, for the relief of the United Company of Merchants of England trading to the East Indies.] London, Charles Eyre and William Strahan, 1773.   G482

Great Britain. Laws, etc. An act for the better ascertaining the tonnage and burthen of ships and vessels importing and exporting goods into and from this kingdom ... London, Charles Eyre and William Strahan, 1773.   G483

The act also covers trade in oak, bark, calicoes, and cordage.

Great Britain. Laws, etc. [An act to allow a drawback of the duties of customs on the exportation of tea to any of His Majesty's colonies or plantations in America; to increase the deposit on bohea tea to be sold at the India Company's sales; and to impower the commissioners of the Treasury to grant licences to the East India Company to export tea duty-free.] London, Charles Eyre and William Strahan, 1773.   G484

Great Britain. Laws, etc. [An act to continue and amend an act ... intituled, An act for opening and establishing certain ports in the island of Jamaica and Dominica, for the free importation and exportation of certain goods and merchandises ...] London, Charles Eyre and William Strahan, 1773. G485

Legislation providing for free export of coffee and cocoa from Dominica, a change in import and export duties on slaves in Dominica and Jamaica, and for the export of wood from Dominica.

Great Britain. Laws, etc. [An act to continue for a further time ... An act for importaton of salted beef, pork, bacon, and butter, from Ireland, for a limited time, and for allowing the importation of salted beef, pork, bacon, and butter, from the British dominions in America, for a limited time.] London, Charles Eyre and William Strahan, 1773. G486

Great Britain. Laws, etc. [An act to encourage the subjects of foreign states to lend money upon the security of freehold or leasehold estates, in any of His Majesty's colonies in the West Indies ...] London, Charles Eyre and William Strahan, 1773. G487

The purpose of the legislation was to make available a larger source of capital for the development of the British West Indian colonies.

Great Britain. Laws, etc. [An act to explain two acts of Parliament, one ... for naturalizing such foreign protestants, and others, as are settled, or shall settle, in any of His Majesty's colonies in America; and the other ... for naturalizing such foreign protestants as have served, or shall serve, as officers or soldiers in His Majesty's Royal American Regiment, or as engineers, in America.] London, Charles Eyre and William Strahan, 1773. G488

Great Britain. Laws, etc. [An act to permit the free importation of cod fish, ling, and hake, caught and cured in Chaleur Bay, or any other part of the Gulph of Saint Lawrence, or on the coast of Labrador.] London, Charles Eyre and William Strahan, 1773. G489

Great Britain. Laws, etc. [An act to restrain the East India Company for a limited time, from making any appointment of commissioners for superintending and regulating the Company's affairs, at their presidencies in the East Indies.] London, Charles Eyre and William Strahan, 1773. G490

Great Britain. Laws, etc. [An act for further continuing so much of two acts, made in the sixth and thirteenth years of the reign of His present Majesty, as relates to the opening and establishing certain free ports in the island of Jamaica.] London, Charles Eyre and William Strahan, 1774. G491

Great Britain. Laws, etc. An act for further continuing two acts ... for punishing mutiny and desertion, and for better payment of the Army and their quarters, in ... America. London, Charles Eyre and William Strahan, 1774. G492

Great Britain. Laws, etc. [An act for granting further time to the United Company of Merchants of England, trading to the East Indies, to expose to sale the singlo and bohea teas remaining in their warehouses unsold ... and for allowing the drawbacks on the exportation of such teas.] London, Charles Eyre and William Strahan, 1774. G493

Great Britain. Laws, etc. [An act for making more effectual provision for the government of the province of Quebec in North America.] London, Charles Eyre and William Strahan, 1774. G494

Great Britain. Laws, etc. [An act for reducing the duty payable upon the exportation of gum senega, granted by an act ... (intituled, An act for laying certain duties upon gum senega and gum arabic, imported into or exported from Great Britain, and for confining the exportation of gum senega from Africa to Great Britain only).] London, Charles Eyre and William Strahan, 1774. G495

Great Britain. Laws, etc. [An act for the better providing suitable quarters for officers and soldiers in His Majesty's service in North America.] London, Charles Eyre and William Strahan, 1774. G496

Great Britain. Laws, etc. [An act for the better regulating the government of the province of the Massachuset's Bay, in New England.] London, Charles Eyre and William Strahan, 1774. G497

Great Britain. Laws, etc. [An act for the impartial administration of justice in the cases of persons questioned for any acts done by them in the execution of the law, or for the suppression of riots and tumults, in the province of the Massachuset's Bay, in New England.] London, Charles Eyre and William Strahan, 1774. G498

Great Britain. Laws, etc. [An act to allow the exportation of a limited quantity of wheat-meal or flour, oats, oatmeal, grotts, barley, pease, beans, malt, and biscuit, to Hudson's Bay Company, and their servants residing there.]

London, Charles Eyre and William Strahan, 1774. G499

Great Britain. Laws, etc. [An act to allow the exportation of a limited quantity of biscuit and pease to the island of Newfoundland, for the benefit of the British fishery there.] London, Charles Eyre and William Strahan, 1774. G500

Great Britain. Laws, etc. [An act to allow the exportation of corn, grain, and other articles to His Majesty's sugar colonies in America; and to extend the provisions of an act ... (intituled, An act to regulate the importation and exportation of corn), allowing the exportation of wheat, meal, flour, rye, barley, or malt, to the islands of Guernsey and Jersey ...] London, Charles Eyre and William Strahan, 1774. G501

Great Britain. Laws, etc. [An act to continue for a further time an act, ... intituled, An act for importation of salted beef, pork, bacon, and butter, from Ireland, for a limited time, and for allowing the importation of salted beef, pork, bacon, and butter, from the British dominions in America, for a limited time.] London, Charles Eyre and William Strahan, 1774. G502

Great Britain. Laws, etc. [An act to continue the several laws therein mentioned, for granting liberty to carry rice from His Majesty's provinces of Carolina and Georgia, in America, directly to any part of Europe, southward of Cape Finisterre; for granting the like liberty to export rice from South Carolina and Georgia directly, to any part of America, to the southward of the said provinces ...] London, Charles Eyre and William Strahan, 1774. G503

Great Britain. Laws, etc. [An act to discontinue, in such manner, and for such time as are therein mentioned, the landing and discharging, lading or shipping, of goods, wares, and merchandise, at the town, and within the harbour, of Boston, in the province of Massachuset's Bay, in North America.] London, Charles Eyre and William Strahan, 1774. G504

Great Britain. Laws, etc. [An act to establish a fund towards further defraying the charges of the administration of justice, and support of the civil government within the province of Quebec, in America.] London, Charles Eyre and William Strahan, 1774. G505

Great Britain. Laws, etc. [An act for amending and explaining an act, passed in the fourteenth year of His Majesty's reign, intituled, An act to establish a fund towards further defraying the charges of the administration of justice, and support of the civil government within the province of Quebec, in America.] London, Charles Eyre and William Strahan, 1775. G506

Great Britain. Laws, etc. [An act to continue for a further time an act ... intituled, An act for importation of salted beef, pork, bacon, and butter, from Ireland, for a limited time; and for allowing the importation of salted beef, pork, bacon, and butter, from the British dominions in America, for a limited time; and for extending the provisions of the said acts to potatoes, and all kinds of pulse.] London, Charles Eyre and William Strahan, 1775. G507

Great Britain. Laws, etc. [An act to continue, for a limited time, so much of an act, ... intituled, An act for granting to His Majesty a sum of money, to be raised by exchequer bills, and to be advanced and applied in the manner upon the terms therein mentioned for the relief of the United Company of Merchants of England trading to the East Indies.] London, Charles Eyre and William Strahan, 1775. G508

Great Britain. Laws, etc. [An act to repeal so much of an act, ... intituled, An act to prevent the exportation to foreign parts of utensils made use of in the cotton, linen, wollen, and silk manufactures of this kingdom, as relates to wool cards used in the woollen manufactures of this kingdom, intended to be exported to any of His Majesty's colonies or plantations in America.] London, Charles Eyre and William Strahan, 1775. G509

Great Britain. Laws, etc. [An act to restrain the trade and commerce of the colonies of New Jersey, Pennsylvania, Maryland, Virginia, and South Carolina, to Great Britain, Ireland, and the British islands in the West Indies, under certain conditions and limitations.] London, Charles Eyre and William Strahan, 1775. G510

Great Britain. Laws, etc. [An act to restrain the trade and commerce of the province of Massachuset's Bay and New Hampshire, and colonies of Connecticut, and Rhode Island, and Providence Plantation in North America, to Great Britain, Ireland, and the British Islands in the West Indies; and to prohibit such provinces and colonies from carrying on any fishery on the banks of Newfoundland ...] London, Charles Eyre and William Strahan, 1775. G511

Great Britain. Laws, etc. A bill to restrain the trade and commerce of the colonies of New Jersey, Pensylvania, Maryland, Virginia, and

South Carolina ... under certain conditions and limitations. [London, 1775.] G512
A draft version of the Restraining Act.

Great Britain. Laws, etc. [An act for allowing the exportation of certain quantities of wheat, and other articles, to His Majesty's sugar colonies in America, and to the island of Saint Helena, and to the other settlements belonging to the United Company of Merchants of England trading to the East Indies, and of biscuit and pease to Newfoundland, Nova Scotia, Bay Chaleur and Labrador ...] London, Charles Eyre and William Strahan, 1776. G513

Great Britain. Laws, etc. [An act for giving a publick reward unto such persons ... as shall discover a northern passage.] London, Charles Eyre and William Strahan, 1776. G514
This act was passed in 1774, promising a reward of twenty thousand pounds to any Englishman who might discover a northwest passage, and five thousand pounds for navigating within one degree of the North Pole.

Great Britain. Laws, etc. [An act for granting further time for allowing the drawback upon the exportation of muslins and callicoes, imported by the East India Company in the years one thousand seven hundred and seventy-three, and one thousand seven hundred and seventy-four; for allowing further time to the said company to expose to sale such bohea and singlo teas and coffee as remained unsold on the fifth day of April ...] London, Charles Eyre and William Strahan, 1776. G515

Great Britain. Laws, etc. An act for making perpetual so much of an act, made in the eighth year of his present Majesty's reign ... as related to the importation of salted beef, pork, bacon, and butter from the British dominions in America ... London, Charles Eyre and William Strahan, 1776. G516
An extension of an earlier act relating to the free importation of cattle from Ireland.

Great Britain. Laws, etc. [An act for the further encouragement of the whale fishery carried on from Great Britain and Ireland, and the British dominions in Europe; and for regulating the fees to be taken by the officers of the customs in the island of Newfoundland.] London, Charles Eyre and William Strahan, 1776. G517

Great Britain. Laws, etc. An act to authorise, for a limited time, the punishment by hard labour of offenders who, for certain crimes, are or shall become liable to be transported to any of His Majesty's colonies and plantations. London, Charles Eyre and William Strahan, 1776. G518
Transportation of criminals to the colonies is here being replaced by sentences at hard labor, primarily dredging the Thames River.

Great Britain. Laws, etc. [An act to continue an act made in the last session of Parliament, ... intituled, "An act for punishing mutiny and desertion, and for the better payment of the army and their quarters;" and for extending the provisions of the said act to His Majesty's marine forces in America.] London, Charles Eyre and William Strahan, 1776. G519

Great Britain. Laws, etc. [An act to prohibit all trade and intercourse with the colonies ... during the continuance of the present rebellion ...] London, Charles Eyre and William Strahan, 1776. G520
An embargo upon trade to the rebellious colonies, authorizing capture of American ships and goods at sea, "for the more speedily and effectually suppressing such wicked and daring designs."

Great Britain. Laws, etc. [An act for enabling the commissioners for executing the office of Lord High Admiral of Great Britain, to grant commissions to the commanders of private ships and vessels, employed in trade, or retained in His Majesty's service, to take and make prize of all such ships and vessels, and their cargoes, as are therein mentioned, for a limited time.] London, Charles Eyre and William Strahan, 1777. G521

Great Britain. Laws, etc. An act for rendering more effectual an act made in the fourteenth year of the reign of His present Majesty, for promoting the discovery of a method for finding the longitude at sea ... London, Charles Eyre and William Strahan, 1777. G522
This act reflects continued interest in perfection of instruments useful in determining longitude at sea.

Great Britain. Laws, etc. [An act for repealing the eleventh rule in the Book of Rates, so far as the same relates to making any allowance upon the importation of damaged currants and raisins, and for making the importer of such goods an abatement in the duties in lieu thereof ...] London, Charles Eyre and William Strahan, 1777. G523

Great Britain. Laws, etc. [An act to amend so much of an act, made in the thirteenth year of the reign of His present Majesty, (intituled An act for establishing certain regulations for the better management of the affairs of the East India Company, as well in India as in Europe), as relates to the day on which the annual elections of directors of the said Company is to be made.] London, Charles Eyre and William Strahan, 1777. G524

Great Britain. Laws, etc. [An act to continue the several laws therein mentioned, relating to encouraging the making of indico in the British plantations in America; to the registering the prices at which corn is sold in the several counties of Great Britain, and the quantity exported and imported; to encouraging the manufacturing of leather ...] London, Charles Eyre and William Strahan, 1777. G525

Great Britain. Laws, etc. [An act to prevent the clandestine unshipping from and receiving goods at sea on board vessels employed in the East India Company's service.] London, Charles Eyre and William Strahan, 1777. G526

Great Britain. Laws, etc. [An act to revive and continue such part of an act, made in the last session of Parliament, intituled, An act for allowing the exportation of certain quantities of wheat, and other articles, to His Majesty's sugar colonies in America, and to the island of Saint Helena ...] London, Charles Eyre and William Strahan, 1777. G527

Great Britain. Laws, etc. [An act for allowing the exportation of certain quantities of wheat-flour, biscuit, and pease, to Newfoundland, Nova Scotia, Bay Chaleur, and Labrador.] London, Charles Eyre and William Strahan, 1778. G528

Great Britain. Laws, etc. [An act for removing all doubts and apprehensions concerning taxation by the Parliament of Great Britain in any of the colonies, and plantations in North America and the West Indies; and for repealing so much of an act, ... as imposes a duty on tea imported from Great Britain into any colony or plantation in America, or relates thereto.] London, Charles Eyre and William Strahan, 1778. G529

Great Britain. Laws, etc. [An act for repealing an act, passed in the fourteenth year of His present Majesty's reign,intituled, An act for the better regulating the government of the province of the Massachusetts Bay in New England.] London, Charles Eyre and William Strahan, 1778. G530

Great Britain. Laws, etc. [An act to enable His Majesty to appoint commissioners with sufficient powers to treat, consult, and agree upon the means of quieting the disorders now subsisting in certain of the colonies, plantations, and provinces of North America.] London, Charles Eyre and William Strahan, 1778. G531

Great Britain. Laws, etc. [An act to explain and amend so much of an act, made in the fourth year of the reign of His present Majesty, as relates to the preventing the clandestine conveyance of sugar and paneles from the British colonies and plantations in America into Great Britain.] London, Charles Eyre and William Strahan, 1778. G532

Great Britain. Laws, etc. [An act to permit the exportation of certain goods, directly from Ireland, into any British plantation in America, or any British settlement on the coast of Africa; and for further encouraging the fisheries and navigation of Ireland.] London, Charles Eyre and William Strahan, 1778. G533

Great Britain. Laws, etc. An act to repeal such part of an act, made in the last session of Parliament, as relates to the manner of discharging bonds given for the due exportation of certain goods from Great Britain to foreign parts; and to extend such part of the same act, as obliges the master of British or Irish ships, sailing from any of His Majesty's dominions into the Baltic, to deliver a manifest of their cargoes to the British Consul ... London, Charles Eyre and William Strahan, 1778. G534

Great Britain. Laws, etc. An act for continuing in the possession of the United Company of Merchants of England trading to the East Indies, for a limited time, and under certain conditions, the territorial acquisitions and revenues lately obtained in the East Indies. [London, 1779.] G535

Great Britain. Laws, etc. An act for discontinuing the duties on cottonwool, the growth and product of the British colonies or plantations in America, exported from this kingdom. [London, 1779.] G536

Great Britain. Laws, etc. An act for further continuing an act ... intituled, an act to impower his Majesty to secure and detain persons charged with, or suspected of, the high crime of treason, committed in ... America ... or the crime of piracy. London, Charles Eyre and William Strahan, 1779. G537

The act is extended for one year, to January 1, 1780.

Great Britain. Laws, etc. An act for granting a drawback of the duties, imposed by an act of the last session of Parliament, upon all foreign wines exported from Great Britain to any British colony or plantation in America or to any British settlement in the East Indies. [London, 1779.] G538

Great Britain. Laws, etc. An act for taking off the duty upon all salt used in the curing of pilchards, and laying a proportional duty upon all pilchards consumed at home only. [London, 1779.] G539

Great Britain. Laws, etc. An act for taking off the duty upon all salt used in the curing of pilchards, and laying a proportional duty upon all pilchards consumed at home only. London, Charles Eyre and William Strahan, 1779. G540

Great Britain. Laws, etc. An act to continue and amend an act, made in the eleventh year of His present Majesty's reign, intituled, An act for the encouragement of the white herring fishery. [London, 1779.] G541

Great Britain. Laws, etc. An act to continue several laws relating to the giving further encouragement for the importation of naval stores from the British colonies in America, to the landing of rum or spirits of the British sugar plantations before payment of the duties of excise; to the discontinuing the duties payable upon the importation of tallow, hogs lard, and grease ... [London, 1779.] G542

Great Britain. Laws, etc. An act to explain so much of an act ... intituled, An act for the encouraging and encreasing of shipping and navigation, as relates to the importation into this kingdom, and other His Majesty's dominions, or goods and commodities of the growth or production of Africa, Asia, or America. [London, 1779.] G543

Great Britain. Laws, etc. An act to repeal so much of several acts of Parliament, as prohibit the growth and produce of tobacco in Ireland; and to permit the importation of tobacco of the growth and produce of that kingdom into Great Britain, under the like duties and regulations as tobacco of the growth of the British colonies in America is permitted to be imported. [London, 1779.] G544

Great Britain. Laws, etc. An act for continuing in the possession of the United Company of Merchants of England trading to the East Indies, for a futher time, and under certain conditions, the territorial acquisitions and revenues lately obtained in the East Indies ... [London, 1780.] G545

Great Britain. Laws, etc. An act for continuing the encouragement and reward of persons making certain discoveries for finding the longitude at sea ... London, Charles Eyre and William Strahan, 1780. G546
  This act reflects continued interest in perfection of instruments useful in determining longitude at sea.

Great Britain. Laws, etc. An act for extending the provisions of two acts, made in the eighteenth year of His present Majesty's reign, and in the last session of Parliament, with respect to bringing prize goods into this kingdom, to Spanish prize goods; and for repealing so much of the said last-mentioned act as relates to the certificates for prize tea and East India goods exported from this kingdom to Ireland ... [London, 1780.] G547

Great Britain. Laws, etc. An act for further continuing an act ... intituled, An act to impower His Majesty to secure and detain persons charged with, or suspected of ... High treason ... or the crime of piracy. London, Charles Eyre and William Strahan, 1780. G548
  The act is continued to 1 January 1782.

Great Britain. Laws, etc. An act for granting further time for allowing the drawback on the exportation of coffee imported by the East India Company, in the ship Europa, in the year one thousand seven hundred and seventy-five. [London, 1780.] G549

Great Britain. Laws, etc. An act to admit to an entry in this kingdom, under certain restrictions, tobacco imported not directly from the place of its growth or produce, and for granting an additional duty on such tobacco, during the present hostilities. [London, 1780.] G550

Great Britain. Laws, etc. An act to allow the exportation of provisions ... to certain towns, ports, or places, in North America. London, Charles Eyre and William Strahan, 1780. G551
  Permits trade in certain American ports certified by one of the secretaries of state to be under British protection.

Great Britain. Laws, etc. An act to allow the trade between Ireland and the British colonies and plantations ... London, Charles Eyre and William Strahan, 1780. G552
  This law restores Ireland's right to ship and receive goods to or from any of the British colonies.

Great Britain. Laws, etc. An act to amend an act ... as relates to the preventing the clandestine conveyance of sugar and paneles ... into Great Britain. London, Charles Eyre and William Strahan, 1780. G553
  The amendment allows for a wider degree of discretion on the part of customs officials in permitting the entry of sugar.

Great Britain. Laws, etc. An act to continue several laws relating to the better securing the lawful trade of His Majesty's subjects to and from the East Indies, and for the more effectual preventing all His Majesty's subjects trading thither under foreign commissions; to the importing salt from Europe into the province of Quebec in America ... [London, 1780.] G554

Great Britain. Laws, etc. An act to explain and amend two acts made in the fifteenth and sixteenth years of the reign of His present Majesty, with respect to the limits of the Greenland seas and Davis's Streights, and the seas adjacent thereto; and to enlarge the time for the return of the vessels employed in the whale fisheries. [London, 1780.] G555

Great Britain. Laws, etc. An act to repeal certain acts made in Great Britain, which restrain the trade and commerce of Ireland with foreign parts. London, Charles Eyre and William Strahan, 1780. G556
Restraints on the export of a variety of cloths, spiritous liquors and glass are removed.

Great Britain. Laws, etc. An act for continuing the encouragement and reward of persons making certain discoveries for finding the longitude at sea ... London, Charles Eyre and William Strahan, 1781. G557
This act reflects continued interest in perfection of instruments useful in determining longitude at sea.

Great Britain. Laws, etc. An act for establishing an agreement with the United Company of Merchants of England trading to the East Indies, for the payment of the sum of four hundred thousand pounds, for the use of the publick, in full discharge and satisfaction of all claims and demands of the publick from the time the bond debt of the said company was reduced to one million five hundred thousand pounds ... [London, 1781.] G558

Great Britain. Laws, etc. An act to explain and amend an act made in the eighth and ninth years of the reign of King William the Third, (intituled, An act for the lessening the duty upon tin and pewter exported, and granting an equivalent for the same by a duty upon drugs), so far as the same relates to the importation of drugs from the Russian dominions ... [London, 1781.] G559

Great Britain. Laws, etc. An act to explain and amend so much of an act, made in the thirteenth year of the reign of His present Majesty, intituled, An act for establishing certain regulations for the better management of the affairs of the East India Company, as well in India as in Europe, as relates to the administration of justice in Bengal ... [London, 1781.] G560

Great Britain. Laws, etc. An act for allowing the importation of goods of the growth, produce or manufacture, of the islands of Saint Christopher, Nevis, and Montserrat, into any ports of His Majesty's dominions ... London, Charles Eyre and William Strahan, 1782. G561
The islands named, lately occupied by French forces, are given the same rights to export to Great Britain as other West Indian islands.

Great Britain. Laws, etc. An act for granting an additional bounty on ships employed in the Greenland and whale fishery, for a limited time. [London, 1782.] G562

Great Britain. Laws, etc. An act for granting an additional duty upon tobacco and snuff; and for repealing certain duties payable upon the importation of brandy and arrack and for granting other duties in lieu thereof. [London, 1782.] G563

Great Britain. Laws, etc. An act to continue several laws therein mentioned, relating to the better encouragement of the making of sail cloth in Great Britain; to the encouragement of the silk manufactures; and for taking off several duties on merchandize exported, and reducing other duties; to the free importation of cochineal and indico ... [London, 1782.] G564

Great Britain. Laws, etc. An act to discharge and indemnify the United Company of Merchants of England trading to the East Indies, from all damage, interests, and losses, in respect to their having made default in certain payments due to the publick, on such payments being made at a future stipulated time; and to enable the said company to continue a dividend of eight pounds per centum to the proprietors of their stock for the present year. [London, 1782.] G565

Great Britain. Laws, etc. An act to enable His Majesty to conclude a peace or truce with certain colonies in North America therein mentioned. [London, 1782.] G566

Great Britain. Laws, etc. An act to extend so much of two acts, of the twentieth and twenty-first years of His present Majesty's reign, as relates to the sale of, and ascertaining the duties upon, East India goods, to tea, and all other goods of the growth, product, or manufacture of China, or any country within the limits of the East India Company's charter ... [London, 1782.] G567

Great Britain. Laws, etc. An act ... for vesting the fort of Senegal, and its dependencies, in the Company of Merchants trading to Africa ... [London, 1783.] G568

Great Britain. Laws, etc. An act for allowing the importation of rice, paddy, Indian corn, Indian meal, and maize, free from duty, for a limited time. London, Charles Eyre and William Strahan, 1783.　　　　　　　　　　G569

Great Britain. Laws, etc. An act for granting relief to the United Company of Merchants of England trading to the East Indies, by allowing further time for payment of certain sums due, and to become due to the publick, and by advancing to the said company, on the terms therein mentioned, a certain sum of money to be raised by loans or exchequer bills ... [London, 1783.]　　　　　　　　　　G570

Great Britain. Laws, etc. An act for preventing certain instruments from being required from ships belonging to the United States of America; and to give to His Majesty, for a limited time, certain powers for the better carrying on trade and commerce between the subjects of His Majesty's dominions and the inhabitants of the said United States. [London, 1783.]　G571

Great Britain. Laws, etc. An act for the further encouraging the growth of coffee and cocoa nuts, in His Majesty's islands and plantations in America. [London, 1783.]　　　　　G572

Great Britain. Laws, etc. An act to allow the drawback of the whole duty of customs upon the exportation of rice. London, Charles Eyre and William Strahan, 1783.　　　　　　G573

Great Britain. Laws, etc. An act to amend an act ... intituled, An act for the more effectual securing the duties upon tobacco; to prohibit the importation of currants into Great Britain in small packages ... [London, 1783.]　　G574

Great Britain. Laws, etc. An act to continue several laws, relating to the regulating the fees of officers of the customs and naval officers in America ... London, Charles Eyre and Wiliam Strahan, 1783.　　　　　　　　　G575
　The act also concerns the export of wheat, pipe clay, and potash to the British West Indies.

Great Britain. Laws, etc. An act to discharge and indemnify the United Company of Merchants of England trading to the East Indies, from all damages, interest, and losses, in respect to their not making regular payment of certain sums due, and to become due, to the publick, and to allow further time for such payment; and to enable the company to borrow a certain sum of money ... [London, 1783.]　　　　　　　G576

Great Britain. Laws, etc. An act to repeal so much of two acts, made in the sixteenth and seventeenth years of the reign of His present Majesty, as prohibits trade and intercourse with the United States of America. [London, 1783.]　　　　　　　　　　　　　　G577

Great Britain. Laws, etc. An act for facilitating the trade and intercourse between this kingdom and the United States of America. Dublin, Executors of David Hay, 1784.　　G578
　A revocation of the many restrictions upon American shipping in Great Britain.

Great Britain. Laws, etc. An act for further continuing, for a limited time, an act ... intituled, An act for preventing certain instruments from being required from ships belonging to the United States of America; and to give to His Majesty, for a limited time, certain powers for the better carrying on trade and commerce between the subjects of His Majesty's dominions, and the inhabitants of the said United States. [London, 1784.]　　　　　　　　　　　　　　G579

Great Britain. Laws, etc. An act for granting to His Majesty certain rates and duties upon bricks and tiles made in Great Britain; and for laying additional duties on bricks and tiles imported into the same. London, Charles Eyre and William Strahan, 1784.　　　　　G580

Great Britain. Laws, etc. An act for regulating and extending the tobacco trade, and for granting to His Majesty, his heirs and successors, the duties therein mentioned. Dublin, Executors of David Hay, 1784.　　　　　　　　G581
　The law provides for the taxing, warehousing, and distribution of tobacco in Ireland.

Great Britain. Laws, etc. An act for the better regulation and management of the affairs of the East India Company, and of the British possessions in India. London, Charles Eyre and William Strahan, 1784.　　　　　G582

Great Britain. Laws, etc. An act to continue, for a limited time, an act made in the last session of Parliament, intituled, An act for preventing certain instruments from being required from ships belonging to the United States of America; and to give to His Majesty, for a limited time, certain powers for the better carrying on trade and commerce between the subjects of His Majesty's dominions, and the inhabitants of the said United States. [London, 1784.]　　G583

Great Britain. Laws, etc. An act to continue so much of an act made in the last session of Parliament, as allows further time for the payment of certain sums due, and to become due to the publick, from the United Company of Merchants of England trading to the East Indies. [London, 1784.]   G584

Great Britain. Laws, etc. An act to extend the powers of an act ... for giving His Majesty certain powers for the better carrying on trade and commerce between ... His Majesty's dominions and ... the United States of America ... London, Charles Eyre and William Strahan, 1784.   G585

The act also covers trade in certain items from the Baltic Sea area.

Great Britain. Laws, etc. An act to revive and continue several laws, relating to the allowing the exportation of certain quantities of wheat and other articles, to His Majesty's sugar colonies in America. London, Charles Eyre and William Strahan, 1784.   G586

Great Britain. Laws, etc. An act for appointing commissioners further to enquire into the losses and services of all such persons who have suffered in their rights, properties, and professions, during the late unhappy dissentions in America, in consequence of their loyalty to His Majesty, and attachment to the British government. [London, 1785.]   G587

Great Britain. Laws, etc. An act for confining, for a limited time, the trade between the ports of the United States of America, and His Majesty's subjects in the island of Newfoundland, to bread, flour, and livestock, to be imported in none but British-built ships ... London, Charles Eyre and William Strahan, 1785.   G588

Great Britain. Laws, etc. An act for further continuing, for a limited time, an act ... intituled, An act for preventing certain instruments from being required from ships belonging to the United States of America; and to give to His Majesty, for a limited time, certain powers for the better carrying on trade and commerce between the subjects of His Majesty's dominions, and the inhabitants of the said United States ... [London, 1785.]   G589

Great Britain. Laws, etc. An act for the better securing the duties payable on tobacco. [London, 1785.]   G590

Great Britain. Laws, etc. An act to repeal the duties upon flasks in which Florence wine and oil is imported; to permit the importation of wines in small casks for private use; to revive, continue, and amend so much of an act made in the sixteenth year of His present Majesty, as allows the exportation of certain quantities of wheat, and other articles, to His Majesty's sugar colonies in America; for disallowing the drawback on the exportation of snuff; for continuing the permission to land rum or spirits of the British sugar plantations ... [London, 1785.]   G591

Great Britain. Laws, etc. An act for appointing commissioners further to enquire into the losses and services of all such persons who have suffered in their rights, properties, and professions, during the late unhappy dissentions in America, in consequence of their loyalty to His Majesty, and attachment to the British government. [London, 1786.]   G592

Great Britain. Laws, etc. An act for appointing commissioners to enquire into the losses of all such persons who have suffered in their properties, in consequence of the cession of the province of East Florida to the king of Spain. [London, 1786.]   G593

Great Britain. Laws, etc. An act for better securing the duties on starch, and for preventing frauds on the said duties. London, C. Eyre and the executors of W. Strahan, 1786.   G594

Great Britain. Laws, etc. An act for confining, for a limited time, the trade between the ports of the United States of America, and His Majesty's subjects in the island of Newfoundland, to bread, flour, Indian corn, and live stock, to be imported in none but British-built ships ... London, C. Eyre and the executors of W. Strahan, 1786.   G595

Great Britain. Laws, etc. An act for further continuing, for a limited time, an act ... intituled, An act for preventing certain instruments from being required from ships belonging to the United States of America; and to give to His Majesty, for a limited time, certain powers for the better carrying on trade and commerce between the subjects of His Majesty's dominions and the inhabitants of the said United States ... [London, 1786.]   G596

Great Britain. Laws, etc. An act for obviating all doubts which have arisen, or might arise, with respect to the exclusive power of the court of directors of the East India Company to nominate and appoint the governor general and council of the presidency of Fort William in Bengal. [London, 1786.]   G597

Great Britain. Laws, etc. An act for the encouragement of the southern whale fishery. [London, 1786.]   G598

Great Britain. Laws, etc. An act for the further regulation of the trial of persons accused of certain offenses committed in the East Indies; for repealing so much of an act, ... (intituled, An act for the better regulation and management of the affairs of the East India Company, and of the British possessions in India ...) [London, 1786.]
G599

Great Britain. Laws, etc. An act for the further support and encouragement of the fisheries carried on in the Greenland seas and Davis's Streights. London, C. Eyre and the executors of W. Strahan, 1786.
G600

Detailed regulations upon ships engaged in whaling in Greenland waters, enabling them to qualify for the bounty of thirty pounds per ton of shipping.

Great Britain. Laws, etc. An act for the more effectual encouragement of the British fisheries. [London, 1786.]
G601

Great Britain. Laws, etc. [An act to amend and render more effectual the several laws now in force for encouraging the fisheries carried on at Newfoundland, and parts adjacent ...] London, C. Eyre and the executors of W. Strahan, 1786.
G602

Detailed regulations for the conduct of the fisheries of the Grand Banks of Newfoundland.

Great Britain. Laws, etc. An act to continue several laws relating to the giving further encouragement to the importation of naval stores from the British colonies in America; to the allowance upon the exportation of British made gunpowder; to the further encouraging the manufacture of British sail cloth; and to the duties payable on foreign sail cloth ... [London, 1786.]
G603

Great Britain. Laws, etc. [An act to continue several laws relating to the giving further encouragement to the importation of naval stores from the British colonies in America ...] London, C. Eyre and the executors of W. Strahan, 1786.
G604

The legislation covers regulations upon the trade in naval stores, gunpowder, sail cloth, sugar, salt, tallow and lard, goat skins, potash, grain, flax, cotton and rum.

Great Britain. Laws, etc. An act to enable the East India Company to raise money by a sale of annuities, and by increasing their capital stock. [London, 1786.]
G605

Great Britain. Laws, etc. An act to explain and amend certain provisions of an act, made in the twenty-fourth year of the reign of His present Majesty, respecting the better regulation and management of the affairs of the East India Company. [London, 1786.]
G606

Great Britain. Laws, etc. A collection of statutes concerning the incorporation, trade, and commerce of the East India Company. London, C. Eyre and S. Strahan, 1786.
G607

Great Britain. Laws, etc. An act for amending an act made in the twenty-sixth year of His present Majesty's reign, for the encouragement of the southern whale fishery; and for making further provisions for that purpose. [London, 1787.]
G608

Great Britain. Laws, etc. An act for appointing commissioners further to enquire into the losses and services of all such persons who have suffered in their rights, properties, and professions, during the late unhappy dissention in America, in consequence of their loyalty to His Majesty, and attachment to the British government. [London, 1787.]
G609

Great Britain. Laws, etc. An act for appointing commissioners further to enquire into the losses of all such persons who have suffered in their properties, in consequence of the cession of the province of East Florida to the king of Spain. [London, 1787.]
G610

Great Britain. Laws, etc. An act for giving relief to such persons as have suffered in their rights and properties, during the late unhappy dissentions in America, in consequence of their loyalty to His Majesty, and attachment to the British government; and for making compensation to such persons as have suffered in their properties, in consequence of the cession of the province of East Florida to the king of Spain. [London, 1787.]
G611

Great Britain. Laws, etc. An act to continue several laws, relating to the free importation of certain raw hides and skins from Ireland and the British plantations in America; to the allowing the exportation of certain quantities of wheat and other articles to His Majesty's sugar colonies in America ... [London, 1787.]
G612

Great Britain. Laws, etc. An act to continue the laws now in force for regulating the trade between ... His Majesty's dominions, and ... United States of America ... London, Charles Eyre and Andrew Strahan, 1787.
G613

Concerns restrictions on trade between the United States and the British West Indies.

Great Britain. Laws, etc. An act to enable His Majesty to make such regulations as may be necessary to prevent the inconvenience which might arise from the competition of His Majesty's subjects and those of the most Christian king, in carrying on the fishery on the coasts of the island of Newfoundland. [London, 1787.] G614

Great Britain. Laws, etc. An act to extend the provisions of an act ... intituled, An act for the more effectual encouragement of the British fisheries. [London, 1787.] G615

Great Britain. Laws, etc. An act for amending an act ... for the encouragement of the southern whale fishery: and for making further provisions for that purpose. London, Charles Eyre and Andrew Strahan, 1788. G616

The act concerns whaling vessels sailing into the South Pacific Ocean which would require license from the East India Company, bounties to be paid to whalers in this area and the licensing of foreign ships sailing from British ports.

Great Britain. Laws, etc. An act for appointing commissioners further to enquire into the losses of all such persons who have suffered in their properties, in consequence of the cession of the Province of East Florida to the King of Spain. London, Charles Eyre and Andrew Strahan, 1788. G617

The act includes provisions for administering claims of landholders.

Great Britain. Laws, etc. An act for regulating the trade between the subjects of His Majesty's colonies and plantations in North America, and in the West India islands, and the countries belonging to the United States of America; and between His Majesty's said subjects and the foreign islands in the West Indies. [London, 1788.] G618

Great Britain. Laws, etc. An act for removing any doubt respecting the power of the commissioners for the affairs of India, to direct that the expence of raising, transporting, and maintaining such troops as may be judged necessary for the security of the British territories and possessions in the East Indies should be defrayed out of the revenues arising from the said territories ... [London, 1788.] G619

Great Britain. Laws, etc. An act for repealing the duties on buck or deer skins undressed, buck or deer skins Indian half-dressed, and elk skins undressed ... London, Charles Eyre and Andrew Strahan, 1788. G620

The act covers duties on a variety of skins and hides, cloth, soap, and alcoholic beverages.

Great Britain. Laws, etc. An act to continue the laws now in force for regulating the trade between the subjects of His Majesty's dominions and the inhabitants of ... the United States of America. [London, 1788.] G621

Great Britain. Laws, etc. An act to enable the East India Company to borrow a further sum of money upon bond. [London, 1788.] G622

Great Britain. Laws, etc. An act for allowing the like drawback on teas, exported to the islands of Guernsey and Jersey, and to Gibraltar, and other places on the continent of Europe, and to Africa as is now allowed on teas exported to Ireland or America. [London, 1789.] G623

Great Britain. Laws, etc. An act for appointing commissioners further to enquire into the losses and services of all such persons who have suffered in their rights, properties, and professions, during the late unhappy dissentions in America, in consequence of their loyalty to His Majesty, and attachment to the British government. [London, 1789.] G624

Great Britain. Laws, etc. An act for explaining and amending an act ... intituled An act for regulating the trade between the subjects of His Majesty's colonies and plantations in North America, and in the West India islands, and the countries belonging to the United States of America; and between His Majesty's said subjects and the foreign islands in the West Indies. [London, 1789.] G625

Great Britain. Laws, etc. An act for granting further time for allowing the drawback upon the exportation of coffee, imported by the East India Company, in the ship Lord Camden, in the year one thousand seven hundred and eighty-six. [London, 1789.] G626

Great Britain. Laws, etc. An act for repealing the duties on tobacco and snuff; and for granting new duties in lieu thereof. [London, 1789.] G627

Great Britain. Laws, etc. An act to continue ... and amend an act ... intituled, An act to regulate ... the shipping and carrying slaves in British vessels from the Coast of Africa. London, Charles Eyre and Andrew Strahan, 1789. G628

Great Britain. Laws, etc. An act to continue the laws now in force for regulating the trade between the subjects of His Majesty's dominions and the inhabitants of the territories belonging to the United States of America, so far as the same relate to the trade and commerce carried on between this kingdom and the inhabitants of the countries belonging to the said United States. London, Charles Eyre and Andrew Strahan, 1789. G629

Great Britain. Laws, etc. An act to enable His Majesty to authorise, in case of necessity, the importation of bread, flour, Indian corn, and live stock, from any of the territories belonging to the United States of America, into the province of Quebec, and all the countries bordering on the gulf of Saint Lawrence, and the islands within the said gulf, and to the coast of Labrador. [London, 1789.]   G630

Great Britain. Laws, etc. An act to enable the East India Company to raise money by further increasing their capital stock. [London, 1789.]   G631

Great Britain. Laws, etc. An act for encouraging new settlers in His Majesty's colonies and plantations in America. [London, 1790.]   G632
An inducement for United States citizens to emigrate to Quebec, Nova Scotia, and Bermuda.

Great Britain. Laws, etc. An act for giving relief to such persons as have suffered in their rights and properties, during the late unhappy dissentions in America, in consequence of their loyalty to His Majesty, and attachment to the British government; for making compensation to persons who furnished provisions, or other necessary articles, to the army or navy in America during the war ... [London, 1790.]   G633

Great Britain. Laws, etc. An act for laying a duty on the importation, from any of the provinces in North America, of rape seed, and all other seeds used for extracting oil; and for allowing the importation from the said provinces of rape cakes, or cakes made of rape seed used for manure, duty-free. [London, 1790.]   G634

Great Britain. Laws, etc. An act for permitting the importation of cashew gum from His Majesty's West India islands. London, Charles Eyre and Andrew Strahan, 1790.   G635

Great Britain. Laws, etc. An act to amend two acts ... the one ... for regulating the trade between the subjects of His Majesty's colonies and plantations in North America, and in the West India islands, and the countries belonging to the United States of America; and between His Majesty's said subjects and the foreign islands in the West Indies; and the other ... to allow the importation of rum ... into the province of Quebec. [London, 1790.]   G636

Great Britain. Laws, etc. An act to continue the laws now in force for regulating the trade between the subjects of His Majesty's dominions and the inhabitants of the territories belonging to the United States of America, so far as the same relate to the trade and commerce carried on between this kingdom and the inhabitants of the countries belonging to the said United States. [London, 1790.]   G637

Great Britain. Laws, etc. An act to exempt goods and chattels imported from the settlement of Yucatan in South America, and sold by auction in Great Britain, from the duty imposed on such sales; and for allowing a drawback of the duties on goods exported to Yucatan. [London, 1790.]   G638

Great Britain. Laws, etc. An act to explain and amend an act, made in the last session of Parliament, intituled, An act for repealing the duties on tobacco and snuff, and for granting new duties in lieu thereof. [London, 1790.]   G639

Great Britain. Laws, etc. An act for altering and amending so much of an act ... intituled, An act for removing any doubt respecting the power of the Commissioners for the Affairs of India, to direct that the expense of raising, transporting, and maintaining, such troops as may be judged necessary for the security of the British territories and possessions in the East Indies ... [London, 1791.]   G640

Great Britain. Laws, etc. An act for establishing a company for carrying on trade between the kingdom of Great Britain and the coasts, harbours, and countries of Africa; and for enabling the said company to hold, by grant from His Majesty, his heirs and successors, and from the native princes of Africa, a certain district of land, commonly called the peninsula of Sierra Leone ... [London, 1791.]   G641

Great Britain. Laws, etc. An act for establishing a court of civil jurisdiction in the island of Newfoundland, for a limited time. [London, 1791.]   G642
The provision for a court was necessitated by conflicts growing out of the fishing trade there.

Great Britain. Laws, etc. An act for granting to His Majesty an additional duty on sugar imported into this kingdom. [London, 1791.]   G643

Great Britain. Laws, etc. An act for removing any doubt respecting the sale or mortgage of annuities, pursuant to an act made in the twenty-sixth year of the reign of His present Majesty, intituled, An act to enable the East India Company to raise money by sale of annuities, and by increasing their capital stock. [London, 1791.]   G644

Great Britain. Laws, etc. An act to continue several laws, relating to the granting a bounty on certain species of British and Irish linens exported ... . London, Charles Eyre and Andrew Strahan, 1791. G645
   The act also concerns the iron, cordage, salt, whaling, and leather industries.

Great Britain. Laws, etc. An act to continue the laws now in force for regulating the trade between ... His Majesty's dominions and ... the United States of America. London, Charles Eyre and Andrew Strahan, 1791. G646
   This act extends regulations upon trade which were originally enacted in 1783.

Great Britain. Laws, etc. An act to prevent other ships than those laden with tobacco from mooring and discharging their lading at the places appointed by an act, ... intituled, An act for repealing the duties on tobacco and snuff, and for granting new duties in lieu thereof; to prohibit the exportation of damaged or mean tobacco; and for permitting the importation of tobacco and snuff into the port of Newcastle upon Tyne. [London, 1791.] G647

Great Britain. Laws, etc. An act to repeal certain parts of an act, passed in the fourteenth year of His Majesty's reign, intituled, An act for making more effectual provision for the government of the province of Quebec, in North America; and to make further provisions for the government of the said province. [London, 1791.] G648

Great Britain. Laws, etc. An act for establishing courts of judicature in the island of Newfoundland, and the islands adjacent. [London, 1792.] G649
   Legislation providing for the civil and criminal courts in Newfoundland.

Great Britain. Laws, etc. An act for regulating the allowance of the drawback and payment of the bounty on the exportation of sugar; and for permitting the importation of sugar and coffee into the Bahama and Bermuda islands, in foreign ships. [London, 1792.] G650

Great Britain. Laws, etc. An act for repealing certain regulations with respect to certificates on exporting tea to Ireland or America. [London, 1792.] G651

Great Britain. Laws, etc. An act to continue and amend several laws relating to the encouragement of the fisheries carried on in the Greenland seas and Davis's Streights; and to amend the laws now in force for the encouragement of the fisheries carried on in the seas to the southward of the Greenland seas and Davis's Streights. [London, 1792.] G652

Great Britain. Laws, etc. An act to continue the laws now in force for regulating the trade between the subjects of His Majesty's dominions and the inhabitants of the territories belonging to the United States of America, so far as the same relate to the trade and commerce carried on between this kingdom and the inhabitants of the countries belonging to the said United States. [London, 1792.] G653

Great Britain. Laws, etc. An act to extend and render more effectual an act ... intituled, An act for enlarging and regulating the trade into the Levant seas. [London, 1792.] G654

Great Britain. Laws, etc. An act to allow to ships carrying on the southern whale fishery to the north of the equator the same premium as they are now entitled to if they do not pass the equator. London, Charles Eyre and Andrew Strahan, 1793. G655
   The act enlarges the scope for Pacific Ocean whaling to British whalers.

Great Britain. Laws, etc. An act to continue the laws now in force regulating the trade between the subjects of His Majesty's dominions and the inhabitants of ... the United States of America, so far as the same relate to the trade and commerce carried on ... London, Charles Eyre and Andrew Strahan, 1793. G656
   Legislation continuing earlier laws dating back to 1783.

Great Britain. Laws, etc. An act for allowing vessels employed in the Greenland and whale fishery to complete their full number of men, at certain ports, for a limited time. [London, 1794.] G657

Great Britain. Laws, etc. An act to continue an act, made in the last session of Parliament, for establishing courts of judicature in the island of Newfoundland ... [London, 1794.] G658
   In addition to the purpose indicated, this legislation renews laws covering taking prize ships at sea, encouragement of indigo cultivation, customs regulations and the whaling industry.

Great Britain. Laws, etc. An act to continue the laws now in force for regulating the trade between the subjects of His Majesty's dominions and the inhabitants of the territories belonging to the United States of America, so far as the same relate to the trade and commerce carried on between this kingdom and the inhabitants of the countries belonging to the said United States. [London, 1794.] G659

Great Britain. Laws, etc. An act for allowing ... the importation of goods from India and China, and other parts within the exclusive trade of the East India Company, in ships not of British-built, nor registered as such; and for the exportation of goods from Great Britain by the same ships, under certain restrictions. [London, 1795.]
G660

Great Britain. Laws, etc. An act for allowing bounties, for a limited time, on the importation into Great Britain of any wheat, wheat flour, Indian corn, Indian meal, or rye, in British ships. London, George Eyre and Andrew Strahan, 1795.
G661

Great Britain. Laws, etc. An act for allowing further time for the payment of the drawback on china ware, imported by the East India Company before the first day of April one thousand seven hundred and ninety-five. [London, 1795.] G662

Great Britain. Laws, etc. An act for charging warehouse rent on wines, in certain cases, secured in His Majesty's warehouses; for equalizing the duties on wines exported to India and China; and for providing warehouses for coffee and cocoa nuts imported into this kingdom. [London, 1795.]
G663

Great Britain. Laws, etc. An act for further continuing an act, made in the thirty-third year of the reign of His present Majesty, intituled, An act for establishing courts of judicature in the island of Newfoundland, and the islands adjacent. [London, 1795.] G664
The continuation of the law is for one year.

Great Britain. Laws, etc. An act for further encouraging and regulating the southern whale fisheries. London, George Eyre and Andrew Strahan, 1795. G665
This legislation contains forty-one provisions concerning premiums to be paid to whalers, numbers of ships qualifying, the use of apprentices on board, keeping of log books, licensing of ships by the South Sea Company and the East India Company, participation of foreign whalers, protection of skilled whalers against impressment, etc.

Great Britain. Laws, etc. An act for the encouragement of the mackarel fishery. [London, 1795.]
G666

Great Britain. Laws, etc. An act to amend an act ... intituled, An act for regulating the allowance of the drawback, and payment of the bounty, on the exportation of sugar; and for permitting the importation of sugar and coffee into the Bahama and Bermuda islands in foreign ships; and for reducing the bounty on refined sugars exported in any other than British ships. [London, 1795.]
G667

Great Britain. Laws, etc. An act to continue and amend ... An act for the more effectual encouragement of the British fisheries. [London, 1795.]
G668

Great Britain. Laws, etc. An act to continue the laws now in force for regulating the trade between the subjects of His Majesty's dominions and the inhabitants of the territories belonging to the United States of America, so far as the same relate to the trade and commerce carried on between this kingdom and the inhabitants of the countries belonging to the said United States. [London, 1795.]
G669

Great Britain. Laws, etc. An act for continuing the encouragement and reward of persons making certain discoveries for finding the longitude at sea ... London, Charles Eyre and William Strahan, 1796.
G670
This act reflects continued interest in perfection of instruments useful in determining longitude at sea.

Great Britain. Laws, etc. An act to continue the laws now in force for regulating the trade between the subjects of His Majesty's dominions and ... the United States of America ... London, George Eyre and Andrew Strahan, 1796. G671
The law covering trade between the United States and the British West Indies, and trade in certain items from the Baltic Sea area is extended to 5 April 1797.

Great Britain. Laws, etc. An act for carrying into execution the treaty of amity, commerce, and navigation concluded between His Majesty and the United States of America. London, George Eyre and Andrew Strahan, 1797. G672
Legislation putting into effect the provisions of the comprehensive Jay Treaty, covering a wide variety of goods traded between Great Britain and the United States.

Great Britain. Laws, etc. An act for preventing the desertion of seamen from British merchant ships trading to His Majesty's colonies and plantations in the West Indies. London, George Eyre and Andrew Strahan, 1797. G673
The act contains twelve provisions covering desertion, hiring, wages, and other aspects of the employment of merchant seamen.

Great Britain. Laws, etc. An act for regulating the height between decks of vessels entered outwards for the purpose of carrying slaves from the coast of Africa. [London, 1797.] G674

Great Britain. Laws, etc. An act for regulating the shipping and carrying of slaves in British vessels from the coast of Africa. [London, 1797.] G675

Size and condition of ships are regulated, awards are to be made to masters and surgeons of ships with low mortality records among slaves.

Great Britain. Laws, etc. An act to continue the laws now in force for regulating the trade between the subjects of His Majesty's dominions and ... the United States of America ... London, George Eyre and Andrew Strahan, 1797. G676

A previous act covering trade between the United States and the British West Indies, and certain goods from the Baltic area is extended to 5 April 1798.

Great Britain. Laws, etc. An act for indemnifying governors, lieutenant governors, and persons acting as such, in the West India islands, who have permitted the importation and exportation of goods and commodities in foreign bottoms. [London, George Eyre and Andrew Strahan, 1798.] G677

Events in the West Indies having made certain laws unworkable, cases brought against officials for violations are dismissed.

Great Britain. Laws, etc. An act for the further encouraging the southern whale fisheries. London, George Eyre and Andrew Strahan, 1798. G678

Premiums to be paid to whalers are limited to twenty-six ships meeting specific qualifications.

Great Britain. Laws, etc. An act to amend an act, passed in the twenty-seventh year of His present Majesty's reign, intituled, An act for allowing the importation and exportation of certain goods ... in the ports of Kingston, Savannah la Mar, Montego Bay and Santa Lucea, in the island of Jamaica ... [London, George Eyre and Andrew Strahan, 1798.] G679

This legislation also includes Grenada, Dominica, and New Providence in the Bahamas. It legalizes the handling of European goods in these islands.

Great Britain. Laws, etc. An act to continue, until the first day of March one thousand seven hundred and ninety-nine ... An act for the more effectual encouragement of the British fisheries. London, George Eyre and Andrew Strahan, 1798. G680

Renewal of an act previously passed in 1787 and 1795.

Great Britain. Laws, etc. An act to continue, until the first day of March one thousand seven hundred and ninety-nine, an act ... for the more effectual encouragement of the British fisheries. London, George Eyre and Andrew Strahan, 1798. G681

The original legislation was made in 1787, with two extensions of it including amendments made subsequently.

Great Britain. Laws, etc. An act to prevent the exportation of base coin to His Majesty's colonies in the West Indies and America. [21st June 1798.] London, George Eyre and Andrew Strahan, 1798. G682

The export of copper coins to the West Indies is prohibited because they have been made in close imitation of gold and silver coins.

Great Britain. Laws, etc. An act for allowing further time for the payment of instalments on certain sums of money advanced by way of loan to several persons connected with trading to the islands of Grenada and Saint Vincent. [London, George Eyre and Andrew Strahan, 1799.] G683

The legislation deals with details of the extension of time made for repayment of the loans.

Great Britain. Laws, etc. An act for indemnifying governors ... in the West India Islands. London, G. Eyre and A. Strahan, 1799. G684

The shortage of necessary provisions made it mandatory to admit goods from the United States, although these had been previously prohibited.

Great Britain. Laws, etc. An act to amend an act ... intituled, An act to enable His Majesty to grant commissions to a certain number of foreign protestants, who have served abroad ... to act and rank as officers or engineers in America only, under certain restrictions and qualifications. [London, George Eyre and Andrew Strahan, 1799.] G685

The purpose of the act is to provide for recruitment of two thousand foreign troops for service in America.

Great Britain. Laws, etc. An act to continue several laws relating to the further support and encouragement of the fisheries carried on in the Greenland seas and Davis's Streights ... and to the discontinuing the duties payable on the importation of tallow, hog's lard, and grease ... [London, 1799.] G686

Great Britain. Laws, etc. An act to continue, until the twentieth day of February one thousand eight hundred, several laws relating to the prevention and punishment of attempts to seduce persons serving in His Majesty's forces ... [London, George Eyre and Andrew Strahan, 1799.] G687

An omnibus act covering various aspects of colonial administration and commerce including importation of goods from the Cape of Good Hope and of grain into Great Britain.

Great Britain. Laws, etc. An act to permit goods the produce of any foreign colony in America, imported directly from thence ... to be entered and landed without payment of the duty granted by an act of the last session of Parliament ...

[London, George Eyre and Andrew Strahan, 1799.] G688

All foreign colonies in North America, and in the United States as well, are included in this act, provided the goods involved are warehoused and exported.

Great Britain. Laws, etc. An act for granting bounties on the importation of wheat, wheaten flour, and rice, until the first day of October one thousand eight hundred. London, George Eyre and Andrew Strahan, 1800. G689

Great Britain. Laws, etc. An act for indemnifying governors, lieutenant governors, and persons acting as such, in the West India islands, who have permitted the importation and exportation of goods and commodities in foreign bottoms. London, George Eyre and Andrew Strahan, 1800. G690

Great Britain. Laws, etc. An act to enable Courts of Equity to compel a transfer of stock in suits, without making ... the Bank of England, or the United Company of Merchants of England trading to the East Indies or the ... Company of Merchants of Great Britain trading to the South Seas or other parts of America party thereto. London, George Eyre and Andrew Strahan, 1800. G691

Great Britain. Laws, etc. An act to permit blubber from the Greenland fishery and Davis's Streights to be boiled into oil after the arrival of the ships from the fishery, and for charging duty thereon. [London, George Eyre and Andrew Strahan, 1800.] G692

The legislation also includes duties on opium, turpentine, and tar.

Great Britain. Laws, etc. An act to permit the importation of goods and commodities from countries in America, belonging to any foreign European sovereign or state, in neutral ships, until the twenty-ninth day of September, one thousand eight hundred and one. London, George Eyre and Andrew Strahan, 1800. G693

Great Britain. Laws, etc. An act for increasing the bounties ... on flour imported from America, in ships which shall have cleared out between certain periods. London, George Eyre and Andrew Strahan, 1801. G694

Great Britain. Laws, etc. An act to render more effectual an act, passed in the fifth year of the reign of His present Majesty, relating to the discovery of the longitude at sea ... London, George Eyre and Andrew Strahan, 1803. G695

This act reflects continued interest in perfection of instruments useful in determining longitude at sea.

Great Britain. Laws, etc. An act to continue ... several laws relating to the encouragement of the Greenland whale fisheries; to the admission to entry in Great Britain of oil and blubber of Newfoundland taken by His Majesty's subjects carrying on the fishery from and residing in the said island ... London, George Eyre and Andrew Strahan, 1808. G696

Great Britain. Laws, etc. An act to continue until the end of this session of Parliament, several acts for carrying into execution the Treaty of amity, commerce, and navigation, between His Majesty and the United States of America. London, George Eyre and Andrew Strahan, 1808. G697

Great Britain. Laws, etc. An act to regulate the trade between Great Britain and the United States of America until the end of the next session of Parliament. London, George Eyre and Andrew Strahan, 1808. G698

Great Britain. Laws, etc. An act for the more effectual recovery of penalties and forfeitures, incurred in the British colonies and plantations in America. London, George Eyre and Andrew Strahan, 1809. G699

Great Britain. Laws, etc. An act to permit the trade between Great Britain and the United States of America to be carried on in ships or vessels belonging to the inhabitants of the said states. London, George Eyre and Andrew Strahan, 1809. G700

Great Britain. Laws, etc. An act to continue the encouragement of persons making discoveries for finding the longitude at sea ... 7th June 1815. London, George Eyre and Andrew Strahan, 1815. G701

This act reflects continued interest in perfection of instruments useful in determining longitude at sea.

Great Britain. Parliament. An abstract of several acts of Parliament ... for ... the Honourable South Sea Company. [London] R. Mount, 1718. G702

An outline of the legislation incidental to the establishment of the South Sea Company.

Great Britain. Parliament. Addresse ... des trèshonourables les seigneurs ... assemblée en Parlement, 13 décembre 1695. [Edinburgh, 1695.] G703

An address to the Parliament regarding The Company of Scotland trading to Africa and the Indies. It is signed Math. Johnson.

Great Britain. Parliament. The answer of the Parliament of the commonwealth of England, to three papers delivered in to the Councel of State by the lords ambassadors extraordinary of the

States General of the United Provinces. As also a narrative of the late engagement between the English fleet ... and the Holland fleet ... London, J. Field, 1652. G704

Great Britain. Parliament. A bill for confining, for a time to be limited, the trade between the ports of the United States of America, and His Majesty's subjects in the island of Newfoundland, to bread, flour, and live stock, to be imported in none but British ships ... [London, 1785.] G705

Great Britain. Parliament. A bill for encouraging the people known by the name Unitas Fratrum or United Brethren, to settle in His Majesty's colonies in America. [London, 1749.] G706

The bill provides for exempting the United Brethren settled in America from taking oaths and from military service.

Great Britain. Parliament. The humble address of the right honourable the lords spiritual and temporal and commons in Parliament assembled, presented to His Majesty on the seventeenth of December, 1695. London, Charles Bill and the executrix of Thomas Newcomb, 1695. G707

Parliament protests the chartering of The Company of Scotland Trading to Africa and the Indies, noting the damage it might do to English trade. The king responds, "I have been ill served in Scotland ..."

Great Britain. Parliament. The humble address of the Right Honourable the Lords Spiritual and Temporal and the Commons, in Parliament assembled, presented to His Majesty, on Tuesday, the eighteenth day of March, 1739. With his Majesty's most gracious answer. London, John Baskett, 1739. G708

A resolution of congratulations on Admiral Vernon's victory at Porto Bello.

Great Britain. Parliament. An order of Parliament, with the consent of His Highness the Lord Protector, for a day of publike thanksgiving within the cities of London and Westminster ... for the great success God hath been pleased to give the navy ... against the Spaniard. London, Henry Hills and John Field, 1657. G709

A document proclaiming a day of thanksgiving for a naval victory over a Spanish fleet near Tenerife on 20 April 1657.

Great Britain. Parliament. A resolution of the Right Honourable the Lords Spiritual and Temporal, and the Commons, in Parliament assembled, presented to His Majesty, on Friday, the twenty third day of November, 1739: with His Majesty's most gracious answer. London, John Baskett, 1739. G710

The resolution promises firm support in the war against Spain, and the sovereign's response is a request for "unanimous and vigorous" backing of the government's policy.

Great Britain. Parliament. A true narrative of the late success which it hath pleased God to give to some part of the fleet of this Common-Wealth, upon the Spanish Coast, against the King of Spains West-India Fleet, in its return to Cadiz. London, Henry Hills and John Field, 1656. G711

A proclamation ordering a day of thanksgiving, 5 November 1656, to commemorate a recent victory by the English fleet against Spain near Cadiz, with some account of the battle.

Great Britain. Parliament. House of Commons. An account of the foreign produce and manufactures, exported from Great Britain to France between the 5th of January, 1714, and the 5th of January, 1787. [London, ca. 1787.] G712

A list of non-English goods that were shipped to France, including many types of woods, dyes, grocery products, and silks.

Great Britain. Parliament. House of Commons. An account of the quantity and value of the imports into Great Britain from France between the 5th of January, 1714, and the 5th of January, 1787. [London, ca. 1787.] G713

An annual listing of some fifty commodities imported from France.

Great Britain. Parliament. House of Commons. An account of the value of all goods, wares, and merchandize exported from, and imported into Great Britain ... from Christmas 1782 to Christmas 1785. [London, 1787.] G714

A survey of England's trade with sixty-nine different countries, islands, and states.

Great Britain. Parliament. House of Commons. A bill for confining, for a time to be limited, the trade between the ports of the United States of America, and ... Newfoundland, to bread, flour, and live stock. [London] 1785. G715

A proposed set of restrictions upon the new nation's trade with Newfoundland which specified that only British ships were to be used.

Great Britain. Parliament. House of Commons. A bill intituled An act for enabling Her Majesty to accept a surrender upon terms of the lands, privileges and rights of the Governor and Company of Adventurers of England trading into Hudson's Bay ... [London] 1868. G716

Great Britain. Parliament. House of Commons. A collection of the debates and proceedings in

Parliament ... upon the inquiry into the late briberies and corrupt practices. London, 1695. G717

Contains the substance of an investigation of the affairs of the East India Company.

Great Britain. Parliament. House of Commons. The debate in the House of Commons, on Friday, June 20, 1794, on the motion of thanks to the managers on the trial of Warren Hastings. London, For J. Debrett, 1794. G718

A minority presented vigorous protests against Edmund Burke's conduct during the trial. Excerpts from his speeches are appended.

Great Britain. Parliament. House of Commons. The debate on the East India Relief Bill in the House of Commons on Monday the 26th of June 1786. London, For John Stockdale, 1786. G719

The debate ranged widely over the East India Company's financial and commercial situation.

Great Britain. Parliament. House of Commons. The debate on the Rohilla War, in the House of Commons, on the 1st and 2d June, 1786. London, For John Stockdale [1786]. G720

This debate relates to Warren Hastings and was concurrent with the impeachment proceedings.

Great Britain. Parliament. House of Commons. A full and complete account of the debates in the House of Commons on Tuesday, November 18, Wednesday, December 17, Friday December 19, Monday December 22, and Wednesday December 24, 1783. London, For J. Stockdale, 1784. G721

An abstract of the debates on the India Bill, an attempt to reform the administration of the East India Company. A copy of the complete bill is included.

Great Britain. Parliament. House of Commons. A list of the minority in the House of Commons who voted against the bill to repeal the American Stamp Act. Paris, J.W., 1766. G722

The Stamp Act was repealed February 21, 1766, with 168 votes against repeal recorded here.

Great Britain. Parliament. House of Commons. Minutes of the evidence taken at the bar of the House of Commons, and of the proceedings of the House, on the hearing of counsel on the second reading of the bill for inflicting certain pains and penalties on Sir Thomas Rumbold ... [London?] 1783. G723

Rumbold (1736-1791) was an administrator for the East India Company, serving in a civil as well as a military capacity during the governorship of Hastings. Sir Thomas came under fire for mismanagement of company affairs in India and Parliament brought this bill against him.

Great Britain. Parliament. House of Commons. Minutes of the evidence taken (in the last session of Parliament) before the Committee of the whole House to whom the bill for providing certain temporary regulations respecting the transportation of the natives of Africa, in British ships, to the West Indies, and elsewhere, was committed. [London, 1789.] G724

Detailed testimony on the slave trade, particularly with reference to conditions aboard ship, supplied by several persons who had engaged in the slave trade between Africa and America.

Great Britain. Parliament. House of Commons. The rates of merchandise ... as they are rated and agreed on by the Commons House of Parliament. London, Edward Husbands and Thomas Newcomb, 1660. G725

A fifty-page list of import and export duties followed by special instructions for merchants engaged in specific branches of commerce.

Great Britain. Parliament. House of Commons. Report of a committee ... relative to the slave trade. [London] 1790. G726

A review of the slave trade in Barbados and its effect upon the economy there, concluding that it "will be the destruction of the cultivation of the lands in this colony."

Great Britain. Parliament. House of Commons. Report upon the petitions relating to the manufacture of hats. London, 1752. G727

A collection of testimony to the effect that the export of unmanufactured beaver created competition abroad and raised the price of beaver in England.

Great Britain. Parliament. House of Commons. Committee appointed to consider of the illicit exportation of wool, live sheep, worsted, and yarn. Report. [London] 1786. G728

Contains testimony from persons who claimed knowledge of the smuggling of wool from England to France, where higher prices were paid for it than on the English market.

Great Britain. Parliament. House of Commons. Committee appointed to enquire into the frauds and abuses in the customs, to the prejudice of trade, and diminution of the revenue. The report ... London, Richard Williamson, 1733. G729

Contains information on the nature and extent of British overseas trade.

Great Britain. Parliament. House of Commons. Committee appointed to enquire into the state and conditions of the countries adjoining to Hudson's Bay. Papers presented to the Committee ... London, 1749. G730

Twenty documents relating to the history of the Hudson's Bay Company.

Great Britain. Parliament. House of Commons. Committee appointed to enquire into the state

272   Great Britain. Parliament

and conditions of the countries adjoining to Hudson's Bay. Report ... London, 1749.   G731

A report on the possibilities of settling the Hudson Bay region and on the means of extending trade and fisheries there.

Great Britain. Parliament. House of Commons. Committee of secrecy. The several reports ... to the honourable House of Commons, relating to the late South-Sea directors. London, For A. Moore, 1721.   G732

A series of seven reports on "this black and destructive South-Sea Scheme."

Great Britain. Parliament. House of Commons. Committee of secrecy on the causes of the war in the Carnatic. First report from the Committee of secrecy. [London] 1781-82.   G733

This and the following three items constitute a series of reports covering the diplomatic, military, and administrative background of conflict in India between the East India Company and Hyder Ali of Mysore.

Great Britain. Parliament. House of Commons. Committee of secrecy on the causes of the war in the Carnatic. Second report from the Committee of secrecy. [London] 1781.   G734

Great Britain. Parliament. House of Commons. Committee of secrecy on the causes of the war in the Carnatic. Appendix to the fifth report from the Committee of secrecy. [London] 1782.   G735

Great Britain. Parliament. House of Commons. Committee of secrecy on the causes of the war in the Carnatic. Appendix to the sixth report from the Committee of secrecy. [London] 1782.   G736

Great Britain. Parliament. House of Commons. Committee of secrecy relating to the negotiations of peace and commerce. A report from the Committee of secrecy ... relating to the late negotiations of peace and commerce etc. London, Jacob Tonson, 1715.   G737

Contains arrangements made between England and France over possessions and trade in America.

Great Britain. Parliament. House of Commons. Committee of secrecy to enquire into the state of the East India Company. Report [and Further reports] from the Committee of secrecy appointed to enquire into the state of the East India Company. [n.p.] 1772-73.   G738

These six reports provide massive information on the financial, military, and political dealings between the East India Company, its officials, and Indian rulers.

Great Britain. Parliament. House of Commons. Committee on impeachment of Warren Hastings. Articles of charge of high crimes and misdemeanors, against Warren Hastings, esq. late governor general of Bengal. London, For J. Stockdale, 1786.   G739

The twenty-two charges against Hastings were presented by Edmund Burke on April 4, 1786.

Great Britain. Parliament. House of Commons. Committee on impeachment of Warren Hastings. The debate on the charge relating to Mr. Hastings's conduct to Cheyt Sing, at Benares, in the House of Commons, on the 13th of June, 1786. London, For John Stockdale, 1786.   G740

This was one of the two most crucial charges in the impeachment proceedings against Hastings.

Great Britain. Parliament. House of Commons. Committee on impeachment of Warren Hastings. The defence of Warren Hastings, esq. (late governor general of Bengal,) at the bar of the House of Commons. London, For J. Stockdale, 1786.   G741

A response to each of the twenty-two charges placed against him, preceded by a general statement of defense.

Great Britain. Parliament. House of Commons. Committee on impeachment of Warren Hastings. Minutes of the evidence taken before a committee of the House of Commons ... appointed to consider the several articles of charge of high crimes and misdemeanors ... against Warren Hastings. London, John Stockdale, 1786.   G742

The questioning primarily concerns Hastings' actions in Benares, Oudh, and in the Rohilla War.

Great Britain. Parliament. House of Commons. Committee on the linen manufactory. Report from the committee appointed to examine ... the matters of fact in the several petitions of the manufacturers of, and traders and dealers in, the linen manufactory. [London] 1751.   G743

This report contains testimony from importers, manufacturers, and exporters of yarn and cloth to explain the reasons for a decline in the linen industry.

Great Britain. Parliament. House of Commons. Committee on the trade to Newfoundland. A brief state of the evidence laid before the Committee of the House of Commons, upon the Newfoundland trade and fishery, in the last session, 1793. [n.p., 1793.]   G744

Testimony to account for the decline in the Newfoundland fishery, most of it attributing the decline to regulatory legislation of 1775.

Great Britain. Parliament. House of Commons. Committee to consider how His Majesty's

navy may be better supplied with timber. Report. London, For J. Whiston [etc.] 1771. G745

A discussion of the means of alleviating a timber shortage through importing from northern Europe and America.

Great Britain. Parliament. House of Commons. Committee to consider measures for the abolition of the trade for the purpose of procuring slaves. Report from the committee ... of measures to be taken for the abolition of the trade ... [London] 1792. G746

This document reports the intentions of the House to slow down the African slave trade pending agreement upon a date for complete abolition.

Great Britain. Parliament. House of Commons. Committee to examine the matter of fact contained in the petition of several merchants of the city of London. Report relating to the finding a north-west passage. [London, ca. 1742.] G747

The summary of an inquiry into Christopher Middleton's 1742 voyage to determine if his efforts to find a northwest passage were genuine.

Great Britain. Parliament. House of Commons. Committee to whom the petition of Benjamin Lacam was referred. Report from the Committee to whom the petition of Benjamin Lacam, sole proprietor of New Harbour in Bengal, was referred. [n.p.] 1783. G748

Results of an inquiry into the revocation of Lacam's license given him for finding and mapping a useful channel and harbor in the Hooghly River.

Great Britain. Parliament. House of Commons. Committee to Whom the Petition of the Deputies of the United Moravian Churches ... was Referred. Report from the Committee ... together with some extracts of the most material vouchers and papers ... London, 1749. G749

A collection of evidence taken before a special committee of the House of Commons in defense of the United Brethren who had encountered problems due to their refusal to take oaths and to bear arms.

Great Britain. Parliament. House of Commons. Committee to whom the petition relating to the Sugar Islands was Referred. Testimony on trade between New England and the French West Indian Islands given before the Committee to whom the Petition Relating to the Sugar Islands was referred: 1730. G750

An account of a hearing before a parliamentary committee inquiring into the trade between the northern American colonies and the French West Indian islands.

Great Britain. Parliament. House of Commons. Select Committee on administration of justice in Bengal, Bahar, and Orissa. Ninth report from the Select Committee. London, For J. Debrett, 1783. G751

This report traces the development of English actions in India and the steady displacement of India merchants by Englishmen. It also cites incidents of corruption in both company and individual transactions.

Great Britain. Parliament. House of Commons. Select Committee on examination of witnesses of the slave trade. Minutes of evidence taken before a committee of the House of Commons ... appointed to take the examination of witnesses respecting the African slave trade. [n.p.] 1791. G752

A continuation of the hearings of 1790.

Great Britain. Parliament. House of Commons. Select Committee on examination of witnesses of the slave trade. Minutes of the evidence taken before a committee of the House of Commons, being a select committee ... to consider further of the circumstances of the slave trade. [n.p.] 1790. G753

A variety of witnesses testify on many aspects of slavery and the slave trade as Parliament considered legislation for the abolition of the slave trade. The committee continued hearings begun by the House of Commons in 1788.

Great Britain. Parliament. House of Commons. Select Committee on the East India Company. The genuine minutes of the Select committee ... to enquire into East India affairs. Containing the most authentic, historical account of the various revolutions and other extraordinary events that have happened in India, from the commencement of Lord Clive's government, to the latest advices received by the honourable English East-India Company. London, T. Evans, 1772. G754

Great Britain. Parliament. House of Commons. Select Committee on the East India Company. Report from the Select committee, appointed to examine the reports of the directors of the East India Company. June 22d 1784. [London] 1784. G755

The parliamentary inquiry resulted from the company's inability to meet certain financial obligations.

Great Britain. Parliament. House of Commons. Select Committee on the Hudson's Bay Company. Minutes of evidence taken before the Select committee ... [London, 1857.] G756

Six parliamentary documents proceeding from hearings held between February 20 and March 9, 1857.

Great Britain. Parliament. House of Commons. Select Committee on the Hudson's Bay Company. Papers. [London, 1857.] G757

Three parliamentary documents dated February 23, March 2, and March 9, 1857.

Great Britain. Parliament. House of Commons. Select Committee on the Hudson's Bay Company. Plans referred to in the Report from the Select committee on the Hudson's Bay Company. [London, 1857.] G758

Three folding maps of northern North America.

Great Britain. Parliament. House of Commons. Select Committee on the Hudson's Bay Company. Report from the Select committee ... together with the proceedings ... minutes of evidence, appendix and index. [London, 1857.] G759

The 547 page report ranges broadly over the activities of the company. It was communicated to the House of Lords.

Great Britain. Parliament. House of Lords. Correct copies of the two protests against the bill to repeal the American Stamp Act ... with lists of the speakers and voters. Paris, J.W., 1766. G760

Arguments advanced during consideration of the repeal of the Stamp Act. This is the minority viewpoint which saw capitulation to American opinion as a threat to orderly government.

Great Britain. Parliament. House of Lords. A full and accurate account of the debates on the East-India bill in the House of Lords, on Tuesday the 9th, on Monday the 15th, Tuesday the 16th, and Wednesday the 17th of December, 1783. London, For J. Stockdale, 1784. G761

The debate cited danger of precedent in which legislation violates the charter of a company. The bill was defeated.

Great Britain. Parliament. House of Lords. The humble address of the ... Lords spiritual and temporal ... to His Majesty on Munday the twelfth day of February, 1699. Edinburgh, Heirs and successors of Andrew Anderson, 1700. G762

The House of Lords reminds the King that the Darien Company's activities will be prejudicial to England's American commerce, He replies that the solution to the problem lies in the union of England and Scotland.

Great Britain. Parliament. House of Lords. The humble address of the right honourable the Lords spiritual and temporal, in Parliament assembled ... With Her Majesties most gracious answer. London, Charles Bill and the executrix of Thomas Newcomb, 1707. G763

An appeal for more and better convoys to protect merchant shipping to America, Russia, and the Mediterranean against marauding French ships.

Great Britain. Parliament. House of Lords. The humble address of the right honourable the Lords spiritual and temporal in Parliament assembled, presented to His Majesty, on Friday the second day of February, 1738. London, John Baskett, 1738. G764

Expresses satisfaction that peace concluded with Spain provides reparations for British losses in American waters.

Great Britain. Parliament. House of Lords. The humble address of the right honourable the Lords spiritual and temporal, and the Commons in Parliament assembled, presented to His Majesty, on Tuesday, the eighteenth day of March, 1739. London, John Baskett, 1739. G765

A message of congratulations upon the victory of Admiral Vernon in the West Indies.

Great Britain. Parliament. House of Lords. The humble address of the right honourable the Lords spiritual and temporal in Parliament assembled, presented to His Majesty, on Friday the second day of March, 1738 ... London, John Baskett, 1738. G766

The address urges that the treaty under consideration with Spain contain guarantees of security of navigation in American seas.

Great Britain. Parliament. House of Lords. The humble address of the right honourable the Lords spiritual and temporal in Parliament assembled, presented to His Majesty, on Friday the second day of March, 1738: with His Majesty's most gracious answer. London, John Baskett, 1738. G767

A statement of gratitude for the position taken by the government in negotiating with Spain over navigation in American waters.

Great Britain. Parliament. House of Lords. The humble address of the right honourable the Lords spiritual and temporal in Parliament assembled, presented to His Majesty, on Friday the second day of February, 1738: with His Majesty's most gracious answer. London, John Baskett, 1738. G768

Parliament assures the sovereign that it will refrain from partisan disagreements while negotiations for a treaty with Spain are in progress.

Great Britain. Parliament. House of Lords. Minutes of the evidence taken at the bar of the House of Lords, upon the order made for taking into consideration the present state of the trade to Africa, and particularly the trade in slaves ... [n.p.] 1792. G769

The testimony given presents a point of view opposed to the abolition of the slave trade because of the damage it would do to the West Indian economy.

Great Britain. Parliament. House of Lords. Proceedings of the House of Lords in relation to the late directors of the South-Sea Company, and others: with the report of their Lordships on the said proceedings: to which is added, the conference with the Commons, relating to Mr. Aislabie and Mr. Craggs ... London, Zachariah Stokey, 1721. G770

A parliamentary inquiry into stock transactions among directors of the South Sea Company.

Great Britain. Parliament. House of Lords. [Reports on the state of England's overseas trade.] Manuscript. [London] 27 November 1704 and 27 November 1707. G771

These two reports cover a wide range of commercial concerns relating primarily to England's Atlantic commerce, with extensive commentary on the American colonies.

Great Britain. Parliament. House of Lords. A resolution of the right honourable the Lords spiritual and temporal, and the Commons in Parliament assembled, presented to His Majesty, on Friday, the twenty third day of November, 1739. London, John Baskett, 1739. G772

States Parliament's support of the war against Spain, and urges security of navigation in American waters as a preliminary to any peace agreement.

Great Britain. Parliament. Joint Committee on African papers. [Abstracts of the minutes of the Committee, April 14-May 17, 1756.] Manuscript. [London] 1756. G773

These minutes cover meetings from April 14 to May 17, 1756, and concern various financial transactions relating to trade in west Africa.

Great Britain. Parliament. Privy Council. Abstract of proceedings in council, relative to the grant, directed to be made of the Jesuits estates, in Canada, to the late Jeffery Lord Amherst. [London, 1803.] G774

A history of proceedings which began in 1770 with the petition of Lord Amherst.

Great Britain. Privy Council. The report of the Lords of the committee, upon Governor Shute's memorial, with His Majesty's order thereupon. London, 1725. G775

The Privy Council is confronted here with several disagreements between Governor Samuel Shute of Massachusetts and the Assembly of that colony.

Great Britain. Sovereign (1603-1625 : James I). The rates of marchandizes, as they are set downe in the Booke of rates, for the custome and subsidie of poundage ... together with the rates of such impositions as are laide upon any commodities, either brought into the realme, or carried out of the same ... [London, 1609.] G776

Great Britain. Sovereign (1603-1625 : James I). A true transcript and publication of His Majesties letters pattent. For ... the Publicke Register for Generall Commerce. London, John Budge, 1611. G777

These letters patent, published with commentary by Sir Arthur Gorges, contain an interesting plan for expediting commercial transactions of all kinds in England, through the use of a central clearinghouse for commercial information.

Great Britain. Sovereign (1603-1625 : James I). The kings letters pattents graunted to the Levant Company. Manuscript. [London, ca. 1620.] G778

A copy of the letters patent of 1605, bearing the ex libris of Lewes Roberts.

Great Britain. Sovereign (1603-1625 : James I). A proclamation declaring His Majesties pleasure concerning Captaine Roger North. London, Robert Barker and John Bill, 1620. G779

An attempt to restrain Roger North from establishing a trading company in Guiana. North had already sailed when the proclamation was issued.

Great Britain. Sovereign (1625-1649 : Charles I). By the King. A proclamation prohibiting the importation of allome, and the buying and spending thereof in any His Majesties dominions. London, B. Norton and John Bill, 1625. G780

Protection from foreign competitors is provided for the English mining industry.

Great Britain. Sovereign (1625-1649 : Charles I). By the King. A proclamation for the better making of saltpeter within this kingdome. London, B. Norton and John Bill, 1626. G781

Gives sole rights for the making of saltpeter to Sir John Brooke and Thomas Russell.

Great Britain. Sovereign (1625-1649 : Charles I). By the King. A proclamation declaring the Kings Majesties royall pleasure touching the inhabitants of Algier, Tunis, Sallie, and Tituan, in the parts of Africa. London, B. Norton and John Bill, 1628. G782

A royal warning against acts of hostility directed toward persons, ships, or goods belonging to English subjects in the places named.

Great Britain. Sovereign (1625-1649 : Charles I). By the King. A proclamation prohibiting the exportation of corne and graine. London, Bonham Norton and John Bill, 1629. G783

Because of bad weather and the probable loss of the harvest, no corn or grain whatsoever is to be allowed out of the kingdom.

Great Britain. Sovereign (1625-1649 : Charles I). By the King. A proclamation reviving and enlarging a former proclamation ... prohibiting the bringing in of any commodities traded by the eastland merchants into this kingdome. London, R. Barker and John Bill, 1629. G784

Restates an earlier proclamation which lists commodities that must be transported in English ships.

Great Britain. Sovereign (1625-1649 : Charles I). By the King. A proclamation touching the importation of French wines. London, Bonham Norton and John Bill, 1629. G785

Because of large stocks of French wines in the country, import of them is forbidden for six months, and thereafter only in English ships.

Great Britain. Sovereign (1625-1649 : Charles I). By the King. A proclamation against the false dying of silke. London, Robert Barker, 1630. G786

Very strict regulations for those dealing in silk, with detailed prohibitions against increasing the weight of silk in the dyeing process.

Great Britain. Sovereign (1625-1649 : Charles I). By the King. A proclamation for preventing the dearth of corne and victuall. London, Robert Barker, 1630. G787

Measures for easing the food shortage, including the forbidding of large company dinners.

Great Britain. Sovereign (1625-1649 : Charles I). By the King. A proclamation for the preventing of exportation of woolles, woolfels, yarne ... London, R. Barker, 1630. G788

Also condemns the use of inferior materials in the dyeing of cloth, which "did exceedingly disgrace and discredit the drapery of this our kingdom."

Great Britain. Sovereign (1625-1649 : Charles I). By the King. A proclamation for the restraining of the importation of iron wyer into this kingdome, and for the support of that manufacture. London, Robert Barker, 1630. G789

Points out the superiority of native wire for many uses, especially in the clothing industry.

Great Britain. Sovereign (1625-1649 : Charles I). By the King. A proclamation prohibiting the exportation of corne and graine. London, Robert Barker, 1630. G790

Earlier proclamations of the same "have not taken such effect as Wee expected."

Great Britain. Sovereign (1625-1649 : Charles I). By the King. A further proclamation prohibiting the exportation of corne and graine. London, R. Barker and the assignes of John Bill, 1631. G791

Reinforces an earlier proclamation of the same kind.

Great Britain. Sovereign (1625-1649 : Charles I). By the King. A proclamation for preventing of deceipt used in the importation of madder. London, Robert Barker and the assignes of John Bill, 1631. G792

Importers of this dye were adding sand to it in order to increase their profits.

Great Britain. Sovereign (1625-1649 : Charles I). By the King. A proclamation for the better ordering of fishing, upon the coasts of His Majesties dominions. London, Robert Barker and the assignes of John Bill, 1631. G793

Enforces regulations for preserving the fish on English coasts, including the ordinances against taking the fry and spawn of fishes.

Great Britain. Sovereign (1625-1649 : Charles I). By the King. A proclamation to restraine the kings subjects departing out of the realme without licence. London, Robert Barker and the assignes of John Bill, 1635. G794

No one except soldiers, mariners, merchants and their assistants may leave the realm without a license.

Great Britain. Sovereign (1625-1649 : Charles I). [Letters patent, granting to John Browne, a monopoly of the sale of cast iron manufactures.] [London, 1635.] G795

The need for support of Browne's industry was brought about by competition from Sweden.

Great Britain. Sovereign (1625-1649 : Charles I). By the King. A proclamation inhibiting the importation of whale finnes, or whale oile, into His Majesties dominions by any, but the Muscovia Company. London, Robert Barker and the assignes of John Bill, 1636. G796

States a monopoly of the northern whale trade for the Muscovy Company.

Great Britain. Sovereign (1625-1649 : Charles I). By the King. A proclamation prohibiting the importation of forraine gun-powder, and that His Majesties subjects may be constantly supplied out of His Majesties store-houses. [London, R. Barker and the assignes of John Bill, 1636.] G797

This proclamation establishes a royal monopoly on the sale of gunpowder.

Great Britain. Sovereign (1625-1649 : Charles I). By the King. A proclamation for allowance of the use of hard silk in some speciall manufactures. London, Robert Barker and the assignes of John Bill, 1638. G798

A modification of an earlier regulation upon the dyeing of silk, with new regulations on its importation.

Great Britain. Sovereign (1625-1649 : Charles I). By the King. A proclamation for reforming sundry abuses in manufactures of silks and stuffs of forrain materials. London, Robert Barker and the assignes of John Bill, 1638. G799

This regulation covers the mixing of foreign materials with English in silk making, evenness in quality of cloth, and prohibits the use of the "great loom" whereby one man could do the work of ten.

Great Britain. Sovereign (1625-1649 : Charles I). By the King. A proclamation for restraining the importation of lattin wire into this kingdome. London, Robert Barker and the assignes of John Bill, 1638. G800

An attempt to protect local manufacturers against inferior wire from abroad.

Great Britain. Sovereign (1625-1649 : Charles I). By the King. A proclamation for restraint of the unlawfull sale and transportation of English horns. London, Robert Barker and the assignes of John Bill, 1638. G801

Tanners and butchers are warned against the sale of horn to foreign merchants.

Great Britain. Sovereign (1625-1649 : Charles I). By the King. A proclamation touching the Corporation of Bever-makers of London. London, Robert Barker and the assigns of John Bill, 1638. G802

This proclamation takes note of the new enthusiasm for beaver hats and seeks to place restraints upon the "bevermakers" who were giving sharp competition to other hat makers.

Great Britain. Sovereign (1625-1649 : Charles I). [License to the East India Company to export gold.] Manuscript. [London, 1639.] G803

A license to carry gold to the East Indies, thereby permitting its sale to the company by English subjects.

Great Britain. Sovereign (1649-1658 : Cromwell). [Proclamation calling for the appointment of British and Dutch commissioners to discuss losses and injuries sustained by both countries in their overseas rivalries.] London, William du-Gard and Henry Hills, 1654. G804

Great Britain. Sovereign (1649-1658 : Cromwell). [Proclamation providing for publication of peace terms between England and the Netherlands and for restitution for damages to each other's shipping after specified dates following publication.] London, William du-Gard and Henry Hills, 1654. G805

Great Britain. Sovereign (1649-1658 : Cromwell). A declaration of His Highness ... setting forth ... the justice of their cause against Spain. London, Henry Hills and John Field, 1655. G806

A statement of English grievances against Spain in the West Indies, believed to have been written by John Milton, who was secretary to Cromwell.

Great Britain. Sovereign (1649-1658 : Cromwell). Declaratie ofte manifest van Syn Hoocheyt door advijs van synen raedt, thoonende uyt de naem van dese Republijck, de rechtveerdicheyt van haer sake tegens Spaengien. [n.p.] 1655. G807

Dutch translation of the preceding work.

Great Britain. Sovereign (1649-1658 : Cromwell). Een manifest ofte een declaratie ... vertoonende in den name van dese republijcque, de gerechtigheyt van hare saeck tegen Spangien. Amsterdam, Jan Hendricks & Ian Rieuwertz, 1655. G808

A Dutch translation of Cromwell's declaration of Spanish depredations against English shipping in the West Indies.

Great Britain. Sovereign (1649-1658 : Cromwell). By the protector. A proclamation ... London, H. Hills & J. Field, 1656. G809

Proclamation for the strict enforcement of laws prohibiting export of wool, wool fels, fullers earth, and other commodities.

Great Britain. Sovereign (1660-1685 : Charles II). By the King. A proclamation declaring the confirmation of the treaties ... between ... England and Portugal ... London, J. Bill and C. Barker, 1660. G810

Great Britain. Sovereign (1660-1685 : Charles II). By the King. A proclamation for the preventing of the exportation of wools, wool-fells, woollen yarn, fullers-earth and other scouring earths. London, J. Bill and C. Barker, 1660. G811

Great Britain. Sovereign (1660-1685 : Charles II). By the King. A proclamation against exportation, and buying and selling of gold and silver at higher rates then in our mint ... London, John Bill and Christopher Barker, 1661. G812

Great Britain. Sovereign (1660-1685 : Charles II). By the King. A proclamation declaring the rates at which gold shall be current in payments, and to prohibite the transportation of the same. London, John Bill and Christopher Barker, 1661. G813

Great Britain. Sovereign (1660-1685 : Charles II). By the King. A proclamation for the encouraging of planters in His Majesties island of Jamaica in the West-Indies. London, John Bill and Christopher Barker, 1661. G814

To encourage settlement of Jamaica, settlers are offered thirty acres of tillable land, are guaranteed the rights of English citizens, and are required to give miltary service in case of insurrection or invasion.

Great Britain. Sovereign (1660-1685 : Charles II). By the King. A proclamation for prohibiting the importation or retailing of any commodities of the growth or manufacture of the States of the United Provinces. London, John Bill and Christopher Barker, 1664-5.　　　　　G815

This action was taken because of increasing problems in relations with the United Provinces, and in reciprocation for legislation passed there.

Great Britain. Sovereign (1660-1685 : Charles II). [Contemporary manuscript copy of letter informing the Council of Massachusetts Bay about commissioners which he proposes to send to New England.] Whitehall, 23 April 1664.
　　　　　G816

The commissioners being sent to New England were a manifestation of the re-establishment of royal authority in the colony.

Great Britain. Sovereign (1660-1685 : Charles II). By the King. A proclamation forbidding foreign trade and commerce. London, John Bill and Christopher Barker, 1665.　　　　　G817

English ships are forbidden to depart for foreign places, presumably because of hostilities at sea with the Dutch.

Great Britain. Sovereign (1660-1685 : Charles II). Antwoort, van Zijn Koninglijke Majesteit van Groot Brittanjen in date den 4 of 14 October 1666. Rotterdam, Joris Grootenhuise, 1666.
　　　　　G818

England's reply to Dutch complaints, with counter claims by the English that the Dutch were interfering with their commerce in various parts of the world.

Great Britain. Sovereign (1660-1685 : Charles II). By the King. A proclamation prohibiting the importation of all sorts of manufactures ... of France. London, Assigns of John Bill and Christopher Barker, 1666.　　　　　G819

The French colonial possessions were also included in this restriction.

Great Britain. Sovereign (1660-1685 : Charles II). By the King. A proclamation prohibiting the importation of all wines of the growth of the Canary Islands. London, Assigns of John Bill and Christopher Barker, 1666.　　　　　G820

This broadside cites high costs, disorderly commercial practices, and mistreatment of English merchants as causes for a general prohibition upon trade to the Canary Islands.

Great Britain. Sovereign (1660-1685 : Charles II). Copie veritable de la lettre de Sa Majesté britannique, du 14 octobre 1666 aux Estats Generaux des Provinces Unies des Pays-Bays, sur l'origine & le progres de la guerre presente, & les moyens d'acheminer à une bonne paix. [n.p., 1666].　　　　　G821

A response to a Dutch statement relative to the causes of the war then in progress between England and the Netherlands. Charles II advances proposals upon which peace could be achieved, and urges their acceptance by the Dutch.

Great Britain. Sovereign (1660-1685 : Charles II). Missive ... met korte aenmerckinge ende aenwysinge op den selfden ingestelt. The Hague, Erfgenamen van H.J. van Wouw, 1666.　　G822

The King's letter and Dutch observations upon it concern the English conquest of New Netherland and Cape Verde.

Great Britain. Sovereign (1660-1685 : Charles II). By the King. A proclamation for recalling dispensations, with some clauses in the acts for encouragement and increasing of shipping and navigation, and of trade. [London] John Bill and Christopher Barker, 1667.　　　　　G823

Notification that six months from the date of this proclamation the parts of this act of 1664 which are still in effect will no longer be enforced.

Great Britain. Sovereign (1660-1685 : Charles II). His Majesties declaration against the States Generall of the United Provinces of the Low-Countreys. London, Assigns of John Bill and Christopher Barker, 1672.　　　　　G824

The declaration of war is preceded by a recitation of Dutch wrongs with respect to English shipping and colonies, and the unwillingness of the Dutch to respect treaty obligations.

Great Britain. Sovereign (1660-1685 : Charles II). Manifest oder Declaration des Krieges wider die Herren General-Staaten von den Vereinigten Provintzien der Nederlande ... Breslau, Gottfried Jonisches Buchladen [1672].　　　　　G825

German translation of the previous item.

Great Britain. Sovereign (1660-1685 : Charles II). Syne Majesteyts declaratie tegens de Staten Generael. The Hague, J. Scheltus, 1672.　　G826

A reply to Dutch accusations that their subjects in Surinam were being denied freedom of movement by the English in violation of agreements between the two countries.

Great Britain. Sovereign (1660-1685 : Charles II). By the King. A proclamation ... London, Assigns of J. Bill and C. Barker, 1674.　　G827

A proclamation announcing the prohibition of African trade to all but the Royal African Company.

Great Britain. Sovereign (1660-1685 : Charles II). By the King. A proclamation for prohibiting the importation of commodities of Europe into any of His Majesties plantations. London, J. Bill and C. Barker, 1675. G828

Great Britain. Sovereign (1660-1685 : Charles II). An act for regulating the plantation trade ... London, Assigns of John Bill [et al.] 1680. G829

A proclamation for the regulation of trade, providing that certain products derived from English plantations in America, Asia, or Africa must be shipped only to England.

Great Britain. Sovereign (1660-1685 : Charles II). At the court at Whitehall the 16th of February, 1680. London, Assigns of John Bill, Thomas Newcomb and Henry Hills, 1680. G830

A decree specifying that certain goods laded in English colonies in America, Asia, and Africa must be bonded to guarantee delivery in England, Wales, or Ireland.

Great Britain. Sovereign (1660-1685 : Charles II). By the King, a proclamation for regulating and encouraging of trade and manufactures in the kingdom of Scotland. Edinburgh, Heir of A. Anderson, 1681. G831

Places protection upon linen, metal, and leather goods, and discriminates against several luxury items.

Great Britain. Sovereign (1685-1687 : James II). By the King, a proclamation for restraining all His Majesties subjects ... to trade in the East Indies. London, J. Bill [etc.] 1685. G832

The prohibition applies to all but the East India Company.

Great Britain. Sovereign (1685-1687 : James II). By the King, a proclamation prohibiting His Majesties subjects to trade within the limits assigned to the Royal African Company ... London, Assigns of John Bill, 1685. G833

An official proclamation published to establish and preserve the monopoly of the Royal African Company upon the African trade.

Great Britain. Sovereign (1685-1687 : James II). By the King. A proclamation for prohibiting the transportation of frames for knitting and making of silk-stockings. London, C. Bill, H. Hills, and T. Newcomb, 1686. G834

Great Britain. Sovereign (1685-1687 : James II). By the King. A proclamation for the recalling all His Majesties subjects from the service of foreign princes in East India. London, Charles Bill, Henry Hills and Thomas Newcombe, 1686. G835

Great Britain. Sovereign (1685-1687 : James II). By the King, a proclamation for the more effectual reducing ... of pirates and privateers in America. London, Charles Bill [etc.] 1688. G836

This proclamation notes the damage piracy is doing to trade in America, and promises pardons to all pirates and privateers who surrender to Sir Robert Holmes.

Great Britain. Sovereign (1685-1687 : James II). By the King. A proclamation for the putting in execution the laws and statutes of this realm. London, C. Bill [etc.] 1688. G837

A ban upon the exporting of wool, partially manufactured woolens, and materials used in the manufacture of woolens.

Great Britain. Sovereign (1688-1694 : William and Mary). By the King and Queen, a proclamation to prohibit the exportation of salt petre. London, C. Bill and T. Newcomb, 1689. G838

A restriction in the interest of national defense.

Great Britain. Sovereign (1694-1702 : William III). By the Lords Justices, a proclamation for publishing the peace between His Majesty and the French King. [London, Charles Bill, and the executrix of Thomas Newcomb, 1697.] G839

Great Britain. Sovereign (1694-1702 : William III). Lettres patentes ou octroi sous le grand seau du royaume d'Ecosse pour la Compagnie du commerce de l'Afrique et des Indes. [Edinburgh] Imprimé pour la Compagnie, 1697. G840

This French edition of the letters patent of the company also contains the *Constitution* of the Scots' Company.

Great Britain. Sovereign (1694-1702 : William III). By the King, a proclamation. William R. Whereas we have been informed, that a false, scandalous and traiterous libel, intituled, An inquiry into the causes of the miscarriage of the Scotch-colony at Darien ... has been printed and dispersed, the design of which libel was to create a misunderstanding between our good subjects of England and Scotland ... London, Charles Bill and the executrix of Thomas Newcomb, 1699. G841

Great Britain. Sovereign (1702-1714 : Anne). Her Majesties most gracious letter ... in relation to the Company trading to Africa and the Indies. Edinburgh, Heirs and successors of A. Anderson, 1702. G842

The Queen announces her desire that ships sailing to Darien should not be molested by English vessels, and states that she will do whatever is possible to aid the Darien settlement.

Great Britain. Sovereign (1702-1714 : Anne). Her Majesty's most gracious speech to both houses of Parliament, on Friday, the sixth day of June, 1712. Dublin, E. Waters [1712].   G843

A review of negotiations leading to the Treaty of Utrecht, covering the transfer of territories in the New World and commercial rights there.

Great Britain. Sovereign (1727-1760 : George II). His Majesty's patent for improving fisheries and manufactures in Scotland. Edinburgh, J. Davidson, 1727.   G844

A law which provides funds to be administered by a board of commissioners, to encourage hemp, woolen, linen, and fishing industries.

Great Britain. Sovereign (1727-1760 : George II). Instructions for such merchants, and others, who shall have letters of marque or commissions for private men of war, against France, from the governor of Gibraltar. Manuscript. [Gibraltar, 1744.]   G845

Royal instructions governing procedures for seizure and disposal of ships and goods by merchantmen holding letters of marque.

Great Britain. Sovereign (1760-1820 : George III). New commission of the governor of Quebec; and other instruments of authority, delivered from the crown relative to America. [London, 1775.]   G846

The commission to Sir Guy Carleton upon his appointment. Other documents include the commission of the governor of New York and the first and second charters of Carolina.

Great Britain. Sovereign (1760-1820 : George III). His Majesty's most gracious speech to both houses of Parliament, on Thursday, November 26, 1778. London, Charles Eyre and William Strahan, 1778.   G847

A call for support of military forces made necessary by French aid to the American rebels and invasion of British colonies in the West Indies and North America.

Great Britain. Sovereign (1760-1820 : George III). His Majesty's most gracious speech to both houses of Parliament, on Saturday, July 3, 1779. London, Charles Eyre and William Strahan, 1779.   G848

Reference is made to hostilities with France and impending difficulties with Spain, and to the rebellion in America which is attributed to foreign influence.

Great Britain. Sovereign (1760-1820 : George III). Instructions for the commanders of such merchant ships and vessels, who shall have letters of marque and reprizals. London the 21 of December 1780. Copenhagen, N.C. Høpffner, 1781.   G849

The instructions are meant to deal with the seizing of ships of the United Netherlands. The English-Danish text reflects concern for the treaty of 1780 between Great Britain and Denmark.

Great Britain. Treaties, etc. [Agreement between the ambassadors of Henry IV and those of the Duke of Burgundy.] Manuscript. Dated Calais, 31 October 1405.   G850

The ambassadors agree to meet again to report on the terms offered for a commercial treaty between England and Burgundy.

Great Britain. Treaties, etc. [Treaty between ambassssadors of England and Burgundy.] Manuscript. [n.p.] 27 May 1411.   G851

Representatives of Henry IV and John the Fearless of Burgundy record agreement on rights of English pilgrims and merchants passing through Burgundy.

Great Britain. Treaties, etc. Articles of peace, entercourse, and commerce, concluded in the names of ... James ... King of Great Britain and ... Philip the third, King of Spaine ... London, Robert Barker, 1605.   G852

Nearly every provision in the treaty relates to the restoration of commerce between England and Spain.

Great Britain. Treaties, etc. Articulen van het contract ende accoort ghemaeckt tusschen ... Enghelandt ende ... Spaengnien. [Middelburg, 1605.]   G853

A Dutch edition of the treaty between James I and Philip III.

Great Britain. Treaties, etc. Capitulaciones de la paz, hecha entre el Rey nuestro señor ... y el serenissimo Rey de la Gran Bretaña ... en Londres, a 18. de Agosto, de 1604. Valladolid. Luis Sāchez, 1605.   G854

This Spanish edition includes introductory material not in the English edition.

Great Britain. Treaties, etc. Articles of peace, entercourse, and commerce, concluded in the names of ... Charles ... and Philip, the Fourth King of Spaine. London, Robert Barker, 1630.   G855

Normal trade between England and Spain is restored, but English shippers are restrained from carrying goods from the Low Countries to Spain.

Great Britain. Treaties, etc. Articles of peace and commerce, between ... Charles ... and John the 4th King of Portugal. London, Robert Barker, 1642.   G856

Normal commercial relations including general freedom of trade are established between the two countries. The treaty notes the inability to conclude terms concerning English trade to Africa, India, and Brazil.

Great Britain. Treaties, etc. Articulen van vrede, unie, ende eeuwich verbondt besloten tusschen ... Engelandt ... ende de ... Staten Generael. The Hague, Weduwe, ende erfgenamen van wylen H.J. van Wouw, 1654.   G857

The treaty of peace ending the Anglo-Dutch war of 1653-54. Terms concerning Dutch fishing rights in the North Sea were left vague, and both parties promised not to carry arms into the harbors of the other.

Great Britain. Treaties, etc. Articuli pacis, unionis, & confoederationis ... inter ... Reipublicae Angliae ... et ... Dominos Ordines Generales ... The Hague, Viduae ac haeredum, H.J. van Wouw, 1654. G858

The treaty ending the first Anglo-Dutch War, calling for resumption of normal commerce.

Great Britain. Treaties, etc. Articles of peace and alliance between Charles II ... and the States General. London, J. Bill and C. Barker, 1662. G859

The treaty provides for free trade between the countries and their colonies, and joint action against pirates.

Great Britain. Treaties, etc. Articulen van 't tractaat ... tusschen ... Groot Brittannien en de Staten Generaal. The Hague, Hillebrandt van Wouw, 1663. G860

A treaty calling for cooperation and friendship between England and the Netherlands, with stipulations for free trade.

Great Britain. Treaties, etc. Articles of peace & alliance, between ... Charles II ... and ... Lewis XIV. [London] Assigns of J. Bill and C. Barker, 1667. G861

Great Britain. Treaties, etc. Articles of peace & alliance, between ... Charles II ... and Frederick III King of Denmark and Norway. [London] Assigns of John Bill and C. Barker, 1667. G862

Great Britain. Treaties, etc. Articles of peace and alliance between ... Charles II ... and States General of the United Netherlands ... 1667. [London] Assigns of J. Bill & C. Barker, 1667. G863

The English edition of the Treaty of Breda, concluding the Second Dutch War. It provided for the transfer of New Amsterdam to English possession, permitted the Dutch to export goods to England, called for joint action against smugglers, and dealt with other commercial problems.

Great Britain. Treaties, etc. Articulen van vrede ende verbondt tusschen ... Karel, de Tweede ... ende de ... Staten Generael. The Hague, H. van Wouw, 1667. G864

A Dutch edition of the Treaty of Breda.

Great Britain. Treaties, etc. Articuli pacis & confoederationis inter serenissimum & potentissimum principem Carolum II ... et celsos ac praepotentes dominos Ordines Generales foederatarum Belgii provinciarum. London, Johannis Bill & Christophori Barker, 1667. G865

Latin edition of the Treaty of Breda, printed in London.

Great Britain. Treaties, etc. Articuli pacis, inter ... Carolum ... & Ordines Generales. The Hague, H. van Wouw, 1667. G866

A Latin edition of the Treaty of Breda, printed in The Hague.

Great Britain. Treaties, etc. Tractaet vande vrede, tusschen ... Karel de Tweede, Konig van Groot Brittannien ... ende ... de Staten Generael der Vereenichde Nederlanden. Rotterdam, J. Redelickhuysen, 1667. G867

Dutch edition of the Treaty of Breda.

Great Britain. Treaties, etc. Articles of peace and commerce, between ... Charles II ... and the Bashaw, Dai, Aga, and governours of ... Algiers. London, Assigns of John Bill and Christopher Barker, 1672. G868

The treaty specifies conditions for English trade in Algiers, and specifies limitations upon Algerian rights of search, seizure, and taking of prizes.

Great Britain. Treaties, etc. Articulen van vrede en verbondt, tusschen ... Groot Brittannien ... ende ... Vereenighde Nederlandtsche Provincien. The Hague, Jacob Scheltus, 1674. G869

The Dutch agree to send a council to London to deal with the problem of East Indian trade.

Great Britain. Treaties, etc. Articuli pacis, inter ... Carolum ejus nominis Secundum Magnae Britanniae Regem ... & ... Ordines Generales Foederati Belgii Provinciarum ... conclusae. The Hague, J. Scheltus, 1674. G870

Great Britain. Treaties, etc. Tractaet van marine, tusschen ... Engelandt ... ende ... Vereenighde Nederlandsche provincien. The Hague, Jacob Scheltum [1674]. G871

The treaty provides for a large measure of free trade between England and the Netherlands.

Great Britain. Treaties, etc. Tractatus de rebus maritimis, inter Serenissimum & Potentissimum Principem Carolum II ... & celsos & praepotentes Dominos Ordines Generales. The Hague, J. Scheltus [1674]. G872

Great Britain. Treaties, etc. Artikel, tusschen ... Carel de II ... ende de ... Staten Generael. [n.p.] 1675. G873

An expansion upon an article of the Anglo-Dutch treaty of 1674, attempting to work out a live and let live policy in the East Indies.

Great Britain. Treaties, etc. A treaty marine between ... Charles II ... and Lewis XIV.

London, Assigns of John Bill and C. Barker, 1677. G874
  The treaty concerns freedom of navigation and trade.

Great Britain. Treaties, etc. Several treaties of peace and commerce concluded between the late King ... and other princes and states. London, Assigns of John Bill, etc., 1685. G875
  A collection of treaties signed during the reign of Charles II, many of which contain commercial agreements with European and African rulers.

Great Britain. Treaties, etc. Several treaties of peace and commerce ... London, Sold by Edward Poole, 1686. G876
  A collection of seventeen treaties between England and other powers, frequently concerning commercial affairs.

Great Britain. Treaties, etc. Treaty of peace, good correspondence and neutrality in America. London, T. Newcomb, 1686. G877
  France and England agree to stay out of each other's colonies, confining their trade and fishing to their own harbors and waters.

Great Britain. Treaties, etc. Articles of peace and commerce between ... James II ... and the Douletli Basha, Aga and governors of ... Algiers. [London] Thomas Newcomb, 1687. G878
  An attempt to establish peaceful commerce between England and Algiers.

Great Britain. Treaties, etc. The assiento; or contract for allowing to the subjects of Great Britain the liberty of importing Negroes into the Spanish America. London, J. Baskett, 1713. G879

Great Britain. Treaties, etc. Tractatus navigationis et commerciorum ... between ... Anne and ... Lewis the XIVth. London, John Baskett and the assigns of Thomas Newcomb and Henry Hills, 1713. G880
  Latin and English text of that portion of the Treaty of Utrecht which related to commercial agreements between the two nations.

Great Britain. Treaties, etc. Tractatus pacis ... between ... Anne ... and Louis XIV. London, J. Baskett, 1713. G881
  Contains the Treaty of Utrecht, Treaty of Navigation and Commerce, and the asiento agreement.

Great Britain. Treaties, etc. Traité de marine et de commerce, entre la Grande-Bretagne & l'Espagne : signé à Utrecht le 9. Decembre 1713. The Hague, T. Johnson, 1714. G882
  This treaty is an aspect of the larger Treaty of Utrecht. It gives the British traders increased privileges to trade in the Spanish-American empire.

Great Britain. Treaties, etc. Tractatus pacis & amicitiae ... Treaty of peace and friendship between ... Anne, by the grace of God Queen of Great Britain ... and Philip the Vth, the Catholick King of Spain, concluded at Utrecht the 2/13th day of July, 1713. London, John Baskett and the assigns of Thomas Newcomb and Henry Hills, 1714. G883
  The treaty prohibits any grant of commercial or territorial advantage in the New World to France by Spain, and includes the asiento agreement giving Great Britain the right to supply slaves to Spanish America.

Great Britain. Treaties, etc. The defensive treaty concluded in the year, 1700. Betwixt His late Majesty King William ... and His present Swedish Majesty King Charles the XII. [n.p., 1717.] G884

Great Britain. Treaties, etc. The treaty of peace, union, and friendship, and mutual defence, between the crowns of Great-Britain, France, and Spain, concluded at Seville on the 9th of November, n.s. 1729. London, S. Buckley, 1729. G885
  With regard to commercial relations between the three nations and their American colonies, arrangements existing in 1725 were to prevail.

Great Britain. Treaties, etc. The convention between the Crowns of Great Britain and Spain, concluded at the Pardo on the 14th of January 1739, n.s. London, Samuel Buckley, 1739. G886
  This convention was an attempt to settle differences over boundaries between Florida and Carolina, seizure of ships, and violations of policies regarding trade in the New World.

Great Britain. Treaties, etc. Treaty between His Britannick Majesty and Her imperial Majesty of all the Russias; together with the four separate articles belonging thereto. Signed at Moscow, December 11, 1742. [n.p., ca. 1742.] G887
  Basically a military treaty, this includes provision for extending the treaty of commerce and navigation made in December, 1734.

Great Britain. Treaties, etc. A treaty concluded and signed at Madrid, on the 5th of October n.s. 1750, between the ministers plenipotentiaries of their Britannick and Catholic Majesties. London, Edward Owen, 1750. G888
  A bilateral arrangement supplementary to the treaty of Aix-la-Chapelle, its primary purpose being a continuation of the asiento agreement.

Great Britain. Treaties, etc. A treaty of peace and friendship between the King of Great Britain and the Emperor of Morocco ... London, Edward Owen, 1751. G889
  Relates to the commerce of England with several North African ports.

Great Britain. Treaties, etc. An extract of the articles of the treaty of commerce, between the crowns of Great Britain and Russia, dated the 2d of December, 1734. [London, ca. 1752.] G890
This extract of the treaty includes provisions of particular interest to English merchants, adding commentary to show the advantages British merchants enjoy over other foreigners trading in Russia.

Great Britain. Treaties, etc. Treaty between His Britannick Majesty, and Her Imperial Majesty of all the Russias. Signed at St. Peterburg, September 19/30, 1755. Together with the two separate and secret articles belonging thereto. [London?, 1755?] G891
A renewal of the Treaty of Defensive Alliance of 1742. The two separate and "secret" articles concern the payment of supplied troops and an agreement to communicate confidentially in time of war.

Great Britain. Treaties, etc. Extracts from the several treaties subsisting between Great Britain and other kingdoms and states, of such articles and clauses, as relate to the duty and conduct of the commanders of His Majesty's ships of war. London, 1758. G892
These extracts are from treaties made between Great Britain and the major powers of Europe, Turkey, and the North African states, going back in some instances to the fifteenth century, and emphasizing commercial relations.

Great Britain. Treaties, etc. Preliminary articles of peace between His Britannic Majesty, the Most Christian King and the Catholick King. London, E. Owen and T. Harrison, 1762. G893
Articles proposing to settle territorial and trading rights among England, France and Spain.

Great Britain. Treaties, etc. A complete collection of all the marine treaties subsisting between Great-Britain and France, Spain, Portugal, ... [etc.] : commencing in the year 1546, and including the definitive treaty of 1763 : with an introductory discourse, explaining the force and meaning of the principal articles. London, J. Millan and D. Steel, 1779. G894
A collection of excerpts from treaties with maritime powers intended for the use of privateers.

Great Britain. Treaties, etc. Authentic copies of the provisional and preliminary articles of peace signed between Great Britain, France, Spain, and the United States of America ... London, For J. Stockdale, 1783. G895
The first published form of the Treaty of Paris concluding the American Revolution and the independence of the United States. The treaty with France includes topics in Asia, that with Spain deals with Florida and the Bahamas.

Great Britain. Treaties, etc. A collection of all the treaties of peace, alliance, and commerce, between Great-Britain and other powers, from the treaty signed at Munster in 1648, to the treaties signed at Paris in 1783. London, For J. Debrett, 1785. G896
A collection of 108 treaties and conventions together with other diplomatic documents through a period "most essentially interesting to the British Nation, as containing the whole of our Trade system."

Great Britain. Treaties, etc. Treaty of navigation and commerce between His Britannick Majesty and the most Christian King. London, T. Harrison and S. Brooke, 1786. G897
Permits considerable freedom of trade, but specifies restrictions on wine, spirits, oil, cloth, hardware, millinery, glass, and porcelain.

Great Britain. Treaties, etc. Convention between His Britannick Majesty and the King of Spain. London, E. Johnston, 1790. G898
Negotiations regarding the Nootka incident resulting from British and Spanish rivalry on the American northwest coast.

Great Britain. Treaties, etc. Convencion entre el Rey nuestro señor y el Rey de la Gran-Bretaña, transigiendo varios puntos sobre pesca, navegacion y comercio en el océano Pacífico ... Madrid, Imprenta Real [1790]. G899
This document represents the beginning of an agreement between the governments of Spain and Great Britain following the Nootka Sound controversy.

Great Britain. Treaties, etc. Convention between His Britannick Majesty and the Empress of Russia : signed at London, the 25th of March, 1793. London, Edward Johnston, 1793. G900
The two nations ally themselves against France, reinvoke a commercial treaty of 1766, and propose to work toward a new commercial agreement.

Great Britain. Treaties, etc. Treaty of amity, commerce, and navigation, between His Britannick Majesty and the United States of America : signed at London, the 19th of November, 1794. London, Edward Johnston, 1795. G901
One of many 1795 editions of the Jay Treaty.

Great Britain's complaints against Spain impartially examin'd. London, For J. Roberts, 1740. G902
A review of Anglo-Spanish relations leading to war, and involving commercial rivalries in the West Indies.

Great Britain's poverty and distress, exemplified by the East-India monopoly. London, For G. Bible, 1755. G903
The author cites the high cost of East Indian goods, the low level of re-export, and the exporting of gold as indictments of the East India Company's monopoly. He proposes a limited free trade to replace it.

The great necessity and advantage of preserving our own manufactures. London, For T. Newborough, 1697. G904

A partisan of the English cloth manufacturers who resented competition from imported Indian cloth replies here to Sir Josiah Child's *The great honour and advantage of the East India trade.*

Green, John. The construction of maps and globes ... London, For T. Horne [etc.] 1717. G905

Apparently intended as an introduction to a two-volume collection of travels, this work provides commentary on the state of geographical knowledge and cartographic technique in addition to its explication of globes.

Green, John. A journey from Aleppo to Damascus: with a description of those two cities, and the neighbouring parts of Syria ... London, For W. Mears [etc.], 1736. G906

An account of the Levant from a variety of sources, including an account of caravans which left Aleppo regularly for Mecca, and a new map of Syria.

Green, John. Remarks, in support of the New chart of North and South America; in six sheets. London, Thomas Jefferys, 1753. G907

Six sheets containing maps of the New World and the Pacific Ocean, accompanied by a detailed commentary of the sources used.

Green, John. A sermon preached before the incorporated Society for the Propagation of the Gospel in Foreign Parts... in the parish church of St. Mary-le-Bow on Friday February 19, 1769. London, E. Owen and T. Harrison, 1769. G908

The annual sermon of the Society, showing concern for the shortage of pastors in America, and the needs of Indians and the slave population of the colonies.

Greene, Thomas. A sermon preached before the incorporated Society for the Propagation of the Gospel in Foreign Parts: at their anniversary meeting in the parish-church of St. Mary-le-Bow, on Friday the 21st of February, 1723 ... London, Joseph Downing, 1723. G909

The sermon is followed by appendices indicating progress of the missions, identity of clerical appointees, names of benefactors, etc.

Grégoire, Henri. Lettre aux philanthropes, sur les malheurs, les droits et les réclamations des gens de coleur de Saint-Domingue, et des autres îles françoises de l'Amérique. Paris, Belin [etc] 1790. G910

An appeal for full recognition of the rights of mulattoes in the French West Indies, with annotations and historical background on the legal position of these people.

Grégoire, Henri. Mémoire en faveur des gens de couleur ou sangmêlés de St.-Domingue, et des autres isles francoises de l'Amérique. Paris, Belin, 1789. G911

A review of race problems in the French colonies with proposals for better relations, beginning with the granting of full citizenship to Mulattoes with all rights of Frenchmen.

Grelot, Guillaume-Joseph. A late voyage to Constantinople. London, John Playford, 1683. G912

A delightfully illustrated general description of Constantinople and the surrounding area, with commentary on the industries and trade of the city.

Grenier, Jacques Raymond, Vicomte de Giron. Mémoires de la campagne de découvertes dans les mers des Indes. Brest, R. Malassis, 1770. G913

The author proposes a new route from Isle de France to Pondichéry by way of the Seychelle Islands, and comments on the winds and currents of the Indian Ocean with respect to navigation.

[Grenville, George.] The regulations lately made concerning the colonies, and the taxes imposed upon them, considered. London, For J. Wilkie, 1765. G914

Recommends stamp duties as a menas of paying for colonial defense, and of regulating the colonial economy for the general good, by the chancellor of the exchequer.

Grenville, George. Tableau de l'Angleterre, relativement à son commerce et à ses finances. Londres & Paris, Desaint, 1769. G915

A discussion of England's declining commercial situation. This French edition contains many notes supplied by the translator, Guyard de Troyes.

Greppi, Paolo. Relazione commerciale: [1776]: di Paolo Greppi, Console Imperiale in Cadice. Manuscript [1776.] G916

Concerns proposals to undertake trade to Spanish America through the port of Trieste.

Greslon, Adrien. Histoire de la Chine sous la domination des Tartares. Paris, Jean Henault, 1671. G917

An account of the attitude toward Jesuits by the Manchu dynasty during the period 1651-69, describing much persecution but with some indications of improved treatment for the missionaries in the future.

[Greville, Charles Francis]. British India analyzed. The provincial and revenue establishments of Tippoo Sultaun and of the Mahomedan and British conquerors in Hindostan, stated and considered. In three parts. London, 1795. G918

An analysis of the ways in which recent British legislation would affect the presence of British authority in India as it sought to relate more closely to local institutions.

[Griffith, Thomas Waters.] l'Indépendance absolue des Américains des Etats-Unis. Paris, Laran, 1798. G919
A reply to J. Fauchet's *Coup d'oeil sur l'etat actuel de nos rapports politiques avec les États-Unis* in which Fauchet contended that the American republic continued to be dependent upon Great Britain.

Grijalva, Juan de. Cronica de la orden de N.P.S. Augustin en las provincias de la Nueva España. [Mexico, Joan Ruyz, 1624.] G920
A history of the Augustinian missions in Mexico, the Philippine Islands and China in the last half of the sixteenth century. The author was born in Mexico and was rector of St. Paul's College in Mexico City.

[Grillo, Domingo.] En la villa de Madrid a cinco dias del mes de Julio de mil y seiscientos y sesenta y dos años ... [Madrid, 1662.] G921
A petition to the King of Spain for asiento rights in exchange for the supplying of ships for the Spanish-American trade.

[Grillo, Domingo and Ambrosio Lomelín.] La experiencia de tantos años quantos ha que se poblaron las Indias ... [n.p., ca. 1660.] G922
An argument for placing the supplying of slaves for Spain's American colonies under Spanish control.

The groans of Ireland: in a letter to a member of parliament. Dublin, George Faulkner, 1741. G923
A description of the disastrous state of the Irish economy, with recommendations for its improvement.

Groeben, Otto Friedrich von der. Orientalische Reise-Beschreibung ... nebst der brandenburgischen Schiffahrt nach Guinea, und der Verichtung zu Morea. Marienwerder, Simon Reinigern, 1694. G924
An account of three voyages to the Levant, to west Africa and to Morea. The second of these was a part of the attempt by the Elector of Brandenburg to establish a trading company on the Gold Coast.

Groningen (Netherlands : Province). Staten Gecommitteerden Tot de Finances. [Letter signed.] Groningen, 19 May 1786. G925
Concerns affairs of the Dutch colony of Surinam.

Gronovius, Jacobus. Geographica antiqua, hoc est: Scylacis Periplus Maris Mediterranei: Anonymi Periplus maeotidis paludis & Ponti Euxini ... Leiden, J. Luchtmans, 1697. G926
A compilation of four geographical works by classical authors. The first three are in Greek and Latin, in parallel columns. The last one in Latin only. Besides his own commentary Gronovius includes the notes of Vossius, Jacques Le Paulmier de Grentemesnil and Samuel Tennulius. This is the first edition.

Gronovius, Jacobus. Geographica antiqua, hoc est: Scylacis Periplus Maris Mediterranei. Anonymi Periplus Maeotidis paludis & Ponti Euxini ... Leiden, Jordanum Luchtmans, 1700. G927
A re-issue of the 1697 edition, with new title and some additional text.

Het groote tafereel der dwaasheid, vertoonende de opkomst, voortgang en ondergang der actie, bubbel, en windnegotie, in Vrankryk, Engeland, en de Nederlanden. [Amsterdam, D. Onder de Linden] 1720. G928
A lampoon of speculative companies, directed particularly against the South Sea Company and John Law's Mississippi Company. Contains eighty-one engravings.

Grose, John Henry. A voyage to the East-Indies with observations on various parts there. London, A. Hooper and A. Morley, 1757. G929
Describes the people, institutions, and trade of western India.

Grose, John Henry. A voyage to the East-Indies, with observations on various parts there. London, For S. Hooper and A. Morley, 1757. G930
A duplicate the previous item but with a manuscript journal bound in.

Grose, John Henry. A voyage to the East Indies; containing authentic accounts of the Mogul government in general, the viceroyalties of the Decan and Bengal with their several subordinate dependances ... With general reflections on the trade of India ... London, S. Hooper, 1772. G931
This third edition includes both the account of the Anglo-French wars in India, and an additional account of travels from Aleppo to Basrah by a Mr. Carmichael in 1771. The illustrations are by Francis Grose.

Grose, John Henry. Voyage aux Indes Orientales ... traduit de l'Anglois par M. Hernandez ... Londres, et se trouve a Lille, Veuve Panckouke; Paris, Desaint & Saillant, Michel Lambert, 1758. G932
The first French translation.

Grosier, J.-B. (Jean-Baptiste). Description général de la Chine. Paris, Moutard [etc.] 1785. G933
This first edition was appended to J.A.M. Moyriac de Mailla's *l'Histoire générale de la Chine*, a translation from the Chinese.

Grosier, J.-B. (Jean-Baptiste). Description générale de la Chine. Paris, Moutard [etc.] 1787. G934
The second edition of a commentary on each of the provinces of China, its outlying areas, and the manners,

customs, religion, science, and natural history of the country as a whole.

Grotius, Hugo. De jure belli ac pacis. Paris, Nicolaum Byon, 1625. G935
The first edition of an examination of the rights of any nation at sea, which to a considerable degree grew out of the author's concern for commercial rivalries.

Grotius, Hugo. De jure belli ac pacis. Amsterdam, Willem Blaeu, 1631. G936
The second authorized edition, with numerous additions and changes in the text from the first edition.

Grotius, Hugo. Drie boecken ... nopende het recht des oorloghs ende des vredes. Haarlem, Adriaen Roman, 1635. G937
The first complete Dutch edition, a fragment having been published in 1626.

Grotius, Hugo. Of the law of warre and peace. London, T. Warren for William Lee, 1654. G938
The first English edition, translated by Clement Barksdale.

Grotius, Hugo. The most excellent Hugo Grotius his three books treating of the rights of war & peace ... London, M.W. for Thomas Basset and Ralph Smith, 1682. G939
The third English edition, a new translation by William Evats.

Grotius, Hugo. The rights of war and peace, in three books ... London, W. Innys [etc.], 1738. G940
This edition contains the annotations of Jean Barbeyrac which make up about half of the text.

Grotius, Hugo. Le droit de la guerre, et de la paix ... Nouvelle traduction par Jean Barbeyrac. Basel, Emanuel Thourneisen, 1746. G941
The third edition of the Barbeyrac translation.

Grotius, Hugo. Mare liberum sive De jure quod Batavis competit ad Indica, na commercia dissertatio. Leiden, Ludovici Elzevirii, 1609. G942
The first published statement of Grotius' argument for freedom of the seas, written as a result of Dutch and Portuguese conflicts in the East Indies.

Grotius, Hugo. De mare libero et P. Merula De maribus. Leiden, Elzevir, 1633. G943
Included in this edition are Paulus Merula, *Navigationibus Hollandorum* and *Tractatus pacis et mutui commercii*.

Grundlage zu einem vollständigen Verzeichnisse aller Schriften die Ostindien und die damit verbundene Länder betreffen. Hamburg, Carl Ernst Bohn [179-?]. G944

An alphabetical listing of 1372 travel narratives and geographies, including material from collected travels.

Grynaus, Simon. Novus orbis regionum ac insularum veteribus incognitarum. Basel, J. Hervagium, 1532. G945
The first edition of a popular collection of voyages compiled by J. Huttich, including accounts of Columbus, Vespucci, Pinzon, Varthema, Marco Polo, and others. Also contains a large world map attributed to Hans Holbein.

Grynaus, Simon. Novus orbis regionum ... Basel, J. Hervagium, 1555. G946
This edition adds the second and third letter of Cortés, and two other letters pertaining to Spanish activities in Central America.

Grynaus, Simon. Die New Welt, der Landschaften unnd Insulen so bis hie her allen Altweltbeschrybern unbekant. Strassburg, Georgen Ulricher, 1534. G947
The first German edition.

Grynaus, Simon. Die nieuwe weerelt der lantschappen ende eylanden die tot hier toe allen ouden weerelt bescrijveren onbekent geweest sijn. Antwerp, Jan vander Loe, 1563. G948
The first Dutch edition.

Guadet, Marguerite-Élie. Opinion de M. Gaudet ... sur les colonies; prononcée dans la séance du 23 mars 1792. [Paris, Imprimerie Nationale, 1792.] G949
A discussion of alleged reasons and real reasons for the slave rebellion in Saint Domingue.

Guadet, Marguerite-Élie. An inquiry into the causes of the insurrection of the Negroes in the island of St. Domingo. London, J. Johnson, 1792. G950
The first English edition.

Gualdo Priorato, Galeazzo, conte. Relatione delle provincie unite del Paese Basso. Cologne, Pietro de la Place, 1668. G951
Accounts of the East and West Indian companies are included in this guidebook, as well as descriptions of the industry and trade of the major cities of the Netherlands.

Guattini, Michele Angelo. Viaggio ... nel regno del Congo. Bologna, Gioseffo Longhi, 1674. G952
This account of Capuchin missionary activity in the Congo and Angola also includes five letters written from Pernambuco by missionaries en route from Lisbon to Africa. Following the author's death in 1668, the account is continued by Dionigi Carli.

Guattini, Michele Angelo. Viaggio nel regno del Congo. Venice, Iseppo Prodocimo, 1679. G953

A close reprinting of the previous work, with some changes in the preliminary material.

Guden, Philipp Peter. Betrachtungen über das Recht bey der Bezahlung in veränderten Münzen. Braunschweig & Hildesheim, Schröderschen Buchladen, 1764. G954

This treatise by Guden on economic matters: gold, currency, exchange rates, prices, banking, etc., makes extensive reference to Cantillon, Forbonnais and Montesquieu. Guden wrote several economic treatises. First edition.

Güldenstädt, Johann Anton. Reisen durch Russland und im caucasischen Gebürge. St. Petersburg, Kayserl. Akademie der Wissenschaften, 1787-1791. G955

A very detailed account of travels from St. Petersburg to Astrakhan, edited by Peter Simon Pallas.

Guéroult du Pas, P. Jacques. Recuëil de veües de tous les differens bastimens de la mer mediterranée, et de l'ocean, avec leurs noms et usages. Paris, Pierre Giffart, 1710. G956

Engravings depicting twenty-nine types of ships used in Atlantic commerce, the same number for the Mediterranean, sixteen used in the coastal fisheries, and six ships of war.

Guerreiro, Bartolomeu. Sermão ... na cidade de Lisboa na Capella Real, dia de São Thome, anno de 1623. Lisbon, Pedro Crasbeeck, 1624. G957

A sermon commemorating Portuguese success in Asia, and a plea for further efforts to defend and extend Christianity there.

Guerreiro, Fernão. Relaçam annual das cousas que fizeram os padres da Companhia de Jesus na India, & Japão nos annos de 600 & 601. Evora, Manoel de Lyra, 1603. G958

An account of recent events relative to Jesuit missions in India and Japan, collected from missionary letters.

Guerreiro, Fernão. Relacion anual de las cosas que han hecho los padres de la Compañia de Jesus en la India Oriental y Japon. Valladolid, Luys Sanchez, 1604. G959

A Spanish translation of the previous work.

Guerreiro, Fernão. Relaçam annual das cousas que fezeram os padres la Companhia de Jesus nas partes da India Oriental, & no Brasil, Angola, Cabo Verde, Guine, nos annos de seiscentos & dous & seiscentos & tres, & do processo da conversam, & Christandade daquellas partes ... Lisbon, Jorge Rodrigues, 1605. G960

This is the second *Relaçam* issued by Guerreiro from reports of Jesuit missionaries in the various Portuguese establishments around the world.

Guerreiro, Fernão. Relaçam annual das cousas que fezeram os padres da Companhia de Jesu nas partes da India Oriental, & em algũas outras da conquista deste reyno nos annos de 604 & 605. Lisbon, Pedro Crasbeeck, 1607. G961

This is the third of Guerreiro's reviews of mission work in the Portuguese empire, covering Japan, China, India, Pegu, Amboyna, Ethiopia, Angola, Guinea and Sierra Leone.

Guerreiro, Fernão. Relaçam annal das cousas que fezeram os padres da Companhia de Jesus nas partes da India Oriental ... no anno de 606. & 607. & do processo da conuersaõ, & Christandade dasquellas partes ... Lisbon, Pedro Crasbeeck, 1609. G962

A digest of Jesuit letters covering Japan, Asia, India, Ethiopia, West Africa, and Brazil.

[Guerreiro, Fernão.] Historischer Bericht, was sich in dem ... Königreich China ... von 1604. und volgenden Jaren, denckwürdigs zugetragen. Augsburg, Chrysostomo Dabertzhofer, 1611. G963

Translation of accounts of missionary progress in China from the collection of letters published in 1605, 1607, and 1609. Appended is a letter from Matteo Ricci.

Guerreiro, Fernão. Relaçam annal das cousas que fizeram os padres da Companhia de Jesus, nas partes da India Oriental ... nos annos de 607. & 608. : & do processo da conuersaõ & Christandade daquellas partes ... Lisboa, Pedro Crasbeeck, 1611. G964

This is the last of Guerreiro's compilations of material on the Jesuits in Africa and the East Indies. This one includes material on Ethiopia, India, China and Japan.

[Guerreiro, Fernão.] Historia y anal relacion de las cosas que hizieron los padres de la Compañia de Jesus, por las partes de Oriente y otras. Madrid, Imprenta Real, 1614. G965

A Spanish translation of the preceding report on Portuguese Jesuit missionary activity in many stations, from Sierra Leone to Japan.

Guiana Company. A breefe relation of the present state of the business of Guiana. [London] 1627. G966

A broadside giving details of a new corporation formed by two previous colonizers, Robert Harcourt and Captain Roger North, for the purpose of settling and exploiting the commercial potential of Guiana.

Guicciardini, Lodovico. Descrittione ... du tutti i Paesi Bassi. Antwerp, Guglielmo Silvio, 1567. G967

This account of the Netherlands contains descriptions of a large number of Dutch and Flemish cities, and includes accounts of the commerce of some of them.

Le guide d'Amsterdam, enseignant aux voyageurs et aux negocians sa splendeur, son commerce, & la description de ses edifices. Amsterdam, Daniel de la Feuille, 1701. G968

An illustrated description of Amsterdam with particular emphasis on its commercial aspects, including its transportation network, mercantile companies, customs regulations, and currency exchange.

Le guide d'Amsterdam, enseignant aux voyageurs, et aux negocians, sa splendeur, son commerce, et la description de ses edifices ... Amsterdam, Paul de la Feuille, 1709. G969
Contains a detailed list of merchandise that flowed through Amsterdam, with amounts of duty paid.

Gumilla, Joseph. Histoire naturelle, civile et géographique de l'Orenoque. Avignon, Desaint & Saillant; Marseilles, Jean Mossy, 1758. G970
A general description of the Orinoco region which emphasizes the products of the area, translated by Marc Eidous from the original edition in Spanish.

Gumilla, Joseph. Historia natural, civil y geografica de las naciones situadas en las riveras del Rio Orinoco. Barcelona, Carlos Gilbert y Tutó, 1791. G971
The third Spanish edition including illustrations not found in earlier editions.

Gunter, Edmund. The description and use of the sector, crosse-staffe, and other instruments: with a canon of artificial sines and tangents ... 2d. ed. much enlarged. London, William Jones for James Bowler, 1636. G972
A landmark book in the history of theoretical navigation, the author's sector and cross-staff being important in locating a ship's position by calculation. It was first published in 1623.

Gusmão, Alexandre de. Obras de Alexandre de Guzmaõ Secretario Particular do gabinete do Fidelissimo Rey o Senhor Dom Joaõ 5°. Manuscript in Portuguese. [n.p., ca. 1752]. G973
The compiler of this manuscript was secretary to the king of Portugal, Dom João V, and a member of the Conselho Ultramarino. A significant part of the work deals with Spanish-Portuguese territorial conflict in America.

Guthrie, William. A new system of modern geography. 2 vols. Philadelphia, Printed by M. Carey, 1794-1795. G974
The first American edition of a work originally published in London, 1770. The maps originally intended for this work were issued separately in the *American Atlas*, 1795, and *General Atlas*, 1796.

Guyenne (France). Chambre de Commerce. Mémoire de la Chambre de Commerce de Guienne, sur le privilege exclusif accordé à une nouvelle Compagnie des Indes. [n.p.] 1786. G975
A criticism of the grant of a charter made to the new Compagnie des Indes the previous year, contending that the company does not have the resources to develop this overseas trade.

Guyenne (France). Directeurs du commerce. Memoire des directeurs du commerce de Guienne : en réponse à celuy de Saint Malo, qui demande au roy la franchise de son port. [n.p., ca. 1770] G976
In contradiction to St. Malo's appeal for special commercial privileges, this memoire cites that port's decline from earlier times and extolls the commerce and prosperity of Bordeaux.

Guyenne (France). Directeurs du commerce. Mémoire des directeurs du commerce de la province de Guienne ... concernant le commerce etranger dans les isles françoises de l'Amérique. [n.p.] 1785. G977
A criticism of the order permitting non-French merchants to trade in the French colonies in America.

Guyon, M. l'abbé (Claude-Marie). Histoire des Indes Orientales, anciennes et modernes. Paris, J. Desaint & C. Saillant, 1744. G978
Traces the history of East Indian trade back to ancient times, and also discusses the contemporary European commerce there.

[Guyon, M. l'abbé (Claude-Marie).] A new history of the East Indies, ancient and modern. London, For R. and J. Dodsley, 1757. G979
This English edition adds extensively to the material on the modern East Indian trade.

Gwagnin, Alexander. Sarmatiæ Europeæ descriptio. [Cracow] Matthias Wierzbieta [1578]. G980
A chronicle and description of Slavic Europe by an Italian who served in the Polish army, drawing in part on the work of the Polish historian Strijkowski.

Gwagnin, Alexander. Sarmatiæ Europeæ descriptio. Speyer, Bernardum Albinum, 1581. G981
Much changed edition.

Haaber, Adam. Proces og dom i sagen imellem factorerne i Bengalen og Capitain Adam Haaber: betreffende skibet Ganges's tilladning paa dets sidste reise fra Bengalen til Kiøbenhavn, &c. Copenhagen, John Frederik Schultz, 1786. H1
 A legal proceeding concerning the management of a cargo ship of the Danish Asiatic Company.

Haarlem. Antwoort ende resolutie by de heeren regierders ende vroetschappen der stadt Haerlem, ghenomen op't stuck vanden treves, op de missive aen haer-lieden ghesonden vande groot mogende Staten van Hollandt ende West-Vrieslandt. [n.p.] 1630. H2
 A reprint of the following item with an additional proposal with respect to relations with Spain.

Haarlem. Resolutie, by de heeren raeden ende vroetschappen der stadt Haerlem, ghenomen op seeckere missive aen haerlieden ghesonden, van d'E. Groot Moghende Heeren Staten van Hollandt end West-Vrieslandt, nopende 't stuck vanden treves. Haarlem, A. Roman, 1630. H3
 The council of Haarlem opposes peace with Spain, giving several reasons including the ruin of the West India Company.

Hacke, William. A collection of original voyages. London, J. Knapton, 1699. H4
 Includes Cowley's circumnavigation, Sharpe's expedition to the South Sea, Wood's voyage through the Straits of Magellan, and Roberts' adventures in the Levant.

Haeghs hof-praetje, ofte 't samen-spraeck tusschen een Hagenaer, Amsterdammer, ende Leyenaer ... Leiden, Christoffel de la Ruelle, 1662. H5
 Concerns the effect on trade of past wars with the English.

Haerlems schuyt-praetjen, op't redres vande West-Indische compagnie. [Amsterdam?] 1649. H6
 Considers the failings of the Dutch West India Company, and possibilities of reforming it.

Hahn, Jonas. Ytterligare tilökning wid den förnyade Johan Månssons Sjö-märkes-bok. Stockholm, Kongl. Tryckeriet [1751]. H7
 An addition to the revised version of Månsson's *Sjö-märkes-bok*, published in 1748.

Hakluyt, Richard. Divers voyages touching the discoverie of America, and the ilands adjacent unto the same, made first of all by our Englishmen, and afterward by the French-men and Britons. London, Thomas Dawson, 1582. H8
 A propaganda publication intended to arouse English interest in overseas enterprise, including accounts of the products of America and the trade goods that would be suitable to the American Indians.

Hakluyt, Richard. The principall navigations, voiages and discoveries of the English nation ... London, George Bishop and Ralph Newberie, 1589. H9
 The second issue of the first edition of this classic in English exploration literature, recording the earliest English travels abroad.

Hakluyt, Richard. The principal navigations, voyages, traffiques and discoveries of the English nation ... London, G. Bishop, R. Newberie, and R. Barker, 1599-1600. H10
 This is the second edition of the greatest English collection of voyages, comprising a history of the expansion of English commercial intercsts in the sixteenth century. It follows the pattern of the 1589 edition, but contains much new information.

Halkett, John. Statement respecting the Earl of Selkirk's settlement upon the Red River in North America. London, John Murray, 1817. H11
 The author was Lord Selkirk's brother-in-law, and his book reports the massacre at Seven Oaks on June 19, 1816.

[Halkett, John.] Statement respecting the Earl of Selkirk's settlement upon the Red River in North America. New York, J. Eastburn, 1818. H12
The first American edition.

[Halkett, John.] Précis touchant la colonie du Lord Selkirk, sur la Riviére Rouge ... Montreal, James Lane, 1818. H13
A translation by Hugues Heney of the second edition of Halkett's *Statement respecting the Earl of Selkirk's settlement upon the Red River.*

Hall, Fayrer. Captain Fayrer Hall's evidence before a committee of the House of Commons, in April 1731, concerning the sugar colony bill. [London, 1732.] H14
A collection of three documents giving the opinions of an experienced merchant captain on a key issue in intercolonial trade relations.

[Hall, Fayrer.] The importance of the British plantations in America to this kingdom. London, For J. Peele, 1731. H15
A review of the commercial situation in the American colonies, with descriptions of several islands and their products, and suggestions for more beneficial regulations of the colonial trade.

Hall, R. (Richard). The history of the barbarous cruelties and massacres, committed by the Dutch in the East-Indies. London and Westminster, 1712. H16
Published at the time of the peace conference at Utrecht, this work seeks to sway English sympathies away from demands of the Dutch by reviewing atrocities committed by them against the English at Amboyna and other East Indian islands.

[Hallager, Morten], compiler. Udførlige og troevaerdige efterretninger om de fra Rusland af langs med kysterne af Iishavet is søes giorte opdagelser; tilligemed de i russiske tienste vaerende danske søe-officerers, Commandeur-Capitain Vitus Berings og Capitain Morten Spangbergs soe-reiser, foretagne i aarene 1728, 1729, 1738, 1741 til 1743 paa des østlige ocean fra Kamtschatka af til Japon og Amerika ... Copenhagen, M. Hallager, 1784. H17
A collection of information on Russian exploration in Siberia and the North Pacific, taken from the writings of Gerhard Friedrich Müller and Peter Simon Pallas.

Hamburg (Germany). Senat. An account of the regulations of the new Hambro' coin as far as concerns the trade of Denmark with this city: Together with the reasons of the present agio of the Danish money. Hamburg, 1734. H18
An essay on the principles of currency exchange in international trade, brought about by disagreements between Denmark and Hamburg with obvious implications for commerce in the Baltic Sea area.

Hamel, Hendrik. Journael van de ongeluckige reyse van't jacht de Sperwer. Amsterdam, G.J. Saagman [1670]. H19
An account of the earliest European contact with Korea resulting from a Dutch shipwreck in 1653.

[Hamel, Hendrick.] Relation du naufrage d'un vaisseau holandois, sur la coste de l'isle de Quelpaerts : avec la description du royaume de Corée / traduite du Flamand, par Monsieur Minutoli. Paris, Louys Billaine, 1670. H20
A translation from the Dutch edition of the same year, this French version adds a description of Korea from an unidentified source.

[Hamilton, Alexander.] A defence of the Treaty of amity, commerce, and navigation; entered into between the United States of America & Great Britain; as it has appeared in the papers under the signature of Camillus. New York, Francis Childs [etc.] 1795. H21
The joint work of Hamilton, Rufus King, and John Jay, this volume collects the first twenty-two essays in defense of the Jay Treaty of a total of thirty-eight which were ultimately published.

Hamilton, Alexander. A new account of the East Indies, being the observations and remarks of Capt. Alexander Hamilton, who spent his time there from the year 1688 to 1723 ... Edinburgh, J. Mosman, 1727. H22
This merchant and adventurer recollects his experience of many years spent trading in ports from the Red Sea to China.

Hamilton, Lord Archibald. An answer to an anonymous libel, entitl'd, Articles exhibited against Lord Archibald Hamilton, late governour of Jamaica. London, 1718. H23
A refutation of charges that Lord Hamilton had encouraged actions against the Spaniards in the West Indies, and allegations of a conspiracy against him.

Hamilton, George, surgeon. A voyage round the world, in His Majesty's frigate Pandora. Berwick, W. Phorson, B. Law and Son, 1793. H24
An account of the voyage undertaken to apprehend the *Bounty* mutineers. It includes descriptions of numerous islands in the South Pacific.

Hamond, Walter. A paradox, prooving, that the inhabitants of the isle called Madagascar ... are the happiest people in the world. London, Nathaniel Butter, 1640. H25
An optimistic picture of Madagascar, designed to gather support for a British colony there which was planned by a group of rivals of the East India Company.

[Hampson, John.] Reflections on the present state of the American war. London, T. Payne, 1776.
H26

The author sees no solution to the colonial conflict other than decisive military action.

Hancock, John. An oration delivered March 5, 1774, at the request of the inhabitants of the town of Boston: to commemorate the bloody tragedy of the fifth of March 1770. Boston, Edes and Gill, 1774. H27

A speech commemorating the Boston Massacre, with confident prediction "that the present struggle for liberty will terminate gloriously for America."

Hane, Laureyns van den. Vlaems recht, dat is costumen ende wetten ... van Vlaenderen. Ghent, Maximiliaen Graet, 1664. H28

A massive compendium of laws of seventy-three jurisdictions in Flanders, also including agreements between jurisdictions. Many of the laws and agreements relate to commercial matters.

Hanno. The voyage of Hanno, translated, and accompanied with the Greek text ... by Thomas Falconer. London, Sold by T. Cadell, jun. and Davies, 1797. H29

An English translation, together with a Greek text, and two arguments favoring the truth of a voyage made in 530 B.C. by a Carthaginian to Cape Palmas.

Hansa Towns. Laws, etc. Der erbaren Hänse Stätte revidirte Schiffs Ordnung und Seerecht. Rostock, M. Sachs, 1614. H30

A compilation of fifteen sea regulations affecting merchants of the Hanseatic League.

Hanway, Jonas. Beschreibung seiner Reisen, von London durch Russland und Persien. Hamburg & Leipzig, Georg Christian Grund und Adam Heinrich Holle, 1754. H31

The first German edition.

Hanway, Jonas. An historical account of the British trade over the Caspian Sea. London, Sold by Mr. Dodsley [etc.] 1753. H32

Includes a history of English commerce in the Caspian area from 1553 to 1743.

Hanway, Jonas. An historical account of the British trade over the Caspian Sea: with a journal of travels from London through Russia into Persia ... Dublin, For William Smith and Richard James, 1754. H33

The text follows closely the London edition of 1753, but the maps and illustrations are fewer and are different.

Hanway, Jonas. An historical account of the British trade over the Caspian Sea ... London, For T. Osborne [etc.] 1762. H34

This appears to be a re-issue of the sheets of the second edition.

Hanway, Jonas. Reize van Londen, door Rusland, nae en in Persie. Amsterdam, K. van Tongerlo en F. Houttuin, 1758. H35

This Dutch edition rearranges much of the material and adds extensively to it with translator's notes.

Harcourt, Robert. A relation of a voyage to Guiana. London, John Beale for W. Welby, 1613. H36

An optimistic appraisal of Guiana by the founder of a short-lived colony there.

Harcourt, Robert. The relation of a voyage to Guiana. London, Edward Allde, 1626. H37

The second edition, published in support of the Guiana colony of Roger North.

Hardoin de la Reynerie, Louis Eugène. Consultation pour les actionnaires de la Compagnie des Indes. Paris, Lottin & Lottin, 1788. H38

Relates to the termination of the old Compagnie des Indes and the creation of the new one.

Hare, Francis. The Negociations for a Treaty of Peace, in 1709 consider'd, in a third letter to a Tory-Member. Part the first. 2d ed. London, A. Baldwin, 1711; The Negotiations for a Treaty of Peace, from the breaking off of the conferences at the Hague, to the end of those at Gertuydenberg, consider'd, in a fourth letter to a Tory-member. Part II. London, A. Baldwin, 1711. H39

A discussion of the ways in which delays in making peace were brought about, stressing England's concern at keeping France out of Spain's affairs in Europe and in the Indies.

Hare, Francis. A sermon preached before the incorporated Society for the Propagation of the Gospel in Foreign Parts, at their anniversary meeting in the parish-church of St. Mary-le-Bow, on Friday the 21st of February, 1734 [i.e. 1735]. London, S. Buckley, 1735. H40

This preacher urges that financial success of the colonies will depend upon good order in them, and the missions were the best means to this end.

[Haren, Onno Zwier van]. The sentiments of a Dutch patriot, being the speech of Mr. V* H**n in an august Assembly on the present state of affairs, and the resolution necessary at this juncture to be taken for the safety of the Republic. Dublin, George Faulkner, 1746. H41

A forceful argument for vigorous Dutch participation in the war against France.

Harmon, Daniel Williams. A journal of voyages and travels in the interiour of North America, between the 47th and 58th degrees of north latitude ... Andover, Flagg and Gould, 1820. H42

The author was a clerk for the North West Company, serving in Manitoba, Saskatchewan, Alberta, and British Columbia for twenty years.

Harris, John. Navigantium atque itinerantium biblioteca. London, T. Woodward [etc.] 1744-48. H43
A collection of about 600 accounts of voyages and travels from 1492 to the early eighteenth century.

[Harris, Walter.] A defence of the Scots abdicating Darien. [n.p.] 1700. H44
A condemnation of the Scottish company responsible for the Darien colony.

[Harris, Walter.] The defence of the Scots settlement at Darien answered, paragraph by paragraph. London, 1699. H45
A spirited defense of the English policy toward the Scottish colony at Darien.

[Harris, Sir Walter.] Remarks on the affairs and trade of Ireland and England. London, For Tho. Parkhurst, 1691. H46
A review of Ireland's economy with a view to proving its importance to the prosperity of England.

Harrison, John. A narrative of the proceedings relative to the discovery of the longitude at sea by Mr. John Harrison's time-keeper, subsequent to those published in the year 1763. London, Printed for the author, and sold by Mr. Sandby, 1765. H47
A pamphlet concerning John Harrison's claim to having developed and perfected a chronometer, the purpose of which was to measure precisely the longitude at sea.

Harte, Walter. Essays on husbandry. London, For W.F. Frederick [etc.] 1770. H48
An eloquent essay on the importance of agriculture as the foundation of an economy, also a technical treatise on the cultivation of alfalfa.

Hartsinck, Jan Jacob. Beschryving van Guiana. Amsterdam, G. Tielenburg, 1770. H49
Describes the commerce of the Dutch West India Company, the Company of Berbice, and the Society of Surinam in Guiana.

Harvest, George. A sermon preached before the Honourable Trustees for Establishing the Colony of Georgia in America ... London, For W. Meadows and M. Cooper, 1749. H50
A laudatory sermon calling attention to the economic development of Georgia as well as its missionary opportunities.

[Hasan ibn Yazīd, Abū Zaid, al-Sīrāfī.] Anciennes relations des Indes et de la Chine. Paris, Chez J.B. Coignard, 1718. H51
French translation by Eusebius Renaudot of ninth-century accounts of China and India.

[Hasan ibn Yazīd, Abū Zaid, al-Sīrāfī.] Ancient accounts of India and China, by two Mohammedan travellers, who went to those parts in the 9th century. London, For S. Harding, 1733. H52
The first English edition.

Hasan ibn Yazīd, Abū Zaid, al-Sīrāfī. Antiche relazioni dell'Indie, e della China, di due Maomettani che nel secolo nono v'andarono, tradotte dall'Araba nella lingua Francese ... fatte Italiane per un'anonimo. Bologna, Tommaso Colli, 1749. H53
The translator adds a six-page preface to this Italian edition.

Hase, Johann Matthias. Sciagraphia integri tractatus de constructione mapparum omnis generis, geographicarum, hydrographicarum, et astronomicarum ... Leipzig, Viduae Mullerianae, 1717. H54
A treatise on cartography, probably a doctoral dissertation at the University of Leipzig.

Haselden, Thomas. The seaman's daily assistant: being a short, easy, and plain method of keeping a journal at sea. London, Mount and Page, 1783. H55
A navigation textbook concluding with "A journal of a voyage from England towards Madeira," presumably putting into use the principles expounded in the previous pages.

Hasselquist, Fredrik. Iter Palestinum eller resa til Heliga Landet, förråttad ifrån år 1749 til 1752. Stockholm, Lars Salvii, 1757. H56
Edited by Linnaeus, this work includes Hasselquist's account of his travels, his descriptions of plants and animals of the Near East, and twelve letters from Hasselquist to Linnaeus.

Hasselquist, Fredrik. Reise nach Palästina in den Jahren von 1749 bis 1752. Rostock, Johann Christian Koppe, 1762. H57
The first German edition, translated by Thomas Heinrich Gadebusch.

Hasselquist, Fredrik. Voyages and travels in the Levant; in the years 1749, 50, 51, 52. London, For L. Davis and C. Reymers, 1766. H58
The first English edition.

Hastings, Warren. The answer of Warren Hastings, esquire, to the articles exhibited by the knights, citizens, and burgesses in Parliament assembled. London, For John Stockdale [etc.] 1788. H59
Hastings' response to the articles of impeachment introduced against him.

Hastings, Warren. Autograph letter signed, dated Fort William, 28 March 1776, concerning affairs in India.   H60

Hastings analyzes the treaty being negotiated with the Mahrattas, comments on affairs in Oudh, and indicates points of difference between him and the Council of the East India Company.

Hastings, Warren. Impeachment trial papers. Manuscript and printed, with indexes. London, 1786-95.   H61

The manuscript of Hastings' defense brief in forty-eight manuscript volumes, with twelve volumes of printed testimony from the trial and from investigations.

Hastings, Warren. Letter : 1777 Mar. 5, Fort William, Bengal, to M.G.S.P.V. e [?] C. [?, England? : with two enclosures]. Bengal, 1777.   H62

Concerns statements in opposition to Hastings which were to be sent to England.

Hastings, Warren. A letter from Warren Hastings, esq. dated 21st of February, 1784. With remarks and authentic documents to support the remarks. London, James Ridgway, 1786.   H63

The letter concerns the possibility of a pension for Hastings upon retirement from East India Company service. It becomes the basis of negative comments on him and his administration by an anonymous editor.

Hastings, Warren. A narrative of the late transactions at Benares. London, For J. Debrett, 1782.   H64

Concerns relations with Chait Singh, an Indian ruler who was opposed to making payments of funds and troops to the East India Company.

Hastings, Warren. The present state of the East Indies ... with notes by the editor. London, For John Stockdale, 1786.   H65

A revised edition of a tract Hastings had issued earlier for private circulation only, according to the editor. Others charged that Hastings had suppressed the earlier edition.

Hastings, Warren. Procès de Warren Hastings, écuyer, ... sur un impeachment délivré à la barre de la Chambre des pairs, contre ledit Warren Hastings, par les communes de la Grande-Bretagne assemblées en Parlement. London, Paris, Desray, 1788.   H66

This French translation by François Soulés of *The trial of Warren Hastings, esq., late governor-general of Bengal* ..., demonstrates the wide publicity of the impeachment charges brought by Edmund Burke against Hastings in the English Parliament. The French also had interests in India and followed the impeachment proceedings closely.

Hastings, Warren. The trial of Warren Hastings, Esq., from February 1788, to June 1793 with a preface containing the history of the origin of the impeachment ... London, 1793.   H67

A summary account of the trial of Warren Hastings, a chronicle of each day's proceedings.

Hauf, Fr. J. Margaritologie vermischt mit conchyliologischen Beyträgen zur Naturkunde von Baiern. Munich, J. Lindauer, 1795.   H68

The history and trade in pearls including a scientific description of oysters and mussels, the qualities pearls must have when evaluated as jewelry, pearl diving in Sri Lanka and India, pearl fisheries, and pearls found California.

Haurisius, Benno Caspar. Nöthige Gründe zur Erlernung der Universal-Historie von Europa, Asia, Africa, und America. Heidelberg, Joh. Jacob Häner, 1741.   H69

An elementary world history and geography.

Hautefeuille, Jean de. La perfection des instrumens de mer. [n.p.] 1715.   H70

Concerns several problems in navigation, particularly determining longitude at sea.

Havart, Daniel. Op-en ondergang van Coromandel. Amsterdam, J. ten Hoorn, 1693.   H71

A history of the Dutch factories on the Coromandel coast.

Haven, Elias Christian von. Priisafhandling over det af Universitet i Kiøbenhavn for aaret 1792 fremsatte spørgesmaal: hvad har Amerikas opdagelse havt for en indflydelse paa menneskeheden i Europa? Copenhagen, 1794.   H72

Examines North and South American commerce.

Haven, Peder von. Reise in Russland. Aus dem Dänischen ins Deutsche übersetzt, von H.A.R. Nebst einem Anhange, darinnen das chinesische und itzo in Russland gebräuchliche Rechen-Bret beschreiben und erkläret wird. Copenhagen, Gabriel Christian Rothe, 1744.   H73

The first German edition, based upon the Danish of the previous year. It includes an account of Russian cities, commerce, social customs and relationships between Russia and her Asiatic neighbours.

Haven, Peder von. Nye og forbedrede efterraetninger om det Russiske rige efter nöyere kundskab som han har indsamlet paa hans sidste reyse. Copenhagen, Paa autors egen bekostning, 1747.   H74

This is an expansion of Haven's account of his travels in Russia, first published in 1743. It includes much more historical and statistical information as well as an account of Bering's second expedition.

Haven, Peder von. Reise udi Rusland. Sorøe, Jonas Lindgren, 1757.   H75

Later Danish edition.

Hawkesworth, John, compiler. An account of the voyages undertaken by the order of His present Majesty for making discoveries in the southern hemisphere. London, For W. Strahan and T. Cadell, 1773. H76
Describes voyages of exploration in the southern hemisphere by Byron, Carteret, Wallis, and Cook.

Hawkesworth, John, compiler. An account of the voyages undertaken by the order of His present Majesty for making discoveries in the southern hemisphere, and successively performed by Commodore Byron, Captain Wallis, Captain Carteret, and Captain Cook ... to which is added a voyage to the north pole by Commodore Phipps. Dublin, James Williams, 1775. H77
While the text is complete in this edition, it omits many of the maps and illustrations, and in the account of the Phipps voyage the numerous appendices are omitted.

Hawkesworth, John, compiler. Relation des voyages enterpris par ordre de Sa Majesté britannique ... pour faire des découvertes dans l'hemisphere méridional. Paris, Saillant et Nyon, & Panckoucke, 1774. H78
In four volumes, the first being given to the voyages of Byron, Wallis, and Carteret, the last three to Cook's first circumnavigation, 1769-1771. The translation is by J.B.A. Suard.

Hawkesworth, John, compiler. Ausfürliche und glabwürdige Geschichte der neuesten Reisen um die Welt, welche auf Befehl und Kosten des jetztreierenden Königs von England in den Jahren 1764 bis 1772. Berlin, Haude und Spener, 1775. H79
The translator, Johann Friedrich Schiller, adds twenty-seven pages of introductory matter and several notes to the text.

[Hawkesworth, John, of Calcutta.] The East Indian chronologist, where the historical events respecting the East India Company are briefly arranged in succession from the date of their charter in 1600 to the 4th of June 1801. Calcutta, Hircarrah Press, 1801 [i.e. 1802]. H80
A year by year account of British activity in India from 1600 to 1802. The author also published many other works under the pseudonym Asiaticus.

Hawkins, Joseph. A history of a voyage to the coast of Africa, and travels into the interior of that country. Philadelphia, For the author by S.C. Ustick, 1797. H81
An account of a slaving expedition to the Ibo tribe in West Africa, with excellent description of their customs, the natural history of the region, and the management of the slave trade.

Hawkins, Sir Richard. The observations of Sir Richard Hawkins, knight, in his voiage into the South Sea. Anno Domini 1593. London, I.D. for J. Jaggard, 1622. H82
Contains extensive observations on the problems of navigation and trade along the coast of South America.

[Hay, Paul, Marquis de Châtelet.] Traitté de la politique de France. Cologne, Pierre Du Marteau, 1669. H83
A survey of France's domestic, military, colonial and foreign policies with recommendations intended for their improvement and for the maintenance of strength and contentment in the country.

[Hayes, Charles.] The importance of effectually supporting the Royal African Company of England. London, E. Say, 1745. H84
Defends the necessity of maintaining forts on the west coast of Africa to protect the trade of the Royal African Company.

Hayes, Charles. A new and easy method to find the longitude at land or sea ... London, 1720. H85
This treatise follows closely the methodology of George Keith's paper, published in 1709.

Haym, Nicola Francesco. Biblioteca Italiana, o sia notizia de' libri rari nella lingua Italiana. Venice, Angiolo Geremia, 1728. H86
Contains lists of books on the Levant, the East and West Indies, and other books of travel.

Hayne, Samuel. An abstract of all the statutes made concerning aliens trading in England ... [London] N.T. for the author, 1685. H87
A tract addressed to the King by a customs officer in Cornwall. After citing instances of the misuse of rights of denization by foreign merchants in England, the author advocates more rigid enforcement of customs regulations.

Haynes, James. Travels in several parts of Turkey, Egypt, and the Holy Land. London, Printed for the Author and sold by J. Axtell, J. Prindden, and G. Redmayne, 1774. H88
A series of fourteen letters describing travels in the Near East, with detailed information on mercantile affairs as well as on the social and religious customs of the region.

Hayter, Thomas. A sermon preached before the incorporated Society for the Propagation of the Gospel in Foreign Parts: at their anniversary meeting in the parish church of St. Mary-le-Bow, on Friday February 21, 1755. London, Edward Owen, 1755. H89
This sermon concerns the slaves in particular, hoping that they will be willing servants and that owners will show prudence in treatment of them.

Hayton, Frère. Les fleurs des hystoires de la terre d'Orient. Paris [1517]. H90
An account of the history of central and western Asia in the last half of the thirteenth century, and a description of

the peoples and institutions of that region also. It was originally written in 1307.

Hayton, Frère. Liber historiarum partium Orientis. Haguenau, Johann Secerius, 1529. H91
The first Latin edition.

Hazart, Cornelius. Kirchen-Geschichte, das ist, catholisches Christenthum durch die gantze Welt ausgebreitet ... der erste Theil in sich begreiffend die asiatische Länder, Japon, China, Tartaria, Mogor, und Bisnagar. Vienna, Leopoldum Voigt, 1678-84. H92
The first German edition of a history of Jesuit missions, describing missions in Africa and America.

Hearne, Samuel. A plan of the Coppermine River. Manuscript. [n.p.] 18 July 1771. H93
The original map of a survey done by Hearne during his expedition to the Arctic Ocean. It contains some variations from the published version.

Hearne, Samuel. A journey from Prince of Wale's Fort in Hudson's Bay to the Northern Ocean. London, A. Strahan and T. Cadell, 1795. H94
An account of an overland journey, 1769-1772, northwestward from Hudson Bay to the Arctic Ocean to determine if a passage to the Pacific Ocean existed in those latitudes.

Hearne, Samuel. Reise von dem Prinz von Wallis-Fort an der Hudsons-Bay bis zu dem Eismeere, in den Jahren 1769 bis 1772. Berlin, Vossischen Buchhandlung, 1797. H95
One of the two 1797 German editions, this text is translated and edited by Johann R. Forster, and it contains several of his own observations.

Hearne, Samuel. Reise vom Fort Prinz Wallis in der Hudsonsbay nach dem nördlichen Weltmeer, aus dem Englischen von M.C. Sprengel. Halle, Rengerschen Buchhandlung, 1797. H96
A translation by Mattias Christian Sprengel.

Hearne, Samuel. Resa til Norra Americas ishaf. Stockholm, Johan Pfeiffer, 1798. H97
An abridged version of Hearne's narrative, this first Swedish edition also contains descriptions of Canada by John Long and Edward Umfreville.

Hearne, Samuel. Landreis van't Prins van Wallis Fort aan Hudsons Baai, naar den Noorder-Oceaan. The Hague, J.C. Leeuwestijn, 1798. H98
This first Dutch edition closely follows the text of the English editions, but adds J. Forster's notes from the 1797 German edition.

Hearne, Samuel. Voyage ... du Fort du Prince de Galles dans la Baie de Hudson, à la Océan Nord. [Paris] Imprimerie de Patris, 1799. H99
The first French edition.

Hearne, Samuel. Dagbog paa en opdagelsereise til lands fra Prinds af Wallis-Fort ... til Jishavet. Copenhagen, J.B. Besony's enke, 1802. H100
The first Danish edition.

[Heath, C.A.] Considerations against laying any new duty upon sugar. London, J. Roberts, 1744. H101
Contends that the proposed increase in the sugar tax would give the French a great advantage in the trade.

Hébert de Rocmont, Abbé. La gloire de Louis le Grand dans les missions estrangeres. Paris, V. Coutelier [1688]. H102
A plea to Frenchmen to support their king in the spread of Christianity abroad which the author considers an important part of the Christian's duty.

Hedendaagsche historie; of Tegenwoordige Staat van Amerika. Amsterdam, I. Tirion, 1766-69. H103
A detailed history and description of America, with numerous maps and charts of ports, harbors, rivers, etc.

Heeren, A.H.L. (Arnold Hermann Ludwig). Ideen über die Politik, den Verkehr und den Handel. Göttingen, Vandenhoek und Ruprecht, 1793-1796. H104
A history of the ancient commerce of the Mediterranean area, including Carthage, Ethiopia and Egypt.

Heiden, Franz Janszoon van der. Vervarelyke schip-breuk van 't Oost-Indisch jacht ter Schelling. Amsterdam, J. Meuss & J. van Someren, 1675. H105
An account of the shipwreck of the Dutch vessel *Ter Schelling* on the coast of Bengal, with observations on that region by survivors.

Heiden, Franz Janszoon van der. Vervarelyke schip-breuk van 't Oost-Indisch jacht ter Schelling. Amsterdam, G. de Groot Keur, 1755. H106
This edition includes descriptions of several East Indian kingdoms not related to the narrative.

Helps to a right decision upon the merits of the late treaty of commerce with France. London, J. Debrett, 1787. H107
The author believes that a treaty with France would benefit both countries.

Helvétius, Adriaan. Recueil des lettres & mémoires ... sur les négociations qui se sont faites entre la France & la Hollande avant la Paix d'Utrecht. Manuscript. [France and Holland] 1704-12. H108
A collection of 950 pages of memoirs and correspondence between Helvetius and others who were engaged in

negotiations involving European and world rivalries preliminary to the Treaty of Utrecht.

[Hely-Hutchinson, John.] The commercial restraints of Ireland considered. Dublin, William Hallhead, 1779. H109
A study of Irish poverty in the seventeenth and eighteenth centuries, attributing it to restraints England laid upon the freedom to export.

Hemmersam, Michael. West-Indianisk reesebeskriffning från åhr 1639 till 1645. ifrån Amsterdam till St: Joris de Mina, itt castell i Africa ... Wijsingzborg, Johann Kankel, 1674. H110
Account written by an employee of the Dutch West India Company who served in Guinea.

Henchman, Thomas. Observations of the reports of the directors of the East India Company, respecting the trade between India and Europe ... 2d ed. London, For J. Wright, J. Debrett, and J. Sewell, 1802. H111
A statement of the issues in a concern of the East India Company over the degree and types of participation in the company's business that was to be allowed to European merchants.

Hendschel, Tobias. Englischen liebbrinnendten S. Francisci Ordens Relations Continuation, oder Volführung angedeuter Excellentz und Fürträffligkeit in nechst aussgefertigter Relation von dess Königreichs Voxu in japonischem Keyserthumb gottselige Bekehrung ... Ingolstadt, Ederischen Truckerey, bey Elisabeth Angermayrin, 1617. H112
A history of the Franciscan Order, including accounts of members who served in Asia and in the New World.

Henin, Jorge de. Discurso de don Jorge de Henin, que trata de los requissitos y ordenes que deve haver en la economia conventua de la monarquia Españo la para que sea perfecta ... Dirigido al Rey, Nr. Sr. Año de 1620. Manuscript. [n.p.] 1620. H113
A memorandum to the King of Spain regarding means to improve the Spanish economy, containing chapters on population, trade, navigation, and precious metals.

Hennepin, Louis. Description de la Louisiane. Paris, Sebastien Huré, 1683. H114
The first edition of Hennepin's account of his travels on the upper Mississippi River.

Hennepin, Louis. Beschryving van Louisania, nieuwelijks ontdekt ten Zuid-Westen van Nieuw-Vrankryk ... mitsgaders de geographische en historische beschrijving der kusten van Noord-America ... door den Heer Denys. Amsterdam, Jan Ten Hoorn, 1688. H115
The first Dutch editions of both works, the former describing the upper Mississippi Valley, the latter the maritime provinces of Canada, with portions of Maine and Quebec included.

Hennepin, Louis. Nouvelle decouverte d'un tres grand pays situé dans l'Amérique, entre le Nouveau Mexique, et la Mer Glaciale. Utrecht, Guillaume Broedelet, 1697. H116
In addition to the account of his own voyage to the upper Mississippi, Hennepin here appropriates Father Membré's account of La Salle's voyage to the mouth of the Mississippi.

Hennepin, Louis. Neue Reise-Beschreibung durch viele Länder weit grösser als gantz Europa ... Bremen, Saurmans, 1698. H117
First German edition of Nouvelle découverte.

Hennepin, Louis. Nouveau voyage d'un pais plus grand que l'Europe avec les reflections des enterprises du Sieur de la Salle. Utrecht, Ernestus Voskuyl, 1698. H118
The first edition of this expansion of the Nouvelle découverte.

Hennepin, Louis. Aenmerckelycke historische reys-beschryvinge door verscheyde landen veel grooter als die van geheel Europa onlanghs ontdekt ... Utrecht, Anthony Schouten, 1698. H119
The first Dutch edition of Nouveau voyage.

Hennepin, Louis. A new discovery of a vast country in America ... between New France and New Mexico. London, For M. Bentley [etc.] 1698. H120
The first English edition, combining translations of the Nouvelle découverte and the Nouveau voyage, Hennepin's expanded accounts of the exploration of the interior of North America.

Hennepin, Louis. A new discovery of a vast country in America ... between New France and New Mexico. London, For M. Bentley [etc.] 1698. H121
The first variant of the second English edition.

Hennepin, Louis. A new discovery of a vast country in America ... between New France and New Mexico. London, For M. Bentley [etc.] 1698. H122
Second variant of the second edition, part two having a different imprint.

Hennepin, Louis. Nieuwe ontdekkinge van een groot land, gelegen in America. Amsterdam, Andries van Damme, 1702. H123
Dutch edition of Hennepin's description of the Mississippi region.

[Hennepin, Louis.] A discovery of a large, rich, and plentiful country, in the North America; extending above 4000 leagues. Wherein, by a very short passage, lately found out, thro' the Mer-Barmejo into the South-Sea; by which a considerable trade might be carry'd on, as well in the northern as the southern parts of America. London, For W. Boreham [1720]. H124

This abridgement of Hennepin's *A new discovery* was undertaken to bolster the sagging stock of the South Sea Company, as it attempted to relate North America's productivity to the supposed discovery of a passage to the Gulf of California.

[Hennepin, Louis.] Charte eines sehr grossen Landes zwischen Neü Mexico und dem Eissmeer &c. Bremen, P.G. Sauermañ, 1699. H125

A map of North America based on Hennepin's *Description of a vast country*, published to accompany the 1698 German edtion of the text.

Hennings, August. Gegenwärtiger Zustand der Besitzungen der Europäer in Ost-indien. Copenhagen, August Friderich Stein, 1784-85. H126

A history of Danish commerce to the East Indies and China in the eighteenth century.

[Hennings, Johann Nicholaus.] Versuch in politischen Schriften, über die Staatswirthschaft, die Handlung und Manufacturen, von einem Kaufmanne. Rostock, Johann C. Koppe, 1762-69. H127

A philosophical discussion of many aspects of trade, including insurance, tariffs, and the wool trade.

Henriques, Aleixo de Miranda. Mandement de M. l'evêque de Miranda en Portugal, qui confirme l'interdit déja porté contre les Jesuites ... [Lisbon, Michel Manescal da Costa, 1759]. H128

This decree appears to isolate the Jesuits in Portugal from all other communication with other members of the church.

Henry, Alexander. Travels and adventures in Canada and the Indian territories, between the years 1760 and 1776. New York, I. Riley, 1809. H129

Details of travel and trade among the Indian nations of the Great Lakes region.

[Henry, David.] An historical account of all the voyages round the world, performed by English navigators. London, For F. Newbery, 1773-74. H130

A collection made up primarily from excerpts from the journals of twelve English circumnavigators from Drake to Cook, and also including accounts of the circumnavigations of Roggeveen and Bougainville and the voyage of Commodore Phipps toward the North Pole in 1773.

Henry, Pierre François. Route de l'Inde, ou, Description géographique de l'Égypte, la Syrie, l'Arabie, la Perse et l'Inde ... traduit en partie de l'Anglais. Paris, Carteret & Dentu, [1799]. H131

A general survey of Near and Middle Eastern countries, reflecting French interest in expanding into those areas.

Herbelot, Barthelémy d'. Bibliotheque orientale, ou Dictionnaire universel, contenant tout ce qui fait connoître les peuples de l'Orient. Paris, Moutard [etc.], 1781-1783. H132

The editor, Nicolas Toussaint Lemoyne Dessarts, states that this edition is both abridged and augmented, comparing it to both the original edition of 1696 and three recent editions.

Herberstein, Sigmund, Freiherr von. Comentari della Moscovia et parimente della Russia. Venice, G.B. Pedrezzano, 1550. H133

The first Italian edition of one of the major sixteenth-century sources on the commerce of Russia, written by a traveler who went to Russia in 1516 and 1519.

Herberstein, Sigmund, Freiherr von. Rerum Moscoviticarum commentarij Sigismundi liberi baronis in Herberstain, Neyperg, & Guettenhag ... Basel, Joannem Oporinum [1551]. H134

The second Latin edition.

Herberstein, Sigmund, Freiherr von. Rerum Moscoviticarum commentarii. Basel, Joannem Oporinum, 1556. H135

The second separately printed Latin edition, including two versions of a map of the Russian river system.

Herberstein, Sigmund, Freiherr von. Rerum Moscoviticarum commentarii. Antwerp, Joannis Steelsii, 1557. H136

This edition also includes Paolo Giovio's account of Muscovy.

Herberstein, Sigmund, Freiherr von. Moscovia der Haupstat in Reissen. Vienna, Michael Zimmerman, 1557. H137

The first German edition, presumably made for friends of the author.

Herberstein, Sigmund, Freiherr von. Moscoviter wunderbare Historien: In welcher dess treffenlichen grossen land Reüssen, sampt der hauptstatt Moscauw ... Basel [Niclauss Brillinger unnd Maxx Russinger] 1563. H138

This translation by Heinrich Pantaleon differs from the earlier German translation made by Herberstein. It is similar in content to the 1556 Latin edition, but contains additional material.

Herberstein, Sigmund, Freiherr von. Die moscouitische Chronica. Das ist, Ein grundtliche Beschreibung oder Historia dess mechtigen und gewaltigen Grossfürsten in der Moscauw ... Frankfurt [Johannem Schmidt in Verlegung Sigmund Feyerabends] 1576. H139

An account of Muscovy derived from the narratives of both Herberstein and Paolo Giovio.

[Herbert, Claude-Jacques.] Essai sur la police générale des grains, sur leurs prix et sur les effets de l'agriculture. Berlin, 1757. H140
The author urges greater freedom in the grain trade.

[Herbert, Claude-Jacques.] Observations sur la liberté du commerce des grains. Amsterdam, Michel Lambert, 1759. H141
This volume, which is concerned with the fluctuation of grain prices and proposes free import of grain, has also been ascribed to C.H. Piarron de Chamousset.

Herbert, Sir Thomas. A relation of some yeares travaile, begunne anno 1626. London, W. Stansby and J. Bloome, 1634. H142
A detailed account of a voyage to India, including information on Africa, Persia, Siam, and Pegu.

Herbert, Sir Thomas. Relation du voyage de Perse et des Indes Orientales ... avec les revolutions arrivées au royaume de Siam l'an mil six cens quarante-sept. Paris, Jean du Puis, 1663. H143
This first French edition includes an account of events in Siam in 1647 following the death of its king, written by Jeremias van Vliet.

Herckmans, Elias. Der zee-vaert lof. Amsterdam, Jacob Pietersz Wachter, 1634. H144
An epic poem celebrating the history of navigation, with major interest in the sixteenth and seventeenth century voyages of the English and Dutch. One of the engravings is by Rembrandt.

[Herfelln, Jacó.] Relaçam verdadeira da tomada das praças que na America fizerão os Francezes aos Inglezes, e noticia certa das grandes, e consideraveis forças militares assim maritimas ... Lisbon, Domingos Rodrigues [1755]. H145
A newsletter apparently based on information gained in England relative to military and naval strength of France and Great Britain and the disposition of forces at the beginning of the Seven Years War.

Herlein, J.D. Beschryvinge van de volk-plantinge Zuriname. Leeuwarden, M. Injema, 1718. H146
A description of the colony of Surinam, including a brief history of its earliest development.

Hermann, Benedict Franz Johann von. Versuch einer mineralogischen Beschreibung des uralischen Erzgebürges. Berlin, Friedrich Nicolai, 1789. H147
A survey of minerals and mineral production in the Ural Mountain region, including statistical tables.

Hernández, Jaime, Father. A philosophical and practical essay on the gold and silver mines of Mexico and Peru ... London, For J. Scott, 1755. H148
An account of mining in Spanish America, of transporting the metals and of minting them into coins, together with a philosophical view of the value of precious metals.

Herodotus. Historia. Rome, Arnoldus Pannartz, 1475. H149
Herodotus is the source of much information on ancient voyages and on the commerce of the peoples he describes.

Herodotus. Libri novem quibus musarum indita sunt nomina. [Venice] Aldus [1502]. H150
The first Greek edition.

Herport, Albrecht. Eine kurtze ost-indianische Reisz-Beschreibung. Bern, Georg Sonnleitner, 1669. H151
Contains descriptions of Formosa, the Cape of Good Hope, Madagascar, Ceylon, and the Indonesian archipelago.

Herrera, Francisco Manuel de. Representación, que la ... ciudad de Cádiz haze al Rey nuestro señor. [n.p.] 1727. H152
Arguments in favor of moving the entrepôt of Spanish South American trade to Cadiz.

Herrera Maldonado, Francisco de. Epitome historial del reyno de la China. Madrid, Andres de Parra, 1620. H153
The text is followed by a listing of seventy-eight sources used by the author.

Herrera y Tordesillas, Antonio de. Historia general de los hechos de los Castellanos ... Madrid, 1601-15. H154
This chronological history of the Spanish explorations and conquests in the New World was written by the first official historian of Spain. It includes the period from 1492 to 1554, and reports Spanish expeditions into the Pacific Ocean also.

Herrera y Tordesillas, Antonio de. Description des Indes Occidentales ... Amsterdam, Michel Colin, 1622. H155
Translation of part of the author's history of Spanish America, with additional material on Jacob Le Maire's circumnavigation.

Herrera y Tordesillas, Antonio de. Nieuwe werelt, anders ghenaempt West-Indien. Amsterdam, Michiel Colijn, 1622. H156
An abridged translation, the first Dutch edition.

Herrera y Tordesillas, Antonio de. Novus orbis, sive Descriptio Indiae Occidentalis. Amsterdam, Michael Colin, 1622. H157
The original Latin edition, the first to include Jacob Le Maire's account of his circumnavigation. It also adds a description of America excerpted from Petrus Bertius' *Tabulis geographicis*.

Herrera y Tordesillas, Antonio de. Histoire generale des voyages et conquestes des Castillans, dans les isles & terre-ferme des Indes Occidentales. Paris, Veuve Nicolas & Jean de la Coste, 1660-71. H158
A three-volume French translation of the first three *Decades* written by this Spanish historian.

Herrera y Tordesillas, Antonio de. The general history of the vast continent and islands of America. London, J. Batley, 1725-26. H159
The first English edition of the famous *Historia general*, translated by John Stevens.

Herring, Thomas. A sermon preached before the incorporated Society for the Propagation of the Gospel in Foreign Parts, at their anniversary meeting in the parish-church of St. Mary-le-Bow, on Friday, February 17, 1737-8. London, J. and J. Pemberton, 1738. H160
"For every convert to Christianity ... is a friend to our country and government as well as to our religion."

Herwyn de Névèle, Pierre-Antoine-Charles, comte. Rapport fait ... sur la franchise de Dunkerque. [Paris, Imprimerie Nationale, 1790.] H161
A defense of the privileges Dunkirk held with regard to the trade with the American colonies, the fishing trade, and commerce with England and the Low Countries. Opposition to these privileges came mainly from Calais.

Hese, Joannes de. Itinerarius ... a Jherusalem per diversas mundi partes. [Cologne, J. Guldenschaff, ca. 1490.] H162
The first edition of an account of travels in the eastern Mediterranean area, including also the fictitious letter from the Sultan of Babylonia to Pope Pius II, and a description of the land of Prester John.

Hese, Joannes de. Itinerarius Joannis de Hese presbiteri a Jherusalem ... [Cologne, C. Zierickzee, ca. 1500.] H163
The second Cologne edition of an account of travels in the eastern Mediterranean area.

Hesse, Elias. Ost-Indische Reise-Beschreibung. Leipzig, Michael Günther, 1690. H164
Deals particularly with Sumatra and the mining operations of the Dutch East India Company there.

Hesselius, Andreas. Kort berettelse om then Swenska kyrkios närwarande tilstånd i America samt oförgripeliga tankar om thess widare förkofring. Norrköping, 1725. H165
"Short account of the present situation of the Swedish church in America, with incontrovertable thoughts on its future progress."

Hestroy, Sieur de la. Mémoires touchant le commerce de la France. Manuscript. [France, ca. 1700.] H166
This work is particularly concerned with France's commerce as it relates to that of the Netherlands.

[Heton, Thomas.] Some account of mines, and the advantages of them to this kingdom. London, W.B. for John Wyat, 1707. H167
A general discussion of mining in England and Wales, by a promoter of the Company of the Mine-Adventurers.

[Heuvell, Hendrik Herman van den.] Onpartijdige raadgevinge tot eensgezinheid en moderatie, van Batavus aan alle waare liefhebberen des vaderlands. Utrecht, B. Wijld, 1779. H168
A caution against getting into war with England.

Hevia Bolaños, Juan de. Labyrintho de comercio terrestre y naval. Lima, Francisco del Canto, 1617. H169
The first edition of an extensive work divided into three parts, the first two dealing with commerce by land, the third concerning navigation.

Hevia Bolaños, Juan de. Laberinto de comercio terrestre y naval. Madrid, Luis Sanchez, 1619. H170
The second edition.

Hevia Bolaños, Juan de. Labyrinthus commercii terrestris et navalis. Florence, Petrus A. Brigonci, 1702. H171
Late edition of a general discussion of commerce, including material on Spanish-American commerce and the slave trade.

Heydt, Johann Wolfgang. Allerneuester geographisch-und topographischer Schau-Platz von Afrika und Ost-Indien. Willhermsdorff, Johann Carl Tetschner, 1744. H172
A series of engravings with text, describing installations of the Dutch East India Company in Africa and the East Indies.

Heylsame raed, in desen tegenwoordige tydt. Dort, J. Claesz, 1652. H173
Discusses the early phase of the Anglo-Dutch War and the commercial rivalry that caused it.

Heylyn, Peter. Cosmographie in four bookes, containing the chorographie & historie of the whole world. London, For Henry Seile, 1652. H174
This description of the known continents contains accounts of exploration and commerce outward from Europe, and includes maps of Europe, Asia, Africa, and the New World.

Heylyn, Peter. Cosmography in four books containing the chorography and history of the whole world. London, Edw. Brewster [etc.] 1703. H175
The final edition, with historical information and maps updated from previous editions.

Heylyn, Peter. Mikrokosmos: A little description of the great world. Oxford, William Turner, 1636.   H176
The seventh edition of a standard English geography text, based upon the author's Oxford lectures.

Hichborn, Benjamin. An oration delivered March 5, 1777, at the request of the inhabitants of the town of Boston; to commemorate the bloody tragedy of the fifth of March, 1770. Boston, Edes and Gill, 1777.   H177
This oration commemorated the anniversary of the "Boston Massacre".

Hickeringill, Edmund. Jamaica viewed: with all the ports, harbors ... towns and settlements. London, B. Bragg, 1705.   H178
The third edition of a propaganda pamphlet, noting the products, facilities for trade, opportunities for settlement, fertility of the soil, etc.

[Hill, Joseph.] Het tegenwoordige interest der Vereenigde Provincien. Amsterdam, 1673.
    H179
A translation of an English pamphlet printed at Middelburg, containing a review of Dutch commercial interests and comparisons with English and French economies.

[Hilliard d'Auberteuil, Michel-René.] Considérations sur l'état présent de la colonie française de Saint-Domingue. Paris, Grangé, 1776.   H180
Full of valuable economic information on Saint Domingue, this scathing attack on the French colonial administration was confiscated and the printer punished.

[Hilliard d'Auberteuil, Michel-René.] Du commerce des colonies, ses principes et ses lois, ... [n.p.] 1785.   H181
Arguments against restrictions on colonial trade.

[Hilliard d'Auberteuil, Michel-René.] Histoire de l'administration de Lord North ... et de la guerre de l'Amérique Septentrionale. Paris, Couturier, 1784.   H182
Contains interesting statistical information on English import duties.

Hinchliffe, John. A sermon preached before the incorporated Society for the Propagation of the Gospel in Foreign Parts, at their anniversary meeting in the parish church of St. Mary-le-Bow, on Friday February 16, 1776. London, T. Harrison and S. Brooke, 1776.   H183
The preacher shows concern for the current enthusiasm for rationalism and science as sources of understanding of justice and morality.

[Hippisley, John.] Essays. I. On the populousness of Africa. II. On the trade at the forts on the Gold Coast. III. On the necessity of erecting a fort at Cape Appolonia. London, For T. Lownds, 1764.   H184
The author's concern is for a reliable supply of slaves for British shippers, and for British dominance of a source of gold near Cape Appolonia.

Histoire abregée des Provinces-Unies des Païs-Bas ... et celui de leure compagnies en Orient & en Occident. Amsterdam, J. Malherbe, 1701.
    H185
A brief history of the Netherlands, emphasizing the importance of the Dutch East and West India companies.

Histoire de la conqueste de la Floride, par les Espagnols, [s]ous Ferdinand de Soto. Ecrite en portugais par un gentil-homme de la ville d'Elvas. Paris, Denys Thierry, 1685.   H186
The first French edition, the source for the English translation issued the following year. The preface indicates it was published as the means to inform Frenchmen about Florida and as an example in the conduct of such expeditions.

Histoire des decouvertes faites par divers savans voyageurs. Bern, Société Typographique; The Hage, Pierre-Frederic Gosse, 1779-91.   H187
A French translation, abridged, of a German travel collection. The material included comes primarily from narratives by Pallas, Gmelin, and Lepekhin.

Histoire des révolutions de l'isle de Haiti ou Saint Domingue ... par un colon. Manuscript. [n.p., ca. 1815.]   H188
An account of the slave rebellion in Saint Domingue with preliminary observations on the settlement, economy and slave-based agriculture of the colony.

Histoire veritable du combat, tant par mer que par terre ... en l'isle de Maragnan. Paris, Y. du Guy, 1615.   H189
A pamphlet describing Portuguese and French rivalry at Maragnan off the coast of Brazil.

Historia cultus Sinensium, seu, varia scripta de cultibus Sinarum, inter Vicarios Apostolicos Gallos aliosque missionarios, & patres Societatis Jesu controversis ... Cologne, 1700.   H190
A large collection of documents going back to the mid-seventeenth century tracing the development of the Chinese Rites controversy.

Historia da muy notavel perda do galeam grande S. Joam em que se contaõ os grandes trabalhos, & lastimosas cousas, que acontecèraõ ao Capitaõ Manoel de Sousa Sepulveda, na terra do Natal onde se perdèraõ a 24. de junho de 1552. Lisbon, Na officina de Antonio Alvares [repr. 1737?].
    H191

Historiae Societatis Jesu, pars prima [-quinta] ..., auctore Nicolao Orlandino, Societatis eiusdem

Sacerdote. Antwerp, Martini Nutii, 1620; Rome, Manelfi, 1649-1652; Rome, Varesii, 1661.   H192

A history of the Society of Jesus to the 1580s, consisting largely of biographical material, and with considerable reference to missions abroad.

An historical account of the proceedings of the last House of Commons. London, T. Boreman, 1735.   H193

An attack on the Walpole ministry and many of its policies respecting England's overseas trade.

An historical account of the voyages and adventures of Sir Walter Raleigh. London, W. Boreham, 1719.   H194

A history of Raleigh's South American projects published to interest the South Sea Company in the same area.

An historical, geographical, political and natural history of North America. London, S. Low, 1805.   H195

The fourth and final printing of this anonymous work and the only one to contain a folding map of North America.

An historical narrative of the discovery of New Holland and New South Wales. London, John Fielding, 1786.   H196

A description of the land, vegetation, animals, and peoples of the Australian coast and adjacent islands, with particular emphasis on Botany Bay.

Historisch-geographische Beschreibung der ... antillischen Inseln. Stuttgart, Johann B. Mezler, 1762.   H197

A history of English and French rivalry in the West Indies, with particular emphasis on Guadeloupe and Martinique.

Historisk-filologiske meddelelser. Historische Abhandlungen der Königlichen Gesellschaft der Wissenschaften zu Kopenhagen. Copenhagen, C.G. Prost, 1787.   H198

Contains a chapter on the commerce of Denmark and Norway from the earliest times. Valentin August Heinze was the editor.

The history of Caledonia: or, the Scots colony in Darien in the West Indies. London, J. Nutt, 1699.   H199

A history of the Darien colony from its earliest roots in 1688.

The history of Captain Cook's three voyages around the world. London, Hodges and Pain, 1784.   H200

A two-volume narrative of Cook's voyages.

The history of the administration of the leader in the India direction. London, For G. Kearsly [1764].   H201

A criticism of Henry Vansittart's administration of the East India Company, particularly of his policy of forcing persons with opposed views from important company positions.

Hitchcock, Robert, Captain. A pollitique platt for the honour of the prince, the greate profite of the publique state, relief of the poore, preservation of the riche, reformation of roges and idle persones, and the wealthe of thousandes that knowes not how to live ... London, Ihon Kyngston, 1580.   H202

An elaborate plan for solving England's social problem of poverty in coastal towns by establishing a fishing industry through construction of four hundred ships, each to employ twenty-four men at sea.

[Hoadly, Benjamin.] A defense of the Enquiry into the reasons of the conduct of Great Britain. London, J. Roberts, 1729.   H203

A reply to a critic of the following work.

[Hoadly, Benjamin.] An enquiry into the reasons of the conduct of Great Britain. London, J. Roberts, 1727.   H204

Primarily concerned with Spanish interference with England's West Indian trade.

Hockin, John Pearce. A supplement to the account of the Pelew Islands: compiled from the journals of the Panther and Endeavour ... and from the oral communications of Captain H. Wilson. London, For Captain Henry Wilson, 1803.   H205

An account of a voyage to the Pelew islands in 1790, with a return voyage by way of China and India.

Hocquart de Turtot. Description et project de commerce à la Calidonie et au golphe du Darien. Manuscript. [France, ca. 1750-55.]   H206

A description of the region bordering on the Gulf of Darien, with recommendations that France attempt to plant a colony there.

Hodges, James. Considerations and proposals for supplying the present scarcity of money, and advancing trade. Edinburgh, Mrs. Ogston, 1705.   H207

Urges credit as an aid to commerce. A sound national credit was to be based on the public revenue and the treasury of the Royal African Company.

[Hodges, James.] The rights and interests of the two British monarchies. London, 1703.   H208

An argument against an "incorporating union" with England, including arguments to show that the Scots would not gain in overseas commerce as a result of the union.

[Hoefnagel, Nicolaas.] Manifest of declaratie van oorlog, gedaan door den autheur van het ... begrafnis-briefje en lees-cedul, tegens de liebel-

schryvers en schenders van staaten, erfstadhouders en magistraaten ... [n.p., 1781.] **H209**
Relates to events following 1778 which led to war with England.

Högström, Pehr. Beskrifning öfwer de til Sweriges krona lydande Lapmarker. Stockhom, Lars Salvii [1747]. **H210**
A description of Lapland by a pastor and member of the Swedish Academy of Science who had served there. It includes extensive commentary on earlier sources.

Högström, Pehr. Beschreibung des der Crone Schweden gehörenden Lapplandes, nebst Arwid Ehrenmalms Reise durch West-Nordland nach der Lappmark Asehle. Copenhagen & Leipzig, Gabriel Christian Rothe, 1748. **H211**
One of two German editions published in 1748, but the only one including Ehrenmalm's account of his travels in Norway and Lapland.

Hoffmann, Johann Christian. Oost-Indianische Voyage. Cassel, Friederich Hertzog, 1680. **H212**
The author, a clergyman in the service of the Dutch East India Company, gives an interesting account of a slave-trading expedition to Madagascar and Mozambique.

Hogendorp, Dirk, Graaf van. Nadere uitlegging en ontwikkeling van het stelsel van Dirk van Hogendorp ... in antwoord op het onlangs uitgekomen werk van den gewezenen commissaris generaal S.C. Nederburgh, getiteld: Verhandeling over de vragen ... The Hague, I. van Cleef, 1802. **H213**
An evaluation of the Dutch commercial position in the East Indies, with some reference to the English trade there also.

Hogendorp, Dirk, Graaf van. Stukken, raakende den tegenwoordigen toestand der Bataafsche bezittingen in Oost-Indie en den handel op dezelve ... The Hague; Delft, J.C. Leeuwestyn en M. Roelofswaert, 1801. **H214**
A review of the Dutch commercial situation in the East Indies following the termination of the Dutch East India Company.

Holberg, Ludvig, baron. Den berømmelige Norske handel-stad Bergens beskrivelse. Copenhagen, Berlingste Arvingers Bogtrykkerie, 1757. **H215**
A history of Bergen describing the city's development as a commercial center and considering its relationship to the other Hanseatic League cities.

Holk, Hans, editor. Dannemarks handels-spiel. Sorøe, Jonas Lindgren, 1766. **H216**
A commercial handbook, noting Denmark's commodities, kinds of merchants, trade regulations, taxes, duties, etc.

Holland (Kingdom). Lodewijk Napoleon, door de gratie Gods en de constitutie des koningrijks, Koning van Holland, connétable van Frankrijk. Wij hebben besloten en besluiten: Art. I. 'Er zal tot nadere order een director der douanes benoemd worden ... [n.p.] Koninklijke Staats-Drukkerij, 1809. **H217**
Relates entirely to administration of customs.

Holland (Kingdom). Lodewijk Napoleon, door de gratie Gods en de constitutie des koningrijks, Koning van Holland, connétable van Frankrijk. Wij hebben besloten en besluiten: Art. I. Onze Staatsraad van Meeuwen wordt benoemd tot directeur der douanes ... [n.p.] Koninklijke Staats-Drukkerij, 1809. **H218**

Holland (Kingdom). Lodewijk Napoleon, door de gratie Gods en de constitutie des koningrijks, Koning van Holland, connétable van Frankrijk. het wetgevend lichaam goedgekeurd hebbende de voordragt door uns toe gedaan, hebben wij besloten en besluiten: I. Wordt gearresteerd de navolgende wet op de zeebrieven en Turksche paspoorten ... [n.p.] Koninklijke Staats-Drukkerij, 1809. **H219**

Holland (Kingdom). Lodewijk Napoleon, door de gratie Gods en de constitutie des koningrijks, Koning van Holland, connétable van Frankrijk. Wij hebben besloten en besluiten: I. Wordt gearresteerd het navolgende reglement, volgens het welke de eigenaars, schippers of directievoerende van alle binnenlandsche schepen en vaartuigen ... zich zullen hebben te gedragen, ten aanzien van den ophef van het binnenlandsch last-geld ... [n.p.] Koninklijke Staats-Drukkerij, 1809. **H220**

Holland (Kingdom). Lodewijk Napoleon, door de gratie Gods en de constitutie des koningrijks, Koning van Holland, connétable van Frankrijk. Wij hebben besloten, en besluiten. I. Wordt gearresteerd het navolgend reglement op het ligten en de behandeling der zeebrieven en Turksche passpoorten ... [n.p.] Koninklijke Staatsdrukkerij, 1809. **H221**

Holland (Kingdom). Lodewijk Napoleon, door de gratie Gods en de constitutie des koningrijks, Koning van Holland, connétable van Frankrijk. Willende daarstellen eenige provisionele maatregelen nopens de manier van procederen in het departement Oostvriesland, in zaken de middelen te water betreffende ... [n.p.] Koninklijke Staatsdrukkerij, 1809. **H222**

Holland (Netherlands : Province). Rade. Sententie by den Hoogen Rade over Hollandt

ende West-Vrieslandt gewesen tot laste van Jacob Syms. [n.p., 1673?] H223
A sentence of banishment and payment of ten thousand guilders is imposed upon Jacob Syms for misuse of East India Company funds.

Holland (Netherlands : Province). Staten. Ratificatie van de Staten van Hollant. Ende de Staten van Vrieslandt: over 't besluyt van den vrede met den coningh van Spangien. [n.p.] 1648. H224
Concerns the Peace of Westphalia.

Holland (Netherlands : Province). Staten. Edele Mogende Heeren, bysondere goede vrunden, nae-gebueren ende bontgenoten. [n.p., 1650]. H225
Relates to the need for a fleet to defend the Dutch holdings in Brazil against the Portuguese.

Holland (Netherlands : Province). Staten. Extract uyt de Resolutien vande Ed. Groot Mo: Heeren Staten van Hollant ende West-Frieslant, genomen den 10 ende 11 November 1650. [n.p.] 1650. H226

Holland (Netherlands : Province). Staten. Missive aende Staten vande provintien van Gelderlandt, Zeelandt, Utrecht, Vrieslandt, Overyssel, Groeningen ... [n.p.] 1650. H227

Holland (Netherlands : Province). Staten. Extract uyt de Resolutien vande heeren Staten van Hollant ende West-Vrieslant. [n.p.] Aert Cornelisz, 1652. H228
Concerns toll duties for ships passing through the Sund carrying goods to Sweden, and the way these duties will be collected.

Holland (Netherlands : Province). Staten. Resolutien van tijdt tot tijdt, genomen ... tegens eenige predicanten vanden Hage, ende specialijcken tegen D. Jac. Stermont. [n.p.] 1652. H229
Resolutions placing restraints upon certain preachers in The Hague for their remarks about the West India Company.

Holland (Netherlands : Province). Staten. Resolutie ... tot antwoort of refutatie vande resolutie vande Heeren Staten van Zeelant. [n.p., 1663.] H230
A reply to Zeeland's protests over import duties on goods sent to Holland from Zeeland.

Holland (Netherlands : Province). Staten. Extract uyt de resolutien ... [n.p.] 1667. H231
Suggests changes in the charter of the Dutch West India Company.

Holland (Netherlands : Province). Staten. Placcaet van de heeren Staten ... op het betalen van den twee-hondersten penningh ... voor den jare 1673. The Hague, J. Scheltus, 1673. H232
A statement of taxes to be levied for defense purposes. Notice is given that financial reports from the East and West India Companies will be called for.

Holland (Netherlands : Province). Staten. Placcaet van de heeren Staten ... op het betalen van eenen hondersten penningh ... op den vijfthienden Junii 1673. The Hague, J. Scheltus, 1673. H233
A statement of taxes being levied with the notation that the stock of the East India Company will be taxed separately.

Holland (Netherlands : Province). Staten. Placaet ... den vijf en twintighsten Januarii 1674. [n.p., 1674.] H234
Pilots are instructed to take to sea for Greenland only those ships bound for Greenland which have permits.

Holland (Netherlands : Province). Staten. Ordonnantie ende instructie ... beroerende het stuck van de pilotage ende aenkleven van dien ... Amsterdam, Abel van der Storck, 1675. H235
Chiefly concerns pilotage fees for incoming ships.

Holland (Netherlands : Province). Staten. Een vertoogh van de considerabele colonie, by ... Hollandt ende West-Vrieslandt, uytgeset op de vaste kust van America. The Hague, Jacobus Scheltus, 1676. H236
A description of Guiana and an appeal for settlers, with detailed statements of the costs involved in equipping settlers and in producing sugar and other crops.

Holland (Netherlands : Province). Staten. A translation of the Dutch placart and ordinance for the government of the great fishery. London, For W. Owen, 1750. H237
A translation of the basic fisheries legislation of Holland in 1651, with later additions. A few notes by the translator, probably William Horsley, point out the precision with which this staple of Dutch trade was regulated.

Holland (Netherlands : Province). Staten. Publicatie ... Doen te weeten: Alsoo wy bevonden hebben, dat seedert veele jaaren op de jaarlyksche keekeningen der vuurgelden telkens zyn gevallen. The Hague, Paulus Scheltus, 1762. H238

Holland (Netherlands : Province). Staten. Publicatie ... Alsoo aan ons nader is gerepresenteert dat de bepaalde tyd van drie jaaren, by onse publicatie van den 28 July 1762 tot het heffen van het vuurgeld ... met de 1 September deeses jaars staat te expireeren, en dat egter noodig is dat de kasse der vuurgelden by continuatie

Holland (Netherlands : Province)

werde ondersteunt en te gemoet gekoomen. The Hague, Isaac Scheltus, 1765. H239

Holland (Netherlands : Province). Staten. [Extracts from the *Resolutiens* of the Staten of Holland, 1770-72 relating to maritime affairs.] [The Hague, 1770-72.] H240
   While these resolutions are from the period 1770-72, they contain frequent reference to earlier legislation concerning pilotage, cargoes, and other maritime matters.

Holland (Netherlands : Province). Staten. Publicatie. De Staaten van Holland en Westvriesland, allen den geenen die deesen sullen sien of hooren leesen, salut: doen te weeten: Alsoo aan ons nader is gerepreseenteert dat de bepaalde tyd van ses jaaren by onse publicatie van den 31 July 1765 tot het heffen van het vuurgeld ... met den 1 September deeses jaars staat te expireeren ... The Hague, Isaac Scheltus, 1771. H241

Holland (Netherlands : Province). Staten. Preparatoirlyk plan, van een tractaat van commercie ... van Holland, en de dertien Vereenigde Staaten van Noord-America. [n.p.] 1780. H242
   A draft of a treaty between the provinces of Holland and the United States which became the basis for the treaty signed between the two nations in 1782.

Holland (Netherlands : Province). Staten. Publicatie. De Staaten van Holland en Westvriesland, allen den geenen die deesen sullen sien of hooren leesen, salut; doen te weeten: Alsoo aan ons nader is gerepresenteert, dat de bepaalde tyd van ses jaaren by onse publicatie van den 22 July 1777 tot het heffen van het vuurgeld ... met den 1 September deeses jaars staat de expireeren ... The Hague, Isaac Scheltus, 1777 [i.e. 1783]. H243

Holland (Netherlands : Province). Staten. Publicatie. De Staaten van Holland en Westvriesland, allen die deezen zullen zien of hooren leezen, salut: doen te weeten, dat wy uit hoofde van de aanmerkelyke voordeelen welke de commercieerende scheepvaart reeds zeedert een geruimen tyd van de haven van het Nieuwe Diep geniet ... en speciaal op de zodanige welke goedvinden van die haven gebruik te maaken op den navolgenden voet. The Hague, Isaac Scheltus, 1788. H244

Hollands ondergang by Vanckrijck vastgesteld, en door desselfs Koningh Lodewyck de XIV. Amsterdam, A.D. Oossaen, 1689. H245
   A complaint against French dominance of Dutch trade, tracing the history of their commercial rivalry for forty years.

Hollandsche sybille. Amsterdam, Roelof Heyndrickz, 1646. H246
   A plea for a treaty with Spain which would enable the Dutch to improve their commercial position in Europe and America.

Den Hollandschen verre-kyker. Utrecht, H. Perfect, 1671. H247
   Particularly concerns the Dutch Baltic and eastern trade just before the outbreak of war with Sweden.

Hollandse Mercurius. Haarlem, Pieter Casteleyn, 1651-77. Abraham Casteleyn, 1678-91. H248
   A news publication recording the events of interest to Dutch readers from 1650 to 1690. Many illustrations and documents are included.

Hollandts praatjen, tusschen vier persoonen, een Geldersman, een Hollander, een Vries, en een Brabander. Brussels, Jan Verdussen, 1650. H249
   A discussion of the extent of Bicker's responsibility for the decline of the Dutch West India Company.

't Hollandts rommelzootje, vertoonende de gantsche ghelegentheyd van het Benaudt, Ontzet, en Gewapent Amsterdam. [n.p., 1650.] H250
   A poem with prose commentary which refers to the capture of two Spanish fleets, and also to the sugar trade of Brazil.

Het Hollants wijve-praetjen ... Haarlem, P. Davidtsz, 1652. H251
   Pamphlet concerning Dutch-English commercial rivalry.

Hollberg, Esaias. Norra Americanska färge-örter. Abo, Johan C. Frenckell, 1763. H252
   A thesis written under the direction of Pehr Kalm which lists various plants in America that yield colors useful for dyes.

[Hollingsworth, S.] An account of the present state of Nova Scotia. Edinburgh, For William Creech, and London, For T. Longman, 1786. H253
   A survey of the economic possibilities of Nova Scotia, with suggestions for the improvement of its various industries.

[Hollis, Thomas] compiler. The true sentiments of America: contained in a collection of letters sent from the House of Representatives of the province of Massachusetts Bay to several persons of rank in this kingdom. London, J. Almon, 1768. H254
   The letters protest British taxation policy in the American colonies. Half of the volume is made up of documents relating to an alleged libel of Governor Bernard by the *Boston Gazette*.

Holm, Thomas Campanius. Kort beskrifning om provincien Nya Swerige uti America. Stockholm, Sal. Wankijfs Änkia, 1702.   H255
An account of the earliest Swedish settlement in America compiled from manuscripts left by the author's grandfather and by Peter Lindström, an engineer and cartographer in the colony, and from oral sources.

Holwell, J.Z. (John Zephaniah). India tracts. London, For T. Becket and P.A. de Hondt, 1764.   H256
A collection of five tracts relating to the East India Company's involvement in political affairs in India. Some of them include statistical information on the company's business there.

Holy, Nicolaas Muys van. Middelen en motiven om het kopen en verkopen van Oost-en West-Indische actien. Amsterdam, 1687.   H257
A plan to bring order into the buying and selling of shares in the Dutch East and West India Companies; it involves a tax on the sale of shares.

Holy Roman Empire. General und Ordnung, wie es hinfüro mit der Traidt, Koll und Kalchmass, auch Elen unnd Gewicht, unnd dann der Goldschmid unnd Zingiesser prob, in dem Ertzhertzogthumb Osterreich ob der Enns gehalten werden solle. Vienna, Caspar Stainhofer, 1570.   H258
A regulatory decree specifying units of weight and measurement for a variety of commodities, including grain, cloth, timber and metals.

Holy Roman Empire. Wir Carl der Sechste, von Gottes Gnaden Erwöhlter Römischer Kayser ... Andertens ihr Compagnia unter dem Namen einer Kayserl. privilegirten Orientalischen Compagnia mit allem dem menschlichen Commercio unterligenden Kauffmanns-Gütern ... Vienna, 1719.]   H259
A charter for an eastern trading company, designed to develop commerce through Turkey.

Holy Roman Empire. Emperor (1576-1612 : Rudolph II). Brief des Keyserlijcke Mayest. van Duytslandt aende E. Mogende Heeren Staten vande Gheunieerde Provintien ... [n.p.] 1608.   H260
A letter from the Emperor of Germany to the States General of Holland. A *Nederlandtschen Bye-Korf* pamphlet.

Holy Roman Empire. Emperor (1711-1740 : Charles VI). Lettres patentes d'octroy accordées par Sa Majesté imperiale et catholique, pour le terme de trente années à la Compagnie generale à établir dans les Pays-Bas aûtrichiens pour le commerce & la navigation aux Indes. Ghent, François & Dominque vander Ween, 1723.   H261
Letters patent establishing the overseas trading company of the Austrian Netherlands, commonly referred to as the Ostend Company.

Holy Roman Empire. Emperor (1711-1740 : Charles VI). Lettere patenti de concessione accordate ... alla Compagnia generale da stabilirsi ne' Paesi Bassi Austriaci per il commerzio, e la navigazione alle Indie. Brussels & Milan, Giuseppe Richino Malatesta, 1724.   H262
An Italian edition of the charter of the Ostend Company.

Holy Roman Empire. Emperor (1711-1740 : Charles VI). Essendosi compiaciuta Sua Maestà Cesarea, e Cattolica, Dio guarda, con sua regal cedola spedita nella imperial corte di Vienna in data de' 9. del corrente mese di febbraro ordinarci la pubblicazione del trattato di pace, e libero commercio avuto trà il supremo Consiglio di Guerra ... [Naples, Secondino Porsile, 1726.]   H263

Holy Roman Empire. Emperor (1711-1740 : Charles VI). Patenti e regole della fiera esente di Trieste, che de' porti Franchi. [n.p., ca. 1729.]   H264
Patent and instructions for the fairs of Trieste and Fiume, including tariff schedules.

Holy Roman Empire. Emperor (1711-1740 : Charles VI). Dimonstrandosi sempre più la Clemenza di S.C. e C.M. che Iddio guardi, propenza ... nel facilitar maggiormente il reciproco universale commercio trà i suoi domini; e che a tale oggetto dopò di avere la M.S. stabiliti, e pubblicati franchi i due porti di Fiume, e Trieste nell' Austria inferiore ... Naples, Secondino Porsile, 1730.   H265

Holy Roman Empire. Emperor (1711-1740 : Charles VI). Essendoci stato rappresentato, cosi per parte de' Mag. governatori, e deputati del regio *Jus prohibendi* di vendere, e far vendere vino a minuto ... in luoghi privati ... [Naples, 1735.]   H266

Holy Roman Empire. Emperor (1765-1790 : Joseph II). Fra le varie benefiche disposizioni emanate dall' augustissima Imperatrice Regina, di sempre gloriosa memoria, a vantaggio del commercio de' suoi amati sudditi su in via internale ordinato al Cap. 13. dell' editto degli 11, Maggio 1775, che i prodotti, e le merci soggette a dazio provenienti da questa Lombardia Austriaca le quali accompagnate dai soliti certificati ... Milan, Giuseppi Richino Malatesta, [1781].   H267

Holy Roman Empire. Laws, etc. Ordnung und Mass, wie die fremden und ausslendischen

Kaufleut iren Kauffschatz unnd kauffmans Waaren, Burgern und Gesten hie zu Wien hingeben unnd verkauffen sollen. [Vienna, ca. 1536.] H268

General regulations upon outside merchants coming to Vienna to trade.

Holy Roman Empire. Treaties, etc. Tractaet van commercie, tusschen ... Karel den VI en ... Philips den V. The Hague, J. Scheltus, 1725. H269

A commercial treaty between Austria and Spain, specifying taxable goods, measures regarding contraband goods, etc.

Holy Roman Empire. Treaties, etc. Tractatus commercii ... Treaty of commerce between ... Charles VI and ... Philip V. [London? ca. 1725.] H270

Nearly all of the forty-seven provisions of this treaty pertain to trade relations between the signatories. The text is in Latin and English.

Homann, Johann Baptist. Generalis totius Imperii Moscovitici, novissima tabula ... Nuremberg, Johannis Baptistae Homann [1704?]. H271

This map was published to accompany the German edition of Isbrand Ides' account of his travels to China in 1692-94.

Homann, Johann Baptist. Generalis totius Imperii Russorum, novissima tabula ... Nuremberg, Johannis Baptistae Homanni [between 1721 and 1723]. H272

This map has important revisions on Homann's earlier depiction of Asiatic Russia.

Homer. La Ulyxea de Homero. Venice, Francisco Rampazeto, 1562. H273

The entire text of the *Odyssey* in blank verse Spanish translation.

Hondius, Jodocus. Tartaria. [Amsterdam, between 1606 and 1628.] H274

This map shows the Strait of Anian between Asia and North America. Korea is portrayed as an island, and Japan is not included.

Honoranda università de mercatanti della inclita città di Bologna. Statuta della honoranda università de mercatanti della inclita citta' di Bologna riformati l'anno M.D.L. [Bologna] Anselmo Giaccarello [1550]. H275

Statutes governing procedures of the regulatory agency for commercial law in Bologna.

Honorius, of Autun. De imagine mundi. [Nuremberg, Anton Koberger, 1472.] H276

The first edition of a basic medieval geography compiled from many sources in the twelfth century.

Honorius, of Autun. Mappa mundi in archiuis romanis reperta. [Italy, early XV century.] H277

This manuscript in semicursive book hand apparently accompanied a map of the world. The text consists of an abridged version of the *Imago Mundi*, and includes brief mention of the island of Atlantis and the island of St. Brendan.

Honorius, of Autun. Mundi synopsis: sive, de imagine mundi. Speyer, Bernardum Albinum, 1583. H278

Apparently the second separately published edition.

Honter, Johannes. Rudimenta cosmographica. Zurich, C. Froschauer, 1548. H279

Among the maps included in this volume is a reproduction of the Waldseemüller world map of 1507.

Honter, Johannes. Rudimentorum cosmographicorum ... libri III. Zurich, Froschauer, 1552. H280

This popular pocket-sized geography is a reprint of the Froschauer edition of 1548.

Honter, Johannes. Rudimentorum cosmographicorum. Zurich, Froschauer, 1565. H281

A poetical description of the world, followed by an atlas of thirteen woodcut maps.

[Hopkins, Stephen.] The rights of colonies examined. Providence, William Goddard, 1765. H282

A challenge to Parliament's right to legislate for colonists who were British subjects, and a demonstration of the harm being done to both the economy and the liberty of the colonies, particularly the author's Rhode Island.

Horn, Georg. Georgi Horni orbis politicus imperiorum, regnorum, principatuum, rerum publicarum. Frankfurt, Fridericum Arnst, 1675. H283

Brief descriptions of various political units throughout the world, with historical and geographical notes.

[Hornot, Antoine.] Anecdotes américaines, ou Histoire abrégée des principaux événements arrivés dans les Nouveau Monde, depuis sa découverte jusqu'à l'époque présente. Paris, Vincent, 1776. H284

A chronological history of European discovery and colonization in America.

Horrebow, Niels. Zuverläsige Nachrichten von Island; nebst einer neuen Landkarte und 2 jährl. meteorologische Anmerkungen. Copenhagen, Leipzig, F.C. Pelt, 1753. H285

A thorough description of Iceland based on a two year residence there, designed to correct and refute information in Johann Anderson's account.

Horsley, William. Serious considerations on the high duties examin'd: address'd to Sir Matthew Decker, by Mr. Horsley. London, For R. Wellington, 1744. H286

A commentary on Decker's proposal that a house tax replace the variety of taxes on commodities. Horsley would refine Decker's proposal with a tax on windows rather than on houses.

Høst, Georg Hjersing. Efterretninger om Marókos og Fes, samlede der i landene fra ao. 1760 til 1768. Copenhagen, N. Möller, 1779. H287

A description of Morocco by a Danish resident there in the service of the Danish Royal African Company.

Høst, Georg Hjersing. Efterretninger om øen Sanct Thomas og dens gouverneurer, optegnede der paa landet fra 1769 indtil 1776, ved Georg Høst ... Copenhagen, Nicolaus Møller og Søn, 1791. H288

A history of the Danish West Indies, chronicling the history of the Danish West India Company from its beginnings in 1671.

Hotham, Sir Richard. Reflections upon East-India shipping. London, Brotherton and Sewel, [1773]. H289

An attack on the directors of the East India Company for employing an excessive number of ships for personal gain.

Houblon, James. [Mercantile accounts, 1667-83.] H290

A manuscript account book, noting costs and profits in trading operations in the Mediterranean and the Levant.

Houghton, John. A collection of letters for the improvement of husbandry & trade. London, For J. Lawrence, 1681-83. H291

A series of articles related to agriculture and trade, including the commerce of the East Indies and Africa.

Houghton, Thomas. Royal institutions: being proposals for articles to establish and confirm laws, liberties, & customs of silver & gold mines. London, For the author, 1694. H292

A collection of ten proposals to be made to Parliament on the subject of mines in the colonies. The author attributes the lack of mining in the colonies to the policy of granting large tracts of land to persons not interested in mining.

[Houstoun, James.] A true and impartial account of the rise and progress of the South Sea Company; wherein the assiento contract is particularly considered. London, T. Cooper, 1743. H293

This pamphlet defends the South Sea Company from accusations made against it in the anonymous *Considerations of the American trade, before and since the establishment of the South Sea Company*, published in 1739. The author had lived in the West Indies.

Houstoun, James. The works of James Houstoun, M.D. containing memoirs of his life and travels in Asia, Africa, America, and most parts of Europe. London, For the author, 1753. H294

The author was a Scottish adventurer, surgeon to the South Sea Company and a trader in Central America and the Spanish Main.

[Hovell, John.] A discourse on the woollen manufactury of Ireland, and the consequences of prohibiting its exportation. [n.p.] 1698. H295

An argument against restricting export of woolens from Ireland, noting that the Protestant proprietors of the industry would suffer, giving rise in Ireland to intrigue against England.

Howel, Thomas. Voyage en retour de l'Inde, par terre, et par une route en partie inconnue jusqu'ici, par Thomas Howel; suivi d'Observations sur le passage dans l'Inde par l'Egypte et le grand désert, par James Capper. Paris, Imprimerie de la République [1797]. H296

A collection of works on overland routes between the Persian Gulf and the Mediterranean Sea, including annotations and commentary by the translator, Théophile Mandar.

Howell, John. The life and adventures of Alexander Selkirk; containing the real incidents upon which the romance of Robinson Crusoe is founded ... Edinburgh, Oliver & Boyd [etc.] 1829. H297

Also contains an appendix describing the island of Juan Fernandez.

Hoyarsabal, Martin de. Les voyages avantureux. Rouen, David du Petit Val, 1632. H298

The second edition of a pilot guide to the areas most frequented by Basque fishermen and merchants, including western European waters and ports and those of Newfoundland.

Hube, Johann Michael. De figura telluris. Göttingen, Schulz, [1761]. H299

Hube discusses the various theories regarding the shape of the earth from ancient times down to his own time. He includes abundant references to other astronomers, ancient and modern.

Hubert, Sieur. Mémoire sur l'etat present de la colonie de la Louisianne. Manuscript. [Louisiana?] 1723. H300

A fifteen-page plea for decisive action in Louisiana to keep the colony from failure. Hubert notes the great economic opportunities of the hinterland, and vehemently criticizes the policies of Bienville that prevent taking advantage of them.

Hubert, Sieur. Mémoire sur la colonie de la Louisianne. Manuscript. [Louisiana] 1722. H301

A fourteen-page report to Maurepas on the dangers faced by Louisiana and the best means of improving the colony. Hubert is very critical of Bienville, and advocates transferring the major French base inland to the vicinity of Natchez.

Huddart, Joseph. The oriental navigator, or, New directions for sailing to and from the East Indies ... Philadelphia, James Humphreys, 1801. H302

A very detailed set of instructions for sailing from Great Britain to China via the Cape of Good Hope, with additional piloting instructions for voyages off the main route.

Hudson's Bay Company. Bye-laws of the Adventurers of England trading into Hudson's Bay, passed at a general court. Held on the 3rd July, 1863. London, Henry Kent Causton and son [1863]. H303

Hudson's Bay Company. [Charter and papers.] Manuscript. London, 1670-80. H304

A collection including a contemporary copy of the company's charter, a memorandum acknowledging that letters patent had been granted to the company in 1680, and a letter concerning a loan granted for an expedition to Hudson Bay in 1676.

Hudson's Bay Company. Correspondence with the Colonial Office. London, H.K. Causton and son, 1868. H305

Relates to the forming of a company for the purpose of opening a route for passenger traffic across Canada to the British colonies on the Pacific coast.

Hudson's Bay Company. [Indentures] Manuscript. London, 1679-80. H306

Ten indentures relating to money lent to the company by several shareholders.

Hudson's Bay Company. List of the Adventurers of England trading into Hudson's Bay. London, H.K. Causton and son, 1865. H307

A list of stockholders.

Hudson's Bay Company. [Memorial to the House of Commons]. [Begins] The Kings of England, by right of discovery ... [London, ca. 1687.] H308

A plea for the building of forts and factories on Hudson Bay, at the public expense, for better execution of the fur trade and for better protection against French and English interlopers.

Hudson's Bay Company. The royal charter ... granted by His Majesty King Charles the Second ... in 1670. London, R. Causton and son, 1816. H309

A reprint of the original charter of the Hudson's Bay Company.

Hudson's Bay Company. Statement of the Hudson's Bay Company, 1857. London, H.K. Causton, 1857. H310

A statement of the history and accomplishments of the Hudson's Bay Company.

Hudson's Bay Company. Upon Wednesday the 18th day of November instant ... London, 1696. H311

A broadside announcing the coming election of officers for the Hudson's Bay Company.

The Hudson's Bay Company. What is it? London, A. H. Baily, 1864. H312

This pamphlet was probably issued by the Canadian government. It implied that the company had no rights to land in Saskatchewan.

Hübner, Johann. De staats-en koeranten-tolk, of woordenboek der geleerden en ongeleerden ... Leyden, Dirk Haak & Samuel Luchtmans, 1732. H313

A massive geographical dictionary containing some thirty thousand entries. The subject matter extends beyond geography into economics, weights and measures, numismatics, heraldry and politics. This is the first Dutch edition.

[Hübner, Martin.] Le politique danois, ou l'Ambition des Anglais démasquée par leurs pirateries. Copenhagen, Frideric Mons, 1756. H314

An anti-British review of the European power struggle at the beginning of the Seven Years War, with particular reference to the Anglo-French conflict in North America.

Hues, Robert. A learned treatise of globes, both coelestiall and terrestriall: with their severall uses. London, T.P. for P. Stephens and C. Meredith, 1639. H315

The first English edition, translated by John Chilmead from the Latin, incorporating the notes to the text by Johannes Isaacus Pontanus from the 1623 Dutch edition.

Hues, Robert. Traicté des globes, et de leur usage. Paris, Abraham Pacard, 1618. H316

The only French edition, translated by D. Henroin.

Huet, Pierre-Daniel. Le grand tresor historique et politique de florissant commerce des Hollandois. Rouen, Ruault, 1712. H317

A review of the history and current status of Dutch commerce, including remarks on Dutch commercial policy.

[Huet, Pierre-Daniel.] Memoires sur le commerce des Hollandois, dans toutes les etats et empires du monde. Amsterdam, Emanuel Du Villard, 1717. H318

This edition has no important differences from the first edition of 1712.

[Huet, Pierre-Daniel.] Comercio de Holanda. Madrid, J. Rodriguez y Escobar [1717]. H319
The first Spanish edition, with additional introductory material.

[Huet, Pierre-Daniel.] Memoires sur le commerce des Hollandois, dans tous les etats et empires du monde. Amsterdam, Du Villard & Changuion, 1718. H320
This edition adds a schedule of rates for Dutch imports and exports to its text about Dutch commercial activity.

[Huet, Pierre-Daniel.] Memoirs of the Dutch trade in all the states, kingdoms, and empires in the world. London, For J. Sackfield [etc., 1718?]. H321
The first English edition.

Huet, Pierre-Daniel. A view of the Dutch trade in all the states, empires, and kingdoms in the world. London, J. Walthoe, jun. and J. Childe, 1722. H322
The same sheets as the previous work, with a new title page.

[Huet, Pierre-Daniel.] Comercio de Holanda. Madrid, Carlos Rey, 1746. H323
The second edition of the Spanish translation with additional material in the introductory section.

[Huet, Pierre-Daniel.] Histoire du commerce et de la navigation des anciens. Paris, François Fournier & Antoine-Urbain Coustelier, 1716. H324
In addition to Greek, Roman and Phoenician commerce, this work includes brief accounts of ancient Chinese, Persian, Indian, Arabian and Ethiopian commerce also.

Huet, Pierre-Daniel. The history of the commerce and navigation of the ancients. London, For B. Lintot and W. Mears, 1717. H325
Translated from the French edition of 1716, this first English edition is dedicated to the directors of the East India Company.

Huet, Pierre-Daniel. Storia del commerzio, e della navigazione degli antichi ... tradotta nell' Italiana Favella sulla seconda edizione di Parigi da Antongiuseppe Belloni. Venice, Francesco Pitteri, 1737. H326
This Italian edition with new introductory material was translated from the second French edition.

Hüttner, Johann Christian. Reize van het Britsch gezantschap door China en een gedeelte van Tartarye. Leiden, A. & J. Honkoop, 1799. H327
An account of China based on the Macartney embassy. This Dutch version is translated from the German edition.

Hulsius, Levinus. Erste Schiffahrt in die orientalische Indien. So die holländische Schiff im Martio 1595, aussgefahren und im Augusto 1597, widerkommen verricht. Frankfurt am Main, Levini Hulsii, 1606. H328
This fourth edition of part one in the Hulsius collection of voyages describes the first Dutch voyage to the East Indies under the command of Cornelis Houtman.

Hulsius, Levinus. Ander Schiffart. In die orientalische Indien. Nuremberg, L. Hulsius, 1602. H329
Part two of the Hulsius series of voyages, describing the Dutch expedition to the East Indies under Neck and Warwick in 1598-1600.

Hulsius, Levinus. Ander Schiffart in die orientalische Indien ... Frankfurt, L. Hulsius, 1605. H330
Second edition of part two.

Hulsius, Levinus. Warhafftige Relation der ... Schiffart gegen Mitternacht ... als Anno 1594, 1595, und 1596. Nuremberg, L. Hulsius, 1598. H331
Part three of the Hulsius series of voyages, containing descriptions of the three voyages of Willem Barents in search of a northeast passage.

Hulsius, Levinus. Vera historia, admirandae cuiusdam navigationis, quam Huldericus Schmidel. Nuremberg, Levinus Hulsius, 1599. H332
Part four of the Hulsius series of voyages, containing the narrative of Ulrich Schmidel's travels in South America. This copy includes illustrations and maps from the subsequent volume in the series which describes Raleigh's travels in Guiana.

Hulsius, Levinus. Kurtze wunderbare Beschreibung. Des goldreichen Königreichs Guianae ... Nuremberg, Hulsius, 1599. H333
Part five of the Hulsius series of voyages in its first German edition. It is a translation of Raleigh's account of Guiana.

Hulsius, Levinus. Brevis & admiranda descriptio regni Guinae ... Nuremberg, L. Hulsius, 1599. H334
Hulsius' Latin edition of the above item.

Hulsius, Levinus. Achte Schiffart. Kurtze Beschreibung, was sich mit den Holländern in den Ost Indien ... zugetragen. Frankfurt, Wolffgang Richtern, 1605. H335
Part eight of the Hulsius series of voyages, giving short accounts of the voyages of Gerard Le Roy, Wolphert Harmensz, Jacob van Heemskerk, Jacob van Neck, and Wybrand van Warwijck in the East Indies.

Hulsius, Levinus. Achte Schiffart, oder kurtze Beschreibung etlicher Reysen so die Holländer

und Seeländer in die Ost Indien ... 1599-1604. Frankfurt, L. Hulsius, 1608. H336
The second edition.

Hulsius, Levinus. Zehende Schiffahrt oder Reyse der Holländer und Seeländer in Ost Indien beschehen under dem Admiral Cornelis Matelief. Frankfurt, Matthis Beckern, 1608. H337
Part ten of the Hulsius series, containing an account of the East Indian voyage of Cornelius Matelief in the years 1605-8.

Hulsius, Levinus. Zehende Schiffart oder Reyse der Holländer und Seeländer in Ost Indien. Frankfurt, E. Kempffern, 1613. H338
The second edition.

Hulsius, Levinus. Eylffte Schiffart, oder kurtze Beschreibung einer Reyse ... in de Ost Indien ... in Jahren 1607, 1608, und 1609. Frankfurt, E. Kempffern, 1612. H339
A description of a voyage to the East Indies for the Dutch East India Company, led by Pieter Willemsz Verhuffen and Johann Verken.

Hulsius, Levinus. Eylffter Schiffart ander Theil ... continuirung der Reyse ... in die Ost Indien mit neun grossen und vier kleinen Schiffen von 1607 bis ... 1612. Frankfurt, Erasmo Kempffer, 1613. H340
Section two of part eleven of the Hulsius series, containing a description of the struggle between the Dutch and Portuguese for control of the East Indies.

Hulsius, Levinus. Zwölffte Schiffahrt oder kurtze Beschreibung der newen Schiffahrt gegen Nord Osten uber die amerische Inseln in Chinam und Japponiam von einem Engellender Heinrich Hudson ... Oppenheim, Hieronymo Gallern in Vorlegung Levini Hulsii, 1614. H341
The twelfth volume in the Hulsius series, containing an account of Hudson's search for a northern passage to Asia.

Hulsius, Levinus. Zwölffte Schiffahrt oder kurtze Beschreibung der newen Schiffahrt gegen Nord Osten. Oppenheim, Hieronymo Gallern, 1627. H342
The second edition of this version of Henry Hudson's voyage.

Hulsius, Levinus. Dreyzehente Schiffahrt darinnen ein warhafftiger und gründtlicher Bericht von dem itzigen Zustandt der Landschafft Virginien. Hanau, In verlegung der Hulsischen, 1617. H343
Hulsius' edition of Ralph Hamor's *True discourse of the present estate of Virginia*. It also includes three additional letters relating to Virginia.

Hulsius, Levinus. Viertzehende Schiffart, oder gründliche und warhaffte Beschreibung dess Neuwen Engellandts. Frankfurt, L. Hulsius, 1617. H344
A translation of Capt. John Smith's *A description of New England*.

Hulsius, Levinus. Fünffzehende Schiffart: warhafftiger und zuvor nie erhorter Bericht eines Engelischen welcher mit einem Schiff die Auffart genandt in Cambaia, dem eussersten Theil Ost Indien ... Hanau, In verlegung der Hulsischen, 1617. H345
Part fifteen of the Hulsius series of voyages, containing the account of Captain Robert Coverte's voyage to India.

Hulsius, Levinus. Die sechtzehende Schiffahrt. Journal oder Beschreibung der wunderbaren Reise Wilhelm Schouten ausz Hollandt im Jahr 1615, 16 und 17. Frankfurt, N. Hoffmann, 1619. H346
Hulsius' edition of Schouten's voyage, with numerous maps and plates depicting the lands and peoples of the South Sea.

Hulsius, Levinus. Die siebenzehende Schiffart ... der wunderbahrē Reise und Schiffart so durch Herr Georgio von Spilbergen glücklichen volbracht. Frankfurt, J. Hofern, 1620. H347
Part seventeen of the Hulsius series, describing the voyage of Spilbergen to the Pacific Ocean by way of the Straits of Magellan.

Hulsius, Levinus. Achtzehender Theil der Newen Welt ... Frankfurt, J.F. Weissen, 1623. H348
Part eighteen of the Hulsius series of travels. Contains an abridgment of Herrera's *Historia general*.

Hulsius, Levinus. Die neuntzehende Schiffarth, inhaltendt, fünff Schiffarthen Samuel Brauns. Frankfurt, H. Palthenio, 1626. H349
The explorations of Samuel Braun, describing the Congo, Angola, and Guinea, and the Dutch, Spanish, and Portuguese trade there.

Hulsius, Levinus. Zwantzigste Schiffahrt, oder gründliche und sattsame Beschreibung dess Newen Engellands. Frankfurt, Wolffgang Hoffmann, 1629. H350
A translation of Whitbourne's *Discourse of Newfoundland*, together with accounts of Virginia and Bermuda, apparently from Smith's *General History of Virginia*.

Hulsius, Levinus. Die ein und zwantzigste Schiffahrt, oder ... Beschreibung der ... Landtschafft Brasilien. Frankfurt, Wolffgang Hoffmann, 1629. H351
An account of the capture of the silver fleet by the Dutch captain Piet Hein as well as a description of Brazil.

Hulsius, Levinus. Die zwey und zwäntzigste Schiffart ... Beschreibung der Schiffart so under

dem Admiral Jacob l'Hermite. Frankfurt, Hulsischen Erben, 1630. H352
Part twenty-two of the Hulsius series, being an account of the circumnavigation by the Nassau Fleet led by Jacques l'Hermite.

Hulsius, Levinus. Chronologia. Das ist, ein kurtze Beschreibung deren Länder, so in diser hierzu gehörigen Landtafel, begriffen seind. Nuremberg, Christopheri Lochneri, 1596. H353
A description of a map issued the same year, encompassing the region from Italy to the Black Sea and north to Poland.

An humble petition and remonstrance presented unto both the High and Honourable Houses of Parliament concerning .... the transportation of leather. [London] 1641. H354
Calls for a restriction upon the exporting of leather, since foreign demand has raised the price of shoes beyond the ability of lower class Englishmen to pay.

Les humbles plaintes et remonstrances n'a gueres faites à messiers les estats d'Hollande, par les marchands & associez de la Compagnie des Indes Orientales. [n.p.] 1623. H355
A French edition of complaints made against the Dutch East India Company, suggesting that the company was of interest to French merchants.

Humboldt, Alexander von. Manuscript map of the Rio Negro & Rio Bravo. [South America, 1800.] H356
The original map drawn by Humboldt of the Rio Negro region of what is now Venezuela showing the connection of the Orinoco and Amazon rivers via the Casiquiare River.

Hume, David. Political discourses. Edinburgh, R. Fleming for A. Kincaid and A. Donaldson, 1752. H357
A collection of twelve essays, some of which deal with economic and commercial policies with implications for British trade.

Hume, David. Political essays on commerce. Venice, Louis Pavini and John Bassaglia, 1767. H358
An English and Italian edition of several essays on topics relating to both domestic and international trade.

Hume, John. A sermon preached before the incorporated Society for the Propagation of the Gospel in Foreign Parts, at their anniversary meeting in the parish-church of St. Mary-le-Bow, on Friday February 19, 1762. London, E. Owen and T. Harrison, 1762. H359
This sermon contradicts the belief that truth is found in the state of nature, contending that good order proceeds from truth which must be taught and enforced.

[Humfrey, John.] A paper to William Penn, at the departure of that gentleman to his territory, for his perusal, in Pensilvania ... London, T.M. for H. Mortlock, 1700. H360
Humfrey states that it was the acceptance of Quakerism by Penn that gave substance to the movement. The text is a doctrinal argument against some of Penn's stated beliefs.

Humphreys, David. An historical account of the incorporated Society for the Propagation of the Gospel in Foreign Parts ... London, Joseph Downing, 1730. H361
This sermon calls attention to efforts being made by the Society among the slaves and the Iroquois Indians.

Hunter, John. An historical journal of the transactions at Port Jackson and Norfolk Island. London, John Stockdale, 1793. H362
An English naval officer describes the first English settlement in Australia.

Hunter, John. Resa til Nya Södra Wallis, åren 1787, följande; jamte nyaste underrättelser om Engelska nybygget i Port Jackson, Nya Holland och Norfoks-Ön, af Capit. Tench och King samt Cap. Edvards resa omkring jorden. Stockholm, Johan Pfeiffer, 1797. H363
A collection of accounts of early voyages to Australia in abridged translation by Samuel Ödmann.

Hurd, Richard. A sermon preached before the incorporated Society for the Propagation of the Gospel in Foreign Parts, at their anniversary meeting in the parish church of St. Mary-le-Bow, on Friday February 16, 1781. London, T. Harrison and S. Brooke, 1781. H364
"We shall make some amends for those multiplied mischiefs ... which our insatiable commerce occasions; and second the designs of an all-wise Providence."

Hushålds-råd. Stockholm, Benjamin G. Schneider, 1734. H365
The first twelve issues of a monthly Swedish journal devoted to current economic and commercial affairs.

[Huske, John.] The present state of North America, &c. London, R. and J. Dodsley, 1755. H366
A review of the British and French positions in North America, with a history of their claims to territory, concluding that only war could settle the conflicting claims and that a war in the immediate future would be most advantageous to the British.

Hutcheson, Archibald. An abstract of all the publick debts. London, Hutcheson, 1723. H367
A view of English public debt, relating to the South Sea Company.

Hutcheson, Archibald. An abstract of an account ... relating to the estates of the directors. London, Hutcheson, 1723. H368

Suggestions for "the consideration of the Gentlemen of the House of Commons, and the Proprietors of the South-Sea stock."

Hutcheson, Archibald. A collection of treatises relating to the national debt & funds ... and also a collection of treatises relating to the South-Sea stock and scheme. London, 1721. H369
The collection encompasses fifteen tracts which were issued as the South Sea Company failure unfolded.

Hutcheson, Archibald. An estimate of the present national debt, to which is added a copy of remarks which were subjoined to some calculations made in April 1717 relating to the publick debts. London, 1718. H370
The computation of the national debt includes amounts owed by the East India and South Sea companies.

Hutcheson, Archibald. Some paragraphs of Mr. Hutcheson's treatises on the South-Sea subject; which relate to the relief of the unhappy traders in South-Sea stock, and to publick credit ... London, 1723. H371
Relates to the South Sea Company, and to the relief of traders in its stock.

Hutchins, Thomas. Copy of letters sent to Great-Britain, by His Excellency Thomas Hutchinson, the Hon. Andrew Oliver, and several other persons, born and educated among us. Which original letters have been returned to America, and laid before the honorable House of Representatives of this province. Boston, Printed by Edes and Gill, 1773. H372
These letters from the colonial governor of Massachusetts were procured in London, probably by Benjamin Franklin, and returned to Boston where their publication did much to arouse a revolutionary spirit.

Hutchins, Thomas. The representations of Governor Hutchinson and others, contained in certain letters transmitted to England ... together with resolves of the two houses thereon. Boston, Edes and Gill, 1773. H373
Another printing of the previous work.

Hutchins, Thomas. An historical narrative and topographical description of Louisiana and West-Florida. Philadelphia, For the author, 1784. H374
A description of the Mississippi valley as far north as the Ohio River and of the northern shores of the Gulf of Mexico, with particular interest in navigational features.

[Hutchins, Thomas.] Strictures upon the Declaration of the Congress at Philadelphia; in a letter to a noble lord. London, 1776. H375
An examination, line by line, of the Declaration of Independence from a hostile point of view by a former governor of Massachusetts.

Hutchins, Thomas. A topographical description of Virginia, Pennsylvania, Maryland, and North Carolina. London, For the author, 1778. H376
An examination of rivers, resources, towns, Indian tribes, and other aspects of the territory between the 34th and 44th degrees of latitude west of the Allegheny Mountains as far as the Mississippi.

Hyde, Thomas. Epistola de mensuris et ponderibus serum seu Sinensium. Oxford, Sheldon, 1688. H377
An essay on the weights and measure used in China, noting their transcriptions into Portuguese, French, and Latin.

Hydra of monster-dier, dat tzedert den jare 1650 in de Vereenigde Nederlanden gewoed heeft, en nu van Hercules is bestreeden in overwonnen. Rotterdam, Willem van Swede, 1672. H378
A review of international and political events, noting French and English harrassment of Dutch shipping, the arrival of Dutch ships, and the improvement in the Baltic trade.

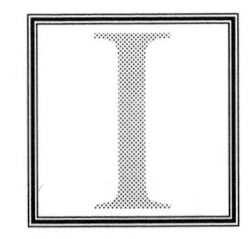

[Ibàñez de Echavarri, Bernardo.] Regno Gesuitico del Paraguay dimostrato co' documenti piu classici de' medesimi padri della Compagnia. Lisbon, Stamperia Reale, 1770. I1
Documents and commentary on the Jesuits' rule of Paraguay before their expulsion in 1769.

Ichthyothera, or the royal trade of fishing. London, J.F. for R. Royston, 1662. I2
Contains a law of 1661 for the encouragement of fishing and an anonymous essay on the means by which England could improve its fishing industry.

Idée de la Chine, ou étrennes Chinoises, et coup d'oeil-curieux sur la religion, les sciences, les arts, les usages, & les moeurs des peuples de la Chine. Pekin [Paris] Valleyre [ca. 1760]. I3
A survey of Chinese history, government, social institutions, learning, natural history and other aspects of the culture, all of it in a favorable vein.

Idée véridique du révérend pere Gabriel de Malagrida, Jésuite italien, exécuté à Lisbonne, par sentence de l'Inquisition ... Liege, Syzime, 1762. I4
An account of the execution of Gabriel de Malagrida, a Jesuit implicated in a plot on the life of the Portuguese king, citing his exemplary service as a missionary in Brazil.

Idées préliminaires sur le privilége exclusif de la Compagnie des Indes. Paris, Lottin & Lottin, 1787. I5
A defense of the Compagnie Nouvelle des Indes and of the idea of privileged companies as the best means to develop overseas trade.

Ides, Evert Ysbrants. Drie-jarige reize naar China. Amsterdam, Francois Halma, 1704. I6
The first Dutch edition of this journal of an embassy from Peter the Great to Peking in 1692-94, together with a description of China by Dionysius Kao.

Ides, Evert Ysbrants. Three years travels from Moscow over-land to China. London, W. Freeman, 1706. I7
The first English edition.

L'Idolatria sostenuta, e difesa nella Cina, e nel Malabar. Lugano, Per gli Agnelli, e comp., 1767. I8
A complaint against the Jesuits for not adhering strictly to papal decrees relative to prohibitions upon Chinese and Malabar rites in Asia.

Idrīsī. De geographia universali. Rome, Typographia Medicea, 1592. I9
The first printing, in Arabic, of the most important work to come from Arab geographers of the Middle Ages. The original work was completed in 1154.

Idrīsī. Geographia nubiensis id est accuratissima totius orbis in septem climata divisi descriptio. Paris, Hieronymi Blageart, 1619. I10
The first Latin edition.

Ilario di Gesù. Relazione della preziosa morte de' padri Bartolomeo Alvarez, Emanuele de Abreu, Vincenzo de Cunha, Gio. Gasparo Cratz, missionarj apostolici della Compagnia di Gesù ... dì 12. di gennajo del 1737. Rome & Milan, Francesco Agnelli, 1739. I11
The author of this account of the execution of Jesuit missionaries in Tonking was vicar apostolic of East Tonking, a member of the Recollect order of Augustinians.

Image du monde. [Myrrour of the world.] [Westminster, W. Caxton, 1481.] I12
The first geography published in English; the text is a compilation sometimes attributed to Gossuin, sometimes to Gautier of Metz.

Imlay, Gilbert. A topographical description of the western territory of North America. London, For J. Debrett, 1793. I13

The second edition of an important work describing the Kentucky area. An account of Kentucky by John Filson is included.

An impartial enquiry into the right of the French king to the territory west of the great river Mississippi ... including a summary account of that river, and the country adjacent. London, W. Nicoll [1762].　　　　　　　　　　　I14
An evaluation of Louisiana, showing a concern for the danger to the Mississippi River commerce if France held any western American lands.

An impartial report of the debates in the House of Commons, on the East India Reform Bills. To which is added, a state of the company's affairs, as delivered to the House by Mr. Nicol, the accountant; and Mr. Annis, auditor of the accounts ... London, For G. Kearlsey, 1783.　　I15
Report on debates over legislation to limit the powers of the East India Company.

An impartial vindication of the English East-India Company, from the unjust and slanderous imputations cast upon them ... London, J. Richardson for Samuel Tidmarch, 1688.　　I16
A reply to *A justification of the directors of the Netherlands East-India Company* published the previous year and relating to commercially inspired hostilities between the two companies in the East Indies.

Impartiality. Impartial observations, to be considered on by the King, his ministers, and the people of Great Britain. [n.p., ca. 1763]　　　　I17
A survey of the British American colonies, noting the major exports of each with a view to proving their ability to pay taxes required by the crown.

Imperatorskaia Akademiia Nauk (Russia). Geograficheskii Department. Rossiiskoi atlas: iz soroka trekh kart sostoiashchii i na sorok odnu guberniiu imperiiu razdieliaiushchii. St. Petersburg, Izdan pri Geograficheskom departmentie, 1800.　　　　　　　　　　　I18
This atlas, edited by Aleksandr Vilbrekht, includes one map of the entire Russian empire, and forty-two others of governmental administrative districts. The final map includes Alaska and the Aleutian Islands in considerable detail.

The importance and management of the British fishery consider'd. London, J. Roberts, 1720.　　I19
A plea for greater English participation in the fishing industry, noting the many benefits its effective prosecution would bring to the country. An appendix describes Dutch methods of curing fish.

The importance of Cape Breton consider'd. London, For R. Dodsley, 1746.　　　　　　I20
Cape Breton is pointed out as the bastion of defense and the free flow of commerce in the northern part of North America.

The importance of Jamaica to Great-Britain, consider'd. London, A. Dodd [ca. 1740].　　I21
A favorable evaluation of Jamaica as a point from which English commerce could dominate North America and the Caribbean region.

The importance of settling and fortifying Nova Scotia. London, For J. Scott, 1751.　　I22
Possibly written by William Bollan, this description of Nova Scotia is aimed at recruiting settlers, and emphasizes the advantage of its farmlands and fisheries.

The importance of the Ostend Company consider'd. London, E. Say for J. Roberts, 1726.　I23
The Ostend Company's commercial aspirations are shown to be in direct competition with Dutch and English overseas trade, and means are suggested for stifling the growth of commerce in the Austrian Netherlands.

The importance of the sugar colonies to Great-Britain stated, and some objections against the sugar colony bill answer'd. London, For J. Roberts, 1731.　　　　　　　　　　　I24
An argument on behalf of the proposal before Parliament to cut off New England's trade with the French sugar-producing islands in the West Indies.

The impracticability of a northwest passage for ships impartially considered. London, A. J. Valpy, 1824.　　　　　　　　　　　　I25
An inquiry into the possible existence and commercial usefulness of a northwest passage.

Inconville, de. [Letter dated Peking, 5 November 1755 to Henri Louis Duhamel du Monceau.] Manuscript in French. [Peking, 1755.]　　I26
A French resident at Peking writes to Henri Louis Duhamel du Monceau recommending adoption in France of Chinese technology for silk-manufacture.

L'Indépendance des Anglo-Américains démontrée utile a la Grande-Bretagne. [n.p., ca. 1782.]　　　　　　　　　　　　　　I27
Two letters, the first a general examination of natural rights as related to property rights and commercial freedom, the second an examination of the nature of commerce.

Indrenius, Andreas Abraham. Specimen academicum de Esquimaux, gente Americana. Abo, Jacob Merckell [1756].　　　　　I28
A dissertation on the American Eskimos written under the direction of Pehr Kalm.

Indulgencias concedidas a las medallas ... concedio a instancia del Padre Gil de la Mata de la Compañia de Jesus Procurador del Japon y China ... [n.p., 1595.]　　　　　　I29

This is a papal bull dated 28 September 1595 issued by Pope Clement VIII granting indulgences for those who worship graven images and reaffirming prior indulgences by other popes. The indulgence was requested by Gil de la Mata, a Jesuit priest and procurator of Japan and China.

Inga, Athanasius. West Indische spieghel. [Amsterdam, B. Jansz & J. Petersz. Wachter, 1624.] I30

Describes in detail the islands and provinces in Spanish America. The work has been attributed to Willem Usselincx.

L'Inganno nascoto nel disinganno, e discoperto da un padre della Compagnia di Giesu', in risposta ad un libro intitolato Il disinganno, composto da un religioso dell' ordine de' Predicatori ... Cologne, 1702. I31

A reply to an anti-Jesuit work, *Il disinganno contraposto da un religioso dell' ordine de' Predicatori*, citing repeated misinterpretation of the Jesuit position with respect to the Chinese Rites.

Ingredienten ende ampliatien van antwoort te geven aen den heer ambassadeur van Vranckryck [de la Tuillerie] op syne propositie van den XVII. Martii 1648. Amsterdam, J. Verny, 1648. I32

Concerns the Peace of Westphalia.

An inquiry into the causes of the insurrection of the Negroes in the island of St. Domingo. London, J. Johnson, 1792. I33

An anonymous author refutes here the arguments in *A particular account of the commencement and progress of the insurrection of the Negroes in St. Domingo*, published the same year.

Insigne victoria que el Señor Marquez de Guadalcazar, Virrey en el Reyno del Pirû, ha alcançado en los puertos de Lima, y Callao, contra vna armada poderosa de Olanda, despachada por orden del Conde Mauricio. Lisbon, 1625. I34

An account of the battle at Callao in the summer of 1624 between Spanish forces there and the raiding Dutch fleet commanded by Jacques L'Hermite.

Instrucçaõ sobre o uso da medida cubica liquida, que por ordem de sua magestade fez ordenar a Junta, que solicita o bem commum do commercio o ... Lisbon, Manoel Coelho Amado, 1756. I35

A treatise on weights and measures used in commerce. This copy has manuscript additions dealing with special regulations pertaining to trade in wine and olives.

Instruction för den unge Polaetus i någre handels-rörelser. Stockholm, Lars Salvii, 1765. I36

An essay on balance of trade and exchange rates, with some history of trade and an account of "new" economic theory.

Instruction, tarifs et pancartes concernant le commerce. Nantes, Nicolas Verger, 1729. I37

A compendium of information on export and import duties for Brittany, with particular reference to Nantes, noting also standards of weights and measures and rates of exchange for foreign currencies.

Instrumento de testemunhas tirado em Goa a pitiçam dos procuradores do Conde Almirante Dom Francisco da Gama despois de haver governdo a quelle estado segunda vez, e se haver partido delle pera Portugal. Nantes, Pedro Dorio [ca. 1646]. I38

A petition concerning commerce in the western Indian Ocean.

Instrumentum pacis. Dat is een kort doch bondig verhael van de vreden-artyckels ... ghesloten ... op den 24 October des jaers 1648. Amsterdam, Cornelis Jansz Stichter [ca. 1648]. I39

A summary of the Treaty of Munster.

The interest of Great Britain, in supplying herself with iron: impartially consider'd. [London? 1738?] I40

A plea for encouragement of British iron manufactures through restrictions upon imports from Sweden and Russia, and restraints upon iron manufacturing in the American colonies.

The interest of these United Provinces. Middelburg, Thomas Berry, 1673. I41

A discussion of the future of the Dutch nation, in which the author prefers to ally the Dutch with the English rather than the French in the event that the homeland cannot be defended. His reasons are largely commercial.

Les interests des princes alliez, proposez à Gertruydemberg renouvellez au congrez d'Utrecht, et autres lieux. Avec le traité de l'assiento, ou du négoce des Négres, entre les couronnes de France & d'Espagne ... Utrecht, G. vande Water et J. van Poolsum, 1713. I42

Interiano, Paolo. Ristretto delle historie Genovesi. [Lucca, Busdrago, 1551.] I43

A history of Genoa compiled from various medieval and early modern chronicles.

Intorcetta, Prospero. Compendiosa narratione dello stato della missione Cinese, cominciãdo dall' anno 1581 fino al 1669, offerta in Roma. Rome, Francesco Tizzoni, 1672. I44

An account of missionary progress in China from its beginnings with extensive comment on the persecutions of the 1660s.

An introduction to the history of the kingdoms and states of Asia, Africa and America, both ancient and modern, according to the method of Samuel Puffendorf ... London, R.J. for T. Newborough [etc.] 1705.   I45

A general history of the areas indicated, with heavy emphasis on classical accounts of western Asia and north Africa. Spanish conquests dominate the history of the Americas. The work has been attributed to Jodocus Crull.

Io. Francisci Buddei p.p. Selecta iuris naturae et gentium. Halae Saxonum, Orphanotrophii, 1748.   I46

A collection of eleven dissertations on international law.

The iron-trade of Great-Britain impartially considered. [London, ca. 1750.]   I47

A review of the threat to the iron, forestry, agriculture, and tanning industries of Britain due to the competition offered to iron manufacturers by their counterparts in Sweden, Russia, and Spain.

An Irregular dissertation, occasioned by the reading of Father Du Halde's description of China ... London, For J. Roberts, 1740.   I48

A comparison of Chinese and British government and institutions claiming British superiority in most instances.

Irwin, Eyles. Begebenheiten einer Reise auf dem Rothen Meer, auf der arabischen und ägyptischen Küste, ingleichen durch die thebaische Wüste. Leipzig, Weidmanns Erben und Reich, 1781.   I49

This German edition is based upon one of the English editions of 1780, with illustrations and maps from that edition, and translator's notes, apparently by Johann Andreas Engelbrecht.

Irwin, Eyles. A series of adventures in the course of a voyage up the Red-Sea. London, J. Dodsley, 1780.   I50

Contains observations on the commerce of the regions visited along the Red Sea and overland to Cairo.

Irwin, Eyles. A series of adventures in the course of a voyage up the Red-Sea, on the coasts of Arabia and Egypt ... with a supplement of a voyage from Venice to Latichea, and ... by Aleppo, Bagdad, and the Tygris, to Busrah, in the years 1780 and 1781. London, J. Dodsley, 1787.   I51

This third edition includes an account of Irwin's overland travel through Persia in 1780-81 with interesting insights on caravan travel at that time.

Irwin, Eyles. Voyage a la Mer rouge, sur les cotes de l'Arabie, en Egypte, et dans les déserts de la Thébaide. Paris, Briand, 1792.   I52

The first French edition. Based upon the third English edition, it includes accounts of travels from Venice to Latichea and from Aleppo to Busrah via Baghdad.

Isert, Paul Erdmann. Reise nach Guinea und den caribäischen Inseln in Columbien, in Briefen an seine Freunde beschreiben. Copenhagen, J.F. Morthorst, 1788.   I53

The first edition of a travel account describing Danish settlements in West Africa and in the West Indies, with particular emphasis on the peoples of West Africa. Included is an account of the slave trade and of the Danish and French West Indies.

Isert, Paul Erdmann. Neue Reise nach Guinea und den Caribäischen Inseln in Amerika, in den Jahren 1783 bis 1787: nebst Nachrichten von dem Negerhandel in Afrika. Berlin und Leipzig, 1790.   I54

This edition differs from the 1788 edition in introductory matter, in the rendition of the text, adds an appendix on the slave trade, but omits a meteorological appendix.

Isert, Paul Erdmann. Reize van Koppenhagen naar Guinea, en van daar naar de Westindiën en de Caribische eilanden in Amerika. Amsterdam, V.D. Burgh [etc.] 1797.   I55

The first Dutch edition, translated from the German edition.

Isert, Paul Erdmann. Voyages en Guinée et dans les îles Caraïbes en Amérique. Paris, Maradan, 1793.   I56

The first French edition.

Isidore, of Seville, Saint. Etymologiae. Augsburg, Günther Ziner, 1472.   I57

The first edition of an important work for the transmission of classical geographic knowledge to medieval Europe. It contains the first printed "T" map of the world.

L'Isle, Guillaume de. Carte de Moscovie. Amsterdam, Jean Covens et Corneille Mortier [1740].   I58

First published in 1706, this map was based on information supplied to De l'Isle from Aldrey Artamonovich, Russian ambassador to the Netherlands from 1699 to 1712.

L'Isle, Guillaume de. Carte des côtes de Malabar et de Coromandel. Amsterdam, Covens & Mortier [1730].   I59

This map was published by Covens and Mortier, part of their edition of Guillaume De l'Isle's *Atlas Nouveau*, the edition of 1730 being their earliest issue of it.

L'Isle, Guillaume de. Hemisphere septentrionale pour voir plus distinctement les Terres arctiques. Paris, Academie royal des Sciences, 1714.   I60

This map of the northern hemisphere contains manuscript additions, anonymous and undated, to eastern Siberia and the north Pacific region.

[Italian mercantile and financial correspondence]. 1436-1576.   I61

Twelve of these letters are from the fifteenth century. They deal with a variety of commercial concerns.

[Italian mercantile and financial correspondence.] Manuscript. Italy, 1426-1486.   I62
Eight of ten letters were dated in various places in Italy. All of them concern mercantile and financial transactions.

Itinerarium Antonini. Itinerarium provinciarum omnium Antonini Augusti, cum fragmento eiusdem. Paris, Henricus Stephanus [after Aug. 1512].   I63
A manual of land and sea routes of the Roman Empire as they existed about 200 A.D.

Itinerarium Orbis Christiani. [Cologne? ca. 1580.]   I64
A collection of eighty-four maps of various parts of Europe, showing roads that linked the major commercial centers.

Ives, Edward. Reizen van Engeland naar Indie, ondernomen in het jaar MDCCLIV. Rotterdam, Hendrik Beman, Bennet en Hake; Utrecht, Abr. van Paddenburg, J. van Schoonhoven, 1776.   I65

The author went to India as surgeon under command of Admiral Watson, British commander in chief in the East Indies. He returned overland through Persia, describing in great detail the country traversed.

J

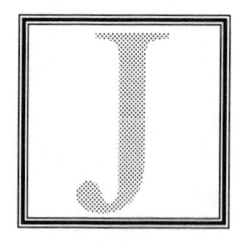

Jacinto de Deus, Padre. Vergel de plantas, e flores da provincia da Madre de Deos dos Capuchos reformados. Lisbon, Miguel Deslandes, 1690. J1

An account of Portuguese missions in India, China, southeast Asia, Indonesia, Ceylon and Mozambique, including biographies of many missionaries who served in these places. The historical section begins in 1540, when the first convent was established in Goa.

Jackson, Randle. The substance of a speech delivered ... at the East-India House, on Wednesday, January 21, 1795, in support of ... conducting the shipping of the East-India Company in future, upon principles of fair and open competition. Reported by William Woodfall ... [London] For J. Debrett [1795]. J2

A statement in favor of open bidding for shipbuilding contracts to be let by the company to avoid the possibilities of collusion or charges of misconduct in this aspect of the company's affairs.

Jacobides, Aquila, pseud. Rechtvaerdige wapenen des Vereenigde Nederlands tegen ... der Fransche en Engelsche koningen. Amsterdam, Winkel-zons Rozalis, 1672. J3

An account of French and English attempts to interfere with Dutch commerce.

Jacobs, Peter. Journal of the Reverend Peter Jacobs, Indian Wesleyan missionary, from Rice Lake to the Hudson's Bay territory. Boston, George C. Rand, 1853. J4

A good general description of the Great Lakes and Hudson Bay regions.

Jacobus Philippus, Bergomensis. Chronicha de tuto el mondo vulgare. Venice, Bernardino Rizo de Novara, 1491. J5

This first Italian edition appends accounts of the lands of Prester John, India, and Scythia to the chronicle of world history.

Jacobus Philippus, Bergomensis. Novissime hystoriarum omnium repercussiones ... Supplementum supplementi Cronicarum nuncupantur ... [Venice, Albertinus de Lissona, 1503.] J6

The first edition to contain material on the voyages of Columbus; it also reports the newly developed trade to Ethiopia and India.

Jacobus Philippus, Bergomensis. Novissime historiarum omnium repercussonies. Venice, G. de Rusconibus, 1506. J7

The second edition.

Jacquemin, Nicolas. Mémoire sur la Guiane française. Paris, Baudelot & Eberhart, 1799. J8

A description of French Guiana and its natural products, with suggestions for encouraging settlement there.

[Jacques, de Vitry.] Divisiones decem nationum totius Christianitatis. [Rome, Eucharius Silber, ca. 1495.] J9

An account of ten Eastern Christian sects, giving commentary on their rites, customs, and religious practices, with geographical and historical information included.

[Jacques, de Vitry.] Divisiones decem nationum totius Christianitatis. [Rome, Eucharius Silber, 1510.] J10

Another printing of this popular work.

Jacques, de Vitry. Libri duo. Quorum prior Orientalis, sive Hierosolymitanae; alter, Occidentalis historiae nomine inscribitur. Douay, Balthazaris Belleri, 1597. J11

Late edition of this work, with a life of the author included.

Jacquinot, Dominique. l'Usage de l'astrolabe, avec un petit traicté de la sphere. Paris, Hierosme de Marnef & Guillaume Cavellat, 1573. J12

A text on the use of the astrolabe for navigation purposes, for geometric problems and including James

Bassantin's *Amplifications* on the use of the astrolabe for computing the location of stars.

Jaillot, Alexis Hubert. Le Neptune françois, ou Atlas nouveau des cartes marines ... Paris, H. Jaillot, 1693. J13

Includes thirty-two sea charts depicting the coast of Europe from North Cape to Gibraltar, including the British Isles and the Baltic Sea.

Jaillot, Bernard. Mappe-monde celeste, terrestre et historique. Paris, Jaillot, 1733. J14

A wall map measuring 42 1/2 x 39 inches containing a double-hemisphere map of the world and numerous inserts of geographical, historical, and astronomical information.

Jamaica. An abridgment of the laws of Jamaica: being an alphabetical digest of all the public acts of Assembly now in force. St. Jago de la Vega, Alexander Aikman, 1793. J15

A digest of the laws of Jamaica passed from 1680 to 1793, arranged by subject and indexed.

Jamaica. An address relating to the African Company to be presented to Her Majesty ... [London? 1711.] J16

The governor, council, and assembly of Jamaica petition for an end to the monopoly of the Royal African Company on the slave trade.

Jamaica. Assembly. To His Excellency Charls Earle of Carlyle Capt Gene[ll] Gouvernour and comand[r] in chief of His Maj[ts] island of Jamaica, &c. Manuscript. [Jamaica, ca. 1678.] J17

The Assembly defends the colonists against charges of unruly behavior and urges that the government of the island not be made more arbitrary, especially in matters of taxation.

Jamaica. Laws, etc. An act for the restraining & punishing privateers & pirates. Manuscript. [Jamaica, ca. 1680.] J18

Offenders against this act were liable to the same processes and punishments as they would be if apprehended in England.

Jamaica. Laws, etc. The laws of Jamaica, passed by the Assembly and confirmed by His Majesty in Council, Feb. 23, 1683. To which is added, a short account of the island and government thereof. With an exact map of the island. London, H. Hills for Charles Harper, 1683. J19

The first publication of Jamaica's laws, together with introductory material promoting settlement on the island.

James, Joseph, and Daniel Moore. A system of exchange with almost all parts of the world. New York, John Furman, 1800. J20

This handbook was designed to acquaint the American merchant with worldwide monetary exchange. Part two, "The India trader's directory," is a description of East Indian goods.

James, Thomas. The strange and dangerous voyage of Captain Thomas James. London, John Legatt for John Partridge, 1633. J21

An account of the first voyage to explore the western coast of James Bay, and a very significant book in the history of the exploration for a northwest passage.

James, Thomas. The dangerous voyage of Capt. Thomas James, in his intended discovery of a northwest passage ... London, O. Payne, 1740. J22

A reprinting of James' narrative of 1633 with some revisions.

James I, King of England. [Manuscript letter signed to the emperor of China.] Westminster, February 7, 1614. J23

A formal diplomatic letter requesting that China open its commerce to English merchants.

James I, King of England. [Manuscript letter signed to the emperor of Japan.] Westminster, January 10, 1612. J24

A formal letter on parchment requesting that the Emperor of Japan receive favorably English merchants wishing to trade there.

Jansen, Jakob. Verhaal der merkwaardige reize ... van Hamburg naar Groenland. Haarlem, Johannes Enschede, 1770. J25

An account of whaling activities in the Greenland area, noting Dutch activities there.

[Janssen, Sir Theodore.] General maxims in trade, particularly applied to the commerce between Great Britain and France. London, S. Buckley, 1713. J26

A comparison of beneficial and non-beneficial trade, with the conclusion that the trade in luxury items from France should be restricted by high duties.

Jansson, Jan. Atlas minor, das ist: Eine kurtze jedoch gründliche Beschreibung der gantzen Weldt. Amsterdam, Joannis Janssonii, 1651. J27

This edition contains 215 maps, reflecting the cartography of the period from 1620 to 1640.

Jansson, Jan. Cinquiesme partie du Grand atlas, contenant une parfaicte description du monde maritime. Amsterdam, Joannem Janssonium, 1650. J28

A sea atlas and an atlas for comparing ancient and current geographical knowledge, with twenty-two maps and charts in all, preceded by an essay on various aspects of navigation.

Jansson, Jan. Nobilis fluvius Albis ... Amsterdam, J. Jansson [ca. 1658]. J29

This map is from the *Atlas Major*.

Jazu, Sieur. Remarques et observations sur le commerce de la Compagnie des Indes a la Chine. Par le Sr Jazu dans son voyage pendant les années 1740 et 1741. Manuscript. [n.p., ca. 1742.] J30
A description of the money, weights and measures and accounting practices used in China and of the various products in the China trade that were of interest to France, addressed to Orry de Fulvy, Intendant of Finances.

Jean, Alexandre. Arithmetique au miroir: par laquelle on peut (en quatre vaccations de demie heure chacune) pratiquer les plus belles regles d'icelle. [n.p.] 1649. J31
A merchant's handbook, with rules for calculating interest and for computing values in money of goods sold by weight and ell-measure, primarily cloth.

Jean Armand, called Mustapha. Voyages d'Afrique faicts par le commandement du Roy. Paris, N. Traboulliet, 1631. J32
An account of Isaac de Razilly's explorations on behalf of the French government to Fez and Morocco in 1629 and 1630.

Jefferson, Thomas. Observations sur la Virginie. Paris, Barrois, 1786. J33
A description of Virginia, its people, natural resources, and government. This translation by André Morellet omits some of Jefferson's political observations.

Jefferson, Thomas. Notes on the state of Virginia. London, John Stockdale, 1787. J34
This first London edition contains material not included in the previous work. It is a reprinting of the first English edition published in Paris ca. 1784.

Jefferson, Thomas. Notes on the state of Virginia. Philadelphia, Prichard and Hall, 1788. J35
The first American edition.

Jefferson, Thomas. Notes on the state of Virginia. Philadelphia, R.T. Rawle, June 1801. J36
This edition includes appendices relating to the geography of the frontier, the murder of the Indian James Logan's family and Jefferson's inaugural address.

Jefferys, Thomas. The American atlas. London, R. Sayer and J. Bennett, 1776. J37
An atlas containing forty-nine copper-engraved maps of America.

[Jefferys, Thomas.] The conduct of the French, with regard to Nova Scotia; from its first settlement to the present time. London, T. Jefferys, 1754. J38
An attempted refutation of French claims to Nova Scotia, drawing upon the early history of its settlement and previously published maps and descriptions of the region.

[Jefferys, Thomas.] Conduite des François, par rapport a la Nouvelle Ecosse, depuis le premier établissement de cette colonie jusqu'à nos jours. London, Freres Vaillant, 1755. J39
A translation of a statement of the British point of view with reference to the dispute over Nova Scotia, with a preface and extensive notes to disprove the British case. The translator and editor was Georges Marie Butel-Dumont.

Jefferys, Thomas. A description of the Spanish islands and settlements on the coast of the West Indies. London, T. Jefferys, 1762. J40
A West Indian gazetteer in which the descriptions of major islands and cities are accompanied by maps and plans. It includes historical information as well as notes on the population, government, climate, and products of the places described.

Jefferys, Thomas. A general map of the middle British colonies in America. London, 1758. J41
This map was first published by Lewis Evans in 1755. In this re-publication of it Jefferys added a line of frontier forts and emphasized internal waterways. It extends from Virginia to Montreal.

Jefferys, Thomas. The great probability of a northwest passage deduced from observations on the letter of Admiral de Fonte. London, T. Jefferys, 1768. J42
The royal geographer of England expresses belief that the de Fonte passage might actually exist. A map shows the suggested passage.

Jefferys, Thomas. The natural and civil history of the French dominions in North and South America. London, Thomas Jefferys, 1760. J43
Extensive descriptions of the French colonies in the New World accompanied by eighteen maps.

Jefferys, Thomas. North America from the French of M^r D'Anville improved with the back settlements of Virginia and course of Ohio. London, Thomas Jefferys, 1755. J44
A brief text describes the English colonies and notes "French incroachments in the north and west."

Jefferys, Thomas. The West-India atlas. London, Robert Sayer and John Bennett, 1775. J45
A collection of thirty-nine very detailed charts of the West Indies, based largely on information captured from the Spaniards, according to the author.

Jenner, Thomas. London's blame, if not its shame. [London] T.J., 1651. J46
A condemnation of the loss of trade to England through the neglect of coastal fisheries.

[Jenyns, Soame.] The objections to the taxation of our American colonies ... briefly consider'd. London, J. Wilkie, 1765. J47

An argument in defense of Parliament's right to tax the American colonies, noting that a lack of representation is no barrier to the taxation of many communities in England.

[Jenyns, Soame.] Thoughts on the causes and consequences of the present high price of provisions. London, J. Dodsley, 1767. **J48**

A commentary on inflation which the author attributed to costs of colonial wars and influx of wealth from colonial enterprise.

SEE ALSO: Andrade, Antonio de; Bartoli, Daniello; Bouvet, Joachim; Biard, Pierre; Carvalho, Valentin; Cassani, José; Dablon, Claude; Du Jarric, Pierre; Ferreira, Manuel; Fleuriau, Bertrand Gabriel; Fróis, Luís; Furtado, Francisco; Guerreiro, Fernão; Kirwitzer, Václav Pantaleon; Le Jeune, Paul; Le Mercier, François; Letras anuas, 1645; Lettere annue del Tibet; Lettre diverse dalle Indie orientali; Lettres annales du Jappon; Lettres edifiantes; Litterae annuae; Litterae Societatis Jesu; López, Gregorio; Maffei, Giovanni Pietro; Magistris, Giacinto; Marini, Gian Filippo de; Martins, Pedro, Bishop of Japan; Matos, Diego de; Moriset, Claude; Nova relatio historica, 1601; Nuove lettere delle cose del Giappone, 1585; Outreman, Pierre d'; Paez, Pedro; Pantoja, Diego de; Pérez de Ribas, Andrés; Pimenta, Nicolau; Pinheiro, Luiz; Quen, Jean de; Rho, Giacomo; Rhodes, Alexandre de; Ricci, Matteo; Rodrigues Girão, João; Rosignoli, Carlo Gregorio; Roth, Heinrich; Ruiz de Montoya, Antonio; Sacchini, Francesco; Salazar, Juan Joseph de; Sanvitores, Diego Luis de; Scelta di lettere edificanti; Schirmbeck, Adam; Semedo, Alvaro; Sepp, Antonio; Sequeira, Luis de; Techo, Nicolás del, *originally* Du Toict; Thomas, Antoine; Toebast, Ignatius; Torres Bollo, Diego de; Trigault, Nicolas; Verbiest, Ferdinand; Victoria, Pedro Gobeo de; Vidal Figueroa, Jose; Villotte, Jacques; Vimont, Barthélemy; Weidenfeld, Adam; Xarque, Francisco.

Jesuits. Annuae litterae Societatis Jesu anni. M.D.LXXXIII ad patres, et fratres eiusdem Societatis. Rome, Collegio eiusdem Societatis, 1585. **J49**

A collection of annual letters covering Jesuit establishments in Europe, a mission at Constantinople, and the provinces of Mexico, Brazil, and the East Indies.

Jesuits. Annuae litterae Societatis Jesu anni M.D.LXXXIX ad patres et fratres eiusdem Societatis. Rome, Collegio Societatis Jesu, 1591. **J50**

These letters include reports from Peru, Angola and Brazil.

Jesuits. Annuae litterae Societatis Jesu anni MDLXXXXII ad patres, et fratres eiusdem Societatis. Florence, Philippum Junctam, 1600. **J51**

These letters do not include any from non-European locations.

Jesuits. Annuae litterae Societatis Jesu anni MDXCIII ad patres, ac fratres eiusdem Societatis. Florence, Philippi Juncte, 1601. **J52**

This collection includes a fifty-page report from Mexico.

Jesuits. Annuae litterae Societatis Jesu anni M.D.XCVI ad patres, & fratres eiusdem Societatis. Neapoli, Tarquini Longi, 1605. **J53**

Non-European areas included in this collection are Mexico, Peru, India, and the Philippine Islands.

Jesuits. Catalogus provinciarum Societatis Jesu, domorum, collegiorum, residentiarum, seminariorum, & missionum, quae in unaquaque provincia numerabantur anno 1679. Rome, Ignatii de Lazaris, 1679. **J54**

A catalog of Jesuit establishments in all parts of the world.

Jesuits. Libro de la caxa dela Casa Professa de Mex.^{co} desde su fundacion q̃ fue a 3. de febrero de 1592 años. Manuscript in Spanish. Mexico City, 1592-1605. **J55**

A record of contributions and disbursements toward the building and maintaining of the "Casa Profesa", a Jesuit establishment in Mexico.

Jesuits. [Manuscripts in French, Italian, and Latin relating to China.] [n.p.] 1725-1732. **J56**

Includes a commentary on the execution of Father João Morão; an eyewitness account of the Chinese government's torture of Chinese converts to Christianity and attempts to expel Europeans; and a translation of Emperor K'ang-hsi's (1662-1722) edict, dictated shortly before his death.

Jesuits. Nouveaux mémoires des missions de la Compagnie de Jésus, dans le Levant. Paris, Nicolas Le Clerc [etc.] 1715-1755. **J57**

A nine-volume set describing Jesuit missions to the Levant.

Jesuits. Reflexions des Jésuites de Rome sur le célèbre jugement rendu à Lisbonne le 12 janvier 1758, qu'ils appellent le Manifeste de Portugal. [n.p., 1758.] **J58**

The Jesuits' response to their condemnation by the king of Portugal, presented here by an anti-Jesuit editor.

Jesuits. Letters from missions. Novi avisi di piu lochi de l'India et massime de Brasil. Rome, Antonio Blado, 1553. **J59**

A collection of letters from Jesuit missions in India, Africa, and Brazil, including one from Francis Xavier.

Jesuits. Letters from missions. Diversi avisi particolari dall' Indie di Portogallo, ricevuti dall' anno 1551 fino al 1558. Venice, Michele Tramezzino, 1565. **J60**

The second edition of a collection of eighty-nine letters from Jesuit missionaries in India, Malacca, the Moluccas, Japan, Africa, and Brazil.

Jesuits. Letters from missions. Lettere dell' India Orientale. Venice, Antonio Ferrari, 1580. J61
A collection of twenty-four letters, chiefly from the period 1568-77, describing Jesuit activity in India, Malacca, the Moluccas, Japan, and Brazil.

Jesuits. Letters from missions. Raggvaglio d'alcune missioni dell' Indie Orientali, & Occidentali. Cavato da alcuni avvisi scritti gli anni 1590 & 1591 ... Rome, Luigi Zannetti, 1592. J62
A collection of letters, and extracts from letters, containing information on the Jesuit missions in India, Ethiopia, Japan, the Philippines, Mexico and Peru.

Jesuits. Letters from missions. Drey newe Relationes. Erste, auss Japon, was sich darinn, so wol in Geist-als weltlichen Sachen im Jahr Christi 1606 denckwürdigs zugetragen. Andere, von Missionibus oder Reisen ... im Jahr 1607 in das Königreich Mexico angestelt. Dritte, von Anbleiben dess mächtigen königs Mogor ... Augsburg, Chrysostomo Dabertzhofer, 1611. J63
A collection of letters from 1606 and 1607 reporting missionary progress in Japan, Mexico, and India, apparently translated from original manuscript sources.

Jesuits. Letters from missions. Ragvali d'alcune missioni fatte dalli padri della Compagnia di Giesu nell' Indie Orientali, cioè nelle provincie di Goa, e Coccino, e nell' Africa in Capo Verde. Rome, Bartolomeo Zannetti, 1615. J64
A series of five reports on mission stations in India and Africa.

Jesuits. Letters from missions. Histoire de ce qui s'est passe en Ethiopie, Malabar, Brasil, et es Indes Orientales. Paris, S. Cramoisy, 1628. J65
Translation, by Jean Darde, of *Lettere annue d'Etiopia, Malabar, Brasil, e Goa*, Rome, 1627.

Jesuits. Letters from missions. Histoire de ce qui s'est passé es royaumes d'Ethiopie, en l'année 1626 jusqu' au mois de mars 1627. Et de la Chine, en l'année 1625 jusques en feburier de 1626. Paris, Sebastien Cramoisy, 1629. J66
Reports from the various residences in Ethiopia and China, with an account of the political situation in China, followed by a description of Tunking by a traveler through that country. Translation of *Lettere dell' Etiopia dell' an. 1626* ... Milan, 1629.

Jesuits. Letters from missions. Edifying and curious letters of some missioners, of the Society of Jesus, from foreign missions. [n.p.] 1707. J67
These Jesuit letters are from the 1690s and up to 1702. They are translations from the *Lettres édifiantes et curieuses*, and all of them pertain to Asiatic missions. Edited by Charles Le Gobien.

Jesuits. Letters from missions. The travels of several learned missioners of the Society of Jesus, into divers parts of the archipelago, India, China, and America. London, R. Gosling, 1714. J68
A collection of Jesuit reports, often in abridged form, noting information of commercial interest in various parts of the world.

Jesuits. Letters from missions. Allerhand so lehr-als geist-reich Brief, Schrifften und Reis-Beschreibungen, welche von denen Missionariis der Gesellschafft Jesu aus beyden Indien, und andern uber Meer gelegenen Ländern, seit an. 1642 bis auf das Jahr 1726 in Europa angelangt seynd ... Augsburg & Grätz, Philipp, Martin, und Johann Vieth, 1728-1736; Vienna, Leopold Johann Kaliwoda, 1748-1755. J69
A collection of Jesuit letters covering the period from 1642 to 1739, 594 items, many of them published from manuscript sources, and frequently written by German, Austrian, and Bohemian missionaries.

Jesuits. Letters from missions. Cartas edificantes, y curiosas, escritas de las missiones estrangeras, por alguno missioneros de la Compañia de Jesus. Madrid, Viuda de Manuel Fernandez, 1753-1757. J70
Spanish translation in sixteen volumes of the *Lettres édifiantes*, newly arranged, and including twenty-one engraved illustrations of Indians and missionaries.

Jesuits. Letters from missions. Lettere edificanti e curiose, scritte da alcuni religiosi della Compagnia di Gesu ... tradotte dall' original Franzese nel volgar nostro Italiano. Venice, Marcellino Piotto e Pietro Valvasense, 1755. J71
This volume represents an attempt at an Italian version of the *Lettres édifiantes*. No subsequent volumes appear to have been issued.

Jesuits. Letters from missions. Lettres édifiantes et curieuses, écrites des missions étrangeres. Paris, J.G. Merigot le jeune, 1780-83. J72
Twenty-six volume collection of Jesuit missionary literature, arranged in sections on the Levant, America, India, China, and "China-India."

Jesuits. Letters from missions. Annuae litterae. Annuae litterae Societatis Jesu anni MDLXXXI. Rome, Collegio eiusdem Societatis, 1583. J73
Includes missionary letters from Mexico, Brazil, and the East Indies.

Jesuits. Letters from missions. Annuae litterae. Annuae litterae Societatis Jesu anni M.D.LXXXIV. Rome, Collegio eiusdem Societatis, 1586. J74
India, Cochin China, Malacca, Peru, Mexico, and Brazil are represented in this collection of letters.

Jesuits. Letters from missions. Annuae litterae.
Litterae Societatis Jesu duorum annorum M.D.LXXXVI et M.D.LXXXVII. Rome, Collegio eiusdem Societatis, 1589. J75
Includes letters from Ethiopia, India, China, Brazil, Peru, Paraguay, Panama, and Mexico.

Jesuits. Letters from missions. Annuae litterae.
Annuae litterae Societatis Jesu anni M.D.LXXXVIII ad patres, et fratres, eiusdem Societatis. Rome, Collegio Societatis Jesu, 1590. J76
Largely concerned with Jesuit activities in Europe, this collection does include material on Mexico, North Africa, Angola, Brazil, and India.

Jesuits. Letters from missions. Annuae litterae.
Litterae Societatis Jesu duorum annorum MDXC e MDXCI. Rome, Collegio eiusdem Societatis, 1594. J77
In addition to letters from the provinces of Europe, this collection includes some from Mexico, Peru, and the East Indies.

Jesuits. Letters from missions. Annuae litterae.
Annuae litterae Societatis Jesu. Anni M.DC.IV. Douay, Viduae Laurentii Kellami, 1618. J78
Letters from Peru, Mexico, and the Philippine Islands are included in this collection.

Jesuits. Letters from missions. Annuae litterae.
Annuae litterae Societatis Jesu, anni [M D]C XII: ad patres, et fratres eiusdem Societatis. Lyons, Claudium Cayne, 1618. J79
Letters from the European establishments predominate, but some information from Mexico, Peru and the Philippine Islands is included.

Jesuits. Letters from missions. Annuae litterae.
Litterae annuae Societatis Jesu, anni M.DC.II. Antwerp, Haerdes Martini Nutii, 1618. J80
Non-European areas reported in these letters are Mexico and the Philippine Islands.

Jesuits. Letters from missions. Annuae litterae.
Litterae annuae Societatis Jesu anni 1606, 1607, & 1608 datae de more ex provinciis ad R.P.N. generalem praepositum, eiusdemq authoritatae typis expresse. Mainz, Joannis Albini, 1618. J81
Actually this is a report for 1608 only, covering all of Catholic Europe, Africa, Mexico, Peru, and the Philippines.

Jesuits. Letters from missions (The East). Nuovi avisi dell' Indie Portogallo, ricevuti dalli reverendi padri della Compagnia de Giesu, tradotta dalla lingua Spagnuola ... [Venice, Michele Tramezzino] 1559. J82
This collection of Jesuit letters includes nine items from Goa, Malacca, Ormuz, Cochin, Travancore, and Calicut, all from the period 1556-1558.

Jesuits. Letters from missions (The East).
Epistolae Indicae de stupendis et praeclaris rebus, quas divina bonitas in India ... Louvain, Rutger Velpius, 1566. J83
A collection of letters written by Jesuit missionaries from India and Persia, including accounts of Portuguese activity in the East.

Jesuits. Letters from missions (The East).
Epistolae Indicae de praeclaris, et stupendis rebus, quas divina bonitas in India, & variis insulis ... Louvain, Rutgerum Velpium, 1566. J84
This edition includes five letters not in the previous edition.

Jesuits. Letters from missions (The East).
Epistolae Japanicae, de multorum gentilium in variis insulis ad Christi fidem. Louvain, Rutgerum Velpium, 1569. J85
A collection of twenty-eight letters from missions in Japan, other parts of Asia, and Brazil from 1552 to 1564, in addition to excerpts from two 1549 letters from Francis Xavier and a summary on Asia based on many sources.

Jesuits. Letters from missions (The East).
Epistolae Japanicae, de multorum in variis insulis gentilium ad Christi fidem conversione. Louvain, Rutgerum Velpium, 1570. J86
This edition rearranges the letters in the 1569 edition, omits introductory matter, but adds an index and a list of authors.

Jesuits. Letters from missions (The East).
Epistolae Indicae et Japanicae. Louvain, Rutgerum Velpium, 1570. J87
A collection of nineteen letters from missionaries in the East, extending from Ormuz to Japan.

Jesuits. Letters from missions (The East).
Recueil des plus fraisches lettres, escrittes des Indes Orientales ... Paris, Michel Sonnius, 1571. J88
Translated from an Italian edition of the previous year, this collection includes letters from Goa, Malacca, Ternate, Cochin, and Madeira from the years 1568-1570.

Jesuits. Letters from missions (The East).
Sendtschreyben und warhaffte Zeytungen, von Auffgang und Erweiterung des Christenthumbs, bey den Hayden inn der newen Welt: auch von Vervolgung unnd Hailigkait der gaistlichen apostolishcen Vorsteher daselbs so erst dieses jar aus den Orientischen Indien kommen ... [Munich, Adam Berg, 1571.] J89
This collection of ten letters from Jesuits in the East is translated from the Rome edition of 1570, and includes an extended preface by the translator-editor, Philip Dobereiner.

Jesuits. Letters from missions (The East).
Warhafftige newe Zeitung, welcher Massen inn

kurtzverschtner Zeit, etliche mahometishe unnd haidnische Künig, Künigreich, Länder und Insuln in India und Aufgang der Sonnen das evangelium unnd christenlichen Glauben angenomen haben. Dilingen, Sebaldum Mayer [1571].   J90

In addition to presenting a copy of a letter from the East detailing progress of the Christian religion there, the author adds a brief geography of the East Indies.

Jesuits. Letters from missions (The East). Rerum a Societate Jesu in Oriente gestarum volumen. Cologne, Gervinum Calenium & haeredes Johannis Quentel, 1574.   J91

The fourth edition of the first attempt at a history of Jesuit missions in the Far East. Maffei was the translator and Manuel da Costa the compiler.

Jesuits. Letters from missions (The East). Cartas que los padres y hermanos de la Compañia de Jesus, que andan en los reynos de Japon escrivieron a los dela misma Compañia, desde el año de mil y quinientos y quarēta y nueve, hasta el de mil y quinientos y setenta y uno ... Alcala, Juan Iñiguez de Lequerica, 1575.   J92

A collection of ninety Jesuit letters and other communications from Japan, in addition to a brief life of Francis Xavier and descriptions of localities in the Indian Ocean and Japan.

Jesuits. Letters from missions (The East). Brevis Japaniae insulae descriptio, ac rerum quarundam in ea mirabilium, à patribus Societatis Jesu nuper gestarum, succincta narratio ... Cologne, Officina Birckmannica, 1582.   J93

A collection of five letters from missions in Japan, four of them from 1577, one from 1580.

Jesuits. Letters from missions (The East). Alcune lettere delle cose del Giappone, dell' anno 1579 infino al 1581. Rome, Francesco Zannetti, 1584.   J94

A collection of seven letters, three by Luis Froes, others by Francesco Carrion, Gregorio de Cespedes, Lorenzo Mexia, and Francesco Cabral.

Jesuits. Letters from missions (The East). Alcune lettere delle cose del Giappone ... dell' anno 1579 infino al 1581. Brescia, Vincenzo Sabbio, 1584.   J95

Another edition of the previous collection.

Jesuits. Letters from missions (The East). Lettera annale delle cose del Giapone del M.D.LXXXII. Rome, Francesco Zannetti, 1585.   J96

A description of progress being made in the establishment of Christian seminaries and other missionary establishments in Japan by Gaspar Coelho, Vice-Provincial of the Society of Jesus.

Jesuits. Letters from missions (The East). Avvisi del Giapone de gli anni M.D.LXXXII. LXXXIII. et LXXXIV. Rome, Francesco Zanetti, 1586.   J97

A collection of eleven letters from Jesuit missionaries in Japan and China. Three letters from Luis Froes dominate the volume.

Jesuits. Letters from missions (The East). Nuovi avvisi del Giapone con alcuni altri della Cina. Venice, I. Gioliti, 1586.   J98

A reprint of the preceding item, set in italics and with the errata corrected.

Jesuits. Letters from missions (The East). Avvisi della Cina et Giapone del fine dell' anno 1586. Naples, Horatio Salviani, 1588.   J99

Includes letters from Alessandro Valignani, Antonio d'Almeida, Luis Froes, and Pedro Gomez. The latter two writers report opposition to missions in Japan.

Jesuits. Letters from missions (The East). Lettere del Giapone, et della Cina de gl'anni M.D.LXXXIX. & M.D.XC. Rome, Luigi Zannetti, 1591.   J100

Eight letters reporting missionary progress in Japan and China, including descriptive material as well.

Jesuits. Letters from missions (The East). Sommaire des lettres du Japon et de la Chine, de l'an M.D.LXXXIX. & M.D.XC. Paris, Leon Cavellat, 1592.   J101

A summary translation of *Lettere del Giapone et della Cina*, Rome, 1591.

Jesuits. Letters from missions (The East). Historica relatio, de potentissimi regis Mogor, a magno Tamerlane oriundi, ... Deinde de omnium Japoniae regnorum ... Mainz, Henrici Breem, 1598.   J102

The first portion of this work is made up of abstracted letters from India of 1582, 1591, and 1595. These are followed by abstracts of six letters from India and Japan, 1594 and 1595.

Jesuits. Letters from missions (The East). Lettera del P. Nicolo Pimenta visitatore della Compagnia di Giesu nell'India Orientale. Rome, Luigi Zannetto, 1601.   J103

A collection of seven letters from various mission stations in India, including one report on Pegu.

Jesuits. Letters from missions (The East). Tre lettere annue del Giappone de gli anni 1603, 1604, 1605 e parte del 1606. Rome, Bartholomeo Zannetti, 1608.   J104

These three letters report secular affairs in Japan, the progress of missions there, and some account of persecutions of Christians.

Jesuits. Letters from missions (The East). Lettere annue del Giapone, China, Goa, et

Ethiopia, scritte ... da padri dell' istessa Compagnia ne gl' anni 1615, 1616, 1617, 1618, 1619. Milan, Pacifico Ontio & Gio. Battista Piccaglia, 1621. J105

This is a rich and diverse collection of Eastern Jesuit material dominated by material from China and Japan, but reports from Goa, Ethiopia, and Macao give insights into some of the lesser missions.

Jesuits. Letters from missions (The East). Relatione delle cose piu notabili scritte ne gli anni 1619, 1620, & 1621 dalla Cina ... Rome, l'Erede di Bartolomeo Zannetti, 1624. J106

Two letters from Macao are by Manuel Dias and Wenceslao Pantaleone; one from Hangchow is by Nicolas Trigault.

Jesuits. Letters from missions (The East). Relatione di alcune cose cavate dalle lettere scritte ne gli anni 1619, 1620, & 1621, dal Giappone. Rome, l'Eredi di Bartolomeo Zannetti, 1624. J107

Includes four letters from various mission stations in Japan reporting largely on the persecution of the missions during these years.

Jesuits. Letters from missions (The East). Lettere annue d'Etiopia, Malabar, Brasil, e Goa. Dall' anno 1620, fin' al 1624. Rome, Francesco Corbelletti, 1627. J108

This collection includes accounts of missions in Ceylon, East Africa, Cochin China, and Tibet, all of which were under Jesuit authority in India.

Jesuits. Letters from missions (The East). Lettere dell' Ethiopia dell' anno 1626, fino al Marzo del 1627 e della Cina dell' anno 1625, fino al Febraro del 1626. Parma, Odoardo Fornovo, 1629. J109

Manuel de Almeida wrote the letter from Ethiopia, and Manuel Dias the letter from China. A letter by Giuliano Baldinetti describes his travels in Vietnam, one of the earliest published descriptions of that country.

Jesuits. Letters from missions (Ethiopia). Nuove, e curiose lettere dell' Ethiopia annualmente, scritte al reverendissimo P. Mutio Viteleschi generale della Compagnia de Geisù ... Florence, Pietro Cecconcelli, 1622. J110

Letters concerning the Ethiopia mission from Pedro Paez and Michele della Pace, the former dated Dambia, 3 July 1617, and the latter Goa, 18 February 1620.

Jesuits. Letters from missions (Ethiopia). Lettere annue di Ethiopia. Rome, l'Herede di Bartolomeo Zannetti, 1628. J111

These letters were written during the early years of the patriarchate of Alphonso Mendez, who attempted reforms of Ethiopian religious practices that resulted in popular revolts.

João José de Santa Thereza, Freire. Istoria delle guerre del regno del Brasile accadute tra la corona di Portogallo, e la republica di Olanda. Rome, Eredi del Corbelletti, 1698. J112

A history of the conflict between the Dutch and Portuguese in Brazil, from the Portuguese point of view. Contains many fine maps of Brazil.

Jobson, Richard. The golden trade: or, A discovery of the River Gambra, and the golden trade of the Aethiopians. London, N. Okes, 1623. J113

An account of a voyage 150 miles inland on the Gambia River on behalf of a group of London merchants seeking to open up trade with Timbuktu.

Jode, Gerard de. Hemispheriū ab aequinoctiali linea ... [Antwerp, 1593.] J114

A north and south polar projection of the earth from the *Speculum orbis terrae* issued by Cornelis de Jode, the cartographer's son.

Jöranson, Christian Ludvig. Försök til et systeme i Sveriges allmänna hushållning och penning-väsende. Stockholm, Anders J. Nordström, 1792-1794. J115

A survey of Swedish economic life in the eighteenth century, including comment and statistics on Swedish commerce.

John, Prester. De ritu et moribus Indorum. [Strassburg, Heinrich Knoblochtzer, ca. 1482.] J116

The third edition of one of the most popular of medieval works of travel and geography, the account of the kingdom of a mythical Eastern Christian ruler.

John, Prester. Prestre Jehan par la grace de Dieu roy tout puissant sur tous les roys chrestiens ... [Paris, Antoine Caillaut, ca. 1483-1505.] J117

A unique copy of an edition of the French text of one of the most persistent medieval legends, describing the fruitfulness and the oddities of the kingdom of Prester John, as well as the power of its ruler.

John III, King of Portugal. Serenissimi atque invictissimi Portugalliae ... ad ... Paulum III. [Venice, J. Singrenium, 1536.] J118

The Portuguese King advises Pope Paul III of the Portuguese military success in India, and the agreement by the King of Cambay to divert more of the commerce of his kingdom to Diu, the Portuguese center.

Johnson, Charles. A general history of the robberies and murders of the most notorius pyrates. London, For Ch. Rivington, J. Lacy, and J. Stone, 1724. J119

A series of biographies of outstanding pirates, together with laws pertaining to piracy and recommendations for reducing the number of English pirates.

Johnson, Charles. Histoire des pirates anglois depuis leur etablissement dans l'isle de la

Providence, jusqu'à present ... Paris, Etienne Ganeau & Guillaume Cavelier, 1726. J120
The second French edition.

Johnson, Charles. Historie der Engelsche zeeroovers. Amsterdam, Hermanus Uytwerf, 1725. J121
The first Dutch edition.

Johnson, James. A sermon preached before the incorporated Society for the Propagation of the Gospel in Foreign Parts: at their anniversary meeting in the parish church of St. Mary-le-Bow, on Friday February 24th, 1758. London, E. Owen and T. Harrison, sold by A. Millar, 1758. J122
This sermon shows a particular concern for conversion of the Indians in the British North American colonies.

[Johnson, Robert.] The new life of Virginea. London, Felix Kyngston for William Welby, 1612. J123
A promotional piece for the Virginia colony, including a history of the efforts there, an account of the present state of the colony, and a projection of success for it.

[Johnson, Robert.] Nova Britannia. Offring most excellent fruites by planting in Virginia. London, Samuel Macham, 1609. J124
A promotional pamphlet calling for widespread participation in supporting the Virginia colony and specifying religion, empire, and wealth, in that order, as motives for the undertaking.

[Johnson, Samuel.] Taxation no tyranny; an answer to the resolutions and address of the American congress. London, T. Cadell, 1775. J125
A reply to American colonial arguments for their rights to representation through natural law, and a general condemnation of colonial actions and attitudes leading to rebellion.

Johnson, Sir William. Relaçaõ de huma batalha, succedida no campo de Lake Giorge na America Septentrionale, entre as tropas Inglezas ... e as Francesas ... Lisbon, 1757. J126
Portuguese translation of an account of Anglo-French military encounter in New Hampshire.

Jolís, José. Saggio sulla storia naturale della provincia del Gran Chaco. Faenza, Lodovico Genestri, 1789. J127
A geography and natural history of the Gran Chaco, with attention also to the peoples of the region. Intended as the first of four volumes, this is the only one published.

Jónsbók. Løgbok Islendinga; hvøria saman hefur sett Magnus Noregs kongur. Holar i Hjaltadal, Marteine Arnoddssyne, 1709. J128
Based on a thirteenth century code of laws which defined the colonial relationship between Iceland and Norway, this edition, apparently the fifth, takes into account subsequent amendments and revisions.

Jónsson, Arngrímur. Brevis commentarius de Islandia: quo scriptorum de hac insula errores deteguntur, & extraneorum quorundam con viciis, ac calumniis, quibus Islandis liberius insultare solent, occurritur ... Copenhagen [Johannes Stockelmannus] 1593. J129
A brief but comprehensive description of Iceland, including its history, published in an attempt to refute other works on that country which the author regarded as unflattering and inaccurate.

Jónsson, Arngrímur. Gronlandia, edur Graenlandz saga. Skalhollte, Hendrick Kruse, 1688. J130
The first published account of Icelandic settlement of Greenland, including also the exploration southward to Vinland. The manuscript was completed about 1605 and was based on various Icelandic sources.

José, de Calasanz, Saint. Storia della vita, virtu, doni, e grazie del venerabile servo di Dio p.f. Pietro di S. Giuseppe Betancur, fondatore dell'Ordine betlemitico nelle Indie Occidentali. Rome, Antonio de Rossi, 1739. J131
A biography of a missionary who served in Guatemala in the mid-seventeenth century.

Josselyn, John. An account of two voyages to New-England. London, Giles Widdows, 1674. J132
An outstanding description of New England, with emphasis on natural history, colonial life, and life at sea, by one who visited Massachusetts and Maine twice, in 1638-39 and 1663-71.

Journaal, ofte Waarchtige beschrijving van de gruwelijke conspiratien der Engelsche ... Amsterdam, H. Stam, 1652. J133
A review of the events of the Amboyna Massacre from the Dutch point of view.

Journael, gehouden op's landts-schip de spiegel ... Amsterdam, Jacob Venckel, 1665. J134
Contains a statement of the relations between the Dutch West India Company and the Royal African Company of England on the west coast of Africa.

Journael, Gehouden op's lants schip de spiegel ... onder ... Michiel de Ruyter. Amsterdam, Pieter la Burgh, 1665. J135
Another edition of the previous item.

Journael of kort verhael van ... oorloghs tusschen ... Macassar en de Oost-Indische Compagnie. Amsterdam, Marcus Doornick [1669]. J136
The King of Macassar and other East Indian princes acknowledge their subservience to the Dutch East India Company.

Journal exact de la situation dans laquelle étoit la Martinique, à l'époque du 18 octobre 1790. [Paris, Imprimerie du Patriote François, 1790.]
J137
An account of the slave rebellion under way in mid-October, 1790 on the island of Martinique.

A journal of a voyage round the world, in His Majesty's ship Endeavour, in the years 1768, 1769, 1770 and 1771. London, T. Becket and P.A. De Hondt, 1771. J138
An account of Cook's first voyage with observations on the soil, products, and peoples of the islands of the South Sea.

A journal of a voyage round the world, in His Majesty's ship the Dolphin. London, M. Cooper, 1767. J139
Contains descriptions of the commerce of various islands and ports visited during Byron's circumnavigation of 1764-66.

A journal of a voyage round the world, in His Majesty's ship the Dolphin, commanded by the Honourable Commodore Byron. London, For A. Millar and J. Hodges, 1784. J140
The second edition of a journal of a "midshipman" on the *Dolphin*.

The journal of a voyage undertaken by order of His Present Majesty, for making discoveries towards the North Pole. London, For F. Newbery, 1774. J141
An anonymous and unauthorized version of the voyage of Phipps and Lutwidge to find a passage eastward toward Japan from a point north of Spitzbergen.

A journal of several remarkable passages, before the Honourable House of Commons ... relating to the East-India trade. [n.p., 1693.] J142
Arguments, decrees, petitions, and other documents concerned with the rivalry between independent merchants and the East India Company.

Journal of the expedition to La Guira and Porto Cavallos in the West-Indies, under the command of Commodore Knowles. London, J. Robinson, 1744. J143
A detailed account of Commodore Knowles' unsuccessful attack on the Venezuelan coast in 1744 by a member of the expedition.

Journal or narrative of the Boscawen's voyage to Bombay in the East-Indies, Benjamin Braund, commander ... also some occasional thoughts on freedom in trade, high duties, smuggling, shipwrecks, &c. by Philalethes. London, For the author, 1750. J144
A good account of life aboard an East Indiaman, followed by essays on various aspects of commercial policy.

Joutel, Henri. Journal historique du dernier voyage que feu M. de la Sale fit dans le Golfe de Mexique ... Paris, Estienne Robinot, 1713.
J145
An account of La Salle's final expedition, which attempted to establish a settlement at the mouth of the Mississippi River.

Joutel, Henri. A journal of the last voyage perform'd by Monsr. de la Sale, to the Gulph of Mexico ... London, A. Bell, B. Lintott, and J. Baker, 1714. J146
This English edition includes a copy of the grant of monopoly to Louisiana made to Antoine Crozat in 1712.

Jouve, Joseph. Histoire de la conquete de la Chine par les Tartares mancheoux. Lyon, Freres Duplain, 1754. J147
A history of the Manchu conquest taken from Mailla's *Histoire generale de la Chine*, with a chronology of China's history appended.

Juan, Jorge. Dissertacion historica, y geographica sobre el meridiano de demarcacion entre los dominios de España, y Portugal. Madrid, Antonio Marin, 1749. J148
The author traveled to South America with a French expedition to make scientific observations. He attempts to invoke the Line of Demarcation to define limits to Portugal's empire in America.

Juan, Jorge. Observaciones astronomicas y phisicas. Madrid, Imprenta Real de la Gazeta, 1773.
J149
Astronomical observations from the expedition of the author and Antonio de Ulloa. See also the account written by de Ulloa.

Julián, Antonio. La perla de la America, provincia de Santa Marta, reconocida, observada, y expuesta en discursos historicos. Madrid, Antonio de Sancha, 1787. J150
This description of a province of New Granada stresses its economic importance, noting the value of mines, pearl fisheries, brazil wood, tobacco, sugar, and other products.

Juridisk undersøgelse, i anledning af de i det Asiatiske Compagnies general-forsamling den 20 Junii faldne resolutioner ... Copenhagen, Gyldendals Forlag, hos M. Hallager, 1738.
J151
A critical analysis of policies set forth by the Danish Asiatic Company in its resolutions of June 20, 1783.

Justi, Johann Heinrich Gottlob von. La chimere de l'equilibre du commerce et du navigation. Copenhagen & Leipzig, Veuve de la Rothe, 1763. J152
A defense of the commercial policies of Great Britain.

The justice and necessity of taxing the American colonies, demonstrated. Together with a vindication of the authority of Parliament. London, J. Almon, 1766.   J153

A defense of the Stamp Act, contending that all funds received from such taxation are essential to the military defense of the colonies.

Justificatie van de resolutien ende proceduren by de ... Stadt Groningen. [n.p.] 1662.   J154

The city of Groningen defends its action in preparing resolutions against Johan Schulemborgh who drew up the peace treaty with Portugal in 1662.

Justificatie vanden doorluchtigen Don Antonio Coninck van Portugael ... nopende d'oorloghe die by ghenootdruct is teghens ... Spaignien. Dordrecht, Peeter Verhagen, 1585.   J155

A discussion of Spanish-Portuguese relations, showing the designs by Spain upon the Portuguese islands in the Atlantic which were of importance to the commerce of both the East and West Indies.

Justification du serenissime Don Antonio roi de Portugal ... touchant la guerre qu'il faict à Philippe roi de Castille. Leiden, Christophle Plantin, 1585.   J156

A French edition of the preceding item.

K

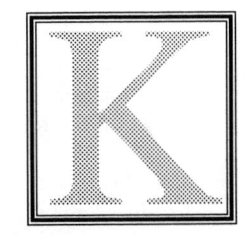

Kaempfer, Engelbert. Amoenitatum exoticarum politico-physico-medicarum. Lemgo, Henric Wilhelm Meyer, 1712. K1
　A survey of Japan, India, and Persia with descriptions of the antiquities, monuments, dress, social customs, animal and vegetable productions, languages, and national characteristics.

Kaempfer, Engelbert. The history of Japan. London, Printed for the publisher, 1727. K2
　The first edition of an extensive collection of observations on the history, culture, natural history, and economy of Japan, based on the author's residence there from 1690 to 1692 as physician to a Dutch embassy.

Kaempfer, Engelbert. Histoire naturelle, civile, et ecclesiastique de l'empire du Japon. The Hague, P. Gosse & J. Neaulme, 1729. K3
　This French translation is based upon the English edition.

Kaempfer, Engelbert. De beschryving van Japan. Amsterdam, J.R. de Jonge, 1733. K4
　The first Dutch edition.

Kaempfer, Engelbert. Geschichte und Beschreibung von Japan. Lemgo, Meyer, 1777-79. K5
　The first German edition, made from the manuscript of the author.

Kaestner, Abraham Gothelf. Weitere ausführung der mathematischen Geographie. Göttingen, Wandenhoef und Ruprecht, 1795. K6
　Gives instructions and equations for measuring the surface of the earth, its diameter and its circumference. Includes six folding plates depicting geometrical figures.

Kalm, Pehr. Enfalliga anmärckningar wid saltkiällor, med wederbörandes tilstädjelse, under oeconomia, professorens ... Abo, Jacob Merckell [1754]. K7
　An academic dissertation surveying the known sources of salt. While emphasis is on Western European suppliers, account is also taken of salt in Egypt, Russia, and North America.

Kalm, Pehr. Histoire naturelle et politique de la Pensylvanie. Paris, Ganeau, 1768. K8
　From the writings of Kalm and Gottlieb Mittelberger the translator has constructed an account of life in Pennsylvania, with considerable emphasis on its natural resources and commerce.

Kalm, Pehr. En resa til Norra America. Stockholm, Lars Salvii, 1753-61. K9
　The first edition of a classic in North American travel literature. Kalm's primary purpose was to discover plants that would be able to thrive in Sweden, but his observations covered a wide range, including comments on the American Indians, the value of colonies, etc.

Kalm, Pehr. Reise nach dem Nordlichen America. Leipzig, Gottfried Kiesewetter, 1754. K10
　A translation by Carl Ernst Klein of the first volume of Kalm's *Travels*. This is the only volume of this translation that was published.

Kalm, Pehr. Travels into North America. Warrington, William Eyres; London, For the editor, 1770-71. K11
　The first English edition, translated and edited by Johann Reinhold Forster. A large map is added, as are a preface and numerous notes by Forster.

Kalm, Pehr. Reis door Noord Amerika. Utrecht, J. van Schoonhoven en G. van den Brink Janz., 1772. K12
　This Dutch edition includes a map and plates not found in the Swedish edition, but it omits Kalm's voyage to England.

Kane, Elisha Kent. Arctic explorations: the second Grinnell expedition in search of Sir John Franklin, 1853, '54, '55. Philadelphia, Childs and Peterson, 1857. K13
　This work is highly regarded for its depiction of arctic life in both text and illustrations.

Karrer, Philipp Jacob. Geographie für Kaufleute, Manufacturisten und Fabrikanten. Leipzig, F. G. Jacobäer, 1799-1800. K14
A description and history of the commerce of Germany, Asia, Africa, and the Levant.

Keate, George. An account of the Pelew Islands, situated in the western part of the Pacific Ocean. London, For G. Nicol, 1788. K15
An account of the products, geography, people, and trade of the islands, based on the journals of Captain Henry Wilson, whose ship was wrecked there in 1783 in a voyage for the East India Company.

Keate, George. An account of the Pelew Islands, situated in the western part of the Pacific Ocean. Philadelphia, Joseph Crukshank, 1789. K16
The first American edition, published without illustrations.

Keate, George. An account of the Pelew Islands, situated in the western part of the Pacific Ocean. Dublin, Luke White, 1793. K17
A reprint of the London 1788 edition, including all of the illustrations, reduced.

Keate, George. An account of the Pelew Islands, situated in the western part of the Pacific Ocean. Boston, Manning & Loring for S. Hall [etc.] 1796. K18
This edition does not include any of the original illustrations, and also omits the Pelew vocabulary.

Keate, George. Relation des îles Pelew, situées dans la partie occidentale de l'Océan Pacifique ... Paris, Le Jay, Maradan, 1788. K19
The first French edition, published the same year as the first English edition. Some translator's notes are added to the text.

Keate, George. Relation des îles Pelew. Paris, Maradan, 1793. K20
A close reprinting of the second French edition of 1792.

Keate, George. Nachrichten von den Pelew-Inseln in der Westgegend des stillen Oceans. Hamburg, Benjamin Gottlob Hoffmann, 1789. K21
The first German edition includes some extensive notes and a preface by the translator, Georg Forster. Includes a map and four illustrations based on the original edition.

Keate, George. Beskrifning om Pelju-Öarne. Norrköping, Jonas Löström; Stockholm, Anders Zetterberg, 1793. K22
An abridged edition, without the plates or map.

Keate, George. Relacion de las islas de Pelew, situadas en la parte occidental del Oceano Pacifico ... traducida al Frances, y de éste al Español con presencia del original Ingles. Madrid, Gomez Fuenenebro, 1805. K23

This first Spanish edition adds a brief preface by the translator.

Keating, William Hypolitus. Narrative of an expedition to the source of St. Peter's River, Lake Winnepeek, Lake of the Woods, &c ... in the year 1823. London, Geo. B. Whittaker, 1825. K24
An excellent source of information on the Dakota and Ojibway peoples of the upper Mississippi Valley by the geologist and historiographer of Stephen Long's second expedition.

Keckermann, Bartholomäus. Systema geographicum duobus libris adornatum & publice olim praelectum ... Adiecta sunt in fine aliquot problemata nautica eiusdem authoris. Hanover, Guilielmi Antonii, 1612. K25
A standard geographical text with a section on navigation.

Keeling, William. Wm. Keelings journall of his 3d voyage to East India as he sent it to the Honble. Compy. Manuscript in English. [n.p.] 20 January 1615 - 9 June 1617. K26
An account of a trading voyage for the English East India Company, descriptive of the commerce of that organization in its second decade.

Keir, Archibald. Thoughts on the affairs of Bengal. London, 1772. K27
A series of proposals for the improvement of government and economy in Bengal, including more Indian participation in the economy, restraint upon English merchants, and an increase in free trade within Bengal.

Keith, George. Geography and navigation compleated: being a new theory and method whereby the true longitude of any place in the world may be found ... London, B. Aylmer, 1709. K28
A theory of determining longitude by fixed stars.

Keith, Sir William. A collection of papers and other tracts, written occasionally on various subjects. London, J. Mechell, 1740. K29
A series of essays displaying concern for English trade in America, Spain, Russia and elsewhere.

Keith, Sir William. The history of the British plantations in America. London, Society for the Encouragement of Learning, 1738. K30
This first and only volume of a projected history of all the British colonies in America deals with Virginia. The author was a former customs official in several colonies and governor of Pennsylvania.

Keller, Heinrich. Erd-Charte nach der Bonneschen Projection, alle für die Erdkunde ergiebigen Entdeckungs-Reisen zu Wasser und zu Lande von der Mitte des 9ten Jahrhunderts bis

jezt darstellend. Weimar, Geographischen Institut, 1814.   K31
A large map depicting routes of famous explorers from the ninth to the nineteenth century.

Kemys, Lawrence. A relation of the second voyage to Guiana. London, T. Dawson, 1596.   K32
The author was an associate of Sir Walter Raleigh's, and headed an expedition to Guiana on Raleigh's behalf in 1596. His description of the country is given chiefly to accounts of rivers, products, and native peoples.

Kennedy, Archibald. Serious considerations on the present state of the affairs of the northern colonies. New York and London, R. Griffiths [1754].   K33
The author advocates policies which would gain the friendship of the Indians as a bulwark of defense against the French.

[Kennett, Basil.] Sermons preached on several occasions to a society of British merchants, in foreign parts. London, S.H. for J. Churchill, 1715.   K34
Most of the sermons pertain to travel abroad and mercantile affairs.

Ker, John. The memoirs ... containing his secret transactions and negotiations in Scotland, England ... and other foreign parts. London, 1726.   K35
Concerns the rise and progress of the Ostend Company, the French in Louisiana, the Newfoundland fishery, and other developments of commercial importance.

Kerguélen-Trémarec, Yves Joseph de. Relation d'un voyage dans la Mer du Nord. Paris, Prault, 1771.   K36
A navigation guide to the waters between Norway and Iceland, with considerable commentary on the peoples, economies, and other aspects of the Atlantic coasts and islands of this area.

Kerguélen-Trémarec, Yves Joseph de. Beschreibung seiner Reise nach der Nordsee. Leipzig, Siegfried Leberecht Crusius, 1772.   K37
This edition adds a translator's introduction, but has only two maps, compared to twelve in the original edition.

Kerguélen-Trémarec, Yves Joseph de. Relation de deux voyages dans les mers Australes & des Indes. Paris, Knapen & Fils, 1782.   K38
An account of Kerguélen's two voyages between 1771 and 1774 in search of a shorter route to China by way of the South Sea.

Keulen, Gerard van. [Coastal navigation charts, black and white photographs of colored manuscript maps in the Collectie Bodel Nijenhuis, Leiden, Universiteitsbibliotheek], tot Amsterdam, bij Gerard van Keulen, aen de Nieuwen Brugh. Leiden, [s.n., 1987?]   K39
These charts were not published in the *Zee atlas* of continents and islands known at that time.

Keye, Otto. Het waere onderscheyt tusschen koude en warme landen ... The Hague, Henricus Hondius [1659].   K40
A comparison of New Netherland and Surinam, both of which were of interest to the Dutch at this time. Surinam is highly favored, in part because the author was a member of a group trying to promote settlement there.

Keye, Otto. Kurtzer Entwurff von Neu-Niederland und Guajana. Leipzig, Ritzschischen Buchladen, 1672.   K41
The first German edition of a Dutch appraisal of New Netherland and Guiana.

Keymor, John. Observation made upon the Dutch fishing, about the year 1601. London, From the original manuscript for Sir Edward Ford, 1664.   K42
An interesting analysis of the way in which the entire Dutch economy was based on its prosperous fishing trade, presenting statistics giving the size and growth of the Dutch fishing fleet, and recommending that their example be copied by the English.

Keyserlicher Majestat Eroberung des Königreychs Thunisi, wie die vergangener tag von Rom, Neaples, und Venedig, gen Augsburg gelangt hat, und von Genua den XII. Augusti hieher geschriben ist. Nuremberg, 1535.   K43
A newsletter based on a series of three letters reporting the victory of Charles V over Haradin at Tunis in the summer of 1535.

Kindersley, Mrs. Letters from the island of Teneriffe, Brazil, the Cape of Good Hope, and the East Indies. London, For J. Nourse, 1777.   K44
This collection of letters ranges widely over social, religious, educational, economic and other matters in the author's comments on the places she visited.

King, Charles, editor. The British merchant; or, Commerce preserv'd. London, John Darby, 1721.   K45
Material relative to restrictiveness toward French commerce. See also entry under *The British merchant*.

[King, Daniel.] The Spaniards cruelty and treachery to the English in the time of peace and war ... London, J.M. for Lodowick Lloyd, 1656.   K46
A strong statement of England's rights to free trade in the West Indies, which, if it cannot be obtained by treaty with Spain, should be taken by war.

King, Richard. Narrative of a journey to the shores of the Arctic Ocean, in 1833, 1834 and 1835. London, R. Bentley, 1836.   K47
Account of an expedition through Canada to the Arctic.

[Kippis, Andrew.] Considerations on the provisional treaty with America. London, For T. Cadell, 1783. K48
   A summary and rebuttal of negative English public reaction to the treaty of 1783, citing the many commercial advantages which may arise from it.

Kippis, Andrew. The life of Captain James Cook. Dublin, For H. Chamberlaine [etc.] 1788. K49
   This biography is essentially an account of Cook's three voyages, with commentary on other voyages to the same regions.

Kippis, Andrew. Leben des Capitain James Cook, von Andreas Kippis. Hamburg, Benjamin Gottlob Hoffmann, 1789. K50
   The first German edition, based on the English edition of the previous year.

Kippis, Andrew. Historia de la vida y viages de Capitan Jaime Cook. Madrid, Imprenta Real, 1795. K51
   The first Spanish edition, translated by Cesareo de Nava Palacio.

Kircher, Athanasius. Tooneel van China ... Amsterdam, J. Jansonius, 1688. K52
   A description of various aspects of Chinese life, with accounts of early travels to China.

Kircher, Athanasius. La Chine ... illustrée de plusieurs monuments, tant sacrés que profanes ... Amsterdam, Jean Jansson à Waesberge, 1670. K53
   The first French edition.

Kirchhof, N. A. J. (Nikolaus Anton Johann). Auszug aus Cook und King's Reise in den Jahren 1776 bis 80 ... Berlin, und Stettin, Friedrich Nikolai, 1794. K54
   An abridged account of Cook's third voyage, with a section on latitude, longitude, and compass variations of landings and sightings.

Kirwitzer, Václav Pantaleon. Histoire de ce qui s'est passé au royaume de la Chine en l'année 1624. Paris, Sebastien Cramoisy, 1629. K55
   After commenting on the events in China in 1624, this writer describes the general progress of Christianity and reviews activities in various residences and missions there.

Klage der West-Indischen Compagnie wider die Ost-Indische. [n.p.] 1664. K56
   A pamphlet attributing the decline of the Dutch West India Company to the stronger position of the East India Company in the Dutch government.

Klare besgryving van Cabo de Bona Esperanca. Amsterdam, Jodocus Hondius, 1652. K57
   A rare pamphlet promoting Dutch colonial enterprise in South Africa, with descriptions of the soil, products, peoples and climate, minerals, vegetables, and animals of the Cape of Good Hope. A very detailed chart of the region is included.

Klare besgryving van't eyland Sanct Helena. Amsterdam, Jodocus Hondius, 1652. K58
   An important pamphlet in the history of Dutch colonial enterprise in South Africa, bound with the previous item.

Klenk, Koenraad van. Historisch verhael, of beschryving van de voyagie ... van Moscovien ... Amsterdam, Jan Claesz ten Hoorn, 1677. K59
   An account of a commercial embassy to Russia by the director of a Dutch trading company seeking to trade in Russia and Persia.

Knox, John. An historical journal of the campaigns in North-America, for the years 1757, 1758, 1759, and 1760: containing the most remarkable occurrences of that period, particularly the two sieges of Quebec ... London, For the Author, 1769. K60

[Knox, John.] A new collection of voyages, discoveries and travels: containing whatever is worthy of notice, in Europe, Asia, Africa and America. London, For J. Knox, 1767. K61
   A seven-volume collection of voyages and travels, containing accounts of the explorations of many Europeans in all parts of the world.

Knox, John. Observations on the northern fisheries. London, For J. Walter [etc.] 1786. K62
   Contends that the only way England can be sure of a supply of competent seamen is through a subsidized fishing industry.

Knox, Robert. An historical relation of the island of Ceylon, in the East-Indies. London, Richard Chiswell, 1681. K63
   The first English book devoted to Ceylon, based upon a twenty-year captivity there by an East India Company captain. It includes an account of French, Portuguese, and Dutch commercial activity there.

Knox, Robert. Ceylanische Reise-Beschreibung, oder, historische Erzehlung von der in Ost-Indien gelegenen Insel Ceylon ... jetzo in Hoch-Teutsche ... übersetzt ... Leipzig, Johann Friedrich Gleditch, 1689. K64
   The first German edition, and the first translation of this narrative from the English.

Knox, Robert. 't Eyland Ceylon in sijn binnenste; of 't koningrijck Candy, geopent, en nauwkeuriger dan oyt te vooren ontdeckt ... Utrecht, Wilhelm Broedelet, 1692. K65
   The first Dutch edition, translated from the English edition of 1681, with illustrations and maps from that edition also.

[Knox, Thomas.] Some thoughts humbly offer'd towards an union between Great Britain and Ireland. London, John Morphew, 1708.   K66
The argument for union is based primarily on the economic advantages of policies that would eliminate Ireland as a competitor and make her a partner instead.

[Knox, William.] The controversy between Great Britain and her colonies reviewed. London, J. Almon, 1769.   K67
A defense of British taxation of the American colonies in which the author examines the reasoning of colonial spokesmen and the constitutional relationship between mother country and colonies.

[Knox, William.] The interest of the merchants and manufacturers of Great Britain, in the present contest with the colonies, stated and considered. London, T. Cadell, 1774.   K68
While conceding the legal equality of the residents of Britain and the American colonials, the author points out the need to differentiate between their economic enterprises as a protection to the British merchant.

[Knox, William.] A letter to a member of Parliament, wherein the power of the British legislature, and the case of the colonists, are briefly and impartially considered. London, W. Flexney, 1765.   K69
A defense of Pariamentary supremacy with respect to legislating taxes in the American colonies.

[Knox, William.] The present state of the nation: particularly with respect to its trade, finances, &c.&c. London, J. Almon, 1768.   K70
A review of Britain's commercial situation noting the expansion of the empire and also the loss of trade to other countries during recent years.

Kolb, Gregor. Compendium totius orbis; partim geographicum, partim genealogicum, partim historicum ... Rottweil, Joannis Georgii Kennerknecht [1726].   K71
A general world geography with a small section given to the non-European areas.

Kolb, Peter. Caput Bonae Spei hodiernum. Nuremberg, Peter Conrad Monath, 1719.   K72
The first edition of a standard work on the Cape of Good Hope, containing information on the history, habits, and customs of the Hottentots and on their commercial and other relations with the Europeans.

Kolb, Peter. Naaukeurige ... beschryving van de Kaap de Goede Hoop. Amsterdam, Balthazar Lakeman, 1727.   K73
The first Dutch edition.

Kolb, Peter. The present state of the Cape of Good Hope. London, For W. Innys, 1731.   K74
The first English edition, somewhat abridged and rearranged, with prefatory sections added by the translator to each of the two volumes.

Kolb, Peter. Description du Cap de Bonne-Esperance. Amsterdam, Jean Catuffe, 1741.   K75
The first French edition with an extensive preface by the translator, giving important information on Kolb, his stay at the Cape, and his literary effort.

Kolb, Peter. Beschreibung des Vorgebürges der Guten Hoffnung, und derer darauf wohnenden Hottentotten. Frankfurt & Leipzig, Peter Conrad Monath, 1745.   K76
This second German edition is actually a translation of a French edition of Amsterdam, 1741, and is not based on the original German edition of 1719.

Korb, Johann Georg. Diarium itineris in Moscoviam. Vienna, Leopoldi Voight [1700].   K77
The report of an embassy sent to the czar of Russia by Emperor Leopold. It includes acounts of Russian court life, geography, popular customs, and religion.

Kort berättelse om Wåst Indien eller America, som elliest kallas Nya werlden. [Wisingsborg, J. Kankel] 1675.   K78
A description of travels to South America, translated by Ambrosius Nidelberg.

Een kort beskriffning uppa trenne reesor och peregrinationer ... Wisingsborg, J. Kankel, 1674.   K79
A collection of voyages in Swedish, containing eight accounts of navigations to China, Japan, Africa, Tartary, and the West Indies.

Een kort beskriffning uppå trenne resor och peregrinationer, sampt konungarijket Japan ... Wisingsborg, Johann Kankel, 1667.   K80
A four-part collection of eastern travels including one by Nils Matson, two by Olof Eriksson Willman, and one anonymous account of travels from Siberia into China.

En kort efterretning om handels-expeditionen til Ostindien med Skibet Dronning Juliane Maria; tilligemend den dertil udgivne subscriptionsplan. Copenhagen, L.N. Svares efterleverske, 1786.   K81
Subscription terms and subscribers to an independent Danish voyage to India are given in this pamphlet, reflecting a lawsuit brought against the promoters of the voyage, Coninck & Reyersen.

Kort en bondigh verhael van't geene in den oorlogh. Amsterdam, Marcus Willemsz. Doornick, 1667.   K82
A major source of information on the causes and operations of the Second Anglo-Dutch War, from the Dutch point of view.

Kort en nauwkeurig verhaal van de reize, door drie schepen in't jaar 1721, gedaan, op ... de West-Indische Compagnie in Holland, om eenige tot nog toe onbekende landen, omtrent de Zuid-Zee gelegen, op te zoeken. Amsterdam, Johannes van Septeren, 1727. K83
The earliest published account of the Pacific Ocean explorations of Jacob Roggeveen, undertaken for the Dutch West India Company.

Kort ende waerachtigh vertoogh ... over ende weder tusschen de respective provincien gepasseert en voorgevallen is ... [n.p.] 1672. K84
Remarks concerning Dutch commerce and the distribution of profits of the East and West India Companies.

Kort verhael gelijck hare Koninckl. Majesteyt tot Denemarken ... Amsterdam, Jan van Hilten [1640?]. K85
Concerns the strained relations between Denmark and the Netherlands over the saltpeter trade, fishing in northern waters, and seizure of Danish ships by the Dutch.

Kort verhael van de gheleghentheyd des Koninghs van Spaignien. The Hague, Aert Meuris, 1628. K86
A survey of the Spanish empire and the ability of Spain to maintain it.

Kort-bondig verhaal van den op en ondergang, van d'heer Constantyn Faulkon ... voornaam gunsteling des konings van Siam. Amsterdam, G. Borstius, 1690. K87
An official of the Dutch East India Company here rejoices over the failure of the Constantine Faulkon to secure for the French a trading base in Siam.

Kortbondige beschryvinge van de colonie de Berbice. Amsterdam, S.J. Baalde, 1763. K88
A short history of the colony of Berbice with a list of its major products. A map identifies the plantations and names the owners.

Korte aenmercking en aenwijsinge op den brief van den Koningh van Groot Britannien, geschreven ... van den 4/14 October 1666. The Hague, Erfgenamen van wijlen H.J. van Wouw, 1666. K89
Refutations of arguments advanced by the English to the effect that their hostilities with the Dutch were due to Dutch aggression against English trade.

Korte deductie van wegen dy vrye Hanse stadt Munster waer uyt te sien is d'ongefondeertheyt vande tewenwoordige belegeringh. The Hague, Johan Veely, 1657. K90
A series of letters indicative of the close commercial relations between Munster, Hamburg, Lübeck, and Bremen.

Kortholt, Matthias Nicolaus. Ad audiendam orationem publicam, de Confutio antiquo Sinensium pilosopho ... Giessen, Viduae B. Ioh. Reinh. Vulpii [1712]. K91
A brief dissertation citing writings on Confucius and his philosophy.

Koster, Henry. Travels in Brazil. London, Longman, Hurst, Rees, Orme, and Brown, 1817. K92
Koster went to Brazil in 1809, traveling mainly in Pernambuco. He rented land and purchased slaves for his sugarcane plantation. He has a full chapter describing Brazilian slavery.

Kotzebue, Otto von. Entdeckungs-Reise in de Sud-See und nach der Berings-Strasse. Weimar, Gebrudern Hoffmann, 1821. K93
A description of life in various Pacific islands, from a circumnavigation of 1815-18.

Kotzebue, Otto von. Ontdekkingsreis in de Zuid-Zee en naar de Berings-Straat, in de jaren 1815, 1816, 1817, en 1818. Amsterdam, Johannes van der Hey, 1822. K94
This edition includes some notes by the translator who worked from the German edition, and a map of the arctic regions not in the Weimar edition of 1821.

Kotzebue, Otto von. A new voyage round the world, in the year 1823, 24, 25, and 26. London, Henry Colburn and Richard Bentley, 1830. K95
Account of the circumnavigation of 1823-6 by the Russians under the author's leadership. Kotzebue provides excellent commentary on several places visited, notably in the South Pacific islands, in Kamchatka, Sitka, and the Ross Colony in California.

Kotzebue, Otto von. Nieuwe ontdekkingreize rondom de wereld, in de jaren 1823, 24, 25, en 26 ondernomen ... Haarlem, De Wed. A. Loosjen, Pz., 1830. K96
This Dutch edition is similar to the English in text, maps and illustrations.

Kotzebue, Otto von. Resa omkring jorden åren 1823, 24, 25, och 26. Stockholm, Johan Hörberg, 1830. K97
The first Swedish edition, translated by Adolf Westin.

Kraak, Ivar. Correspondance historique et critique entre deux Suedois, au sujet de la bataille de Pultava ... & le commerce de la Compagnie orientale hollandoise. Lund, Charles Gustave Berling, 1775. K98
This correspondence includes descriptions of Pacific islands, Asia, and South Africa, and of the operations of the Dutch East India Company.

Kragh, Otthe. Propositie by Hare Excellentien de Heeren Otthe Kragh, ende Gotsche Buchwalt ... [n.p.] 1660. K99

The Danish ambassadors praise the Netherlands for help given in the war with Sweden, and propose an alliance between the two countries for the future.

Kramer, Johann Matthias. Neueste und richtigste Nachricht von der Landschaft Georgia in dem Engelländischen Amerika. Göttingen, Johann Peter Schmid, 1746. K100

This German translation appears to be based on Oglethorpe's *A new and accurate account of the provinces of South Carolina and Georgia*, although it is sometimes attributed to a similar tract by Benjamin Martyn.

Krasheninnikov, Stepan Petrovich. Opisanie zemli Kamchatki. St. Petersburg, Akademii Nauk, 1755. K101

The first edition of a detailed description of Kamchatka, written by a member of a scientific expedition. The concluding chapters deal with commerce, including notice of the Russian fur trade in the Aleutian Islands.

Krasheninnikov, Stepan Petrovich. The history of Kamtschatka and the Kurilski Islands. Glocester, R. Raikes for T. Jefferys, 1764. K102

The first English edition.

Krasheninnikov, Stepan Petrovich. Histoire de Kamtschatka, des isles Kurilski, et des contrées voisines ... Lyons, Benoit Duplain, 1767. K103

This translation is from the English edition of 1764, and is much abridged, compared to the French editon of 1770 which is translated from the Russian.

Krasheninnikov, Stepan Petrovich. Histoire et description du Kamtchatka ... Amsterdam, Marc Michel Rey, 1770. K104

The second French edition of the unabridged text. The map of Kamchatka is by Chappe d'Auteroche.

[Krasheninnikov, Stepan Petrovich.] Aardrykskundige en natuurlyke beschryving van Kamtschatka, en de Kurilsche Eilanden. Haerlem, Joh. Enschede, 1770. K105

The first Dutch edition. Another issue was published at Amsterdam in 1770 also.

Krebs, Johann Friedrich. Dissertatione geographica aestumatas dierum inaequalitates, superiorum benevolo indulto placido eruditorum examini submittit ... Conrado Hackero, Monachomontano, respondente ... Jena, Literis Krebsianis, 1672. K106

An academic dissertation, presumably from the University of Jena on the variation of the length of the day from pole to equator and its effect on plants, animals, climate and geology.

Der Krieg zwischenn dem groszmechtigen Propheten Sophi, Türcken, und dem Soldan, alla die Ding die do geschehen seind in Auffgäng der Sonnen ... im Jahr MCCCC und XVII. [Nuremberg, F. Peypus, 1517.] K107

A newsletter reporting conquests in Syria and Egypt by Selim I, sultan of Turkey.

Kristnisaga. Christendoms saga. Skalholt, H. Kruse, 1688. K108

A history of the Icelandic church, with emphasis on missionary activity, probably written in the thirteenth century from oral sources. In chapter eleven there is mention of Leif Ericson's discovery of Vinland.

Kruse, Jürgen Elert. Allgemeiner und besonders hamburgischer Contorist ... Berlin & Hamburg, Christian Moritz Vogel, 1762-1765. K109

A commercial handbook noting units of weight, measurement and coinage used in various places, and a table of exchange rates containing some six thousand entries.

Kruzenshtern, Ivan Fedorovich. Beyträge zur Hydrographie der grössern Ozeane als Erläuterungen zu einer Charte des ganzen Erdkreises nach Mercator's Projection. Leipzig, Paul Gotthelf Kummer, 1819. K110

The map described here was not included in the volume, but is to be found in Kruzenshtern's *Reise um die Welt*, St. Petersburg, 1810-12.

Kruzenshtern, Ivan Fedorovich. Reize om de wereld, gedaan in de jaren 1803, 1804, 1805 en 1806, op bevel van Alexander den Eersten, Keizer van Rusland ... Haarlem, A. Loosjes, 1811. K111

This Dutch edition includes a folding map of Japan and the adjacent ocean, a folding plate and a journal of the *Nadesha* and *Neva* in tabular form.

Kruzenshtern, Ivan Fedorovich. Resa omkring jorden, förrättad åren 1803, 1804, 1805, och 1806 på Hans Maj:ts keisarens af Ryssland befallning ... Örebro, Nils Magnus Lindh; Jönköping, Joh. Pehr Lundstrom, 1811-12. K112

This Swedish edition is abridged and is without maps, illustrations or tables.

Kruzenshtern, Ivan Fedorovich. Voyage round the world in the years 1803, 1804, 1805, & 1806. London, C. Roworth and T. Davison for John Murray, 1813. K113

The official report on the 1803-6 Russian circumnavigation, in its first English edition.

Kruzenshtern, Ivan Fedorovich. Viaggio intorno al mondo, fatto negli anni 1803-4-5 e 1806 d'ordine di sua maesta' imperiale Alessandro Primo ... tradotto dal tedesco dal Sig. Angiolini ... Milan, Giambattista Sonzogno, 1818. K114

The first Italian edition, translated from the German.

Kryger, Johan Fredrik. Åminnelse-tal, öfver ... Magnus Lagerström. Stockholm, Lars Salvius, 1760.   K115

   A speech given in memory of Magnus Lagerström, director of the Swedish East India Company, containing information on the history of the company and its trade.

Kryger, Johan Fredrik. Åminnelse-tal öfver framledne Kongl. Maj:ts troman, directeur vid Ost-Indiska Compagniet ... Claes Grill. Stockholm, Lars Salvius, 1768.   K116

   An essay in praise of a director of the Swedish East India Company.

Kuricke, Reinhold. Jus maritimum Hanseaticum. Hamburg, Z. Hertel, 1667.   K117

   Latin and German text of Hanseatic sea laws, and comparison with earlier Mediterranean and Baltic sea laws.

Kurze geographisch-historische Erläuterungen des Handels und der jezigen Lage der Oesterreichischen und denen Vereinigten Niederlanden wegen Eröfnung der Schelde nebst den hieher gehörigen drey Artikeln des münsterischen Friedens 1648 und einer Special-Karte von Zeeland und der Schelde. Hamburg, 1785.   K118

   A discussion of the geography of the Scheldt River, its economic significance, and the history of the closing of that river to oceanic commerce.

Kurze Geschichte des neuen Reichs der Britten am Ganges seit dem J. 1756: aus dem Englischen. Göttingen, Vandenhoek, 1780.   K119

   A translation of an anonymous work published at Cambridge, England calling attention to the damage which the East India Company had done in India and predicting divine retribution if India is not released from the company's control.

L

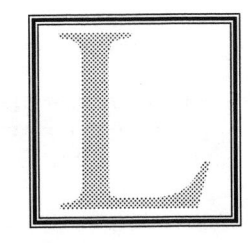

Labarbinais, Le Gentil. Nouveau voyage au tour du monde. Amsterdam, Pierre Mortier, 1728.   L1

A recounting of travels to South America, China, South Asia, and the East Indies, with numerous accounts of the products, merchants, and commerce of port cities visited by the author.

La Barre, Antoine Joseph Le Febure de. Description de la France equinoctiale, cydevant appellee Guyanne. Paris, I. Ribov, 1666.   L2

A guide for those who would establish colonies on the north coast of South America, listing products, describing the inhabitants, and noting the difficulties to be encountered. The author went there in 1664.

Labarthe, Pierre. Voyage a la côte de Guinée. Paris, Debray [etc.] 1803.   L3

Labarthe describes the commerce of the region as well as the Danish colony, Christianbourg. The book was published in German in the same year. Includes a hand colored map of the coast.

Labat, Jean Baptiste. Nouveau voyage aux isles de l'Amerique. Paris, Pierre-François Giffart, 1722.   L4

A description of the Lesser Antilles with particular emphasis on the natural history and commercial products of the islands. The author resided there from 1694 to 1705.

Labat, Jean Baptiste. Nieuwe reizen naar de Franse eilanden van America ... Amsterdam, Balthasar Lakeman, 1725.   L5

The first Dutch edition.

Labat, Jean Baptiste. Nouveau voyage aux isles de l'Amerique. Paris, Guillaume Cavelier, 1742.   L6

This edition is extensively augmented, both in text and illustrations, over that of 1722.

Labat, Jean Baptiste. Nouvelle relation de l'Afrique occidentale. Paris, Theodore Le Gras, 1728.   L7

A description of West Africa between Cape Blanc and the Sierra Leone River, with comments on the activities of the various European trading companies there.

Labat, Jean Baptiste. Voyage de chevalier Des Marchais en Guinée, isles voisines, et à Cayenne. Paris, Chez P. Prault, 1730.   L8

An account of travels to Guiana and the neighboring islands in 1725-27, describing the commerce and other aspects of life in that region.

Labbé, Marin, bishop of Tilopolis. Lettre ... au Pape, sur le certificat de l'Empereur de la Chine, et sur la necessité de condanner sans delai toutes les superstitions chinoises. Antwerp, Heritiers de Jean Keerberg, 1702.   L9

An anti-Jesuit commentary on the November 30, 1700 letter of Emperor K'ang Hsi which affirmed that the veneration of Confucius and of the dead were customs of no religious significance.

Labbé, Marin, bishop of Tilopolis. Lettre ... au Pape, sur le certificat de l'Empereur de la Chine et sur la necessité de condanner sans delai toutes les superstitions chinoises. Antwerp, Heritiers de Jean Keerberg, 1702.   L10

This edition contains a four-page "avertissement" by the publisher.

Labillardière, Jacques Julien Houten de. Relation du voyage a la recherche de La Pérouse. Paris, H.J. Jansen, 1799.   L11

A naturalist's account, accompanied by an atlas, of the expedition sent to the South Pacific to try to discover the fate of La Pérouse's expedition.

La Caille, Nicolas Louis de. Journal historique du voyage fait au Cap de Bonne-Esperance. Paris, Guillyn, 1763.   L12

Voyage to the Cape of Good Hope via Brazil, with observations on the commerce of places visited.

La Clède, Nicolas de. Histoire generale de Portugal. Paris, Rollin, 1735.   L13

Nearly half of this two volume work is given to tracing the rise and fall of the Portuguese empire in the East and in Africa. Much less attention is given to Brazil.

[Lacombe de Prézel, Honoré.] Dictionnaire du citoyen, ou Abrégé historique, théorique et pratique du commerce. Paris, Grangé [etc.] 1761. L14

A commercial handbook, describing briefly products, places of importance, and commercial terms.

[Lacombe de Prézel, Honoré.] Dictionnaire du citoyen, ou Abregé historique, theorique et pratique du commerce. Amsterdam, Aux depens de Compagnie, 1762. L15

A reprint of the 1761 Paris edition.

Lacombe de Prézel, Honoré. Dizionario del cittadino osia ristretto istorico, teorico e pratico del commerzio. Naples, Benedetto Gessari, 1765. L16

A translation by Francesco Alberti of an elementary French commercial dictionary dealing with products, business terms, and other commercial matters.

[Lacombe de Prézel, Honoré.] Les progrès du commerce. Amsterdam [etc.] A.-M. Lottin, 1760. L17

A history of commerce from earliest times, followed by commentary on contemporary trade.

Lacombe Frères & Compagnie. A collection of twenty-eight letters written by correspondents in Santo Domingo regarding the commerce of that island. The letters are dated at Port au Prince, from 30 September 1784 to 13 February 1791. L18

La Condamine, Charles-Marie de. Relation abrégée d'un voyage fait dans l'interieur de l'Amérique méridionale. Paris, La Veuve Pissot, 1745. L19

Account of a scientific expedition containing information on the commerce and absence of it in parts of South America.

La Condamine, Charles-Marie de. Relation abrégée d'un voyage fait dans l'interieur de l'Amerique méridionale ... Nouvelle édition augmentée ... Maestricht, Jean-Edme Dufour & Philippe Roux, 1778. L20

This edition includes the account of the riot against the expedition on August 29, 1739 and Jean Godin's letter to La Condamine of July 28, 1773 recounting the remarkable voyage of Madame Godin down the Amazon River.

La Condamine, Charles-Marie de. Extracto del diario de observaciones hechas en el viage de la provincia de Quito al Para, por el Rio de las Amazonas; y del Parà a Cayana, Surinam y Amsterdam ... Amsterdam, Joan Catuffe, 1745. L21

This translation was made by La Condamine from the French edition of the same year.

La Condamine, Charles-Marie de. Bekort verhaal van een reyze gedaan in 't binnelands gedeelte van Zuyd America. Amsterdam, Dirk Sligtenhorst, 1746. L22

The first Dutch edition.

La Condamine, Charles-Marie de. Mesure des trois premiers degrés du méridien dans l'hemisphere austral, tirée des observations de M.^{rs} de l'Académie Royale des Sciences, envoyés par le Roi sous l'équateur. Paris, Imprimerie Royale, 1751. L23

The official publication of the method used to measure the length of arc of a degree of longitude at the equator to determine the shape of the earth.

[Lacoste, Jean.] Lettre de m. D*** à D*** au sujet de La noblesse commerçante. Paris, 1756. L24

Discusses the means to improve French commerce, particularly with America.

Lacoste, Jean. Mémoire pour le citoyen Lacoste ex-Ministre de la Marine. [Paris, J. Girould, 1793.] L25

The author gives his self-defense for actions in the Windward Islands during colonial troubles.

Lacretelle, Pierre-Louis de. Mémoire a consulter, et consultation pour les négocians faisant commerce des marchandises des Indes; contre la nouvelle Compagnie des Indes. [Paris, Couturier] 1786. L26

An argument against the recently chartered Compagnie Nouvelle des Indes as the holder of a monopoly on French trade east of the Cape of Good Hope, including related documents.

La Croix, A. Phérotée de. Algemeene weereldbeschryving ... In de Hoogduitsche tael overgebracht, met veel' aenmerkingen en verbeteringen, door ... Hieronymus Dicelius. Amsterdam, François Halma, 1705. L27

A compendium of historical and geographical knowledge, with maps from Nicolas Sanson.

La Croix, A. Phérotée de. Relation universelle de l'Afrique, ancienne et moderne. Lyons, Thomas Amaulry, 1688. L28

The text, maps, and illustrations owe much to Dapper's description of Africa.

La Croze, Maturin Veyssière. Histoire du Christianisme des Indes. The Hague, Vaillant & N. Prevost, 1724. L29

This history is particularly concerned with Eastern Christians and their conflict with the Roman Rite through the establishment of Portuguese missions in India.

La Croze, Maturin Veyssière. Abbildung des indianischen Christen-Staats. Halle, Johann Adam Spörl, 1727.   L30
The German translator, Georg Christian Bohnstedt, adds an extensive preface and some notes to the text.

La Croze, Maturin Veyssière. Abbildung des indianischen Christen-Staats ... Leipzig, Samuel Benjamin Walther, 1739.   L31
Similar to the preceding work, but with a map added.

Laet, Joannes de. Niewe Wereldt, ofte beschrijvinghe van West-Indien. Leiden, Isaack Elzevier, 1625.   L32
A detailed description of the Americas, compiled from a variety of sources and including numerous maps.

Laet, Joannes de. Novus Orbis, seu descriptionis Indiae occidentalis Libri XVIII. Leiden, Isaack Elzevier, 1633.   L33
The first Latin edition.

Laet, Joannes de. l'Histoire du Nouveau Monde ou description des Indes Occidentales. Leiden, Bonaventure & Abraham Elsevier, 1640.   L34
The first French edition, with additional material not included in the Dutch edition.

Laet, Joannes de. Histoire ofte jaerlijck verhael van de ... West-Indische Compagnie ... Leiden, Bonaventuer and Abraham Elsevier, 1644.   L35
A yearly account of the activities of the Dutch West India Company from 1623 to 1636, the years of its greatest strength in the West Indies.

Laet, Joannes de. Notae ad dissertationem Hugonis Grotii de origine gentium Americanarum. Amsterdam, Ludovicum Elzevirium, 1643.   L36
A statement on the origins of the American Indian inspired by Hugo Grotius' publication the previous year of his theories on that subject.

La Fillière, Alain Nogeret de. Journal de ma campagne sur la fregatte du Roy la Dianne, commandée par monsieur Duvigneau, capitaine de vaisseau, pour Quebec en 1750. Manuscript. Louisbourg, 1750.   L37
The background of this voyage is the treaty signed by France and Great Britain in 1748, the Treaty of Aix-la-Chapelle. The *Diane's* mission was to reinforce French garrisons. Included in the manuscript are calculations of longitude, estimates of latitude, descriptions of harbors and islands en route.

Lafitau, Joseph-François. De zeden der wilden van Amerika. The Hague, G. Vander Poel, 1731.   L38
The first Dutch edition of a work descriptive of the Indians of America, their customs, religion, etc.

Lafitau, Joseph-François. Histoire des decouvertes et conquestes des portugais dans le nouveau monde. Paris, Saugrain pere and Jean-Baptiste Coignard fils, 1733.   L39
A history of Portuguese discoveries from 1412 to 1581.

Lafitau, Joseph-François. Mémoire presenté a son Altesse royale Monseigneur le Duc d'Orleans ... concernant la précieuse plante du gin seng de Tartarie, découverte en Canada. Paris, Joseph Mongé, 1718.   L40
The author claims to have discovered in Canada ginseng of a quality equal to that found in China. The plant was highly valued for medicinal properties.

Lafitau, Joseph-François. Moeurs des sauvages ameriquains, compare'es aux moeurs des premiers temps. Paris, Saugrain l'aîné & Charles Estienne Hochereau, 1724.   L41
The American Indians are compared to peoples of antiquity in an attempt to prove that the Indians had Tartar origins.

La Flotte, de, M. Essais historique sur l'Inde, précédés d'un journal de voyages et d'une description géographique de la côte de Coromandel. Paris, Herissant le fils, 1769.   L42
An account of a voyage to India, with brief histories of the establishments of the Portuguese, French, Danes, and English on the Coromandel coast.

Lagerström, Magnus. Undersöking om den Ostindiske handelens. Stockholm, Schneider, 1738.   L43
A historical survey of the East Indian trade with an account of current commerce there, written by a director of the Swedish East India Company.

Lagrange and Boice (Firm). [Account book of Lagrange and Boice, wine merchants.] Manuscript in English. New Brunswick; New York, 1772-1783.   L44
This account book records the types of transactions which were a part of the wine trade in colonial America including commodities incidental to that trade such as lumber for casks, beeswax, etc.

Lahontan, Louis Armand de Lom d'Arce, baron de. Nouveaux voyages ... dans l'Amerique Septentrionale. The Hague, Fréres l'Honoré, 1703.   L45
Lahontan was employed in various military positions in New France, serving in the Great Lakes area with Duluth and Tonti. His description of the "Long River" has discredited his book, despite much valuable information in it.

Lahontan, Louis Armand de Lom d'Arce, baron de. New voyages to North America. London, For H. Bonwicke [etc.] 1703.   L46

The first English edition, with maps and plates re-engraved, and including a series of letters written by Lahontan after his return from America.

Lalemant, Jérôme. Relation de ce qui s'est passé de plus remarquable és missions des peres de la Compagnie de Jesus, en la Nouvelle France, es annees 1645 & 1646. Paris, Sebastien Cramoisy, 1647. L47

Lalemant was Superior General of the Canadian mission, and the first part of this report covers Quebec in general. The second part contains Father Paul Ragueneau's account of the Huron mission. This is the first issue.

Lalemant, Jérôme. Relation de ce qui s'est passé de plus remarquable és missions des peres de la Compagnie de Jesus, en la Nouvelle France, es annees 1645 & 1646. Paris, Sebastien Cramoisy, 1647. L48

The second issue, with the reading "Tapoué Nama Nitirinisin" on line 10, p. 176 of Part I.

Lalemant, Jérôme. Relation de ce qui s'est passé de plus remarquable és missions des peres de la Compagnie de Jesus, en la Nouvelle France, es anees 1645 & 1646. Paris, Sebastien Cramoisy, 1647. L49

An issue composed of parts of the two preceding items.

Lalemant, Jérôme. Relation de ce qui s'est passé de plus remarquable és missions des peres de la Compagnie de Jesus, en la Nouvelle France, sur le grand fleuve de S. Laurens en l'annee 1647. Paris, Sebastien Cramoisy et Gabriel Cramoisy, 1648. L50

Reports the establishment of a mission among the Abenakis, missionary work among other Canadian Indians, settlement of the Isle de Miskou, and the hostility of the Iroquois who put to death Father Isaac Jogues.

Lalemant, Jérôme. Relation de ce qui s'est passé de plus remarquable és missions des peres de la Compagnie de Jesus, en la Nouvelle France, sur le grand fleuve de S. Laurens en l'annee 1647. Paris, Sebastien Cramoisy et Gabriel Cramoisy, 1648. L51

A variant issue of the previous item.

Lalemant, Jérôme. Relation de ce qui s'est passé de plus remarquable és missions des peres de la Compagnie de Jesus, en la Nouvelle France, es annees 1647 & 1648. Paris, Sebastien Cramoisy et Gabriel Cramoisy, 1649. L52

Includes a general report on the Canadian missions by Lalemant and one on the Huron mission by Paul Ragueneau. The latter contains geographical details of the Great Lakes region.

Lalemant, Jérôme. Lettres envoiées de la Nouvelle France au R.P. Jacques Renault provincial de la Compagnie de Jesus en la province de la France. Paris, Sebastien Cramoisy, 1660. L53

This volume contains three letters, all from Quebec, dealing with the arrival of a bishop, the mission to the Hurons and Algonquins, and the mission to Acadia.

Lalemant, Jérôme. Relation de ce qui s'est passé de plus remarquable aux missions des peres de la Compagnie de Jesus, en la Nouvelle France, és années mil six cent cinquante neuf & mil six cent soixante. Paris, Sebastien Cramoisy, 1661. L54

Includes discussion of the customs and political organization of the Iroquois, Algonquin, and Huron nations as well as consideration of a northwest passage and the Hudson Bay region.

Lalemant, Jérôme. Relation de ce qui s'est passé de plus remarquable aux missions des peres de la Compagnie de Jesus, en la Nouvelle France, és années mil six cent cinquante neuf & mil six cent soixante. Paris, Sebastien Cramoisy, 1661. L55

Identical to the above item, but with manuscript notations in the margin to the text describing the Hudson Bay area.

Lalemant, Jérôme. Relation de ce qui s'est passé de plus remarquable aux missions des peres de la Compagnie de Jesus, en la Nouvelle France, és années 1661 & 1662. Paris, Sebastien Cramoisy et Sebast. Mabre-Cramoisy, 1663. L56

Contains Iroquois accounts of the natural history of southern North America, reports of Father Pierre Balloquet's winter among the Montagnais and the Algonquins, Father Simon Le Moine's journey to Onondaga, and Father André Richard's account of the Micmac war at Gaspé.

Lalemant, Jérôme. Relation de ce qui s'est passé de plus remarquables aux missions des peres de la Compagnie de Jesus en la Nouvelle France, es années 1662 & 1663. Paris, Sebastien Cramoisy, et Sebast. Mabre-Cramoisy, 1664. L57

Three major subjects dealt with in this relation include reverses suffered by the Iroquois at the hands of the Algonquins, the earthquake of 1663, and the death of Father René Ménard.

Lalemant, Jérôme. Relation de ce qui s'est passé de plus remarquables aux missions des peres de la Compagnie de Jesus. En la Nouvelle France, és années 1662 & 1663. Paris, Sebastien Cramoisy, et Sebast. Mabre-Cramoisy, 1664. L58

A variant issue of the previous item.

Lalemant, Jérôme. Relation de ce qui s'est passé aux missions des peres de la Compagnie de Jesus, en la Nouvelle France, és

annees 1663 & 1664. Paris, Sebastien Cramoisy & Sebast. Mabre-Cramoisy, 1665. L59
Notes the decline of Iroquois strength, appeals for more missionaries, and reports attempts by the Iroquois to send an embassy to the French to seek peace.

Lalemant, Jérôme. Relation de ce qui s'est passé de plus remarquable aux missions des peres de la Compagnie de Jesus, en la Nouvelle France, és années 1663 & 1664. Paris, Sebastien Cramoisy & Sebast. Mabre-Cramoisy, 1665. L60
A variant issue of the above item.

Lally, Thomas-Arthur, comte de. Mémoire pour le comte de Lally ... contre monsieur le Procureur-Général. Paris, Guillaume Desprez, 1766. L61
The defense of the commander of France's land forces in India who had lost Madras and Pondichery, bringing on charges of treachery by various persons who had observed or participated in the defense of those cities.

La Loubère, Simon de. Du royaume de Siam. Paris, La Veuve J.B. Coignard, 1691. L62
Includes descriptions of products of Thailand and means of trading there.

La Loubère, Simon de. A new historical relation of the kingdom of Siam ... wherein a full and curious account is given of the Chinese way of arithmetick, and mathematick learning ... London, Printed by F.L. for Tho. Horne [etc.] 1693. L63
A description of Thailand, including its economy, education, popular customs, government, etc. The second part is a survey of Chinese science and mathematics.

Lalourcé, Jean Charlemagne. Mémoire a consulter, et consultation pour Jean Lioncy ... [Paris] P.A. le Prieur, 1761. L64
Members of the Jesuit Society are accused of participating in illicit commerce.

La Luzerne, César Henri, comte de. Eclaircissements sur la demande de messieurs les députés de Saint-Domingue. [n.p., ca. 1789.] L65
A discussion of restrictions upon free trade in flour in Saint Domingue in view of the French government's refusal to open the trade in time of shortage.

La Mardelle, Guillaume Pierre François de. éloge funèbre du comte d'Ennery, et Réforme judiciare a Saint-Domingue. [Paris, Imprimerie Nationale, ca. 1790.] L66
A funeral eulogy for a former governor general of the French West Indies used as a means for publishing a reform in the administration of St. Domingue.

La Martinière, Pierre Martin de. Voyage des pais septentrionaux. Paris, Louis Vendosme, 1671. L67

First edition of a popular account of a trading voyage along the Scandinavian coast, the north coast of Russia, and Greenland by a Danish trading company.

[La Martinière, Pierre Martin de.] Nouveau voyage du nort. Amsterdam, E. Roger [ca. 1700]. L68
The third French edition.

[La Martinière, Pierre Martin de.] Nouveau voyage vers le septentrion. Amsterdam, Estienne Roger, 1708. L69
This edition contains several illustrations of northern peoples, animals, implements, etc.

[La Martinière, Pierre Martin de.] A new voyage into the northern countries. London, J. Starkey, 1674. L70
The first English edition.

[La Martinière, Pierre Martin de.] A new voyage to the north. London, T. Hodgson and A. Barker, 1706. L71
The second English edition.

La Martinière, Pierre Martin de. Neue Reise in die nordischen Landschafften. Hamburg, Johann Nauman und Georg Wolff, 1675. L72
The first German edition, translated from the English.

[Lambert, Claude-François.] A collection of curious observations on the manners, customs, usages ... and sciences of the several nations of Asia, Africa, and America. London, For the Author, 1750. L73
The eighty-four chapters cover a great range of topics including languages, social customs, production methods, laws, religion, and other aspects of life in many countries.

[Lambert, W.] Bengal sugar. An account of the method and expense of cultivating the sugarcane in Bengal. London, For Debrett, 1794. L74
A review of sugar production methods and costs in Bengal, implying that East Indian sugar could replace the product of British plantations in America.

Lamberti, Arcangelo. Relatione della Colchide hoggi detta Mengrellia, nella quale si tratta dell'origine, costumi e cose naturali di quei paesi. Naples, C. Cavalli, 1654. L75
A description of present day Georgia Republic by a Jesuit missionary. Includes information on geography, natural history, agriculture and religion. The work was later reprinted in M. Thevenot's *Relation de divers voyages curieux*.

Lamiral, Dominique Harcourt. L'Affrique et le peuple affriquain, considérés sous tous leurs rapports avec notre commerce & nos colonies. Paris, Dessenne, 1789. L76

Discusses the people and commerce of West Africa, the Compagnie du Sénégal, and the importance of gum in trade.

Lamoignon de Basville, M. de (Nicholas). Memoires pour servir à l'histoire de Languedoc. Amsterdam, Pierre Boyer, 1734. L77
This general history of Languedoc contains some sections dealing with the commerce of the region and the trade of its major cities.

Lamont, Isaac. Memorie ... gepresenteert aan de ... Westindische Compagnie. [n.p., ca. 1706.] L78
Defense against a charge of maladministration in the Dutch West Indies, by Isaac Lamont, governor of two of the islands.

La Mottraye, Aubry de. Travels through Europe, Asia, and into part of Africa. London, 1723-1732. L79
An account of travels from 1696 to 1729, describing commerce as well as other aspects of life in Greece, Turkey, Russia, and Scandinavia.

La Mottraye, Aubry de. Voyages ... en Europe, Asie & Afrique; ou l'on trouve une grande varieté de recherches geographiques, historiques & politiques. The Hague, T. Johnson & J. Van Duren, 1727. L80
The first French edition.

Lampsins, Adriaan. Notificatie. De Heeren Adriaen ende Cornelis Lampsins ... inviteeren alle de gene die lust hebben haer to begeven op het eylandt Nieuw Walcheren alias Tobago ghenaemt ... Vlissingen, Jacob Pick, 1656. L81
A broadside soliciting interest in a West Indian colonial undertaking.

Lande, Lawrence M. The development of the voyageur contract (1686-1821). Montreal, McGill University, 1989. L82
A listing, with many facsimiles, of 111 fur trade contracts noting the outfitter, voyageur, place and date, destination, and other particulars of the engagement.

Landnámabók. Sagan Landnama um fyrstu bygging Islands af Nordmønnum. Skalhollte, Hendr. Kruse, 1688. L83
A record of the earliest Norse settlements on Iceland. It preserves the history of the first families there, noting their origins, the places they settled, and their manner of living.

Lando, Gio. Giacomo (Giovanni Giacomo). Aritmetica mercantile. Venice, G. Imberti, 1640. L84
First published in 1604 in Naples, Lando's work went through at least three more editions, all published in Venice. Concerns the economic relationship between the "principal cities of Christianity", including Rome, Naples, Genoa, Milan, etc.

Lange, Lorenz. Journal de la residence du Sieur Lange, agent de Sa Majesté imperiale de la Grande Russie à la cour de la Chine; dans les années 1721 & 1722. Leiden, Abraham Kalleweir, 1726. L85
The first and only separately published account of this embassy, with a preface indicating the nature of commercial and political problems between Russia and China that brought it about.

Langham, Thomas. The neat duties ... of all merchandize, specified in the Book of Rates. London, For the author, J. Brotherton and W. Meadows, 1717. L86
The third edition of a handbook for merchants which lists some 2,500 commodities, indicates duties on them, and also explains certain features of laws pertaining to imports and exports.

Langhanss, Christoph. Neue ost indische Reise. Leipzig, Michael Rohrlachs, 1705. L87
An extensive account of the commerce of the East Indies by a German who went there with the Dutch East India Company.

[Langrishe, Sir Hercules.] Considerations on the dependencies of Great Britain. London, For J. Almon, 1769. L88
The author discusses the Irish and colonial trade problems, suggesting greater commercial liberty for the colonies.

Langsdorff, G. H. von (Georg Heinrich). Voyages and travels in various parts of the world. London, H. Colburn, 1813-1814. L89
Contains well-illustrated accounts of life in the islands of the Pacific, with particular interest in the Russian activities in Alaska.

Lannux, Mr. de. Oraison funebre de tres-haut, tres-puissant et tres-auguste prince Louis XIV ... Toul, C. Vincent, 1716. L90
A eulogy for Louis XIV delivered by Lannux on February 6, 1716 at the Toul cathedral. It mentions Louis' influence in the French colonies.

Lansel, J.-Ant. Nécessité d'un régime, pour conserver et faire fleurir le commerce et les manufactures ... Paris, Boulard [1791]. L91
An argument in favor of encouragement and regulation of industry and commerce, with a brief history of French and English experience in this regard.

Lanthenas, François. M. Lamiral, réfuté par lui-même, ou réponse aux opinions de cet auteur, sur l'abolition de la traite des noirs. Paris, L. Potier de Lille, 1790. L92
L'Amiral's book *l'Affrique et le peuple affriquain* is used in this publication of the Amis des Noirs to condemn the entire slave trade and the institution of slavery.

Laon, Jean de, sieur d'Aigremont. Relation du voyage des François fait au Cap de Nord en Amérique. Paris, A. de Sommaville, 1654. L93
An account of the French expedition under General Royville to French Guiana in 1652.

La Pérouse, Jean-François de Galaup, comte de. Voyage de la Pérouse autour du monde. Paris, Imprimerie de la Republique, 1797. L94
Although the Lapérouse expedition disappeared after it left Botany Bay in 1788 the reports sent back previously with De Lesseps contained an abundance of scientific information on the Pacific Ocean, its coasts, and islands.

La Pérouse, Jean-François de Galaup, comte de. Relation abrégée du voyage de La Pérouse, pendant les années 1785, 1786, 1787, 1788; ... Leipzig, 1799. L95
An abridgement of the four volume work above, with an introductory commentary on it.

La Pérouse, Jean-François de Galaup, comte de. A voyage round the world. London, G.G. and J. Robinson [etc.] 1798-99. L96
Most of the English editions are based on this translation which includes prefaces by the translator and the editor.

La Pérouse, Jean-François de Galaup, comte de. Resa omkring jorden af Herr De La Perouse. Åren 1785 och följande. Sammandrag. Stockholm, Johan Pfeiffer, 1799. L97
An abridged translation by Samuel Ödmann.

La Pérouse, Jean-François de Galaup, comte de. Reize van de La Perouse, in de jaaren 1785, 1786, 1787, en 1788. Amsterdam, Johannes Allart, 1801-1804. L98
A translation of the 1799 abridgement.

La Pérouse, Jean-François de Galaup. Viaggio di La Perouse intorno al mondo ... Milan, Sonzogno, 1815. L99
The first Italian edition, an abridged translation by Angelo Petracchi which is part of a series, *Raccolta de' viaggi.*

[La Peyrère, Isaac de.] Relation du Groenland. Paris, A. Courbe, 1647. L100
A description of the geography, population, history, and commerce of Greenland, based in part on early chronicles.

[La Peyrère, Isaac de.] Bericht von Gröhnland, gezogen aus zwo Chroniken: Einer alten ihslandischen und einer neuen danischen. Hamburg, Johan Nauman & Jurhen Wolf, 1674. L101
The first German edition.

La Peyrère, Isaac de. Ausführliche Beschreibung des Theils bewohnt, Theils unbewohnt, so genannten Grönlands. Nuremberg, C. Riegel, 1679. L102
The second German edition.

[La Peyrère, Isaac de.] Nauwkeurige beschrijvingh van Groenland. Amsterdam, Jan Claesz ten Hoorn, 1678. L103
The first Dutch edition.

La Peyrère, Isaac de. Relation de l'Islande. Paris, Chez L. Billaine, 1663. L104
A description of the geography, population, government, and commerce of Iceland.

La Popelinière, Lancelot-Voisin, sieur de. L'Amiral de France. Paris, T. Perier, 1584. L105
A history of the French navy and naval affairs from the earliest times, with details of navy regulations.

La Popelinière, Lancelot-Voisin, sieur de. Les trois mondes. Paris, L'Olivier de Pierre L'Huillier, 1582. L106
A history of ancient navigation and of Renaissance discoveries and explorations.

Larchevêque-Thibault, Gabriel Jean-Baptiste. Mémoire et pieces justificatives adressés a la Convention nationale. Paris, Testu, 1793. L107
An account of the author's arrest and subsequent treatment at the hands of the colonial administration in Saint Domingue.

La Rochelle (France). Chamber of Commerce. Mémoire ... sur le project d'introduction des guildives en France. La Rochelle, P. Mesnier [1765]. L108
A statement of opposition to the importing of rum from the colonies and the trade in molasses with England and the Netherlands.

La Rochelle (France). Chamber of Commerce. Mémoire ... sur les permissions accordées aux etrangers de faire la commerce dans nos colonies. La Rochelle, P. Mesnier, 1765. L109
The merchants of La Rochelle are concerned about English cod fishing and trade among France's North American islands.

La Rochelle (France). Chamber of Commerce. Observations ... sur un mémoire qui a pour titre "Sur les retour des colonies." [La Rochelle, ca. 1784.] L110
An objection to foreign interference in French trade with her American colonies.

La Rochelle (France). Chamber of Commerce. Réponse ... a un mémoire ... sur l'éntendue & les bornes des boix ... dans les colonies. [La Rochelle, ca. 1784.] L111
A defense of the metropolitan merchants in their conduct of commerce with the French American colonies.

La Roque, Captain de. Manuscript letter to Louis Phelypeaux, comte de Pontchartrain. Canton, 19 February 1699. L112
The captain of the *Amphitrite* describes the route from the Cape of Good Hope to Canton, his dealings with the mandarins there prior to beginning trade, and the opportunities for commerce in China.

[La Roque, Jean de.] Voyage de l'Arabie Heureuse. Paris, André Cailleau, 1716. L113
An account of the coffee trade of Yemen and the slave trade of East Africa, relating to an attempt by a mercantile company of St. Malo to establish trade there.

[La Roque, Jean de.] Reise nach dem glücklichen Arabien, durch die Morgenländische See, und die Enge des Rothen Meeres, nebst einer aüsfuhrlichen Beschreibung der berühmten Stadt Moka ... Leipzig, Braunischen Buchladen, 1740. L114
This German edition was published without the section on the origin and history of coffee.

[La Roque, Jean de.] Viaggio nell' Arabia felice per l'Oceano Orientale. Venice, Sebastian Coleti, 1721. L115
The first Italian edition.

Larruga, Eugenio. Historia de la Real y General Junta de Commercio. [Madrid, 1779-89.] L116
A twelve-volume collection of materials for the history of the Spanish Junta de Commercio. The first four volumes contain a manuscript history, and the remainder contain manuscript and printed documents supporting the text.

[La Salle de l'Etang, Simon Philibert de.] Dictionnaire Galibi ... Precédé d'un essai de grammaire. Paris, Bauche, 1763. L117
This dictionary is seen as a first step toward success for the French colony at Cayenne in Guiana.

Lasnier de Vaussenay, François-Pierre. Rapport fait a l'Assemblée nationale sur la franchise de Bayonne. Paris, Imprimerie Nationale [ca. 1790]. L118
A presentation of the cases for and against the commercial privileges formerly held by the towns of Bayonne and Saint Jean de Luz.

Late newes out of Barbary. In a letter written of late from a merchant there, to a gentl. not long since impolyed into that countrie from His Majestie. London, Arthur Jonson, 1613. L119
An account of a revolution in Morocco. The author is concerned with continued commercial relations with Morocco and finds them secure.

The late occurrences in North America, and policy of Great Britain considered. London, J. Almon, 1766. L120
A well reasoned and clearly written analysis of the causes of mutual distrust between Britain and her American colonists.

[La Trobe, Benjamin.] A brief account of the mission established among the Esquimaux Indians, on the coast of Labrador. London, M. Lewis for the Brethren's Society for the Furtherance of the Gospel, 1774. L121
An account of the early efforts of the Moravian Brethren's mission in Labrador, indicating initial success in spite of great hardship.

La Trobe, Benjamin. A succinct view of the missions established among the heathen by the church of the Brethren, or Unitas fratrum. In a letter to a friend. London, M. Lewis, sold by Dilly and Beckett, 1771. L122
A report on the methods and progress of the missions of the United Brethren in Surinam, the Danish West Indies, British West Indies, Tranquebar and the Nicobar Islands, Ceylon, Persia, Guinea, South Africa, Egypt, and Greenland.

Lattré, Jean. Carte des Etats-Unis de l'Amerique suivant le traité de paix de 1783. Dédiée et présentée a S. Excellence Mr Benjamin Franklin. Paris, Chez Lattré, 1784. L123
The official French version of the boundaries of the United States at the conclusion of the American Revolution.

[Laudivio, de Vezzano]. Turcorum imperatoris epistolae aliquot ad varios Christianae ac suae etiam ditionis principes, populos, ac civitates, lectu sane dignissimae. Antwerp, J. Steelsmano, 1533. L124
Translation of letters supposedly written by Sultan Mehmed II but actually written by Laudivio, a member of the Order of the Knights of Malta. They concern the raging European wars and commercial activities of the time.

Laudonnière, Renè Goulaine de. l'Histoire notable de la Floride situee es Indes Occidentales. Paris, Guillaume Auvray, 1586. L125
Records the four expeditions between 1562 and 1567 which attempted to establish a French colony in Florida.

Laujon, Alexandre P.M. Précis historique de la dernière expédition de Saint-Domingue, depuis le départ de l'armée des côtes de France, jusqu' à l'évacuation de la colonie; ... Paris, Delafolie & LeNormant [1805]. L126
An account by a witness of the French expedition to Saint Domingue in 1802 which was defeated by rebellious former slaves and decimated by disease.

Lauraguais, Louis-Léon-Félicité, comte de. Mémoire sur la Compagnie des Indes, dans lequel on établit les droits & les intérêts des actionnaires. [n.p.] 1770. L127

The author is at pains to point out differences between his views and those of André Morellet with respect to the Compagnie des Indes.

Lauraguais, Louis-Léon-Félicité, comte de. Mémoire sur la Compagnie des Indes, précédé d'un discours sur le commerce en général. Paris, Lacombe, 1769. L128

Anti-Physiocratic discussion of French economic life and a condemnation of the Compagnie des Indes.

Laval, Antoine François. Voyage de la Louisiane. Paris, Jean Mariette, 1728. L129

A French mathematician's account of his voyage, containing sailing directions for the West Indies, and maps of many islands and harbors.

Lavanha, João Baptista. Navfragio da nao Santo Alberto, e itenerario da gente, que delle se salvou. Lisbon, Alexandre de Siqueyra, 1597, [repr. 1737]. L130

Lavanha, João Baptista. Relação do naufragio da nao S. Alberto, ne penedo das fontes no anno de 1593: e itinerario da gente, que delle se salvou, athè chegarem a Moçambique. Lisbon, 1736. L131

Laveaux, Etienne Magneaud Bizefranc de. Discours prononcé par Laveau. [Paris, Imprimerie Nationale, 1799.] L132

A speech celebrating the abolition of slavery in the French colonies.

Law, Edmund. A sermon preached before the incorporated Society for the Propagation of the Gospel in Foreign Parts: at their anniversary meeting in the parish church of St. Mary-le-Bow, on Friday February 18, 1774. London, T. Harrison and S. Brooke, 1774. L133

This sermon expresses a concern for the Society's possibilities in India, reflecting military success there.

Law, John. Considérations sur le commerce et sur l'argent. The Hague, Jean Neaulme, 1720. L134

The first French edition of *Money and trade considered*, including a brief and laudatory biography of Law.

Law, John. Manuscript letter signed. Paris, 30 January 1720. L135

Concerns posting of information on a law of the previous day concerning fiscal matters.

Law, John. Manuscript letter signed. Paris, 10 April 1720. L136

The letter concerns French fiscal legislation.

[Law, John.] Money and trade considered, with a proposal for supplying the nation with money. Edinburgh, Heirs and successors of Andrew Anderson, 1705. L137

This is the first publication of John Law's economic theories on the use of land as a base for value of paper currency, making possible a larger supply of money and thereby an increase in trade and industry.

Law, John. Oeuvres de John Law. Paris, Buisson, 1790. L138

Discourses on banks, banking, finance, commerce, and currency.

[Law suit between Nicolás Echezarreta and his cousin, Domingo de Olea: an exchange of pamphlets.] [n.p., 1734?] L139

The lawsuit concerns investments in trade between Cadiz and Buenos Aires.

Lawrence, Richard. The interest of Ireland in its trade and wealth stated. Dublin, Jos. Ray, 1682. L140

Contains suggestions for the improvement of manufactures and trade in Ireland.

Lawson, John. The history of Carolina. London, For W. Taylor and J. Baker, 1714. L141

The second English edition of a book describing prospects of colonizing in Carolina, with an account of trade with the Indians and many citations of products and commodities available for commercial development.

Lawson, John. Allerneuste Beschreibung der Provinz Carolina in West-Indien. Hamburg, Thomas von Wierings Erben, 1712. L142

The first German edition.

Lawson, John. Allerneueste Beschreibung der gross-britannischen Provintz Carolina in West-Indien. Hamburg, Thomas von Wierings Erben, 1722. L143

The second German edition.

Lazzero Recanti, Salvatore. Four autographed letters signed addressed to P.H. Roux from Leghorn, May 27, 1746-October 4, 1748. L144

This correspondence concerns the French Compagnie d'Afrique.

Leake, Stephen Martin. Nummi Britannici historia, or, An historical account of English money ... with particular descriptions of each piece, and illustrated with cuts of the more antient ... London, For W. Meadow, 1726. L145

A review of the history of monetary values in England, with descriptions of techniques of coinage and illustrations of early coins.

Leardo, Giovanni. [Facsimile of world map of 1452. New York, American Geographical Society, 1928.] L146

This circular world map shows the known or imagined land mass of the world on a circular plane surrounded by ocean.

Le Beau, Claude. Avantures du Sr. C. Le Beau ... ou voyage curieux et nouveau, parmi les sauvages de l'Amérique Septentrionale. Amsterdam, Herman Uytwerf, 1738. L147

The author traveled among the Iroquois, Huron, and Algonquin Indians primarily, noting all aspects of their life and customs.

Le Beau, Claude. Geschichte des Herrn C. Le Beau ..., oder, Merckwürdige und neue Reise zu denen Wilden des nordlichen Theils von America ... Erfurt, Joh. David Jungnicol, 1752. L148

One of two German editions issued in 1752, translated from the French.

Le Blanc, François. Traité historique des monnoies de France, depuis le commencement de la monarchie jusques a present. [Paris, C. Robustel, 1690.] L149

A history of French coinage including hundreds of illustrations, indicating content of the various coins as well as regulations upon French coinage for about a thousand years.

Leblanc, Vincent. Les voyages fameux du sieur Vincent Le Blanc. Paris, Gervais Clousier, 1648. L150

An extensive travel narrative encompassing travels in the Levant, Asia, Africa, and America.

Leblanc, Vincent. De vermaarde reizen ... in der vier delen des werrelts. Amsterdam, Jan Hendriksz & Jan Rieuwertsz, 1654. L151

First Dutch edition.

Leblanc, Vincent. The world surveyed. London, For J. Starky, 1660. L152

The first English edition.

[Leboucher, Odet Julien.] Histoire de la derniere guerre, entre la Grande-Bretagne, et les États-Unis de l'Amérique, la France, l'Espagne et la Hollande, depuis son commencement in 1775, jusqu'a sa fin en 1783. Paris, Brocas, 1787. L153

A detailed account of the naval aspects of the war primarily, with the American phase seen as a part of the larger world-wide conflict between France and Great Britain.

[Le Candele, P.] Wel-vaert vande West-Indische Compagnie. [n.p., 1646.] L154

A pamphlet dealing with the financing and commerce of the Dutch West India Company, including its trade in sugar and gold in Brazil and Angola.

Le Clercq, Chrestien. Histoire des colonies françoises et les fameuses découvertes depuis le fleuve de S. Laurent, la Loüisiane & le fleuve Colbert jusqu'au Golphe Mexique, achevées sous la conduite de feu Monsieur de la Salle. Lyon, Thomas Amaulry, 1692. L155

This work is critical of Jesuit publications relating to North America. It contains the first published account of the discoveries of La Salle on the Mississippi.

Le Clercq, Chrestien. Nouvelle relation de la Gaspesie, qui contient les moeurs & la religion des sauvages gaspasiens ... Paris, Amable Auroy, 1691. L156

A thorough description of the manners and customs of the Indians of the Gaspé area in Canada, with particular interest in a group which used the cross as a religious symbol.

Le Cointe-Marsillac. Le more-lack, ou essai sur les moyens les plus doux & les plus équitable d'abolir le traite & l'esclavage des Nègres d'Afrique, en conservant aux colonies tous les avantages d'une population agricole. Londres, et se trouve a Paris, Prault, 1789. L157

An argument in favor of abolishing the slave trade as a means of improving the conditions of slaves through the increased value they would have.

Le Comte, Louis. Nouveaux memoires sur l'état present de la Chine. Paris, Jean Anisson, 1697-1698. L158

A series of twenty-two letters to important persons in France describing China and the progress of the Jesuit mission there.

Le Comte, Louis. Nouveaux memoires sur l'etat present de la Chine. Amsterdam, Henri Desbordes & Antoine Schelte, 1698-1701. L159

The third edition.

Le Comte, Louis. Memoirs and observations ... made in a late journey through the empire of China. London, B. Tooke, 1697. L160

The first English edition

Le Comte, Louis. Beschryvinge van het machtige keyserryk China. The Hague, E. Boucquet, 1698. L161

The first Dutch edition.

Le Comte, Louis. Lettre a Monseigneur le duc du Mayne sur les ceremonies de la Chine. [n.p.] 1700. L162

An explanation of the Jeusit point of view on the Chinese Rites controversy, a defense of their position, and a plea for an understanding of Chinese history and culture.

Le Comte, Louis. Réponse a la lettre de messieurs des missions étrangeres, au Pape, sur les ceremonies chinoises. [n.p., ca. 1700.] L163

A review of recent writings and events relating to the controversy between the Jesuits and the Séminaire des missions étrangères over the acceptance of certain Chinese rites in religious practices of Chinese converts.

Le Comte, Louis. A compleat history of the empire of China ... the 2d ed. London, Printed for James Hodges, 1739. L164
A translation of *Nouveau memoires sur l'état présent de la Chine.*

Ledru, André Pierre. Reise nach den Inseln Teneriffa, Trinidad, St. Thomas, St. Crux und Porto-Rico; auf Befehl der französischen Regierung, vom 30 Sept. 1796 bis zum 7 Juni 1798, unter der Leitung des Capitain Baudin unternommen. Leipzig, Heinrich Büschler, 1811. L165
An account of a natural history expedition sent out by the French government. Includes notes by Sonnini de Manoncourt from the original French and notes by Eberhard August Wilhelm von Zimmermann, the translator.

Ledyard, John. Methods for improving the manufacture of indigo. Devizes, T. Burrough, 1776. L166
Contains suggestions to planters in Georgia, Florida, Carolina, and Jamaica for the better cultivation of indigo.

Lee, Arthur. An appeal to the justice and interests of the people of Great Britain, in the present disputes with America, by an Old Member of Parliament. London, For J. Almon, 1774. L167
An argument in favor of the American colonists' position with respect to the rights of Parliament to tax them, using Ireland as an example.

Lee, Arthur. A second appeal to the justice and interests of the people, on the measures respecting America. London, For J. Almon, 1775. L168
A review of colonial policy leading toward the outbreak of revolution in America, attributing the outcome to the lack of a conciliatory attitude in Parliament and the failure to understand the motives of the colonists.

Leeward Islands (Federation). Laws, etc. Acts of Assembly, passed in the Charibbee Leeward Islands, from 1690 to 1730. London, John Baskett, 1734. L169
This collection of legislation focuses on Antigua and Nevis, covering forty years, and deals with all aspects of economic, social and civil life in those islands. Presumably laws of this type were applied to other islands in the Leeward group as well.

[Le François, A., abbé.] Methode abrégée et facile pour apprendre la géographie. Paris, Libraries Associés, 1758. L170
A popular French geography textbook with 17 maps by cartographer Gilles Robert de Vaugondy. Includes a section on astronomy, tables of longitude and latitude, and a listing of the principal cities of the world.

Legal, G. Observations sur tout ce qui concerne les colonies d'Amérique, notamment celle de Saint-Domingue. [n.p., 1789?] L171
A former resident in the French West Indies contradicts the views of Henri Gregoire who had called for improving the legal position of mulattoes there in his *Memoire en faveur des gens de couleur.*

Legatio David Aethiopiae Regis, ad Clementem Papa VII. Bologna, I. Remolen, 1533. L172
Contains copies of letters that passed between the Negus of Ethiopia, the Pope, and King Manuel of Portugal, as well as an account of Francisco Alvares' expedition to Ethiopia.

Le Gobien, Charles. Acte de protestation signifié aux sieurs, syndic, doyen & docteurs de la Faculté de Theologie de Paris le dix-huitiéme jour d'octobre 1700 ... [n.p., 1700.] L173
A protest against the censure upon the books of Le Gobien and Louis Daniel Le Comte by the Faculty of Theology at Paris.

Le Gobien, Charles. Histoire de l'edit de l'empereur de la Chine, en faveur de la religion chrestienne: avec un eclaircissement sur les honneurs que les Chinois rendent à Confucius & aux morts. Paris, Jean Anisson, 1698. L174
A history and justification of the Jesuit mission in China, answering critics of Jesuit methods and acceptance of Chinese Christians who continued certain Confucian rites.

Le Gobien, Charles. Istoria dell' editto dell' imperatore della Cina in favore della religione Christiana. Turin, Gio. Battista Zappata, 1699. L175
The first Italian edition.

Le Gobien, Charles. Histoire des isles Marianes. Paris, N. Pepie, 1700. L176
A history of the Christian missions in the Marianas, with reprintings of several letters from the early missionaries.

[Le Gobien, Charles.] Jugement d'un grand nombre de docteurs des universitez de Castille et d'Arragon sur les propositions censurées en Sorbonne le 18. d'octobre, 1700. Liege, Guillaume Henry Streel, 1701. L177
A strong statement in support of the Jesuit position regarding Chinese rites by ninety-one churchmen and scholars in Spain. It is also an attack on Louis Ellies DuPin's book, *Defense de la censure de la Faculté de Théologie de Paris.*

[Le Gobien, Charles.] Lettre a un doctor de la faculté de Paris, sur les propositions deferées en Sorbonne par Monsieur Priou. [n.p.] 1700.
L178
    A defense primarily of Louis Daniel Le Comte's *Nouveaux memoires sur l'etat present de la Chine.*

[Le Gobien, Charles.] Parallele de quelques propositions, dont les unes ont esté déferées au S. Siege & à la Sorbonne, les autres ne l'ont pas esté, quoy qu'elles meritassent beaucoup plus de l'estre. [n.p., 1700.]
L179
    A more extended version of the arguments presented in the previous item.

[Le Gobien, Charles.] Second parallele des propositions du P. Le Comte, avec quelques autres propositions, adressé à Monsieur le Syndic de la Faculté de Theologie de Paris. [n.p., 1700.]
L180
    A comparison of texts between Le Comte's *Nouveaux memoires* and Paul Beurrier's *La perpétuitéde la foy* in their treatment of Chinese approaches to Christianity, the latter work having drawn no criticism from the Sorbonne faculty of theology.

[Le Gobien, Charles.] Propositions soutenues, ou autorisées par quelques docteurs de la Faculté de Theologie de Paris. [n.p., 1701?]
L181
    Not directly related to the Chinese Rites controversy, arguments on other theological questions appear to be directed against the opponents of the Jesuits, probably Jansenists.

Legouvé, Jean Baptiste. Plaidoyer pour le syndic des créanciers des sieurs Lioncy Freres & Gouffre, négocians a Marseille. Paris, D'Houry, 1761.
L182
    A complaint against the Society of Jesus, accusing its members of participating illegally in trade in America.

Le Gouz de la Boullaye, François. Les voyages et observations du sieur de la Boullaye le Gouz. Paris, F. Clousier, 1653.
L183
    A description of the peoples, governments, natural products, and customs of Levant and the East Indies as well as some European countries.

Le Guat, François. De gevaarlyke en zeldzame reyzen ... naar twee onbewoonde Oostindische eylanden. Utrecht, W. Broedelet, 1708.
L184
    The first Dutch edition of a narrative, alleged to be fictional, of an attempted French settlement of the Mascarene Islands. Translated from the French, it contains useful information on the plant and animal life of the islands.

Le Guat, François. A new voyage to the East-Indies. London, For R. Bonwicke [etc.] 1708.
L185
    The first English edition, translated from the Dutch.

Le Havre (France). Merchants. Mémoire ... pour qu'il ne soit plus accordé de passeports aux etrangers pour introduire des Négres de leur traite dans les colonies françoises de l'Amérique. [Havre, P.J.D.G. Fauré, ca. 1760.]
L186
    A plea for restricting trade with the Guinea coast to French merchants only.

Le Havre (France). Merchants. Mémoire des négocians du Havre. [n.p., ca. 1784.]
L187
    The merchants of Le Havre urge withdrawal of a proclamation of August 30, 1784, because of the damage it may do to French-American trade.

Leibniz, Gottfried Wilhelm, Freiherr von. Novissima Sinica historiam nostri temporis illustrata ... [n.p.] 1697.
L188
    Writings on China based on the author's connections with missionaries of the Society of Jesus.

Leiden (Netherlands). Gemeente-Archief. Leyden documents relating to the Pilgrim fathers ... facsimile, transcript, translation and annotations by Dr. D. Plooij of Leyden and Dr. J. Rendel Harris of Manchester. Leyden, E.J. Brill, Ltd., 1920.
L189
    A colleciton of documents in facsimile, translation, and transcription relating to the residence of the Pilgrims in the Netherlands prior to their departure for America.

Leiden (Netherlands). Laws, etc. Gilde-brief, van de neeringhe der boomgaert-luyden, ende andere ... [Leyden] Raedthuys, 1610.
L190
    A set of rules for the fruit vendors' guild of Leyden.

Leiden (Netherlands). Laws, etc. Keuren der stadt Leyden des graefschaps van Holland. [Leyden] 1583.
L191
    The privileges of the city of Leyden, introduced by references to earlier grants of privilege for the city, and containing reference to various aspects of the city's commercial life.

Leiden (Netherlands). Laws, etc. Oflezinghe aengaende tmarctghelt vande warmoefluyden. [Leyden, 1609.]
L192
    Merchants bringing wares to Leyden are to pay fees which will be used to pay those who clean the streets.

Leiden (Netherlands). Laws, etc. Ordinantien op het laden by gheburten van de groote schipperye aende craen. Leyden, Raedthuys, 1609.
L193
    Three ordinances regulating the water traffic of Leyden.

Leiden (Netherlands). Laws, etc. Verhoginghe ven tloon van de bierdraghers. [Leyden, 1609.]
L194
    Specifies an increase in fees for brewery delivery men.

Leighton, Sir Elisha. [Autograph letter to the earl of Lauderdale.] [n.p.] December 29, 1668. L195
A reminder to the earl of Lauderdale that his subscription to the Company of Merchant Adventurers was not paid, with specifications for its payment in installments and penalties for late payment.

Leiste, Christian. Beschreibung des brittischen Amerika zur Ersparung der englischen Karten. [Wolfenbüttel] 1778. L196
A survey of British North America in which the author describes the geography, population, and production of the individual colonies. A map of the middle colonies is included.

Leitão, Francisco de Andrade. Discurso politico sobre o se aver de larger a coroa de Portugal, Angola, S. Thome, & Maranhaõ, exclamado aos altos, & poderosos estados de Olanda. Lisbon, A. Alvarez, 1642. L197
A translation of Leitão's *Copia primae allegationis* from the Latin published the same year in The Hague. A protest against Dutch attacks on Portuguese possessions in Angola, St. Thomé, Maranhao and Pernambuco.

Le Jeune, abbé Pierre Claude. Observations critiques et philosophiques sur le Japon. Paris, Knapen & fils, 1780. L198
A review of the Japanese economy, noting the opportunities for foreign trade in Japan.

Le Jeune, Paul. Brieve relation du voyage de la Nouvelle France, fait au mois d'avril dernier ... Paris, Sebastien Cramoisy, 1632. L199
This is the first of the *Jesuit Relations* of New France, covering the period from April 18, 1632 to the end of August. It concerns the author's work in the vicinity of Tadoussac and his travels to Quebec.

Le Jeune, Paul. Relation de ce qui s'est passé en la Nouvelle France en l'anneé 1633. Paris, Sebastien Cramoisy, 1634. L200
This second *Jesuit Relation* for New France reports the first full year of the mission's activity there, and also the activities of Champlain and other events in the colony.

Le Jeune, Paul. Relation de ce qui s'est passé en la Nouvelle France, en l'année 1634. Paris, Sebastien Cramoisy, 1635. L201
This *Relation* stresses the problems of the missionaries due to the difficulty in learning the languages of the Indians.

Le Jeune, Paul. Relation de ce qui s'est passé en la Nouvelle France, en l'annee 1634. Paris, Sebastien Cramoisy, 1635. L202
The second edition, with numerous typographical variations, but no significant change in text.

Le Jeune, Paul. Relation de ce qui s'est passé en la Nouvelle France, en l'annee 1634. Paris, Sebastien Cramoisy, 1635. L203
A variant of the first and second editions.

Le Jeune, Paul. Relation de ce qui s'est passé en la Nouvelle France en l'année 1635. Paris, Sebastien Cramoisy, 1636. L204
In addition to the reports of missionary progress in both the Huron country and in lower Canada, this *Relation* has a section titled "Divers sentimens & advis des peres qui sont en la Nouvelle France."

Le Jeune, Paul. Relation de ce qui s'est passé en la Nouvelle France en l'année 1635. Paris, Sebastien Cramoisy, 1636. L205
A variant issue of the previous item.

Le Jeune, Paul. Relation de ce qui s'est passé en la Nouvelle France, en l'année 1634 & 1635. Avignon, Jaques Bramereau, 1636. L206
The text follows closely the Paris editions, but this Avignon edition was printed with ecclesiastical authority rather than the authority of state.

Le Jeune, Paul. Relation de ce qui s'est passé en la Nouvelle France en l'année 1636. Paris, Sebastien Cramoisy, 1637. L207
This *Relation* notes the death of Champlain, gives details of Huron life and customs and reports further missionary travels among the Indians by the Jesuits.

Le Jeune, Paul. Relation de ce qui s'est passé en la Nouvelle France en l'annee 1637. Rouen, Jean le Boulenger, 1638. L208
This *Relation* is largely concerned with missionary successes in lower Canada, and with preparation for expansion of the Huron mission.

Le Jeune, Paul. Relation de ce qui s'est passé en la Nouvelle France en l'année 1637. Rouen, Jean Boulenger, 1638. L209
A second copy, with variants.

Le Jeune, Paul. Relation de ce qui s'est passé en la Nouvelle France en l'année 1637. Rouen, Jean le Boulenger, 1638. L210
A variant issue with the first state of the cancel title page.

Le Jeune, Paul. Relation de ce qui s'est passé en la Nouvelle France en l'année 1637. Rouen, Jean Le Boulenger, 1638. L211
Another variant, with the second state of the cancel title page.

Le Jeune, Paul. Relation de ce qui s'est passé en la Nouvelle France en l'année 1638. Paris, Sebastien Cramoisy, 1638. L212
This *Relation* is largely concerned with the increasing opposition to the Jesuits by the Indians, the establishment of a new residence near Three Rivers, and the steadfastness of the Jesuits in the face of their difficulties.

Le Jeune, Paul. Relation de ce qui s'est passé en la Nouvelle France en l'année 1638. Paris, Sebastien Cramoisy, 1638.   L213
   The second edition.

Le Jeune, Paul. Relation de ce qui s'est passé en Nouvelle France en l'année 1639. Paris, Sebastien Cramoisy, 1640.   L214
   This *Relation* gives considerable attention to the religious and other customs of the Indians which made the Jesuits' progress slow. It also reports the founding of the Ursuline convent at Quebec and some reorganization of the mission to the Hurons.

Le Jeune, Paul. Relation de ce qui c'est passé en la Nouvelle France en l'année 1639. Paris, Sebastien Cramoisy, 1640.   L215
   The second edition.

Le Jeune, Paul. Relation de ce qui s'est passé en la Nouvelle France en l'annee M.DC.XL. Paris, Sebastien Cramoisy, 1641.   L216
   Reports the arrival of additional priests and nuns at the Canadian mission, enumerates Indian tribes throughout the eastern half of North America, notes the arrival of an unnamed Englishman in search of a northwest passage, and indicates numerous baptisms.

Le Jeune, Paul. Relation de ce qui s'est passé en la Nouvelle France en l'annee M.DC.XL. Paris, Sebastien Cramoisy, 1641.   L217
   A variant issue of the previous item.

Le Jeune, Paul. Relation de ce qui s'est passé en la Nouvelle France, es années 1640 et 1641. Paris, Sebastien Cramoisy, 1642.   L218
   Part I, written by Father Le Jeune, commends the work of the Ursuline nuns, notes the progress of a settlement of Indian converts, and the hostility of the Iroquois. Part II, by Father Lalemant, provides reports on seven missions.

Le Jeune, Paul. Relation de ce qui s'est passé de plus remarquable aux missions des peres de la Compagnie de Jesus, en la Nouvelle France, es années mil six cens cinquante six & mil cens cinquante sept. Paris, Sebastien Cramoisy et Gabriel Cramoisy, 1658.   L219
   Summarizes the work of recently established missions among the Iroquois with optimistic views of the prospects for success.

Le Jeune, Paul. Relation de ce qui s'est passé de plus remarquable aux missions des peres de la Compagnie de Jesus en la Nouvelle France, és années mil six cens cinquante sept. Paris, Sebastien Cramoisy et Gabriel Cramoisy, 1658.   L220
   A variant of the previous item.

Le Jeune, Paul. Relation de ce qui s'est passé de plus remarquable aux missions des peres de la Compagnie de Jesus, en la Nouvelle France, és années 1660 & 1661. Paris, Sebastien Cramoisy, 1662.   L221
   This *Relation* emphasizes the growing violence of the Iroquois wars and notes the expansion of missionary activity to the north, toward Hudson Bay.

Le Maire, Jacques. Spieghel der Australische navigatie. Amsterdam, Michiel Colijn, 1622.   L222
   The first account by Le Maire of a voyage around Cape Horn in an attempt to establish a new route from Europe to the East Indies.

Le Maire, Jacques-Joseph. Les voyages ... aux Isles Canaries, Cap-Verd, Senegal, et Gambie. Paris, Jacques Collombat, 1695.   L223
   The author was a physician in the service of the Compagnie d'Afrique, and reported on the peoples and products of the places he visited. Illustrations depict African customs and industries.

[Le Marchant, William.] The rights and immunities of the Island of Guernsey: most humbly submitted to the consideration of government, in a speech of one of the magistrates of that island to the royal court there. London, 1771.   L224
   An argument on behalf of Guernsey's ancient rights and privileges as a province of Normandy in the face of British establishment of a customs house on the island.

Le Mercier, François. Relation de ce qui s'est passé en la mission des peres de la Compagnie de Jesus, au pays de la Nouvelle France, depuis l'eté de l'année 1652 jusques à l'eté de l'année 1653. Paris, Sebastien Cramoisy et Gabriel Cramoisy, 1654.   L225
   This *Relation* shows concern for relations with the Iroquois, reports the arrival of a group of a hundred settlers at Montreal, and contains three letters of Mother Marie de l'Incarnation from Quebec.

Le Mercier, François. Relation de ce qui s'est passé en la mission des peres de la Compagnie de Jesus, en la Nouvelle France, es annees 1653 & 1654. Paris, Sebastien Cramoisy et Gabriel Cramoisy, 1655.   L226
   Contains an account of treaty negotiations with the Iroquois, and includes a letter and prayer in the Huron language and in French translation.

Le Mercier, François. Relation de ce qui s'est passé en la mission des peres de la Compagnie de Jesus, en la Nouvelle France, es annees 1653 & 1654. Paris, Sebastien Cramoisy et Gabriel Cramoisy, 1655.   L227
   The second issue.

Le Mercier, François. Relation de ce qui s'est passé en la Nouvelle France, és années 1664 & 1665. Paris, Sebastien Cramoisy & Sebastien Mabre-Cramoisy, 1666.   L228

A plea is made for more missionaries; the arrival of the Marquis de Tracy as lieutenant-general is noted. A folding plan gives the layout of three French forts and a map of Lake Ontario and the upper St. Lawrence River.

Le Mercier, François. Relation de ce qui s'est passé en la Nouvelle France, és années 1664 & 1665. Paris, Sebastien Cramoisy & Sebast. Mabre-Cramoisy, 1666. L229
A variant issue of the above item.

Le Mercier, François. Relation de ce qui s'est passé de plus remarquable aux missions des peres de la Compagnie de Jesus, en la Nouvelle France, aux années mil six cent soixante cinq, & mil six cent soixante six. Paris, Sebastien Cramoisy & Sebastien Mabre-Cramoisy, 1667. L230
Describes favorable results of expeditions against the Iroquois, and includes a letter from the Mother Superior of the hospital at Quebec which lists the hospital's needs.

Le Mercier, François. Relation de ce qui s'est passé de plus remarquable aux missions des peres de la Compagnie de Jesus en la Nouvelle France, les années mil six cens soixante sept. Paris, Sebastien Cramoisy et Sebastien Mabre-Cramoisy, 1668. L231
Notes the favorable turn of events in Canada due to peace with the Iroquois and the greater interest being taken in the colony by Louis XIV. The result is increased settlement and an improved economy.

Le Mercier, François. Relation de ce qui s'est passé de plus remarquable aux missions des peres de la Compagnie de Jesus, en la Nouvelle France, les années mil six cens soixante six & mil six cens soixante sept. Paris, Sebastien Cramoisy et Sebast. Mabre-Cramoisy, 1668. L232
This copy has appended the "Lettre de la Reverende Mere Superieure des Religieuse Hospitalieres de Kebec en la Nouvelle France", by Marie de S. Bonaventure, October 20, 1667.

Le Mercier, François. Relation de ce qui s'est passé de plus remarquable aux missions des peres de la Compagnie de Jesus, en la Nouvelle France, aux années mil six cens soixante-sept & mil six cens soixante-huit. Paris, Sebastien Mabre-Cramoisy, 1669. L233
This *Relation* is primarily concerned with the mission to the Iroquois. It includes a letter from François de Petrée, the first bishop of New France.

Le Mercier, François. Relation de ce qui s'est passé de plus remarquable aux missions des peres de la Compagnie de Jesus. En la Nouvelle France, les années 1669 & 1670. Paris, Sebast. Mabre-Cramoisy, 1671. L234
Missionary efforts are reported, indicating optimism for the future. The Lake Superior region is described and a letter from Father Jacques Marquette describes his travels among the Illinois and other western Indians.

Le Moine de L'Espine, Jacques. Le negoce d'Amsterdam, ou traité de sa banque ... des compagnies orientales & occidentales. Amsterdam, P. Brunnel, 1710. L235
A merchant handbook describing Dutch commerce.

Le Moine de L'Espine, Jacques. De koophandel van Amsterdam, en andere Nederlandsche steden, naar alle gewesten der waereld. Amsterdam, Dordrecht, Leiden, & Harlingen, J. de Groot [etc.] 1801-2. L236
The tenth edition.

Lemoyne, Simon Sylvestere Clément. Idées préliminaires, et prospectus d'un ouvrage sur les pêches maritimes de France. Paris, Imprimerie Royale, 1777. L237
A prospectus for a book designed to promote the French fishing industry, noting the benefits it would bring to several aspects of the French economy. The book itself does not appear to have been published.

Le Moyne d'Iberville, Pierre. Relation de la prise et capitulation de l'isle Nieve appartenant aux Anglois. Manuscript. Nevis, 1706. L238
A manuscript account of the day by day activities from March 26-April 6, 1706 in planning and accomplishing the caputure of Nevis by the French.

Lempriere, William. Resa uti Marocco, åren 1789 och 90. I sammandrag. Stockholm, Johan Pfeiffer, 1795. L239
The translator of this Swedish edition was Samuel Lorens Ödmann.

Lempriere, William. A tour from Gibraltar to Tangier, Sallee, Mogodore, Santa Cruz, Tarudant; and thence, over Mount Atlas, to Morocco: including a particular account of the royal harem, &c. London, J. Walter [etc.] 1791. L240
An English physician's travels in Morocco, with reports on the people, economy, and social customs of the country, including an account of the pilgrimage to Mecca and the trade with Timbuktu.

[Lemström, Henric.] Erhindringar. Wid de under riksdagen utkomne skrifter, rörande det allmänna. No. 1-16. Stockholm, Kongl. Finska Boktryckeriet, 1765. L241
A collection of writings published in connection with Parliamentary debates, some of which refer to Swedish trade and to the East India Company.

Leng, John. A sermon preached before the incorporated Society for the Propagation of the Gospel in Foreign Parts: at their anniversary meeting in the parish-church of St. Mary-le-

Bow, on Friday the 17th of February, 1726 [i.e. 1727] ... London, J. Downing, 1727. L242
This sermon emphasizes the duty of merchants who have profited from New World commerce to assist in improvement of the lives of non-Christian peoples.

Lenglet Dufresnoy, Nicolas. Geografia de' fanciuli ovvero metodo di geografia. Venice, Luigi Pavini, 1749. L243
The third Italian edition of an elementary geography text, translated from the French.

Lenglet Dufresnoy, Nicolas. Méthode pour étudier la geographie. Paris, N.M. Tilliard, 1768. L244
A ten-volume set, one volume of which contains an extensive bibliography and map list for the study of geography. Ancient, Biblical and modern geography are all included.

Leningradskii gornyi institut im. G. V. Plekhanova. Rossīiskoi atlas: iz soroka chetyrekh kart sostoiashchīi i na sorok ... St. Petersburg, 1792. L245
An atlas of forty-four maps of the provinces of the Russian empire, with three additional maps, one of western Russia dated 1793, and two French maps, one of St. Petersburg and environs, the other of Bering Sea and Strait, with the tracks of major expeditions from the first Bering voyage to the last voyage of Cook.

Leo, Africanus. De totius Africae descriptione. Antwerp, Joannes Latium, 1556. L246
The first Latin edition of the earliest modern description of Africa.

Leo, Africanus. Description de l'Afrique. Lyons, Jean Temporal, 1556. L247
Also includes translations from Ramusio of the travel narratives of Varthema, Cadamosto, Corsali, and others.

Leo, Africanus. A geographical historie of Africa. London, George Bishop, 1600. L248
The first English edition of a description of Africa, especially useful for its account of the interior of the continent.

Leo, Africanus. Africae descriptio. Leiden, Elzevir, 1632. L249
This edition is from the "Elzevir Republics" series.

León Pinelo, Antonio de. Epitome de la biblioteca oriental i occidental, nautica i geographica. Madrid, Juan Gonzalez, 1629. L250
This is one of the earliest bibliographies of exploration literature, and is considered the first bibliography of America. It is divided into four sections: the East, Spanish America, navigation, and geography. All titles are translated into Spanish.

León Pinelo, Antonio de. Tratado de confirmaciones reales de encomiendas, oficios, i casos, en que se requieren para las Indias Occidentales. Madrid, Juan Gonzalez, 1630. L251
A compilation of royal decrees concerning powers granted to colonial officials in Spanish America from the beginnings of Spanish colonial activity to the time of publication.

León Pinelo, Antonio de. Vida del illustrissimo i reverendissimo d. Toribio Alfonso Mogrovejo. [Madrid] 1653. L252
Mogrovejo was the archbishop of Lima and was recognized for his support of the rights of the Indians of Peru. Leon Pinela was the official historian of the Indies and this work seems to be the earliest source of Mogrovejo's life in Peru.

[Leonard, Daniel.] The origin of the American contest with Great-Britain, or the present political state of the Massachusetts-Bay, in general, and the town of Boston in particular. New York, James Rivington, 1775. L253
The first eight letters of "Massachusettenis" which had been published previously in the *Massachusetts Gazette and Postboy* setting forth the Loyalist position.

Leonardo de Argensola, Bartolomé. Conquista de las islas Malucas. Madrid, A. Martin, 1609. L254
A history of the Moluccas, with particular interest in the Spanish commercial activity there during the reign of Philip III.

Leonardo de Argensola, Bartolomé. Histoire de la conquète des isles Moluques par les Espagnols, par les Portugais, & par les Hollandois. Amsterdam, Jacques Desbordes, 1706. L255
This first translation from the Spanish edition of 1609 adds an extensive history of the Dutch in the Moluccas in the seventeenth century, including accounts of their conflicts there with the English.

Leonardo de Argensola, Bartolomé. The discovery and conquest of the Molucco and Philippine islands. London, 1708. L256
The first English edition.

Leonardo de Argensola, Bartolomé. Beschreibung der Molukischen insuln. Franckfurt und Leipzig, M. Rohrlachs, 1710-1711. L257
This is the first German translation.

Leonardo de Argensola, Bartolomé. Primera parte de los anales de Aragon; que prosigue los del secretario Geronimo Çurita, desde el año M.D.XVI. Saragossa, Juan de Lanaia, 1630. L258
This volume covers the period 1516-1520, and includes accounts of Spanish conquest in Mexico and the preparation of Magellan's fleet.

Leopold, Carl Fridric. Korta frågor angående nyttan af wåre inländska wäxter, med wederbörandes tilstädielse. Abo, Jacob Merckell [1753].   L259

A comparison of the uses and values of domestic and imported goods.

Le Page du Pratz. Histoire de la Louisiane. Paris, DeBure [etc.] 1758.   L260

A description of the geography, natural history, and peoples of the lower Mississippi valley, based on a residence of fifteen years.

Le Page du Pratz. The history of Louisiana. London, T. Becket and P.A. de Hondt, 1763.   L261

This first English edition includes a forty-two page preface discussing England's interest in the interior of North America.

Le Pelletier, Jean de. Memoires pour le retablissement du commerce en France. [n.p.] 1701.   L262

Proposals for placing merchants on the Conseil du Commerce, and for simplification of taxes in the interest of stimulating French trade.

Le Rahier, Christophe. Memoire, ou l'on propose de tenter la découverte du passage du nordest, pour frayer une nouvelle route aux Indes Orientales & Occidentales. Manuscript. [n.p., ca. 1750].   L263

A proposal made, apparently to a naval official, citing previous experience in China and India by the author, and noting types of equipment and men needed.

Le Roy, Pierre Louis. Kort, naauwkeurig en echtrelaas van het gebeeurde aan vier Russische zeelieden, welke by ongeluk geraakt zyn op het onbewoond eiland Oost-Spitzbergen ... Amsterdam, Petrus Conradi, 1768.   L264

An account of the survival of four Russian sailors who were shipwrecked on Spitzbergen where they remained more than six years.

Le Roy, Pierre Louis. A narrative of the singular adventures of four Russian sailors ... on the desert island of East-Spitzbergen. London, C. Heydinger, 1774.   L265

English edition of the previous item.

Léry, Jean de. Histoire d'un voyage fait en la terre du Bresil, autrement dit Amerique. La Rochelle, Antoine Chuppin, 1578.   L266

An observer's account of the French colony attempted at Rio de Janeiro in 1557-60. The author presents views differing from those of André Thevet, who also described this colony.

Léry, Jean de. Histoire d'un voyage fait en la terre du Bresil, autrement dite Amerique. [Geneva] Pour les heritiers d'Eustache Vignon, 1594.   L267

The fourth French edition.

Léry, Jean de. Historia navigationis in Brasiliam, quae et America dicitur. Geneva, Eustatius Vignon, 1586.   L268

The first Latin edition.

Léry, Jean de. Historia navigationis in Brasiliam quae et America dicitur. Geneva, Haeredes Eustatius Vignon, 1594.   L269

The second Latin edition.

Le Sage, Alain René. Les avantures de Monsieur Robert Chevalier, dit de Beauchêne, capitaine de filibustiers dans la Nouvelle France. Paris, Etienne Ganeau, 1732.   L270

Despite the author's well known talents for fiction, most critics of this work attribute its origins to an actual narrative of piracy and adventure.

Lescallier, Daniel, baron. Exposé des moyens de mettre en valeur et d'administrer la Guiane. Paris, Du Pont [1798].   L271

A survey of French Guiana, its commerce, inhabitants, administration, etc.

[Lescallier, Daniel, baron.] Mémoire sur la Marine. Paris, Clousier, 1790.   L272

A proposal for a new administration of French maritime affairs with the primary motive of improving overseas trade.

Lescallier, Daniel, baron. Réflexions sur le sort des noirs dans nos colonies. [n.p.] 1789.   L273

An examination of attitudes towards slavery in the French colonies by an opponent of slavery, Daniel Lescallier, who proposes eight policies for the eventual elimination of slavery in French possessions.

Lescallier, Daniel, baron. Traité pratique du gréement des vaisseaux et autres batimens de mer. Paris, Clousier, F. Didot; London, P. Elmsly; Amsterdam, G. Dufour, 1791.   L274

This treatise on masts and rigging includes 34 engraved plates detailing everything from sails to anchors to knots to cannons. The text gives exact instructions on rigging for ships of all sizes, with tables of cordage required.

Lescallier, Daniel, baron. Vocabulaire des termes de marine anglois et françois, en deux parties: orné de planches, avec une explication des figures qui y sont contenues, & des définitions de quelques termes de marine, principalement ceux de gréement. Paris, Imprimerie royale, 1777.   L275

This maritime vocabulary is accompanied by a collection of some three hundred illustrations of various parts of a ship.

Lescarbot, Marc. Histoire de la Nouvelle France. Paris, Jean Milot, 1609. L276
Includes the accounts of North American exploration by Verrazano, Laudonnière, Cartier, and Roberval, as well as details of the De Monts colony and reasons for its failure.

Lescarbot, Marc. Histoire de la Nouvelle France. Paris, Jean Milot, 1612. L277
The second edition.

Lescarbot, Marc. Histoire de la Nouvelle France. Paris, A. Perier, 1618. L278
The third and most complete edition.

Lescarbot, Marc. Nova Francia. Augsburg, C. Dabertzhofer, 1613. L279
The first German edition.

[Lescarbot, Marc.] Les muses de la Nouvelle France. Paris, Jean Millot, 1609. L280
A dramatic production alleged to have been performed in a short-lived French settlement on an island in the St. Croix River.

[Lescarbot, Marc.] Les muses de la Nouvelle France. Paris, Jean Millot, 1612. L281
The second edition.

[Lescarbot, Marc.] Les muses de la Nouvelle France. Paris, A. Perier, 1618. L282
The third edition.

Lescarbot, Marc. Relation derniere de ce qui s'est passé au voyage du sieur de Poutrincourt en la Nouvelle France depuis 20 mois ença. Paris, Jean Millot, 1612. L283
An account of a voyage to Port Royal, Acadia, in 1611.

[Leslie, Charles.] Of Jamaica. A new history of Jamaica. London, J. Hodges, 1740. L284
Thirteen letters form this history of Jamaica, with especially interesting discussions of the constitution and economy of that island.

Lesseps, Jean-Baptiste-Barthélemy, baron de. Journal historique du voyage de M. de Lesseps. Paris, Imprimerie Royale, 1790. L285
De Lesseps served as an interpreter in the Lapérouse expedition, and in 1787 he was landed at Kamchatka with the responsibility of delivering a report on the expedition overland to Paris. His narrative records much of the plant and animal life and commercial possibilities of Siberia.

Lesseps, Jean-Baptiste-Barthélemy, baron de. Travels in Kamtschatka, during the years 1787 and 1788. London, For J. Johnson, 1790. L286
A slightly abridged translation from the first French edition.

Lesseps, Jean-Baptiste-Barthélemy, baron de. Herrn von Lesseps, Gefährten des Grafen de la Perouse, Reise durch Kamtschatka und Sibirien nach Frankreich, aus dem Französischen übersetzt, mit Anmerkungen von Johann Reinhold Forster ... Berlin, Vossischen Buchhandlung, 1791. L287
This translation by Johann Reinhold Forster contains extensive notes by him.

Lesseps, Jean-Baptiste-Barthélemy, baron de. Historisch dagverhaal der reize van den Heer de Lesseps. Utrecht, B. Wild en J. Altheer, 1791-92. L288
The first Dutch edition.

Lesseps, Jean-Baptiste-Barthélemy, baron de. Resa genom Kamtschatka och Sibirien år 1787 och 1788. Upsala, Joh. Edmans Enka, 1793. L289
An abridged Swedish edition with introduction and notes by Samuel Ödmann.

Lest over-gelevert geschrift vande heeren extraordinaire afgesanten der Vereenichde Nederlanden, aenden koninck van Franckryck ... Haarlem, Christiaen Christiaensen, 1622 [i.e. 1662]. L290
Concerns negotiations between France and the Netherlands for a commercial treaty. Text is in French and Dutch.

L'Estra, François. Relation ou journal d'un voyage fait aux Indes Orientales. Paris, E. Michallet, 1677. L291
An account of a voyage from France to the East Indies in the years 1671-75, containing observations on the trade carried on there by other European nations.

Le Tellier, Michel. Carta de un doctor en theologia à un missionero de la China, que le ha propuesto diversas dudas sobre el camino que ha de seguir en estas missiones ... [n.p., 1687.] L292
This work is introduced with a survey of missionary activities and problems in various parts of the world. Le Tellier enumerates works translated into Chinese by the missionaries and points out the need for proficiency in science and mathematics among missionaries sent to China.

Lethinois, André. Avvenimenti memorabili del Principe Baldassare figlio primogenito del Re di Timor e Solor nell' isole Molucche esposti a sua Maesta' Cristianissima. Paris, Knapen, 1769. L293
An appeal to the French king to make en effort to increase French influence and trade in the Moluccas.

Letras anuas dela Compañia de Iesus dela prouincia del Nueuo Reyno de Granada: desde el año de mil y seyscientos y treinta y ocho, hasta el año de mil y seys cientos y quarenta y tres. Zaragoza, 1645. L294
This annual letter from New Granada describes the missions in the province, noting difficulties in making con-

verts, dealing with an epidemic and other problems, but envisions an expanding effort into Ecuador.

Letter book concerning British commerce with Malaga. Manuscript. London, July 24, 1793 to May 20, 1794. **L295**
Concerns the trade in fruit and wine from Malaga to London.

A letter concerning the consequence of an incorporating union, in relation to trade. [Edinburgh] 1706. **L296**
An argument opposing the proposed union of England and Scotland on the basis that it would not be commercially advantageous to Scotland.

A letter concerning the East-India trade, to a gentleman. [London, 1698.] **L297**
An attack on the monopoly of the East India Company.

A letter from a gentleman at Bengal to his friend in London; dated Calcutta, Sept. 8, 1787. London, For John Stockdale, 1788. **L298**
Hastings' successes in India are contrasted with the losses sustained under Parliament's management of affairs in North America.

A letter from a gentleman at London to his friend at Edinburgh. [n.p.] 1700. **L299**
An attempt to convince the Scottish Parliament that it would be wise to avoid pressing claims to the Darien colony.

A letter from a gentleman in America to his friend in Scotland. [n.p., 1699.] **L300**
The author was a Boston merchant who laments the decline of the Scots' colony at Darien. He indicates that there was considerable interest in the Darien venture in Boston.

A letter from a gentleman in the country to his friend at Edinburgh. Edinburgh, G. Mosman, 1696. **L301**
The anonymous author of the letter argues that the Company of Scotland trading to Africa & the Indies will serve both England and Scotland well.

A letter from a gentleman of the Lord Ambassador Howard's retinue ... dated at Fez, Nov. 1, 1669. London, W.G. for Moses Pitt, 1670. **L302**
A narrative of a voyage from London to Morocco, including an appendix describing the products of that country.

A letter from a lawyer of the inner temple, to his friend in the country, concerning the East-India stock, and ... uniting the new and old companies. London, 1698. **L303**
The author analyzes the actions of both the new and the old East India companies, cites improper actions by the new company, and questions the legality of its stock.

A letter from a member of Parliament to his friend in the country, containing his reasons for being against the late act for preventing the retail of spirituous liquors. London, H. Haines [1736]. **L304**
The author states that his opposition was based on his belief that passage of the act would increase imports of French brandy at the expense of rum from the British colonies in the West Indies.

A letter from a member of the last Parliament ... concerning the conduct of the war with Spain. London, T. Cooper, 1742. **L305**
Contains observations on the American commerce of the major European powers.

A letter from a merchant at Jamaica to a member of Parliament in London, touching the African trade. London, For A. Baldwin, 1709. **L306**
An appeal for a more humane treatment of the Negro slaves; a number of cases of extreme cruelty are cited.

A letter from a merchant in the city of London, to the R____t H_____ble W____ P____ esq: upon the affairs and commerce of North America, and the West Indies. London, For J. Scott, 1757. **L307**
A review of England's commercial position in America and Africa, with suggestions for the better securing of the American trade against French competition.

A letter from a merchant of London to a member of Parliament: in answer to a letter from a member of Parliament to his friends in the country, concerning duties on wine and tobacco. London, For A. Dodd, 1733. **L308**
A criticism of an earlier publication by Sir Robert Walpole in which he favored the excise tax.

A letter from a proprietor of India stock, in town, to a proprietor in the country. London, W. Nicoll, 1769. **L309**
A criticism of the directors of the East India Company for refusing to declare an increased dividend.

A letter from a West-India captain, to a merchant in London. London, For J. Nutt, 1703. **L310**
An attempt to promote an English settlement in Darien, to the east of the Scottish colony there. It was to be settled largely from New England.

A letter from a West-India merchant to a gentleman at Tunbridg, concerning that part of the French proposals, which relates to North America ... London, 1712. **L311**
A pamphlet dealing with the British rights to trade in Newfoundland and the West Indies, as opposed to the French rights in those areas.

A letter from an English merchant at Amsterdam, to his friend at London, concerning the trade and coin in England. London, 1695. **L312**

A discussion of England's unfortunate plight in international trade due to the decline of her coinage through clipping.

A letter from some merchants in the out-ports, relating to ... the tobacco trade. [n.p., ca. 1720.]
L313
Arguments against a bill which would limit the importing of poor grades of tobacco.

A letter to a friend, concerning a late pamphlet, entituled, Angliae tutamen, or The safety of England ... London, 1696. L314
A response to a pamphlet which was concerned with banks, lotteries, monopolies, and other aspects of England's financial situation.

A letter to a friend concerning the present proposal of the old East India Company. [n.p., ca. 1699.] L315
A protest against the monopoly of the East India Company, and against the company's loan of 700,000 pounds to the government at eight per cent.

A letter to a friend, in which some account is given of the Brethren's Society for the Furtherance of the Gospel among the Heathen. London, 1769. L316
A description of the Society which was the means for sending Moravian Brethren to the British colonies as missionaries to the Indians, together with some history of those missions.

A letter to a member of Parliament concerning clandestine trade. London, A. Baldwin, 1700.
L317
The author contends that smuggling is aided by cumbersome customs regulations, inadequacy of officials, and frequent changes in inspection practices.

A letter to a member of Parliament concerning the free British fisheries. London, For R. Spavan, 1750. L318
A proposal for improving the British fishery, designating particular ports advantageous for fisheries, costs to be anticipated, and a company with some government investment to encourage private investors.

A letter to a member of Parliament, concerning the importance of our sugar-colonies to Great Britain. London, J. Taylor, 1745. L319
A pamphlet arguing that an increased sugar tax in Great Britain would pose a threat to the prosperity of the Jamaica sugar industry as well as to a number of British industries which sold heavily in Jamaica or in Africa as a part of the Atlantic trade in which Jamaica was a keystone.

A letter to a member of Parliament, concerning the naval store-bill brought in last session: with observations on the plantation-trade ... London, 1720. L320

A comprehensive review of national and colonial trade policies indicating the interrelation of trade from many countries.

A letter to a member of Parliament, concerning the present state of affairs at home and abroad. London, T. Cooper, 1740. L321
Among various issues addressed are Britain's rivalry with Spain and the related issue of trade in the West Indies.

A letter to a member of Parliament, concerning the South-Sea Company: with proposals for settling a certain annual dividend. London, 1720.
L322
Proposes strict controls on the company lest it bring upon the nation's trade the same catastrophic results it was bringing to national finance.

A letter to a member of Parliament, occasion'd by a bill now depending ... to repeal part of the act of navigation. [London, ca. 1719.] L323
The anonymous author contends that the Levant Company had not proved its allegations that Leghorn was a source of raw silk coming into England.

A letter to a member of Parliament, occasion'd by the South Sea Company's scheme for reducing the publick debts. London, J. Roberts, 1720.
L324
A criticism of the policy of granting wide commercial privileges to the company in the West Indies and Africa.

A letter to a member of Parliament on the settling a trade to the South Sea of America. [London] J. Phillips [1711]. L325
An enthusiastic approval of the establishment of the South Sea Company, with plans for an active commerce to South America.

A letter to a member of Parliament, relating to the bill for the opening of a trade, to and from Persia through Russia. London, T. Cooper, 1741.
L326
The view is presented here that establishing a route through Russia would deprive Great Britain of its profitable market for woolens in Turkey which could not be replaced by the woolen trade in Russia and Persia.

A letter to a member of Parliament. Shewing the injustice ... of the proposal lately made by the old East India Company. London, 1701. L327
A condemnation of the old East India Company for securing Parliament's consideration of a proposal to loan the government two million pounds in return for a continuation of its monopoly of the East Indian trade.

A letter to a member of the Honourable House of Commons, on the present important crisis of national affairs. London, Printed for W. Morgan [1762]. L328

A consideration of the progress of the war against France in North America, with the recommendation that no peace be made without Britain's retention of Louisiana, Florida, and Havana.

A letter to a member of the P__t of G__t B____n, occasion'd by the priviledge granted by the French king to Mr. Crozat. London, J. Baker, 1713. L329

A review of the dangers inherent in France's apparent intent to develop the trade of the Mississippi valley. The Mississippi region is described as to size, natural resources, Indian population, and commercial potential.

A letter to a west-country clothier and freeholder, concerning the Parliament's rejecting the French treaty of commerce, by the way of advice, in the ensuing elections ... [n.p.] 1713. L330

A defense of those who voted against the treaty with France because of the adverse effect it would have on England's trade with Portugal which took large quantities of English woolen goods.

A letter to Caleb D'Anvers, esq; occasioned by the depredations committed by the Spaniards in the West-Indies. London, For H. Whitridge, 1729. L331

Observations on recent writings in *The Craftsman*, relative to the British government's inaction in the face of Spanish interruption of British trade in the West Indies.

A letter to Mr. Fox, on the duration of the trial of Mr. Hastings. London, For J. Owen, 1794. L332

This anonymous author points out that the charges against Hastings could not be divorced from England's position as sovereign in part of India, or from Parliament's policies which, in the main, endorsed Hastings' actions.

A letter to Richard Brinsley Sheridan, esq. on the proposed renewal of the charter of the East India Company. London, For J. Debrett, 1793. L333

A reminder of the evils in the East India Company complained of by Burke and Sheridan ten years earlier and an attempt to embarrass them for not opposing these evils as the charter of the company was being considered for renewal.

A letter to Sir John Eyles, baronet, sub-governour of the South-Sea Company. London, For R. Knite, 1722. L334

The author, who signs himself A.B., makes it clear that he expects Eyles' influence to bring about an improvement in the company's affairs.

A letter to Sir R____ H____ wherein is considered, what effect the repeal of those laws which now regulate our commerce with France are likely to have ... London, For A. Baldwin, 1713. L335

A review of England's export situation, with particular emphasis on the cloth trade. R.H. is Sir Robert Harley.

A letter to Sir William Robinson, in relation to a proposal for a trade to the Spanish West-Indies. London, 1707. L336

A discussion of the advantages and disadvantages of certain proposals stated in a previous pamphlet which supported free trade with Spanish possessions in the West Indies.

A letter to the Honourable A____r M____r com___ner of trade and plantation. London, For J. Roberts, 1714. L337

This letter to Arthur Moore is a criticism of the Treaty of Utrecht for its concessions to French trade which the author feels will hinder British manufactures.

A letter to the Lords Commissioners for Trade and Plantations, concerning the advantage of Gibraltar to the trade of Great Britain. London, J. Roberts, 1720. L338

Gibraltar is viewed as essential to England's trade in time of war, and of great value in promoting trade in time of peace.

A letter to the proprietors of East India stock. London, W. Nicoll, 1769. L339

A consideration of the policies and government of the East India Company, reflecting also some concern for the good government of the American colonies.

A letter to the proprietors of East-India stock. Containing a brief relation of the negotiations with government. London, For B. White, 1769. L340

A history of the negotiations between the government and the directors of the East India Company over the amount to be paid to the government and the manner of payment of the company's debt.

A letter to the proprietors of East-India stock, relative to some propositions intended to be moved at the next general court, on Wednesday the 12th of July. London, W. Nicoll, 1769. L341

An appeal to stockholders to insist on policies which will give greater stability to the price of company stock.

A letter to the proprietors of East-India stock, upon the question to be balloted for on Tuesday the 23d day of March ... London, W. Nicoll, 1767. L342

A protest against granting Lord Clive 300,000 pounds for another voyage to India.

A letter to the proprietors of East India stock, upon the question to be ballotted for on Tuesday the 24th day of March ... London, W. Nicoll, 1767. L343

A re-issue of the previous work, with the date in the title altered and "second edition" inserted.

A letter to the proprietors of India stock: containing a reply to some insinuations in an old proprietor's letter to the proprietors on the 13th instant, relative to the ballot of that day ... by a Steady Proprietor ... London, W. Nicoll, 1769.   L344

A survey of the business of the East India Company, setting it in a favorable light.

A letter to the proprietors of India stock, relative to the critical situation of their affairs. London, For A. Hunt, 1767.   L345

The author defends the right of the East India Company to assume the functions of revenue collector in India as opposed to those who saw this activity as a sovereign function to be administered by Parliament.

A Letter to the Right Honourable the Earl of B***, on a late important resignation and its probable consequences ... London, For J. Coote, 1761.   L346

A comprehensive review of the Seven Years War, anticipating peace negotiations in which something must be given up, and it is suggested that commercial concessions would be preferable to territorial.

A letter to the West-India merchants, in answer to their petition ... praying for a prohibition of the trade carried on from the Northern Colonies, to the French and Dutch West India settlements. London, For H. Whitridge & G. Woodfall, 1751.   L347

Points out the advantage to Great Britain of trade between British and other colonies in the New World.

Lettera a' signori del Seminario delle missioni straniere sù le accuse, che danno a' Gesuiti, di non essersi sottomessi sinceramente al nuovo decreto circa gli affari della Cina. [n.p., 1709.]   L348

Although this defense of the Jesuits claims to be translated from the French, there does not appear to have been a French edition.

Lettera d'informazione in cui si spiegano i sentimenti de PP. Gesuiti sopra le controversie della Cina. [n.p.] 1710.   L349

An argument favorable to the Jesuits' cause in the Chinese Rites controversy.

Lettera di risposta ad un' amico del Padre Ivo Anani: sopra la lettera concernente i riti del la China del R. Padre Luigi le Comte ... Cologne, Heredi d'Egmond, 1700.   L350

A commentary on Louis Le Comte's *Lettere ... a Monseigneur le Duc du Maine*, supporting the Jesuit position on the Chinese Rites controversy from the writings of patristic sources.

Lettere annue del Tibet del MDCXXVI e della Cina del MDCXXIV [i.e. 1625]: scritte al M.R.P. Mutio Vitelleschi, generale della Compagnia di Giesu. Rome, Francesco Corbelletti, 1628.   L351

This collection of missionary reports includes Antonio Andrade's account of his mission to Tibet in 1624 and Václav Pantaleone Kirwitzer's report on the political and missionary situation in China.

Letters, containing a correct and important elucidation of the subject of Mr. Hastings's impeachment. London, J. Bell, 1790.   L352

The first and second of an intended series of letters friendly to Warren Hastings, reprinted from *The Oracle*.

Letters, containing a correct and important elucidation of the subject of Mr. Hastings's impeachment, which originally appeared in the Oracle. Second part. London, Printed by and for J. Bell, 1790.   L353

Lettre a Monsieur ** * docteur de Sorbonne. Au sujet de la révocation fiat par M. l'Abbé de Brisacier de son approbation ... au livre intitulé, Defense des nouveaux Chrestiens ... [n.p.] 1700.   L354

This work includes Jacques Charles de Brisacier's approbation of Michel Le Tellier's book, *Defense des nouveaux Chrestiens*, and his subsequent revocation. The point at issue is the acceptance by Jesuit missionaries of Chinese Rites within Christianity.

Lettre a Monsieur ** * docteur de Sorbonne au sujet de la révocation fait par M. l'Abbé de Brisacier de son approbation donnée en 1687 au libre intitulé, Défense des nouveaux Chrétiens & des missionnaires de la Chine. [n.p.] 1700.   L355

Another edition of the previous item.

Lettre a Monsieur ** * touchant les honneurs que les Chinois rendent au philosophe Confucius & à leurs ancêtres. [n.p.] 1700.   L356

Includes also a "second letter" and a letter from the king of Portugal to Cardinal Barberin.

Lettre à un ami en Hollande au sujet de la Nouvelle Compagnie Imperiale des Indes. [Ostend, 1724.]   L357

The right of the Ostend Company to participate in the East Indian trade is defended on the basis that the poverty of the southern Netherlands requires revival of trade.

Lettre a un prelat, sur un ecrit intitulé, Lettre de M. le Cardinal de Tournon, patriarche d'Antioch, &c. à m. Maigrot evêque de Conon, &c. [n.p., 1708.]   L358

A reply to Tournon's letter of 6 October 1706 to Charles Maigrot, vicar apostolic to China.

Lettre d'un ami a un ami; sur l'établissement des fabriques en Dannemarc. [Copenhagen] 1740.   L359

A recommendation that Denmark follow the example of England and Holland and build factories to improve her commercial position.

Lettre d'un cultivateur à son ami, sur la Compagnie des Indes. [Paris, 1769.]   L360

Discusses complaints and charges against the company, concluding that it has perpetrated an injustice upon France.

Lettre d'un docteur de Louvain, a un jeune seigneur flamant, au sujet du differend du Seminaire etranger, & des Jesuites. Brussels, 1700.   L361

An attempt at a balanced presentation of the case between the Jesuits and their critics with respect to the Chinese Rites.

Lettre d'un gentil-homme francois à un de ses amis d'Amsterdam, où il donné des aduis tres-importans sur les desseins de Cromwel, & de sa Republique. [Paris?] 1653.   L362

This pamphlet illustrates French concern regarding Cromwell's intentions, specifically dealing with his policy toward British naval power and any attempt by the English to gain dominance of the high seas.

Lettre diverse dalle Indie orientali de nuovo venute: le quali narrano molte cose notabili del gran regno del Giappone, ne gli anni, 74. 75. & 76 ... Turino, 1579.   L363

Five letters reporting missionary progress in Japan and Goa. The authors are Francisco Cabral, Monsignor Carnero, and Gomez Vaz.

Lettres annales du Jappon, des années M.DC.XIII. & M.DC.XIV: où plusieurs choses d'edification sont racontees fidelement, & les martyres arrivez durant la persecution desdictes annees. Lyon, Claude Morillon, 1618.   L364

The authors of the letters are Sebastião Vieira and Gabriel de Matos. They report active repression of the missions by the authorities. Brief news from the Philippines, Madagascar, and Mozambique is included.

Lettres d'un actionnaire sur le commerce de la Compagnie des Indes. Avignon, 1764.   L365

A defense of the Compagnie des Indes as France's dominant overseas trading company.

Lettres d'un François à un Hollandois, au sujet des differends survenus entre la France & la Grand-Bretagne, touchant leurs possessions respectives dans l'Amérique septentrionale. [n.p.] 1755.   L366

A review of the causes of Anglo-French hostilities in America, from a French point of view, and with the intention of persuading the Dutch correspondent of England's aggressiveness.

Lettres d'un François à un Hollandois, au sujet des differends survenus entre la France et la Grande-Bretagne, touchant leurs possessiones respectives dans l'Amerique septentrionale. Paris, P. La Rive, 1755.   L367

Another edition of the foregoing item, without significant change in text.

Lettres edifiantes et curieuses: ecrites des missions etrangeres par quelques missionnaires de la Compagnie de Jesus. Paris, 1703-1776.   L368

This series reflects the continued interest in France in the progress of the Jesuit missions in various parts of the world. The termination of the series reflects the suppression of the Society of Jesus by papal decree.

Lettres et pieces, concernant les changemens actuels de Portugal, à l'égard des Jésuites, envoyées par le nonce résident à Lisbonne, à la Secrétairerie de l'État ecclésiastique ... [n.p., 1758].   L369

These are the charges made against the Jesuits in Paraguay as presented at the Holy Office in Rome, together with the deliberations and responses of the cardinals.

Le Vaillant, François. Voyage ... dans l'intérieur de l'Afrique. Paris, Chez Leroy, 1790.   L370

An account of sixteen months of travel in Kaffirland, with eleven illustrations by the author.

Le Vaillant, François. Travels into the interior parts of Africa, by the way of the Cape of Good Hope. London, For G.G.J. and J. Robinson, 1790.   L371

The first English edition.

Le Vaillant, François. Resa uti Södra Africa, åren 1780 til 1783. Åbo, J.C. Frenckells, 1795.   L372

An abridged Swedish translation by Samuel Ödmann.

Le Vaillant, François. Second voyage dans l'intérieur de l'Afrique, par le Cap de Bonne-Espérance. Paris, H.J. Jansen, 1794-95.   L373

Describes a second journey into the African interior during the years 1783-85, giving informative material on the country of Namaqualand.

Le Vaillant, François. New travels into the interior parts of Africa, by the way of the Cape of Good Hope, in the years 1783, 84, and 85. London, For G.G. and J. Robinson, 1796.   L374

The first English edition, adding a map of southern Africa which shows the routes of the author's two trips into the interior.

Le Vaillant, François. Sednare resa uti Södra Africa, åren 1784 och 1785, fran Goda Hopps Udden jämte Atlantiska Hafwet til och innom Wändkresten. Stockholm, Kongl. Ordens Boktryckeriet, hos Assessoren Johan Pfeiffer, 1798.   L375

The Swedish translation does not include the illustrations found in the French and English editions.

Lévis, Pierre-Marc-Gaston, duc de. [Papers on Saint Domingue.] Manuscript. 1816-[182-].
L376
  Letters, memoranda, mémoires, and observations made during a time of continuing unrest in the former French colony by Frenchmen intent on restoring their authority there.

Le Wright, J. (John). Two proposals becoming England at this juncture to undertake ... a collony in the West-Indies. [London] 1706. L377
  A proposal for a commercial colony on the Isthmus of Darien, near the defunct Scots' colony. This was to be an English enterprise, linking American and East Indian commerce.

[Leyden, John.] A historical and philosophical sketch of the discoveries & settlements of the Europeans in northern and western Africa. Edinburgh, J. Moir [etc.] 1799. L378
  This work is a survey of the knowledge Europeans had acquired about north and west Africa by the end of the eighteenth century, and includes considerable information on the efforts of the Danes, Swedes, and English to establish colonies in Africa.

Leydts praetjen, van desen tegenwoordige tyt en gelegendheydt. Leyden, P. Claesz, 1652. L379
  A conversation concerning the possibilities of peace with England in which it is made clear that peace would not be to the advantage of Dutch trade.

L'Hermite, Jacques. Breeder verhael ende klare beschrijvinge van tghene den Admirael Cornelis Matelief de Jonge inde Oost-Indien. Rotterdam, Jan Janssz., 1608. L380
  An account of Dutch victories in the East Indies, as they began to establish themselves firmly in the markets there at the expense of the Portuguese.

L'Hermite, Jacques. Journael vande Nassausche Vloot ofte beschryvingh vande voyagie om den gantschen aerdt-kloot. Amsterdam, Hessel Gerritsz ende Jacob Pietersz Wachter, 1626.
L381
  An account of a Dutch attempt to molest the Spanish on the coast of Peru, in Chile, and at Acapulco in order to gain a foothold on the western coast of South America.

Libro di conventioni et de debbitori & altre cose ... et salariati. Manuscript. [Italy, ca. 1590.]
L382
  An account book of an Italian merchant covering the years 1542 to 1590.

Lierzang op de verklaarde onafhanglijkheid der Noord-Amerikaansche Staaten. [Dordrecht, 1782.] L383
  A lyric poem celebrating the independence of the United States.

Lieudé de Sepmanville, François Cyprien Antoine, Baron. Détail particulier pour la carte de la Gonave, ajoutée en 1788 au pilote de l'isle de Saint-Domingue. [Paris, Imprimerie Royale, 1788.] L384
  A correction to cartographical and navigational information published previously relative to the harbor at Gonave and nearby points on the island of Santo Domingo.

Liewen, Carl Gustaf. [Circulare-bref til Krigsrätterne. November 8, 1799.] Stockholm, Kongl. Tryckeriet, 1799. L385
  Concerns disposition of cases when military personnel have been attacked while assisting customs officials in their duties.

Ligon, Richard. A true & exact history of the island of Barbadoes. London, H. Moseley, 1657.
L386
  A description of Barbados, with special emphasis on the sugar trade.

Lilio, Zaccaria, Bishop. Orbis breviarium. Florence, Antonio di Bartolommeo Miscomini, 1493. L387
  A compendium of geographical information taken from a large number of classical sources. The material is arranged in alphabetical dictionary fashion.

Lilio, Zaccaria, Bishop. Orbis breviarium. Venice, Johannes & Gregorius de Gregoriis, de Forlivio [after 1500.] L388
  A better-indexed but otherwise little changed edition.

Lilio, Zaccaria, Bishop. Breve descrittione del mondo. Venice, Gabriel Giolito de Ferrari, 1552.
L389
  The first translation of this gazetteer.

Liljencrantz, Johan, greve. Tal, om Sveriges utrikes handel i allmånhet, och den Levantiska. Stockhom, L. Salvius, 1770. L390
  Count Johan Liljencrantz (formerly Johan Westerman) was the royal advisor on trade to Adolphus Frederick II. The work is an account of Swedish foreign trade in general with the Levant and Asia Minor receiving specific mention.

Lille (France). La compagnie me marque, Monsieur, par sa lettre du 10 de ce mois, qu' elle veut bien consentir que les tabacs en côtes restés en dépôt dans les bureaux ... [Lille, 1754.]
L391

Lille (France). La compagnie, Monsieur, par sa lettre du 22 de ce mois, nous marque qu'elle est enformée que les receveurs des fermes en Flandres & en Haynaut, ont fait jusqu'à présent une distinction entre les feüilles & les côtes de tabac ... [Lille, 1749.] L392

Lille (France). Nous ne doutons pas, Monsieur, que vous n'ayes eû connoissance de la Déclaration du Roy du 4 may dernier, qui impose un droit de trente sols par livre sur tous les tabacs étrangers ... [Lille, 1749.]   L393

Lille (France). Directeur des Fermes du Roi. Copie d'une lettre de messieurs les Fermiers Généraux du Roy, à M. Aubourg Directeur à Lille. A Paris le 16 janvier 1738. [Lille, 1738.]   L394
   This letter contains instructions relative to the collection of taxes.

Lille (France). Directeur des Fermes du Roi. M. De La Motte, Monsieur, me marque par sa lettre du 26 de ce mois, que par l'examen qu'il fait de la régie de mon département ... [Lille, 1751.]   L395

Lille (France). Directeur des Fermes du Roi. Nous sommes prévenus depuis longtemps, Monsieur, de la négligence des Commis aux Huiles de votre Département ... [Lille, 1752.]   L396

Lille (France). Directeur des Fermes du Roi. Nous vous avons marqué le 11. de ce mois Monsieur, rélativement à notre délibérations du 22 septembre dernier, que les frais de transport des tabacs de saisie ... [Lille, 1751.]   L397

[Lilly, Christian.] S.ʳ Francis Wheler's expedition in the West Indies. With his return into England. Manuscript. [1693.]   L398
   An account of a naval expedition against the French in Martinique and Newfoundland, which failed to accomplish anything but the destruction of French settlements on St. Pierre. The author was the military engineer with the expedition, and his account includes six maps and plans of harbors in Martinique and Newfoundland.

Lima (Peru). Tribunal del Consulado. Memorial del Tribunal del Consulado de Lima ... [Lima? ca. 1750.]   L399
   The maritime council in Lima petitions for commercial prerogatives similar to those of Seville.

[Lind, John.] A letter to the right honourable Willoughby Bertie ... in which His Lordship's candid and liberal treatment of the now earl of Mansfield is fully vindicated. London, For T. Payne and son, T. Cadell, and J. Sewell, 1778.   L400
   A pamphlet concerned with the argument over initial causes of the American Revolution, whether they were American or British in origin.

[Lind, John.] Remarks on the principal acts of the thirteenth Parliament of Great Britain. London, For T. Payne, 1775.   L401
   The acts examined relate to the American colonies.

Lindner, Cornelius. Gründliche Anleitung zum nützlichen Gebrauche der Erd-u. Himmels-Kugeln: den Anfängern in Erlernung der Geographie und Astronomie zum Besten ... Nürnberg, Peter Conrad Monath, 1726.   L402
   A manual on the construction and use of terrestrial and celestial globes.

Lindsay, John. A voyage to the coast of Africa. London, S. Paterson, 1759.   L403
   A description of Senegal and Gorée by the chaplain of one of the ships sent there to fight the French.

Lindsay, Patrick. The interest of Scotland considered. Edinburgh, R. Fleming, 1733.   L404
   A treatise on the agriculture, trade, manufacture, and fisheries of Scotland.

The linen spinster, in defense of the linen manufactures, &c. To be continued as Mrs. Rebecca Woollpack gives occasion. Number I. London, J. Roberts, 1720.   L405
   An argument against restraints upon imported cloths, and against the violence with which some had attempted to show their displeasure at the wearing of imports which tended to replace domestic manufactures. A response to Sir Richard Steele's *The spinster*.

[Linguet, Simon Nicolas Henri.] Lettre de mr. De** a mr. R** en reponse a la sienne sur la liberté de l'Escaut. Amsterdam, 1781.   L406
   The author contends that freedom of navigation of the Scheldt River would not restore the former commercial prominence of Antwerp.

The linnen and woollen manufactory discoursed: with the nature of companies and trade in general. London, For Geo. Huddleston, 1698.   L407
   A criticism of the joint stock company as the most effective type of enterprise for organizing and directing commerce, particulary in the linen industry.

Linschoten, Jan Huygen van. Itinerario, voyage ofte schipvaert, van Ian Huygen van Linschoten naer Oost ofte Portugaels Indien ... Amsterdam, Cornelis Claesz, 1595-96.   L408
   This is the first edition of a comprehensive guide to the commerce and navigation of the East Indies and the South Atlantic Ocean, including thirty-six illustrations and six maps.

Linschoten, Jan Huygen van. Itinerarium ofte schipvaert naer Oost ofte Portugaels Indien. Amsterdam, Jan Evertsz Cloppenburch, 1623.   L409
   The third Dutch edition.

Linschoten, Jan Huygen van. Discours of voyages into ye Easte & West Indies. London, John Wolfe, 1598. L410
The first English edition.

Linschoten, Jan Huygen van. Navigatio ac itinerarium. The Hague, A. Henricus, 1599. L411
The first Latin edition.

Linschoten, Jan Huygen van. Histoire de la navigation ... aux Indes Orientales. Amsterdam, Jean Evertsz Cloppenburgh, 1619. L412
The second French edition which was the first to be fully translated and to make use of the illustrations and maps of the original Dutch issue.

Linschoten, Jan Huygen van. Histoire de la navigation ... aux Indes Orientales. Amsterdam, Evert Cloppenburgh, 1638. L413
The third edition in French.

Linschoten, Jan Huygen van. Voyagie ofte Schipvaert ... by noorden om lange Noorvvegen ... Franeker, Gerard Ketel [1601]. L414
Accounts of Dutch voyages in search of a northeast passage in 1594 and 1595. The author was a member of the expeditions, and his description is accompanied by fifteen maps and charts.

Linschoten, Jan Huygen van. Twee journalen van twee verscheyde voyagien gedaen door ... Norwegen, de Noordt-Caep, Laplandt, Finlandt ... Amsterdam, G.J. Saeghman [1663?]. L415
An abridged version of Linschoten's northern voyages.

Linton, Anthony. Newes of the complement of the art of navigation. And of the mightie empire of Cataia ... London, Felix Kyngston, 1609. L416
An attempt to encourage English interest in the discovery of a northeast passage to China.

Lionne, Artus de, Bishop of Rosalie. Lettre ... a Monsieur Charmot, Directeur du Seminaire des Missions Etrangeres de Paris, a Canton. [n.p.] 1700. L417
The author responded to Jesuit assertions that he had misused his source material by presenting here in their original languages letters from which he had translated in his earlier edition.

Lionne, Artus de, Bishop of Rosalie. Lettre ... a Monsieur Charmot, Directeur du Seminaire des Missions Etrangeres de Paris, a Canton. Rome, 1700. L418
A critique of Michel Le Tellier's *Défense des nouveaux Chrestiens* which was a defense of Jesuit missionary policies in China.

Lionne, Artus de, Bishop of Rosalie. Lettre ... a Monsieur Charmot, Directeur du Seminaire des Missions Etrangeres de Paris, a Canton. [n.p.] 1700. L419
A reprint of the Rome edition above.

Lionne, Paule Payen de. Lettre de Madame de Lionne aux Jesuites. [n.p., 1701.] L420
A defense of Bishop Artus Lionne by his mother against attacks by the Jesuits for his stand on the Chinese Rites.

Lipen, Martin. Navigatio Salomonis Ophiritica illustrata. Wittenberg, A. Hartmann, 1660. L421
In this work the author attempts to locate the elusive gold-rich kingdom of Ophir in South America.

L'Isle, Claude de. Relation historique du royaume de Siam. Paris, G. de Luyne, 1684. L422
A description of Siam, its rulers and people, inspired by the interest of the French East India Company in that area.

L'Isle, Guillaume de. Atlas nouveau, contenant toutes les parties du monde. Amsterdam, Jean Cóvens & Corneille Mortier [ca. 1741]. L423
This large atlas is made primarily from the works of de l'Isle, but also includes maps of Henry Popple, Placide, Jaillot, Sanson, and G. Laws.

L'Isle, Guillaume de. Carte de la Louisiane et du cours du Mississippi. Paris, Chez l'Auteur, 1718. L424
A map of the Mississippi and its tributaries in considerable detail, with Indian tribes and villages, French forts, and the routes of explorers indicated.

L'Isle, Guillaume de. Carte du Canada ou de la Nouvelle France. Paris, Chez l'Auteur, 1703. L425
This North American map shows possible passages westward out of Hudson Bay; it also includes Lahontan's Long River, but notes that it may not be accurately placed.

L'Isle, Guillaume de. Carte du Canada qui comprend la partie septentrionale des Etats Unis d'Amèrique. Paris, Dezauche, 1783. L426
A re-issue of a map first published in 1703, with few alterations except for insertion of "Etats Unis" on both the cartouche and on the map.

L'Isle, Joseph Nicolas de. Explication de la carte des nouvelles decouvertes au nord de la Mer du Sud. Paris, Desaint et Saillant, 1752. L427
A pamphlet and map depicting discoveries along the northwest coast of North America, including the de Fonte passage.

L'Isle, Joseph Nicolas de. Nouvelles cartes des decouvertes de l'Amiral de Fonte et autres navigateurs Espagnols, Portugais, Anglois, Hollandois, François & Russes. Paris, 1753. L428

A survey of the entire northwest passage problem, including the narrative of the fictious voyage of Admiral de Fonte.

A list of copies of charters, from the Commissioners for Trade and Plantations, presented to the Honourable the House of Commons ... the 25th of April 1740. London, 1741. L429
Includes the charters of Maryland, Connecticut, Rhode Island, Massachusetts, Pennsylvania, and Georgia.

A list of merchant-ships taken by the Spaniards. [n.p., 1742.] L430
A record of 335 ships taken by the Spaniards between September 12, 1739, and January 11, 1742. Included are names of the captains, port of embarkation and destination, date of capture, and the names of Spanish ports to which the ships were taken.

List of the members of Parliament who voted for an act for asserting the Indian and African Company's right to their colony of Caledonia. Manuscript. [n.p.] January 14, 1701. L431
A manuscript listing the advocates of rights for the Company of Scotland, as shown by their voting for a resolution favorable to that company.

Lithander, Daniel. Oförgripeliga tankar om nödwändigheten af skogarnas bettre wård ock ans i Finland. Åbo, Jacob Merckell [1753]. L432
In addition to discussing the preservation of forests in Finland, this thesis considers the value of Great Britain's colonies to the mother country.

Lithgow, William. The totall discourse, of the rare adventures, and painefull peregrinations of long nineteen yeares travayles, from Scotland, to the most famous kingdomes in Europe, Asia, and Africa. London, Nicholas Okes, 1632. L433
The first edition of the full text, recounting the author's three travels abroad, including extensive experience in the Near East and in North Africa.

Lithgow, William. 19 jaarige lant-reyse, uyt Schotlant nae de vermaerde deelen werelts Europa, Asia en Africa. Amsterdam, J. Benjamin, 1653. L434
The second Dutch edition.

Litterae annuae Societatis Jesu anni MDC. Antwerp, Heredes Martini Nutii & Joannem Meursium, 1618. L435
These reports included European establishments only.

Litterae annuae Societatis Jesu anni MDCI. Antwerp, Heredes Martini Nutii & Joannem Meursium, 1618. L436
The only non-European report included is a brief one from Angola.

Litterae Societatis Jesu, anno MDCII. et MDCIII. e Sinis, Molucis, Japone ... Mainz, Balthasari Lipii, 1607. L437
A collection of five letters from Jesuit missions, including two from China, two from the Moluccas, and one from Japan.

Litterae Societatis Jesu annorum duorum MDCXIII, et MDCXIV ad patres, et fratres eiusdem Societatis. Lyons, Claudium Dayne, 1619. L438
This collection includes reports from Mexico, Peru, and the Philippine Islands.

Litterae Societatis Jesu duorum annorum M.D.XCIIII et M.D.XCV. ad patres et fratres eiusdem Societatis ... Naples, Tarquinium Longum, 1604. L439
This collection includes reports from missions in Mexico, Peru, Brazil, and the East Indies.

Little, Otis. The state of trade in the northern colonies considered. London, G. Woodfall, 1748. L440
The author's purpose was to encourage settlement and improve the commerce of North America.

Littleton, Edward. The groans of the plantations: or, A true account of their grievous and extreme sufferings by the heavy imposition upon sugar. London, M. Clark, 1689. L441
A criticism of taxes and regulations upon the sugar trade of Barbados, urging England to observe the methods and profitability of the Dutch sugar trade.

[Livingston, Philip.] The other side of the question: or, A defence of the liberties of North-America. In answer to a late friendly address to all reasonable Americans, on the subject of our political confusions. New York, James Rivington, 1774. L442
An attack upon *A late friendly address to all reasonable Americans* by Thomas Bradbury Chandler, also published in 1774. Livingston's argument is based largely on natural rights which governments could confirm but not deny.

Livorno (Italy). Laws, etc. Collezione degl' ordini municipali di Livorno. Livorno, Carlo Giorgi, 1798. L443
A collection of commercial regulations going back to the sixteenth century, and including also the *Statuti de Mercanzia* of Florence.

Livro das cidades, portos, e fortalezas da conquista da India Oriental. Manuscript. [Portugal? ca. 1750.] L444
A book of twenty-three water-color plans of harbors, forts, and cities in Portuguese India.

[Lloyd, Charles.] The conduct of the late administration examined. Boston, Edes and Gill, 1767. L445

A case against the Rockingham Ministry that failed to adequately explain or enforce the Stamp Act. Appendices include letters, extracts from newspapers and other documentary material.

[Lobo, Jerónimo.] Neue Beschreibung und Bericht der wahren Beschaffenheit 1. Des Mohrenlandes, sonderlich des abyssinischen Käyserthums. 2. Des Ursprungs Nyli ... Nuremberg, Johann Hoffmanne Kunsth, 1670. L446

This German edition of Lobo's description of Ethiopia is based upon the English translation by Peter Wyche, for the Royal Society.

[Lobo, Jerónimo.] Relazioni varie cavate da una traduzione Inglese dell' originale Portoghese. Florence, Piero Matini, 1693. L447

An Italian edition of Peter Wyche's English translation.

Lobo, Jerónimo. Voyage historique d'Abissinie. Paris & The Hague, P. Gosse & J. Neaulme, 1728. L448

This first complete edition contains Lobo's narrative, and a series of dissertations on Ethiopia added by the translator, Joachim Legrand.

Lobo, Jerónimo. A voyage to Abyssinia ... With a continuation of the history of Abyssinie down to the beginning of the eighteenth century, and fifteen dissertations on various subjects ... by Mr. Le Grand. London, A. Bettesworth and C. Hitch, 1735. L449

This English edition is a translation by Samuel Johnson from the French edition.

Lobo, Jerónimo. Reise nach Habessinien, und zu den Quellen des Nils ... Zürich, Orell, Geszner, Fuszli, 1793. L450

Edited by Theophil Friedrich Ehrmann, this edition includes material from Giacomo Baratti, Charles Jacques Poncet, and al-Maqrizi, all earlier authors of observations on Ethiopia. Ehrmann also adds extensive notes of his own.

Loccenius, Johan. De iure maritimo & navali libri tres. Stockholm, Joannis Janssonii, 1651. L451

A text in maritime law covering such topics as shipwrecks, piracy, marine contracts, fishing rights, etc. Apparently the second issue of the first edition.

[Locke, John.] Histoire de la navigation, son commencement, son progrès & ses découvertes jusqu' à présent. Paris, Etienne Ganeau, 1722. L452

Includes historical and statistical information on the West Indies, a critical bibliography of contemporary geographical literature, and a catalog of the map collection of Theodorus Boendermaker.

[Lockman, John.] The vast importance of the herring fishery, etc. to these kingdoms. London, For W. Owen [ca. 1750]. L453

A collection of three letters addressed to a member of parliament urging policies which would encourage the fishing industry.

Lockman, John. The vast importance of the herring fishery, etc., to these kingdoms. London, For W. Owen, 1750. L454

The second edition.

Lockyer, Charles. An account of the trade in India. London, S. Crouch, 1711. L455

A very detailed record of commercial opportunities and practices encountered on the author's voyage from Madras to Achin, Malacca, Condore, Canton, Persia, the Malabar Coast, and the Cape of Good Hope.

Lodewijcksz, Willem. Prima pars descriptionis itineris navalis in Indiam Orientalem ... Amsterdam, C. Nicolai, 1598. L456

An account of the first Dutch expedition into the East Indies under Cornelius Houtman in the years 1595-97. The author was a commissary with the fleet.

Lodewijcksz, Willem. 'Teerste boeck—Historie van Indien: waer inne verhaelt is de avonturen die de Hollantse schepen bejegent zijn: oock een particulier verhael der conditien religien, manieren eñ[de] huys-houdinge der volckeren ... Amsterdam, Michiel Colijn, 1617. L457

The third edition in oblong quarto.

Lodewijcksz, Willem. Nova tabula, insularum Javae, Sumatrae, Borneonis et aliarum Malaccam ... Amsterdam, Cornelius Nicolai, 1598. L458

A detailed map of some of the East Indian islands, the first Dutch mapping of that area.

Löfling, Per. Iter hispanicum, eller, Resa til spanska länderna uti Europa och America ... Stockholm, Lars Salvii, 1758. L459

Löfling was a student of Linnaeus who botanized in Spain and in South America where he died. The book includes a brief biography and two letters to Linnaeus.

Löw, Conrad. Meer oder Seehanen Buch. Cologne, B. Buchholtz, 1598. L460

A collection of voyages, including accounts of Spanish and Portuguese explorations and distinctive accounts of the first northeastern voyage of Barents and the first East Indian voyage of Houtman.

[Logan, John.] Considérations générales sur le procès intenté a W. Hastings, écuyer, ancien gouverneur-général de Bengale. Londres, et se trouve à Paris, Buisson, 1788. L461

A translation of the above item with a fifty-two page preface introducing the impeachment to French readers, and thirteen pages of explanatory notes following the text.

[Logan, John.] A review of the principal charges against Warren Hastings. London, John Stockdale and John Murray, 1788. L462
   A defense of Hastings by a clergyman who contends that expediency and the national interest were responsible for many of Hastings' actions in India.

Lombard, Ezechiel. Antwoorden op de vraage. Middelburg, P. Gillissen, 1780. L463
   A treatise on the three-master merchant ships used by the Dutch in the East India trade. Included are two large engraved illustrations showing cutaway views of the ships and the sailing of the vessels on the ocean.

London, John. An answer to the pretended remarks on Mr. Webber's scheme, and the Draper's pamphlet. London, J. Robinson [etc.] 1741. L464
   A response to arguments against Webber's proposal for restrictions on the export of unmanufactured wool.

London. Committee of Tea Dealers. A narrative of the conduct of the tea-dealers, during the late sale of teas at the India House. London, For T. Cadell, 1785. L465
   A discussion of the difficulties between the tea dealers and the East India Company officials over the manner in which the company chose to market its tea.

London. Shoemakers. To the honourable House of Commons. The humble petition of the poor journeymen shooe-makers of the city of London, Westminster and Southwark, and their brethren of the countrey. [London, ca. 1689.] L466
   A complaint against a law that had favored the export of leather and had resulted in a reduced demand for English shoes from abroad.

[Long, Edward.] The history of Jamaica. London, T. Lowndes, 1774. L467
   An account of the major economic activities on Jamaica with descriptions of its cities, harbors, and natural productions.

Long, J. (John), Indian trader. Voyages and travels of an Indian interpreter and trader, describing the manners and customs of the North American Indians. London, For the Author, 1791. L468
   A graphic record of Indian life and customs and of the fur trade in the Hudson Bay and Great Lakes regions. Includes an Ojibway vocabulary.

Long, J. (John), Indian trader. J. Long's ... Reisen, enthaltend: eine Beschreibung de Sitten und Gewohnheiten der nordamerikanischen Wilden: der englischen Forts oder Schanzen längs dem St. Lorenzflusse, dem See Ontario, u.s.w. ... Hamburg, Benjamin Gottlob Hoffmann, 1791. L469
   One of two German editions issued in 1791, this one has an introduction describing the geography of Canada and several explanatory footnotes.

Long, J. (John), Indian trader. Voyages chez différentes nations sauvages de l'Amérique septentrionale. Paris, Prault & Fuchs, 1794. L470
   The first French edition, omitting the vocabulary in various Indian languages, but adding notes by the translator.

Long, Richard. Manuscript letter signed, to James Vernon, dated 8 January 1700. L471
   A covering letter to the following item. James Vernon was secretary of state.

Long, Richard. Manuscript letter signed, to William III, dated 8 January 1700. L472
   A reporting of information gained from Spanish and Portuguese seamen to the effect that the Plate River reached inland near to the sources of silver which would afford the Spaniards a new outlet for exporting it.

Long, Richard. Manuscript letter to William III, dated 23 November 1700. L473
   This manuscript relates to a proposal current in England for the establishment of an English colony on the Isthmus of Darien. The author presents information on the geography of this region and on the river route by which the English could reach the rich inland city of Santa Fe.

Longhead, Waitwell. A letter from Waitwell Longhead, Esq; of Freeland-Manor in the county of Bucks, to his friend Sir Politick Wou'd-Be ... Wherein the late circumstances of the nation, with respect to foreign-affairs, are set in a true light. London, J. Roberts, 1731. L474
   A defense of the Walpole ministry for its diplomatic skill in building an alliance that forced the dissolution of the Ostend Company at the Treaty of Vienna.

Lopes, Duarte. Relatione del reame di Congo et delle circonvicine contrade. Rome, B. Grassi, 1591. L475
   A very inclusive description of Africa edited by Filippo Pigafetta. Portuguese commerce in western Africa is described in detail, and two outstanding maps of Africa are included.

Lopes, Duarte. A report of the kingdome of Congo, a region of Africa. And of the countries that border rounde about the same. London, John Wolfe, 1597. L476
   The first English edition.

[Lopes, Duarte.] Beschrijvinge van't koningkrijck Congo. Amsterdam, J.J. Bouman, 1658. L477
   This Dutch edition has illustrations differing from those in the Rome edition of 1591.

Lopes Serra, João. Vida o paneguirico funebre. Al senor Alfonso Furtado Castro do Rio de Mendoncà. Manuscript. Brazil, 1676.   L478
A funeral oration celebrating the life and achievements of a colonial governor of Brazil.

López, Gregorio. Lettera annua della prouincia delle Filippine dell'anno M.DC.VIII. Rome, Bartolomeo Zannetti, 1611.   L479
An annual report from Jesuit missions in the Philippines, with separate reports on nine individual mission locations.

López, Juan Luis. Discurso juridico, historico-politico, en defensa de la jurisdicion real ilustracion de la provision de veinte de febrero del año passado de 1684 ... Lima, 1685.   L480
A defense of the decree of February 20, 1684 in which the crown had ordered the church to observe the government's position of priority with respect to governing the Indians. The original decree is included also.

Lopez de Cogolludo, Diego. Historia de Yucathan. Madrid, Juan Garcia Infanzon, 1688.   L481
An authoritative history of Yucatan from the earliest Spanish incursions to 1665. The author used major published sources and manuscript materials not published previously.

López de Gómara, Francisco. Hispania victrix. Primera y segunda parte de la historia general de las Indias cō todo el descubrimiento, y cosas notables que han acaescido dende que se ganaron hasta el año de 1551. Medina del Campo, Guillermo de Millis, 1553.   L482
The second edition of one of the major chronicles of Spanish discovery, exploration and conquest in the New World.

López de Gómara, Francisco. La historia general de las Indias. Antwerp, Juan Steelsio, 1554.   L483
One of three editions published in Antwerp in 1554.

López de Gómara, Francisco. Historia de las Indias. Madrid, 1749.   L484
A part of a collected work edited by Barcia Carbillido y Zúñiga.

López de Gómara, Francisco. Historia del illustriss. et valorosiss. capitano Don Ferdinando Cortes ... et quando discoperse, et acquisto la Nuova Hispagna. Rome, Valerio & Luigi Dorici, 1556.   L485
The first Italian edition of the second part of Gomara's history of the West Indies, dealing primarily with the conquest of Mexico.

López de Gómara, Francisco. La seconda parte delle historie generali dell' India ... si tratta particolarmente della presa del Re Atabalippa, delle perle, dell' oro, delle spetierie, ritrovate alle Malucche, & delle guerre civili tra gli Spagnuoli. Venice, Andrea Arrivabene, 1557.   L486
A different translation from that of Cravaliz, published in 1555.

López de Gómara, Francisco. Historia, delle nuove Indie Occidentali. Venice, Giovanni Bonadio, 1564.   L487
A translation by Agostino di Cravaliz of the first part of Gómara's history, covering the discovery, early exploration, and first settlement of the New World by the Spaniards.

López de Gómara, Francisco. La historia generale delle Indie Occidentali. Rome, Valerio & Luigi Dorici, 1556.   L488
The first separate Italian edition of the first part of this history of Spanish America.

López de Gómara, Francisco. Historia delle nuove Indie Occidentali. Venice, Camillo Franceschini, 1576.   L489
This edition follows closely the text of the 1564 edition.

López de Gómara, Francisco. The pleasant historie of the conquest of the Weast India, now called New Spayne. London, Henry Bynneman [1578].   L490
The first English edition.

López de Gómara, Francisco. Histoire generalle des Indes Occidentales. Paris, Michel Sonnius, 1587.   L491
The second French edition.

Lopez Ruiz, Santiago José. Propuesta politico-moral: sobre varias reflexiones, en que se hace entenden la razon de un individuo, amante del buen orden, y celoso de los altos derechos de la religion y del estado. Manuscript. [n.p., 1789.]   L492
A review of all aspects of religious, civil, and economic life in Peru by a prominent churchman of Quito.

Losa, Francisco de. La vida, que hizo el siervo de Dios Gregorio Lopez, en algunos lugares de esta Nueva España. Lisbon, Pedro Crasbeeck, 1615.   L493
The biography of a Spanish hermit who lived in Mexico from 1562 to 1596, by one who spent eight years with him.

Losa, Francisco de. La vie du bienheureux Gregoire Lopez ... de la traduction de Mr Arnauld d'Andilly ... Paris, Pierre le Petit, 1674.   L494
French edition of the preceding biography.

Loskiel, George Henry. Geschichte der Mission der evangelischen Brüder unter Indianern in Nord-Amerika. Barby, Brüdergemeinen; Leipzig, Paul Gotthelf Kummer, 1789. L495
An account of the missionary activities of the Evangelical Brethren among the American Indians, chiefly in New York and Pennsylvania, but also as far west as Detroit.

Loskiel, George Henry. Historiske beskrifning öfwer Evangeliska Brödernes missions-arbete ibland Indianerne uti Norra America. Stockholm, Joh. Christ. Holmberg, 1792. L496
Swedish edition of the previous item.

Lotter, Matthäus Albrecht. Mappemonde ou carte générale de l'univers ... avec le tour du monde du Lieut. Cook et tous les découvertes nouvelles. Augsburg, M.A. Lotter, 1782. L497
This map records the routes of Captain Cook on all three of his circumnavigations.

Lotter, Tobias Conrad. America Septentrionalis, concinnata juxta observationes Dnn Academiae Regalis Scientiarum et nonnulorum aliorum, et juxta annotationes recentissimas. Augsburg, Tobiam Conr. Lotter [ca. 1763]. L498
Based on a map from early in the eighteenth century, the coloring added suggests political changes occurring during the Seven Years War.

Lotter, Tobias Conrad. Mappa geographica regionem Mexicanam et Floridam terrasque adjacentes. Augsburg [ca. 1756]. L499
Based indirectly upon the de l'Isle map of North America of 1703, through intermediate issues by Homann and Seutter, with small modifications.

[Louis de la Mere de Dieu.] Relation du martyre au' ont souffert aux Indes deux religieux Carmes deschaussez. Paris, François Pelican, 1647. L500
A celebration and description of the deaths of Denys de la Nativité and Redempt de la Croix, Carmelites serving in Achin.

Louis XIV, King of France. De par le Roy. Extrait des registres du Conseil d'Estat. Sur ce qui a esté representé au Roy estant en son Conseil, par le sieur Marquis de Feuquires, viceroy de l'Amerique. Fontainebleau, Aug. 16, 1661. L501
A proclamation, published in the form of a broadside, revoking earlier patents for colonizing in North and South America, Africa, and the East Indies. Its purpose was to assure future settlers that they would not be troubled by earlier claims.

Louis XIV, King of France. Document signed and countersigned by Colbert, Richer, and d'Hozier. Manuscript. Versailles, 6 March 1689. L502
This document contains the appointment of the Marquis d'Esragny as Inspector-General and second in command of French troops destined for Siam as the French East India Company contemplated dominance there.

Louvet, Pierre. Le mercure hollandois, ou l'Histoire de la republique des Provinces Unies de Pays-Bas. Lyons, Estienne Baritel, 1673. L503
A history of the Netherlands, with primary focus on the century preceding 1671, which emphasizes Dutch commercial expansion overseas.

Love, John. Geodaesia, or, the Art of surveying and measuring of land made easie. 3rd ed. London, W. Taylor, 1720. L504
A standard surveying book, used in the eighteenth century and on into the nineteenth. This edition contains many fine illustrations, a number of tables, and a chapter on laying out lands in America.

Lover of his Country. The South-Sea scheme detected, and the management thereof enquir'd into ... in answer to a pamphlet entitled, The South-Sea scheme examin'd. London, W. Boreham, 1720. L505

Lowndes, Thomas, of Liverpool. The merchants guide: consisting of tables for the computation of the duties, and directions for transacting the business of the custom-house. Liverpool, Printed by William Nevett, 1774. L506
A manual for use in the Liverpool customs office, informative on British commerce and on customs administration.

Lowndes, William. Some remarks on a report containing an essay for the amendment of the silver coin. London, W. Whitlock, 1695. L507
Remarks on a published report dealing with clipping and counterfeiting the currency.

Lowth, Robert. A sermon preached before the incorporated Society for the Propagation of the Gospel in Foreign Parts: at their anniversary meeting in the parish church of St. Mary-le-Bow, on Friday February 15, 1771. London, E. Owen and T. Harrison, 1771. L508
While noting the Society's success in maintaining religion among the colonists, this preacher is not optimistic about its expansion among the Indians.

Loyer, Godefroy. Relation du voyage du royaume d'Issyny, Côte d'Or, pais de Guinée, en Afrique. Paris, A. Seneuze & J.R. Morel, 1714. L509
An account of western Africa by a missionary, based on his experiences there from 1687 to 1703.

Lozano, Pedro. Copia de carta, escrita por un missionero de la Compania de Jesus del Paraguay. [Cordoba? 1740?] L510

The letter is to the procurator general, Juan Joseph Rico, and covers events of the late 1730s in Paraguay.

Lozano, Pedro. Descripcion chorographica ... de las dilatadissimas provincias del gran Chaco, Gualamba. Cordova, Joseph Santos Balbàs, 1733. L511
A Jesuit missionary's account of a relatively unknown area, including descriptions of plants and animals of great economic value.

Lubin, Augustin. Mercure geographique, ou, Le guide du curieux des cartes geographiques. Paris, Christophle Remy, 1678. L512
A dictionary of cartographic and geographic terms, with explanations of their origins and translations into several languages.

Lucas, Paul. Voyage du sieur Paul Lucas au Levant. Paris, Nicolas Simart, 1731. L513
An account of travels up the Nile and into Persia undertaken in 1699, reporting on the cataracts of the Nile and on caravan travel and commercial life in the Middle East.

Lucca (Republic). Corte de' Mercadanti. Li statuta de la Corte de Mercadanti delle 'eccellentiss. repub. di Lucca. Lucca, Ottaviano Guidoboni, 1610. L514
Statutes governing the mercantile community of Lucca, dealing largely with the cloth trade since silk manufacture and trade was the city's major industry.

Lucca (Republic). Laws, etc. Gli statuti della citta di Lucca. Nuovamente corretti, con molta diligentia stampati. [Lucca, Giovambattista Phaello Bolognese, 1539.] L515
A collection of almost seven hundred laws regulating commerce and other aspects of life in Lucca.

Lucena, João de. Historia de vida do Padre Francisco Xavier e do que fizerão na India os mais religiosos da Companhia de Jesu. Lisbon, Pedro Crasbeeck, 1600. L516
An extensive biography, including material descriptive of political conditions, missionary activity, and places visited by Xavier in the Far East.

Lucena, Vasco Fernandes de. Ad Innocentium octavum pontificem maximū de obedientia oratio. [Rome, Stephan Plannck, ca. 1486.] L517
An oration of obedience delivered to Pope Innocent VIII on behalf of John II of Portugal. It announces Portuguese success in exploring the western coast of Africa, and expresses optimism for finding a water route to India shortly.

Lucena, Vasco Fernandes de. Ad Innocentiū viii pontificē maximū de obedientia oratio. [Rome or Gaeta, Andreas Freitag, 1487-1492.] L518
The second edition.

Lucidarius. Von allerhand geschöpffen Gottes, den Engeln, den Himmeln, Gestirn, Planeten, und wie alle Creaturen geschaffen seynd auff Erden. Frankfurt, Sigismund Latomus, 1609. L519
A German chapbook containing outdated geographical information in the medieval tradition.

Lucino, Luigi Maria. Esame, e difesa del decreto pubblicato in Pudisceri da Monsignor Carlo Tommaso di Tournon ... approvato, e confermato con breve dal sommo Pontefice Benedetto XIII ... Rome, Stamperia Vaticana, 1729. L520
A defense of the 1704 decree of Carlo Tomasso Maillard de Tournon in which he proscribed sixteen specific practices of the Jesuits in India, a part of the Malabar Rites controversy.

Ludolf, Hiob. Nouvelle histoire d'Abissinie, ou d'Ethiopie. Paris, C. Cellier, 1693. L521
Ludolf, who never visited Africa, used information from an Ethiopian monk who spent time in Rome. Includes a folded map, done by Ludolf's son, which is the first map to show the source of the Blue Nile at Lake Tana.

Ludolf, von Sachsen. De Terra Sancta et itinere Jherosolomitano. [Strassburg, Heinrich Eggestein, ca. 1475.] L522
The first edition of this pilgrimage book, containing information on the geography and commerce of the Mediterranean as well as an account of Palestine.

Ludolf, von Sachsen. Prologus in librum domini Ludolphi de Suchen ... [Gouda, G. Leeu, 1483-85.] L523
The second Latin edition.

Lübeck (Germany). Laws, etc. Statuta und Stadt Recht, sampt angehengter Schiffs: und Hochzeiten Ordnung. Lübeck, Laurentz Albrechts Sel. Erben, 1608. L524
One part of the statutes is given entirely to regulations upon maritime commerce. Another section of the book contains shipping regulations of the Hanseatic League from 1591.

[Lütken, Frederik Christopher.] Oeconomiske tankar til høsiere efter-tanke. Copenhagen, C.G. Glasings [etc.] 1756-59. L525
A commentary on the economies of Denmark and Norway, with material on manufacturing, taxation, overseas trade, commercial companies, etc.

Luillier-Lagaudiers. Voyage du sieur Luillier aux Grandes Indes, avec une instruction pour le commerce des Indes Orientales. Paris, Claude Cellier, 1705. L526
An account of travels to India, with particular emphasis on Bengal and Pondichery, and a section on the commerce of the East Indies.

Luillier-Lagaudiers. Voyage du sieur Luillier aux grandes Indes. The Hague, J. Clos, 1706.　　L527
　The second edition.

[Luillier-Lagaudiers.] Nouveau voyage aux grandes Indes. Rotterdam, J. Hofhout, 1742.　　L528
　A later edition with an additional chapter describing diseases encountered en route to the East Indies, and remedies against them.

Lulius, Didericus. Rechtsgeleerde memorie: waar in onzydig onderzogt word de gegrondheid der klagten van den Koning van Groot-Brittannien, over de geheime correspondentie tusschen Amsterdam en de Americaansche colonien. [n.p.] 1781.　　L529
　A pamphlet relating to secret negotiations between the United States and the Netherlands during the American Revolution.

Lumnius, Joannes Fredericus. De extremo Dei iudicio et Indorum vocatione libri II. Antwerp, A. Tilenius, 1567.　　L530
　The first edition. Lumnius was the pastor of the Beguine at Antwerp.

Lumnius, Joannes Fredericus. De extremo Dei iudicio, et Indorum vocatione libri II. Venice, Dominicum de Farris, 1569.　　L531
　From Old Testament theory the author postulates that the American Indians were the lost tribe of Israel, and anticipates that they will be united into Christendom through the mission of the Society of Jesus.

Lundius, Carolus, Praeses. Dissertatio de Sveonum cum gentibus Europaeis, secundum leges & pacta, commerciis ... Uppsala, Typis Keyserianis, 1699.　　L532
　A history of Swedish commerce, submitted as a thesis at Uppsala University by Olaus Benzelius. The work discusses Swedish commerce with major European nations.

Lushington, Sir Stephen. The correspondence between Sir Stephen Lushington, baronet, and Warren Hastings, Esq. on the statement alluded to in both letters. London, J. Debrett, 1795.　　L533
　An examination of the financial situation of Warren Hastings, including his trial expenses and his financial dealings on behalf of the East India Company.

Lusignan, Sauveus. A series of letters, addressed to Sir William Fordyce, M.D. F.R.S. containing a voyage and journey from England to Smyrna ... London, For the author, 1788.　　L534
　A travel narrative written by an English merchant with extensive experience as a free-lance entrepreneur in the Near East.

Luther, Martin. Lutheri Catechismus, öfwersatt på American-Virginske språket. Stockholm, Burchardi Tryckeri af J.J. Genath, 1696.　　L535
　In addition to the translation of the Lutheran Shorter Catechism into the Delaware language, this work also includes a glossary of Delaware words.

Lycke, Christian Jacob. Noget til publikum i en bekiendt sag fra Christian Jacob Lycke. Copenhagen, Johan Friderich Morthorst, 1789.　　L536
　Presents Coninck & Reiersen's position in the lawsuit brought against them concerning a trading expedition of the ship *Princess Frederika*.

[Lycke, Christian Jacob.] Unpartheyische Darstellung der Process-Sache welche die Herren Stats-Räthe de Coninck & Rejersen im Juny 1789 vor dem höchsten Gericht zu Copenhagen verloren haben. [n.p.] 1789.　　L537
　German translation of the preceding item.

[Lyschander, C.C. (Claus Christoffersen).] Dend Grølandske chronica. [Copenhagen] hans Kongl. Majestets privil. Bogtrykkerie, 1726.　　L538
　Prefaced by a rhymed chronicle of Eric the Red's Norse Greenland settlement, this reprint is an account in poetry of three Danish voyages to the Greenland area in 1605, 1606, and 1607.

Lysten van de Hollandsche scheepen, zo veel deeze Stadt Amsteldam betreft. Welke op hunne reisen, naar of van de West-Indiën, door de Engelschen in weerwil van de subsisterende tractaten genomen, ipgebragt, en onregtmatig geconfisqueert zyn ... Amsterdam, Jacob Hoff [1758].　　L539
　A catalog of ships, their captains, cargoes and values which were taken or otherwise molested by British ships in the period just prior to publication. One hundred ships are thus identified.

[Lyttelton, George Lyttelton, baron.] Considerations upon the present state of our affairs at home and abroad. London, T. Cooper, 1739.　　L540
　The author's principal concern is the interruption of Britain's West Indian trade by the Spanish.

[Lyttelton, George Lyttelton, baron.] Farther considerations on the present state of affairs, at home and abroad. London, For T. Cooper, 1739.　　L541
　Concerns the rivalry with Spain in the West Indies.

M

Månsson, Johan. Sjö-märkes-bok öfwer farwatnen inom Öster-sjön. Stockholm, Lars Salvius, 1748.   M1

A revision of a pilot guide to the Baltic Sea, originally issued in 1644. The editor is Jonas Hahn, an Admiralty officer.

Maatrozen saamenspraak te port a port ... [n.p.] 1701.   M2

A conversation between a Frenchman, a Dutchman, an Englishman, and a Portuguese with reference to their commerce in the East and West Indies.

Mably, abbé de. Brieven over de regeeringsvorm en wetten der Vereenigde Staaten van Noord-America aan zyne excellentie John Adams ... Amsterdam, W. Holtrop, 1785.   M3

A commentary on the outcome of the American Revolution, congratulating the Americans on their insistence on natural rights, but holding some reservations about the states' constitutions.

[Macarty, Captain.] An appeal to the candour and justice of the people of England, in behalf of the West India merchants and planters, founded on plain facts and incontrovertible arguments. London, J. Debrett, 1792.   M4

A defense of slavery in the British West Indian colonies together with a report on the debate in the House of Commons relative to motions for the abolition of slavery on April 2, 1792.

Macaulay, Kenneth. Histoire de Saint-Kilda, imprimée en 1764, traduite de l'Anglois, contenant la description de cette isle remarquable. Paris, Knapen, 1782.   M5

To the account of St. Kilda are appended French translations of Staehlin von Storcksburg's *New northern archipelago* and Petr Ludovik Le Roy's *Narrative of ... four Russian sailors, who were cast away on ... East-Spitzbergen.*

[McCulloh, Henry.] A miscellaneous essay concerning the courses pursued by Great Britain in the affairs of her colonies. London, R. Baldwin, 1755.   M6

A commentary on problems relating to the governing of the American colonies, and the regulation of their commerce.

[McCulloh, Henry.] Proposals for uniting the English colonies on the continent of America so as to enable them to act with force and vigour against their enemies. London, For J. Wilkie, 1757.   M7

A proposal for a uniform tax and currency among all of Britain's American colonies to give them the needed unity and finances to provide for adequate military strength to resist the French in North America.

McCulloh, Henry. [Treatise on American colonial administration.] Manuscript. [n.p., ca. 1755.]   M8

A study of colonial governmental, economic, and diplomatic problems, with proposals for policy, addressed to the Earl of Granville.

[McCulloh, Henry.] The wisdom and policy of the French in the construction of their great offices, so as best to answer the purposes of extending their trade and commerce ... London, For R. Baldwin, 1755.   M9

The French Council of Commerce is favorably compared to the British Council of Trade and Plantations. The author also urges a more aggressive policy toward the French in America.

[MacDonald, Thomas.] A brief statement of opinions, given in the Board of Commissioners, under the sixth article of the Treaty of amity, commerce, and navigation, with Great Britain ... Philadelphia, James Humphreys, 1800.   M10

Decisions and discussion relating to claims made by British subjects for payment of debts owed by Americans, as provided for in the Treaty of amity, commerce and navigation of 1794.

MacDonell, Alexander Greenfield. A narrative of transactions in the Red River country; from the commencement of the operations of the Earl of Selkirk, till the summer of the year 1816. London, B. McMillan, 1819. M11
 An account of the conflict between the Red River settlers and the North West Company from the latter's point of view. Includes a map of the region in question.

Macedo, Duarte Ribeiro de. Observação sobre a transplantação de fructos da India ao Brazil. Pelo dezembargador Duarte Ribeiro de Macedo. No anno de 1782. Manuscript in Portuguese. [n.p., 1782.] M12
 A copy of a manuscript originally written about 1675 by a Portuguese diplomat and economist interested in the transplanting of plants between Asia and America.

Macer, Joannes. Les trois livres de l'histoire des Indes. Paris, Guillaume Guillard, 1555. M13
 An early French geography, with particular emphasis on Japan and China. The material on Japan was apparently taken from missionary letters of Francis Xavier.

MacFait, Ebenezer. A new system of general geography, in which the principles of that science are explained ... Edinburgh, J. Balfour, W. Creech [etc.] 1780. M14
 The first and only volume of a projected larger geographical text modeled on Varenius.

McGillivray, Simon. A narrative of occurrences in the Indian countries of North America, since the connexion of the Right Hon. the Earl of Selkirk with the Hudson's Bay Company, and his attempt to establish a colony on the Red River. London, B. McMillan, 1817. M15
 A review of the Red River controversy from an anti-Selkirk position, with supplementary documents.

[McGillivray, Simon.] Notice respecting the boundary between his Majesty's possessions in North America and the United States. London, B. McMillan, 1817. M16
 Contains a map showing the main trading stations of the Northwest Company.

Maciej, z Miechowa. Tractatus de duabus Sarmatiis Asiana et Europiana ... [Cracow, J. Haller, 1517.] M17
 The first edition of one of the earliest printed accounts of travel into Russia from the west. The author, a Polish physician, describes the people, cities, rivers, and other aspects of Russia.

Maciej, z Miechowa. Tractatus de duabus Sarmatiis. [Augsburg, Auguste Vindelicon, 1518.] M18
 The second edition.

Maciej, z Miechowa. Tractat von baiden Sarmatien und andern anstossenden Landen, in Asia und Europa. [Augsburg, 1518.] M19
 The first German edition.

Mackenzie, Sir Alexander. Voyages from Montreal on the River St. Laurence through the continent of North America, to the frozen and Pacific oceans; in the years 1789 and 1793. London, T. Cadell and Davies [etc.] 1801. M20
 The author was in the service of the North West Company, and explored the region to the north and west of Lake Athabasca.

Mackenzie, Sir Alexander. Voyages from Montreal, on the River St. Lawrence, through the continent of North America, to the frozen and Pacific oceans; in the years 1789 and 1793. London, T. Cadell and W. Davies [etc.] 1802. M21
 The second edition.

Mackenzie, Sir Alexander. Voyages ... dans l'intérieur de l'Amérique Septentrionale, faits en 1789, 1792 et 1793. Paris, Dentu, 1802. M22
 This first French edition adds a number of translator's notes, some of them based on the papers of Bougainville.

Mackenzie, Sir Alexander. Reisen von Montreal durch Nordwest-Amerika nach dem Eismeer und der Süd-See in den Jahren 1789 und 1793. Nebst einer Geschichte des Pelzhandels in Canada. Berlin und Hamburg, 1802. M23
 This is the first full German edition. The anonymous translator adds a preface which reviews recent explorations in northwestern Canada and books and maps related to them.

[Mackenzie, J.] A woolen draper's letter on the French treaty, to his friends and fellow tradesmen all over England. London, For the Author, 1786. M24
 An appeal to cloth merchants to rally against a proposed commercial treaty which would allow increased importation of cloth from France.

Mackenzie, Roderick. Now or never, or, a familiar discourse concerning the two schemes for restoring the national credit. London, W. Boreham, 1721. M25
 This pamphlet attacks the established trading companies for not allowing competition and supports the South Sea Company. Has been attributed to Richard Martin.

Mackworth, Sir Humphrey. An answer to several queries relating to the proposal ... for the relief of the South Sea Company ... London, W. Boreham, 1720. M26
 An explanation of the South Sea Company's plan for stimulating trade through inflation.

Mackworth, Sir Humphrey. A proposal for payment of the publick debts for relief of the South Sea Company. London, W. Boreham [1720].
M27
Proposes a new currency equal to the debt of the company, and secured by Parliament.

Mackworth, Sir Humphrey. Sir H. Mackworth's proposal in miniature. London, W. Boreham, 1720.
M28
A defense of a proposal to establish a new currency, following the failure of the South Sea Company.

Mackworth, Sir Humphrey. To the honourable the knights, citizens, and burgesses of Great Britain, in Parliament assembled, the humble proposal of Sir Humphrey Mackworth, for restoring the national credit ... London, H. Meere, 1721.
M29
A proposal to create financial stability and assist investors in South Sea Company stock through the issue of a "new species of money."

McLean, John. Notes of a twenty-five years' service in the Hudson's Bay territory. London, Richard Bentley, 1849.
M30
The author's intention is to give a picture of the privations of the trader in the service of the Hudson's Bay Company and of the degradation by the company of the Indians in that area.

[Macneny, Patrick.] Refutation des argumens avancés de la ... Compagnies d'Orient & Occident des Provinces Unies contre la liberté du commerce des habitants des Pais-bas ... The Hague, P. and I. Scheltus, 1723.
M31
An argument on behalf of the Ostend Company, contending that the Treaty of Munster did not prevent Ostend trade in the East and West Indies.

Macneny, Patrick. The freedom of commerce of the subjects of the Austrian Netherlands asserted and vindicated. [Brussels] Eugene Henry Fricx [1723].
M32
Translation of the above item.

[Macneny, Patrick.] Wederlegginge van de argumenten opgestelt ... teegens de vryheyt van commercie van de inwoonders der Nederlanden. The Hague, Paulus & Isaac Scheltus, 1723.
M33
The first Dutch edition.

Macpherson, Charles. Memoirs of the life and travels of the late Charles Macpherson. Edinburgh, A. Constable, 1800.
M34
Set mainly in Guadeloupe, Macpherson's book gives an account of life there and ends the narrative with a discussion of slavery. This work is part of the responses arising out of Pitt's attempt to introduce the abolition of the British slave trade in Parliament.

[Macpherson, James.] The rights of Great Britain asserted against the claims of America: being an answer to the Declaration of the general Congress. London, T. Cadell, 1776.
M35
A response to the July 6, 1775 declaration by Congress of the reasons for taking up arms against Great Britain, apparently published at the instance of the British government.

Macrobius, Ambrosius Aurelius Theodosius. Somnium Scipionis cum interpretatione et Saturnaliorum libri VII. Brescia, Boninus de Boninis, 1485.
M36
A fifth century *Commentary on Scipio's dream* incorporating a view of the universe and of the earth which divided the latter into climatic zones and allowed for the existence of antipodean peoples. The text is illustrated by a mappemonde.

Macrobius, Ambrosius Aurelius Theodosius. [Somnium Scipionus, Saturnaliorum.] Venice, Agostino de Zanni, 1513.
M37
This is the first edition prepared by Joannes Rivius of Venice.

Macrobius, Ambrosius Aurelius Theodosius. Macrobius integer nitidus ... a Joanne Rivio restitutus. [Paris] Jehan Petit [1515].
M38
One of two Rivius editions from this year.

Macrobius, Ambrosius Aurelius Theodosius. [Somnium Scipionis ex Ciceronis libro de Republica excerptum.] Paris, Badius, 1519.
M39
A reprint of the 1515 Paris edition.

Macrobius, Ambrosius Aurelius Theodosius. In somnium Scipionis libri duo: et septem eiusdem libri Saturnaliorum. Cologne [Eucharium Cervicornum] 1521.
M40
The first edition, under the editorship of Arnoldus Versaliensis and Gottried Hittorp, with a long commentary on the Saturnalia.

M'Tavish, Frobisher & Co. [Fur trade contract] 1801 Jan. 23, Montreal [with] Jean Baptiste Boucher [and his brother] Jean Marie Boucher: M'Tavish, Frobisher & Co. [Montreal, 1801.]
M41
Contract engaging a fur trader for service in the west.

Maddison, Sir Ralph. Great Britains remembrancer, looking in and out. Tending to the increase of the monies of the commonwealth. London, Tho. Newcomb, to be sold by Humphrey Moseley, 1655.
M42
The author of this work was concerned about the effect on values in England of a debased currency. He also proposes reform of the mint and the establishing of a national bank to replace the foreign bankers who dominated that aspect of the economy.

Madrid, Agustin de. Relacion, del viage que hizo el abad Don Juan Bautista Sydot, desda Manila al imperio del Japon, embaiado por nuestro Santissimo Padre Clemente XI. [n.p., ca. 1717.] M43

An account of the adventures of an envoy of the Pope who spent four years in Japan at a time when few Westerners were received there.

Maetroosjes Op-wecker. [n.p.] 1618. M44

This "Sailor's awakening" dramatizes the unrest in the Netherlands over the peace with Spain.

Maffei, Giovanni Pietro. Rerum a Societate Jesu in Oriente gestarum volumen. Naples, Horatius Salvianus, 1573. M45

Reports and letters by various Jesuit missionaries from Ethiopia, India, and Japan.

Maffei, Giovanni Pietro. Historiarum Indicarum libri XVI. Selectarum item ex India epistolarum eodem interprete libri IV. Florence, Philippus Juncta, 1588. M46

A history of European penetration of the East Indies.

Maffei, Giovanni Pietro. Historiarum Indicarum libri XVI. Cologne, Birckmann, 1589. M47

This edition is notable for its inclusion of a large world map.

Maffei, Giovanni Pietro. Historiarum Indicarum libri XVI. Cologne, Birckmann, 1590. M48

This Cologne edition compares with the 1589 Birckmann edition in text, but is an octavo and does not include the world map.

Maffei, Giovanni Pietro. Historiarum Indicarum libri XVI. Bergamo, Comini Venturae, 1590. M49

This edition does not include the Jesuit letters appended to some editions. It does include a table of contents.

Maffei, Giovanni Pietro. Historiarum Indicarum. Antwerp, Martinus Nutius, 1605. M50

This copy includes John Hay's *De rebus Japonicus, Indicis, et Peruanis epistolae*, frequently cited on the title page but often lacking.

Maffei, Giovanni Pietro. Historiarum Indicarum libri XVI. Antwerp, Martini Nutii, 1605. M51

This edition includes 187 pages of letters from missionaries in the Far East.

Maffei, Giovanni Pietro. Joannis Petri Maffeii, Bergomatis e Societate Jesu, Historiarum Indicarum libri XVI. Vienna, Trattner, 1751. M52

A late edition indicating continued popularity of this history of Jesuit missions.

Maffei, Giovanni Pietro. Le istorie delle Indie Orientali. Florence, Filippo Giunti, 1589. M53

The first Italian edition.

Maffei, Giovanni Pietro. Le historie delle Indie Orientali. Venice, Damian Zenaro, 1589. M54

This is the same translation as the Florence edition of 1589.

Maffei, Giovanni Pietro. Le istorie dell' Indie Orientali. Bergamo, Pietro Lancelotti, 1749. M55

This edition has a biography of the author.

Maffei, Giovanni Pietro. Histoires des Indes ... où il est traicté de leur descouverte, navigation, & conqueste. Lyons, Jean Pillehotte, 1604. M56

This French edition does not include the Jesuit letters appended to some of the earlier editions.

Maffei, Giovanni Pietro. De vita et morib. Ignatii Loiolae. Rome, F. Zannettum, 1585. M57

The first edition of Maffei's classic biography of Ignatius Loyola.

Maffei, Giovanni Pietro. Ignatii Loiolae vita qui Societatem Jesu fundavit. Rome, Jacobum Tornerium, 1587. M58

A biography of the founder of the Society of Jesus.

Maffei, Giovanni Pietro. Selectarum epistolarum ex India libri quatuor. Vienna, Trattneriana, 1751. M59

A late printing of a group of letters from the 1560s and 1570s, including two from 1570 and 1571 noting Jesuit presence in Brazil.

Maffei, Raffaele. Commentariorum urbanorum. Rome, J. Besicken, 1506. M60

A chapter entitled "Loca nuper reperta" contains an account of the voyage of Cabral and subsequent Portuguese fleets to India, with reference to early voyages to the New World also.

Maffei, Raffaele. Commentariorum urbanorum Raphelis Volaterrani, octo & triginta libri. Basel, Hieronymus Froben, 1530. M61

The second edition.

Maffei, Raffaele. Comme[n]tarioru[m] urbano[rum]. Paris, Jodoco Badio [1515]. M62

The third edition.

Maffei, Raffaele. Commentariorum urbanorum Raphaelis Volaterrani, octo & triginta libri. Basel, Froben, 1544. M63

A reprint of the 1530 edition.

Magazin von merkwürdigen neuen Reisebeschreibungen, aus fremden Sprachen übersetzt und mit erlauternden Anmerkungen begleitet. Berlin, Voss, 1790-1793. M64

A ten volume collection of voyage literature.

Magazin von merkwürdigen neuen Reisebeschreibungen: aus fremden Sprachen übersetzt ... Berlin, Vossischen Buchhandlung, 1794-1800. M65
These volumes, 11-17 complete the set, except for the index which is wanting.

Magen, Nikolaus. Die gute Nachbarschaft durch die Zunahme von Handlung und Reichtum ... erwogen von einem Kaufmann. London, J.C. Haberkorn und J.N. Gussen, 1751. M66
Advocates the free flow of goods between neighboring states.

Magistris, Giacinto. Relatione della Christianità di Madure fatta da padri missionarij della Compagnia di Giesù della provincia del Malavàr ... Rome, Angelo Bernabò del Verme, 1661. M67
A report on progress of the Madure mission in southern India, a point of some conflict between Jesuits and their critics within the church.

Magistris, Giacinto. Relation derniere de ce qui s'est passé dans les royaumes de Maduré, de Tangeor, & autres lieux ... aux Indes Orientales. Paris, Sebastien Cramoisy & Sebastien Mabre Cramoisy, 1663. M68
French edition, translated by Jacques de Machault.

Maguelonne de Courtaulin, Jean de. [Letter.] Manuscript. Paris, Oct. 11, 1686. M69
An eight-page letter in Latin, written to a bishop in China concerning missionary affairs there.

Maigrot, Charles. Copie d'une lettre de Monsieur Maigrot à Monsieur Charmot, du 11 janvier 1699 ... touchant la religion ancienne des Chinois. [n.p.] 1700. M70
An attack upon Louis Daniel Le Comte's *Nouveaux mémoires sur l'état present de la Chine* for its description of Chinese religious practices.

Maigrot, Charles. Lettera di monsig. Maigrot, vescovo Cononense, e vicario apostolico della provincia di Fokien nella China al signor Nicolo' Charmot ... tradotta dal Francese nell' Italiano. Cologne, Cornelio d'Egmond [1700]. M71
An Italian translation of the previous item.

Maillard de Tournon, Carlo Tommaso. Lettres de l'eminentissime Cardinal de Tournon, ... au comte de Lizarraga, Gouverneur de Manile, capitale des Isles Philippines. [n.p.] 1712. M72
The Cardinal's letters concern the capture of a ship carrying five missionaries en route to the Philippines. The governor of Manila replies, and writes also to the Emperor of China to secure release of the ship.

Maille, Jean. Exposition des propriétés du spalme: considéré comme courroi ... comme enduit ... comme mastic ... avec la maniere de l'employer sous ces trois rapports. Paris, Le Breton, 1763. M73
A treatise on tar and its various uses in shipbuilding and maintenance with a history of the author's involvement in its manufacture and trade.

Maino, Giasone dal. Oratio habita apud Alexandrum sextum Pont. [Pavia, Ant. de Carcano, 1493.] M74
The oration contains an imprecise reference to lands in the Atlantic although it was delivered before the return of Columbus.

Mainoldus, Jacobus. De titulis Philippi Austrii regis catholici liber. Bologna, Peregrinum Bonardum, 1573. M75
An elaboration upon the titles of the Hapsburg rulers of Spain and Austria noting the characteristics of each area ruled by them including New World possessions. These are accompanied by a history of their exploration.

Maiollo, visconte di. Atlas of portolan charts: facimile of manuscript in British Museum: edited by Edward Luther Stevenson, Ph.D. New York, The Hispanic Society of America, 1911. M76
A facsimile of an atlas, Egerton Ms. 2803 in the British Library, from the second decade of the sixteenth century.

Maiollo, visconte di. Map of the world, 1527. [Facsimile.] New York, The Hispanic Society of America, 1905. M77
A facsimile of a world map of the portolan type based upon an original which was destroyed in 1944.

Mair, John. A brief survey of the terraqueous globe. Edinburgh, J. Bell and W. Creech, 1775. M78
This is the second edition of this work, the first published in 1762, with additions, amendments, and improvements; two of which include maps engraved by Thomas Kitchin.

Mairan, Dortous de. Lettres de M. de Mairan au R.P. Parrenin, missionnaire de la Compagnie de Jesus, à Pekin. Contenant diverses questions sur la Chine. Paris, Desaint & Saillant, 1759. M79
The letters between Mairan and Dominique Parrenin concern problems of China's history, science, and language. They are from the period 1728-1740.

[Mairobert, Mathieu François Pidanzat de.] Discussion sommaire sur les anciennes limites de l'Acadie, et sur les stipulations du traite d'Utrecht qui sont relatives. Stockholm, Kongl. Tryckeriet, 1755. M80
The problem of giving boundaries to Acadia is dealt with here in French and Swedish.

Majelli, Carlo. Oraison funebre de l'eminentissime Charles-Thomas Maillard, cardinal de

Tournon, legat apostolique dans la Chine .... [n.p.] 1712. **M81**
The text is in French and Latin. A second section is a commentary on the Chinese Rites controversy with which Cardinal de Tournon was closely associated just prior to his death.

Malagrida, Gabriel. Procés-verbal de condamnation de Gabriel Malagrida, Jésuite, par l'Inquisition de Portugal ... Lisbon, Antoine Rodrigues Galhardo, 1761. **M82**
A review of the case of Gabriel de Malagrida, an Italian Jesuit, from the point of view of his religious ideas which led to his conviction as a heretic.

[Maldonado de Saavedre, Melchor.] [Two documents concerning the Ocloya Indians.] Manuscript. [Santiago del Estero, 8 October 1638 and Tucumán, 26 May 1639.] **M83**
By a decree of 1634 all Indians were supposed to gather together in *reducciones*. The issue in these documents is whether the Jesuits or the Franciscans should be responsible for the area inhabited by the Ocloya Indians. The decision was made in favor of the Franciscans.

Malipetro, Ambrogio. (Recipient). [Sixteen holograph letters from various merchants. Aleppo, 3 June 1484 to 13 June 1486.] **M84**
The recipient of these letters was presumably a merchant in Tripoli. The contents are almost entirely commercial, dealing with shipments of specific products, arrival of caravans, sailings of ships, etc.

Mallet, Paul Henri. Northern antiquities: or, A description of the manners, customs, religion and laws of the ancient Danes, and other northern nations. London, T. Carnan, 1770. **M85**
This two volume work was intended as a preface to the author's history of the Danes. It includes an interesting commentary on the Norse settlements in Greenland and Vinland.

Mallet, Paul Henri. Nouveau recueil de voyages au nord de l'Europe et de l'Asie. Geneva, Paul Barde, Manget & Compagnie; Paris, Moutard, Mérigot, et Buisson, 1785-86. **M86**
This collection of voyages in the northern regions of Europe contains travels to Scotland and the northern coastal islands of Great Britain, and Mallet's translation of Coxe's travels.

Malouet, Pierre-Victor, baron. Lettre à M.S.D., Membre du Parlement, sur l'intérêt de l'Europe, au salut des colonies de l'Amérique. [London] Baylis, et se trouve chez J. Deboffe & Dulau, 1797. **M87**
From his temporary exile in England Malouet considers the importance of the West Indies to all of Europe, and recommends that in time of European war this area be declared neutral.

Malouet, Pierre-Victor, baron. Opinion de M. Malouet, sur le projet de décret relatif à l'etat des personnes dans les colonies. [n.p., 1791.] **M88**
A warning against applying the Declaration of the Rights of Man to the French colonies in America because of the differences between society there and in France.

Malouet, Pierre-Victor, baron. Rapport ... sur les dépenses & le régime économique de la marine. Paris, Baudouin, 1790. **M89**
A detailed discussion of the expenses of the navy in protecting French coasts and French colonies, with proposals for reducing this amount.

Malynes, Gerard. The center of the circle of commerce. London, William Jones, 1623. **M90**
A commentary on *The circle of commerce* by Edward Misselden, emphasizing the importance of a correct rate of exchange between nations, asserting that the regulation of these rates gives governments power over commerce.

Malynes, Gerard. The maintenance of free trade. London, I.L. for William Sheffard, 1622. **M91**
This economist sees the lack of flexibility in the value of England's money in international exchange as a major cause of the decline in her trade.

Mamerot, Sebastien. Les passages de oultre mer. [Paris, Antoine and/or Nicholas Couteau for François Regnault, ca. 1525.] **M92**
Mamerot traveled to Jerusalem and translated many of the works on the Holy Land into French. This is the story of Godfrey of Bouillon and his exploits of the First Crusade, including the establishment of Christian settlements in Syria and Palestine.

Mandelslo, Johann Albrecht von. Morgenländische Reyse-Beschreibung. Schleswig, Johan Holwein, 1658. **M93**
An account of travels to Persia and India by a member of a commercial embassy sent out by the Duke of Holstein in 1633.

Mandelslo, Johann Albrecht von. Beschryvingh van de gedenkwaerdige zee-en landt-reyze, deur Persien naar Oost-Indien ... Amsterdam, Jan Hendricksz. en Jan Rieuwertsz, 1658. **M94**
Based on the first separate edition in German published in Schleswig the same year.

Mandeville, Sir John. [Travels.] Milan, Petrus de Corneno, 1480. **M95**
The first Italian edition. This account of the Near East and Asia was written in the fourteenth century, based on the travel narratives of others.

Mandeville, Sir John. Tractato de le piu marauegliose cose piu notabile che si trouino in le parte del mondo ... [Venice, Zuan Baptista Sessa, 1504.] **M96**

376   Mandeville, Sir John

A reprint of the Italian edition of Milan, 1480, with numerous variations in spelling and contractions.

Mandeville, Sir John. Qual tratta delle piu maruegliose cose e piu notabile ch[e] si trouino: e come presentialmente ha cercato tutte le parte habitabile del mõ[n]do: & ha notato alcune degne cose che ha vedute in esse parte. Venice, Alvise di Torti, 1534.   M97

A small-format Italian edition without illustrations.

Mandeville, Sir John. Reysen und Wanderschafften durch das gelobte Land. Augsburg, A. Sorg, 1481.   M98

The first German and the first illustrated edition, containing 121 hand-colored woodcuts.

Mandeville, Sir John. [Travels.] Manuscript. Germany, 1455.   M99

The Velser German translation. It is abridged in some sections.

Mandeville, Sir John. [Itinerarium. Gouda, Gerard Leeu, 1483-85.]   M100

The second Latin edition.

Mandeville, Sir John. Itinerarius. [Strassburg, Printer of the 1483 "Vitus Patrum," ca. 1484.]   M101

The third Latin edition.

Mandeville, Sir John. Itinerarius in partes Iherosolimitanas. Et in ulteriores transmarinas. [Cologne, Cornelis de Zierikzee, ca. 1500.]   M102

The fourth Latin edition.

Mandeville, Sir John. Libro de las maravillas del mũndo. Valencia, Jorge Costilla, 1531.   M103

The third Spanish edition.

Mandeville, Sir John. The voiage and travaile of Sir John Maundevile, Kt. which treateth of the way to Hierusalem; and of marvayles of Inde, with other ilands and countreys. London, J. Woodman, D. Lyon, and C. Davis, 1725.   M104

The most complete edition to its time; the editor said he used seven English, French, and Latin manuscripts and four published editions in Latin, English, and Italian in its preparation.

[Mandrillon, Joseph.] Révolutions des Provinces Unies sous l'étendard des divers stadhouders. Nijmegen, 1788.   M105

A history of the Netherlands with particular emphasis on the origins and growth of Dutch overseas commercial interests.

Mandrillon, Joseph. La spectateur américain, ou remarques générales sur l'Amérique septentrionale et sur la république des treize-états-unis. Amsterdam; Brussels, De la Haye, 1785.   M106

A survey of the natural history and economy of the thirteen states, their reasons for seeking independence, and their commercial potential, with comments by the author on revolutionary principles of the time.

Manesson-Mallet, Allain. Description de l'univers, contenant les differents systêmes du monde, les cartes generales & particulieres de la geographie ancienne & moderne. Paris, Denys Thierry, 1683.   M107

A richly illustrated world geography, including numerous city plans, maps, pictures of various peoples, ceremonies, buildings, ships, etc.

Manesson-Mallet, Allain. Beschreibung des gantzen Welt-Kreisses, in sich begreiffend verschiedene Vorstellungen der Welt, allgemeine und besondere Land-Charten der alten und neuen Erd-Beschreibung ... Frankfurt, Johann David Zunner, 1684-1685.   M108

The illustrations for this German edition were entirely re-engraved after the originals in the 1683 French edition.

Manifest door d'inwoonders van Parnambuco uytgegeven tot hun verantwoordinge op't aennemen der wapenen tegens de West-Indische Compagnie. Antwerp, P. van den Cruyssen, 1646.   M109

"Manifest published by the inhabitants of Pernambuco in defense of their having taken up arms against the West India Company."

Manifest ende redenen van oorloge, tot Lisbona uytghegheven ... [n.p.] 1658.   M110

Portuguese reasons for war against the Dutch in the West Indies. Also contains a history of the Dutch colony at Pernambuco in its last years.

Manifest ofte summarische onderrechtinghe, waer uyt onder anderen te sien is, hoe syne Coninckliijcke Majesteyt in Denemarcken, Norwegen ... [n.p.] 1644.   M111

Indicates Dutch concern for Scandinavian rivalries, potentially involving the Baltic trade of the Netherlands.

Het manifest van Engelant, waer in verhaelt worden de reden en motiven die sy sustineren te hebben, om ons rechtvaerdighlijck den oorlogh aen te doen ... Amsterdam, K. de Pas, 1652.   M112

Contains English charges of Dutch restriction upon East Indian commerce.

Manifest van't Koninghrijck van Portugael. [n.p.] Broer Jaensz [etc.] 1641.   M113

Announces the reasons why the Portuguese have overthrown their Spanish rulers, noting how Spanish administration resulted in great loss to Portugal's earlier prominence.

Manila (Philippines). Señor ... la ... ciudad y commercio de Manila en las Islas Philipinas ... [Manila? 1738.] M114
Deals with the commerce of the Philippines with China, Spain, and America.

Manila (Philippines). Señor. La ciudad y comercio de Manila ... de las Islas Philipinas ... [Manila? ca. 1720.] M115
A memorandum on Philippine commerce, describing its precarious position and urging more direct trade with New Spain.

Mannert, Konrad. Imperii Russici pars Orientem Spectans ... Nuremberg, A. G. Schneideriana, 1794. M116
The map includes an inset depicting the Aleutian Islands, part of Alaska, and islands off the Siberian coast.

Manoel, de Monforte, frei. Chronica da Provincia da Piedade: primeira Capucha de toda a ordem, & regular observancia de nosso seraphico padre S. Francisco. Lisbon, Miguel Deslandes, 1696. M117
A history of a group of Discalced Franciscans based in Portugal which maintained missions in India, Malacca, and in west Africa.

Manoel da Encarnação, frei. Sermam que pregou o P. Fr. Manoel da Encarnaçam, presentado em S. Theologia, da Ordem dos Pregadores. No auto da fee que se celebrou em a cidade de Goa na India Oriental ... 7 de Fevereiro de 1617. Lisbon, Pedro Crasbeeck, 1628. M118
The earliest printed sermon of an auto-da-fe preached in Portuguese India.

Manoel da Rainha dos Anjos, freire. Vida tragica, e relaçao mavioza dos trabalhos, e perseguiçoes, que desde Portugal athe a Turquia padeceu ... Manuscript. [n.p., ca. 1790.] M119
A narrative of travels and religious controversy in Turkey and eastern Europe by a Portuguese Franciscan.

Manrique, Sebastião. Itinerario de las missiones del India Oriental. Rome, Guillelemo Halle, 1653. M120
The second issue of the first edition. The author was an Augustinian missionary in India. He also traveled to Indo-China and Siam, returning to Rome via Persia and Palestine.

[Mant, Richard]. An essay on commerce. [Oxford, 1799.] M121
A philosophical and historical essay on the benefits which commerce may bring to a nation, but noting also the evils that it has brought because of greed.

Mantegazza, Gaetan. [Description of Burma.] Manuscript. [France?] 1784. M122
This Barnabite missionary describes the economic geography, the towns, the river systems, markets, etc., of Burma at a time when few Europeans were active there. Written in French, it also includes a large manuscript map.

Mantegazza, Stefano. Relatione tripartita del viaggio di Gierusalemme ... Milan, Per l'her. di Pacifico P. & Gio. Battista Piccaglia, 1616. M123
A pilgrimage book that pays some attention to commercial life of Levantine cities.

Manucci, Niccolò. Histoire generale de l'empire du Mogol depuis sa fondation. The Hague, Guillaume de Voys, 1708. M124
A history of the nine Mogol emperors preceding Aurangzeb, taking note of the European presence in the empire also.

[Manuel I, King of Portugal.] Abtruck ains lateinischen Sandtbrieves an babstliche Heiligkeit von künigklicher Wurde zů Portegall dis Jars ausgangen von d' eroberē Stadt Malacha anderen Künigreychen unnd Herschaftn in India ... [Augsburg, Erhard Öglin, 1513.] M125
This is one of two German translations of a newsletter issued in 1513, announcing the conquest of Malacca by the Portuguese, and describing its rich potential as a commercial center.

Manuel I, King of Portugal. Epistola ... ad Juliam papam secundum de victoria contra infidiles habita. Paris, G. Eustace [ca. 1507]. M126
A letter from King Manuel of Portugal to Pope Julius II, announcing the victories of Lorenço Almeida against the Moslems in naval engagements in the Indian Ocean.

Manuel I, King of Portugal. Epistola ... de victoriis in India & Malacha: Ad ... Leonem X Pont. Max [Rome, Marcellus Silber for Jacobus Mazochius, ca. 1513.] M127
An account of the conquest of Malacca by Afonso d'Albuquerque and the subsequent establishment of Portuguese commercial supremacy there, noting that merchants from many eastern islands and countries come to Malacca to trade.

Manuel I, King of Portugal. Epistola ... de victoriis nuper in Africa habitis. [Rome, Marcellus Silber, 1513.] M128
A newsletter relating to Portuguese victories in Morocco.

Manuel I, King of Portugal. Epistola potentissimi ac invictissimi Emanuelis Regis Portugaliae & Algarbiorum &c. De victoriis habitis in India & Malacha. [Rome, Iacobum Mazochium, 1513] M129
One of two Latin editions of a newsletter published in 1513 describing the Portuguese victory at Malacca in 1511.

Manuel I, King of Portugal. Gesta proxime per Portugalenses in India, Ethiopia et alliis orientalibus terris. [Cologne, Joannes Landen, 1507.]
M130
A newsletter describing the establishment of Portuguese supremacy over the route to India through the capture of such important African cities as Sofala, Kilwa, and Mombasa.

Manufest ofte redenen van justificatie vande ... Staten Generael aen den Koninck van Groot-Brittangien. Schiedam, P. Verschuyr, 1664.
M131
Relates to Anglo-Dutch commercial rivalry in the West Indies and Guinea.

[Manuzio, Antonio, ed.] Viaggi fatti alla Tana, in Persia, in India et in Constantinopoli ... Venice, Aldus, 1543.
M132
A collection of fifteenth-century Italian voyages to Persia, Ethiopia, and India.

Manwayring, Sir Henry. The sea-mans dictionary, or, An exposition and demonstration of all the parts and things belonging to a shippe ... London, G.M. for John Bellamy, 1644.
M133
A compendium of seaman's technology and vocabulary, some 600 terms being described in detail, intended for the instruction of gentlemen who went to sea in positions of authority but with little basic knowledge of seamanship.

Mapa do ouro de s. mag. e partes, que vem nos cofres da nau n.s. do livramento e S. Jozé, capitania da frota do Rio de Janeiro que sahiu em 6 de junho deste anno ... como tamben da carga dos navios mercantes da dita frota. [n.p., 1755.]
M134
This broadside records amounts and types of gold being returned to Portugal from Brazil, and also lists other commodities returned in a recent fleet, including items from Madeira.

Mappa das merces, e patentes, que el Rey n.s. Fez, e mandou aos officiaes, e mais pessoas que na presente Monção de 1748 vaõ servir ao estado da India. [n.p., 1748.]
M135
A listing of the officers of the Portuguese military administration in India.

Mappemonde. [A fragment of a world map showing southern Europe and most of Africa.] Manuscript. [n.p., ca. 1450.]
M136
This fragment of an unknown planisphere is of special interest for its portrayal of Africa.

[Marbault.] Essai sur le commerce de Russie, avec l'histoire de ses découvertes. Amsterdam, 1777.
M137
A general discussion of eighteenth-century Russian commerce, domestic and foreign.

The marchants humble petition and remonstrance ... with an accompt of the losses of their shipping and estates, since the war with Spain. London, Joseph Moxon, 1659.
M138
Discusses the importance to England of her trade with Spain, and how during the war with Spain, the French and Dutch "have benefitted to our disadvantage."

Marchetty, François. Discours sur le negoce des gentilshommes de la ville de Marseille et sur la qualité des nobles marchands qu'ils prenoient il y a cent ans. Marseilles, C. Brebion and J. Penot, 1671.
M139
A defense of the participation in trade practiced by the nobility of Marseilles.

[Marchmont, Hugh Hume, earl of.] A state of the rise and progress of our disputes with Spain. London, T. Cooper, 1739.
M140
The British view of the history of their own and Spanish trade in the West Indies and the rivalries and breaches of peace there.

[Marees, Pieter de.] Beschryvinge ende historische verhael, van gout koninckrijck van Gunea, anders de Gout-custe de Mina genaemt, liggende in het deel van Africa ... Amsterdam, Cornelis Claesz voor Jan Arentsz Chaalon, 1602.
M141
The first edition of an account of the first Dutch voyage to Guinea, 1600-1602, with extensive descriptions of the people and productions of that area.

[Marees, Pieter de.] Description et recit historial du riche royaume d'or de Gunea. Amsterdam, Cornille Claesson [1605].
M142
The first French edition.

Mariani, Giovanni. Tariffa perpetua: con le ragion fatte per scontro de qualunque mercadante si uoglia. Venice, Francesco Rampazetto da Lona, 1553.
M143
A commercial handbook with particular emphasis on currency conversion, adapted primarily for use in northern Italy.

Marie, Jean. Laus tabaci, sive chymici metamorphosis tabacum. [Paris, J. Quillau, 1718.]
M144
A Latin poem celebrating tobacco.

Marie de l'Incarnation, Mère. Lettres de la venerable Mère Marie de l'Incarnation, premiere superieure des Ursulines de la Nouvelle France. Paris, Pierre de Bats, 1684.
M145
The letters describe aspects of French missionary efforts in Canada. They were edited by Claude Martin, the author's son.

Marie de l'Incarnation, Mère. Lettres spirituelles et historiques de la venerable Mère de l'Incarnation. Paris, A. Warin, 1696.
M146

The second part, *Lettres Historiques*, contains comments on the relations between the French and Indians of Canada from 1640 to 1670.

Marie de l'Incarnation, Mère. Retraites de la venerable Mère Marie de l'Incarnation religieuse Ursuline. Paris, Veuve Louis Billaine, 1682.
M147

A series of religious exercises used in New France.

Marien, Thomas Antoine de. Tableau des droits & usages de commerce relatifs au passage du Sund. Copenhagen, Nicolas Möller, 1776.
M148

A summary of duties and controls imposed by Denmark on trade ships passing through the Sund and a description of Danish trade relations with other European countries.

Marin, Carlo Antonio. Storia civile e politica del commercio de' Veneziani. Venice, Coleti, 1798-1808.
M149

An eight volume set recording the commercial history of Venice from its beginnings to the end of the eighteenth century. The major emphasis is in the period from 1100 to 1500. A number of documents are found in the footnotes and in the appendices.

[Marine insurance records.] 1574-1577. M150

Eight manuscript documents, three in Latin, and three Italian translations from French, all pertaining to European coastal shipping.

Marini, Gio. Filippo de. Delle missioni de' padri della Compagnia di Giesu nella provincia del Giappone, e particolarmente di quella di Tunkino. Venice, Heredi di Francesco Storti, 1665.
M151

The material on Japan is brief, as the work is almost entirely a description of Indo-China and the history of the Jesuit mission there.

Marini, Gio. Filippo de. Histoire nouvelle et curieuse des royaumes de Tunquin et de Lao. Paris, Gervais Clouzier, 1666.
M152

A description of the geography, social customs, religions, laws and other aspects of life in Indo-China.

Marini, Gio. Filippo de. Nouvelle relation des Indes orientales ... Paris, G. Clouzier, 1683.
M153

The third French edition, translated from the Italian. The original Italian edition was published in 1663.

Mariti, Giovanni. Johan Maritis resa uti Syrien, Palästina och på Cypern. Stockholm, Kongl. Ordens Tryckeriet, 1790.
M154

An abridged translation by Samuel Ödmann of an extensive account of travels and residence in the Near East by an Italian merchant.

[Maritime contracts for the sloop Neptune: one engaging a sailor and one for the transport of cargo.] Manuscript in French. 1802. M155

The sailor engaged is Joseph Melon. The cargo material is unclear.

Maritime documents. [A collection of 23 manuscript letters and documents concerning the capture of the French ship *Comte de Virlande* with its cargo by English corsairs.] Manuscripts. [n.p.] January 30, 1744, to November 22, 1748.
M156

[Maritime insurance document.] Manuscript. Venice, December 10, 1426. M157

An insurance policy to cover a cargo proceeding from Venice to Valencia.

[Maritime shipping contract.] Manuscript. Bruges, June 8, 1370. M158

A detailed maritime contract for the shipment of wool from Sluys to Porto Pisano.

Mariz, Pedro de. Dialogos de varia historia. Coimbra, Antonio de Mariz, 1597 [i.e. 1599].
M159

The second edition of a chronicle of the kings of Portugal, containing significant information on Portuguese expansion to both the New World and Asia.

Mármol Carvajal, Luis del. Primera - [Segunda] parte de la descripcion general de Affrica, con todos los successos de guerras que avido entre los infieles, y el pueblo Christiano ... Granada, Rene Rabut, 1573; Malaga, Juan Rene, 1599.
M160

An extensive history and geography of Africa, including relations of European countries to that continent, and a history of Moslem Africa as well.

Mármol Carvajal, Luis del. l'Afrique de Marmol. Paris, Louis Billaine, 1667. M161

French translation of the above item.

[Marmont du Hautchamp, Barthélemy.] Histoire du systeme des finances, sous la minorité de Louis XV pendant les années 1719 & 1720. The Hague, Pierre de Hondt, 1739.
M162

A documentary history of the rise and fall of John Law's bank, trading company, and influence in France.

[Marmont du Hautchamp, Barthélemy.] Histoire générale et particulîere du visa en France. The Hague, F.H. Scheurleer, 1743.
M163

A history of French finances from 1715, with a discussion of various proposals to improve finances and commerce.

Marperger, Paul Jacob. Die neu-eröffnete Kauffmans-Börse ... Hamburg, Benjamin Schillern, 1704. M164

A commercial handbook by the leading German economist of the period, noting leading centers of commerce, major commodities in international trade, money exchange, instructions for bookkeeping, etc.

[**Marperger, Paul Jacob.**] Fortsetzung der Remarquen über den noch immer anhaltenden weltberühmten missisippischen Actien-handel in Paris. [n.p., ca. 1720.] M165

A commentary on the Mississippi Company, including a map of North America.

[**Marperger, Paul Jacob.**] Historische und geographische Beschreibung des an dem grossen Flusse Mississippi ... [Leipzig] Leipziger Neu-Jahrs-Messe, 1720. M166

A description of Louisiana and the proposed French commercial enterprises there under direction of John Law.

[**Marperger, Paul Jacob.**] Kurtze Remarques über den jetziger Zeit weitberuffenen missisippischen Actien-Handel in Paris, und andere grotze Unternehmungen des Herrn Laws. [n.p., ca. 1720.] M167

A commentary on the Mississippi Company and its prospects for success, noting the history of other overseas trading companies, the background of this one, and the geography of the Mississippi Valley.

Marperger, Paul Jacob. Moscowitischer Kauffmann. Lübeck, Peter Böckmann, 1723. M168

A survey of Russian commerce. The author was the financial adviser to the Elector of Saxony.

Marperger, Paul Jacob. Neu-eröffnetes Handels-Bericht, oder, Wohlbestelltes Commercien-Collegium. Hamburg, Benjamin Schiller [1709]. M169

A massive handbook in commercial law, including history, principles, and current usages in many aspects of merchandising, banking and other commerical enterprises.

Marperger, Paul Jacob. Neu-eröffnete Wasser-Fahrt auf Flüssen und Canälen. Dresden & Leipzig, J.C. Krause, 1723. M170

A treatise on the utilization of Europe's waterways to facilitate commerce.

Marperger, Paul Jacob. Nutz-und lustreicher Plantagen-Tractat, oder Gründlicher Beweisz, was die Cultur fremder und auch einheimischer Plantagen an Bäumen, Kräutern und andern Gewächsen unsern Teutschland ... bringen könne, wie die Populosität, samt denen Manufacturen dadurch könte gemehret ... Dresden, Johann Christian Büttnern, 1722. M171

A survey of plants the world over with a view to incorporating them into Germany's economy through transplanting and producing them in Germany.

Marperger, Paul Jacob. Schwedischer Kauffmann. Wismar & Leipzig, Johann Christian Schmidt, 1706. M172

A review of Swedish commerce, noting its products, manufactures, major cities commercial relations with other countries, cutoms, regulations, shipping facilities, etc.

Marperger, Paul Jacob. Vorausgefertiger Entwurff seines künfftig zu erwartenden vollkommenen Commercien-Rahts. [n.p., ca. 1720]. M173

Outlines the qualifications and duties of an ideal future minister of trade.

Marquart, Johann. Tractatus politico-juridicus de jure mercatorum et commerciorum singulari. Frankfurt, Thomas M. Götzius, 1662. M174

A compendium of commercial and legal information relating to European commerce, with particular emphasis on Germany, Holland, and Sweden.

Marqui, Jean. [Letter signed to Régiste Robichaux.] Manuscript. [Lestele, 27 September 1793.] M175

A statement concerning the author's attempts to sell furs in New Brunswick.

[**Marra, John.**] Journal of the Resolution's voyage, in 1772, 1773, 1774, and 1775, on the discovery to the southern hemisphere ... London, F. Newbery, 1775. M176

The author, a gunner aboard the *Resolution*, includes here the events of the *Adventure's* voyage also.

[**Marra, John.**] Journal of the Resolution's voyage, in 1772, 1773, 1774, and 1775, on discovery to the southern hemisphere. Dublin, Caleb Jenkin and John Beatty, 1776. M177

This Dublin edition includes the map, but not the illustrations found in the London edition.

Marriott, Sir James. The case of the Dutch ships, considered. London, For R. and J. Dodsley, 1758. M178

A contention that the Dutch had forfeited claims to neutrality by trading with French colonies and by allowing Dutch territory to be used by France in its war against Great Britain.

[**Marriott, Sir James.**] A letter to the Dutch merchants in England. London, For M. Cooper, 1759. M179

An appeal to the Dutch merchants in England to use their influence to prevent Dutch commerce with France's American colonies.

Marsden, William. The history of Sumatra. London, For the Author [etc.] 1783. M180

The writer, an official of the East India Company, lived for eight years in Sumatra and provides a general description of the island as well as information on commercial relationships between it and nearby regions.

Marsden, William. Histoire de Sumatra, dans laquelle on traite du gouvernement, du commerce, des arts, des loix, des coutumes & des moeurs des habitans ... de cette isle. Paris, Buisson, 1788. M181

This French edition adds numerous notes by the translator, J.P. Parraud.

Marsden, William. Voyage a l'isle de Sumatra. Paris, Buisson, 1794. M182

The second French edition.

Marshall, Charles. Description of Messrs Marshall's grand peristrephic panorama of the polar regions; which displays the north coast of Spitzbergen, Baffin's Bay, Arctic Highlands, &c. Now exhibiting in the large new circular wooden building in George's Square, Glasgow. Leith, William Heriot, 1821. M183

The panorama contained eight views, six devoted to the Polar Expedition of 1818 and two to Ross' attempt to discover the Northwest Passage in the same year.

Marsillac, Jean. La vie de Guillaume Penn, fondateur de la Pensylvanie ... Ouvrage contenant l'historique des premiers fondemens de Philadelphie, des loix et de la constitution des États-Unis de l'Amerique ... Paris, Imprimerie du Cercle Social, 1791. M184

A laudatory biography used as a vehicle for promoting democratic ideas in France.

Martellus, Henricus. Christoforo Ensenii Florentini sacerdotis dignissimi descriptio arcipelagi et cicladum aliarum que insularum. [Florence, ca. 1475.] M185

A manuscript atlas on vellum, reproducing Buondelmonte's *Liber Insularium*. It contains eighty-five colored maps, including very interesting portrayals of England and Constantinople.

Martens, Friedrich. Spitzbergische oder groenlandische Reisebeschreibung. Hamburg, G. Schultz, 1675. M186

An account of a whaling voyage with observations on arctic plant and animal life.

Martens, Friedrich. Naukeurige beschryvinge van Groenland of Spitsbergen ... Dordrecht, Hendrik Walpot [ca. 1710]. M187

This Dutch version adds extensive information on whaling voyages prior to the 1671 voyage of Martens.

Martin, Benjamin. New principles of geography and navigation. In two parts. Part I. containing the theory of the true figure and dimensions of the earth ... Part II. containing a table of meridional parts ... London, For the Author and J. Newbery, 1758. M188

A study of the problem of determining the degree of arc of a meridian in the interest of more correct charting and navigation.

Martin, Claude. La vie de la venerable Mère Marie de l'Incarnation première superieure des Ursulines de la Nouvelle France. Paris, Louis Billaine, 1677. M189

The subject of this biography became an Ursuline nun when widowed at age nineteen. She subsequently emigrated to Canada where she lived for thirty-two years and served as head of the Ursuline convent.

Martin, François, de Vitré. Description du premier voyage faict aux Indes Orientales par les François en l'an 1603. Paris, Laurens Sonnius, 1604. M190

An account of the earliest French commercial voyage to the East Indies undertaken by merchants of St. Malo, Vitré, and Val. The author was physician to the voyage and includes among other topics a Malaysian dictionary.

Martin, Robert Montgomery. The Hudson's Bay territories and Vancouver's Island. London, R. and W. Boone, 1849. M191

Includes a map locating the trading stations of the Hudson's Bay Company.

Martines, Joan. Portolan atlas Joan Martines en Messina, añy 1582. New York, Hispanic Society of America, 1915. M192

A facsimile of a manuscript atlas with introduction by Edward Luther Stevenson.

Martinez de la Puente, José. Compendio de las historias de los descubrimientos, conquistas, y guerras de la India Oriental y sus islas. Madrid, Viuda de J. Fernandez de Buendia, 1681. M193

A history of discovery in Africa, Asia, and the Spice Islands.

Martini, Martino. Breve historia delle guerre seguite in questi ultimi anni tra Tartari, e Cinesi ... tradotta in Italiano dal Sig. Climaco Latini. Milan, Heredi Battista Bidelli, 1654. M194

The first vernacular edition of a popular history of the decline and fall of the Ming dynasty in China by a Jesuit who witnessed many of the events he describes. It was first published in Latin the same year.

Martini, Martino. Historische Beschreibung des tartarischen Kriegs in Sina. Munich, Lucas Straub, 1654. M195

The first German edition.

Martini, Martino. Historische Beschreibung dess tartarischen Kriegs in Sina ... Munich, Lucas Straub, 1654. M196

Martini, Martino. An entirely different translation and arrangement of text from the other German editions of 1654.

Martini, Martino. Histori von dem tartarischen Kriege ... Amsterdam, Iohan Blaeu, 1654. M197
One of three German editions issued in 1654.

Martini, Martino. Historie van den Tartarschen oorloch, in dewelcke wert verhaelt, hoe de Tartaren in dese onse eew in't Sineesche rijck sijn gevallen. Delft, Jacob Jacobsz Pool, 1654. M198
The first Dutch edition.

Martini, Martino. Historie van den Tartarschen oorloch. Utrecht, Gerard Nieuenhuysen, 1655. M199
The third Dutch edition, including a map and illustrations as well as a commendatory poem by Simon de Vries not included in previous editions.

Martini, Martino. Bellum Tartaricum, or the conquest of the great and most renowned empire of China, by the invasion of the Tartars ... London, John Crook, 1654. M200
The first English edition.

Martini, Martino. Tartaros en China. Madrid, Joseph Fernandez de Buendia, 1665. M201
The second Spanish edition.

Martini, Martino. De bello Tartarico historia; in qua, quo pacto Tartari hac nostra aetate Sinicum Imperium invaserint. Amsterdam, Johannem Janssonium Junioram, 1655. M202
This edition includes illustrations.

Martini, Martino. Sinicae historiae decas prima. Amsterdam, Joannem Blaeu, 1659. M203
The first volume, all that was ever published, of a planned complete history of China.

Martini, Martino. Histoire de la Chine. Paris, C. Barbin et A. Seneuze, 1692. M204
The first French edition.

Martinique (French colony). Laws, etc. Proclamation [offering amnesty to rebelling slaves if they will return to their masters]. St. Pierre, Martinique, P. Richard & Le Cadre, 1791.
M205

Martinius, Franciscus. Argo-nauta Batavus, sive expeditionis navalis, quam alter noster Jason, & heros fortissumus, Petrus Heinius, sub auspiciis illustrissimorum & potentissimorum ... Societatis Indiae Occidentalis ... et victoriae in Sinu Matanzae divinitus reportate historia. Kampen, Petri Henrici Wyringani, 1629. M206
A Latin poem of twenty-eight pages commemorating the capture of the Spanish Silver Fleet in 1628 by a Dutch force under Piet Hein.

Martins, Pedro, Bishop of Japan. Raguaglio d'un notabilissimo naufragio, cavato da una lettera ... scritta da Goa. Venice, Gioliti, 1588. M207
An account of a shipwreck on the east coast of Africa by one of a group of Jesuits bound for India.

[Martyn, Benjamin.] An impartial inquiry into the state and utility of the province of Georgia. London, W. Meadows, 1741. M208
A defense of Georgia as a great potential producer of silk, cotton, cochineal, olives, and other products.

[Martyn, Benjamin.] Reasons for establishing the colony of Georgia with regard to the trade of Great Britain. London, W. Meadows, 1733. M209
Georgia is valued for its apparent ability to replace Italy as a source of raw silk, and Russia as a source of flax, hemp, and potash.

[Martyn, Henry.] The advantages of the East-India trade to England, consider'd. London, J. Roberts, 1720. M210
The author attempts to disprove contentions that the exporting of gold to India and the importing of cheap cloths are a disadvantage to the British economy. He compares the India trade favorably with Britain's fishing trade and the importing of Irish cattle.

[Martyn, Henry.] Considerations upon the East-India trade. London, A. and J. Churchill, 1701. M211
A supporter of the East India trade, the author believes it would be of greater benefit to the nation if it were opened to all merchants. This work is sometimes attributed to Sir Dudley North.

Mascarenhas, José Freire de Monterroyo. Epanaphora Indica: na qual se dà noticia da viagem, que o illustissimo, e excellentissimo senhor Marquez de Castelo Novo fez com o cargo de vice-rey ao estado da India. Lisbon, 1746-1750. M212
Parts I-V of a history of Portuguese victories in India during the viceroyalty of the Marquez de Castelo Novo, a brief episode of success during a time of decline in Portuguese power in India.

[Mascarenhas, José Freire de Monterroyo.] Manifesto ou combinaçam do procedimento de sua magestade catholoca com a delrey da Gram Bretanha, assim no que sucedeu antes da convençam de 14 de janeiro do anno de 1739. Lisbon, A. Correa Lemos, 1740. M213
A discussion of the conflicts between Spain and Great Britain, centering on British activity against Spain in America.

Mascarenhas, José Freire de Monterroyo. Novo triunfo da religiam serafica: ou noticia summaria do martyrio, e morte que padeceram ... o veneravel Padre Fr. Liberato Weis com dous companheyros seus ... Lisbon, Paschoal da Sylva, 1718. M214

An account of the martyrdom of three Franciscan missionaries in Ethiopia in 1716, including some account of the political situation in the country at that time.

Mascarenhas, José Freire de Monterroyo. Os Orizes conquistados, ou Noticia da conversam dos indomitos Orizes Procazes, povos barbaros, & guerreros do Certaõ do Brasil. Lisbon, Antonio Pedrozo Galram, 1716. M215

An account of conquest and conversion leading to the baptism of 3,700 Brazilians who had been most troublesome to the Portuguese.

[Mascarenhas, José Freire de Monterroyo.] Queyxas de Hespanha, & Inglaterra, e reciprocas justificaçoens de ambas estas coroas, representadas em varias cartas, & memoriaes que se escreveraõ, & appresentáraõ nas duas cortes. Lisbon, Pascoal da Sylva, 1719. M216

A collection of diplomatic correspondence between Spanish, British, and Dutch officials, concerning various overseas matters, including Britain's South Sea Company.

Mascarenhas, José Freire de Monterroyo. Relaçam da embayxada, que o poderoso Rey de Angome Kiay Chiri Broncom, senhor dos dilatadissimos sertoēs de Guiné mandou ... D. Luiz Peregrino de Ataide ... vice-rey do estado Brasil ... Lisbon, Francisco da Silva, 1751. M217

An account of an embassy from the King of Angome in West Africa to the viceroy of Brazil, negotiating on behalf of the King of Portugal.

[Mascarenhas, José Freire de Monterroyo.] Relaçam do verdadeiro estado do imperio do Preste Joam. Lisbon, Officina da Gazeta, 1759. M218

This author identifies the legendary Prester John with the Dalai Lama.

Massachusetts (Colony) Governor, 1760-1770 (Francis Bernard). Letters to the Ministry from Governor Bernard, General Gage, and Commodore Hood, and also memorials to the Lords of the Treasury, from the Commissioners of the Customs. Boston, Edes and Gill, 1769. M219

Most of the letters are from Francis Bernard, governor of Massachusetts, and they comprise an interesting history and interpretation of events in the colony from January 21 to October 14, 1768.

Massachusetts (Colony) Governor, 1760-1770 (Francis Bernard). Letters to the Right Honourable the Earl of Hillsborough, from Governor Bernard, General Gage, and the honourable His Majesty's council for the province of Massachusetts-Bay. London, For J. Almon, 1769. M220

A different group of letters from the previous item, covering the period November, 1768 to June 1769 and including an appendix containing documents relating to their publication.

Massei, Giuseppe. Vita di S. Francisco Saverio, della Compagnia di Gesù, apostolo dell'Indie ... Venice, Nicolo Pezzana, 1712. M221

The seventh edition of a biography of St. Francis Xavier first published in 1681.

Massie, J. (Joseph). Considerations on the leather trade of Great Britain. London, Thomas Payne, 1757. M222

An argument favoring restriction on the export of unmanufactured leather.

[Massie, J. (Joseph).] A letter to Bourchier Cleeve, Esq.; concerning his calculations of taxes. London, Thomas Payne, 1757. M223

A discussion of how duties and excise taxes on fish, wool, furs, and other goods and commodities would affect the taxes paid by a family with an average income.

[Massie, J. (Joseph).] Observations upon Mr. Fauquier's *Essay on ways and means for raising money to support the present war without increasing the public debts.* London, Thomas Payne, 1756. M224

The author contends that there is insufficient coin in Britain to support war taxes as Fauquier had proposed, and that the war would not bring in sufficient fund from prizes, etc. to offset the loss of money taken out of the country to support it.

[Massie, J. (Joseph).] Reasons humbly offered against laying any further British duties on wrought-silks of the manufacture of Italy, the kingdom of Naples and Sicily, or Holland. London, T. Payne, 1758. M225

A series of ninety-eight arguments to prove that British industry, land values, and naval strength are all helped by the importing of silks from Italy and Sicily, whereas silk imported from Turkey and India results in loss to the nation.

Massie, J. (Joseph). A representation concerning the knowledge of commerce as a national concern. London, T. Payne, 1760. M226

The author attempts to prove that England's trade can best prosper if some fundamental rules for commercial development are discovered and made known.

Massie, J. (Joseph). A state of the British sugar-colony trade. London, T. Payne, 1759. M227

Contains a comparison in efficiency of production between French and British sugar-producing islands.

Masso, Antonius. Orationes duae, comitiis consularibus, Lugduni habitae. Lyons, G. Rovill, 1556. M228
A complaint against subsidies levied upon the commerce of Lyons, noting the decline it will bring on the fairs of the city.

Master, Elizabeth, Lady. The case of Lady Elizabeth Master. [n.p., 1721.] M229
A plea for compassion by the wife of a director of the South Sea Company, who lost heavily in the collapse of the company.

Mata, Pedro de. Relation de las grandes perdidas de naos y galeones, que han tenido los Portugueses en la India Oriental ... [Madrid, Julian de Paredes, 1651.] M230
This newsletter was written from Macassar and reports heavy Portuguese losses by storms in the Indian Ocean in 1649, along with accounts of riots in Goa and famine in Macao, as well as major losses in both cities by storms.

Matelief, Cornelis. An historicall and true discourse, of a voyage made ... into the East Indies. London, For William Barret, 1608. M231
A report on the activities of Matelief's fleet which sought to establish Dutch supremacy at Malacca and in the Moluccas. It was translated from the Dutch the same year it was first published.

Mather, Cotton. India Christiana: a discourse delivered unto the Commissioners for the Propagation of the Gospel among the American Indians ... Boston, B. Green, 1721. M232
A plea and justification for Christian missions in the New World and in the East Indies. It includes a letter to Bartholomeus Ziegenbald, leader of a Protestant mission in India, and a reply from John Ernst Grundler from that mission.

[Mather, Increase.] A brief relation of the state of New England, from the beginning of that plantation to this present year, 1689. London, Richard Baldwine, 1689. M233
An entirely favorable picture of New England, noting its economic and strategic importance to England, its educational and religious advances. The author's purpose was to assure England of the wisdom of respecting the constitutional rights of the New Englanders.

Mather, Increase. De successu evangelii apud Indos Occidentales in Novâ-Angliâ: epistola ad cl. virum d. Johannem Leusdenum ... Utrecht, Wilhelmum Broedeleth, 1699. M234
A collection of missionary letters reporting the work of John Eliot, John Cotton and an Indian named Hiacomes in Massachusetts and in addition two letters from Ceylon and two from Amboyna.

Mather, Samuel. An attempt to shew, that America must be known to the ancients; made at the request, and to gratify the curiosity of an inquisitive gentleman. Boston, J. Kneeland for T. Leverett, 1773. M235
Classical and Biblical scholarship are employed to demonstrate the knowledge of America in ancient times. The final chapter is a defense of colonial rights in matters of taxation.

[Mathias de Saint-Jean, Père.] Le commerce honorable. Nantes, Guillaume le Monnier, 1646. M236
A survey of French commerce with suggestions for its improvement, including the idea of establishing a bourse to permit wider participation in trade.

Matienzo, Juan de. Commentaria Ioannis Matienzo regii senatoris in cancellaria Argentina regni Peru in librum quintum Recollectionis legum Hispaniae. Madrid, Ludouicus Sanctius, 1613. M237
A commentary on Spanish law and its applicability to Spain's American colonies.

Matos, Diego de. Copia de una carta que el padre Diego de Matos de la Compañhia de Jesus escrieve ... del estado de la conversion a la verdader religion Christiana Catolica Romana, del gran Imperio de Etiopia ... en veinte de juneo de 1621. Madrid, Luis Sanchez, 1624. M238
An early report on Jesuit progress in Ethiopia following the temporary acceptance of Roman Catholic jurisdiction by the king. The author arrived there in March, 1621.

Matos, Gabriel de. Lettera annua di Giappone del M.DC.III. Rome, Luigi Zannetti, 1605. M239
Added to the letter from Japan are two letters from the Moluccas and one from China.

Matter of fact; or the arraignment and tryal of the Di____rs of the S____ S__ Company. London, J. Applebee, 1720. M240
A mock trial in which various views regarding the South Sea Company are set forth.

Matthews, John. A voyage to the River Sierra-Leone. London, B. White & Son, 1788. M241
A series of eight letters describing the commerce of the Sierra Leone region.

Matthews, John. A voyage to the River Sierra-Leone on the coast of Africa. London, B. White and Son, 1791. M242
A re-issue of the 1788 sheets, with illustrations and introductory material added.

Matthews, John. Voyage a la rivière de Sierra-Leone, sur la côte d'Afrique. Paris, Hautbout l'aîné, l' an V [1797]. M243
Nicolas François Bellart, the translator of this French edition, takes issue with the author in his preface and in translator's notes, showing a more negative attitude toward the slave trade than Matthews had.

[Mauduit, Israel] ed. The letters of Governor Hutchinson, and Lieut. Governor Oliver, &c. Printed at Boston. And remarks theron. With the Assembly's address, and the proceedings of the Lords Committee of Council ... London, J. Wilkie, 1774. M244

These are the letters which Franklin procured in London and published in Boston.

[Mauduit, Israel.] Some thoughts on the method of improving and securing the advantages which accrue to Great-Britain from the northern colonies. London, J. Wilkie, 1765. M245

The author urges increased trade rather than taxation as the means to increase income from the colonies.

Maupertuis. Astronomie nautique: ou Élémens d'astronomie, tant pour un observatoire fixe, que pour un observatoire mobile. Paris, Imprimerie Royale, 1751. M246

The second edition of a work given largely to the problem of determining latitude.

Maupertuis. La figure de la terre. Paris, Imprimerie Royale, 1738. M247

An account of an expedition sent to Lapland to measure the degree of arc of a meridian in order to determine the true shape of the earth.

Maupertuis. Jordens figur, upfunnen af Herrar de Maupertuis, Clairaut, Camus, Lemonnier, ledamöter af Kongl. Vetenskaps Academien i Paris ... samt af H. Celsius, Kongl. Astron. Professor i Upsala ... Översat af Fransyskan. Stockholm, Joh. Laur. Horrns, 1738. M248

Translated from the French edition of the same year.

Maupertuis. Ouvrages divers de Mr. de Maupertuis ... Amsterdam, Aux depens de la Compagnie, 1744. M249

Includes: *Discourse sur les* and *Lettre sur la comete.*

Maurepas, Jean Frédéric Phélypeaux, comte de. [Letter signed, addressed to Hubert de Saint Menien.] Manuscript. Versailles, 4 January 1739. M250

Concerns affairs in Louisiana.

Mauricius, Johannes. Afgoden-dienst der Jesuiten in China waar over sy nog heden beschuldigt worden aan het hof van Romen. Amsterdam, Jacobus Borstius, 1711. M251

An anti-Jesuit work relating to the Chinese Rites controversy, written by a Dutch Dominican priest.

Maurile de Saint Michel. Voyage des isles Amériques. Mans, Hierôme Olivier, 1653. M252

Observations made by a missionary on the French colonies in the West Indies.

Mauro, Fra. Il mappamundo. [Venice, Istituto Poligrafico dello Stato, 1956.] M253

A facsimile in forty-eight sheets, with an introduction by Roberto Almagia.

Maurolico, Francesco. Cosmographia Francisci Maurolyci ... in tres dialogos distincta ... Venice, 1543. M254

A collection of three cosmographical treatises by one of the leading geometricians of the sixteenth century.

Maury, Jean Siffrein. Opinion sur le droit d'initiative que réclament les assemblées coloniales pour toutes les loix relatives à l'état des personnes dans les colonies. Paris, Imprimerie Nationale, 1791. M255

A cautious approach to the problem of slavery in French colonies, recognizing the abuses of it but also suggesting that action concerning it be delayed for consideration by colonial legislative bodies.

Maux et remedes. Ou Memoire contenant des reflections sur l'etat present de la France et l'exposition d'un sisteme d'administration. Manuscript. [France, ca. 1780.] M256

An analysis of France's economic problems shortly prior to the Revolution with particular reference to trade, and with recommendations for its improvement.

Maximilianus, *Transylvanus*. Maximiliani Transylvani Caesaris a secretis epistola, de admirabili & novissima Hispanorū in Orientem navigatione ... Rome, F. Minitii Calvi, 1523. M257

The first printed account of the first circumnavigation, written by a student who interviewed sailors from the fleet who had come to Valladolid to report to Charles V.

Maximilianus, *Transylvanus*. De Moluccis insulis ... Cologne, E. Cervicornus, 1523. M258

Another edition of the above item. The order of priority is uncertain.

Maximilianus, *Transylvanus*. Il viaggio fatto da gli spangnivoli atorno a'l mondo. Venice, 1536. M259

This volume includes the first Italian edition of Maximilianus' account of Magellan's voyage, and a short account from the manuscript journal of Pigafetta. The latter professes to be a translation of Fabre's French abridgment published in Paris about 1525.

[Maxwell, Henry.] An essay towards an union of Ireland with England. London, Timothy Goodwin, 1703. M260

The case of Ireland is examined with respect to the principles of colonial government, and specifically considering the economic benefits that would come to both countries through union.

[Maya, Matias de.] Relação da conversão anossa Sancta Fè da rainha, & principe da China, & de outras pessoas da casa real, que baptizarão o anno de 1648. [Lisbon, Crasbeeck, 1650.] M261
An account of conversion and baptism of members of the Ming dynasty which was at that time being overthrown by the Manchu. Events of this displacement are also reported, with their consequences for Christian missions in China.

Meares, John. An answer to Mr. George Dixon. London, Logographic Press, 1791. M262
Dixon had charged Meares with illegal trading on the northwest coast of North America, with tampering with charts, and with misrepresenting the fur trade there. In this work, Meares presents his defense and attacks Dixon.

Meares, John. Authentic copy of the memorial respecting the capture of vessels in Nootka Sound. London, J. Debrett, 1760 (i.e. 1790). M263
Memorial to William Grenville concerning incidents at Nootka Sound in the course of opening trade between China and the western coast of America.

Meares, John. Voyages made in the years 1788 and 1789, from China to the north west coast of America. London, Logographic Press, 1790. M264
Contains observations on the possibility of finding a northwest passage and on the fur trade between the North American coast and China.

Meares, John. Voyages de la Chine à la côte nord-ouest d'Amérique. Paris, F. Buisson, 1792. M265
The first French edition, with extensive commentary by the translator.

Meares, John. Viaggi dalla China alla costa nord-ouest d'America fatti negli anni 1788 e 1789. Florence, Giovacchino Pagini, 1796. M266
The first Italian edition contains notes by the translator and geographical vocabulary of Pacific and North American names.

Meares, John. Tvänne resor från Ostindien till Americas nordvästra kust. Stockholm, J.S. Ekmanson for Mag. I. Utter, 1797. M267
An abridgment by Samuel Ödmann, this first Swedish edition includes no illustrations.

Mechlin, Christian. Flambeau de la mer et plan des ports de la Mediterannee. Manuscript. France [ca. 1708]. M268
A collection of 119 manuscript maps and charts in color, showing the major ports of the Mediterranean.

Meder, Lorenz. Handel Buch. Nuremberg, J. von Berg unnd U. Newber, 1558. M269
A survey of Europe's major commercial centers, reporting the commerce, business methods, markets, currencies, and other pertinent information.

Mediation emellan Ostindiska Compagniet, och des motståndare, af en opartisk auctor proponerad, i Stockholm den 19 novemb. 1734. Stockholm, B.G. Schneider [1734]. M270
A short proposal for mediation between those demanding the abolition of the Swedish East India Company and those supporting the organization.

Medici, Niccolini, merchants. [Letterbook of the Florentine mercantile company of Medici-Beroardi and its successors in Lisbon, 1726-1742.] Manuscript in Portuguese and Italian. Lisbon, 1726-1742. M271
The letterbook includes 284 copies of letters relating to Portuguese commerce, many of them concerning Brazil and the Atlantic islands.

Medina, Baltasar de. Chronica de la santa provincia de San Diego de Mexico, de religiosos desçalsos de N.S.P.S. Francisco e la Nueva-España. Mexico, Juan de Ribera, 1682. M272
The provincial for the Franciscan Order in New Mexico reports the activities of members of his order in that province. An engraved map of the province is included.

Medina, Pedro de. Arte de navegar. [Valladolid, F. Fernandez de Cordua, 1545.] M273
This is the first practical treatise on navigation, based on the experiences of Spanish pilots in transatlantic voyages. It contains a rare map of the New World, embodying the results of Spanish exploration to about the year 1540.

Medina, Pedro de. L'Arte del navegar. Venice, G. Pedrezano, 1554. M274
The first Italian edition.

Medina, Pedro de. Libro de grandezas y cosas memorables de España. Alcala de Henares, Pedro de Robles y Juan de Villanueva, 1566. M275
This history of Spain contains an account of the voyage of Columbus and includes Medina's map of the American continents.

Meditationes super problemate nautico, de implantatione malorum ... Paris, Claudium Jombert, 1728. M276
A prize-winning essay of the French Royal Academy of Science for 1727, addressing the question, "what is the best way to mast ships with respect to the number and height of masts." It was written by Pierre Bouguer, but published anonymously in this Latin version.

Megiser, Hieronymus. Warhafftige ... Beschreibung der uberausz reichen, mechtigen und weitberhümbten Insul Madagascar. Altenburg in Meissen, 1609. M277

A brief description of Madagascar and an account of its discovery by the Portuguese.

Meirelles, Manoel Antonio de. Relaçaõ da conquista das praças de Alorna, Bicholim, Avaro, Morly, Satarem, Tiracol, e Rary. Lisbon, Manoel Coelho Amado, 1747. M278

An account of a series of Portuguese military victories in the vicinity of Goa. The author was a military engineer who participated in the campaigns.

Meirelles, Manoel Antonio de. Relaçam dos felices successos da India desde 20 de Dezembro de 1746 até 28 do dito de 1747 ... Parte terceira. Lisbon, Francisco Luiz Ameno, 1748. M279

A continuation of a news publication reporting on Portuguese military actions and negotiations in the vicinity of Goa under the viceroyalty of the Marquez de Castello Novo, subsequently Marquez de Alorna.

Meirelles, Manoel Antonio de. Relaçaõ dos felices successos da India desde o primeiro de Janeiro até o ultimo de Dezembro de 1748 ... Parte quarta. Lisbon, Francisco Luiz Ameno, 1749. M280

A report on Portuguese military actions and negotiations in the vicinity of Goa under the viceroyalty of the Marquez de Castello Novo, subsequently Marquez de Alorna.

Meirelles, Manoel Antonio de. Relacaõ dos felices successos da India desde Janeiro de 1749 até o de 1750, no governo do illustris ... D. Pedro Miguel de Almeida de Portugal ... Parte quinta. Lisbon, Francisco Luiz Ameno, 1750. M281

The fifth and final newsletter in a series that reported Portuguese successes against the Mahrattas in the 1745-1750 period.

Meister, Georg. Der orientalisch-indianische Kunst-und Lust-Gärtner. Dresden, Johann Riedel, 1692. M282

Describes the plants of the East Indies, parts of the Asiatic mainland, Japan, and the Cape of Good Hope.

Mela, Pomponius. Cosmographi geographia ... Venice, E. Ratdolt, 1482. M283

The sixth incunabular edition of the work of a first-century geographer which was widely read in the fifteenth and sixteenth centuries.

Mela, Pomponius. Cosmographia. Venice, Christophorus de Pensis, de Mandello, ca. 1493. M284

The first edition to be edited by Ermolao Barbaro.

Mela, Pomponius. Pomponius Mela cosmographus De situ orbis Hermolai Barbari fideliter emendatus. [Venice, Albertinus de Lisona, 1502.] M285

Ermolao Barbaro's version of Mela's text without editorial commentary.

Mela, Pomponius. De situ orbis, libri tres. [n.p., ca. 1512.] M286

This edition by Joannes Camers is based on the earlier Ermolao Barbaro edition. It includes an index.

Mela, Pomponius. Pomponii Melae Hispani, Libri de situ orbis tres: adiectis Ioachimi Vadiani Heluetii in eosdem scholiis ... [Vienna Pannoniae, Lucae Alantse, 1518]. M287

The first edition of the Vadianus commentary on Pomponius Mela's text.

Mela, Pomponius. Pomponius Mela. Julius Solinus. Itinerarium Antonini Aug. Vivius Sequester. De regionibus urbis Rom[a]e: P. Victor. Dionysius Afer De situ orbis Prisciano interprete. [Toscolano, Alexander Paganinus, 1521.] M288

A collection of five Roman geographies which were popular in the sixteenth century, published in near-miniature format.

Mela, Pomponius. De orbis situ libri tres ... Basel, Andream Cratandrum, 1522. M289

In this edition the commentator, Vadianus compares Mela with other classical geographers and refers to modern discoveries.

Mela, Pomponius. De situ orbis. Paris, 1530. M290

A reprint of the 1522 edition.

Mela, Pomponius. De situ orbis. Paris, Michaelis Faizandat, 1539. M291

This edition has commentary on the text by Pedro Juan Oliver, and supplies new place names and terms to supplement the original text.

Mela, Pomponius. De orbis situ libri tres. Paris, Joannem Roigny, 1540. M292

This edition was prepared by Joachim Vadianus.

Mela, Pomponius. De situ orbis libri tres. Paris, Jacobum Kerver, 1557. M293

This edition was prepared by Pedro Juan Oliver. It includes diagrams and index.

Mela, Pomponius. De situ orbis libri tres ... Antwerp, Christophori Plantini, 1582. M294

The editor Andreas Schottus incorporates the commentary of two previous editors, Ermolao Barbaro and Fernando Nuñez de Guzman.

Mela, Pomponius. The worke of Pomponius Mela, the cosmographer, concerning the situation of the World. London, For Thomas Hacket, 1585. M295

The first edition of Arthur Golding's English translation.

Mela, Pomponius. La geographia de Pomponio Mela, que traduxo de Latin en Castellano ... Madrid, Diego Diaz de la Carrera, 1642. M296
The first Spanish edition.

Mela, Pomponius. Isaaci Vossii Observationes ad Pomponium Melam De situ orbis. The Hague, Adrianum Vlacq, 1658. M297
Mela's text is followed by the commentary of Vossius, which is about five times the length of the original text.

Mela, Pomponius. De situ orbis. Leiden, Luchtmanniana, 1743. M298
A small pocket-sized volume, edited by Abraham Gronovius. Includes the work of other editors and a comprehensive index.

Mela, Pomponius. De situ orbis libri III. Leiden, Samuelem Luchtmans, 1748. M299
This edition by Abraham Gronovius incorporates the notes of all previous editors.

Mela, Pomponius. De situ orbis libri tres. Eton, J. Pote, 1775. M300
The second edition of the Eton printing.

Mela, Pomponius. De situ orbis libri III. Leiden, Samuelem et Johannem Luchtmans, 1782. M301
A reprint of the 1748 edition.

Mello, Francisco Manuel de. Epanaphoras de varia historia Portugueza. Ao excellentissimo senhor Dom Joaõ da Sylva ... Em cinco relaçoens de sucessos pertencentes a este reyno. Lisbon, Antonio Craesbeeck de Mello, 1676. M302
An account of five episodes of importance to Portuguese history, including the discovery of Madeira and the return of Pernambuco to Portuguese control at the end of the wars with the Dutch in Brazil.

Melon, Jean François. Essai politique sur le commerce. [n.p.] 1734. M303
The author was an advocate of a mercantilist system which did not support protective legislation and favored the interests of the consumer over the producer.

Melon, Jean François. Essai politique sur le commerce. [n.p.] 1736. M304
This is an augmented edition, adding seven chapters.

[Melon, Jean François.] Essai politique sur le commerce. Amsterdam, François Changuion, 1754. M305
The fifth edition.

Melon, Jean François. Essai politique sur le commerce. [n.p.] 1761. M306
The most complete edition of this work, in which the author discusses critically all aspects of French economy, including agriculture, manufactures, monopolies, colonies, and overseas trading companies.

Melon, Jean François. A political essay upon commerce. Dublin, Philip Crampton, 1738. M307
A translation from the French with notes in which principles relating to the French economy are applied to the British and Irish situations.

Melville, Henry Dundas, viscount. [A collection of five documents relating to commercial and military affairs in the West Indies.] Manuscript. London and West Indies, 1793-1804. M308
Military affairs are dominant, but one memorial relates to a sugar act of 1792 and reflects the sugar merchants' point of view.

Mémoire. Manuscript. France, 1795. M309
A treatise on Europe's commerce, with particular attention to that of England.

Mémoire contenant les moyens de continuer le commerce, et de maintenie l'abondance dans les colonies françoises malgré les opérations de la guerre. Manuscript. France [ca. 1790]. M310
Especially concerns the means of protecting French commerce in the New World from the English, the Dutch, and privateers.

Mémoire du commerce particulier d'Amsterdam et de sa banque, année 1699. Manuscript. [n.p., ca. 1699.] M311
This manuscript was made for Charles-Jean Baptiste Fleurieu d'Armenonville, secretary of state to Louis XIV. It is a detailed report on the commerce of Holland, Leghorn, and the West Indies.

Mémoire historique des dernieres révolutions des provinces de l'ouest et du sud de la partie françoise de Saint-Domingue. Paris, Imprimerie du Patriote François, 1792. M312
A lengthy description of the revolutionary problems in Santo Domingo, written from the viewpoint of the revolutionists.

Memoire instructif, concernant la saisie faite dans une salle des grands Augustins. [Paris, ca. 1720.] M313
A memoir about a voyage to China in a ship belonging to the newly established Compagnie de la Chine.

Memoire instructif sur le privilege du vin. Marseilles, Pierre Penot [1719]. M314
A history of the wine trade of Marseilles, with a discourse on the regulations necessary to protect that city's interest in the trade.

Mémoire pour le Sieur de Bussy. Paris, L. Cellot, 1764. M315
A collection of seven documents concerning the case of the Compagnie des Indes against Sieur Bussy.

Mémoire pour les habitans de la colonie de l'isle de Bourbon. [n.p., ca. 176-?] M316
A complaint against the management of the colony on Mauritius by the Compagnie des Indes. Specifically it is charged that there is a lack of justice, irregularity of supply, lack of market for locally produced goods, and a lack of concern for the public welfare.

Mémoire pour servir de breve instruction tant aux directeurs & commissionaires provinciaux de la grande Compagnie de l'Amérique. Paris, G. de Luyne, 1653. M317
An outline of the plans of Siegneur de Royville for the establishment of a colony on the north coast of South America.

Memoire servant de remonstrance a nosseigneurs du Parlement, pour la Compagnie du Nort, establie en France pour la pesche des ballaines. [n.p., ca. 1645.] M318
A defense of the monopoly held by a French whaling company against criticism by others who sought to engage in that trade.

Mémoire sur l'admission des navires étrangers dans les colonies de l'Amérique. Manuscript. France [1776?]. M319
Proposes the establishment of two depots in the West Indies to receive French commerce, and thus control smuggling and trade there by foreigners.

Mémoire sur le commerce des États-Unis de l'Amérique. Manuscript. France [1789]. M320
Advocates close commercial relations with the United States, contemplating the establishment of warehouses in France for American goods.

Mémoire sur le conférences chez Mr. G. de B. remis le 7 avril 1779. Manuscript. France, April 7, 1779. M321
A criticism of a report showing excessive profits made by farmers general on the sale of salt, salt taxes, tobacco, real estate, etc.

Mémoire sur le prix de grains en France, et sur les avantages et désavantages de l'exportation. Manuscript. France, 1767. M322
The author approves of exporting grain, but only in connection with a storage program to insure an adequate supply of grain in France.

Memoire touchant le Canada. Manuscript. [n.p., ca. 1728.] M323
Calls for the colonization of Detroit and the establishment of French bases at Green Bay and "Chicagou."

Mémoire ultérieur, dans lequel les négocians de Marseille exposent le préjudice qui doit être apporté à leur commerce particulier. Marseilles, Jean Mossy, 1782. M324
The reaction to a decree which granted the right of free entry of goods in transit for re-export to cities other than Marseilles.

Memoires des deputés du commerce des villes de France. Manuscript. [n.p., ca. 1750.] M325
Deputies from Bordeaux, Languedoc, Bayonne, Nantes, Paris, La Rochelle, Rouen, Lyon, and Lille comment on the commerce of their respective areas and on the nation as a whole.

Mémoires historiques et géographiques sur les pays situés entre la mer noire et la mer Caspienne. Paris, H.J. Jansen & Perronneau, 1797. M326
A collection of three essays, with maps, on the geography, peoples, cities, and commerce of southern Russia, with information drawn from both ancient and modern sources.

Mémoires historiques sur la minorité de Louis XV. Manuscript. France, 1718-21. M327
A journal concerning the financial and commercial undertakings of John Law, whose bank established in 1716, came to be the major financial institution in the country.

Memoires pour Rome, sur l'etat de la religion chretienne dans la Chine. [n.p.] 1710. M328
These *Memoires* were compiled by Maillard de Tournon to document his actions with regard to the Chinese Rites controversy.

Mémoires pour servir a l'histoire de la Compagnie des Indes de France ... Manuscript. France, 1759. M329
Not a narrative history, but a series of twenty-six chapters dealing with the history of the various companies which were merged into the Compagnie des Indes in 1719.

Memoires sur le commerce de la concession du Senegal, et sur celui des François á la coste de Guinée, jusqu'a riviere du Bénin inclusivement: contenant des plans de régie pour les comptoirs et l'historique de ce que l'on a cru utile a l'intelligence des commerces locaux ... Manuscript. [n.p., between 1752 and 1770]. M330
A report on the commerce of Senegal by an anonymous official who notes the major products, problems of dealing with local people, the slave trade, presence of European rivals in the area, with recommendations for improvement.

Mémoires sur Sete et le Languedoc. Manuscript. [n.p., ca. 1780.] M331
A survey of the commerce of Sete, serving the Languedoc region, noting its active participation in the wine, tobacco, and fishing trades, among others.

Memoirs of a French officer who escaped from slavery. Oxford, Clarendon Press, 1786. M332
An account of travel and adventure in western Africa.

Memoirs of the principal transactions of the last war. London, Green and Russell, 1758. M333
A tract concerned chiefly with showing the importance of Nova Scotia to the British Empire in America.

Memoria abreviada, em que se descreve a grande, e importante ilha de Cuba: seu celebre porto, e famoso cidade da Havana. [Lisbon] Miguel Rodriegues, 1762. M334
A history and description of Cuba, with particular emphasis on the arrival of Columbus there and on the early organization of it as a Spanish Colony.

Memorial for the linen-manufacturers of Scotland. [n.p., 1742.] M335
The Scottish linen manufacturers call for protective legislation similar to that in effect for the encouragement of the woolen industry in England.

Memorial for the linen-manufacturers of Scotland. [n.p., 1745.] M336
A proposal for an increased tax on foreign linens of one penny per ell to encourage local manufacturers, with answers to objections likely to be raised by the American colonies which received much of this product.

Memorial of the agents of the West India sugar colonies; presented to the chancellor of the exchequer and the secretary of state. [London] 1792. M337
The petitioners urge that high taxes on East Indian sugar be continued, and that lowering them would not reduce the price of sugar in England, and could ruin the West Indian plantations.

Memorias do estado prezente, e comercio de Mossambique. Manuscript. [n.p., ca. 1760.] M338
A survey of the Portuguese colony of Mozambique, covering the years 1753-1758 and containing both statistical and historical information.

Memorie, aen de Hoogh Mogende Heeren Staten Generael der Vereenighde Nederlanden. [n.p.] 1668. M339
A memorandum pointing out the wisdom of a further subsidy to the Dutch West India Company.

Memorie over de achterstallighe subsidien by den staet geconsenteert aen de West-Indisch Compagnie. [n.p., ca. 1665.] M340
A memorandum concerning subsidies granted by the States General to the Dutch West India Company.

Memorie wegens het commercieele belang deezer republicq in het sluiten van een tractaat van commercie met de Vereenigde Staaten van Noord-Amerika. Rotterdam, D. Vis [etc.] 1781. M341
This tract presents the view that when the United States are free their trade may be diverted to the Netherlands.

Mendonça, Jeronymo de. Jornada de Africa. Lisbon, Pedro Crasbeeck, 1607. M342
The author was captured in a battle with Mohammedans in North Africa in 1578. This report on events preceding and during his captivity contains accounts of the major commercial centers of Morocco and Barbary and their commercial activity.

Mendonça, Jeronymo de. Jornada de Africa composta por Hieronimo de Mendonça ... Copiado fielemente da ediçaõ de Lisboa de 1607 por Bento Joze de Souza Farinha ... Lisbon, Joze da Silva Nazareth, 1785. M343
A very close reprint of the 1607 edition.

Mendosse, Tristan de. Le bon advis mesprisé, ou, La lettre de monsr. Tristan de Mendosse Jadis, ambassadeur pour le nouveau eletto don Joan el Quarto, par grace de trahison roy de Portugal: escrite à son successeur l'ambassadeur de Portugal, Francisco de Sousa Continho, presente a la Haye. [n.p.] 1649. M344
A satirical piece about Portuguese-Dutch diplomacy relating to their war in Brazil.

Mendoza, Fernando. Advis de ce qu'il reformer en la Cöpagnie des Jesuites, presenté au Pape & à la congregation generale ... [n.p.] 1615. M345
The first part of the book concerns the inner management of the Society of Jesus, and this is followed by four letters from various stations in India, dated 1608 and 1609.

Mendoza, Lourenço de. Suplicacion a Su Magestad Catolica ... en defensa de los Portugueses. Madrid, 1630. M346
A Portuguese priest's petition demanding equal treatment for the Portuguese living in South American areas ruled by Spain.

Mennander, Carl Fredrik. Anmärckningar samlade under en resa til China: och med wederbörandes tilstädielse. Abo, Joh. Rumpe [1794] M347
An account of a voyage to China by Israel Reinerius, a Swedish botanist, the first Swedish scholar to go to China. His work includes a detailed enumeration of the natural history of China and of places visted en route.

Mentzel, Christian. Kurtze chinesische Chronologia ... nebst einem ... moscowitischen Reisebeschreibung zu Lande nach China. Berlin, J.M. Rüdiger, 1696. M348
An appendix contains the first published notice of the travels of Evert Ysbrandszoon Ides from Muscovy to Peking, which were undertaken in 1693-95.

Mercado, Thomas de. Tratos y contratos de mercaderes. Salamanca, Mathias Gast, 1569. M349
A treatise on Spanish political economy, including discussion of commercial relations with the Indies, the slave

trade, currency exchange, fairs, and commercial and banking law.

Mercado, Thomas de. Summa de tratos y contratos. Seville, H. Diaz, 1571. M350
The second edition, augmented.

Mercator, Gerhard. Atlas sive cosmographicae meditationes de fabrica mundi et fabrica figura. Amsterdam, H. Hondij, 1628. M351
An atlas with hand-colored maps and French text based on Mercator's *Atlas* of 1585-95, and added to by Jodocus Hondius and his son Henry Hondius.

Mercator, Gerhard. Atlas. Amsterdam, H. Hondius, 1633-38. M352
The first English edition of Mercator's *Atlas*.

Mercator, Gerhard. Atlas Minor. Amsterdam, J. Hondius, 1607. M353
The first edition of Hondius' pocket-sized Mercator *Atlas*, with maps re-engraved on a small scale.

Mercator, Gerhard. Septentrionalium terrarum descriptio. Duisburg, 1595. M354
A north polar projection of the earth from the 1595 edition of Mercator's *Atlas*.

The merchant's complaint against Spain. London, W. Lloyd, 1738. M355
Shows merchant hostility to Spain based upon rivalry in the West Indies.

Mercier, Louis-Sébastien. Mon bonnet de nuit. Neuchatel, Société Typographique, et se vend a Versailles, chez Poinçtot, 1784-85. M356
A collection of writings on many subjects by a popular playwright, covering politics, economics, free trade, war, taxation, and the independence of the United States.

[Mercier de la Rivière, Pierre François Joachim Henri.] l'Interêt général de l'état; ou, La liberté du commerce des blés ... Amsterdam, et se trouve à Paris, Chez Desaint, 1770. M357
A discussion of free trade in grain by one of the leading physiocrats.

Meredith, Sir William. Historical remarks on the taxation of free states, in a series of letters to a friend. London, 1778. M358
A refutation of William Barron's *History of colonization of free states of antiquity*, taking the position that the British government's taxing policies were not justified by historical precedent.

Meres, Sir John. The equity of parliaments and publick faith, vindicated. London, C. Coningsby, 1720. M359
Advocates action by Parliament in the interest of annuitants to the South Sea Company.

Merolla, Girolamo. Breve, e succinta relatione del viaggio nel regno di Congo ... Naples, Per F. Mollo, 1692. M360
A Capuchin missionary's account of the flora, fauna, peoples, activities, and trade at Bahia, Brazil, and the Congo-Angola region.

Mesa, Sebastian de. Jornada de Africa por el Rey Don Sebastian, y union del reyno de Portugal a la corona de Castilla. Barcelona, Pedro Lacavalleria, 1630. M361
A review of the events leading up to the defeat of the Portuguese in Morocco in 1578 and the subsequent proclamation of the dual monarchy with Spain.

Mesquita Perestrello, Manoel. Relaçaõ summaria da viagem que fez Fernaõ d'Alvares Cabral, desde que partio deste reyno por capita` mór da armada que foy no anno de 1553: às partes da India athê que se perdeo no Cabo de Boa Esperasnça no anno de 1554. Lisbon, 1735. M362

Meteren, Emanuel van. Commentarien ofte memorien van-den staet. Amsterdam, 1609. M363
This is the first edition of this chronicle to contain considerable information on the Dutch in the East Indies and the English in America.

Meteren, Emanuel van. Niederländische Historien oder Geschichten aller deren Händel ... bis auff das Jahr 1611. Arnheim, J. Jansen, 1612. M364
This German edition is apparently a translation of the 1610 Dutch edition, and contains an account of Hudson's voyage into the Hudson River, and also a lengthy description of the English settlement in Virginia.

Meteren, Emanuel van. Belgica ... Historie der Neder-landscher ende haerder na-buren oorlogen ende geschiendenissen, tot den jare 1612. The Hague, H. van Wouw, 1614. M365
This edition published after the author's death adds to the information on American settlements included in the editions of 1609 and 1612.

Meteren, Emanuel van. l'Histoire des Pays-Bas. The Hague, Hillebrant Jacobsz Wouw, 1618. M366
A translation of the 1614 Dutch edition, the last to which the author contributed.

Metius, Adriaan Adriaansz. Institutiones astronomicae & geographicae: fondamentale ende grondelijcke onderwysinghe van de sterrekonst, ende beschryvinghe der aerden, door het ghebruyck van de hemelsche ende aerdtsche globen. Amsterdam, Willem Jansz, 1621. M367
An instruction book in cosmography, enhanced by illustrations depicting instruments designed by the author.

Metius, Adriaan Adriaansz. Nieuwe geographische ondervvysinge: waer in ghehandelt werdt de beschryvinghe ende afmetinghe des aertsche globe ende van sijn ghebruyck. Amsterdam, Willem Jansz, 1621. M368
A companion volume to Metius's cosmography, with emphasis on the practical aspects of celestial navigation.

Metrà, Andrea. Il mentore perfetto de negozianti. Trieste, Giovanni Tommaso Hoechenberger; Wage, Fleis & Co., 1793-97. M369
A five volume commercial handbook which describes the trade of the major cities of the world and includes commentary on the trade of islands and colonies as well.

[Metre, Alexander Christian de.] De Metrens remonstrantie, op't woord van de kaas-verkoopers. Amsterdam, 1673. M370
A defense of Dutch commercial inclinations. The author was offended by the French who had referred to the Dutch as a nation of cheese merchants.

Mexia, Pedro. Viluältige Beschreibung, christenlicher unnd heidnischer Keyseren, Künigen, weltweiser Männeren gedächtnuss wirdige Historien ... Basel, Henricum Petri, 1564.
M371
An encyclopedic work which enjoyed great popularity in the sixteenth century. It includes astronomical, geographical and historical information.

Mexía, Pedro. Selva rinovata di varia lettione ... diuisa in cinque parti ... aggiuntovi di nuovo alcuni Raggionamenti, filosofici in dialogo ... Venice, Ghirardo Imberti, 1638. M372
A much published collection of essays on several subjects including geography and a discussion of Magellan's circumnavigation.

Mexia, Pedro. Selva di varia lettione ... Nella quale si contiene histoire memorabili; antiche, e moderne ... delle quattro parti del mondo Asia, Africa, Europa, Mondo Nouvo ... Venice, Iseppo Prodocimo, 1682. M373
A late edition of this compendium of knowledge.

Meyerberg, Augustin, Freiherr von. Al'bom Meierberga: vidy i bytovyia kartiny Rossīi XVII vieka. St. Petersburg, Izd. A.S. Suvorina, 1903.
M374
A facsimile of a manuscript sketchbook depicting rural, village, court, and other scenes from Russia based on travels of German ambassadors in 1661 and 1662. The text is in German.

Meyerberg, Augustin, Freiherr von. Iter in Moschoviam. [n.p., ca. 1680.] M375
This account of an embassy to Czar Alexis from the Holy Roman Emperor Leopold describes many Russian cities and provinces and includes a section on the laws of the country.

Meyerberg, Augustin, Freiherr von. Voyage en Moscovie. Leiden, F. Harring, 1688. M376
A much abridged edition.

Meynier de Salinelles, Étienne David. Rapport fait a l'Assemblée nationale au nom du comité d'agriculture et de commerce, sur la régime à donner au port et au territoire de Marseille, quant aux droits de douane. Paris, Imprimerie Nationale [1791]. M377
A consideration of the benefits Marseilles had received from a situation of protected commerce, with the conclusion that it should be continued.

Michaelis, Johann David. Recueil de questions, proposées à une société de savants, qui par ordre de Sa Majesté danoise font le voyage de l'Arabie. Amsterdam, S.J. Baalde; Utrecht, J. van Schoonhoven & Comp., 1774. M378
One hundred questions put to the members of the Danish expedition which explored Arabia in 1761-67. The author was an orientalist and one of the key figures in organizing the expedition.

Michaelis, Johann David. Vragen aan een gezelschap van geleerde mannen, die op bevel Zyner Majesteit des Konings van Deenmarken naar Arabie reizen. Amsterdam, S.J. Baalde; Utrecht, J. van Schoonhoven, 1774. M379
The first Dutch edition, edited by J. van Ekers.

Michelet, Jacques. Discours de geographie contenant les principales pratiques pour les descriptions de la terre, et de la mer ... Paris, Chez Hierosme Drovart, 1615. M380
A textbook in mathematical geography, instructing in methods of depicting the earth or portions of it in various projections.

[Michell, Abraham Ludwig.] Exposition of the motives ... which have determined the King (of Prussia) ... to lay an attachment upon the capital funds, which His Majesty had promised to reimburse to the subjects of Great-Britain. London, For J. Raymond [1752]. M381
This document notes the violations of the freedom of the seas by British privateers against Prussian ships. It includes extensive arguments from international law and identifies the Prussian and British ships involved.

Michelot, Henry, and L. Bremond. [Atlas of Mediterranean maps. Marseilles, 1715-26.]
M382
A collection of sixteen charts of coasts and ports of the Mediterranean and its islands. Major harbors are shown in considerable detail.

[Middelgeest, Simon van.] Nootwendich discours oft Vertooch aan de hooch-mogende heeren Staaten Generaal van de participanten der Ost-Indische Compagnie. [n.p.] 1622. M383

A protest against the extension of the charter of the Dutch East India Company because of the arbitrariness of the directors.

[Middelgeest, Simon van.] Tweede noot-wendiger discours ofte Vertooch aan alle lant-lievende. [n.p., 1622.] M384
A second complaint by the stockholders against the directors of the Dutch East India Company.

Middleton, Charles Theodore. A new and complete system of geography. London, J. Cooke, 1778-1779. M385
A general geography which includes information on the commerce of most of the known regions of the earth.

Middleton, Christopher. To the King: This chart of Hudson's Bay & Straits, Baffin's Bay, Strait Davis & Labrador coast &c. is most humbly dedicated. [London] C. Middleton, 1743. M386
This chart resulted from Middleton's voyage along the west coast of Hudson Bay in 1742. It indicates no westward passage out of the bay, and includes much navigational information.

Middleton, Christopher. A vindication of the conduct of Captain Christopher Middleton, in a late voyage ... for discovering a north-west passage ... London, For the Author, 1743. M387
A reply to the accusations of Arthur Dobbs that Middleton sought to prevent a discovery of the passage.

Middleton, Christopher. A reply to the Remarks of Arthur Dobbs on Captain Middleton's Vindication ... London, G. Brett, 1744. M388
A continuation of Middleton's defense.

[Miege, Guy.] Des Graffen Carlile nahmens Sr. Königl. Maj. von Gross-Britannien abgelegte drey Gesandtschafften, an Alexium Michaelowitz, Tzaaren und Gross-Fürsten in Mosskau, &c. ... Samt einer curieusen Beschreibung des Landes Moscovien, ingleichen Liefflands und deren beyderseits Einwohner ... Frankfurt und Leipzig, Joh. Gabriel Ehrt, 1701. M389
An account of Charles II's embassy to Moscow, Sweden, and Copenhagen. This German edition includes an extensive description of Muscovy not found in the English or French editions.

Mijdregt, Heer van. Consideration ... wegens de Caep de Goede Hoop. Manuscript. Netherlands, 1692. M390
A series of extracts from six letters dated October 6, 1688, to December 19, 1691, containing complaints against the administration of the Dutch settlement at the Cape by Governor Simon Vander Stel.

Milan (Italy). Laws, etc. [Statutorum inclite civitatis Mediolani.] Milan, Joannes Antonius de Honate, 1482. M391
The statutes of Milan, containing laws governing commerce and a section on the *Statuta mercatorum*.

Milan (Italy). Laws, etc. Statuta Mediolani. Milan, Jo. Antonium Castellionaeum, 1552. M392
A new edition with extensive commentary by C. Cotta, a student of Roman law, followed by a section *Novissima Mediolani statuta* reflecting Milan's sixteenth century dependent status.

Milan (Italy). Laws, etc. Statuta mercatorum auri, argenti, et serici Mediolani. [Milan?] 1610. M393
A collection of documents containing regulations on various aspects of Milan's commercial life from 1501 to 1575.

[Miller, Gerard Fridrikh.] A letter from a Russian sea-officer, to a person of distinction at ... St. Petersburgh. London, A. Linde, 1754. M394
Contains the first English account of the second Bering expedition, and material on the mapping of northwestern North America. French and German editions were published in 1753.

Miller, Gerard Fridrikh. A new map of the north east coast of Asia, and the north west coast of America, with the late Russian discoveries. [London, 1764.] M395
This map is removed from *London Magazine*, May, 1764, where it illustrated a communication on the migration of people from Asia to America.

Miller, Gerard Fridrikh. Nouvelle carte des decouvertes faites par des vaisseaux russes aux côtes inconnues de l'Amerique septentrionale avec les pais adiacentes. St. Petersburg, l'Academie Imperiale des Sciences, 1754. M396
The earliest map to show the routes of Bering and Chirikov to Alaska during the second Bering expedition.

Miller, Gerard Fridrikh. Nouvelle carte des decouvertes faites par des vaisseaux russiens aux côtes inconnues de l'Amerique septentrionale avec les pais adiacents. St. Petersburg, Academie Imperiale des Sciences, 1784. M397
This edition of the map shows the Aleutian Islands in more realistic form than earlier editions, and changes the representation of the northwest coast of America radically.

Miller, Gerard Fridrikh. Opisanie morskikh puteshestvii po ledevitomu i po vostochnomu moriiu s Rossiiskoi storony uchinennykh. St. Petersburg, Imperial Academy of Sciences, 1758. M398

The first Russian account of Vitus Bering's voyage through the Bering Strait, from the third volume of *Sochineniia i perevody*.

Miller, Gerard Fridrikh. The Russian discoveries, from the map published by the Imperial Academy of St. Petersburg. London, For Robert Sayer, 1775. M399

The original edition was published in 1773. It shows the tracks of Bering and Chirikov to the coast of North America in 1741 as well as routes of earlier explorers along the northeast coast of Siberia.

Miller, Gerard Fridrikh. Voyages from Asia to America, for completing the discoveries of the north-west coast of America. London, T. Jefferys, 1761. M400

Accounts of voyages made by the Russians to the west coast of North America and to the Aleutian Islands.

Miller, Gerard Fridrikh. Voyages from Asia to America, for completing the discoveries of the North West Coast of America ... London, T. Jefferys, 1764. M401

The second edition of this English translation, with corrections in the text, several large notes to the text, and an index.

Miller, Gerard Fridrikh. Voyages et découvertes fiates par les Russes le long des côtes de la Mer glaciale. Amsterdam, Marc-Michel Rey, 1766. M402

The first French edition.

Millet, T. (Thomas). Nouvel examen du rapport de M. Barnave sur l'affaire de Saint-Domingue, d'après celui qu'il a fait imprimer. Paris [ca. 1790]. M403

Barnave's report, it is stated here, was based on insufficient information on the true motives and the true situation in Saint Domingue which produced rebellion.

Milner, James. Three letters relating to the South-Sea Company and the bank. London, J. Roberts and A. Dodd, 1720. M404

The author condemns the company for stock-jobbing and falsely raising the value of the stock.

Milscent, Claude-Louis-Michel. Du régime colonial. Paris, Imprimerie du Cercle Social, 1792. M405

Comments on the situation in the French colonies, with particular reference to Saint Domingue by a Creole who presents the case for that element in the colonial population.

Milton, John. A brief history of Moscovia and of the less-known countries lying eastward of Russia as far as Cathay. London, M. Flesher for Brabazon Aylmer, 1682. M406

A description of eastern Europe and western Asia from a variety of sources.

Minadoi, Giovanni Tommaso. Historia de la guerra entre Turcos y Persianos. Madrid, F. Sanchez, 1588. M407

This is a firsthand account of approximately the first ten years of Turkey's war with Persia. Minadoi was in Turkey and Syria until 1585 as part of the Venetian consulate.

Ministerial prejudices in favour of the convention examin'd and answer'd. London, T. Cooper, 1739. M408

An examination of the public opposition to the policy of continued peace with Spain.

Mirabeau, Honoré-Gabriel de Riquetti, comte de. De la Banque d'Espagne, dite de Saint-Charles. [n.p.] 1785. M409

A vigorous attack on the recently-formed Bank of St. Charles which was in effect a national bank of Spain. The author notes its close connection to the Philippine Company, a new trading venture.

Mirabeau, Honoré-Gabriel de Riquetti, comte de. Discours de m. Mirabeau l'ainé, concernant le revenu public à établir sur la consommation du tabac dans le royaume. [Paris, Imprimerie Nationale, 1791.] M410

Discusses the effects of national control over the tobacco trade, including the rights to trade, manufacture, distribute, and sell the tobacco.

Mirabeau, Honoré-Gabriel de Riquetti, comte de. Opinion de M. de Mirabeau l'aîné, sur les retours de l'Inde: imprimée par ordre de l'Assemblée nationale. Paris, Imprimerie Nationale, 1790. M411

An examination of the current declaration of free trade to the East Indies, and a plea for further liberalization.

[Mirabeau, Victor de Riquetti, marquis de.] l'Ami des hommes, ou Traité de la population. Hamburg, Chrétien Herold, 1758. M412

An examination, by an early Physiocratic writer, of economic and political questions focusing on population as the significant consideration in the economy.

[Mirabeau, Victor de Riquetti, marquis de.] Philosophie rurale, ou Économie générale et politique de l'agriculture, reduite à l'ordre immuable des loix physiques & morales, qui assurent la prospérité des empires. Amsterdam, Libraires Associés, 1763. M413

This classic of Physiocratic thought was inspired by François Quesnay who also wrote the seventh chapter. It contains the most complete version of the thinking of Quesnay and Mirabeau on political economy.

Mirbeck, Ignace-Frédéric. Lettre a m. Bertrand, ci-devant ministre de la marine. [Paris, Clousier, 1792.] M414

An attack upon Bertrand's publication *Observations, addressées à l'Assemblée nationale, sur les discours prononcés par MM. Gensonné et Brissot*, which Mirbeck regarded as libellous.

Mirbeck, Ignace-Frédéric. Lettre a m. de la Coste, ministre de la marine. [Paris, Clousier, 1792.] M415
  A letter from a colonial official clarifying some of his activities in the Leeward Islands.

Misselden, Edward. Free trade. Or, the meanes to make trade florish. London, John Legatt for Simon Waterson, 1622. M416
  A survey of England's unsatisfactory trade situation, with remedies suggested, including better regulations and royal assistance to the East India Company.

Missive inhoudende den aerdt vanden treves tusschen den koninck van Spaengien ende de Gheunieerde Provincien. [n.p.] 1630. M417
  An analysis of the truce between Spain and the Netherlands based largely on the writings of Emanuel van Meteren.

Missive uyt Middelburgh aen syn vrient in Hollandt. Middelburg, G. Verdussen, 1647. M418
  Favors peace with Spain because of the threat to Dutch trade from Swedish domination of the Baltic.

Mitchell, Archibald. India courier extraordinary. Proceedings of Parliament relating to Warren Hastings, Esq. [London] 1786-87. M419
  A collection of speeches, charges, evidence, and testimony presented in the House of Commons, leading to the impeachment of Warren Hastings.

Mitchell, John. The contest in America between Great Britain and France ... London, A. Millar, 1757. M420
  A description of British and French colonies in America, their plantations, trade, etc.

Mitchell, John. A map of the British and French dominions in North America. London, J. Mitchell for Jefferys and Faden [1774?]. M421
  A later impression of an important map in American history, giving British and French political divisions, and much historical, descriptive, and geographical data, including information on Indian tribes.

Mitchell, John. Present state of Great Britain and North America. London, T. Becket and P.A. de Hondt, 1767. M422
  An account of the scarcity of staple commodities, decline in trade, overpopulation, and need for manufactured goods in England.

Mittelberger, Gottlieb. Gottlieb Mittelbergers Reise nach Pennsylvanien im Jahr 1750. und Rükreise nach Teutschland im Jahr 1754 ... Frankfurt und Leipzig, 1756. M423
  A German immigrant's account of his experiences in settling in Pennsylvania, noting recruitment of settlers in Europe, the trans-atlantic voyage, settlement processes and life on the frontier.

Mizauld, Antoine. Cosmographiae, seu Mundi sphaerae, libri tres, nova methodo & dilucida conscripti. Paris, Federicum Morellum, 1567. M424
  A cosmographical treatise in Latin verse, anti-Copernican in tone.

Mocquet, Jean. Voyages en Afrique, Asie, Indes Orientales & Occidentales. Paris, J. De Heuqueville, 1617. M425
  An account of experiences during five voyages made between 1601 and 1612.

Mocquet, Jean. Reysen in Afrique, Asien, Oosten West-Indien. Dordrecht, Abraham Andriessz, 1656. M426
  The first Dutch edition.

Mocquet, Jean. Wunderbare jedoch gründlich- und war-haffte Geschichte und Reise Begebnisse in Africa, Asia, Ost-und West-Indien. Lüneberg, Johann Georg Lippers [1688]. M427
  The first German edition, substantially enlarged through commentary by the translator, Johann Georg Schoch.

Mocquet, Jean. Travels and voyages into Africa, Asia and America, the East and West-Indies; Syria, Jerusalem, and the Holy-Land. London, For W. Newton [etc.] 1696. M428
  The first English edition.

Modena (Duchy). Tariffa quale di presente si osserva sopra l'estima di quanto hanno da pagare le mercantie nella gabella di Modona. Cosi per il terriero, com per il forestiero. Modona, Antonio, e Filippo fratelli de' Gadaldini, 1615. M429

A modern universal table: the most copious and authentick that ever was published, of the present state of the real and imaginary monies of the world. [n.p., 1770?] M430
  A broadside giving values of currencies for Europe, Asia, Africa and America.

A modest and just apology for: or, defence of the present East-India-Company. London, 1690. M431
  A defense of the East India Company against charges that it had acted illegally in supressing interlopers and had been at fault in hostilities that occurred in India in 1686.

Modest offer of some meet considerations ... particularly to East India. [London, 1695.] M432
  Proposes opening the East Indian trade to all English subjects.

[Moerbeeck, J.A.] Spaenschen raedt. Om die Geunieerde Provincien. The Hague, A. Meuris, 1626. M433
The author attempts to show the damage that would come to the Netherlands, including its West India Company, by concluding peace with Spain.

Moitoiret de Blainville, Antoine. Traité du jauge de la marine et de la navigation. Rouen, Jean-B. Besogne, 1698. M434
A discourse on the measuring of a variety of types of ships, and also some information on methods of navigation.

Moitoiret de Blainville, Antoine. Traité du jauge universel. Rouen, Jean-B. Besogne, 1698. M435
A treatise on measurement, applied particularly to commercial shipping.

[Molesworth, Robert Molesworth, viscount.] An account of Denmark, as it was in the year 1692. London, 1694. M436
This history of Denmark contains information on imports, exports, tariffs, and commercial relations. Special mention is made of the Sund tolls and the history of their development.

[Molina, Giovanni Ignazio.] Compendio della storia geografica, naturale, e civile del regno del Chile. Bologna, S. Tommaso d'Aquino, 1776. M437
This natural and civil history of Chile is illustrated by ten engravings and a map. It includes statistical data on the European settlements there.

[Molina, Giovanni Ignazio.] Des herrn abts Vidaure Kurzgefasste geographische, natürliche und bürgerliche Geschichte des Königreichs Chile. Hamburg, C.E. Bohn, 1782. M438
The first German edition.

Molina, Giovanni Ignazio. Saggio sulla storia naturale del Chili del signor abate Giovanni Ignazio Molina. Bologna, Stamperia di S. Tommaso d'Aquino, 1782. M439
The first edition of the *Natural history of Chile*.

Molina, Giovanni Ignazio. Saggio sulla storia civile del Chili del signor abate Giovanni Ignazio Molina. Bologna, Stamperia di S. Tommaso d'Aquino, 1787. M440
Part II, a companion to the above item.

Molina, Giovanni Ignazio. Compendio de la historia geografica, natural y civil del reyno de Chile. Madrid, Antonio de Sancha, 1788-95. M441
The first Spanish edition.

Molina, Giovanni Ignazio. Essai sur l'histoire naturelle du Chili. Paris, Née de la Rochelle, 1789. M442
A French translation of Part I of Molina's enlarged compendium of information on Chile. Part II of the work was not published in French.

Moll, Herman. Atlas minor. London, H. Moll, 1729. M443
A set of sixty-two maps of various countries.

Moll, Herman. A system of geography. London, Timothy Childe, 1701. M444
A world geography heavily weighted toward Europe, but with good descriptions and maps of Asia, Africa, and America.

Møller, Niels Christian C. Bidrag eller udkast til Frederiks-Øernes eller de Nikobariske Øers, indbyggeres, producters, o.s.v. Copenhagen, Mathias Seest, 1799. M445
An account of the Nicobar Islands, noting natural history, economic products, inhabitants, and missionary activity, reflecting Danish interest in those islands in the Indian Ocean.

Molloy, Charles. De jure maritimo et navali, or, A treatise of affairs maritime and of commerce. London, Abel Swalle, 1690. M446
A standard text in maritime law in its fifth edition, but with a title page from the fourth.

Monardes, Nicolás. Brief traité de la racine mechoacan, venue de l'Espagne nouvelle. Rouen, Martin & Mallard, 1588. M447
Monardes hails mechoacan, the "rhubarb of the Indies," as being much more effective and less painful than rhubarb as a medicine. It was brought back to Spain and sold at a high price.

Monardes, Nicolás. De simplicibus medicamentis ex Occidentali India. Antwerp, Christopher Plantin, 1574. M448
The first Latin edition of a work written by a Spanish physician, describing medicinal plants found in America. This is the first translation from the original Spanish edition of 1569.

Monardes, Nicolás. Delle cose che vengono portate dall' Indie Occidentali pertinenti all' uso della medecina. Venice, Giordano Ziletti, 1575. M449
The first Italian edition.

Monardes, Nicolás. Delle cose che vengono portate dall' Indie Occidentali pertinenti all' uso della medicina. Venice, F. Ziletti, 1582. M450
The second Italian edition.

Monardes, Nicolás. Joyfull newes out of the new-found worlde. London, E. Allde by the assigne of Bonham Norton, 1596. M451

The third English edition of a popular herbal, first published in English in 1577.

Monconys, Balthasar de. Journal des voyages. Lyons, H. Boissat & G. Remeus, 1665-66. M452

Contains observations on natural and scientific phenomena in the Levant area.

Moniz de Carvalho, António. Francia interessada con Portugal ... con noticias de los intereses comunes de los principes, y estados de Europa. Paris, Miguel Blageart, 1644. M453

An appeal to Anne of Austria, mother and guardian of the young Louis XIV of France, for continued close relations between France and Portugal.

A Monsieur le cher. d'entrecasteaux, brigadier des armées navales, gouverneur général des isles de France et de Bourbon et autres isles voisines; et a Monsieur Motais de Narbonne, commissaire général de la marine ... Paris, Imprimerie de Monsieur, 1789. M454

A petition from the colonists and merchants of French possessions in the Indian Ocean noting the damage that is done to their commerce by the monopolistic position of the Compagnie des Indes.

Montagu, Mary Wortley, lady. Brieven van de hoogëdele vrouwe Maria Worthly Montague. Amsterdam, P. Meijer, 1765. M455

The first Dutch edition of Lady Mary's *Letters from the East*, describing travels from Vienna to Constantinople in 1717 and 1718.

Montanus, Arnoldus. Gedenkwaerdige gesantschappen der Oost-Indische maetschappy in't Vereenigde Nederland, aen de Kaisaren van Japan. Amsterdam, Jacob Meurs, 1669. M456

More than an account of an embassy, this work is a compilation of information on the religion, commerce, politics, geography, and history of Japan and other regions of eastern Asia.

Montanus, Arnoldus. Atlas japannensis: being remarkable addresses by way of embassy from the East-India Company of the United Provinces, to the Emperor of Japan. London, Tho. Johnson, 1670. M457

The first English edition.

Montanus, Arnoldus. Ambassades mémorables de la Compagnie des Indes Orientales des Provinces Unies, vers les emperours du Japon. Amsterdam, J. de Meurs, 1680. M458

The first French edition.

Montanus, Arnoldus. Atlas chinensis ... London, T. Johnson, 1671. M459

An account of two voyages from Batavia to China by the Dutch East India Company, describing the commerce of China.

[Montanus, Arnoldus.] Die unbekante Neue Welt; oder, Beschreibung des Welt-teils Amerika, und Sud-Landes: darinnen vom Uhrsprunge der Ameriker und Sudländer, und von den gedenckwürdigen Reysen der Europer darnach zu ... Amsterdam, Jacob von Meurs, 1673. M460

The first German edition of an extensive compilation of geographical, historical, and natural history information on the New World.

Montanus, Arnoldus. De wonderen van 't Oosten. Amsterdam, C. Jansz., 1651. M461

A history of early Dutch activities in the East Indies.

[Montaran, de.] Memoire sur les tarifs des droits de traites en général. Paris, Prault, 1762. M462

A discussion of import and export duties with a view to improving them through a national rather than regional tariff system.

Montefiore, Joshua. An authentic account of the late expedition to Bulam, on the coast of Africa: with a description of the present settlement of Sierra Leone, and the adjacent country. London, For J. Johnson, 1794. M463

An account of the attempt to settle a colony on the west African island of Bulam to demonstrate the possibilities of developing agricultural colonies in Africa as an alternative to the slave trade.

Montgomery, Sir Robert. A discourse concerning the design'd establishment of a new colony to the south of Carolina. London, 1717. M464

A promotion piece describing the writer's colonizing plans for his property in Georgia. The proposal was never acted upon but is extremely interesting as an idealized blueprint for New World settlement.

Montstopping aende vrede-haters. Leiden, Cornelis M. van Schie, 1647. M465

In urging peace with Spain on the basis of expediency, the author absolves Spain of blame in the decline of the West India Company.

Montvert, m. de (Pierre-Esprit Sambuc). Observations sur le système de l'Angleterre, pour réduire dans sa dépendance le commerce maritime de l'univers. [Paris, Herissant] 1790. M466

Evaluates England's political and economic system as a means to further its commercial ambitions, and notes what resources Spain and France can use to prevent English domination of world trade.

Moore, Francis. Travels into the inland parts of Africa. London, E. Cave, 1738. M467

The journal of an officer of the Royal African Company, describing the Gambia River region.

Moore, Francis. Travels into the inland parts of Africa ... London, E. Cave [1740]. M468

The second edition.

Moore, Francis. A voyage to Georgia. London, For Jacob Robinson, 1744.   M469
The record of the progress of the Georgia colony from October 1735 to June 1736. It describes flora and fauna in detail and praises the colony and its management.

Mooy, Maarten. Omstandig journaal van de reize naar Groenland. Amsterdam, David Weege, 1787.   M470
An account of a Dutch whaling voyage lasting from April 1786 to February 1787. It describes the equipping and victualing of the ship, gives a list of its crew, and notes other ships met near Greenland.

Moracin correspondence. [A collection of eleven letters and one document.] Manuscript. Pondichery, 1741-93.   M471
Leon de Moracin was an official of the Compagnie des Indes.

La morale pratique des Jesuites. Cologne, 1689-1695.   M472
A collection of anti-Jesuit materials containing criticism of their conduct of missions abroad as well as their theological doctrines.

Morden, Robert. Geography rectified: or A description of the world. London, R. Morden and T. Cockerill, 1700.   M473
Descriptions of many countries, their peoples, commodities, coins, customs, etc.

Moreau, Jacob Nicolas. O observador Hollandez, ou, Primeira carta de Mons. van ** a Mons. H. ** da Haya: sobre o estado presente dos negocios da Europa: traduzido da lingua Franceza ... Lisbon, Na Officina patriarcal de Francisco Luiz Ameno, 1757.   M474
A commentary on the French and Indian wars in North America with some additional account of the Anglo-French conflict in India as well. It is dated September 1, 1755, and is based on *l'Observateur hollandais*, a Paris newspaper.

[Moreau, Jacob Nicolas.] O observador Hollandez, ou, Segunda carta de Mons. van ** a Mons. H. ** da Haya: sobre o estado presente dos negocios da Europa: traduzido da lingua Franceza na Portugueza ... Lisbon, Na Officina Patriarcal de Luiz Ameno, 1758.   M475
This newsletter dated October 1, 1755 is concerned primarily with Anglo-French warfare in the interior of North America, including Washington's defeat at Fort Necessity.

[Moreau, Jacob Nicolas.] O observador Hollandez, ou, Terceira carta de Mons. Van ** a Mons. H. ** da Haya: sobre o estado presente dos negocios da Europa: traduzido da lingua Franceza na Portugueza ... Lisbon, Na Officina Patriarcal de Francisco Luiz Ameno, 1758.   M476
A general review of the Anglo-French war, dated October 15, 1755.

Moreau, Pierre. Histoire des derniers troubles du Bresil, entre les Hollandois et les Portugais. Paris, A. Courbe [1651].   M477
An account of the struggles for Brazil between the Portuguese and Dutch, with emphasis on the period from 1644 to 1648.

Moreau, Pierre. Klare en waarachtige beschryving van de leste beroerten en asval der Portugezen in Brasil. Amsterdam, Jan Hendriksz & Jan Rieuwertsz, 1652.   M478
The first Dutch edition.

Moreau de Saint-Méry, M. L. E. (Médéric Louis Elie). Considérations présentées aux vrais amis du repos et du bonheur de la France, a l'occasion des nouveaux mouvemens de quelques soi-disant Amis-des-Noirs. Paris, Imprimerie Nationale, 1791.   M479
An argument against the extreme actions of the Amis de Noirs, a group trying to bring an end to French participation in the slave trade.

Moreau de Saint-Méry, M. L. E. (Médéric Louis Elie). Description topographique, physique, civile, politique et historique de la partie française de l'isle Saint-Domingue. Philadelphia, l'Auteur; Paris, Dupont; Hamburg, Libraries, 1797-98.   M480
A very complete description of the French holdings on the island just before the insurrection by one who knew the French West Indies from long experience.

Moreau de Saint-Méry, M. L. E. (Médéric Louis Elie). Loix et constitutions des colonies françoises de l'Amérique sous le vent. Paris, Quillau [1784].   M481
A subscription proposal for an eight volume work on the French West Indian Colonies.

Moreau de Saint-Méry, M. L. E. (Médéric Louis Elie). Opinion de m. Moreau de S. Méry, député de la Martinique. Paris, Impr. Nationale [1789].   M482
Relates to a motion of L. Curt concerning the appointment of a committee to examine colonial policy.

Moreira, João Marques. Relação da magestosa, misteriosa, e notavel acclamaçam que se fez a Magestade d'El Rey Dom Joam o IV ... na cidade do nome de Deos do grande imperio da China ... Lisbon, Lopes Roza, 1644.   M483
An essay in honor of Portugal's King João IV, written at Macao and presenting a description of Portuguese presence in that area.

Morejon, Pedro. A briefe relation of the persecution lately made against the Catholike Chris-

tians, in the kingdome of Japonia. [S. Omer] 1619. M484
The first English edition. Part one only was published.

Morejon, Pedro. Relacion de la persecucion que huuo estos años contra la Iglesia de Iapon, y los ministros della ... Saragossa, Iuan de Larumbe, 1617. M485
An account of the Jesuit mission in Japan at a time when it was being repressed by government authority.

Morejon, Pedro. Relacion de los martyres del Japon del año de 1627. Por el padre Pedro Moreion, rector del collegio de la Compañia de Jesus de Macan ... Mexico, Juan Ruyz, 1631. M486
An account of Japanese suppression of Christian missions, with martyrdoms of Jesuits, Franciscans, and Dominicans noted, as well as Japanese Christians.

Morel de la Durantaye, Olivier. [Quittance acknowledging payment of debt by Sieur Perrot.] Manuscript in French. Michilimackinac, Aug. 16, 1690. M487
The quittance calls for Perrot to be responsible for transporting beaver pelts to Montreal, specifying quality and value.

Morellet, André. Examen de la Réponse de m. N** au Mémoire de m. l'Abbé Morellet sur la Compagnie des Indes. Paris, Desaint, 1769. M488
A reply to Necker's criticism of Morellet's attack upon the privileged position of the Compagnie des Indes.

Morellet, André. Mémoire sur la situation actuelle de la Compagnie des Indes. Paris, Desaint, 1769. M489
An argument supported by statistics against the continued monopoly by the Compagnie des Indes over much of France's trade.

Morellet, André. Mémoires relatifs a la discussion du privilége de la Nouvelle Compagnie des Indes. Amsterdam, et se trouve a Paris, Demonville, 1787. M490
A collection of arguments, pro and con, regarding the chartering of a monopolistic company to carry on French trade to Asia.

Morellet, M. Nottes sur le commerce qui se fait dans l'empire du grand Mogol. Manuscript. [France? ca. 1725.] M491
A report to the Comte de Maurepas on the East Indian commerce, noting nations engaged in it, the products involved, the trade between the eastern countries, etc.

Moresini, Alessandro. Tariffa del pagamento di tutti i dacii di Venetia. [Venice, ca. 1525-1530.] M492
A commercial handbook listing tariffs, financial regulations of Italian cities, fairs, etc.

Morier & Wilkinson. [Letter to Isaac Rogers in London.] Manuscript. Smirna, Sept. 27, 1799. M493
The letter is addressed to Isaac Rogers of London, and notes products available for export pending receipt of funds to purchase them.

Morin, Thomas and Nicholas Jennings. A proposal for the incouragement of seamen. [London] 1697. M494
This proposal recommends establishing a fund for disabled sailors and widows and children of men who died in service, thereby making seamen duty more attractive.

Moriset, Claude. [Autograph letter, signed.] Manuscript. Surat, April 20, 1696. M495
The author, a Jesuit missionary in India, comments chiefly on the commercial rivalry among European nations in the Indian Ocean.

Morisot, Claude-Barthélemy. Orbis maritimi sive Rerum in mari et littoribus gestarum generalis historia. Dijon, P. Palliot, 1643. M496
A compendium of maritime matters, with accounts of the voyages of Raleigh, Cavendish, and others.

Morisot, Claude-Barthélemy. Relations veritables et curieuses de l'isle de Madagascar, et du Bresil. Paris, A. Courbé, 1651. M497
Contains the relations of explorers to Madagascar, Brazil, Egypt, and Persia, as well as a history of the hostilities between the Dutch and Portuguese in Brazil.

Moro, Michiel. [Letter to Laurenzius Dolpfino.] Manuscript. London, Sept. 25, 1444. M498
The letter concerns market and shipping information with respect to Venice.

Morocco. Sovereign (1636-1654 : Muhammad Al-Shaykh Al-Saghir). A letter from the King of Morocco, to His Majesty the King of England Charles I. For the reducing of Sally, Argiers, &c ... with an account of the execution of the pyrats, and the number of Christian captives sent to His Majesty. London, For Rowland Reynolds, 1680. M499
The King of Morocco offers an alliance with Great Britain whereby the latter would supply the sea forces in a joint attack on Tunis and Algiers, citing earlier success against Salé.

Morosini, Zuan Alvise. [Letter to Marino qm. Domenico.] Manuscript. Venice, April 5, 1483. M500
A letter of mercantile interest, received in Venice 7 June 1483.

[Morris, Corbyn.] An essay towards deciding the important question, whether it be a national advantage to Britain to insure the ships of her enemies? London, J. Robinson [1747]. M501

The author answers various arguments by private interests who see no harm in insuring French ships; the author believes that because of this practice French trade in the West Indies is kept alive.

Morris, Corbyn. An essay towards deciding the question, whether Britain be permitted by right policy to insure the ships of her enemies? London, A. Millar, 1758. M502
The second edition, with *Further considerations on our insurance* and an index added.

Morse, Jedidiah. The American geography. London, John Stockdale, 1792. M503
The second edition of the first geography of the United States to be written by a native-born scholar. The volume contains two maps showing the northern and southern states, westward to just beyond the Mississippi.

Morse, Jedidiah. The American geography. London, John Stockdale, 1794. M504
This enlarged edition includes a map of Kentucky by John Filson.

Morse, Jedidiah. Tegenwoordige staat der Verëenigde Staaten van Amerika ... Amsterdam, Pieter den Hengst, 1793-1796. M505
The first Dutch edition.

Mortier, Pieter. Carte particuliere de Isthmus, ou Darien, qui comprend le Golfe de Panama &c. Cartagene, et les isles aux environs. Amsterdam, Pierre Mortier [ca. 1698]. M506
Map showing the area of the Scots' colony of Darien.

Mortimer, George. Observations and remarks made during a voyage ... in the brig Mercury. London, For the Author, 1791. M507
An account of a voyage to China by way of Amsterdam and St. Paul Islands, Tahiti, Hawaii, Unalaska, and Tinian, written by a marine on board.

Mortimer, George. Engelsmannen Joh. Hindric Cox resa genom Söderhafvet till ön Amsterdam, Marien-Öarna, O-Tahiti, Sandvichs-och Räf Öarna, Tinian, Unalaska och Canton in China. Nyköping, Peter Winge, 1798. M508
This Swedish edition adds a brief preface and several notes by the translator, but does not include the maps found in the English editions.

Morton, Thomas, 1575-1646. New English Canaan or New Canaan. Amsterdam, Jacob Frederick Stam, 1637. M509
An account of Massachusetts written by a fur trader who found himself at odds with the Puritans for his boisterous way of living. Includes an excellent account of the Indians and of the natural history of the area.

Morton, Thomas, 1764-1838. Columbus, or, A world discovered: an historical play: as it is performed at the Theatre-Royal, Covent-Garden. London, W. Miller, 1792. M510
A drama, the author's first, based in part on Marmontel's *Les Incas*.

Mosheim, Johann Lorenz. Historia Tartarorum ecclesiastica: adiecta est Tartariae Asiaticae secundum recentiores geographos in mappa delineatio. Helmstedt, Fridericum Christianum Weygand, 1741. M511
An academic dissertation, the respondent being Hermannus Christianus Paulsen, dealing with the history of Christianity in central Asia during and after the time of Ghengis Khan.

Mosneron de Launay, Jean Baptiste, baron. Discours sur les colonies et la traite des Noirs, prononcé le 26 fevrier 1790 ... [n.p., 1790.] M512
This tract concerns the suppression of the monopoly of the Compagnie des Indes and of the Senegal Company, and opposes the extension of the Rights of Man to the colonies where it would mean the end of slavery.

Mossel, Jacob. [Collection of private papers.] Manuscript. Negapatnam, 1738. M513
Mossel was governor of the Dutch trading stations on the Coromandel coast. He includes reports on the commerce of the region as far back as 1613.

The most important transactions of the sixth session of the first Parliament of His Majesty King George II. London, W. James [1733]. M514
The principle concern in this résumé is the Excise Bill which removed import duties on tobacco, replacing them with an inland duty.

Un mot sur les noirs: a leurs amis. [n.p., ca. 1790.] M515
This anonymous author rejects the idea that slavery is against nature, contending that it is a part of nature, deriving from the rights of war and of conquest.

[Moxon, Joseph.] Ein kurtzer Discours von der Schiff-fahrt by dem Nord-pol nach Japan, China und so weiter. Hamburg, J. Naumann & G. Wolff, 1676. M516
A German translation of a paper written in 1674 in which it was held that the search for a northeast passage should be continued.

Moxon, Joseph. A tutor to astronomy and geography. Or an easie and speedy way to know the use of both globes. London, S. Roycroft for Joseph Moxon, 1686. M517
A textbook on the use of terrestrial and celestial spheres by a globe-maker. Also contains legends explaining the constellations and a history of astronomy.

Müller, Andreas. Hebdomas observationum de rebus sinicis ... Berlin, Georgi Schultzi, 1674.
M518
The major work of a noted orientalist containing the history of China from 300 B.C. as well as recent information including the evangelization of China by the Jesuits.

Müller, Johann Bernhard. Leben und Gewohnheiten der Ostjacken, eines Volcks dass bis unter dem Polo Arctico wohnet, wie selbiges aus dem Heydenthum in diesen Zeiten zur Christl. griechischen Religion gebracht ... Berlin, Christ, Gottlieb Nicolai, 1720.
M519
An account of a central Siberian people and the region in which they lived together with a report on the progress of Greek Christian missions among them.

Müller, Wilhelm Johann. Die africanische auf der guineischen Gold-Cust gelegene Landschafft Fetu. Nuremberg, Johann Hoffmann, 1675.
M520
A description of Fetu on the Gold Coast by a clergyman in the service of the Danish African Company. Danish, Dutch, and English commercial activities are discussed, and some references to the slave trade are included.

Münster, Sebastian. Cosmographia. Beschreibung aller Lender. Basel, Henric Petri, 1544.
M521
The first German edition of one of the most popular geographies of the sixteenth century.

Münster, Sebastian. Cosmographia. Beschreibung aller Lender. Basel, Henric Petrus, 1546.
M522
The woodcut illustrations in this copy are hand-colored.

Münster, Sebastian. Cosmographiae universalis. [Basel, Henric Petri, 1550.]
M523
The first Latin edition, with an outstanding collection of woodcuts which supplemented the illustrations found in the earlier editions.

Münster, Sebastian. La cosmographie universelle. [Paris, Henric Petri, 1568.]
M524
The third French edition, containing the same maps and views as the 1550 Latin edition.

Münster, Sebastian. Erclerung der newen Landtaffeln unnd des Instruments der Sonnen. Mainz, Peter Jordan, 1534.
M525
This little volume deals with problems of astronomy related to geography and the instruments used in making calculations in such studies. Includes a description of an unidentified map.

Münster, Sebastian. Germaniae atque aliarum regionum, quae ad imperium usque Constantinopolitanum protenduntur, descriptio. [Basel, A. Cratander, 1531.]
M526
A description of a map made by Nicolaus de Cusa and published by Conrad Peutinger about 1530, including a discussion of some scientific problems in geography and cartography.

Muentzer, Wolffgang. Reyszbeschreibung ... von Venedig auss nach Jerusalem, Damascum und Constantinopel. Nuremberg, Ludwig Lochner, 1624.
M527
An account of travels in the Near East in 1556 and 1557.

Mulgrave, Constantine John Phipps, baron. A voyage towards the North Pole undertaken by His Majesty's command, 1773. London, W. Bowyer and J. Nichols, 1774.
M528
The journal of an expedition to determine how far north it was possible to sail, undertaken as a result of renewed English interest in the northeast passage.

Mulgrave, Constantine John Phipps, baron. Voyage au Pole Boréal. Paris, Saillant & Nyon, Pissot, 1775.
M529
The first French edition.

Mulgrave, Constantine John Phipps, baron. Reise nach dem Nordpol. Bern, Typographischen Gesellschaft, 1777.
M530
The German edition adds arguements for a navigable northern route by the Swiss geographer Samuel Engels.

Mulgrave, Constantine John Phipps, baron. See-Reisen von Engländern, Holländern, Franzosen, Spaniern, Dänen, und Russen auf dem Nordmeer. Bern, Typographischen Societät, 1795.
M531
A re-issue of the 1777 edition, but with the material rearranged.

[Mun, Thomas.] A discourse of trade, from England unto the East-Indies: answering to diverse objections which are usually made against the same. London, Nicholas Okes for John Pyper, 1621.
M532
The author, an economist and director of the East India Company, answers critics of the India trade.

Mun, Thomas. England's treasure by forraign trade. London, J.G. for T. Clark, 1664.
M533
The classic on the balance of trade theory. "We must ever observe this rule, to sell more to strangers than wee consume of theirs in value."

Mun, Thomas. Traite du commerce, dans lequel tous les marchands trouveront les moyens dont ils se peuvent legitiment servir pour s'enrichir. Paris, Jacques Morel, 1700.
M534
The second French edition of *England's treasure by foreign trade*, basic to the philosophy of mercantilism.

Muncaster, John Pennington, baron. Historical sketches of the slave trade, and of its effects in Africa. London, John Stockdale, 1792.
M535
A critical view of the African slave trade.

Munk, Jens. Navigatio septentrionalis. Det er: Relation eller bescriffuelse om seiglads oc reyse pas denne Nordvestiske Passagie. Copenhagen, Heinrich Waldkirch, 1624. M536

The first edition of Munk's account of his attempt in 1619-20 to find the northwest passage. In this attempt sixty-one of the sixty-four crew members perished.

Munk, Jens. Navigatio septentrionalis. Det er Relation eller beskrivelse om seiglads og reyse paa denne Nordvestiske Passage som nu kaldes Nova Dania. Copenhagen, Kongl. Majestets privilegerede bogtrykkerie, 1723. M537

This second Danish edition includes a twenty-four page biography of Munk not present in the 1624 edition.

Muñoz, Juan Bautista. Discurso sobre la navegacion al Occeano Pacifico, i particularmente a las islas Filipinas, por los transitos descubiertos al medio-dia dela America. Manuscript. [n.p.] 12 October 1779. M538

A memorandum by a prominent Spanish historian for a more systematic program of navigation and trade between Spain and the Philippines.

Muñoz de Castro, Pedro. Exaltacion magnifica de la Betlemitica Rosa de la mejor Americana Jerico ... Mexico, Doña Maria de Benavides, Viuda de Juan Ribera, 1697. M539

An account of the Bethlehemite order of Guatemala, a nursing order founded in 1650 which subsequently spread throughout Central America and Mexico.

Munsters Praetie. [n.p.] 1646. M540

A discussion of the merits of peace with Spain, in which a merchant points out the benefits that would come to the Dutch West India Company from such a peace.

Muratori, Lodovico Antonio. Il cristianesimo felice nelle missioni de' padri della Compagnia de Gesù nel Paraguai. Venice, Giambatista Pasquali, 1743. M541

This work, called volume one, is considered complete separately from the second volume, published in 1749.

Muratori, Lodovico Antonio. Il cristianesimo felice nelle missioni de' padri della Compagnie de Gesù nel Paraguai. Venice, Giambatista Pasquali, 1752. M542

A two-volume history of the growth of Jesuit dominance in Paraguay, with descriptions of other aspects of the country as well, and also including some reference to other Jesuit missions in America.

Muratori, Lodovico Antonio. Relation des missions du Paraguai. Paris, Bordelet, 1754. M543

The first French edition.

Murchio, Vincenzo Maria. Il viaggio all' Indie Orientali. Rome, Filippomaria Mancini, 1672. M544

An account of travels to India by way of Turkey and Persia, with particular attention to the religious practices of the St. Thomas Christians.

Murchio, Vincenzo Maria. Il viaggio all' Indie Orientali. Venice, Giacomo Zattoni, 1678. M545

The second edition.

Muriel, Domingo. Fasti novi orbis et ordinationum apostolicarum ad Indias pertinentium breviarium cum adnotationibus. Venice, Antonium Zatta, 1776. M546

A collection of 605 documents and a commentary relating to papal concerns with European overseas activity.

Murillo Velarde, Pedro. Historia de la provincia de Philipinas de la Compañia de Jesus. Manila, Nicolas de la Cruz Bagay, 1749. M547

This work was intended as a continuation of Francisco Colin's *Labor evangelica*, bringing the history of the Philippines up to 1716.

Murr, Christoph Gottlieb von. Histoire diplomatique du chevalier portugais Martin Behaim de Nuremberg. 3rd ed. Strasbourg et Paris, Treuttel et Würtz, 1802. M548

A French translation of Murr's book on Martin Behaim and his famous globe. The book's other illustration is a woodcut of Vespucci's fleet off the coast of South America, dated 1522.

Murray, Charles. [Letter to an unnamed Portuguese official.] Manuscript in Portuguese. Madeira, 1779. M549

Murray was British Consul General in Madeira, and he writes to an unnamed correspondent concerning a British pirate ship.

Murray, Mungo. A treatise on ship-building and navigation. London, D. Henry and R. Cave, 1754. M550

A largely theoretical work with a mathematical emphasis, but also giving practical advice on the laying down of a ship and on navigation.

Murray, Robert. A proposal for the better securing our wooll against exportation. [London, ca. 1695.] M551

A proposal for a national wool staple in London from which supplies could be sent out to individual merchants under license, or used as a means of providing employment in poverty-stricken areas.

[Mylius, Arnold.] compiler. De rebus Hispanicis, Lusitanicis, Aragonicis, Indicis & Aethiopicis. Cologne, In officina Birckmannica, sumptibus Arnoldi Mylij, 1602. M552

A collection of historical works of Damião de Goes, Diogo de Teive, Jerónimo Pau, and Gerónimo Blancas y Tomás, dealing with aspects of Spanish and Portuguese history, including Portuguese overseas interests.

Myne Heeren van den Gerechte der Stad Amsterdam hebben goedgevonden de Keure van dato 16 April 1745 : raakende den tyd van het betaalen der premien van assurantie te abrogeeren ende wyders de volgende articulen uit de ordonnantie op de assurantie en avaryen binnen deese Stad den 28 April 1744 geëmaneert te altereeren en te ampliëeren in maniere als volgt ... Amsterdam, Samuel Lamsveld ..., 1756.
M553

Myrtius, Joannes. Opusculum geographicum rarum. Ingolstadt, W. Eder, 1590. M554
Contains a world map on which Greenland, North America, and Asia appear as parts of the same continent.

N

N.L.P. Lettre d'un missionnaire apostolique, qui donne connoissance des belles ouvertures, qu'il y a dans l'empire de la Chine, & les royaumes voisins pour la publication de l'Evangile ... Paris, 1665.　　N1

An optimistic view of missionary possibilities in China and Cochin China, with theological arguments for promoting the Christian faith abroad.

N. N. Missive aen een heer der regeringe, door eenen welmenenden Hollander: over het tegenwoordig tydsgewrigt geschreeven bevattende eenigen der voornaemste motiven, om welken de geunieerde provincien geen deel in de tegenwoordigen oorlog van Groot-Brittanje voor als nog behooren te nemen. [n.p.] 1741.　　N2

An extended review of Anglo-Dutch commercial and naval rivalry with a view to establishing policy with respect to the war between Spain and Great Britain.

Na conferensia qu se teue em Badajos a 3 di Dez. de 681 ... : [n.p., after Dec. 3, 1681].　　N3

A report on a conference between Spanish and Portuguese geographers and diplomats trying to establish the boundary between their possessions in Uruguay with particular reference to the town of Colonia do Sacramento.

Nachricht von der neuesten Entdeckungen der Engländer in der Süd-See. Berlin, Haude und Spener, 1772.　　N4

A translation of the anonymous and unauthorized *A Journal of a voyage round the world*, the first published account of Cook's first circumnavigation.

[Naeranus, Johannes.] Hollandsche oprechtigheid tegen de Engelse ... Amsterdam, 1665.　　N5

A conversation between citizens of The Hague, Amsterdam, and Zeeland relative to the commercial troubles with England.

Naerder aenwysinghe der bewinthebbers regieringe. [n.p., ca. 1622.]　　N6

A criticism of the directors of the Dutch East India Company for their management of the company's affairs.

Nærmere oplysninger henhørende [t]il de Hrr. Revisorers betænkning over directionens besvarelse paa revisorernes erindringer ... fra 1ste April 1774 til ultim. Martii 1775. Copenhagen, Lauritz Simmelkiaer, 1775.　　N7

An accounting of the affairs of the Danish East India Company.

Nagaev, Aleksei Ivanovich. Atlas vsego Baltiiskago moria. [St. Petersburg, 1757.]　　N8

A collection of twenty-eight maps of the Baltic Sea and adjacent bodies of water. The maps are based on the author's observations and on Danish and Swedish sources.

Nairac, Pierre-Paul. Discours ... sur le commerce de l'Inde. [Paris, Imprimerie Nationale, 1790.]　　N9

A review of French trade in the East Indies, with recommendations for its improvement.

Nantes (France). Merchants. Mémoire des négociants de Nantes, contre l'admission des étrangers dans nos colonies. [Nantes, Imprimerie de Brun, l'aîne, 1784.]　　N10

The merchants of Nantes present a petition asking the King to prohibit all foreigners from trading in French colonies.

Nantes (France). Merchants. Observations des négocians de Nantes, sur un ecrit qui a pour titre, Mémoire en réponse a celui du commerce de France ... [Nantes, Imprimerie de ve. Brun, 1774.]　　N11

A critical response to a writer who touted the benefits of free commerce.

A narrative of affairs lately received from His Majesties island of Jamaica. London, Randal Taylor, 1683.　　N12

Three speeches by the governor of the colony and one by the speaker of the assembly.

The nation preserved, or, The plot discovered: containing an impartial account of the secret pol-

icy of some of the South-Sea directors ... London, For the Author, 1720. **N13**
   The anonymous author describes the motives of the South Sea Company directors as "covetousness degenerated into ambition," with the desire to control Parliament to their own advantage.

The nature of contracts consider'd, as they relate to ... the South Sea Company. London, J. Roberts [etc.] 1720. **N14**
   Deplores the purchases of South Sea Company stock at reduced prices.

Navarrete, Martín Fernández de. Colección de los viages y descubrimientos ... Madrid, Imprenta Real, 1825-1837. **N15**
   A collection of sources including manuscripts and rare printed works relating to early Spanish explorations.

De na-ween vande vrede. Ofte ontdekkinge vande kommerlijcke ghelegentheydt onses lieven Vaderlants. [n.p.] 1650. **N16**
   This pamphlet reflects dissatisfaction with the peace of 1648, noting that Dutch commerce has declined everywhere since the treaty was signed.

Neal, Daniel. The history of New-England. London, For J. Clark [etc.] 1720. **N17**
   This work places a heavy emphasis on the religious history of the New England colonies, but it is also concerned with relations between the colonists and the Indians, with education, and with government.

Neale, Thomas. To preserve the East-India trade. [London, Freeman Collins, 1695.] **N18**
   In an apparent attempt to get merchants and landowners united in their concern for overseas trade, the author proposes that profits of the East India Company above five per cent a year be divided between shareholders and landowners.

Neander, Michael. Orbis terrae partium succincta explicatio. Leipzig, Abrahami Lambergi, 1589. **N19**
   A world geography based on both ancient and modern authorities. Includes accounts of the Near East, Ethiopia, and Russia by sixteenth-century writers.

Neander, Michael. Vom Zustand, Leben, Thun, Wesen, Lere und Glauben der Christen in der Türcken zu itzigen Zetten ... Eisleben, Urban Gaubisch, 1589. **N20**
   A description of Turkey with particular reference to Christians living there. Included also is a collection of letters from Martin Crusius of Tübingen giving information on Christians living in Moslem areas.

Nécessité absolue de l'union de la liberté avec la bonne foi dans le commerce. Amsterdam; Paris, Desenne, 1787. **N21**
   An essay on the meaning of free trade.

The necessity of repealing the American Stamp-Act demonstrated. London, For J. Almon, 1766. **N22**
   An excellent summary of colonial objections to the Stamp Act of 1765, with strong arguments for its repeal.

Neck, Jacob Cornelissoon van. Historiale beschrijvinghe ... vande reyse ghedaen met acht schepen van Amsterdam. Amsterdam, Michiel Colijn, 1619. **N23**
   Describes the second Dutch voyage to the East Indies, and reports East Indian mercantile methods.

Neck, Jacob Cornelissoon van. Journal ou comptoir, contenant le vray discours et narration historique, du voiage ... Amsterdam, Corneille Nicolas, 1601. **N24**
   The first French edition of an account of a voyage which established Dutch commerce in Mauritius, Bantam, Madura, Celebes, Amboyna, and Ternate.

Necker, Jacques. Réponse au mémoire de M. l'abbé Morellet, sur la Compagnie des Indes. Paris, Imprimerie Royale, 1769. **N25**
   A defense of this particular company, and an argument in favor of monopolistic trading companies in general.

Necker, Jacques. Sur la législation et le commerce des grains. Paris, Pissot, 1775. **N26**
   A consideration of the decline of the French grain trade and agriculture.

Necker, Jacques. Sur le compte rendu au roi en 1781. Nouveaux éclairissemens. Paris, Hotel de Thou, 1788. **N27**
   An expansion upon his *Compte rendu* of 1781, with commentary on the remarks of his major critic, Charles Alexandre de Calonne.

Nederlandsche Oost-Indische Compagnie. Aende e. vermogende heeren burgemeesteren ... [n.p., 1623]. **N28**
   A series of requests from the major shareholders of the Dutch East India Company for the alteration of their charter, especially with respect to the rendering of accounts.

Nederlandsche Oost-Indische Compagnie. Antwoort, van de vergaederingh van de seventiene. Amsterdam, P. Matthysz [1683]. **N29**
   The Dutch reply to English protests at being excluded from trade at Bantam.

Nederlandsche Oost-Indische Compagnie. Artikel-brief van de geoctroyeerde Nederlandsche Oost-Indische Compagnie. Amsterdam, J. van Egmont en Zoon [1742]. **N30**
   Regulations on all aspects of the management of the company's affairs, with particular emphasis on shipping.

Nederlandsche Oost-Indische Compagnie. Artikel-brief van de geoctroyeerde Nederlandsche Oost-Indische Compagnie ... Den vierden

Nederlandsche Oost-Indische Compagnie

September, 1742, gearresteert. By de resolutie 11 Oct. ... Amsterdam, J. van Egmont en Zoon [1747]. N31

Reprinting of the previous item.

Nederlandsche Oost-Indische Compagnie. Artyckel-brief. Middelburg, Pieter van Goetthem, 1669. N32

An instruction book prescribing the duties and conduct of various types of employees going to the East Indies for the Dutch East India Company.

[Nederlandsche Oost-Indische Compagnie.] An authentick copy of the acts of the processe against the English at Amboyna. London, John Dawson, For the East India Company, 1632. N33

A statement of the investigatory and judicial proceedings by which the Dutch arrived at the conclusion that several Englishmen and their Japanese servants had plotted the overthrow of the Dutch in Amboyna, thereby justifying the "Amboyna Massacre."

Nederlandsche Oost-Indische Compagnie. Beschrijving van ... handel in Japan. Manuscript. [Batavia?] 1756. N34

A copy of an offical report on the Dutch trade with Japan, Siam, and Macassar.

Nederlandsche Oost-Indische Compagnie. Carga of lading van elf Oost-Indische retourscheepen ... Amsterdam, Nicolaas Byl, 1777. N35

The cargoes cover a variety of products, including spices, coffee, wood, indigo, and precious stones.

Nederlandsche Oost-Indische Compagnie. [Collection of papers issued under the governorship of Jacob Mossel.] Batavia, 1750-58. N36

Mossel was governor of the Dutch trading stations on the Coromandel coast. See also the entry under his name in this catalog.

Nederlandsche Oost-Indische Compagnie. Corte aenwijsinghe van de redenen daer door de misnoegende participanten inde Oost-Indische Compagnye. [n.p.] 1623. N37

Complaints against the articles of the company's charter relating to accounts, dividends, and naming of replacements to the board of directors.

Nederlandsche Oost-Indische Compagnie. Een korte wederlegginge van de langhe deduction der bewinthebberen. [n.p., 1624?]. N38

A defense by the directors against criticisms of the shareholders.

Nederlandsche Oost-Indische Compagnie. Eenighe protesten der dolerande participanten. [n.p., 1623?]. N39

An announcement by some of the more important shareholders of their resignations from the board of directors because of dissatisfaction with the rendering of accounts.

Nederlandsche Oost-Indische Compagnie. [Instruction book for the China trade.] Manuscript. Netherlands, 1759-1766. N40

A letter book giving instructions to captains and merchants engaging in trade with China via the Dutch factory at Bantam.

Nederlandsche Oost-Indische Compagnie. Journael ... des oorlaghs tusschen Macassar, en den ... Oost-Indische Compagnie. Amsterdam, M. Doornick [1670]. N41

A description of the war by which the Dutch gained supremacy in the island of Celebes.

Nederlandsche Oost-Indische Compagnie. A justification of the directors of the Netherlands East-India Company. As it was delivered over unto ... the States General ... the 22d of July, 1686. London, S. Tidmarsh, 1688. N42

The report is signed P. van Dam. It concerns Dutch activities in Bantam.

Nederlandsche Oost-Indische Compagnie. Memorandum book of the factory of the Dutch East India Company at Canton, 1758-59. Manuscript. [Canton, ca. 1760.] N43

Contains information on the commodities handled by the Canton factory, the arrival and departure of ships, etc.

Nederlandsche Oost-Indische Compagnie. A translation of the memorial presented to the States General of the United Provinces, the 15th day of March, 1722/3. [London? 1723?]. N44

A plea from the directors of the Dutch East India Company for special treatment on account of the economic "damages" suffered by the company from competition of the Ostend Company.

Nederlandsche Oost-Indische Compagnie. Vermeerdert journal of kort verhael van 't begin, voortgangh en eynde des oorloghs tusschen ... Macassar, en de Nederlandtsche Geoctroyeerde Oost-Indische Compagnie. Amsterdam, Marcus Doornick [1670]. N45

An account of hostilities between the Dutch East India Company and the King of Celebes during 1666-69. This edition contains a list of rulers of Macassar who were defeated by the Dutch, taken from a letter of Admiral Cornelis Janszoon Speelman.

Nederlandsche reizen, tot bevordering van den koophandel na de meest afgelegene gewesten des aardkloots. Amsterdam, P. Conradi, 1784-87. N46

A collection of accounts of Dutch voyages which were instrumental in the expansion of Dutch trade, chiefly to the East Indies.

Nederlandsche reizen, tot bevordering van den koophandel, na de Westindien. Amsterdam, P. Conradi, 1787. N47
   A series of accounts of Dutch activities in the West Indies.

Nederlandse Hervormde Kerk. Synode van Zuid-Holland. Berigt, en onderrigtinge, nopens en aan de colonie en kerke van Pensylvanien : opgestelt en uytgegeven door de gedeputeerden van de E. Christelyke Synodus van Zuyd-Holland, benevens de Gecommitteerden van de E. Classis van Delft en Delfsland, en Shieland. [Netherlands, 1730?]. N48
   A brief history of the colony of Pennsylvania and of the Dutch Reformed Church there is followed by an appeal for assistance to some of the congregations.

Negri, Francesco. Viaggio settentrionale fatto, e descritto. Padua, Stamperia del Seminario, 1700. N49
   An account of travels in Scandinavia, with observations on the customs and natural history of Lapland.

Neitzschitz, Georg Christoph von. Sieben-Jährige und gefährliche Welt Beschauung durch die vornehmsten drey Theil der Welt Europa, Asia und Africa. Budissin, Barthol. Kretzschmarn, 1666. N50
   An account of travels primarily in the Near East.

Nemours (France). Assemblée des trois ordres, 1789. Procès-verbal de l'Assemblée baillivale de Nemours pour la convocation des États-Généraux; avec les cahiers des trois ordres. Paris, Pierre J. Duplain, 1789. N51
   These deliberations include discussion of major economic, political, and social problems confronting France. The points of view of the third estate are given the most extensive treatment.

Netherlands (before 1581). Laws, etc. Nyeuwe ordinantie ende mandement ... hoe ende in wat manieren zijnder Maiesteyt ondersaten, coopluyden, scippers, visschers en bootsgezellen gehouden zijn voirtaene heure scepen toe te reedene, equipperen, ende versien ... Mit diversche andere puncten en articlen aengaende den zeerechten ... Louvain, Servaes van Sassen [1551]. N52
   This ordinance covers many aspects of maritime commerce, and includes a section on sea law.

Netherlands (before 1581). Laws, etc. Ordonnancien, statuten, edicten ende placcaten ... van weghen der Keyserlicker ende Conijnglicker Majesteyten. Ghent, Jan van Steene, 1559. N53
   A collection of laws for the governing of the Low Countries, some of them going back as far as 1366. Many of them relate to maritime affairs and trade.

Netherlands (before 1581). Laws, etc. Placcart du Roy nostre sire, touchant la denunciation des biens arrestez au royaulme Dangleterre, appertenans aux subjectz de pardeça. Brussels, Michiel de Hamont, 1570. N54

Netherlands (before 1581). Laws, etc. Placcart et ordonnance ... pour obuyer aux fraudes & abuz, que se commettent sur le faict & transport des drapz & aultres denrees & marchandises Dangleterre, & aultrement. Brussels, Michiel de Hamont, 1570. N55

Netherlands (before 1581). Laws, etc. Ordinancie gemaect op tstuck van dexecutie, ende avancement vant recolement vanden quohieren vanden hondertsten penun. Brussels, Michiel van Hamont, 1572. N56
   A decree announcing the imposition of a one per cent capital levy on the Netherlands by the Spanish administration.

Netherlands (before 1581). Laws, etc. Placcaet ende ordinancie onss heeren des Conincx, daerby verboden ende geinterdiceert wordt, soe wel den vremdelingen als ondersaten van zijnder Maiesteyt, met eenige rebelle ende wederspennige te tracteren, oft coopmanschapsche wijse te handelen ... Brussels, Michiel van Hamont, 1572. N57

Netherlands (before 1581). Laws, etc. Placcart et ordonnance du Roy nostre sire, touchant l'annotation, saissement & denunciatiō des biens meubles & immeubles, ensemble des droitz & actions, competans aux rebelles & aultres. Brussels, Michiel de Hamont, 1572. N58

Netherlands (before 1581). Laws, etc. Placcaet ende ordinancie onssheeren des Conincx ... van't tcooren ende graen. Brussels, M. van Hamont, 1573. N59
   A royal decree forbidding independent exporting of grain from the Spanish Netherlands, and requiring that all grain be brought to the central government market.

Netherlands (before 1581). Laws, etc. Ordonnance et instruction du Roy ... de la collectation de certains moyens generaux ... mis sur les marchandises. Antwerp, C. Plantin, 1579. N60
   A list of import and export duties on a wide variety of commodities.

Netherlands. (Southern Provinces, 1581-1793). [A collection of thirteen documents relating to the grain trade.] Namur: Chez Jean François Lafontaine, 1730-1789. N61
   The regulations concern importing and exporting, monopolies, and internal trade.

Netherlands. (Southern Provinces, 1581-1793). Conc[ep]t o[p]te v[or]ghinge vander see: 1599 Dec. 7. Manuscript. [n.p., 1599.]   N62
   The regulations cover shipping to Western European ports, Italy, and North America.

Netherlands. (Southern Provinces, 1581-1793). Conseil des Domaines & Finances. Tariffe des droits d'entrée et sortie ... Brussels, H.A. Velpius, 1664.   N63
   Import and export duties on about 300 items in the Austrian Netherlands.

Netherlands. (Southern Provinces, 1581-1793). Laws, etc. Placcaet ende ordonnantie vande eertshertoghen. Op den prijs ende evaluatie van sekere nieuwe silveren stucken die haere hoocheyden teghenwoordelijcken doen munten met henne titulen ende wapenen. Brussels, Rutgert Velpius; Antwerp, Hieronimus Verdussen, 1599.   N64

Netherlands. (Southern Provinces, 1581-1793). Laws, etc. Nouveau placcart et ordonnance du Roy nostre sire. Pour plus pres pourveoir contre les apparentes chiertez du grains. Brussels, R. Velpius, 1587.   N65
   A decree limiting the abuses of the monopoly which caused grain to be excessively priced.

Netherlands. (Southern Provinces, 1581-1793). Laws, etc. Placcaet ende ordonnantie ons heeren des Conincx. Op den treyn vande negociatie ende coopmanshandel, met die van Hollant, Zeelant ende ander, soo wel te water als te lande. Antwerp, Weduwe van Guilliaem van Pariis, 1592.   N66

Netherlands. (Southern Provinces, 1581-1793). Laws, etc. Placcaet ons genaedichs heeren des Conincx. Daermede eenen yegelycken soo coopluyden, scheppers als voerluyden, verbodē wort den vyant aen te voeren oft aff te haelen, eeninge waeren oft coopmanschappen ... Brussels, Rutgheert Velpius, 1593.   N67

Netherlands. (Southern Provinces, 1581-1793). Laws, etc. Ordonnance et placcart du Roy ... sur le faict du redressement des minerailles d'alluns, soulffres & coperoses. Antwerp, Pierre van Tongheren, 1594.   N68
   A decree granting rights to mine for sulphur, alum and similar materials, and restricting free trade in these commodities.

Netherlands. (Southern Provinces, 1581-1793). Laws, etc. Ordonnantie ende placcaet ... van het redressement vande mijneralen soo vande alluynen, solffer, als coperoose. Antwerp, Peter van Tongheren, 1594.   N69
   A Dutch edition of the previous item.

Netherlands. (Southern Provinces, 1581-1793). Laws, etc. Placcaet ende ordinantie ons heeren des Conincx. Op tseyt vande schulden ghemaeckt ende ghecontracteert by de Generaele Staeten van dese Nederlandē zedert de doot van wylē de Groot-Commandeur van Castillien, &c. in zynen leven Stadthouder, Gouverneur ende Capiteyn generael vande voornoemde Nederlanden. Brussels, Rutgeert Velpius, 1594.   N70

Netherlands. (Southern Provinces, 1581-1793). Laws, etc. Placcaet ende ordonnantie, ons genadichs heeren des Conincx ... vanden coopmans handel ... Hollant, Seelant, ende andere landen. Antwerp, Weduwe van Guiliam van Pariis, 1594.   N71
   A decree restricting commerce between the southern provinces of the Netherlands and those to the north which were rebelling against their Spanish rulers.

Netherlands. (Southern Provinces, 1581-1793). Laws, etc. Placcaet ende ordinantie ons genaedichs heeren des Conincx ... van de coopmans handel ende traffyck ... met Hollandt, Zeelandt ende andere landen. Brussels, R. Velpius, 1595.   N72
   Further restrictions upon the trade between southern and northern provinces of the Netherlands.

Netherlands. (Southern Provinces, 1581-1793). Laws, etc. Nieuwe liste van het recht van licenten, datmen voortaen betalen sal voor alle toegelaten ende ghepermitteerde waeren, ende coopmanschappen, varende naer de landen gehouden by den vyantende rebellen ... Brussels, Rutgeert Velpius, 1597.   N73

Netherlands. (Southern Provinces, 1581-1793). Laws, etc. Nouvelle liste du droict des licentes que se payera d'oresenavant sur toutes marchandises licites. Antwerp, H. Verdussen, 1597.   N74
   A schedule of duties on those goods which were permitted to enter the southern provinces of the Netherlands from the provinces in rebellion to the north.

Netherlands. (Southern Provinces, 1581-1793). Laws, etc. Placcart sur le faict des avant-acheteurs, marchandz en groz et monopoliers de toutes sortes de vivres victuailles. Brussels, H. Antoine, 1598.   N75
   A decree placing a restriction upon the transporting and sale of food to nearby cities outside of the southern Netherlands.

Netherlands. (Southern Provinces, 1581-1793). Laws, etc. Placcart et ordonnance des archiducqz noz soverains seigneurs et princes. Par laquelle leurs Altezes deffendent le transport des salpetres, & pouldres, hors des pays de pardeça, & donnent reglement sur la recerce, negociation, & confection desdictes denrées. Brussels, Rutgert Velpius, 1599. N76

Netherlands. (Southern Provinces, 1581-1793). Laws, etc. Ordinantie ende placcaet vande eertzhertoghen, teghens alle de ghene die niewe valsche inventie vinden, ende ghebruycken om herwertsovere te bringen abbordaen, haerinck, gesouten visch, ende alle andere sorten van coopmanschappen, gaende ende commende naer den vyandt ende rebellen. Brussels, Rutgert Velpius, 1600. N77

Netherlands. (Southern Provinces, 1581-1793). Laws, etc. Ordonnantie ende instructie daer opmen van wegen die dry Staeten des lants ende hertochdoms van Brabant collectern ... Brussels, Rutgeert Velpius, 1601. N78
An announcement of special taxes levied on all goods and on the importing of wine and beer. These taxes were to support soldiers stationed in Brabant.

Netherlands. (Southern Provinces, 1581-1793). Laws, etc. Placcart ... par laquelle leurs altezes deffendent le transport des salpetres & pouldres. Brussels, R. Velpius, 1601. N79
A prohibition upon the export of saltpeter and powder from the southern Netherlands.

Netherlands. (Southern Provinces, 1581-1793). Laws, etc. Ordinancie ... vande schepen, wagens, kerren, coopmanschappen ende persoonen comende ... deur die stadt van Antwerpen. Brussels, R. Velpius, 1602. N80
Provides for the inspection of ships, carts, and other vehicles carrying merchandise into Antwerp.

Netherlands. (Southern Provinces, 1581-1793). Laws, etc. Placcaet ... belangende de oepeninge ende restauratie vanden traffyck ... van Spaignien. Brussels, R. Velpius, 1603. N81
Provides for the restoration of traffic between Spain and the Low Countries.

Netherlands. (Southern Provinces, 1581-1793). Laws, etc. Placcart et ordonnance sur l'ouverture et restauration du trafficq & commerce d'Espaigne avec les pays de pardeça, encores qu'ilz soyent distraictz de l'obeyssance des Serenmes. Archiducqz noz princes souverains & naturelz. Brussels, Rutger Velpius, 1603. N82

Netherlands. (Southern Provinces, 1581-1793). Laws, etc. Ordonnance ... sur le faict des pouldres et salpetres. Brussels, R. Velpius, 1604. N83
A broadside containing a series of regulations on the production and sale of saltpeter and powder.

Netherlands. (Southern Provinces, 1581-1793). Laws, etc. Ordonnance ... sur le faict des pouldres et salpetres. Brussels, R. Velpius, 1604. N84
Identical to the previous decree, but in pamphlet rather than broadside format.

Netherlands. (Southern Provinces, 1581-1793). Laws, etc. Placcaet ... soo op de revocatie van sekere voorgaende placcaet vanden vyfden Aprilis 1603. Brussels, R. Velpius, 1605. N85
Revocation of an earlier decree which reestablished commercial relations between Spain and the Netherlands.

Netherlands. (Southern Provinces, 1581-1793). Laws, etc. Placcaet ... aengaende de coopmanschappen ende manufacturen gemaect inde ghehoorsaeme provincien ... Brussels, R. Velpius, 1606. N86
Regulations on the commerce between the southern provinces and the rebellious provinces to the north.

Netherlands. (Southern Provinces, 1581-1793). Laws, etc. Placcart ... par lequel est tresexpressement deffendu ... de transporter ... aucunes laines crues & non filées. Brussels, R. Velpius & H. Anthoon, 1610. N87
A series of restrictions upon the export of non-manufactured wool from the southern provinces.

Netherlands. (Southern Provinces, 1581-1793). Laws, etc. Placcaet ende ordonnantie ons ghenaedichs heeren desConincks. Inhoudende den voet ende orden diemen voirtaen binnen Wesel ende Rynberck houden sal int lichten vande licenten vande coopmans-handel te waeter ende te lande op den Rhyn, ende andere daer van dependerende stroomen. Brussels, Huybrecht Anthoon, 1622. N88

Netherlands. (Southern Provinces, 1581-1793). Laws, etc. Ordinantie ons heeren des Conincx. Inhoudende verbodt vanden coophandel mette gherebelleerde provincien. Brussels, Huybrecht Anthoon, 1625. N89

Netherlands. (Southern Provinces, 1581-1793). Laws, etc. Nederlandtsche placcaet-boeck: waerinne alle voornaemste placcaten, ordonnantien, accorden, ende andere acten ende munimenten, uyt-ghegeven by de ... Vereenigde Nederlantsche Provintien ... Amsterdam, Jan Janssen, 1644. N90
A collection of more than 1100 pages of laws issued from 1581 to 1644, many of them relating to the formation of the Dutch East and West India companies and other aspects of Dutch commerce.

Netherlands. (Southern Provinces, 1581-1793). Staten-Generaal. Placcaet—Die Staten Generael der Vereenichde Nederlanden—Allen den genen die dese jegenwoordige sullen sien oft hooren lesen saluyt, Doen te weeten—Also alle die werelt kennelijck is, dat die vereenichde

Nederlanden onder de jegenwoordige regeringe ... The Hague, Hillebrant Iacobsz, 1608. **N91**
A collection of political tracts which agitated for the formation of a Dutch West India Company.

Netherlands. (Southern Provinces, 1581-1793). Treaties, etc. Spain, 1714 June 26. Traité de paix et de commerce, entre le roy d'Espagne, et les Etats-Generaux des Provinces-Unies des Pays-Bas. Conclu à Utrecht le 26 Juin 1714. Paris, François Fournier, 1714. **N92**
A general settlement of trade between Spain and the Netherlands with special mention of Spain's exclusive rights in the West Indies.

Neu-entdecktes Norden, oder gründliche und warhaffte Reise-beschreibung, aller mitternächtigen und nordwärtsgelegenen Länder, Städte, Vestungen und Insulen, samt der darinnen sich befindlichen Nationen, Lebens-art, Sitten und Religion ... Frankfurt & Leipzig, Johann Albrecht, 1727. **N93**
A collection of northern travels, descriptive of Iceland, Greenland, Novaya Zemlya, and Siberia, and also including accounts of voyages in search of the northeast and northwest passages.

Neu-entdecktes Norden, oder gründliche und warhaffte Reise-beschreibung, aller mitternächtigen und nordwärtsgelegenen Länder, Städte, Vestungen und Insulen, samt der darinnen sich befindlichen Nationen, Lebens-art, Sitten und Religion ... Frankfurt und Leipzig, Johann Albrecht, 1728. **N94**
A page for page reprint, entirely reset, of the 1727 edition.

Neue Nachrichten von den Missionen der Jesuiten in Paraguay und von andern damit verbundenen vorgängen in der Spanischen Monarchie. Hamburg, Typographischen Gesellschaft, 1768. **N95**
Materials pertaining to the Jesuits in Paraguay, collected, according to the preface, from Andrès Marcos Burriel, a Spanish Jesuit.

Neuvialle, Jean Sylvain de. Relaçaõ da jornada, que fez ao imperio da China, e summaria noticia da embaixada que deo na corte de Pekim em o primeiro de Mayo de 1753, o Senhor Francisco Xavier Assiz de Pacheco e Sampayo, escrita a hum padre da Companhia de Jesus ... pelo Reverendo Padre Newiehle, francez, da mesma Companhia ... Lisbon, Antonio Pedrozo Galram, 1754. **N96**
An account of an embassy from the Jesuit mission on Macao to the Chinese Emperor at Peking with particular emphasis on its ceremonial aspects.

Neville, Henry. Wahrhafftige Beschreibung des neu erfundenen Pineser Eylands. [n.p., 1668.] **N97**
A fictitious account of the discovery and settlement of an island somewhere east of Africa.

A new and correct map of North America. [n.p.] Mathew Albert and G.F. Lotter, 1784. **N98**
This map is made up of four sheets showing boundaries based on the Treaty of Paris, 1783. It includes the West Indies, Central America, and the northern portion of South America.

A new, authentic, and complete collection of voyages round the world ... containing a new, authentic, entertaining, instructive, full, and complete historical account of Captain Cook's first, second, third and last voyages ... London, Alex Hogg [1784?]. **N99**
Large folio compilation of voyages by English navigators (including Lord Byron, Samuel Wallis, Philip Carteret, Lord Mulgrave, Lord Anson and Sir Francis Drake). George William Anderson, the editor, gives either complete accounts or edited versions of the voyages.

New discoveries concerning the world and its inhabitants. London, J. Johnson, 1778. **N100**
A collection of accounts of South Pacific voyages, with considerable emphasis on the smaller islands and groups of islands.

New France. Laws, etc. Édits, ordonnances royaux, déclarations et arrêts du Conseil d'État du Roi, concernant le Canada. Quebec, P.E. Desbarats, 1803-06. **N101**
A reprinting in chronological arrangement of legislation, letters patent, commissions, and other documents pertinent to the establishment and continuance of the government of New France.

New France. (Viceroyalty). Autographs and portraits of viceroys of New France, 1612-1737. Manuscript. [Various places and dates]. **N102**
Autograph documents of ten viceroys of New France, with portraits of nine of them.

A new general collection of voyages and travels. London, T. Astley, 1745-47. **N103**
A collection of travel narratives from merchants and explorers, beginning with the early Portuguese voyages.

New Spain. [License for a Discalced Carmelite mission to California.] Manuscript in Spanish. Mexico City, Nov. 24, 1601. **N104**
An order by the viceroy taking note of an intended voyage to the coast of California and that the Franciscan missions in Mexico were not strong enough to evangelize in California, therefore the Carmelites were authorized to find friars to accompany the voyage.

New Spain. Proponense por su mag[esta]d y el Virrey en su nom[br]e a la prove[nci]a de St.

A[l]berto de los p[adr]es descalcos Carmelitas los puntos siguientes ... Manuscript. Mexico City, Nov. 18, 1601.   N105

   A contemporary copy of a viceregal memorandum to the Discalced Carmelite missionaries in Mexico and their response. The viceroy complains of inadequate efforts to establish missions in New Mexico, and the Carmelites respond with various explanations and indicate their greater interest in California as a missionary objective.

New Spain. Vu excellencia manda à las justicias, y ofiziales reales foraneos, que cada uno en su respetiva jurisdiccion notifique à todos los Colectores de Rentas Reales, que en ella huviere, hagan los enteros en las caxas, à que son obligados en las monedas de oro, y plata del antiguo cuño, esquinadas, y angulares, reservando en si las circulares de la nueva estampa ...: Don Juan Francisco de Guemes, y Horcasitas, Conde de RevillaGigedo [sic] ... Virrey ... de esta Nueva España ... [Mexico? Virrey? 1752?]   N106

   The conde de Revillagigedo, 41st viceroy of Mexico, issues regulations governing the melting down of objects made of gold and silver from Peru, Ecuador, and Guatemala.

New Spain. D. Joachin Monserrat, Ciurano, Cruíllas, Crespì de Valldaure ... Marqueés de Cruíllas ... Virrey, Gobernador, y Capitàn General de Nueva-España ... Haviendo llegado â Vera-Cruz el dia 15. de Mayo proximo la flota del mando del Gefe de Esquadra D. Augustin de Ydiaquez ... [Mexico City? 1765?]   N107

   This decree of 10 July 1765 concerns a fleet commanded by Augustin de Ydiaquez, and is a reiteration of an earlier decree of 20 May.

New Spain. El B[aili]o. Fr[ey]. D[on]. Antonio Maria Bucareli, y Ursúa, Henestrósa, ... Virrey, Governador y Capitan General de esta Nueva España ... Por quanto en veinte y cinco de Junio del año passado de mil setecientos setenta y dos madné promulgar el vando del tenor siguiente ... [Mexico? 1776.]   N108

   The decree calls attention to losses in revenue sustained by the crown through importation of cotton made by foreign weavers.

New Spain. Don Martin de Mayorga ... Virrey, Gobernador y Capitan General del Reyno de Nueva España ... [twelve regulations by the Spanish crown for the tobacco industry in Spain's American colonies] ... Mexico, 1783.   N109

New Spain. Reales ordenanzas para la direccion, régimen y gobierno del importante Cuerpo de la Minería de Nueva-España, y de su Real Tribunal General. Madrid, 1783.   N110

   A collection of laws arranged under nineteen sections covering the exploring, development, working and administering of mines in Mexico.

New Spain. Real ordenanza para el establecimiento é instruccion de intendentes de exército y provincia en el reino de la Nueva-España. Madrid, 1786.   N111

   The basic legal structure for the governing of Mexico by the Spanish crown, including geographical divisions, administrative hierarchy, manner of electing or appointing officials, etc.

New Spain. Reales ordenanzas para la direccion, regimen y gobierno del importante Cuerpo de la Mineria de Nueva-España, y de su Real Tribunal General. Lima, Casa Real de los Niños Huerfanos, 1786.   N112

   A collection of regulations for governing the administration of mines in Mexico.

New Spain. D. Manuel Antonio Florez Maldonado ... Virrey ... de Nueva España ... de 28 de Febrero próximo anterior la Real Cédula ... El Rey— ... Producir el fomento de la agricultura ... para la introduction de Negros en las islas de Cuba, Santo Domingo, Puerto-Rico, y Provincia de Caracas ... [Mexico? 1789?]   N113

   A decree designed to improve Spanish West Indian agriculture through the importation of slaves.

New Spain. Reglamento, u ordenanzas de ensayadores: formadas en virtud de lo mandado ... Mexico, Don Felipe de Zuñiga y Ontiveros, 1789.   N114

   An extensive compilation of regulations concerning all aspects of processing precious metals in Mexico, including administrative as well as technical aspects.

New Spain. Don Juan Vicente de Guemez Pacheco de Padilla Horcasítas y Aguayo, Conde de Revilla Gigedo ... Virrey, Gobernador y Capitan general de Nueva España ... De resultas de haber solicitado licencia de este Superior Gobierno para pasar à España, el Indio Juan de Aguilar ... con el objeto de hacer por sí en aquella península el comercio de la grana de su cosecha ... [n.p.] Mexico, 1792.   N115

   The applicant, Juan de Aguilar from the province of Oaxaca is authorized to go to Spain to engage in grain trade.

New Spain. Laws, etc. D. Joachin de Monserrat, ... Segun lo acordado en junta ... he resuelto se arrienden los tabacos de polvo, y oja por obispados ... bajo las reglas siguientes ... [Mexico, 1765.]   N116

   Twenty articles governing the wholesale and retail distribution of tobacco.

New Spain. Laws, etc. D. Joachin Monserrat ... Estando ya recogidos los tabacos de polbo, y oja, que se hallaban en poder de varios sugetos de esta capitàl, para dàr principio â su expendio de quenta de la real hacienda ... [n.p., 1765.] N117

New Spain. Laws, etc. D. Joachin Monserrat ... Explicados yá por el vando de 14. de Diciembre del año proximo los justos motivos con que la piedad de su Magestad, ha resuelto estancar el fruto del tabaco en polvo, y rama, por evitar â sus amados vassallos la imposicion de otras gavelas ... [n.p., 1765.] N118

New Spain. Laws, etc. D. Joachin Monserrat ... Haviendose reconocido, que muchos gobernadores, corregidores, alcaldes mayores de este reyno, equivocando el articulo 4. del Vando del 14. septiembre, no han procedido en la paga de tabacos ... [n.p., 1765.] N119

New Spain. Laws, etc. D. Joachin Monserrat ... Por un efecto del paternal amor, con que el Rey se desvela en atender â el bien de sus vassallos, y â la mayor seguridad ... que se estableciesse en ellos el estanco del tabaco en oja, y polvo, como lo està en los demás reynos, y provincias de su corona ... [n.p., 1765]. N120

New Spain. Laws, etc. Don Carlos Francisco de Croix ... Estando prevenido por el capitulo 45. de las ordenanzas de la real fabrica, y assiento de polbora, que ninguna persona de qualesquier estado, condicion, ó dignidad que sea, pueda fabricar, introducir, vender, ni comprarla, no siendo sacada con la correspondiente guia de esta real fabrica ... [n.p., 1768.] N121

New Spain. Laws, etc. Ordenanzas, methodo, o regla que se ha de observar a efecto de cerrar la puerta à la perpetracion de fraudes en la grana cochinilla, que en universal daño del comercio de este reyno, y el de Europa se han experiementado ... Mexico, D. Felipe de Zuñiga y Ontiveros, 1773. N122

New Spain. Laws, etc. Continuando el rey los generosos efectos de su piedad por adelantar la industria y felicidad de sus vasallos ... se ha servido habilitar el puerto de S. Blas para comercio con los del Sur del Peru ... Mexico, 1796. N123

The port of San Blas was opened to commerce with the ports of Spanish America by this decree.

New Spain. Laws, etc. Miguel la Grua Talamanca y Branciforte ... El rey nuestro Señor ... permitió la entrada en la plaza de la Havana de las harinas y otros víveres á los Anglo-Americanos ... [Mexico, 1796.] N124

An edict allowing American ships the right to carry flour and other necessities to Havana, a concession resulting from Spain's war with France.

New Spain. Laws, etc. Miguel la Grua Talamaca y Branciforte ... Por quanto el Exmô. Señor Don Diego de Gardoqui se ha servido comunicarme con fecha de 8 de octubre del año proxîmo pasado la real orden del tenor siguiente ... Dade en Orizava á 16 de junio de 1797. [n.p.] 1797. N125

To encourage trade, exemptions of duties are granted on agricultural products, exported from the Philippines and coming through Acapulco.

New Spain. Laws, etc. D. Joseph de Yturrigaray ... Virrey ... El Exmô. Señor Don Miguel Cayetano Soler, Secretario de Estado ... me ha comunicado con fecha de 24 de julio último la Real Orden del tenor siguiente ... Dado en México á [18?] de enero de 1804. [n.p., 1804.] N126

Regulations to avoid illegal production, contraband sales, and improper accounting.

New Spain. Real Audiencia (Mexico City). En la ciudad de Mexico, â veinte, y nueve de abril, de mil setecientos, sesenta, y cinco años: los señores alcaldes de corte de la Real Audiencia de esta Nueva-España ... [Mexico, 1765.] N127

Outlaws the practice of confiscating the property of Indians accused of criminal activity and turning it over to third parties for "safe keeping."

Newe Relation wie Don Sebastian Gonzales, ein Portugeser wider den gewaltigen indianischen König von Arracam ... die berümbte Insul Sundiva erobert hat. Augsburg, Chrysostomo Dabertzhofer, 1611. N128

A newsletter describing the victory of a Portuguese force over a ruler in Indo China, resulting in the capture of the island of Sundiva.

Newe und gründtliche Relation von der mercklichen Victori oder Sig welchen Herz Joannes de Sylua ... den 24. Aprill dess 1610. Jars wider etliche hollendische Raubschiff ... Augsburg, Chrysostemo Dabertzhoffer [1616?]. N129

A newsletter reporting Dutch attacks on the Spanish Philippines in 1610.

Newes of Sr. Walter Rauleigh. With the true description of Guiana. London, For H.G. to be sold by I. Wright, 1618. N130

The account of Raleigh's last Guiana venture, giving hope for the establishment of an active trade in the products of that region.

Newes out of Holland, of the East Indie trade there. London, J.D. for Nicholas Bourne and Thomas Archer, 1622. N131
An early example of English hostility to the Dutch in the East Indies, in which the corruption of Dutch officials, rather than their success, is emphasized.

News from the East-Indies. [London, 1691.] N132
A commentary on the terms by which the East India Company would be readmitted to trade with the Mogul's dominions.

News from the East-Indies. [London, 1691.] N133
Similar to the above in content, but with an added warning against the stockjobbers seeking to raise money to pay indemnities called for by the Mogul's terms.

Newton, Samuel. An idea of geography and navigation. London, For Christopher Hussey, 1695. N134
A textbook in navigation and related mathematics.

Newton, Thomas. On the imperfect reception of the Gospel: A sermon preached before the incorporated Society for the Propagation of the Gospel in Foreign Parts ... in the parish church of St. Mary-le-Bow, on Friday February 17, 1769. London, E. Owen and T. Harrison, 1769. N135
The annual sermon, urging the appointment of a bishop for the American colonies, indicating concern for the slave population, and the political discontent in the American colonies.

Nichols, Harley B. Journal of a voyage from New York to Java and return in the bark Verona, 17 July 1875 to 29 December 1876. Manuscript. [various places] 1875-76. N136

Nicholson, William. [Letter book.] Manuscript. London; Senegal, Jan. 14, 1774-Aug. 16, 1774. N137
Nicholson was victualler to the British military base at the mouth of the Senegal River where he oversaw the export of slaves for a London company.

[Nickolls, Sir John.] Remarques sur les avantages et les désavantages de la France et de la Gr. Bretagne, par rapport au commerce. Leiden, [Paris] 1754. N138
The author criticizes French commercial policy.

Nickolls, Sir John. Remarques sur les avantages et les desavantages de la France et de la Grande-Bretagne ... augmentée d'un essai sur la police & le commerce des grains. Dresden, 1754. N139
This edition adds for the first time another separately published piece, *Essai sur la police generale des grains*.

[Nickolls, Sir John.] Remarks on the advantages and disadvantages of France and Great-Britain with respect to commerce. London, T. Osborne, 1754. N140
The first English edition.

Nickolls, Sir John. Anmärkningar öfwer Frankrikes och Englands större eller mindre förmåner ... öfwersatt af Franska originalet efter den nyaste uplagan af år 1754. Stockholm, Pet. Hesselberg, 1761. N141
The first Swedish edition.

Nickolls, Robert Boucher. A letter to the treasurer of the Society Instituted for the Purpose of Effecting the Abolition of the Slave Trade. London, James Phillips, 1787. N142
An argument on behalf of ending the trade in slaves, tending to prove that it is economically disadvantageous as well as a violation of human principles.

Nicolai, Eliud. Newe und warhaffte Relation, von deme was sich in beederley, das ist, in den West- und Ost-Indien ... Munich, N. Henricum, 1619. N143
A collection of voyages by various European navigators, particularly to the East Indies.

Nicolay, Nicolas de. Les quatre premiers livres des navigations et peregrinations Orientales ... Lyons, G. Roville, 1568. N144
One of the earliest French description of the lands and peoples of the Near East, with sixty full-page copper engravings.

Nicolay, Nicolas de. Discours et histoire veritable des navigations, peregrinations et voyages, faicts en la Turquie. Antwerp, Arnould Coninx, 1586. N145
This edition has sixty-one woodcut illustrations that appear to be from the same blocks as the Antwerp edition of 1576.

Nicolay, Nicolas de. Le navigationi et viaggi nella Turchia. Antwerp, Guiglielmo Silvio, 1576. N146
The first Italian edition, including sixty woodcuts depicting the peoples of the Near East.

Nicolay, Nicolas de. Le navigationi et viaggi, fatti nella Turchia. Venice, Francesco Ziletti, 1580. N147
The second Italian edition, with eight engravings not included in earlier editions.

Nicolay, Nicolas de. Vier Bucher von de Raisz und Schiffart in die Turckey ... Antorff, Wilhelm Silvium, 1576. N148
The first German edition.

Nicolay, Nicolas de. De schipvaert ende reysen gedaen int landt van Turckyen. Antwerp, Willem Silvius, 1577.　　　　　　　　　　　　　N149
　The first Dutch edition.

Nicolay, Nicolas de. The navigations, peregrinations and voyages, made into Turkie by Nicholas Nicholay ... devided into foure bookes, with threescore figures ... translated out of the French by T. Washington the younger. London, Thomas Dawson, 1585.　　　　　　　　　　　　　N150
　The first and only English edition.

[Nicolini, Alfonso.] Sposizione letterale delle notizie anecdote giustificative della condotta de MM. RR. PP. Gesuiti nel Paraguai, e nel Portogallo ... Barcelona, Antonio Michele Cervello, 1759.　　　　　　　　　　　　　N151
　Relates to the settlement of Colonia del Sacramento and to the position of the Jesuits in that part of South America.

Nicoll, John. The advantage of Great Britain consider'd in the tobacco trade. London, 1727.
　　　　　　　　　　　　　　　　　　　　　N152
　Advocates making potash of poor grades of tobacco instead of using it for snuff and "old Spanish."

Nicolosi, Giovanni Battista. Dell' Hercole e studio geografico. Rome, V. Mascardi, 1660.
　　　　　　　　　　　　　　　　　　　　　N153
　An atlas containing twenty-two double-page maps, including lesser known areas such as the Maldive Islands and the supposed land of Jesso.

Nider, Johannes. De contractibus mercatorum. [Cologne, Ulrich Zell, ca. 1468.]　　　N154
　The first edition of a work on morality in commerce.

Nider, Johannes. De contractibus mercatorum. Cologne, Conrad Winters [ca. 1479].　　N155
　The second Cologne printing.

Niebuhr, Carsten. Beschreibung von Arabien aus eigenen Beobachtungen und im Land selbst gesammleten Nachrichten abgefasset. Copenhagen, Nicolaus Möller, 1772.　　　　　N156
　The first edition of an account of a Danish scientific expedition to Egypt, Arabia, India and Persia from 1761-1767. The author was the only survivor of the expedition.

Niebuhr, Carsten. Description de l'Arabie. Copenhagen, Nicolas Möller, 1773.　　　N157
　The first French edition.

Niebuhr, Carsten. Description de l'Arabie, d'après les observations et recherches faites dans le pays même. Paris, Brunet, 1779.　　N158
　This Paris edition was intended to supply French readers with an edition in acceptable French since the earlier Copenhagen edition was regarded as an unfortunate translation.

Niebuhr, Carsten. Voyage en Arabie & en d'autres pays circonvoisins. Amsterdam, S.J. Baalde; Utrecht, J. van Schoonhoven & Barthelemy Wild, 1776-80.　　　　　　　N159
　This French edition is illustrated with 124 copper engravings.

Niebuhr, Carsten. Voyage de M. Niebuhr en Arabie et en d'autres pays de l'Orient. Avec l'extrait de sa description de l'Arabie & des observations de Mr. Forskal. Switzerland, Chez les Libraires Associés, 1780.　　　　　N160
　An abridgement of Niebuhr's two works on Arabia with additional observations of Petter Forskål, one of the original members of the expedition.

Niebuhr, Carsten. Beschryving van Arabie, uit eigene waarnemingen en in't land zelf verzamelde narigten opgesteld. Amsterdam, S.J. Baalde; Utrecht, J. van Schoonhoven, 1774.
　　　　　　　　　　　　　　　　　　　　　N161
　This first Dutch edition is superior to the preceding editions in the quality of its illustrations. It also adds an index.

Niebuhr, Carsten. Reize naar Arabië en andere omliggende landen. Amsterdam, S.J. Baalde; Utrecht, J. van Schoonhoven, 1776-1780.
　　　　　　　　　　　　　　　　　　　　　N162
　This Dutch edition was published concurrently with the French edition by the same publisher.

Niebuhr, Carsten. Sammandrag af Justitiae-rådets Herr Casten Niebuhrs resa i Levanten och beskrifning om Arabien ... af Samuel Ödmann. Stockholm, Kongl. Ordens-Tryckeriet, 1787.
　　　　　　　　　　　　　　　　　　　　　N163
　An abridgment of Niebuhr's *Travels* with a seventeen page introduction by Samuel Ödmann, the editor.

Niebuhr, Carsten. Travels through Arabia and other countries in the East ... Edinburgh, R. Morrison and son [etc.] 1792.　　　　N164
　The first English-language edition, an abridged version.

Niebuhr, Carsten. Travels through Arabia and other countries in the East. Perth, R. Morison, 1799.　　　　　　　　　　　　　　　　N165
　An abridged edition, with notes added by Robert Heron, the translator.

Niekamp, Johann Lucas. Kurtzgefasste Missions-Geschichte; oder, Historischer Auszug der evangelischen Missions-Berichte aus Ost-Indien von dem Jahr 1705 bis zu Ende des Jahres 1736, mit zwey dazu nöthigen Land-Charten ... Halle, Wäysen-Hauses, 1740-1772.
　　　　　　　　　　　　　　　　　　　　　N166
　The first of these two volumes is the first edition of Niekamp's history of the Tranquebar mission. The second volume is a continuation of that history to 1767.

Niekamp, Johann Lucas. Histoire de la mission danoise dans les Indes Orientales. Geneva, Henri-Albert Gosse, 1745. N167
The first French edition, translated by Benjamin Gaudard.

[Niekamp, Johann Lucas.] Histoire des voyages, que les Danois ont fait dans les Indes Orientales. Geneva, Henri-Albert Gosse & Comp., 1747. N168
Second French edition of the Gaudard translation.

Niekamp, Johann Lucas. Historia missionis evangelicae in India Orientali. Halle, 1747. N169
Latin edition of the preceding item, also translated from the German.

Niekamp, Johann Lucas. Kort forfattet missionshistorie eller historisk udtog af de fra Ost-Indien indkomne Evangeliske missions-beretninger fra aar 1705 til 1736 aars udgang ... Copenhagen, Gottmann Friderich Risel, 1755. N170
The first Danish edition.

Nieremberg, Juan Eusebio. Ideas de virtud en algunos claros varones de la Compañia de Jesus ... Madrid, Maria de Quiñones, 1643. N171
A collection of biographies of thirty members of the Society of Jesus during its first century. Many of these Jesuits had served as missionaries abroad.

Nierop, Dirk Rembrantsz van. By-voeghsel op eeninge oefeningen welcke sijn eeninge aenteyckeningen ... Amsterdam, A. van der Storck, 1678. N172
Includes material on the geography and natural history of the Americas, as well as an account of explorations of the west coast of North America.

Nierop, Dirk Rembrantsz van. Tweede deel van enige oefeningen 't welk is in geographia ofte aertkloots-beskrijvinge ... Amsterdam, A.S. van der Storck, 1674. N173
Contains the first account of the voyage of Tasman in which he circumnavigated Australia. Also includes an account of the voyage of Martin Vries in the northern Pacific Ocean.

Nieuhof, Johannes. l'Ambassade de la Compagnie orientale ... vers l'empereur de la Chine. Leiden, J. de Meurs, 1665. N174
An account of an embassy to China by the Dutch East India Company from 1655 to 1657, containing an extensive description of China and many illustrations.

Nieuhof, Johannes. Die Gesantschaft der Ost-Indischen Geselschaft ... an den Tartarischen Cham. Amsterdam, Jacob Mörs, 1666. N175
The first German edition.

Nieuhof, Johannes. Legatio Batavica ad magnum Tartariae Chamum Sungteium. Amsterdam, Jacobum Meursium, 1668. N176
The first Latin edition.

Nieuhof, Johannes. An embassy from the East-India Company of the United Provinces, to the Grand Tartar Cham, Emperour of China. London, John Macock, 1669. N177
The first English edition.

Nieuhof, Johannes. Gedenkwaerdige Brasiliaense zee-en lant-reize ... een bondige beschrijving van gantsch Neerlants Brasil. Amsterdam, Weduwe van J. van Meurs, 1682. N178
A well-illustrated history and description of Brazil including many documents relating to Dutch possessions and commerce there.

Nieuhof, Johannes. Zee en lant-reize door verscheide gewesten van Oostindien. Amsterdam, Weduwe van J. van Meurs, 1682. N179
A description of eastern lands and islands, with accounts of leading products and commerce. The author lived in Ceylon and Batavia from 1655 to 1671.

Nieuwe commertie-compagnie tusschen de rijcken vranckryck ende Sweden opgerecht. [n.p.] 1663. N180
Announces the formation of a new French-Swedish trading company with proposed stations in London, Amsterdam, Bordeaux, Nantes, Rouen, and Paris.

Nieuwe ende extraordinare praemien ofte prijsgelderen. [n.p.] 1665. N181
Announces prizes to be given to Dutch sailors who show unusual bravery in conflicts with the English.

Nieuwe tydingen ut den conseio ofte secreten raedt van Spangien. Amsterdam, J. Wachter, 1621. N182
An attack upon Spain's power in the East and West Indies.

Niño de Guzman, Pedro. Copia de villete, que el señor Don Pedro Niño de Guzman ... escriuio al M.R.P.M. Fr. Iuan de San Augustin ... para que disponga se cante el Te Deum Laudamus en la Capilla ... Madrid, Julian de Paredes, 1655. N183
An order from the president of Casa de Contratación in Seville directing the celebration with religious activities of the successful voyage of the treasure fleet in 1655.

Nishikawa, Joken. Zōho Kai tsūshō kō. Kyoto, 1708. N184
A revised edition of a geographical compendium first published in Japan in 1695. It briefly describes the location, products and inhabitants of each country discussed, and includes maps of the world and of China.

Nispen, Adriaan van. Dan kaizarlijkken gezant, Aug. Gisleen Busbeeq, aan de grooten Soliman. Dordrecht, A. Andriessz, 1652. N185
The first edition of an account of a Dutch embassy to Turkey under the leadership of August Busbeeq.

Nispen, Adriaan van. Verscheyde voyagien. Dordrecht, V. Caeymacx, 1652. N186
Contains an account of Jan Danckaerts' travel to Russia about 1605.

[Noble, Charles Frederick.] A voyage to the East Indies in 1747 and 1748. London, T. Becket and P.A. Dehondt [etc.] 1762. N187
The narrative of an East Indian voyage given primarily to descriptions of Java and China.

Nodal, Bartolomé García and Gonzalo de. Relacion del viaje que por orden de Su Magd. y acuerdo del Real consejo de Indias. Madrid, F. Correa de Montenegro, 1621. N188
An account of the first Spanish exploration of the route around Cape Horn. A better route than the Straits of Magellan offered was sought to facilitate Spanish commerce with western South America and the South Pacific.

Nodal, Bartolomé García and Gonzalo de. Relacion del viage ... al descubrimiento del estrecho nuevo de San Vincente ... reconocimiento del de Magallanes. Cadiz, Manuel Espinosa de los Monteros, 1766. N189
The second edition.

Noels de la Chine. [n.p., ca. 1701.] N190
Two poems celebrating the condemnation by the faculty at the Sorbonne of books intending to justify the Chinese rites within Christian practice.

Nolin, Jean Baptiste. Amérique ou nouveau continent dréssée sur les nouvelles relations découvertes et observations. Paris, Daumont, 1754. N191
This map of the Western Hemisphere by a leading French cartographer is of particular interest because of its inclusion of an inset depicting two presumed passages between Hudson Bay and the Pacific Ocean.

Nolin, Jean Baptiste. Carte du Canada et de la Louisiane que forment la Nouvelle France et des colonies angloises. Paris, Daumont, 1756. N192
This map was published to illustrate the Anglo-French war in North America. It is similar in scope to the 1755 maps of Mitchell and d'Anville, but comprises only one sheet.

Noort, Olivier van. Description du penible voyage faict entour de l'univers ou globe terrestre. Amsterdam, C. Claessz., 1602. N193
An account of the circumnavigation of the globe by Olivier van Noort in the earliest French edition.

Noort, Olivier van. [Letter to the burgomaster of Utrecht.] Manuscript. [Utrecht, ca. September 1601.] N194
The letter refers to the author's voyage around the world, the first made by a Dutch navigator.

Nootwendich bericht ende memorien ... rakende het oorloch by zyne majesteyt van Dennemarken ... Middelburg [1658]. N195
Memorials of the ambassadors of France, England, and Denmark, with a reply by the Swedish ambassador to Denmark concerning the closing of the Baltic to western European trade.

Nootwendige aenmerkinge op een fameuse libel, ghenaemt de *Bickerse beroerte, ofte den Hollantsen eclipsis.* Antwerp, Jan van Waesbergen, 1650. N196
A defense of Bicker against those who blamed him for the decline of the Dutch West India Company.

Norbert de Bar-le-Duc. Memoires utiles et necessaires, tristes et consolans, sur les missions des Indes Orientales, &c. Lucca, Antoine Rossi, 1742. N197
A collection of documents relating primarily to Capuchin missions, but with frequent reference to Jesuits also. Much of the text is in both French and Italian.

Norbert de Bar-le-Duc. Memorie istoriche presentate al sommo pontefice Benedetto XIV, intorno alle missioni dell' Indie Orientali ... Lucca, Salvatore e Gian-Domenico Marescandoli, 1744. N198
The first Italian edition of a documentary history of Roman Catholic missions in Malabar from a Capuchin point of view which is often critical of the Jesuit missions in the East.

Norbert de Bar-le-Duc. Memorie storiche sopra le missioni dell' Indie Orientali. Nuremberg, M. Vaillant, 1754. N199
The author was a Capuchin priest whose experience in India between 1736 and 1740 produced an extreme hostility toward the Jesuits there, and these four volumes largely concern his case against them with respect to the Malabar rites controversy.

Norden, Frederik Ludvig. Voyage d'Egypte et de Nubie. Copenhagen, La Maison Royale des Orphelines, 1755. N200
An account of travels in Egypt in 1737-38 by a protégé of Denmark's King Christian VI, including 159 engravings made from drawings by the author.

Norden, Frederik Ludvig. Voyage d'Egypte et de Nubie, par Frédéric-Louis Norden. Nouvelle édition, soigneusement conférée sur l'original, avec des notes et des additions tirées des auteurs anciens et modernes, et des géographes arabes ... Paris, Pierre Didot l'aine, 1795-1798. N201

This is the second edition in French, edited by Louis Matheu Langlès, who adds extensive commentary to the text.

Nordenanker, Johan. Tal, om strömgångarne i Öster-Sjön; hållet för Kongl. Vetenskaps Academien ... den 18 Jan. 1792 ... Stockholm, Anders Zetterberg, 1792.   N202
A discussion of the currents in the Baltic Sea.

Nordencrantz, Anders. Arcana oeconomiae et commercii, eller Handelens och hushåldningsmärkets hemligheter. Stockholm, Joh. Laur. Hoorn, 1730.   N203
A survey of economic history, ancient and modern, and a discussion of economic theory and policies with respect to Sweden's economy.

Nordencrantz, Anders. Hwad rätte och förmögne köpmän i ett land uträtta kunna, samt nyttan och nödwändigheten af deras contoirs uprätt-och wid magt hällande i riket, uti twenne til riksens höglostige ständer på Riksdagen år 1726 ingifne memorialer ... Stockholm, Kongl. Tryckeriet, 1765.   N204
A memorial on the benefits to be derived from the functions of businessmen, at home and abroad, abstracted from the author's *Arcana oeconomiae et commercii*.

Nores, Giasone de. Discorso di Iason Denores intorno alla geographia ... Padua, Paolo Meietti, 1589.   N205
An elementary treatise on world geography, divisions of the earth, climates, and locations, by a Cypriot author.

Nores, Giasone de. Breve trattato del mondo, et delle sue parti. Venice, Andrea Muschio, 1571.   N206
A treatise on cosmography and geography.

Nores, Giasone de. Tavole ... del mondo, et della sphera ... Padua, Paulo Meietto, 1582.   N207
An elementary text on the sphere, including the earth, celestial sphere and the zodiac.

Normandy (France). Chambre du Commerce. Observations de la Chambre du Commerce de Normandie, sur le traité de commerce entre la France & l'Angleterre. [n.p., ca. 1786.]   N208
An unfavorable view of the recent commercial treaty because of the disadvantage it brought to the French cloth trade.

Norris, Sir John. Ephemeris expeditionis Noreysii et Draki in Lusitanium. London, T. Woodcocke, 1589.   N209
An account of an English expedition against the shipping of Spain and Portugal under the command of Drake and Norris in 1589.

Norris, Robert. Memoirs of the reign of Bossa Ahádee, king of Dahomy ... to which are added, the author's journey to Abomey, the capital: and a short account of the African slave trade. London, For W. Lowndes, 1789.   N210
An account of the history, social and political structure of Dahomey and its relationship to the slave trade that had long been practiced there, along with the author's justification of it.

Norris, Robert. Resa på Neger-Kusten til Kongl. Hofvet i Dahomej, af Ängelske handels agenten Norris, år 1772. Götheborg, Sam. Norbert, 1792.   N211
Samuel Ödmann's Swedish translation is from the German version of Johann Reinhold Forster. The text is a narrative of travels with an account of social and political life in Dahomey.

North, Brownlow. A sermon preached before the incorporated Society for the Propagation of the Gospel in Foreign Parts: at their anniversary meeting in the parish church of St. Mary-le-Bow, on Friday February 20, 1778. London, T. Harrison and S. Brooke, 1778.   N212
The revolutionary conflict in North America is noted as a detriment to mission work as the church was seen as an agent of government rather than a teacher of peace and charity.

[North, Sir Dudley.] Discourses upon trade; principally ... interest, coynage, clipping, increase of money. London, T. Basset, 1691.   N213
A free trade argument, discussing trade from the standpoint of the effects of coinage and interest upon it.

North American Land Company. Plan of association of the North American Land Company, established February, 1795. Philadelphia, R. Aitken & Son, 1795.   N214
The company held six million acres of land in Pennsylvania, Virginia, North and South Carolina, Georgia and Kentucky.

North West Company. [Draft of an agreement between the partners of the Northwest Company in preparation for the merger with the Hudson's Bay Company.] Manuscript. [n.p., 6 April 1821.]   N215
The agreement contained in this document anticipates the merger of the two great fur-trading companies of Canada, bringing an end to their intense rivalry.

[North West Company.] Report of the proceedings connected with the disputes between the Earl of Selkirk and the Northwest Company. London, B. McMillan, 1819.   N216
Report of the trial held at York, in Upper Canada.

The North-American and the West-Indian gazetteer. London, For G. Robinson, 1776.   N217

An alphabetical guide to American places and a handbook on America, published so that Englishmen may be better acquainted with their colonies.

A nosseigneurs de l'Assemblée nationale. [Paris, P. Fr. Didot jeune, 1790.] N218

The National Assembly is reminded of several problems relating to Indian Ocean commerce, including the evacuation of Pondichery and the damaging effects of the monopoly of the Compagnie des Indes.

A nosseigneurs de l'Assemblée nationale. Nosseigneurs, nous soussignés habitans de Pondichéry, de l'île-de-France et de l'île-de-Bourbon ... [Paris, 1789.] N219

A protest against the evacuation of Pondichery by the French government, citing its importance to French prestige and commerce in the Indian Ocean.

Notice historique, sur les désastres de St. Domingue, pendant l'an XI et l'an XII. Paris, Pillot [ca. 1804]. N220

The anonymous author was a French officer who was taken prisoner by the rebels. He points out the part Britain played in aiding the rebellion.

Noticia breve de la expedicion militar de Sonora y Cinaloa, su exîto feliz, y ventajoso estado en que por consecuencia de ella se han puesto ambas provincias. [Mexico City, 1771.] N221

This is a short account of Gálvez's military expedition against the Indians of Sonora, written by Gálvez himself or one of the expedition members.

Noticia certa da grande batalha, que houve na America entre os Francezes, e Inglezes, em cujo conflicto forão estes derrotados ... Importantissima expedição, intenta a França contra Inglaterra, e outras cousas concernentes a presente guerra. Lisbon, Domingos Rodrigues, 1756. N222

An account of the Anglo-French conflict in America, with mention of Braddock's defeat.

Noticia certa de hum successo acontecido no imperio da China, aonde se referem os tormentos, trabalhos, e martyrios que alli padessem os Catholicos. [Lisbon, 1757.] N223

A commentary on the opposition of the Chinese authorities to Christianity there, noting two martyrdoms in particular.

Noticia de hum notavel successo acontecido em Africa no paiz de Constantina, em o mez de janeiro do prezente anno. Lisbon, 1758. N224

An account of an earthquake near Tunis.

Noticia do grande assalto, e batalha, que os Mouros derão a Praça de Mazagam, em o mez de junho do presente anno de 1756 ... Lisbon, Domingos Rodrigues, 1756. N225

A newsletter account of a Portuguese victory over Morocco in a battle for possession of Mazagan.

Noticia verdadeira da guerra da America ... a tomada do forte de Sam Jorze ganhado pelos Francezes &c. [Lisbon, ca. 1757.] N226

A newsletter describing the capture of Ft. George by the French during the Anglo-French war in North America.

Noticia verdadeira das heroicas acçoens dos valerozos Portuguezes na tomada das praças, e terras no estado da India ... [Lisbon, Domingos Gonsalves, 1785.] N227

An account of Portuguese military actions in India, chiefly against the Indian leader Bonsulo in the vicinity of Bicholim.

Notificazione della Nuova Compagnia del Commercio di Tutti li Paesi dell' Indie Orientali, e China ... Genoa, Paolo Scionico, 1754. N228

Italian translation of the terms and conditions of establishment of a new commercial company in Lisbon called the New Company for Commerce and the East Indies.

Notizia alla santita di N[ost]ro Signore P.P. Benedetto XIV. per riassumere il carteggio co[n] gl[i] Imperatore della Cina. Manuscript. [n.p., ca. 1740.] N229

An anonymous memorandum intended for Pope Benedict XIV urging a papal legation to the emperor of China to restore the steadily weakening relationship between Rome and China.

[Nougaret, P. J. B. (Pierre Jean Baptiste).] Voyages intéressans dans différentes colonies françaises, espagnols, anglaises, &c. London; Paris, Jean-François Bastien, 1788. N230

A collection of geographical, historical and anecdotal material on several American colonies, including Curaçao, Santo Domingo, Martinique, Louisiana, and Mexico.

Nourse, Mr. A defence of the resolutions and address of the American Congress: in reply to Taxation no tyranny ... London, J. Williams, [1775]. N231

A reply to Dr. Johnson's *Taxation no tyranny* in which the author examines the sources of power for any governing body.

Nouvelle Compagnie des Indes. Mémoire pour les actionnaires de la Compagnie des Indes. Paris, J.R. Lottin, 1790. N232

An explanation of commercial procedures used by the company in its India trade.

Nouvelle Compagnie des Indes. Précis pour les actionnaires de la Compagnie des Indes, en réponse à l'adresse présentée à l'Assemblée Nationale par les députés extraordinaires des manufactures & du commerce du royaume. [n.p.] 1790. N233

La nouvelle conversion du roy de Perse. Avec la deffette de deux cents mil Turcs apres sa conversion. Paris, François Hyby, 1606. N234

An attribution of Persian victories over the Turks and improved relations between Europe and Persia to the conversion of the Persian king to Christianity.

Nouvelles de Saint-Domingue. No. [1] - 26. [Paris] Quillau [1790]. N235

Twenty-six issues of a leaflet reporting events in Saint Domingue during a time of tension between the revolutionary government in Paris and the colonists, who did not want to grant political rights to Mulattoes.

Nouvelles des missions orientales: reçues à Rome depuis l'an 1794, jusqu'en 1807 inclusivement. Paris, Société Typographique, 1808. N236

A collection of missionary reports, in extracted form primarily, from missions in China and southeast Asia.

Nova e curiosa relaçam da embaixada, que mandou o Graõ Mogor, ao Rey de Inglaterra: tirada de varias cartas fidedignas, que fizeraõ varios aleados aos correspondentes, que tem nesta cidade. Lisbon, 1757. N237

A newsletter reporting a possible embassy from the Grand Mogul in India to Great Britain.

Nova relação das grandes mortandades, ruinas, e assolações, que tem sausado os grandes, e horriveis terremotos, que tem havido neste presente anno de 1751 em Africa. Lisbon, Miguel Manescal da Costa, 1751. N238

A newsletter describing an earthquake in northern Africa.

Nova relatio historica de rebus in India Orientali à patribus Societatis Jesu, anno 1598. & 99. gestis. Mainz, Joannis Albini, 1601. N239

A later edition of this collection of seven letters from various places in the East.

Novo, e publico manifesto, ou declaraçam da guerra, que por ordem da corte de França se publicou contra a Gram Bretanha, em dezaseis de Junho ... Lisbon, Domingos Rodrigues, 1756. N240

A newsletter reporting the declarations of war by France and Great Britain against each other.

Nuix, Juan. Reflexîones imparciales sobre la humanidad de los Españoles en las Indias, contra los pretendidos filósofos y políticos. Para ilustrar las historias de MM. Raynal y Robertson. Madrid, Joachin Ibarra, 1782. N241

An attempt to improve the image of Spanish colonial policy in America, particularly with respect to treatment of the Indians.

Nunes, Pedro. De arte atque ratione navigandi. Coimbra, Antonii à Marijs, 1573. N242

Includes *Eiusdem in theoricas planetarum Georgii Purbachii*, *Eiusdem de erratis Orontii Finaei*, and *De crepusculis*, published together for the first time.

Nunes, Pedro. Petri Nonii Salaciensis opera. Basel, Henric-Petrina, 1566. N243

This volume contains two works by Nunes: *De duobus problematis circa navigandi artem* and his commentary on *In theoricas planetarum* by Georg von Peurbach.

Nuove lettere delle cose del Giappone, paese del mondo novo, dell'anno 1579. infino al 1581 ... Venice, Gioliti, 1585. N244

A collection of seven letters from Jesuit missionaries in Japan, three of them by Luís Fróis.

Nuyts, Pieter A. Cort verhael ... van den Chineeschen & Japanschen handel. Manuscript. Zeelandia [Formosa] 10 February 1629. N245

The author was governor of Dutch holdings on Formosa, and this manuscript describes the commerce of the island, noting the necessary expenditures if the Dutch trade there was to continue.

[Nyercke, Joost Willemsz.] Klaer-Bericht ofte aenwysinge ... Hoorn, M. Gerbrantsz., 1630. N246

Concerns the grain trade of the Netherlands.

O

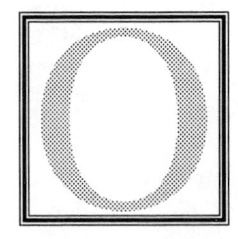

Obando y Solís, José Francisco de. Manifiesto, en que succintamente se exponen los motivos, y feliz exito de la embajada à la isla, y corte de Borney ... [Manila, 1752.]   O1
Concerns an attempt to re-establish commercial relations between the Philippines and Borneo.

[O'Beirne, Thomas Lewis.] A candid and impartial narrative of the transactions of the fleet under the command of Lord Howe ... with observations ... London, For J. Almon, 1779.   O2
A defense of Howe by one who served in his command. This second edition includes a map showing the positions of the French and English fleets off Sandy Hook.

Oberti, Finetto. Aggiustamento universale di pesi, e misure de panni di lana, seta, lino, & vittouaglie ... Venice, Turini, 1643.   O3
A manual of weights and measures for use by merchants trading in Europe, Asia, and Africa.

[O'Brien, Sir Lucius Henry.] Letters concerning the trade and manufactures of Ireland, principally so far as the same relate to the making iron in this kingdom. Dublin, Luke White, 1785.   O4
The author contends for greater uniformity in duties between Ireland and Great Britain, and an end to restrictiveness on that trade as an aid in encouraging iron manufacture in Ireland.

Observatien op de brief van A. de Bruyn. Deventer, Jacob Verworen, 1647.   O5
The author agrees with the Spanish emissary, and fears France and Sweden. "Our flourishing state, welfare, and commerce are the golden fleece they seek."

Observations arising from the declaration of war against Spain, and the future management of it on the part of Great Britain: with some considerations on the consistency of the M-----y and their arguments. In a letter to ---------. London, T. Gardner, 1739.   O6
An attack on the Ministry for delaying so long in declaring war on Spain and following a policy of weakness in the West Indies.

Observations concerning indigo and cochineal. London, 1746.   O7
Detailed instructions for the production of these two products with brief comments on silk, rice, and tar.

Observations critiques et politiques sur le commerce maritime: dans lesquelles on discute quelques points relatifs à l'industrie & au commerce des colonies françoises. Amsterdam; Paris, Jombert, 1755.   O8
An attack upon the proposal to destroy the sugar refineries in St. Domingue, and of the defense of that proposal as enunciated by Pierre André O'Heguerty in his *Essai sur les intérets du commerce maritime*.

Observations des négocians de Bordeaux, sur l'arrest du conseil, du 30 août 1784. Paris, 1784.   O9
A critical reaction to a new law admitting foreign merchants to the American trade.

Observations d'un actionnaire, sur le mémoire de M. L. M. contre la Nouvelle Compagnie des Indes. Paris, Gattey, 1788.   O10
Refutes an earlier tract which denounced the new Compagnie des Indes and insisted that French commerce to the East would prosper better under a system of free trade.

Observations d'un habitant des colonies, sur le Mémoire en faveur des gens de couleur, ou sang-mêlés, de St-Domingue & des autres isles françoises de l'Amérique ... par M. Grégoire ... [n.p., 1789.]   O11
The author of this work is Moreau de Saint-Mery, and he responds to an address by Henri Grégoire to the National Assembly urging greater recognition of the rights of the people in the French West Indies.

Observations générales et impartiales sur l'affaire de Scioto. [Paris, P.F. Didot le Jeune, 1790.]   O12
A defense of the Scioto Land Company against charges of mismanagement and misrepresentation by its agents in Paris.

Observations générales sur les causes des maladies du blé, et sur l'inefficacité des moyens employés jusqu'à present pour l'en garantir. Londres, et se trouve à Paris, J.B.G. Musier, 1788.   O13
An account of a wheat blight in France and the means to control it.

Observations importantes et d'intérêt public, sur les colonies françaises en Amérique. [n.p., ca. 1792.]   O14
An expression of fear lest the excesses of the revolutionary governments in the West Indies create a counterrevolution which would re-establish the earlier forms of oppression.

Observations occasion'd by reading a pamphlet, intitled, A discourse concerning the currencies of the British plantations in America. London, For T. Cooper, 1741.   O15
"I agree with the author, 'That our colonies have defrauded more in a few years by their paper emissions, and other currencies, than bad administrations ... have formerly done...'"

Observations on British wool, and the manufacture of it in this kingdom. London, H. Kent, 1738.   O16
A discussion of the various types and qualities of British and foreign wool, the illicit trade in wool, and the damage it does to Britain while bringing advantage to other countries.

Observations on the case of the northern colonies. London, J. Roberts, 1731.   O17
An attempt to effect the passage of a bill pending in Parliament which would prohibit the North American colonies from trading with the French West Indies and require the colonies to obtain their wants from the British.

Observations on the commerce of Great Britain with the Russian and Ottoman empires, and on the projects of Russia against the Ottoman and British dominions. London, J. Debrett, 1801.   O18
A tract concerned with the perceived threat of Russian expansion in India, the Far East and North America to as far as Mexico, to the disadvantage of Great Britain's commerce in those regions. The introduction is signed W.B.

Observations on the conduct of Great Britain with regard to the negociations and other transactions abroad. London, J. Roberts, 1729.   O19
A defense of Sir Robert Walpole against charges of willfully neglecting England's West India commerce.

Observations on the present state of Denmark, Russia, and Switzerland. London, For T. Cadell, 1784.   O20
A series of letters describing in some detail the economy, taxation, government, and social structure of Denmark and Russia.

The observations on the Treaty of Seville examined. London, For R. Francklin, 1730.   O21
An attack upon Walpole's defense of the Treaty of Seville. The treaty is seen as an action against Britain's most natural allies.

Observations physiques et mathematiques pour servir a l'histoire naturelle, & à la perfection de l'astronomie & de la geographie: envoyées de Siam à l'Academie Royale des Sciences à Paris ... Avec les reflexions de messieurs de l'Academie & quelque notes du P. Goüye, de la Compagnie de Jesus. Paris, Veuve d'Edme Martin, Jean Boudot & Estienne Martin, 1688.   O22
In addition to observations of eclipses and other astronomical phenomena in the East this work also includes attempts at fixing the longitude of certain places, and also a section on crocodiles and other animals of Asia.

Observations physiques et mathematiques, pour servir a l'histoire naturelle & à la perfection de l'astronomie & de la geographie: envoyées des Indes et de la Chine à l'Academie Royale des Sciences à Paris, par les peres Jesuites. Avec les ... notes du P. Goüye, de la Compagnie de Jesu. Paris, Imprimerie Royale, 1692.   O23
The observations of Jesuits in Asia include determination of latitude and longitude, eclipses, tides, and climate. Maps of parts of India and Burma are included.

Observations sommaires sur le mémoire publié pour la colonie de l'Isle-de-France, relativement au commerce de l'Inde. [n.p.] 1790.   O24
Twenty-three accusations against the Compagnie des Indes made by the colony on Mauritius, with the reply of the company.

Observations sur le commerce de la Mer Noire. Amsterdam, Libraires Associés, 1787.   O25
A compendium of commercial information identifying products available in specific places, conditions for carrying on business, import and export duties, rates of exchange, and other information of value to merchants.

Observations sur le commerce entre l'Angleterre à la France. Manuscript. [Paris?] 1788.   O26
Relates particularly to the cloth and wine trades, and advocates greater reciprocity between the two countries.

Observations sur le livre entitulé *De l'Inde, ou reflexions sur les moyens que doit employer la France relativement à ses possessions en Asie.* Paris, P. Fr. Didot le jeune, 1790.   O27

The work under criticism was written by J.A. Le Brasseur, and concerned French interests in the Indian Ocean.

Observations sur le memoire concernant le commerce de France avec les Etats Unis. Manuscript. France, ca. 1790.　　　　　　　O28
A response to criticism of the contract between the Farmers General of France and Robert Morris, whereby Morris was given the monopoly for supplying American tobacco to France.

Observations upon the laws of excise. London, J. Wilford [1733].　　　　　　　　　　　　O29
Declares that excise taxes will be destructive of trade and liberty.

Observations upon the manifesto of his catholic majesty. London, T. Cooper, 1739.　　　　O30
A refutation of Spanish arguments attempting to justify their refusal to pay for damages done to the South Sea Company.

O'Connor, M. Considerations on the trade to Africa. London, J. Barnes, 1749.　　　　O31
A last-minute appeal to Parliament and the public for funds to prevent the failure of the Royal African Company.

Odorico, da Pordenone. Elogio storico alle gesta del beato Odorico ... con la storia da lui dettata de' suoi viaggi Asiatici. Venice, Antonio Zatta, 1761.　　　　　　　　　　　　　O32
A critical edition by Guiseppe Venni, with Latin text and notes in Italian, preceded by a biographical introduction.

Ödmann, Samuel. Ängelsmannens, W.G. Brownes resa til Africanska kunnunga-riket Fur, och Frantsmannens, Follies, genom Africanska öknen Sahara. Jämte bihang af den förres försök at uptäcka läget af Jupiter Ammons fordna tempel. Stockholm, Johan Pfeiffer, 1801.　　　O33
Abridgments of African travels by William George Browne and Louis-Guillaume Follie.

Ödmann, Samuel. Beskrifning om Kamtschatka des invånare och physiska mårkvårdigheter. Upsala, Joh. Edman, 1787.　　　　O34
Selections, primarily from Steller and Krasheninnikov, presenting a history and description of Kamchatka.

Ödmann, Samuel. Donald Campbells land-resa til Indien, och Fra Paolinos da San Bartolomeo resor til Indien. Sammandrag. Stockholm, Johan Pfeiffer, 1801.　　　　　　　　　O35
Abridged translations of two popular travels to India. Campbell was a British soldier, Paulinus was a Carmelite priest.

Ödmann, Samuel. Lion Wafers Dagbok och beskrifning af Americanska nåset, dess invånare och physiska märkvärdigheter. Upsala, Johan Edman, 1788.　　　　　　　　　　　O36
Abridged edition of Lionel Wafer's description of the Isthmus of Panama, first published in an English edition of 1699.

Ödmann, Samuel. Sammandrag af Herr Sonnerats resa till Nya Guinea. Upsala, Joh. Edman, 1786.　　　　　　　　　　　　　O37
A summary of Sonnerat's voyage to the South Pacific, with an introduction and commentary by the editor.

Örnheilm, Claudius Arrhenius, Praeses. Dissertatio de origine gentium Novi Orbis prima. Strengnaees, Zacharias Asp, 1676.　　　O38
An academic dissertation in which the origins of the American Indians are traced to the time of the Flood.

The offers of France explain'd ... London, A. Baldwin, 1712.　　　　　　　　　　O39
The anonymous author reviews with alarm the terms of peace offered by France, noting the damage that would result to the British trade in America.

Ogden, James. The British lion rous'd; or Acts of the British worthies, a poem in nine books. Manchester, R. Whitworth, 1762.　　　O40
A long poem dealing with the Seven Years' War, some of the poetry alluding to events in North America.

Ogden Colony (New York). Judgment book. Manuscript. New York, 1820-1848.　　　O41
The ledger pertains particularly to transactions of George Redington. The Ogden Colony was settled in 1790 on a land grant made by President Washington.

Ogilby, John. Africa. London, Thomas Johnson for the Author, 1670.　　　　　　　O42
A compilation based largely on Olfert Dapper's description of Africa published in 1668. It includes historical, geographical, and commercial information, and contains numerous maps and illustrations.

Ogilby, John. America: being the latest and most accurate description of the New World. London, Printed by the Author, 1671.　　　O43
A description of the New World from earlier and contemporary authors, particularly Arnoldus Montanus.

Ogilby, John. Asia. London, The Author, 1673.　　　　　　　　　　　　　O44
A well-illustrated survey of Persia and India compiled from a variety of sources.

[Oglethorpe, James Edward.] A new and accurate account of the provinces of South-Carolina and Georgia. London, J. Worral [etc.] 1732.　　　　　　　　　　　　　O45
An appeal for colonists based upon the idea that both England and her more unfortunate citizens could profit from the removal of the latter to this promising colony.

[O'Heguerty, Pierre-André.] Des pescheries. [n.p.] 1757.   O46
A survey of French whaling and fishing industries, with recommendations for their improvement, and observations on those industries in the Netherlands and Great Britain.

O'Heguerty, Pierre-André. Essai sur les intérêts du commerce maritime. The Hague, 1754.   O47
A discussion of France's overseas trade, including East and West Indian commerce, and the Baltic trade.

[O'Heguerty, Pierre-André.] Remarques sur plusieurs branches de commerce et de navigation. [n.p.] 1757.   O48
Discusses primarily the grain trade, fishing and whaling, the cloth trade to the Levant, and the sugar and indigo trade to America.

Óláfs saga Tryggvasonar. Saga thess Haloplega Herra Olafs Tryggvasonar Noregs Kongs ... Skalhollte, Jone Snorrasyne, 1689-1690.   O49
This saga describes the reign of King Olav I Tryggvason who was accepted as king of all Norway in 995, and whose reign coincided with active missionary efforts in Iceland and the Faroe Islands as well as the early voyages to Greenland, all of which are related in the saga.

Olaus, Magnus, Archbishop of Uppsala. [Carta Marina.] Rome, Antoine Lafreri, 1572.   O50
The second edition of an unusual map of the Scandinavian area, showing numerous details of the economy, history, and commerce of that region.

Olaus, Magnus, Archbishop of Uppsala. Carta marina et descriptio septemtrionalium terrarum. [Facsimile.] Malmö, AB Malmö, Ljustrycksanstalt, 1949.   O51
Hand-colored facsimile of a map of Scandinavia originally published in 1539.

Olaus, Magnus, Archbishop of Uppsala. Opera breve, laquale demonstra ... la charta over delle terre frigidissime. Venice, Giovan Thomaso, 1539.   O52
A guide to the author's map of the Scandinavian regions, identifying the many figures on the map and giving their importance.

Olaus, Magnus, Archbishop of Uppsala. Historia de gentibus septentrionalibus. Rome, 1555.   O53
A history and geography of Scandinavia, with a map and numerous illustrations depicting the history and folklore of that region.

Olaus, Magnus, Archbishop of Uppsala. Historia de gentibus septentrionalibus. Antwerp, Christopher Plantin, 1558.   O54
The first edition of the Latin abridgment.

Olaus, Magnus, Archbishop of Uppsala. Historia de gentibus septentrionalibus. Antwerp, Joannem Bellerum, 1562.   O55
The fourth Latin edition.

Olaus, Magnus, Archbishop of Uppsala. Historia ... de gentium septentrionalium. Basel, Henric-Petrina, 1567.   O56
This edition includes a folding map, much more complete than that found in earlier and subsequent editions.

Olaus, Magnus, Archbishop of Uppsala. De gentibus septentrionalibus historia. Antwerp, Ex typographeio Forsteriano, 1599.   O57
This edition was published without illustrations.

Olaus, Magnus, Archbishop of Uppsala. Historiae septentrionalium gentium breviarium libri XXII. Leiden, Adrianum Wyngaerde et Franciscum Moiardum, 1645.   O58
The text follows that of the 1558 Plantin edition, but this edition does not include the illustrations.

Olaus, Magnus, Archbishop of Uppsala. Historien der mittnächtigen Länder. Basel [Henric Petri, 1567].   O59
The first German edition, translated by Johann Baptiste Ficker, containing the map and an explanatory section describing it.

Olaus, Magnus, Archbishop of Uppsala. Beschreibung allerley Gelegenheyte, Sitten, Gebräuchen und Gewonheyten, der mitnächtigen Völker. Strassburg, Theodosium Rihel [1567].   O60
This second German edition, translated by Israel Achatius, does not include the map.

Olaus, Magnus, Archbishop of Uppsala. Storia ... de' costumi de' popoli settentrionali. Venice, Francesco Bindoni, 1561.   O61
The first Italian edition, published without illustrations.

Olaus, Magnus, Archbishop of Uppsala. Historia delle genti et della natura delle cose settentrionali. Venice, Giunti, 1565.   O62
The first illustrated Italian edition. The illustrations include a map of Scandinavia.

Olaus, Magnus, Archbishop of Uppsala. Histoire des pays septentrionaus. Paris, Martin le Jeune, 1561.   O63
This French edition was based on the 1558 Antwerp abridgment.

Olaus, Magnus, Archbishop of Uppsala. De vvonderlijcke historie vande noordersche landen ... Antwerp, Willem Silvius, 1562.   O64
The first Dutch edition, based on the abridgment of 1558 made by Cornelius de Schryver.

Olaus, Magnus, Archbishop of Uppsala. Toonneel der noordsche landen ... met een korte en klare beschryvingh van Yslandt en Groenlandt. Amsterdam, Nicolaes van Ravensteyn, 1652. O65
This edition includes Dithmar Blefken's description of Iceland and Greenland.

Olaus, Magnus, Archbishop of Uppsala. Toonneel der noordsche landen. Amsterdam, Hieronymus Sweerts, 1665. O66
This edition was published without illustrations.

Olaus, Magnus, Archbishop of Uppsala. A compendious history of the Goths, Swedes, and Vandals, and other northern nations. London, J. Streater, 1658. O67
The first English edition.

Olavius, Ólafur. Oeconomisk reise igiennem de nord-vestlige, nordlige, og nordostlige kanter af Island, ved Olaus Olavius ... Copenhagen, Gyldendals Forlag, 1780. O68
An economic survey of northern Iceland with particular reference to mining, fishing, and shipping. Maps, illustrations, and statistical tables supplement the text.

Oldenbarnevelt, Johan van. Remonstrantie aende Hooghe ende Moghende Heeren Staten vande landen van Hollant ende West-Vrieslant. [n.p.] Ghedruckt nae de copye van Hillebrant Jacobsz, 1618. O69
An exhortation recalling the Dutch struggle for independence, with frequent reference to aid from England.

Oldendorp, C. G. A. (Christian Georg Andreas). Geschichte der Mission der evangelischen Brüder auf den caraibischen Inseln S. Thomas, S. Croix und S. Jan. Barby, Christian Friedrich Laur; Leipzig, Weidmanns Erben und Reich, 1777. O70
An account of missionary activity in the Danish West Indies by the Moravian Brethren. The islands are also described in terms of people, wildlife, vegetation, and climate.

Oldendorp, C. G. A. (Christian Georg Andreas). Historiska beskrifning öfwer ewangeliske brödernas mission-sarbete på ... St. Thomas, St. Croix och St. Jan. Stockholm, P.A. Brodin, 1786-88. O71
The first Swedish edition.

Oldendorp, C. G. A. (Christian Georg Andreas). Tillförlåtlig underrättelse om Negrerne på Guinea Kusten, samt de derifrän hämtade slafvars närvarande belägenhet, medfart, seder och sinnelag ... Utdragen ur Herr Oldendorps Missions historia. Uppsala, Johan Edman, 1784. O72
A description of West African peoples, the slave trade, the situation of slaves in the West Indies, with a brief section on sugar culture.

Oldmixon, Mr. (John). The British Empire in America. London, John Nicholson [etc.] 1708. O73
A detailed account of the country, soil, climate, products, and trade of the British colonies in America, with some information on their historical development and a map of each.

[Oldmixon, Mr. (John).] Gross-Brittannisches America nach seiner Erfindung, Bevölkerung und allerneuestem Zustand. Hamburg, Zacharias Hertels, 1710. O74
This is the first German translation from the original English edition of 1708. It does not include maps found in the earlier edition.

[Oldmixon, Mr. (John).] Het Britannische ryk in Amerika. Amsterdam, Rudolf en Gerard Wetstein, 1721. O75
This first Dutch edition contains an added essay on the coffee plant and introductory matter encouraging the planting of coffee in Surinam.

Olearius, Adam. Beschrijvingh wande nieuwe Parciaensche, ofte orientaelsche reyse: welck door gelegentheyt van een Holsteynsche Ambassade, aen den Koningh in Persien geschiet is ... Amsterdam, Jacob Benjamyn, 1651. O76
One of two Dutch editions of the most popular work on Russia in the 17th Century, published in 1651 and including the Persian travels of Johann Albrecht von Mandelslo.

Olearius, Adam. Vermehrte newe Beschreibung der muscowitischen und persischen Reyse; so durch Gelegenheit einer holsteinischen Gesandschafft an den russischen Zaar und König in Persien geschehen ... Schleswig, Fürstl. Druckery durch Johan Holwein, 1656. O77
The first enlarged edition.

Olearius, Adam. Relation du voyage de Moscovie, Tartarie, et de Perse ... traduite de l'Alleman du sieur Olearius ... par L.R.D.B. Paris, Pierre Aubovin, 1656. O78
The first French edition.

Olearius, Adam. Relation du voyage d'Adam Olearius en Moscovie ... contenant le voyage de Jean Albert de Mandelslo aux Indes Orientales. Paris, Jean du Puis, 1666. O79
The second French edition.

[Olearius, Adam.] Viaggi di Moscovia de gli anni 1633, 1634, 1635, e 1636. Viterbo, 1658. O80
The first Italian edition.

Olearius, Adam. The voyages and travels of the ambassadors sent by Frederic Duke of Holstein, to the Great Duke of Muscovy and the King of Persia, etc. London, For John Starkey and Thomas Basset, 1669.　　　　　　　　O81
　The second English edition.

Olearius, Adam. Des Welt-berühmten Adami Olearii colligirte und viel vermehrte Reise-Beschriebungen bestehend in der nach Muskau und Persien ... Hamburg, Zacharias Herteln und Thomas von Wiering, 1696.　　　　　O82
　This edition includes the *Morgenlandische Reise-Beschreibung* of Mandelslo, eastern travels by one Sanson, Volquard Iverson, Jürgen Andersen, and the description of the Tartar conquest of China by Martini.

Olivier, Guillaume Antoine. Voyage dans l'empire Othoman, l'Égypte et la Perse. Paris, H. Agasse, 1801-1807.　　　　　　　　O83
　An account of a French naturalist's six years of travel in the Near and Middle East. An atlas accompanying the text depicts towns, harbors, people, vegetation, and wildlife of the regions visited.

Olmo, José Vincente del. Nueva descripcion del orbe de la tierra. Valencia, Joan Lorenço Cabrera, 1681.　　　　　　　　　O84
　A general geography with sections on the history of cartography, on methods of making navigation charts and their use, and on various types of map projections.

Olrik, Christian Magnus. Forsøg om Bergens handel. Sorøe, Jonas Lindgren, 1764.　　O85
　A review of Bergen's commerce, both local and overseas, for the years 1755, 1756, and 1757.

Den ommegank van Amsterdam. Breda, 1650.　　　　　　　　　　　　　　　O86
　This tract accuses prominent persons of Amsterdam of sabotaging the Dutch West India Company in Brazil.

Den omsigtigen Hollander vertoond in een t'samenspraek. Holland, Gerrits de Vredesockers, 1667.　　　　　　　　　　　O87
　A warning against the peaceful approach of the English just before the Treaty of Breda.

Omstandig en allernaeuwkeurigst verhaal van den oorsprong, begin, voortgang en gelukkige ontdekkinge van het vervloekt en schelms verraadt. Utrecht, Johannes Evelt [1741].　O88
　An account of the rebellion by Chinese merchants at Batavia.

Omstandigh verhael van de Fransche rodomontade voor het Fort Curassau. [n.p., 1673.]　O89
　Concerns rivalry between the French and Dutch in the West Indies.

Onderdanig dank-adres, aan alle heeren koopleiden en handelaars, &c. &c. der Nederlandsche steeden, als voorstanders en beschermers onzer commercie ... [n.p., ca. 1782.]　O90
　A tract in verse, dedicated to John Adams, acknowledging the independence of the United States.

Den ongeveynsden Nederlandtschen patriot. Alckmaer, J. Claesz, 1647.　　　　O91
　A conversation between a Dutchman and a Frenchman concerning the negotiations at Munster, and the relative trustworthiness of the French and Spanish.

Den ongeveynsden Nederlantschen patriot. Middelburgh, S. Verhoeven [1647].　　O92
　Expansion of the previous item.

Onpartijdich oordeel over de deductie ende contra-deductie, op het stuck van 'tvinden vande redemtie-penningen. Rotterdam, Pieter de Claer, 1650.　　　　　　　　　　　　　　O93
　Relates to commerce in the Baltic.

Onpartydig onderzoek nopens het voordeel en nadeel, het welk de republiek ... The Hague, J.F. Jacobs de Agé, 1782.　　　　　　　O94
　A consideration of the commercial advantages the Dutch may hope to obtain through the independence of the American colonies.

d'Onstelde Amsterdammer, met sijn trouwe waerschouwinghe, raed en antwoort op bickers beroerten. Brussels, Symon, Vermeer, 1650.　　　　　　　　　　　　　　　O95
　A reply to an earlier tract which blamed the mayor of Amsterdam for the decline of the Dutch West India Company.

Onstelde-zee, oft zee-daden voorgevallen tusschen de ... Staten Generael ... en die van de tegenwoordige regeringh van Engelant ... Amsterdam, J. Hondius, 1654.　　　　O96
　A Dutch view of the causes and early events of the war with the English, which grew primarily from commercial rivalries.

d'Ontmaskerde Fransman. Keulen, Pieter Hamer, 1701.　　　　　　　　　　O97
　An analysis of the power of France, noting that control of Spain would give France control over the wealth of the East and West Indies.

Het ontroerd Holland. Of kort verhaal van de voornaamste onlusten, oproeren en oneenigheden, die in de Vereenigde Nederlanden ... in deze laatste jaaren zyn voorgevallen. Harderwijk, Willem Brinkink [ca. 1750].　　　　　O98
　An account of popular unrest in the Netherlands in the late 1740s, with repercussions for the East and West India Companies. Accounts of related events in Batavia, the Cape of Good Hope and Curaçao are included.

d'Ontroerden leeuw, tweede deel. Vervolgende de voornaamste voorvallen deses tijts. Amsterdam, Steven Swart, 1673. O99

A news publication covering the period from December 1, 1672, to April 1, 1673, including reports of the establishment of a French base on Ceylon against the wishes of the Dutch East India Company.

Onverwachte tijdingen uyt Vlaenderen, voorgestelt in een t'samen spraecke tusschen een paepschen Hollander en Vlamingh. [n.p.] 1647. O100

Concerns peace with France and Spain, with particular reference to Roman Catholic religious influence.

Oogh-teecken der inlantsche twisten ende beroerten, onder t'seghel van Henrick van Nassau. The Hague, 1620. O101

Concerns the expansion of Dutch trade, with particular respect to that of France, England, and Spain.

Ooghen-salve tot verlichtinghe, van alle participanten so vande Oost ende West-Indische Compaignien. The Hague, L. de Lange, 1644. O102

"Eye salve to clear the eyes of all shareholders of both the East and West India Companies, together with notable considerations regarding the union of the two companies."

Oost-Indisch-praetjen, voorgevallen in Batavia, tusschen vier Nederlanders. [n.p.] 1663. O103

Two conversations, both critical of the management of the East India Company.

Open-hertige en trou-hertige requeste, gepresenteert ende overgegeven aen de Ed. Mog. Heeren Staten van Zeelandt ... [n.p.] 1648. O104

Concerns peace negotiations with Spain.

Opmerckinghe vanden Dertigjarigen Duytschen Krygh welcke haer begin ghenomen heeft anno 1618 ende door Gods genade anno 1648 ghe-eyndight is ... Amsterdam, Jan van Hilten, 1648. O105

A chronicle of events of the Thirty Years War.

Ordóñez de Ceballos, Pedro. Viage del mundo. Madrid, L. Sanchez, 1614. O106

The author of this work had traveled to the Near East, Africa, Asia, Oceania, and the New World in addition to Europe. He describes the regions he visited, and includes comments on their peoples and products.

Ordóñez de Ceballos, Pedro. Eyghentlijcke beschryvinghe van West-Indien. Amsterdam, Michiel Colijn, 1621. O107

A Dutch translation of the part of the preceding work relating to Spanish America.

Ordóñez de Ceballos, Pedro. Historia, y viage del mundo del clerigo agradecido Don Pedro Ordoñez de Zevallos ... Madrid, Juan Garcia Infanzon, 1691. O108

The fourth edition. The text does not appear to vary significantly from the first edition of 1614.

O'Reilly, Bernard. Greenland, the adjacent seas, and the north-west passage to the Pacific Ocean. London, For Baldwin, Cradock, and Joy, 1818. O109

O'Reilly describes Greenland and adjacent islands, proposes means for discovering a north-west passage, and suggests that Disko Island be used as a British trade depot if the passage is found.

Origen de la Real Compañia de San Christoval de la Habana ... Madrid, 1749. O110

Details on the production and commerce of the company.

El origen, y fundaciónes de las Inquisiciones de España fueron como le síguen. Manuscript. [n.p.] 1652. O111

A brief history of the Inquisition in Spain, including its manifestations in the American colonies.

[Original minutes of meetings of the council of the combined Anglo-Dutch "Fleet of Defence."] Manuscript. Hirado, July 15, 1620-October 16, 1622. O112

The "Fleet of Defence" was an Anglo-Dutch effort to disrupt Spanish commerce in the Far East and divert it to Formosa and Japan. This manuscript records the council's deliberations in Hirado, Japan, where both countries had factories.

Original papers transmitted by the Nabob of Arcot to his agent in Great Britain: comprehending the transactions on the coast, down to the 10th of October, 1776. London, For T. Cadell, 1777. O113

This volume was designed to influence British public opinion in favor of the Nabob who was objecting to the violation of his suzerainty by the East India Company.

Orizant, Jan. Naerder openbaringe, van Nederlants Engelschen oorloge ... Leiden W.C. vander Box, 1653. O114

A view of the cause of Anglo-Dutch hostilities, with reference to commercial rivalries in the West Indies.

Orlandini, Nicolò. Historiæ Societatis Jesu pars prima [secunda]. Antwerp, Martini Nutii, 1620. O115

The first part of this work is a history of the Jesuits, covering the years 1540 to 1556, including accounts of missionary undertakings in Ethiopia, India, and other points in the East. Part two is by Francesco Sacchini.

Orléans, Pierre Joseph d'. La vie du pere Matthieu Ricci de la Compagnie de Jesus. Paris, George & Louis Josse, 1693. O116

This work goes beyond the life of Ricci to include accounts of the Jesuit mission in China under the leadership of Adam Schall and Ferdinand Verbiest, concluding with a general description of China.

[Orlers, Jan Janszn.] Wilhelm en Maurits van Nassau ... haer leven en bedrijf. Amsterdam, J. Jansz., 1651. O117
A history of the rise of Dutch power in the late sixteenth and early seventeenth centuries, including Dutch maritime expansion.

[Orme, Robert.] A history of the military transactions of the British nation in Indostan, from the year MDCCXLV ... London, For John Nourse, 1775. O118
The second edition of a history of the wars between the French and English, and their various Indian allies in the period from 1745-1763. The set includes numerous maps and plans of the major commerical and administrative centers of the English and French East India establishments.

Orosius, Paulus. Historiae. Venice, Christoforum de Pensis de Mandello, 1499. O119
A popular medieval history and geography written in the fifth century. This printing was edited by Aeneas Vulpes.

Orpheus. Orphei poetarum vetustissimi Argonauticon opus Graecum cum interpretatione Latina incerti autoris, recens addita, & diligentius quàm hactenus emendata. [Basel, Andreae Cratandri, 1523.] O120
A version of the voyage of the Argonauts resulting from the religious influence of Orphism in the sixth century.

Orta, Garcia de. Due libri dell'historia de i semplici, aromati, e altre cose, che vengono portate dall' Indie Orientali. Venice, 1576. O121
The first Italian edition of the earliest work on East Indian medicinal products. Portions of it are from Nicolás Monardes, the Spanish physician who first cataloged New World medicinal plants.

Orta, Garcia de. Due libri dell'historia de i semplici, aromati, e altre cose ... dall'Indie Orientali pertinenti all' uso della medicina. Venice, Francesco Ziletti, 1582. O122
The second Italian edition.

Orta, Garcia de. Aromatum et simplicium aliquot medicamentorum apud Indos nascentium historia. Antwerp, Christopher Plantin, 1579. O123
The third Plantin Latin edition, edited by Charles de l'Écluse with the text much reduced from the Goa edition of 1563.

Orta, Garcia de. Histoire des drogues espiceries, et de certains medicamens simples, qui naissent des Indes, tant Orientales que Occidentales: divisée en deux parties ... Lyon, Jean Pillehotte, 1602. O124

This volume also includes first editions in French of the works on medicinal plants by Christovam da Costa and Nicolas Monardes, all with annotations by Charles l'Écluse.

[Ortega, José de.] Apostolicos afanes de la Compañia de Jesus, escritos por un padre de la misma sagrada religion de su provincia de Mexico. Barcelona, Pablo Nadal, 1754. O125
The author worked for thirty years in the Jesuit mission in Nayarit, Mexico, and this book describes the missionary work there as well as episodes in California and Arizona.

Ortelius, Abraham. Abraham Ortelius his epitome of the theater of the worlde. London, Jeames Shawe, 1603. O126
A pocket-size atlas, the first in English, containing 123 maps with accompanying text.

Ortelius, Abraham. Abrege du theatre d'Ortelius. Antwerp, Jean Baptiste Vrients, 1602. O127
A French edition of the *Epitome*, an abridgment of *Theatrum orbis terrarum*, containing 125 maps.

Ortelius, Abraham. Synonymia geographica ... Antwerp, C. Plantini, 1578. O128
The first edition. Later editions published under the title *Thesaurus geographicus*.

Ortelius, Abraham. Theatro del mondo, di Abraamo Ortelio. Nel quale si dà notitia distinta di tutte le provincie, regni, & paesi del mondo ... Venice, Steffano Curti, 1683. O129
This Italian edition of the *Epitome* contains four maps.

Ortelius, Abraham. Theatrum orbis terrarum. Antwerp, C. Diesth, 1570. O130
The second issue of the first edition of the first modern atlas.

Ortelius, Abraham. Theatrum orbis terrarum. London, J. Norton, 1606. O131
The earliest English edition of the first general atlas to be printed in England.

Ortelius, Abraham. Thesaurus geographicus, recognitus et auctus. Antwerp, Ex officina Plantiniana, 1596. O132
A gazetteer of geographical terms, compiled by the famous Dutch cartographer and map publisher.

Orth, Mr., Secretary to Sir Paul Rycaut. Autograph letter signed, to William Blathwayt. Hamburg, 20 August 1697. O133
This letter comments on preparation of ships in Hamburg for the Scots' attempt to establish a settlement at Darien, and on the decline of interest in the enterprise in Hamburg.

Ortiz, Alonso. Los tratados. Seville, Tres alemanes compañeros, 1493. O134

Ortiz, Lorenzo.
A collection of orations and writings of a canon of Toledo in which allusion is made to the Spanish discoveries in the New World.

Ortiz, Lorenzo. El principe del mar, San Francisco Xavier, de la Compañia de Jesus ... Seville, Tomas Lopez de Haro, 1714.   O135
A commemorative biography of St. Francis Xavier, celebrating him as a man of the sea through his extensive travels in the East Indies.

Osbeck, Pehr. Anledningar til nyttig upmärksamhet under Chinesiska resor. Stockholm, Lars Salvius, 1758.   O136
An essay presented to the Swedish Academy of Science describing the author's travels in China and the commercial opportunities in the East for the Swedish East India Company.

Osbeck, Pehr. Dagbok öfwer en Ostindisk resa åren 1750, 1751, 1752. Stockholm, Lor. Ludv. Grefing, 1757.   O137
Reports, by two students of Linnaeus, on the natural history of China and the East Indies, with observations on the peoples and commerce of the regions visited. The other author is Olof Torén.

Osbeck, Pehr. Reise nach Ostindien und China. Rostock, Johann Christian Koppe, 1765.   O138
This German edition includes the letters and observations of Karl Gustaf Ekeberg, describing China from his travels there in 1751-52.

Osbeck, Pehr. A voyage to China and the East Indies. London, Benjamin White, 1771.   O139
The first English edition, translated by Johann Reinhold Forster. Appended to the account of the plant life of China and the East Indies are similar studies by Olof Torén and Carl Gustaf Ekeberg.

Osório, Jerónimo. De rebus, Emmanuelis regis Lusitaniae. Lisbon, A. Gondisalvus, 1571.   O140
A history of the reign of Manuel I of Portugal, containing accounts of the voyages of Da Gama, Cabral, Cortereal, Magellan, and others. The author was the son of one of the participants in Da Gama's voyages.

Osório, Jerónimo. De rebus Emmanuelis regis ... libri duodecim. Cologne, Arnold Birckmann, 1574.   O141
The first Cologne printing of this popular history.

Osório, Jerónimo. De rebus; Emmanuelis, Lusitaniae regis invictissimi ... Cologne, Birckmann, 1586.   O142
This Latin edition has an introduction and commentary by Jean Matal.

Osório, Jerónimo. Histoire de Portugal. [Geneva] F. Estienne, 1581.   O143
The first French edition.

Osório, Jerónimo. The history of the Portuguese, during the reign of Emmanuel. London, A. Millar, 1752.   O144
The first English edition.

[Otis, James.] Considerations on behalf of the colonists. In a letter to a noble lord. London, J. Almon, 1765.   O145
A reply to Soame Jenyns' *Objections to the taxation of the colonies by the legislature of Great Britain briefly considered.*

Otis, James. A vindication of the British colonies. London, J. Almon, 1769.   O146
A reply to Martin Howard's *A letter from a gentleman at Halifax* which had been critical of *The rights of the colonies examined*, by Stephen Hopkins, all relating to the Stamp Act.

Ottsen, Hendrick. Journael oft daghelijcx-register van de voyagie na Rio de Plata. Amsterdam, Michiel Colijn, 1617.   O147
The second edition of the only source of information on one of the earliest Dutch experiences in the West Indian trade, a voyage which failed but foreshadowed Dutch commercial enterprise in the Atlantic.

Outreman, Pierre d'. Tableaux des personnages signalés de la Comp.ie de Jesus: exposés en la solennité de la canonization des SS. Ignace. & Franc. Xavier celebree par le College de la Comp. de Jesus. Douay, Baltazar Bellere, 1623.   O148
A collection of 233 biographies of Jesuits, many of whom had served abroad, in celebration of the canonization of Ignatius Loyola and Francis Xavier.

Ovalle, Alonso de. Historica relacion del reyno de Cile. Rome, Francisco Cavallo, 1646.   O149
The first Spanish edition of an authoritative history of Chile written by one who spent most of his life there. This edition contains twenty-one full page portraits of Chilean governors and other Spanish-American administrators and military commanders.

Ovalle, Alonso de. Historica relatione del regno di Cile ... Rome, Francisco Cavalli, 1646.   O150
The first Italian edition of the preceding history of Chile, well illustrated with fourteen engravings, eighteen woodcuts, and a folding map.

Overbeke, Aernout van. Geestige en vermaeckelicke reys-beschryvinge van den Heer Aernout van Overbeke. [Amsterdam] Jan Joosten, 1672.   O151
A humorous recounting of a voyage to the East Indies with a stop at the Dutch settlement on the Cape of Good Hope.

Overture concerning the debts of the African and Indian Company. [n.p., 1707?]   O152

Proposals for the Company of Scotland Trading to Africa and the Indies to set forth all aspects of its financial condition.

Ovington, J. (John). An essay upon the qualities of tea. London, R. Roberts, 1699.   O153

A description of tea, its culture and uses, at that time little known in England or Europe.

Ovington, J. (John). A voyage to Suratt, in the year 1689. London, Jacob Tonson, 1696.   O154

The author, a chaplain to the English factory at Surat, gives a detailed description of mercantile activity there.

Oxenden, Sir George. Indenture between George Oxenden, Thomas Burton, and William Parker, for a voyage to India by two merchant ships. Manuscript. [n.p.] Jan. 29, 1655.   O155

An agreement between Oxenden and Thomas Breton, merchants, and William Parker of London to engage in sending two trading ships to India.

Oxenstierna, Axel, greve. Wir Burgermeister und Raht desz heiligen Reichs Stadt Nürnberg ... [Nuremberg, 1633.]   O156

A broadside inviting German investors to interest themselves in the Swedish South Sea Company.

Oxholm, Peter Lotharius. Charte over den Danske Øe St. Croix i America. [Copenhagen] P.L. Oxholm, 1799.   O157

A large scale map of St. Croix, in the Virgin Islands, giving topographic and hydrographic information, political divisions, population statistics, production and other economic information.

Oxholm, Peter Lotharius. Charte over den Danske Øe St. Jan i America. [Copenhagen] P.L. Oxholm, 1800.   O158

A map of St. John in the Virgin Islands, drawn on a large scale and containing excellent topographic-hydrographic and economic information.

Oxholm, Peter Lotharius. De Danske Vestindiske öers tilstand i henseende til population, cultur og finance-forfatning ... Copenhagen, Johan Frederik Schultz, 1797.   O159

A description of the Danish West Indies, relying largely on statistics, but with illustrations of natural history and plantation life.

Pacheco, Diogo. Emanuelis Lusitan: Algarbior: Africae, Aethiopiae, Persiae, Indiae, reg. invictiss: Obedientia. [Rome, E. Silver, 1514?] P1
    An oration to Pope Leo X on behalf of King Manuel of Portugal in which attention is called to Portuguese acquisitions of territory in Africa, Asia, and America.

Pacheco, Diogo. Obedientia potentissimi Emanuelis Lusitaniae regis ... ad Julium II, pont. max. [Rome? 1505.] P2
    An oration delivered to Pope Julius II on behalf of King Manuel of Portugal, calling attention to Portuguese advances in Africa and India.

Pacifique, de Provins, père. Relation du voyage de Perse ... Lille, Pierre de Rache, 1632. P3
    An account of two travels, the first to Constantinople, Egypt and Palestine, the second to Persia, both apparently in the interest of establishing Capuchin missions in those areas.

Pacifique, de Provins, père. Brieve relation du voyage des isles de l'Amérique. Paris, Nicholas & Jean de la Coste, 1646. P4
    A report on the various French West Indian settlements by one who had spent ten years there. He describes the products and the commerce of the various islands.

Padua (Italy). Laws, etc. Statuta Patavina noviter impressa cum diligenti cura & castigatione: & cum additionibus necessariis. [Venice, Guilielmum de Fontaneto, 1528.] P5
    The first printing of the laws of Padua, reflecting the economic life of this inland city which came under the control of Venice in 1405.

Paduani, Giovanni. De compositione [et] vsu multiformium horologiorum solarium ad omnes totius orbis regiones, ac situs in qualibet superficie: ... Venice, Franciscum Franciscium Senensem, 1582. P6
    A treatise on sundials and their use in establishing relations between place and celestial time when making observations.

Paes, Leonardo. Promptuario das diffiniçoens Indicas. Lisbon, Antonio Pedrozo Galram, 1713. P7
    A description and history of India, with particular attention to the history of Christianity in Portuguese India.

Paez, Pedro. Zwey Schreiben, das eine zu Dambia in Ethiopia, vnnd das ander zu Goa inn India verfasst ... Augsburg, Sara Mangin, 1622. P8
    The letters are from 1617 and 1619, reporting significant progress by the Jesuits.

Pagan, Blaise François, comte de. Relation historique et geographique de la grande riviere des Amazones dans l'Amerique. Paris, Cardin Besogne, 1655. P9
    An account of the Amazon River region published with the intent to encourage the French government to take an active interest in developing that area.

Pagan, Blaise François, comte de. An historical and geographical description of the great country and river of the Amazones in America. London, John Starkey, 1661. P10
    The first English edition.

Paganino, Jacinto Joseph. Compendio das observações, e calculo para achar a longitude pela distancia da lua ao sol, usando das taboadas do conhecimento dos tempos. Lisbon, Francisco Luiz Ameno, 1783. P11
    A review of the problem of determining the longitude at sea with a discussion of a method using lunar distances and altitude of the sun.

Paganino, Jacinto Joseph. Roteiro do Neptuno oriental. Lisbon, Francisco Luiz Ameno, 1783. P12
    A guide to navigation in the East Indies, including the coast of China.

Paganino, Jacinto Joseph. Roteiro occidental para a navegaçaõ da costa, e portos do Brasil. Lisbon, Francisco Luiz Ameno, 1784. P13
A pilot guide to the Brazilian coast with some information on west Africa as well.

Paganino, Jacinto Joseph. Roteiro oriental para a navegaçaõ das costas do grande oceano Atlantico, e oriental, desde o cabo de Finisterrae ate' o fundo do golfo de Bengala. Lisbon, Francisco Luiz Ameno, 1783. P14
A pilot guide for sailing from Europe to Bengal with detailed directions for the east and west coasts of Africa and the Indian Ocean.

Paganino, Jacinto Joseph. Uso da agulha azimutal reflexa de nova invençaõ, para achar a variaçaõ, e altura do sol no mar, e na terra ... Lisbon, Francisco Luiz Ameno, 1783. P15
A description of a new type of compass with instructions for its use.

[Paganucci, Jean.] Manuel historique, géographique et politique des négocians. Lyons, Jean-Marie Bruyset, 1762. P16
A commercial handbook of broad scope, including technical, geographical, historical and other information useful to the contemporary French merchant.

Page, P. F. (Pierre François). Discours historique sur la cause des désastres de la partie française de Saint-Domingue. [Lille, L. Potier, 1793?]. P17
A survey of the problems of Saint Domingue by a member of the colonial assembly.

Page, P. F. (Pierre François). Notes fournies au Comité de Salut public par les Commissaires de Saint Domingue. [n.p., ca. 1794.] P18
This is primarily a criticism of the administration of Polverel, Sonthonax, and Ailhaud in Saint Domingue in 1792 and 1793.

Page, P. F. (Pierre François). Précis analytique des pièces fournies au comité colonial par les commissaires de Saint-Domingue. Page & Brulley, contre les déportés de cette colonie. [Lille, L. Potier, 1793?]. P19
Charges against various citizens involved in the Saint Domingue revolts.

Page, P. F. (Pierre François). Réponse ... aux calomnies qu'on a fait signer au citoyen Belley. [Paris] Laurens [1794]. P20
The author places most of the blame for the events in Saint Domingue on the policies of Commissioners Sonthonax and Polverel.

Page, P. F. (Pierre François). Sentinelle, garde a vous! a J.B. Louvet. Paris, Cretot [1793]. P21
An attack upon the policies of Jacques-Pierre Brissot with respect to the rebellion in Saint Domingue by a commissioner for the colony there.

Pagès, Monsieur de, (Pierre Marie François). Voyages autour du monde et vers les deux poles. Paris, Moutard, 1782. P22
A two-volume work by an author who describes such diverse places as Cuba, New Orleans, Mexico, the Philippines, India, Persia, Madagascar, and Spitzbergen.

Pagès, Monsieur de, (Pierre Marie François). Voyages autour du monde, et vers les deux poles. Berne, Nouvelle Société Typographique; Lausanne, Jean-Pierre Heubach, 1783. P23
The second edition, published without the maps found in the earlier edition of Paris, 1782.

Pagès, Monsieur de, (Pierre Marie François). Reisen um de Welt und nach den beiden Polen. Frankfurt & Leipzig, Johann Georg Fleischer, 1786. P24
The first German edition.

Pagès, Monsieur de, (Pierre Marie François). Franska sjo-capitaines De Page's resa genom öde Arabien, emellan Bassora och Damas, år 1770. Upsala, Joh. Edman, 1788. P25
An excerpt from De Pages *Voyage autour du monde* in its 1784 edition, covering overland travels in Arabia and Persia, translated by Samuel Lorens Ödmann.

Pagès, Monsieur de, (Pierre Marie François). Travels round the world, in the years 1767, 1768, 1769, 1770, 1771. London, J. Murray, 1791. P26
The first English edition.

Pagès, Monsieur de, (Pierre Marie François). Travels round the world, in the years 1767, 1768, 1769, 1770, 1771. The second edition, corrected and enlarged. London, For J. Murray, 1792-93. P27
This appears to be a re-issue of the second edition.

Pagnini, Giovanni Francesco. Della decima e di varie altre gravezze imposte dal comune de Firenze della moneta e della mercatura de' Fiorentini fina al sec. XVI ... [Florence] G. Bouchard, 1765-66. P28
A four-volume work containing information on the commerce of Italy in the fourteenth century, including descriptions of trade routes to China.

Pagnini, Guglielmo. Pratica mercantile moderna. Lucca, Busdragho, 1562. P29
A commercial arithmetic concerning problems of money and exchange, particularly with reference to the trade of Lucca.

Paine, Thomas. Lettre adressée a l'Abbé Raynal, sur les affaires de l'Amérique Septentrionale. [Paris?] 1783. P30
 Raynal is corrected in his interpretation of the causes of the Revolution, some of its events, and the motivations of American monetary and foreign policy.

Paine, Thomas. A letter addressed to the Abbe Raynal, on the affairs of North-America ... London, R. Ridgway, 1791. P31
 English edition of the previous item.

Paine, Thomas. Remarques sur les erreurs de l'*Histoire philosophique et politique* de Mr. Guillaume Thomas Raynal. Amsterdam, J.A. Crajenschot, 1783. P32
 Another edition of the previous item, with a preface and translator's notes by Antoine M. Cerisier.

Paine, Thomas. Rights of man: being an answer to Mr. Burke's attack on the French Revolution. Dublin, G. Burnet [etc.] 1791-92. P33
 The first Dublin edition of a book relating the American Revolution to the French and to the art of governing everywhere.

Paine, Thomas. Droits de l'homme; en reponse a l'attaque de M. Burke sur la révolution francois. Paris, Buisson, 1791. P34
 The first French edition.

Paine, Thomas. Het gezond verstand ... Dordrecht, De Leeuw en Krap, 1794. P35
 The first Dutch edition of *Common Sense*, including an appendix and the "Address to the Quakers" from the English edition. A translator's introduction and notes are also included.

Paine, Thomas. Additions to Common Sense; addressed to the inhabitants of America. London, For J. Almon, 1776. P36
 The additions were not made by Paine, but were collected from various sources by the Philadelphia publisher Bell, whose edition was the basis for this first London printing.

[Palafox y Mendoza, Juan de.] Al Rey nuestra señor. Satisfaction al memorial de los religiosos de la Compañia del nombre de Jesus de la Nueve-España. [n.p.] 1652. P37
 Concerns the author's conflict with the Jesuits in the management of church matters in Mexico.

Palafox y Mendoza, Juan de. Briefe an Pabst Innocenz X. Seine Streitigkeiten mit den Jesuiten betreffend. Frankfurt & Leipzig, 1772. P38
 The two letters state Palafox's anti-Jesuit position. They are accompanied by an introduction and notes to the text.

Palafox y Mendoza, Juan de. Cartas del venerable siervo de Dios D. Juan de Palafox y Mendoza, ... a el rme. Padre Andres de Rada, ... con la verdad desnuda ... Madrid, Manuel Martin, 1768. P39
 This collection of letters also includes a eulogy to Palafox by Rodrigo Serrano y Trillo.

Palafox y Mendoza, Juan de. Don Johann von Palafox Bischof anfanglich zu Engelstadt in Mexico, hernach zu Osma in Spanien. Nach seinem Werthe. Salem, Daniel Hachoze, 1774. P40
 This volume contains two letters from Palafox y Mendoza to Pope Innocent X, and another by one Peter Aurel Armakanus, probably a pseudonym, dated Lyon, 29 November 1771.

Palafox y Mendoza, Juan de. Histoire de la conqueste de la Chine par les Tartares. Paris, Antoine Bertier, 1670. P41
 The first French edition of an account of the fall of the Ming and rise of the Manchu dynasty, with descriptions of Manchu customs and hope expressed for progress by Christian missions.

Palafox y Mendoza, Juan de. Nuove lettere ... scritte a' superiori della' Compagnia del Messico. Venice, Giuseppe Bettinelli, 1760. P42
 Three of the letters are to Palafox's superiors in Mexico, two are to Pope Innocent X, and one is from Andrés de Rada to Palafox. All are from the period 1647-49.

Palairet, Jean. A concise description of the English and French possessions in North America. London, J. Haberkorn, 1755. P43
 The author was an agent of the States General of the United Netherlands.

Palairet, Jean. Kurzgefasste Beschreibung der engländischen und französischen Besitzungen auf ... America. Leipzig, Peter Schenck, in Amsterdam, 1755. P44
 German translation of the previous item.

Palairet, Jean. Nouvelle introduction à la géographie moderne. London, J. Haberkorn, 1754-55. P45
 A geography text, including an introduction to historical geography and descriptions of the major countries, islands, towns, and colonies of the world.

Palerne, Jean. Peregrinations du S. Jean Palerne ... où est traicté de plusieurs singularités, & antiquités remarquées és provinces d'Egypte, Arabie deserte, & pierreuse, Terre Saincte, Surie, Natolie, Grece, & plusiers isles tant la Mer Mediterranee ... Lyon, Jean Pillehotte, 1606. P46
 An account of travels in the Near East between 1581 and 1583, including a polyglot dictionary of terms considered useful for travelers to that area.

Palladius, Bishop of Aspuna. De gentibus Indiae et Bragmanibus. London, T. Roycroft, 1665. P47

An account of Brahman thought based upon the presumed contact with Brahman leaders by Alexander the Great.

Pallas, Peter Simon. [Collection of seventeen manuscript letters and memoranda addressed to Thomas Pennant.] Manuscript. St. Petersburg, January 18, 1766-October 5, 1781. P48

Written in English, this correspondence discusses many aspects of natural history, exploration, and commerce in the northern regions.

Pallas, Peter Simon. [Collection of accounts of Russian voyages in the Bering Sea area.] Manuscript. St. Petersburg, 6 November 1779, 8 March 1781. P49

This collection includes accounts of the voyages of Nitkita Shalaurov, Dmitri Bragin, and that of Petr Kumich Krenitzin and Mikhail Dmitrevich Leväshev. The narrative accompanied correspondence to Thomas Pennant.

Pallas, Peter Simon. Lettera ... che contiene un ragguaglio autentico delle ultime scoperte e morte del capitano Cook. [Milan, 1780.] P50

The news of Cook's death in Hawaii came first to Europe via the overland route from Siberia, while the expedition was still at sea. This letter from Pallas to a friend in Berlin was rapidly translated into other languages.

Pallas, Peter Simon. Neue nordische Beyträge zur physikalischen und geographischen Erd-und Völkerbeschreibung, Naturgeschichte und Oekonomie. St. Petersburg und Leipzig, Johann Zacharias Logan, 1781-1796. P51

A seven-volume scientific journal relating particularly to exploration and observations in Siberia and the northern Pacific Ocean, containing accounts of contemporary and earlier expeditions.

Pallas, Peter Simon. Reise durch verschiedene Provinzen des russischen Reichs. St. Petersburg, Kayserliche Academie der Wissenschaften, 1771-1776. P52

A detailed study of Siberia based upon a six-year expedition, including accounts of native peoples, geography, natural history, and commerce.

Pallas, Peter Simon. Reise durch verschiedene Provinzen des russischen Reichs in einem ausführlichen Auszuge. Frankfurt & Leipzig, Johann Georg Fleischer, 1776-1778. P53

This second German edition has significant variations from the St. Petersburg edition of 1771-1776, in general containing omissions from the earlier version. There are also differences in the illustrations.

Pallas, Peter Simon. Voyages ... en différentes provinces de l'empire de Russie. Paris, La Grange, 1788, Maradan, 1789-93. P54

The first complete French edition.

Pallas, Peter Simon. Voyages ... dans plusieurs provinces de l'empire de Russie et dans l'Asie septentrionale. Paris, Maradan, 1794. P55

A translation from the original German edition, with notes added by Lamarck and Langlès. The eight volumes of text are supplemented by an atlas volume with one hundred plates and ten maps.

Pallas, Peter Simon. Viaggi del Signor Pallas in diverse province dell' Imperio Russo sino al confini della China. Milan, Sonzogno, 1816. P56

The first and only Italian edition, with fine hand-colored illustrations.

Pallas, Peter Simon. Bermerkungen auf einer Reise in die südlichen Statthalterschaften des russischen Reichs. Leipzig, Gottfried Martini, 1799-1801. P57

The first edition of Pallas' classic description of the Crimea and Caucasia, which contains information on the economy and natural history of these regions.

Pallas, Peter Simon. Bemerkungen auf einer Reise in die südlichen Statthalterschaften des russischen Reichs. Leipzig, Gottfried Martini, 1803. P58

The second German edition.

Pallas, Peter Simon. Observations faites dans un voyage entrepris dans le gouvernements méridionaux de l'empire de Russie. Leipzig, Godefroi Martini, 1799-1801. P59

The first French edition.

Pallas, Peter Simon. Second voyage de Pallas, ou Voyages entrepris dans les gouvernemens méridionaux de l'empire du Russie, pendant les années 1793 et 1794 ... Paris, Guillaume & Deterville, 1811. P60

This edition of Pallas's southern expedition is not the same translation as that issued in 1799-1801. The atlas volume includes 55 plates which are the same as those in the earlier edition.

Pallas, Peter Simon. Travels through the southern provinces of the Russian empire in the years 1793 and 1794. London, A. Strahan for T.N. Longman [etc.] 1802-3. P61

The first English edition, a translation by Francis William Blagdon.

Pallas, Peter Simon. Tableau physique et topographique de la Tauride, tiré du journal d'un voyage fait en 1794. St. Petersbourg, 1795. P62

A description of Taurida, a Russian province that included Crimea and a part of Ukraine. It contains a detailed account of the geography, geology, and natural history of the region.

Pallu, François. [Letter signed.] Manuscript in Latin. Fogan, in the province of Fokien, 29 September 1684. P63
This letter was presumably addressed to the Seminaire des Missions etrangères, and concerns the problem of Chinese rites in the conversion of Chinese to Christianity.

Pallu, François. Relation abregée des missions et des voyages des evesques francois, envoyez aux royaumes de la Chine, Cochinchine, Tonquin, & Siam. Paris, Denys Bechet, 1668. P64
An account of the author's three years in Siam, with recommendations for further development of the Christian missions there.

[Palma-Cayet, Pierre-Victor.] Chronologie septenaire de l'histoire de la paix entre les roys de France et d'Espagne ... Paris, J. Richer, 1605. P65
This chronological history contains details of voyages to the East and West Indies, and accounts of French and Indian relations in Canada.

Palmquist, Erich. Någre widh sidste kongl. ambassaden till Tzaren Muskou giorde observationer ofwer Rysslandh, des wäga, pass meds fastningar och Brantzer ... anno 1674. Stockholm, Generalstabens Litografiska [ca. 1898]. P66
Facsimile of observations and drawings made during an embassy to Russia by a Swedish ambassador, depicting Russian towns, military equipment, punishment of criminals, and maps of the interior.

Palóu, Francisco. Relacion historica de la vida y apostolica tareas del venerable padre fray Junipero Serra, y de las misiones que fundó en la California Septentrional, y nuevos establecimientos de Monterey. México, Don Felipe de Zúñiga y Ontiveros, 1787. P67
An account of the beginnings and early progress of Franciscan missions in California under the direction of Junípero Serra.

Paludanus, Bernard. [A letter to Abraham Ortelius.] Manuscript in Latin. Enkhuizen, 22 March, 1596. P68
A letter confirming the return of one Dutch ship from the northeast passage expedition and stating Linschoten's persistent belief that a passage could be located in the vicinity of Vaygach.

Paludanus, Bernard. [A letter to Abraham Ortelius.] Manuscript in Latin. Enkhuizen, 20 December 1596. P69
A report of the failure of the first Dutch expedition in search of a northeast passage to China. Reasons are given for the optimistic opinion that the strait could still be found.

Panciroli, Guido. Rerum memorabilium sive deperditarum. Frankfurt, Godefridi Tampachii [1629]. P70
A comparison of ancient and modern knowledge of many subjects by a sixteenth century scholar, with commentary by the editor, Heinrich Salmuth.

Panciroli, Guido. Nova reperta sive rerum memorabilium recens inventarum, & veteribus incognitarum ... Frankfurt, Godefredi Tampachii, 1631. P71
A new edition of the previous item.

Panciroli, Guido. The history of many memorable things lost, which were in use among the ancients: and an account of many excellent things found, now in use among the moderns, both natural and artificial. London, John Nicholson, 1715. P72
This edition includes commentary by the English translator.

Panckoucke, A. J. (André-Joseph). Elemens d'astronomie et de geographie a l'usage des negotians. Lille, Jean-Baptiste Brovellio, 1739. P73
An elementary text dealing with the sphere, the stars, the zodiac, winds, horizon, etc.

Panckoucke, A. J. (André-Joseph). Elemens de geographie a l'usage des négocians. Lille, Veuve Danel, 1740. P74
An elementary text in geography, about two thirds of it being devoted to Europe. The descriptions of many places contain information of mercantile interest.

The pangs of credit: or, an argument to shew where it is most reasonable to bestow the two millions. London, J. Roberts, 1722. P75
An argument that those who were forced to exchange government annuities for stock in the fradulent South Sea Company should get a larger share of the money confiscated from the directors.

Pantoja, Diego de. Relacion de la entrada de algunos padres de la Compañia de Iesus en la China, y particulares sucessos que tuuieron ... Valencia, Iuan Chrysostomo Garriz, 1606. P76
The second edition of Pantoja's letter to Luigi di Guzman, provincial of Toledo, written from China, 9 March 1602.

Pantoja, Diego de. Relatione dell' entrata d'alcuni padri della Compagnia di Giesu nella China ... Rome, Bartolomeo Zannetti, 1607. P77
A report of the author's travels in China, of events relating to other Jesuits there, and on the prospects for the Christian mission in China.

Papel nuevo ... y veridica relacion todas las presas, que han hecho los armadores Españoles. Madrid, V. Jordan, 1741. P78
 Enumerates ships and cargoes seized during naval war with England.

Papel que expresa la causa de la ruina des comercio de las Indias. Manuscript. [Spain, ca. 1740.] P79
 Attributes the decline of Spain's American commerce to free trade and importation of commodities from the Philippines.

Papers relative to the rupture with Spain, laid before both houses of Parliament, on Friday the twenty-ninth day of January, 1762, by His Majesty's command. London, Mark Baskett and the assigns of Robert Baskett, 1762. P80
 Correspondence relating to negotiations for peace between France and Great Britain in which Spain inserted demands concerning disputes with Great Britain over the fishing rights at Newfoundland, border conflicts in Honduras and on the Logwood Coast (Nicaragua).

[Papi, Lazzaro.] Lettere sull' Indie Orientali. Filadelfia [Pisa] Stamperia Klert, 1802. P81
 An account of India with emphasis on religious, social, and legal subjects by an Italian who served as a soldier there from 1792 to 1802.

Papillon, Thomas. The East-India-trade: a most profitable trade to the kingdom. [n.p., 1680.] P82
 A director of the East India Company describes the benefits of the company's trade to many segments of England's economy.

Papillon, Thomas. A treatise concerning the East-India-trade. London, 1696. P83
 A reprint of the previous item.

Paradin, Guillaume. Memoires de l'histoire de Lyon. Lyons, Antoine Gryphius, 1573. P84
 This history of Lyons contains references to the history of the fairs of the city.

Paredes, Buenaventura de, fray. Petition. Manuscript in Spanish. [Mexico City, after 29 November 1601]. P85
 The Franciscans raise objections to the idea of a Carmelite mission in California, stating their opinion that both Mexico and California had been allotted to them.

Paris (France). Lieutanant Général de Police. Ordonnance de police, qui fait très-expresses défenses à tous les marchands de courir les uns sur les autres pour le débit de leurs marchandises, ni d'user d'aucun artifice pour surprendre les acheteurs, & se les ménager au préjudice de la liberté du commerce. [Paris, L.F. Delatour, 1776.] P86

Paris (France). Lieutanant Général de Police. Ordonnance rendue par Monsieur Herault ... qui condamne plusieurs particulieres trouvées vétuës de toiles peintes, en deux cens livres d'amende chacune. Du dix-neuf avril mil sept cens trente. [Paris] P.J. Mariette [1730]. P87

Paris (France). Lieutanant Général de Police. Ordonnance rendue par Monsieur Herault ... qui condamne plusieurs particuliers trouvez vétus de toiles peintes, en deux cens livres d'amende chacun. Du 29. juillet mil sept cens trente. [Paris] P.J. Mariette [1730]. P88

[Pâris-Duverney, Joseph.] Examen du livre intitulé *Reflexions politiques sur les finances et le commerce*. The Hague, V. & N. Prevôt, 1740. P89
 A critique of a book written by John Law.

Parival, Jean-Nicolas de. Kort verhael der beroerten en ellendigheden, welcke in weynige jaren voorgevallen zijn. Amsterdam, 1653. P90
 A review of events of the 1650-53 period, including the Dutch loss of Brazil.

Park, Mungo. Travels in the interior districts of Africa. London, W. Bulmer, for the author, 1799. P91
 The first edition of a classic of travel literature, describing Park's attempts to explore the Niger River.

Park, Mungo. Travels in the interior districts of Africa. London, W. Bulmer, for the Author, 1807. P92
 This edition includes only one map and omits the appendix by Major Rennell.

Park, Mungo. Resa i det inre af Africa, åren 1795 til 1797. Sammandrag. Stockholm, Johan Pfeiffer, 1800. P93
 This Swedish abridgment by Samuel Ödman is much reduced from the original edition.

Park, Mungo. Reize en entdekkingen in de binnenlanden van Africa, gedaan door den Majoor Houghton en den Heer Mungo Park ... verrijkt met eenige aardrijkskundige ophelderingen van den Majoor J. Rennell. Haarlem, François Bohn, 1800. P94
 A collection of information on Africa based on the works of Daniel Houghton, James Rennell, and Mungo park.

Park, Mungo. Reise i det indere Afrika. Copenhagen, A. Soldin, 1800. P95
 The first Danish edition, a translation by C.C. Boeck.

Park, Mungo. Voyage dans l'intérieur de l'Afrique, fait en 1795, 1796 et 1797. Paris, Dentu, Carteret, Tavernier [1805]. P96
 The second French edition of the complete text.

Parker, Henry. Of a free trade. London, F. Neile for Robert Bostock, 1648. P97
A defense of commerce through licensed companies in general and of the Merchant Adventurers in particular, by the secretary of that group residing in Hamburg.

Parker, Mary Ann. A voyage round the world, in the Gorgon man of war: captain, John Parker. London, John Nichols, 1795. P98
A woman's account of her travels to the Cape of Good Hope and New South Wales.

Parker, of Lincoln's Inn. Evidence of our transactions in the East Indies, with an enquiry into the general conduct of Great Britain to other countries. London, For Charles Dilly, 1782. P99
A history of the growth of English power in India, with a view that gains there will be offset by losses in America.

Parkinson, Sydney. A journal of a voyage to the South Seas. London, For Stanfield Parkinson, 1773. P100
The author of this journal sailed with Cook in his voyage of 1768-71 and died during the voyage. His brother published the journal with a preface in which he criticized Sir Joseph Banks, and the edition was suppressed.

Parkinson, Sydney. A journal of a voyage to the South Seas, in His Majesty's ship the Endeavour. London, Charles Dilly and James Phillips, 1784. P101
The second edition contains introductory matter relating to the dispute over the author's journal and other effects.

Parkinson, Sydney. Voyage autour du monde sur le vaisseau de sa Majesté britannique l'Endeavour. Paris, Guillaume, 1797. P102
This French edition is based on the 1784 English edition, but omits material relating to the controversy over Parkinson's papers and their publication. It adds a preface on recent exploration in the Pacific.

Parma (Italy). Laws, etc. Statuta. Parma, Angelus Ugoletus, 1494. P103
The earlist edition of the laws of this important north Italian city, including those regulating mercantile activity.

Parra, Antonio. Descripcion de diferentes piezas de historia natural las mas del ramo maritimo, representadas en setenta y cinco laminas. Havana, Capitania General, 1787. P104
A survey of the natural history of the waters around Cuba commissioned by the Spanish government and the Botanical Garden of Madrid. Fishes and crustaceans are the most numerous specimens, but sponges and marine plants are also included.

Parraud, J.P. Voyages au Thibet, faits en 1625 et 1626, par le père d'Andrada, et en 1774, 1784, et 1785, par Bogle, Turner et Pourunguir. Paris, Hautbout l'Ainé, 1796. P105
Narratives of both of Andrade's missionary travels to Tibet, and several accounts of the Bogle and Turner embassies on behalf of the English East India Company. A preface contains comments on onther descriptions of Tibet.

Parthey, Daniel. Ost-Indianische und persianische neun-jährige Kriegs-Dienst und warhafftige Beschreibung. Nuremberg, Johann Hoffmann, 1697. P106
Describes various eastern regions, and contains thirty plates portraying them.

A particular state of the receipts and issues of the publick revenue, taxes, and loans from Lady Day 1702 to Michaelmas 1710. Manuscript. England, ca. 1710. P107
Records the sources of British revenue, including information on income from taxes on imports.

The Particulars and inventories of the estates of the late Sub- Governor, Deputy-Governor, and Directors of the South-Sea Company, and of Robert Surman, late Deputy-Cashier, and of John Grigsby, late Accomptant of the said company, together with abstracts of the same ... London, Printed for J. Tonson, B. Lintot, and W. Taylor, 1721. P108
This is a complete set of financial statements, inventories of properties and possessions, and related records of all of the directors of the South Sea Company. These were drawn up in preparation for assessment of penalties to the directors for stock-manipulation which caused the failure of the company in the famous South Sea Bubble.

Paruta, Paolo. Historia Vinetiana ... divisa in due parti. Venice, Domenico Nicolini, 1605. P109
This history of Venice is a continuation of Pietro Bembo's *Rerum Veneticarum*, published in 1551, and is given largely to the diplomacy and wars that were a part of Venice's decline in the sixteenth century.

Paschoud, Reverend Mr. Historico-political geography: or, A description of the names, limits, capitals, divisions ... of the several countries in the world. London, J. Read, 1722-24. P110
A detailed text of world geography with an entertaining introduction on the values of studying geography for a variety of professions and classes of people.

Pasi, Bartolommeo di. Tariffa de i pesi, e misure corrispondenti dal Levante al Ponente. Venice, Pietro di Nicolini da Sabbio, 1540. P111
This edition contains material not included in the editions of 1503 and 1521.

Pasi, Bartolommeo di. Tariffa de i pesi, e misure corrispondenti dal Levante al Ponente. Venice, Paolo Gherardo, 1557. P112
The fourth edition, revised from earlier printings.

Pasi, Bartolommeo di. Tariffa de pesi e mesure correspondenti dal Levante al Ponente. Venice, Alessandro de Bindoni, 1521.   **P113**
   An augmented edition noting commodities, commercial centers, weights, and values, and other information of use to merchants.

Pasi, Bartolommeo di. Tariffa de pexi e mesure. Venice, Albertin da Lisona, 1503.   **P114**
   A handbook of coinage, exchange, customs duties, etc., pertaining to Mediterranean trade.

Pasqualigo, Pietro. Petri Paschalici Veneti oratoris ad Hemanuelem Lusitaniae regem oratio. [Venice, Berardinus Venetus de Vitalibus, 1501.]   **P115**
   An oration by the Venetian ambassador to Portugal requesting assistance against the Turks. The orator refers to the commercial importance of recent Portuguese eastern voyages.

Passe, Crispijn van de. Effigies regum ac principum, eorum scilicet, quor[um] vis ac potentia in re nautica seu marina prae caeteris spectabilis est ... [Cologne, Theophoriae Coloniensis, 1598]   **P116**
   A celebration of the history of navigation, with a text by Matthias Quad, supplemented by portraits of leading explorers including Columbus, Magellan, Vespucci, Laudonnière, Pizarro, Cavendish, and Drake, etc.

Passerone, Lodovico. Guida geografica; overo, Compendiosa descrittione del globo terreno: premessa una breve notitia di tutto l'universo. Venice, Nicolò Pezzana, 1706.   **P117**
   An elementary text in geography and cosmography.

Passi, Carlo. La selva di varia istoria. Venice, Giorgio Cavalli, 1564.   **P118**
   An abridgment of Paolo Giovio's *Historiarum sui temporis*, a history of medieval and renaissance Europe, noting relations with China, Persia, the Levant, and the discovery of America.

Pastoret, Claude Emmanuel Joseph Pierre, marquis de. Motion d'ordre d'Emm. Pastoret sur l'état actuel de nos rapports ... avec les Etats-Unis ... Paris, Imprimerie Nationale, 1797.   **P119**
   A survey of Franco-American relations, with particular interest in commerce between the two countries in time of war.

Pastorius, Francis Daniel. Umständige geographische Beschreibung der zu allerletzt erfundenen Provintz Pensylvaniae, in denen endgräntzen Americae in der West-Welt gelegen ... Frankfurt & Leipzig, Andreas Otto, 1700.   **P120**
   The author was the founder of Germantown, Pennsylvania, having led a group of German settlers there in 1683. He describes the opportunities for an improved economic and spiritual life in the colony, encouraging other settlers to emigrate.

Paterson, William. A narrative of four journeys into the country of the Hottentots, and Caffraria. London, J. Johnson, 1789.   **P121**
   A description of the flora and fauna, and observations on the manners and customs of the Boers, Hottentots, and Bushmen inhabiting the coastal area of South Africa.

Paterson, William. Voyages dans le pays des Hottentots a la Caffrerie, a la Baye Botanique, et dans la Nouvelle Hollande. Paris, Letellier, 1790.   **P122**
   This edition does not include the map and illustrations from the English edition of the previous year. The title and preface imply that Watkin Tench's narrative of travels to Australia was to be included, which it is not.

Patin, Charles-Philippe, vicomte de. Le commerce maritime fondé sur le droit de la nature & des gens ... Malines, Laurent van der Elst, 1727.   **P123**
   An essay on the freedom of commerce, supporting the Ostend Company in its contentions for the right of free trade in the East Indies.

Paulinus, a S. Bartholomaeo. Viaggio alle Indie Orientali umiliato alla santità di n.s. papa Pio Sesto, pontefice massimo, da fra Paolino da S. Bartolomeo Carmelitano scalzo. Rome, A. Fulgoni, 1796.   **P124**
   The first edition of observations by a Carmelite missionary on many aspects of life in India based upon travels there between 1776 and 1789.

Paulinus, a S. Bartholomaeo. A voyage to the East Indies. London, J. Davis, 1800.   **P125**
   The first English edition.

Paulli, Simon. Orbis terraqueus in tabulis geographicis et hydrographicis descriptus. Strassburg, Libraria Editoris, 1670.   **P126**
   A catalog of maps of all parts of the known world.

Paulus Middleburgensis. Paulina de recta paschae celebratione. Fossombrone, O. Petrucius, 1513.   **P127**
   Contains mention of the discoveries in the New World by Columbus and Vespucci.

Pausanias. Commentarii Graeciam describentes ... Venice, Aldi, 1516.   **P128**
   The first edition of a Greek travel book from the second century A.D. It includes an account of a voyage into the ocean and the discovery of the "Isles of Satyrs."

Pausanias. Veteris Graeciae descriptio. Florence, L. Torrentinus, 1551.   **P129**
   This second Latin edition was edited by Romolo Amaseo.

Pausanias. Descrittione della Grecia. Mantua, Francesco Osanna, 1594. P130
   The first vernacular translation, by Alfonso Buonacciuoli. An extensive index is included in this edition.

Pauw, Cornelius. Recherches philosophiques sur les Américains, ou Mémoires interessants pour servir a l'histoire de l'espece humaine. Cleves, J.G. Baerstecher, 1772. P131
   This edition includes the author's *Défense*, but does not include the *Dissertation* of Pernety. See the following edition.

Pauw, Cornelius. Recherches philosophiques sur les Américains ... augmentée d'une *Dissertation critique* par Dom Pernety, & de la *Défense de l'auteur des Recherches contre cette Dissertation*. Berlin, 1777. P132
   The three works included here comprise the major items in a controversy over the American Indians with respect to their comparability to other races.

Pauw, Cornelius. Selections from M. Pauw, with additions by Daniel Webb, Esq. Bath, R. Crutwell, 1795. P133
   The commentary of Daniel Webb tends to confirm the observations of de Pauw on the inferiority of all things native to America when compared to Europe.

Pavia (Italy). Laws, etc. Statuta Papia et comitatus. [Pavia, Jacobus de Burgofrancho et Phillippus de Cassano, 1505.] P134
   The laws of this city, which was once a flourishing commercial center for trade between France and Italy.

Paxton, P. (Peter). A discourse concerning the nature, advantage, and improvement of trade: With some considerations why the charges of the poor do and will increase. London, E.P. for R. Wilkins, 1704. P135
   A broad view of the English economy with particular interest in the balance of trade, which the author sees as being dependent upon cheaply maintained work force which would enhance England's competitive position abroad.

Payne, John. Universal geography formed into a new and entire system describing Asia, Africa, Europe, and America. Dublin, Zachariah Jackson, 1792-1794. P136
   The work is in four books: Asia, Africa, Europe, and America, beginning with an introductory geography lesson, and a glossary of geographical terms. The main text comments on the history, politics, and social life and customs of the various peoples of the earth.

Peace and no peace: or an enquiry whether the late convention with Spain will be more advantageous to Great Britain than the Treaty of Seville. London, R. Chissen [1739?]. P137
   The author is not optimistic about negotiating a favorable settlement with Spain.

Pechberty, Jean. Extrait d'une lettre ecritte de Canton le 17^e fevrier 1699 a la Compagnie des Indes. Manuscript. [n.p., 1699.] P138
   A description of the *Amphitrite's* voyage from the Cape of Good Hope to Canton, its reception there, opportunities for trade, and rates of exchange prevailing in Canton.

Pechberty, Jean. Extrait de la lettre ecrite ... sur la navire la Amphetritte de Canton le 17^e fy. 1699. Manuscript. [n.p., 1699.] P139
   An abridgement of the preceding item.

Peck, Pierre. V. Cl. Petri Peckii in titt. Dig. & Cod. ad rem nauticam pertinentes, commentarii ... Amsterdam, Viduam Joannis Henrici Boom, 1688. P140
   A treatise on maritime law first published in 1556 and here commented on by Arnoldus Vinnius, a Dutch jurist. His commentary on the Law of Rhodes is also included.

Peckham, Sir George. A true reporte, of the late discoveries, and possession, taken in the right of the crowne of England, of the New-found landes. London, I.C. for John Hinde, 1583. P141
   A promotion piece urging settlement in the New World, an attempt to demonstrate that noblemen and merchants might find profit in participating in development of a colony, and that unemployed persons in England would find a good life there.

Pedraza, Juan. Relacion cierta y verdadera que trata de la vitiori y toma de la Parayua que el yllustre señor Diego Flores de Baldes tomo con la armada ... en la jornada de Magallanes. Seville, Fernãdo Maldonado, 1584. P142
   A poem of twenty-four ten-line stanzas, relating an encounter in the vicinity of Paraiba between French interlopers and a Spanish fleet commanded by Diego Flores de Baldez.

Pedro de San Francisco de Asís, padre. La Reyna de la America, Nuestra Señora del Pilar de Zaragoza, sermon panegyrico, que en la Iglesia del Hospicio de San Nicolas de Tolentino de Augustinos Descalzos de Mexico, y en la Dominica occurrente XXII. post Pentecosten ... Mexico, Joseph Bernardo de Hogal, 1739. P143
   In addition to a religious interpretation of the Spanish conquests in America, this tract includes a history of the Augustinian mission on the island of Calamianes in the Philippines.

Peifer, David. Imperatores Turcici, libellus de vita, progressu, & rebus gestis principum gentis Mahumeticae, elegiaco carmine conscriptus. Basel, Joannem Oporinum [1550]. P144
   A series of neo-Latin poems, the purpose of which was to incite European sovereigns to wage war on the Turks.

Peleus, Julien. Les questions illustres de ... advocat en Parlement. Paris, N. Buon, 1608. P145

A collection of legal cases, including the case of a French merchant named Boyer who was employed by Sieur de Monts. In connection with Boyer's case the conditions of de Mont's monopoly are published for the first time.

Pelleprat, Pierre. Relation des missions. Paris, S. Cramoisy & G. Cramoisy, 1655. P146

Describes the establishment of Jesuit missions in the West Indies and Central and South America from 1638-1654.

Pellham, Edward. Gods power and providence: shewed, in the miraculous preservation and deliverance of eight Englishmen, left by mischance in Greenland. London, J. Partridge, 1631. P147

An account of Greenland, particularly its animal and vegetable products, and the means of survival in the far north.

[Pellissery, Roch-Antoine de.] Le caffé politique d'Amsterdam, ou Entretiens familiers d'un François, d'un Anglois, d'un Hollandois, et d'un cosmopolite, sur les divers intérêts économiques & politiques de la France, de l'Espagne, & de l'Angleterre. Amsterdam, 1778. P148

A mock-conversation, traditional among Dutch publishers, in which the affairs of Europe's major powers are discussed, including colonial and commercial interests.

Pelsaert, Francisco. Ongeluckige voyagie, van't schip Batavia, nae de Oost-Indien. Amsterdam, Jan Jansz, 1647. P149

An account of a mutinous East India voyage in 1628-29, together with a description of troubles of the East India Company in Siam.

Pemberton, Ebenezer. A sermon preach'd in New-Ark, June 12, 1744, at the ordination of Mr. David Brainerd, a missionary among the Indians ... Boston, Rogers and Fowle for J. Pemberton, 1744. P150

The sermon concerns the value of missions. An appendix contains reports of missionary work by Azariah Horton on Long Island and by David Brainerd near Albany.

Penaguião, João Rodrigues de Sá e Meneses, conde de. Rebelion de Ceylan, y los progressos de su conquista en el gobierno de Constantino de Saa, y Noronha. Lisbon, Antonio Crasbeeck de Mello, 1681. P151

Notes the beginning of Dutch trade in Ceylon and describes Portuguese East Indian commerce in general.

Peñalosa y Mondragón, Benito de. Libro de las cinco excelencias del Español que despueblan a España para su mayor potencia y dilatacion. Pamplona, Carlos de Labàyen, 1629. P152

This is a defense of Spain's American empire against its critics, noting the wealth it produced which enabled Spain to support religious work in the New World.

Penn, William. Missive van William Penn, eygenaar en gouverneur van Pennsylvania ... Amsterdam, J. Claus, 1684. P153

The second Dutch edition of Penn's account of the opportunities for settlement, trade, and freedom in Pennsylvania.

Penn, William. Some account of the province of Pennsilvania in America. London, Benjamin Clark, 1681. P154

The first publication relating to this colony, containing a plea for settlers, and information about the land, constitution, conditions governing settlement, etc.

Penna di Billi, Francesco Orazio della. Missio apostolica, Thibetano-Seraphica, das ist, neue durch päbstliche Gewalt in dem grossen thibetanischen Reich ... Munich, Johann Jacob Vötter, 1740. P155

A description of Tibet, its geography, climate, people, religions and economy as well as the progress of the Christian missions there by an author who lived there for some thirty years.

Pennant, Thomas. Inleiding tot de kennis der Noorder-Poollanden; getrokken uit de dierkunde der Noorder-Poollanden. Amsterdam, Wessin en Van der Heij, 1789. P156

A translation of the two-hundred page introduction to the *Arctic Zoology*. Apparently the only Dutch edition.

[Pennant, Thomas.] Le nord du globe; ou, Tableau de la nature dans les contrées septentrionales. Paris, Théophile Barrois le jeune, 1789. P157

A translation of Pennant's *Arctic Zoology*, describing the plants, animals, and peoples of the northern regions of Europe, Asia, and North America.

Pennant, Thomas. Outlines of the globe. London, Henry Hughes, 1798-1800. P158

Imaginary travels to India, the Far East, and Australia containing information on a wide variety of subjects, from natural history to trade and the history of its development.

Pennsylvania (Colony). Treaties, etc. Minutes of conferences, held at Easton, in October, 1758. Philadelphia, B. Franklin and D. Hall, 1759. P159

Sixteen Indian nations were involved in these conferences, some of them presenting grievances against the colonists. The conferences involved discussions for peaceful relations on the frontier and ended in a spirit of amity.

Pennsylvania (Colony). Treaties, etc. Minutes of conferences, held with the Indians, at Easton, in the months of July and August, 1757. Philadelphia, B. Franklin, 1757. P160

Negotiations with Teedyuscung, Chief of the Delawares, and representatives of other Indian nations.

Pennsylvania (Colony). Treaties, etc. Minutes of conferences, held with the Indians, at Harris's Ferry, and at Lancaster, in March, April, and May, 1757. Philadelphia, B. Franklin, 1757.
P161
The conferences were held to determine French strength in the west and to keep the Indians of that region loyal to the English.

Pennsylvania (Colony). Treaties, etc. The treaty held with the Indians of the Six Nations, at Philadelphia, in July, 1742. Philadelphia, B. Franklin, 1743. P162
Contains the speeches of several Indian chiefs and of the governor of Pennsylvania, together with terms agreed upon for cession of lands along the Susquehanna River. This copy of it has contemporary manuscript annotations.

Pennsylvania (Colony). Treaties, etc. A treaty held with the Ohio Indians at Carlisle, in October, 1753. Philadelphia, B. Franklin, 1753.
P163
The negotiations are described in terms of the commercial and diplomatic relations desired by both sides.

The Pennsylvania magazine: or, American monthly museum. For January, [-July] 1776. Philadelphia, R. Aitken, 1776. P164
The "Monthly Intelligence" section in the July issue contains the Declaration of Independence.

Penrose, Bernard. An account of the last expedition to Port Egmont, in Falkland's Islands, in the year 1772. London, J. Johnson, 1775. P165
The author describes plant and animal life in the area of the Falkland Islands, and suggests that the whaling methods used by the Portuguese off the coast of Brazil could possibly be used there.

Pereira, António Pinto. Historia da India, no tempo em que a governovo visorey Dom Luis d'Ataide, composta por Antonio Pinto Pereyra. Dirigida a el Rey Dom Sebastião ... Coimbra, Nicolao Carvalho, 1617. P166
A chronicle of the first viceroyalty of Luiz de Ataide, 1568-1572, recording extensive military activity in India, and including also a history of early Portuguese administration of the Moluccas.

Pereira, Marques Nuno. Compendio narrativo do peregrino da America. Lisbon, Francisco Borges de Sousa, 1765. P167
A survey of Brazilian morality, covering such topics as witchcraft, treatment of Jews and slaves, concubinage, and robbery.

Pérez, Antonio. Cort-begryp vande stucken der gheschiedenissen vā Antonio Perez, onlancx verdreven secretaris vanden teghenwoordighen Coninck van Spagnien, Philips de Twede: waerinne de Spaensche practijcken, tot een spiegel van alle menschen, nuttelick ende naecktelick ontdeckt werden ... The Hague, Aelbrecht Heyndricxzoon, 1596. P168
An account of the life of a controversial person who fled Spain and whose writings were instrumental in developing anti-Spanish sentiments in England and the Netherlands.

Pérez de Ribas, Andrés. Historia de los triumphos de nuestra santa fee entre gentes las mas barbaras y fieras del Nuevo Orbe ... Madrid, Alōso de Paredes, 1645. P169
A history of Jesuit missions in the American southwest.

Perez del Christo, Christoval. Excelencias, y antiguedades de las siete islas de Canaria. Jerez de la Frontera, Juan Antonio Tarazona, 1679.
P170
A discussion of the Canary Islands as they figured in the geographical and imaginative literature of the ancients, with reference to modern geography as well.

Peri, Gio. Domenico (Giovanni Domenico). Il negotiante. Venice, G. G. Hertz, 1682. P171
A merchant handbook containing a survey of prices, duties, etc., chiefly for the Mediterranean trade.

Periplus Ponti Euxini. Arriani historici et philosophi Ponti Euxini & Maris Erythraei Periplus. Lyons, Bartholomaeum Vincentium, 1577. P172
An edition by Johann Wilhelm Stuck of the survey of the Black Sea made for the Roman emperor Hadrian by Flavius Arrianus in 131 A.D. It contains Greek and Latin text in parallel columns.

Pernety, Antoine-Joseph. Dissertation sur l'Amérique et les Américains, contre les *Récherches philosophiques* de Mr. de P. Berlin, Samuel Pitra [1769]. P173
A response to a work by Cornelius de Pauw in which he alleges the inferiority of everything American, especially its inhabitants.

Pernety, Antoine-Joseph. Journal historique d'un voyage fait aux Iles Malouïnes en 1763 & 1764. Berlin, Etienne de Bourdeaux, 1769. P174
The first edition of the earliest account of the attempted colonization on the Falkland Islands by Bougainville. The author was a Prussian scientist, and his book contains much natural history of the South Atlantic.

Pernety, Antoine-Joseph. Histoire d'un voyage aux Isles Malouines, fait en 1763 & 1764. Paris, Saillant & Nyon, 1770. P175
The second French edition.

Pernety, Antoine-Joseph. The history of a voyage to the Malouine (or Falkland) Islands. London, For T. Jefferys, 1771. P176
The first English edition.

Péron, Captain M. Memoires du Capitaine Péron sur ses voyages ... Paris, Brissot-Thivars, 1824. P177
Contains accounts of numerous trading voyages to Asia, Africa, and the East Indies. Most significant is the account of the first American vessel to call at a California port. The author died in 1769, and this text was prepared from his manuscripts by L.S. Brissot-Thivars.

Perrin, William. The present state of the British and French sugar colonies. London, T. Cooper, 1740. P178
A review of England's sugar trade, with recommendations for its improvement.

Perrin du Lac, François Marie. Voyages dans les deux Louisianes et chez les nations sauvages du Missouri ... Lyons, Bruyset et Buynand, 1805. P179
A description of western America, with the earliest published map of the trans-Missouri region to show considerable accuracy.

Perrot, Nicolas. [Contract signed between Nicolas Perrot and Jean Baptiste Duchene.] Manuscript in French. Rivière du Loup, Quebec, 28 July 1688. P180
A voyageur contract for western fur trade.

Perrot, Nicolas. [Contract signed, between Nicolas Perrot and Louis Juillet and Louis des Carry.] Manuscript in French. Rivière du Loup, Quebec, 3 July 1688. P181
A contract for fur trade in the country of the Ottawa, and nations "more or less distant."

Perrot, Nicolas. [Contract signed between Nicolas Perrot and Pierre Rivard, François Rivard, Vivien Jean, etc.] Manuscript in French. Cap de la Madeline, Quebec, 4 April 1685. P182
A contract between Perrot and a group of fur traders for their going westward from Green Bay and returning furs to Montreal.

Perrot, Nicolas. [Petition signed.] Manuscript in French. Trois Rivières, Quebec, 12 February 1685. P183
A petition for command at Green Bay, an important fur trade post.

Pertinente beschrijving van Guiana. Gelegen aen de vaste kust van America. Amsterdam, Jan Claesz ten Hoorn, 1676. P184
Based on earlier writers, this is an invitation to colonists to participate in a settlement being undertaken by the provinces of Holland and West Friesland.

Peru. Don Manuel de Guirior ... Virrey Governador, y Capitan General de las Provincias del Reyno del Perù, y Chile &c., Por quanto el Real Tribunal del Consulado de estos Reynos, me ha hecho presente, que con ocasion del arrivo del Navio las Mercedes al Puerto del Callao ... [Lima, 1778.] P185
A decree concerning duties on imports into Peru from the Spanish colony of Argentina.

Peru. [Records of the investigation of the administration of Viceroy Manuel de Amat.] Manuscript in Spanish. [Lima, ca. 1776?-1777.] P186
Four documents dealing primarily with the financial aspects of the administration of the viceroyalty of Peru.

Peru. Laws, etc. Tomo primero de las ordenanzas del Peru ... Lima, Francisco Sobrino y Bados, 1752. P187
The second edition augmented and newly arranged.

Peru shipping and commercial records. Manuscript in Spanish. [n.p., ca. 1778.] P188
These documents illustrate the controversy wherein the Spanish colonies in America complained that trade policy in effect made commerce between colonies more expensive than trade with Spain.

Perugia (Italy). Laws, etc. Statutorum auguste Perusie. Perugia, Girolamo di Francesco Cartolaro, 1528. P189
This collection of laws of Perugia supplies information on the commercial life of that city.

Peruschi, Giovanni Battista. Informatione del regno e stato del gran Rè di Mogor. Brescia, P.M. Marchetti, 1597. P190
This is the second Italian edition, the first being published in Rome in the same year. This Brescia edition does include a folded map of Asia (the East Indies) which is lacking in the Rome edition.

Peruschi, Giovanni Battista. Advis moderne de l'estat et grand royaume de Mogor, situé entre la Tartarie, l'Inde & la Perse ... Paris, Phillipe du Pré, 1598. P191
The first French edition.

[Peters, Benoni.] Occurrences in a voyage to Bombay & Surat in ye East Indies, in ye yeares 1741, 2, & part of 1743, perform'd by ye Porto-Bello Indiaman. Manuscript. En route, 1741. P192
A portion of a journal to the East Indies, covering the route from England to Sumatra, reporting natural phenomena, events aboard ship, medical matters, and other items of interest to the author who was the ship's surgeon.

Peters, C. (Charles). Two sermons preached at Dominica, on the 11th and 13th of April, 1800; and officially noticed by His Majesty's privy council in that island. London, John Hatchard, 1802. P193
The sermons were tinged with anti-slavery sentiments. They are followed here by an appendix concerning the condition of slaves on the island of Dominica.

Pétion, J. (Jérôme). Discours sur la traite des noirs, par M. Pétion de Villeneuve, membre de l'Assemblée nationale. Paris, Desenne, 1790. P194

To the author's own anti-slave trade views are added those of Jean Louis Carra, whose "Observations" are appended.

Pétion, J. (Jérôme). Opinion sur le commerce du tabac. [Paris, Imprimerie Nationale, 1791.] P195

This writer expresses his opinions on the tobacco trade and suggests that there be no distinction between French and foreign tobacco, and also that only French or American ships should bring American tobacco to France.

Petit, Pierre. De Amazonibus dissertatio. Amsterdam, J. Wolters & Y. Haring, 1687. P196

This second edition was enlarged and corrected over the first. The work by the French philosopher Petit was used in discussions regarding Amazons in South America.

Pétition à l'Assemblée nationale, par les propriétaires de Saint-Domingue, residans à Paris. [Paris, Imprimerie Nationale, 1791.] P197

A plea for assistance in the face of a slave revolt in St. Domingue.

Petrarca, Francesco. Chronica delle vita pontefici et imperatori Romani ... Venice, J. de Pinci de Lecco, 1507. P198

A history of the Roman emperors and popes from Julius Caesar to Pius III. Contains mention of Columbus being sent by Ferdinand and Isabella across the Western Ocean.

Petrejus, Petrus. Historien und Bericht von dem Gross-fürstenthumb Muschkow. Leipzig [Tipis Bavaricis] 1620. P199

The first German edition of a description of the provinces, lakes, rivers, peoples, and commerce of Russia.

Petrejus, Petrus. Regni Muschovitici sciographia. Thet är Een wiss och egentelich beskriffning om Rydzland, med thes många och stora furstendömers, provinciers, befestningars, städers, siögars och elfwers tilstånd, rum och lägenheet ... Stockholm, Ignatium Meurer, 1614-15. P200

The first edition of a comprehensive history of Russia. Each of the six books has its own title page.

Petty, Sir William. Handgreiffliche Demonstration, dass die Stadt London ... grösser und volckreicher sey ... als die Städte Parise und Rome. Danzig, David Friedrich Rheten, 1693. P201

This comparison of London, Paris, and Rome is based upon Petty's English editions, but contains material not found in the English versions.

[Petyt, William.] Britannia languens, or A discourse of trade. London, T. Dring and S. Crouch, 1680. P202

A study of England's commercial situation with respect to the competition offered by France and the Netherlands. The author recommends more government regulation of trade in the national interest.

Peucer, Kaspar. De dimensione terrae et geometrice numerandis locorum particularium intervallis ex doctrina triangulorum sphaericorum & canone subtensarum liber. Wittenberg, Johannes Crato, 1554. P203

A review of ancient methods and results in the measurement of the earth, followed by the author's own theories. Also includes the description of Palestine by Burchardus de Monte Sion.

Peuchet, J. (Jacques). Dictionnaire universel de la géographie commerçante. Paris, Blanchon, 1799-1800. P204

A five-volume commercial dictionary, which gives particular emphasis to the produce and commerce of cities, countries, and islands in all parts of the world.

Peutinger, Konrad. Sermones convivales. Strassburg, Joannes Priis, 1506. P205

The last of these four essays contains remarks on the early commercial voyages of the Portuguese to India, making this book one of the earliest of such commentaries.

Peutinger, Konrad. De mirandis Germaniae antiquitatibus, sermones conuiuales. Strassburg, Christianum Egenolphum [1530]. P206

The second edition.

Peutinger table. Peutingeriana tabula itineraria. Vienna, Typographia Trattneriana, 1753. P207

The first complete printing of this fifth-century map of Roman roads, with commentary comparing the map with other ancient authorities in geography.

Peyssonel, Claude Charles de. Traité sur le commerce de la Mer Noire. Paris, Chez Cuchet, 1787. P208

Notes the major nations and products in the commerce of the Black Sea.

Pezenas, père (Esprit). Elementi dell' arte nautica. Leghorn, Anton Santini, 1754. P209

This work was written by a Jesuit physicist, hydrographer, and astronomer. First published in French in 1733, its text is supplemented with numerous tables, charts, and diagrams.

Pflaum, Jacob. [Kalendarium, 1477-1552.] Ulm, Johannem Zainer, 1478. P210

This calendar includes tables for phases of the moon, solar eclipses, and movements of the planets, and text explaining astronomical phenomena.

Philippe de la Très Sainte Trinité, père. Viaggi orientali del p. Filippo della SS. Trinita, Generale de'Carmelitani Scalzi. Venice, Antonio Tiuanni, 1683.   P211
   The first Italian edition.

Philippe de la Très Sainte Trinité, père. Voyage d'Orient. Lyons, Antoine Jullieron, 1652.   P212
   An account of missionary travels to the Levant, Persia, and Goa in the 1630s by the general of the Carmelite order. It was first published in a Latin edition of 1649.

Philippe de la Très Sainte Trinité, père. Voyage d'Orient. Lyons, A. Jullieron, 1669.   P213
   A later reprinting of the previous work.

Philippines. Ordenanzas de marina, para los navios del rey, de las islas Philipinas, que en guerra, y con reales permissos hacen viages al reyno de la Nueva España, u otro destino del real servicio. [Manila, 1757.]   P214
   A set of maritime regulations for Spanish ships sailing in convoy from the Philippines to Acapulco, detailing means of communication between ships, duties of officers, amount and type of armament, rations for crew, etc.

Philipps, J. T. (Jenkin Thomas). An account of the religion, manners, and learning of the people of Malabar in the East-Indies. London, W. Mears and J. Brown, 1717.   P215
   A collection of letters supposedly written by natives of India to Danish missionaries, describing the religion, social life, and customs of Malabar.

[Philips, Erasmus.] The state of the nation in respect to her commerce, debts, and money. London: Printed for J. Woodman and D. Lyon, 1725.   P216
   A review of British commerce since 1688, taking into account the impact of wars with France upon it and the effect of the Treaty of Utrecht.

Philips, John. An authentic journal of the late expedition under the command of Commodore Anson. London, J. Robinson, 1744.   P217
   The earliest account of the *Centurion's* circumnavigation, written by a midshipman.

Philipucci, Francis Xavier. De Sinensium ritibus politicis acta ... Paris, Nicolaum Pepié, 1700.   P218
   A collection of arguments in the Chinese Rites controversy from the Jesuit point of view.

Phillip, Arthur. Extracts of letters, &c. from Governor Phillip, relating to New South Wales. [London] 1792.   P219
   Extracts from four letters, dated March 4 to November 5, 1791. They trace the progress of the settlements at Sydney and at Norfolk Island.

Phillip, Arthur. Extracts of letters from Arthur Phillip, Esq. London, J. Debrett, 1791.   P220
   Letters written to Lord Sydney by the first governor of Australia, noting the progress and condition of the colony and stating the need for settlers.

Phillip, Arthur. Reise nach der Botany-Bay. Hamburg, Benjamin Gottlob Hoffmann, 1791.   P221
   A German translation of the account written by the first governor of New South Wales. It contains a supplementary section on the voyage of Thomas Gilbert from Port Jackson to Canton, and a map.

Phillip, Arthur. The voyage of Governor Phillip to Botany Bay. London, John Stockdale, 1789.   P222
   A description of the beginnings of English settlement in Australia, including accounts of voyages to various Pacific islands.

Phipps, Thomas. Mr. Phipps's speech to a committee ... concerning the African trade. London, H. Parker, 1712.   P223
   Defends the Royal African Company and argues that only such a company can maintain the necessary forts on the Guinea coast.

Piacenza (Italy). Capitoli, et ordini delle fere di Bezensone; che si fanno al presente in la citta di Piacenza, con li quali dette fere, e li negotii de cambii che si fanno in esse, si doveranno reggere, e governare, & da tutti i banchieri trattanti ... [Piacenza, 1595.]   P224
   A collection of regulations dealing primarily with banking and exchange.

Piacenza (Italy). Nuovo avviso per la fiera. [Piacenza] Salvoni [1752].   P225
   A broadside setting forth regulations for merchants attending the fair at Piacenza.

[Piarron de Chamousset, Claude-Humbert.] Vues d'un citoyen. Paris, Lambert, 1757.   P226
   This work by a French reformer includes his proposal for improving French Louisiana with a colony which would receive France's homeless children.

Piccolomini, Alessandro. Della grandezza terra et dell' acqua. Venice, Giordano Ziletti, 1558.   P227
   A consideration of Aristotle's theory regarding the relative amounts of land and water in the earth, including arguments of other ancient geographers and the facts of recent navigation and discoveries.

Piccolomini, Alessandro. La prima parte dele theoriche ò vero speculationi dei pianeti. Venice, Giordano Ziletti, 1558.   P228
   An explanation of the apparent motion of the planets, accompanied by numerous diagrams.

[Pichon, Thomas.] Genuine letters and memoirs, relating to the natural, civil, and commercial history of the islands of Cape Breton and Saint John. London, J. Nourse, 1760. P229

The first English edition. The author knew Cape Breton as secretary to the French governor there, and provided the English with information which was helpful to them in the capture of Fort Beauséjour.

Pico della Mirandola, Giovanni Francesco. De animae immortalitate digressio. Bologna, Hieronymo de Benedictis, 1523. P230

A treatise on the immortality of animals.

Pico della Mirandola, Giovanni Francesco. Dialogus in tres libros divisus—titulus est Strix, sive de ludificatione daemonum ... Bologna, Hieronymo de Benedictis, 1523. P231

The author's earlier concern for the location of demons in various places and times is brought up to date with application of this interest to the New World and Portuguese discoveries in Asia.

Pico della Mirandola, Giovanni Francesco. Examen vanitatis doctrinae gentium et veritatis Christianae disciplinae ... Mirandola, Joannes Mazochius, 1520. P232

A conservative philosopher examines various types of learning in comparison to Scripture, and notes the differences between European and American peoples.

Pico della Mirandola, Giovanni Francesco. Hymni heroici tres ... Milan, A. Minutianus, 1507. P233

Contains allusions to the New World, which the author believed to be farther south and connected with an Antarctic continent.

Pictet de Rochemont, Charles. Tableau de la situation actuelle des États-Unis d'Amérique, d'après Jedidiah Morse et les meilleurs auteurs américains. Paris, Du Pont, 1795. P234

In addition to Morse the author drew upon Jefferson, Cooper, Franklin, Tench Coxe, etc. The introductory matter praises the new republic for its adherence to liberty.

Pidou de Saint-Olon, Monsieur (François). The present state of the empire of Morocco. London, R. Bently, 1695. P235

A translation of the French ambassador's report in which he describes the major imports and exports of the realm.

Pierre de Sainte Marie Madelaine, Dom. Traitté d'horlogiographie, contenant plusieurs manieres de construire sur toutes surfaces, toutes sortes de lignes horaires, & autres cercles de la sphere ... Paris, Melchior Tavernier, 1641. P236

A treatise on sundials and their relationship to astronomy and navigation, with fifty-nine pages of places depicting instruments and diagrams for their use.

Pigafetta, Antonio. Magellan's voyage: A narrative account of the first circumnavigation. Translated by R.A. Skelton. New Haven, Yale University Press, 1969. P237

The annotated translation is accompanied by a facsimile reproduction of the manuscript in Yale University's Beineke Library. Pigafetta accompanied the Magellan expedition, and was one of the eighteen survivors.

Pigafetta, Antonio. Primo viaggio intorno al globo terracqueo. Milan, G. Galeazzi, 1800. P238

From an Italian manuscript of the sixteenth century in the Ambrosian Library in Milan. Includes reproductions of fourteen maps and designs which relate to the manuscript.

Pigafetta, Filippo. Discorso ... d'interno all' historia della Aguglia, et alla ragione del muoverla ... Rome, Bartolomeo Grassi, 1586. P239

A description of an obelisk in Rome which included many geogarphical references based on Pliny, Strabo, Ptolemy and other ancient authorities.

Pigafetta, Filippo. Discorso di Filippo Pigafetta sopra l'ordinanza dell' Armata Catholica ... Rome, Apresso il Santi ad instanza di Nicolò Picoletti [1588]. P240

A description of the Spanish Armada of 1588, its armament, and probable deployment in battle.

Pighius, Albertus. De aequinoctiorum solsticiorūque inventione Ad R. in Christo patrem, D. Frāciscum Molinium Abbatem. S. Maximini, a secretis & cōsilio. R. Francorum Christianiss. & pijs largitionibus eiusdem praepositum primarium. Basel [1520]. P241

A discussion of problems in astronomy relating to the reforming of the calendar. The voyages of discovery are mentioned as a part of the necessity for a uniform celebration of Easter.

Pighius, Albertus. De Moscovia, ad Clementem VII., Pont. Max., Albertus Campensis. Venice, Paulum Girardum, 1543. P242

An account of Muscovy written in the early 1520s, based in part on information supplied by members of the author's family who were merchants in Russia.

Pimenta, Nicolau. Cartas que o padre Nicolao Pimenta ... escreueo ao Géral della à 26. de Noue[m]bro do ano de 1599. & ao 1. de Dezembro de [1]600 ... Lisbon, Pedro Crasbeeck, 1602. P243

A report of Jesuit missionary progress in India and Burma, with particular emphasis on northern India.

Pimenta, Nicolau. Copia d'una del p. Nicolo Pimenta, visitatore della provincia d'India Orientale, al molto reuerendo p. Claudio Acquaviva, preposito generale della Compagnia di Giesù, del primo di decembre, 1600. Rome, Luigi Zannetti, 1602. P244

This report contains letters from six mission stations in India as well as an account of Pimenta's travels in northern India.

Pimenta, Nicolau. Exemplum epistolae P. Nicolai Pimentae, provinciae Orientalis Indiae visitatoris. Mainz, Joannem Albinum, 1602. P245
The author was Visitor for Jesuit missions in India, and reports here on missionary concerns in India, Pegu, Cambodia, and the Moluccas.

Pimentel, Manuel. Arte practica de navegar, & roteiro das viagens, & costas maritimas do Brazil, Guine, Angola ... Lisbon, Bernardo da Costa de Carvalho, 1699. P246
Prepared by his son, this new edition of Serraõ Pimentel's navigation guide contains many alterations and adds a pilot guide to the Mediterranean from Cadiz to Malta.

Pimentel, Manuel. Arte de navegar ... & roteiro das viagens, et costas maritimas de Guinè, Angola, Brasil, Indias & ilhas occidentaes, & orientaes. Lisbon, Officina Real Deslandesiana, 1712. P247
An edition with additional illustrations in the navigation section and maps in the roteiro which were not included in the previous editions.

Pimentel, Manuel. Arte de navegar, em que se ensinão as regras praticas, e os modos de cartear, e de graduar a balestilha por via de numeros, e muitos problemas uteis á navegaçao, e roteiro das viagens, e costas maritimas de Guiné, Angola, Brazil, Indias, e ilhas occidentaes, e orientaes, novamende emendado, e accrescentadas muitas derrotas ... Lisbon, Miguel Manescal da Costa, 1762. P248
The fourth edition of the basic navigation text for use by Portuguese seamen in the eighteenth century.

Pina, Rui de. Chronica do muito alto, e muito esclarecido principe D. Affonso II terceiro Rey de Portugal ... fielemente copiada de su original, que se conserva no Archivo Real da Torre do Tombo. Lisbon, Officina Ferreyriana, 1727. P249
The reign of Affonso II, 1211-1223, was characterized by continued expansion at the expense of the Moors, and by conflicts with the papacy and the nobility.

Pina, Rui de. Chronica do muito alto, e muito esclarecido principe D. Affonso III. quinto Rey de Portugal ... fielemente copiada do seu original, que se conserva no Archivo Real da Torre do Tombo. Lisbon, Officina Ferreyriana, 1728. P250
Affonso III, 1245-1279, was one of the weaker Portuguese kings of the medieval period. His reign saw an increase in the power of the Cortes which came to have representation from the commons for the first time.

Pina, Rui de. Chronica do muito alto, e muito esclarecido principe D. Sancho I segunda Rey de Portugal ... fielemente copiada de seu original, que se conserva no Archivo Real da Torre do Tombo. Lisbon, Officina Ferreyriana, 1727. P251
A chronicle of Portugal's second king, 1185-1211, a reign which saw increased unity within Portugal as territories taken from the Moors were settled.

Pina, Rui de. Chronica do muito alto, e muito esclarecido principe D. Sancho II quarto Rey de Portugal ... fielemente copiada do seu original, que se conserva no Archivo Real da Torre do Tombo. Lisbon, Officina Ferreyriana, 1728. P252
The reign of Sancho II, 1223-1245, witnessed continued religious strife, leading to his being deposed by the Pope.

Pina, Rui de. Chronica do muito alto, e muito esclarecido principe Dom Diniz sexto Rey de Portugal ... fielemente copiada do seu original que se conserva no Archivo Real da Torre do Tombo. Lisbon, Ferreyriana, 1729. P253
Diniz, 1279-1325, is the best known of the Portuguese medieval monarchs. He was interested in cultural development, in improving the agriculture and economy of Portugal, and in maritime affairs. He concluded an important treaty with England in 1294.

Piña y Mazo, Pedro de. Respuesta fiscal que en 16. de Agosto de 1774. dio D[o]n Pedro de Piña, y Mazo, Fiscal del Consejo, y Camara de Indias, en vista de 4°. Concilio Provincial de Mexico ... Manuscript. [n.p.] 1774. P254
An extensive analysis of the reports on the proceedings, decisions and deliberations of the Fourth Provincial Council of Mexico, including conduct of churchmen, administration of justice, teaching and missionizing among the Indians, etc.

Pinargenti, Simon. Isole che son de Venetia nella Dalmatia e per tutto l'Arcipelago, fino à Constantinople ... Venice, Simon Pinargenti, 1573. P255
A collection of fifty-two maps of the major commercial centers between Venice and Constantinople, showing harbors, rivers, and islands of importance.

Pinckney, Philip. An index to the statutes now in force, relating to the stamp-duties. London, J. Tonson, 1722. P256
A subject index published for the use of merchants and customs officials who would find it necessary to search the laws for commercial regulations.

Pinheiro, Luiz. Relacion del sucesso que tuvo nuestra santa fe en los reynos del Japon, desde el año de seyscientos y doze hasta el de seyscientos y quinze. Madrid, Alonso Martin de Balboa, 1617. P257

An account of the last years of the Roman Catholic missions in Japan before their expulsion in 1614.

Pinto, Fernão Mendes. Peregrinaçam. Lisbon, P. Crasbeek, 1614. P258
An account of twenty-one years of travel in the East Indies in the mid-sixteenth century. The author visited various Portuguese trading stations, and was the first European to visit Japan.

Pinto, Fernão Mendes. Peregrinaçam. Lisbon, Antonio Crasbeeck de Mello, 1678. P259
The second Portuguese edition.

Pinto, Fernão Mendes. Peregrinaçaõ ... agora novamente correcta, e emendada. Accrecentada com o itinerario de Antonio Tenreiro, que da India veio por terra a este reyno de Portugal ... Lisbon, Joam de Aquino Bulhoens, 1762. P260
The itinerario of Antonio Tenreiro included here is an account of an overland journey from India to Portugal, ending in 1529.

Pinto, Fernão Mendes. Historia oriental de las peregrinaciones ... Madrid, Tomas Junti, 1620. P261
The first Spanish edition.

Pinto, Fernão Mendes. Historia oriental de las peregrinaciones de Fernan Mendez Pinto. Madrid, M. Sanchez, 1664. P262
The fourth Spanish edition.

Pinto, Fernão Mendes. Les voyages advantureux de Fernand Mendez Pinto. Paris, Arnould Cotinet & Jean Roger, 1645. P263
The second French edition. It is dedicated to Cardinal Richelieu.

Pinto, Fernão Mendes. De wonderlyke reizen ... die hij in eenentwintig jaren deur Europa, Asia, en Afrika gedaan heeft ... Amsterdam, Jan Hendriksz & Jan Rieuwertsz, 1652. P264
The first Dutch edition, and the first illustrated edition.

Pinto, Fernão Mendes. The voyages and adventures, of Fernand Mendez Pinto. London, J. Macock for Henry Cripps and Lodowick Lloyd, 1653. P265
The first English edition.

Pinto, Fernão Mendes. Wunderliche und merkwürdige Reisen ... durch Europa, Asia, und Africa. Amsterdam, Henrich & Dietrich Boom, 1671. P266
The first German edition.

Pinto, Isaac de. Letters on the American troubles. London, J. Boosey and J. Forbes, 1776. P267
In this tract Pinto defends Great Britain's policy regarding the American colonies and criticizes Josiah Tucker's acquiescence in the separation between Britain and the thirteen colonies.

[Piossens, Chevalier de.] Memoires de la regence de S.A.R. Mdr. le Duc Dorléans, durant la minorité de Louis XV Roi de France. The Hague, Jean van Duren, 1729. P268
The regency years encompassed the time in which John Law's financial program operated in France, and this and other matters of commercial importance are covered in this account of the regency.

[Piossens, Chevalier de.] Memoirs of the regency of His Royal Highness the late Duke of Orleans, during the minority of his present most Christian Majesty Lewis the XVth. London, R. Montagu [etc.] 1732. P269
This English edition includes only the first of the three volumes from the French edition above.

Pirckheimer, Willibald. Germaniae ex variis scriptoribus per brevis explicatio. Nuremberg, Jo. Petreium, 1530. P270
The description of Germany is followed by comparisons of Ptolemaic and modern place names and by a brief description of Spanish discoveries in America.

Pirî Reis. Kitabi Bahriye ... Istanbul, Devlet Basimevi, 1935. P271
A modern edition of a sixteenth-century Turkish navigation book, including a facsimile of the version in the St. Sophia Museum at Istanbul.

Pirî Reis. Pirî Reis Haritasi. Istanbul, Devlet Basimevi, 1935. P272
A facsimile of the map of 1513 with a brief monograph by Yusuf Akçura. The text is published in Turkish, German, English, and French.

Pisa (Italy). Provisione della fiera da farsi nella citta di Pisa dua volte l'anno con sue franchigie, & essentioni riconcessa dal Serenissimo Card. Gran Duca di Toscana. Florence, Giorgio Marescotti, 1588. P273
Eighteen regulations upon the fair of Pisa with numerous marginal manuscript insertions, and seventy-two leaves of manuscript additions.

Pisa (Italy). Stratto, tassa, e tariffa, di quello, come e quanto si debbe pagare di gabella delle grascie, mercanzie, bestie, & robe, che si metteranno in qual si voglia modo nella città è contado di Pisa, ò d'essi luoghi si caveranno. Pisa, Giovanni Fontani, 1614. P274
A listing of the duties on goods at Pisa, apparently based on a code of 1592, with twenty-two leaves of manuscript additions.

Piso, Willem. Historia naturalis Brasiliae ... In qua non tantum plantae et animalia, sed et indigenarum morbi, ingenia et mores describuntur et

iconibus supra quingentas illustrantur. Leiden, F. Hackium; Amsterdam, L. Elzevirium, 1648.
P275

Pistoia (Italy). Tariffa delle gabelle per Pistoia. Florence, Gaetano Cambiagi, 1791. P276
A schedule of duties on a large number of provisions for the city of Pistoia.

Pistorius, Thomas. Korte en zakelyke beschryvinge van de colonie van Zuriname ... Amsterdam, T. Crajenschot, 1763. P277
A description of the plantations and colony of Surinam.

Pitman, Henry. A relation of the great sufferings, and strange adventures of Henry Pitman. London, A. Sowle, 1689. P278
Contains descriptions of islands in the West Indies visited by the author.

Pitt, William. The speech of the right honourable William Pitt, in the House of Commons, on Friday, February 21, 1783. London, J. Debrett, 1783. P279
A defense of the peace treaty being negotiated between Britain and her enemies, including recognition of American independence.

Pittman, Philip, Captain. The present state of the European settlements on the Mississippi. London, J. Nourse, 1770. P280
This account is based on the author's five years of experience in exploring and surveying the Mississippi River area. Many maps of the river are included.

Pitts, Joseph. A true and faithful account of the religion and manners of the Mohammetans ... Exeter, S. Farley for Philip Bishop and Edward Score, 1704. P281
The author was captured at sea by Algerian pirates and sold into slavery in Algeria, subsequently traveling to Egypt and Mecca. His narrative is rich in description of the private social customs as well as piracy.

Pius II, Pope. Asiae Europae que elegantissima descriptio ... Accessit Henrici Glareani, Helvetij, poetae laureati compendiaria Asiae, Africae, Europaeque descriptio. Paris, Galeotum a Prato, 1534. P282
Edited by Henricus Glareanus, this edition adds brief notes on Africa as well as Europe and Asia, and contains a mention of the New World.

Pius II, Pope. Cosmographia Pii Papae in Asiae & Europeae eleganti descriptione ... [Paris, Henricum Stephanum, 1509.] P283
This edition combines the previous work with the author's description of Europe, first published in 1490.

Pius II, Pope. La discrittione de l'Asia, et Europa de papa Pio II. Venice, V. Vaugris, 1544. P284
A late edition of this collection of the writings of Aeneas Sylvius.

Pius II, Pope. Epistola di papa Pio II. a Mahometto II. Gran Turco. [Venice? ca. 1540.]
P285
A long and powerful letter to the Turkish emperor, Mohammed II, urging his conversion to Christianity as a means of bringing peace to these warring religious communities.

Pius II, Pope. Epistolae in Pontificatu editae. Milan, Antonius Zarotus, 1487. P286
The third edition of this series of fifty-two letters by Pope Pius II, the Humanist pope. The letters are addressed to the major rulers of Europe and concern the perceived Turkish threat to European Christianity.

Pius II, Pope. Historia rerum ubique gestarum. Cum locorum descriptione non finita Asia Minor incipit. [Venice, Johannem de Colonia and Johannem Manthen de Gherretzem, 1477.]
P287
This account of Asia incorporates material on the Far East from Poggio-Bracciolini's *De varietate fortunae* which contained information from Nicolo Conti's travels in the first half of the fifteenth century.

Pizarro y Orellana, Fernando. Varones ilustres del Nuevo Mundo. Madrid, Diego Diaz de la Carrera, 1639. P288
Contains the lives of Columbus, Cortés, the four Pizarros, Diego de Almagro (father and son), and Diego Garcia de Paredes, together with comments on their activities that tend to justify Spanish conquest in America.

Pizzigano, Zuane. The 1424 Nautical Chart. Manuscript. Portugal, 1424. P289
A portolan chart of western Europe and the Atlantic Ocean. A group of islands, including "Antylia," are the earliest known portrayal of land in the western Atlantic.

A plain and seasonable address to the freeholders of Great-Britain on the present posture of affairs in America. London, Richardson and Urquhart, 1766. P290
An attack upon Pitt for his advocacy of repeal of the Stamp Act, and a warning against leniency toward the colonies which would prompt further resistance to Parliamentary authority.

The plain reasoner. Wherein the present state of affairs are set in a new, but very obvious light: the separate and connected interests of Great-Britain and Hanover consider'd ... London, M. Cooper, 1745. P291
A pessimistic view of Great Britain's situation, particularly with respect to its competitive relationship with France.

Plainte de la nouvelle France dicte Canada, a la France sa germaine. Pour servir de factum en une cause pandente au conseil. [n.p., 1620?]
P292

An anonymous and undated protest by a member of a religious group in New France against uncooperative officials in the colony.

Plaisted, Bartholomew. A journal from Calcutta in Bengal ... to Aleppo. London, J. Newberry, 1757. P293
Chiefly an account of an overland journey from the Persian Gulf to Aleppo, with many interesting observations on caravan travel and trade.

Plan for relieving the East-India Company, from the present temporary distress. [n.p., 1774.] P294
Concerns the India tea trade.

Het plan of ontwerp tot bevordering van den algemenen vrede in Europa. [n.p., 1735.] P295
A plan for the re-establishment of peace in Europe, stipulating that the King of Naples and Sicily reinstate and maintain trade with the Dutch and the English.

[Plancius, Petrus.] Haec tabella hydrographicè oras maritimas Africae. [Amsterdam, Cornelis Claesz, 1592.] P296
Based on Iberian sources, this map shows the west coast of Africa from Morocco to Angola and the northeast coast of Brazil as well as the major island groups lying between Africa and South America.

[Plancius, Petrus.] Insulae Moluccae celeberrimae sunt ob maximam aromatum copiam quam per totum terrarum orbem mittunt ... [Amsterdam, Cornelis Claesz, 1592.] P297
A map of the East Indies, one of eight regional maps known to have been published by Cornelis Claesz in 1592, a reflection of emerging Dutch commercial interests in that region.

Plans and proposals transmitted to the committee on the British fishery. London, 1750. P298
A series of twelve proposals designed to reduce the restrictions upon British fishermen, enabling them to compete more effectively with the Dutch.

Plantation justice. Shewing the constitution of their courts. London, B. Barker [etc.] 1702. P299
A criticism of the courts in Barbados, charging that "The merchants of England are grown too cautious to ventur much" and commercial decline has resulted.

Platoe, William. An extraordinary craftsman. London, R. Franklaine, 1729. P300
Protests against the manner in which the government allows the Spaniards to molest English shipping.

[Plautius, Caspar, Abbot of Seitenstetten.] Nova typis transacta navigatio. [Munich] 1621. P301
Contains an account of early Spanish colonization in the New World, dealing with Columbus' second voyage and his unhappy relations with Father Buil.

Playfair, William. Strictures on the Asiatic establishments of Great Britain. London, For the Author by Bunney and Gold, 1799. P302
A thorough study of the East India Company's trade and its value to England, concluding that the nation would benefit from greater free trade to India.

Playters, Sir William. [Petition to the Lords Commissioners for the Great Seal of England to recover proceeds from a partnership engaged in naval activities under letters of marque.] Manuscript. [n.p., ca. 1651.] P303
The partners included the petitioner's late son Thomas, and the letters of marque were granted by the King of Spain.

Plessen, Christian Siegfried. De foederibus commerciorum. Leipzig, Breitkopfianis [1735]. P304
A dissertation on commercial law, including discussion of piracy, commercial agreements, restraint of trade, shipwreck, the laws of various cities.

Pliny, the Elder. Historia naturalis. Treviso, Michael Mansolus, 1479. P305
This work had a strong influence on medieval geographic thought and on the beginnings of the Age of Discovery. It appeared in many editions, this one prepared by the Bolognese scholar Philippus Beroaldus.

Pliny, the Elder. Naturalis hystoriae. [Venice, Rainaldi di Nouimagio, 1483]. P306
This edition was also prepared by Philippus Beroaldus.

Pliny, the Elder. Naturalis hystoriae. Venice, Marinuum Saracenum, 1487. P307
Like the preceding work, this Beroaldus edition contains lists of authorities used.

Pliny, the Elder. De naturali hystoria diligentissime castigatus. Brescia, Angeli & Jacobi de Britannicorum, 1496. P308
The only edition of Pliny's *Natural History* published in Brescia and the first edited by Giovanni Britannico.

Pliny, the Elder. Naturae historiarum. Venice, Bernardinus Benalius [1498]. P309
This edition was edited by Hermolaus Barbarus and revised by Joannes Baptista Palmarius.

Pliny, the Elder. Naturae historiarum. Venice, Joannem Alvisium, 1499. P310
A near reprint of the 1498 edition.

Pliny, the Elder. Historiae naturalis libri XXXVII ab Alexādro Benedicto ... emendatiores redditi. [Venice, Ioānnem Rubeum & Bernardinum fratresq Vercellensis, 1507.] P311
The first edition prepared by Alessandro Benedetti, Veronese physician. Subsequent editions appeared in 1510 and 1513.

Pliny, the Elder. Naturalis hystoriae libri xxxvii. [Paris] Ioannis Frellon [1511]. P312

This edition of Pliny's *Naturalis historia* was edited by Nicolaus Maillard and is very much in keeping with the body of classical scholarship using Renaissance techniques coming from the University of Paris.

Pliny, the Elder. Naturae historiarum libri XXXVII è castigationibus Hermolai Barbari, quam emendatissimo editi ... [The Hague, Joannis Kobergii, ac Lucae Alantsee, 1518.] P313

The text follows closely the edition of 1498, but an index of some twenty thousand entries by Joannes Camers is added.

Pliny, the Elder. Naturalis historie. Venice, Melchiore Sessam & Petrus Serenae, 1525. P314

The chapters in this edition are introduced by a set of thirty-seven interesting woodcut illustrations. The index by Camers is included.

Pliny, the Elder. Liber secundus de Mundi historia ... Frankfurt, Betrum Brubachium, 1553. P315

A commentary by Jakob Milich on the second book of Pliny's *Historia naturalis* which deals with cosmography.

Pliny, the Elder. Historiae mundi libri XXXVII, denvo ad vetustos codices collati, et plurimis locis iam iterum post cunctorum editiones emendati, adiunctis Sigismundi Gelenij Annotationibus ... Basel, Froben, 1554. P316

This edition was prepared by Sigismund Gelen. It contains a massive 210 page index compiled by Johann Herold.

Pliny, the Elder. Historia natural. Madrid, Luis Sanchez, 1624; Madrid, Juan Gonçalez, 1629. P317

Jerónimo Gómez, editor of this first Spanish edition of Pliny's *Natural History*, adds extensive commentary and six full-page woodcuts to the text.

Pliny, the Elder. Historiae naturalis libri XXXVII. 3 vols. Leiden, Elzeviriana, 1635. P318

Edited by Joannes de Laet.

Pliny, the Elder. Historiae naturalis libri XXXVII, quos interpretatione et notis illustravit Joannes Harduinus ... Paris, Antonii-Urbani Coustelier, 1723. P319

A heavily annotated edition, bringing to bear the commentaries of many sixteenth and seventeenth century sources, and providing a massive index.

Plumer, H. Journal of a voyage from London to Madras. Manuscript. [n.p.] 1769. P320

Plumer was an East India Company clerk and this is his account of a voyage under the command of Captain Buggin. It began in January of 1769 and reached India in June of the same year. Plumer describes shipboard life and describes the Comoro Islands.

Pluquet, François-André-Adrien. Philosophisch-politischer Versuch über den Luxus. Leipzig, Schwickertschen Verlage, 1789. P321

First German edition of Pluquet's book originally published in Paris in 1786. He takes a stand against the pursuit of luxury, viewing it as being harmful to the individual and the state.

Plymouth Company (1749-1816). A patent for Plymouth in New-England, to which is annexed, extracts from the records of that colony, &c. &c. Boston, John Draper, 1751. P322

A collection of documents beginning with the original grant to the Plymouth colony and subsequent documents pertaining to grants of land along the Kennebeck River. These were issued preparatory to granting land along the river to settlers.

Poincten van consideratie raeckende de vrede met Portugal. Amsterdam, 1648. P323

A recognition of the necessity of peace between the Dutch and Portuguese in Brazil, with recommendations for an improved administration of Dutch holdings in Brazil.

Poiret, Jean Louis Marie. Herr Poirets Bref om Numidien. I sammandrag. Stockholm, Kongl. Ordens-Tryckeriet, 1792. P324

This Swedish abridgment differs from the English in that it includes four more letters, and several footnotes by the translator-editor, Samuel Lorens Ödmann.

Poiret, Jean Louis Marie. Travels through Barbary; in a series of letters, written from the ancient Numidia, in the years 1785 and 1786 ... London, C. Forster [ca. 1790]. P325

Poiret was a French botanist whose observations included information on the economic and social life of the Arabs. In this translation the botanical material is not included.

Poivre, Pierre. Oeuvres complettes de P. Poivre, Intendant des Isles de France et de Bourbon, correspondent de l'Académie des Science, etc.; précédés de sa vie, et accompagnées de notes. Paris, Fuchs, 1797. P326

A collection of ten works preceded by a life of the author, written by Pierre Samuel Du Pont de Nemours. Poivre's dominant concern in his travels and colonial administration was agriculture.

Poivre, Pierre. Travels of a philosopher. London, T. Becket, 1769. P327

Poivre's views on agriculture were first read at the Royal Society of Agriculture at Lyons in 1764-65 and again at the Royal Society of Paris in 1766, and were finally published in 1768 and translated into English the following year. He presents China as an idealized agrarian society and Asian agricultural practices are compared to European methods.

Poivre, Pierre. Voyages d'un philosophe, ou Observations sur les moeurs & les arts des peuples de l'Afrique, de l'Asie & de l'Amérique. Maestricht, Jean-Edme Dufour & Philippe Roux, 1779. P328
A survey of agriculture principally in southern Asia and in the islands of the Indian Ocean colonized by France.

Poland. Treaties, etc. Articulen van accord gemaeckt den 1 July ... wegen het overgeven der stadt Warsaw. [n.p.] 1656. P329
Terms agreed upon at the surrender of Warsaw by the Swedes to Poland.

The politician's dictionary: or A compendium of political knowledge: containing historical remarks on the interests, connections, forces ... commerce, manufactures, &c. of the different states of Europe. London, William Lane [etc.] 1776. P330
Information on a variety of subjects including several aspects of exploration, colonies, commerce of many countries, naval matters, etc.

Politicq discours, over den wel-standt van dese vereenichde provincien ... [n.p.] 1622. P331
This tract stresses the importance of the West India Company to the homeland, looking to the ruin of Spanish enterprise in the West Indies.

Politike Aanmerkingen op de propositie van de Franche ambassadeur ... aan ... de Konink van Sweden. [n.p.] 1674. P332
The French appeal to Sweden for further help against the Dutch, and the Swedish respond with a refusal.

[Pollexfen, John.] England and East-India inconsistent in their manufactures. Being an answer to a treatise intituled, An essay on the East-India trade. London, 1697. P333
The East India trade is described as one which does not enrich England, but only the monopolists of the East India Company.

Polo, Marco. [Buch des edlen Ritters und Landfahrers Marco Polo. Nuremberg, F. Creussner, 1477.] P334
The first edition of one of the most famous of all travel books, recording the author's travels to China by land and return by sea in the thirteenth century.

Polo, Marco. Incipit prologus in libro domini Marci Pauli ... [Gouda, G. Leeu, 1483-85.] P335
This is the first Latin edition of the *Travels* of Marco Polo. It was this edition which Columbus is known to have read prior to his voyage to America.

Polo, Marco. Libro del famoso Marco Polo Veneciano de las cosas maravillosas que vido en las partes orientales. Logroño, Miguel de Eguia, 1529. P336
The third Spanish edition, including Fernández de Santaella's "Cosmographia introductia" and Book Four of Poggio Bracciolini's *De varietate fortunae*.

Polo, Marco. Opera stampata novamēte delle maravigliose cose del mondo. [Venice, Paulo Danza, 1533.] P337
The fourth Italian edition, a reprint of the 1496 edition.

Polo, Marco. La description géographique des provinces & villes plus fameuses de l'Inde Orientale. Paris, Vincent Sertenas, 1556. P338
The first French edition.

Polo, Marco. The most noble and famous travels of Marcus Paulus. London, Ralph Newbery, 1579. P339
The first English edition, a translation from the Spanish by John Frampton.

Pombal, Sebastião José de Carvalho e Melo, Marquês de. Elogio de D. Luiz Carlos Ignacio Xavier de Menezes, quinto conde da Ericeira, primeiro marquez do Louriçal ... Lisbon, Miguel Rodrigues, 1757. P340
A eulogy on the life of the marquez do Louriçal who served as Portuguese viceroy of India in 1717-21 and 1740-42, concerned primarily with administrative and military events in Portuguese India.

Pombal, Sebastião José de Carvalho e Melo, Marquês de. Instrucçoens que El Rey meu senhor manda dar pelo real erário ao governador, e capitaõ general da capitania de Sao Paulo ... Manuscript. [Lisbon] 7 January 1775. P341
Concerns primarily economic matters in the administration of the capitania of Sao Paulo.

Pombal, Sebastião José de Carvalho e Melo, Marquês de. Relaçaõ abbreviada da republica, que os Religiosos Jesuitas das Provincias de Portugal, e Hespanha, estabeleceraõ nos Dominios Ultramarinos das duas Monarchias, e da Guerra ... [Paris? 1758?] P342
A bill of particulars against the Jesuits in Paraguay citing deeds considered against the interests of the Portuguese, the Spanish, and the Indians. The text is in Portuguese and French.

Pomet, Pierre. Histoire generale des drogues. Paris, Jean-Baptiste Loyson, & Augustin Pillon, 1694. P343
A well-illustrated catalog of spices and drugs, chiefly of the East and West Indies, and a guide to trade in medicinal products.

Ponce, Nicolas. Recueil de vues des lieux principaux de la colonie françoise de Saint-Domingue, gravées par les soins de M. Ponce ... le tout principalement destiné à l'ouvrage intitulé: Loix et constitutions des colonies françoises de l'Amerique sous le vent ... Paris, M. Moreau de Saint-Méry, M. Ponce, M. Phelipeau, 1791.   P344

A superb collection of maps, plans, and views of the French colony at Saint Domingue prior to the rebellions of the 1790s which destroyed much of it.

[Poncelin de La Roche-Tilhac, Jean-Charles.] Tableau du commerce, et des possessions des Européans en Asie et en Afrique ... Ouvrage destiné à servir de suite à l'État physique, politique, ecclesiastique & militaire de l'Amérique. Paris, l'Auteur & Lamy, 1783.   P345

Includes geographical, historical, and commercial information, with particular reference to European holdings in Asia and Africa.

Poncino, Alvise. Autograph letter signed to Guiscardo da Carminate. Manuscript in Italian. Lodi, 21 September 1503.   P346

A letter of mercantile interest, received in Venice 25 September 1503.

Pontanus, Johannes Isacius. Rerum et urbis Amstelodamensium historia. Amsterdam, J. Hondius, 1611.   P347

A history of Amsterdam which contains accounts of Dutch explorations in the East Indies and also reports of the attempts to find a Northeast Passage.

Pontanus, Johannes Isacius. Historische beschrijvinghe der seer wijt beroemde coop-stadt Amsterdam. Amsterdam, Jodocus Hondius, 1614.   P348

The first Dutch edition.

Pontanus, Johannes Isacius. Joh. Isacii Pontani Discussionum historicarum libri duo, quibus praecipuè quatenus & quodnam mare liberum vel non liberum clausumque accipiendum dispicitur expenditurque ... Hardewijck, Nicolaus à Wieringen, 1637.   P349

A treatise on maritime law based primarily on Scandinavian medieval maritime experience. Also included is a discussion of the location of Ophir.

Pontoppidan, Carl. Hval-og robbefangsten udi Strat-Davis, ved Spitsbergen, og under Eilandet Jan Mayn. Copenhagen, F.W. Thiele, 1785.   P350

A summary of the whaling and seal-hunting industries of Denmark by the government official in charge of that branch of the nation's economy.

Pontoppidan, Carl. Magazin for almeenyttige bidrag till kundskab om indretninger og forfatninger i de Kongelige Danske stater. Copenhagen, Sebastian Popp, 1792.   P351

An extensive coverage of Danish trade with Greenland, Iceland, the Faero Islands and other aspects of the Danish economy.

Pontoppidan, Erich. Det første forsøg paa Norges naturlige historie. Copenhagen, Berlingske Arvingers Bogtrykkerie, 1752; Kongelige Wäysenhuses Bogtrykkerie, 1753.   P352

An extensive survey of the plant and animal life of Norway with chapters also on the climate, minerals, and people.

[Pontoppidan, Erich.] Eutropii Philadelphi oeconomiske balance eller uforgribelige overslag paa Dannemarks naturlige og borgerlige formue ... Copenhagen, Andreas Hartvig Godiche, 1759.   P353

Pontoppidan comments on the products Denmark exports and which it imports. He stresses the improvement of agriculture and livestock as necessary for Denmark's economic health.

Pope, Charles. A practical abridgment of the laws of the customs, relative to the import, export, and coasting trade of Great Britain and her dependencies. London, For the compiler by A. Strahan, 1813.   P354

A digest of the customs laws for the convenience of merchants.

Popery and tryanny: or, The present state of France: in relation to its government, trade, manners of the people, and nature of the countrey. London, 1679.   P355

The author apparently lived in France. He describes many aspects of French commercial policy, but is particularly interested in the situation of the nobility, bourgeoisie, and peasantry with respect to the French economy.

Popple, Henry. A map of the British Empire in America ... London, S. Harding, 1733.   P356

Depicts in great detail the French and Spanish holdings in the New World as well as British possessions.

[Popple, William.] Respondent's further answer. Manuscript. [London] 5 June, 1753.   P357

A defense of the administration of Governor William Popple of Bermuda against accusations by the Assembly of that colony.

Popular prejudices against the convention and treaty with Spain. London, T. Cooper, 1739.   P358

Concerns the possible results to English trade of a treaty of peace with Spain.

Por el commercio de la ciudad de Sevilla, á cuyo cargo està la renta del almojarifazgo mayor, y demas derechos menores de aquella ciudad, y su partido, en el pleyto con Fernando Cardoso, y Diego Rodriguez Luis. [n.p., 1647?]   P359

Records of a dispute between the authorities of the city of Seville and Fernando Cardoso, a merchant, on the subject of commerce and duties for import and export.

Porcacchi, Thomaso. L'isole piu famose del mondo. Venice, Simon Galignani & Girolamo Porro, 1572. P360

The first edition of a popular island book, containing thirty copper-engraved maps.

Porcacchi, Thomaso. L'isole piu famose del mondo. Venice, Simon Galignani & Girolamo Porro, 1576. P361

The second edition, with seventeen additional maps.

Porcacchi, Thomaso. L'isole piu famose del mondo. Venice, Heredi di Simon Galignani, 1605. P362

The fourth edition of this famous "island book" which relates primarily to the Mediterranean but does include maps and descriptions of Cuba, Hispaniola, Jamaica, Madagascar, Ceylon, and the East Indian archipelago.

Porter, Sir James. Observations on the religion, law, government, and manners of the Turks, to which is added the state of the Turkey trade from its origin to the present time. London, For J. Nourse, 1771. P363

An extensive description of Turkish institutions and social life. The section on trade describes its decline in the eighteenth century, noting as principal cause the change in the charter of the Levant Company.

Porteus, Beilby. A sermon preached before the incorporated Society for the Propagation of the Gospel in Foreign Parts, at their anniversary meeting in the parish church of St. Mary-le-Bow, on Friday, February 21, 1783. London, J.F. and C. Rivington, 1784. P364

The chief concern of this sermon is the missionizing of slaves in the West Indies.

Portlock, Nathaniel. A voyage around the world. London, J. Stockdale and G. Gouldring, 1789. P365

An account of a circumnavigation of 1785-88, including descriptions of trade with North American Indians.

Portlock, Nathaniel. Reis naar de noord-west kust van Amerika. Amsterdam, Matthijs Schalekamp, 1795. P366

A Dutch translation of the account of the Portlock-Dixon circumnavigation. The maps and illustrations, as well as the introduction, are from the account of this voyage by William Beresford.

[Portolan chart of South Atlantic area. Portugal, ca. 1524.] P367

This chart shows the eastern coast of Brazil, including some forty place names, and the coast of Africa from Morocco to the Cape of Good Hope, with about 125 place names.

Portolano del Adriatico e Mediterra. [Italy, XIV century.] P368

A manuscript book of sailing instructions for the Mediterranean Sea, from Constantinople to Lisbon.

Portolano per tutti i navichanti. Venice, B. Rizus, 1490. P369

The first printed book on navigation. The colophon states: "Composed by a Venetian gentleman for the use of all navigators who wish to travel safely."

Portugal. Dom Joam por graça de Deos Rey de Portugal ... faço saber a vòs que eu pasley ora huma ley por min assinada ... Lisbon [s.n.] 1713. P370

A decree by the King stating that all shipwrecks upon the coasts of His dominions shall be the property of the King and under jurisdiction of the royal estate as represented by local authorities.

Portugal. Dom Joseph por graça de Deos Rey de Portugal ... Faço saber aos que esta ley virem, que, mandando examinar ... as verdadeiras causas com que desde o descobrimento do Grão Pará, e Maranhão até agora não só se não tem multiplicado, e civilisado os Indios ... [Lisbon, 1755.] P371

A proclamation from King Joseph (1750-1777) of Portugal restoring the right to liberty, property and the freedom to engage in trade back to the Indians of Grão Pará and Maranhão, Brazil.

Portugal. Dom Phelippe per graça de Deos, Rey de Portugal ... faço saber ... que sendo informado que pellos julgadores ... Lisbon [s.n.] 1607. P372

A law concerning the sentencing of criminals in which no magistrate shall sentence an offender to the galleys unless the gravity of the crime merits a sentence of at least two years.

Portugal. Edit d'expulsion des Jésuites de tous les Etats de la Couronne de Portugal. [Lisbon, 1759.] P373

This is a legalistic yet eloquent statement of the causes of the expulsion of the Jesuits from Portugal including as a major cause their management of the colony in Paraguay.

Portugal. Edit de Sa Majesté Trés-Fidéle la roi de Portugal, par lequel Elle abolit les ecoles d'humanités des Jésuites, défend de se servir de leur méthode d'enseigner, & en prescrit une nouvelle. Lisbon, Michel Rodriguez, 1759. P374

This decree dissolves the Jesuit schools and sets forth a new system of higher education.

Portugal. Eu El Rey faço saber aos que este meu Alvará viré ... Lisbon, Antonio Alvarez, 1643. P375

A charter concerning the minting of patacas (silver currency) and authorizing their minting in several places, including overseas possessions, and standardizing the stampmark and value of the pataca.

Portugal. Eu El Rey faço saber aos que este Alvará com força de lei virem ... [Lisbon?, s.n., 1761] P376
A charter stating the negative influence of the Jesuits on the politics and economy of India.

Portugal. Lettre du roi de Portugal, qui ordonne le séquestre de tous les biens des Jésuites de ses royaumes. Lisbon, Michel Rodregues, 1759. P377
A recitation of the Jesuits' misdeeds in Portugal precedes the announcement of the sequestering of their goods.

Portugal. Ley, porque V. Mag[estade] ha por bem prohibir, q[ue] nenhum Navio, ou Embarcação, de qualquer lote que seja, q[ue] vier do Estado do Brasil, Maranhão, & mais Conquistas, para esta Regno, possa tomar, sem evidente perigo, Porto algu[m] estranho ..., por decreto de Sua Mag[estade] de 27. de Outubro de 684. Lisbon, 1684. P378
Ships sailing to Brazil are not to stop at foreign ports except under stress of storm or pirates.

Portugal. Ley porque V. Magestade ha por bem que na ciudade da Bahia se abra Casa de Moeda, & se lavre nella com novo cunho, & corra sòmente naquelle estado, sem que se possa tirar delle para este reyno, com as penas nella declaradas, pela maneira que acima se declara. [Lisbon, 1694.] P379
A law concerning coinage produced at Bahia from local precious metals.

Portugal. Ley porque Vossa Magestade ha por bem que todo o assucar, que vier das conquistas para este reyno, se peze em hum trapiche, donde haverà ver-o-pezo, & que nas caixas se ponha marca de fogo para se conhecer a qualidade de que he o assucar, na fórma acima declarada, com as penas conteudas nella. [Lisbon, 1688.] P380
A law regulating the price and quality of sugar produced in Brazil.

Portugal. Ley porque Vossa Magestade manda que o estanque do pao brasil corra por conta da fazenda, que se administra pela Junta, na fórma que até agora, & que daqui em diante todo o pao brasil venha nos navios da junta, & não tenha jurisdição para o mandar vir em outros, & que qualquer embarcação, que o trouxer, seja confiscada, & o mesmo pao, & encorra nas mais penas, que nella se declara. [Lisbon, 1697.] P381
The monopoly on brazil wood is reserved to the Junta de Comercio.

Portugal. Ley sobre se nam dar dinheiro, nem quaisquer outras mercadorias arisco das naos da India, aos homés do mar, & officiaes dellas. Lisbon, 1609. P382
A law regulating shipping and merchant ships to India.

Portugal. Manifeste du roi de Portugal, contenant les erreurs impies & séditieuses que les religieux de la Compagnie de Jesus ont enseignées aux criminels qui ont été punis, & qu'ils se sont efforcés de répandre parmi les peuples de ce royaume. Lisbon, Miguel Rodriguez [1759]. P383

Portugal. Regimento da Junta da administraçam do tabaco. Lisbon, Domingos Gonsalves, 1741. P384
A collection of laws indicating new guidelines and procedures for administering the tobacco trade, much of it pertaining to Brazil.

Portugal. Regimento dos contos do reyno, e casa, nesta nova impressam a crescentado com hum alphabeto para nelle se achar com muita facilidade o que contem todos os capitulos. Lisbon, Officina de Valentim da Costa Deslandes, 1708. P385
The work is in 127 chapters which contain a great deal of information regarding Portuguese colonial matters in Africa, India, Brazil, the Azores and Madeira.

Portugal. Casa dos contos. Regimento dos contos. Lisbon, Joam da Costa, 1669. P386
A collection of 127 regulations concerning the treasury of Portugal, with some provisions referring to import and export taxes and regulations.

Portugal. Conselho de estado. Jugement du Conseil Souverain, chargé par Sa Majesté trés-fidéle d'instruire le procès au sujet de l'attentat commis sur sa personne sacrée ... du douze janvier 1759. [n.p., 1759.] P387
The report of a commission of inquiry into a plot on the life of José I of Portugal, implicating the Jesuits whose involvement related to their troubles with the Portuguese government over their mission in Paraguay.

Portugal. Direcção Geral das Alfândegas. Pauta que ha de servir para o despacho da alfandega, e no fim se trata das fazendas ... Lisbon, Bernardo da Costa de Carvalho, 1727. P388
A very extensive table of customs duties to be paid on goods imported into Portugal.

Portugal. Junta de Missoes. Livro dos termos das Juntas de Missoes ... em que se julgavam as liberdades dos Indios ... Manuscript. Para, 1759. P389
A record book consisting chiefly of the minutes of the council which administered the district of Misiones in Brazil and decided cases relating to Indians who were allotted for service to the landowners.

Portugal. Laws, etc. Ordenacam da defeza dos veludos & sedas. [n.p.] 1535. P390

Portugal. Laws, etc.

The king orders that the people of his kingdom, of whatever quality, are not to use cloth containing gold or silver, nor are they to use gold or silver in ornaments or paintings, except in specified cases.

Portugal. Laws, etc. Ley sobre as veias de ouro, prata e outros metaes. [n.p.] 1557. P391
A law setting forth the conditions under which Portuguese citizens could mine for gold.

Portugal. Laws, etc. Ley sobre o nao comprar pao para o tornar a vender. Lisbon, G. Galharde, 1557. P392
A law regulating the sale of grain in Portugal, and in the Azores and Madeira as well.

Portugal. Laws, etc. Ley sobre os arcabuzes pequenos. Lisbon, G. Galharde, 1557. P393
Restricts the importation of small arms.

Portugal. Laws, etc. O Primeiro - [quinto] livro das ordenaçoes. [Lisbon, Manuel Joam, 1565.] P394
The final edition of Portugal's basic code of laws, promulgated in 1521, and remaining relatively unchanged until 1603.

Portugal. Laws, etc. Artigos das sisas novamente emendados per mandado del rei nosso senhor. Lisbon, Manuel Joam, 1566. P395
A statement of Portuguese excise taxes in force under Sebastian, with a section indicating taxes on cloth put into effect by his predecessors, John II (1481-95) and Manuel I (1495-1521).

Portugal. Laws, etc. Leis extravagantes. Lisbon, Antonio Gonçalvez, 1569. P396
A collection of Portuguese laws, mostly from the first half of the sixteenth century, including provisions relating to Guinea, India, and Brazil.

Portugal. Laws, etc. Ley sobre os vestidos de seda, & feytios delles. Lisbon, 1570. P397
Regulates the wearing of cloth with silk, gold, or silver ornaments.

Portugal. Laws, etc. Leys, e provisoes, que el rey dom Sebastiã nosso senhor fez depois que começou á governar. Lisbon, Francisco Correa, 1570. P398
The laws of Sebastian contain several relating to Portuguese overseas enterprises, including the Indian drug trade, missionary activity in China and Japan, and fortifications in Africa.

Portugal. Laws, etc. Dom Philippe per graça de Deos, Rey de Portugal ... Faço saber aos que esta ley ... no principio contra os degradados que não cumprem o degredo em que forão cõ[n]denados para sempre para o Brasil, auia tambem lugarnos degradados para sempre para as Galés ... Lisbon, 1603. P399

The law states that persons exiled to Brazil must comply with the sentence or face execution.

Portugal. Laws, etc. Provisam para nam virem escravos da India. Lisbon, 1618. P400
Includes three laws relating to trade with India.

Portugal. Laws, etc. Ley sobre nam dar dinheiro a risco dos navios que navegam para as partes ultramarinas. [Lisbon, ca. 1623.] P401
A law preventing the insuring of ships sailing from Lisbon, since it had been discovered that these ships did not defend themselves.

Portugal. Laws, etc. Eu Elrey faço saber aos que este meu Alvara virem, que considerando o damno, que se me representou recebe minha fazenda real, & os homes de negocio ... [Lisbon, 1655.] P402
Records are to be kept in the Lisbon customs house of all proposed overseas voyages, and a commission of three men must keep account there of all moneys taken out of the country.

Portugal. Laws, etc. Dom João por graça de Deos, Rey de Portugal ... na navegaçaõ das ilhas adjacentes ao reyno para o Brazil ... [Lisbon, 1736.] P403
A royal decree placing restrictions upon the commerce between Brazil and the Portuguese Atlantic Islands due to the loss of gold to other countries through this trade.

Portugal. Laws, etc. Dom João por graça de Deos, Rey de Portugal ... que no regimento da Junta da Administraçaõ do Tabaco ... [Lisbon, 1736.] P404
A decree prohibiting the introduction of foreign tobacco into Portugal and her possessions, with particular emphasis on Brazil.

Portugal. Laws, etc. Collecção das leys, decretos, e alvarás. Lisbon, Antonio Rodrigues Galhardo [etc.] [1750-1800]. P405
A collection of 964 documents bound in six volumes. Included are numerous items relating to Portuguese overseas commerce.

Portugal. Laws, etc. Alvará de ley, porque V Magestade ha por bem tomar debaixo da sua real protecçaõ o contrato dos diamantes do Brasil, e fazer exclusivo o comercio das referidas pedras, na forma, que nelle se declara. [Lisbon, 1753.] P406

Portugal. Laws, etc. El rey nosso senhor, attendendo às representaçoes dos moradores das Ilhas dos Açores, que lhe tem pedido mande tirar dellas o numero de cazaes, que for servido, e transportallos a America ... [Lisbon, ca. 1755.] P407
A decree setting forth conditions under which persons would be encouraged to emigrate from the Azores to Brazil.

Portugal. Laws, etc. Estatutos da Junta do Commercio ordendos por el Rey ... Lisbon, Miguel Rodriguez, 1756. P408
   Statutes regulating the trade of Portugal with its overseas colonies and companies.

Portugal. Laws, etc. Alvará ... pelo qual V Magestade he servida mandar estabelecer huma prompta, e segura communicaçao deste reino com os dominios ultramarinos do Brazil, e das ilhas, por meio de paquetes. [Lisbon, 1798.] P409

Portugal. Laws, etc. Alvará, por que Vossa Magestade ... he servida erigir em villa o Araial da Campanha do Rio Verde na capitanía de Minas Geraes, e crear nella o Lugar de Juiz de Fóra, Civel, Crime e Orfãos, com os ordenados, e emolumentos ... [Lisbon, 1799.] P410

Portugal. Laws, etc. Alvará com força de lei, pelo qual Vossa Alteza Real, tendo consideraçao ao abatimento, e decadencia em que achão as mina de ouro e diamantes no Brazil ... [Lisbon] Regia Officina Typographica [1803]. P411
   Provides for the reorganization of the administration of gold and diamond production in Brazil.

Portugal. Sovereign (1598-1621 : Philip II). Treslado do regimento, que Sua Magestade passou, por el le assinado, & passado pella Chãcellaria, para o novo tribunal, do conselho do estado da India, & dos mais ultramarinos: & foy concertado com o proprio original. [Lisbon, 1604.] P412
   This is an order from Philip III of Spain and Portugal in which he sets forth the administrative machinery for a new agency for managing most of the Portuguese overseas territories.

Portugal. Sovereign (1598-1621 : Philip II). Dom Phelippe per graça de Deos Rey de Portugal ... Faço saber a vós Corregedor da Comarqua, & Correyção de cidade de Coimbra; que eu passey ora hũ meu Aluará per mim assignado ... [Lisbon, 1605.] P413
   Portuguese shippers, because of the hostilities between Spain and the Netherlands, were forbidden to trade with Holland or Zeeland, to employ Dutch sailors, or to trade with the Dutch in Brazil, since Portugal was then under Spanish domination.

Portugal. Sovereign (1598-1621 : Philip II). Sobre os oficiaes da justiça que cometerem erros em seu oficio. Lisbon, 1614. P414
   Concerns delinquency among Portuguese officials.

Portugal. Sovereign (1640-1656 : John IV). Brief van credentie ... ghesonden ... aende staten van Catalogne. Middelburg, Weduwe ende erffghenamen van Symon Moulert [1640]. P415
   The independence of Portugal from Spain was of interest to the Dutch West India Company due to their rivalry in Brazil. This interest undoubtedly accounts for this translation of a letter from the Portuguese King to the Catalonians, who also wished independence.

Portugal. Sovereign (1640-1656 : John IV). Que eu passei ora hũa ley por mi assinada, & passada por minha Chancellaria, da qual o treslado he o seguinte. [Lisbon, 1648.] P416
   This law prohibited the export of money to Brazil without license and registration.

Portugal. Sovereign (1656-1683 : Alfonso VI). Acte van authorisatie voor Don Ferdinando Telles de Faro on de vrede ... Dordrecht, Pieter Verstraten, 1658. P417
   A letter from the Portuguese queen to her ambassador in the Netherlands, urging him to conclude peace as quickly as possible.

Portugal. Sovereign (1656-1683 : Alfonso VI). Alvarà virem ... para entregar seis mil moyos de trigo, & onze mil de cevada. Lisbon, 1663. P418
   Provision for the importing of grain.

Portugal. Sovereign (1683-1706 : Pedro II). Alvarà virem ... sobre a prohibição do dinheiro, prata, & ouro para o estado do Brazil. Lisbon, 1695. P419
   Regulations upon coinage in Brazil.

Portugal. Sovereign (1683-1706 : Pedro II). Ley virem ... pela Junta da Administração do Tabaco. Lisbon, 1700. P420
   A law designed to prevent embezzling of tobacco.

Portugal. Sovereign (1683-1706 : Pedro II). Alvarà de ley virem ... a introducção dos tabacos estrangeiros. Lisbon, 1706. P421
   A law designed to prevent smuggling of tobacco.

Portugal. Sovereign (1706-1750 : John V). Eu el-Rey faço saber ãos que este meu alvará em forma de ley ... que a junta de Companhia Gèral do Commercio do Brasil. [n.p., ca. 1720.] P422
   This document appears to divest the directors of the company of some of their responsibilities, particularly with respect to the maintenance of convoys.

Portugal. Sovereign (1706-1750 : John V). Alvarà em fórma de ley, pelo qual V. Magestade ha por bem ordenar se naõ abraõ novos caminhos, ou picadas para as minas em que jà houver fórma de arrecadaçaõ du sua real fazenda, nem por estes caminhos, ou picadas, prohibidas por esta ley ... [Lisbon, 1733.] P423
   The law prohibits new roads which were giving illegal access to the mines in Brazil.

Portugal. Sovereign (1706-1750 : John V). Dom Joaõ por graça de Deos, Rey de Portugal ... Faço saber aos que esta minha ley virem ... em que fuy servido supprimir o tribunal da junta do commercio, que todo o ouro, que viesse do Brasil ... Lisbon, 1735. P424
Regulation concerning gold mined in Brazil.

Portugal. Sovereign (1706-1750 : John V). Carta do lugar de corregedor do civel da rellaçam da Bahia deque Magestade merce an Doutor Bento da Costa de Oliveyra Sam Payo dezembargador da mesma Rellaçam ella maneyra que aüme Se declara, 1740 Nov. 23. Manuscript. Portugal, 1740. P425

Portugal. Sovereign (1750-1777 : Joseph). Decreto sobre os direitos, que deve pagar o assucar nas alfandegas deste reino. [Lisbon, 1751.] P426
Noting abuses in the tobacco and sugar trades in Brazil, the king decrees reform in their management.

Portugal. Sovereign (1750-1777 : Joseph). Regimento das cazas de inspecção. Lisbon, 1751. P427
A law establishing centers for inspection of ships at Bahia, Rio de Janeiro, Pernambuco, and Maranhao.

Portugal. Sovereign (1750-1777 : Joseph). Regimento das intendencias, e casas de fundição. Lisbon, 1751. P428
Regulations upon mining in Brazil.

Portugal. Sovereign (1750-1777 : Joseph). Alvará ... que aos donos engenhos, e lavradores de assucar, e tabaco do estado do Brasil. Lisbon, 1756. P429
A regulation upon the trade in sugar and tobacco in Brazil.

Portugal. Sovereign (1750-1777 : Joseph). Instructions de Sa Majesté Tres-Fidele, a son ministre en cour de Rome, du 8 octobre 1757, du 10 février 1758 & du 20 avril 1759. [n.p., 1759.] P430
Letters from the Portuguese minister to the Papacy and from the Portuguese king, José I, comprising indictments against the Jesuits in Paraguay and Brazil.

Portugal. Sovereign (1777-1816 : Maria I). [Alfandega de Lisboa e Casa da India.] Manuscript. [Lisbon, 1780.] P431
A compilation of Portuguese laws going back to the fourteenth century, relating to the development of customs regulations for Lisbon's trade and the commerce with Portugal's overseas empire.

Portugal. Treaties, etc. Accort ende articulen tusschen de croone van Portugal ende de Staten Generael. Amsterdam, F. Lieshout, 1641. P432
An addition to the truce between the Dutch and Portuguese, settling the right of free trade between the territories of the two countries, chiefly in Brazil.

Portugal. Treaties, etc. Extract uyt d'articulen van het tractaet van bestant ... tusschen ... Portugael ... ende de ... Staten Generael. Amsterdam, F. Lieshout, 1641. P433
Terms of the truce between the Dutch and Portuguese, calling for the restoration of normal commercial relations.

Portugal. Treaties, etc. Trattado das tregoas suspensão de todo o acto de hostilidade ... a XII de Junho 1641. The Hague, H.J. van Wouw, 1642. P434
The treaty was designed to end hostilities in Brazil, but delay in ratification enabled the Dutch to continue the war which was largely in the interests of the West India Company.

Portugal. Treaties, etc. Translaet uyt het Latijn inde Nederlandsche tale. Provisioneel ende particulier tractaet. The Hague, Weduwe ende erfgenamen van wijlen H.J. van Wouw, 1645. P435
A treaty between the Netherlands and Portugal resolving differences growing out of trade rivalry in the East Indies.

Portugal. Treaties, etc. Articulen van vrede ende confoederatie gheslotten tusschen ... Portugael ... ende de ... Vereenighde Nederlanden. The Hague, Hillebrandt van Wouw, 1663. P436
A series of agreements concerning commerce, chiefly in the colonial possessions of the signatories.

Portugal. Treaties, etc. Articuli pacis et confoederationis, inter ... Lusitaniae ... & ... Foederati Belgii Ordines ... The Hague, H. J. van Wouw, 1663. P437
A treaty involving France, the Netherlands, and Portugal concerning the sugar, tobacco, and other colonial trades.

Portugal. Treaties, etc. Tratado de limites das conquistas entre os muito altos, e poderosos senhores D. Joaõ V Rey de Portugal e D. Fernando VI Re de Espanha ... Assignado em Madrid a 13 de Janeiro de 1750. Lisbon, 1750. P438
The Treaty of Madrid set forth the boundaries in disputed areas between Spanish and Portuguese possessions in South America. The volume also includes earlier treaties, including the Treaty of Tordesillas, 1494.

Portugal. Treaties, etc. Tratado preliminar de paz, e de limites na America Meridional, relativo aos estados que nella possuem as coroas de Portugal, e de Hespanha ... assinado em Madrid pelos plenipotenciarios de Suas Magestades ... em o primeiro de Outubro de MDCCLXXVII, e ratificado por ambas as Maestades. Lisbon, Regia Officina Typografica, 1777. P439
The treaty settling disputes between Spain and Portugal over territories lying between Brazil and Paraguay.

Portugal. Treaties, etc. Tratado de alliança defensiva entre os muito altos, e podersos senhores Dona Maria Rainha de Portugal e Dom Carlos III Rei de Hespanha, assinado em Madrid ... em onze de Março de MDCCLXXVIII ... Lisbon, Regia Officina Typografica, 1778. P440

This treaty reaffirms some of the articles of treaties made in 1668, 1715, and 1763. It also concerns the commercial rights of the two countries in South America and in West Africa, and trade in slaves and tobacco.

Portugal. Treaties, etc. Tratado de amizade, navegaçao, e commercio entre as muito altas, e muito poderosas senhoras Dona Maria I Rainha de Portugal e Catharina II Imperatriz de todas as Russias, assinado em Petersburgo ... em 9/20 de Dezembro de MDCCLXXXVII e ratificado por ambas as magestades. Lisbon, Regia Officina Typographica, 1789. P441

This treaty between Portugal and Russia covers the normal matters of customs duties, consular affairs, shelter from storm and pirates, neutrality, etc., and also contains specific provisions for trade in salt, wine, indigo, tobacco, olive oil and cloth.

Portugal. Treaties, etc. Tractado de paz e amizade entre ... Dom João Principe Regente de Portugal, e o illustrissimo senhor Jusef Bax Carmanaly, Regente, e Governador de Tripoli, assignado em Tripoli, em 14 de Maio de M.DCC.XCIX. [Lisbon] Regia Officina Typografica, 1799. P442

This treaty establishing peace between Portugal and Tripoli was negotiated on behalf of the Regent, João, who was then living in Brazil, by Donald Campbell, a British naval officer.

Portugal. Treaties, etc. Tratado de amizade, de navegação, e de commercio renovado entre Portugal e a Russia, e assignado em Petersburgo aos 27/16 de Dezembro de 1798. St. Petersburg, Typographia Imperial, 1799. P443

Renewal of a treaty of 1787, with provision for exchange of consular officers and other matters to facilitate trade between two countries.

Portugalesische Schlacht und gewisse Zeitung aus Madrill und Lisabona samt leidigem Fall dem König aus Portugal den fünfften Augusti dieses lauffenden 1578. Leipzig [Johannem Beyer] 1578. P444

An account of the battle of Alcácer-Kebir in 1578 in which the Portuguese monarch Sebastian I was killed, along with two north African rulers who were his allies on this occasion.

Poser und Gross Nedlitz, Heinrich von. Tage Buch seiner Reise von Constantinopel aus durch die Bulgarey, Armenien, Persien und Indien. Jena, Samuel Krebsen, 1675. P445

This account of travel into Asia during the years 1621-24 contains numerous observations on eastern cities and their commerce.

Possevino, Antonio. Antonii Possevini Mantuani Societatis Jesu, Apparatus ad omnium gentium historiam ... Venice, J. Bapt. Ciottum, 1597. P446

A reference work on classical, medieval and early modern universal histories, with a section on writings on Asia, Africa, and America and a study of geography and navigation.

Possevino, Antonio. Moscovia. Vilna, Joannem Velicensem, 1586. P447

One of the most important sixteenth-century accounts of Russia, written by a papal legate to Ivan the Terrible who traveled to Russia in 1581-82. This account is his report to Pope Gregory.

Possevino, Antonio. Moscovia. Antwerp, Christophori Plantini, 1587. P448

The second edition.

Postel, Guillaume. Cosmographicae disciplinae compendium, in suum finem, hoc est ad Divinae Providentiae certissimam demonstrationem conductum. Basel, Joannem Oporinum, 1561. P449

A compendium of renaissance geography, noting some of the new discoveries, the peoples of the world, the extent of Christendom, and descriptions of the continents and major islands.

Postel, Guillaume. De originibus, seu, de varia et potissimum orbi latino ad hanc diem incognita. Basel, Joannes Oporinus, 1553. P450

A description of the peoples of the Near East and parts of Asia by a traveler learned in eastern languages.

Postel, Guillaume. Syriae descriptio. [Paris] Hieronymus Gormont, 1540. P451

A pilgrimage book with considerable geographical information written by a student of eastern cultures.

[Postlethwayt, Malachy.] The African trade, the great pillar and support of the British plantation in America. London, J. Robinson, 1745. P452

A plea for an increased annual subsidy to the African Company, guaranteed by Parliament, in order to save the African trade and thus prohibit "the total ruin of all the British Plantations in America."

Postlethwayt, Malachy. Britain's commercial interest explained and improved, in a series of dissertations on several important branches of her trade and policy. London, D. Browne [etc.] 1757. P453

A review of the commercial situation of Great Britain, particularly with respect to the challenge of France, taking into account the economies of the North American

Postlethwayt, Malachy colonies, the East India Company, and the African trade, as well as the economic problems of the British Isles.

Postlethwayt, Malachy. Great-Britain's true system. London, A. Millar, J. Whiston, B. White, and W. Sandby, 1757. P454

The author proposes close relations with the Netherlands and the German states through commercial connections. He favors a program of payment for war supplies on a yearly basis so as to avoid a large national debt with heavy interest payments which would be injurious to trade.

Postlethwayt, Malachy. In honour to the administration. The importance of the African expedition considered: with copies of the memorials, as drawn up originally, and presented to the ministry ... To which are added observations, illustrating the said memorials ... London, C. Say, 1758. P455

A plan for destroying French commercial power by striking at West Africa which the author believes is the source of much French trade because of the dependence of other French overseas territories upon it.

[Postlethwayt, Malachy.] The national and private advantages of the African trade considered. London, J. and P. Knapton, 1746. P456

An expansion of arguments in a previous pamphlet asking for Parliament's aid in saving the African trade, with the addition of descriptions of the Guinea area and forts and settlements there.

Postlethwayt, Malachy. A short state of the progress of the French trade and navigation. London, J. Knapton, 1756. P457

A detailed look at French industry and commerce with a view to the ways in which they support French maritime and naval power.

[Potgieter, Barent Jansz.] Journael van 't geene vijf schepen, van Rotterdam, in 't jaer 1598, den 27 Juny, na de Straet Magalanes varende, over gekomen is, tot den 21. January 1600 ... Amsterdam, Gillis Joosten Saeghman, [1663?]. P458

An account of an abortive voyage to the East Indies by one of a fleet of five ships, the ship commanded by Seebald de Weert going no further than the Strait of Magellan.

[Pottier de La Hestroye.] Réfléxions sur la traité de la dîme royale. [n.p.] 1716. P459

A criticism of Marshal Vauban's "royal tithe." An essay on means to improve French trade to Africa and the West Indies is also included.

Pouchot, François. Mémoires sur la derniere guerre de l'Amerique Septentrionale. Yverdon, 1781. P460

A description of the hostilities between the French and English in North America, 1754-60, with accounts of the natural resources and topography of Canada.

Pouchot de Chantassin, Claude-Michel. Des königl. frantzösischen Admirals Herrn du Quesne Reise nach Ost-Indien. Hamburg, Gottfried Liebernickel, 1696. P461

An account of a French fleet's actions in the Indian Ocean against Dutch and English shipping. It also includes descriptions of French establishments in India.

[Pouchot de Chantassin, Claude-Michel.] Relation du voyage et retour des Indes Orientales, pendant les années 1690 & 1691. Paris, Veuve Coignard; Brussels, George de Backer, 1692. P462

An account of naval actions against Dutch and English ships by a fleet commanded by Abraham DuQuesne, the Younger. The author, a seaman, describes Pondichéry, Ceylon, and several small islands in the Indian Ocean.

Poullain, Henri. Traitez des monnoyes. Paris, Frederic Leonard, 1709. P463

Written in the early seventeenth century, this treatise comments on the problem of maintaining values between gold and silver due to the influx of silver from South American mines.

Poullet. Nouvelles relations du Levant. Paris, L. Billaine, 1668. P464

Contains accounts of mercantile activity in the Levant, particularly by Dutch traders.

Pownall, Thomas. The administration of the colonies, wherein their rights and constitution are discussed and stated. London, For J. Walter, 1768. P465

An extensive treatise urging a union between Great Britain and her American colonies which would take account of the economic realities which make them essential to each other, with plans for setting up and administering such a union.

Pownall, Thomas. A letter from Governor Pownall to Adam Smith, L.L.D. F.R.S. Being an examination of several points of doctrine, laid down in his "Inquiry into the nature and causes of the wealth of nations." London, J. Almon, 1776. P466

A thoughtful critique, taking issue with Smith on several major points, particularly with respect to the application of Smith's ideas to British policy in America.

[Pownall, Thomas.] A memorial, most humbly addressed to the sovereigns of Europe, on the present state of affairs between the Old and the New World. London, J. Almon, 1780. P467

The author urges acceptance of the fact that America was indeed an independent force in the world, made so by its geography and the individual freedoms prevailing there. He predicts that Europe's commerce will be greatly influenced by the American market.

[Pownall, Thomas.] Pensées sur la révolution de l'Amérique-Unie, extraites de l'ouvrage anglois,

intituleé Mémoire, adressé aux souverains de l'Europe, sur l'état présent des affaires de l'Ancien & du Nouveau-Monde. Amsterdam, Harreveld [etc.] [1781]. P468
  The French translation, brought out at the instance of John Adams, of a version of Pownall's book published by Edmund Jenings, which version was repudiated by Pownall. This translation contains an extended preface by the editor.

Pownall, Thomas. The right, interest, and duty of the state, as concerned in the affairs of the East Indies. London, S. Bladon, 1773. P469
  An analysis of the relationship of the East India Company to the British government at a time when the company was bankrupt.

Pownall, Thomas. A topographical description of ... North america. London, J. Almon, 1776. P470
  Contains a map portraying central North America as far west as the Mississippi River.

Poyntz, John. The present prospect of the famous and fertile island of Tobago. London, George Larkin, 1683. P471
  An evaluation of the productivity of Tobago and its aptness for settlement.

Poyntz, John. The present prospect of the famous and fertile island of Tobago. London, J. Astwood, 1695. P472
  The second edition.

Poyntz, John. Proposals offered ... for the incouragement of settling a joint stock of 40000 acres in the island of Tobago in America. [n.p., 1695.] P473
  This broadside invites subscribers for a colonial undertaking, with grants of land promised and opportunity for trade in goods and slaves.

Praatje in't ronde, of verhaal van een gesprek voorgevallen in Den Hage ... Dordrecht, J. Redelijckhuisen, 1669. P474
  A discussion of the various Dutch trading companies and their relations with the English.

Prade, Jean Le Royer, sieur de. Discours du tabac, où il est traité particulierement du tabac en poudre. Paris, Jean Jombert, 1693. P475
  A discourse on the growing of tobacco, its manufacture into snuff, and the medicinal effects of its use.

Prahl, B. De Nicobariske Øers naervaerende tilstand samt rytten for den Danske handel at befolde samme. Copenhagen, J.F. Schultz, 1804. P476
  The Danes maintained a mission in the Nicobar Islands, and this book is an attempt to interest Danish merchants in trade there.

Pray, György. Georgii Pray Historia controversiarum de ritibus Sinicis ab [ear]um origine ad finem compendio deducta. Budapest & Kassa, Bibliopolio Strohmayeriano, 1789. P477
  A documentary history of the Chinese Rites controversy.

Précis pour les grands propriétaires des colonies françaises de l'Amérique. [n.p., 1785.] P478
  An argument on behalf of free trade in the French colonies of North America.

Préfontaine, Chevalier de. Maison rustique, a l'usage des habitans de la partie de la France équinoxiale, connue sous le nom de Cayenne. Paris, Cl. J.B. Bauche, 1763. P479
  A handbook of information on the products, agriculture, and techniques for settlement and administration of plantations in Guiana by a long-time resident of that country.

Prejugez legitimes en faveur du decret de N.S. pere le pape Alexandre VII. et de la pratique des Jesuites, au sujet des honneurs que les Chinois rendent a Confucius et a leurs ancestres ... [n.p.] 1700. P480
  A collection of statements relating to the Chinese Rites controversy from Dominican and Franciscan sources.

The preliminaries productive of a premunire. London, H. Carpenter [1748]. P481
  A protest against England's negotiations in the treaty of Aix la Chapelle. Preliminary terms appeared to be detrimental to England's trade.

[Prescott, Benjamin.] A free and calm consideration of the unhappy misunderstandings and debates ... between the Parliament of Great Britain and these American colonies. Salem, S. and E. Hall, 1774. P482
  A statement of colonial grievances, including both political and economic complaints, contained in eight letters to persons in England.

The present state of Holland, or a description of the United Provinces. London, For a company of booksellers; Leyden, J. Arnold Langerak, 1745. P483
  A detailed and approving description of the Netherlands by an Englishman long resident there, noting antiquities, buildings and monuments, economic, religious, and political institutions as well as cultural aspects.

The present state of politicks in Europe. With some observations on the present posture of our own affairs. London, T. Cooper, 1739. P484
  Largely concerned with overseas matters, notably British relations with Spain and Russia.

The present state of Scotland consider'd. Edinburgh, W. and T. Ruddimans, 1745. P485

460 Present state of

A cure for Scotland's impoverished state is seen in a greater awareness on the part of the upper classes to encourage the development of manufactures.

The present state of the British and French trade to Africa and America consider'd and compar'd ... London, E. Comyns, 1745.   P486
A booklet written to encourage the British government to adopt trade policies which would encourage commerce. Heavy duties upon trade are especially deplored.

The present state of the British Empire in Europe, America, Africa, and Asia. London, W. Griffin [etc.] 1768.   P487
A survey of the entire British Empire, in which each region is described with respect to land, inhabitants, industry, and natural products.

The present state of the country and inhabitants, Europeans and Indians, of Louisiana. London, J. Millan, 1744.   P488
A description of the Mississippi valley by a Frenchman living in New Orleans. The many products of the region are described, as are trade connections with Canada and the West Indies.

The present state of the revenues and forces, by sea and land, of France and Spain. Compar'd with those of Great Britain ... London, Tho. Cooper, 1740.   P489
The anonymous author contends that the combined forces of France and Spain are not equal to those of Britain, and therefore a more forceful policy toward them in America is justified.

The present state of the West-Indies. London, R. Baldwin, 1778.   P490
A description of the West Indies, noting historical, geographical, economic, and political features of Spanish, English, French, and Danish possessions.

[Pretty, Francis.] Beschryvinge vande overtreffelijcke ende wijdtvermaerde zeevaerdt vanden ... Meester Thomas Candish. Amsterdam, Cornelis Claesz, 1598.   P491
The first published account of the circumnavigation of the earth by Cavendish, including also the narrative of Drake's and Hawkins' West Indian voyage of 1595.

[Prévost, abbé.] Histoire générale des voyages, ou Nouvelle collection de toutes les relations de voyages, par mer et par terre, qui ont été publiées jusqu'a present ... Paris, Didot [etc.] 1746-1770.   P492
A nineteen-volume collection of exploration literature.

[Prévost, abbé.] Voyages du capitaine Robert Lade en differentes parties de l'Afrique, de l'Asie et de l'Amerique. Paris, Didot, 1744.   P493
Probably an account of an imaginary voyage describing Dutch, English, and Spanish colonies.

[Preyel, Adam.] Abentheur von allerhand Mineralien, Wurzeln, Kraütern, Stauden, Blumen, Rohren und Baümen ... von Gebäwen, Sitten und Geschichten, welche in dem uhralten Königreich Sina, auch in Europa gefunden werden ... Frankfurt, Wilhelm Serlin und George Fickwirth, 1656.   P494
A vast compendium of information on China, making comparisons with Europe, and including some information pertaining to other areas.

Price, Charles. Case of Charles Price, merchant, and others; owners and freighters of the ship *Andaluzia*. [London, ca. 1689.]   P495
A review of a case in which the defendants were accused of interloping upon the East India trade and were forced to make settlement with the East India Company.

Price, Joseph. Five letters from a free merchant in Bengal to Warren Hastings. London [J. Williams] 1778.   P496
This is an attack on the East India Company's polices and practices, though Price argues the advantages of the company's monopoly and supports its charter renewal. He gives a history of European actions in India and is particularly concerned about the growing French influence.

Price, Joseph. A short commercial and political letter to Charles James Fox on the subject of his Asiatic bills, now pending in parliament. London, J. Stockdale, 1783.   P497
A criticism of bills then pending in Parliament which would promote free trade in opium and restrict the import of salt into Bengal.

[Price, Joseph.] A vindication of Gen. Richard Smith, chairman of the Select Committee of the House of Commons. London, For the Author, 1783.   P498
This tract is primarily concerned with the manner in which British East Indian commerce is to be governed, and defends Warren Hastings' administration in India against attacks by Burke and others.

Price, Richard. Observations on the importance of the American Revolution, and the means of making it a benefit to the world. To which is added, a letter from M. Turgot ... with an appendix containing the will of M. Fortuné Ricard, lately published in France. Dublin, For L. White [etc.] 1785.   P499
Price sees in the American Revolution the best hope of the world for liberal government, and offers advice to Americans on how to preserve their freedom and develop liberal institutions.

Price, Richard. Aanmerkingen over de gewigtigheid der staatsomwenteling in Noord-Amerika ... uit het Fransch vertaald. Amsterdam, Johannes Weppelman, 1785.   P500
Dutch edition of Richard Price's *Observations on the importance of the American Revolution*, including

Turgot's letter to Price which was a response to his *Observations on the nature of civil liberty*.

Price, Richard. Aanmerkingen over den aart der burgerlyke vryheid, over de gronden der regeering, en over de regtveerdigheid en staatkunde van den oorlog met Amerika. Leiden, L. Herding, 1776.　　　　　　　　　　P501
Dutch edition of *On the nature of civil liberty* which had strong influence on behalf of the American Revolution. This fifth edition is dated only five weeks after the first.

Price, Richard. Nadere aanmerkingen over den aart en de waarde der burgerlyke vryheid en eener vrye regeering ... uit het Engelsch vertaald ... door Johan Derk baron van der Capellen ... Leyden, Herdingh, 1777.　　　　P502
The first Dutch edition of Price's *Observations on civil liberty*.

[Price lists. Various places of publication, 1700-1800.]　　　　　　　　　　　　　P503
A collection of published price lists noting East and West Indian goods for sale by different companies in various European ports.

Prices current. Kingston, Jamaica, 26 June 1803.
　　　　　　　　　　　　　　　　　　P504
The printed form lists thirty-two exports and twelve imports with prevailing prices supplied in manuscript. An autographed letter from James M. Henry to merchants in Portsmouth, N.H. commenting on the depressed state of the market in Jamaica is appended.

[Prices current for cotton and indigo on Isle de France.] Port Nord-Ouest, Isle de France, F.N. Bolle [1796].　　　　　　　　　　　P505
A monthly statement of prices for cotton and indigo on Mauritius from January, 1792 to September, 1796.

Primor e honra da vida soldadesca no estado da India. Lisbon, Jorge Rodrigues, 1630.　　P506
This eulogy to the soldiers of empire apparently was written long before it was published. It contains numerous accounts of service by individuals in the establishment and maintenance of the Portuguese possessions in India.

Prince, Thomas. A chronological history of New-England in the form of annals ... Boston, Kneeland and Green for S. Gerrish, 1736.
　　　　　　　　　　　　　　　　　　P507
This chronology takes the history of New England to 1630. It is preceded by a general chronological history which includes European and English colonization in the New World.

Prince, Thomas. Extraordinary events in the doings of God, and marvellous in pious eyes. Illustrated in a sermon at the South Church in Boston, N.E. on the general thanksgiving, Thursday, July 18, 1745. Boston, D. Henchman, 1745.　　　　　　　　　　　　　P508
The sermon commemorated the taking of Louisbourg by New England troops and a British naval force.

Principale puncten, die inde voor der handelinghe van den vrede van weghen de E. vermoghende Heeren Staten Generael ... onbegrijpelick sullen geproponeert werden ... [n.p.] 1608.　　　　　　　　　　　　　P509
A list of twenty-eight points to be presented by the Dutch negotiators for peace with Spain. The first demand is reciprocal trade.

Prinsep, John. A letter to the proprietors of East India stock, on the present crisis of the company's affairs. London, J. Debrett, 1793.　　P510
A recommendation that the company's land revenue incomes be kept separate from the commercial account of the company, and that dividends be limited to eight percent.

Prinsep, John. Representation of Mr. John Prinsep, candidate for the succession to the post of superintendant of Bengal cloth investments vacated by Mr. Jacob Blaquiere. [London, 1789.]
　　　　　　　　　　　　　　　　　　P511
In addition to reviewing the case of John Prinsep, a servant of the East India Company, this petition shows the procedures that prevailed in appointments and succession to important positions in the company.

[Prinsep, John.] The right in the West-India merchants to a double monopoly of the sugar market of Great Britain, and the expedience of all monopolies examined. London, Debrett and Heather [1793].　　　　　　　　　　P512
An attack on the sugar monopoly held by the West Indian planters and merchants, and a proposal to supplant it by opening up the British sugar trade to the East India Company, which would bring cheaper supplies from Bengal.

Prinsep, John. Strictures and observations on the Mocurrery system of landed property in Bengal. London, For Debrett [1794].　　　　P513
An argument against allowing lands in Bengal to be administered by Zamindars and favoring a more direct relationship between British authority and landowners.

[Prinsep, John.] Strictures and occasional observations upon the system of British commerce with the East Indies. London, J. Debrett, 1792.
　　　　　　　　　　　　　　　　　　P514
The author's main concern is the establishing of sugar production in Bengal by the East India Company.

[Prior, Matthew.] Memoire ... au sujet de la démolition de Dunkerque, & du canal de Mardyck. [The Hague, T. Johnson, 1714.]
　　　　　　　　　　　　　　　　　　P515
The poet-diplomat requests that France abide by her agreement in the Treaty of Utrecht to destroy canals lead-

ing from Dunkirk to the sea, a move which was to have implications for British commerce.

Prior, Thomas. A list of the absentees of Ireland ... with observations on the present trade and condition of that kingdom. Dublin, R. Gunne, 1745. P516

The author sees absentee landlords as a great drain on Ireland's economy, and urges instead more investment in Irish industry as a means of enabling the British to compete with Continental producers.

Pritchard, John. Narratives of John Pritchard [et al.] respecting the aggressions of the Northwest Company against the Earl of Selkirk's settlement upon Red River. London, J. Murray, 1819. P517

A pro-Selkirk account of the hostilities between the rivals for the Red River region.

The privileges of an Englishman in the kingdoms and dominions of Portugal. London, For the Translator, 1736. P518

Contains a treaty of 1652 which guarantees English merchants favored treatment in the Portuguese empire.

Procedure og dom ved Kiøbenhavns Hof- of Stadsret i sagen mellem agenterne Zinn og Erichsen, samt Banco-Commissair Cramer paa den eene og Etatsraad Friderich de Coninck paa den anden side. Copenhagen, Johan Frederik Schultz, 1791. P519

Relates to a legal case brought against the firm of Coninck and Reyersen by the Danish Asiatic Company.

Procés en reglement de jurisdiction entre les prevost des marchands & eschevins juges conservateurs des privileges des foires de la ville de Lyon ... Paris, P. Le Petit, 1669. P520

A collection of documents concerned with governing the fairs at Lyons.

Proclus. Procli Diadochi Sphaera, astronomiam. Discere incipientibus utilissima, noviter ex graeco recognita. [Bologna, Cynthii Achillini, 1526.] P521

This is Thomas Linacre's translation, supplemented by extensive commentary by Lodovico Vitali.

Proclus. Sphaera [in Greek]. Paris, Christianus Wechelus, 1531. P522

An apparently unrecorded first separate printing of this elementary astronomy text.

Proclus. Procli Sphaera, Thoma Linacro Britanno interprete, cum annotatiunculis, ex publicis praelectionibus Iacobi Tusani ... exceptis. Paris, Apud Martinum Iuuenem, 1556. P523

A translation by Thomas Linacre, with notes by Jacques Toussain incorporating material on the sphere by Peter Apianus.

Proclus. Procli Sphaera, cum annotatiunculis ex publicis praelectionibus Jacobi Tusani ... exceptis. Paris, Apud Martinum Iuuenem ..., 1557. P524

Greek text and commentary.

Proclus. Procli De sphaera liber I. Cleomedis de mundo, sive circularis inspectionis meteororum libri II. Arati Solensis Phaenomena, sive Apparentia. Dionysii Afri Descriptio orbis habitabilis. Basel, Henric Petri [1561]. P525

A collection of five cosmographies, four ancient and one modern, the latter being Johannes Honter's *Cosmographiae rudimentis.*

Proclus. La sfera di Proclo Liceo tradotta da maestro Egnatio Danti; cosmografo del serenissimo Gran Duca di Toscana. Con le annotazioni, & con l'uso della sfera del medesimo. Florence, Giunti, 1573. P526

The commentary on Proclus's *Sphere* is followed by the editor's own *Trattato dell' uso della sfera.*

Proeve, over eenen rypen-raet, ende zalige resolutie, onlangs uytghegheven door een lief-hebber des Vaderlants ... Toulon, Christoffel Speeckaert, 1636. P527

A moralistic tract, calling on the East and West India Companies to discontinue their piracy.

The profit and loss of the East-India-trade, stated, and humbly offer'd to the consideration of the present Parliament. London, 1700. P528

The anonymous author opposes rechartering of the East India Company, citing as arguments the reduction in trade to the Levant, the Mediterranean, and the West Indies, as well as reduced cloth production in England.

Proisy, Vincent-René de. État des finances de Saint-Domingue, contenant le résumé des recettes & dépenses de toutes les caisses depuis le 1er janvier 1789 jusqu'au 31 décembre de la même année ... Paris, Imprimerie Royale, 1790. P529

A survey of the financial administration and of the financial condition of the French colony of Saint Domingue just prior to the slave rebellion there.

Project middelen tot redres van de finantie van de respective Admiraliteiten. Manuscript. [n.p., ca. 1720.] P530

A discussion of ways and means to finance convoys for Dutch shipping, with reference to earlier policy on the same subject and concern for the decline in the Dutch trade.

Projet d'une compagnie pour l'Amerique. [n.p., ca. 1651.] P531

This eight-page tract relates to a plan for a French settlement on the north coast of South America in the mid-seventeenth century. Originator of the venture was Estienne le Roux, Seigneur de Royville.

A proposal for humbling Spain. Written in 1711 by a person of distinction. London, J. Roberts, 1739. P532
A proposal for sending an expedition against Spanish holdings in America for the increase of England's trade.

A proposal for uniting the kingdoms of Great Britain and Ireland. London, A. Millar, 1751. P533
The advantages of union to both England and Ireland are enumerated, England's chief gain being a renewed ability to compete in the woolen and linen industries.

Proposals for an equivalent for the intended wine duties. [London, 1695.] P534
A broadside offering alternatives to the proposed wine tax which petitioners contend would ruin the wine trade, thereby hurting the export trade to Spain.

Proposals for raising a new company for carrying on the trade of Africa ... under the title of The United Company. London, J. Morphew, 1709. P535
Outlines a proposed company to unite the trade of the Royal African Company with that of the West Indies.

Proposals for settling the East-India trade. London, E. Whitlock, 1696. P536
Advocates free participation by Englishmen in the East Indian trade.

Propositie van Syne Hoogheid ter vergaderingen van haar H.M. ... tot redres en verbeeteringe van den Koophandel ... The Hague, J. Scheltus, 1751. P537
A discussion of the decline of Dutch commerce, with suggestions for improving it.

Propositie vanden Heere vander Horst, ghedaen ... den XII en Januarij 1607. Midtsgaders d'antwoort ... [n.p.] 1608. P538
A proposal that peace be established with Spain, and with the concurrence of the Estates General.

Propositions du sieur Jacques Auriol & associez pour se charger de la Compagnie d'Afrique pendant dix années ... Paris, Pierre Simon, 1730. P539
A proposal by a group of merchants to acquire for ten years the right to trade on the Barbary coast, replacing the Compagnie des Indes there.

Prospectus d'un plan d'envoyer des colons suisses et allemands à la belle et fertile colonie de la Rivière-Rouge, dans l'Amérique septentrionale. [n.p.] 1821. P540
An appeal for immigrants to settle in the Red River Colony of Canada, with costs and conditions set forth.

The provisions made by the treaties of Utrecht, for separating Spain for ever from France, and for preventing France from enjoying any separate exclusive commerce with the Spanish dominions in America ... London, S. Baker, 1762. P541
A reminder to the British negotiators of the forthcoming treaty with France of these earlier provisions against any union of France and Spain.

Proyart, abbé. Histoire de Loango, Kakongo, et autres royaumes d'Afrique. Paris, C.P. Berton, N. Crapart [etc.] 1776. P542
This account of the Loango-Congo region was compiled from the memoirs of French missionaries who had directed a mission there in the years 1766-73.

Proyart, abbé. Rese-beskrifning innehällande märkwärdiga underrättelser om Loango, Kakongo, och nagre andre riken uti Afrika ... Stockholm, Holmberg och Wennberg, 1780. P543
A translation from the French edition of 1776. This Swedish edition does not include the map.

Proyecto del Sr. Macanas a la Magestade Phelipe Quinto par el govierno de la Compañia de Commercio de Indias. Manuscript. Spain [1737-61]. P544
An advisor to Philip V presents plans for a monopoly company and discusses other commercial affairs. This manuscript is followed by nine others on various subjects.

[Prudhomme, Louis Marie.] Voyage à la Guiane et a Cayenne, fait en 1789 et années suivantes. Paris, Chez l'editeur, 1798. P545
Describes the commerce and spheres of influence of France, Spain, Portugal, and the Netherlands in Guiana.

Pruneau de Pommegorge, Antoine Edme. Description de la Nigritie. Amsterdam; Paris, Maradan, 1789. P546
A description of the Niger and Senegal River areas and the Guinea coast by a servant of French commercial companies who had resided there for twenty-two years.

Prussia (Kingdom). Sovereign (1740-1786 : Friedrich II). Quod Deus bene vortat. Octroy accordé par Sa Majesté le Roy de Prusse, pour faire commerce à Bengale, et aux cotes voisines. Du consentement, de la Royale Compagnie de la Chine, etablie à Emden. [n.p., 1753.] P547
The charter of a Prussian trading company to trade in Bengal, the company to be headquartered in Emden.

[Prynne, William.] An humble remonstrance to His Majesty, against the tax of ship-money imposed, laying open the illegalitie, abuse, and inconvenience thereof. [London] 1641. P548
The author argues against the Crown's right to impose a tax allegedly for defense purposes when there is no war, and to tax without the consent of Parliament.

Ptolemy. Almagestum. Venice [Johannes Hamman] 1496. P549

The first edition of Ptolemy's major work in astronomy. This is an epitome begun by Georg von Peurbach and completed by Johannes Mueller.

Ptolemy. Almagestum. Venice, Petrus Liechtenstein, 1515. P550

The first complete edition of the *Almagest*, incorporating many geographic concepts of interest to explorers and geographers of the early sixteenth century.

Ptolemy. Almagestum. Venice, Lucantonio Giunta, 1528. P551

This is the first edition of the *Almagest* to be translated from the Greek. The translator was George of Trebizond.

Ptolemy. Almagestum. Manuscript in Greek. Italy, ca. 1535. P552

Although the date and editor are unknown, this manuscript probably precedes the first published Greek edition of 1538.

Ptolemy. Almagestum. Basel, Joannem Walderum, 1538. P553

The first Greek edition, prepared by Simon Grynaeus.

Ptolemy. Almagestum. Basel, Henric Petri, 1543. P554

The second edition of the epitome version.

Ptolemy. Almagestum. Nuremberg, Joannem Montanum & Ulricum Neuberum, 1550. P555

The third edition of the epitome version.

Ptolemy. Geographia. Vincenza, Hermanus Levilapis, 1475. P556

The first edition, which was published without maps.

Ptolemy. Geographia. [Florence, Nicolo Todescho, ca. 1480-82.] P557

This edition has thirty-one copperplate maps, and the text is a metrical paraphrase by Francesco Berlinghieri.

Ptolemy. Cosmographia. Ulm, L. Hol, 1482. P558

This is the first edition of Ptolemy to be printed in Germany, and the first edition in which woodcut maps appear.

Ptolemy. Geographia. Rome, Petri de Turre, 1490. P559

The twenty-seven copperplate maps are from the same plates as those used in the 1478 Rome edition. Textual additions are based on the 1486 Ulm edition, including the "Registrum alphabeticum" and "De locis ac mirabilibus mundi."

Ptolemy. Geographia. Rome, B. Venetus de Vitalibus, 1508. P560

This is the first edition of Ptolemy to contain a description of the New World. The atlas volume contains the famous Ruysch map, which for nearly 400 years was considered the first map to show the New World.

Ptolemy. Geographia. Venice, J. Pentius de Leucho, 1511. P561

This edition of Ptolemy has twenty-eight maps, including a double-page cordiform map of the world, which contains one of the early representations of America.

Ptolemy. Geographia. Strassburg, J. Schott, 1513. P562

This edition was begun in 1505 by Martin Waldseemüller and was completed by Jacobus Eszler and Georgius Ubelin in 1513. It contains twenty modern maps in addition to the traditional ones from new woodcuts.

Ptolemy. Geographia. Strassburg, J. Schott, 1520. P563

The forty-seven maps are identical to those in the 1513 edition, but there are some alterations in text.

Ptolemy. Geographia. Strassburg, J. Grueninger, 1522. P564

This edition was edited by Lorenz Fries. It contains forty-nine double-page maps. The three showing the New World illustrate the slow progress being made in establishing the proper geographic relationships between North and South America and Asia.

Ptolemy. Geographia. Strassburg, Joannes Grüninger, 1525. P565

The translator of this edition was Willibald Pirckheimer, one of the foremost humanists of the early sixteenth century. The maps are the same as in the 1522 edition.

Ptolemy. Geographia. Lyons, Michiel and Gaspar Treschel, 1535. P566

The fifty woodcut maps are from the same blocks as those in the 1522 and 1525 editions. This edition was prepared by Michael Servetus.

Ptolemy. Geographia. Basel, Hieronymus Froben, 1533. P567

The first edition of the Greek text. It was published without maps.

Ptolemy. Geographia à Graeco denuo traducti. Cologne, Joannes Ruremundanus, 1540. P568

Published without maps, this edition is a new translation by Johann Bronchorst from Greek manuscripts.

Ptolemy. Geographia universalis, vetus et nova. Basel, Henricum Petrum, 1540. P569

A new edition prepared by Sebastian Münster, who designed forty-eight new woodcut maps and a geographical appendix.

Ptolemy. Geographicae enarrationis, libri octo. [Vienna, G. Treschel, 1541.] P570

The second edition of the Servetus text. The maps are the same as those in the editions of 1522, 1525, and 1535.

Ptolemy. Geographia universalis. Basel, Henricus Petri, 1542. P571

The second edition of the Münster version, with some alterations in the maps.

Ptolemy. Geographia. Basel, Henric Petrus, 1545.
P572
The third Münster edition, with six new maps and with some alteration to text describing maps.

Ptolemy. La geographia. Venice, G.B. Pedrezano, 1548. P573
The first Italian edition, with maps by Giacomo Gastaldi. The translation is by Pietro Andrea Mattioli.

Ptolemy. La geografia. Venice, Vincenzo Valgrisi, 1561. P574
Translated from Greek, this new Italian edition contains sixty-four maps arranged so that the traditional Ptolemaic maps are juxtaposed to modern ones. Girolamo Ruscelli, editor and translator, provides extensive commentary.

Ptolemy. Geographia. Venice, Vincentium Valgrisium, 1562. P575
Based on the Willibald Pirckheimer edition of 1525, this Latin edition was edited, with commentary, by Giuseppe Moleto. It contains the same maps as the 1561 Ruscelli edition.

Ptolemy. Geographia. Venice, Jordani Zileti, 1564. P576
A reprint of the 1562 edition, with a new title page and a slightly altered preface.

Ptolemy. La geografia. Venice, Giordano Ziletti, 1574. P577
The third edition of the Ruscelli translation, edited by Giovanni Malombra. One new map is added.

Ptolemy. Tabulae geographicae. Cologne, Godefridi Kempensis, 1578. P578
Edited by Gerard Mercator, this edition has no text other than a brief preface. It includes twenty-eight maps, and brief annotations on the verso of the maps.

Ptolemy. Geographiae universae. Venice, Haeredes Simonis Galignani de Karera, 1596.
P579
An edition in two parts; the first presents the *Geographia* with a commentary by editor Giovanni A. Magini and the second contains a modern atlas, independent of Ptolemaic tradition.

Ptolemy. Geografia cioè descrittione universale della terra. Venice, Gio. Battista & Giorgio Galignani Fratelli, 1597-98. P580
The first Italian translation from Magini's 1596 Latin edition.

Ptolemy. Geografia. Venice, Heredi di Melchior Sessa, 1598-99. P581
This edition has five more maps than the Italian edition of 1574 and added editorial commentary by Giuseppe Rosaccio.

Ptolemy. Geographiae libri octo Graeco-Latini. Amsterdam, Cornelii Nicolai & Judoci Hondii, 1605. P582
This edition with Greek and Latin text was edited by Petrus Montanus, contains a preface by Jodocus Hondius, and includes twenty-eight maps by Mercator, identical to those in the 1578 edition.

Ptolemy. Geography. New York, The New York Public Library, 1932. P583
Edited by Edward Luther Stevenson from Greek and Latin manuscripts as well as printed editions, this is the only English edition. It includes reproductions of maps from a manuscript of ca. 1460.

Ptolemy. Ptolemaei planisphaerium. Jordani planisphaerium. Federici Commandini Urbinatis in Ptolemaei planisphaerium commentarius. Venice, Aldus, 1558. P584
The first publication of two works demonstrating the stereographic projection—the sphere at the equator seen from a polar position—by Ptolemy and Jordan of Saxony, a thirteenth century scholar, with commentary by Commandino.

A publication of Guiana's plantation. Newly undertaken by ... the Earle of Barkshire. London, William Jones for Thomas Paine, 1632. P585
An appeal for support and settlers for a colony to be established near the mouth of the Amazon River.

Puckle, James. England's interest: or, A brief discourse of the Royal Fishery. London, J. Southby, 1696. P586
An account of England's fishing industry and goods for which fish can be exchanged, and a suggestion for the establishment of a new fishing company for the benefit of English commerce.

Puckle, James. England's path to wealth and honour, in a dialogue between an Englishman and a Dutchman. London, For F. Cogan, 1750. P587
The dialogue concerns the economies of both nations, but with particular reference to the superiority of the Dutch fishing trade in the North Sea.

Puget-Bras, Chevalier de. Instructions génerralles données a tous les bâtimens du roy en station au isles Sous le Vent. Manuscript. Port-au-Prince, 1784-86. P588
These instructions are intended to specify treatment of American ships attempting to trade in French colonial ports in the West Indies. Also included are abbreviated journals of eighteen French ships operating in these waters.

Puget-Bras, Chevalier de. [Letter book.] Manuscript in French. Port-au-Prince, 1784-86.
P589
Letters by a French official assigned the duty of keeping American traders out of Saint Domingue written to Marechal de Castries, minister of war.

Pullein, Samuel. The culture of silk: or, An essay on its rational practice and improvement. London, A. Millar, 1758. P590
A detailed treatise on all aspects of silk culture for the benefit of American colonists intending to develop a silk industry.

Pullen, John. Memoirs of the maritime affairs of Great Britain. London, T. Astley, 1732. P591
Contains a number of items, all relating to the South Sea trade.

Pulteney, William. The effects to be expected from the East India Bill, upon the constitution of Great Britain, if passed into a law. London, J. Stockdale, 1783. P592
A protest against Pitt's India Bill which the author believes might give excessive power to a few aristocrats, who would have a personal interest distinct from that of the nation.

[Pulteney, William, Earl of Bath.] The budget opened: or, An answer to a pamphlet intitled, *A letter from a member of Parliament to his friends in the country, concerning the duties on wine and tobacco*. London, Printed by H. Haines, 1733. P593
An argument against converting the duties on tobacco and wines from a customs duty into an excise on the grounds that it would curtail individual liberties and eventually lead to a general excise.

[Pulteney, William, Earl of Bath.] The case of the revival of the salt duty, fully stated and considered; with some remarks on the present state of affairs. London, H. Haines, 1732. P594
This pamphlet reflects the search for a taxation policy that would be acceptable and that would support Britain's overseas commitments.

[Pulteney, William, Earl of Bath.] The late excise scheme dissected. London, J. Dickenson, 1734. P595
This writer argues against an excise tax on tobacco.

[Pulteney, William, Earl of Bath.] A review of all that hath pass'd between the courts of Great Britain and Spain. London, H. Goreham, 1739. P596
An account of Anglo-Spanish trade rivalry from 1721-1739.

[Pulteney, William, Earl of Bath.] A review of the excise-scheme; in answer to a pamphlet .... With some proper hints to the electors of Great Britain. London, H. Haines, 1733. P597
An attack upon the proposed excise tax, and upon a pamphlet defending it, as well as a condemnation of the ministry for its use of the post office to disseminate propaganda favorable to the excise proposal.

Purchas, Samuel. Purchas his pilgrimage. London, William Stansby for Henry Fetherstone, 1613. P598
An account of the religions of various parts of the world in all ages.

Purchas, Samuel. Purchas his pilgrimage, or, Relations of the world and the religions observed in all ages and places discouered, from the creation unto this present ... 2d ed. London, William Stansby for Henrie Fetherstone, 1614. P599
The second edition, with text enlarged by about fifteen per cent.

Purchas, Samuel. Purchas his pilgrimage, or Relations of the world and the religions observed in all ages ... London, William Stansby for Henry Fetherstone, 1617. P600
When considering some of the less known areas such as Africa and America, Purchas is largely concerned with the history of European overseas acitivity, the commercial and strategic opportunities afforded by each region, and descriptions of their geography and populations.

Purchas, Samuel. Purchas his pilgrimage. London, William Stansby for Henry Fetherstone, 1626. P601
Included as volume five of the *Pilgrimes* of 1625, it is the fourth edition of the 1613 work.

Purchas, Samuel. Purchas his pilgrimes. London, William Stansby for Henry Fetherstone, 1625. P602
A five-volume collection of voyages, including numerous accounts of English East Indian and American exploration.

Purry, Jean Pierre. Kurtze jedoch zuverlässige Nachricht von den gegenwärtigen Zustand und Beschaffenheit des Mittägigen Carolina in America ... Leipzig, Samuel Benjamin Walthern, 1734. P603
A prospectus designed to attract settlers to Purry's intended colony on the Savannah River.

Purry, Jean Pierre. Mémoire sur les pais des Cafres et la Terre de Nuyts. Amsterdam, Pierre Humbert, 1718. P604
The first French edition of a recommendation that the Dutch East India Company establish a colony on the west coast of Australia, called Nuytsland. It compares this region favorably with South Africa.

[Puységur, A.-H.-A. de Chastenet (Antoine-Hyacinthe-Anne), comte de.] Détail sur la navigation aux côtes de Saint-Domingue et dans ses débouquemens. Paris, Imprimerie Royale, 1787. P605
A pilot guide to the coast of the French colony and to the adjacent islands.

Pyrard, François. Voyage ... contenant sa navigation aux Indes Orientales, aux Moluques & au Bresil. Paris, Samuel Thiboust & Remy Dallin, 1615. P606

The second edition of the earliest account of a French commercial expedition to the East Indies.

Pyrard, François. Voyage ... contenant sa navigation aux Indes Orientales, Maldives, Moluques, Bresil. Paris, Samuel Thiboust & Remy Dallin, 1619. P607

This third edition has a vocabulary of the people of the Maldive Islands not included in the previous editions.

Pyrard, François. Voyage ... contenant sa navigation aux Indes Orientales, Maldives, Moluques, & au Bresil. Paris, Louis Billaine, 1679. P608

The fourth edition, edited by P. Du Val, Geographer Ordinary to the King.

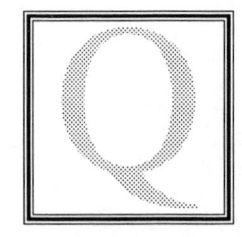

Quando las Indias no deuieran otra cosa a España ... [n.p., 1626.]   Q1
A report on events in the Spanish empire with particular attention to the war with the Dutch and English.

Queirós, Pedro Fernandes de. Copie de la requeste presentee au Roy d'Espagne ... sur la descouverte de la cinquiesme partie du monde. Paris, 1617.   Q2
A French edition of the first proposal for colonizing in the South Pacific. It is the eighth memorial presented to the Spanish King by the author who believed he had found the Great Southern Continent.

Quelen, Augustus van. Kort verhael vanden staet van Fernabuc. Amsterdam, 1640.   Q3
A pamphlet reviewing the administration of commerce, justice, and the military in Pernambuco under the governorship of Johan Maurits.

Quellenburgh, Henrik van. Vindiciae Batavicae, ofte, Refutatie van het tractaet van J.B. Tavernier ... Amsterdam, Jan Bouman, 1684.   Q4
A response to Jean Baptiste Tavernier's account of his eastern travels in which he had made some observations on the Dutch in the East Indies which were not acceptable to this author.

Quen, Jean de. Relation de ce qui s'est passé en la mission des peres de la Compagnie de Jesus, au pays de la Nouvelle France, és années 1655 & 1656. Paris, Sebastien Cramoisy et Gabriel Cramoisy, 1657.   Q5
Among topics covered in this *Relation* are the visits of several missionaries to the Mohawk and Onondaga Indians, the war of the Iroquois against the Eries, and an attack by the Iroquois on a Huron party resulting in the death of Father Leonard Garreau.

[Quesnay, François.] Physiocratie, ou Constitution naturelle du gouvernement le plus avantageux au genre humain. Pekin [Paris] Merlin, 1767.   Q6
A collection of writings on government and economy by Quesnay, edited by Du Pont de Nemours who provides an introduction of one hundred pages.

Questie tusschen de bewinthebbers van de Geoctroyeerde Oost-Indische Compagnie, ende hare participanten ... [n.p.,ca. 1624.]   Q7
A broadside dealing with complaints by the stockholders of the Dutch East India Company against mismanagement by the directors.

Questions to be proposed to such gentlemen as have been resident on the coast of Africa ... or have been in the slave trade. London, J. Phillips, 1788.   Q8
A collection of 146 questions to be asked of persons engaged in the slave trade or on plantations in the West Indies in hearings to be conducted by a committee of the Privy Council.

Queyroz, Fernão de. Historia da vida do veneravel Irmaõ Pedro de Basto ... e de variedade de sucessos que Deos ilhe manifestou. Lisbon, Miguel Deslandes, 1689.   Q9
The subject of this biography served in civil and ecclesiastical positions in India from 1586 to 1645, and commented extensively on Portuguese imperial problems during that period in his autobiography, which is the major source for this work.

Quincy, Josiah. Observations on the act of Parliament commonly called the Boston Port-Bill; with thoughts on civil society and standing armies. Boston, Edes and Gill, 1774.   Q10
A justification of Boston's hostile attitude toward British policy, and a call for resistance to the occupation of the town by troops.

Quintilian. M. Fabii Quintiliani Oratoriarum institutionum lib. XII, una cum Declamationibus eiusdem argutissimis, ad horrendae vetustatis exemplar repositis, diligenterq[ue] impressis. Cologne [Eucharii Cervicorni & Heronis Fuchs, 1521.]   Q11
The work of an important Roman rhetorician, born in the first century A.D.

R. S. Some neutral considerations, with relation to two printed papers.... The committee of Parliament's Report concerning the Indian and African Company, and an Overture, concerning the debts of the said Company. [n.p., 1707.] R1

A commentary on proposals in Parliament over the compensation to be paid to stockholders of the failed Company of Scotland Trading to Africa and the Indies.

Rålamb, Claes, friherre. Observationes juris practicae ... Beskriffning om thess Constantinopolitaniske resa och legation til Portam Ottomannicam bifogad är. Stockholm, Henrich Keyser, 1679. R2

The author was ambassador extraordinary from Charles X of Sweden to the Turkish Porte, seeking to keep Turkey neutral in the power struggle between Sweden and other European powers.

Raccolta di tutte le controversie seguite in varii tempi intorno a i ritti Chinesi divisa in piu' tomi. Augusta, 1756. R3

A two volume work, the first volume contains excerpts from sixteenth century writers on China, and the second consists of documents chiefly from the late seventeenth century relating to the Chinese Rites controversy.

Radoteur, pseud. Relazione d'una nuova generazione d'uomini scoperta dal Capitano Radoteur presso il fiume Marannon, ossia delle Amazzoni, da lui scritta a un suo amico, e transportata dal Franzese in Italiano. Bergamo, Francesco Locatelli, 1770. R4

A fictitious account of travels in northern Brazil involving the "discovery" of a race of four-legged people.

Rae, John. Narrative of an expedition to the shores of the Arctic Sea in 1846 and 1847. London, T. & W. Boone, 1850. R5

The expeditions explored Melville and Simpson peninsulas, King William Land and Adelaide Peninsula.

Ragionamento sopra il commercio generale. Manuscript. Vienna, 1750. R6

A 430-page review of the commerce of the major European countries, including their trade with overseas areas. It appears to have been prepared for an Italian official of the Austrian government.

Ragueneau, Paul. [Autograph letter signed, addressed to Vincentia Caraffa.] Manusript in French. House of St. Mary with the Hurons, New France, 1 March 1649. R7

The head of the Huron mission writes of events there: 1700 baptisms, eleven new missions, the constant threat of war which made impossible all of the work he would like to undertake. The letter was written to the Intendant General of the Society of Jesus in Rome.

Ragueneau, Paul. Relation de ce qui s'est passé en la mission des peres de la Compagnie de Jesus aux Hurons, pays de la Nouvelle France, és années 1648 & 1649. Paris, Sebastien Cramoisy et Gabriel Cramoisy, 1650. R8

This *Relation* is primarily concerned with the destruction of the Huron missions, the Iroquois and the martyrdom of three Jesuit priests.

Ragueneau, Paul. Relation de ce qui s'est passé en la mission des peres de la Compagnie de Jesus aux Hurons, pays de la Nouvelle France, és années 1648 & 1649. Paris, Sebastien Cramoisy et Gabriel Cramoisy, 1650. R9

The second edition, entirely reset.

Ragueneau, Paul. Narratio historica eorum, quae Societatis Jesu in Nova Francia fortiter egit, & passa est, annis M.DC.XLIIX & XLIX. Innsbruck, Hieronymi Agricolae, 1650. R10

The first Latin edition.

Ragueneau, Paul. Relation de ce qui s'est passé en la mission des peres de la Compagnie de Jesus, aux Hurōs, & aux païs plus bas de la Nouvelle France, depuis l'esté de l'année 1649 jusques à l'esté de l'anné 1650. Paris, Sebastien Cramoisy et Gabriel Cramoisy, 1651. R11

A report of continuing troubles for the Huron mission because of the Iroquois Wars. Some survivors were removed to the Isle d'Orleans in the St. Lawrence, two priests were killed, yet the writer notes great zeal for the Faith on the part of many Hurons.

Ragueneau, Paul. Relation de ce qui s'est passé en la mission des peres de la Compagnie de Jesus, aux Hurons, & aux païs plus bas de la Nouvelle France, depuis l'esté de l'année 1649 jusques à l'esté de l'année 1650. Paris, Sebastien Cramoisy et Gabriel Cramoisy, 1651. R12
The second edition.

Ragueneau, Paul. Relation de ce qui s'est passé de plus remarquable és missions des peres de la Compagnie de Jesus, en la Nouvelle France, es annees 1650 & 1651. Paris, Sebastien Cramoisy et Gabriel Cramoisy, 1652. R13
In addition to reports from the individual missions, this *Relation* includes journals of travel by Father Jacques Buteux and by Martin Lyonne.

Ragueneau, Paul. Relation de ce qui s'est passé en la mission des peres de la Compagnie de Jesus, au pays de la Nouvelle France, depuis l'eté de l'année 1651 jusques à l'eté de l'année 1652. Paris, Sebastien Cramoisy et Gabriel Cramoisy, 1653. R14
In addition to Father Ragueneau's report on the various missions this *Relation* contains an account of the martyrdom of Father Jacques Buteux at the hands of the Iroquois and a eulogy to Mother Marie de St. Joseph.

Ragueneau, Paul. Progressus fidei catholicae in Novo Orbe. I. in Canada, sive Nova Francia. II. in Cochinchina. III. in magno Chinensi regno. Cologne, Joannem Kinchium, 1653. R15
The information on the Jesuit missions in the East was supplied by Nicolas Trigault.

Raimond, Julien. Veritable origine des troubles de S.-Domingue. Paris, Desenne, Bailly [etc.] 1792. R16
A discussion of the problems of Saint Domingue, by a representative of the black population.

Raisonnement einiger curiösen Personen, über das ungemein-reiche Gold-Bergwerck in Africa. Leipzig, G.C. Wintzern, 1720. R17
An account of English trade and gold mining on the west African coast.

Raleigh, Sir Walter. The discoverie of the large, rich, and bewtiful empire of Guiana. London, Robert Robinson, 1596. R18
Raleigh's earliest appraisal of Guiana was optimistic in its belief in the fertility of the soil and the value of its products as the basis for an English colony there.

Raleigh, Sir Walter. An essay on ways and means to maintain the honour and safety of England ... London, 1701. R19
Sheeres claims to have found Raleigh's essay "among the rubbish of old papers while I had the honour to serve in the Office of the Ordnance...." He suggests that the essay could have been written by Sir Dudley Digges.

Raleigh, Sir Walter. Grondige ende waerachtige beschrijvinge van ... Guiana. [Amsterdam] 1644. R20
An account of the Raleigh-Keymis Guiana enterprise.

Raleigh, Sir Walter. Judicious and select essays and observations. London, T.W. for H. Moseley, 1650. R21
Contains Raleigh's *Apologie for his voyage to Guiana* as well as other essays of commercial and colonial interest.

Raleigh, Sir Walter. Observations on the British fishery ... presented to King James I. London, J. Roberts, 1720. R22
The unnamed editor believed Raleigh's comparison of English and Dutch fishing and commerce was still pertinent a century later.

Raleigh, Sir Walter. Three discourses of Sir Walter Raleigh. London, Benjamin Barker, 1702. R23
Published by his grandon Phillip Raleigh, these tracts were designed to keep alive an active hostility to Spain.

Raleigh, Sir Walter. Warachtighe ende grondige beschryvinghe van het groot en gout-rijck coningrijck van Guiana, gelegen zijnde in America ... Mitsgaders de beschrijvinge vande omliggende rijcke lantschappen Emeria, Arromaia, Amapaia, eñ Topago ... door den E. Heere Walter Ralegh ... ende den vermaerden zeevaerder Capiteyn Laurens Kemis. Amsterdam, Michiel Colijn, 1617. R24
The third Dutch edition of the descriptions of Guiana by Raleigh and Kemys, resulting from their exploratory expeditions there in 1595-96.

Rallier, Louis-Antoine Esprit. Nouvelles observations sur Saint-Domingue. Paris, Baudoin [ca. 1796]. R25
An analysis of events during the rebellion in Saint Domingue, entirely favorable to the rebels' cause.

Rallier, Louis-Antoine Esprit. Observations sur Saint-Domingue. Paris, Imprimerie Nationale [1797]. R26
The author advocates policies of liberation and enfranchisement, beginning with the Mulattoes in the French colony.

Rallier, Louis-Antoine Esprit. Suite des observations sur Saint-Domingue. Paris, Baudoin [1797]. R27

A thoughtful examination of the differences between France and Saint Domingue and an attempt to provide answers to the question of how both can be governed by the laws of the French Republic.

[Ramberti, Benedetto.] Delle cose de Turchi. Libri tre. Venice, Bernardin, 1541. R28
A description of the sailing route from Venice to Constantinople, including a guide to the latter, and noting its important commercial activity.

Ramel, Jean Pierre. Journal ou temoignage de l'Adjudant Général Ramel, Commandant de la Garde du corps legislatif de la Republique Française ... Leipzig, 1799. R29
A prisoner's account of life in the French prison colony in Guiana. A map of the Guiana coast is included.

Ramel, Jean Pierre. Narrative of the deportation to Cayenne, of Barthélemy, Pichegru, Willot, Marbois, La Rue, Ramel, &c. &c. ... London, J. Wright, 1799. R30
The first English edition.

Ramel, Jean Pierre. Dagverhaal der lotgevallen van Pichegru, Barthelemy, Villot, Aubry Dossonville, Le Tellier, La Rue en Ramel, uitgebannen uit Frankrijk naar Guijane. Utrecht, G.T. van Paddenburg en zoon, 1799. R31
A narrative of exile to Guiana that befell victims of the French Revolution, and some account of travel in that colony.

Ramsay, David. Histoire de la révolution d'Amérique, par rapport a la Caroline Méridionale ... Londres, et se trouve à Paris, 1787. R32
The first French edition of the first history of the American Revolution to be published. A physician in South Carolina, the author shows the social and economic impact of the war in that area. The French translator celebrates the war as a triumph of liberty.

Ramsay, James. An inquiry into the effects of putting a stop to the African slave trade, and of granting liberty to the slaves in the British sugar colonies. London, James Phillips, 1784. R33
The author sees the inevitability of the loss of the British West Indian colonies, and urges that plantations in West Africa could supplant them and provide an alternative to the slave trade there.

Ramusio, Giovanni Battista. Delle navigationi et viaggi. Venice, Heredi di Lucantonio Giunti, 1550. R34
The first edition of the first volume of a projected three-volume collection of voyages.

Ramusio, Giovanni Battista. Delle navigationi et viaggi. Venice, L.A. Giunti, 1556-88. R35
This three-volume set is one of the most important collections of voyages. The first volume concerns Asia and Africa primarily; the second contains accounts of Russia, Central Asia, and the northern regions; volume three is devoted to the exploration of America.

Ramusio, Giovanni Battista. [Abridgment of Delle navigationi et viaggi, vol. II.] Manuscript. [Italy, ca. 1560.] R36
The text pertains to Asiatic travels primarily.

Ramusio, Giovanni Battista. Delle navigationi et viaggi. Venice, Giunti, 1606. R37
This edition adds to the text the narratives of Willem Barents to the arctic and Cesare Federici to the East Indies.

Rangel, Manuel. Relaçam do lastimozo naufragio da nao Conceiçam chamada algaravia a nova de que era Capitaõ Francisco Nobre. Lisbon, A. Álvares [1699?]. R38
This is an account of a Portuguese shipwreck in the Indian Ocean in 1555. Rangel eventually reached China in 1557.

Rangel, Manuel. Relaçam do lastimozo naufragio da nao Conceiçam chamada algaravia a nova de que era Capitaõ Francisco Nobre a qual se perdeo nos bayxos de Pero dos Banhos em 22. de Agosto de 1555. Lisbon, Antonio Alvares [repr. 1737]. R39

Rangel, Manuel. Relaçaõ do naufragio da nao Conceyçaõ de que era capitaõ Francisco Nobre, a qual se perdeo nos baixos de Pero dos Banhos aos 22. dias do mez de agosto de 1555: escrita por Manoel Rangel ... Lisbon, 1735. R40

Raphael de Jesus, Frei. Castrioto Lusitano. Lisbon, Antonio Craesbeeck de Mello, 1679. R41
A history of the Portuguese recovery of Pernambuco from the Dutch, with special emphasis on the role played by Joaõ Fernandes Vieira in that campaign.

Les raretés des Indes, "Codex Canadensis." Paris, M. Chamonal, 1930. R42
A volume of facsimile reproductions of 180 drawings illustrating plant and animal life as well as native costumes of seventeenth-century Canada.

Rask, Johannes. En kort og sandferdig rejsebeskrivelse til og fra Guinea ... Trondhiem, Jens Christensen Winding, 1754. R43
An account of a voyage to Guinea and a four-year residence there by a clergyman in the service of the Danish Guinea and West India Company.

Rasmussen, Jens Lassen. Det under Kong Frederik den Femte oprettede Danske Afrikanske Kompagnies historie, af arkivsdocumenter udarbeidet ven Dr. J.L. Rasmussen. Copenhagen, Fr. Brummer [1818]. R44

An account of a Danish trading company operating in Morocco, between 1749 and 1767, compiled from contemporary sources.

Rauwolf, Leonhard. Aigentliche Beschreibung der Raisz ... inn die Morgenländer fürnemlich Syriam, Judeam, Arabiam ... Laugingen, Georgen Willers, 1583. R45

The first complete edition of this doctor's account of his travels in the Levant, giving a picture of the near Eastern trade before the English became active there. Contains forty-two woodcuts of eastern plants.

Raven, Christopher Indise. Consideratie op de middelen tot voordeel van de staat ende aufbreuk vanden vyand, aengewesen en bewaerheyt. Amsterdam, Pieter Rotterdam, 1691. R46

Proposals to discontinue the importing of goods from France, supported by arguments to the effect that this would hurt France, but not the Netherlands.

Raven, Dirk. Journael ofte beschrijvinge vande reyse ... nae Spitsbergen. Hoorn, Isaac Willemsz, 1646. R47

An account of a whaling voyage undertaken by the Greenland Company of Hoorn, with remarks on whalers from other countries engaged in whaling there.

Ravenna (Italy). Laws, etc. Capitolatione sopra la grassa, e d'altre cose spettanti all' officio de gli edili ... Ravenna, Pietro de Paoli & G.B. Giovannelli, 1649. R48

A collection of regulations concerning the economic activities of the craftsmen of Ravenna.

Ravn, Wilhelm Frederik. Kort underretning om det Maroccanske slaverie i aarene 1751, 1752 og 1753. Copenhagen, 1754. R49

A journal of travels in Morocco, written in verse.

Rawlin, William. To the Kings most excellent Majesty in Council. The humble petition and appeal of William Rawlin Esq. one of the searchers of His Majestys dutys and customs of 4½ p cent at Bridge Town in the island of Barbados. Manuscript. [Barbados, 1736.] R50

A petition by a customs official in Barbados, seeking reversal of a judgement favoring Henry Warren, who had been accused of seeking to evade customs duties on sugar.

Ray, John. A collection of curious travels & voyages ... London, S. Smith and B. Walford, 1693. R51

Includes travels in Africa and the Levant.

Raynal, abbé (Guillaume-Thomas-François). Histoire philosophique et politique, des établissemens & du commerce des Européens dans les deux Indes. Amsterdam, 1770. R52

The first edition of the most widely-published eighteenth century critique of European overseas expansion, published in six volumes.

Raynal, abbé (Guillaume-Thomas-François). Histoire philosophique et politique des établissmens & du commerce de Européens dans les deux Indes. The Hague, Gosse, 1774. R53

A revised and expanded edition, with maps added.

Raynal, abbé (Guillaume-Thomas-François). Histoire philosophique et politique des établissemens et du commerce des Européens dans les deux Indes. Geneva, Jean-Leonard Pellet, 1781. R54

The second of the ten-volume Geneva editions.

[Raynal, abbé (Guillaume-Thomas-François).] A philosophical and political history of the settlements and trade of the Europeans in the East and West Indies. London, T. Cadell, 1776. R55

The first English edition.

Raynal, abbé (Guillaume-Thomas-François). A philosophical and political history of the settlements and trade of the Europeans in the East and West Indies. London, T. Cadell, 1777. R56

The third English edition, in five volumes, translated by John Obadiah Justamond.

Raynal, abbé (Guillaume-Thomas-François). A philosophical and political history of the settlements and trade of the Europeans in the East and West Indies. Dublin, John Exshaw and Luke White, 1784. R57

Based on the 1780 Geneva edition, this Dublin edition includes four maps by Thomas Kitchen.

Raynal, abbé (Guillaume-Thomas-François). A philosophical and political history of the settlements and trade of the Europeans in the East and West Indies. London, A. Strahan and T. Cadell, 1788. R58

The translator states that this edition is based on a recent French edition which varies notably from earlier printings, containing new calculations and new maps.

[Raynal, abbé (Guillaume-Thomas-François).] Philosophische und politische Geschichte der europäischen Handlung und Pflanzörter in beyden Indien. Copenhagen & Leipzig, Johann Friedrich Heineck und Faber, 1774-78. R59

The first German edition. The translation is accompanied by observations by the translator who is unidentified.

[Raynal, abbé (Guillaume-Thomas-François).] Historia politica de los establecimientos ultramarinos de las naciones Europeas. Madrid, Antonio de Sancha, 1784-90. R60

This first Spanish translation is an abridgment.

Raynal, abbé (Guillaume-Thomas-François). Révolution de l'Amerique. London, Lockyer Davis; The Hague, P.F. Gosse, 1781. R61

An analysis of the causes of the American Revolution together with a history of its progress, from a pro-Colonial point of view.

Raynal, abbé (Guillaume-Thomas-François). Tableau et révolutions des colonies angloises dans l'Amérique septentrionale. Amsterdam, Compagnie des Libraires, 1781. R62
A survey of the American colonies, their economies, populations, etc., with an account of events leading to the American Revolution and a history of the military campaigns.

Raynal, abbé (Guillaume-Thomas-François). The revolution of America. Dublin, C. Talbot, 1781. R63
One of eleven editions published in 1781.

Raynal, abbé (Guillaume-Thomas-François). Staatsomwenteling van Amerika, uit het Fransch ... Amsterdam, Willem Holtorp, 1781. R64
The first Dutch edition.

[Raynal, abbé (Guillaume-Thomas-François).] Tableau de l'Europe, pour servir de supplément à l'histoire philosophique & politique les etablissements & du commerce des Européens dans les deux Indes. Amsterdam, 1774. R65
This supplement to the author's *Histoire ... des etablissements et du commerce des Européens dans des deux Indes* notes the effect, or lack of it, of overseas expansion upon European institutions.

Raynal, abbé (Guillaume-Thomas-François). Storia dell' America Settentrionale del signor abate Raynal, continuata fino al presente, con carte geografiche rappresentanti il teatro della guerra civile tra la Gran Bretagna, e le Colonie Unite ... Venice, Antonio Zatta, 1778-1779. R66
The first volume includes descriptions of each of the American colonies and a set of fifteen double-page maps based on Mitchell's map of North America. The second volume is a history of the American Revolution to 1779.

Raynal, abbé (Guillaume-Thomas-François). A philosophical and political history of the British settlements and trade in North America ... Aberdeen, J. Boyle, 1779. R67
An excerpt from the *Histoire philosophique et politique* with a concluding part on the British social taxation policies.

Raynal, abbé (Guillaume-Thomas-François). Esprit et genie de m. l'abbé Reynal tiré de ses ouvrages. Geneva, Jean Léonard, 1782. R68
A summary of the views of Abbé Raynal on many topics, including those on the expansion of European commerce abroad and on colonization.

Real Academia de la Historia (Spain). Mapas españoles de America ... Madrid, 1951. R69
A collection of reproductions of early Spanish maps of America.

Real Compañia de Comercio, Barcelona. Real Compañia de Comercio para las islas de Santo Domingo, Puerto Rico, y la Margarita ... Madrid, Joseph Rico, 1755. R70
Regulations and privileges for a new company established by citizens of Barcelona to engage in West Indian trade.

Real Compania de San Christoval de la Habana. Manifest que el establecimento y manejo de la Real Compania de la Habana ... Havana, 1747. R71
Details on production and commerce of the company.

Real Compañía Guipuzcoana de Caracas. Manifiesto, que con incontestables hechos prueba los grandes beneficios, que ha producido el establecimiento de la Real Compañia Guipuzcoana de Caracas ... [Madrid? 1749?] R72
A defense of the company as a source of great benefits to the Venezuela colony. Also included is a brief history of the company.

Real Compañía Guipuzcoana de Caracas. Noticias historiales practiques de los sucessos ... de esta compañia. [Madrid?] 1765. R73
Outlines the value to Spain of the commerce of a Venezuelan trading company, stating objections to a free trade in that area.

Real Compañía Guipuzcoana de Caracas. [Records of the rebellion against its commercial monopoly in Venezuela, 1750.] Manuscript in Spanish. [Spain, ca. 1750.] R74
A collection of four items all relating to the place of the Royal Guipuzcoana Company in the commerce of Venezuela.

Reasons against establishing an African Company at London, exclusive to the plantations, and all the out-ports ... [n.p., 1711.] R75
A repudiation of a plan to form a new African Company, tracing the history of the failures of monopolies in the West African trade.

Reasons against making the present East-India Company the root for carrying on the future trade. [London, ca. 1698.] R76
It is asserted here that the East India Company cannot trade effectively in India because it is in ill favor with the people there.

Reasons against the renewal of the sugar act, as it will be prejudicial to the trade, not only of the northern colonies, but to that of Great Britain also. Boston, Thomas Leverett, 1764. R77
A series of nine arguments tending to show that the Sugar Act will reduce fishing and other industries related, through exchange of commodities, to the sugar trade.

Reasons for a war against Spain. In a letter from a merchant of London trading to America. London, J. Wilford, 1737. R78

"'Tis to protect and secure our trade that we are pushed to the dilemma either of giving it up, or engaging in a just and necessary war for its defence."

Reasons for improving the fisheries and linnen manufacture of Scotland. London, J. Roberts, 1727. R79

A survey of Scottish economic affairs, noting that the union with England did not produce the happy results expected. Commercial relations between Scotland and other countries are described.

Reasons for keeping Guadaloupe at a peace, preferable to Canada ... London, M. Cooper, 1761. R80

The commercial potentialities of Guadeloupe are compared to those of Canada, to the advantage of Guadeloupe.

Reasons for the present conduct of Sweden, in relation to the trade in the Baltick. London, For the Author, 1715. R81

A translation of a tract that purports to be a letter from a gentleman in Danzig to his friend in Amsterdam. It defends the Swedes in their interference with Dutch ships trading to Russian ports on the Baltic, for the Dutch were supplying arms to the Russians with whom the Swedes were at war.

Reasons grounded on facts, shewing, I. That a new duty on sugar must fall on the planter, II. That the liberty of a direct exportation to foreign markets will not help him in this case, III. That a new duty will not certainly increase the revenue, and IV. That it will probably occasion the desertion of our sugar islands. London, M. Cooper, 1748. R82

A forecast of ruin for many sugar plantations in the British West Indies if sugar taxes are increased.

Reasons humbly offer'd against grafting upon or confirming the present East India Company. [London, ca. 1689.] R83

A proposal that the old East India Company be abolished and a new one created by act of Parliament.

Reasons humbly offer'd to ... the Commons of England assembled in Parliament, shewing the great loss that accrues to their Majesties ... by the African Company's ingrossing the sole trade of Africa. [London, ca. 1695.] R84

Independent traders charge that the monopoly held by the Royal African Company keeps the price of slaves high, causing underdevelopment of West Indian plantations, and loss of revenue through diminished exports.

Reasons humbly offered against the bill for repealing part of the Act of Navigation. [London, ca. 1719.] R85

This broadside asserts that the importation of drugs grown in Asia and Italy would be prohibited by repealing the section of the Act of Navigation under consideration.

Reasons humbly offered for passing the bill for enlarging the trade to Russia. [London, 1698.] R86

It is suggested that the trade to Russia could be improved through wider participation in it, and this could be achieved by a lower fee for admission to the Russia Company.

Reasons humbly offered for restraining the wearing of wrought silks, bengals, and dyed, printed, and stained callicoes, of the product and manufacture of Persia and the East-Indies ... London [1699?]. R87

These restraints upon other cloths were apparently in the interest of the woolen industries of Great Britain.

Reasons humbly offered to ... Parliament for laying an easie duty on whalefinns of the fishery of New-England, New York, and Pensilvania ... [London, ca. 1688.] R88

A plea for more favorable rates on whalebone exported from the American colonies to England.

Reasons humbly offered to the honourable House of Commons for encouraging of the English manufacture of earthen ware ... [London, ca. 1688.] R89

A plea for protection against foreign imports.

Reasons offered to the court of proprietors, and to the court of directors, for the management of the East India Company's affairs, why they never should permit a scheme ... for establishing ... a new harbour, in Channel Creek. London, 1780. R90

Criticism of a proposal for a new harbor on the Hooghly River involving a grant to Benjamin Lacam to administer and collect fees.

Reasons to shew, that there is a great probability of a navigable passage to the western American ocean, through Hudson's Streights, and Chesterfield Inlet ... London, J. Robinson, 1749. R91

Observations and affidavits by two persons who had been in the Dobbs expedition of 1747 testify to the likelihood of a passage to the Pacific through Chesterfield Inlet.

[Rebus engravings.] Britannia to America; and America to her mistaken mother. London, M. Darly, 1778. R92

Mother Britannia warns of the dangers of a French alliance, and Daughter America responds that she is old enough to know her own interests.

Recherches curieuses des mesures du monde. Paris, Martin Collet, 1625. R93

A treatise on the measurement of the earth, the size of the continents and distances between various places.

Een recht-tijdich expostulatie ofte klachte over de Nederlanders ... Rotterdam, I. Gerritsz, 1652.
R94
The Dutch are reminded of ther dependence upon England in trade, and that a closer union between them would be advantageous to both.

Het rechte tweede deel van't Engelsche praetjen, tusschen vier personen ... Rotterdam, G. Iansz, 1652.
R95
The Dutch government is criticized for talking peace with the English while English are taking Dutch merchant ships at sea.

Den rechtē weg ausz zu faren von Liszbona gen kallakuth vō meyl zu meyl. [Nuremberg, G. Stuchs, 1505.]
R96
This rare news tract describes "The right way to sail from Lisbon to Calicut," and contains the first printed map to show the all-water route to India.

Den rechten ommeganck vande gevioleerde stadt van Amsterdam. [n.p., ca. 1650.] R97
A reply to *Den ommeganck van Amsterdam*.

Reck, Philipp Georg Friedrich von. An extract of the journals of Mr. Commissary Von Reck, who conducted the first transport of Saltzburgers to Georgia, and of the Reverend Mr. Bolzius, one of their ministers. London, M. Downing, 1734.
R98
These two journals cover the period of the voyage to Georgia and early settlement of emigrants from Salzburg in 1734.

Réclamations de la Compagnie de la Guyanne [et] observations sur les réclamations de la Compagnie de la Guyanne. Manuscript. France, 19 Sept. 1785.
R99
A detailed statement of the expenses incurred by the government of the colony of Goree, with complaints against the management of the colony.

Recopilacion sumaria de todos los autos acordados de la Real Audiencia y Sala del Crimen de esta Nueva España, y providencias de su superior gobierno. Mexico, Felipe de Zuñiga, 1787.
R100
A compilation of royal proclamations and laws together with judicial decrees and court decisions which had the force of law. This collection is supplementary to its predecessor, issued in 1722.

Recüeil de diverses pieces, concernant la Pensylvanie. The Hague, Abraham Troyel, 1684.
R101
A collection of five pieces describing conditions, government, opportunity for settlement, and indicating types of settlers most wanted in Pennsylvania.

Recueil d'actes et pièces concernant le commerce de divers pays de l'Europe. London, 1754.
R102
A series of eight speeches debating the question of free trade in the eastern Mediterranean where the Levant Company was dominant.

Recueil d'ordonnances, déclarations, arrests, et décisions concernant les consuls ... dans les echelles du Levant. Manuscript. [France, ca. 1750.]
R103
A handbook of instructions for French consuls and their secretaries and assistants in the commercial ports of the Near East.

Recueil de divers voyages faits en Afrique et en l'Amerique. Paris, L. Billaine, 1674. R104
A collection of accounts of several regions of Africa and America, with descriptions of peoples and products of those areas.

Recueil de diverses pieces ... que les françois ont droict de chasser & pescher les baleines és pays du nord. [n.p.] 1635.
R105
A collection of documents from 1613 to 1634 to prove the French whaling rights in certain parts of Spitsbergen which were being contested by the Dutch.

Recueil de memoires, arrets, etc., concernant les soyes etrangères ... qui vennent des Indes et de la Chine. Manuscript. France, ca. 1719.
R106
This is a collection of memorials, opinions, letters, petitions, etc., regarding the establishment of a new China Company, and the effect that it would have on French industry, particularly the manufacturing of silk.

Recueil de pieces, contenant les brefs, au roi de France, aux cardinaux, aux evêques, & celui à l'evêque de Nole, la lettre du genéral des Jésuites, en leur envoyant la Bulle Apostolicum ... France, 1765.
R107
A collection of letters reflecting an anti-Jesuit position and dealing with the suppression of the Jesuits in France and the consideration of certain missionaries in Japan and the Philippines for canonization.

Recueil de pieces en faveur des compagnies hollandoises pour le commerce des Indes Orientales et Occidentales et contre ... la nouvelle Compagnie d'Ostende. Rotterdam, T. Johnson, 1728.
R108
An introduction to a series of tracts issued in opposition to the Ostend Company by Dutch and English East Indian interests.

Recueil de pieces, pour servir d'addition & de preuve à la Relation abregée concernant la République établie par les Jésuites dans les Domaines d'outre-mer des Rois d'Espagne & de Portugal, & la guerre qu'ils y soutienent contre les armées de ces deux monarques. [n.p.] 1758.
R109

A collection of documents supporting the cause against the Jesuits in the Portuguese and Spanish possessions.

Recueil de pièces utiles pour l'instruction de l'affaire de la Compagnie des Indes. [Paris? 1769?] R110

Contains several documents relating to the opening of the eastern trade to all French subjects.

Recueil de plusiers mémoires touchant la finance et la Compagnie des Indes. Manuscript. France, ca. 1727. R111

A manuscript of 323 pages concerning the finances of France in the period 1720-27, including much information on John Law and his Compagnie des Indes.

Recueil des déclarations, arrêts et réglemens, rendus sur le tabac. [n.p.] 1786. R112

A handbook to aid those trying to locate information in the numerous royal decrees, ordinances, and regulations concerning the importation and sale of tobacco.

Recueil des loix constitutives des colonies Angloises, confédérées sous la dénomination d'États-Unis de l'Amerique-septentrionale. Philadelphia; Paris, Cellot & Jombert, 1778. R113

A collection of documents relating to American independence, including the Declaration of Independence, the Articles of Confederation, and the consititutions of six states.

Recueil des mémoires sur le commerce des Pays-Bas autrichiens. [Brussels] Imprimerie des Nations, 1787. R114

An attempt to arrive at a conclusion about the national economic interest of the Austrian Netherlands through a collection of statements on the economic interests of the major cities.

Recueil des ordres donnés pour le bannissement des religieux de la Compagnie de Jesus, d'Espagne, & des isles adjacentes. Madrid, 1767. R115

A collection of decrees, laws, letters, and other documents relating to the suppression of the Jesuits in Spain and all her overseas dominions.

Recueil des représentations, protestations et réclamations faites à S.M.I. par les représentans & etats des provinces des Pays-Bas autrichiens. Contenant la joyeuse entrée, avec ses additions, edits, & divers traités de paix, sur lesquels les mêmes réclamations sont étayées ... [Brussels] Imprimerie des Naitons, 1788. R116

A collection of documents comprising responses to the proposed reforms of Joseph II for the Austrian Netherlands which had major implications for the economic, political and ecclesiastical administration of those provinces.

Reden van dat die West-Indische Compagnie ofte handelinge ... is tot behoudenisse van onsen staet. [n.p.] 1636. R117

A defense of the West India Company as a great contributor to the prosperity of the Netherlands.

Redenen waerom het oorbaerder is dat de vereenichde Nederlanden haer met de republyq van Engelandt verbinden ... Rotterdam, Anthony van Lusthof, 1651. R118

Advocates alliance between the English and Dutch in the interest of their American trade.

Redenen, waeromme dat de vereenighde Nederlanden, geensints eenighe vrede met den koningh van Spaignien konnen, mogen, noch behooren te maecken. The Hague, Aert Meuris, 1630. R119

A series of ten reasons, supported by lengthy arguments, why the Dutch should not make peace with Spain. The reasons concern both religion and trade.

Redenkundig berigt wegens de ware oorzaak van 't bederf, mitsgaders de middelen van redres der Nederlandsche Oost-Indischen Compagnie, door den Indischen patriot ... [n.p., ca. 1773.] R120

A resident at Batavia for thirty years criticizes the management of the East India Company there.

Redern, Sigismund Ehrenreich de. Hemisphere Septentionale ... Berlin, 1762. R121

This is a polar projection of the northern hemisphere. Included are tracks of explorations, across the Pacific and one across the Arctic. The latter (if it did take place) was from Japan to Portugal by one David Me[l?]quei? in 1660.

Redi, Francesco. Esperienze intorno a diverse cose naturali, e particolarmente a quelle, che ci son portate dall' Indie. Florence, Insegna della Nave, 1671. R122

Written in the form of a letter to the Jesuit scholar Athanasius Kircher, this work discusses broadly the natural history of the East Indies.

Reflections on the importation of bar-iron from our own colonies of North-America. [London, 1757.] R123

States that the importing of American iron would not be in the interest of Britain, and favors continued use of Swedish and Russian sources to supplement the English supply.

Reflections on the present state of our East-India affairs. With many interesting anecdotes, never before made public. By a gentleman long resident in India. London, T. Lownds, 1764. R124

A review of the East India Company's position at a time when its emphasis was being diverted from commercial to military objectives.

Reflections on the present state of the East-India trade; and proposals to render it of more general benefit to the British nation. [London, 1779.] R125

An attempt to interest British merchants in the spice trade by taking advantage of the declining position of the Dutch in the Spice Islands. It appears to have been written in 1769 but not issued then.

Reflexien over de jegenswoordige situatie van de Oost-Indische Compagnie. [n.p., 1791.]   R126
A review of the affairs of the Dutch East and West India companies.

Réflexions d'un vieillard du pays de Médoc sur l'arrêt ... qui permet l'admission des etrangers dans nos colonies. [n.p.] 1785.   R127
A criticism of the policy of opening the French colonies in America to foreign merchants.

Reflexions generales sur la lettre qui paroît sous le nom de Messieurs du Seminaire des missions étrangères, touchant les cérémonies chinoises. [n.p.] 1700.   R128
A pro-Jesuit response.

Réflexions sur différens objets du commerce, et en particulier sur la libre fabrication des toiles peintes. Geneva, 1759.   R129
A discussion of free manufacture and import of colored cloths and the innumerable regulations on such trade, partly to protect the interests of the Compagnie des Indes.

Reflexions sur la censure, publiée sous le nom de la Faculté de Theologie de Paris, contre les livres intitulés, Nouveaux memoires sur l'etat present de la Chine: Histoire de l'edit de l'empereur de la Chine: Lettre des ceremonies de la Chine. [n.p.] 1700.   R130
A critic of the Faculty of Theology's action in censuring LeGobien's and Le Comte's books, noting the irregular procedure that was followed and the strong anti-Jesuit sentiment involved in the deliberations.

Réflexions sur la situation des affaires présentes entre la France et la Grande-Bretagne. Leipzig, Lankisch et heritiers, 1756.   R131
A review of the points at issue at the beginning of the Seven Years's War, with the advice that France would do well to avoid attempts to expand her overseas holdings.

Réflexions sur le commerce. [Paris, ca. 1790.]   R132
A survey of France's commerce with her colonies, with recommendations for its development.

Réflexions sur un mémoire présenté au conseil, où on demande que les Anglois soient admis à commerce librément dans les colonies françoises. Manuscript. [France, ca. 1784.]   R133
Arguments opposing the opening of French West Indian commerce to foreign ships, especially English ones.

Reflexions über Mr. Laws neues systema der financen. Leipzig, G.C. Wintzern, 1720.   R134

A discussion of John Law's financial program for France.

Reftelius, Carl. Historisk och politisk beskrifning, öfwer riket och staden Algier, ifrån år 1516 til och med år 1732. Stockholm, Peter Jör. Nyström, 1737-39.   R135
A history and description of Algiers, reflecting Sweden's newly established commercial interest there.

Regalia, Antonio José Alvarez de Abréu, marques de la. Victima real legal, discurso unico juridico-historico-politico sobre que las vacantes mayores y menores de las Iglesias de las Indias Occidentales pertenecen à la corona de Castilla y Leon con pleno y absoluto dominio. Madrid, Andres Ortega, 1769.   R136
A legal treatise claiming that the church has a right to one tenth of the revenues of Spanish colonies, tracing the origins of that principle. The enlarged second edition.

Reggio di Calabria (Italy). Laws etc. [Statuta. Ferrara, Belfortis Andreas Gallis, ca. 1478.]   R137
A collection of statutes which gives heavy emphasis to commercial regulations.

Reggio Emilia (Italy). Laws, etc. Statuta magnifice communitatis Regii. [Reggio, Vincentius Bertochus, 1501.]   R138
Many of the laws in this collection show a concern for commercial affairs. Reggio Emilia, a small town near Bologna, was a flourishing community in the late medieval period.

Regiomontanus, Joannes. Calendarium magistri Joannis de Monteregio viri peritissimi. [Augsburg, Erhard Ratdolt, 1499.]   R139
This calendar covers the period 1475-1531.

Regiomontanus, Joannes. Ephemerides, 1484-1506. Venice, E. Ratdolt, 1484.   R140
A copy of this work in Columbus' possession enabled him to predict an eclipse of the moon for February 29, 1504, which caused the Jamaican Indians to consider him supernatural.

Registre de polices maritimes. Manuscript. [France] 1734-43.   R141
Manuscript documents relating to commerce between Smyrna and various Mediterranean ports, chiefly Marseilles.

Registro de cartas para procuradores da Bahya, Rio de Janeiro, Pernambuco ... Manuscript. [n.p.] 1749-1753.   R142
Copies of more than one hundred letters dealing with commerce, slavery, settlement and other aspects of colonial Brazil.

Rego, Francisco Xavier do. Tratado completo da navegaçaõ. Lisbon, Joaõ Antonio da Silva, 1779.
R143
A textbook on navigation, with maps and illustrations of nautical instruments.

Rehbinder, Johan Adam, friherre. Nachrichten und Bemerkungen über den algierschen Staat. Altona, Johann Friedrich Hammerich, 1798.
R144
An exhaustive description of Algeria, covering history, geography, economy, peoples, etc., including a map and twelve illustrations.

Rehn, Carl Johan, respondent. Historia vectigalis öresundensis. Uppsala, J. Edman, 1783.
R145
An academic dissertation on the history of the administration of tolls in the Sund, including statistics for shipping from 1781-82.

Reichel, Carl Gotthold. Statistisk og historisk jordbeskrivelse, efter en Indsk laerebog. Copenhagen, C.L. Buch, 1793.
R146
A school text in geography, a country by country survey of the world.

Reiffenberg, Friedrich von. Critische Jesuiter-Geschichte, worinn alles aus ächten Quellen kurz hergeleitet, die sogenannte Pragmatische Historie des Herrn Professor Harenbergs stark beleuchtet ... Frankfurt und Mainz, Varrentrappischen Buchhandlung, 1765.
R147
A defense of the Society of Jesus against attacks by a protestant theologian, Johann Christoph Harenberg. It contains a review of Jesuit missions in both Asia and the New World.

Reinel, Jorge. [Portolan chart of southern Atlantic Ocean including western Africa and Brazil.] Manuscript. [Portugal, ca. 1534.]
R148
A brilliantly-colored portolan chart, with many place names on the Brazilian and African coasts. The cartographer was from a family of distinguished Portuguese mapmakers.

Reisch, Gregor. Margarita philosophica. [Freiburg, Joannes Schott, 1503.]
R149
The first edition of one of the most important encyclopedic works of the sixteenth century, including a treatment of world geography and an important world map.

Reisch, Gregor. Margarita philosophica. Strassburg [Johannes Grüninger] 1512.
R150
This edition includes an appendix concerning instruments for surveying and for making astronomical observations.

Reisch, Gregor. Margarita philosophica. Basel, Henric Petri, 1535.
R151
This edition was prepared by Oronce Fine who added nearly 400 pages, including some material on geography, and a new world map.

Reisen nach Peru, Acadien und Egypten, worin die Merkwürdigkeiten der Natur und Kunst in diesen Ländern, nebst den Sitten und Gewohnheiten der Einwohner beschreiben werden. Göttingen, Abraham Vandenhoeks seel. Wittwe, 1751.
R152
This volume includes Bouguer's voyage to Peru, Diéreville's account of Acadia and Granger's travels in Egypt, being part three of *Sammlung neuer und merkwürdiger Reisen zu Wasser und zu Lande*.

Reitz, Johan Frederick. Oude en nieuwe staat van't Russische of Moskovische Keizerryk. Utrecht, Johannes Broedelet, 1744.
R153
An account of Russia, including information on its commerce with a chart of import and export duties.

Reize naer de Zuidzee, met het schip de Wager, onder het opzicht van den Heere George Anson. Ondernomen in den jaere 1740. Leiden en Amsterdam, J. Le Maire, S.J. Baalde, C. van Hoogeveen, junior, 1766.
R154
A translation from the French of the account of the survivors aboard the *Wager*, with illustrations added.

Reize rondom den aardkloot door den Kommandeur Byron, aan boord van het Engelsch schip den Dolphin, gedaan. Haarlem, Joh. Enschede, 1767.
R155
The first Dutch edition of the narrative of the *Dolphin*'s voyage by "an officer on board," translated from the English edition of the same year.

Relaçam curiosa das grandezas do reino da China, noticia da sua situaçam, fortalezas, rios, e lugares notaveis. Lisbon, Pedro Ferreira, 1762.
R156
A brief description of China, its geography, history, cities, religion, etc.

Relaçam do combate, que tiveraõ com os Francezes com os Inglezes, aonde se referem as proezas, que estes tem feito, com algũas noticias da América, e tomada do Forte Bull ... Lisbon, Domingos Rodrigues, 1756.
R157
A newsletter account of Anglo-French hostilities in Europe and North America, with a description of the French capture of Fort Bull between Albany and Oswego in February 1756.

Relaçam do navfragio qve fizeram as naos Sacramento, & Nossa Senhora da Atalaya, vindo da India para o reyno, no Cabo de Boa Esperança: de que era Capitaõ mòr Luis de Miranda Henriques, no anno de 1647. Lisbon, P. Craesbeeck, 1650 [repr. 1737].
R158

Relaçam verdadeira dos felices sucessos da India, e victorias que alcansaram as armas portuguezas naquelle estado ... Primeira parte. [n.p.] 1753. R159
A newsletter reporting a minor military engagement in the vicinity of Goa, and a naval battle near the mouth of the Persian Gulf. A second part does not appear to have been published.

Relaçaõ curiosa, e descripçam geographica das terras de Moçambique, rios Sena, e interesses, que podem tirar das mesmas terras, os que povoarem, e cultivarem, segundo as muitas experiencias, que tem feito varias pessoas, que nellas tem habitado, e commerciado ... as ditas terras. [Lisbon, 1755.] R160
A highly favorable account of Mozambique as an encouragement to Portuguese settlers, together with a statement of benefits guaranteed to settlers by the crown.

Relacaõ da jornada que fes o governador Antonio de Sousa Coutinho ao estreito de Ormus, & do successos della. [Lisbon] Domingos Lopes Rosa, 1653. R161
A report of an encounter between the Portuguese fleet sent from India and the Arabian fleet of Muscat in 1652.

Relacaõ da muy notavel perda do galeaõ grande S. Joaõ em que se contaõ os grandes trabalhos, e lastimosas cousas que acontecèraõ ao capitaõ Manoel de Sousa Sepulveda, 1552. Lisbon, 1735. R162

Relaçaõ da viagem, e successo que tiveraõ as naos Aguia, e Garça vindo da India para este reyno no anno de 1559: com huma discriçaõ da cidade de Columbo: pelo padre Manoel Barradas da Companhia de Jesus. Lisbon, 1735. R163

Relação da viagem e successos da Armada do estreito de Ormus ... Lisbon, A. Craesbeeck de Mello, 1670. R164
A description of a punitive expedition against brigands at Muscat and Ormuz, regions of great importance to the Portuguese Indian trade.

Relaçaõ do forte combate, que tiveram duas naos de guerra inglezas, com a náo da India franceza, que no dia dois de junho do presente anno sabio do porto desta ciudad. Lisbon, 1757. R165
A Portuguese reference to the naval battles between the English and French off the coast of India.

Relação do modo com que desempenhou o chéfe de divisão, Donald Campbell, a commissão de que o encarregou, o almirante Lord Nelson, na viagem ao porto de Tripoli, a fim de effeituar a paz entre o baxá daquella regencia, e a coroa de Portugal. Lisbon, Simao Thadeo Ferreira, 1799. R166
An account of the negotiations leading to a treaty between Portugal and Tripoli in which British diplomacy was instrumental.

Relaçaõ do naufragio da nao Santa Maria da Barca de que era capitaõ D. Luis Fernandes de Vasconcellos: A qual se perdeo vindo da India para Portugal no anno de 1559. Lisbon, 1735. R167

Relaçaõ marcial do plausivel, e affortunado sucçesso, que nas partes da India tiveraõ as armas Portuguezas contra o Bonsuló nosso inimigo em o conflicto com elle havido em o dia nove de mayo do anno passado de 1758. [n.p., 1759.] R168
A newsletter recording the success of the Portuguese against a local Indian ruler known as the Bonsuolo, preventing him from joining forces with the Mahrattas.

Relacion breve de los grandes y rigurosos martirios que el año passado de 1622 dieron en el Iapon ... Madrid, Por Andres de Parra, 1624. R169
A record of 118 martyrdoms in Japan based on reports by Jesuit missionaries, some of whom had escaped to Manila.

Relacion cierta y verdadera de la feliz vitoria y prosperos successos q̃ en la India Oriental, dicha del Brasil, han conseguido los Portugueses, contra armadas muy poderosas de Olanda, y Persia, este año de 1624. Barcelona, Estevan Liberos, 1625. R170
One of four editions of a newsletter published in four different cities in Spain reporting primarily Portuguese success in naval conflict in the Persian gulf.

Relacion de la valerosa defensa de los naturales Bisayas del pueblo de Palompong en la ysla de Leyte ... en las yslas Philipinas, que hicieron contra las armas Mahometanas de Ylanos, y Malanaos, en el mes de Iunio de 1754. [Manila, Compañia de Jesus, 1755?]. R171
An account of a Moslem raid on the town of Palompong on Leyte by a small fleet of junks which was repulsed by the local population.

Relacion de los felices sucessos que han renido las armas del exercito de su Magestad ... en el reino de Chile ... [Madrid, ca. 1663.] R172
An account of wars against the Indians, the population of Valdiva, and of the presidio of Chiloe.

Relacion nueva de lo que son las Filipinas que trae el pe P. Chirino de la Compa de Jus que partio dellas en jullio de 1602. Manuscript. [Madrid, ca. 1603.] R173
Concerns questions of Philippine trade and navigation, and other aspects of the Spanish presence there.

Relacion que embio Diego Ruyz, Teniente de maestre de campo, General y natural de la ciudad de Granada ... del armada y exercito que fue al socorro del Brasil, desde que entrò en la Bahia de Todos Santos. Madrid, Imprenta Real, 1625.
R174
A newsletter announcing the reconquest of Bahia in 1625 from the Dutch who had taken it a year earlier.

Relacion verdadera de la famosa vitoria que ha tenido el marques de Cadereita, capitan general de los galeones, en la isla de San Martin ... Seville, Juan Gomez de Blas, 1633. R175
Describes the naval battle between the Spanish and Dutch at St. Martin Island in the Caribbean in 1633. The Spanish victory is celebrated here.

Relacion verdadera de la ingsine y milagrosa vitoria, que don Iorge de Mendoça Passaña ... con setecientos y cincuenta Portuguese, ciento y cincuenta de a cauallo, y seiscientos de a pie, alcanço en siete del mes de iunio deste año de 1629, contra el Cacis Cid Mahamet Laex, el qual traya mil de a cauallo, y seis mil de a pie. [Lisbon, Antonio Aluarez, 1629.] R176
An account of a Spanish victory over Moroccans in a battle for Ceuta.

Relacion verdadera de la memorable hazaña de los nueve invencibles martes portugueses, y de la insigne vitoria que con su Capitan Antonio de Pina alcançaron de treze galeones de holandeses, y otras naves enemigas, y de la rica presa que cogieron en la India Oriental este año de 1621. [Barcelona, Estevan Liberos, 1621.] R177
An account of a Portuguese victory in the Moluccas over a combined Dutch-Ambonese fleet.

Relacion verdadera de la refriega que tuvieron nuestros galeones de la plata en el Cabo de San Anton ... Madrid, Diego Diaz de la Carrera, 1638. R178
A newsletter reporting a naval battle off Cape San Antonio in Cuba, August 1638, in which a Dutch fleet of forty ships was defeated with a loss of four hundred men and their admiral, Cornelis Jol.

Relacion y declaracion de la mercaderias prohibidas, y de contravando contenidas en las cedulas reales ... [n.p., 1650?]. R179
Lists commodities from France and Portugal which were subject to special import restrictions.

Relatio triplex de rebus indicis: I. R.P. Cornelii Beudinii, dicti Godinez, martyrium. II. Caaiguarum gentis mores coepta conversio. III. R.P. Adriani Knudde, dicti crespi, elogium. Antwerp, Jacobum Meursium, 1654. R180
The three parts all relate to Jesuit missions and missionaries in the New World.

Relation contenant ce qui s'est passé depuis peu pour l'établissement de la religion chrétienne dans le grand empire de la Chine. [Paris, 1692.]
R181
A newsletter containing the Edict of Toleration promulgated by emperor K'ang Hsi in 1692, with introductory text noting the change from hostility to tolerance toward Christianity in China.

Relation d'un voyage aux Indes Orientales, par un gentil-homme françois arrivé depuis trois ans. Paris, Pierre Villery & Jean Guignart, 1645.
R182
An anonymous Frenchman's account of travels to Java, Formosa, China, and the Americas.

Relation de ce qui s'est passé au Fort S. Pierre, isle de la Martinique, au sujet des ordres donnés par le général anglois au missionnaires, de laisser leurs eglises libres a certaines heures les jour de dimanche, pour que ses troupes pussent y faire les exercises de leur culte ... [n.p., ca. 1763.] R183
An account of events on Martinique after the British occupation in 1762 when Dominican clergymen resisted General Monckton's order to permit use of the churches by his troops for religious services.

Relation de ce qui s'est passé cette année en Canada. [Paris, Galleries du Louvre, ca. 1755.]
R184
A newsletter reporting recent events of the French and Indian War in North America.

Relation de ce qui s'est passé dans les Indes Orientales en ses trois provinces de Goa, de Malabar, du Iapon, de la Chine, & autres païs nouvellement descouuerts ... Paris, Sebastien Cramoisy et Gabriel Cramoisy, 1651. R185

Relation de ce qui s'est passé de plus remarquable aux missions des peres de la Compagnie de Jesus en la Nouvelle France, les années 1668 & 1669. Paris, Sebast. Mabre-Cramoisy, 1670.
R186
This relation is chiefly concerned with the news from recently established missions among the Iroquois. A letter from Governor Lovelace at New York complains about the sale of intoxicants to the Indians.

Relation de ce qui s'est passé de plus remarquable aux missions des PP. de la Compagnie de Jesus en la Nouvelle France, és années 1657 & 1658. Paris, Sebastien Cramoisy, 1659. R187
This *Relation* contains a variety of sources, among them two letters from Paul Ragueneau, an anonymous journal of events between the Indians and the French, and a description of routes to the "sea of the north."

Relation de l'autho-da-fé de Lisbonne, 20 septembre 1761. [n.p., 1761.] R188

An account of the life, actions, conviction, and execution of Gabriel de Malagrida for his complicity in a plot on the life of the Portuguese king, Jose I.

Relation de la découverte que vient de faire Mr. de Bougainville, d'une isle qu'il a nommée La Nouvelle Cythere. [n.p., 1769.] R189

A newsletter announcing the return of Bougainville from his circumnavigation of the earth, with detailed descriptions of the people and products of Tahiti.

Relation de tout ce qui s'est passé de plus memorable en la guerre que les Hollandois de la Compagnie des Indes Orientales ont euë contre le roy et les autres regens de Macassar, depuis l'an 1666 jusques a l'année 1669 ... Paris, Frederic Leonard, 1670. R190

The French edition of an account of a victory of the Dutch over the king of Celebes.

Relation des revolutions arrivées a Siam, dans l'année 1688. Amsterdam, Pierre Brunel, 1691. R191

The introduction to this account claims it was written by the French commandant in Thailand during the revolution in which French interests in Thailand were defeated.

Relation du royaume de Lassa au Thibet ou pays de Boutant, par le p. Dominique de Fano, Cap. Manuscript. [n.p., ca. 1710.] R192

The author was a Capuchin missionary to Tibet. He describes the geography, social life, economy, religion, and language of the country.

Relation eller berättelse, om then ädle och högwelborne herres, Herr Bengt Oxenstiernas ... höga förfarenheet, och widtkring om werlden giorda reesor. [Stockholm, ca. 1644.] R193

An account of travels in the Mediterranean, the Levant, and as far east as Ormuz, one of the earliest accounts of Swedish travels in these areas.

A relation of the invasion and conquest of Florida by the Spaniards. London, John Lawrence, 1686. R194

Contains accounts of the exploration of De Soto, of a journey by the Chinese Emperor into East Tartary in 1682, and of Spanish landings on the coast of California in 1683.

Relation véritable de huict navires venus des Indes Orientales & Occidentales. Lyons, C. Armand dit Alphonse, 1628. R195

Identifies eight ships and describes cargoes brought from the East and West Indies.

Relatione breve del tesoro grandissimo. Milan & Bologna, Benacci, 1614. R196

A poem loosely based on an historical event. In the late 1500's Felipe de Brito, a mercenary in Burma attempted unsuccessfully to take over Pegu with the help of the Portuguese in Goa. The poem emphasizes his victories.

Relatione della solenne entrata fatta in Roma da D. Filippo Francesco Faxicura, con il reverendiss. padre, Fra Luigi Sotelo ... ambasciadori per Idate Massamune, re di Voxu nel Giapone ... Rome, Giacomo Mascardi, 1615. R197

An account of a visit to Rome in 1613 of a Japanese embassy which also visited Spain and Genoa in the hope of closer relations between Japan and Europe.

Relatione sommaria, mandata alla Maesta del re di Spagna, della vittoria, che Dio N.S. ha concessa nell'impresa della fortrezza, & porto della Mamora, alla sua reale armata ... Venice, Giacomo Violati, 1614. R198

A newsletter translated from a previous Spanish edition announcing a Spanish victory over local rulers in Morocco.

Relatione vera dell' Armata, la quale per commandamento de Rè Catolico Don Filippo si congregò nel porto della città di Lisbona l'anno M.D.LXXXVIII ... Rome, Vincenzo Accolti, 1588. R199

A listing of Spanish ships that made up the Armada of 1588, noting captains, numbers of men, and armament for each.

Relazione della presa de' forti dell' isola de Gorea et anche al Capo Verde presa dell' isola de Tabago. Lucca, Salvatore Marescandoli, 1678. R200

A newsletter recounting the French conquest of the island of Goree off the Senegal coast from the English, and the subsequent taking of Tobago from the Dutch by the same fleet.

Relazione della preziosa morte dell' Eminentiss. & Reverendis. Carlo Tomaso Maillard di Tournon ... seguita nella città di Macao li 8 del mese di Giugno dell' anno 1710. Rome & Turin, Gio. Battista Fontana, 1712. R201

A eulogy including several funeral orations, recounting Cardinal Maillard de Tournon's service to the church in India and China.

Relazione della preziosa morte dell'eminentiss. & reverendiss. Carlo Tomaso Maillard di Tournon ... Rome, Francesco Gonzaga, 1711. R202

Maillard de Tournon, as vicar apostolic to China, was a central figure in the Chinese Rites controversy.

Relazione delle cose di Modon. Manuscript. [n.p.] September 1686. R203

A description of a military-diplomatic event involving the duchy of Modena.

Relazione o sia lettera scritta da un missionario abitante in Macao nella Cina in cui si danno recenti notizie dell' accadutone i regni di Siam, del Pegu, di Bracma, o sia di Bengala, di

Concinkina, di Tunkin, e l'impero stesso della Cina. Rome, Chracas, 1768. R204
A report on missionary activities and other events in southeast Asia.

Remarkable shipwrecks, or, A collection of interesting accounts of naval disasters. Hartford, Andrus and Starr, 1813. R205
A collection of thirty-one shipwreck narratives, mostly from the seventeenth and eighteenth centuries, from many places, and involving the ships of several nations.

Remarks occasioned by the late conduct of Mr. Washington, as president of the United States. Philadelphia, Benjamin Franklin Bache, 1797. R206
"The design of these remarks is to prove the want of claim in Mr Washington either to the gratitude or confidence of his country ..."

Remarks on a scandalous libel, entitl'd A letter from a member of Parliament, &c. relating to the bill of commerce ... London, A. Baldwin, 1713. R207
A vociferous attack on the writings of Daniel Defoe with respect to economics and trade between France and Great Britain.

Remarks on the administration of the East-India Company's affairs in India. [London, 1781.] R208
Observations on economic conditions in India, on inadequacies of East India Company rule there, and particularly on the failures of Warren Hastings' administration.

Remarks on the French memorials concerning the limits of Acadia. London, T. Jefferys, 1756. R209
The text and two maps show the rival claims of the French and English in Nova Scotia.

Remarks on the new sugar-bill, and on the national compacts respecting the sugar-trade and slave-trade. London, Printed for J. Johnson and J. Debrett, 1792. R210
Two pamphlets in support of West Indian sugar planters and against the sugar refiners, brought about by the passage of the sugar bill in the House of Commons. The planters saw the bill as a way to forcibly lower prices for their product.

Remarks on the supplement to the African Company's case. [n.p., ca. 1730.] R211
Independent traders' reply to a Royal African Company publication in which the company sought to establish the necessity of military garrisons in West Africa.

Remarks on those passages of the letters of the Spanish ministers ... which relate to the hostilities committed by the Spanish Guarda-costas, in the West-Indies. London, J. Peele, 1727. R212
A protest against the refusal of Spain to take seriously the British claims of Spanish interference with British West Indian trade.

Remarks on trade in a dialogue between a committee-man and an interloper. London, Joseph Hindmarsh, 1683. R213
A single leaf containing a supposed conversation relating to stock manipulations by the governing body of the East India Company.

Remarks upon a book entituled, The present state of the sugar colonies consider'd. London, J. Peele, 1731. R214
Advocates a relaxing of regulations requiring American exporters of sugar to call at England with their cargoes.

Remarks upon a late pamphlet intitul'd, *The two great questions consider'd*. London, 1700. R215
A reply to a pamphlet by Defoe which had advocated a large standing army for England and a system of alliances to counterbalance the growing strength of France.

Remarks upon Colonel Fullarton's "View of the English interests in India." By an officer, late in the company's service in Bengal. London, For John Stockdale, 1788. R216
An anonymous attempt to answer the charges, set forth by a distinguished commander, of the miserable state of English possessions in India through bad government.

Remarks upon Mr. Webber's scheme and the draper's pamphlet. London, J. Roberts, 1741. R217
This author agrees that there must be an improvement in trade and an increase in English wool manufacture, but strongly disagrees with Webber's plan to effect these goals.

Remarks upon several pamphlets writ in opposition to the South-sea scheme. London, J. Roberts, 1720. R218
A criticism of three pamphlets which had espoused a conservative position regarding the national debt taken by the Bank of England.

Remarks upon the Scotch act, in a letter to a friend. [London] John Whitlock, 1695. R219
This author is alarmed about allowing the Company of Scotland to trade with Africa and the Indies, believing that such trade could make Scotland a great free port for American, Asian, and African goods.

Remarques d'un docteur en théologie, sur la protestation des jesuites; avec un réponse au nouveau libelle de ces peres contre le censure de Sorbonne. [n.p., 1700.] R220
This is a rebuttal to Le Gobien's *Acte de protestation* and a rejoinder to the *Censure de quelques propositions*.

Remarques, of aenmerckingen, op de missive laetstleden geschreven van den koning van Engelandt, tot antwoort van den brief door de Ho: Mo: Heeren Staten Generael der Vereenigde Nederlanden gesonden aen Sijn Majesteyt door een trompetter. Amsterdam, Hieronymus Sweerts, 1673. R221
A commentary on Charles II's reply to a previous letter from the States General leading toward settlement of the third Anglo-Dutch War in 1674.

Remarques plus particulieres, ou Replique à la duplique, publiée par le Sieur Downing. The Hague, H. van Wouw, 1666. R222
The Dutch reply to the English ambassador, Downing, the purpose of this edition being to convince the French king of the justice of the Dutch cause in their war with England.

Remonstrance charitable a M. Louis de Cicé ... Avec quelques reflexions sur la censure de l'Assemblée du Clergé. Cologne, Pierre Marteau, 1700. R223
A criticism of Bishop Cicé for his negative comments on Jansenism while condemning Jesuit policies in their China missions.

Remonstrantie aen ... Karel de II. Koningh van Groot Brittangien ... Delft, Jan Hendricks van der Hoeve, 1661. R224
A translation of an English criticism of the policy of letting the Dutch build their commercial strength on the herring fisheries near England.

Renard, Louis. Atlas van zeevaert en koophandel door de geheele weereldt. Amsterdam, Reinier & Josua Ottens, 1745. R225
An impressive atlas combining the nautical and the commercial with maps drawn by such men as DeLisle, Halley, and Witsen. The text contains statements about products, prices, export and import statistics, etc.

Rennefort, Souchu de. Histoire des Indes Orientales. Paris, A. Seneuze et D. Nortemels, 1688. R226
Describes the East Indies and commercial opportunities there, and also gives information on the establishment of the Compagnie des Indes Orientales.

Rennefort, Souchu de. Relation du premier voyage de la Compagnie des Indes Orientales en l'isle de Madagascar ou Dauphine. Paris, Jean de la Tourette, 1668. R227
Observations on the East Indian trade.

Rennell, James. Memoir of a map of Hindoostan, or the Mogul's empire. M. Brown for the author and W. Faden, 1783. R228
The first edition of commentary and a definitive map of India following the British conquests there.

Rennell, James. Memoir of a map of Hindoostan. London, For the Author by M. Brown, 1785. R229
The second edition, with additions and alterations, of a volume describing a map of India. The map itself is included only in a reduced form.

Rennell, James. Memoir of a map of Hindoostan. London, W. Bulmer & Co. for the Author, 1792. R230
This edition is extensively revised and augmented. Although it claims to be the second edition, it is the fourth English edition.

Rennell, James. A map of Hindoostan, or the Mogul Empire. London, J. Rennell, 1788. R231
The first nearly correct map of India in its third edition, the first having been published in 1783. The map is in four sheets with a total dimension of 106 x 124 cm.

[Rennell, James.] Index to the memoir [and map of Hindoostan]. [London, 1788.] R232

Rennell, James. A Bengal atlas: containing maps of the theatre of war and commerce on that side of Hindoostan. [London] 1780. R233
This first issue contains thirteen maps including Bengal and Bahar.

Rennell, James. Description historique et géographique de l'Indostan. Paris, Imprimerie de Poignée, 1800. R234
The third French edition, including an atlas with eleven maps, and additional text translated by Jean Henri Castéra.

[Renneville, Constantin de, editor.] A collection of voyages undertaken by the Dutch East-India Company, for the improvement of trade and navigation. London, W. Freeman, J. Walthoe [etc.] 1703. R235
The first English edition, largely a translation of Izaak Commelin's *Begin ende voortgangh van de ... Oost Indische Compagnie*.

[Renneville, Constantin de, editor.] Recueil des voyages qui ont servi a l'etablissement et aux progrez de la Compagnie des Indes Orientales. Rouen, Pierre Cailloue, 1725. R236
The first French edition, with some additional material and newly engraved maps and plates.

Replique à l'auteur du pour et contre. London, 1785. R237
A defense of the policy of exclusiveness in the French colonies.

The reply of a member of Parliament to the mayor of his corporation. London, J. Roberts, 1733. R238

An argument favoring the excise tax on wine and tobacco, stating that it will produce a relief of some 500,000 pounds on the land tax.

A reply to the vindication of the representation of the case of the planters of tobacco in Virginia. London, For R. Charlton, 1733. R239
A reply to a portion of *The case of the planters of tobacco in Virginia* which had criticized certain laws and commission merchants in Great Britain.

Réponse à la brochure intitulée *Le pour et le contre*. [n.p.] 1785. R240
Vindication of the policy of excluding foreign commerce from the French American colonies.

Reponse a la lettre des Jesuites a un prelat, touchant les cérémonies chinoises. [n.p.] 1709. R241
A refutation of the Jesuits' position, including French and Latin texts of six basic documents in the Chinese Rites dispute.

Réponse au plan d'imposition économique. Amsterdam & Paris, Couturier, 1774. R242
A proposed tax reform for France, with city dwellers paying a consumer's tax and farmers paying a *taille* based on the amount of land held.

Reponse aux remarques de M*** sur la protestation de Pere Le Gobien. [n.p.] 1700. R243
A rejoinder to the *Censure de quelques propositions*, alleging it was written with a venemous spirit toward the Jesuits, and therefore was inadequate as an argument against the writings of Le Comte and LeGobien.

The representations of Governor Hutchinson and others, contained in certain letters transmitted to England ... and laid before the General-Assembly of the Massachusetts-Bay, together with the resolves of the two Houses thereon. Boston, Edes and Gill, 1773. R244
This edition adds introductory material, some additional letters, and the response of the Massachusetts General Assembly.

Rerum à Carolo V. Caesare Augusto in Africa bello gestarum commentarij, elegantissimis iconibus ad historiam accommodis illustrati ... Antwerp, Joan Bellerum, 1555. R245
A collection of histories of military expeditions of Charles V against Algiers, Tunis, and other North African cities which Spain sought to dominate as a base against Moslem pirates in the Mediterranean.

Rerum memorabilium in regno Japoniae gestarum, litterae an. M.DC.XIX, XX, XXI, XXII, Societatis Jesu. Antwerp, Hieronymi Verdussii, 1625. R246
A collection of three letters plus an addendum. The authors are Gasparo Ludovico, Giovanni Battista Bonelli, and Girolamo Maiorica. Their reports cite repression of Jesuit missions by Japanese authorities.

Rerum Moscoviticarum auctores varii unum in corpus nunc primum congesti. Frankfurt, Haeredes Andreae Wecheli, Claud. Marnium & Joan Aubrium, 1600. R247
A collection of most of the important western accounts of Russia from the sixteenth century, including Herberstein, Fabri, Giovio, Miechowita, and Chancellor.

En resa til Africa och Ost-Indien; eller berättelse om atskilligt som blifwit i akttagit, hos Hottentotterne, uti flere delar af Ost-Indien, och på Japan ... Stockholm, Kongl. Tryckeriet, 1764. R248
An account of the East Indies and Africa by a Swedish traveler who accompanied a ship of the Dutch East India Company. It is particularly concerned with the commercial products of Asia and the East Indies.

Resende, André de. Epitome rerum gestarum in India a Lusitanis. Louvain, Servatius Zassenum, 1531. R249
An account of Portuguese conquests in India, frequently noting the commodites of Indian and Arab merchants that were seized or burned.

Resende, Garcia de. Livro das obras de Garcia de Resende. [Evora, Andre de Burgos] 1554. R250
A rhymed chronicle of events of the first half of the sixteenth century, with considerable mention of Portuguese discoveries in the East.

Résumé de mon avis au Comité du commerce avec les États-Unis lorsque la question des tabacs nous a été presénté. Manuscript. France [1780]. R251
The author is favorable to commerce with the United States, particularly the importing of tobacco.

Résumé sur le commerce libre ou privilégié de l'Inde. [Paris, Imprimerie Nationale, 1790.] R252
An argument favoring suppression of the monopoly of the Compagnie des Indes.

Resumen de la pretension, que tiene en el supremo consejo de las Indias. [Lima? ca. 1715.] R253
Concerns citizens of Spain, who, along with French and British subjects, are introducing prohibited merchandise into Peru.

Reutenfels, Jacobus. De rebus Moschoviticis, ad Serenissimum Magnum Hetruriae Ducem Cosmum Tertium. Padua, Petri Mariae Frambotti, 1680. R254
A general history and description of Russia based on many sources and apparently not on the author's own observations.

A review of the principal proceedings of the Parliament of 1784. London, R. Edwards, 1792. R255
This review notes contributions to colonial policy in India, commercial improvement in Ireland, beneficial trade policies at home, and the beginnings of debate on the slave trade.

Revius, Jacobus. Daventriae illustratae, sive historiae urbis Daventriensis, libri sex. Leiden, P. Leffen, 1651. R256
A history of Deventer, a city important to the Hanseatic trade in the fifteenth and sixteenth centuries.

Rey, Claudius. Observations on Mr. Asgill's Brief answer to a brief state of the question between the printed and painted callicoes. London, W. Wilkins [etc.] 1719. R257
The author, a weaver, argues for greater limitation of the importation of East Indian calicoes.

Reyd, Everhard van. Historie der Nederlantscher Oorlogen begin ende voortganck tot den jaere 1601 ... Daer bÿ gevoegt de Nederlandsche geschiedenissen dienende voor continuatie tot ... 1640. Beschreven door wijlen Johan van Sande ... Leeuwarden, Gijsbert Sybes, 1650. R258
A chronicle of Dutch history to 1640. It includes numerous references to events in the East and West Indies involving Dutch commercial interests.

Reynaud de Villeverde, Jean-François, comte de. Motion de M. le comte de Reynaud, Député de Saint-Domingue, a la séance du 31 août. [Versailles, Baudoin, 1789.] R259
An argument against the monopoly by France on grain and flour trade to the colony in Saint Domingue.

Reynell, Carew. The true English interest; or An account of the chief national improvements. London, G. Widdowes, 1674. R260
A review of England's economic position with respect to how it might be improved through a greater encouragement of trade.

Reyszbuch desz heyligen Lands ... Frankfurt am Main, Johannes Saurn, 1609. R261
A collection of eighteen travel accounts describing the Holy Land, ranging from narratives of the First Crusade to travels that were undertaken only decades before the collection was published.

Rho, Giacomo. Lettere del Padre Giacomo Ro della Compagnia di Giesù, doppò la sua partenza di Lisbona per Cina, che fu alli 6 d'Aprile 1618 ... Milan, Battista Bidelli, 1620. R262
An account of a missionary's travels to China, with particular interest for his description of Goa.

Rhode, Johann Christoph. Theatrum belli in America Septentrionali ... [n.p., ca. 1755.] R263
A map in two sheets depicting North America from James Bay southward to Cape Fear and westward beyond the Mississippi.

Rhodes, Alexandre de. Relazione de' felici successi della Santa Fede ... nel regno di Tunchino. Rome, Giuseppe Luna, 1650. R264
A description of Vietnam and an account of missionary activity there from 1627 to 1646 by the founder of the Roman Catholic church in that country.

Rhodes, Alexandre de. Histoire du royaume de Tunquin. Lyons, Jean Baptiste Devenet, 1651. R265
While the main purpose of this book is to report the activities of Jesuits, the first part of it contains an excellent description of the land, people, products, and commerce of Tonking.

Rhodes, Alexandre de. Tunchinensis historiae libri duo quorum altero status temporalis huius regni. Altero mirabiles evangelicae praedicationis progressus referuntur. Coeptae per patres Societatis Iesu, ab anno 1627. ad annum 1646 ... Leiden, Ioan. Bapt. Devenent, 1652. R266
The first Latin edition.

Rhodes, Alexandre de. Divers voyages et missions du P. Alexandre de Rhodes en la Chine, & autres royaumes de l'Orient, avec son retour en Europe par la Perse & l'Armenie, le tout divisé en trois parties. Paris, Sebastien Cramoisy et Gabriel Cramoisy, 1653. R267
An account of the author's missionary work in the Far East from his departure in 1619 to his return to Rome in 1648.

Rhodes, Alexandre de. Histoire de la vie, et de la glorieuse mort de cinq péres ... dans le Japon. Paris, S. & G. Cramoisy, 1653. R268
An account of the persecution of the Jesuits in Japan in the seventeenth century, due in part to commercial rivalry of European powers there.

Rhodes, Alexandre de. Relatione della morte di Andrea Catechista, che primo de Christiani nel regno di Cocincina è stato ucciso da gl'infideli in odio della fede. Rome, Heredi del Corbelletti, 1652. R269
This account of the martyrdom of a Vietnamese Christian is accompanied by a general review of the progress of Christian missions there.

Rhodes, Alexandre de. Sommaire des divers voyages. Paris, Florentin Lambert, 1653. R270
An account of travels by a Jesuit missionary in the East from 1618 to 1653. The book contains an excellent map of the Indo-Chinese coast.

Ribeiro, João. Histoire de l'isle de Ceylan. Paris, Jean Boudot, 1701. R271

This translation by Joachim Legrand of a Portuguese manuscript is the first published edition. It includes numerous additions by the translator.

Ribera, Juan de. Lettera annua della v. provincia delle Filippine, dal Giugno del 1602. al seguente giugno del 1603. Rome, Luigi Zannetti, 1605. R272
A brief but detailed report of the state of Jesuit missions in the Philippines, noting eleven establishments and a resident population of sixty-one.

Ricard, Samuel. Traité général du commerce. Amsterdam, D.J. Changuion, 1781. R273
A comprehensive picture of Europe's commerce, country by country.

Ricard, Samuel. Traité general du commerce, ... contenant les reductions des mesures, poids & monnoyes de la Hollande et d'Amsterdam, reduites aux mesures, poids & monnoyes des principales places de l'Europe, savoir pour les mesures des corps etendus, liquides & ronds ..., par Samuel Ricard. Amsterdam, Paul Marret, 1700. R274
A handbook containing tables and comparisons of weights, measures, currencies, etc. in use throughout Europe.

Ricci, Matteo. Annua della Cina del M.DC.VI. e M.DC.VII. Rome, Bartolomeo Zannetti, 1610. R275
This letter reports on missionary activity at four Jesuit establishments in China.

Ricci, Matteo. De Christiana expeditione apud Sinas suscepta ab Societatis Jesu, ex P. Matthaei Riccii eiusdem Societatis commentariis, libri V ... Auctore P. Nicolao Trigautio ... Leiden, Horatii Cardon, 1616. R276
The second edition of Ricci's memoirs, translated by Nicolas Trigault, and recording the early history of the Jesuit mission in China.

Ricci, Matteo. Entrata nella China de' padri della Compagnia del Gesu ... Opera del p. Nicolao Trigauci, padre di detta compagnia, & in molti luoghi, da lui accresciuta, e revista ... Naples, Lazzaro Scoriggio [1622]. R277
The first Italian edition.

Ricci, Matteo. Istoria de la China i cristiana empresa hecha en ella, por la Compañia de Jesus. Seville, Gabriel Ramos Veiarano, 1621. R278
The first Spanish edition.

Ricci, Vincenzo. Ragionamento intorno alla navigazione, ed al commerzio. Padua, Giovambatista Penada, 1755. R279

A survey of the history of navigation and its relation to commerce, including a discussion of the benefits of commerce.

Ricci, Vittorio. Copye van eenen brief, gheschreven van ... Sina, aen P.F. de Los Angelos procureur vande Philippinen uyt de orden vanden H. Dominicus. Antwerp, Michiel Cnobbaert, 1667. R280
An account of Christian missionary progress in China, with particular reference to the work of Adam Schall.

Ricci, Vittorio. Les dernieres nouvelles de la Chrestienté de la Chine. Paris, Denys Bechet, 1668. R281
Extracts from three missionary letters from China, with some reference to the mission in Cochin China as well.

Riccioli, Giovanni Battista. Geographiae et hydrographiae reformatae libri duodecim quorum argumentum sequens pagina explicabit ... Bologna, Haeredis Victorii Benatii, 1661. R282
An extensive mathematical geography given primarily to all aspects of measurement of the earth.

[Richardson, Joseph.] A complete investigation of Mr. Eden's treaty, as it may affect the commerce, the revenue, or the general policy of Great Britain. London, J. Debrett, 1787. R283
A review of England's commercial history precedes an analysis of trade in specific products, noting the negative effect the recent treaty would have on trade.

Rickman, John. Journal of Captain Cook's last voyage to the Pacific Ocean. London, E. Newberry, 1781. R284
The author notes the interest in European goods among people of the various Pacific islands, and also describes relations with Russian merchants in the Bering Strait region.

[Rickman, John.] Tagebuch einer entdeckungs Reise nach der Südsee in den Jahren 1776 bis 1780 unter Anführung der Capitains Cook, Clerke, Gore und King. Berlin, Haude und Spener, 1781. R285
This German translation by Johan Reinhold Forster adds numerous anotations, some containing reference to Zimmerman's account of the voyage. An improved map is included, but not the illustrations from the English edition.

[Rickman, John.] Troisieme voyage de Cook; ou, Journal d'une expédition faite dans la Mer Pacifique du Sud & du Nord, en 1776, 1777, 1778, 1779, & 1780. Paris, Pissot & Laporte, 1782. R286
This French edition adds a translator's preface and several explanatory footnotes, but includes only one illustration, along with the folding map.

Ricoul, François. Procès-verbal de M. Ricoul, de la visite dans le département de La Rochelle, 1687-1688. Manuscript. France [ca. 1689]. R287

A report on the commerce within the jurisdiction of the customs inspector of La Rochelle, including information on the privileges of the vaious trading companies.

The right of the crown of Great Britain to Hudsons Bay and Streights, in North-America, asserted: and some account of the violences committed by the French, upon the English there in time of peace. [n.p., ca. 1702.] R288

A chronological history of British claims to Hudson Bay, from 1497-1689.

The rights of the British colonies considered. London, W. Flexney [1765?]. R289

A criticism of English colonial policy with respect to colonial trade.

Rio de la Plata. Real ordenanza para el establecimiento é instruccion de intendentes de exército y provincia en el virreinato de Buenos-Aires, año de 1782. Madrid, Imprenta Real [1783?]. R290

A fundamental collection of laws for governing colonial Argentina, intended as the legal structure for its administration.

Rio de la Plata. Administración de correos. Conocimientos para el despacho de las naos, que van à los Reynos de Castilla. [n.p.] 1750-1803. R291

The documents concern goods that entered through the postal service at Rio de la Plata.

Risingh, Joh. Cl. (Johan Classon). Itt uthtogh, om kiöp-handelen eller commercierne. Stockholm, Nicolas Wankijff, 1669. R292

A general treatment of Sweden's commerce, divided into twenty-one topics including companies, monopolies, manufactures, duties, and imports. The author was the last governor of New Sweden.

Ristretto o compendio del giornale fatto nel viaggio alle Antisole e principalmente a la Martinique l'anno 1660. Manuscript. [n.p., 17th century.] R293

An account of French settlements on Martinique, with information on tobacco, cotton, and sugar production.

Rivadeneira y Barrientos, Antonio Joaquin de. Disertaciones que asistente real ... escrivio sobre los puntos que se le dieron a consultar por el Concilio Mexicano, 1770. Manuscript. [n.p.] 1770. R294

A report by the representative of the crown on the fourth Mexican Provincial Council concerning problems of governance between church and state.

Robbe, Jacques. Methode pour apprendre facilement la geographie ... Paris, Michel David, 1714. R295

The sixth and final edition of a popular geography text, including a section on navigation.

Robert de Vaugondy, Didier. Abregé des differens systêmes du monde; de la sphere, et des usages des globes, suivant les hypothèses de Ptolomée & de Copernic. Paris, Durand, 1745. R296

An instruction book for the use of terrestrial and celestial globes with explanations of the astronomical systems of Ptolemy, Copernicus and Tycho Brahe.

Robert de Vaugondy, Didier. Essai d'une carte polaire arctique. Paris, Chéz l'Auteur, 1774. R297

This polar projection extends to sixty degrees north latitude, and shows Vaugondy's belief in the probability of a northwest passage.

Robert de Vaugondy, Didier. Essai sur l'histoire de la géographie, ou sur son origine, ses progrès & son état actuel. Paris, Antoine Boudet, 1755. R298

A history of geographic knowledge, technique, and cartography intended as an introduction to the *Atlas universel* published in 1757 by the author and his father.

Robert de Vaugondy, Didier. Institutions géographiques. Paris, Boudet, Desaint, 1766. R299

A survey of the theory and history of geography, encompassing discussion of the sphere, latitude and longitude, globes, astronomy, etc.

Robert de Vaugondy, Didier. Mappemonde, ou Description du globe terrestre. Paris, Boudet, 1752. R300

Shows the tracks of several explorers of the south Atlantic and Pacific oceans.

Robert de Vaugondy, Didier. Mémoire sur les pays de l'Asie et de l'Amérique, situés au nord de la Mer du Sud. Paris, A. Boudet, 1774. R301

A study of the problem of the northwest passage with text and maps in which earlier theories are measured against recent discoveries.

Robert de Vaugondy, Didier. Orbis vetus in utrâque continente. Paris, Ant. Boudet, 1752. R302

A world map in which the American continents are related to the legend of the island of Atlantis.

Robert de Vaugondy, Didier. Partie méridional de Russie européene, ou sont distinguées exactement toutes les provinces, d'aprés le detail de l'Atlas russien. [Paris, ca. 1770.] R303

Apparently a later version of a map included in the Robert de Vaugondy atlas as it appears to incorporate border adjustments with Turkey.

Robert de Vaugondy, Didier. Partie occidentale de l'empire de Russie ... [Paris, Robert de Vaugondy, 1750.] R304

From Vaugondy's *Atlas Universel*, 1757, based on a Covens and Mortier map of 1748 which was adapted from Bering expedition maps and from De L'Isle's Akademiia Nauk atlas of 1745.

Robert de Vaugondy, Didier. Partie orientale de l'empire de Russie en Asie ... [Paris] Robert de Vaugondy, 1750. R305

An eastward extension of the previous item, but a separate map with its own cartouche and borders.

Robert de Vaugondy, Didier. Usages des globes celeste et terrestre ... Paris, Antoine Boudet, 1751. R306

This text on the use of globes as instruments of geography, astronomy and navigation is prefaced by a discussion of the history of geography.

Robert de Vaugondy, Gilles. Atlas universel. Paris, Les auteurs et Boudet [1758]. R307

This collection of 108 maps is prefaced by a history of geography and some commentary on the maps. Twelve of the maps deal with ancient knowledge, seventeen with non-European areas.

Roberts, Henry. Chart of the N.W. coast of America and the N.E. coast of Asia, explored in the years 1778 and 1779. London, Wm. Faden, 1784. R308

The chart depicts the northern voyages of Captain Cook and his successor, Captain Clerke. It also includes the overland expedition of Samuel Hearne in 1771-72.

Roberts, Henry. Karte von den N.W. amerikanischen und N.Oe. asiatischen Küsten, nach den Untersuchungen des Kapit: Cook in den Jah: 1778 und 1779. Vienna, F.A. Schraemble, 1788. R309

This edition follows that of 1784 closely.

[Roberts, J.] The trades increase. London, Nicholas Okes, 1615. R310

An early argument for free trade and wider participation in overseas trade, with the encouragement of fishing proposed as the best means to build up a merchant fleet.

Roberts, Lewes. The merchants mappe of commerce. London, R. Mabb, 1638. R311

A commercial directory for "all merchants or their factors that exercise the arte of merchandiseinge in any part of the habitable world."

Roberts, Lewes. The merchants map of commerce: wherein the universal manner and matter relating to trade and merchandize, are fully treated of ... London, Thomas Horne, 1700. R312

The fourth and last edition, a reprint of the second but without the maps, and adding *Advice concerning bills of exchange* by John Marius and Thomas Mun's *England's treasure by foreign trade*.

Roberts, Lewes. The treasure of traffike, or A discourse on forraigne trade. London, E.P. for N. Bourne, 1641. R313

A treatise on trade policy in which the author deplores the bullion theory and favors a council of merchant advisors to the king to create a "well ordered traffike."

Roberts, William. An account of the first discovery and natural history of Florida. London, T. Jefferys, 1763. R314

An attempt to acquaint English merchants and navigators with the history and geography of Florida shortly after it had been acquired from Spain.

[Robertson, Robert.] A detection of the state and situation of the present sugar planters of Barbadoes and the Leward Islands. London, J. Wilford, 1732. R315

A detailed survey of the cost and profit figures of the sugar industry, including a discussion about the social conditions on Barbados and the Leeward Islands which shows that the situation there was critical.

[Robertson, Robert.] A supplement to the detection of the state and situation of the present sugar planters of Barbadoes and the Leeward-Islands. London, J. Wilford, 1733. R316

Expansion of the previous work, highlighting the wide variety of marketable goods produced by the North American colonies and the poor condition of the sugar islands.

Robertson, William. The history of America. London, W. Strahan and T. Cadell; Edinburgh, J. Balfour, 1777. R317

Intended as the first portion of a history of European colonization of America, these two volumes deal with Spanish activity in the New World. A bibliography of 224 books and manuscripts used by the author is included.

Robertson, William. The history of America. London, W. Strahan, T. Cadell, and J. Balfour, 1778. R318

This copy includes "Additions and corrections to the former editions," 1788, and Books IX and X, edited by William Robertson the Younger, and published in 1796, bringing the history of Virginia to 1688 and New England to 1652.

Robertson, William. The history of America. London, W. Strahan, T. Cadell; Edinburgh, J. Balfour, 1780. R319

The third edition, with no significant alteration from the first.

Robertson, William. The history of America. London, A. Strahan, T. Cadell and J. Balfour, 1788-1796. R320

The fifth edition. Volume four of this set is the first edition of Robertson's *History of America books IX and X, containing the history of Virginia, to the year 1688, and the history of New England, to the year 1652.*

Robertson, William. The history of America. London, Printed by A. Strahan for A. Strahan, T. Cadell and W. Davies, and E. Balfour, Edinburgh, 1803. R321

The tenth edition, in four volumes. This edition includes the separate histories of New England and Virginia, four maps by Kitchin and a folded plate depicting Indian art.

Robertson, William. Histoire de l'Amérique. Maestricht, Jean-Edme Dufour & Philippe Roux; The Hague, Detune, 1777. R322

One of two French editions issued in 1777.

Robertson, William. l'Histoire de l'Amerique ... Paris, Panckoucke, 1778. R323

One of two editions published by Panckouke in 1778, apparently the first complete editions of this translation by Jean Baptiste Antoine Suard.

Robertson, William. Geschichte von Amerika. Leipzig, Weidmanns Erben und Reich, 1777. R324

The first German edition, following the English text and maps closely.

Robertson, William. Americas historia. Stockholm, Johan Pehr Lindh, 1796-97. R325

The first Swedish edition, a translation from the French.

Robertson, William. An historical disquisition concerning the knowledge which the ancients had of India. London, A. Strahan and T. Cadell; Edinburgh, E. Balfour, 1791. R326

A survey of early knowledge of the East in Europe, showing how European demand for eastern products was the major factor in the growth of geographic knowledge to the time of the earliest Portuguese voyages to India.

Robertson, William. An historical disquisition concerning the knowledge which the ancients had of India; and the progress of trade with that country prior to the discovery of the passage to it by the Cape of Good Hope ... Dublin, John Ershaw for G. Burnet [etc.] 1791. R327

Published the same year as the first edition without significant changes in text or maps.

Robertson, William. Recherches historiques sur la connoissance que les anciens avoient de l'Inde et sur les progrès du commerce avec cette partie du monde avant la découverte du passage par le Cap de Bonne-Esperance ... Paris, Buisson, 1792. R328

The first French edition, without apparent additions by the translator and with maps similar to the London, 1791 edition.

Robertus Remensis, monk. Bellum Christianorum principum ... Basel, Henric Petrus, 1533. R329

A contemporary account of the first crusade, including also the Columbus Letter.

Robichaud, Regis. [Autograph letter signed.] Manuscript in French. [n.p.] 21 September 1793. R330

Letter to Jacque Lanas concerning the writer's sale of pelts as a fur trader in New Brunswick.

Robichaud, Regis and Anselm. Fournitures faites à Jacob Hautaonais - sauvage. Manuscript. [n.p.] 5 aout 1780. R331

A list of trade goods supplied to an Indian fur trader.

[Robins, Benjamin.] Observations on the present convention with Spain. London, T. Cooper, 1739. R332

Includes the text of the treaty of El Pardo in which Spain promised to pay 95,000 pounds for damage done to the South Sea Company.

Robinson, Henry. Certain proposalls in order to the peoples freedome and accommodation ... with the advancement of trade and navigation of this commonwealth. London, M. Simmons, 1652. R333

The author suggests protection of forests useful for shipbuilding, stimulation of the fishing trade, improvement of woolen manufactures, and other measures for improvement of the nation's commerce.

Robinson, Henry. England's safety, in trades encrease. London, Nicholas Bourne [1641]. R334

A series of recommendations for the improvement of English trade, with particular interest in fishing and the East Indian commerce.

Robortello, Francesco. Oratio in funere Imp. Caroli V. Augusti, in ampliss. Hispanorum collegio Bonon. habita. Bologna, Alexandrum Benacium, 1559. R335

An oration in tribute to Charles V who is praised for his defense of Christendom against the Turks and for expanding its realm into the New World.

Robson, Joseph. An account of six years residence in Hudson's-bay, from 1733 to 1736, and 1744 to 1747. London, J. Payne [etc.] 1752. R336

An employee of the Hudson's Bay Company, Robson was critical of it, particularly its trading relationships with the northern Indians.

Rocamora y Torrano, Ginés. Sphera del universo. Madrid, Juan de Herrera, 1599.   R337
A general survey of cosmographical knowledge, including a translation of Sacrobosco's *Sphera Mundi* and a table of locations by latitutde and longitude.

Rocha, Manuel Ribeiro. Ethiope resgatado, empenhado, sustentado, corregido, instruido, e libertado. Lisbon, Officina Patriarcal de Francisco Luiz Ameno, 1758.   R338
A very early call for the abolition of the African slave trade. Rocha was a lawyer in Bahia and argues from a legal as well as a religious standpoint, stating that all slaves should be freed and their owners compensated.

Rocha e Mello, Caetano Joseph de. Naufragio Carmelitano, ou Relaçaõ do notavel successo, que aconteceo aos padres missionarios Carmelitas descalços na viagem, que faziaõ para o reyno de Angola no anno de 1749. Lisbon, Manoel Soares, 1750.   R339
An account of shipwreck and capture on the Angola coast.

Rocha Pita, Sebastião da. Historia da America Portugueza, desde o anno de mil e quinhentos do seu descobrimento, até o de mil e setecentos e vinte e quatro ... Lisbon, J.A. da Sylva, 1730.   R340
The author, a Brazilian, writes his history in the form of a chronicle, with details on early settlement, political affairs, the church, and wars with the Dutch.

Rochefort, Charles de. Histoire naturelle et morale des iles Antilles de l'Amerique. Rotterdam, A. Leers, 1658.   R341
An account of the Antilles, with numerous plates, depicting its natural history as well as the culture of the Caribs.

[Rochefort, Charles de.] Histoire naturelle et morale des iles Antilles de l'Amerique ... Rotterdam, Arnout Leers, 1665.   R342
This is the second French edition, with a new dedication, additional introductory matter and additions to both text and illustrations over the first edition of 1658.

Rochefort, Charles de. Histoire naturelle des iles Antilles de l'Amerique. Lyons, Christophle Fourmy, 1667.   R343
This edition includes the letters to the author first published in the Dutch edition of 1662. It also adds illustrations not included in the earlier editions.

Rochefort, Charles de. Histoire naturelle et morale des iles Antilles de l'Amérique. Rotterdam, R. Leers, 1681.   R344
A reissue of the edition of 1665, with a new title page and the addition of a supplement.

Rochefort, Charles de. Natuurlyke en zedelyke historie van d'eylanden de vooreylanden van Amerika. Rotterdam, Arnout Leers, 1662.   R345
This Dutch edition contains letters to the author from America, probably included here to bolster the author's case against charges of plagiarism made by Jean Baptiste Du Tertre who had also written on the West Indies.

[Rochefort, Charles de.] The history of the Caribby-Islands ... rendered into English by John Davies. London, Printed by J.M. for Thomas Dring and John Starkey, 1666.   R346
An English translation intended to attract colonists to an area of increasing interest to the British.

Rochefort, Charles de. Relation de l'isle de Tabago, ou de la Nouvelle Oüalcre, l'une des isles Antilles de l'Amerique. Paris, Louys Billaine, 1666.   R347
A promotion piece for settlement under the leadership of the Lampsins family of the Netherlands under the protection of both the Dutch and French governments. Begun in 1654, the settlement ended with an attack by the English in 1666.

Rochon, Alexis. Voyage à Madagascar et aux Indes Orientales. Paris, Prault, 1791.   R348
A description of the geography and natural history of Madagascar and adjacent islands, including also a brief account of Cochin China, with proposals to develop the commerce of Madagascar.

Rochon, Alexis. A voyage to Madagascar, and the East Indies ... to which is added a memoire on the Chinese trade. London, G.G.J., and J. Robinson, 1792.   R349
The first English edition.

Rochon, Alexis. Reis door Madagascar en de Oostindiën. Dordrecht, De Leeuw en Krap, 1793.   R350
The first Dutch edition.

Rochon de Chabannes, Marc Antoine Jacques. La noblesse oisive. [n.p.] 1756.   R351
A chastisement of the idle French nobility in answer to Coyer's *Noblesse commerçante*.

Rodero, Gaspar. Hechos de la verdad, contra los artificios de la calumnia, representados ... [n.p., ca. 1733.]   R352
A defense of the Jesuit mission in Paraguay against published attacks on it.

Rodrigues, João. Lettera di Giappone dell' anno M.DC.VI. Rome, Bartolomeo Zannetti, 1610.   R353
A statement of the secular situation in Japan, the progress of Christianity and reports on twenty-one separate missionary establishments there.

Rodrigues, João. Lettera annua del Giappone del' anno 1624. Rome, Erede di Bartolomeo Zannetti; Naples, Egidio Longo, 1628. R354

The author was a priest in Japan at least since 1614, and had written several earlier letters. This letter contains accounts of the Japanese persecutions of Christians.

Rodrigues, João. Litterae annuae Japoniae anni M.DC. XXIV. Dillingen, Caspari Sutoris, 1628. R355

Latin edition of the previous work.

[Rodrigues da Costa, Antonio.] Conversam de el Rei de Bissau conseguida pelo illustrissimo senhor Dom Frei Victoriano Portuense bispo de Cabo Verde ... Lisbon, Antonio Manescal, 1695. R356

This conversion of the King of Bissau in Portuguese Guinea was followed by Portuguese commercial and religious establishments there.

Rodriguez, Manuel. El Marañon, y Amazonas. Madrid, Antonio Gonçalez de Reyes, 1684. R357

An account of the discovery and exploration of the Amazon River and adjacent regions.

Roe, Sir Thomas. Journael van de reysen ghedaen door den Ed. Heer en Ridder Sr. Thomas Roe, ambassadeur van Sijn Coninckljjcke Maejesteyt van Groot-Brittanje, afgevaerdicht naer Oost-Indien aen den Grooten Mogol ... Amsterdam, Jacob Benjamin, 1656. R358

This Dutch edition, based on the account in *Purchas his pilgrimes*, is the only separately published edition of that version of Roe's journal.

Roe, Sir Thomas. Sir Thomas Roe, his speech in Parliament. Wherein he sheweth the cause of the decay of coyne and trade in this land. London, 1641. R359

Advocates improvement of the wool trade by diversion to lighter cloths and government intervention for more favorable duties abroad.

Roedere, Pierre Louis. Discours sur la prohibition de la culture du tabac, et le privilége exclusif de la fabrication et du débit. Paris, Imprimerie Nationale, 1791. R360

A discussion of the tobacco raising, manufacturing, and selling in France, with arguments for keeping them free to everyone.

Roef-praatje, tusschen verscheiden persoonen, over de tegenswoordige staat van Surinamen, en de laage prys der producten. Amsterdam, H. Selleger, 1774. R361

An imaginary conversation concerning the coffee trade of Surinam.

Roger, José. Relaçaõ dos successos prosperos, e infelices do illust. e excellent. senhor D. Luiz Mascarenhas, Conde de Alva, Vice-Rey em os estados da India, referida a todo o tempo de seu governo, e ao acomettimento da fortaleza da Pondá aonde perdeo a vida ... Lisbon, Francisco Luiz Ameno, 1757. R362

An account of the battle for Ponda in which Dom Luiz Mascarenhas, the Portuguese viceroy, was killed and the fortress lost to the Mahrattas.

[Roger, Urbain.] Lettres sur le Dannemarc. Geneva, Fréres Philibert, 1757-64. R363

A series of letters about Denmark, some of which contain material on Danish trade to the East and West Indies and to Africa.

Rogerius, Abraham. Offne Thur zu dem verborgenen Heydenthum: oder, Warhaftige Vorweisung dess Lebens und Sittens samt der Religion und Gottesdienst der Bramines auf der Cust Chormandel, und denen herumligenden Ländern. Nuremberg, Johann Andreas Endter und Wolfgang dess jüng seel. Erben, 1663. R364

The author was a Dutch missionary who served some fifteen years in the East. His well-annotated description of Eastern religion is augmented in this German edition by accounts of African, Asiatic and American religions by Christoph Arnold.

Rogers, Robert. A concise account of North America: containing a description of the several British colonies on that continent. London, For the Author and sold by J. Millan, 1765. R365

The first half of the book consists of descriptions of each of the colonies; the latter part describes the interior, the rivers, lakes and the habits and customs of the Indians.

Rogers, Robert. Journals of Major Robert Rogers: containing an account of the several excursions he made under the generals who commanded upon the continent of North America, during the late war. London, For the Author, 1765. R366

Records the author's activities in campaigns against the Indians from 1755 to 1761, beginning with an attack on them in 1755 at Crown Point, New York.

Rogers, Woodes. A cruising voyage round the world. London, A. Bell and B. Lintot, 1712. R367

Based on a privateering voyage, this work also contains material on the South Sea trade.

Rogers, Woodes. Nieuwe reize naa de Zuid Zee, van daar naa Oost-Indien, en verder rondom de waereld ... Amsterdam, Johannes Oosterwyk en Hendrik van de Gaete, 1715. R368

The first Dutch edition, the first translation from the English, with some new engravings added.

Rogers, Woodes. Voyage autour du monde, commencé en 1708 & fini en 1711. Amsterdam, Veuve de Paul Marret, 1716. R369

This French edition adds material on the Amazon from Gomberville's translation of Acūna published in 1682, and also includes a coastal pilot for the west coast of Spanish America, supposedly taken from a Spanish ship.

Roggeveen, Arent. La primera parte del Monte de Turba ardiente allumbrando con la claridad de su fuego todas la India-Occidental. Amsterdam, Peter Goos, 1680. R370

A detailed atlas of the West Indies containing thirty-three maps. While the text is in Spanish, the legends and place names on the maps are in the Dutch of the original edition.

Rohr, Julius Philipp Benjamin von. Anmerkungen über den Cattunbau ... zum nuzen der dänischen westindischen Colonien auf allerhöchsten koniglichen Befehl geschrieben ... Mit einer Vorrede von Herrn D. Philipp Gabriel Hensler. Altona und Leipzig, Johann Friedrich Hammerich, 1791-93. R371

An essay on cotton culture and manufacture in the West Indies with a view to developing that industry in the Danish West Indies.

Roke, George. Journaal van ... die, voor admirael het esquader gedestineerd na Cadix ... [n.p.] 1693. R372

An account of a voyage of several Dutch ships bound for Cadiz which was interrupted by an attack by French ships.

[Rokeby, Matthew Robinson-Morris, baron.] Considerations on the measures carrying on with respect to the British colonies in North America. Boston, Edes and Gill, 1774. R373

An argument on behalf of colonial opposition to the tea tax, based on the natural right of all peoples to govern themselves, and on the essential difference between American and English societies.

[Rokeby, Matthew Robinson-Morris, baron.] A further examination of our present American measures and of the reasons and the principles on which they are founded. Bath, R. Cruttwell, 1776. R374

A long and caustic review of British colonial policy in North America with predictions that attempts to retain the colonies through military action were destined to failure.

Rolt, Richard. A new and accurate history of South-America. London, T. Gardner, 1756. R375

A systematic description of South America drawn from many sources. It presents detailed information on the commerce of all parts of the continent.

Roma, J.P. Essai de l'histoire du commerce de Venise. Paris, P.G. Le Mercier fils & A. Morin, 1729. R376

A general discussion of the history of Venice and its trade from the foundation of the city to the year 1300.

Romanus, Adrianus, of Louvain. Parvum theatrum urbium sive Urbium praecipuarum totius orbis ... descriptio. Frankfurt, Nicolai Bassaei, 1595. R377

Primarily a collection of brief descriptions of European cities, but it includes some information on non-European areas.

[Rømer, Ludvig Ferdinand.] Tilforladelig efterretning om negotien paa kysten Guinea. Copenhagen, Ludolph Henrich Lillie, 1756. R378

This history of European commerce in Guinea describes the region's peoples and products in terms of their relationship to the activities of the Danish West India Company and the Guinea Company.

Rømer, Ludvig Ferdinand. Tilforladelig efterretning om kysten Guinea. Copenhagen, Ludolph Henrich Lillies Enke, 1760. R379

The second Danish edition.

[Rømer, Ludvig Ferdinand.] Die Handlung verschiedener Völker auf der Küste von Guinea und in Westindien aus dem Dänischen übersetzt. Copenhagen, Rothenschen Buchhandlung, 1758. R380

The first German edition.

Rømer, Ludvig Ferdinand. Nachrichten von der Küste Guinea, mit einer Vorrede D. Erich Pontoppidan. Copenhagen & Leipzig, Friederich Christian Pelt, 1769. R381

This German edition was based on the second Danish edition, with the preface by Eric Pontoppidan.

Romieu de Sorgues. [Instructions for the administration of French tariffs.] Manuscript. France [ca. 1770]. R382

A collection of information on tariffs, including the history of much tariff legislation of the seventeenth and eighteenth centuries. It appears to have been intended for use by customs officials.

Romieu de Sorgues. Tarif alphabetique des droits de la douanne de Valence. Manuscript. France [ca. 1800]. R383

A schedule of tariff regulations, with histories of most regulations appended, as they apply to the city of Valence. Other regulatory legislation is also included and some of it pertains to nearby cities, including Lyons.

Rooke, Henry. Travels to the coast of Arabia Felix. London, R. Blamire, 1783. R384

This account of travels through Arabia and Egypt includes observations on Arabian navigation and commerce, and a translation of a decree forbidding Christians to trade in the Red Sea.

Rooke, Henry. Voyage sur les côtes de l'Arabie heureuse, sur la Mer rouge et en Egypte ... Londres, & se vend a Paris, Chez Royez, 1788. R385

This French translation contains extensive notes by the translator. It was based on the London edition of 1784.

Rosaccio, Giuseppe. Il mondo e sue parti. Florence, Francesco Tosi, 1595. R386
A pocket-size atlas containing eighteen maps accompanied by a text and gazetteer material.

Rosaccio, Giuseppe. Teatro del mondo e sue parti ... Bologna, Constantino Pisarri, 1724. R387
An elementary world geography text, with numerous woodcut maps.

Roselli, Petrus. [Portolan chart.] Manuscript. Italy, 1466. R388
A brilliantly colored portolan including the area from the Red Sea westward to Antilia, and from the Canary Islands northward to the Baltic Sea.

Rosenstand Goiske, Peder. Til interessentskabet i expeditionen med skibet Juliana Maria. Copenhagen, Johan Frederik Schultz, 1790. R389
Relates to a law case brought by the Danish East India Company against private merchants in 1781.

Rosignoli, Carlo Gregorio. Vite e virtu di D. Paolo Siu, colao della Cina, e di D. Candida Hiu, gran dama cinese ... Milan, Giuseppe Malatesta, 1700. R390
A Jesuit author presents biographies of Paul Siu and his niece Candida Hiu, prominent Chinese who had become Christians.

Rosnel, Pierre de. Le mercure indien, ou, Le tresor des Indes. Paris: Aux dépens de l'autheur, 1668. R391
A discourse on gold, silver, quicksilver and precious stones, with a description of the mine at Potosí and details on the properties and values of the metals and stones identified.

Rossi, Domenico de. La guida del mercurio geografico. Rome, Domenico de Rossi, 1692-1714. R392
A fine example of Italian map-making, this atlas contains many detailed maps of Europe as well as some maps by Sanson and Cantelli of areas outside Europe.

Roth, Heinrich. Relatio rerum notabilium regni Mogor in Asiâ. Aschaffenburg, Joannis Michaelis Straub, 1665. R393
A report on Christianity in Asia as well as descriptions of the religions, government, and social customs in the country of the Great Mogul by a Jesuit missionary.

Rotterdams zee-praatjen, tusschen een koopman, een borger en een stierman. Schiedam, Rechte Lief-Hebbers, 1653. R394
A description of Dutch-English hostilities growing out of commercial rivalry.

Roukonen, David Davidson. Oförgripelige tankar, öfwer den Ost-Indiska handelens nytta uti Swea rike ... Stockholm, Kong. Tryckeriet, 1765. R395
An appraisal of the Swedish East India Company's value to the national economy, with comparisons to the West Indian trade.

Roume, Philippe Rose. Mémoire de M. Roume, commissaire et ordonnateur de l'île de Tabago ... qui réfute des représentations faites par les créanciers anglais des colons de Tabago, aux comités réunis du commerce et des colonies, du 15 juin 1791. Paris, Mignerit, 1791. R396
An analysis with negative comment on a proposed international financial enterprise to be headquartered on Tobago and under British leadership.

Roume, Philippe Rose. Mémoire de M. Roume, commissaire et ordonnateur de l'isle de Tabago. Paris, Imprimerie Nationale, 1790. R397
A French reply to English complaints of disruption of settlements and trade on Tobago in violation of surrender terms.

Rous, Thomas Bates. An explanation of the mistaken principle on which the Commutation Act was founded: and the nature of the mischiefs that must follow from a perseverance in it ... London, For J. Debrett [ca. 1790]. R398
A discussion of property versus consumption taxes, with particular reference to tea, presenting interesting information on the tea trade.

Rous, Thomas Bates. Observations on the commutation project. London, J. Debrett, 1786. R399
An argument against the removal of the tax on tea because of the loss of income, increase in consumption, and consequent danger to England's malt trade.

Rousillon, Pierre. Rapport ... sur le commerce du Sénégal. Paris, Imprimerie Nationale [1790]. R400
A history of the failure of French trade in West Africa under monopolistic companies, and a suggested remedy of free trade there for all French subjects.

Rousillon, Pierre. Rapport ... sur les droits à imposer sur les denrées coloniales. Paris, Imprimerie Nationale [1790]. R401
Report on colonial trade, with recommendations for its improvement through lower duties on colonial exports.

Rousillon, Pierre. Rapport, projet de loi et tarif pour le commerce du Levant. Paris, Imprimerie Nationale [1790]. R402
A review of the Levant trade, with a series of recommendations for its improvement.

[Rousselot de Surgy, Jacques-Philibert]. Mélanges interessans et curieux, ou abrégé d'histoire naturelle morale, civile, et politique de l'Asie, l'Afrique, l'Amerique et des Terres polaires. Yverdon, 1764-1767. R403

Geographic, economic and ethnographic information from a variety of sources, with comments by the author. In spite of the title there is no material on America.

[Rousselot de Surgy, Jacques-Philibert.] Memoires géographiques, physiques et historiques. Sur l'Asie, l'Afrique & l'Amerique. Paris, Durand, 1767. R404

A collection of information gathered from the *Lettres édifiantes*, with matters concerning religion deleted by the editor.

Roy, Jacob Jansz de. Voyagie ... na Borneo en Atchin, in't jaar 1691 en vervolgens. [n.p., ca. 1700.] R405

The author visited Siam and Malaya also, and includes in this work copies of his correspondence with officials of the Dutch East India Company.

Royal African Company. An abstract of the case of the Royal African Company of England. [London, 1730.] R406

Lists the forts maintained by the Royal African Company and the products taken to and from West Africa.

Royal African Company. An answer of the Company ... to the petition and paper of certain heads and particulars ... [London] 1667. R407

A reply to charges that the company's monopoly on slave trade had deprived American plantations of needed slaves.

Royal African Company. An antidote to expel the poison contained in an anonymous pamphlet ... London, J. Roberts, 1749. R408

An answer to a previously published pamphlet criticizing the directors, policies, and financial transactions of the Royal African Company.

Royal African Company. The case of the Royal-African Company. [London, ca. 1709.] R409

A review of the trade to West Africa, pointing out its decline since the admission of independent traders to it in 1698, and calling for a return to its management by a joint stock company.

Royal African Company. The case of the Royal African Company of England. London, S. Aris, 1730. R410

A history and defense of the monopoly of the Royal African Company on the West African trade.

Royal African Company. The case of the Royal African Company of England and their creditors. London, 1748. R411

The author proposes that a portion of the excessive profits of pawnbrokers be directed to the support of the Royal African Company.

Royal African Company. An explanation of the African-Company's property in the sole trade to Africa. London, 1712. R412

An argument for the company, showing why Parliament should modify the Act of 1698 to be more favorable to it.

Royal African Company. Instructions for keeping the accounts of the Royall African Company of England on the Gold Coast. Manuscript. London, 13 July 1730. R413

The instructions cover thirty-six topics. Books are to be balanced every six months.

Royal African Company. A memorial touching the nature and present state of the trade to Africa. [n.p., 1709.] R414

A review of the history of England's trade to West Africa, with recommendations for its prosecution through a joint stock company with a monopoly and freedom to negotiate with African rulers.

Royal African Company. Reasons for settlement of the trade to Africa, in a joynt-stock, with the arguments of the separate-traders against it answer'd. [London, ca. 1711.] R415

Twelve arguments to demonstrate that a joint stock company, here meaning the Royal African Company, is the best way for Great Britain to carry on trade to West Africa.

Royal African Company. The several declarations of the Company of Royal Adventurers of England trading into Africa. [London] 1667. R416

This pamphlet marks the beginning of the direct English trade in slaves for the supply of the American plantations. A list of adventurers of the company is also included.

Royal African Company. Some observations on extracts taken out of the report from the Lords Commissioners for Trade and Plantations. [London, 1708.] R417

Detailed investigation into the statistics furnished by private traders to prove that they had transported more slaves to the West Indies, Virginia, Maryland, Carolina, and New York than the company had.

Royal African Company. A supplement to The case of the Royal African Company of England. London, S. Aris, 1730. R418

Answers allegations made against the African Company in a previously published pamphlet.

Royal African Company. That the trade to Affrica, is only manageable by an incorporated company and a joynt stock, demonstrated in a letter to a member of the present House of Commons. [London, 1690.] R419

A review of the Royal African Company, showing how it was established by a joint stock subscription and attempting to prove that independent traders could not carry on the trade to West Africa in a satisfactory manner.

The royal fishing revived. London, 1670. R420
Suggestions to improve England's fishing trade, most of them modeled on the Dutch fishing industry.

Rubys, Claude de. Les privileges, franchises et immunitez octroyees par les roys treschrestiens, aux consuls, exchevins, manans & habitans de la ville de Lyon. Lyons, Antoine Gryphius, 1574. R421
A commentary on the privileges of Lyons and their renewals from 1485 to 1570.

[Rudolphinus de Passageriis, Rolandinus.] Suma notariae. Manuscript. Ferrara, 1465. R422
A handbook for notaries, written in 1255, containing instructions for the administration of mercantile affairs.

Rudolphinus de Passageriis, Rolandinus. Summa artis notariae. [Venice, Andrea de Bonetis, 1483.] R423
Early printed edition of the previous work, which was a standard text on its subject from the thirteenth to the sixteenth centuries.

Rudyerd, Sir Benjamin. A speech concerning a West Indie association, at a committee of the whole house in the Parliament. [London] 1641. R424
A plea for increased participation in colonizing activities in the West Indies, and more trade in the area, so that Britain could supplant Spain there.

Ruelle, Pieter. Le flambeau reluisant, ou proprement, Thresor de la navigation ... traduit du Flamend en François par J. Viret. Amsterdam, Henri Doncker, 1667. R425
A text on practical navigation, with tables of geographical coordinates for ports in all parts of the world. It also includes a section on the marine quadrant.

Ruiz de Montoya, Antonio. Conquista espiritual hecha por los religiosos de la Compañia de Jesus, en las provincias del Paraguay, Parana, Uruguay, y Tape. Madrid, Imprenta del Reyno, 1639. R426
A history of early Jesuit efforts in Paraguay and Uruguay, including reports on the condition of the various Christian Indian settlements, and adverse comments on the treatment of the Indians by the Spaniards.

Ruiz, Hipólito. Della China e delle altre sue specie nuovamente scoperte e descritta da D. Ippolito Ruiz ... Rome, Giunchiana, a spese di Venanzio Monaldini, 1792. R427
A discussion of quinoa, an herb native to Chile and Peru, with particular reference to its medicinal properties. The author was a Spanish botanist, and this text is a translation from the Spanish edition of the same year.

The rules of the water-side; or, The general practice of the customs. London, A. Bell, J. Baker, and W. Taylor, 1715. R428
A merchant's handbook, explaining customs procedures, identifying customs offices, indicating units of measurement, and providing information essential to unloading commodities at an English port.

Rundle, Thomas. A sermon preached at St. George's Church, Hanover Square, on Sunday February 17, 1733/4, to recommend the charity for establishing the new colony of Georgia. London, For T. Woodward and J. Brindley, 1734. R429
An appeal for funds to support the beginnings of the Georgia colony.

[Rush, Benjamin.] Observations upon the present government of Pennsylvania. In four letters to the people of Pennsylvania. Philadelphia, Styner and Cist, 1777. R430
A criticism of Pennsylvania's Revolutionary government by an ardent patriot who feared the development of a tyranny within Pennsylvania.

Russell, Francis. A short history of the East India Company. London, John Sewell and J. Debrett, 1793. R431
An examination of the financial structure, trade, and semi-governmental activities of the company.

Russell, William. The history of America, from its discovery by Columbus to the conclusion of the late war. London, Fielding and Walker, 1778. R432
The first edition of a text describing the discovery, conquest, settlement, and progress of America. Contains numerous references to trade and includes many maps.

Russell, William. Geschichte von Amerika von dessen Entdeckung an bis auf das ende des vorigen Krieges. Nebst einem Anhang, welcher eine Geschichte des Ursprunges und des Fortganges des gegenwärtigen unglücklichen Streites zwischen Gross-Britannien und seinen Colonien enthält ... Leipzig, Schwickertschen Verlage, 1779-1780. R433
The only translation of the previous work.

Russia. Laws, etc. Russisch-Kaiserliche Ordnung der Handels-Schiffahrt auf Flüssen Seen und Meeren. St. Petersburg, Weitbrecht und Schnoor, 1781. R434
A collection of 298 ordinances put into effect for the regulation of many aspects of Russia's maritime trade.

Russia. Laws, etc. [Der Stadt Riga Handels-Ordnung.] Riga, ca. 1778. R435
An extensive ordinance regulating Riga's trade, differentiating between Baltic ports and more distant connections, and listing taxes upon imports and exports.

[Russian composite atlas. n.p., 1728-83.] R436
A collection of sixty-two maps of the Russian Empire collected by Lord Malmsbury, British ambassador to the court of Catherine II.

[Ryberg, Neils.] Til interessenterne udi det Asiatiske Compagnie. Copenhagen, N. Møller, 1784. R437

A critical review of a report by the Danish Asiatic Company, including statistical tables.

Ryberg, Neils. An die interessenten der Königl. dänischen asiatischen Compagnie. Copenhagen, N. Møller, 1784. R438

Translation of the previous work.

Rycaut, Sir Paul. The history of the Turkish Empire from the year 1623 to the year 1677. London, J.M. for John Starkey, 1680. R439

The second section of this chronicle was written with a view to the relationship of English trade in Turkey to the government of that country.

Rychkov, Nicolai P. Tagebuch über seine Reise durch verschiedene Provinzen des russischen Reichs in den Jahren 1769. 1770. und 1771. Riga, Johann Friedrich Hartknoch, 1774. R440

An account of travels from Simbirsk on the Volga River to Orenburg on the Ural, with commentary on the land, people, and natural history. Translated from the Russian, with notes, by Christian Heinrich Hase.

Ryves, Sir Thomas. Historia navalis antiqua, libris quatuor. Londini, Robertum Barker, 1633. R441

This work incorporates the author's earlier *Historia navalis*, continuing it to the establishing of the Roman Empire.

Sá, Diogo de. De navigatione libri tres: quibus mathematicae disciplinae explicantur ... Paris, Reginaldi Calderii, & Claudii eius filii, 1549.
S1
A general work of cosmography by a Portuguese mathematician.

Sá, Joachim Francisco de. Nova relaçaõ da victoria, que alcançaram as bandeiras portuguezas em Moçambique, e como se houveram as companhias que em duas náos partiraõ para aquella terra, e sahiraõ desta corte em o dia 16 Abril de 1751 ... [n.p., ca. 1751.]
S2
A newsletter announcing military victories against the peoples of Mozambique, including some statement on the importance of that colony in the Portuguese empire.

Saar, Johann Jacob. Ost-Indianische funfzehenjährige Kriegs-Dienst. Nuremberg, W.E. Felszecker, 1662.
S3
A German in the service of the Dutch East India Company comments on East Indian trade.

Sabellico, Marco Antonio. Croniche che tractano de la origine de Veneti, e del principio de la cita. Milan, Gottardo da Ponte [ca. 1510].
S4
The first Italian edition, including a funeral oration by the translator in honor of the author.

Sabellico, Marco Antonio. Decades rerum Venetarum. Venice, Andreae de Toresanis de Asula, 1487.
S5
A history of Venice from its founding to the author's own time, by a prominent Venetian scholar.

Sabellico, Marco Antonio. Secunda pars Enneadum ... usque ad annum M.D.IIII. cum epitome omnium librorum et indice litterarum ordine diggesto. [Venice, B. Vercellensis, 1504.]
S6
A chronicle history with considerable material on the discovery of America and early voyages to India, including discussions of the products of the two regions.

Sabido el comercio que la Europa tiene en las Indias. [Madrid, 1699.]
S7
Commercial information on numerous Spanish-American ports.

Saccheri, Girolamo. Continuazione dell' Esame teologico, in cui si risponde a due libri, l'uno intitolato Lettera ad un' amico ... l'altero intitolato Brevissima controversia ... [n.p., 1709.]
S8
A response to other tracts in the Chinese Rites controversy including the *Difesa del Giudizio* by Jacques Hyacinthe Serry.

Sacchini, Francesco. Historiae Societatis Jesu pars secunda. Antwerp, Martini Nutii, 1620.
S9
A continuation of Nicolaus Orlandino's history of the Jesuits, this second part covers the period from 1557 to 1564, noting missionary activities in the eastern and western hemispheres.

Sacro Bosco, Joannes de. Tractatus de sphera. Manuscript. England, 15th century.
S10
An English manuscript version of Sacro Bosco's great work on the sphere. The scribe appears to have been one Robertus Cornyssh.

Sacro Bosco, Joannes de. Sphera mundi. [Venice, Franciscus Renner de Hailbrun, 1478.]
S11
The first edition in which diagrams are used.

Sacro Bosco, Joannes de. [Sphaera mundi.] Venice, E. Ratdolt, 1485.
S12
This is apparently the seventh edition. It is also the first book to be printed in more than two colors.

Sacro Bosco, Joannes de. Sphaera mundi. Venice, Octaviani Scoti, 1490.
S13
This edition includes the commentary of Georg Peurbach and Johann Regiomontanus.

Sacro Bosco, Joannes de. Sphera mundi. Paris, Guidus Mercator, 1498.
S14

Includes a statement on the discovery of America by Columbus.

Sacro Bosco, Joannes de. Sphera mundi. Venice, Simon Bevilaqua, 1499. S15
This edition includes commentaries by Cecco d'Ascoli, Franciscus Capuanus, and Jacques LeFèvre. Also included are a table, by LeFèvre, of latitude and longitude for locations of cities.

Sacro Bosco, Joannes de. Sphaera mundi. Venice, Joannes Baptista Sessa, 1501. S16
The text is presented without commentary, but appended to it are Johannes Mueller's comments on the theory of the planets by Gerard of Cremona and a new theory of planets by Georg Peurbach.

Sacro Bosco, Joannes de. Nota eorum quae in hoc libro continentur. Oratio de laudibus astrologiae habita a Bartholomeo Vespucio ... Textus sphaerae Joannis de Sacro Busto ... Venice, J. & B. de Rebeis, 1508. S17
A number of treatises on cosmography, including a commentary by Bartholomeo Vespucci, nephew of the explorer, stating that he does not believe the theory that the torrid zone is inhabitable.

Sacro Bosco, Joannes de. Textus de sphera ... cum additione (quantum necessarium est) adiecta. Paris, Henrici Stephani, 1511. S18
This is Jacques LeFèvre's commentary, with a description of Bonet de Lates' astronomical ring and a summary of Euclid's geometry.

Sacro Bosco, Joannes de. Sphera materialis. Nuremberg, Jobst Gutknecht, 1516. S19
This first German edition is presented without commentary by the translator.

[Sacro Bosco, Joannes de.] Sphera cum commentis in hoc volumine contentis. Venice, Heredum quondam Bomini Octaviani Scoti, 1518. S20
This edition includes a collection of commentaries, similar to the edition of 1499, but adding those by Pierre d'Ailly, Michael Scoti, and Robert of Lincoln.

Sacro Bosco, Joannes de. Sphaera mundi. Venice, Jacobus Petius de Leucho, 1519. S21
A near reprint of the 1501 edition, with a few alterations in the diagrams.

Sacro Bosco, Joannes de. Textus de sphaera. Paris, Simonem Colinaeum, 1521. S22
A close reprint of earlier Paris editions, but with illustrations by Oronce Finé.

Sacro Bosco, Joannes de. Opusculum de sphera mundi. [Alcalá de Henares, Michael d'Eguia, 1526.] S23
The editor, Pedro Sanchez Cirvelo, adds his interpretation to this basic text, including references to recent discoveries.

Sacro Bosco, Joannes de. Sphaera Jani de Sacrobusto astronomiae ac cosmographiae ... per Petrum Apianum accuratissima diligentia denuo recognita ac emendata. Ingolstadt, Apianis aedibus, 1526. S24
This edition was edited by Petrus Apianus, a noted German astronomer and geographer, and was printed at his press.

Sacro Bosco, Joannes de. Textus de sphaera ... Cum compositione annuli astronomici Boneti Latensis: et geometria Euclidis Megarensis. Paris, Simonem Colinaeum, 1538. S25
The edition prepared by Jacques LeFèvre d'Étaples, with woodcuts by Oronce Finé.

[Sacro Bosco, Joannes de.] Sphera volgare novamente tradotta con molte notande additioni. Venice, Bartholomeo Zanetti, 1537. S26
The first Italian edition to which Fiorentino Mauro, the editor, has added chapters on cosmography and the art of navigation.

Sacro Bosco, Joannes de. Sphaera ... emendata. Cum additionibus in margine, & indice rerum & locorum memorabilium, & familiarissimis scholiss. Lyons, Haeredes Jacobi Junctae, 1567. S27
Edited by Francesco Giuntini, with commentary by Élie Vinet, and including passages from Pedro Nunes, Valeriano Bolzani, Alfraganus, and Proclus.

Sacro Bosco, Joannes de. Libellus de sphaera. Wittenberg, Petrus Seitz, 1574. S28
This edition includes two prefaces by Philipp Melanchthon, written in 1531 and 1538.

Sacro Bosco, Joannes de. Trattato della sphera. Venice, F. Brucioli, 1543. S29
This Italian translation is by Antonio Brucioli.

Sacro Bosco, Joannes de. Annotationi sopra la lettione della spera del Sacro Bosco. Florence, 1550. S30
This edition of Mauro's translation adds some studies on the sphere according to Platonic thought and Christian theology.

Sacro Bosco, Joannes de. La sfera ... tradotta emendata ... con molte et utili annotazioni. Florence, Giunti, 1571. S31
This translation by Pier Vincenzo Dante was made in 1498. It was edited in this translation's first edition by Ignazio Dante.

Sacro Bosco, Joannes de. Sfera di Gio. Sacro Bosco. Siena, S. Marchetti, 1604. S32
This is the final edition of Pifferi's translation of and commentary on Sacro Bosco's *Sphaera mundi*, the first translation appearing in 1537. This edition is considerably augmented and has many illustrations.

Sacro Bosco, Joannes de. Tractado de la sphera. Seville, J. de Leon, 1545. S33
This first Spanish edition contains a small woodcut map of the Western Hemisphere.

Sacro Bosco, Joannes de. La sphere de Jean de Sacro-bosco, augmentee de nouveaux commentaires, et figures servant grandement pour l'intelligence d'icelle. Paris, Hierosme de Marnef & Guillaume Cavellat, 1576. S34
This first French edition has many comments by the translator, Guillaume des Bordes.

Saeghman, Gillis Joosten. De groote Spaensche tiranye of het kleine martelaers-boeck, waer in te sien zijn de barbare onmenschelijke wreetheden der Spanjaerden gedaen in Nederlant ... Amsterdam, Gillis Joosen Saagman, 1667. S35
A collection of accounts of Spanish atrocities in the Netherlands during their rule there and during the Dutch war of liberation.

Sagard, Gabriel. Le grand voyage du pays des Hurons, situé en l'Amerique vers la Mer douce, és derniers confins de la Nouvelle France, dite Canada. Paris, Denys Moreau, 1632. S36
Sagard was a Recollet who spent a few months in Canada in 1623. He is a principal source of non-Jesuit information on the Indians of the Georgian Bay area.

Sagard, Gabriel. Histoire du Canada. Paris, C. Sonnius, 1636. S37
A history of the Recollet missionary activity in Canada from 1614 to 1629. Includes an extension of Sagard's previous work, *Le grand voyage du pays des Hurons.*

[Sahlmoon, Isaac.] Hollands stats-och commercie-spegel, föreställande, under wisse anmärkningar, de förente Nederländers republique. Stockholm, Benjamin Gottlieb Schneider, 1731. S38
A survey of Dutch commercial affairs, with considerable emphasis on its overseas companies and alliances.

[Sahuguet, Marc René Sahuguet, abbé d'Espagnac.] Précis pour les actionnaires de la Nouvelle Compagnie des Indes. [n.p., 1787.] S39
The company defends its exclusive trading privilege, noting the losses and corruption arising from free competition.

St. John de Crèvecoeur, J. Hector. Lettres d'un cultivateur américain, écrites a W.S. Ecuyer, depuis l'Année 1770, jusqu'à 1781. Paris, Cuchet, 1784. S40
The first French edition of one of the classic idyllic descriptions of life in rural colonial America, adding four letters and some additional descriptive material.

St. Lo, George. England's safety: or, A bridle to the French King. London, W. Miller, 1693. S41
Proposals for the improvement of England's navy and maritime trade.

Saint Pierre (Martinique). Adresse des deputés de la ville de S. Pierre Martinique, a la Assemblée nationale. [Paris, 1790.] S42
An account of revolutionary outbreaks on Martinique.

Saint Pierre (Martinique). Extrait des registres de délibérations de la commune de la ville Saint-Pierre, isle-Martinique, du dimanche 18 avril. [n.p., 1790.] S43
A documented history of unrest on Martinique.

Saint-Cyran, m. de (Paul-Edme Crublier). Refutation du projet des Amis des Noirs, sur la suppression de la traite des Négres & sur l'abolition de l'esclavage dans nos colonies ... [Paris, Devaux] 1790. S44
Contends that slaves in the French plantations were happier than French laborers and that their liberation would mean the massacre of white settlers in the West Indies.

Saint-Domingue. Copie d'une note remise au comite de salut-public, par la députation de Saint-Domingue. [n.p., 1795.] S45
A request from members of the Saint Domingue delegation for time to answer charges made against them by their opponents.

Saint-Domingue. Assemblée générale. Les Américains réunis à Paris, & ci-devant composant l'Assemblée générale de la partie françoise de Saint-Domingue, a l'Assemblée nationale. Paris, Imprimerie Nationale, 1791. S46
A response from the Assembly of Saint Domingue to the National Assembly's decree of October 12, 1790 stating that no change in the status of persons in the colonies would be made without a request from colonial assemblies.

Saint-Domingue. Assemblée générale. A particular account of the commencement and progress of the insurrection of the Negroes in St. Domingo. London, J. Sewell, 1792. S47
This description of the slave rebellion was intended to throw discredit upon the Amis des Noirs.

Saint-Domingue. Commissaires. Lettre des commissaires de la colonie de Saint-Domingue, au Roi. [Paris, Clousier, 1788.] S48
The commissioners extoll the virtues of the colony preparatory to an election of deputies to the Estates General in France, and they approve the method of franchise proposed by the king.

Saint-Domingue. Conseil supérieur. Arrest du Conseil supérieur du Cap-François, isle Saint

Domingue, qui condamne la morale & doctrine des soi-disans Jésuites, &c. Du 13 décembre 1762. S49
A decree prohibiting the importing of Jesuit texts into Saint Domingue, noting that Jesuit teaching could be a danger to relationships between slaveowners and slaves.

Saint-Domingue. Députés. Requête présentée aux États-Généraux du royaume, le 8 juin 1789. [n.p., 1789?]. S50
A plea by the Députés of Saint Domingue to the Etats-généraux du royaume for representation of colonial interests in the French government.

Saint-Domingue. Laws, etc. Ouverture de tous les ports de la colonie aux étrangers. Port-au-Prince, Mozard, 1790. S51
With famine threatening French Saint Domingue and the mother country unable to lend any aid, the local authorities proclaimed freedom for ships of any country to bring goods to them.

Saint-Gervais. Mémoires historiques qui concernent le gouvernement de l'ancien & du nouveau royaume de Tunis. Paris, Ganeau & Henry, 1736. S52
Describes the commerce of Tunis.

Saint-Ignace, Mère. Histoire de l'Hôtel Dieu de Quebec. Montauban, J. Legier, 1751. S53
A history of missionary activity at Quebec in the seventeenth century.

Saint-Léger. Compte rendu a l'Assemblée nationale ... le 2 juin 1792. [Paris, 1792.] S54
A report by a civil commissioner to Saint Domingue, noting the hostilities on the island, and his inability to bring peace between rebellious slaves and the planters.

[**Saint-Pierre, Bernardin de.**] Voyage a l'Isle de France, a l'Isle de Bourbon, au Cap de Bonne-Esperance, &c. Neuchatel, Imprimerie de la Société Typographique, 1773. S55
Written in the form of letters to a friend, this volume primarily describes the island of Mauritius and evaluates the French settlement there.

[**Saint-Pierre, Bernardin de.**] A voyage to the island of Mauritius. London, W. Griffin, 1775. S56
Though somewhat abridged from the original French, this first English edition was annotated by the translator.

Saint-Vallier, Jean Baptiste de la Croix Chevrières de. Estat present de l'eglise et de la colonie françoise dans la Nouvelle France. Paris, Denis Langlois, 1688. S57
A description of the bishop's voyage out to Canada and back, containing an account of the missions there with considerable attention to relations between the French and the Indians, including troubles with the Iroquois.

Saint-Vallier, Jean Baptiste de la Croix Chevrières de. Relation des missions de la Nouvelle France. Paris, Robert Pepie, 1688. S58
Same as the previous item, but with a new title page.

[**Saintard, P.**] Essai sur les colonies françoises. [n.p.] 1754. S59
This author uses the French colony of Saint Domingue as the basis for a general discussion of the relationship between colonies and their mother countries.

[**Saintard, P.**] Essai sur les interets du commerce national pendent la guerre ... [n.p.] 1756. S60
A collection of twelve letters concerning the commerce of Bordeaux, Nantes, the colonies, and the slave trade.

[**Saintard, P.**] Roman politique sur l'état présent des affaires de l'Amerique, ou Lettres de M***. a M***. sur les moyens d'établir un paix solide & durable dans les colonies, & la liberté générale du commerce extérieur. Amsterdam, Paris, Duchesne, 1757 [i.e. 1756]. S61
A consideration of Europe's involvement in North America with a view to establishing a balance of power among the colonizing nations which would eliminate war and encourage commerce.

Sainte-Croix, Guillaume-Emmanuel-Joseph Guilhem de Clermont-Lodève, baron de. De l'etat et du sort des colonies des anciennes peuples. Philadelphie [Paris] 1779. S62
A study of ancient commercial empires and a comparison of them with eighteenth century imperialism, chiefly the British in North America.

Sainte-Maure, Charles de. A new journey through Greece, Aegypt, Palestine, Italy, Swisserland [sic], Alsatia, and the Netherlands ... now first done into English. London, For J. Batley, 1725. S63
This work includes a good survey of the commerce of the Levant.

Salamanca, Antonio. [World map in double cordiform projection.] Rome, Antonio Salamanca, ca. 1550. S64
This map is a very close copy of the double cordiform world map of Mercator, published in Louvain in 1538.

[**Salander, Erik.**] Then dyra tiden i Swerige. Stockholm, Kongl. Tryckeriet, 1745. S65
This pamphlet names foreign trade as the cause of Swedish economic problems, and suggests promotion of domestic industry through restriction of foreign imports.

Salazar, Juan Joseph de. Vida del V.P. Alonso Messia de la Compania de Jesvs, fervoroso missionero, y director de almas en la Ciudad de Lima. Lima, Imprenta nueva de la Calle de S. Marcelo, 1733. S66

A biography of a Peruvian Jesuit who served sixty-one years as missionary, teacher, and administrator. The story of his life reflects Jesuit institutions and progress in Peru.

Saldanha, Francisco de. Decret du Card. Saldanha, pour la réforme des Jésuites de Portugal & des domaines qui en dépendent, du 15 mai 1758. [n.p.] 1758. S67
The decree orders the Jesuits to discontinue most of their economic activities in Portuguese territories and deliver up their possessions. An introductory statement concerns Jesuit activity in Martinique.

Saldanha, Francisco de. Mandement de S.E. Monseigneur le Cardinal de Saldanha, patriarche de Lisbonne, au sujet de l'expulsion des Jésuites. [Lisbon, 1759.] S68
Cardinal Saldanha reports his concurrence with the expulsion of the Jesuits from Portugal and its overseas possessions.

[Sales, Luis.] Noticias de la provincia de Californias en tres cartas de un sacerdote religioso hijo del real convento de predicadores de Valencia a un amigo suyo. Valencia, Hermanos de Orga, 1794. S69
Provides information on the California missions after the expulsion of the Jesuits in 1767.

[Salīm Allāh, Munshī.] A narrative of the transactions in Bengal, during the soobahdaries of Azeem us Shan, Jaffer Khan, Shuja Khan, Sirafraz Khan, and Alyvirdy Khan, translated from the original Persian, by Francis Gladwin, Esq. Calcutta, Stuart and Cooper, 1788. S70
An account of the history of Bengal during much of the eighteenth century, noting local political rivalries and the impingement of European trading companies on them.

Salinas, Marqués de. Manuscript letter signed. [n.p.] 1623. S71
This letter to the Duke of Medina Sidonia urges the destruction of the English colony on Bermuda and calls attention to the threat to Philippine commerce posed by the presence of Dutch ships there.

Salmeron, Marcos. Recuerdos historicos y politicos de los servicios que los generales, y varones ilustres de la religion de Nuestra Señora de la Merced ... Valencia, Chrysostomo Garriz por Bernardo Nogues, 1646. S72
A history of the Order of Our Lady of Mercy which originated in Spain in the thirteenth century and was involved in establishing missions in various parts of Spain's New World empire.

[Salmon, Thomas.] Hedendaagsche historie of tegen-woordige staat van Afrika ... Amsterdam, Isaak Tirion, 1763. S73
Based upon the *Modern history*, first published in London in 1739, the Dutch edition includes forty-four parts, this being the fortieth and including much additional material and maps by d'Anville.

[Salmon, Thomas.] Hedendaagsche historie of tegen-woordige staat van Spanje en Portugal. Behel ende ... den koophandel en manufakturen; vaart op de Oost-en Westindien; de natuurlyk historie, enz ... Amsterdam, Isaak Tirion, 1759. S74
One of forty-four parts of a Dutch translation from the English, with considerable emphasis on the commerce of each country and with a section on the East Indian trade of Portugal.

Salmon, Thomas. Lo stato presente di tutti i paesi, e popoli del mondo ... Volume II del Giappone, isole Ladrone, Filippine, e Molucche, regni di Kochinchina, e Tonkino e della provincia di Quansi. Venice, Giambatista Albrizzi, 1738. S75
Second Italian edition of a volume on the Far East translated from the London, 1725-39 edition. The maps are after the Dutch edition.

Salzade, Mr. de. Recueil des monnoies, tant anciennes que modernes, ou, Dictionnaire historique des monnoies ... Brussels, Jean-Joseph Boucherie, 1767. S76
Organized into essays on gold, silver, copper, nickel, lead, tin and shells followed by a dictionary for each. Also includes a section on European currencies. This is the first edition; the work was reprinted at least twice.

Samen-spraeck tusschen Warnaer en Frederyck ... Amsterdam, I. Teelman, 1648. S77
The author favors peace with Spain, noting that France is becoming a greater threat to Dutch commerce.

t'Samenspraeck gehouden tusschen twee reysigers; zynde de een Haegenaer en de andere een Amsterdammer. [n.p., 1690.] S78
A discussion of taxes assessed on merchants and the eventual unfortunate effect they will have on commerce.

Sampaio, Emmanuel Pereira de. Memoriale informativo per la supplica dell'erezione delli trè vescovadi di Cochinchina, Siam, e Tunkino, presentato a nostro signore Benedetto, Papa XIV ... [n.p., ca. 1746.] S79
An appeal by the Portuguese ambassador in Rome to papal authority for establishing three new bishoprics in southeast Asia.

[Samwell, David.] Détails nouveaux et circonstanciés sur la mort du Capitaine Cook, traduits de l'anglois. Londres, et se trouve a Paris, Née de la Rochelle, 1768. S80
A detailed account of the death of Captain Cook by a witness to the event. Also included is Dr. Samwell's view against the idea that Cook's voyages introduced venereal disease into the Hawaiian Islands.

San Antonio, Juan Francisco de. Chronicas de la apostolica provincia de S. Gregorio de religiosos descalzos de N.S.P. S. Francisco en las Islas Philipinas, China, Japon, &c. Parte primera ... Manila, Juan del Sotillo, 1738. S81
 This first part of a series of three (the others published in 1741 and 1744) describes the geography, natural history, and people of the Philippines, and also recounts the history of Franciscan missionaries there as well as missions to the Asian mainland from the Philippines.

San Roman de Ribadeneyra, Antonio. Historia general de la Yndia Oriental. Valladolid, Luis Sanchez, 1603. S82
 Relates chiefly to eastern discoveries of the Portuguese.

San Vitores, Diego Luis de. Noticia de los progressos de nuestra Santa Fe en las Islas Marianas. [Spain, ca. 1671.] S83
 The author was a missionary in the Marianas, and he describes the commercial opportunities afforded by those islands, both as stopping points for ships passing from the Philippines to Mexico and as producers of goods. He also presents a good description of the people of the Marianas.

Sánchez, Alonso. Relacion de las cosas de Filipinas ... Manuscript. Madrid [1588?]. S84
 Contemporary copy of a report to Phillip II of Spain by the procurator general of the Jesuits in the Philippines.

[Sande, Johan van den.] Trouhertighe vermaninghe aen het Vereenichde Nederlandt, om niet te luysteren na eenige ghestroyde ende versierde vreed-articulen ... [n.p.] 1605. S85
 Concerns relations with Spain in the Low Countries.

Sandi, Vettor. Principi di storia civile della repubblica di Venezia. Venice, Sebastian Coletti, 1769-1772. S86
 This edition includes material through 1767.

Sandi, Vettor. Principi di storia civile della repubblica di Venezia. Venice, Sebastian Coleti, 1755-56. S87
 A general chronicle of Venice from its beginnings, recording much of the commercial growth of the city.

Sandoval, Alonso de. De instauranda Aethiopum salute Historia de Aethiopia, naturaleça, policia sagrada y profana, costumbres, ritos, y cathecismo evangelico, de todos los Aethiopes cõ que se restaura la salud desus almas ... Madrid, Alonso de Paredes, 1647. S88
 Intended primarily as a description of black people in all parts of the world, this work extends beyond into material of geographical and natural history interest, particularly relating to Asia and Africa.

Sandys, George. A relation of a journey begun An: Dom: 1610. London, Ro: Allot, 1627. S89
 The third edition.

Sandys, George. A relation of a journey begun An: Dom: 1610. London, W. Barren, 1615. S90
 An account of travels in the Near East, with references to the commerce carried on there, and important contributions to the geography and ethnology of the Levant.

Sanson, Nicolas. Amérique septentrionale. Paris, N. Sanson & Pierre Mariette, 1650. S91
 The earliest printed map to show the western Great Lakes, although Lakes Superior and Michigan have incomplete western shorelines.

Sanson, Nicolas. Atlas de la geographie ancienne, sacre, ecclesiastique et profane ... Amsterdam, Jean Covens & Corneille Mortier, 1721. S92
 Contains maps of the ancient and medieval worlds as well as contemporary maps, showing the extent of geographical knowledge in the eighteenth century.

Sanson, Nicolas. Cartes generales de toutes les parties du monde. Paris, Pierre Mariette, 1666. S93
 An atlas of ninety-three maps, divided between detailed modern portrayals and ancient concepts of geography.

Sanson, Nicolas. Die gantze Erd-Kugel, bestehend in den vier bekannten Theilen der Welt. Frankfurt am Main, Johann David Zunners, 1679. S94
 This German edition has an expanded text, and maps that vary significantly from the French editions.

Sanson, Nicolas. L'Europe, [l'Asie, l'Afrique, l'Amerique] en plusiers cartes et divers traittés de geographie et d'histoire. Paris, Chez l'Autheur, 1683. S95
 An atlas containing sixty-one maps.

Sanson, Nicolas. Introduction a la geographie. Paris, Chez l'Auteur, 1681-1686. S96
 An elementary textbook in geography including an exhaustive collection of definitions of terms.

Sanson, Nicolas. Introduction a la geographie, où sont la geographie astronomique, qui explique la correspondance du globe terrestre avec la sphere ... Amsterdam, Pierre Mortier, 1708. S97
 An elementary geography textbook.

Sanson, Nicolas. Tabula nova totius Regni Poloniae ... [Amsterdam, ca. 1702.] S98
 This map of Poland and adjacent areas was based on a map of Nicolas Sanson, 1655. It does not appear to have been included in the earlier issues of Visscher's atlas.

Sanson, Missionary. The present state of Persia. London, M. Gilliflower, 1695. S99
 A translation from the French, with reference to the treatment accorded merchants and an account of trade regulations as well as a description of the people and government of Persia.

Santa Cruz de Marcenado, Alvaro Navia Osorio, marqués de. Comercio suelto, y en compañias general y particular en Mexico, Peru, Philipinas, y Moscovia. Madrid, Antonio Marin, 1732. S100
Comments on propositions to revitalize Spanish commerce at home and abroad, taken from a number of unpublished manuscripts.

Santo-Domingo, M. de. Conduite de M. de Santo-Domingo, lui par lui-même à l'Assemblée Nationale, le 7 octobre 1790. [Paris?] De l'Imprimerie de Didot fils [1790?]. S101
A review of events surrounding the mutiny of the crew of the *Leopard*, a crucial event in the early stages of the revolution in the French colony of Saint Domingue.

Santos, João dos. Ethiopia oriental, e Varia historia de cousas, notaveis do Oriente. Evora, Convento de S. Domingos de Evora, 1609. S102
The author lived at various places on the east African coast from 1586 to 1597, and presents a history of the development of Portuguese administration and commerce in that area.

Santos, José Lopes. Carta individual geografica, emparte de Guianna Portugueza, e foz do Rio Amazonna athe os limites da colonia Franceza. Manuscript. Brazil, 1795. S103
A chart of the Brazilian coast from Salinópolis to the border of French Guiana, indicating soundings, anchorages, cities, and fortified places.

Sanuti Pellicani, Giovanni Battista. Illustrissime Domine. Cum ab immemorabili honoranda Societas Strazzarolorum. Bologna, J. Montij, 1675. S104
A series of proposals relating to the use of gold and other metals and to relationships with artisans working with these materials.

Sanuto, Giulio. Globe gores, Sanuto. Chicago, The Newberry Library, 1987. S105
A facsimile of gores from one of the largest surviving complete sets of globe gores produced in the sixteenth century. The gores are accompanied by an explanatory text by David Woodward.

Sanuto, Livio. Geografia. Venice, Damiano Zenaro, 1588. S106
An atlas of Africa containing twelve double-page maps and text, in the style of a gazetteer, that describes the places named on the maps. Two preliminary chapters discuss theoretical geography.

Saravia, Juan. Institutione de mercanti che tratta del comprare et vendere, et della usura che puo occorrere nella mercantia, insieme con un trattato de cambi. Venice, Bolognino Zaltieri, 1561. S107
This work was previously published in Spanish editions of 1544 and 1547. It is a response to the price revolution resulting from Spanish import of precious metals from America.

Sardi, Alessandro. De moribus et ritibus gentium, libri Alexandri Sardi Ferrariensis & Olai Magni Gothi. Antwerp, Forsteriana, 1662. S108
A re-issue of the sheets of the 1599 edition of Magnus and probably also of Sardi.

Sardinha Mimoso, João. Relacion de la real tragicomedia con que los padres de la Compania de Jesus en su Colegio de S. Anton de Lisboa recibieron a la Magestad Catolica de Felipe II de Portugal, y de su entrada en este reino. Lisbon, Jorge Rodriguez, 1620. S109
A dramatic presentation commemorating the expansionist theme during the reign of Manuel I, staged for the arrival in Portugal of Philip III of Spain (II of Portugal) in 1619.

Sardinia (Kingdom). Sovereign (1730-1773 : Charles Emmanuel III). Degnatasi Sua Maestà con sua reale dispacio del dì 9. del caduto mese di Settembre sù le rappresentazioni dell' Eccelsa Real giunta di Governo, e della Congregazione dello Stato di acconsentire, ed ordinare, che si rimetta in prattica lo stabilimento del Provveditor Generale, che somministri li generi, e robbe necessarie alla suffistenza dell' armata ... Milan, Giuseppe Richino Malatesta, Stampatore Regio Camerale [1735]. S110

Sardinia (Kingdom). Sovereign (1730-1773 : Charles Emmanuel III). Edit du Roy, portant l'établissement d'une compagnie de commerce ... avec le titre de Compagnie Royale de Piédmont ... Chambery, Marc-François Gorrin [1752]. S111
This is the charter establishing the new Royal Company of Piedmont, the purpose of which was to improve the silk trade of that state.

Sarmiento de Gamboa, Pedro. Viage al Estrecho de Magallanes en los años de 1579 y 1580. Madrid, Imprenta Real de la Gazeta, 1768. S112
The account of a navigation of the Strait of Magellan from west to east and of the establishment of settlements there for the defense of the Strait.

Sarychev, Gavriil Andreevich. Puteshestvie flota Kapitana Sarycheva ... St. Petersburg, Schnor, 1802. S113
The first edition of an account of the Siberian expedition of Joseph Billings which lasted from 1785 to 1794, ordered by Catherine II to secure more accurate knowledge of Russian dominions in North Pacific.

Sarychev, Gavriil Andreevich. Achtjährige Reise im nordöstlichen Sibirien, auf dem Eismeere und

dem nordöstlichen Ozean. Leipzig, Wilhelm Rein und Comp., 1805-6.   S114
The first German edition. It contains an excellent map of the North Pacific region.

Sarychev, Gavriil Andreevich. Account of a voyage of discovery to the north-east of Siberia. London, J.G. Barnard for Richard Phillips, 1806-7.   S115
The first English edition.

Sarychev, Gavriil Andreevich. Reis in het noordoostelijke Siberie, en op de ijszee en den Noordoostelijken Oceaan ... Amsterdam, Johannes Allart, 1808.   S116
This Dutch edition includes the large folding map of Siberia, ten folding plates and five colored costume plates. It adds a preface and appendix by the translator, N. Messchaert.

Sauer, Martin. An account of a geographical and astronomical expedition to the northern parts of Russia. London, A. Strahan for T. Cadell, Jun. and W. Davies, 1802.   S117
An account of the activities and achievements of expeditions in eastern Siberia and the Aleutian Islands from 1785 to 1794.

Sauer, Martin. Voyage ... dans le nord de la Russie asiatique ... et sur les côtes de l'Amerique. Paris, F. Buisson, 1802.   S118
A French edition, translated from the English and annotated by J. Castéra.

Sauer, Martin. Viaggio fatto per ordine dell'Imperatrice di Russia Caterina II nel nord della Russia Asiatica, nel Mare Glaciale, nel Mare d'Anadyr, e sulla costa Nord-Ouest dell'America, dal 1785 fino al 1794 dal Commodoro Billings. Milan, Sonzogno, 1816.   S119
This Italian edition includes numerous notes to the text by the translator, Luigi Bossi.

Saugnier. Relations de plusieurs voyages a la cote d'Afrique, a Maroc, au Sénégal, a Gorée, a Galam, etc. Avec des détails intéressans pour ceux qui se destinent à la traite des Nègres, de l'or, de l'ivoire, etc. Paris, Gueffier, 1791.   S120
An account of travel and trade in West Africa, with interesting specifics as to commodities, prices, manner of doing business, etc.

Saugnier. Voyages to the coast of Africa by Mess. Saugnier and Brisson: containing an account of their shipwreck on board different vessels, and subsequent slavery, and interesting details of the manners of the Arabs of the desert, and of the slave trade, as carried on at Senegal and Galam. London, G.G.J. and J. Robinson, 1792.   S121
The first English edition.

Saugrain, Claude Marin. Dictionnaire universel de la France, ancienne et moderne, et de la Nouvelle France ... Paris, Saugrain [etc.] 1726.   S122
A gazetteer of France and New France, giving details of geographical, historical, economic and other information on political and geographic divisions.

Saunders, W. An essay towards the establishing the fishery of Great Britain. London, J. Morphew, 1708.   S123
An improved fishing trade is seen as a means to employ the poor and a support to English navigation in general.

[Saunier de Beaumont.] Allerneuste Reisen eines Portugiesen, Innigo von Biervillas, nach denen malabarischen Cüsten ... und andern ost-indianischen Orten. Berlin, Johann Peter Schmid, 1736.   S124
The first German edition.

[Saunier de Beaumont.] Voyage d'Innigo de Biervillas à la côte de Malabar, Goa, Batavia & autres lieux des Indes Orientales ... Paris, G.A. Depuis, 1736.   S125
An imaginary voyage with considerable information on the geography, customs, and commerce of Brazil, the Cape of Good Hope, India, Ceylon, and Java.

Savage, Thomas. An account of the late action of the New Englanders. London, T. Jones, 1691.   S126
An account of the assault upon Quebec by a force of 2000 men who sailed from Boston in 1690. This force, under the command of Sir William Phips, was quickly repulsed by the French.

Savary des Brûlons, Jacques. Dictionnaire universel de commerce. Amsterdam, Jansons à Waesberge, 1726-32.   S127
Includes information on trading companies, fairs, consulates, products and their sources, prices, and a vast range of other information of value to merchants.

Savary des Brûlons, Jacques. Dictionnaire universal de commerce: d'histoire naturelle, & des arts & metiers. Contenant tout ce qui concerne le commerce qui se fait dans les quatre parties du monde. Copenhagen [i.e. Geneva] Freres Cl. & Ant. Philibert, 1759-1765.   S128
The best of the French editions, this much expanded edition takes into account important economic writings of the mid-eighteenth century.

[Savary des Brûlons, Jacques.] Dictionnaire portatif de commerce, contenant la connoissance des marchandises de tous les pays. Bouillon, Société Typographique, 1770.   S129
An abridged edition.

Savary des Brûlons, Jacques. The universal dictionary of trade and commerce ... with large additions and improvements incorporated throughout the whole work ... by Malachy Postlethwayt. London, For John Knapton, 1757. S130

The second English edition, adapted from the French edition to serve British interests primarily.

Savary des Brûlons, Jacques. The universal dictionary of trade and commerce. London, H. Woodfall [etc.] 1766. S131

The third English edition, including a description of British affairs in North America since 1763.

Savary des Brûlons, Jacques. Dizionario di commercio. Venice, Giambatista Pasquali, 1770-1771. S132

An abridged Italian edition, with adaptations to make it particularly suitable for Italian merchants.

Savary, Jacques. Parères ou avis et conseils sur les plus importantes matières du commerce. Paris, Jean Guignard, 1688. S133

A collection of seventy opinions on matters of commercial law arising out of specific cases in French trade.

Savary, Jacques. Le parfait negociant. [Der vollkommene Kauff-und Handelsmann.] Geneva, Jean Herman Widerholt, 1676. S134

The text is in French and German, the first appearance of a German translation of this compendium of information useful in all aspects of trade.

Savary, Jacques. Le parfait negociant, ou Instruction generale pour ce qui regarde le commerce des marchandises de France, & des pays estrangers. Lyon, Jacques Lyons, 1700-1701. S135

The fifth edition, in which two treatises on exchange by Jacques de La Serra and Claude Noret are added.

Savary, Jacques. Le parfait negociant. Paris, Freres Estienne, 1757-70. S136

An augmented edition.

Savérien, M. (Alexandre). Dizionario istorico, teorico, e pratico di marina. Venice, Gio. Battista Albrizzi Q. Girolamo, 1769. S137

A dictionary of nautical terms, translated from the French.

Savonarola, Raffaello. Universus terrarum orbis scriptorum calamo delineatus. Padua, Jo. Baptistae Conzatti, 1713. S138

A geographical dictionary of bibliographical importance, since it contains extensive bibliographies on the more important places listed.

Savoy (Duchy). Laws, etc. [Statutorum Sabaudiae liber.] Turin, Bernardinum de Sylva, 1530.
S139

The laws of Savoy were first promulgated in 1430 by Amadeus VIII, and are published here with additions made subsequently.

Saxby, Henry. The British customs: containing an historical and practical account of each branch of that revenue. London, Thomas Baskett [etc.] 1757. S140

A statement of the duties payable on imports, exports, and coastal shipping with historical information on the establishment of such duties from 1672 to 1757.

Sayer, Robert. A new map of Africa wherein are particularly express'd the European forts and settlements. Drawn from the most approved geographers, with great improvements from the sieurs of d'Anville & Robert. London, R. Sayer, [ca. 1765]. S141

Particularly rich in coastal place names, this map also includes the east coast of Brazil and islands of the Indian Ocean as far east as the Maldives.

Sayer, Robert. The Russian discoveries, from the map published by the Imperial Academy of St. Petersburg. London, 1775. S142

A map of the northern Pacific Ocean showing the tracks of Bering's and Chirikov's ships.

Sayer, Robert, and John Bennett. The theatre of war in North America, with the roads, and tables, of the superficial contents, distances, &ca. London, R. Sayer and J. Bennett, 1776.
S143

The second issue, following the Declaration of Independence. The explanatory text is titled "A compendious account of the British colonies in North America."

Scaccia, Sigismondo. Tractatus de commerciis et cambio. Frankfurt, 1648. S144

A legal and theoretical treatment of trade and exchange.

Scali, Pietro Paolo. Introduzione alla pratica del commercio ovvero notizie necessarie per l'esercizio della mercatura. Livorno, Gio. Paolo Fantechi, 1751. S145

A handbook for the use of merchants doing business in Livorno, with a discourse on the general principles of money and commerce followed by tables of exchange of the major European commercial centers.

Scelta di lettere edificanti scritte dalle missioni straniere, preceduta da quadri geografici storici, politici, religiosi et letterari dei paesi di missione ... Milan, Ranieri Fanfani, 1825-1829. S146

The first Italian edition of the *Lettres édifiantes*, based on the *Choix des lettres édifiantes* edited in 1808 by J.B. Montmignon, and enlarged in 1824.

Schaede die den staet der Vereenichde Nederlanden. The Hague, Jan Veeli, 1644. S147

Urges the uniting of the East and West India commerce of the Netherlands under one company.

Schall von Bell, Johann Adam. Historica narratio de initio et progressu missionis Societatis Jesu apud Chinenses. Vienna, Matthaei Cosmerovii, 1665. S148
  The author was instrumental in assisting with the reform of the Chinese calendar. This book deals largely with that subject, but includes other matter relating to Christian missions in China.

Schall von Bell, Johann Adam. Historica relatio de ortu et progressu fidei orthodoxae in regno Chinensi per missionarios Societatis Jesu. Ratisbon, Augusti Hanckwitz, 1672. S149
  This edition includes a map of China.

Schamp & Dewinter. Mémoires sur le commerce des etats hereditaires. Manuscript. Netherlands [ca. 1753]. S150
  A discussion of European commerce, with particular emphasis on the trade of the United Provinces and the Austrian Netherlands.

Schedel, Hartmann. Registrum huius operis libri cronicarum cū figuris et ÿmagïbus ab inicio mūdi. [Nuremberg, A. Koberger, 1493.] S151
  The Latin edition of the *Nuremberg Chronicle*, which includes a Ptolemaic world map.

Scheffer, Johannes. Lapponia id est, Regionis Lapponum et gentis nova et verissima descriptio ... Frankfurt, Christiani Wolffii, 1673. S152
  The first edition of the most basic work on Lapland for this period, describing the land and its products, the people and their customs, religion, economy, etc.

Scheffer, Johannes. The history of Lapland. Oxford, At the theater, 1674. S153
  The first English edition.

Scheffer, Johannes. Lappland, das ist: neue und wahrhafftige Beschreibung von Lappland und dessen Einwohnern. Frankfurt am Main & Leipzig, Martin Hallervorden, 1675. S154
  The first German edition.

Scheffer, Johannes. Histoire de la Laponie. Paris, Olivier de Varennes, 1678. S155
  The first French edition.

Scheffer, Johannes. Waarachtige en aen-merkenswaardige historie van Lapland ... Amsterdam, Jan ten Hoorn, 1682. S156
  The first Dutch edition, translated from the French.

Scheibler, Carl Friedrich. Capitain John Smiths Reiser oprindelsen til de Engelske colonier i Nordamerica. Odense, Iversen, 1783. S157
  A Danish translation from the 1782 German edition.

Scheibler, Carl Friedrich. Reisen, Entdeckungen und Unternehmungen des Schifs-Capitain Johann Schmidt, oder John Smith ... grösten theils aus desselben eigenen Schriften beschrieben von Carl Friedrich Scheibler. Berlin, Siegismund Friedrich Hesse, 1782. S158
  A brief account of the earliest English colonial efforts in North America, chiefly Virginia and New England, based on the writings of Captain John Smith.

A scheme for raising 3,200,000 l. for the service of the government, by redeeming the fund and trade now enjoy'd by the East-India Company. [London, 1730.] S159
  A proposal for breaking the monopoly of the East India Company through a loan of 3,200,000 pounds to the government from private sources.

Schérer, Jean-Benoît. Histoire raisonnée du commerce de la Russie. Paris, Cuchet, 1788. S160
  A detailed discussion of historic and current Russian trade.

Schillinger, Franz Caspar. Persianische und ostindianische Reis. Nuremberg, Johann Christoph Lochner, 1709. S161
  Commercial activities of Europeans in the Near and Middle East are noted particularly in this account of overland travels which also comments on the cities visited en route.

Schiltberger, Johannes. Ein wunderbarlicher unnd kurzweylige Histori wie Schildtberger ... von den Türken gefangen, in die Heydenschafft defüret, und wider heim kommen. Nuremberg, Johann vom Berg & Ulrich Newber [ca. 1548]. S162
  Memoires of more than thirty years' residence in western and central Asia between 1396 and 1427, including information on the silk trade.

Schiltberger, Johannes. Ein wunderbarliche und kurtzweilige History, wie Schildtberger, einer auss der Stad München inn Beyern, von den Türcken gefangen. Frankfurt am Main, Herman Gülfferich, 1549. S163
  An illustrated edition.

Schirmbeck, Adam. Messis Paraquariensis a patribus Societatis Jesu per sexennium in Paraquaria collecta, annis videlicet M.DC. XXXVIII. XXXIX. XL. XLI. XLII. XLIII. Munich, formis Lucae Straubii, impensis Joannis Wagneri, 1649. S164
  A report on Jesuit installations in Paraguay for the years 1638 to 1643, published by the Jesuit college in Landshut.

Schlatter, Michaël. Getrouw verhaal van den waren toestant der meest herderloze gemeentens in Pensylvanien. Amsterdam, Jacobus Loveringh, 1751. S165
  An appeal for financial support for the Dutch Reformed churches in Pennsyvlania.

Schlegel, Johann Heinrich. Samlung zur dänischen Geschichte, Münzkenntnisz, Oekonomie und Sprache. Copenhagen, 1771-76. S166
Contains material on the history of the Danish East India Company.

Schlözer, August Ludwig von. Briefwechsel meist statistischen Inhalts. Göttingen, Johann Christian Dieterich, 1775 [i.e. 1774-1775]. S167
A collection covering a wide variety of topics such as commerce in the East Indies, Spanish sea power, the French East India Company, and a detailed account of Madame des Odonais's travels through South America.

[Schmid, Georg Ludwig.] Principes de la législation universelle. Amsterdam, Marc-Michel Rey, 1776. S168
A Swiss Physiocrat's discourse on many aspects of government, society, and liberty, with comment on overseas trading companies, colonies, and commercial freedom.

[Schmid, Georg Ludwig.] Traités sur divers sujets intéressans de politique et de morale. [n.p.] 1760. S169
A collection of five essays, two decidedly physiocratic in tone, dealing with the historic and current place of agriculture and commerce in the economy of a nation.

Schmidt, Jacob Christian. Fuldstaendigt udtog af den Engelske Admiral Lord Ansons og adskillige andres reyser omkring verden, fra det aar 1577 indtil 1744 ... Kiøbenhavn, 1760. S170
Inspired by Richard Walter's account of Anson's circumnavigation, this work goes beyond it to report in considerable detail and with extensive notes earlier voyages in the South Pacific.

[Schmidt, Johann Peter.] Allgemeine Geschichte der Handlung und Schiffahrt, der Manufacturen und Künste, des Finanz- und Cameralwesens, zu allen Zeiten und bey allen Völkern. Breslau, Johann Jacob Korn, 1751-54. S171
The first two volumes of an intended larger work. These cover ancient and medieval commerce, European, Asian, and African.

[Schnitscher, J. Christ.] Berättelse om Ajuckinska Calmuckiet eller om detta folkets ursprung, huru de kommit under Ryssarnas lydno, deras gudar, gudsdyrkan och prester ... Stockholm, Lars Salvius, 1744. S172
A general description and history of the Kalmucks, a Siberian people, and the means by which they came under Russian domination.

Ein schöne newe Zeytung so kayserlich mayest ausz India yetz nemlich zukommen seind. [Augsburg, Sigmund Grimm, 1522.] S173
A newsletter containing brief descriptions of the discovery of America and the Spanish conquest of Mexico. Near the end of the tract is a mention of the return of the one ship from Magellan's fleet. It is the earliest known printing of this news.

Schöner, Johann. Ephemeris pro anno Domini M.D.XXXII. accuratissime supputata. Nuremberg, J. Petreium [1532]. S174
This work of the well-known geographer deals entirely with astronomy.

Schöner, Johann. Johann Schöner ... a reproduction of his globe of 1523. London, Henry Stevens and Son, 1888. S175
A facsimile reproduction of the globe with a historical account of it.

Schöner, Johann. Luculentissima quaedam terrae totius descriptio. Nuremberg, J. Stuchs, 1515. S176
The first edition of Schöner's description of his first globe, made in 1515, the earliest to depict completely the northern and southern halves of the Western Hemisphere. The globe and book contain information on a strait at the southern tip of South America.

Schöner, Johann. Opusculum geographicum ex diversorum libris. Nuremberg, 1533. S177
This book was designed to accompany a globe which is pictured on the verso of the title page. The globe indicates Schöner believed the New World to be part of Asia.

Schöner, Johann. Tabulae astronomicae. Nuremberg, Jo Petreium, 1536. S178
Astronomical tables and text by an important mathematician and globe-maker.

Schöpf, Johann David. Reise durch einige der mittlern und südlichen vereinigten nordamerikanischen Staaten nach Ost-Florida den Bahama-Insuln unternommen in den Jahren 1783 und 1784 ... Erlangen, Johann Jacob Palm, 1788. S179
An account of travels in the United States at the conclusion of the American Revolution, with detailed observations of scientific, social, and economic nature.

Schomburg, L. H. v. (Leopold Heinrich von). Reise, von Kopenhagen nach Lissabon, dem Vorgebürge der Guten Hofnung und den Azorischen Inseln ... Odense, Königlich Buchdruckerey, 1784. S180
A travel journal with folding tables recording directions, distance, places visited, etc.

Schorer, Jacob Hendrik, and J. van den Houte. Missive .. wegens Zeeland tot de zaaken der O.I. Compagnie ... [Middelburg, 1794.] S181
Deals with the last years of the Dutch East India Company and how it should avoid the complete loss of its capital.

Schottus, Andreas. Hispaniae illustratae. Frankfurt, Claudium Marnium & Haeredes Johannis Aubrij, 1603-08. S182
 A history of Spain and Portugal, containing accounts of their overseas explorations and trade.

Schouten, Willem Corneliszoon. Journal ou relation exacte du voyage ... dans les Indies. Paris, M. Gobert, 1618. S183
 An account of a voyage for discovering a new passage from the Atlantic to the Pacific around Cape Horn, sponsored by a group of Dutch merchants.

Schouten, Willem Corneliszoon. Diarium vel descriptio laboriosissimi & molestissimi itineris facti à Guilielmo Schoutenio, Hornano. Amsterdam, P. Kaerium, 1619. S184
 Latin edition of the previous item.

Schouten, Wouter. Oost-Indische voyagie. Amsterdam, Jacob Meurs & Johannes van Someren, 1676. S185
 An extensive account of seven years of travel in the East Indies, with numerous engravings depicting the people, cities, ships, and harbors of that region.

Schouten, Wouter. Ost-Indische Reyse. Amsterdam, Jacob von Meurs en Johannes von Sommern, 1676. S186
 The first German edition, with illustrations superior to those in the Dutch edition.

Schram, Wybrant. Journael ende verhael vande Oost-Indische reyse ... Amsterdam, H. Doncker, 1650. S187
 An account of an East Indian voyage of 1626, including a meeting with the famous pirate of the African coast, Claes Compaen.

Schreiben eines englischen Negotianten an einen Kaufmann in Berlin die Königl. Preussische Handlungscompagnie betreffend. Nebst der Antwort. London, 1750. S188
 The English merchant raises questions about the advisability of establishing a Prussian trading company, and the respondent presents information to show that companies have been prominent in all countries that have achieved commercial prominence.

Schreyer, Johann. Neue ost-indianische Reise-Beschreibung. Saalfeld, Johann Rittern, 1679. S189
 Although the author dwells chiefly on the peoples, flora, and fauna of Africa, he does extend his descriptions to Persia, India, Siam, Formosa, and other eastern regions.

Schroeder, Johann Heinrich. Der Seefahrer, oder ... merkwürdige Reisen nach Ost-Indien. Leipzig und Gotha, Christian Mevius, 1749. S190
 An account of travels in the East Indies by a German employee of the Dutch East India Company, with particular emphasis on Ceylon and Java.

Schröter, Johann Friedrich. Algemeine Geschichte der Länder und Völker von America. Halle, Johann Justinus Gebauer, 1752. S191
 An extensive survey of the history, native peoples, natural resources, and colonies of the New World. It is edited by Sigmund Jacob Baumgartner.

Schultze, Eberhard. Geographisches Handbuchlein ... Tübingen, J. Cellius, 1655. S192
 A brief geographical handbook, describing various parts of the earth.

Schulze, J. L. (Johann Ludwig). Neue Nachrichten von denen neuentdekten Insuln in der See zwischen Asien und Amerika. Hamburg und Leipzig, Friedrich Ludwig Gleditsch, 1776.
 S193
 This work discusses the subject of Russian explorations in Alaska, specifically the Aleutian Islands from 1745 to 1770. Johann Benedikt Scherer and August Ludwig von Schlözer have also been suggested as possible authors. The source of information was probably Gerhard Müller.

Schuyt-praetje, gehouden tusschen een Student een Geldersman, en een Vlaming. Utrecht, S. van Korteweg, 1666. S194
 A conversation concerning the sea war with the English.

Schuyt-praetjen, aengaende sekeren brief geschreven uyt landes Kroom op Schoonen den 19. May 1658 ... Amsterdam, B. van Wesel [1658]. S195
 Concerns tolls and the free passage of ships through the Sound.

Schwartz, Georg Bernhardt. Reise in Ost-Indien. Heilbronn, Franz Joseph Eckebrecht, 1751. S196
 This narrative is particularly concerned with Java, describing its products and people, as well as foreign merchants trading there.

Schweigger, Salomon. Ein newe Reyssbeschreibung auss Teutschland nach Constantinopel und Jerusalem. Nuremberg, Caspar Fulden, 1619.
 S197
 Travels through eastern Europe, illustrated with many woodcuts.

Schweigger, Salomon. Ein newe Reiss Beschreibung auss Teutschland nach Constantinopel und Jerusalem. Nuremberg, Wolffgang Endters, 1639. S198
 The fourth edition.

Schweighofer, Johann Michael. Einleitung zur Kenntniss der Staatsverfassung beider vereinigten Königreiche Maroko und Fes. Vienna, Sebastian Hartl, 1783. S199
 A brief general survey of the geography, economy, and culture of Morocco arranged topically.

Schweitzer, Christophorus. Journal und Tage-Buch seiner sechs-jährigen ost-indianischen Reise. Tübingen, Johann Georg Cotta, 1688. S200

An account of seven years in the Dutch East India Company. Much of the narrative is given to descriptions of Java and Ceylon.

Scioto Land Company. Nouveau prospectus de la Compagnie du Scioto, avec plusieurs extraits de lettres, écrites du Scioto même. Paris, Clousier, 1790. S201

A second prospectus issued by the company through its Paris agent who was seeking to interest French emigrants in a land speculation venture in Ohio.

[Scioto Land Company.] Observations générales et impartiales sur l'affaire du Scioto. [Paris, 1790.] S202

A defense of the Scioto Land Company and its activities in attempting to sell Ohio lands to prospective emigrants.

Lo scoprimento dello stretto artico et di meta incognita. Naples, Gio. Battista Cappelli, 1582. S203

An Italian edition of the narratives of Dionyse Settle and Henry Ellis describing Frobisher's second and third voyages.

Score, Richard. A guide to the customers and collectors clerks: or, A new index to the Book of rates ... London, Charles Bill and the executrix of Thomas Newcomb, 1699. S204

In addition to the extensive index to customs laws, this work also includes recent changes in rates and other information of use to merchants.

Scotland. Act of Parliament for erecting a bank in Scotland, Edinburgh, July 17, 1695. Edinburgh: Printed by the Heirs and successors of Andrew Anderson, 1695. S205

The Bank of Scotland was closely related to the Company of Scotland Trading to Africa and the Indies, both reflecting Scotland's desire to get into international commerce.

Scotland. Commission for Communication of Trade. Act of the commission for communication of trade. Edinburgh, Heirs and successors of A. Anderson, 1699. S206

A document calling "unfree traders" to attend the commission, apparently for taxation purposes.

Scotland. Commissioners and trustees for improving fisheries and manufactures. Plan by the commissioners and trustees for improving fisheries and manufactures in Scotland. Edinburgh, James Davidson, 1727. S207

Governing regulations and conditions for the disbursement of funds appropriated under the act of 1727 which sought to encourage and promote the fisheries and the manufacturing of linen and wool.

Scotland. Laws, etc. Act for a company trading to Africa and the Indies. June 26th, 1695. Edinburgh, Heirs and successors of Andrew Anderson; London, John Whitlock, 1695. S208

Enabling legislation prepatory to the creation of the Company of Scotland Trading to Africa and the Indies.

Scotland. Laws, etc. Act of Parliament in favours of John Adair and Captain Slazer. At Edinburgh the sixteenth day of July, one thousand six hundred and ninty five years. [Edinburgh, 1695.] S209

The act provides a subsidy for the mapping of the Scottish coasts, resulting in 1703 in publication of Adair's *The description of the sea-coast of Scotland*.

Scotland. Laws, etc. An act of the Parliament of Scotland for erecting an East-India Company in that kingdom. Edinburgh, Heirs and successors of Andrew Anderson; London, Reprinted for Sam. Manship and Hugh Newman, 1695. S210

The act indicates the form the company is to take and the regulations upon subscriptions; it authorizes actions by the company in promoting commerce and settlement abroad.

Scotland. Parliament. Address to His Majesty by the Parliament. [Edinburgh? 1698.] S211

A protest against a memorial by the English consul in Hamburg, including a copy of that memorial which had sought to induce citizens of Hamburg not to invest in the Company of Scotland.

Scotland. Parliament. Minutes of the proceedings in Parliament. Edinburgh, Heirs of A. Anderson, 1700-07. S212

Minutes of the Scottish Parliament which contain material relating to the Company of Scotland Trading to Africa and the Indies and other Scottish commerce.

Scott, David, agent to the gov.-gen. of India. Remarks and ideas upon the export trade from Great Britain to India ... [London, 1787.] S213

The author feels that exports to India could be increased, and urges that exports to China be carried in company ships.

Scott, Edmund. An exact discourse of the subtilties, fashishions, pollicies, religion, and ceremonies of the East Indians. London, W.W. for Walter Burre, 1606. S214

The author was the first English factor in the East Indies, and he reports on the commercial activities of Eastern peoples as well as the Dutch in Bantam.

Scott, Jonathan. An historical and political view of the Decan, &ca. Manuscript. [n.p., ca. 1791.] S215

An appraisal of the lands under domination of Tipoo Sultan, "to estimate the actual resources of our nearest actual enemy."

Scott, Major (John). Major Scott's speech in the House of Commons, on the 1st and 3d of July 1789; upon the state and finances of India. London, John Stockdale, 1789. S216
A defense of Warren Hastings and his administration in India.

Scott, Major (John). Observations upon Mr. Sheridan's pamphlet, intitled, "Comparative statement of the two bills for the better government of the British possessions in India". London: Printed for John Stockdale, 1789. S217
A highly partisan tract critical of Richard Brinsley Sheridan's pamphlet which had favored an India bill proposed by Fox and opposed by Pitt.

Scott, Major (John). The conduct of His Majesty's late ministers considered, as it affected the East-India Company and Mr. Hastings. London, J. Debrett, 1784. S218
Warren Hastings' chief defender notes the improvement of the East India Company under Hastings' direction while the government was losing an empire in North America.

Scylax. Periplus Scylacis Caryandensis. Amsterdam, J. & C. Blaeu, 1639. S219
Descriptions of the Mediterranean and Black seas from ancient sources. The Mediterranean periplus is believed to date from 350 B.C.

[Seabury, Samuel.] A view of the controversy between Great-Britain and her colonies: including a mode of determining their present disputes, finally and effectually ... New York, James Rivington, 1774. S220
A response to a pamphlet by Alexander Hamilton in which the author states the position of the conservative who sees danger in the emerging government for the colonies as a violation of their established governments.

Seasonable observations on the trade to Africa. London, 1748. S221
Suggests a plan to use profits of pawnbrokers to finance a new trading company which would protect and maintain British rights in West Africa, and reduce the debts of the Royal African Company.

Seasonal observations on the present fatal declension of the general commerce of England. In which ... plain and practicable methods are proposed for retrieving the national trade, before it is past recovery. London, J. Huggonson, 1737. S222
An analysis of England's commercial problems, charging most of them to excessive luxury and burdensome taxes. Encouragement of the woolen trade is seen as the major need in reversing the decline, but reforms in taxation and in colonial government are also advocated.

Sebastiani, Giuseppe Maria, Bp. of Castello. Prima speditione all' Indie Orientali ... Rome, Nella Stamperia di Filippo Maria Mancini, 1666. S223
The author was apostolic legate to Malabar, where he attempted to bring the St. Thomas Christians into conformity with the Roman rite. He also reports news from China and Japan.

Sebastiani, Giuseppe Maria, Bp. of Castello. Seconda speditione all' Indie Orientali ... Rome, Nella stamperia di Filippo M. Mancini, 1672. S224
The second embassy to Malabar with the same purpose as the previous one, with additional observations on religious and political matters.

Sebastiani, Giuseppe Maria, Bp. of Castello. Seconda speditione all' Indie Orientali. Venice, Antonio Tivani, 1683. S225
An account of travels between 1660 and 1664 in western India, the author's chief concern being religious affairs among differing groups of Christians there.

Sebastião dos Santos. Relaçam de huma gloriosa victoria que alcançou o senhor Ioão da Silua Tello de Menezes, Governador da villa de Mazagão cõ[n]tra os mouros de Azamor, & seu alcaide 4 feira tres de Outubro de 1635. Lisbon, Antonio Alvarez, 1636. S226
An account of a Portuguese military victory over a Moroccan force at Mazagan, a city in Morocco frequently contested between them.

Secker, Thomas. A sermon preached before the incorporated Society for the Propagation of the Gospel in Foreign Parts, at their anniversary meeting in the parish-church of St. Mary-le-Bow, on Friday, February 20, 1740-1. London, J. and H. Pemberton, 1741. S227
The success of the SPG is reported in the building of 100 churches in forty years, the distribution of 10,000 prayer books and 100,000 religious tracts, with seventy people in the mission field supported by the Society.

A second courante of newes from the East India in two letters. The one written by master Patricke Copland then preacher to the English in the East India .. the other written by master Thomas Knowles factor there, &c. [London] 1622. S228
Copland's letter is to Adrian Jacobson Hulsebus, dated 20 April 1619, in which he laments the growing hostility between English and Dutch in the East Indies. Knowles' letter is dated 25 February 1621 and describes Dutch actions against the English, reporting also on a voyage from Java to Japan.

A second letter from a gentleman in town to his friend in the country about the fishing-copartnery in North-Britain. Edinburgh, 1724. S229

An analysis of the prospects for a more active British fishery in the North Sea, in which the author proposes government subsidization of individual fishermen rather than of a large company.

Second recueil de pieces concernant les usurpations des Jésuites dans l'Amérique espagnole & portugaise. [n.p.] 1758. S230

A second collection of indictments against the Jesuits in Paraguay, calling attention to omissions in the previous collection, and supplying missing sections.

A second voyage around the world in the years MDCCLXXII, LXXIII, LXXIV, LXXV, by James Cook, esq. London, For the Editor; sold by J. Almon [etc.] 1776. S231

An anonymous and perhaps unreliable account of Cook's second voyage.

Het secreet des Conings van Spangien, Philippus den Tweeden, achter-gelaten aen ziinen lieven sone, Philips de Derde ... [n.p., ca. 1599.] S232

A Dutch-inspired pamphlet showing Philip II of Spain advising his son to join with the Dutch to prevent French and English expansion in America.

Sedes & origo belli dano-suecici. Amsterdam, 1658. S233

Relates events leading up to the conflict between Sweden and Denmark which brought about the closing of the Sound to Dutch commerce.

Sefström, Erik. Handels-Bibliothek, innehållande relationer och afhandlingar om in-och utrikes handelen. Stockholm, Andreas Holmerus, 1772. S234

A survey of Swedish commerce.

Seixas y Lovera, Francisco de. Descripcion geographica, y derrotero de la region austral Magallanica. Que se dirige al Rey nuestro señor, gran monarca de España, y sus dominios en Europa, Emperador del Nuevo Mundo Americano, y Rey de los reynos de la Filipinas y Malucas ... Madrid, Antonio de Zafra, 1690. S235

A history of the exploration of the southern extremity of South America, a listing of authors who have dealt with it, and a general geography of the area.

Seixas y Lovera, Francisco de. Theatro naval hydrographico, de los fluxos, y refluxos, y de las corrientes de los mares, estrechos, archipielagos, y passages aquales del mundo. Madrid, Antonio de Zafra, 1688. S236

A survey of tides and currents with regard to their importance for navigation.

Seizure of the ship Industry by a conspiracy and the consequent sufferings of James Fox and his companions. London, T. Tegg, 1810. S237

An account of a seventeenth-century voyage to the Hudson Bay region.

Selden, John. Mare clausum seu De dominio maris libri duo. London, Will. Stanesbeius, pro Richard Meighen, 1635. S238

The first edition of a classic in maritime law, growing out of Anglo-Dutch commercial rivalry at sea.

Selden, John. Mare clausum seu De dominio maris libri duo. London, Will. Stanesbeii for Richard Meighen, 1636. S239

The second London edition, including Marcus Zuerius Boxhorn's *Apologia pro navigationibus Hollandorum adversus pontum Heuterum* and also a copy of a treaty of commerce and navigation between Henry VII and the archduke of Austria in 1495.

Selden, John. Mare clausum seu De dominio maris libri duo. Leiden, J. & T. Maire, 1636. S240

The first edition published in the Netherlands.

Selden, John. Mare clausum; the right and dominion of the sea in two books. London, Andrew Kembe and Edward Thomas, 1663. S241

This edition contains a thirty-seven page supplement, *Dominium maris*, concerning the rights of Venice over the Adriatic Sea, translated by James Howell.

Select tracts relating to colonies. London, J. Roberts [ca. 1720]. S242

A collection of quotations from Sir Francis Bacon, John De Witt, William Penn, Machiavelli, and Sir Josiah Child on the benefits arising from colonies to the nation establishing them.

Selkirk, Thomas Douglas, Earl of. A letter to the Earl of Liverpool from the Earl of Selkirk. [London, J. Brettell, 1819.] S243

Relates to Lord Selkirk's Red River colony and its conflicts with the Northwest Company.

Selkirk, Thomas Douglas, Earl of. Observations on the present state of the highlands of Scotland. Edinburgh, J. Ballantyne & Co., 1806. S244

A statement of the reasons for and consequences of emigration of people from Scotland to Canada.

Selkirk, Thomas Douglas, Earl of. A sketch of the British fur trade in North America; with observations relative to the North-West Company of Montreal. London, James Ridgway, 1816. S245

A history and criticism of the Northwest Company's fur trading operations, concluding, "it is evident that the national interest will not be promoted by an adherence to the system of the North-West Company."

Selkirk, Thomas Douglas, Earl of. Esquisse du commerce de pelleteries ... Montreal, J. Brown, 1819. S246
French edition of the foregoing item.

Seller, John. Practical navigation: or, An introduction to the whole art ... London, J.D. for the author and Richard Mount, 1694. S247
The seventh edition of a popular navigation textbook.

Semedo, Alvaro. Imperio de la China. Madrid, Juan Sánchez, 1642. S248
The first edition of this description of China, published by Manuel de Faria y Sousa from the memoirs of the author, a Portuguese Jesuit.

Semedo, Alvaro. Relatione della grande monarchia della Cina. Rome, Hermanni Scheus, 1643. S249
The first Italian edition.

Semedo, Alvaro. Histoire universelle du grand royaume de la Chine. Paris, Sebastien & Gabriel Cramoisy, 1645. S250
The first French edition.

Semedo, Alvaro. Histoire universelle de la Chine. Lyon, Hierosme Prost, 1667. S251
This edition adds Martino Martini's *Histoire de la guerre des Tartares contre la Chine*.

Semedo, Alvaro. The history of the great and renowned monarchy of China. London, E. Tyler for John Crook, 1655. S252
The second English edition containing as well Martino Martini's *Conquest of the ... empire of China by the invasion of the Tartars*.

Séminaire des missions étrangères. Reponse de M^rs des missions etrangeres, a la protestation et aux reflexions des Jesuites. [n.p.] 1710. S253

Séminaire des missions étrangères. Relation des missions des evesques françois aux royaumes de Siam, de la Cochinchine, de Camboye, & du Tonkin. Paris, Pierre Le Petit, Edme Couterot, & Charles Angot, 1674. S254
A report on early French missions in south-east Asia, published as an appeal for further support in France.

Séminaire des missions étrangères. Relation des missions et des voyages des evesques vicaires apostoliques, et de leurs ecclesiastiques és années 1672, 1673, 1674, & 1675. Paris, Charles Angot, 1680. S255
A report covering primarily the progress of missions in Siam, Indo China and India, reflecting French interests there.

Séminaire des missions étrangères. Relation des missions et des voyages des evesques vicaires apostoliques et de leurs ecclesiastiques és années 1676 & 1677. Paris, Charles Angot, 1680. S256
A summary of news from the missions in Cochin China, Tonkin, Cambodia, Siam, China and other places in the East.

[Sénac de Meilhan, Gabriel.] Considérations sur les richesses et le luxe. Amsterdam; Paris, Veuve Valade, 1787. S257
A condemnation of luxury goods because of their tendency to deplete a nation of its capital, which ought to be invested in productive enterprises.

Sendschreiben eines Portugiesen aus Lissabon an einen seiner Freunde in Rom über das von den Jesuiten an den regierenden Pabst Clemens XIII übergebene memoire ... Frankfurt und Leipzig, 1759. S258
An anti-Jesuit piece, relating particularly to financial dealings of the Jesuits in various parts of the Portuguese empire.

Senex, John. A map of the world, corrected from the observations communicated to the Royal Societys of London and Paris. London, John Senex, 1725 [i.e. ca. 1730]. S259
A double-hemisphere world map including information on winds, compass variation, and historical data, with significant new knowledge on the northern Pacific Ocean.

Senex, John. A treatise of the description and use of both globes ... London: Printed for John Senex, 1718. S260
A brief textbook in astronomy and geography including a catalog of books, maps, and globes sold by Senex.

Señor. La ciudad y provincia de ... la Assumpcion del Paraguay. [n.p., ca. 1750.] S261
Considers the possibilities of finding an outlet for the products of Paraguay, chiefly with other Spanish-American countries.

Sentiment de la députation de la province de Bretagne sur le commerce de l'Inde. [n.p., ca. 1789.] S262
Favors free trade in commerce to India, but wants it to pass through the port of Orient.

Sepp, Antonio. Reissbeschreibung ... aus Hispanien in Paraquariam kommen. Nuremberg, Joh. Hoffmann, 1697. S263
An account of travels by two German Jesuit missionaries to Buenos Aires and up the Plate, Paraná, and Uruguay rivers.

Sepúlveda, Juan Ginés de. Dialogo llamado Democrates ... [Seville, Juan Cromberger, 1541.] S264
A justification of aggression toward the American Indians, a point of view that brought the author into conflict with Bartolomé de las Casas.

[Sequeira, Luis de.] Relação summaria da prizam, tormentos, e glorioso martyrio dos veneraveis padres Antonio Joseph, Portuguez, e Tristam de Attimis, Italiano, ambos da Companhia de Jesus, da V. Provincia da China. Lisbon, Francisco de Silva, 1751. S265

An account of the capture, torture, and death of two Jesuit missionaries in China who violated the decree against preaching.

[Sequeira, Luis de.] Compendiosa relazione della prigionia, de tormenti, e della gloriosa morte de' due padri Antonio Joseph Portoghese, e Tristano d'Attimis Italiano ... Portoghese tradotta nell' Italiano. Venice, Tommaso Bettinelli, 1752. S266

Italian edition of the foregoing item.

Serafins, Angelo dos. Relação da viagem, que o illustrissimo, e excellentissimo Marquez de Tavora, vice-rey do estado da India, fez do porto desta cidade de Lisboa ... ao da cidade de Goa ... Lisbon, Miguel Rodrigues, 1751. S267

An account of the voyage to India of the Marquez de Tavora who arrived there in 1750, serving as viceroy for the next four years.

[Séras, P.] Le commerce ennobli. Brussels, 1756. S268

A defense of the French nobility engaged in commerce.

Serrano, Andrés. Los siete principes de los angeles, validos del Rey del Cielo ... Brussels, Francisco Foppens, 1707. S269

Principally concerned with the activities of seven missionaries in the Philippine Islands, but also contains a section on new discoveries in the Pacific, and a map of the Philippines.

Serrano, Francisco, bishop of Tiposa. La Christiandad de Fogan, en la provincia de Fokien, en el imperio de China, cruelmente perseguida del impio Cheu-Hio-kien virrey de dicha provincia. Barcelona, Heredos de Bartholomè y Maria Angela Giralt, 1750. S270

Principally an account of the martyrdom of Pedro Martir Sanz, Bishop of Mauricastro, and the accompanying persecution of Christian missions. This edition includes accounts of four additional martyrdoms in China.

Serrão Pimentel, Luiz. Arte practica de navegar e regimento de pilotos. Lisbon, Antonio Craesbeeck de Mello, 1681. S271

A pilot guide and textbook on navigation for the use of Portuguese navigators sailing to the East and West Indies and the coasts of Africa and Brazil.

Sertomontanus, Joannes Augutus. Astronomia & geographia practica. Lubeck, U. Wetsteinii, 1668. S272

A discussion of astronomical measurements including the mathematics involved, complete with diagrams and tables. Perhaps the author was a teacher as his book is very much a practical astronomy textbook of the seventeenth century.

Sessé y Piñol, José de. Libro de la cosmographia universal del mundo, y particular descripcion de la Syria y tierra Santa. Saragosa, Juan de Larumbe, 1619. S273

The main portion of the text is the recounting of a travel in the Near East by Juan Perera, the author's uncle, in 1552.

Settle, Dionyse. De Martini Forbisseri Angli navigatione in regiones occidentis et septentrionis. Nuremberg, Catharinae Garlachin & Johannis Montani, 1580. S274

Latin edition of the first published account of Martin Frobisher's first voyage in search of a northwest passage, undertaken in 1576.

Settle, Dionyse. Historia navigationis Martini Forbisseri. Hamburg, Joh. Naumann & George Wolff, 1675. S275

The second Latin edition, with commentary by Rudolph Capell.

Seutter, Matthaeus. Accurata delineatio celeberrimae regionis Ludovicianae vel Gallice Louisiane al Canadae et Floridae adpellatione in Septentrionali America descriptae ... [Augsburg, ca. 1725.] S276

A map of North America emphasizing French possessions, undoubtedly inspired by the failure of the Louisiana Company.

Seutter, Matthaeus. Accurater geographischer Entwurf der ... Trankebar. [Augsburg, 1744.] S277

A map of the town of Trankebar and its hinterland on the Coromandel coast. The major factory of the Danish East India Company was located there.

Several arguments proving, that our trade to Africa, cannot be preserved ... by any other method, than that of a considerable joint-stock, with exclusive privileges. [London, ca. 1710.] S278

Earlier Dutch and English experience is used to point to the necessity of a joint stock company for the carrying on of trade between West Africa and the American colonies.

Several examinations taken before once of His Majesty's principal Secretaries of State: together with two letters referred to in some of the said examinations. London, Jacob Tonson, Bernard Lintot and William Taylor, 1723. S279

The persons examined in these documents are Philip Carlyll, William Beasing, and Thomas Yalden.

Seville (Spain). Señor ... Sevilla postrada à los reales pies ... [Seville, 1726.] S280

A collection of documents on the rivalry of Cadiz and Spain for predominance in the West Indian trade.

Seville (Spain). Real junta particular de commercio. En papel de 12 del correinte, me dice el Señor Marquès de Grimaldi ... [Seville, 1771.]
S281
An attempt to limit undesirables coming to Seville under the guise of merchants.

Sharp, Granville. A declaration of the people's natural right to a share in the legislature; which is the fundamental principle of the British constitution of state. London; Boston, Edes and Gill, 1774. S282
An argument on behalf of colonial representation in the British Parliament, based on the natural right of people to share in legislation in matters concerning them.

Sharp, Granville. A declaration of the people's natural right to a share in the legislature: which is the fundamental principle of the British constitution of state. London, For B. White, 1775.
S283
The second edition.

Sharp, Granville. The law of retribution; or, A serious warning to Great Britain and her colonies, founded on unquestionable examples of God's temporal vengeance against tyrants, slave-holders and oppressors. London, W. Richardson for B. White and E. and C. Dilly, 1776. S284
England's earliest anti-slavery spokesman predicts dire consequences will result from participation in the slave trade by Britain and the American colonies.

[Sharp, Granville.] A short sketch of temporary regulations ... for the intended settlement on the grain coast of Africa. London, H. Baldwin, 1788. S285
A proposed structure of government and economy for the colony being established in Sierra Leone, primarily for freed slaves.

Shaw, Thomas. Reisen oder Anmerkungen verschiedene Theil der Barbarey und der Levante betreffend. Leipzig, Bernh. Christoph Breitkopf und Sohn, 1765. S286
This German edition is based on the enlarged English edition of 1757. It includes many maps and illustrations relating to the author's studies in northern Africa and the Near East from 1720 to 1733.

Shaw, Thomas. Reizen en aanmerkingen, door en over Barbaryen en het Ooste door Dr. Thomas Shaw. Utrecht, J. van Schoonoven, 1773. S287
Based on the second English edition, but with new maps and illustrations, this edition adds editorial comment by Pieter Boddaert.

Shaw, Thomas. Voyages ... dans plusieurs provinces de la Barbarie et du Levant. The Hague, Jean Neaulme, 1743. S288
The anonymous translator indicates that changes were made in the text with the approval of Shaw, which would make this edition a transition between the first and second English editions.

Sheffield, John Holroyd, Earl of. Observations on the commerce of the American states. With an appendix ... London, J. Debrett, 1783. S289
A survey of the American economy, noting natural products, manufactures, exports, imports, and the impact of all of these on British commerce.

Sheffield, John Holroyd, Earl of. Observations on the commerce of the American states. London, J. Debrett, 1784. S290
A much expanded edition.

Shelikhov, G.I. (Gregorii Ivanovich). Russischen Kaufmanns erste und zweite Reise von Ochotsk in Siberien ... nach ... Amerika. St. Petersburg, J.Z. Logan, 1793. S291
The report of a Russian merchant and colonizer who engaged in the fur trade in eastern Siberia and the islands of the northern Pacific Ocean as well as on the coast of Alaska.

Shelvocke, George. A voyage round the world by way of the great South Sea, perform'd in the years 1719, 20, 21, 22. London, J. Senex [etc.] 1726. S292
An account of an expedition sent against Spanish shipping in the Pacific Ocean which suffered shipwreck on Juan Fernandez Island, was continued in a captured Spanish ship, and ended with Shelvocke's return to England in a ship of the East India Company.

Shelvocke, George. Reise um die Welt. Bremen, Georg Ludewig Förster, 1787. S293
The only translation of Shelvocke's account, apparently inspired by Cook's voyages.

Sheridan, Richard Brinsley. A comparative statement of the two bills for the better government of the British possessions in India. London, J. Debrett, 1788. S294
A comparison of bills introduced by Pitt and Fox relating to British affairs in India.

Shipley, Jonathan. A sermon preached before the incorporated Society for the Propagation of the Gospel in Foreign Parts ... in the parish church of St. Mary-le-Bow, on Friday February 19, 1773. London, T. Harrison and S. Brooke, 1773.
S295
This annual sermon has a strong political flavor, proposing that the SPG might be a bridge for bringing the American colonists and Britain to more cordial relations.

A short abstract of a case which was last session presented to the Parliament. [London, ca. 1700.]
S296

Examples are given here of East India imports, particularly cloth, which have worked to the disadvantage of English industry.

A short account of the African slave trade. Seven-oaks, Printed for a Society and sold by T. Clout, 1791. S297

Advocates ending the slave trade by boycotting West Indian products.

A short account of the late application to Parliament made by the merchants of London upon the neglect of their trade. London, T. Cooper, 1742. S298

A petition with supporting evidence showing the loss to English merchants from the Spanish attacks on their ships.

A short account of the Marratta state. Written in Persian by a Munshy, who accompanied Col. Upton on his embassy to Poonah. Calcutta printed, London reprinted for Geo. Kearsley, 1787.
S299

The history, economy, geography and social customs of the Marhattas are included. The Asian travel narrative of Caesar Frederici is included, from the 1588 London edition.

A short address to the chartered companies of England: calculated to point out the tendency of the bill brought into Parliament by Mr. Fox. [n.p., 1783.] S300

The author points out dangers in the bill which would give seven parliamentary appointees governing authority over the East India Company. He notes also the danger of the precedent of parliamentary abrogation of a charter.

A short essay upon trade in general, but more enlarged on that branch relating to the woolen manufactures of Great Britain and Ireland. London, J. Huggonson, 1741. S301

A review of the woolen trade noting the loss of revenue to the treasury through smuggling, and the industry's position in overseas commerce, particularly the trade with India and with France.

A short history of English transactions in the East-Indies. Cambridge, For the Author by Fletcher and Hodson, 1776. S302

A compilation of reports of English activities in India which the compiler says is impartial, but which results in an extreme condemnation of English policies toward the people of India.

A short history of the conduct of the present ministry, with regard to the American Stamp Act. London, J. Almon, 1766. S303

A criticism of the Rockingham ministry for the unwillingness of its members to speak out against the Stamp Act when it was passed, and their timidity in having it repealed, allowing relations between Britain and her American colonies to deteriorate.

A short narrative and justification of the proceedings of the committee appointed ... to prosecute the discovery of the passage to the western ocean of America. London, J. Robinson, 1749.
S304

A review of events surrounding a voyage organized by Arthur Dobbs for the double purpose of exploring for the Northwest Passage and destroying the monopoly of the Hudson's Bay Company.

Short notes and observations drawn from the present decaying condition of this kingdom in point of trade. London, 1662. S305

A series of twelve recommendations to rescue England from her commercial depression caused primarily by the strong competition of the Dutch. It contains such novel suggestions as the burning of surplus wool.

A short review of the British government in India: and of the state of the country before the company acquired the grant of the Dewanny. London, John Stockdale, 1790. S306

While the East India Company is defended, the anonymous author sets its actions in a context of declining Moghul power and the need for some form of governance to provide order.

A short state of the countries and trade of North America. Claimed by the Hudson's Bay Company, under pretence of a charter ... London, J. Robinson, 1749. S307

A criticism of the Hudson's Bay Company, questioning the legality of its charter, the authenticity of its reports, and attacking its policies.

A short state of the war and the peace, with additions. [London, ca. 1751.] S308

A defense of the terms of peace, noting Britain's great sacrifices during the War of the Spanish Succession, and approving particularly the gains made in territory and trade in the New World.

A short view of the dispute ... concerning the regulation of the African trade. London, 1750.
S309

An argument against the creation of a joint stock company to handle the slave trade in west Africa.

Sierra Leone Company. An account of the colony of Sierra Leone from its establishment in 1793. London, James Phillips, 1795. S310

A reprint of the report published the previous year.

Sierra Leone Company. Substance of the report delivered by the court of directors ... the 27th March, 1794. London, James Phillips, 1794.
S311

A financial report and description of the company's settlement, which was to be populated by freed slaves.

Sierra Leone Company. Substance of the report of the court of directors of the Sierra Leone Company ... the 26th of February, 1795. London, James Phillips, 1795.　　　　　　　　S312
　　An account of losses sufffered by the company's settlement at Freetown when it was attacked by a French squadron.

Sievers, Johann August Carl. Briefe aus Sibirien an seine Lehrer. St. Petersburg, Zacharias Logan, 1796.　　　　　　　　　　　　　　　　　　S313
　　Letters from a German scientist in Siberia dating from 1790 to 1794, giving information on the peoples, places, and natural products he observed there.

Silva, Antonio da. Sol do oriente S. Francisco Xavier da Companhia de Jesu. Lisbon, A. Craesbeeck de Mello, 1665.　　　　　　　　　　S314
　　An account of Saint Francis Xavier's ten years in Asia by a Portuguese Jesuit.

Silva y Figueroa, García de. l'Ambassade de D. Garcias de Silva Figueroa en Perse. Paris, Jean du Puis, 1667.　　　　　　　　　　　　　　S315
　　An account of an unsuccessful Spanish embassy to Persia which gives a detailed description of numerous trading centers in that country.

Silva y La Vanda, Manuel. Consulta y representacion hecha ... Marques de Villa Garcia ... [Lima? ca. 1745.]　　　　　　　　　　　　　S316
　　A discussion of the South American cloth trade and the extent to which the English are engaged in it.

Silveira, Simão Estaço da. [Recommendations for improving navigation from Peru to Spain.] [Madrid, 1626?]　　　　　　　　　　　　　　S317
　　This sea captain proposes that the Marañon River be used as the means for exporting silver from Peru to Spain, hoping that this route might enable the Spanish to escape the raids of Dutch and English pirates.

Silveira, Simão Estaço da. Relacaõ sūmaria das cousas do Maranhão. Lisbon, Geraldo da Vinha, 1624.　　　　　　　　　　　　　　　　　　S318
　　A brief history of the Portuguese occupation of Maranhão, with a description of the products of the region.

Simler, Johann Wilhelm, ed. Vier loblicher Statt Zürich verbürgerter Reissbeschreibungen ... [Zürich, M. Schauffelbergers seligen Erbin, 1677-1678.]　　　　　　　　　　　　　　S319
　　In addition to Hans J. Amman's account of Palestine, this volume contains records of travelers to Jamaica, the Caribbean, New England, and the Gold Coast.

Simón, Pedro. Primera parte de las Noticias historiales de las conquistas de tierra firme en las Indias Occidentales. Cuenca, Domingo de la Yglesia [1627].　　　　　　　　　　　　　S320
　　This history of discovery and conquest in Venezuela includes a narrative of the expedition of Pedro de Ursúa and Lope de Aguirre in 1560-61, and a Spanish view of Raleigh's search for El Dorado in 1618.

Simpson, Thomas. Narrative of the discoveries on the north coast of America; effected by the officers of the Hudson's Bay Company during the years 1836-39. London, Richard Bentley, 1843.　　　　　　　　　　　　　　　　　　S321
　　The author was an officer in an expedition sent from the Red River to explore the Arctic coast east and west of the Mackenzie River.

Since there have been made severall voyages to the north of Russia, to finde a passage through the frozen sea & so to make a shorter way to China ... Manuscript. [n.p., 18th century.]
　　　　　　　　　　　　　　　　　　　　S322
　　A proposal made to the Commissioners of the Admiralty for an expedition to explore the Arctic coast of Siberia.

Sir Francis Drake revived, who is or may be a pattern to stirre up all heroicke and active spirits of these times, to benefit their countrey and eternize their names by like noble attempts ... London, For Nicolas Bourne, 1653.　　　　S323
　　The first collected edition of Drake's voyages, including the first publication of the account of his final voyage.

[Skinner, Joseph.] The present state of Peru. London, R. Phillips, 1805.　　　　　　　　　S324
　　Skinner translated portions of *El Mercurio Peruano* for this compilation on physical geography. Includes twenty hand colored stippled engravings.

The skreen removed, in a list of all the names mention'd in the report of the Committee of Secrecy, with the sums wherewith they are charged, in relation to South-Sea stock ... London: Printed for J. Lapworth, 1721.　　S325
　　An abridgment of the committee's report on the financial manipulations of the directors of the South Sea Company.

[Sloane, Sir Hans.] Histoire de la Jamaique. London, Nourse, 1751.　　　　　　　　　　　S326
　　A history of Jamaica which contains a survey of its natural resources, agriculture, production, commerce, etc.

Smalbroke, Richard. A sermon preached before the incorporated Society for the Propagation of the Gospel in Foreign Parts: at their anniversary meeting in the parish-church of St. Mary-le-Bow, on Friday, February 16, 1732 [i.e. 1733]. London, J. Downing, 1733.　　　　　　　S327
　　The preacher sees the best means of expanding Christianity in the New World in improving the example given by the colonists.

Smallegange, Matthijs. Nieuwe cronyk van Zeeland. Middelburg, Joannes Meertens; Amsterdam, Abraham Someren, 1696.　　　　S328

Contains histories of the major commercial cities of this province of the Netherlands.

Smelt, Leonard. The speech of Leonard Smelt, Esq. delivered by him at the meeting of the county of York, December 30 1779. York, A. Ward and R. Faulder, 1780. S329

A speech made in opposition to the continuation of the war in America.

Smith, Adam. An inquiry into the nature and causes of the wealth of nations. London, W. Strahan and T. Cadell, 1776. S330

First edition of the classic of eighteenth-century thought on economics and trade.

Smith, Adam. Recherches sur la nature et les causes de la richesse des nations. The Hague, 1778-1779. S331

The first French edition.

Smith, Adam. Recherches sur la nature et les causes de la richesses des nations. Paris, Buisson, 1790. S332

A new translation of *The Wealth of Nations* by Jean Antoine Roucher intended for the enlightenment of France's revolutionary government.

Smith, Adam. Undersøgelse om national-welstands natur og aarsag. Copenhagen, Gyldendal, 1779. S333

The first Danish edition of the *Wealth of Nations*, appending to it Thomas Pownall's *Letter ... to Adam Smith* in translation.

Smith, Adam. Ricerche sulla natura, e la cagioni della ricchezza delle nazioni. Naples, Giuseppe Policarpo Merande, 1790-91. S334

The first Italian edition.

Smith, Adam. Investigacion de la naturaleza y causas de la riqueza de las naciones. Valladolid, Vidua é Hijos de Santander, 1794. S335

The first Spanish edition, with extensive commentary by the translator, Josef Alonso Ortiz.

Smith, Albertus Gerhardus. Dissertatio juris publici Belgici de privilegiis Societatis Indiae Orientalis, quam auspice deo optimo maximo, ex auctoritate rectoris magnifici, Isbr. van Hamelsveld ... Utrecht, Abrahamum à Paddenburg, 1786. S336

An academic dissertation on the beginnings of European trade with the East Indies and the formation of the Dutch East India Company.

[Smith, Charles.] Three tracts on the corn-trade and corn-laws. London, J. Brotherton, 1766. S337

An examination of the English grain trade for the previous two centuries, and a comparison with the grain trade of France.

Smith, John. England's improvement revived. London, Thomas Newcomb for the Author, 1670. S338

This work on forestry sprang from the author's concern for the timber trade as a major source of strength to England's overseas trade.

Smith, John. The generall history of Virginia, New-England, and the Summer Isles. London, I.D. and I.H. for Michael Sparkes, 1627. S339

Includes writings of Smith and others, as well as maps, documents, lists of colonists, and other source materials for the history of English exploration and settlement.

[Smith, Matthew.] A declaration and remonstrance of the destressed and bleeding frontier inhabitants of the province of Pennsylvania. [Philadelphia, W. Bradford?] 1764. S340

A complaint against the provincial government's lenient attitude toward Indians on the frontier, a policy attributed to unequal representation of the frontier counties in the assembly.

Smith, Samuel. This history of the colony of Nova-Caesaria, or New Jersey ... Burlington, James Parker, David Hall, 1765. S341

The first general history of New Jersey contains numerous documents in the text, in notes and in a series of appendices.

[Smith, Simon.] The golden fleece: or the trade, interest, and well-being of Great Britain considered. London, R. Viney, 1736. S342

A survey of the losses incurred to Britain through sale of raw wool abroad and through smuggling of finished Irish woolens. Close regulation of the export trade is urged as a solution.

Smith, Simon, Agent for the Royall Fishing. The herring-busse trade: expressed in sundry particulars. London, E.P. for Nicholas Bourne, 1641. S343

In an effort to improve England's herring fishing trade, the author sets forth the Dutch manner of building and equipping ships for this trade, and observes that the herring trade brings in a variety of commodities which in turn can be exchanged for gold.

Smith, Simon, Agent for the Royall Fishing. A true narration of the royall fishings of Great Britaine and Ireland. London, E.P. for N. Bourne, 1641. S344

The author advocates reform in England's fishing methods, in the belief that an improvement in the fishing trade would benefit the entire maritime economy.

Smith, Sir Thomas. Sir Thomas Smithes voiage and entertainment in Rushia. London, N. Butter, 1605. S345

The author went to Russia as ambassador in 1604 in the interest of improving commerce between the two countries.

[Smith, William] 1727-1803. An answer to Mr. Franklin's Remarks, on a late protest. Philadelphia, William Bradford, 1764. S346

Franklin's appointment as colonial agent to England by the Pennsylvania Assembly brought a protest in print from ten prominent Pennsylvanians. When he replied to their protest, Smith defended the protesters, and attacked Franklin further.

[Smith, William] 1727-1803. A briefe state of the province of Pennsylvania, in which the conduct of their assemblies for several years past is impartially examined, and the true cause of the continual encroachments of the French displayed. London, R. Griffiths, 1755. S347

The failure of Pennsylvania to vote military appropriations is ascribed to the Quaker power structure which is maintained in government through its alliance with German settlers. Loyalty oaths and restrictions upon voting are presented as remedies.

[Smith, William] 1727-1803. An historical account of the expedition against the Ohio Indians, in the year MDCCLXIV, under the command of Henry Bouquet, esq. ... Dublin, John Milliken, 1769. S348

In addition to the account of Colonel Bouquet's expedition, this work contains a section of commentary on frontier warfare.

[Smith, William] 1727-1803. Relation historique de l'expédition contre les Indiens de l'Ohio en MDCCLXIV. Commandée par le chevalier Henry Bouquet ... Amsterdam, Marc-Michel Rey, 1769. S349

This French edition adds a preface by the translator, C.G.F. Dumas, and a brief biography of Bouquet.

Smith, William, 1727-1803. A sermon on the present situation of American affairs. Preached in Christ-Church, June 23, 1775. London, Edward and Charles Dilly, 1775. S350

The provost of the College of Philadelphia contends that American insistence upon free institutions was designed to reflect honor upon the parent nation.

Smith, William, 1728-1793. Histoire de la Nouvelle-York ... London, 1767. S351

This French edition has an abridged preface and also abridged final chapters.

Smith, William, 1728-1793. The history of the province of New-York. London, Thomas Wilcox, 1757. S352

This history of the province of New York includes a detailed description of New York City and of many of the counties.

Smith, William, 1769-1847. History of Canada; from its first discovery, to the peace of 1763. Quebec, For the Author by John Neilson, 1815. S353

Includes much documentation from French sources.

Smith, William, rector of St. John's, Nevis. A natural history of Nevis, and the rest of the English Leeward Charibee Islands in America. Cambridge, J. Bentham, 1745. S354

In addition to a major concern with natural history, the author writes of American Indians and their treatment by colonial governors and of the conditions of slaves in the West Indies.

Smith, William, Surveyor. A new voyage to Guinea. London, John Nourse, 1745. S355

A survey of the regions in which the Royal African Company of England had trading stations.

Smith, William, Surveyor. Nouveau voyage de Guinée. Paris, Durand & Pissot, 1751. S356

The first French edition.

Smollet, Tobias George. A compendium of authentic and entertaining voyages. London, R. and J. Dodsley [etc.] 1756. S357

A seven-volume collection of major voyages, edited and abridged for the general reader.

The snake in the grass discover'd, or, Observations on a late pamphlet, intituled Considerations on the present state of the nation ... London, W. Boreham and A. Dod, 1720. S358

An attack upon proposed monetary policies which are represented as the schemes of stock jobbers and other selfish interests.

Snelgrave, William. A new account of some parts of Guinea, and the slave-trade. London, James, John and Paul Knapton, 1734. S359

A slave trader's general yet vivid account of his experiences as captain of a number of ships sailing the England-Guinea-West Indies route.

Snelgrave, William. Nouvelle relation de quelques endroits de Guinee, et du commerce d'esclaves qu'on y fait. Amsterdam, Aux dépens de la Compagnie, 1735. S360

This first French edition contains an enlarged map of the coastal area of Guinea prepared by Jean Baptiste d'Anville.

Snelling, Thomas. Snelling's seventy-one plates of gold and silver coin, with their weight, fineness and value. London, For H. Chapman, W. Collins, and T. King [1757]. S361

The coins are both British and continental. Weight, fineness, and value are attached to each coin. There is no other text.

Snellius, Willebrord. Tiphys Batavus, sive, Histiodromice, de navium cursibus, et re navali. Leiden, Elzeviriana, 1624. S362

This book on navigation concerns the study of Pedro Nunes's rhumb lines. It is illustrated and includes a substantial section of tables. This is the first edition.

Sobre la poblacion del puerto de Sn Julian. Manuscript. [n.p., ca. 1730.] S363

This manuscript is an expression of concern over the threat of a British colonial establishment in southern South America, an idea championed by Daniel Defoe and the South Sea Company. The author urges a Spanish counter position at Port St. Julian.

Société des Amis de la République Française & de la Convention Nationale, Fort-de France, Martinique. Adresse. La Société des amis de la République-Française & de la Convention nationale, section du Fort de la République-ville, a l'armée de la Martinique. Fort de la République, Martinique, J.F. Willox, [1793]. S364

The letter congratulates the army for victories over French royalist and British forces and for re-establishing order.

Société des amis des noirs. Lettres de la Société des Amis des Noirs a m. Necker, avec la réponse de ce ministre. [n.p.] 1789. S365

The Society wrote to the Director-General of Finances soliciting his interest in their cause on 6 June 1789. He responded on June 14, and they commented upon his response on June 24.

Société des amis des noirs. Réflexions sur le Code Noir, et dénonciation d'un crime affreux, commis a Saint-Domingue: adressées à l'Assemblée Nationale, par la Société des Amis des Noirs. Paris, Imprimerie Patriote François, 1790. S366

A single crime committed against a slave in the colony of Saint Domingue is seen as a part of the larger crime of slavery, with the argument urging its abolition.

Société des amis des noirs. Réglemens de la Société des Amis des Noirs. [Paris, 1788.] S367

The constitution for France's anti-slavery organization is preceded by an introduction indicating the reasons for its establishment.

Société royale de médecine (France). Projet d'instruction sur une maladie convulsive, fréquente dans les colonies de l'Amérique, connue sous le nom de tétanos. Paris, Imprimerie royale, 1786. S368

Tetanus was a problem for the French in Louisiana and for their West Indian sugar colonies. Most of this book concerns treatment among the slave population.

Societeit van Suriname. Accord met de Staaten van Zeeland ... wegens de koop en overneminge van de colonie van Surinam. Amsterdam, Societeyt van Suriname [1713?]. S369

A collection of documents recording the early history of the Society of Surinam, a Dutch trading organization.

Societeit van Suriname. Berigt door directeuren van de Societeit. [Amsterdam, 1746.] S370

Gives commercial statistics and trade policies of the Society from 1683 to 1744.

Societeit van Suriname. Conventie tusschen de directeuren van de geoctroyeerde Societeyt van Suriname. The Hague, J. Scheltus, 1734. S371

An agreement between the Society of Surinam and the government regarding protection of the colony.

Societeit van Suriname. Project van inschryvinge, in een generaal fonds van beleningen op plantagien in de colonie Suriname. Amsterdam, P. Schouten [1779]. S372

An attempt to secure a public loan for the Dutch plantations at Surinam.

Society for the Propagation of the Gospel in Foreign Parts (Great Britain). An account of the propagation of the gospel in foreign parts, what the Society establish'd in England by Royal Charter hath done since their incorporation, June the 16th 1701, in Her Majesty's plantations, colonies, and factories ... [London, Joseph Downing, 1704.] S373

The first report of the Society, surveying the state of religion among the colonists in North America, noting the achievements of the Society in its first years, and presenting a request for financial support.

Society for the Propagation of the Gospel in Foreign Parts (Great Britain). An account of the Society for Propagating the Gospel in Foreign Parts, established by the royal charter of King William III, with their proceedings and success, and hopes of continual progress under the happy reign of Her most Excellent Majesty Queen Anne. London, Joseph Downing, 1706. S374

A review of the founding and early early years of the SPG and its purposes, emphasizing the need for missions to the Indians and African slaves.

Society for the Propagation of the Gospel in Foreign Parts (Great Britain). A collection of papers, printed by order of the Society for the Propagation of the Gospel in Foreign Parts ... London, Joseph Downing, 1706. S375

This collection includes requests sent to bishops for recruiting instructions for clergy admitted to the society and for schoolmasters employed in the mission schools.

Society for the Propagation of the Gospel in Foreign Parts (Great Britain). Standing orders of the Society for the Propagation of the Gospel in Foreign Parts. [London, 1706.] S376

The orders pertain to the governmental structure of the Society, describing the duties of the various officers.

Society of Friends. London Yearly Meeting. Meeting for Sufferings. The case of our fellow-creatures, the oppressed Africans, respectfully

recommended to the serious consideration of the legislature of Great-Britain, by the people called Quakers. London, J. Phillips, 1783. S377
Urges the abolition of the slave trade.

Society of Friends. London Yearly Meeting. Meeting for Sufferings. The case of our fellow-creatures, the oppressed Africans : respectfully recommended to the serious consideration of the legislature of Great-Britain / by the people called Quakers. London, Printed by James Phillips ..., 1784. S378
A plea to Parliament for undertaking legislation to prohibit the slave trade, and for the ultimate relief of slaves held, "as justice and mercy may dictate, and their particular situations may admit." This work has been attributed to Anthony Benezet.

Söder compagniet (Sweden). Capitulatie van de compagnie van de Indies. Manuscript. [Netherlands or Sweden, ca. 1633.] S379
This manuscript substitutes the "Ampliato" or extension of privileges of 1633 for article thirty-seven of the company's charter.

Söder compagniet (Sweden). Instruction oder Anleitung: welcher Gestalt die Einzeichnung zu der newen Süder Compagnie durch Schweden und nunmehr auch Teutschland ... Heilbronn, Christoff Klausen, 1633. S380
An appeal for German capital for the Swedish South Sea Company.

Söder compagniet (Sweden). Manifest und Vertragbrieff der Australischen Companey im Königreich Schweden auffgerichtet. [n.p.] 1624. S381
The announcement of the formation of a Swedish company to trade in "Africa, Asia, America, and Magellanica."

Solinus, C. Julius. Rerum memorabilium. [Rome, J. Schurener, de Bopardia, 1474-75.] S382
The second edition of the work of a third-century geographer whose popularity in Europe continued into the sixteenth century.

Solinus, C. Julius. Rerum memorabilium collectaneae. [Parma, Andreas Portilia, 1480.] S383
The fifth edition.

Solinus, C. Julius. De memoralibus mundi. Venice [Joannes Rubeus Vercellensis] 1498. S384
The twelfth edition.

Solinus, C. Julius. De memorabilibus mundi. Paris, Denis Roce [1503]. S385
This edition was edited by Jodicus Badius Ascensius.

Solinus, C. Julius. De memorabilibus mundi diligenter annotatus et indicio alphabetico prenotatus. Speier, C.H., 1512. S386
The second printing of the edition prepared by Jodocus Badius Ascensius, the earlier one having been published in 1502.

Solinus, C. Julius. De situ orbis terrarum. Pesaro, Hieronymo Soncino, 1512. S387
In this edition Alexander Gabuardus, the editor, adds a listing of rivers, mountains, lakes, and peoples of the world compiled by Vibius Secquester, as well as a listing of the provinces of the world from an unknown source.

Solinus, C. Julius. De memorabilibus mūdi diligenter annotatus et indicio alphabetico prenotatus. [Speyer, Conrad Hist, 1515.] S388
This is the second Speyer edition, which like its predecessor of 1512 is based on the 1503 Paris edition of Jodocus Badius Ascensius.

Solinus, C. Julius. Polyhistor. Vienna, J. Singrenius, 1520. S389
Contains the world map of Peter Apian which is one of the earliest to designate the New World "America."

Solinus, C. Julius. Rerum toto orbe memorabilium thesaurus locupletissimus. Basel, M. Ising & Henric Petri, 1538. S390
The editor, Pedro Juan Oliver has included Pomponius Mela's *De situ orbis*, as well as maps of Africa and Asia. He adds extensive commentary to the text.

Solinus, C. Julius. Rerum toto orbe memorabilium thesaurus locupletissimus. Basel, M. Isingrinium, 1543. S391
A reprint of the foregoing edition.

Solinus, C. Julius. Commentaria in C. Julii Solini Polyhistoria. Basel, Henric Petri, 1557. S392
Commentaries on Solinus and Pomponius Mela by Joannes Camers and Joachim Vadianus, respectively, and additional material by an unknown scholar. A letter is included from Vadianus to Rudolph Agricola, dated Vienna, 1512, referring to the discovery of America.

Solís, Antonio de. Historia de la conquista de Mexico, poblacion, y progressos de la America Septentrional, conocida por el nombre Nueva España. Madrid, Bernardo de Villa-Diego, 1684. S393
The first edition of a classic history of the conquest of Mexico by Cortés, as much renowned for its literary quality as for its recording of the events of the conquest.

Solís, Antonio de. Historia de la conquista de Mexico. Barcelona, F. Oliver, y Martí, 1770. S394
This edition includes a short biography of the author.

Solís, Antonio de. Histoire de la conquête du Mexique ou de la Nouvelle Espagne. Paris, Antoine Dezallier, 1691. S395
The first French edition, including maps and illustrations not present in the previous Spanish editions.

Solís, Antonio de. Istoria della conquista del Messico, della popolazione, e de' progressi nell' America Settentrionale conosciuta sotto nome di Nuova Spagna, scritta in castigliano ... Firenze, Gio. Filippo Cecchi, 1699. S396
The first Italian edition.

Solís, Antonio de. Istoria della conquista del Messico della popolazione, e de' progressi nell' America Settentrionale conosciuta sotto nome di Nuova Spagna. Venice, Andrea Poletti, 1715. S397
The third Italian edition. The translation is attributed to Filippo Corsini.

Solís, Antonio de. The history of the conquest of Mexico by the Spaniards. London, For T. Woodward, J. Hooke, and J. Peele, 1724. S398
The first English edition, a translation by Thomas Townshend, with illustrations and maps.

Solís, Antonio de. Historie om conquêten af Mexico eller om indtagelsen af det Nordlige America bekiendt under navnet Nye Spanien. Copenhagen, Andreas Hartvig, 1747. S399
The first edition in a Scandinavian language, translated by Birgitte Lange.

Solis, Duarte Gomes. Alegacion en favor de la Compañia de la India Oriental. [Lisbon] 1628. S400
This author spent many years in the East before returning to Portugal with his ideas for improving the East Indian trade, stressing the need to reorganize it through the formation of an overseas trading company.

Solis, Duarte Gomes. Discursos sobre los commercios de las Indias. [Madrid] 1622. S401
A treatise on Spanish trade policies and the means to their improvement by a merchant and economist of Lisbon. He deals primarily with the East Indian trade.

Solórzano Pereira, Juan de. Disputationem de Indiarum iure, sive, De iusta Indiarum Occidentalium inquisitione, acquisitione, et retentione. Madrid, Franciscio Martinez, 1629. S402
The dominant work on the legal right of Spain in the New World, relative particularly to the conquest and enslavement of Indians.

Solórzano Pereira, Juan de. D. Philippo IV. Hispaniarum, et Indiarum, regi. Opt. Max ... Disputationem de Indiarum jure. Madrid, 1653. S403
The second Latin edition.

Solórzano Pereira, Juan de. De Indiarum jure. Lyons, Laurentii Anisson, 1672. S404
The third Latin edition.

Solórzano Pereira, Juan de. Politica Indiana. Madrid, Diego Diaz de la Carrera, 1648. S405
The first Spanish edition.

Solórzano Pereira, Juan de. Politica Indiana ... Madrid, M. Sacristan, 1736-1739. S406
The third Spanish edition, the first to be edited by Ramirez de Valenzuela.

Solórzano Pereira, Juan de. Obras varias. Recopilacion de diversos tratados, memoriales, y papeles, escritos algunos en causas fiscales, y llenos todos de mucha enseñança, y erudicion, cuyo indice se verà en la ultima hoja ... Saragossa, Heredos de Diego Dormer [1676]. S407
A collection of eight works by a leading Spanish legal authority, some of which pertain to laws governing Spanish conquest and settlement in America.

Some considerations humbly offer'd on behalf of Jamaica ... with relation to a bill now depending, whereby thirty per cent is intended to be charg'd on all East India prohibited goods ... [London, 1705.] S408
The trade of Jamaica is said to be threatened by legislation which would increase competition from the Dutch at Curaçao.

Some considerations offered touching the East-India affairs. [London, ca. 1698.] S409
A plea for a stronger East India Company more independent of control from London.

Some considerations on the consequences of the French settling colonies on the Mississippi, with respect to the trade and safety of the English plantations in America and the West Indies. London, J. Roberts, 1720. S410
The author views with alarm the possibility of large French colonies on the Mississippi which might link up with the French in the St. Lawrence region and drive the English out.

Some considerations on the importation and exportation of beaver; with remarks on the Hatter's case. [London, 1752.] S411
A reply to the complaining hatters which points out that their trade has not declined, and that a restriction on the export of beaver would seriously depress the trade.

Some considerations on the nature and importance of the East-India trade. London, John Clarke, 1728. S412
A strong argument in support of the East Indian trade as managed by the East India Company.

Some considerations relating to the trade to Guiny. [n.p., ca. 1690.] S413
An advocate of free trade to Africa denounces the Royal African Company for failure to prosecute the wool trade, for not exploring inland, and for not supplying adequate numbers of slaves to America.

Some considerations shewing the justice and equity of the present intended establishment of the East-India trade ... [London, ca. 1698.] S414
A favorable view of the chartering of a new East India Company upon condition of its loaning the government two million pounds.

Some considerations upon the late act of Parliament of Scotland, for constituting an Indian Company. London, 1695. S415
The anonymous author urges the English to have no serious concern about the harm that might be done to English commerce by the Scottish Company, and indicates that the English will profit from its success.

Some equitable considerations, respecting the present controversie between the present East India Company, and the new subscribers or petitioners against them. [London, ca. 1691.] S416
An argument in favor of the continuation of the old East India Company, contending that its critics would not likely manage the trade any better than the old company under proper regulation.

Some general considerations offered, relating to our present trade. And intended for its help and improvement. London, J. Harris, 1698. S417
A survey of commercial problems relating largely to England's ability to trade successfully abroad.

Some neutral considerations, with relation to two printed papers, which are cry'd about the streets, viz. the committee of Parliament's report concerning the Indian and African Company, and an overture, concerning the debts of the said Company. [n.p., 1707?]. S418
Concerns the disposition of the Scottish company's affairs following the union of Scotland and England.

Some observations on the assiento trade, as it hath been exercised by the South-Sea Company; proving the damage which will accrue thereby to the British commerce and plantations in America, and particularly to Jamaica. London, H. Whitridge, 1728. S419
A criticism of the South Sea Company's monopoly on the slave trade centered at Jamaica.

Some observations shewing the danger of losing the trade of the sugar colonies ... London, 1714. S420
The writer feels that England's position in the sugar trade is endangered by the higher price of slaves resulting from the repeal of the Royal African Company's monopoly.

Some observations upon a late pamphlet, intitled, A modest representation of the past and present state of Great Britain, occasion'd by the late change in the administration. London, A. Baldwin, 1711. S421
Proponents of the South Sea Company are reminded of the limitations upon its trade by the lack of British bases in South America and the prohibition upon their ships returning by way of the East Indies.

Some observations upon a paper, intituled, The list, that is, of those who voted for and against the excise-bill. London, For J. Peele, 1733. S422
The issue of who voted for and against the wine and tobacco excise bill was interpreted as either undue influence by the Ministry or disloyalty to the monarchy.

Some queries relating to the present dispute about the trade to Africa. [n.p., 1711.] S423
A series of twenty-one questions on the advisability of creating another monopolistic Africa Company to the disadvantage of free traders.

Some reflections on the trade between Great Britain and Sweden, humbly submitted to the consideration of the Legislature, by a Gentleman who resided some years in Sweden. London, For the Author and sold by J. Robinson, 1756. S424
The author urges a cutback in iron imports from Sweden through increased duties, with proceeds from them going to encourage iron production in the American colonies.

Some remarks on a late pamphlet intituled, Reflections on the expediency of opening the trade to Turky. London, 1753. S425
Critics of the Levant Company had accused it of being a monopoly and of permitting the French to share in the trade to Turkey. This rebuttal attributes the French Levant trade to the excellence of French cloth.

Some remarks on a pamphlet, call'd Reflections on the constitution and management of the trade to Africa. [London] 1709. S426
A protest against the monopoly of the Royal African Company on the slave trade.

Some remarks upon the present state of the East-India Company's affairs ... London, 1690. S427
A condemnation of Sir Josiah Child's management of the company's affairs, with suggestions that the company be terminated and a new one established.

Some remedies to prevent mischiefs from the late act of Parliament made in Scotland in relation to the East-India trade. [London, ca. 1697.] S428

It is proposed that English investment in the Darien Company be prohibited, and that measures be taken to make possible wider participation in the East India trade.

Some seasonable and modest thoughts ... concerning the Scots East-India Company. Edinburgh, G. Mosman, 1696. S429

Presents the Darien colony as being of potential benefit to England's trade.

Some seasonable animadversions on excise: occasion'd by a pamphlet lately publish'd entituled, Considerations occasion'd by the Craftsman. London, J. Wilford, 1733. S430

A refutation of the defense of the excise tax on wine and tobacco.

Some short and necessary observations ... in the settlement of the African trade. [London, ca. 1711.] S431

Includes a petition by eighty-five planters in Barbados requesting the strengthening of the Royal African Company against the independent traders.

Some thoughts concerning the better security of our trade and navigation, and carrying on the war against France more effectually. London, 1695. S432

The author advocates a vigorous commerce as the best defense against France and proposes measures to protect England's Atlantic trade.

Some thoughts on the present state of our trade to India. London, M. Cooper, 1754. S433

An indictment of the East India Company for its monopoly, the losses in gold it entailed for England, the involvement in foreign wars which it caused, and the useless products it returned.

Some thoughts on the present state of our trade to India; with a dedication, humbly addressed to the freeholders of Great-Britain. London, J. Brotherton, 1758. S434

A criticism stating that the East India Company is illegal, financially disadvantageous, and monopolistic.

Some thoughts on the woolen manufactures of England: in a letter from a clothier to a member of parliament. Dublin, R. Gunne, &c., 1731. S435

An argument in favor of encouragement for Irish woolen exports to England as the means of keeping their yarns from going to England's competitors.

Somer, Jan. Wasser und Land-Reyse gethan nach der Levante, oder Morgen-Ländern ... Amsterdam, Christoffel Cunradus, 1664. S436

One of two German editions published this year of a Near Eastern travel narrative previously published in a Dutch edition of 1661.

Somerville, Thomas. A discourse on our obligation to thanksgiving, for the prospect of the abolition of the African slave-trade. Delivered ... on April 15. Kelso, J. Palmer, 1792. S437

A sermon occasioned by the passage in the House of Commons of a resolution for the abolition of the slave trade by January 1, 1796.

Sonnerat, M. (Pierre). Voyage à la Nouvelle Guinée. Paris, Ruault, 1776. S438

Sonnerat's journal was concerned primarily with the plant and animal life of the Philippine Islands; it has many illustrations.

Sonnerat, M. (Pierre). Voyage aux Indes Orientales et a la Chine. Paris, l'Auteur, 1782. S439

An account of travels to India, China, and the East Indies, treating chiefly natural history but including much information on the topography, commerce, and peoples of these regions.

Sonnerat, M. (Pierre). Reise nach Ostindien und China. Zürich, Orell, Gessner Füssli, 1783. S440

The first German edition.

Sonnini, C. S. (Charles Sigisbert). Voyage dans la haute et basse Égypte, fait par ordre de l'ancien gouvernement, et contenant des observations de tous genres ... Paris, F. Buisson, [1799]. S441

This description of Egypt was based upon the author's travels there in the late 1770s. Its purpose was to stimulate French interest in Egypt, reflecting French imperial ambitions of that time. The atlas volume includes forty plates.

Sonnini, C. S. (Charles Sigisbert). Travels in upper and lower Egypt: undertaken by order of the old government of France. London, For J. Stockdale, 1799. S442

The first English edition, a translation by Henry Hunter whose preface indicates English concern over French ambitions in the Near East.

Sonnini, C. S. (Charles Sigisbert). Resa i ofra och nedra Egypten. Stockholm, Johan Pfeiffer, 1801. S443

This Swedish translation by Samuel Ödmann is an abridged version, without illustrations, but with notes by the translator.

Sotelo, Luis. Lettera di Fra Lodovico Sotelo, Francescano, Legato del Re Ossense del Giappone alla Sede Appostolica. Venice, Giuseppe Bettinelli, 1760. S444

Apparently the only vernacular edition of a report on the state of the church in Japan, written in January, 1624, a time when it was under intense opposition from Japanese authorities.

Soto y Marne, Francisco de. Copia de la relacion, y diario critico-nautico, de el viage, que desde la ciudad de Cadiz à la de Cartagena de Indias ... Madrid, Imprenta de Musica de D. Eugenio Bieco, 1753. S445
A ship's log for a voyage from Cadiz to Cartagena with particularly detailed accounts of Martinique and the coast of Venzuela.

Sotomaior, Francisco. Relaçam da milagrosa victoria que alcansou Dom Francisco Souto Mayor, governador da fortaleza de S. Iorge da Mina contra os rebeldes, & inimigos Olandeses, de dezanoue naos, o anno de mil seiscentos & vintecinco, aos vintecinco de Octoubro ... Lisbon, Iorge Rodrigues, 1628. S446
A report of a Portuguese defeat of an attacking Dutch fleet at St. Jorge da Mina on the west coast of Africa in 1625.

Sousa, Fernando de. [Financial papers]. Manuscripts in Portuguese. [Various places, 1617-1666.] S447
Financial records of Fernão de Sousa and his family. He was governor of Angola from 1624 to 1630, and the documents include transactions in Tangiers, Goa, Angola, Africa, and various places in Europe.

Sousa, João de, comp. and tr. Documentos Arabicos para a historia Portugueza copiados dos originaes da Torre do Tombo. Lisbon, Academia Real das Sciencias, 1790. S448
A collection of fifty-eight letters from the first half of the sixteenth century relating to Portuguese commerce and diplomacy. The text is in Arabic and Portuguese.

Sousa, José Roberto Monteiro de Campos Coelho e. Remissoens das leys novissimas, decretos, avisos, e mais disposiçoens ... de el Rei Dom Jozé o I ... e ... Dona Maria I ... Lisbon, Joaõ Antonio da Silva, 1778. S449
A subject guide to Portuguese laws enacted during the reign of José I, 1750-77, and the first year of the reign of Maria I.

Sousa, Manuel Caetano de. Oraçaõ funebre nas exequias do reverendissimo padre Antonio Vieira da Companhia de Jesu. Lisbon, Joseph Antonio da Sylva, 1730. S450
An oration celebrating the life and work of Antonio Vieira, a prominent figure in the Jesuit mission to Brazil.

Sousa Coutinho, Francisco de. Propositie ghedaen ter vergaderinge van ... Staten Generael der Vereenigde Nederlanden, in's Graven-Hage den 16 Augusti, 1647. [n.p.] 1647. S451
Arguments of the Portuguese ambassador to the Netherlands concerning hostility between Portuguese settlers and the Dutch West India Company in Brazil.

Sousa de Macedo, Antonio de. Razon de la guerra entre Portugal, y las provincias unidas de los Paizes baxos ... [Madrid, 1657.] S452
An enumeration of the causes of war between the Dutch and Portuguese.

South Sea Company. Abstract of the charter of the Governour and Company of Merchants of Great Britain, trading to the South Seas. [London] J. Barber, 1711. S453
An explanation of the purposes of the South Sea Company, a list of its directors, a statement of their powers, and a statement of restrictions upon the company.

[South Sea Company.] [A collection of fourteen broadsides relating to the South Sea Company.] London, 1720-21. S454
These broadsides concern stock manipulation primarily.

[South Sea Company.] [A collection of seventeen broadsides.] London, 1721. S455
These broadsides are publications of the individual directors, seeking to deny responsibility for the fraudulent dealings of the company.

[South Sea Company.] [Inventories of the directors.] London, Jacob Tonson, Bernard Lintot, and William Taylor, 1721. S456
A Parliamentary investigation into the affairs of the South Sea Company found duplicity among the directors, and in preparation for further action against them inventories of the property of thirty-five officials were published.

South Sea Company. A list of the names of the corporation of the Governor and Company of Merchants of Great Britain trading to the South-Seas. [London, J. Barber, 1717.] S457
The list of shareholders includes 2,500 names.

South Sea Company. The report of the committee appointed to inspect and examine the several accompts of the South-Sea Company, laid before the general court of the said Company the 16th of June, 1732; and added to the special committee for law-suits, for the prosecution of Mr. James Dolliffe, and Captain William Cleland. Made to a general court held the 9th of May, 1733. London, W. Wilkins, 1733. S458
A series of accountings under thirty headings detailing commercial and financial information on the activities of the South Sea Company from 1720 to 1732.

The South-Sea scheme detected; and the management thereof enquir'd into ... London, W. Boreham, 1720. S459
An attack upon the South Sea Company in the form of a reply to a previously published pamphlet, *The South Sea scheme examin'd*.

The South-Sea scheme examin'd and the reasonableness thereof demonstrated. London, J. Roberts, 1720. S460

Despite the general loss of faith in the South Sea Company, the author urges investors to be calm, assuring them that the value of the stock will be restored.

Spaensche vosse-vel; ofte copye van een missive, die gehouden mach werden seer avontuyrlijck in de handen van een oprecht patriot ... ghekomen. Leeuwaerden, Claude Fonteyne, 1631. S461

Refers to the capture of the Spanish silver fleet by Piet Heyn, and discusses dangers inherent in the power held by the merchants of the Dutch East and West India Companies.

Spain. Coleccion general de las providencias hasta aqui tomadas por el gobierno sobre el estranamiento y ocupacion de temporalidades de los regulares de la Compañia, que existian en los dominios de S.M. de España, Indias, e islas Filipinas. Madrid, Imprenta real de la Gazeta, 1769-69. S462

These documents relate to the expulsion of the Jesuits from Spain and her colonies.

Spain. Ordenanzas generales de la armada naval. Madrid, La Vidua de Don Joachin Ibarra, 1793. S463

A collection of Spanish naval law, covering duties and procedures of all major officers, and extensive references on procedures for conducting voyages to America, Asia, and the Pacific Ocean.

Spain. Para que se guarde, y cumpla el capitulo sexto de la transaccion del assiento de Negros, que estuvo à cargo de la Compañia de Guinea de Portugal, en la forma que se expressa. [Spain, 1703?] S464

The law appears to attempt to provide relief to the Guinea Company for losses suffered in the slave trade.

Spain. Real cedula de S. M. y Señores del Consejo, en que se declara y manda quéde solo á cargo de las justicias remitir los reos rematados, aunque sean los destinados para Filipinas, hasta la respectiva Cabeza de Partido ... Madrid, Pedro Marin, 1788. S465

A royal order to keep the garrison at Manila filled by sending deserters and other criminal types there in preference to their being sent to garrisons in Puerto Rico or Africa.

Spain. Real cedula de S.M. en que manifestando los justos motivos de su real resolucion de 21. de junio de este año, autoriza á sus vasallos Americanos, para que por via de represalias y desagravio hostilicen por mar y tierra á los súbditos del rey de la Gran Bretaña. Madrid, Pedro Marin, 1799. S466

A recitation of British depredations against Spanish possessions and interests in the western hemisphere with royal authorization to take whatever measures necessary to restore peace.

Spain. Real cédula de incorporacion de el Banco de Potosi á la Real hacienda y ordenanzas para su regimen y gobierno, con arreglo á las leyes de Indias ... Madrid, Don Benito Cano, 1795. S467

Regulations for incorporating and governing the bank of Potosí.

Spain. Real decreto ... He venido en mandar se estrañen de todos mis dominios de España, é Indias, Islas Filipinas, y demás adyacentes à los religiosos de la ... Compañia de Jesus ... [Madrid?, 1767?] S468

Royal decree of 1 March 1766 proclaiming expulsion of the Society of Jesus from all Spanish territories and colonies, together with instructions for executing the decree.

Spain. Recopilacion de leyes de los reynos de las Indias ... Madrid, Antonio Balbas, 1756. S469

An abstract of statutes pertaining to the governing of Spanish America.

Spain. Resolucion del rey, comunicada por el Excmo. Señor Don Miguel de Muzquiz á la Direccion General de Rentas, en Aviso de veinte y tres de abril de mil setecientos setenta y quatro, mandando que á las embarcaciones, que salgan para las islas de Barlovento, Yucatán, y Campeche, no se las precise á desembarcar los efectos en el puerto ... [n.p., 1774.] S470

An order enlarging the opportunity for shippers to unload goods at various ports in the Caribbean area.

Spain. La reyna governadora—Por quanto aviendo publicado en Paris el Rey Christianissimo la guerra contra esta corona ... [Madrid, 1674]. S471

The Queen Mother, regent for her son Charles II, issued this proclamation forbidding all trade with France and its overseas possessions because France had invaded Spain's territories in Flanders.

Spain. Archivo General de Indias, Seville. Comercio ilicito en el Mar del Sur. Manuscript. Seville, 1914. S472

A collection of papers copied for E.W. Dahlgren.

Spain. Consejo Real de Castilla. Real provision del supremo Consejo de Castilla ... que estaban confirmadas por los señores del mismo Consejo en dos de diciembre, de mil setecientos y treinta y siete, sin embargo de contradiccion, que pusieron diferentes comerciantes de la potencias de Francia, Inglaterra, y Olanda ... Bilboa, Viuda de A. de Zafra, 1741. S473

Spain. Laws, etc. Libro en q̄ esta copila dal alguna bullas ... Alcala de Henares, Lancalao Polonus, 1503. S474

Spain. Laws, etc.

A collection of Spanish laws, one of which is the first published law for the establishment of Spanish colonies in America.

Spain. Laws, etc. Ordenanças reales, para la Casa de la Contractacion de Sevilla, y para ótras cosas de las Indias. Madrid, Francisco Sanchez, 1585. S475

Compiled in 1552, these rules governing the administration of the Casa de Contratación, and setting forth its powers in the regulation of Spanish trade to America, are published here for the first time.

Spain. Laws, etc. Ordenanzas para el prior y consules della universidad de las mercaderes de la ciudad de Sevilla. Madrid, Francisco Sanchez, 1585. S476

Relates to the management of the Spanish West Indian trade.

Spain. Laws, etc. Ordenes ... se ha servido expedir, y se han de executar en el recibo de la Capitane de Barlovento ... Madrid, A. Bizarron [ca. 1630]. S477

Regulations for the handling of Spanish cargo from the West Indies.

Spain. Laws, etc. Cedula real y vando publico ... contra los introduciones de las mercaderias ... Madrid, Andres de Parras, 1647. S478

A prohibition against importing goods from Portugal.

Spain. Laws, etc. Recopilacion de differentes resoluciones ... sobre si la Casa de Contratacion ... Madrid, J. de Ariztia, 1722. S479

A collection of orders and decrees in connection with commerce and navigation between Spain and America.

Spain. Laws, etc. Real cedula ... para el comercio-libre á Indias ... Madrid, Pedro Marin, 1778. S480

A decree extending free trade with South America.

Spain. Laws, etc. Real cedula de S.M. y señores del Consejo, en que se estienda el commercio-libre ... Madrid, Pedro Marin, 1778. S481

A decree relating to the freedom of commerce between Spain, the Canary Islands, and South America.

Spain. Laws, etc. Reglamento y aranceles reales para el comercio libre de España a Indias. Madrid, P. Marin [1778]. S482

Articles defining import and export regulations for trade to America, the Philippines, and the Canary Islands.

Spain. Laws, etc. Real ordenanza para el establecimiento é instruccion de intendentes de exèrcito y provincia en el virreinato de Buenos-Aires. Madrid, Imprenta Real [1782]. S483

A basic collection of laws for governing Argentina.

Spain. Laws, etc. Reales ordenanzas para la direccion, régimen y gobierno del importante cuerpo de la minería de Nueva-España, y de su real tribunal general. Madrid, 1783. S484

A collection of laws and regulations governing mining in New Spain.

Spain. Laws, etc. Real ordenanza para el establecimiento é instruccion de intendentes de exèrcito y provincia en el reino de la Nueva-España. Madrid, 1786. S485

A collection of laws for the governing of Mexico.

Spain. Laws, etc. Ordenanzas para el prior y consules de la Universidad de Cargadores à Indias de la ciudad de Cadiz. Cadiz, Don Juan Ximinez Carreño, 1787. S486

These ordinances are a collection, the only one printed, of regulations issued by various Spanish sovereigns for governance of the Consulado of Cadiz, which had largely to do with the commerce between Spain and America.

Spain. Sovereign (1556-1598 : Philip II). Esta es un traslado ... de una carta ... de su Magestad ... de sus contadores mayores y de otros officiales de su casa ... [Madrid] 1567. S487

A royal decree raising import duties on items coming from the West Indies and on goods reaching Spain from Asia via Mexico.

Spain. Sovereign (1556-1598 : Philip II). Cedula, 1595 Nov. 19, El Pardo [España, a la] Casa de la Contratación, Seville, yo El Rey. Manuscript. El Pardo, Spain, 19 November 1595; Seville, 30 April 1596. S488

This decree informs the president and officials of the Casa de la Contratación of the king's license to Fray Jusepe de Jesús Maria to take fifteen members of the Discalced Carmelites to Mexico where as missionaries they were to be supplied with provisions.

Spain. Sovereign (1556-1598 : Philip II). Cedula, 1595 Nov. 26, El Pardo [Espanã, a los] Officiales de mi Real hasienda de la nueva Spaña que Ressidis en la ciudad de México [ordering that medicines be provided to the future Carmelite mission in New Mexico for six years]. Manuscript. El Pardo, Spain, 26 November 1595. S489

Philip II directs the treasury in New Spain to supply medicines for sick missionaries for a period of six years.

Spain. Sovereign (1556-1598 : Philip II). Cedula, 1595 Nov. 26, El Pardo [Espanã, a los] Officiales de mi Real hassienda del a nueva Spaña que residis en la ciudad de Mexico [ordering chalices, patens, crucifixes and bells to be supplied to churches to be founded in New Mexico by the Carmelites]. Manuscript. El Pardo, Spain, 26 November 1595. S490

In response to Fray Joseph de Jesus Maria's petition, Philip II orders officials in the Mexican treasury to use crown funds to provide chalice, paten, crucifix, and bell for each mission church founded by the Carmelites.

Spain. Sovereign (1556-1598 : Philip II). Cedula, 1595 Nov. 26, El Pardo [España, a los] Officiales de mi Real hasienda de la nueva Spaña que rresidis [sic] en la ciudad de Mexico [ordering that wine, oil for lamps, and wax for candles be supplied to the mission churches to be founded by the Carmelites in New Mexico]. Manuscript. [El Pardo, Spain] 26 November 1595. S491

Philip II directs the Mexican treasury to supply Carmelite mission churches with candles, oil and wine, all for liturgical use.

Spain. Sovereign (1556-1598 : Philip II). Cedula, 1595 Nov. 26, El Pardo [España, a el Don Gaspar de Zúñiga y Acevedo] conde de Monterrey, virrey ... del a nueva aña ..., yo El Rey. Manuscript. [El Pardo, Spain] 26 November 1595. S492

An order to the viceroy calling for construction of monasteries for the Carmelites in New Mexico.

Spain. Sovereign (1598-1621 : Philip III). Recomendacion, 1598 Dec. 16 Aranxuez [España, a el] conde de Monterey, ... virrey ... de la nueva España. Manuscript. Aranxuez, 16 December 1598. S493

Philip III notes the Carmelites' complaint that they have been excluded from missionary work in New Mexico by the priority of the Franciscans, and commends their interest in California to the viceroy of Mexico.

Spain. Sovereign (1598-1621 : Philip III). El Rey. Lo que por mi mandado se assienta y concierta con Juan Nuñez Correa Portugues ... sobre la haberia, q̃ en las ciudades de Sevilla y Cadiz, y otras partes se cobra, de todo el oro y plata, piedras, perlas, y joyas, y otras cosas, que vienen de las Indies. [Madrid, 1603.] S494

A contract containing fifty-seven provisions, granting trading rights in Spanish America to Juan Nuñez Correa for a period of ten years.

Spain. Sovereign (1598-1621 : Philip III). Cedula, 1605 May 3, Vall[adoli]d [a los] Officiales de mi Real hazienda de la nueva España que rresidio [sic] en la ciudad de Mex[i]co. Manuscript. 3 May 1605. S495

Philip III renews the gift of wine and oil for liturgical purposes to the Camelite missions in Mexico.

Spain. Sovereign (1598-1621 : Philip III). Verclaringhe ghedaen uyt den naem des Coninck van Spaengnien, tot waerschouwinghe aen alle de coopleiden ende negotianten in zijne rijcken ende landen van Spaengnien ende Portugael van date den elfsten November 1607. Middelburgh, Richaerd Schilders [1608?]. S496

Spain. Sovereign (1598-1621 : Philip III). Missive ofte placcaet van den Conink van Spagnien ... Enkhuisen, J. Lenaertsz Meyn, 1609. S497

In his instructions to the Duke of Lerma to destroy and banish the Moors under Muley Cidan, King Philip warns that they are receiving commercial aid from "northern lands on the sea," an apparent reference to Dutch-African trade.

Spain. Sovereign (1598-1621 : Philip III). Procuratie oft bevestinghe der Concincklijcke Ma. van Spaignien. Brussels, R. Velpius, 1609. S498

A proclamation of recognition of the Spanish-Dutch truce of 1608.

Spain. Sovereign (1621-1665 : Philip IV). Prematica en que se amplia la ley ... de la nueva Recopilacion ... Madrid, Dona Teresa Iunti, 1626. S499

An extension of a law requiring the investment of money earned in foreign trade in further commercial enterprises.

Spain. Sovereign (1621-1665 : Philip IV). Versaminge van de memorien ende klachten van den Ambassadeur van Spagnien ... Antwerp, Jan van Linthout, 1653. S500

The Spanish ambassador complains of Dutch interference in Spain's commerce, chiefly in the West Indies.

Spain. Sovereign (1621-1665 : Philip IV). Almoxarifazgo de Indias. [n.p., 1663?]. S501

A grant of monopoly to Don Francisco Vaez on the exporting of certain West Indian products, and also a permit to trade directly with China and the Philippines.

Spain. Sovereign (1665-1700 : Charles II). Resolucion de la Reyna nuestra señora, en orden al establecimiento de una Compañia Española para el Comercio Armado. [n.p., 1669.] S502

An attempt, apparently unsuccessful, to launch a new type of trading company modeled somewhat on Dutch and English companies.

Spain. Sovereign (1665-1700 : Charles II). A los virreys del Perù, Nueva-España, y Santa Fè presidentes, audiencias, y oficiales reales de los puertos ... [n.p., 1680.] S503

Authorities in Spanish America are informed of the establishment of a squadron in the Atlantic to combat smugglers and pirates.

Spain. Sovereign (1665-1700 : Charles II). Der Königl Majest. von Spanien placat, worinnen begriffen, welcher gestalten deroselben Lande und Königreiche gegen denen frantzösischen Unterthanen des Commercii und Kauffhandels halber sich zu verhalten. Madrid, 1689. S504

A statement of Spanish commercial interests in its war with France.

Spain. Sovereign (1665-1700 : Charles II).
Octroy de Sa Majesté, pour l'establissement de la Compagnie Royale des Pays Bas. Brussels, E.H. Fricx, 1698. S505
A document announcing the formation of a trading company of the Spanish Netherlands.

Spain. Sovereign (1700-1746 : Philip V).
Proyecto para el despacho preciso de una flotilla para las provincias de Nueva España. [n.p.] 1711. S506
An ordinance providing for a fleet of seven ships, five being merchantmen, to sail from Cadiz to Vera Cruz and Havana.

Spain. Sovereign (1700-1746 : Philip V).
Declaration de los derechos que por razon de Alcavala ... deben satisfacer en Cartagena & Portovelo ... de Lima e Panama. Madrid, Juan de Ariztia, 1720. S507
Contains lists of merchandise shipped from Spain to America.

Spain. Sovereign (1700-1746 : Philip V).
Resolucion de su Magested expedida a consulta de Su Real y Supremo Consejo de India. [Madrid, 1722.] S508
Special measures for naturalized foreigners and Spanish citizens trading in the Spanish colonies.

Spain. Sovereign (1700-1746 : Philip V). Don Phelipe ... establecer y formar una compania para el commercio de dichas mis Islas Philipinas. [Madrid? ca. 1733.] S509
Contains regulations on the Spanish Philippine Company, noting the products in which it trades, and the duties on each.

Spain. Sovereign (1700-1746 : Philip V). His Catholick Majesty's manifesto, justifying his conduct in relation to the late convention. London, R. Amey and A. Dodd, 1739. S510
Spain accuses England of bad faith in negotiations which affect the trade of both countries in America.

Spain. Sovereign (1700-1746 : Philip V). The King of Spain's declaration of war against Great-Britain. Done at Buen Retiro, on the 28th of November ... London, For R. Amey [1739]. S511
The King's declaration prohibits all commercial relations between Spain and England. The text is in Spanish and English.

Spain. Sovereign (1700-1746 : Philip V). [Proclamation prohibiting trade with England and her "vassals."] Madrid, Gomez, 1739. S512
During the War of Jenkins' Ear, Philip V severed all trade relations with England as well as England's "vassal", Portugal.

Spain. Sovereign (1700-1746 : Philip V). Copia de la real cedula de su Magestad expedida para que en la ciudad de San Christoval de la Habana se forme una compañia ... Madrid, Antonio Sanz, 1740. S513
A decree establishing a company at Havana to monopolize the commerce in tobacco, sugar, and other products.

Spain. Sovereign (1700-1746 : Philip V). Manifesto, ou combinaçam do procedimento de Sua Magestade catholica com a del Rey da Gram Bretanha. Lisbon, Antonio Correa Lemos, 1740. S514
A statement of Spain's grievances against Great Britain leading to war in 1739, in a Portuguese translation.

Spain. Sovereign (1700-1746 : Philip V). El Rey. Por quanto el Infante D. Phelipe, mi muy caro, y amado hijo almirante generale de todas mis fuerzas maritimas de Espana, y las Indias ... [Madrid? 1741?]. S515
A set of regulations concerning the building and provisioning of ships in Havana.

Spain. Sovereign (1700-1746 : Philip V). Decreto de la Magestad del Rey catholico Phelipe V sobre varias acusacions dadas en su Real Consejo de Yndias contra los Jesuitas del Paraguay ... Naples, 1744. S516
The result of an inquiry into the administration of Paraguay with reference to Jesuit authority there and to economic matters also.

Spain. Sovereign (1700-1746 : Philip V). Decreto di Sua Maestà il Re cattolico Filippo V sopra varie accuse portate al suo Real consiglio delle Indie contro i Gesuiti del Paraguay ... Naples, 1744. S517
Italian translation of the previous item apparently published at the same time, and adding a two-page "avvertimento".

Spain. Sovereign (1700-1746 : Philip V). Real despacho ... por inquisicion general, aun en los casos en que interesse la real hacienda, ò mire à descubrir fraudes ... [Bilbao, 1745.] S518
Royal instructions applicable to merchants of Bilbao and the neighboring territory, calling for inspection of records to detect frauds in the collection of taxes.

Spain. Sovereign (1746-1759 : Ferdinand VI).
Real cedula de la Compañia Real de Fabricas, y Comercio de Sevilla. Madrid, Gabriel Ramierez, 1747. S519
A royal decree authorizing commerce with America to be carried on by this new company.

Spain. Sovereign (1759-1788 : Charles III). Real cedula ... para impedir la extracion de oro, y plata de estos dominios ... Saragossa, Imprenta de Rey, 1768. S520

Regulations upon the exploitation of gold and silver mines.

Spain. Sovereign (1759-1788 : Charles III). Real decreto en que S.M. ha resuelto ampliar la concesion del comercio libre de 16 octubre de 1765. Madrid, Juan de San Martin, 1778. S521
A royal decree extending the right of free trade between Spanish possessions in America so as to include the Rio de la Plata region, Chile, and Peru.

Spain. Sovereign (1759-1788 : Charles III). Real decreto en que S.M. ha resuelto ampliar la concesion del comercio libre ... de 16. de octubre de 1765. Barcelona, Eulalia Piferrer vidua [1778]. S522
Another edition of the foregoing item.

Spain. Sovereign (1759-1788 : Charles III). Real cedula de S.M. y señores del consejo, por la qual se crea, erige y autoriza un banco nacional y general para facilitar las operaciones del comercio y el beneficio publico de estos reynos y los de Indias, con la denominacion de Banco de San Carlos baxo las reglas que se expresan. Madrid, Pedro Marin, 1782. S523
The Banco de San Carlos was established to facilitate Spain's West Indies trade.

Spain. Sovereign (1759-1788 : Charles III). Real derecho de alcavala de la primera y demàs ventas de todos los frutos, generos, y mercaderias que se llevaren de estos reynos de España para comerciar en aquellos dominios. [Cadiz, 1782.] S524
A group of nine regulations pertaining to Spanish West Indian trade.

Spain. Sovereign (1759-1788 : Charles III). Real cedula de ereccion de la Compañia de Filipinas. Madrid, Joachin Ibarra [1785]. S525
The Real Compañia de Filipinas was licensed to trade between Spain, South America, the Philippine Islands, and the Asiatic mainland.

Spain. Sovereign (1759-1788 : Charles III). Real cedula de S.M. y señores del consejo, en que se declara y manda quéde solo á cargo de las justicias remitir los reos remetados, aunque sean los destinados para Filipinas ... Madrid, Don Pedro Marin, 1788. S526
Concerns the need for troops to fill up the Manila regiment.

Spain. Sovereign (1788-1808 : Charles IV). Real cedula de Su Magestad concediendo liberdad para el comercio de Negros con las islas de Cuba, Santo Domingo, Puerto Rico, y provincia de Caracas, á Españoles y extrangeros, baxo las reglas que se expresan. Madrid, La viuda de Ibarra, 1789. S527
The slave trade is opened in the interest of improving agriculture in the places named.

Spain. Sovereign (1788-1808 : Charles IV). Real cedula en ereccion del Consulado de Vera-Cruz ... Madrid, Benito Cano, 1795. S528
Regulations for the development and protection of commerce and manufactures at Vera Cruz.

Spain. Sovereign (1788-1808 : Charles IV). El Rey. Uno de los principales motivos que me determináron a concluir la paz con la Republica Francesa ... [n.p., 1796.] S529
A decree announcing the reasons for the severance of peaceful relations between Spain and Britain, citing British interference with commerce in America and the Mediterranean.

Spain. Sovereign (1788-1808 : Charles IV). [A royal decree authorizing duty-free trade in fruits and other produce between Manila and Acapulco. Dated in Orizava, 16 June 1797.] [n.p.] 1797. S530

Spain. Treaties, etc. Articles of a treatie of truce made and concluded in the towne and citie of Antwerp, the 9. of April 1609. London, George Potter and Nicholas Brown, 1609. S531
The first English edition.

Spain. Treaties, etc. Artijckelen van't bestandt ghesloten ende geconcludeert voor XII jaren tusschen ... Spanien, ... ende de staten van de ... Nederlanden. Antwerp, Joachim Trognesius [1609]. S532
The truce of 1609 brought to an end the war between Spain and the Netherlands, resulting in independence for the northern provinces.

Spain. Treaties, etc. Verconderinge van het bestandt tusschen Zijne Maiesteyt ... ende de Staten Generael. Antwerp, P. Stroobant, 1609. S533
The text of the treaty concluded with Spain in 1609, with an additional commentary on the reaction of the people of Antwerp to it.

Spain. Treaties, etc. Tractaet van vrede, beslooten den dertichsten Januarij deses tegenwoordigen jaers ... The Hague, Weduwe ende erfgenamen van wijlen, H.J. van Wouw, 1648. S534
A portion of the Treaty of Westphalia in which three provisions relate to the continued activity of the Dutch East and West India companies.

Spain. Treaties, etc. Tratados, privilegios, y preeminencias, hechos, y concedidos a las ciudades Anseaticas ... Madrid, Domingo Garcia Morràs, 1648. S535
A collection of agreements between Spain and the cities of the Hanseatic League confirmed at the Treaty of Westphalia.

Spain. Treaties, etc. Tractaet vande marine ... tusschen ... Spaigne ... ende de ... Vereenighde Nederlanden. The Hague, Weduwe ende erfgenamen van wijlen H.J. van Wouw, 1651. S536
A supplement to the Treaty of Westphalia, dealing with shipping and fishing.

Spain. Treaties, etc. Traicté de paix entre les couronnes d'Espagne et de France. Brussels, Hubert Anthoine Velpius, 1660. S537
A large part of the treaty deals with trade between the two countries and their colonies.

Spain. Treaties, etc. Tratado de navegacion, y comercio adjustado entre esta corona y el emperador de Romanos. Madrid, J. de Ariztia [1725?]. S538
An agreement between Philip V and Holy Roman Emperor Charles VI regarding rights of navigation and commerce.

Spain. Treaties, etc. Tratado definitivo de paz concluido entre Sus Magestades Christianissima, y Britanica, y los Estados Generales de las Provincias Unidas, en Aix la Chapelle à 18 de octubre de 1748 ... Madrid, Imprenta del Mercurio, 1749. S539
The treaty of Aix la Chapelle provided for the mutual restoration of conquests in North America and in Asia by France and Great Britain. Text in French and Spanish.

Spain. Treaties, etc. Tratado definitivo de paz concluido entre el Rey nuestro señor y S.M. Christianisima ... y S.M. Británica ... en Paris á 10 de febrero de 1763. Madrid, Imprenta Real de la Gaceta, 1763. S540
This Spanish edition of the Treaty of Paris includes both the preliminary articles and the definitive treaty.

Spain. Treaties, etc. Tratado definitivo de paz, e uniaõ entre ... Portugal ... Gram Bretanha ... França, e ... Hespanha ... assignado em Pariz a dez de fevereiro de mil setecentos sessenta e tres. Lisbon, Miguel Rodrigues, 1763. S541
This edition has the text in French and Portuguese.

Spain. Treaties, etc. Tratado definitivo de paz concluido entre el Rey nuestro señor ye el Rey de la Gran Bretaña firmado en Versailles á 3 de septiembre de 1783, con sus artículos preliminares. Madrid, Imprenta Real, 1783. S542
Signed the same day as the Anglo-American and Anglo-French treaties, this third part of the diplomatic trilogy ceded East and West Florida to Spain in exchange for the Bahamas.

Spain. Treaties, etc. Convencion para explicar, ampliar, y hacer efectivo lo estipulado en el artículo sexto del tratado definitivo de paz del año de 1783 ... firmada en Lóndres á 14 de julio de 1786. Madrid, Imprenta Real [1786]. S543
This convention, signed in 1786 between Great Britain and Spain, clarifies and provides means of implementing article six of the 1783 Treaty of Paris which provided for English evacuation of Belize.

Spain. Treaties, etc. Tratado definitivo de paz, concluido entre El Rey nuestro Señor y la República Francesa, firmado en Basilea á 22 de Julio de 1795. Madrid, Imprenta Real [1795]. S544

Spain. Treaties, etc. Tratado de amistad, límites y navegacion concluido entre el Rey nuestro señor y los Estados Unidos de América. Madrid, Imprenta Real, 1796. S545
The treaty between the United States and Spain, negotiated by Thomas Pinckney, which established the boundary of Florida, freedom of navigation on the Mississippi, and numerous other commercial provisions.

Spaniens och Portugalls besittningar uti America, statistisk afhandling, förra delen. Linköping, Groth och Petrie, 1809. S546
The first volume of an intended survey of Spanish and Portuguese colonies in America, this volume covering Mexico, Peru, and Chile.

[Spanish manuscript documents. n.p., 17th and 18th centuries.] S547
A miscellaneous collection containing items dealing with church, political, naval, and international affairs.

[Spanish manuscript documents. n.p., ca. 1800.] S548
These documents concern primarily Spanish trading companies in South America and the Philippine Islands and other economic matters.

[Spanish political and economic correspondence.] Proyecto del S[r] Macanas a la Magestade Felipe Quinto pa el govierno de la compania de comercio de Indias. Manuscript. Spain, 1737-1761. S549

[Spanish shipbuilding records.] Manuscript. [Bilbao] 1628. S550
Six ships are described as to construction, tackle, rigging and provisioning. These ships were constructed for use in the Spanish-American trade.

Spanish treachery, baseness, and cruelty, displayed from 1588 to 1739. London, J. Brett, 1739. S551
Attempts to show the necessity of war with Spain.

Sparrman, Anders. Resa till Goda-Hopps-udden, Södra pol-kretsen och omkring jordklotet, samt till Hottentott-och Caffer-Landen, åren 1772-76. Stockholm, Anders J. Nordström, 1783. S552
The first edition of a major work on the geography, natural history and ethnology of South Africa.

Sparrman, Anders. A voyage to the Cape of Good Hope, towards the antarctic polar circle, and round the world. London, G.G.J. and J. Robinson, 1786. S553
The second English edition.

Sparrman, Anders. A voyage to the Cape of Good Hope, towards the antarctic polar circle, and round the world. Perth, R. Morison junior, for R. Morison and son [etc.] 1789. S554
This is a new translation from the Swedish.

Sparrman, Anders. Voyage au Cap de Bonne-Espérance, et autour du monde avec le Capitaine Cook. Paris, Buisson, 1787. S555
The first French edition.

Sparrman, Anders. Reise nach dem Vorgebirge der guten Hoffnung, den südlischen Poländern und um die Welt, hauptsächlich aber in den Ländern der Hottentotten und Kaffern in den Jahren 1772 bis 1776. Berlin, Haude und Spener, 1784. S556
This German edition is introduced by Georg Forster who was also on the voyage with Sparrman. He alludes to small changes he has made in the text.

Sparrman, Anders. Tal, om den tilväxt och nytta, som vetenskaperne i allmänhet, färdeles naturalhistorien, redan vunnit och ytterligare kunna vinna, genom undersökningar i Söder-hafvet ... Stockholm, Johan Georg Lange, 1778. S557
An oration based on observations Sparrman made during Cook's second voyage in which he had taken part.

Sparrman, Anders. En upptäckts-resa till Norra Stilla hafvet och kring jordklotet. Stockholm, Anders Zetterberg, 1800-01. S558
An abridged account of Vancouver's voyage, translated and edited by Anders Sparrman.

A specimen towards a new and complete plan for regulating and settling the military power of Great Britain, in concert with commerce. London, Weaver Bickerton, 1730. S559
Although representing himself to be an advocate of free trade, the author makes many proposals involving restrictions upon free commerce in the English colonies.

Speed, John. Asia, with the islands adjoyning ... London, G. Humble, 1626. S560
This map appeared in Speed's *A prospect of the most famous parts of the world*, 1627.

Speed, John. England Wales Scotland and Ireland described and abridged ... London, John Speed, 1666. S561
The plates are the same as those in the 1620 edition. The text is abridged from Speed's *Theatre of the empire of Great Britain*.

Speed, John. A mapp of the Sommer Ilands, once called the Bermudas. London, G. Humble, 1626. S562
From Speed's *A prospect of the most famous parts of the world*. The map, originally drawn by Abraham Goos, contains the names of Bermuda landholders.

Speed, John. A new and accurat map of the world. London, T. Basset and R. Chiswell, 1676. S563
A hand-colored world map, drawn in 1651, and published with Speed's *The theatre of the empire of Great Britain*, 1676.

Speer, Joseph Smith. The West-India pilot: containing piloting directions for Port Royal and Kingston harbours in Jamaica, in and out of the kays &c. ... London, For the Author, 1771. S564
The second edition, containing twenty-seven charts, and in addition piloting information and text describing various islands, cities and trading opportunities in the West Indies.

Spencer, Thomas, Secretary to Sir Timothy Thornhill. A true and faithful relation of the proceedings of the forces of their Majesties K. William and Q. Mary, in their expedition against the French, in the Caribby Islands in the West-Indies ... London, Robert Clavel, 1691. S565
An account of naval and military operations at St. Christophers, Nevis, St. Martins, Mariagalante, St. Bartholomews, and St. Eustace, in most of which the English forces prevailed.

Spilbergen, Joris van. Oost ende West-Indische spiegel. Leiden, Nicolaes van Geelkercken, 1619. S566
This account of Spilbergen's circumnavigation of the earth in 1614-18 also includes the *Australische navigatien* of Jacob Le Maire.

Spilbergen, Joris van. Speculum orientalis occidentalisque Indiae navigationum. Leiden, Nicolaes van Geelkercken, 1619. S567
The first Latin edition.

Spilbergen, Joris van. Miroir Oost & West-Indical, auquel sont descriptes les deux dernieres navigations, faictes es années 1614, 1615, 1616, 1617, & 1618. Amsterdam, Jan Jansz, 1621. S568
The first French edition.

Spilbergen, Joris van. Copye van een brief ... tracterende van't veroveren ... der Spaensche armade. [n.p., 1607.] S569
An account of a Dutch victory over the Spaniards in a naval battle near Gibraltar.

Spilman, James. A journey through Russia into Persia. London, R. Dodsley, 1742. S570

An account of a trade mission to Persia undertaken for the purpose of securing trading privileges. It includes descriptions of commercial opportunities in several Persian cities.

Spirit Merchant. Account book. [England, 8 August 1749 to 19 July 1754.] S571
Records prices and transactions with clients in the West Country of England.

Spon, Jacob. Italianische, dalmatische, griechische und orientalische Reise-Beschreibung. Nuremberg, Johann Hofmann, 1681. S572
Descriptions of the cities and islands in the eastern Mediterranean, with major interest in the areas under strong Venetian influence.

Spon, Jacob. Italiänische, dalmatische, griechische und orientalische Reise- Beschreibung ... aus dem Französischen ins Teutsche übersetzt durch J. Menudier ... Nuremberg, Johann Hofmanns, 1690. S573
A re-issue of the sheets of the 1681 edition.

Sprengel, M. C. (Matthias Christian). Alexander Mackenzie's Reise nach dem nördlichen Eismeere vom 3. Jun. bis 12. September 1798. Weimar, Landes, Industrie-Comptoirs, 1802. S574
This is a brief account of the 1789 and 1792-1793 Mackenzie expeditions, with a short history of the Canadian fur trade and commentary on Mackenzie's travels in relation to it.

Sprengel, M. C. (Matthias Christian). Allgemeines historisches Taschenbuch, oder, Abriss der merkwürdigsten neuen Welt-Begebenheiten, enthaltend für 1784 die Geschichte der Revolution von Nord-America. Berlin, Haude und Spener [1784]. S575
A history of the American Revolution for German readers, including descriptions of each of the colonies, background of the conflict, seventeen plates depicting events, and a map.

Sprengel, M. C. (Matthias Christian). Geschichte der Europäer in Nordamerica. Erster Theil. Leipzig, Weygandschen Buchhandlung, 1782. S576
Intended as a larger work, this history is almost entirely conerned with British colonization in North America.

Sprengel, M. C. (Matthias Christian). Vom Ursprung des Negerhandels. Halle, Johann Christian Hendel, 1779. S577
A history of the slave trade, with major emphasis on the African slave trade prior to the discovery of America.

Sprenger, Johann Theodor. Succincta praxis & usus globi coelestis & terrestris. Jenae, Henr. Christophori Crökeri, 1691. S578

A description of celestial and terrestrial globes and their uses.

Squire, Jane. A proposal for discovering our longitude. London, For the Author, sold by P. Vaillant and F. Needham, 1742. S579
The second edition of a work written in 1731. This edition includes letters from the author charging that the work was not properly considered by the appropriate authorities for the prize offered for solving the problem of determining longitude at sea.

Squire, Jane. A proposal to determine our longitude. London, For the Author and sold by S. Cope, 1743. S580
This edition incorporates additions in manuscript from a previous edition.

Staat der generale Nederlandsche Oost-Indische Compagnie. Amsterdam, J. Allart, 1792. S581
A 525-page report on the conditions of the Dutch East India Company.

Staatkundige aanmerkingen over het gehouden gedrag der Engelschen, op den 9 augustus 1780 in de groote baay van het eiland St. Martin. [n.p.] 1780. S582
A discussion of the right of seizure of commercial ships growing out of the English seizure of an American ship at St. Martin.

Stadel, Johann Karl von. Compendium cosmo-et geographiae, nec non chronologiae summorum pontificum, cardinalium, imperatorum, regum, ducum, & principum. Rome, Typis Bernabo, 1712-1713. S583
A biographical and geographical dictionary of wide scope, drawing upon the major geographical writers of the time.

Staden, Hans. Warhaftig Historia und Beschreibung einer Landtschafft ... in der Newenwelt America gelegen. Marburg, Andres Kolben, 1557. S584
An early account of Brazil by one who was a captive of the Tupinamba tribe for about two years. Includes woodcut illustrations and a map showing the coast of Brazil.

Staden, Hans. Warhafftig Historia unnd Beschreibung einer Lantschafft ... in der Newen Welt America gelegen. Frankfurt am Main, Weygant Han [1557]. S585
The second edition.

Staehlin, Jakob von. An account of the new northern archipelago lately discovered by the Russians. London, C. Heydinger, 1774. S586
An account of the islands, people, and products in the Aleutian region.

Staehlin, Jakob von. Das von den Russen in den Jahren 1765, 66, 67 entdekte nordliche Insel-

Meer, zwischen Kamtschatka und Nordamerika. Stuttgart, Christoph Friedrich Cotta, 1774. S587
Contains the controversial map that frustrated Cook on his voyage to find the Northeast Passage. The map is in French, text in German. Most copies of this book were destroyed by order of the Russians.

Stafford, Cornelius William. The Philadelphia directory, for 1797 ... [Philadelphia] William W. Woodward, 1797. S588
Includes a plan of the city of Philadelphia, and a table of duties on imports.

Stair, John Dalrymple, Earl of. The state of the national debt, the national income, and the national expenditure. Edinburgh, John Wood, 1776. S589
"It is ... hoped that this State of the National Situation may tend to open the Nation's Eyes to the indispensable Necessity of putting an End to this unnatural Civil War with America ..."

Stamp Act Congress (1765 : New York, N.Y.). Authentic account of the proceedings of the congress held at New-York, in MDCCLXV, on the subject of the American stamp act. [London, For J. Almon, 1767.] S590
An account of the Stamp Act Congress, recording the resolution of the Massachusetts Assembly which invited the delegates, the names of the delegates and an account of their deliberations.

Stanton, Daniel. A journal of the life, travels, and gospel labours, of a faithful minister of Jesus Christ, Daniel Stanton. Philadelphia, J. Crukshank, 1772. S591
A Quaker's account of travels to Ireland, the West Indies and the American Colonies, noting conditions of slavery and relations of colonists with Indians.

A state of the allegations and evidence produced ... upon the representation of the West-India planters. [London, 1784.] S592
Complaints by British West Indian planters and merchants against restrictions upon their trade with the United States, together with opposing arguments urging that trade be oriented to Britain and Canada.

A state of the annuities pertaining to the South Sea Company. Manuscript. England. January 5, 1714. S593
Tables and computations to prove that by retiring certain government annuities early, sufficient money could be saved to provide the South Sea Company with funds to pay interest on stock, the public could be relieved of duties on malt and the fisheries, and the East India Company of duties on salt.

State of the British and French colonies in North America. London, A. Millar, 1755. S594
A description of English and French colonies in North America, and the means of checking the French there without going to war.

The state of the British trade to the coast of Africa considered. [n.p., ca. 1730.] S595
This résumé of the history of British trade to West Africa reflects the dissatisfaction of independent traders who resented the authority given to the Royal African Company.

The state of the island of Jamaica ... address'd to a member of Parliament. London, H. Whitridge, 1725. S596
Suggests the consideration of means to alleviate problems concerning Jamaica's commerce.

The state of the nation consider'd, in a letter to a member of Parliament. London, W. Webb [1747]. S597
A criticism of Britain's management of its war with France which had resulted in the loss of British trade.

The state of the nation with a general balance of the public accounts. Dublin, S. Powell, 1749. S598
A complaint against terms of the treaty of Aix-la-Chapelle for the adverse effect they might have on the English position in America and the East Indies.

The state of the sugar-trade; shewing the dangerous consequences that must attend any additional duty thereon. London, E. Say for R. Willuck, 1747. S599
A statistical comparison of the French and British sugar trade, attempting to prove that additional duties on sugar from the British plantations would place it at a disadvantage compared to sugar from the French colonies.

A state of the trade carried on with the French on the island of Hispaniola, by merchants in North-America, under colour of flags of truce. London and New York, H. Gaine, 1760. S600
A defense of the trade carried on between the American colonies and the French in Hispaniola, pointing out its values to both the colonial and the British economies.

Status quaestionis Romae nunc temporis habitae circa honores a Sinensibus exhibitos Confucio et progenitoribus fato functis. Brussels, Danielem Wattier, 1700. S601
A description of the Chinese Rites, so controversial to the Jesuits' missionary work in China, based on a manuscript sent to Rome and presented here in Latin and French texts. Five related pamphlets are included.

Staunton, Sir George. An historical account of the embassy to the Emperor of China. London, John Stockdale, 1797. S602
The first edition of an account of Lord Maccartney's embassy to China which was designed to improve Britain's commercial relations there. The author was sec-

retary to the ambassador, and his book includes engravings depicting many aspects of Chinese culture.

Staunton, Sir George. An authentic account of an embassy from the King of Great Britain to the Emperor of China. London, W. Bulmer and Co. for G. Nicol, 1798. S603

The second edition. It includes an atlas volume containing a detailed set of maps depicting the regions through which the embassy passed.

Staunton, Sir George. An authentic account of an embassy from the King of Great Britain to the Emperor of China ... Dublin, P. Wogan [etc.] 1798. S604

This Dublin edition follows the text of the 1798 London edition, with illustrations similar to those found in the text of the London edition, but generally of poorer quality.

Staunton, Sir George. An authentic account of an embassy from the King of Great Britain to the Emperor of China ... Philadelphia, Robert Campbell by John Boiren, 1799. S605

The first American edition, with text based on the London edition of 1798, but with fewer illustrations.

Staunton, Sir George. Des Grafen Macartney Gesandschaftsreise nach China. Frankfurt & Leipzig, 1798. S606

One of three German editions published in 1798.

Staunton, Sir George. Reis van Lord Macartneij naar China. Amsterdam, J. Allart, 1798-1801. S607

The first Dutch edition, in seven volumes, of Staunton's account of Lord Macartney's embassy to China.

Staunton, Sir George. Viaggio nell' interno della China e nella Tartaria. Venice, Sebastiano Valle, 1799. S608

The first Italian edition, based on the 1798 English edition.

Stavorinus, Johan Splinter. Reize van Zeeland over de Kaap de Goede Hoop, naar Batavia, Bantam, Bengalen, enz. gedaan in de jaaren MDCCLXVIII tot MDCCLXXI. Leiden, A. en J. Honkoop, 1793. S609

An account of a voyage to various trading stations of the Dutch East India Company, with extensive observations on Bengal and the Cape of Good Hope.

Stavorinus, Johan Splinter. Voyage par le Cap de Bonne-Espérance a Batavia, a Bantam et au Bengale, en 1768, 69, 70 et 71 ... Paris, H.J. Jansen, 1798. S610

This French edition contains a brief note by the translator, Hendrik Jansen, relating the interest of revolutionary France to overseas interest.

Stavorinus, Johan Splinter. Voyages to the East-Indies. London, G.G. and J. Robinson, 1798. S611

This English edition includes an account of a second voyage by Stavorinus to the East Indies in 1774-75, with many observations on the trade of the Dutch East India Company.

Stebbing, Henry. A sermon preached before the incorporated Society for the Propagation of the Gospel in Foreign Parts, at their anniversary meeting in the parish-church of St. Mary-le-Bow, on Friday, February 19, 1741-2. London, E. Owen, 1742. S612

The reverend Stebbing asserts that the miracles which were the means to the earliest spread of Christianity must in a more enlightened age be supplanted by energetic support of missionary work.

Steck, Johann Christoph Wilhelm von. Essai sur les consuls. Berlin, Frederic Nicolai, 1790. S613

Describes the consular office and service in general, its history, purpose and general procedures.

Steck, Johann Christoph Wilhelm von. Essais sur divers sujets relatifs à la navigation et au commerce pendant la guerre. Berlin, Frederic Nicolai, 1794. S614

Concerns embargoes, seizure of goods, blockade, letters of marque, reprisal, etc.

Stedman, C. (Charles). The history of the origin, progress, and termination of the American war. London, For the Author, 1794. S615

A history of the American Revolution from the British point of view by a participant. It includes eight maps and plans, mostly of battle sites.

Stedman, John Gabriel. Narrative of a five years expedition against the revolted Negroes of Surinam ... Manuscript. England [ca. 1790]. S616

The original manuscript account of Stedman's travels and service in Guiana as an officer in the force recruited to suppress the slave rebellion. It differs substantially from the published version.

Stedman, John Gabriel. Narrative of a five years' expedition, against the revolted Negroes of Surinam. London, J. Johnson and J. Edwards, 1796. S617

The first edition of Stedman's narrative, including seventy-six plates, four maps, and many alterations from the original manuscript.

Stedman, John Gabriel. Narrative of a five years' expedition, against the revolted Negroes of Surinam, in Guiana, on the wild coast of South America; from the year 1772, to 1777. London, For J. Johnson and J. Edwards, 1796. S618

The first edition, with illustrations in color.

Stedman, John Gabriel. Narrative of a five years' expedition, against the revolted Negroes of Surinam, in Guiana, on the wild coast of South America; from the year 1772, to 1777. London, J. Johnson and Th. Payne, 1806. S619

The second English edition.

Stedman, John Gabriel. Voyage a Surinam et dans l'intérieur de la Guiane. Paris, F. Buisson, 1798. S620

The first French edition.

Stedman, John Gabriel. Reize naar Surinamen. Amsterdam, Johannes Allart, 1799-1800. S621

This first Dutch edition includes translator's notes and notes taken from the French edition. The number of plates is reduced to forty-six.

Stedman, John Gabriel. Dagbok öfwer sina fälttåg i Surinam. Stockholm, Johan Pfeiffer, 1800. S622

The first Swedish edition, an abridged version.

Stedman, John Gabriel. Viaggio al Surinam e nell' interno della Guiana. Milan, Giambattista Sonzogno, 1818. S623

The first Italian edition of Stedman's account of the slave rebellion in Guiana, with an appendix on the geography of the region.

Stedman, John Gabriel. Reisen in Surinam. Berlin, Schüppelschen Buchhandlung [1799]. S624

An abridged German edition for children.

Stedman, John Gabriel. Journals, diaries, correspondence. Manuscript. Surinam, Netherlands, England, 1772-1796. S625

A collection of manuscript material which includes an autobiographical sketch and miscellaneous Stedman-related materials as well as journals, diaries and correspondence, forty-seven items in all.

Steel, David. The art of sail-making. London, D. Steel, 1796. S626

Originally published in volume one of Steel's *The elements and practice of rigging, seamanship and naval tactics*, 1794, this book has a dictionary of terms, a description on the use of sails and instructions on sail making, with many illustrations.

[Steele, Joshua.] An account of a late conference on the occurrences in America. London, J. Almon, 1766. S627

An imaginary discussion in which five Englishmen explore ideas for colonial representation in Parliament, including one plan based upon payment of taxes which would give North America 93 seats.

Steenis, Hendrick Cornelis. Journaal wegens de rampspoedige reystocht ... op de Moorsche kust in Africa ... Amsterdam, B. Mourik [1753]. S628

Includes an account of Dutch East India Company losses due to shipwreck, with a list of all ships lost from 1688 to 1752.

Steller, Georg Wilhelm. Beschreibung von dem Lande Kamtschatka. Frankfurt und Leipzig, Georg Fleischer, 1774. S629

A general survey of Kamchatka including descriptions of the products and economy of the peninsula.

Steller, Georg Wilhelm. Reise von Kamtschatka nach Amerika mit dem Commandeur-Capitän Bering. St. Petersburg, Johann Zacharias Logan, 1793. S630

Edited by Peter Simon Pallas, this book is by a naturalist who traveled with Bering on his second expedition.

Stephanus, of Byzantium. De urbibus. Venice, Aldus, 1502. S631

The first edition of a lexicon from the late fifth or early sixth century, locating cities and tribes known to antiquity. The text is in Greek.

[Stephen, James]. The crisis of the sugar colonies, or, An enquiry into the objects and probable effects of the French expedition to the West Indies ... in four letters to the Right Hon. Henry Addington ... London, For J. Hatchard, 1802. S632

The author takes alarm at Napoleon's expedition to Santo Domingo, fearing the restoration of slavery there and the threat to British West Indian possessions.

[Stephen, James.] The opportunity, or, reasons for an immediate alliance with St. Domingo. London, C. Whittingham for J. Hatchard, 1804. S633

Stephen calls for the recognition by the British government of Haiti's independence and urges the formation of a commercial alliance between the two countries.

[Stephens, Thomas.] A brief account of the causes that have retarded the progress of the colony of Georgia. London, 1743. S634

This tract, prepared by the leader of a group of malcontents, points out the oppressions and injustices suffered by them under Oglethorpe and his administration.

Stephens, Thomas. To the King's Most Excellent Majesty in Council, the humble petition of Thomas Stephens, agent for the people of Georgia in America. Manuscript. London, 26 March 1742. S635

The petition requests changes in the structure of Georgia's economy: larger land grants, the use of slave labor, and the end of a requirement to produce wine and silk.

Stephens, William. A state of the province of Georgia. London, W. Meadows, 1742. S636

Stepney, George

A favorable description of Georgia by the secretary of the province, to counteract the criticism of Patrick Tailfer and his associates.

[Stepney, George.] An essay upon the present interest of England. London, J. Nutt, 1701. S637

The author shows concern for England's trade in Europe and the West Indies if France should increase her influence in Spain.

Stevens, Robert, Merchant in Bombay. The new and complete guide to the East-India trade. London, D. Steel and S. Bladon, 1775. S638

A comprehensive guide to doing business in the East Indies, noting weights, measures, coinage, duties, shipping costs, etc.

Stewardson, William. A letter to the Hon. the Commissioners of His Majesty's customs ... containing an account of the detection of frauds at the custom-house. London, By the Author [1763]. S639

An attack upon two customs officials for their failure to prosecute smugglers.

[Stiessius, Christian.] Relation von dem gegenwärtigen Zustand des moscowitischen Reichs. Frankfurt, Thomas Fritischen, 1706. S640

An account of the history, geography, social and political aspects of Russian life, inspired by the visit of Peter the Great to Germany.

Stillman, Samuel. Good news from a far country, a sermon preached at Boston, May 17. 1766, upon the arrival of the important news of the repeal of the Stamp-Act. Boston, Kneeland and Adams for Philip Freeman, 1766. S641

A patriot and Baptist preacher ties the Stamp Act issue to the larger concern of civil and religious liberty.

Stith, William. The history of the first discovery and settlement of Virginia: being an essay towards a general history of this colony. Williamsburg, William Parks, 1747. S642

The early history of Virginia is examined in early documents which the author felt might in time disappear. He also used Smith's history of Virginia and other published sources.

[Stobniczy, Jan ze.] Introduction in Ptolomei Cosmographiam. [Cracow, Hieronymum Vietorem Calcographum, 1519.] S643

Contains commentary on places located by Ptolemy, and includes mention of the discovery of the New World.

Stochove, Vincent. Voyage du sieur de Stochove faict es années 1630, 1631, 1632, 1633. Brussels, Hubert Anthoine Velpius, 1643. S644

An account of travels in the Near East noting economy, government, and religious and social customs.

Stockholm (Sweden). Laws, etc. Athskillighe Stockholm stadz ordinantier. Stockholm, Ignatium Meurer, 1646. S645

This collection of ordinances for the city of Stockholm is primarily concerned with shipping regulations and duties on incoming merchandise.

Stockholm (Sweden). Överståthållarämbetet. Publication, huru med skieps afmätningarne och lästetalets jemkande hädan efter förhållas skal. Stockholm, Kongl. Tryckeriet, 1726. S646

Concerns the measurement of ships and the determination of their capacity.

Stockholm (Sweden). Överståthållarämbetet. Publication, ut ingen må understå sig at wid stadsens hamnar och strander. Stockholm, Kongl. Boktryckeriet [1732]. S647

No one may stock building materials at the harbor of Stockholm without permission from the city council.

Stockholm (Sweden). Överståthållarämbetet. Publication, och förbud, ut spannemåls handlare och hökare societeten eimå tilfogas något intrång uti des handel och näring. Stockholm, Kongl. Bok-tryckeriet [1739]. S648

The trade in grain, meat, and cheese is reserved to a particular group of merchants.

Stockholm (Sweden). Överståthållarämbetet. Kungörelse, angående tilstånd för tobaksspinneri idkarne, at få tilwerka tobaksrullar, til halft skålpunds wigt, eller nåot deröfwer. Stockholm, Lars Salvius, 1756. S649

The lowest allowed weight on tobacco rolls is now reduced from one pound to one-half pound, especially because of requests from the western Norwegian border.

Stockholm (Sweden). Överståthållarämbetet. [Decree about tobacco products. September 19, 1757.] [Stockholm, 1757.] S650

Tobacco products are to be stamped at the place of manufacture by authorized representatives of the town market office.

Stockholm (Sweden). Överståthållarämbetet. Kungörelse och förbud, emot inrikes tilwerkad såpas forsål-jande af obehörige personer. Stockholm, Lars Salvius, 1771. S651

The governor general's proclamation prohibiting sale of locally-produced soap by unauthorized persons.

Stockholm (Sweden). Överståthållarämbetet. Kungörelse til förekommande af hinder och olägenhet för fiskköpare och then til staden ankommande landtmannen, at wid stadsens bryggor anlägga. Stockholm, Kongl. Boktryckare, 1774. S652

A proclamation for the prevention of obstacles or difficulties when fish buyers and peasants coming to the city wish to anchor at the quays and bridges.

Stockholm (Sweden). Överståthållarämbetet.
Kungörelse om tiden til the wid skeppsbroen för the siö-farande inrättade kok-husens öpnande och tilslutande. Stockholm, H. Foutt, 1775.
S653
Specifies the hours of opening of the cooking houses for seamen at the Skeppsbroen.

Stockholm (Sweden). Överståthållarämbetet.
Kungörelse, angående månglerie accisens upbärande här i staden för innewarande år. Stockholm, Kongl. Tryckeriet, 1777. S654
Gives collection procedure and year's rates for goods sold by female retailers.

Stockholm (Sweden). Överståthållarämbetet.
Kungörelse angående klädmäkleriidkarne här i staden. Stockholm, Kongl. Tryckeriet, 1779.
S655

Stockholm (Sweden). Överståthållarämbetet.
Kungörelse, angående wissa trägårdswäxters och frugters försäljande efter wigt. Stockholm, Kongl. Tryckeriet, 1779. S656

Stockholm (Sweden). Överståthållarämbetet.
Kungörelse och förbud för obehörige personer til tobaks-handels idkande. Stockholm, Kongl. Tryckeriet, 1779. S657
Prohibits participation in the tobacco trade by unauthorized persons.

Stockholm (Sweden). Överståthållarämbetet.
Kungörelse, angående then skyldighet, som här i staden boende coopvaerdie-siöfolk böra i akt taga ... Stockholm, Kongl. Tryckeriet, 1780.
S658
Procedures necessary for seamen if they are to avail themselves of a special tax exemption.

Stockholm (Sweden). Överståthållarämbetet.
Kungörelse, angående theras skyldighet, som reda dref eller handla med dref eller gammalt tågwirke. Stockholm, Kongl. Tryckeriet, 1782.
S659
The governor general's proclamation concerning the obligations of those who pick or sell oakum or old ropes.

Stockholm (Sweden). Överståthållarämbetet.
Kungörelse, huruledes hamn-penningarne för de ifrån inrikes orter hit til staden kommande fartyg och båtar ... Stockholm, Kongl. Tryckeriet, 1783.
S660
The port charges for ships coming to Stockholm are the same as other Swedish ports, based on the size of the ship.

Stockholm (Sweden). Överståthållarämbetet.
Kungörelse och förbud, emot handelsmanufactur-och hantwerkeriwarors obehöriga afsalu. Stockholm, Kongl. Tryckeriet [1783]. S661

Stockholm (Sweden). Överståthållarämbetet.
Kungörelse och warning emot gatu-köp, olaga handel och för-köp. Stockholm, Kongl. Tryckeriet, 1783. S662
A proclamation and warning concerning street sales, illegal commerce, and preclusive buying.

Stockholm (Sweden). Överståthållarämbetet.
Kungörelse, angående klädmäklerie idkande här i staden. Stockholm, Kongl. Tryckeriet, 1784.
S663
The governor general's proclamation concerning the registration of all who engage in the sale of clothing goods.

Stockholm (Sweden). Överståthållarämbetet.
Kungörelse, angående then ordning, som wid försälgningen och uphandligen af the hit til staden från andra städer ankommande lärfts-krämare-waror bör i akt tagas. Stockholm, Kongl. Tryckeriet, 1787. S664
The procedure which is to be followed at the time of selling or buying of clothing goods which have been brought to Stockholm from other towns.

Stockholm (Sweden). Överståthållarämbetet.
Kungörelse, angående aflossningen af det hit til staden ankommande lakegods och packbare waror ... Stockholm, Kongl. Tryckeriet, 1793.
S665
Directs the discharge of goods arriving from lakes or the coast, and defines those which may or may not be packed on board ships.

Stockholm (Sweden). Överståthållarämbetet.
Kungörelse, angående spisqwarters-och klädmäkleri-idkares styldighet at uti denna stadens handels Collegio ... Stockholm, Kongl. Tryckeriet, 1793. S666
Obliges inn-keepers and clothing merchants to present themselves at the city's chamber of commerce for taxation purposes.

Stockholm (Sweden). Överståthållarämbetet.
Kungörelse, angående den ordning, som wid försälgningen och uphandligen af de hit til staden från andre städer ankommande lärftskrämare-waror, bör i akt tagas. Stockholm, Kongl. Tryckeriet, [1794]. S667

Stockholm (Sweden). Överståthållarämbetet.
Kungörelse, angående förekommande af gatuhandel, förköp och otidigt mangleri m.m. Stockholm, Kongl. Tryckeriet, 1795. S668
Concerns prevention of street selling or buying, and unauthorized peddling.

Stockholm (Sweden). Överståthållarämbetet.
Kungörelse, angånde spisqwarters-idkares, klädmäklares, caffée-kokares och nipper-handlares ... Stockholm, Kongl. Tryckeriet, 1799. S669

Keepers of eateries and coffeehouses, clothes and trinket sellers, with the exception of burghers, are to appear at specified times before the city's Trade Commission for taxation purposes.

Stockholm (Sweden). Överståthållarämbetet. Kungörelse, angående det salt, som af ständiga uplaget härstädes kommer at allmänheten tilhanda hållas. Stockholm, Kongl. Tryckeriet, 1801. S670
A proclamation from the governor of Stockholm indicating that salt will be provided for the public from reserve stocks.

Stöffler, Johann. Sphaeram mundi, omnibus numeris longè absolutissimus commentarius ... [Tübingen, Hulderichi Morhart, 1534.] S671
A commentary on Proclus, a fifth century Neo-platonist, drawing upon classical, Christian, and Moslem scholarship.

Stokes, Anthony. A view of the constitution of the British colonies in North-America and the West Indies, at the time the civil war broke out on the continent of America. London, B. White, 1783. S672
The author had resided in several of the North American colonies and in the West Indies, and was favorable to the British cause during the American Revolution.

Stokram, Andries. Korte beschryvinghe van de ongeluckige wederom-reys van het schip Aernhem ... van Batavia na het vaderlandt. Amsterdam, G.J. Saeghman [1663]. S673
An account of a shipwreck on Mauritius and the rescue of the crew by a privateer.

Stonhouse, John. Thoughts on the expedience of setting permanent leases with the landholders in Bengal, Bahar, and Orissa. London, J. Stockdale, 1792. S674
Stonhouse calls for turning over land the East India Company farms to the Indians under long term leases at moderate, fixed prices.

Storia di Don Bernardino de Cardenas, vescovo del Paraguai. Lugano, Suprema Superiorità Elvetica, 1760. S675
A collection of documents recording the conflict between the Society of Jesus in Paraguay and the bishop who held nominal jurisdiction over that colony.

Storia di Don Filippo Pardo, Arcivescovo di Manile nell'Isole Filippine. Lugano, Suprema Superioritá Elvetica, 1760. S676
An extract of two works by Alfonso Sandin and Cristobal Pedroche, both published in Madrid, 1683 concerning disputes in Manila between the Jesuits and the archbishop there.

Stork, William. An account of East-Florida. London, For G. Woodfall [etc.] [1766]. S677
A propaganda piece directed toward prospective settlers of English colonies in Florida.

Stork, William. An extract from the account of East Florida. London, 1766. S678
A pamphlet promoting Denys Rolle's Florida settlement. In addition to extracts from Stork's book there are letters testifying to the fruitfulness of Florida.

Strabo. Geographia. Manuscript. Italy [ca. 1460-1470]. S679
One of two known copies made of the first Latin translation of this work. This copy contains a unique life-size portrait of the translator, Guarino of Verona.

Strabo. Geographia. [Venice] Vindelinus de Spera, 1472. S680
The second edition of the most comprehensive geographical work to come from antiquity.

Strabo. Geographia. [Treviso] Joannes (Rubeus) Vercellensis, 1480. S681
The fourth edition.

Strabo. Geographia. [Venice] Joannes (Rubeus) Vercellensis, 1494. S682
The fifth edition.

Strabo. De situ orbis. [Venice] Joannes (Rubeus) Vercellensis, 1495. S683
This sixth edition is the second prepared by Antonio Mancinelli.

Strabo. De situ orbis. Venice, Bertholomeum de Zanus, 1502. S684
Based on the 1494 edition of Antonio Mancinelli, with new introductory material.

Strabo. De situ orbis. [Venice, Philippo Pincio Mantuano, 1510.] S685
A reprint of the 1502 edition.

Strabo. Geographia. Paris, Hemon Le Fevre, 1512. S686
The eighth edition, first non-Italian printing.

Strabo. Geographicorum commentarios. Basel, Valentin Curio, 1523. S687
An early attempt at a critical edition, edited by Conrad Heresbach.

Strabo. Geographicorum libri xvii. Basel, J. Vualder, 1539. S688
The second edition of Conrad Heresbach's translation. It includes an epitome of the *Geographia* not in earlier editions, and a list of Strabo's sources.

Strabo. Rerum geographicarum. Basel, Henric Petrina, 1571. S689
The maps included in this edition are the same as those in the 1545 edition of Ptolemy's *Geography*.

Strabo. Rerum geographicarum. Geneva, Eustathius Vignon, 1587. S690

This edition includes a double-hemisphere map by Rumold Mercator and a commentary on Strabo by Isaac Casaubon.

Strabo. Strabonis de situ orbis libri XVII ... Amsterdam, Johannem Janssonium Juniorem, 1652. S691

This is Guarino of Verona's translation of Strabo, edited by Gregorio Trifernate. It features an index of some 5,300 entries.

Strabo. De situ orbis. [Venice] Aldus [1516]. S692

The first Greek edition, edited by Benedictus Tyrrhenus.

Strabo. Strabonis de situ orbis libri XVII. Grecè & Latine simuliam ... Basel, Henrichum Petri, 1549. S693

A new translation from the Greek by Conrad Heresbach, with both Greek and Latin texts included.

Strabo. La ... geografia di Strabone. Venice, Francesco Senese, 1562; Ferrara, 1565. S694

The first translation of Strabo's *Geographia* into a vernacular language, with a glossary of place names in both ancient and modern usage.

Stracca, Benvenuto. De mercatura, seu mercatore tractatus. Venice [Aldus] 1553. S695

A treatise on commercial law, encompassing a wide variety of subjects relating to trade.

Stracca, Benvenuto. Tractatus de mercatura, seu mercatore omnia ... Lyons, Haeredes Jacobi Junte, 1556. S696

This edition includes the *Tractatus de assecurationibus et sponsionibus* of Pedro Santarem.

Stracca, Benvenuto. Tractatus de mercatura seu mercatore. Cologne, I. Gymnicum, 1576. S697

This edition contains a treatise on the *Contractibus mercatorum* of Johannes Nider.

Strahlenberg, Philipp Johann von. Das nord- und ostliche Theil von Europa und Asia ... in einer historisch-geographischen Beschreibung ... Stockholm, In Verlegung des Autoris, 1730. S698

The first edition of an extensive description of Siberia based on the author's thirteen years' residence and travel there. A map to accompany this edition was issued separately. See S703.

Strahlenberg, Philipp Johann von. An historico-geographical description of the north and eastern parts of Europe and Asia. London, J. Brotherton [etc.] 1738. S699

A survey of land, resources, peoples, and cultures of portions of Russia, Siberia, and Tartary based upon thirteen years of residence there.

Strahlenberg, Philipp Johann von. Description historique de l'empire Russien. Amsterdam, Desaint & Saillant, 1757. S700

The first French edition, with extensive annotations and additions. Maps by D'Anville have been added also.

[Strahlenberg, Philipp Johann von.] Nueva descripcion geographica del imperio Ruso. Valencia, Francisco Burguete, 1780. S701

The first Spanish edition, based on the French edition.

Strahlenberg, Philipp Johann von. Vorbericht eines zum Druck verfertigten Werckes von der Grossen Tatarey und dem Königreiche Siberien. Stockholm, Benjamin G. Schneider, 1726. S702

This is an announcement that the author is preparing his great work on Siberia, stating his interests in many aspects of that land and commenting on others who have written about it.

Strahlenberg, Philipp Johann von. Nova descriptio geographica Tattariae Magnae tam orientalis quam occidentalis in particularibus et generalibus territoriis una cum delineatione totius Imperii Russici imprimis Siberiae accurate ostensa. [Stockholm, 1730]. S703

This map was intended to accompany the author's *Das nord und ostliche Theil von Europa und Asia*, but was too large to be bound in. It extends from Japan on the east to west of Moscow, also including northern China, Tibet and Turkestan.

Strahlenberg, Philipp Johann von. Carte nouvelle de tout l'Empire de la Grand Russie ... [Amsterdam, Covens & Mortier, ca. 1740]. S704

This map is based on the one which accompanied Stralenberg's book, *Das nord-und ostliche Theil von Europa und Asia*, 1730.

[Strahlenberg, Philipp Johann von]. Spatiotissimum Imperium Russiae Magnae, juxta recentissimas observationes mappa geographica ... Augustae Vindel, Matthaei Seutteri [ca. 1740]. S705

Suetter's version of Stralenberg's map of Russia published in 1730.

[Strahlenberg, Philipp Johann von]. Spatiotissimum Imperium Russiae Magnae, juxta recentissimas observationes mappa geographica ... Augustae Vindel, Tobiae Conradi Lotteri [ca. 1760]. S706

A re-issue of the previous item by Lotter who inherited Suetter's plates of the map.

Stratto delle porte de Firenze ridotto da moneta bianca à neral, le 28 febbraio 1544 per le mercantie ... Florence, Giorgio Marescotti, 1579. S707

A booklet of fifty-five pages filled with import and export duties for the city of Florence.

Stringer, Moses. Opera mineralia explicata: or The mineral kingdom, within the dominions of Great Britain, display'd. London, Jonas Brown [1713]. S708
A history of and commentary on the mining industry in England, with a defense of the Society of the Mines Royal and the Society of the Mineral and Battery Works.

[Strömberg, A. J.] Anmärkningar angående handelen och sjö-farten, författade wid besökande af utrikes hamnar och handelsstäder. Stockholm, Nyström och Stolpe, 1760. S709
This Swedish commercial handbook describes the commercial situation and navigation of five harbors of interest to Swedish trade: Tripoli, Bengazi, Morea, Galipoli, and Bremen, with maps of the harbors.

Strongcastle, Cornelius. An essay to prevent the exportation of wool, and retrieve the woollen manufacture of England. London, J. Watson for the Author, 1741-42. S710
The author proposes that importation of competing cloths be restricted, and that the government become a buyer of raw wool at fixed prices to prevent exportation at low prices.

Struys, Jan Janszoon. Drie aanmerkilijke en seer ramspoedige reysen door ... Moscovien, Tartarijen, Meden, Persien, Oost-Indien, Japan ... Amsterdam, J. van Meurs en J. van Someren, 1676. S711
Observations on travels through the Near East, Russia, Persia, and eastern Asia.

Struys, Jan Janszoon. Sehr schwere wiederwertige und denckwerdige Reysen durch Italien, Griechenland, Lifland, Moscau, Tartarey, Meden, Persien, Türkey, Ost-Indien, Japan, und unterschiedliche andere Länder. Amsterdam, Jacob von Meurs & Johannes von Sommern, 1678. S712
The first German edition.

Struys, Jan Janszoon. Les voyages. Amsterdam, La veuve J. van Meurs, 1681. S713
The first French edition.

Struys, Jan Janszoon. The voyages and travels of John Struys. London, Abel Swalle, 1684. S714
The first English edition.

Stuart, John Ferdinand Smyth. Voyage dans les États-Unis de l'Amérique, fait en 1784. Paris, Buisson, 1791. S715
An abridged translation of an Englishman's narrative of travels in the United States, noting the natural resources, economy, political situation, and Indian tribes in the regions he visited which extended as far West as the Mississippi River.

Stuart, Peter. Letter to Mssrs. Davison and Lee. Manuscript copy signed. Beauport, 5 September 1788. S716
This letter concerns debts to the Northwest Company at the post of Domain and Mingan which were carried over through the reorganization of the company in 1787.

Stubbe, Henry. A further justification of the present war against the United Netherlands. London, H. Hills and J. Starkey, 1673. S717
A review of Anglo-Dutch commercial hostilities of the seventeenth century.

[Stubbe, Henry.] A justification of the present war against the United Netherlands ... London, H. Hill and J. Starkey, 1672. S718
A response to an earlier publication titled *Considerations upon the present state of the United Netherlands.*

Stubenberg, Johann Wilhelm von. Thesaurus mundi das ist Eine kurtze doch gründliche Anweisung, wo der Schatz der Welt in hundert und mehr Jahren hingekommen ... [n.p.] 1689. S719
A discussion of the impact fluctuations in gold and silver have upon the economy of Europe.

Stuck, Gottlieb Heinrich. Gottlieb Heinrich Stuck's Nachtrag zu seinem Verzeichnis von aeltern und neuern Land-und Reisebeschreibungen. Ein Versuch eines Hauptstücks der geographischen Litteratur... Halle, Johann Christian Hendel, 1784. S720
An exhaustive bibliography of travel literature, covering all western European languages.

Stüven, Johann Friedrich. De vero Novi Orbis inventore. Dissertatio historico-critica. Frankfurt, Dominicum à Sande, 1714. S721
The author was an advocate of the theory that Martin Behaim had discovered America.

Stukken raakende de vaart van de Spagnaarden op de Philippynsche Eilanden. [n.p., ca. 1790.] S722
A series of documents, memoranda, and letters from 1732, 1768, and 1786, relating to Spanish-Philippine commerce.

Sturmy, Samuel. The mariners magazine. London, Anne Godbid for William Fisher [etc.] 1679. S723
The second edition of a work covering all aspects of navigation, theoretical and practical.

Suarez, Josephus. La libertad de la ley de Dios, en el imperio de la China. Lisbon, Miguel Deslandes, 1696. S724
The author was rector of the Jesuit college in Peking, and he describes the opposition met by the Jesuits while propagating the faith there.

Suárez de Figueroa, Cristóval. Hechos de Don Garcia Hurtado de Mendoza, quarto Marques de Cañete. Madrid, Imprenta Real, 1613. S725
 The author, a distinguished poet and novelist, describes Mendoza's governorship of Chile, his campaign against the Araucanian Indians, and his viceroyalty of Peru.

De substantie van't gene heere Conradus van Beuningen, Afgesonden ... aen den koning van Vrankryck. [n.p.] 1665. S726
 The Dutch ask for assistance from France in their rivalry with England, reminding the French of the treaty which binds them in matters of commerce and navigation.

Sucre rafiné à Marseille, sujet au droit de la douane ... de sept livres par quintal. [n.p., ca. 1760.] S727
 Concerns the difference in duties on sugar refined in Marseilles and shipped to other French ports, and that coming from foreign countries.

Sulivan, Sir Richard Joseph. A letter to the honorable the Court of Directors of the East-India Company, from Richard Joseph Sulivan Esq., November 15, 1784. S728
 The author contests his dismissal from the East India Company for taking a position with the Nabob of the Carnatic, contending that their interests were similar.

Summaria relaçam dos prodigiosos feitos que as armas Portuguezas obràraõ na ilha de Ceilaõ cõtra os Olandezes, & Chingala no anno passado de 1655. [Lisbon, Crasbeek, 1656.] S729
 A report sent by Jesuits in Ceylon, describing victories by the Portuguese over the Dutch there in 1655, and noting also gains made by the Dutch elsewhere in the East Indies.

Summary observations and facts collected from late authentic accounts of Russian and other navigators, to show the practicability and good prospect of success in enterprises to discover a northern passage for vessels by sea ... London, J. Nourse, 1776. S730
 The author advocates attempting to find a route from Spitzbergen to the Bering Strait, contending it would be ice-free and with mild temperatures in summer.

A summary view of the East-India company of Great Britain. Dublin, W. Porter, 1784. S731
 A tract reviewing the history of events in India that led up to the crisis of 1783.

Sunderman, Isaac. De werken van Isaac Sunderman ... zyne tweemalige reisen naer Oost-Indien. [n.p.] Voor den Autheur, 1711. S732
 This writer made two trips to the East Indies, in 1696 and 1700. His book includes information on Dutch mercantile activity there, as well as observations on native life and customs.

Suplique des citoyens de couleur des isles et colonies françoises, tendante à obtenir un jugement, 30 janvier 1790. [n.p., 1790.] S733
 An appeal to the National Assembly to consider citizens of color for full citizenship.

Supplément au voyage de M. de Bougainville, ou Journal d'un voyage autour du monde, fait par MM. Banks & Solander. Neuchatel, La Société Typographique, 1773. S734
 A translation of the first account of Cook's voyage of 1768-71, with supplementary material on the Isle de Bourbon.

Supplement des pieces, en faveur des Compagnies Hollandoises pour le commerce des Indes Orientales et Occidentales. [n.p., 1728.] S735
 Includes the King of Spain's declaration in favor of the Dutch East India Company, and his later concessions to the Ostend Company.

A supplement to the reports of the Committee of Secrecy. London, For A. Moore, 1721. S736
 A part of the investigation of the directors of the South Sea Company.

Suriano, Francesco. Opera nova chiamata Itinerario de Hierusalem: overo dele parte orientale. [Venice, Francesco Bindoni, 1524.] S737
 A pilgrimage book noting places of religious significance, but also including much information of geographical and commercial interest.

Sutton, Sir Robert. A true and exact particular and inventory of all and singular the lands, tenements and hereditaments, goods, chattels, debts and personal estate whatsoever, of the right honourable Sir Robert Sutton ... London, S. Buckley, 1732. S738
 Sutton was a director of the Charitable Corporation for the Relief of Industrious Poor when a major embezzlement occurred.

Los suzesos de el Reyno de tierra firme en los años de setenta y nuebe, y ochenta por hauersido adversos, y que preusan el que de ellos se tenga noticia en los Reynos de España ... Autograph manuscript in Spanish, unsigned. [n.p., 1680.] S739
 A report by an anonymous government official calling for more military assistance to Panama, citing Indian rebellions and incursions by Europeans.

Svedelius, Jacob Michael. Dissertatio. De effectu detectae Americae in Europam ... Upsala, Johann Fred. Edman [1800-1802]. S740
 An academic dissertation on the topic then popular among philosophers: the positive and negative effects of the discovery of America upon Europe.

[Swaine, Charles.] An account of a voyage for the discovery of a north-west passage by

Hudson's streights, to the western and southern ocean of America. London, Jolliffe, 1748-49.
S741
Taken in part from the log of the *California*, commanded by Captain Francis Smith. The voyage was undertaken in 1746-47.

Swan, James. Causes qui se sont opposées aux progrès du commerce, entre la France, et les États-Unis de l'Amérique. Paris, L. Potier de Lille, 1790. S742
A series of six letters, written to Lafayette, considering potential commercial relations between the United States and France and proposing a French North American Company.

Swan, John. Speculum mundi or A glasse representing the face of the world. Cambridge, T. Buck and R. Daniel, 1635. S743
An account of the creation, incorporating classical and Renaissance learning with respect to geography and astronomy.

Swartz, Olof. Inträdes-tal, innehållende anmärkningar om Vestindien; hållet för Kongl. Vetenskaps Academien, den 18 martii 1789, af Olof Swartz ... Stockholm, J. G. Lange, 1790.
S744
A survey of the West Indies, noting climate, geography, peoples and economies of the various islands. The author was a Swedish botanist.

Swedberg, Jesper. America illuminata. Skara, Herm. A. Moeller [1732]. S745
This extensive history of the Swedish colonies in America contains numerous documents which passed between the colonials and the homeland.

Swedberg, Johannes Dan., respondent. Dissertatio gradualis de Svionum in America colonia. Upsala, Werneriana, 1709. S746
This thesis by Petrus Elvius reviews the history of Scandinavian enterprise in America, beginning with the Vikings and continuing through the colony of New Sweden.

Sweden. Octroi accordé par le roi pour la continuation de la navigation & du commerce aux Indes-Orientales, fait à Stockholm, au Senat, le 7. de Juillet 1762. [Stockholm] Imprimerie Royale, 1762. S747
This is the third charter of the Swedish East India Company.

Sweden. Wij Carl Gustaff medh Gudz nåde, Sweriges .... Stockholm, 1654. S748
A broadside proclamation granting the company of New Sweden a monopoly on the tobacco trade.

Sweden. Kommerskollegium. Kundgiörelse, angående den föklaring ... uppå general tull-arrende societentens förfragan. Stockholm, Kongl. Boktryckeriet [1736]. S749
A detailed explanation of the status of certain goods under import restriction.

Sweden. Kommerskollegium. Kundgörelse, til förekommande af de inträng, som tobaksspinnerierne uti afsättningen as theras tilwärkningar, genom obehörige personer tilfogas, undantagande Stockholm, hwarom särskilt kundgjordt är. Stockholm, Kongl. Tryckeriet, 1754. S750
The right of sale is restricted to those having right of production, except where the right of sale was obtained before the restrictions were placed on spices, etc.

Sweden. Kommerskollegium. Circulaire bref, angående the til Spanska och Medelländska Siön gaende coopvaerdie-fartygs bestyckande och förseendemed nödige hand-och andre gewär, samt ammunitions persedlar. [Stockholm] Kongl. Tryckeriet [1755]. S751

Sweden. Kommerskollegium. ... Krigs-cammer- och Commerce-Collegiers samt stats contoirs kundgiörelse, angående tiden, när then af Riksens ständer ... Stockholm, Kongl. Tryckeriet [1757]. S752
Announces the date when new internal customs rates will become effective.

Sweden. Kommerskollegium. [Proclamation. October 24, 1757.] [Stockholm, 1757.] S753
Concerns the stamping of previously-bought unstamped tobacco and sugar.

Sweden. Kommerskollegium. Kungiörelse, angående ... landt-tulls och accisordnings ... Stockholm, Kongl. Tryckeriet [1758]. S754
An explanation of an earlier law on customs and excise taxes.

Sweden. Kommerskollegium. Kundgiörelse ... rörande tullens erläggande för inkommande wahror. Stockholm, Kongl. Tryckeriet [1759].
S755
Clarifies an earlier resolution concerning duties on imported goods.

Sweden. Kommerskollegium. Kungiörelse, angående förekommandet af åtskillige hos en del Swenskt coopvaerdie siöfolk försporde missbruk och oordenteligheter. Stockholm, Kongl. Tryckeriet [1763?]. S756
Seamen without gainful and appropriate work during the sailing season will be removed from the rolls and lose their privileges.

Sweden. Kommerskollegium. Författade reglemente, hwarefter spannemåls-minut-och victualie-handels-societeten här i staden har sig at rätta. Stockholm, Nyström och Stolpe, 1765.
S757

The constitution and bylaws of the grain and food association of Stockholm.

Sweden. Kommerskollegium. Kundgörelse angående nederlags frihet på tjenligit salt wid sill-salterierne. Stockholm, Kongl. Tryckeriet, 1766. S758
The herring salteries on the North Sea are given free port privileges to stock Spanish and Portuguese salt for their own use or re-export.

Sweden. Kommerskollegium. Kundgörelse, ut snus och carduser får i städerne, undantagande Stockholm, äfwen af andra än tobaks-spinneri-idkare tilwärkas. Stockholm, Kongl. Tryckeriet, 1766. S759
An extension of licenses for the manufacture of tobacco products, excluding Stockholm.

Sweden. Kommerskollegium. Kundgörelse, angående coopvaerdie-skeppares skyldighet, at på utrikes orter ... Stockholm, Kongl. Tryckeriet [1767]. S760
Requires Swedish captains and their crews to present themselves to the Swedish consul or some other official when arriving in a foreign port.

Sweden. Kommerskollegium. [Proclamation. June 5, 1767.] [Stockholm, Kongl. Tryckeriet, 1767.] S761
Instructions concerning placement of customs stamps and town market stamps on cane sugar and tobacco.

Sweden. Kommerskollegium. [Proclamation. June 18, 1767.] [Stockholm, Kongl. Tryckeriet, 1767.] S762
A decree stating that town market officials are to license tobacco manufacture.

Sweden. Kommerskollegium. [Proclamation. n.p., August 10, 1767.] S763
A request for submission of proposals regarding the duties and taxes which can be considered applicable to raw materials.

Sweden. Kommerskollegium. Kundgörelse, af Kongl. Majs:ts nådige förbud, rörande utländske tobaks bladers försälgning i minut. Stockholm, Kongl. Tryckeriet, 1768. S764
The retail sale of tobacco leaves is forbidden to all except authorized merchants.

Sweden. Kommerskollegium. Kundgörelse, angående huru tullstämplingen af inrikes tåpp-säcker, samt spunnen och cardus-tobak hädanefter bör förrättas. Stockholm, H. Fougt, 1773. S765
Concerns the administration of customs duties on cane sugar and tobacco produced in Sweden.

Sweden. Kommerskollegium. Kungörelse, angående förbud emot utländske tobaks-bladers försäljning. Stockholm, H. Fougt, 1773. S766
Retail sale of foreign tobacco leaves except to authorized manufacturers is forbidden; violators will be fined and their goods confiscated.

Sweden. Kommerskollegium. Kungörelse om segelduks tilwerkningens befrämjande i riket. Stockholm, Kongl. Boktryckare, 1774. S767
A proclamation regarding the encouragement of production of sailcloth in the realm.

Sweden. Kommerskollegium. Kungörelse ut salt-tullen wid inträffade banqueroutter. Stockholm, Kongl. Boktryckare, 1775. S768
A proclamation declaring that duty fees on salt shall have priority in the assessment of liens in cases of bankruptcy.

Sweden. Kommerskollegium. Kungörelse, angående then ed skepps-nederierne böra afläg-ga wid uttagande af fri-bref och Turkiska siö-pass. Stockholm, Kongl. Tryckeriet, 1777. S769
A proclamation regarding the oath ship owners are to take when receiving free letters and Turkish sea passes.

Sweden. Kommerskollegium. Kungörelse, angående böternes förhöjande för skeppare, som lemna siöfolk tilfälle at rymma ... Stockholm, Kongl. Tryckeriet [1778]. S770
Fines are increased on captains who allow seamen to escape service; wives of seamen are to be allowed preference in certain types of employment.

Sweden. Kommerskollegium. Kungörelse, angående rittonde anmärknings-puncten wid 1771 års inkommande siö-tull-taxa. Stockholm, Kongl. Tryckeriet, 1778. S771
Notes some exceptions to 1771's sea-customs tariff for imported goods.

Sweden. Kommerskollegium. Kungörelse, angående bewillningens beräknande för erhållne caracterer. Stockholm, Kongl. Tryckeriet, 1779. S772
A proclamation about the computation of grants for achieved ranks and grades.

Sweden. Kommerskollegium. Kungörelse, angående the Swenska städernes handel på tyska orterne. Stockholm, Kongl. Tryckeriet, 1779. S773
A proclamation concerning the Swedish cities' trade in German localities.

Sweden. Kommerskollegium. Skrifwelse til ... Carl Sparre rörande salt-nederlaget och salt-importen ... Stockholm, Kongl. Tryckeriet, 1781. S774

Sweden. Kommerskollegium

A letter from the king and the commerce commission to the government of Stockholm relative to salt supplies for the city and district.

Sweden. Kommerskollegium. Kungörelse, angående fri handel med sill-tran. Stockholm, Kongl. Tryckeriet [1785]. S775

Sweden. Kommerskollegium. Kungörelse, angående hwad wid Swenska skepps befraktande för de nu frigande magters räkning i akt tagas bör. Stockholm, Kongl. Tryckeriet, 1788. S776
A proclamation concerning procedures to be followed when Swedish ships are chartered by the warring powers.

Sweden. Kommerskollegium. Kungörelse, angående ut skilnaden emellan hel-och ofria tullen så wäl för neutrale utländningar som inhemske handlande tils widare uphörer. Stockholm, Kongl. Tryckeriet, 1788. S777
The differences in duties for foreign and local merchants shall be removed, for the time being, in the case of foreign merchants from neutral countries.

Sweden. Kommerskollegium. Kungörelse, angående förändring med tull-afgifterne för åtskillige sidentyger m.m. Stockholm, Kongl. Tryckeriet, 1792. S778
A proclamation concerning changes in the duties for several silk cloths, etc.

Sweden. Kommerskollegium. Kungörelse, angående frihet för tobaks-fabriques idkare at få infor-skrifwa tobaksstjelkar. Stockholm, Kongl. Tryckeriet, 1792. S779
Swedish merchants are permitted to import any quantity of tobacco stalks, but must pay the regular duty on them.

Sweden. Kommerskollegium. Kungörelse, angående tiden til återsökande och restitution, ... Stockholm, Kongl. Tryckeriet, 1793. S780
A proclamation concerning the time limit for restitution of excess duties paid to the customs office.

Sweden. Kommerskollegium. Kungörelse och förbud, emot införsel hit i riket af alt mångfärgadt sattineradt flor. Stockholm, Kongl. Tryckeriet, 1793. S781
Prohibits the import of multi-colored satin veils.

Sweden. Kommerskollegium. Kungörelse, angående förbud emot inrikes transport af caffé m.m. Stockholm, Kongl. Tryckeriet, 1794. S782
All products, including coffee, which have been prohibited as of August 1, are no longer to be transported into or within the country.

Sweden. Kommerskollegium. Kungörelse, angående förbud emot så kallat Swenskt caffé. Stockholm, Kongl. Tryckeriet, 1794. S783
The general prohibition against foreign coffee is extended to cover the so-called Swedish coffee or anything that might smell, taste, or be made the same way as coffee.

Sweden. Kommerskollegium. Kungörelse, rörande utgående tullens nedsättande å Swensk bergmåssa. Stockholm, Kongl. Tryckeriet, 1794. S784
A proclamation concerning the reduction of export duties on Swedish rock moss.

Sweden. Kommerskollegium. Kungörelse, angående anstalter til förekommande af brist och dyrhet på victualie-waror. Stockholm, Kongl. Tryckeriet, 1795. S785
Measures for preventing shortage and dearness of dry goods and foodstuffs.

Sweden. Kommerskollegium. Kungörelse, angående beslagare andelens beräknande hädanester, af til införsel i riket förbudne och confiscable dömde waror. Stockholm, Kongl. Tryckeriet, 1798. S786
Concerns the computation of the confiscator's part in goods which are considered forbidden to import and are confiscated.

Sweden. Kommerskollegium. [Instruction concerning the use of prisoners in fortress building.] Stockholm, Kongl. Tryckeriet, 1799. S787

Sweden. Kommerskollegium. Kungörelse, angående en wiss faststäld lindring i tullen för de waror, som från America och West-Indien med Swenska skepp inkomma. Stockholm, Kongl. Tryckeriet [1799]. S788

Sweden. Kommerskollegium. Kungörelse, angående frihet för ... införa salt. Stockholm, Kongl. Tryckeriet, 1799. S789
A proclamation granting permission to Swedish and foreign merchants to import salt from any port until the end of the year.

Sweden. Kommerskollegium. Kungörelse, angående hwad i akt tagas bör i anseende til nederlag och utförsel af caffé ... Stockholm, Kongl. Tryckeriet, 1799. S790
Concerns what is to be done with stockpiles and export of coffee which can be shown to have been imported before the prohibition announced in the proclamation of April 6, 1799.

Sweden. Kommerskollegium. Kungörelse angående frihet från passtagande och dubbel siötull för salt ... Stockholm, Kongl. Tryckeriet, 1802. S791

A proclamation concerning small quantities of salt which are exempt from double import duties and other requirements.

Sweden. Kommerskollegium. Kungörelse angående tullen på utrikes ifrån inkommande tobaksstjelkar. Stockholm, Kongl. Tryckeriet, 1803. S792

Importers declaring tobacco leaves to be stalks will lose the right to import stalks.

Sweden. Kommerskollegium. Kungörelse, angående widtagen anstalt til förekommande af underslef wid utförsel af nederlags-salt. Stockholm, Kongl. Tryckeriet, 1803. S793

Exporters of salt are required to present within six months of export proof from the port of discharge of the quantity exported.

Sweden. Kommerskollegium. Kungörelse, angående widtagen anstalt til förekommande af tull-försnillning å utländske tobaksblad, som på landtullssidan i Finland införas. Stockholm, Kongl. Tryckeriet, 1804. S794

Persons bringing tobacco leaves through customs must have proof that they are homegrown, or pay the higher rate for imports.

Sweden. Kommerskollegium. Kungörelse, angående förbud tils widare emot utförsel af salt til utrikes ort. Stockholm, Kongl. Tryckeriet, 1806. S795

Renewal of a temporary restriction against exporting salt.

Sweden. Kommerskollegium. Kungörelse, angående försälining af waror, som för enskildte handlandes räkning införas från West-Indien och Norra America. Stockholm, Kongl. Tryckeriet, 1806. S796

Sweden. Kommerskollegium. Kungörelse, angående frihet til export af Liverpools salt. Stockholm, Kongl. Tryckeriet, 1809. S797

Importers of Liverpool salt are forbidden to re-export more than two-thirds of the imported quantity.

Sweden. Kommerskollegium. Kungörelse, angående widtagen särskild anstalt för at bereda tilgång på salt wid strömmings-fisket i rikets skärgårdar. Stockholm, Kongl. Tryckeriet, 1809. S798

Concerns special measures taken to provide a salt supply for herring fishing.

Sweden. Kommerskollegium. Kungörelse, angående förbud tils widare emot utförsel af salt utan undantag. Stockholm, Kongl. Tryckeriet, 1810. S799

A temporary prohibition of export of any salt, because of the decline in stockpiles.

Sweden. Kommerskollegium. Kungörelse, angående uphäfwandet af nu gällande förbud emot utförseln af salt. Stockholm, Kongl. Tryckeriet, 1812. S800

Current restrictions are removed, and regulations for salt from May 28, 1806, are again effective.

Sweden. Kommerskollegium. Kungörelse, angående tillåten utförsel till Finland af salt från nederlagen i rikets stapel-städer. Stockholm, Kongl. Tryckeriet, 1816. S801

Since the stockpiles of salt are so great that the ship owners are losing money, they are authorized to export excess salt to Finland.

Sweden. Kommerskollegium. Kungörelse angående de i Norra America utbrustne farsoter. Stockholm, Kongl. Tryckeriet, 1819. S802

Sweden. Kommerskollegium. Kungörelse, angående quarantaine för fartyg, kommande ifrån Södra America. Stockholm, Kongl. Tryckeriet, 1819. S803

Sweden. Kommerskollegium. Kungörelse, angående de i Norra America utbrustne farsoter. Stockholm, Kongl. Tryckeriet, 1821. S804

Sweden. Kommerskollegium. Kungörelse, angående tullen för salt, som på Cap Verds öarne intages af Swenska skepp, kommande från Brasilien. Stockholm, Kongl. Tryckeriet, 1821. S805

Salt brought from the Cape Verde Islands on Swedish ships will be subject to the same customs fees as that from Portugal and Brazil.

Sweden. Kommerskollegium. Kungörelse, angående handeln emellan Swerige och fasta landet af Södra America. Stockholm, Kongl. Tryckeriet, 1822. S806

Sweden. Kommerskollegium. Kungörelse, angående quarantaines-skyldighetens upphörande för fartyg, kommande ifrån Södra America. Stockholm, Kongl. Tryckeriet, 1822. S807

Sweden. Kommerskollegium. Kungörelse, angående upphörande af nederlagsränta för salt. Stockholm, Kongl. Tryckeriet, 1822. S808

A proclamation concerning discontinuance of stockpile rent for salt.

Sweden. Kommerskollegium. Wi, chef och ledamöter uti Kongl. Maj:ts ... aflåten nådig skrifwelse till Kongl. Collegium af den 15. i denna månad, funnit godt i nåder förklara: att det är Kongl. Maj:ts undersåtare obetaget, att drifwa handel på alla orter å fasta landet af Södra America ... [Stockholm, 1822.] S809

Sweden. Kommerskollegium. Kungörelse, i anledning af cholerans utbrott i Australien samt i atskilliga hamnar wid Lorenzo-floden och i staterne New-York och Pensylvanien. Stockholm, Kongl. Tryckeriet, 1832. S810

Sweden. Kommerskollegium. Kungörelse, i anledning af pestens utbrott å ön Syra i archipelagen, samt gula feberns utbrott i Havana å ön Cuba. Stockholm, Kongl. Tryckeriet, 1832.
S811

Sweden. Kongl. Slotts Kansleri. Publication, angående cauffardie och private fartygs angifwande wid Danska tull-cammaren. Stockholm, Kongl. Tryckeriet [1739]. S812
Discusses the duty of merchant and private ships to call at the Danish customs when passing through Oresund.

Sweden. Kongl. Slotts Kansleri. Kungiörelse huru the Ryske kiöpmän, som här på Stockholm handel drifwa, sit gods sälja skola, och hwad provision Ryska tolken eller inspectoren theraf bör bekomma. Stockholm, Kongl. Tryckeriet, 1746. S813
Concerns Russian merchants in Stockholm and stipulates fees to be paid by buyers and sellers of Russian goods.

Sweden. Kongl. Slotts Kansleri. Kungiörelse om torghandelen med spannemål miöl, gryn och ärter ... Stockholm, Kongl. Tryckeriet [1760].
S814
Removes restrictions on the trade in grain, meal and peas.

Sweden. Kongl. Slotts Kansleri. Kundgiörelse, at inwånare i städerne, som begifwa sig med waror til försälgning å marknader ... Stockholm, Kongl. Tryckeriet, 1769. S815
Residents in cities who venture forth with goods to sell at markets are to supply themselves with the appropriate magistrates' proof of their right to do so.

Sweden. Kongl. Slotts Kansleri. Kungörelse angående skeps-rederiernes åliggande i anseende til coopvaerdie-siöfolkets personelle kronoutskylder. Stockholm, H. Fougt, 1774. S816
Shipowners and the Seaman's House are required to inform collectors of the whereabouts of seamen, and to pay the debts of those at sea.

Sweden. Laws, etc. Konung Kristoffers landslag. Manuscript. Sweden, ca. 1550. S817
This set of laws was promulgated in 1442 and remained in effect until 1734. The laws include a section covering aspects of Sweden's economy and trade.

Sweden. Laws, etc. Samling utaf Kongl. bref, stadgar och förordningar etc. angående Sweriges rikes commerce, politie och oeconomie. Stockholm, Kongl. Tryckeriet, 1747-75. S818
A compilation of reprinted Swedish documents concerned with commercial and economic affairs from 1523 to 1718.

Sweden. Riksdagen. Instruction, hwarefter hallrätternes deputerade, så wäl som manufactur contoirets advocat fiscal och samtelige ombudsmän hafwa sig et rätta ... Stockholm, Kongl. Tryckeriet, 1763. S819
Instructions for unloading and recording cargoes of sugar and tobacco.

Sweden. Riksdagen. Utdrag af protocollet, hållit uti Riksens ständers secreteutskott den 17 Julii 1765. Stockholm, Kongl. Tryckeriet, 1765.
S820
Concerns bank loans and the issue of bonds, lotteries, rates of interest, and questions of collateral.

Sweden. Riksdagen. Continuation af Riksens högloflige ständers deputationers, wid 1769 ars Riksdag ... Stockholm, C. Stolpe, 1769. S821
Questions and comments addressed by the delegates of the Estates of the Realm to the General Customs-Directorate at the 1769 Riksdag, and the Directorate's answers.

Sweden. Sovereign (1594-1632 : Gustavus II Adolphus). Ordinantie huruledes köphandelen aff rijksens inbyggiare så wäl som fremmande drifwas skal. Stockholm, Ignatio Heurer [1617].
S822

Sweden. Sovereign (1594-1632 : Gustavus II Adolphus). Octroy eller privilegium som then stormechtigste högborne furste och herre, Herr Gustaff Adolph, Sweriges Göthes och Wendes Konnung etc. Stockholm, Ignatius Meurer, 1626.
S823
Royal privileges granted to the Swedish South Sea Company.

Sweden. Sovereign (1594-1632 : Gustavus II Adolphus). Ampliatio oder Erweiterung desz Privilegii so der allerdurchleuchtigste, grozmächtigste Fürst und Herr, Herr Gustavus Adolphus, etc. Heilbronn, Christoff Klausen, 1633. S824
An enlargement of the original privileges of the Swedish South Sea Company, designed to attract German capital.

Sweden. Sovereign (1632-1654 : Kristina). Tullordning för inländske och fremmande uthi siöstäderne. Stockholm, Heinrich Kayser, 1636.
S825
A schedule of duties with other commercial regulations.

Sweden. Sovereign (1632-1654 : Kristina).
Tullordning för inländske och fremmande uthi siöstäderne. Stockholm, Heinrich Kayser, 1637.
S826
A schedule of duties with other commercial regulations.

Sweden. Sovereign (1632-1654 : Kristina).
Tullordning för inländske och fremmande uthi siöstäderne. Stockholm, Heinrich Kayser, 1639.
S827
A schedule of duties together with other regulations.

Sweden. Sovereign (1632-1654 : Kristina).
[Broadside concerning the sale of tobacco.] Stockholm, 1641.
S828
A regulation curtailing the importation of tobacco to a small quantity to be handled exclusively by the Swedish South Sea Company.

Sweden. Sovereign (1632-1654 : Kristina).
Förordning huru medh tobaks handelen skal blifwa hällit. [Stockholm, 1641.]
S829
All tobacco trade must be through the Söderländske Compagniet.

Sweden. Sovereign (1632-1654 : Kristina).
[Proclamation.] [Stockholm, 1650.]
S830
A broadside proclamation concerned with the suppression of illegal trade.

Sweden. Sovereign (1632-1654 : Kristina).
Placat, betreffende die freyheit auff schiffsbaw ... Stockholm, H. Keyser [1652].
S831
A royal edict permitting Swedish citizens to build or buy ships in the provinces.

Sweden. Sovereign (1654-1660 : Charles X).
Brief ... aende burgemeesters raedt, schepenen, ende ganscher gemeente der stadt Danzick. The Hague, Christianus Calaminus, 1656.
S832
The Swedish King warns the people of Danzig to cooperate with him, or he will take the city and destroy what trading privileges they have.

Sweden. Sovereign (1660-1697 : Charles XI).
Placat, öfwer tobackz handelen. Stockholm, Kongl. Booktr., 1665.
S833
Sets prices of tobacco and gives tobacco traders, accompanied by government officials, the right to search dwellings thought to hold illegal tobacco.

Sweden. Sovereign (1660-1697 : Charles XI).
Ordningh och taxa oppå lille tullen och accijsen ... Stockholm, Ignatio Meurer, 1666.
S834
A schedule of small customs and taxes, originally made in 1655, containing instructions on difficult cases for officials.

Sweden. Sovereign (1660-1697 : Charles XI).
Placat, angående någon frijheet på salltsiuderijt. Stockholm, Kongl. Booktr., 1666.
S835
Promotes salt factories by exempting imports of raw salt and exports of the finished product from customs duties. Workers are exempt from military service.

Sweden. Sovereign (1660-1697 : Charles XI).
Placat, angående någon tull-frijheet på salltetz införszel. Stockholm, Kongl. Booktr., 1666.
S836
Low import duties on salt, usually applying to Swedish ships only, are extended to all importers for about one year.

Sweden. Sovereign (1660-1697 : Charles XI).
Niederlags Ordonnance auff allerhand Wahren, nembl. Saltz, Wein, Brandtwein und Pappier, so mit schwedischen Schiffen nacher Stockholm geführet werden; item russisch; und leiflandische wahren ins gross. Stockholm, Ignatius Meurer, 1667.
S837

Sweden. Sovereign (1660-1697 : Charles XI).
Ordning, ofwer siö-tullen, hwar effter then samma på uth-och ingående wahror ... Stockholm, Kongl. Booktr., 1667.
S838
A customs regulation and tariff table.

Sweden. Sovereign (1660-1697 : Charles XI).
Placat, angående priset aff Spanskt salt som för närwarande tijdh skal acktas. Stockholm, G. Hantsch, 1667.
S839
Sets a maximum price for salt until the economy improves.

Sweden. Sovereign (1660-1697 : Charles XI).
Förordning öfwer tobaakz handelen, nu mehra renoverat. Stockholm, Kongl. Booktr., 1670.
S840
The tobacco trade is made into a state monopoly.

Sweden. Sovereign (1660-1697 : Charles XI).
Påbudh och förordningh emoot allehanda extorsioner uthaff the siöfarende. Stockholm, Kongl. Booktr., 1671.
S841
A decree specifying severe penalties for officials extorting money from merchant seamen.

Sweden. Sovereign (1660-1697 : Charles XI).
Placat, angående huru stoore-siötullen aff all koppar skal clareras. Stockholm, Kongl. Booktr., 1671.
S842

Sweden. Sovereign (1660-1697 : Charles XI).
Handels-ordinantie, hwar effter alla the som medh handel och wandel umgås, hafwe sigh at effterrätta. Stockholm, Niclas Wankijff, 1673.
S843
Only Swedish subjects are to enjoy privileges in trade, and no dual citizenships are allowed. If a subject acts as a cover for a foreigner to gain privileges for him, both parties will be punished.

Sweden. Sovereign (1660-1697 : Charles XI).
Placat, angående heel frijheet i tullen aff alt thet salt som införes uthi innewarande åhr. Stockholm, Kongl. Booktr. [1674]. S844
A lower customs rate for salt is applicable this year.

Sweden. Sovereign (1660-1697 : Charles XI).
Placat och förordning, angående handhafwandet aff stora siöö tulls wåsendet ... Stockholm, Kongl. Booktryckiare, 1678. S845
Customs officials are permitted to search any ship or building believed to contain undeclared goods, and penalties for officials failing to carry out their duties are cited.

Sweden. Sovereign (1660-1697 : Charles XI). [A broadside proclamation relating to the sale of mastwood in Riga. n.p., August 5, 1680.] S846

Sweden. Sovereign (1660-1697 : Charles XI).
Förordning och stadga, hwar effter medh Swenske skepp och godz ... Stockholm, Kongl. Booktryckiare [1680]. S847
This royal ordinance concerns regulations on Swedish ships and goods passing through Oresund.

Sweden. Sovereign (1660-1697 : Charles XI).
Förordningh, huru med clarerandet för inkommande skepp och fahrtyg skal förhållas. Stockholm, Kongl. Booktr. [1681]. S848
Relates to the clearing of ships to and from Swedish ports.

Sweden. Sovereign (1660-1697 : Charles XI).
Placat, och protectorial för tull-accijs ock quarne tulls betiente i Swerige, Finland och the ther onderliggiande provincier. Stockholm, Kongl. Booktr. [1681]. S849
Concerns customs officials in Sweden, Finland, and other provinces.

Sweden. Sovereign (1660-1697 : Charles XI).
Placat och protectorial för tull-accis och quartie-tulls betiente i Swerige, Finland och the ther underliggiande provincier. [Stockholm, 1681.] S850
Another edition of the preceding item.

Sweden. Sovereign (1660-1697 : Charles XI).
Förbudh om olofligit månglerij och landskiöp. Stockholm, Niclas Wankijff, 1682. S851

Sweden. Sovereign (1660-1697 : Charles XI).
Nådigste notification om Tiäru Compagniets uphäfwande. Stockholm, Niclas Wankijff [1682]. S852
The royal notification of the dissolution of the Tar Company's monopoly and the general opening of the trade.

Sweden. Sovereign (1660-1697 : Charles XI).
Placat öfwer dhet miszbruk och undersleff som medh tobackz olåstiga införande och impracticerande brukat warder. Stockholm, Kongl. Booktr. [1685]. S853
An edict dealing with the illegal import and use of tobacco; a reward is offered to informers.

Sweden. Sovereign (1660-1697 : Charles XI).
Förordning angående store siötullens clarerande ... Stockholm, Kongl. Booktr. [1686]. S854
Concerns clearing customs; the coinage used, and foreign and domestic rates of exchange.

Sweden. Sovereign (1660-1697 : Charles XI).
Ordning och taxa, oppå lille tullens och accijsens opbärande ... Stockholm, Kong. Booktryckare [1686]. S855
A tariff schedule with instructions to be followed at customs.

Sweden. Sovereign (1660-1697 : Charles XI).
Stadga och förordning, hwareffter extraordinarie pass-penningar och andredes lijke expenser ... Stockholm, Kongl. Booktr. [1686]. S856
Requires travelers to pay certain fees to customs officials.

Sweden. Sovereign (1660-1697 : Charles XI).
Förordning, angående nederlagz frijhetens myttiande på salt uti staden Stockholm. Stockholm, Kongl. Booktr. [1687]. S857
Announces free port rights for salt in the city of Stockholm.

Sweden. Sovereign (1660-1697 : Charles XI).
Placat, emoot tobakz införande, sampt angående tobaks bläders införskrifwande och spinnerijers inråttande. Stockholm, Kong. Booktryckiare [1687]. S858
Prohibits importing finished tobacco products.

Sweden. Sovereign (1660-1697 : Charles XI).
Resolution angående främmande handelsmän och expediter, sampt deras handels frijheet. Stockholm, Niclas Wankijf [1687]. S859
Foreign merchants will no longer be subject to special discrimination in Swedish cities; laws which apply to Swedish merchants will apply to them.

Sweden. Sovereign (1660-1697 : Charles XI).
Förordning, huru store siö-tullen skal clareras med wisse mynte sorter eller ock med sölfwer in natural. Stockholm, Kongl. Booktryckiare [1688]. S860
Instructions for payment of clearing customs.

Sweden. Sovereign (1660-1697 : Charles XI).
Förordning, at de, som hafwa liquiderade fordringar för frackter ... Stockholm, Kongl. Booktr. [1689]. S861
Persons having claims against the government for ships and goods used during the war are given a reduction in customs duties on salt.

Sweden. Sovereign (1660-1697 : Charles XI).
Förnyade och prolongerade placat, vär uti allom, utan åtskilnad, af hwad nation eller på hwad skiep det hälst wara må ... Stockholm, C.N. Wankijf [1691].   S862
Concerns a low customs rate on salt from any nation.

Sweden. Sovereign (1660-1697 : Charles XI).
Nådigste förordning, huru med all mäldz både angifwande och afmalande, sampt quarn-tulls och acciis-zedlarne skall förhållas. Stockholm, S. Niclas Wankijf [1691].   S863
States regulations for the grinding of grain and the payment of taxes on it in the cities.

Sweden. Sovereign (1660-1697 : Charles XI).
Placat, vär uti allom utan åtskilnad, af hwad nation ... hela frijheten i tullen på inkommande salt ... Stockholm, C.N. Wankijff [1691].   S864
Concerns a temporary low customs rate on salt from any nation.

Sweden. Sovereign (1660-1697 : Charles XI).
Förnyad ordning och reglement, hwar effter Tzariske May:ts här traffiquerande undersåtare sig med deras warors försålliande skola hafwa at rätta. Stockholm, Sal Wankijfs effterlefwerska [1692.]   S865

Sweden. Sovereign (1660-1697 : Charles XI).
Förnyade placat och stadga angående förbudne sijden=tyg och andre slijke wahrur. Stockholm, Kongl. Booktryckerijet [1693].   S866
Strengthens the previous decrees of 1690 and 1688 banning the sale and manufacture of silk cloth.

Sweden. Sovereign (1660-1697 : Charles XI).
Placat, och förordning, angående åtskillige slags sortementer af lärefft. Stockholm, Kongl. Booktr. [1694].   S867
Continental linens are prohibited and duties are raised on other types of linen.

Sweden. Sovereign (1660-1697 : Charles XI).
Förordning angående lootswäsendet i Swerige och Finland. Stockholm, S. Niclas Wankijf [1696].   S868
A royal regulation for pilots, giving their responsibilities in Sweden and Finland.

Sweden. Sovereign (1660-1697 : Charles XI).
Nådigste stadga och förordning angående nederlags frijheten på Spanskt och Franskt wijn, som uti Swänske skepp directe föras från Spanien och Franckrijke till Stockholm. Stockholm, Kongl. Booktr. [1696].   S869
Gives the responsibilities and privileges of shipping pilots, and includes taxes and customs fees.

Sweden. Sovereign (1660-1697 : Charles XI).
Reglemente och instruction för loots-inspectoren i Stockholm. Stockholm, S. Wankifs Enckia [1696].   S870
A royal regulation and instruction for the pilot inspector and local officials in Stockholm and Finland.

Sweden. Sovereign (1660-1697 : Charles XI).
Stadga och förordning, angående fördelningen uppå samptel. lootsarnes börder och hwad styrning dem hwar i synnerheet tilkommer, med bijfogad tax, huru lootspenningarne öfwer alt af de traffiquerande betalas böre. Stockholm, Sahl. Wankifs Änckia [1697].   S871

Sweden. Sovereign (1660-1697 : Charles XI).
Stadga och förordning, angående fördelningen uppå samptel. Lootsarnes börder och hwad styrning den hwar i synnerheet tilkommer, med bijfogad taxa. Stockholm, Kongl. Booktr. [1697].   S872
A royal decree concerning the pilots and their responsibilities, with instructions for merchants paying them.

Sweden. Sovereign (1697-1718 : Charles XII).
Placat och påbudh, angående öfwerwåld och röfwerij, som föröfwas på skeppsbrutne och strandade fahrkoster. Stockholm, S. Wankijfs Enckia [1697].   S873
A decree forbidding maltreatment of shipwrecked persons and confiscation of shipwrecked goods. The removal of warning lights and the setting out of false lights is prohibited.

Sweden. Sovereign (1697-1718 : Charles XII).
Placat och förbud, angående åthskillige slags sijdentygs och brocaders bärande och brukande til kläde-drächter, wid alfwarsamt straff tilgiörandes. Stockholm, S. Wankif Enkia [1699].   S874
A decree concerning the control and prohibition of importing, manufacturing, and wearing certain silk, gold, and silver brocade cloth.

Sweden. Sovereign (1697-1718 : Charles XII).
Samtel. härwarande råds yterligare förklaring och bref til ... Herr Grefwe Knut Posse ... Stockholm, Kongl. Boktr. [1710].   S875
Letter to Count Knut Posse regarding freedom from customs, port costs, and excises for those who bring foodstuffs to besieged Riga.

Sweden. Sovereign (1697-1718 : Charles XII).
[Leaflet relating to clearing of customs duties through the banks. July 30, 1712.] [Stockholm, 1712.]   S876

Sweden. Sovereign (1697-1718 : Charles XII).
Tull-taxa på uthgående wahror, wid stora siötullen ... Stockholm, J.H. Werner, 1715.   S877
A new schedule of duties on exports by which all ships will pay the same rate, in many cases lower than before.

Sweden. Sovereign (1697-1718 : Charles XII). Placat och forbud at inge priser fä ranconera eller utlösa sig uti siön. Stockholm, Kongl. Tryckeriet [1716]. S878

Sweden. Sovereign (1718-1720 : Ulrika Eleonora). Förordning angående små-tullarnes och accisens betalande i godt och redbart mynt. Stockholm, Kongl. Boktr., 1719. S879
An ordinance about the payment of internal customs and excises in coin rather than in paper money.

Sweden. Sovereign (1718-1720 : Ulrika Eleonora). Förordning, om handelens obehindrade lopp. Stockholm, Kongl. Tryckeriet, 1719. S880
An ordinance concerning free trade in Sweden.

Sweden. Sovereign (1718-1720 : Ulrika Eleonora). Nådigste förordning, hwar efter commiss-farare hädan efter, så länge detta kriget påstår, skola wara skyldige sig at rätta. Stockholm, Kongl. Tryckeriet, 1719. S881
Regulation of commercial travelers during wartime.

Sweden. Sovereign (1718-1720 : Ulrika Eleonora). Taxa, hwar efter tullen och licenten för utgående och inkommande waror wid stora siö-tullen ... Stockholm, Kongl. Tryckeriet, 1719. S882
A tariff, according to which the customs and license fees are to be paid on all listed imported or exported goods at the main sea-customs.

Sweden. Sovereign (1720-1751 : Fredrik I). Förnyade protectorial för tull-betienterne. Stockholm, Kongl. Boktryckeriet, 1721. S883
A declaration of protection by the crown for customs officials who were not actually full-fledged civil servants.

Sweden. Sovereign (1720-1751 : Fredrik I). Protectorial för tull-betienterne, dat. Stockholm, den 3 Augusti 1721. Stockholm, 1721. S884
Indicates penalties for all who hinder or do not assist the customs officials in their duties.

Sweden. Sovereign (1720-1751 : Fredrik I). Förordning angående hämmandet af alt okiöp med de hit til staden kommande victualie persedler och andra wahror. Stockholm, Kongl. Boktryckeriet, 1722. S885
Restrictions on purchase and sale of food, to prevent speculation by merchants.

Sweden. Sovereign (1720-1751 : Fredrik I). Förklaring, huruledes med handelen och siöfahrten ifrån utrikes orter på Swerige och des underliggande provincier, ... Stockholm, Kongl. Boktryckeriet, 1723. S886
Explains how to deal with ships arriving in Sweden, in order to control contagious diseases.

Sweden. Sovereign (1720-1751 : Fredrik I). Förordning, angående skeps-clarerare ... Stockholm, Kongl. Boktryckeriet, 1723. S887
Ordinance stating that ship clearers are not allowed to engage in commerce or to own ships.

Sweden. Sovereign (1720-1751 : Fredrik I). Förordning, angående waror, hwilka så wäl af kiöpmän ... Stockholm, Kongl. Boktryckeriet, 1723. S888
Discusses the computation of interest on debt resulting from credit purchases of goods.

Sweden. Sovereign (1720-1751 : Fredrik I). Förordning angående de fremmandes fahrt på Swerige och Finland. Stockholm, Kongl. Boktryckeriet [1724]. S889

Sweden. Sovereign (1720-1751 : Fredrik I). Förordning, huru med confiscerade warors lystande emot caution, samt för auctionerande bädanefter förhållas bör. Stockholm, Kongl. Boktryckeriet [1724]. S890
Concerns the disposal of confiscated goods, procedures of release for bail, and the auction of such goods when bail is given.

Sweden. Sovereign (1720-1751 : Fredrik I). Förordning, hwarefter kiöpmän och skeppare, som på Swerige och Finland handla och fahra. Stockholm, Kongl. Tryckeriet, 1724. S891
Procedures for entry and exit in the ports of Sweden and Finland.

Sweden. Sovereign (1720-1751 : Fredrik I). Förklaring öfwer förordningen af den 10 Nov. 1724 ... Stockholm, Kongl. Tryckeriet, 1726. S892
Explanation of ordinance of November 10, 1724, regarding foreigners sailing to Sweden and Finland.

Sweden. Sovereign (1720-1751 : Fredrik I). Taxa, hwar efter tullen och licenten för utgående och inkommande waror wid stora siö-tullen, ... Stockholm, Kongl. Tryckeriet, 1726. S893
A tariff, according to which the customs and license fees are to be paid on all listed imported and exported goods at the main sea-customs.

Sweden. Sovereign (1720-1751 : Fredrik I). Förordning hwarefter wisse inkommande wahror, utom den wanlige tullen och umgialderne, med 5 pro cent ... Stockholm, Kongl. Tryckeriet, 1728. S894
A special tax of five per cent will be levied on certain imported goods, primarily luxury, exotic, and manufactured foreign articles, in addition to the usual customs duties.

Sweden. Sovereign (1720-1751 : Fredrik I). Påbud huru de handlandes inlagor hädanefter

skola inrättas. Stockholm, Kongl. Boktryckeriet [1728].   S895
A decree pertaining to the manner in which merchants are to declare goods to customs officials, with penalties prescribed for falsification.

Sweden. Sovereign (1720-1751 : Fredrik I).
Publication och förbud angående tobaksstielkars införsel. Stockholm, Kongl. Tryckeriet, 1728.   S896
A decree forbidding the importation of tobacco stalks in the interest of encouraging the Swedish tobacco industry.

Sweden. Sovereign (1720-1751 : Fredrik I).
Publication angående ett rytt generalt tullarrende. Stockholm, Kongl. Tryckeriet [1729].   S897
A date is set for the application for leases on the collection of certain types of customs duties.

Sweden. Sovereign (1720-1751 : Fredrik I).
Förordning angående salthandelen. Stockholm, Kongl. Boktr., 1731.   S898
A royal proclamation concerning the salt business.

Sweden. Sovereign (1720-1751 : Fredrik I).
Förordning om Swenska heelfrihetens uphörande för utrikesbygde skep. Stockholm, Kongl. Boktryckeriet, 1731.   S899
A royal ordinance about the cessation of special privileges for foreign-built Swedish ships.

Sweden. Sovereign (1720-1751 : Fredrik I).
Påbut angående dem, som fara siö-tullarne förbi, utan at sig dersammastädes behörigen anmäla. Stockholm, Kongl. Tryckeriet [1731].   S900
A royal decree concerning those who fail to report to customs offices for inspection when sailing or rowing by them.

Sweden. Sovereign (1720-1751 : Fredrik I).
Privilegium för commissarien Hindrich König & Compagnie, angående en fart och handel på Ost-Indien. Stockholm, Hartwig Gercken, 1731.   S901
The first charter of privileges of the Swedish East India Company.

Sweden. Sovereign (1720-1751 : Fredrik I).
Förordning, angående rote-och indelnings båtsmäns öfwande i siöwäsendet, igenom coopvaerdie fart. Stockholm, Kongl. Boktryckeriet [1733].   S902
The training of seamen for war service is to take place on merchant vessels.

Sweden. Sovereign (1720-1751 : Fredrik I).
Förklaring öfwer förordningen af den 25. October 1733. Stockholm, Kongl. Tryckeriet, 1734.   S903
High-ranking seamen are not permitted to use their official uniforms when serving on merchant vessels.

Sweden. Sovereign (1720-1751 : Fredrik I).
Allmän förordning, hwarefter alle de, som här i riket handeln wilja lära ... Stockholm, Kongl. Tryckeriet, 1735.   S904
A general ordinance according to which all those who wish to learn commerce, and later engage in it, are to proceed.

Sweden. Sovereign (1720-1751 : Fredrik I).
Taxa hwarefter landthielpen ifrån den 1 Januarii 1735 ... af de inkommande wahror. Stockholm, Kongl. Tryckeriet [1735].   S905
A special government tax is to be collected on imports in addition to the regular duties.

Sweden. Sovereign (1720-1751 : Fredrik I).
Nådiga resolution angående Sweriges ... handel på Levanten. Stockholm, J.L. Horrn, 1738.   S906
Royal resolutions setting forth the conditions under which Swedish trade to the Levant is to be carried on.

Sweden. Sovereign (1720-1751 : Fredrik I).
Förordning, angående theras straff, som efter ett års förlopp ifrån then 19. i thenne månad här i riket handla eller försälja någon utrikes spunnen tobak. Stockholm, Kongl. Tryckeriet, 1739.   S907
Cites the punishment for illegal trade in foreign tobacco: landowners will lose property and civil rights, non-landowners will be sentenced to physical labor.

Sweden. Sovereign (1720-1751 : Fredrik I).
Nådige förklaring öfwer dykeriförordingen af then 18 Novemb. 1734. Stockholm, Kongl. Tryckeriet [1739].   S908
An explanation of decrees of November 18, 1734, concerning diving for salvage, with the intent to correct abuses of the salvage commission.

Sweden. Sovereign (1720-1751 : Fredrik I).
Taxa, hwarefter stora siö-tullen uppå alla inkommande wahror. Stockholm, Kongl. Tryckeriet, 1739.   S909
A schedule of tariff duties on imported goods which also includes a list of goods which could not be imported.

Sweden. Sovereign (1720-1751 : Fredrik I).
Taxa hwarefter stora siö-tullen uppå alla utgående wahror bör ärlaggas och upbäras. Stockholm, Kongl. Tryckeriet [1739].   S910
Provides for duties on exports and includes special instructions for collecting them.

Sweden. Sovereign (1720-1751 : Fredrik I).
Brev til öfwer-ståthållaren och samtelige landshöfdingarne angående förekommande af brist och dyrhet på salt. Stockholm, Kongl. Tryckeriet, 1741.   S911
A royal letter to the chief city governors and all county sheriffs about the causes of shortage and high cost of salt, and the prevention of this.

Sweden. Sovereign (1720-1751 : Fredrik I).
Förbud, angående siöfarit manskaps begifwande utom riket. Stockholm, Kongl. Tryckeriet [1742]. S912
Men with sea training are forbidden to leave the country for the purpose of manning warships.

Sweden. Sovereign (1720-1751 : Fredrik I).
Förklaring, öfwer thes genom trycket nyligen utfärdade reglemente ... Stockholm, Kongl. Tryckeriet, 1741. S913
An explanation of the recently printed regulations pertaining to Swedish ships during the prevailing war with Russia.

Sweden. Sovereign (1720-1751 : Fredrik I).
Förordning angående främmande köpmän eller handels expediter. Stockholm, Kongl. Tryckeriet, 1741. S914
Regulations upon foreign merchants resident in Sweden.

Sweden. Sovereign (1720-1751 : Fredrik I).
Förordning, angående nederlags frihet, uppå then spanmål, som med Swenske skepp ifrån utrikes orter hit införes. Stockholm, Kongl. Tryckeriet [1741]. S915

Sweden. Sovereign (1720-1751 : Fredrik I).
Förordning, til hämmande af lurendrägerier och inpracticeringar af utrikes waror. Stockholm, Kongl. Tryckeriet, 1741. S916
A royal ordinance for prevention of fradulent sales or usage of foreign goods.

Sweden. Sovereign (1720-1751 : Fredrik I).
Reglemente, hwarefter thes örlogs-skiepp ... under påstående kriget emot Ryssland. Stockholm, Kongl. Tryckeriet, 1741. S917
A regulation according to which war ships as well as commissioned ships are to proceed during the prevailing war with Russia.

Sweden. Sovereign (1720-1751 : Fredrik I).
Resolution uppå åtskillige handlandes ifrån stapel-och siö-städerne i storförstendömet Finland giorde underdånige ansökning ... Stockholm, Kongl. Tryckeriet [1742]. S918
Finnish seamen in Sweden are granted freedom from recruitment and draft, but may enlist if they wish.

Sweden. Sovereign (1720-1751 : Fredrik I).
Kungiörelse angående praemier för them, hwilka uptäcka sådane lurendrägerier ... Stockholm, Kongl. Tryckeriet, 1745. S919
A reward is offered for reporting foreign goods fraudulently declared to be of Swedish production.

Sweden. Sovereign (1720-1751 : Fredrik I).
Privilegium, på en handels och siö-farts inrättande på America, för handelsmännerne Abraham och Jacob Arfwedson & Companie. Stockholm, Kongl. Tryckeriet [1745]. S920

Sweden. Sovereign (1720-1751 : Fredrik I).
Förbud emot införsel af chocolade, arrachs och andre fremmande liqueurer. Stockholm, Kongl. Tryckeriet, 1746. S921
Prohibits the importation of cacao, arrack, and other foreign liquors, imposing a fine of six times the value of the product if it is imported.

Sweden. Sovereign (1720-1751 : Fredrik I).
Förnyade privilegium angående fartens och handelens fortsättiande på Öst Indien. Stockholm, Kongl. Tryckeriet [1746]. S922
The second charter of privileges of the Swedish East India Company.

Sweden. Sovereign (1720-1751 : Fredrik I).
Förordning, om skuld-sedlars bruk och rättighet wid rudemateriers och manufactur warors köpande och säljande. Stockholm, Kongl. Tryckeriet [1746]. S923
Concerns the use of promissory notes in the purchase of raw materials and manufactures.

Sweden. Sovereign (1720-1751 : Fredrik I).
Privilegium, angående fartens och handelens forsättiande på Öst-Indien. Stockholm, Kongl. Tryckeriet, 1746. S924
Second royal charter giving exclusive twenty-year trading rights in East India to the Swedish East India Company, exempting company employees from military service, customs, taxes, etc., and granting the company rights to have its own judiciary and accounting system.

Sweden. Sovereign (1720-1751 : Fredrik I).
Privilegium, die Fortsetzung der Fahrt und des Handels nach Ost-Indien betreffend. Stockholm, Königl. Buchdruckerey, 1746. S925
This is an extension of the charter of the Swedish East India Company, which was originally granted in 1731.

Sweden. Sovereign (1720-1751 : Fredrik I).
Påbud, angående en consumtions accis erläggande af thé, caffé, rök-och snus-tobak samt puder. Stockholm, Kongl. Tryckeriet, 1747. S926
Tax regulations for tea, coffee, smoking tobacco, snuff, and powder, rated according to social group.

Sweden. Sovereign (1720-1751 : Fredrik I).
Förnade nådige privilegium för Levantiske Compagniet. Stockholm, Kongl. Tryckeriet [1748]. S927
A renewal of the charter of the Swedish Levant Company.

Sweden. Sovereign (1720-1751 : Fredrik I).
Förordning, angående lotsmärket i riket för wisse delar. Stockholm, Kongl. Tryckeriet [1748]. S928
A table of pilot rates for various parts of Sweden.

Sweden. Sovereign (1720-1751 : Fredrik I). Förordning för skepps-clarerare. Stockholm, Kongl. Tryckeriet, 1748. **S929**
Qualifications and duties of ship clearers.

Sweden. Sovereign (1720-1751 : Fredrik I). Reglemente hwarefter coopvaerdie-skeppare och skeppsfolk hafwa sig at rätta. Stockholm, Kongl. Tryckeriet, 1748. **S930**
Royal regulations of conduct for merchant skippers and seamen.

Sweden. Sovereign (1720-1751 : Fredrik I). Förordning, angående straff för then, som syrer eller förderfwar maste-och storwerks trä, eller ämne thertil. Stockholm, Kongl. Tryckeriet, 1749. **S931**
States penalties for unauthorized persons cutting certain kinds of wood, especially that used for masts.

Sweden. Sovereign (1751-1771 : Adolph Fredrik). Nådige stadfästelse uppå directionens af Ost-Indiske Compagniet avertissement, angående thenne handelens inrättand med en ständig fonds. Stockholm, Kongl. Tryckeriet [1753]. **S932**
Thirteen provisions regarding the administration of the Swedish East India Company.

Sweden. Sovereign (1751-1771 : Adolph Fredrik). Publication, angående et nytt general-tull-arrende. Stockholm, Kongl. Tryckeriet [1753]. **S933**
A new general customs lease.

Sweden. Sovereign (1751-1771 : Adolph Fredrik). Stadfästelse uppå directionens af Ost-Indiske Compagniet avertissement. Stockholm, Kongl. Tryckeriet [1753]. **S934**
An announcement of the sale of subscriptions to the Swedish East India Company.

Sweden. Sovereign (1751-1771 : Adolph Fredrik). Förklaring, öfwer thess then 19 sistledne Februarii utfärdade förbud emot Ost-Indiske sidentygers införsel och försälgning i riket ifrån början af år 1755. Stockholm, Kongl. Tryckeriet, 1754. **S935**
A proclamation and explanation of prohibition against the import and sale of East Indian silk cloth in the realm.

Sweden. Sovereign (1751-1771 : Adolph Fredrik). Kungiörelse, hwarefter the handlande och sjöfarande ... Stockholm, Kongl. Tryckeriet, 1756. **S936**
Instructions for merchants and traders during the present war between France and England.

Sweden. Sovereign (1751-1771 : Adolph Fredrik). Land-tulls och accis-ordning. Stockholm, Kongl. Tryckeriet, 1756. **S937**
Specific instructions for assessing and collecting various taxes, including customs duties and excise taxes.

Sweden. Sovereign (1751-1771 : Adolph Fredrik). Reglemente, för land-tulls och accis-kamrarne i riket. Stockholm, Kongl. Tryckeriet, 1756. **S938**
A handbook for officials at customhouses that covers procedures on operation, reports to be submitted, etc.

Sweden. Sovereign (1751-1771 : Adolph Fredrik). Taxa på inrikes land-tullen. Stockholm, Kongl. Tryckeriet [1756?]. **S939**
A schedule of duties for items carried in overland trade.

Sweden. Sovereign (1751-1771 : Adolph Fredrik). Brev til öfwer-ståthållaren och samtelige landshöfdingarne ... Stockholm, Kongl. Tryckeriet, 1757. **S940**
A royal letter to the chief governor and all sheriffs about the taxing of the privilege to use tea, coffee, and cocoa. It notes that since the importation of these items will soon cease, no special additional tax will be levied at this time.

Sweden. Sovereign (1751-1771 : Adolph Fredrik). Förklaring öfwer wisse stycken uti förordningen af then 27 Januarii 1757 ... Stockholm, Kongl. Tryckeriet [1757]. **S941**
A document containing the explanation of parts of an earlier ordinance concerning fradulent declaration of imports.

Sweden. Sovereign (1751-1771 : Adolph Fredrik). Nädiga publication, angående Levantiske handelen. Stockholm, Kongl. Tryckeriet [1757]. **S942**
A renewal of the charter of the Swedish Levant Company.

Sweden. Sovereign (1751-1771 : Adolph Fredrik). Publication, angående Levantiske handelen. Stockholm, Kongl. Tryckeriet, 1757. **S943**
A royal publication concerning the Levant trade.

Sweden. Sovereign (1751-1771 : Adolph Fredrik). Ytterligare kungiörelse, pa Kongl. Maj:ts nådigste befalning, angående uphandling af inkommande spannemål, miöl, gryn och ärter på torgen här i staden. [Stockholm] Kongl. Tryckeriet [1757]. **S944**

Sweden. Sovereign (1751-1771 : Adolph Fredrik). Kundgiörelse, angående the friheter och förmåner ... Levantiska handelen. Stockholm, Kongl. Tryckeriet, 1759. **S945**
A proclamation concerning the exemptions and privileges which the Swedish staple cities hereafter will enjoy in the free Levant trade.

Sweden. Sovereign (1751-1771 : Adolph Fredrik). Förklaring öfwer Kongl. förordningen af then 11. Martii 1748. [Stockholm] Kongl. Tryckeriet [1761]. S946
The royal explanation of an ordinance concerning ship clearers and their fees.

Sweden. Sovereign (1751-1771 : Adolph Fredrik). Bref til samtelige land-shöfdingarne, angående noga handhofwande ... Stockholm, Kongl. Tryckeriet [1762]. S947
A royal letter to sheriffs urging vigilance to prevent hoarding of grain or the use of it for illegal manufacture of liquor.

Sweden. Sovereign (1751-1771 : Adolph Fredrik). Frikallelse-bref för general tull-arrende-societeten. Stockholm, Kongl. Tryckeriet [1762]. S948
Concerns the lease of customs during 1748-55.

Sweden. Sovereign (1751-1771 : Adolph Fredrik). Kundgiörelse och påbud, til hämmande af landsköp med spannemäl, och olofligit brännewins brännande. [Stockholm] Kongl. Tryckeriet [1762]. S949

Sweden. Sovereign (1751-1771 : Adolph Fredrik). Octroi accordé par le roi pour la continuation de la navigation & du commerce aux Indes-Orientales. [Stockholm] Imprimerie Royale, 1762. S950
A continuation of the license of the Swedish East India Company for twenty years.

Sweden. Sovereign (1751-1771 : Adolph Fredrik). Privilegium angående fartens och handelens fortsättande på Ost-Indien. Stockholm, Kongl. Tryckeriet, 1762. S951
A royal charter concerning the continuation of commerce to the East Indies.

Sweden. Sovereign (1751-1771 : Adolph Fredrik). Stadfästelse uppå directionens af thet nya Ost-Indiska Compagniet avertissement, angående subscriptionernes emottagande och thenne handelens widare fortsättande med en ständig fond. Stockholm, Kongl. Tryckeriet, 1762. S952
The royal confirmation of the directorate of the new East-India Company's advertisement concerning acceptance of subscriptions and the continuation of this trade with a constant fund.

Sweden. Sovereign (1751-1771 : Adolph Fredrik). Brev til öfwer-ståthållaren och samtelige landshöfdingarne, angående taxerings längdernes noga granskning. Stockholm, Kongl. Tryckeriet, 1763. S953
A letter to the governor general and all sheriffs concerning careful perusal of the tax returns.

Sweden. Sovereign (1751-1771 : Adolph Fredrik). Brev til samtelige consistorierne, angående, huruwida en prestman, som blifwit upförd på förslag til någon ledig lägenhet ... Stockholm, Kongl. Tryckeriet, 1763. S954
Concerns whether a priest who has been recommended for a vacancy may be allowed to refuse appointment, and stipulates that when a priest has applied for a position he may not refuse it later.

Sweden. Sovereign (1751-1771 : Adolph Fredrik). Förordning, angående stora sio-tullens betalande hädanefter. Stockholm, Kongl. Tryckeriet, 1765. S955
Payment of the great sea customs may be made only in gold or silver or coins of those metals.

Sweden. Sovereign (1751-1771 : Adolph Fredrik). Förklaring, angående then genom förordningen af then 19 Junii. Stockholm, Kongl. Tryckeriet, 1766. S956
The explanation of an ordinance giving rules for clearing of the sea customs.

Sweden. Sovereign (1751-1771 : Adolph Fredrik). Förordning, angående landt-tulls-och accis-märket. Stockholm, Kongl. Tryckeriet, 1766. S957
A rather detailed description of changes in procedures, fines, and clarification of conflicting statements in earlier ordinances and decrees.

Sweden. Sovereign (1751-1771 : Adolph Fredrik). Förordning, angående straff för them, som wid timande sjöskador icke lemna skyndesam hjelp och handräckning. Stockholm, Kongl. Tryckeriet, 1766. S958
An ordinance concerning penalties for those who do not give immediate aid and help at the time of sea mishaps.

Sweden. Sovereign (1751-1771 : Adolph Fredrik). Förordning, til lurendrägeriers hämmande. Stockholm, Kongl. Tryckeriet, 1766. S959
Restricts fraudulent activities, with more severe measures prescribed for the control of illegal entry or sale of goods which are forbidden.

Sweden. Sovereign (1751-1771 : Adolph Fredrik). Kundgiörelse, angående then landtmannen i gemen förundte seglations friheten innom riket til thess warors och afwels, afsättande. Stockholm, Kongl. Tryckeriet, 1766. S960
Gives generally extended freedom of movement by sea within the realm for the sale of goods and animals by the peasants.

Sweden. Sovereign (1751-1771 : Adolph Fredrik). Ytterligare kundgiörelse, angående gatukiöp och olaga handel, samt förkiöp och mångleri jemte the för wederbörande utfärdade taxors nogare efterlefnad. [Stockholm] Kongl. Tryckeriet [1767].   S961

Sweden. Sovereign (1751-1771 : Adolph Fredrik). Kundgiörelse, angående inkommande stora siö-tullens erläggande och clarerande i Swenska specie riksdaler. Stockholm, Kongl. Tryckeriet, 1768.   S962
A proclamation for payment of customs duties in Swedish rather than foreign currency.

Sweden. Sovereign (1751-1771 : Adolph Fredrik). Kundgiörelse, ut inwånare i städerne, som begifwa sig med waror til försälgning å marknader, böra förse sig med wederbörande magistraters bewis om theras rättighet thertil. [Stockholm] Kongl. Tryckeriet [1769].   S963

Sweden. Sovereign (1751-1771 : Adolph Fredrik). Förklaring, angående then tull-frihet ... Stockholm, Kongl. Tryckeriet, 1770.   S964
An explanation of the customs exemptions which foreign ministers and ambassadors who arrive at court are to receive.

Sweden. Sovereign (1751-1771 : Adolph Fredrik). Kundgörelse, angående låne-banco attesters på courant silf:mt emottagande i betalning ... Stockholm, Kongl. Tryckeriet, 1770.
S965

Sweden. Sovereign (1751-1771 : Adolph Fredrik). Taxa, hwarefter stora siö-tullen uppå alla utgående waror bör erläggas och upbäras. Stockholm, Grefingska Tryckeriet [1770].
S966
A schedule of tariffs for goods leaving Sweden by sea.

Sweden. Sovereign (1751-1771 : Adolph Fredrik). Hamm-ordning. Stockholm, Grefingska Tryckeriet, 1771.   S967
A regulation covering procedures and penalties to be used by court authorities in fishing ports.

Sweden. Sovereign (1771-1792 : Gustaf III). Taxa, hwarefter stora siö-tullen uppå alla inkommande waror bör erläggas och upbäras. Stockholm, Grefingska Tryckeriet [1771].   S968
A schedule of tariffs on imports by sea, with instructions and official correspondence relating to this schedule.

Sweden. Sovereign (1771-1792 : Gustaf III). Instruction, hwarefter thess och riksens Cammar-Collegium, uti thet, som tull-werket angå kan, har sig at rätta. Stockholm, Kongl. Tryckeriet, 1772.   S969
A royal instruction according to which the government authorities are to act, with regard to the customs administration.

Sweden. Sovereign (1771-1792 : Gustaf III). [Circulair om förtekningar på tienste befordringar med accord wid militairen.] [Stockholm, 1773.]   S970
A circular and attached form for reporting payments to the pension fund for officers with the military.

Sweden. Sovereign (1771-1792 : Gustaf III). Förordning, huru förhållas bör med utgående tullens och öfrige afgifters beräknande ... Stockholm, Kongl. Boktryckare, 1773.   S971
An ordinance concerning procedures for the assessment of duties on goods which are being exported on locally built ships, when these ships depart from the country the first time.

Sweden. Sovereign (1771-1792 : Gustaf III). Förordning, huru förhållas bör med utgående tullens och öfrige afgifters beräknande för the waror, som utföras med här i riket för främmandes räkning bygda fartyg; när thesse fartyg första gången härifrån afgå m.m. Stockholm, Henr. Fougt, 1773.   S972

Sweden. Sovereign (1771-1792 : Gustaf III). Kongl. Maj:ts nädiga privilegium för et compagnie ... hwalfisk-fange wid Grönland och Straet Davis. Stockholm, H. Fougt, 1774.   S973
A charter issued to the Greenland and Davis Strait Whaling Company of Sweden.

Sweden. Sovereign (1771-1792 : Gustaf III). Kungörelse, angående tiden til muntring meddem, som ärhållit tillstånd, at idka månglerie-handel. Stockholm, Lars Salvius [1774].   S974

Sweden. Sovereign (1771-1792 : Gustaf III). Förordning, rörande hwad i akttagas bör, wid inhemska fartygs, farkosters och båtars passerande förbi rikets större och mindre fästningar. Stockholm, Kongl. Boktryckare, 1775.
S975
An ordinance regarding procedures to be followed by Swedish ships and boats when passing the fortresses of the realm.

Sweden. Sovereign (1771-1792 : Gustaf III). Circulaire-bref til Öfwer-ståthållaren och samtelige collegier, landshöfdingar och chefer, angående thet nya general tull-arrendet. Stockholm, Kongl. Boktryckare, 1776.   S976
A royal circular letter regarding the new general customs lease.

Sweden. Sovereign (1771-1792 : Gustaf III). Förnyade nådige land-tulls-och accis-taxa. Stockholm, Kongl. Boktryckare, 1776.   S977
The renewal of a schedule of duties on goods carried overland, with exchange rates for money.

Sweden. Sovereign (1771-1792 : Gustaf III).
Kungörelse, angående et nytt general-tull-arrende. Stockholm, Kongl. Boktryckare, 1776.
S978
Concerns a new general customs lease.

Sweden. Sovereign (1771-1792 : Gustaf III).
Förnyade nådige taxa, hwarefter landt-tullen och accisen kommer at upbäras. Stockholm, Kongl. Tryckeriet [1777].
S979
The renewal of a tariff on goods shipped overland, with exceptions noted.

Sweden. Sovereign (1771-1792 : Gustaf III).
Kungörelse och förbud emot owarsamt umgäende med eld och tobaks rökande pa wissa ställen här i staden. Stockholm, Kongl. Tryckeriet [1777].
S980

Sweden. Sovereign (1771-1792 : Gustaf III).
Kungörelse och förklaring, angående siö-mäns befrielse ifrån personelle utskylder. Stockholm, Kongl. Tryckeriet [1777].
S981
As an encouragement for seamen to remain in Sweden, the king exempts them from personal taxes.

Sweden. Sovereign (1771-1792 : Gustaf III).
Förordning, angående uphörandet af finska allmogens seglations frihet på Revel. Stockholm, Kongl. Tryckeriet, 1779.
S982
An ordinance concerning the termination of freedom for the Finns to sail to Revel.

Sweden. Sovereign (1771-1792 : Gustaf III).
Förordning och påbud, angående Swenska coopvaerdie skeppares skyldighet ... Stockholm, Kongl. Tryckeriet, 1779.
S983
A proclamation requiring all merchant shippers to have actual residence in Sweden, indicating that those who have attained rights of citizenship are to bring their families to Sweden, or forfeit those rights.

Sweden. Sovereign (1771-1792 : Gustaf III).
Kungörelse, om tiden infrån hwilken thy förnyade siö-tulls taxorne komma at taga theras början. Stockholm, Kongl. Tryckeriet, 1782.
S984
A proclamation about the time when the renewed sea-customs tariffs will become effective.

Sweden. Sovereign (1771-1792 : Gustaf III).
Taxa, hwarefter afgiften til Kongl. Maj:t och Kronan, uppå de waror, som ifrån Ost-Indien med Swenska skepp ... Stockholm, Kongl. Tryckeriet, 1782.
S985
A customs tariff according to which goods from the East Indies which have arrived on Swedish ships and which will remain in the realm will be counted and paid for.

Sweden. Sovereign (1771-1792 : Gustaf III).
Taxa, hwarefter stora siö-tullen uppå alla inkommande waror beräknas och erlägges. Stockholm, Kongl. Tryckeriet, 1782.
S986
A schedule of import duties.

Sweden. Sovereign (1771-1792 : Gustaf III).
Taxa, hwarefter stora siö-tullen uppå alla utgående waror, beräknas och erlägges. Stockholm, Kongl. Tryckeriet, 1782.
S987
A schedule of export tariffs.

Sweden. Sovereign (1771-1792 : Gustaf III).
Kungörelse, angående befrielse infrån land-tull å tak-skiffer, samt rå och obränd kakl-sten. Stockholm, Kongl. Tryckeriet, 1783.
S988
A proclamation concerning exemption of roofing stone and raw, unburned chalkstone from internal customs duties.

Sweden. Sovereign (1771-1792 : Gustaf III).
Taxa, hwarefter tullen uppå utgående och inkommande waror. Stockholm, Kongl. Tryckeriet, 1783.
S989
A schedule of import and export duties for goods entering or leaving at the Russian and Norwegian borders.

Sweden. Sovereign (1771-1792 : Gustaf III).
Förordning, angående nederlagsfriheten å salt och spannemål. Stockholm, Kongl. Tryckeriet, 1785.
S990
A proclamation concerning free port privileges for salt and grains.

Sweden. Sovereign (1771-1792 : Gustaf III).
Förordning, til hämmande af lurendrägerier. Stockholm, Kongl. Tryckeriet, 1785.
S991
A royal ordinance concerning the prevention of illegal commercial activities.

Sweden. Sovereign (1771-1792 : Gustaf III).
Kungörelse, som förklarar ön St. Barthelemy i Westindien för en fri hamn eller Porto Franco. Stockholm, Kongl. Tryckeriet [1785].
S992

Sweden. Sovereign (1771-1792 : Gustaf III).
Nådiga reglemente, angående styrelsenå ön St. Barthelemy i West-Indien. Stockholm, Kongl. Tryckeriet [1786].
S993
Nine provisions concerning the government and commerce of the Swedish colony on St. Barthélemy.

Sweden. Sovereign (1771-1792 : Gustaf III).
Nådige kungörelse, til hämmande af obetänkte utflyttningar til ön St. Barthelemy. Stockholm, Kongl. Tryckeriet [1786].
S994
Because of the meager resources of the island of St. Barthélemy in the West Indies, efforts should be made to discourage Swedes from settling there.

Sweden. Sovereign (1771-1792 : Gustaf III).
Seglations-ordning; gifwen i lägret wid

ladugårdsgärdet then 15 Junii 1774. Stockholm, Kongl. Tryckeriet, 1787. S995
Quite detailed instructions and regulations pertaining to sailing and navigation.

Sweden. Sovereign (1771-1792 : Gustaf III). Kungörelse, angående förmoner för them, som godwilligt antaga tienst på Kongl. Maj:ts orlogsskepp och fartyg ... Stockholm, Kongl. Tryckeriet, 1789. S996
A proclamation concerning special privileges for those who voluntarily serve on royal warships in the forthcoming sea expedition.

Sweden. Sovereign (1771-1792 : Gustaf III). Reglemente, hwarefter upbördsmän och redogörare wid alla kronans magaziner, samt under sjo-expeditioner om skeppsbord, måge sig til godo beräkna afgången å the under händer hafwande upbörder af spanmål och proviantversedlar, samt huru förhållas bör wid skeende gryn-och miölförmalning. Stockholm, Kongl. Tryckeriet [1790]. S997

Sweden. Sovereign (1771-1792 : Gustaf III). Förordning, angående tiden så wäl för borgenårer å öen St. Barthelemy at bewaka deras fordringar uti de inom Sweriges rike sig yppande concurs-twister, som ock för borgenärer här inom riket at likaledes deras rätt i akt taga uti dylika å berörde ö förefallande mål. Stockholm, Kongl. Tryckeriet, 1791. S998

Sweden. Sovereign (1771-1792 : Gustaf III). Kungörelse, angående den af win, bränwin och caffé bestådde skepps-provision. Stockholm, Kongl. Tryckeriet, 1791. S999
Concerns the amounts of wine, liquor, and coffee allowable as ships' stores.

Sweden. Sovereign (1792-1809 : Gustaf IV Adolph). Kungörelse, hwarefter Swenske handlande och skepps-rederier ... Stockholm, Kongl. Tryckeriet, 1793. S1000
A proclamation according to which Swedish merchants and ship owners are to conduct trade and shipping in order to utilize Swedish neutrality during present war activities.

Sweden. Sovereign (1792-1809 : Gustaf IV Adolph). Kungörelse, angående dels förbud emot införsel af wisse utländske waror. Stockholm, Kongl. Tryckeriet [1794]. S1001
Prohibition of some imports and higher duties on some others.

Sweden. Sovereign (1792-1809 : Gustaf IV Adolph). Kungörelse, angående caffés införande och nyttjande tils widare. Stockholm, Kongl. Tryckeriet, 1796. S1002
Temporarily at least, the use of imported coffee will be allowed, subject to old customs rates.

Sweden. Sovereign (1792-1809 : Gustaf IV Adolph). Förordning angående hwad bolag i akt taga böra ... Stockholm, Kongl. Tryckeriet, 1798. S1003
A proclamation concerning what those companies which are incorporated or have special signatures should consider when engaged in commerce and factory business.

Sweden. Sovereign (1792-1809 : Gustaf IV Adolph). Kungörelse angående dels et lättare och säkrare beräknande af den tull-förhögning, som, til Medelländska Sjo-fartens fredande, den 2 Februarii 1797 blifwit i nåder påbuden, och dels en widare tilökning i denna inkomst, til bestridande af de kostnader som för den innewarande år anbefaldte convoy-expedition äro af nöden. Stockholm, Kongl. Tryckeriet [1798]. S1004

Sweden. Sovereign (1792-1809 : Gustaf IV Adolph). Kungörelse, angående förbud emot oloflig handel och uplag af lurendrägade waror i rikets skärgårdar. Stockholm, Kongl. Tryckeriet, 1798. S1005
Prohibits illegal commerce and storing of smuggled goods in the archipelagoes of the realm.

Sweden. Sovereign (1792-1809 : Gustaf IV Adolph). Kungörelse angående tullens nedsättande a hwita Bomullslärfter, som från Ost-Indien och Bengalen ankomma. Stockholm, Kongl. Tryckeriet, 1798. S1006
A general levy of import duties on goods brought into Sweden from the East Indies.

Sweden. Sovereign (1792-1809 : Gustaf IV Adolph). Kungörelse, om pensioner för sådane afskedstagande civile embets-och tjenstemän ... Stockholm, Kongl. Tryckeriet, 1798. S1007
A proclamation concerning pensions for civil servants and officials who retire before reaching the age of seventy.

Sweden. Sovereign (1792-1809 : Gustaf IV Adolph). Kungörelse, angående den förledit år å convoyafgisten utsatte tilöknings fortfarande. Stockholm, Kongl. Tryckeriet, 1799. S1008
Continues the increased convoy charge of the previous year.

Sweden. Sovereign (1792-1809 : Gustaf IV Adolph). Kungörelse, angående förnyande af det uti förordningen under den 1 Januarii 1794 stadgada förbud emot caffés införsel och bruk. Stockholm, Kongl. Tryckeriet, 1799. S1009
Concerns renewal of prohibition against the import and use of coffee as established in the proclamation of January 1, 1794.

Sweden. Sovereign (1792-1809 : Gustaf IV Adolph). Taxa ... som infrån Ost-Indien med

Swenska skepp inkomma

Swenska skepp inkomma ... Stockholm, Kongl. Tryckeriet, 1799. S1010
A list of products from the East Indies, and the duties they must pay on entry into Sweden in Swedish ships.

Sweden. Sovereign (1792-1809 : Gustaf IV Adolph). Taxa, hwarefter afgiften til Kongl. Maj:t och Kronan uppå de waror, som ifrån Ost-Indien med Swenska skepp ... Stockholm, Kongl. Tryckeriet, 1799. S1011
A tariff according to which the customs to His Majesty will be counted and paid on goods imported from the East Indies on Swedish ships.

Sweden. Sovereign (1792-1809 : Gustaf IV Adolph). Taxa, hwarefter stora siö-tullen uppå alla inkommande waror beräknas och erlägges. Stockholm, Kongl. Tryckeriet, 1799. S1012
A schedule of import duties with special instructions for irregular cases.

Sweden. Sovereign (1792-1809 : Gustaf IV Adolph). Taxa, hwarefter stora siö-tullen uppå alla utgående waror beräknas och erlägges. Stockholm, Kongl. Tryckeriet, 1799. S1013
A schedule of export duties with instructions for making exceptions on certain items.

Sweden. Sovereign (1792-1809 : Gustaf IV Adolph). Warning och förbud, emot gemenskap och handel met utländske kapare. Stockholm, Kongl. Tryckeriet, 1799. S1014
Prohibits commerce with foreign pirates.

Sweden. Sovereign (1792-1809 : Gustaf IV Adolph). Kongl. Maj:ts nådiga reglemente för Swenska handelssjöfarten under krigstider; gifwid St. Petersburg den 23 December 1800. Stockholm, Kongl. Tryckeriet, 1801. S1015
Regulations governing Swedish commercial shipping in time of war.

Sweden. Sovereign (1792-1809 : Gustaf IV Adolph). Privilegium, til befrämjande af Swenska handelsfarten på Ost-Indien. Stockholm, Kongl. Tryckeriet [1806]. S1016

Sweden. Sovereign (1809-1818 : Charles XIII). Nådiga kungörelse angående Ost-Indiska Compagniets uplösning, och handelns på Ost-Indien öpnande för en hwar, som deruti wil deltaga. Stockholm, Kongl. Tryckeriet, 1814. S1017
A proclamation concerning the dissolution of the Swedish East India Company, removing its exclusive privileges and opening the trade to any merchant.

Sweden. Sovereign (1809-1818 : Charles XIII). Privilegium för ett bolag, kalladt Östersjö Compagniet. Stockholm, Kongl. Tryckeriet, 1815. S1018

Sweden. Sovereign (1809-1818 : Charles XIII). Reglor för det genom Kongl. Maj:ts nådiga privilegium af den 25 Januarii 1815 octroyerade bolag, kalladt Östersjö-Compagniet. Stockholm, Kongl. Tryckeriet, 1815. S1019

Sweden. Sovereign (1818-1844 : Charles XIV John). Kungörelse, angående särskilde föreskrifter i afseende å den stapel städernas handlande och skeppsredare åliggande skyldighet ... Stockholm, Kongl. Tryckeriet, 1828. S1020
A special regulation pertaining to the responsibility of merchants and ship owners in staple towns to keep and import certain quantities of salt.

Sweden. Sovereign (1818-1844 : Charles XIV John). Kungörelse, angående skeppsredares och handlandes i stapelstäderna skyldighet ... Stockholm, Kongl. Tryckeriet, 1829. S1021
Ship owners and merchants in staple towns are responsible for importing, producing, and maintaining certain quantities of salt.

Sweden. Treaties, etc. Instrumentum pacis ... tusschen beyder zijts plenipotentiairen, keyserlijck en Koncklijcke Zweetsche. Amsterdam, Jan van Hilten, 1648. S1022
Articles of peace between the Holy Roman Empire and Sweden, with provision for restoration of trade between them.

Sweden. Treaties, etc. Tractaet van elucidatie of nader verklaringe. Middelburg, F. Croock, 1660. S1023
A treaty between the Netherlands and Sweden, containing schedules of duties on a variety of goods.

Sweden. Treaties, etc. Tractatus, inter regem Sueciae ... atque Ordines Generales Foederati Belgi ... The Hague, Vidua ac haeredum Hillebrandi Jacobi à Wouw, 1661. S1024
A commercial treaty of 1659 between Sweden and the Netherlands defining duties on Swedish goods imported into the Netherlands.

Sweden. Treaties, etc. Tractaet, tusschen den Coninck van Sweeden, ende de ... Staten Generael. The Hague, Hillebrandt van Wouw, 1662. S1025
A Dutch edition of the treaty of 1659 between Sweden and the Netherlands.

Sweden. Treaties, etc. Extract och uthtog uthaff ... Swerige och ... Store Britannien angående commereierne är affhandlat och bewiliat ... Stockholm, Georg Hantsch, 1666. S1026
Extracts of the commercial agreement between Sweden and Britain.

Sweden. Treaties, etc. Tractat van navigatie en commercie tusschen ... Sweeden ... ende ...

Vereenighde Nederlanden. The Hague, Jacob Scheltus, 1676. S1027
An agreement on commercial matters, contraband, etc.

Sweden. Treaties, etc. Tractatus de commerciis et navigatione ... The Hague, Jacob Scheltus, 1676. S1028
Latin edition of the above treaty.

Sweden. Treaties, etc. Tractatus de commerciis, inter ... Carolum Suecorum ... regem, &c. ab una & ... Ordines Generales Foederatarum Belgii Provinciarum ... The Hague, J. Scheltus, 1676. S1029
A treaty of commerce between Sweden and the Netherlands.

Sweden. Treaties, etc. Tractaat van commercie, navigatie en marine ... tusschen ... Sweden ... en ... Vereenigde Nederlanden. The Hague, Jacob Scheltus, 1681. S1030
A naval and commercial treaty between the Netherlands and Sweden, setting forth commercial restrictions and specifying a large measure of free trade.

Sweden. Treaties, etc. Tractatus de commerciis et navigatione ... The Hague, J. Scheltus, 1681. S1031
Latin edition of the treaty of Nijmegen.

Sweden. Treaties, etc. Handels-och navigations tractat, emellan Kongl. Maj:t och Kronan Swerige, och then Turchl. Ottomanniske Porten; afhandlad och sluten i Constantinopel then 10 Januarii, åhr 1737. Stockholm, Kongl. Tryckeriet [1737]. S1032

Sweden. Treaties, etc. Freds och handels tractat, emellan ... Swerige och Republiquen Tripolis. Stockholm, Kongl. Tryckeriet, 1741. S1033
A treaty of peace and trade between Sweden and the Republic of Tripoli.

Sweden. Treaties, etc. Préliminaire handels och navigations convention, emellan Kongl. Maj:t och Cronan Swerige, och hans aller Christeligaste Maj:t Konungen i Frankrike. Afhandlad och sluten i Versailles then 25 April 1741 och ratificerad i Stockholm then 4 Maii samma år. Stockholm, Kongl. Tryckeriet [1741]. S1034

Sweden. Treaties, etc. Handels tractat emmellan Kongl. Maj:t och Cronan Swerige och Kongl. Majestät af Bägge Sicilierne. Afhandlad och sluten i Paris then 30 Junii år 1742. Stockholm, Kongl. Tryckeriet, 1744. S1035

Sweden. Treaties, etc. Provisionelle convention, til förklarande af préliminaire conventionen, rörande handeln och siöfarten, af then 25 April år 1741, emellen Hans Kongl. Maj:t af Swerige och Hans Aldrachristligaste Maj:t Konungen af Frankrike. Stockholm, Kongl. Tryckeriet, 1785. S1036

Sweden. Treaties, etc. Wänskaps och handels tractat emellan ... Swerige och the Förente Staterne i Norra America. Stockholm, Kongl. Tryckeriet, 1785. S1037
A treaty of amity and commerce between Sweden and the United States. It was negotiated in Paris by Benjamin Franklin in 1783.

Sweden. Treaties, etc. Wänskaps-handels-och sjöfarts förbund emellan Hans Maj:t Konungen af Swerige å ena, samt Hans Maj:t Keisaren af Ryssland å andra sidan; afhandladt och afslutit i S:t Petersburg den 1/13 Martii 1801 ... Stockholm, Kongl. Tryckeriet, 1801. S1038

Sweden. Treaties, etc. Convention de commerce & de navigation, entre Sa Majesté le Roi de Suède & de Norvège, & le Roi du royaume uni de la Grande Bretagne & de l'Irlande, conclue à Londres, le 18 Mars 1826. Stockholm, l'Imprimerie Royale, 1826. S1039

Sweden. Treaties, etc. Handels-och sjöfarts-tractat emellan Hans Maj:t Konungen af Swerige och Norrige, å ena, samt Hans Maj:t Konungen af det förenade riket Stora Britannien och Irland, å andra sidan, afhandlad och sluten i London den 18 Martii 1826 ... Stockholm, Kongl. Tryckeriet, 1826. S1040

Sweden. Treaties, etc. Handels-och sjöfarts-tractat emellan Hans Maj:t Konungen af Swerige och Norrige, å ena, samt Hans Maj:t Konnugen af Dannemark, å andra sidan, afhandlad och sluten i Stockholm den 2 November 1826 ... Stockholm, Kongl. Tryckeriet, 1826. S1041

Sweden. Treaties, etc. Handels-och wänskapsconvention emellan Hans Maj:t Konungen af Swerige och Norrige, å ena, samt Hans Majestät Keisaren af Rysland, å andra sidan, afhandlad och sluten i S:t Petersburg den 26/14 Februarii 1828 ... Stockholm, Kongl. Tryckeriet, 1828. S1042

Sweerts, Pierre François. Insignium huius aevi poetarum lacrymae in obitum Cl. V. Abrahami Orteli Antverpiani ... Antwerp, Joannem Keerbergium, 1601. S1043
Poems in honor of Abraham Ortelius, cartographer.

Symes, Michael. An account of an embassy to the kingdom of Ava, sent by the governor-general of India, in the year 1795. London, W. Bulmer, 1800. S1044

An extensive account of Burma, illustrated by twenty-six copperplate engravings.

Symes, Michael. Relation de l'ambassade anglaise, envoyée en 1795 dans le royaume d'Ava. Paris, F. Buisson, 1800.　　S1045
The first French edition.

Symes, Michael. Relazione dell'ambasciata Inglese spedita nel 1795 nel regno d'Ava, o nell'impero dei Birmani. Naples, Nuovo Gabinetto Letterario, 1832.　　S1046
The second Italian edition, with hand-colored illustrations.

Symes, Michael. Resa till konungariket Ava, år 1795. Af Major M. Symes, Brittiska Ostindiska Compagniets sändebud. Stockholm, Henrik A. Nordström, 1805.　　S1047
An abridged edition, translated from the German edition of 1801.

Symonds, John. Remarks upon an essay intituled, The history of the colonization of the free states of antiquity, applied to the present contest between Great Britain and her American colonies. London, J. Nichols, 1778.　　S1048
Symonds attacks his opponent, William Barron, on numerous points of fact and interpretation, contending above all that the ancients had no pretense at establishing governments based on freedom of their subjects.

Sympson, Anthony. A short, easy, and effective method to prevent the running of wool, etc., from Great Britain and Ireland to foreign parts. London, 1741.　　S1049
Advocates a more effective supervision of wool producers, a higher export duty, and more diligent patrol of the coast.

Synod of Diamper. Synodo diocesano da igreia e bispado de Angamale dos antigos Christiãos de Sam Thome das serras do Malavar das partes da India Oriental. Coimbra, Diogo Gomez Loureyro, 1606.　　S1050
A statement of religious observances and practices to be put into effect among the St. Thomas Christians of India.

Syria, Pedro de. Arte de la verdadera navegacion. Valencia, Juan Chrysostomo Garriz, 1602.
　　S1051
A navigation text in the tradition of the sixteenth-century cosmographies, including geographical and astronomical information.

T

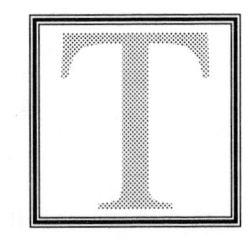

[T. S. (Thomas Smith).] England's danger by Indian manufactures. [n.p., 1693?]   T1
    The work is an attack on Indian manufactures and the harm they cause domestic industries.

Tabago: or A geographical description ... together with a full representation of the produce and other advantages ... of that famous island. London, W. Reeves [1753].   T2
    A description of Tobago with respect to its commercial advantages. Also a history of the European settlements on the island.

Tableau général du commerce de l'Europe, avec l'Afrique, les Indes Orientales et l'Amérique. London; Paris, Desenne, 1787.   T3
    General survey of world commerce, noting particularly the major regions with which European merchants traded.

Tabula Christiane religionis valde utilis et necessaria cuilibet Christiano quam omnes scire tenentur. [Rome, Stephan Plannck, ca. 1495.]   T4
    A handbook of Christian doctrine, undoubtedly published for use by pilgrims to the Holy Land.

[Tachard, Guy.] Voyage de Siam ... Paris, A. Seneuze et D. Horthemels, 1686.   T5
    Observations made by a member of a commercial mission from France to Siam.

[Tachard, Guy.] A relation of the voyage to Siam. London, Printed by T.B. for J. Robinson and A. Churchil, 1688.   T6
    The first English edition.

Tachard, Guy. Second voyage ... au royame de Siam. Paris, D. Horthemels, 1689.   T7
    An account of a voyage to Siam undertaken in 1687.

Tailfer, Patrick. A true and historical narrative of the colony of Georgia in America. London, Printed for P. Timothy, in Charles-Town, South-Carolina [1741].   T8
    A criticism of the governors of the Georgia settlement for unwise policies in regard to government and trade there.

Taisnier, Joannes. Opusculum perpetua memoria dignissimum, de natura magnetis, et eius effectibus. Cologne, J. Birckmannum, 1562.   T9
    Taisnier believed that the magnet could cause perpetual motion and includes a plan for a perpetual motion machine. Tides and the relation of a ship's hull to its speed are discussed.

[Taitbout.] Essai sur l'isle d'Otahiti, située dans la Mer du Sud; et sur l'esprit et les moeurs de ses habitans. Avignon; Paris, Froullé, 1779.   T10
    A description of Tahiti taken from the accounts of Cook and Bougainville with a view to comparing the civilizations of Europe and Tahiti, to the latter's advantage.

Tamayo de Vargas, Tomás. Restauracion de la ciudad del Salvador ... en la provincia del Brasil. Madrid, Viuda de Alonso Martin [1628].   T11
    An account of the struggle between the Dutch and the Portuguese in Brazil as well as a commentary on Dutch commercial ambitions there.

Tamburini, Michel Angelo. Declaration ou soumission ... des Jesuites assemblés à Rome l'an mil sept cens onze aux decrets du Pape Clement XI qui condamnent les ceremonies chinoises. [n.p.] 1712.   T12
    Includes four documents relative to the submission of the Jesuits to Papal authority in the matter of the Chinese Rites.

Tankar om fri handel. Götheborg, Lars Wahlström, 1779.   T13
    The notes to this brief essay on free trade indicate that it was inspired by Adam Smith's *Wealth of Nations*, and Raynal's *Tableau de l'Europe*.

Tankar om Swenska sjöfarten, eller den så kallade kraft-handeln. Stockholm, Grefingska Tryckeriet, 1771. T14
Discusses the Swedish economic system and the importance within it of shipping and trade.

Tankar, om tobaks-planteringens nytta och skada. Stockholm, Kongl. Tryckeriet, 1748. T15
An argument, pro and con, relative to the economic advantage of trying to produce tobacco in Sweden, possibly at the expense of other crops.

Tanner, John. A narrative of the captivity and adventures of John Tanner ... during thirty years residence among the Indians in the interior of North America. New York, G. & C. & H. Carvill, 1830. T16
Tanner's captivity covered the period 1790 to 1820, and took him into the Red River district where he noted the activities of the Hudson's Bay Company and the Northwest Company and the conflicts between them.

Tapp, David. Funffzehen Jährige curiöse und denck-würdige ... ost-indianische Reise-Beschreibung. Hanover & Wolffenbüttel, Gottfried Freytag, 1704. T17
The author was in the East Indies from 1667 to 1682. He describes the regions he visited and the commodities they produced, and gives a picture of life aboard a ship in the trade.

Tarbé, Charles. Rapport sur les troubles de Saint-Domingue, fait à l'Assemblée nationale ... au nom de Comité colonial, le 10 décembre 1791. Paris, Imprimerie Nationale, 1791. T18
A history of events in the French colony of Saint Domingue through 1791, a narrative history followed by extensive "pieces justificatives" describing the origins and development of the rebellion.

Targa, Carlo. Ponderazioni sopra le contrattazioni marittime. Leghorn, Giovanni Paolo Fantechi, 1755. T19
A collection of essays on numerous topics relating to maritime commerce and law.

Targowissko, Johannes de. Oratoris ad Innocencium octauum pō[n]tificem. [Rome: Printed by Bartholomaeus Guldinbeck, after 26 May 1486.] T20
An oration made on behalf of King Casimir of Poland and Lithuania announcing that monarch's intentions to forestall Turkish advances from the east by an expedition into Moldavia.

The tarif settled by the French king and council, September 18, 1664. Edinburgh, George Stewart, 1713. T21
This tariff, relating to goods shipped from Great Britain to France, is extracted from Colbert's tariff of 1664.

Tarih-i Hind-i garbî veya Hadîs-i nev : A history of the discovery of America. [Istanbul, Turkey] Historical Research Foundation, Istanbul Center, 1987. T22
A facsimile of the Ottoman Turkish manuscript work compiled from various European sources to inform Sultan Murad III (1546-1595) of the European discoveries in North and South America. There is an English translation of the second part, covering the discoveries.

Tarleton, Lieutenant-General (Banastre). A history of the campaigns of 1780 and 1781, in the southern provinces of North America. London, T. Cadell, 1787. T23
A history of the final stages of the American Revolution, with maps depicting the major battles.

Tasca, Giovanni Pietro. Relatione del viaggio d'Alessandria d'Egitto: Con il negotiati, chi Mons. di Breves seco ne' regni di Tunisi, e d'Algieri; l'anno 1606. Manuscript. [Italy, ca. 1606.] T24
This is an account of the embassy of François Savary de Brèves to Tunis and Algiers in 1606. The author of the manuscript accompanied him from Alexandria to his destination and thence to Marseille the following year.

Tatarinov, Mikhail. Okuratnaia karta chasti Kamchatki. Manuscript. [Irkutsk, 1781.] T25
This map appears to have been made as a means for Russian authorities to record the voyage of Captain Cook in the Bering Sea area, 1779. It has additions in English attributed to Peter Simon Pallas.

Taube, Friedrich Wilhelm von. Geschichte der engländishcen Handelschaft, Manufacturen, Colonien, und Schiffarth. Leipzig, Johann Paul Kraus, 1776. T26
In addition to being a history of English commerce, this is a commentary on the causes of the outbreak of the American Revolution.

Taube, Friedrich Wilhelm von. Abschilderung der engländischen Manufacturen, Handlung, Schiffahrt und Colonien, nach ihrer jetzigen Einrichtung und Beschaffenheit. Vienna, Johann Paul Kraus, 1777-78. T27
First published in 1774, this is a larger work than the previous title, and notes the major products and the structure of British overseas commerce.

Tausia-Bournos, M. Coup-d'oeil impartial sur les décrets de l'Assemblée national, relativement aux colonies. [Paris, L. Pottier de Lille, 1791.] T28
Calls attention to the inconsistencies between the laws relating to Saint Domingue and their interpretation to the detriment of stability in the colony.

Tavares de Vellez Guerreiro, João. Jornada, que Antonio de Albuquerque Coelho ... na China ... Lisbon, Officina da Musica, 1732. T29

A description of a journey into the interior of India with comments on the relation of this area to both Portuguese and English trade.

Tavernier, Jean-Baptiste. Les six voyages ... en Turquie, en Perse, et aux Indes. Paris, Gervais Clouzier & Claude Barbin, 1676. T30
The author was one of the most active French mercantile travelers of the seventeenth century, and reports extensively on the trade of places he visited in Asia.

Tavernier, Jean-Baptiste. Suite des voyages de Mr. Tavernier ... ou Nouveau recüeil de plusiers relations et traitez. Paris, Gervais Clouzier, 1679. T31
A supplement to the preceding work, with additional material on Japan, Indo-China, Persia and the Dutch management of trade in the East Indies. Contains numerous maps and views.

Tavernier, Jean-Baptiste. The six voyages of John Baptista Tavernier through Turky into Persia, and the East-Indies. London, R.L. and M.P., 1678. T32
The first English edition, translated by John Phillips.

Tavernier, Jean-Baptiste. Beschreibung der sechs Reisen ... in Türckey, Persien und Indien ... in der Hoch-Teutschen Sprach ans Liecht gestellt durch Johann Herman Widerhold. Geneva, 1681. T33
One of two German editions published in 1681. This edition includes Sir John Chardin's description of the coronation of Suliman III.

Tavernier, Jean-Baptiste. De zes reizen van de Heer J. Bapt. Tavernier. Amsterdam, Weduwe van Johannes van Someren, 1682. T34
The first illustrated edition of Tavernier's Asiatic travels. The translator was Jan Hendrik Glazemaker.

Tavernier, Jean-Baptiste. Recüeil de plusiers relations et traitez singuliers et curieux. Paris, Gervais Clouzier, 1679. T35
Another printing of the *Suite des voyages* of the same year.

Tavernier, Jean-Baptiste. A collection of several relations & treatises singular and curious. London, A. Godbid and J. Playford for M. Pitt, 1680. T36
The first English translation.

Tavernier, Jean-Baptiste. Vierzig-Jährige Reise-Beschreibung. Nuremberg, Johann Hofmann, 1681. T37
The first German edition, translated by Jean Menudier.

Tavernier, Jean-Baptiste. Viaggi nella Turchia, nella Persia, e nell' Indie ... Bologna, Gioseffo Longhi, 1690. T38
The second Italian edition.

Távora, Francisco de Assis de Távora, Marquês de. Proposta aos deputados da Junta ordenada por S. Mag[estad]e para dizerem os seus pareceres sobre a permissaó de possuirem Cafres os Mouros moradores de Mossambique com as condiçoens e obrigaçoens dispostas na provizaó de 24 de Janeiro de 1751. Manuscript. Mozambique, 4 August 1750; Goa, 23 January 1751, 23 November 1753. T39
These papers concern the legislation passed in Lisbon on 24 January 1751 which attempted to resolve the question of whether Moslem subjects of Portugal in Mozambique should be allowed to own slaves.

Taylor, John. Letters on India. London, S. Hamilton, 1800. T40
A series of twenty-six letters warning of the dangers to England's eastern trade, and suggesting means to improve it.

Taylor, John. Voyage dans l'Inde, au travers du grand désert, par Alep, Antioche, et Bassora ... traduit et enrichi de notes explicatives et critiques par L. de Grandpré. Paris, Genet, 1803. T41
A description of travels in the Near and Middle East with particular emphasis on routes, currencies, equipment, clothing, illnesses to be expected, and mercantile opportunities, with extensive notes by the translator.

Techo, Nicolás del, *originally* **Du Toict.** Historia provinciae Paraquariae Societatis Jesu. Liége, Joan. Mathiae Hovii, 1673. T42
In addition to describing the Jesuit mission in Paraguay, Techo also deals extensively with Chile and Argentina, portraying social life, growth of cities, war between indigenous peoples, etc.

Tegenwoordigen staat van Sweden. Antwerp, Stoffel Michiels, 1695. T43
An account of Sweden, discussing its commerce with various European countries, as well as giving a brief history of Swedish trade.

Tegucigalpa (Honduras). Real Aduana. [Collection of documents relating to customs duties collected in the jurisdiction of Tegucipalpa, Honduras.] Manuscript. Honduras, ca. 1788-1790. T44
Approximately 200 folio sheets (and smaller) concerning customs duties on chocolate, sugar, liquor, cheese, hogs, tobacco, sugar, fish, and soap. Includes salaries paid to the customs agents and references to the shipping between Honduras and Havana.

Teive, Diogo de. Commentarius de rebus in India ... Coimbra [Joannes Barreruis & Joannes Alvarus] 1548. T45
A history of the second siege of Diu in 1546.

Teixeira, Bento. Naufragio que passou Jorge de Albuquerque Coelho vindo do Brazil para este reyno no anno de 1565. Lisbon, 1736. T46

Teixeira, Pedro. Relaciones de ... un viage hecho ... dende la India oriental hasta Italia por tierra. Antwerp, H. Verdussen, 1610. T47
   Describes travel and trade in India, Persia, Africa, Mexico, and other regions in the period 1586 to 1604. It includes a history of the city of Ormuz.

Teixeira, Pedro. The history of Persia. London, Jonas Brown, 1715. T48
   A translation by Captain John Stevens of the previous work.

Temple, Sir William. Observations upon the United Provinces of the Netherlands. London, A. Maxwell for Sa. Gellibrand, 1673. T49
   An appraisal of Dutch commercial power, relating it to the geography of the region and the character of the people. An extensive historical background is also provided.

Temple, Sir William. Aenmerckingen over de Vereenighde Nederlandtsche provintien. Amsterdam, Jacob Vinckel, 1673. T50
   Dutch translation of the previous work.

Temple, Sir William. Brieven van de Heer William Temple; geschreven gedurende syne ambassade in 'sGravenhage, aan den grave van Arlington, en den ridder Jean Trevor ... The Hague, Meindert Uitwerf en Englebregt Boucquet, 1700. T51
   A collection of fifty letters, nearly all from 1668 to 1669, relating to Anglo-Dutch diplomacy involving overseas possessions and trade.

Templeman, Daniel. The secret history of the late directors of the South-Sea-Company. London, For the Author, 1735. T52
   Urges an inquiry into the affairs of the company.

Ten considerations in favour of the East-India Company. [London, ca. 1691.] T53
   Reasons for the continuation of the East India Company, noting that it had operated with considerable expense and risk.

Tench, Watkin. A narrative of the expedition to Botany Bay. London, J. Debrett, 1789. T54
   An account of the beginnings of the English settlement at Port Jackson by a captain of the marines who gives a careful evaluation of the prospects for success in the colonization of Australia.

Tench, Watkin. Voyage à la Baie Botanique; avec un description du nouveau pays de Galles meridional, de ses habitans, de ses productions, &c. & quelques détails relatifs a M. de la Peyrouse, pendant son séjour à la Baie Botanique ... Paris, Letellier, 1789. T55
   This edition includes a history of the discovery and exploration of Australia not found in the English edition.

Ternaux-Compans, Henri. Voyages, relations et mémoires ... de la découverte de l'Amérique ... Paris, Librarie de la Societé de Geographie de Paris, 1837. T56
   A twenty-volume set of translations of the early accounts of the explorers of Central and South America.

Terni. (Italy). Capitoli della fiera ... di Santa Lucia di Terni. Terni, Tomasso Guerrieri, 1638. T57
   A collection of regulations governing the fairs of Terni, first issued in 1594.

Terra Rossa, Vitale. Riflessioni geografiche circa le terre incognite ... Padua, Per il Cadorino, 1686. T58
   A glorification of Venetian contributions to the age of discovery, including accounts of Marco Polo, the Zeno brothers, and Cadamosto.

Terrick, Richard. A sermon preached before the incorporated Society for the Propagation of the Gospel in Foreign Parts, at their anniversary meeting in the parish church of St. Mary-le-Bow, on Friday February 17, 1764. London, E. Owen and T. Harrison, 1764. T59
   The sermon notes British commercial and military success as a great opportunity for the expansion of Christianity.

Terry, Edward. A voyage to East-India. London, T. W. for J. Martin and J. Allestrye, 1655. T60
   The author was chaplain to Sir Thomas Roe, and remained in India from 1616 to 1619. He comments on the peoples and products of the regions he visited, including South Africa.

Texeron, Melchor. [Autograph letter signed.] Cadiz, November 26, 1797. T61
   Texeron's account of his crossing from Puerto Rico to Cadiz in a Spanish commercial ship, including descriptions of evading British warships, the serious miscalculation of course, and news of the blockade of Cadiz by the British.

Thailand. Embassy. France. Harangue faite a Sa Majesté par les ambassadeurs du Roy de Siam le mardy 14 janvier 1687 à leur audience de Congé. Lyons, Antoine Jullieron [1687]. T62
   The speech was delivered at the conclusion of ambassador Kōsā Pan's visit.

Thelaus, Johann Christian. Dissertatio ... De Piratica. Uppsala, Werner, 1716. T63
   A legal study that considers the role of governments in matters of piracy and covers questions of jurisdiction and hostage taking. Viking and African piracy are specifically mentioned.

Thevenet, Father. [Exhortations in the Algonquian language.] Manuscript. [n.p.] 1806-1808.
T64
A handbook carried by missionaries for use in preaching to the Indians.

Thévenot, Jean de. Reisen in Europa, Asia und Africa, worinnen gehandelt wird von der morgenländischen Reise, und unter andern denen unterthänigen Herrschafften des Gross-Türcken denen Sitten, Religionen, Machten ... dieses grossen Reichs ... Frankfurt am Mayn, Philipp Fievet, 1693.
T65
The first German edition of all three parts of Thévenot's travels.

Thévenot, Jean de. Relation d'un voyage fait au Levant. Paris, L. Billaine, 1665.
T66
Contains observations on the peoples of Turkey, Palestine, and North Africa.

Thévenot, Jean de. The travels of Monsieur de Thevenot into the Levant. In three parts. Viz. into I. Turkey. II. Persia. III. The East Indies. London, H. Clark for H. Faithorne [etc.] 1687.
T67
The first English translation of the previous work.

Thévenot, Jean de. Voyages de Mr. de Thévenot tant en Europe qu'en Asie & en Afrique divisez en trois parties, qui comprement cinq volumes ... Paris, Charles Angot, 1689.
T68
The first French edition under one imprint, including the accounts of travel in the Levant, India, and Persia published separately in 1664, 1674, and 1684.

Thévenot, M. (Melchisédech). Recueil de voyages de Mr Thévenot. Paris, Estienne Michallet, 1682.
T69
Among the accounts of travel and discovery collected here is the account of the exploration of Marquette and Joliet in which they reached the Mississippi River.

Thévenot, M. (Melchisédech). Relations de divers voyages curieux qui n'ont point este publiees. Paris, T. Moette, 1696.
T70
An enlarged edition of this collection of voyages to America, Asia, Africa, Russia, and the East Indies. Many maps and plates are included.

Thevet, André. Cosmographie de Levant. Lyons, Ian de Tournes & Guil. Gazeau, 1554.
T71
Observations on the people and on the animal and vegetable products of Levant by the French royal cosmographer.

Thevet, André. La cosmographie universelle. Paris, P. l'Huilier, 1575.
T72
A two-volume work with numerous maps and plates in which the author describes the known parts of the world.

Thevet, André. Les singularitez de la France antarctique. Paris, Heritiers de Maurice de la Porte, 1557.
T73
The author was a participant in Admiral Coligny's unsuccessful Huguenot colony in Brazil. His description includes both North and South America.

Thevet, André. Les singularitez de la France antarctique. Paris, Heritiers de Maurice de la Porte, 1558.
T74
A re-issue of the 1557 edition, with a new title page.

Thevet, André. Les singularitez de la France antarctique. Antwerp, Christophle Plantin, 1558.
T75
This edition has no significant alterations from the first edition.

Thevet, André. Historia dell' India America. Venice, Gabriel Giolito de' Ferrari, 1561.
T76
The first Italian edition.

Thevet, André The New found worlde, or Antarctike, wherin is contained wõderful and strange things ... London, Henry Bynneman, for Thomas Hacket, 1568
T77

[Thiberge, Louis.] Lettre de messieurs des Missions etrangeres au Pape sur les idolatries et sur les superstitions chinoises. [Paris? 1700?]
T78
A documented history of the Chinese Rites controversy, including complete texts of many of the documents.

[Thiberge, Louis.] Lettre de messieurs des missions etrangeres, au Pape. Sur le decret de Sa Sainteté rendu en 1704 & publié en 1709 contre les idolatries & les superstitions chinoises. [n.p.] 1710.
T79
The pope is urged to take a strong stand in forcing Jesuit compliance with the policy banning Chinese Rites in Christian practice.

Thiery de Menonville, Nicolas Joseph. Traité de la culture du nopal ... dans les colonies françaises de l'Amérique. Paris, Delalain; Bordeaux, Bergert, 1787.
T80
A discussion of the possibilities of establishing a cochineal industry in Santo Domingo, through the cultivation of the nopal cactus and the introduction of the insect which feeds upon it.

Thoman, Mauriz. Mauriz Thomans, ehemaligen Jesuitens und Missionars in Asien und Afrika, Reise-und Lebensbeschreibung. Augsburg, Matthäus Riegers sel. Söhnen, 1788.
T81
An account of missionary work in Mozambique, including its termination there when the Jesuits were suppressed.

Thomas, Antoine. Relazione delli padri della Compagni di Gesu di Pekin intorno a quanto opero e fece l'Illṁo Revṁo Patriarca Monsignore Carlo Tommaso Maillard di Tournon legato a latere nell' imperio della Cina, e poi Em̃o Prete Cardinale della S.R. Chiesa morto relegato in Macao li otto del mese di Guigno 1710. Manuscript. [Italy, ca. 1710.] T82

An Italian translation of a letter describing events in China, particularly with reference to the Chinese Rites controversy about 1706.

Thomas, Antoine. Lo stato presente della chiesa cinese rappresentato a Monsignor Vescovo di ... [n.p., 1707.] T83

Italian translation from the French of a response to an anti-Jesuit publication relating to the Jesuit mission in China.

[Thomas, Sir Dalby.] An historical account of the growth of the West-India collonies, and of the great advantages they are to England, in respect to trade. London, J. Hindmarsh, 1690. T84

A practical economic treatise, giving arguments for emigrating to America and the West Indies.

Thomas, Gabriel. Continuatio der Beschreibung der Landschafft Pensylvaniae en denen endgräntzen Americae. Frankfurt and Leipzig, Andreas Otto, 1702. T85

Appended to Thomas's entirely optimistic account of Pennsylvania, translated from the English edition of 1698, is Daniel Falckner's *Curieuse Nachricht von Pensylvania*, including answers to 103 questions about the province addressed to him upon his return from there.

Thomas, John. A sermon preached before the incorporated Society for the Propagation of the Gospel in Foreign Parts, at their anniversary meeting in the parish church of St. Mary-le-Bow, on Friday February 15, 1750 [i.e. 1751]. London, Edward Owen, 1751. T86

The thesis of this missionary sermon is the unity of all humanity and the diversity of gifts and opportunity which are all intended to serve that unity.

Thomas, M. (Antoine Léonard). Eloge de René Duguay-Trouin. Paris, B. Brunet, 1761. T87

Thomas was a University of Paris professor. Includes much on the French navy, and twenty pages of historical notes.

Thomas, Pascoe. A true and impartial journal of a voyage to the South-Seas, and round the globe. London, S. Birt [etc.] 1745. T88

An account of Anson's circumnavigation with numerous observations on the geography, natural history, and economic opportunities of the Pacific area.

[Thomas, S.] The British negociator, or, Foreign exchanges made perfectly easy. London, M. Richardson, L. Hawes, and T. Slack, 1765.
T89

Tables and explanations of foreign exchange.

Thompson, Charles. The travels of the late Charles Thompson, Esq.: containing his observations on France, Italy, Turkey in Europe, the Holy Land, Arabia, Egypt, and many other parts of the world ... Reading, J. Newbery and C. Micklewright, 1744. T90

A collection of descriptions of many places, none of them east of the Red Sea, but not actually a travel narrative.

Thompson, Edward. Sailor's letters, written to his select friends in England, during his voyages and travels in Europe, Asia, Africa, and America, from the year 1754 to 1759. London, T. Becket [etc] 1767. T91

A highly literate, informative and entertaining collection written from India, North America and the West Indies, with extensive comments on English life in all of these places as well as local customs, education, religion, etc.

[Thompson, Thomas.] Considerations on the trade to Newfoundland. London, Andrew Bell [1711]. T92

Urges clearly defined British claims to Newfoundland to forestall French advances there.

[Thomson, Charles.] An enquiry into the causes of the alienation of the Delaware and Shawanese Indians from the British interest ... London, J. Wilke, 1759. T93

An analysis of British-Indian relations in Pennsylvania. Includes an account of the travels of Christian Frederic Post and his diplomacy among the Indians.

Thomson, P. A new description of America. Falkirk, 1787. T94

This short chapbook describes South America and gives information of interest to persons considering emigrating there.

[Thomson, William.] Travels in Europe, Asia, and Africa. London, J. Murray, 1782. T95

Written by a cultured gentleman who gives excellent insights into problems of the British Empire, and especially valuable economic information on India.

[Thomson, William.] Voyages en Europe, en Asie et en Afrique. London; Paris, Regnaut, 1786.
T96

This French edition adds maps of India and the Middle East, as well as the travels of James Capper and Anders Sparrman, which are not found in earlier editions.

Thoughts on a question of importance proposed to the public, whether it is probable that the immense extent of territory acquired ... will operate towards the prosperity or the ruin of the island of Great-Britain? London, J. Dixwell, 1765. T97

The author foresees the possibility of labor shortage and high prices resulting from the establishment of colonies abroad, and these colonies threaten to become competitors on the world market.

Thoughts on commerce and liberty. London, S. Hooper [1786]. T98
A discussion of the reciprocal benefits conferred upon each other by liberty and commerce.

Thoughts on the question proposed to be discussed in the general court of proprietors of East-India stock. London, For the Author, 1794. T99
" ... namely, whether the directors of the company may, in the future act as agents for private persons engaged in the trade to or from India."

Thunberg, Carl Peter. Inträdes-tal, om de myntsorter, som i äldre och sednare tider blifvit slagne och varit gängbare uit kejsaredömet Japan ... Stockholm, Johan Georg Lange, 1779. T100
A lecture to the Swedish Academy of Science on the manners and customs of the Japanese people, including an account of Japanese coinage.

Thunberg, Carl Peter. Resa uti Europa, Africa, Asia, förrättad ären 1770-1779. Upsala, Joh. Edman, 1788. T101
An account of travels to South Africa, Java, Ceylon, and Japan by a Swedish naturalist. His observations extend beyond plant life, including comments on the social life and customs as well as the economies of areas he visited.

Thunberg, Carl Peter. Voyages de C.P. Thunberg, au Japon, par le Cap de Bonne-Espérance, les Isles de la Sonde, &c. Paris, Benoît Dandré [eyc.] 1796. T102
The second French edition of this travel account, adding a bibliogrpahy of works cited by the editor, J.B. Lamarck.

Thurlow, Thomas. A sermon preached before the incorporated Society for the Propagation of the Gospel in Foreign Parts: at their anniversary meeting in the parish church of St. Mary-le-Bow, on Friday February 17, 1786. London, T. Harrison and S. Brooke, 1786. T103
This preacher directs some attention to the need to carry Christianity to Moslems and others in India.

[Tickell, Richard]. Anticipation, containing the substance of His M---------y's most gracious speech to both H------s of P----l-----t, on the opening of the approaching session, together with a full and authentic account of the debate which will take place ... on the motion for the address, and the amendment. London, For T. Becket, 1778. T104
The ficticious speech and debate relate to matters concerning the American Revolution, particularly the supplying of ships participating in it.

Til interessentskabet i den particulaire expedition til Ostindien med skibet Dronning Juliana Maria, fört af Capitaine Peter Holm. Copenhagen, M. Hallager, 1783. T105
A pamphlet relating to the ship *Princess Juliana Maria* which was chartered by independent merchants for a voyage to the East Indies which brought a lawsuit from the Danish East India Company.

Tillard, William. The case of William Tillard, one of the late directors of the South-Sea-Company. [n.p., 1721.] T106
Tillard claims absence due to illness from the crucial deliberations of the company and notes a loss of six thousand pounds from his own subscriptions to company stock.

Tilleman, Eric. En liden enfoldig Beretning om det landskab Guinea. [Copenhagen, Hans Pedersen, 1697.] T107
A description of west Africa, reflecting Danish commercial interests there.

Timberlake, Henry. Voyages du Lieutenant Henri Timberlake, qui fut chargé, dans l'année 1760, de conduire en Angleterre trois sauvages, de la tribu des Cherokees. Paris, Hautbot l'Aine, 1797. T108
The author had served in the British army in North America. His travels enabled him to make observations on the land, products, and peoples of the interior of North America.

[Tinne, A.] Brief van een Amsterdams koopman te Petersburg geëtablisseert; houdende een relaas van de impressie aldaar veroorzaakt door de papieren van de Heer Laurens. Amsterdam, 1780. T109
The letter concerns commercial and diplomatic relations with Great Britain, relating to the problem of armed neutrality and the American Revolution.

Tirion, Isaak. Nieuwe kaart van de Noord Pool na de alderlaatste ondekking int licht gebracht. Amsterdam, J. Keyser, 1735. T110
The Dutch edition of Tirion's polar projection of the northern hemisphere.

Tirion, Isaak. Nuova carta del polo Artico secondo l'ultime osservazioni. [Venice, 1738]. T111
This polar projection of the northern hemisphere is very similar to the preceding, showing the source of the Mississippi River as a 500 mile lake in northwestern North America, California as an island, etc.

Titulos primordiales de la Hacienda de S. Estevan Tiripitio, 1562-1786. [A collection of 983 documents relating to land management and sugar culture in southeastern Michoacan province, Mexico, covering the period 1562-1786.] Manuscript in Spanish and Tarascan. Mexico, 1562-1786. T112
Eighty-three of the documents are in Tarascan from the 1560s. The remaining documents date from 1588. In addi-

tion to records of land sales, the collection includes transfer of equipment and slaves, and records dealing with local government.

[Tixedor, François Xavier.] Nouvelle France ou France commerçante. London, 1765. T113
A general discussion of French commerce.

Tjassens, Johan. Zee-politie der Vereenichde Nederlanden. The Hague, Johan Veely, 1652. T114
A survey of Dutch commercial and maritime laws and regulations, including an overview of Dutch overseas administration and documents regulating its trading companies.

To the Right Honourable the Committee for Forraign Affaires ... on the behalf of the merchants ... trading to Spain. [London, 1652.] T115
English merchants petition the committee to obtain satisfaction from Spain for violation of peace and losses to their trade.

[Tod, Thomas.] Consolatory thoughts on American independence. Edinburgh, James Donaldson, 1782. T116
The author predicts that the new American nation will be predominantly agricultural, and consequently a consumer of English manufactured goods rather than a competitor.

Todeschi, Claudio. Saggi di agricoltura, manifatture, e commercio, coll' applicazione di essi al vantaggio del Dominio Pontificio. Rome, Arcangelo Casaletti, 1770. T117
A brief economic history as preface to an essay on the free trade movement and its potential implications for the Papal States.

Toebast, Ignatius. Wonderbaere reyze na d'uytterste paelen van America, door den zeer errw. pater Ignatius Toebast, Jesuit, en missionaris in d'Indien ... Gendt, J. F. Vander Schueren & Joseph Bogaert [1786?]. T118
A collection of letters, possibly published to commemorate the centenary of the death of their author, a Belgian priest who served as a missionary in Central America.

Den toestantder swevende verschillen, tusschen de Oost, end West-Indische compagnien ... [n.p.] 1664. T119
A commentary on the Anglo-Dutch differences in the East and West Indies, which were primarily commercial rivalries.

Tollenaer, Arend. Remonstrantie ofte vertoogh, inhoudende verscheyden schatten van groote consideratie ... van Hollandt ende West-Vrieslandt. The Hague, J. Scheltus, 1672. T120
A series of laws, both Dutch and English, pertaining to the commerce of both countries.

Tolosani, Giovanni Maria. Compendio di sphera et machina del mondo nuovamente composto. [Florence, Bernardo Zucchetta, 1515.] T121
A booklet which possibly is related to old skipper charts of medieval Europe; a cosmographical poem in Italian verse.

Tommaso di Tommasuccio da Piombino. Vita di Maometto e descrizione dei paesi d'Oriente. Manuscript. Italy, 15th century. T122
Contains an account of an unknown traveler in the Near East. The author claims to have gone to sea at the age of fifteen and been taken by pirates to various eastern Mediterranean countries.

Tonti, Henri de. Dernieres decouvertes dans l'Amerique Septentrionale de M. de La Sale. Paris, Jean Guignard, 1687. T123
Tonti was La Salle's chief aid who assumed command in the Illinois country during La Salle's absences, and assisted him in exploring the Mississippi in 1682. Tonti disclaimed authorship of this work.

Tonti, Henri de. Dernieres decouvertes dans l'Amerique Septentrionale de M. de La Sale. Paris, Jean Guignard, 1697. T124
A variant of the preceding item, with several canceled leaves.

Tonti, Henri de. An account of Monsieur de la Salle's last expedition and discoveries in North America. London, J. Tonson, S. Buckley, and R. Knapton, 1698. T125
The first English edition.

[Tooke, William.] Varieties of literature. London, J. Debrett, 1795. T126
Contains the first English account of the first permanent Russian settlement in America, from the journal of Gregory Shelekof of the Russian American Company.

[Torcia, Michele.] Appendice contente une breve difesa della nostra nazione contro le incolpe attribuitele da alcuni scrittori esteri. Naples, 1783. T127
A defense of Italy and Italians against detractors, among them William Robertson, the Scottish historian, who wrote unfavorably about Gemelli-Careri, an Italian traveler.

[Torcia, Michele.] Sbozzo del commercio di Amsterdam. Naples, 1782. T128
A survey of Amsterdam's commerce, with extensive shipping statistics and tables recording the trade of the East India Company.

Torén, Olof. Voyage ... fait à Surate, à la Chine, &c. depuis le prémier avril 1750 jusqu'au 26 juin 1752. Milan, Freres Reycends, 1771. T129

The first French edition of a journal recording the natural history, products, commerce, social life, and customs of Surat, other regions in India, and China.

Torén, Olof. Reise des Herrn Olof Toree nach Surate und China ... Leipzig, Christian Gottlob Hilschern, 1772. T130

This edition is supplemented by Karl Gustaf Ekeberg's, "Kurze Beschreibung der chinesischen Feldökonomie," Blackford's account of England's North American colonies based on Kalm and Douglass, and Franklin's answers before the House of Commons in 1766 concerning political affairs and attitudes in America.

Torfæus, Thormodus. Commentatio historica de rebus gestis Faereyensium seu Faröensium. Copenhagen, Justini Hög, 1695. T131

A history of the Faeroe Islands, compiled by an Icelandic scholar.

Torfæus, Thormodus. Gronlandia antiqua, seu veteris Gronlandiae descriptio. Copenhagen, Typographéo Regiae Majest. & Universit., 1706. T132

A history of early Scandinavian colonization of Greenland.

Torfæus, Thormodus. Historia rerum Norvegicarum. Copenhagen, Joachimi Schmitgenii, 1711. T133

This history of Norway includes events to the mid-fourteenth century and contains much material on Iceland with some references to Greenland and Vinland.

Torfæus, Thormodus. Historia Vinlandiae antiquae, seu partis Americae septentrionalis. Copenhagen, Typographéo Regiae Majest. & Universit., 1705. T134

A collection of sources relating the Scandinavian discovery of Vinland, with reference also to the supposed discovery of America by the Welsh in the twelfth century.

Torfæus, Thormodus. Orcades seu rerum Orcadensium historiae. Copenhagen, Justini Hög, 1697. T135

This history of the Orkney Islands from the ninth to the seventeenth centuries is based on Norse sagas.

Torism and trade can never agree. London, A. Baldwin [1713?]. T136

Cites the history of England's growth in wealth and liberty despite Tory opposition to both.

Torquato, Antonio. Prognosticon de eversione Europae, & alia quaedam, quorum catalogum sequens do cebit pagina. Antwerp, Martinum Nutium, 1552. T137

A collection of geographical and ethnographic information with particular emphasis on the East, including Ethiopia and Turkey.

Torquemada, Juan de. Primera [segunda, tercera] parte de los veinte i un libros rituales i monarchia indiana, con el origen y guerras, de los Indios Occidentales, de sus poblaçones descubrimiento, conquista, conversion, y otras cosas maravillosas de la mesma tierra. Madrid, Nicolas Rodriguez Franco, 1723. T138

The second edition of a classic in Hispanic Americana, chronicling the conquest of Mexico and the progress of Christian missions there as well as giving descriptions of the peoples of Mexico.

Torre Miranda, Antonio de la. Noticia individual, de las poblaciones nuevamenta, fundadas en la provincia de Cartagena ... Puerto de Santa Maria, D. Luis de Luque y Leyva, 1794. T139

A compendium of information of the province of Cartagena, covering population, geography, agriculture, mining, commerce, etc.

Torre y Sevil, Francisco de la. El peregrino atlante S. Francisco Xavier apostol del oriente epitome historico, y panegyrico de su vida, y prodigios ... Lisbon, 1674. T140

An account of Saint Francis Xavier's life, with particular emphasis on his organization of missionary work in the Far East, noting numerous mission stations in India, the Indonesian archipelago, and Japan.

Torres Bollo, Diego de. Breve relatione del P. Diego de Torres della Compagnia di Giesù ... Doue si raccontano anche alcuni particolari notabili successi gli anni prossimi passati. Per consolatione de i religiosi di detta Compagnia in Europa. Al fine s'aggiunge la lettera annua dell'Isole Filippine del 1600. Venice, Gio. Battista Ciotti Sanese, 1604. T141

A collection of reports on the progress of Jesuit missions in Peru and the Philippines.

Torrubia, José. Disertacion historico-politica en que se trata de la extencion de el Mahometismo en las islas Philipinas. Madrid, A. Balvàs, [1736]. T142

The author is concerned with the spread of Islam in the islands and presents the topic in the rather interesting form of a dialogue between a Spanish courtier and a Filipino.

Torrubia, José. La gigantologia Spagnola vendicata ... Naples, Muziana, 1760. T143

Drawing on early travel and natural history literature as well as recent publications of scientific academies, the author supports the theory of the previous existence of giants in South America.

Torsellino, Orazio. De vita Francisci Xaverii, qui primus e Societate Jesu in Indiam & Japoniam evangelium invexit, libri sex. Liege, Henrici Houji, 1597. T144

This biography of St. Francis Xavier is given almost entirely to his missionary travels in the East.

Tosi, Clemente. Dell' India Orientale descrittione geografica, et historica. Rome, Michele Ercole, 1669. T145
 A two-volume work comprising a vast gathering of information on the geography of the area from Persia to China with a confutation of the religions of the East.

Tosi, Clemente. L' India orientale, descrittione geografica & historica ... Rome, Felice Cesaretto, 1676. T146
 An exhaustive study of Asiatic religions and the impact made upon them by European Christianity. An extensive geography of Asia is also included.

Tott, François, baron de. Mémoires ... sur les Turcs et les Tartares. Amsterdam, 1785. T147
 Commentary on many aspects of Turkish and Tartar life by a diplomat who had served in the Near East for sixteen years.

Tournefort, Joseph Pitton de. Relation d'un voyage du Levant. Paris, Imprimerie Royale, 1717. T148
 The first edition of a popular account of travels in the Near East, based on an expedition led by the author in 1700-1702. It includes 150 plates.

Tournefort, Joseph Pitton de. Relation d'un voyage du Levant. Lyons, Freres Bruyset, 1727. T149
 The third French edition.

Tournefort, Joseph Pitton de. A voyage into the Levant. London, D. Browne [etc.] 1718. T150
 The first English edition.

Tournefort, Joseph Pitton de. Beschryving van eene reize naar de Levant. Amsterdam, Janssoons van Waesberge, 1737. T151
 The first and only Dutch edition, translated by Pieter le Clercq.

Tournefort, Joseph Pitton de. Beschreibung einer auf königlichen Befehl unternommenen Reise nach der Levante. Nürnberg, Gabriel Nicolaus Raspe, 1776-77. T152
 The first German edition, translated from the French.

Touron, A. (Antoine). Histoire des hommes illustres de l'ordre de Saint Dominique; c'est a dire, des papes, des cardinaux, des prélates éminens en science & en sainteté; des célébres docteurs, & des autres grandes personages, qui ont le plus illustré cet ordre, depuis la mort du saint fondateur, jusqu'au pontificat de Benoît XIII. Paris, Babuty, Quillau, 1743-49. T153
 This is primarily a collection of biographies of notables of the Dominican order, including many who had served in Asia and America.

Touron, A. (Antoine). Histoire générale de l'Amérique depuis sa découverte ... Paris, Jean-Thomas Hérissant, fils, 1768-1770. T154
 A history of Spanish discovery and conquest in the New World from a Dominican point of view, stressing treatment of Indians, slavery, and missionary progress.

La trā q̄ comunmente lamamos China, llamaron por ao nombre el reyno del Catay ... Manuscript. [Spain, ca. 1575.] T155
 A brief description of China, probably originating in Manila where Spanish merchants and missionaries were attempting to make contact with the mainland.

Tractaet tegens pays, treves, en onderhandelinge met den Koningh van Spaignien. The Hague, Aert Meuris, 1629. T156
 Arguments against peace with Spain, which it was believed would be against the interests of Dutch commerce.

The trade granted to the South-Sea-Company: considered with relation to Jamaica. London, Samuel Crouch, 1714. T157
 A pamphlet concerned with the monopoly on the slave trade to Spanish America received by the South Sea Company, and the place Jamaica would have in that trade.

Traité, dans le quel on approfondit les funestes suites ... de la Compagnie d'Ostende. Amsterdam, J. van Septeren, 1726. T158
 A statement of the reasons why the continuance of the Ostend Company would ruin the commerce of England and the Netherlands.

Tramezini, Michele. Septemtrionalium regionum Svetiae Gothiae Norvegiae Daniae et terrarum adiacentium. Venice, 1558. T159
 A chart of the Baltic and North Sea regions based upon the first chart of this area made by Cornelis Anthonisz in 1543.

Travels of the Jesuits, into various parts of the world: particularly China and the East-Indies. London, T. Pieys, 1762. T160
 A collection of missionary letters and reports, taken from the *Lettres édifiantes*, and commented on extensively by the editor, John Lockman.

A treatise of the description and use of both globes. To which is annexed, A geographical description of our earth. London, John Senex and W. Taylor, 1718. T161
 An instruction book on the use of globes, undoubtedly intended to accompany one of Senex's globes listed in an advertisement in the volume.

A treatise upon the trade from Great Britain to Africa. London, R. Baldwin, 1772. T162
 Notes the advantages to Britain of the trade with Africa, and also presents a history of the African trade.

The treaty of Seville, and the measures that have been taken for the four last years, impartially considered. London, J. Roberts, 1730. T163
A defense of the Treaty of Seville as the best means of avoiding war and a combination of powers united against British interests in Europe.

Eene treffelijcke t'zamensprekinghe tusschen den Paus ende coninck van Spaengnien belangende den peys met ons lieden aen te gaene. [n.p., 1607.] T164
An imaginary conversation between the pope and the King of Spain, interrupted by news of rebellion in the Low Countries and the intention of the rebels to start a Dutch West India Company.

Tregoas entre o prudentissimo rey Dom Joam o IV de Portugal, & os poderosos estados das provincias unidas. Lisbon, A. Alvarez, 1642. T165
The terms of peace between Portugal and the "powerful states of the United Provinces."

[Trenchard, John.] A comparison between the proposals of the bank and the South-Sea Company. London, J. Roberts, 1720. T166
The proposals relate to the reduction of the national debt; the author favors the proposal of the bank.

Trenchard, John. An examination and explanation of the South-Sea Company's scheme for taking in the publick debts. London, J. Roberts, 1720. T167
A warning to persons considering purchase of additional stock in the South Sea Company.

[Trenchard, John.] A letter to a member of Parliament. London, J. Roberts, 1720. T168
The author views the scheme of the South Sea Company as "injurious and destructive to the trade and navigation of Great Britain."

Tres-humbles remonstrances sur l'estat des affaires chrestiennes dans les mers de Levant, Midi & Ponant. Paris, Abraham Saugrain, 1618. T169
An exhortation to Louis XIII to proceed with vigor against the Turks in the Mediterranean, with an appended poem celebrating victories in Barbary.

Trigault, Nicolas. De Christianis apud Japonios triumphis sive de gravissima ibidem contra Christi fidem persecutione exorta anno MDCXII usq. ad annum MDCXX libri quinq. Munich, 1623. T170
An account of persecution of Christian missionaries in Japan.

Trigault, Nicolas. Due lettere annue della Cina del 1610 e del 1611. Milan, Per l'her. di Pacifico Pontio, & Gio. Battista Piccaglia, 1615. T171
The two letters are dated Nanking, August 1612, and Coccino, May 1613.

Trigault, Nicolas. Litterae Societatis Jesu e regno Sinarum annorum MDCX. & XI. Ad R.P. Claudium Aquavivam eiusd. societatis praepositum generalem. Augsburg, Christophorum Mangium, 1615. T172
An account of missionary progress in China based on two letters by Trigault.

Trigault, Nicolas. Rei Christianae apud Japonios commentarius ex litteris annuis Societatis Jesu annorum 1609, 1610, 1611, 1612 collectus. Augsburg, Christophorum Magnium, 1615. T173
An account of the Jesuit missions in Japan, undoubtedly published as a part of the author's purpose in returning from the East to promote the Jesuits' missionary effort there.

Trigault, Nicolas. Rerum memorabilium in Regno Sinae gestarum, litterae annuae Societatis Jesu. Antwerp, Hieronymi Versussii, 1625. T174
A general report on the Jesuit missions in China, noting also the progress of the Tartar wars.

Trigault, Nicolas. Vita Gasparis Barzaei, Belgae e Societate Iesu B. Xaverii in India Socij. Antwerp, Ioach. Trognaesii, 1610. T175
A life of Kaspar Berse, a Jesuit missionary from Belgium who was successor to St. Francis Xavier as leader of the Asia mission. The biography records his work in Mozambique and in India.

Trindade, Antonio de. Serman pregado em dia do Seraphico Padre Sam Francisco em o convento de Goa. Lisbon, Paulo Craesbeeck, 1645. T176
The author was a Franciscan in the province of St. Thomas in India.

Tripoli (Libya). Capitulatie van Tripoli. The Hague, P. Scheltus, 1713. T177
Contains stipulations regarding tolls, procedure in event of shipwreck, and other navigational matters.

Troef grooten troef, tusschen Engelandt en Hollandt. [n.p.] 1664. T178
The major commercial powers of Europe are portrayed as card players at a table. All of them, especially the Netherlands, are losing to England.

Troil, Uno von, Archbishop of Uppsala. Bref rörande en resa til Island. Upsala, Magnus Swederus, 1777. T179
Letters written to Troil and others interested in Iceland, covering such subjects as geography, geology, history, literature, and printing. An Icelandic bibliography is included.

Troil, Uno von, Archbishop of Uppsala. Lettres sur l'Islande. Paris, P. Fr. Didot, 1781. T180
The first French edition.

Troilo, Franz Ferdinand von. Orientalische Reise-Beschreibung; wie er zu dreyen unterschiedenen mahlen nach Jerusalem, von dannen in Egypten auf den Berg Sinai, und ferner nach Constantinopel sich begeben ... Dresden, Melchior Bergen, 1676. T181

An account of travels in the eastern Mediterranean from 1666 to 1670, noting places of biblical, historical and commercial interest.

Trou-hertighe onderrichtinge, aen alle hooft participanten en lief-hebbers vande ge-octroyeerde West-Indische Compagnie ... [Amsterdam] 1643. T182

"Well meant advice to all the great shareholders and friends of the authorized West India Company, concerning the opening of trade to the Africa coast...."

Trouloosheyt der Engelsche, van eenige jaren herwaerts aengewesen. [n.p.] 1672. T183

A defense of Dutch actions on the west coast of Africa as hostilities with the English were reopened.

A true and exact description of the Island of Shetland, containing an account of its situation, trade, produce, and inhabitants. London, T. James [etc.] 1753. T184

Designed to interest English fishermen in Shetland as a base for an enlarged herring fishery.

A true and particular relation of the dreadful earthquake which happen'd at Lima, the capital of Peru, and the neighbouring port of Callao, on the 28th of October, 1746 ... London, Printed for T. Osborne..., 1748. T185

The description of the earthquake is a vehicle for a general compilation of information on Peru, including navigational, historical, geographical and economic material.

A true declaration of the news that came out of the East-Indies with the pinace called the Hare ... [n.p.] 1624. T186

An English version of the Amboyna Massacre in which the author attempts to prove that the incident was being used by the Dutch to take over English East Indian bases.

A true historicall discourse of Muley Hamets rising to the three kingdomes of Moruecos, Fes, and Sus. London, Thomas Purfoot for Clement Knight, 1609. T187

An account of the struggle for political power over Morocco by the three sons of Muley Hamet. Contains an interesting description of the traffic in gold and salt.

The true interest of Great-Britain, in regard to the trade and government of Canada, Newfoundland, and the coast of Labrador. London, J. Williams, 1767. T188

An essay on the best means of governing the colonies so as to secure the maximum commercial benefits to England.

The true relation of that worthy sea fight, which two of the East India shipps, had with 4 Portingals, of great force and burthen, in the Persian Gulph. With the lamentable death of Captaine Andrew Shilling. London, I.D. for Nathaniel Newbery and William Sheffard, 1622. T189

Describes a naval engagement on December, 1620, in which the English secured a foothold on the Persian Gulf for the advantage of the East India Company's trade.

A true relation of the reasons which necessitated His Majesty of Sweden to continue the war with Denmark. London, T. Pierrepont, 1658. T190

The major point at issue was the control of the Sund and the commerce passing through it.

A true relation of the unjust, cruel and barbarous proceedings against the English at Amboyna. London, H. Lownes for Nathaneal Newberry, 1624. T191

Includes an English view of the trial and execution of ten Englishmen accused of trying to overthrow the Dutch in Amboyna, a Dutch version of the same events, and an English answer to the Dutch interpretation.

A true relation of what has passed between the English Company Trading to the East-Indies and the Governor and Company of Merchants of London Trading into the East-Indies ... [London, 1698.] T192

An agreement between the Company of Merchants of London trading to the East Indies and the old East India Company.

A true relation without all exception, of strange and admirable accidents, which lately happened in the kingdome of the great Magor, or Magull, who is the greatest monarch of the East Indies. London, I.D. for Thomas Archer, 1622. T193

An account of the court of the Great Mogul, followed by brief notes on a voyage to Ceylon and Japan.

A true state of the case between the British northern-colonies and the sugar islands in America. [London] 1732. T194

A review of the decline of English commerce in the American colonies, charging that it resulted from excessive regulations.

A true state of the present difference between the Royal African Company, and the separate traders. London, 1710. T195

A defense of free trade to West Africa as the best means of adequately supplying the American plantations with slaves.

Trumbull, Jonathan. Brieven van hunne excellenties de Heeren Jonathan Trumbull, en William Livingston ... aan Johan Derk Baron van der Capellen. Amsterdam, Conradi [etc.] [1780]. T196

Concerns Dutch-American relations during the American Revolution. The authors were governors of Connecticut and New Jersey respectively.

Trusler, John. A descriptive account of the islands lately discovered in the South-Seas ... With some account of the country of Camchatca, a late discovery of the Russians. London, Printed for the Author, 1778. T197
A survey of the major islands and island groups of the South Pacific with respect to geography, products, climate, and populations, including a map of the South Pacific and an account of Kamchatka.

Trutfetter, Jodocus. Summa in totā physicen: hoc est philosophiam naturalem conformiter siquidem vere sophie ... [Erfurt, Matthaeum Maler, 1514.] T198
An encyclopedic work, with a section on astronomy and geography. The author is often cited as Jodocus Isenacensis.

Truth, truth, truth. London, J. Roberts [etc.] 1715. T199
A vicious attack upon the ministry for its concluding a treaty at Utrecht which allowed France a continued presence in the West Indies, perceived to be a source of great wealth.

Tuba pacis, ofte Basuyne des vredes. Gestelt door een oprecht patriot ... Tegen het suchtigh ende trouhertigh discours van E.P. zijnde een t'samenspraeck tusschen Nederlander, Spaenjaert, Fransman ende Sweed. [n.p.] 1647. T200
This expression of concern for the forthcoming peace of Wesphalia deals primarily with the freedom of religion.

Tucker, Josiah. A brief essay on the advantages and disadvantages which respectively attend France and Great Britain, with regard to trade. London, T. Trye, 1750. T201
A greatly expanded second edition containing proposals for improving Britain's trade position, emphasizing the harm done by monopolistic trading companies.

[Tucker, Josiah.] The case of going to war, for the sake of procuring, enlarging, or securing of trade. London, R. and J. Dodsley, 1763. T202
A forceful declaration of the author's beliefs that there are no benefits to be derived from going to war, and why apparent gains from an expansion of trade as a consequence of war are false and momentary.

Tucker, Josiah. Cui bono? or, An inquiry, what benefits can arise ... in the present war? Gloucester, R. Raikes for T. Cadell, 1781. T203
In a series of letters to Necker, the French minister of finance, this author argues against wars and commercial restriction as a means to national prosperity.

Tucker, Josiah. Cui bono? ou Examen des avantages que les plus grandes victoires, ou les succès les plus completes, dans la guerre actuelle, pourroient porcurer aux Anglois ou aux Americains ... Rotterdam, Bennet et Hake, 1782. T204
French translation of the preceding work.

Tucker, Josiah. Four tracts, together with two sermons, on political and commercial subjects. Gloucester, R. Raikes, 1774. T205
The author discusses the relationship of wealth, wars, and colonies to the well-being of a country.

Tucker, Josiah. An humble address and earnest appeal to those respectable personages in Great-Britain and Ireland ... whether a connection with, or a separation from the continental colonies of America, be most for the national advantage. Gloucester, R. Raikes, 1775. T206
A booklet suggesting that the best solution for the uprising in America would be to exclude the rebellious colonies entirely from British sovereignty, maintaining only mutually beneficial commercial and treaty relations.

Tucker, Josiah. An humble address and earnest appeal to those respectable personages in Great-Britain and Ireland ... Gloucester, R. Raikes, 1775. T207
"Second edition, corrected."

[Tucker, Josiah.] Reflections on the expediency of opening the trade to Turkey. London, T. Trye, 1753. T208
The author argues that the monopoly of the Levant Company deprives Britain of both exports and imports, thereby weakening the entire economy and giving an advantage to France in the Levant trade.

Tucker, Josiah. Reflections on the present low price of coarse wools, its immediate causes, and it probable remedies. London, T. Cadell, 1782. T209
Tucker observes the decline in sale of coarse woolen cloth and urges bounties for its export to the Baltic region and to Russia. He also suggests it be provided to persons of marginal economic status in Great Britain.

Tucker, Josiah. Tract V. The respective pleas and arguments of the mother country, and of the colonies. Gloucester, R. Raikes, 1775. T210
The author examines the positions of Parliament and of the American colonies following the meeting of the Continental Congress.

Tucker, Josiah. Tract V. The respective pleas and arguments of the mother country, and of the colonies, distinctly set forth ... Gloucester, R. Raikes, 1776. T211
The second edition.

Tucker, Josiah. Verhandeling over het recht van het Britsche Parlement om belastingen te leggen op de Noord Amerikaansche Volkplanters, voorgesteld in eenen brief van een' koopman te Londen aan zyn' neef in Amerika. Utrecht, J. van Schoonhoven, 1775. T212

The introduction to this translation calls attention to Europe's interest in the developing conflict in America.

Tucker, St. George. A dissertation on slavery: a proposal for the gradual abolition of it, in the state of Virginia. Philadelphia, Mathew Carey, 1796. T213

The plan for ending slavery was to declare all females born after a certain date free, and thus also their children, in the hope that this would induce a gradual migration of Blacks from Virginia.

[Turgot, Anne-Robert-Jacques, baron de l'Aulne.] Lettres sur les grains. [n.p., 1770?]. T214

A selection of three letters from a group of six written to Joseph Marie Terray on the subject of freedom of the grain trade.

Turgot, Anne-Robert-Jacques, baron de l'Aulne. Mémoire sur les colonies américaines; sur leurs relations politiques avec leurs métropoles, et sur la maniere dont la France et l'Espagne ont dû envisager les suites de l'independance des Etats-Unis de l'Amérique. Paris, DuPont, 1791. T215

Originally written in 1776, this is an extended essay in which Turgot calls for no active intervention against Great Britain in America, but a policy of watchfulness and preparation.

The Turkey merchants and their trade vindicated. [London] 1720. T216

A denunciation of English merchants buying Turkish silk in Italy which was brought there by French merchants who bought the silk with French wool.

[Turnbull, Gordon]. A narrative of the revolt and insurrection of the French inhabitants in the island of Grenada. Edinburgh, Arch. Constable; London, Vernor & Hood, 1795. T217

A history of a slave rebellion in the British colony of Grenada, noting the influence of French revolutionary ideas there.

Turner, Samuel. An account of an embassy to the court of the Teshoo Lama, in Tibet; containing a narrative of a journey through Bootan, and part of Tibet ... To which are added, views taken on the spot, by Lieutenant Samuel Davis; and observations botanical, mineralogical, and medical, by Mr. Robert Saunders. London, W. Bulmer, 1800. T218

An account of an embassy to Tibet, containing detailed descriptions of the people, land, plants and animals of Bhutan also.

Turpin, François Henri. Histoire civile et naturelle du royaume de Siam, et des revolutions qui ont bouleversé cet empire jusqu'en 1770. Paris, Costard, 1771. T219

The account of military events in Siam are preceded by a long historical background and are followed by discussion of regions near Siam which might make an acceptable alternative for French commercial interests.

Tvende breve fra s. til u - - ; angaaende tvistighederne i det Asiatiske Compagnie. Copenhagen, Gyldendals Forlag, hos J.R. Thiele, 1785. T220

Two letters continuing the controversy about the management of the Danish Asiatic Company.

Twee deductien, aen-gaende de vereeninge van d'Oost ende West-Indische Compagnien ... The Hague, Jan Veeli, 1644. T221

An argument on behalf of uniting the Dutch East and West India companies, contending that English competition could be more easily met in this way.

Tweede discoers over het Deensche manifest, ende den aengevangenen oorloch van den coninck van Dennemarcken tegens den coninck van Sweeden. Rotterdam, I. Pietersz, 1657. T222

A statement of the reasons for the war between Sweden and Denmark, a major one being disagreements over Baltic commerce.

Tweejaarige reyze rondom de wereld ... met drie schepen, in het jaar 1721 ondernemen. Dordrecht, Joannes van Braam, 1728. T223

An anonymous account of the voyage of Jacob Roggeween into the South Pacific and around the world in the interests of the Dutch West India Company.

Twining, Richard. Observations on the tea and window act, and on the tea trade. London, T. Cadell, 1785. T224

A tea merchant defends legislation designed to protect the East India Company against tea smugglers.

Twining, Richard. Remarks on the report of the East India directors ... London, T. Cadell, 1784. T225

A criticism of the East India Company's management of the tea trade.

Twist, Johan van. Beschrijving van Guseratte ... Amsterdam, Henderick Doncker, 1647. T226

A factor of the East India Company describes the geography, people, products, and commerce of the major towns of Gujarat.

Twist, Johan van. Generale beschrijvinge van Indien. Amsterdam, J. Hartgerts, 1648. T227

The author was director of the Dutch factory at Surat. He describes the products of Gujarat, and gives instructions for navigating the Indian coast.

Two addresses to the King against an excise on wine and tobacco. London, J. Roberts, 1733.
T228

Two letters concerning the East-India Company. [London?] 1676.
T229

An early pamphlet on the question of whether the East India Company is a sound place for investment. The pamphlet argues that it is not and calls for free trade.

Two papers on the subject of taxing the British colonies in America. London, J. Almon, 1767.
T230

Proposes a tax be levied on the colonies for the support of troops to protect their trade.

U

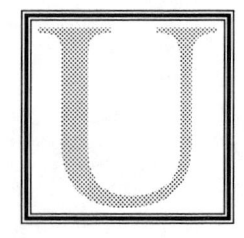

Uberti, Fazio Degli. Opera di Faccio Degliuberti Fiorentino lhiamato ditta mundi : vuolgare. [Venice, Christofaro di Pensa da Mandelo, 1501.] U1

A poem based upon the *Rerum memorabilium* of Solinus, a third-century Roman geographer.

Uchteritz, Heinrich von. Kurtze Reise-Beschreibung ... auf der Insul Barbados. Weissenfels, Johann Christian Wohlfarten, 1712. U2

The third edition of a narrative first published in 1666, recounting the experiences of a German nobleman who was held as a slave on Barbados.

Udemans, Godefridus. 't Geestelyck roer van't coopmans schip. Dordrecht, Françoys Boels, 1638. U3

The author of this "spiritual rudder" was a Calvinist preacher who wrote it as a manual of conscience for merchants and employees of the Dutch West India Company, justifying some of their practices which were being criticized.

Udemans, Godefridus. 't Geestelyck roer van't coopmans schip. Dordrecht, F. Boels, 1640. U4

The second edition.

Udemans, Godefridus. Geestelick compas. Dordrecht, Françoys Boels, 1647. U5

This fourth edition contains a treatise on commerce and trade not included in earlier printings.

Udemans, Godefridus. Koopmans jacht. Dordrecht, Françoys Boels, 1647. U6

"The merchant's yacht, bringing good news ... for all pious merchants in order to get or to preserve the wished for blessing upon their business."

Uhrbrock, Andreas Christian. Mere til publikum i en ikke nok bekiendt sag, fra Andreas Christian Uhrbrock ... Copenhagen, Gyldendals Forlag, 1789. U7

Pertains to a lawsuit of the Danish Asiatic Company against merchants violating its monopoly of trade in the East Indies.

Ulloa, Alfonso de. Vita dell' invittissimo e sacratissimo imperator Carlo V ... Di nuouo ristampata, & con molta diligenza ricorretta ... Venice, Heredi di Francesco Rampazetto, 1581. U8

A general history of the time of Charles V, noting European expansion in both the eastern and western hemispheres and its impact in Europe.

Ulloa, Antonio de. Noticias americanas: entretenimientos phisico-historicos sobre la América meridional, y la septentrional oriental. Madrid, Francisco Manuel de Mena, 1772. U9

This survey of Spanish America includes comments on the plants, animals, minerals, and climate. Particular attention is given to the Indians and their origins.

Ulloa, Antonio de. Noticias americanas: entretenimientos fisico-históricos sobre la América meridional, y la septentrional oriental. Madrid, Imprenta Real, 1792. U10

The second edition.

Ulloa, Antonio de. Historische reisbeschryving van geheel Zuid-America; gedaan op bevel des Konings van Spanje. Goes, Jacobus Huysman, 1771-1772. U11

The first Dutch edition, including twenty-five maps and illustrations.

Ulloa, Antonio de. Physikalische und historische Nachrichten vom südlichen und nordöstlichen America. Leipzig, Weidmanns Erben und Reich, 1781. U12

The first German edition, with an extensive section of annotations by the German naturalist, Johann G. Schneider.

Ulloa, Antonio de. Mémoires philosophiques, historiques, physiques, concernant la découverte de

l'Amérique, ses anciens habitans, leurs moeurs, leurs usages ... Paris, Buisson, 1787. U13
This French translation by Jean Baptiste Lefebvre de Villebrune includes observations and additions from the German edition of 1781 by Johan Gottlob Schneider.

Ulloa, Antonio de. Relacion historica del viage a la America meridional. Madrid, Antonio Marin, 1748. U14
The observations made on this scientific expedition include many relating to the major commercial centers of northern South America.

Ulloa, Antonio de. Voyage historique de l'Amérique meridionale. Amsterdam & Leipzig, Arkstée & Merkus, 1752. U15
The first French translation.

Ulloa, Antonio de. A voyage to South America. London, L. Davis and C. Reymers, 1758. U16
The first English edition.

Ulloa, Antonio de. A voyage to South America. Describing at large, the Spanish cities, towns, provinces, &c ... London, L. Davis and C. Reymers, 1760. U17
This second English edition has minor changes in the text.

Ulloa, Antonio de. A voyage to South America. Describing at large, the Spanish cities, towns, provinces, &c. on that extensive continent. London, L. Davis, 1772. U18
This third English edition has illustrations different from those in the first edition, and significant notes are added by John Adams of Waltham Abbey.

Ulloa, Bernardo de. Restablecimiento de las fabricas, y comercio Español. Madrid, Antonio Marin, 1740. U19
This work may be considered a supplement to Gerónimo de Uztáriz, *Theorica y practica de comercio de marina*, first published in 1724.

Ulloa, Bernardo de. Retablissement des manufactures et du commerce d'Espagne. Amsterdam [Paris] Chez les Freres Estienne, 1753. U20
An examination of the causes for the low state of Spanish manufacturing and commerce, both in Spain and her American colonies, with a discussion of means to restore it.

Umfreville, Edward. The present state of Hudson's Bay. Containing a full description of that settlement, and the adjacent country; and likewise of the fur trade, with hints for its improvement &c. &c. London, Charles Stalker, 1790. U21
A criticism of the Hudson's Bay Company by one who was in its service from 1771 to 1782, and who subsequently was employed as a trader by the Northwest Company.

Umfreville, Edward. Den gegenwärtigen Zustand der Hudsonsbay, der dortigen Etablissements und ihres Handels, nebst einer Beschreibung des Innern von Neu Wallis, und einer Reise von Montreal nach New York. Helmstädt, Fleckeisen, 1791. U22
This first German edition, prepared by Eberhard August Wilhelm von Zimmermann, contains extensive introductory material and editorial notes by him and a map of the northern regions of North America adapted from an Arrowsmith map of 1791.

Underricht von Pflantzung dess Maulbeer-Baums, Unterhaltung der Seidenwürm, wie auch von der Weiss die Seiden zu bereiten und zu spinnen. [n.p.] 1669. U23
A handbook of instruction for producing silk, detailing the entire process of raising mulberry plants, caring for silkworms and harvesting the finished product.

Ungern Sternberg, Mathias Alexaner von, Baron. Tankar om sveriges handel och allmänna hushållning. Stockholm, Lars Salvius [1752]. U24
Ideas about Sweden's commerce and general economy as presented in a speech by the outgoing president of the Royal Academy of Science.

United Provinces of the Netherlands. Missive van sijn Hoogheid met een nader reglement omtrent de vaart en handel op de colonie van Essequebo en Demerary, dat. 15, rec. 16 January 1772. [n.p., 1772.] U25
An amplification and extension of the following legislation.

United Provinces of the Netherlands. Missive van zyn Hoogheid met een reglement omtrent den vaart en handel op Essequebo en Demerary, rec. 6 Dec. 1770. [n.p., 1770.] U26
Five points of regulation upon West India Company shipping to the Essequebo River region of Guiana.

United Provinces of the Netherlands. Octroy ofte conditien ... van de colonie de Berbice. Amsterdam, G. en J. Broen [1732]. U27
Proclamation announcing the freedom of commerce in the colony of Berbice.

United Provinces of the Netherlands. Verbael gehouden door de Heeren H. van Beverningk, W. Nieupoort, J. van de Perre en A. P. Jongestal. The Hague, H. Scheurleer, 1725. U28
Minutes of Anglo-Dutch negotiations regarding various commercial disputes, chiefly in North America, during 1653-54.

United Provinces of the Netherlands. Ambassader (Great Britain). d'Ambassade van Nederlant aen Engelandt, met alle voorgevallen audientien, propositien, en responsiven van den koninck en sijne ministers. [n.p.] 1664. U29

Contains five reports by the Dutch envoy, M. van Goch, concerning English attacks on the forts and trading-posts of the Dutch West India Company on the West Coast of Africa.

United Provinces of the Netherlands. Magistrates. Memorie overgegeven by de heeren gedelegeerde rechteren aen ... de Heeren Staten Generael. [n.p.] 1688. U30
A report by a panel of magistrates on various economic matters, including laws regulating trade.

United Provinces of the Netherlands. Stadholder (1747-1751 : William IV). Proposals made by His late Highness the Prince of Orange, to their High Mightinesses the States-General, and to the States of Holland and West Friesland, for redressing and amending the trade of the republick. London, H. Kent, 1751. U31
A reduction of import duties and the creation of free ports are among the recommendations designed to stimulate Dutch commerce.

United Provinces of the Netherlands. Stadholder (1747-1751 : William IV). Proposals made by His late Highness the Prince of Orange, to their High Mightinesses the States-General ... London, H. Kent, 1751. U32

United Provinces of the Netherlands. Stadholder (1751-1795 : William V). Missive van Zyne Hoogheid met een reglement omtrent den vaart en handel op Essequebo en Demerary. Rec. Dec. 1770. [n.p., 1770.] U33
Five points of regulation upon West India Company shipping to the Essequebo River region of Guiana.

United Provinces of the Netherlands. Stadholder (1751-1795 : William V). Missive van Sijn Hoogheid met een nader reglement omtrent de vaart en handel op de colonie van Essequebo en Demerary. Dat. 15 Rec. 16 January 1772. [n.p., 1772.] U34
An amplification and extension of the previous legislation.

United Provinces of the Netherlands. Stadholder (1751-1795 : William V). Missive en memorie door Zyne Hoogheid den Heere Prince van Orange en Nassau aan Hun Hoog Mogende op den 7 October 1782 overgegeven. [The Hague, 1782?] U35
A collection of documents dealing with the deployment of Dutch naval forces during the American Revolution as a part of its "armed neutrality" policy.

United Provinces of the Netherlands. Stadholder (1751-1795 : William V). Missive en memorie, door Zyne Hoogheid, den Heere Prince van Orange en Nassau, aan hunne Hoog Mog. op den 7 October 1782 overgegeeven ... als admiral generaal van de unie. [n.p., 1782.] U36

A collection of materials relating to the actions of the Dutch fleet during hostilities with the English in the West Indies, actions in which St. Eustache, Demerary, Essequebo and Berbice were lost by the Dutch.

United Provinces of the Netherlands. Stadholder (1751-1795 : William V). Missive en memorie, door Zyne Hoogheid, den Heere Prince van Orange en Nassau, aan Hunne Hoog Mog. op den 7 October 1782 overgegeeven [sic]. [n.p., 1782?] U37
A report on the conduct of the Dutch navy in actions against the British in the West Indies and in an expedition against Brest.

United Provinces of the Netherlands. Stadholder (1751-1795 : William V). Vervolg van de Missive en memorie door Zyne Hoogheid den Heere Prince van Orange en Nassau ... [n.p., 1783.] U38
An addition to the Missive of the previous year, covering events and correspondence to November 1782, and reporting extensively on the supplying and equipping of Dutch fleets.

United Provinces of the Netherlands. Staten Generaal. Lijste der licenten, ghemaeckt by mijnen heeren de Generaele Staten vande gheunieerde Nederlandtsche provincien, vanden goederen die zullen moghen ghevoert worden naer vyanden landt, nae die rivieren vander Mase, Rhijn, Wael ende dYssel ... Delft, Aelbrecht Hendricksz., 1588. U39

United Provinces of the Netherlands. Staten Generaal. Lijste der convoyen vande goederen ghevoert werende naer neutrael landen, als op Bremen ende oostwaerts, op Diepen ende westwaerts, eñ voorts op Ingelāt, Schotlant ende andere coninckrijcken, mitsgaders van alle incomende goederen ... The Hague, Aelbrecht Heyndricksz., 1596. U40

United Provinces of the Netherlands. Staten Generaal. Octroi van Oost Indische Compagnie. Manuscript. Netherlands [ca. 1602]. U41
An early draft of the Dutch East India Company's charter, containing generally the same material as the official published version, but differing in the number and arrangement of paragraphs.

United Provinces of the Netherlands. Staten Generaal. Placcaet ende ordonnantie opte wapeninghe ende manninghe vande schepen, soo ter coopvaerdije als visscherije ... varende. The Hague, Hillebrandt Jacobsz, 1607. U42
Instructions for the arming and conduct of merchant and fishing vessels of the Netherlands.

United Provinces of the Netherlands. Staten Generaal. Ordre, By de Hoog, Mogende Heeren

Staten Generael der Vereenichde Nederlanden ghemaeckt op het bevaren vande Middelantsche Zee ende het Sout halen in West-Indien. Amsterdam, M. Colijn, 1621.　　　　　　U43
　Concerns the Dutch West India Company's fleet of 100 vessels to acquire salt at Ponto del Reye in the West Indies and to be accompanied by Dutch ships of war.

United Provinces of the Netherlands. Staten Generaal. Placcaet by de Hooghmo: Heeren Staten Generael ... vande West-Indische Compagnie. The Hague, H. Jacobssz, 1621.　U44
　A five-page proclamation by the United Provinces government, announcing the establishment of the West India Company, and defining its purposes and the limitations on its operations.

United Provinces of the Netherlands. Staten Generaal. Lyste der convoyen ende licenten, ghemaeckt by mijne heeren de Generale Staten vande Vereenighde Nederlandtsche Provintien, van alle inkomende goederen, soo uyt vyande landen, de Mase, als uyt neutrale landen ... The Hague, Hillebrant Jacobssz, 1622.　　U45

United Provinces of the Netherlands. Staten Generaal. Placcaet teghens seecker fameus libel geintituleert Nootwendigh discours ofte vertoogh aende Hog: Mog: Heeren Staten Generael vande participanten der Oost-Indische Compagnie tegens bewinthebberen. The Hague, Weduwe en erfgenamen van wijlen Hillebrant Jacobssz van Wouw, 1622.　　U46
　A decree proscribing the *Nootwendich discourse*, attributed to Simon Middelgeest, which was critical of the directors of the Dutch East India Company.

United Provinces of the Netherlands. Staten Generaal. Octroy by de Hooghe Mogende Heeren Staten Generael verleent aende West-Indische Compagnie. The Hague, Weduwe, en erfghenamen van wijlen H.J. van Wouw, 1623.　　　　　　　　　　　U47
　"Patent granted by their High Mightinesses the States General to the West India Company."

United Provinces of the Netherlands. Staten Generaal. Octroy de ... Heeren Staten Generael, verleent aende West-Indische Compagnie ... Middelburg, Symon Moulert [1623?].　U48
　This edition was published for the Zeeland chamber of the company.

United Provinces of the Netherlands. Staten Generaal. Ordonnances, privileges, franchises, et assistances octroyez & concedez ... a la Compagnie des Indes Occidentales. Paris, Jean Anthoine Joallin, 1623.　　　　　U49
　The translator's preface notes the fact that Paris has been placarded by Dutch promoters of the West India Company, seeking to encourage French investment in the enterprise.

United Provinces of the Netherlands. Staten Generaal. Placcaet ... van 't verkoopen, ende transporteren van actien inde Oost-Indische Compagnie. The Hague, Weduwe en erfghenamen van wijlen H.J. Wouw, 1623.　　U50
　A government order to prevent manipulation of the value of shares of the Dutch East India Company.

United Provinces of the Netherlands. Staten Generaal. Placaet ... op't stuck van 't verkoopen ende transporteren van actien inde West Indische Compagnie. The Hague, Weduwe ende erfghenamen van wijlen H.J. van Wouw, 1624.　U51
　Regulations for the buying and selling of shares in the West India Company.

United Provinces of the Netherlands. Staten Generaal. Instructie ... reguleren, in 't visiteren, meten ende tarren vande Engelsche lakenen. The Hague, Weduwe ende erfgenamen H.J. van Wouw, 1630.　　　　　　　　　U52
　Regulations upon the import of English woolen cloth.

United Provinces of the Netherlands. Staten Generaal. Placcaet ... op't stuck vanden tarra vande Enghelsche lakenen. The Hague, Weduwe ende erfgenamen H.J. van Wouw, 1630.　U53
　A series of eleven regulations on English cloth coming into the Netherlands.

United Provinces of the Netherlands. Staten Generaal. Placaet ... op het heffen end betalen der last ghelden, over schepen varende door de Strate van Gibraltar naar ... Levanten. The Hague, Weduwe en erfgenamen wan wijlen H.J. van Wouw, 1633.　　　　　　　　U54
　A fee is levied on each Dutch ship passing through the Strait of Gibraltar, probably to defray costs of defense against Mediterranean pirates.

United Provinces of the Netherlands. Staten Generaal. Placaet ... op het heffen ende betalen der last-ghelden, over de schepen varende door de Strate van Gibraltar ... The Hague, Weduwe ende erfgenamen H.J. van Wouw, 1636.　U55
　Instructions for Dutch ships sailing through the Strait of Gibraltar.

United Provinces of the Netherlands. Staten Generaal. Lyste der convoyen ende licenten, ghemaeckt by mijne heeren de Generale Staten vande Vereenichde Nederlantsche Provintien, van alle inkomende goederen, soo uyt vyande landen, de Maze, als uyt neutrale landen ... Middelburgh, Weduwe ende erffgenamen van Symon Moulert, 1640.　　　　　U56

United Provinces of the Netherlands. Staten Generaal. Placaet ... om de kruyssers werder in zee te brenghen. The Hague, Weduwe, ende erf-

genamen van wijlen Hillebrandt Jacobssz van Wouw, 1643. U57
Fighting ships are ordered out to defend Dutch shipping.

United Provinces of the Netherlands. Staten Generaal. Extract, uyt het boeck vande vredehandelingh vande ... Staten Generael der Vereenichde Nederlanden. [n.p.] 1647. U58
A pamphlet noting that a fleet will be sent to Brazil soon to protect the interests of the Dutch West India Company.

United Provinces of the Netherlands. Staten Generaal. Poincten der artijckelen ... in het tractaet van vreden tot Munster. Dordrecht, Symon Moulaert, 1647. U59
Instructions for the Dutch negotiators at Munster, including insistence upon freedom of the East and West India companies to trade according to their charters.

United Provinces of the Netherlands. Staten Generaal. Placaet ... The Hague, Weduwe ende erfgenamen Hillebrandt Jacobssz van Wouw, 1651. U60
A proclamation forbidding the import of dyed woolen cloth.

United Provinces of the Netherlands. Staten Generaal. Placaet ... The Hague, Weduwe ende erfgenamen van wijlen Hillebrandt Jacobssz van Wouw, 1651. U61
Provides for increased convoys for the protection of Dutch merchant shipping.

United Provinces of the Netherlands. Staten Generaal. Placaet ... The Hague, Weduwe ende erfgenamen van wijlen Hillebrandt Jacobssz van Wouw, 1651. U62
Restrictions upon the shipping of gold, silver, and other goods to foreign countries where they might serve to the disadvantage of the Netherlands.

United Provinces of the Netherlands. Staten Generaal. Placaet ... The Hague, Weduwe ende erfgenamen van wijlen Hillebrandt Jacobssz van Wouw, 1651. U63
A broadside proclamation granting pardon to pirates who render a service to the nation at sea.

United Provinces of the Netherlands. Staten Generaal. Copie vande commissien ... aen de capiteynen ter zee, tegens alle oorloch-schepen ... Delft, Ian Pietersz, 1652. U64
Authorizes Dutch captains to attack English ships in response to England's Navigation Act of 1651.

United Provinces of the Netherlands. Staten Generaal. Lyste ... waer op ende waer naer ontfanghen ende gecollecteert sal worden een per cento op de uptgaende ... goederen. The Hague, Jacobus Scheltus [1652]. U65
A charge of one per cent was to be made on goods listed here, and two per cent on exported imports.

United Provinces of the Netherlands. Staten Generaal. Placaet ende ordonnantie, nae de welcke hier te lande het last-geldt geheben sal worden ... [n.p.] 1652. U66
Instructions for collecting tolls on ships leaving and arriving at Dutch ports.

United Provinces of the Netherlands. Staten Generaal. Placaet ende ordonnantie. Tegens het onachtsaem ende reuckeloos varen der coopvaerdye-schippers dieser landen ... The Hague, Weduwe ende erfgenamen van wijlen Hillebrant Jacobsz van Wouw, 1652. U67
Concerns the necessity of, and instructions for, shipping in convoys for defense.

United Provinces of the Netherlands. Staten Generaal. Placaet. Opte grootte, equipagie, monture, manninge ende admiraelschappen der schepen, varende door de Strate van Gibralter. The Hague, Weduwe ende erfgenamen van wijlen Hillebrant Jacobsz van Wouw, 1652. U68
Instructions for Dutch ships trading in the Mediterranean.

United Provinces of the Netherlands. Staten Generaal. Placcaet ... noopende de commercie ende navigatie ter zee, by haer beraemt ende besloten den 5 December 1652. The Hague, Weduwe ende erfgenamen van Hillebrant Jacobsz van Wouw, 1652. U69

United Provinces of the Netherlands. Staten Generaal. Placaet opte groote equipagie, monture, manninge ende admiraelschappen der schepen, varende ... naer de Middelandtsche Zee, ende op Levanten. The Hague, Weduwe ende erfgenamen van wylen Hillebrandt Jacobsz van Wouw, 1655. U70
Instructions regarding the lading, arming, and navigation of Dutch ships in the Mediterranean.

United Provinces of the Netherlands. Staten Generaal. Placaet ende ordonnantie ... aengaende de kortingen die op de comptoiren der convoyen ende licenten geschieden sullen, op het recht vande goederen ter zee in komende ... The Hague, Weduwe ende erfgenamen van wylen Hillebrandt Jacobsz van Wouw, 1657. U71
Contains a schedule of convoy money owed to seamen engaged in that work.

United Provinces of the Netherlands. Staten Generaal. Publicatie. The Hague, Weduwe ende erfgenamen van wylen H.J. van Wouw, 1657. U72
Contains news of a treaty between France and the Hanseatic League in which France agreed to receive Hanseatic merchants.

United Provinces of the Netherlands. Staten Generaal. Publicatie. The Hague, Weduwe ende erfgenamen van wylen H.J. van Wouw, 1657.
U73
Diplomatic correspondence between France and the Netherlands relating to the treaty between France and the Hanseatic cities, including the text of the treaty, signed in 1655.

United Provinces of the Netherlands. Staten Generaal. Missive ... aen Syn. Kon. Maj. van Denemarck. Amsterdam, Coenraet Jansz., 1659.
U74
The Dutch government replies to a complaint from the Danish King, stating that it can do little against the Swedes without more help from the Danes.

United Provinces of the Netherlands. Staten Generaal. Verscheyde brieven, antwoorden en andere documenten van ... der Vereenigde Nederlanden. Amsterdam, Pieter C. van Leeuwen, 1662.
U75
Correspondence concerning the taking of a Dutch ship by the English and the taking of two English ships by the Dutch.

United Provinces of the Netherlands. Staten Generaal. Placaet, opte groote equipagie, monture, manninge ende admiraelschappen der schepen, varende ... naer de Middelandtsche Zee, ende op Levanten. The Hague, Hillebrandt van Wouw, 1663.
U76
A set of twelve instructions regarding the lading, arming, and navigation of Dutch ships in the Mediterranean.

United Provinces of the Netherlands. Staten Generaal. Publicatie. The Hague, Hillebrandt van Wouw, 1663.
U77
A proclamation urging compliance with the preceding earlier regulations for the benefit of Dutch commerce in the Mediterranean.

United Provinces of the Netherlands. Staten Generaal. Waerschouwinge. The Hague, Hillebrandt van Wouw, 1663.
U78
A warning urging compliance with the instructions set forth in the preceding proclamation.

United Provinces of the Netherlands. Staten Generaal. Missive aen den Koninck van Groot-Brittangien. Amsterdam, Jan Gerritsen, 1664.
U79
The Dutch call attention to the growing troubles between themselves and the English, and hope the English king will do all in his power to avoid war.

United Provinces of the Netherlands. Staten Generaal. Verklaringe ... op de declaratie van Syne Majesteyt van Groot Bretagne. Utrecht, Jeremias de Bol, 1664.
U80
The Dutch deny that their East India Company had refused entrance and loading to two English ships in the East Indies.

United Provinces of the Netherlands. Staten Generaal. Wederlegginge van 't gesustineerde van den Coningh van Groot Brittannien ... The Hague, 1664.
U81
A protest against English interference in Dutch West African trade. The text is in French and Dutch.

United Provinces of the Netherlands. Staten Generaal. Naeder placaet ende verbodt, tegens de vaert ende visscherye op ende ontrent Groenlant. [n.p., 1665].
U82
A third notice forbidding travel and fishing in the waters about Greenland.

United Provinces of the Netherlands. Staten Generaal. [Publicatie.] The Hague, Hillebrandt van Wouw, 1665.
U83
Requires removal of all alien residents from the Netherlands except those with permission to remain.

United Provinces of the Netherlands. Staten Generaal. Resolutie vande Ed. Groot Mo. Heeren staten van Hollandt ende West Vriesland. The Hague, H.J. van Wouw, 1665.
U84
A protest against English interference with the Dutch trade to Guinea.

United Provinces of the Netherlands. Staten Generaal. Sommierre aenteyckeninge ende deductie ... op de lest-ingediende Memorie van ... George Downing. The Hague, 1665.
U85
A repudiation of English claims to monopoly in Gambia.

United Provinces of the Netherlands. Staten Generaal. Antwoort van de ... Staten Generael ... aen de Heer Downing. Middelburg, J. Fierens, 1666.
U86
A list of the current differences existing between the English and Dutch governments, chiefly concerning East and West India trade.

United Provinces of the Netherlands. Staten Generaal. Nieuwe ende naedere gecorrigeerde lyste van de gemeene middelen ... van alle inkomende ofte uytgaende waren ... The Hague, H. van Wouw, 1666.
U87
A new list of import and export duties in effect in the Netherlands.

United Provinces of the Netherlands. Staten Generaal. Placaet. The Hague, Hillebrandt van Wouw, 1667.
U88
A proclamation requiring the removal from the Netherlands of all alien merchants except those with express permission to remain.

United Provinces of the Netherlands. Staten Generaal. Placaet. The Hague, Hillebrandt van Wouw, 1667. U89
  A broadside proclamation containing a series of regulations about sailors serving on Dutch ships.

United Provinces of the Netherlands. Staten Generaal. d'Antwoort van de Staten Generael ... op de declaratie van oorlogh des Konings van Groot Britanien. [n.p., 1672.] U90
  A reply to the English declaration of war. The Dutch accuse the English of interfering with the management of the Surinam colony.

United Provinces of the Netherlands. Staten Generaal. Placaet ende ordonnantie op het heffen ende betalen ... over de schepen, varende door de Strate van Gibraltar ... [The Hague, ca. 1673.] U91
  Instructions for Dutch ships sailing through the Strait of Gibraltar.

United Provinces of the Netherlands. Staten Generaal. Verteütschtes Send-Schreiben, an den König von Gross-Britannien, abgangen wegen Ihrer Hochmög: der Hn. General-Staten der Vereinigten Niederlanden. [n.p.] 1673. U92
  Official correspondence relating to differences between the Dutch and English, leading to a peace settlement at the end of the third Anglo-Dutch War, 1674.

United Provinces of the Netherlands. Staten Generaal. Octroy, by de ... Staten Generael, verleent aen de West-Indische Compagnie. The Hague, J. Scheltus, 1674. U93
  The new charter given to the Dutch West India Company following the loss of New Netherland.

United Provinces of the Netherlands. Staten Generaal. Ordonnantie ende waerschouwinge. The Hague, J. Scheltus, 1677. U94
  A notice by the Dutch government that there is to be unrestricted freedom of fishing along the coasts of France, Spain, the Low Countries, to the north of England, and near Greenland and North America.

United Provinces of the Netherlands. Staten Generaal. Concept. Nieuwe gedresseerde lyste van de gemeene middelen ... van alle inkomende ende uytgaende waren ende koopmanschappen. [n.p., ca. 1681.] U95
  A list of more than five hundred commodities, indicating the import and export duties to be paid on each.

United Provinces of the Netherlands. Staten Generaal. Octroy ofte fondamentele conditien, onder de welcke haer Hoogh Mog. ten besten ende voordeele van de ... colonie van Suriname. The Hague, J. Scheltus, 1682. U96
  A decree outlining the rights of the Dutch West India Company in the colony of Surinam.

United Provinces of the Netherlands. Staten Generaal. Declaratie van oorlogh, mitsgaders placaet ... raeckende de navigatie en commercie van neutralen ... The Hague, Jacobus Scheltus [1689]. U97
  Along with their declaration of war against France, the Dutch spell out their interpretation of the rights of neutrals to trade in French ports.

United Provinces of the Netherlands. Staten Generaal. Octroy ... verleent aen de Oost-Indische Compagnie. The Hague, J. Scheltus, 1689. U98
  A new charter for the Dutch East India Company which was to continue until 1700.

United Provinces of the Netherlands. Staten Generaal. Octroy ... verleendt aen de Oost-Indische Compagnie. The Hague, P. Scheltus [1696]. U99
  A review of earlier charter provisions, and adding provisions to be in effect until 1740.

United Provinces of the Netherlands. Staten Generaal. Octroy by de Hoogh. Mog. Heeren Staten Generael verleent aen de West Indische Compagnie. The Hague, P. Scheltus, 1701. U100
  The first edition of the third patent granted to the Dutch West India Company.

United Provinces of the Netherlands. Staten Generaal. Manifest ... der Vereenighde Nederlanden, genoodtsaeckt zijn tegens de koningen van Vranckryck en Spaigne den oorlogh te declaren. The Hague, Paulus Scheltus, 1702. U101
  Declaration of war against France and Spain, noting the actions taken by the French king to damage Dutch commerce in Europe and in America.

United Provinces of the Netherlands. Staten Generaal. Ampliatie van het placaet van den sesden Junii 1702 over de proemien voor de commissie-vaerders deser landen. Den twintighsten Junii 1704. The Hague, Paulus Scheltus, 1704. U102

United Provinces of the Netherlands. Staten Generaal. Placaet. De Staten Generael der Vereenigde Nederlanden, allen den geenen die desen sullen sien ofte hooren lesen, salut: Doen to weten: Dat wy by resumptie van voorige ordres op het stuck van de commissie-vaert deser landen goedtgevonden hebben tot het weeren van onordentelijckheden ende om voor te komen de klachten van de ingezetenen van desen staet van onse geallieerden en neutralen ... The Hague, Paulus Scheltus, 1705. U103

United Provinces of the Netherlands. Staten Generaal. Placaet. De Staten Generael der Vereenigde Nederlanden. Allen den geenen die desen sullen sien ofte hooren lesen, saluyt. Doen te weten. Dat wy by resumptie van de ordres in voorige tijden en onlangs gestelt op het stuck van waren van contrabande, en commercie op's vyandts landen goedtgevonden hebben te ordonneren en te statueren ... Den acht en twintighsten Julii 1705. The Hague, Paulus Scheltus, 1705.
U104

United Provinces of the Netherlands. Staten Generaal. Placaet. De Staten Generael der Vereenighde Nederlanden, allen den geenen die desen sullen sien of hooren lesen, salut. Doen te weten: Dat wy tot meerder protectie van de commercie, navigatie, en visscherye en tot beveylinge van de zeegaten deser landen goetgevonden hebben de proemien by ons placaet van den sesden Junii des jaers 1702 gestelt te verhoogen in dier voegen. The Hague, Paulus Scheltus, 1705.
U105

United Provinces of the Netherlands. Staten Generaal. Placaet, van elucidatie, ampliatie ende veranderinge, op het stuck van praemin voor de commissievaerdens ... die eenige vyandtlijcke schepen van oorlogh ofte commissie-vaerders komen te veroveren ofte te vernielen ... The Hague, Paulus Scheltus, 1709.
U106

United Provinces of the Netherlands. Staten Generaal. Nieuwe ende nadere gecorrigeerde lyste, van de gemeene middelen die door ordre ... geheben sullen werden van alle inkomende of uytgaende waren en koopmanschappen ... Middelburg, Bartholomeus de Later [1711].
U107

The tariff on incoming and outgoing goods, an excellent indicator of the commodities traded by Dutch merchants. The basic list was established in 1655, but is updated to 1711 here.

United Provinces of the Netherlands. Staten Generaal. Placaet. De Staten Generaal der Vereenigde Nederlanden, allen den geenen die desen sullen sien ofte hooren lesen, salut; doen de weten: Nademael sedert eenigen tijd van wegens de maghten in den oorlogh tegens den Koningh van Spagne begrepen, diversse klaghten aan ons zijn voorgekomen, over den toevoer van waaren van contrabande uyt dese landen naar Spagne ... The Hague, Paulus Scheltus, 1719.
U108

United Provinces of the Netherlands. Staten Generaal. Placaat. De Staaten Generaal der Vereenigde Nederlanden, allen den geenen, die desen sullen sien of gehooren lesen, salut, doet te weeten: Alsoo wy meer en meer ondervinden, dat zedert eenige weynige jaaren diversche ordonnantien of edicten in Zweeden uytgekoomen zijn, tot versperring of bezwaaring van de navigatie en commercie deser landen ... The Hague, Jacobus Scheltus, 1729.
U109

United Provinces of the Netherlands. Staten Generaal. Nader prolongatie van het octroy ... The Hague, J. Scheltus, 1730.
U110

An extension of the charter of the Dutch West India Company through 1760.

United Provinces of the Netherlands. Staten Generaal. Octroi of conditien, waar by hunne Hoog. Mog. de Heeren Staaten Generaal aan de directeuren van de colonie de Berbice ... The Hague, J. Scheltus [1733].
U111

A proclamation authorizing the directors of the colony at Berbice to open free trade in that colony.

United Provinces of the Netherlands. Staten Generaal. Naader reglement op het subject van de vrye vaart op de kust van Africa ... The Hague, Jacob Scheltus, 1734.
U112

A document regulating the trade of Dutch merchants to West Africa, with particular reference to the Dutch West India Company and the slave trade.

United Provinces of the Netherlands. Staten Generaal. Placaat van de praemie voor commissie vaarders deeser landen, dewelke eenige oorlogscheepen van de Franschen sullen koomen te veroveren, in dato dan 11 December 1747. The Hague, Jacobus Scheltus, 1747.
U113

United Provinces of the Netherlands. Staten Generaal. Placcaat tegens het inloopen van kaapers ... Den 11 December 1747. The Hague, Jacobus Scheltus, 1747.
U114

United Provinces of the Netherlands. Staten Generaal. Octroy ... verleend aan de Oost-Indische Compagnie. The Hague, J. Scheltus, 1748.
U115

A copy of the original charter of the East India Company, with all additions and continuations, as well as a renewal of the charter to 1774.

United Provinces of the Netherlands. Staten Generaal. Extract uyt het Register der resolutien ... den 26 November 1749. [n.p., ca. 1750.]
U116

Notes that William, Prince of Orange and Nassau, will preside at all meetings of the management of the Dutch West India Company, and will direct the company's stations in Guinea.

United Provinces of the Netherlands. Staten Generaal. Octroi of fondamenteele conditien ...

van ... de colonie van Suriname ... The Hague, J. Scheltus, 1752. U117
   States the rights of the West India Company to trade in Surinam.

United Provinces of the Netherlands. Staten Generaal. Publicatie ... Doen te weeten; also wy tot verval der onkosten van de extraordinaris equipagien, die tot meerder beveyliging en bescherming der koopwaardyscheepen deeser landen, souden werden gedaan ... een extraordinaris middel van belasting uit to vinden. The Hague, Isaac Scheltus, 1760. U118

United Provinces of the Netherlands. Staten Generaal. Nader prolongatie van het octroy voor de Westindische Compagnie. The Hague, I. Scheltus, 1761. U119
   A further prolongation of the charter of the Dutch West India Company, together with a history of the company.

United Provinces of the Netherlands. Staten Generaal. Publicatie. De Staaten Generaal der Vereenigde Nederlanden: Allen den geenen die deese jeegenwoordige sullen sien of hooren leesen, salut: Doen te weeten; alsoo de reedenen, welke ons gemoveert hadden, om by onse publicatie van den 29 Mey deeses jaars, alle vaart en handel uit en over deesen staat ... in desselfs landen van Gulik en Berg, te verbieden ... The Hague, Isaac Scheltus, 1770. U120

United Provinces of the Netherlands. Staten Generaal. Publicatie. De Staaten Generaal der Vereenigde Nederlanden; allen den geenen die deese jeegenwoordige sullen sien of hooren leesen, salut; doen te weeten: Alsoo wy met de uiterste bevreemding vernoomen hebben ... om sonder eenig beklag repraesentatie of warrschouwing den handel en vaart van de commercieerende ingezeetenen der steeden Dordrecht en Rotterdam langs den Rhyn te belemmeren ... The Hague, Isaac Scheltus, 1770. U121

United Provinces of the Netherlands. Staten Generaal. Publicatie. De Staaten Generaal der Vereenigde Nederlanden; allen den geenen die deesen sullen sien of hooren leesen salut; doen to weeten: Alsoo tot onse kennis is gekoomen dat de ordre by ons op den 11 September 1765 gestelt dat de boekhouders der Scheepen van deese landen, vaarende af en aan Ostende, verpligt souden zyn t' elkens by het invallen van het schip aldaar, hunne Turksche pasporten te rug te brengen ... The Hague, Isaac Scheltus, 1775. U122

United Provinces of the Netherlands. Staten Generaal. Publicatie, De Staaten Generaal der Vereenigde Nederlanden, allen den geenen die deesen sullen sien of hooren leesen, salut: Doen te weeten; nademaal de reedenen, welke ons tot het primitive verbod van uitvoer van Ammunitie van Oorlog na de Engelsche Colonien hebben gepermoveert, als nog subsisteeren ... The Hague, Isaac Scheltus, 1777. U123
   The proclamation calls for fines and confiscation for offenders and provides for wide distribution on the order so that none can pretend ignorance of it.

United Provinces of the Netherlands. Staten Generaal. Publicatie. De Staten Generaal der Vereenigde Nederlanden ... verbod van uitvoer van ammunitie van oorlog na de Engelsche colonien ... The Hague, Isaac Scheltus, 1777. U124
   Proclamation forbidding export of munitions of war to the British colonies in North America.

United Provinces of the Netherlands. Staten Generaal. Placaat van de Hoog Mogende Heeren Staaten Generaal der Vereenigde Nederlanden, houdende verbod van uitvoer uit deese landen en van toevoer na het ryk van Groot-Brittannien van oorlogs-ammunitie en eenige andere specien by het placaat breeder beschreeven, als mede waarschouwing tegens den vervoer van contrabande goederen na het voorszryk. The Hague, Isaac Scheltus, 1781.
U125

United Provinces of the Netherlands. Staten Generaal. Placaat van de praemie voor de commissievaarders deser landen, dewelke eenige oorlog-scheepen van de Engelsche sullen koomen te veroveren, in dato den 12 January 1781. The Hague, Isaac Scheltus, 1781. U126

United Provinces of the Netherlands. Staten Generaal. Placaat. De Staaten Generaal der Vereenigde Nederlanden; allen den geenen die deesen sullen sien of hooren lesen, salut; doen te weeten: Nademaal het den Koning van Engeland goedgedagt heeft, sonder eenige wettige reeden, den staat deeser landen vyandelyk aan te tasten door het verleenen van brieven van marque ... The Hague, Isaac Scheltus, 1781. U127

United Provinces of the Netherlands. Staten Generaal. Rapporten van de Heeren Haar Ed. Groot Mog. Gecommitteerden G.J. Doys baron van der Does, Heer van Noordwyk, Mr. P.H. van de Wall, J. Rendorp, Heer van Marquette, en Mr. H. van Straalen, over den staat der Generaal Nederlandsche Oost-Indische Compagnie. Dunkirk, 1791. U128
   A report of a committee of inquiry into the financial state of the Dutch East India Company.

United Provinces of the Netherlands. Staten Generaal. Publicatie. De Staaten Generaal der

Vereenigde Nederlanden, allen den geenen, die deeze zullen zien, ofte hooren leezen, heil en broederschap. Doen te weeten: Dat wy meermaalen by de repraesententen van de Fransche natie en meer bepaaldelyk ... van den vryen uitvoer van alle goederen hier te lande ... The Hague, Isaac Scheltus, 1795.   U129

United Provinces of the Netherlands. Treaties, etc. Bysonder artijckel, raeckende de scheepvaert ... volgens tractaet vande vrede besloten. Amsterdam, C. Iansz, 1648.   U130
    A separate printing of the article of the Treaty of Munster which related to the freedom of the Dutch to trade abroad.

United Provinces of the Netherlands. Treaties, etc. Tractaet van vruntschap ende verbintenisse ... tusschen ... Staten Generael ... ende de Heeren gouverneurs ... van de Steden van Salé ... The Hague, Weduwe ende erfgenamen van wylen H.J. van Wouw, 1651.   U131
    The treaty was to put an end to African privateering and set free Dutch sailors being held by the African state of Salé.

United Provinces of the Netherlands. Treaties, etc. Conditien ende artikulen van't verdrag van Amboyna ... The Hague, Wilhelm Breeckevelt, 1654.   U132
    A commercial treaty providing for peaceful trade between England and the Netherlands in the East Indies.

United Provinces of the Netherlands. Treaties, etc. Nader tractaet van vreede ende vrundtschap ... tusschen ... Staten Generael ... ende den prince ... van Salé. The Hague, Weduwe ende erfgenamen van H.J. van Wouw, 1659.   U133
    Treaty with the Moroccan city of Salé with provision for commerce between the signatories.

United Provinces of the Netherlands. Treaties, etc. Tractaet van vrede ende van commercie. The Hague, J. Scheltus, 1680.   U134
    A treaty of peace and commerce between the Netherlands and the ruler of Algiers.

United Provinces of the Netherlands. Treaties, etc. Traitté de paix & de commerce, entre ... Provinces Unies ... & de Royaume d'Alger. The Hague, J. Scheltus, 1680.   U135
    A treaty allowing free trade between the Dutch and four North African countries.

United Provinces of the Netherlands. Treaties, etc. Tractaet van commercie, navigatie en marine ... tusschen den Koningh van Sweden ... ende de Heeren Staten Generael. The Hague, J. Scheltus, 1681.   U136
    Articles of the Treaty of Nijmegen, 1679, which included a free trade agreement between the Netherlands and Sweden.

United Provinces of the Netherlands. Treaties, etc. Tractaet van commercie, navigatie en marine. The Hague, P. Scheltus, 1697.   U137
    A commercial treaty between France and the Netherlands, attempting to restore normal commercial relations.

United Provinces of the Netherlands. Treaties, etc. Tractaat tusschen ... de Heeren Staaten Generael ... en de regeeringe van Algiers. The Hague, P. Scheltus, 1713.   U138
    The treaty provides for a reduction from twenty to ten per cent on duties payable by the Dutch in Algerian ports.

United Provinces of the Netherlands. Treaties, etc. Tractaet tusschen ... de Heeren Staten Generael ... ende de regeeringe van Tunes. The Hague, P. Scheltus, 1713.   U139
    The treaty promises unhindered access to Tunisian ports for Dutch ships.

United Provinces of the Netherlands. Treaties, etc. Tractaet van commercie, navigatie en marine ... tusschen ... Vranckryck ... ende ... de Staten Generael. The Hague, P. Scheltus, 1713.   U140
    A treaty of commerce and navigation between France and the Netherlands, a portion of the Treaty of Utrecht.

United Provinces of the Netherlands. Treaties, etc. Tractaet van de vreede, commercie, navigation, ende marine ... tusschen ... Philippus V ... ende ... de Staten Generael ... The Hague, P. Scheltus, 1714.   U141
    A treaty of commerce and navigation between the Netherlands and Spain, a part of the Treaty of Utrecht.

United Provinces of the Netherlands. Treaties, etc. Tractaat tusschen ... de Heeren Staaten Generael ... en de regeeringe van Algiers. The Hague, J. Scheltus, 1726.   U142
    Confirms terms of the 1713 treaty, and reduces duties from ten to five per cent on goods brought into Algerian ports.

United Provinces of the Netherlands. Treaties, etc. Tractaat tusschen de Heeren Staten Generael en de regeeringe van Tripoli. The Hague, J. Scheltus, 1728.   U143
    The Dutch were authorized to trade in Tripoli, paying three per cent duty on all goods sold there.

United Provinces of the Netherlands. Treaties, etc. Tractaat van vreede en commercie geslooten tusschen ... den Keiser van Marocco en de ... Heeren Staaten Generael. The Hague, J. Scheltus, 1753.   U144

A confirmation of the normal rights and privileges for Dutch merchants trading in Moroccan ports.

United Provinces of the Netherlands. Treaties, etc. Tractaat tusschen ... de Heeren Staaten Generael ... en de regeeringe van Algiers. The Hague, J. and I. Scheltus, 1758. U145

Provides for free Dutch access to Algerian ports, with payment of duty not to exceed five per cent.

United Provinces of the Netherlands. Treaties, etc. Tractaat van vreede en commercie, geslooten tusschen ... den Keiser van Marocco en de ... Heeren Staaten Generael. The Hague, J. Scheltus, 1777. U146

A renewal of the treaty of 1752 between the Netherlands and Morocco.

United States. Continental Congress. A declaration by the representatives of the United Colonies of North-America ... setting forth the causes and necessity of their taking up arms. Philadelphia, William and Thomas Bradford, 1775. U147

"We are reduced to the alternative of chusing an unconditional submission to the tyranny of irritated ministers, or resisting by force—the latter is our choice." The declaration was written by John Dickinson.

United States. Continental Congress. Extracts from the votes and proceedings of the American Continental Congress, held at Philadelphia, on the fifth of September, 1774. London, J. Almon, 1774. U148

A statement of the complaints of the American colonies, a prelude to the Declaration of Independence.

United States. Continental Congress. Journal of the proceedings of the congress held at Philadelphia, September 5th, 1774. London, J. Almon, 1775. U149

"Containing, the Bill of Rights; a list of grievances, occasional resolves; the Association; an address to the people of Great Britain; a memorial to the inhabitants of the British American colonies; and, an address to the inhabitants of the province of Quebec."

United States. Continental Congress. Lettre circulaire du congrès des États-Unis de l'Amérique. Paris, Pougin [1795]. U150

A French translation of a proclamation made by the Continental Congress concerning the value of paper money and debts of the country.

United States. Dept. of State. Authentic copies of the correspondence of Thomas Jefferson, esq. the Secretary of State to the United States of America, and George Hammond, esq. Minister Plenipotentiary of Great-Britain, on the non-execution of existing treaties ... between Great Britain and the United States. Philadelphia, printed: London, reprinted for J. Debrett, 1794. U151

Diplomatic correspondence leading to settlement of differences between Great Britain and the United States going back to the treaty of 1783. Also included is some correspondence between American officials and Citizen Genêt.

United States. Dept. of State. Report of the Secretary of State, on the privileges and restrictions on the commerce of the United States in foreign countries, published by order of the House of Representatives. Philadelphia, Childs and Swaine, 1793. U152

This report prepared by Thomas Jefferson is a survey of the overseas commerce of the United States, noting the value of each of the fifteen major commodities and the nations most prominent as importers of these goods.

United States. Dept. of the Treasury. Report of the Secretary of the Treasury of the United States, on the subject of manufactures, presented to the House of Representatives, December 5, 1791. Dublin, P. Byrne, 1792. U153

Alexander Hamilton's survey of the economy of the American republic with particular emphasis on the possibilities for developing manufacturing industries.

The Universal pocket-book: being the most comprehensive, useful and compleat book of the kind ever yet publish'd ... London, For T. Cooper, 1740. U154

A commercial and domestic handbook, including geographical and historical material, methods of record-keeping, weights and measures, wages of craftsmen, etc., including a good plan of London.

Universidad y Casa de Contratación de la M.N. y M.L. Villa de Bilbao. Ordenanzas de la ilustre Universidad, y Casa de Contratacion de la ... villa de Bilbao. Bilbao, Viuda de Antonio de Zafra y Rueda, 1738. U155

A code of maritime and commercial law which dates from 1511, and evolved to its final form in 1737. It was widely used as a basis for mercantile law in South America.

Universidad y Casa de Contratación de la M.N. y M.L. Villa de Bilbao. Ordenanzas de la ilustre Universidad, y Casa de Contratacion de la M.N.Y M.L. villa de Bilbao. Madrid, Sancha, 1796. U156

A reprint of the 1738 *Ordenanzas* with only slight alterations.

Università de' mercanti (Siena, Italy). Li statuti del Universita de mercanti e della corte de Signori uffitiali della Mercantia. Siena, Luca Bonetti, 1572. U157

A collection of statutes relating to the commercial life of Siena.

Università de' mercanti (Siena, Italy). Statuti dell' Uniuersità de' mercanti, e della Corte de gl'offiziali della mercanzia della città di Siena. Siena, Bonetti, 1619. U158
A revision of the *Statuti* issued in 1572.

Université de Cahors. Le manifest du Scindic de l'Université de Cahors. Contre les peres Iesuites. Pour estre veu devant Messieurs du Conseil Privé du Roy. [n.p.] 1624. U159
A pamphlet charging that the Jesuits had infiltrated the intellectual life of France through the universities and the bishoprics.

Université de Paris. III. Requeste de l'Universite de Paris, presentée a la Cour de Parlement. Le 7 decembre 1644. Contre les libelles que les Jesuites ont publiez. Paris, 1644. U160
Arguments against the granting of certain academic recognition to Jesuits, with reference to accusations made against them for their traffic with the Indians in New France.

Université de Paris. Faculté de Théologie. Censure de la sacree Faculte de Theologie de Paris portée contre les propositions extraites des livres intitulez *Nouveaux memoires sur l'état present de la Chine. Histoire de l'edit de l'empereur de la Chine. Lettre des ceremonies de la Chine.* [n.p., 1700.] U161
The statement of censure is followed by an *Act de protestation* (4 pages in folio) defending the authors of the books, Louis Daniel Le Comte and Charles Le Gobien.

Université de Paris. Faculté de Théologie. Reponse de cent trente-deux docteurs de la Faculté de Theologie de Paris, sur les questions de la Chine. Dressées en l'année 1699 par les eminentissimes Cardinaux deputés ... [n.p., 1700.] U162
The discussions of the Faculty of Theology and the orders of vicar apostolic, Charles Maigrot, relative to the Chinese Rites controversy.

Unprejudiced observer. A letter to a great M_____r, on the prospect of a peace: wherein the demolition of the fortifications of Louisbourg is shewn to be absurd: the importance of Canada fully refuted ... London, G. Kearsley, 1761. U163
Reviews the possible territorial settlements upon conclusion of peace with France and several pamphlets on that subject. This anonymous author favors acquiring French West Indian islands in preference to Canada.

Unverzagt, Georg Johann. Die Gesandschafft ... von Gross-Russland an den sinesischen Käyser. Lübeck, Johann C. Schmidt, 1725. U164
An account of an embassy from Peter the Great to the Emperor of China which includes descriptions of Siberia, parts of Mongolia, and China.

Uring, Nathaniel. A history of the voyages and travels of Captain Nathaniel Uring. London, W. Wilkins for J. Peele, 1726. U165
Contains numerous accounts of mercantile activities in the West Indies and West Africa.

[Uring, Nathaniel.] A relation of the late intended settlement of the islands of St. Lucia and St. Vincent, in America. London, J. Peele, 1725. U166
Includes documentary material pertaining to an attempted English settlement which was frustrated by the French.

Urreta, Luis de. Historia de la sagrada orden de predicadores, en remotos reynos de la Etiopia. Valencia, Juan Chrysostomo Garriz, 1611. U167
An account of a Dominican group's missionary work in Ethiopia.

Usselincx, Willem. Aggreatie des grootmachtichsten Coninck van Hispagnien, Philips den Derden ... Ghesonden aen de groot-moghende Heeren den Staten Generael vande Gheunieerde Provintien. [n.p.] 1608. U168
"Agreement of the King of Spain to treat with the States General."

Usselincx, Willem. Argonautica Gustaviana. Frankfurt am Main, Caspar Rödteln, 1633. U169
A collection of documents and promotional material issued in the interest of establishing an international overseas trading company.

Usselincx, Willem. Articulen van het contract ende accort ghemaeckt tusschen Jacobus den Ersten ... ende Philips den Derden ... Na de copie ghedruckt tot Londen by Robert Barker. [n.p., 1608.] U170
"Articles of the contract made between James I and Phillip III."

Usselincx, Willem. De artijckelen ende besluyten der Inquisitie van Spaegnien, om die vande Nederlanden te overvallen ende verhinderen. [n.p., 1608.] U171
"The articles and conclusions of the Inquisition of Spain."

Usselincx, Willem. Bedenckinghen over den staet vande Vereenichde Nederlanden. [n.p.] 1608. U172
"Considerations on the state of the United Netherlands, on navigation and commerce and on trade in general in those lands ... "

Usselincx, Willem. Brief des Keyserlijcke Majest. van Duytslandt aende E. Mogende Heeren Staten vande Gheunieerde Provintien gheschreven ... [n.p.] 1608. U173

"Letter of the Emperor of Germany to the States General."

Usselincx, Willem. Brief van hare Hoocheden aende E. Moghende Heeren Staten der vrye Vereenichde Nederlantsche Provintien ghesonden, gedateert binnen Brussel den 13 Martij, anno 1607. [n.p.] 1607.   U174
"Letter of Albert and Isabella to their High Mightinesses the States General of the United Netherlands."

[Usselincx, Willem.] Bulle oft mandaet des Paus van Roomen, aende gheestelicheyt al om bevolen ... [n.p., 1608.]   U175
A poem entitled "The Pope's Bull to the clergy for their advice on peace with the Heretical Hollanders."

Usselincx, Willem. Buyr-praetjen: Ofte tsamensprekinge ende discours op den brief vanden agent Aerssens uyt Vranckrijck aende ... Staten Ghenerael geschreven ... [n.p., 1608.]   U176
"Dialogue between two neighbors on the letter of the agent Aerssens."

Usselincx, Willem. Codicille van de Nederlandsche oorloghe ... Tot Franc end al, by Frederijck de Vrije [1609].   U177
"Codicil of the Dutch war."

Usselincx, Willem. Consideratien vande vrede in Nederlandt gheconcipieert, anno 1608. [n.p., 1608.]   U178
"Considerations on the peace proposed in the Netherlands, 1608."

[Usselincx, Willem.] Copye van een discours tusschen een Hollander ende een Zeeuw. [n.p., 1608.]   U179
"Copy of a discourse between a Hollander and a Zeelander."

Usselincx, Willem. Copye vande brieven der Heeren General Staten vande Gheunieerde Provintien. Gheschreven aen den Heeren Staten van Hollandt ende West-Vrieslandt. Delft, Jan Andriesz. [1608].   U180
"Copy of the letter of the States General to the States of Holland and West-Vriesland."

Usselincx, Willem. Copye vande namen der coninclicke, ende andere potentaten ghesanten van weghen de ... Staten Generael versocht omme mede te staen over de vredehandelinghe tusschen de vereemschde Nederlantsche Provintien ... ende den Coninc van Spaegnien ... [n.p.] 1608.   U181
"Copy of the names of the diplomatic agents sent to take part in the negotiations for peace between the Netherlands and the King of Spain."

Usselincx, Willem. Copye vanden brieff gheschreven van Zijn Hoocheyt aen Graeff Herman vanden Bergh gouverneur van't Hertochdom van Geldre ... [n.p.] 1607.   U182
"Copy of a letter to Count Herman van den Bergh."

[Usselincx, Willem.] Dees wonder-maer end' prophetsije wis, door's geests gesicht, gebooren is ... [n.p., 1609.]   U183
"A dream" beginning with eight lines of verse.

Usselincx, Willem. Dialogus oft tzamensprekinge, gemaect op den vredehandel. Gestelt by vraghe ende antwoordt. [n.p.] 1608.   U184
"Dialogue or conversation on the negotiations for peace."

Usselincx, Willem. Discours by forme van remonstrantie: vervatende de noodsaeckelickheyd vande Oost-Indische navigatie ... [n.p.] 1608.   U185
"A discourse in form of a remonstrance showing the necessity of navigation to the East Indies."

Usselincx, Willem. Discours van Pieter en Pauwels, op de handelinghe van den vreede. Anno 1608. [n.p., 1608.]   U186
"Discourse of Peter and Paul on the peace negotiations."

Usselincx, Willem. Echo ofte galm, dat is Wederklinckende gedichte van de teghenwoordighe vredehandelinghe. [n.p.] 1608.   U187
"Echo or sound: a reverberating poem on the impending peace negotiations."

Usselincx, Willem. Grondich discours over desen aenstaenden vrede-handel. [n.p., 1608.]   U188
"Appropriate discourse on these impending negotiations," meaning peace negotiations with Spain.

Usselincx, Willem. Memorie vande ghewichtighe redenen die de Heeren Staten Generael behooren te beweghen om gheesins te wijcken vande handelinghe ende vaert van Indien. [n.p., 1608.]   U189
"An advertisement of the weighty reasons which ought to determine ... the States General not to give up the commerce and navigation to India ... "

Usselincx, Willem. Naerder bedenkingen over de seevaerdt, coophandel ende neeringhe, als mede de versekeringhe vanden staet deser vereenichde landen ... [n.p.] 1608.   U190
"Further reflections on the navigation, commerce, and trade, as well as the security of these united lands in the present treaty of peace."

[Usselincx, Willem.] Den Nederlandtschen byekorf. [n.p., ca. 1608.]   U191
The title-piece for a collection of thirty-eight pamphlets favoring a continuation of the war with Spain rather than a peace that would be injurious to Dutch commerce in the

East and West Indies. Usselinx probably did not write all of them, but he was the leader of the anti-peace party.

Usselincx, Willem. Nootelijcke consideratien die alle goede liefhebbers des Vaderlants behooren rijpelijck te overwegen, opten voorgeflagen tractate van peys met den Spaengiaerden. [n.p.] 1587. [1608]. U192
"Necessary considerations on the peace treaty, to be maturely considered by all good patriots."

Usselincx, Willem. Onpartydich discours opte handelinghe vande Indien. [n.p., 1608.] U193
"Impartial treatise on the Indian commerce."

[Usselincx, Willem.] Een oud schipper van Monickendam, Daer ons den vromen held uyt quam ... [n.p., 1608.] U194
An anti-Spanish tract opening with four lines of poetry.

Usselincx, Willem. Placcaet van de Staten Generael van de Gheunieerde Nederlanden, by de welcken, mits den redenen in't lange int self begrepen, men verclaert den Coninck van Spaegnien vervallē vande overheyt ende heerschappie van dese voorsz Nederlanden ... [n.p., 1608.] U195
"Proclamation by which the King of Spain is declared to have forfeited his right and dominion over these Netherlands."

Usselincx, Willem. Principale puncten, die inde voorder handelinghe vanden vrede van weghen de E. vermoghende Heeren Staten General der Vereenichde Provintien onbegriipipelick sullen geproponeert werden ... [n.p.] 1608. U196
"Principal points which in the present negotiations will be presented by the States General."

Usselincx, Willem. Proeve des nu onlangs uytghegheven drooms oft t'samen spraack tusschen den Coning van Hispanien ende den Paus van Roomen ... [n.p.] 1608. U197
"Specimen of a lately published discourse between the King of Spain and the Pope of Rome."

Usselincx, Willem. Raedtsel. [n.p., 1608.] U198
A discussion of the peace terms in form of a conversation.

Usselincx, Willem. Schuyt-praetgens op de vaert naer Amsterdam, tusschen een lantman, een hovelinck, een borgher, ende schipper. [n.p., 1608.] U199
"Ferry-talk on the canal to Amsterdam."

Usselincx, Willem. Het secreet des Conings van Spangien, Philippus den Tweeden, achter-gelaten aen zijnen lieven zoone, Philips de Derde ... [n.p., 1608.] U200
"The secret of Philip II of Spain given to his son Philip III."

Usselincx, Willem. Sendbrief in forme van supplicatie aen de Coninncklijcke Majesteyt van Spaengien: van wegen des Princen van Oraengien ... [n.p., 1608.] U201
"Letter in form of a supplication to the King of Spain."

Usselincx, Willem. Sommaire recueil des raisons plus importantes, qui doivent mouvoir Messiers des Estats des Provinces unies du Pays bas, de ne quitter point les Indes. [n.p.] 1608. U202
A French edition of the previous item.

Usselincx, Willem. Stucken gemencioneert in den Bycorff. The Hague, H. Jacobsz., 1608. U203
Reprints of twelve "Bycorff" pamphlets not censored by the government.

Usselincx, Willem. Sweriges rijkes general handels companies contract. Stockholm, 1625. U204
The charter of the Swedish South Sea Company, authorizing Swedish commerce to America, Africa, Asia, and Magellanica.

Usselincx, Willem. Het testament ofte wtersten wille vande Nederlandsche oorloghe ... Door Yemand van Waer-mond. Tot Franc end al, By Frederijck de Vrije. [1609]. U205
"The testaments or last will of the war."

Usselincx, Willem. Het testament vande oorloghe ... [n.p.] 1608. U206
In poetic format like the previous item, but with entirely different text.

Usselincx, Willem. Trouhertighe vermaninghe aende verheerde Nederlantsche Provintien ... Anno 1586. [n.p., 1608.] U207
"Candid admonition to the devastated Dutch provinces."

Usselincx, Willem. Uthförligh förklaring öfwer handels contractet angäendes thet Södre Compagniet ... Stockholm, I. Meurer, 1626. U208
"Further explanation of the agreement concerning the South Company of the Kingdom of Sweden." This book was published as an advertisement in an attempt to induce Swedes to invest in the company. The author was appointed head of the company by Gustavus Adolphus.

Usselincx, Willem. Vanden spinnekop ende t'bieken ofte droom ghedicht. [n.p., 1608.] U209
A poem employing plays upon words.

Usselincx, Willem. Verhael vande occasie en oorsaeck waer door de Nederlanden gecommen zijn aenden vreede handel. [n.p., 1608.] U210
"Account of the occasion and reasons by which the Dutch have come to the present negotiations for peace."

Usselincx, Willem. Vertoogh, hoe nootwendich, nut ende profijtelijck het zy voor de Vereenichde Nederlanden te behouden de vryheyt van te handelen op West-Indien, inden vrede met den Coninck van Spagnien. [n.p., 1608.] U211
    A dissertation to prove how "necessary, useful, and profitable it is for the United Provinces to preserve the freedom of trading to the West Indies in the peace with the King of Spain."

[Ussieux, Louis d'.] Compendio historico del descubrimiento, y conquista de la India Oriental ... Cordoba, D. Juan Rodriguez, 1773. U212
    First published in France in 1770, this is an account of Portuguese expansion in India to 1515. This Spanish translation is by Manuel Antonio Ramirez y Gongora.

Usticke, William, and Peter Marette. A copy of a letter from James Island in the river of Gambia the 1st of May 1661. Manuscript copy signed. James Island, Gambia, 1 May 1661. U213
    The writers were factors for the group which became the Royal African Company of England, and they report on their establishment in the Gambia River, noting efforts to trade in ivory, wax, hides, and slaves, while hoping for trade in gold, and cultivation of land near the river.

Uyt-vaert vande West-Indische Compagnie. Met een propositie ende vertooninghe ghedaen door een seker heere, aenden Coninck van Castilien, teghens de West-Indische Compagnie. [The Hague?] Gedruckt voor den Autheur, 1645. U214
    "Departure of the West India Company, with a proposal and demonstration by a certain gentleman to the King of Castile against the West India Company."

Uztáriz, Gerónimo de. Theorica, y practica de comercio, y de marina. Madrid, Antonio Sanz, 1742. U215
    This work concerns the importance of manufacturing, commerce, navigation, and administration to any state, and also reviews the causes of Spain's commercial decline.

Uztáriz, Gerónimo de. Theorica, y practica de comercio, y de marina, en diferentes discursos, y calificados exemplares. Madrid, Antonio Sanz, 1757. U216
    A near reprint of the 1742 edition.

Uztáriz, Gerónimo de. The theory and practice of commerce and maritime affairs. London, John and James Rivington and John Crofts, 1751. U217
    The first English edition, translated by John Kippax.

Uztáriz, Gerónimo de. The theory and practice of commerce and maritime affairs. Dublin, G. Faulkner, 1752. U218
    First edition to be published in Ireland.

Uztáriz, Gerónimo de. Theorie et practique du commerce et de la marine. Hamburg, Chrétien, 1753. U219
    A "traduction libre" with numerous editorial comments by François Véron Duverger de Forbonnais.

Vadianus, Joachim. Epitome trium terrae partium, Asiae, Africae et Europae. Zurich, C. Froschauer, 1534. V1

The first edition of this geography, with descriptions of various regions of Asia, Africa, and America. It contains a map in which South America is drawn with relative accuracy and North America is named "Terra de Cuba."

Vadianus, Joachim. Epitome topographica totius orbis. Antwerp, Joannes Grapheum, 1535. V2

This is actually an edition of the foregoing work, under a new title.

Vadianus, Joachim. Epitome trium terrae partium, Asiae, Africae et Europae. Zurich, C. Froschauer [1546]. V3

In this copy are bound proof sheets of the maps subsequently published in Honter's *Rudimenta cosmographica*.

Vaillant, Jan Olphert. Werktuigkundige beschouwing van de uitwerking der wind en zee op een schip, deszelfs zeilen en roer. Amsterdam, Hendrik Arends, 1786. V4

A textbook on sailing, with illustrations of shipboard instruments and equipment essential to the operation of a sailing ship.

[Vairasse, Denis.] Histoire des Severambes. Amsterdam, E. Roger, 1716. V5

A description of imaginary peoples supposedly inhabiting a continent in the southern hemisphere.

[Vairasse, Denis.] History of the Severambians: a people of the south-continent. London, J. Noon, 1738. V6

The second English edition.

Valadés, Diego. Rhetorica Christiania ad concionandi et orandi usum accommodata, utriusq facultatis exemplis suo loco insertis; quae quidem ex Indorum maximè deprompta sunt historiis ... [Perugia, apud Petrumiacobum Petrutium, 1579.] V7

The author, a Franciscan missionary, was the son of a Spanish father and Tlaxacaltec mother. This is one of the earliest books by a Mexican to interpret the Mexican culture to Europeans. It is particularly renowned for its illustrations drawn and engraved by the author.

Valckenburgh, Johan. Brief ... geschreven aen de Heeren Staten Generael. The Hague, Hillebrant van Wouw, 1665. V8

The author, governor of the Dutch West India Company, reports English raids upon company trading stations in Guinea.

Valdés, Manuel Antonio. Tribulaciones de los fieles en la parte oriental de la Asia. Mexico, D. Mariano Joseph de Zúñiga y Ontiveros, 1803.
V9

A report on missions in eastern Asia with particular emphasis on Korea.

Valerius Flaccus, Gaius. Argonautica. Io. Baptistae Pij carmen ex quarto Argonauticon Apollonij. Orphei Argonautica innominato interprete. [Venice, Aldus, 1523.] V10

This text of the *Argonautica* was the principal alternative to the earlier version by Apollonius of Rhodes.

Valerius Flaccus, Gaius. Argonauticon. Antwerp, Plantin, 1565. V11

The first Plantin edition, edited by Louis Carrion.

Valignano, Alessandro. Lettres du pere Alexandre Valignan, visiteur de la Compagnie de Jesus au Jappon & en la Chine, du 16 octobre, 1599, et du p. Valentin Caravaille de la mesme Compagnie du 25 feburier, 1601, au reverend p. Claude Aquaviva, general de la mesme Compagnie. Arras, Robert Maudhuy, 1604. V12

These letters note the impact on the Jesuit missions of political unrest in Japan following the death of the ruler Taicosama.

Vallejo, Thomas. [Letter, 1680 June 14, Isla de San Juan, pueblo de San Ignacio de Agadñe to

Padre Thyrso Gonzalez de la Comp'a de JHS, Salamanca.] Manuscript in Spanish. Agaña, Guam, 14 June 1680. V13

The author was a Jesuit missionary in the Mariana Islands. He writes to his superior at Salamanca, noting that he encloses some verses from Father Diego Luis de Sanvitores, urges that books be sent for the mission, and sends greetings from Father Antonio de Xaramillo in the Philippines.

[**Vallette Laudun.**] Journal d'un voyage a la Louisiane fait en 1720. The Hague, et se trouve a Paris, Musier, 1768. V14

An account of a voyage from France to the French West Indies, the Gulf of Mexico, and Louisiana, noting the French settlements there and describing in detail life aboard ship. The narrative is presented in 132 letters to a French lady.

Van Braam Houckgeest, André Everard. Voyage de l'ambassade de la Compagnie des Indes Orientales Hollandaises, vers l'empereur de la Chine. Philadelphia, l'Editeur, 1797-98. V15

The author traveled in China for the Dutch East India Company in 1794 and 1795. This French translation of his manuscript was made by Moreau de Saint-Méry, and is accompanied by numerous illustrations of various aspects of Chinese life.

Van Braam Houckgeest, André Everard. An authentic account of the embassy of the Dutch East-India Company, to the court of the emperor of China. London, For R. Phillips, 1798. V16

This English edition is based upon the pirated French translation of 1798 which actually includes only the first volume of the original two-volume Philadelphia edition.

Vancouver, George. Voyage de découvertes, a l'océan Pacifique du nord, et autour du monde. Paris, Didot Jeune, 1802. V17

The first French edition.

Vancouver, George. A voyage of discovery to the North Pacific Ocean, and round the world. London, G.G. and J. Robinson, and J. Edwards, 1798. V18

A detailed reporting of the Pacific coast of Canada based on a voyage of 1792-94. It includes an atlas volume of maps and plates.

[**Vandebergue-Seurrat, Claude.**] Voyages de Geneve et La Touraine, suivis de quelques opuscules. Orléans, Rouzeau-Montaut, 1779. V19

The author supplements his travels with a concern for improving French commerce. He advocates a royal Order of Commerce to entice the nobility, and a chair of Consular Law at the University.

Vansittart, Henry. A narrative of the transactions in Bengal, from the year 1760, to the year 1764. London, J. Newbery [etc.] 1766. V20

Contains accounts of the activities of the English East India Company in Bengal during these years.

Varenius, Bernhardus. Geographia generalis. Amsterdam, Ludovicum Elzevirium, 1650. V21

The first edition of a geography that was to become a standard text.

Varenius, Bernhardus. Geographia generalis. Cambridge, Joann. Hayes, 1672. V22

This edition was edited by Isaac Newton.

Varenius, Bernhardus. Geographia generalis. Cambridge, Cornelii Crownfield, 1712. V23

This edition contains an appendix by James Justin dealing with geographical measurements and winds in the various oceans.

Varenius, Bernhardus. A compleat system of general geography: Explaining the nature and properties of the earth ... London, Stephen Austin, 1734. V24

A new English translation which incorporates the work of previous editors Isaac Newton and Jacob Jurin, the translation by Dugdale being overseen by Peter Shaw, M.D.

[**Vargas Ponce, José.**] Relacion del último viage al Estrecho de Magallanes ... en los años de 1785 y 1786. Madrid, Por la Viuda de Ibarra, Hijos y Compañia, 1788. V25

A scientific survey of the Strait, to determine how passable it really was, and of the plant and animal life in the region, with a view toward colonization.

Varios comercio y fabricas. [Reports on the commerce and industry of Spain and her colonies, to or from Spanish commercial institutions or governmental agencies.] Manuscripts in Spanish. [n.p.] 1728-1789. V26

The documents reflect Spanish concern with reforming the economies and commerce of the colonies.

Varthema, Lodovico de. Itinerario ... nello Egypt ... Surria ... Arabia ... Persia ... India & nella Ethiopia. Rome, Stephano Guillireti de Loreno & Hercule de Nani, 1510. V27

An account of travels in the Levant, India, the East Indian islands, and Ethiopia, describing numerous aspects of commerce as well as the peoples of those areas.

Varthema, Lodovico de. Itinerario ... nello Egitto, nella Soria, nella Arabia deserta, & felice ... & nella Ethyopia. Venice, Matthio Pagan [ca. 1550]. V28

This is the fourth of the Italian editions to contain the account by Juan Diaz of Grijalva's expedition to Yucatan in 1518.

Varthema, Lodovico de. Novum itinerarium Aethiopiae ... ac Indiae. [Milan, 1511.] V29

The first Latin edition.

Varthema, Lodovico de. Die ritterlich und lobvirdig Rayss ... von den Landen Egypto, Syria, von bayden Arabia, Persia, India, und Ethiopia ... [Augsburg, H. Miller, 1515.]   V30
   The first German and first illustrated edition. It contains forty-six woodcuts.

[Varthema, Lodovico de.] Itinerario ... en el qual cueta mucha parte dela Ethiopia Egipto: y entrābas Arabias: Siria y la India. Seville, Jacobo Cromberger, 1520.   V31
   The first Spanish edition.

Vasconcelos, Agostinho Manuel de. Vida de Don Duarte de Meneses, terce conde de Viana. Lisbon, Pedro Crasbeeck, 1627.   V32
   This biography is concerned primarily with Portuguese expansion in North Africa in the mid-fifteenth century.

Vasconcelos, Agostinho Manuel de. Vida y acciones del rey Don Juan el Segundo. Madrid, Maria de Quiñones, 1639.   V33
   A chronicle of the reign of John II of Portugal containing a review of the preceding reign. The author makes numerous references to Portuguese expansion in Africa as well as to the immediate consequences of Columbus' first voyage to America.

Vasconcelos, Simão de. Chronica de Companhia de Jesu do estado do Brasil. Lisbon, Henrique Valente de Oliveira, 1663.   V34
   A history of Jesuit missions in Brazil from 1549 to 1570, preceded by a history of the discovery and settlement of Brazil by the Portuguese and a description of the country, its peoples, and products.

De vast-gekuypte loevesteynsche ton aen duygen. Snavelenburgh, Jan Verkeer-bort, 1672.   V35
   A lament over the decline of the East India Company because of alleged mismanagement, recalling happier times when Holland was the warehouse of Europe.

Vauban, Sébastien Le Prestre de. Projet d'une dixme royale. [n.p.] 1707.   V36
   An early revolutionary work which is sharply critical of France's tax structure and advocates an income tax as the basis for French revenues.

Vauban, Sébastien Le Prestre de. Projet d'une dixme royale. [n.p.] 1708.   V37
   The second edition.

Vauban, Sébastien Le Prestre de. An essay for a general tax; or A project for a royal tithe. London, John Matthews for George Strahan, 1710.   V38
   The second English edition of Vauban's book in which an income tax is proposed as the basis for French revenues.

Vaudreuil, Pierre de Rigaud, marquis de. Mémoire pour le marquis de Vaudreuil ... ci-devant gouverneur & lieutenant général de la Nouvelle-France. [Paris, Imprimerie de Moreau, 1763.]   V39
   The testimony given here is an indictment of the system of governance which it is alleged led to the French defeat in North America.

Vaughan, William. The Golden Fleece divided into three parts ... errours of religion ... vices and decays of the kingdome, and lastly the ways to get wealth and to restore trade ... London, Francis Williams, 1626.   V40
   The author was interested in colonizing Newfoundland, and this work describes its many commercial advantages.

Vaz de Almada, Francisco. Tratado do svcesso qve teve a naos S. Joam Baptista, e iornada que fez a gente que della escapou, desde trinta & tres graos no Cabo de Boa Esperança, onde fez naufragio, atè Sofala, vindo sempre marchando por terra. Lisbon, Pedro Craesbeck, 1625, [repr. 1737].   V41

Veer, Gerrit de. Diarium nauticum seu vera descriptio trium navigationum admirandarum ... Amsterdam, C. Nicolaij, 1598.   V42
   The first Latin edition of de Veer's chronicle of three attempts by the Dutch to find a northeast passage. The expeditions took place in 1594, 1595, and 1596, and were led by Willem Barendsz and Jacob Heemskerk.

Veer, Gerrit de. Tre navigationi fatte dagli Olandesi, e Zelandesi ... Venice, Gio. B. Ciotti, 1599.   V43
   The first Italian edition.

Veer, Gerrit de. Viaggio primo del mare aghiacciato fatto da Wihelmo Bernardo 1594. Manuscript. Italy, ca. 1599.   V44
   This manuscript version includes only the first of Barendsz's three voyages, and does not conform to the printed version of the text.

Veer, Gerrit de. Trois navigations admirables faictes par les Hollandoies & Zelandois au septentrion. Paris, Guillaume Chaudiere, 1599.   V45
   One of two French editions published in this year.

Veer, Gerrit de. Waerachtighe beschrijvinghe van drie seylagien ... deur de Hollandtsche ende Zeelandtsche schepen by noorden Noorweghen, Moscovia ende Tartaria, na de coninckrijcken van Catthai ende China. Amsterdam, Cornelis Claesz, 1599.   V46
   The second Dutch edition.

[Veer, Gerrit de.] The true and perfect description of three voyages ... by the ships of Holland and Zeland. London, T. Pauier, 1609. V47
The first English edition.

Vega, Garcilaso de la. Primera parte de los Commentarios reales, que tratan del origen de los Yncas. Lisbon, Pedro Crasbeeck, 1609. V48
A classic history, written by the son of a Spanish captain and an Inca woman, of the reigns of twelve Inca rulers. It comments on the lands, peoples, government, religion, and economy of the empire they ruled.

Vega, Garcilaso de la. Primera parte de los Commentarios reales, que tratan, de el origen de los Incas. Madrid, Oficina Real, 1723. V49
The second Spanish edition, with a prologue by the editor, Andrés González de Barcia Carballido y Zuñiga.

Vega, Garcilaso de la. Le commentaire royal, ou l'Histoire des Yncas, Roys du Peru ... traduitte sur la version Espagnolle, par I. Baudoin ... Paris, Augustin Courbe, 1633. V50
The first French edition of the first part of the *Commentarios Reales*, first published in Lisbon, 1609.

Vega, Garcilaso de la. Histoire des guerres civiles des Espagnols dans les Indes ... Escritte en Espagnol par l'Ynca Garcilasso de la Vega. Et mise en François, Par I. Baudoin. Paris, Augustin Courbé et Edme Couterot, 1650. V51
This is the first issue of the first edition of a translation of the second part of the *Commentariòs reales*.

Vega, Garcilaso de la. Histoire des guerres civiles des Espagnols dans les Indes. Paris, Simeon Piget, 1658. V52
This apparently is a second issue of the French translation first published in 1650, but with a new title page.

Vega, Garcilaso de la. Histoire des Incas, rois de Perou. Amsterdam, Jean Frederic Bernard, 1737. V53
This is a French edition of the *Royal Commentaries* and the *History of Florida*, containing more illustrations than most editions. It also contains Hennepin's account of his travels in North America.

Vega, Garcilaso de la. The royal commentaries of Peru. London, Miles Flesher, for Samuel Heyrick, 1688. V54
This first English edition is a translation by Paul Rycaut. It is somewhat abridged and includes ten plates in addition to a portrait of the translator.

Vega, Garcilaso de la. Historia general del Peru trata el descubrimiento del, y como la ganaron los Españoles. Cordova, Viuda de Andres Barrera, 1617. V55
A fundamental source for the history of the Spanish conquest of Peru.

Vega, Garcilaso de la. Historia general del Peru. Madrid, Nicolas Rodriguez Franco, 1722. V56
The second Spanish edition, edited by Andrés González de Barcia Carballido y Zuñiga, with emendations and a detailed index.

Vega, Garcilaso de la. Histoire de la Floride ... Paris, G. Clouzier, 1670. V57
A French edition of the account of the explorations of De Soto in North America.

Vega, Garcilaso de la. La Florida del Inca. Madrid, Nicolas Rodriguez Franco, 1723. V58
The second Spanish edition, edited by Andrés González de Barcia Carballido y Zuñiga. It recounts the exploits of De Soto and Louis de Moscoso as well as other Spaniards and Indians who figured prominently in the conquest of Florida by Spain.

Vega, Garcilaso de la. Authentische Geschichte der Eroberung von Florida durch Ferdinand von Soto. Leipzig, Christ. Willh. Schubarths des ältern, 1794. V59
The German translator adds extensive notes to the text and to the preface of the previous French publisher.

Veiga, Manoel da. Relaçam geral do estado da Christandade de Ethiopia. Lisbon, Mattheus Pinheiro, 1628. V60
An account of the attempt to install the Latin rite in the Ethiopian church during the early years of Affonso Mendes's "patriarchate". Also included is an account of the early progress of missions in Tibet.

Veitia Linage, Joseph de. Norte de la contratacion de las Indias Occidentales. Seville, I.F. de Blas, 1672. V61
A history of Spanish colonial commerce by an official of the Casa de Contratacion.

Veitia Linage, Joseph de. The Spanish rule of trade to the West Indies. London, For S. Crouch, 1702. V62
This translation contains lists of commodities passing between Europe and the West Indies.

Velasco, Diego de. Descubrimiento del camino que la ciudad de Quito ... ha pretendido abrir para el Puerto, y Baya de Caracas. [Madrid? ca. 1617.] V63
An account of an expedition of 1616 to reopen the old Indian road from Caracas to the Pacific Ocean, mentioning advantages the road would give to the Spanish trade.

Velásquez de Cárdenas y León, Carlos Celedonio. Breve practica y regimen del confessionario de Indios, en Mexicano, y Castellano ... Mexico, Bibliotheca Mexicana, 1761. V64

General instructions in the Christian faith for Mexican Indians.

Velius, Theodorus. Chronyk van Hoorn. Hoorn, Jacob Duyn, 1740. V65
Notes the participation by merchants of Hoorn in the Dutch East and West India companies.

Velle, Nicasius Martens van. De oprechte waegschaele der Vereenighde Neder-landen, in de welcke gerechticheydt ende ongerechticheydt wyt heyt en dwaes heyt vrede ende oorloge volkomentlijck bewogen worden ... Antwerp, Peter den Hollander, 1647. V66
Concerns the Peace of Westphalia.

Velle, Nicasius Martens van. De oprechte waegschaele der Vereenighde Neder-landen, in de welcke gerechticheydt ende ongerechticheydt wyt heyt en dwaes heyt vrede ende oorloge volkomentlijck bewogen worden ... Arhem, Ioos Thijssens van Westerloo, 1647. V67
Reprint of the foregoing item.

Velloso, José Mariano da Conceição. Cultura americana que contem huma relação do terreno, clima, producçao, e agricultura das colonias Britanicas no Norte da America, e nas Indias Occidentaes ... Por hum Americano. Lisbon, Antonio Rodrigues Galhardo, 1799. V68
Based upon an unknown English or American source from the pre-Revolutionary period, this is a description of each of the colonies under British governance, with the emphasis on economic activities.

Velloso, José Mariano da Conceição. Memoria sobre a cultura do loureiro cinamomo, vulgo, canelleira de Ceilão, que acompanhou a remessa das plantas da mesma feita de Goa para o Brazil. [Lisbon] Simão Thaddeo Ferreira, 1798. V69
A dissertation on the properties of the Brazilian cinnamon laurel, relating it to East Indian cinnamon.

Venault de Charmilly. Lettre à M. Bryan Edwards ... en réfutation de son ouvrage, intitulé Vues historiques sur la colonie française de Saint-Domingue. London, T. Baylis, 1797. V70
A page by page citation of statements made by Edwards which are called incorrect, in fact or interpretation.

Venegas, Miguel. Noticia de la California. Madrid, Viuda de Manuel Fernandez, 1757. V71
The first edition of the most basic source for the early appreciation of the nature of the soil, peoples, and products of California, as well as for the history of the settlement and colonization of that area by the Spanish.

Venegas, Miguel. A natural and civil history of California. London, James Rivington and James Fletcher, 1759. V72
This English edition contains an unsigned preface emphasizing the strategic importance of California to Spain, and advocating an English search for the northwest passage as a means of establishing English dominance in Pacific trade routes.

Venegas, Miguel. Natuurlyke en burgerlyke historie van California. Haarlem, Johannes Enschede, 1761. V73
The first Dutch edition.

Venegas, Miguel. Histoire naturelle et civile de la Californie. Paris, Durand, 1767. V74
A translation from the English edition by Marc Antoine Eidous without significant additions.

Venegas, Miguel. Natürliche und bürgerliche Geschichte von Californien. Lemgo, Meyerschen Buchhandlung, 1769. V75
The first German edition.

Venegas, Miguel. Vida y virtudes del V. P. Juan Bautista Zappa, de la Compañía de Jesús ... Barcelona, Pablo Nadal, 1754. V76
This biography of Father Zappa provides a comprehensive picture of the Jesuit mission in Mexico, and makes reference to the California mission.

Venegas de Busto, Alejo. Primera parte de las diferencias de libros que ay en el universo. Toledo, Juā de Ayala, 1540. V77
A general philosophical work, with a section on cosmography which includes commentary on the discovery of America and the origins of its native peoples as descendants of the Phoenicians and Carthaginians.

Venegas de Busto, Alejo. Primera parte de las diferencias de libros que ay en el universo. [Toledo, J. de Ayala, 1546.] V78
"Newly improved and corrected" edition.

Venice (Republic : To 1797). [A collection of 110 broadside decrees relating to Venetian trade in the second half of the eighteenth century.] Venice, Z. Antonio Pinelli, 1753-88. V79
These decrees frequently contain grants or withdrawals of privileges to engage in particular aspects of trade or manufacture, immunity from certain customs duties, and prohibitions upon specific imports and exports.

Venice (Republic : To 1797). Consiglio dei Rogati. Parti prese nell' eccellentiss. Conseglio di Pregadi. Con diverse legge cavate dal statuto. [Venice] G.P. Pinelli [after 1632]. V80

Venice (Republic : To 1797). Laws, etc. [Collection of 129 decrees. Some printed, some in manuscript. Venice, 16th-18th centuries.] V81

A collection of laws relating in part to the commercial life of Venice.

Venice (Republic : To 1797). Laws, etc. Statuta Venetorum. [Venice, D. Bertochus, 1492.] **V82**
Contains the nine major changes in the merchant code of Venice made after 1477, the date of the first edition. These changes concern cargo regulations, sentences upon sailors, payment of customs dues, etc.

Venice (Republic : To 1797). Senato. Codice per la Veneta mercantile marina approvato dal decreto dell' eccellentissimo Senato 21. settembre 1786. [Venice] Figliuoli del qu: A.A. Pinelli, 1786. **V83**
This maritime code covers thirty-two topics, including shipwreck, maritime personnel, contracts, shipbuilding, etc.

Venice (Republic : To 1797). Senato. Polizza d'incanto formata dalla conferenza ... per la deliberazione dell' impresa generale de tabacchi. Venice, Figliuoli del qu. Z. Antonio Pinelli, 1784. **V84**
Concerns revenues to be collected from exporters of Dalmatian tobacco.

[Vento des Pennes, marquis de.] La noblesse ramenée a ses vrais principes ... Paris, Desaint & Saillant, 1759. **V85**
A criticism of Coyer's *Noblesse commerçante*, and also a criticism of French commercial policy.

Ventura de Argumossa, Theodoro. Erudiccion politica, despertador sobre el comercio, agricultura, y manufacturas, con avisos de buena policia, y aumento del real erario. Madrid, 1743. **V86**
A review of Spain's economy and a consideration of means to improve it, based upon the author's wide travels in Europe.

Venusti, Antonio Maria. Compendio utilissimo di quelle cose, le quali a nobili e christiani mercanti appartengono ... Milan, Giovan' Antonio degli Antonii, 1561. **V87**
This work by a Milanese physician is a wide-ranging discussion of commerce from theoretical, ethical, and functional standpoints gathered in part from the writings of others.

Verardi, Carlo. Historia Baetica. [Basel, Johann Bergmann, de Olpe, 1494.] **V88**
This volume includes a prose drama celebrating the capture of Granada from the Moors and a Latin version of the Columbus Letter which contains four woodcuts.

Verax, Philanax, pseud. A letter from a member of the Parliament of Scotland ... concerning their late act for establishing a company of that kingdom trading to Africa and the Indies. [London, Printed; Edinburgh, Heirs and successors of Andrew Anderson, 1696.] **V89**
This pamphlet contains a criticism of influential men in England for their opposition to the Darien Colony. This opposition is allegedly due to fear of competition and to foreign influence.

Verbiest, Ferdinand. Astronomia Europaea sub imperatore Tartaro Sinico Cám Hy appellato ex umbra in lucem revocata à P.R. Ferdinando Verbiest Flandro-Belga e Societate Jesu ... Dillingen, Joannis Caspari Bencard, per Joannem Federle, 1687. **V90**
An account of the European system of astronomy installed in China by the emperor K'ang Hi, through the assistance of Verbiest. A picture of the observatory is included.

[Verbiest, Ferdinand.] Voyages de l'empereur de la Chine dans la Tartarie. Ausquels on a joint une nouvelle découverte au Mexique. Paris, Estienne Michallet, 1685. **V91**
Verbiest accompanied the emperor of China on tours of Tartary in 1682 and 1683. Also included here is an anonymous account of the expedition to Lower California of Isidro de Atondo y Antillòn in 1683.

Verclaringe ende verhael hoe de Heere Wouter Raleighe, Ridder, hem ghedreghen heeft, soo wel in sijne voyaghe al in ende sedert sijne wedercomste ... The Hague, Aert Meuris, 1619. **V92**
A collection of three pamphlets relating to the trial and execution of Sir Walter Raleigh.

Das verdächtige Pineser-Eyland. Hamburg, Johann Naumann [1668]. **V93**
A refutation of the possibility of the Isle of Pines story being true; it is made out to be a farce.

Verdere aenteyckeninge of duplyque, op seeckere replyque vanden heer George Downing. The Hague, H. van Wouw, 1666. **V94**
The Dutch reply to Ambassador Downing of England, presenting numerous documents in favor of the Dutch cause in their war with England.

Verdun de la Crenne, Jean René Antoine, marques de. Voyage fait par ordre du roi en 1771 en 1772, en diverses parties de l'Europe, de l'Afrique et de l'Amérique; pour vérifier l'utilité de plusiers méthodes et instrumens, servant à determiner la latitude & la longitude ... Paris, Imprimerie Royale, 1778. **V95**
An account of an expedition commissioned for the purpose of establishing more precise locations of coasts and islands in the North Atlantic. Jean Charles de Broda and Alexander Guy Pingre were also leaders of this expedition and co-authors of the book.

Vergelyckinge tusschen Claudius Tiberius, kayser van Romen, en Olivier Cromwell, protector ... van Engelandt. Brussels, 1657. V96
A severe criticism of Cromwell, whose navigation acts had been very harmful to Dutch trade.

Verhael van de Nederlantsche vreede handeling. The Hague, Jan Veely, 1650. V97
This collection of diplomatic documents relates to European affairs between 1621 and 1648, frequently involving overseas trading privileges.

Verhael van het geene gepassert is wegens 't innemen van Bantem. [n.p.] 1683. V98
An account of difficulties and rivalry between the Dutch and English at Bantam.

Verhael vande rechte middelen, om soo wel den standt vande ghemeyne saecke, als de religie in den Nederlanden te moghen behouden. [n.p.] 1584. V99
A consideration of the Dutch position, particularly with reference to guaranteeing religious freedom, as to whether close relations with France or Spain would serve better. The author is inclined toward France. The tract contains reference to navigation to the East by way of the Cape of Good Hope.

Verhandelinge, daarin ontdekt worden ... van de oprechtingen der Compagnie van Oostende te vreesen hebben. Amsterdam, Johannes van Septeren, 1726. V100
The author shows the interdependence of the Dutch and English trade, and urges the English to show no favor to the new Company of Ostend, for this would injure Dutch commerce and ultimately that of the English as well.

[Verheiden, Jacob.] Oratie, of wtspraecke van het recht der Nederlandtsche oorloghe teghen Philippum ... Amsterdam, Michiel Colijn, 1608. V101
A translation of a Latin oration of 1596 defending the Dutch war against Spain as a part of the anti-truce party's effort to continue the war.

Verheiden, Willem. Nootelijcke consideratien die alle goede liefhebbers des vaderlandts behooren rijpelijck te ouerwegen opten voorgheslagen tractate van peys met den Spaengiaerden. [Netherlands?] 1587. V102
This pamphlet is a variant of one that appears as number 17 in *Den Nederlandsche Bye-korf*, 1608. The contents suggest that it was published in 1608.

Les veritables motifs de messieurs et dames de la Société de Nostre Dame de Montreal. Paris, 1643. V103
An explanation of the reasons for the founding of the Société de Notre Dame de Montreal, stressing that the interest in Canada was something of a more mystical nature than interest in beaver skins.

La verité du fait, du droit, et de l'interêt dé tout ce qui concerne le commerce des Indes, établi aux Païs Bas autrichiens par Sa Maj. imper. et catholique. [n.p.] 1726. V104
A review of the entire controversy over the attempts of the Ostend Company to establish commerce in the East Indies.

Vermeulen, Gerret. De gedenkwaerdige voyagie ... naar Oost-Indien. Amsterdam, J. Claesz. ten Hoorn, 1677. V105
Contains descriptions of Java, Sumatra, Celebes, Macassar, Bali, and other East Indian islands.

Vermuyden, Sir Cornelius. A coppy of a breefe summary of the voyage unto Gambia, from Jan. ye 27th 1660 untill March 21st 1660. Manuscript copy signed. Elephant Island, Gambia River, 22 March 1660 [i.e. 1661]. V106
A copy of a report, presumably to the directors of a new company for trading to west Africa, describing the geography, productivity, and chances for commercial success in the Gambia River area.

[Vernon, Edward.] Considerations upon the white herring and cod fisheries. London, M. Cooper, 1749. V107
A defense of a joint-stock company for the improvement of British fisheries, contending that it would help the entire British economy.

[Vernon, Edward.] Original papers relating to the expedition to Panama. London, M. Cooper, 1744. V108
An account of the problems and progress of the British fleet in the West Indies, operating from Jamaica against the Spaniards in 1741-42.

Vernon, S. [Letter to William Vernon.] Manuscript. Newport, 20 July 1785. V109
Samuel Vernon was William Vernon's son. The family was a successful Rhode Island trading firm in the eighteenth century involved in the commercial triangle trade. In this letter William's son describes the cargo of one of their ships: " ... he had about seventy negroes on board and a large qty. of gold ... and supposes he would leave the coast [Africa] about the middle of April ..."

Verona (Italy). Laws, etc. Statuta civitatis Veronae. Venice, Hermannus Liechtenstein, 1475. V110
Among the statutes are regulations on the commercial life of the city.

Verovering van de silver-vloot inde Bay Matanca. A°. 1628. Amsterdam [1629]. V111
A broadside news sheet giving a picture, map, and details of the Dutch victory over the Spanish in the Bay of Matanca in 1628. A list of the cargo taken is included.

Verscheyde stucken raeckende de vrede-handelinghe. Amsterdam, I. van der Ast, 1647. V112

A series of arguments in support of peace with Spain. The editor states that he favors peace, as it has always been more favorable to trade than war.

Vertooch aen de ... Staten Generael, aengaende de tegenwoordige regeringe van de bewinthebbers van het Oost-Indische Compagnie. [The Hague? 1622.] V113

Complaints of the shareholders against the management of the East India Company.

Vertooch aen de ... Staten Generael der Vereenichde Nederlanden. Amsterdam, J. van Marel, 1647. V114

A pamphlet advocating the termination of the Dutch West India Company's activities in Brazil.

Vertoog van de algemeene vryheydt der staten van Hollandt ende West-Vrieslandt, onder ende gedurende de bedieninge onser graaven. [n.p.] 1684. V115

A review of the manner of levying taxes throughout the earlier periods of Dutch history.

Vertoogh, over den toestant der West-Indische Compagnie. Rotterdam, J. van Roon, 1651. V116

A critical history of the Dutch West India Company, noting the reasons for its decline, and recommending that it be united with the East India Company.

Vervolg van het Rotterdams zee-praatje. Middelburg, Gerrit Jansz. van Hoorn, 1653. V117

A conversation between a merchant, a citizen, and a helmsman regarding English inroads on Dutch commerce in Africa.

'T vervolgh op de t'samen-spraeck ... verhalende hoe dat sommige persoonen haer begeven in den dienst vande West-Indische Compagnie ... [n.p., 1647.] V118

A discussion of the possibility of serving in the West India Company.

Vervolgh van de t'Samenspraeck gehouden tusschen twee reysigers. [n.p., 1690.] V119

Concerns taxes assessed on merchants and their eventual effect on commerce.

Vervolgh-troef grooten troef tusschen Engelant en Hollandt. [n.p.] 1664. V120

A discussion in the form of a card game between England and the Netherlands, calling attention to the points of conflict between them, many of which are commercial.

'T verwaerloosde Formosa, of Waerachtig verhael ... der Nederlanders in Oost-Indien. Amsterdam, J.C. ten Hoorn & M. Pieters, 1675. V121

A description of Formosa in the seventeenth century, together with an account of Dutch commerce there.

A very new pamphlet indeed! Being the truth: addressed to the people at large ... respecting the slave trade. London, 1792. V122

"It may be asked, by what motives the promoters of the Abolition have been actuated? the answer is plain, Fanaticism and False Philosophy had exalted their imagination and obscured their reason ..."

Verzameling ... van alle de projecten en conditien van de compagnien van assurantie, commercie en navigatie, &c. The Hague, Cornelis Hoffeling, 1721-22. V123

A collection of documents relating to speculative and commercial enterprises in vogue at the time and documents concerning earlier overseas trading companies as well.

Vespucci, Amerigo. De ora antarctica per regem Portugallie pridem inventa. Strassburg, M. Hupfuff, 1505. V124

An account of the third voyage of Vespucci, previously published under the title of *Mundus Novus*.

Vespucci, Amerigo. Facsimile of the "Dutch Vespucius." Providence, 1874. V125

One of twenty-five copies of a facsimile of the Dutch translation of Vespucci's letter describing his third voyage.

Vespucci, Amerigo. Mundus novus. [Augsburg, Johannes Otmar, 1504.] V126

The first dated edition of the letter to Vespucci's patron, Lorenzo di Piero Francesco de Medici, describing the author's voyage of 1501-02.

[Vespucci, Amerigo.] Woodcut showing Vespucci's ships entering the Plate River in South America. [Nuremberg, G. Stuchs, 1505-06.] V127

This is believed to be one of the earliest representations of the exploration of South America. It appears to portray Vespucci's fleet, sailing under the Portuguese flag at the mouth of the Plate River.

Veydt, F. Essai sur les douanes, et sur l'intérét national du commerce des Pays-bas autrichiens. Brussels, Emmanuel Flon, 1788. V128

A discussion of commercial policy in which the author's purpose is to demonstrate the effect of tariffs on various industries in the Austrian Netherlands and to prove their general advantage over free trade.

Viage del Commandante Byron al rededor del mundo. Madrid, Don Francisco Mariano Nipho, 1769. V129

The first Spanish edition of an official account of Byron's circumnavigation of 1764-66, with a description of the Patagonians.

Viage del Commandante Byron al rededor del mundo. Madrid, Imprenta real de la Gazeta, 1769. V130
The second Spanish edition.

Viaggio intorno al mondo fatto dalla nave Inglese il Delfino comandata dal capo-squadra Byron. Florence, Giuseppe Allegrini, 1768. V131
The first Italian edition of the narrative of the *Dolphin*'s voyage by "an officer on board," translated from the English edition of 1767.

Viani, Servite. Istoria delle cose operate nella China da Monsignor Gio. Ambrogio Mezzabarba, patriarca d'Alessandria, legato appostolico in quell' impero, e di presente vescovo di Lodi. Paris, Monsù Briason [1739]. V132
The mission of legate Mezzabarba was to secure obedience to papal decrees among the Jesuit missionaries in China with respect to rites practiced by Chinese Christians. The author of this account of the legation was Mezzabarba's confessor on the voyage.

[Viau, Théophile de.] Le tableau satyrique, des peres de la Societé. [n.p., ca. 1620.] V133
A satire in rhymed couplets, portraying the Jesuits as heretics and traitors, working in the interests of Spain.

Viciana, Raphael Martin de. Chronyca de la inclita y coronada ciudad de Valencia y de su reyno. [Valencia, J. Navarro, 1564.] V134
This chronicle includes accounts of the voyages of Columbus, Cortes, and Pizarro as well as histories of important cities of Valencia.

[Vickaris, A.] An essay for regulating of the coyn. London, James O. for R. Cumberland, 1696. V135
Advocates a new coinage system to alleviate the shortage of money and to improve trade.

Victoria, José. [Petition concerning a religious festival.] Manuscript in Spanish. [n.p., 1745?] V136
The person to whom the petition is addressed is unclear.

Victoria, Pedro Gobeo de. Joannis Bisselii, è Societate Jesu, Argonauticon Americanorum, sive, Historiae periculorum Petri de Victoria, ac sociorum eius. Munich, Lucae Straubii, 1647. V137
An account of travels in Central and South America in the late sixteenth or early seventeenth century. This edition contains commentary by the translator, Johann Bissel, who apparently worked from the German edition of 1622.

Victorien der Nederlandsche Geoctroyeerde Oost-Indische Compagnie op het koninkryck van Macassar. [n.p., ca. 1670.] V138
A pictorial broadside, portraying Cornelis Speelman's victory over the King of Macassar, with a brief text describing the event.

Vidal de Figueroa, Jose. Carta escrita en la Ciudad de Mexico por el Padre Ioseph Vidal, de la Compañia de Iesvs ... a D. Geronimo Sanvitores ... [Madrid, 1674.] V139
A letter from the procurator of the Society of Jesus in the Mariana Islands reporting the death of Diego Luis de Sanvitores who founded the mission there.

Vielheuer, Christoph. Gründliche Beschreibung fremder Materialien und Specereyen Ursprung ... Leipzig, J. Fritzsche, 1675. V140
A compilation of information on various Indian and American commodities.

A view of the coasts, countries and islands within the limits of the South Sea Company. London, J. Morphew, 1711. V141
Describes the people, products, and commerce of South America and the South Pacific.

A view of the depredations and ravages committed by the Spaniards on the British trade and navigation. London, W. Hinchliffe, 1731. V142
Describes Spanish raids on English shipping, and advocates reprisals.

A view of the internal policy of Great Britain. London, For A. Millar, 1764. V143
A discussion of the economic and political history of Great Britain, noting external and internal forces that shaped it, with some emphasis on the development of colonies and colonial policy.

A view of the political transactions of Great Britain. London, T. Cooper, 1739. V144
An account of British policies from the Treaty of El Pardo to the outbreak of the war.

A view of the present state of Ireland, containing observations upon ... its dependance, linen trade, provision trade, woolen manufactory, coals, fishery, agriculture ... intended for the consideration of Parliament. London, R. Faulder, 1780. V145
An attempt to convince the British Parliament that past policies of restraint upon Irish commerce have not been productive and that changes in the direction of free trade for Irish goods must be made.

A view of the state of the trade to Africa. London, A. Baldwin, 1708. V146
A pamphlet discussing the poor financial state and malpractices of the Royal African Company.

A view or state of James Campbell merchant in London his case touching his sufferings & services on acc[t] of ye colony & trade of Newfoundland ... Manuscript. [n.p., 1710.]   V147

A petition to the queen for relief in the amount of 10,737 pounds which Campbell claimed had been lost due to French and Indian incursions in Newfoundland. He had warned the government in London, urging certain actions to prevent such incursions but the government had not acted upon his advice.

Villaret de Joyeuse, Louis Thomas. Discours de Villaret-Joyeuse ... sur l'importance des colonies & les moyens de les pacifier. [Paris] Imprimerie Nationale, 1797.   V148

A short discussion of the importance of colonies to the entire French economic system, and a plea for caution in handling the affairs of Saint Domingue, especially in the matter of slavery.

Villault, Nicolas, Sieur de Bellefond. Relations des costes d'Afrique appellées Guinée. Paris, D. Thierry, 1669.   V149

A description of West Africa by a French observer who notes the natural products of the region and the commercial activity of European nations there.

Villault, Nicolas, Sieur de Bellefond. A relation of the coasts of Africk called Guinee. London, John Starkey, 1670.   V150

The first English edition.

Villavicencio, Juan José de. Vida, y virtudes de el venerable, y apostolico padre Juan de Ugarte de la Compañia de Jesus. Mexico, Colegio de San Ildefonso, 1752.   V151

Father Ugarte was the procurator of the California mission. His activities also included an expedition to find a port for use of the Manila Galleon and research into the geography of California.

Villegaignon, Nicolas Durand de. Ad articulos Calvinianae, de sacramento Eucharistiae, traditionis, ab eius ministris in Francia Antarctica ... Venice, Gasparem Bindonum, 1562.   V152

A statement of theological conflicts between the author and the Calvinist ministers he had invited to Brazil and with whom he had quarreled.

Villegaignon, Nicolas Durand de. Caroli V. Imperatoris expeditio in Africam ad Argieram. Paris, Joannem Lodoicum Tiletanum, 1542.   V153

An account, by a participant, of the attempt by Charles V of Spain to strengthen his North African empire by an attack on Algiers.

Villotte, Jacques. Voyages d'un missionaire de la Compagnie de Jesus, en Turquie, en Perse, en Armenie, en Arabie & en Barbarie. Paris, Jacques Vincent, 1730.   V154

The author's travels began in 1688 and continued until 1709. His narrative includes description of caravan life, the commerce of various cities, state of the Jesuit missions, and political events in the Middle East.

Vimont, Barthélemy. Relation de ce qui s'est passé en la Nouvelle France en l'année 1642. Paris, Sebastien Cramoisy, 1643.   V155

This *Relation* records the arrival of military aid from France, the founding of Montreal, increasing trouble from the Iroquois including the capture of Father Jogues, and the decline of the smallpox epidemic among the Hurons.

Vimont, Barthélemy. Relation de ce qui s'est passé en la Nouvelle France en l'année 1642. Paris, Sebastien Cramoisy, 1643.   V156

A variant issue of the previous item.

Vimont, Barthélemy. Relation de ce qui s'est passé en la Nouvelle France en l'année 1642. Paris, Sebastien Cramoisy, 1643.   V157

A copy made up of parts of the two issues above.

Vimont, Barthélemy. Relation de ce qui s'est passé en la Nouvelle France en l'annee 1642 & 1643. Paris, Sebastien Cramoisy & Gabriel Cramoisy, 1644.   V158

Includes letters from Father Jogues concerning his captivity and escape, reference to Jean Nicolet's westward exploration to Green Bay, and a declaration by the Jesuits of their independence of the Company of New France.

Vimont, Barthélemy. Relation de ce qui s'est passé en la Nouvelle France en l'annee 1642 & 1643. Paris, Sebastien Cramoisy & Gabriel Cramoisy, 1644.   V159

A variant issue of the previous item.

Vimont, Barthélemy. Relation de ce qui s'est passé en la Nouvelle France es annees 1643 & 1644. Paris, Sebastien Cramoisy & Gabriel Cramoisy, 1645.   V160

The report from Quebec describes conflict with the Iroquois and their capture of both Jesuit and Indian prisoners. The report from the Huron mission details progress of the individual stations.

Vimont, Barthélemy. Relation de ce qui s'est passé en la Nouvelle France es annees 1643 & 1644. Paris, Sebastien Cramoisy et Gabriel Cramoisy, 1645.   V161

A variant of the above item.

Vimont, Barthélemy. Relation de ce qui s'est passé en la Nouvelle France, és années 1644 & 1645. Paris, Sebastien Cramoisy & Gabriel Cramoisy, 1646.   V162

Most of Vimont's report relates to attacks on the Canadian Indians by Iroquois from the south. A letter from Father Lalemant describes the progress of the Huron mission.

Vimont, Barthélemy. Relation de ce qui s'est passé en la Nouvelle France, és années 1644 &

1645. Paris, Sebastien Cramoisy & Gabriel Cramoisy, 1646. V163
A variant issue of the above item.

Vimont, Barthélemy. Relation de ce qui s'est passé en la Nouvelle France, és années 1644 & 1645. Paris, Sebastien Cramoisy & Gabriel Cramoisy, 1646. V164
A copy made up from the above two issues.

Vincent, of Beauvais. Speculum historiale. Manuscript on vellum, written and signed by Jean de Rebais. [Flanders, ca. 1280.] V165
Contains accounts of Tartary from John de Piano Carpini and Simon of St. Quentin who traveled there in the mid-thirteenth century.

A vindication of the conduct of the ministry, in the scheme of the excise on wine and tobacco. London, J. Roberts, 1734. V166
An explanation of the ministry's unfavorable attitude toward the new excise bill, including further suggestions for improving the collection of duties on wine and tobacco.

The vintner and tobacconist's advocate, being remarks upon, and a full answer to those scandalous papers published in The Daily Courant, under the title of The Occasional Financer, and under the names of Carus and Meanwell. London, T. Reynolds, 1733. V167
A rebuttal to writings by advocates of changing the customs duty on tobacco and wine to an excise tax as proposed in a bill before Parliament.

Violet, Thomas. An appeal to Caesar: wherein gold and silver is proved to be the Kings Majesties royal commodity ... London, 1660. V168
A plea for action against an act pending in Parliament which would make possible the export of gold and silver without license from the Crown, together with the author's plea for a position of enforcer of the non-export laws in effect.

Violet, Thomas. Mysteries and secrets of trade and mint-affairs. London, William Du-Gard, 1653. V169
A series of recommendations for legislation to improve England's commercial position. In general they favor free trade, but call for encouragement and regulation of specific branches of commerce.

Violet, Thomas. A petition against the Jewes, presented to the Kings Majestie and the Parliament. Together with several reasons, proving the East-India trade, the Turkey trade, and east-country trade, may all be driven without transporting gold or silver out of England ... London, 1661. V170
The Jews invited into England during the Commonwealth period are seen as a threat to both religion and trade. The proposal to trade in the East Indies without gold or silver calls for a substitution of goods instead.

Violet, Thomas. To the Right Honourable the Lords in Parliament assembled. The humble petition of Tho. Violet goldsmith. [London, 1660.] V171
Violet is petitioning for personal losses suffered due to services performed for Charles I in 1643.

Violet, Thomas. A true narrative of some remarkable proceedings concerning the ships *Samson*, *Salvador*, and *George*. London, William Du-Gard, 1653. V172
The author, a government informer on merchants and customs officials who exported precious metals illegally, was instrumental in recovering large amounts of treasure. This volume contains documents relating to his activities.

Violet, Thomas. A true narrative of the proceedings in the court of admiraltie, against the ships *Sampson*, *Salvador*, and *George*. London, 1659. V173
Relates to the importation of silver and gold into England.

Visei, Giovanni Battista. Portolano. Manuscript. Italy, 17th century. V174
A description of the Mediterranean area.

Visscher, Jacobus Canter. Mallabaarse brieven, behelzende eene naukeurige beschryving van de kust van Mallabaar. Leeuwarden, Abraham Ferwerda, 1743. V175
A collection of thirty-seven letters dealing with the economy, religion, and history of the Malabar Coast and with the interests of the Dutch East India Company there.

Visschers-praetjen, over de tegenwoordigen staet der Nederlanden met het Parlement van Engelandt. Rotterdam, K. Robbersz, 1652. V176
This "fishermen's talk" discusses the Anglo-Dutch war and the commercial rivalries that brought it about.

Viverius, Jacobus. Hand-boeck, of Cort begrijp der caerten ende beschryvinghen van alle landen des werelds. Amsterdam, Cornelis Claesz, 1609. V177
This edition contains a completely new Dutch text by Jacobus Viverius. The maps are the same as in the 1603 Latin edition.

Den vlaamsen achitoffel vertoont onder den schijn en tijtel van Hollandsen raatsheer. Rotterdam, Joannes Naeranus, 1666. V178
Contains accounts of Anglo-Dutch commercial rivalry and naval warfare on the west coast of Africa.

Vliet, Jeremias van. Beschryving van het Koningryk Siam; mitsgaders het verhaal van den oorsprong, onderscheyd, politjke regering, d'ec-

clesiastique, en costuymelijke huyshoudinge van d'edelen en borgerlijke lieden ... Leiden, Frederik Haaring, 1692. V179
An account of the geography, economy, politics, diplomatic situation and other aspects of Siam at a time when the Dutch were attempting to expand commerce there.

Vogel, Johann Wilhelm. Zehen-Jährige ost-indianische Reise-Beschreibung. Altenburg, Johann Ludwig Richter, 1704. V180
An account of a voyage to the East Indies, with considerable information on the commerce of both mainland areas and islands.

[Vogel, Paul Joachim Siegmund, translator.] Gegenwärtiger Zustand der Besitzungen der Holländer in Ostindien. Nuremberg, Ernst Christoph Grattenauer, 1781. V181
A translation with extensive annotation of *Etat présent des Indes Hollandaises*.

[Voltaire.] Fragments sur l'Inde, sur le Général Lalli, et sur le Comte de Morangiés. [n.p.] 1773. V182
The second edition, adding a "Precis du procès de Mr. le comte de Morangies contra la famille Verron."

Voor-looper an het Sweedsche manifest. Amsterdam, Leenaerd de Bondtwercker, 1644. V183
Concerns hostility between Sweden and Denmark which would interrupt free trade in Baltic areas.

Het voordeel, dat Spanjen sal veroorsaeken door het breeken met Vranckryck, vertoont aen eenige van de hooge ministers der selver kroone, met de korte noodsaekelijkheden uyt de staets-kunde. Antwerp, Jan Cnobbaert, 1673. V184
Concerns European diplomatic matters involving both the East and West Indies.

Voortganck vande West-Indische Compaignie. Amsterdam, M. Brandt, 1623. V185
A report to the shareholders on the condition of the company. Authorship has sometimes been attributed to Willem Usselinx.

Vos, Jan. Vreede tusschen Filippus de Vierde Koning van Spanje; en de Staaten der vrye Neederlanden. Amsterdam, J. Lescaille, 1648. V186
Concerns the Treaty of Westphalia.

Vosgien. Dictionnaire géographique portatif. Paris, Didot, 1755. V187
This geographical dictionary was based on Laurent Echard's *The gazetteer's or newsman's interpreter* and on Bruzen de la Martinère's *Le grand dictionnaire géographique*, but differs from both of them in content.

Vossius, Isaac. Dissertation touchant l'origine du Nil et autres fleuves ... Paris, Louis Billaine, 1667. V188
The author places the origins of the Nile in Ethiopia, and provides a description and map of that country. This edition includes material not in the Latin edition of 1666 from which it was translated.

Vossius, Isaac. Variarum observationum. London, Robert Scott, 1685. V189
A collection of essays including one on the cities of China and another on the northeast passage.

Vous laisserez vous écorcher sans rien dire? [n.p., Imprimerie des droits du peuple, 1790?] V190
Strong criticism of the actions of Sonthonax and Polverel in Saint Domingue, written in the form of a dialogue between a colonist and a person from Nantes.

Voyage a la mer du sud, fait par quelques officiers commandants le vaisseau le Wager. Lyons, Freres Duplain, 1756. V191
This account of the wreck of the *Wager* and of the travels of its survivors is compiled from the narratives of Bulkeley and Cummins, Alexander Carpenter, Isaac Morris, and an anonymous writer.

A voyage round the world, in His Majesty's ship the Dolphin. London, J. Newbery, 1767. V192
An account of the exploration of the South Seas and portions of the South American coast by two ships under the command of John Byron during a circumnavigation from 1764-66.

Voyages and discoveries in South-America. London, S. Buckley, 1698. V193
Contains the narratives of Cristobal de Acuna, Acarete du Biscay, Jean Grillet, and Francis Bechamel, all of which pertain to little-known areas of South America.

Voyages aux côtes de Guinée & en Amérique. Par Mr. N***. Amsterdam, Etienne Roger, 1719. V194
The anonymous author's commentary on his travels in Guinea and the West Indies is largely confined to natural history.

Voyages chez les peuples Kalmouks et les Tartares. Berne, Société Typographique, 1792. V195
A three-part compilation of travels in Russia, taken from the works of Pallas, Gmelin, and Lepechin. The third section concerns the Tartars and Kalmucks. Part of this work is a new edition of *Histoire des decouvertes faites par divers savans voyageurs*, 1779.

Les voyageurs modernes, ou Abrégé de plusieurs voyages faits en Europe, Asie & Afrique. Paris, Nyon [etc.] 1760. V196
Translations from the English of several voyage narratives, primarily in Africa and the Near East. The translator and editor is Philippe Florent de Puisieux.

Vrankryk verduurt en overwonnen, door de band van de unie deser Staten. Amsterdam, Pieter Rotterdam [1690].   V197

A commentary on trade between France and the Netherlands, noting the overbalance of imports from France and restrictions designed to restore the balance.

Vremde geschiedenissen in ... Cambodia en Louwen-lant, in Oost-Indien. Haarlem, Pieter Castelyn, 1669.   V198

An account of the attempt by the Dutch East India Company to penetrate Cambodia during the period 1635-44.

Vries, David Pietersz de. Korte historiael, ende journaels aenteyckeninge, van verscheyden voyagiens ... Hoorn, Voor D.P. de Vries by S.C. Brekegeest, 1655.   V199

The author made six voyages, and describes the trade of the East Indies as well as that of America. He claims to have been the first Dutch patroon to go to Staten Island.

Vries, Nicolaas de. Schat-kammer, ofte kunst der stuurlieden, inhoudende de arithmetica of rekenkunde, beneevens een duidelyke onderwysinge in de navigatie ... Amsterdam, Gerard Hulst van Keulen, 1786.   V200

This was a popular navigation instruction text in the Netherlands during the eighteenth century, first published in 1702. This edition adds a section on general mathematics.

Vries, S. de (Simon). Oude en nieuwe-tijds wonder-toneel: vertonende de vorige en hedendaagze vreemde gewoonten van veelerlei volkeren in de bekende deelen des werelds ... Den tweden druk verzierd met kopere plaaten. Leeuwarden, Meindert Injeme, 1717.   V201

A work of general ethnological interest, with particular emphasis on marriage customs in non-European societies.

Vries, S. de (Simon). Curieuse aenmerckingen der bysonderste Oost en West-Indische verwonderens-waerdige dingen. Utrecht, Johannes Ribbius, 1682.   V202

A collection of voyages with extensive and well-illustrated descriptions of the products of America, Asia, and Africa.

Vries, S. de (Simon). De noordsche weereld; vertoond in twee nieuwe, aenmercklijcke, derwaerts gedaene reysen: d'eene, van de Heer Martiniere, door Noorweegen, Lapland, Boranday, Siberien, Samojessie, Ysland, Groenland en Nova Zembla ... Amsterdam, A.D. Ooszaen, 1685.   V203

A collection of travels in the north.

De vruchten van't monster van den treves ... [n.p.] 1630.   V204

Opposes the proposed truce with Spain which would enable that country to consolidate its strength in the East and West Indies where the Dutch companies were gaining.

Vrye gedachten van een jong welmeenend patriot, over het berugte Advys van jonkheer Johan Derk van der Capellen tot den Pol. Beneffens eenige aanmerkingen over den Brief van een vyand van kwaadspreekendheid. The Hague, J. Thirry [etc.] [1776].   V205

A commentary on two pamphlets of opposing views regarding Anglo-Dutch relations during the American Revolution.

De vrye zee, aengaende haere vryheyt in 't varen en visschen voor de vereenichde Nederlanden ... [n.p.] 1652.   V206

A discussion of the freedom of the seas, with particular reference to England's attempts to exclude the Dutch from fishing and whaling in the Spitzbergen and Greenland areas and the trade to Russia.

Den vryen handel ter zee ... The Hague, Johannes Tongerloo, 1666.   V207

Maintains the necessity for free use of the seas, with particular emphasis on the fishing and whaling regions of the Atlantic.

Vrymoedich discours, op de tegenwoordighe handelingh van Treves ... [n.p.] 1633.   V208

An anti-peace tract considering the implications of Dutch trade in the Spanish war.

Vrymoedige aanmerkingen op de memorie den 9 April 1779 gepresenteerd aan ... den Staaten Generaal der Vereenigde Nederlanden, door den Heer Ridder Yorke. [n.p., 1779.]   V209

A response to the British ambassador concerning Dutch trade with France and the American rebels.

Vrymoedigh discours tusschen twee paepsche Hollanders, over de tegenwoordige Munstersche vrede-handelinge. [n.p.] 1647.   V210

Concerns the Treaty of Westphalia.

W

Het Waare en nauwkeurige journael der reize, gedaan door drie schepen op ordre van de Ed. Heeren bewindhebberen van de West-Indische Compagnie. Amsterdam, Johannes van Septeren, 1727.   W1
An account of Jacob Roggeveen's expedition to the South Sea, in its third enlarged edition.

Wadström, Carl Bernhard. Adresse au Corps législatif et au Directoire exécutif de la République française. [Paris, Imprimerie des Sciences et Arts, 1795.]   W2
A prominent anti-slavery advocate here urges France to join with Great Britain in a plan to make the economy of Europe more responsive to human needs than to purely economic considerations.

Wadström, Carl Bernhard. An essay on colonization, particularly applied to the western coast of Africa, with some free thought on cultivation and commerce. London, For the Author by Darton and Harvey, 1794.   W3
An argument on behalf of making agriculture a profitable occupation in West Africa, thereby supplanting the purely commercial exploitation of it practiced by participants in the slave trade. Includes documentary histories of the Sierra Leone Company and the Bulama colony.

Wadström, Carl Bernhard. Observations on the slave trade, and a description of some part of the coast of Guinea. London, James Phillips, 1789.   W4
The author suggests alternatives to the slave trade in Guinea, noting the possibilities of agriculture, mining, and fishing.

Waerachtich verhael, belanghende de aenkomste tot Constantinoplen van den ambassadeur der ... Vereenighde Nederlanden: midtsgaders het goede tractement ende onthael den selven Heere Ambassadeur Cornelis Haga met sijn gheselschap aldaer ten hove aengedaen ende de groote vryheden by hem aldaer verkreghen. [n.p.] Jacob Harmansz Verblack, 1612.   W5
An account of the embassy of Cornelis Haga to Turkey, his friendly treatment there, and translations of letters from the Sultan and other Turkish officials offering friendly relations with the Dutch.

Waerachtich verhael, vande handelinghe tot Munster, tusschen de Majesteyten van Vranckrijck ende Spagnien, sedert dat de pleinpotentiarijsen vande Heeren Staten Generael der Vereenighde Nederlanden als middelaers daerinne sijn gebruyckt. Amsterdam, S. vander Made, 1647.   W6
Concerns the Treaty of Westphalia.

Waerachtich verhael vande tijdinghen gecomen uut de Oost-Indien, met het jacht ghenaemt de Haze. [n.p.] 1624.   W7
A Dutch version of the trials of English conspirators on Amboyna in which it is stated that they confessed freely.

Waerdenburgh, Dirk van. Copie de la lettre escrite a messieurs les Estats Generaux ... touchant la prise de la ville de Olinda de Fernabouc. Paris, Jean Bessin, 1630.   W8
A report of the taking of Pernambuco by the Dutch, written by an officer in charge of the Dutch troops.

Het waere interest vande Vereeningde Provintien en bysonderlijck dat van Hollandt ... vanden tegenwoordigen tijdt gestelt. [n.p.] 1690.   W9
An appraisal of Holland's situation, noting the profits that would come in from overseas trading companies.

Wafer, Lionel. A new voyage and description of the isthmus of America. London, J. Knapton, 1699.   W10
A description of the Isthmus of Panama by one who lived there among the natives in the 1680s.

Wafer, Lionel. A new voyage and description of the isthmus of America. London, James Knapton, 1704.   W11
This second edition includes an introduction calling for increased English interest in Panama, and adds Nathaniel

Davis' narrative of a privateering venture against the Spaniards on the isthmus in 1702.

Wagenaar, Jan. Amsterdam in zyne opkomst ... Amsterdam, Isaak Tirion, 1760-1802. W12
A history of Amsterdam, with accounts of the city's participation in the Dutch East and West India companies.

Wagenaar, Jan. Brief van een koopman te R. aan een zyner vrinden te A. Ter gelegenheid der overgeleverde memorien van de Heeren D'Affry en Yorke. Amsterdam, Jan Kamers [etc.] [1756]. W13
The author contends that the Dutch are not obliged to assist Great Britain in its war with France since the war is not in Europe, but in America.

Waghenaer, Lucas Janszoon. Spieghel der zeevaerdt. Leiden, C. Plantijn, 1584-85. W14
The first edition of the earliest published sea atlas. It contains navigation charts for the coast of Europe from the Arctic to Gibraltar, including the British Isles. The text describes the charts and gives navigational instructions.

Wahlstedt, Jacob J. Iter in Americam. Upsala, Literis Wernerianus [1725]. W15
An academic dissertation discussing the location of Vinland and its relationship to Greenland and North America.

Wakely, Andrew. The mariner's compass rectified ... with the description and use of those instruments most in use in the art of navigation. London, W. and J. Mount and T. Page, 1749. W16
A popular navigation textbook first published in 1663. It contains navigation tables, descriptions of instruments, and locations of major harbors and coastal promontories.

Waldseemüller, Martin. [The 1507 globular map of the world.] [St. Die, 1507.] W17
This is the first globular map to use the term "America" in designating the continents of the New World. It was originally published to accompany Waldseemüller's *Cosmographiae introductio*.

Waldseemüller, Martin. Cosmographiae introductio. St. Die, April 25, 1507. W18
This treatise on cosmography contains the earliest known suggestion that the continents of the New World be called America. The accounts of the four voyages of Vespucci are also included in this volume which was designed to accompany the globular map described above.

Waldseemüller, Martin. Cosmographiae introductio. St. Die, August 29, 1507. W19
A later edition of the preceding item.

Waldseemüller, Martin. Cosmographiae introductio. [Strassburg, I. Grüninger, 1509.] W20
The third printing.

Waldseemüller, Martin. Carta marina de 1516. Madrid, Gráficas Yagües, 1959. W21
A facsimile with commentary by Carlos Sanz.

Waldseemüller, Martin. Mapa universel de 1507. Madrid, Gráficas Yagües, 1959. W22
A facsimile of the wall map with commentary by Carlos Sanz.

Walerande, J.B. de. Le plaidoyer de l'Indien hollandois contre le pretendu pacificateur espagnol. [n.p.] 1608. W23
A plea to the governors of the Netherlands not to accept the Spanish demands calling for discontinuance of Dutch trade in the West Indies.

Wales, William. The original astronomical observations, made in the course of a voyage towards the South Pole, and round the world. London, W. and A. Strahan, 1777. W24
In addition to the astronomical and meteorological data recorded in this account of Cook's second voyage, an extensive introduction describes the instruments used in making the observations.

Walker, Sir Hovenden. A journal: or Full account of the late expedition to Canada. London, D. Browne, W. Mears, and G. Strahan, 1720. W25
An account of the author's unsuccessful military expedition against Quebec in 1711, with an introduction concerning the criticism he had received.

Wallace, James. Jurnall of our intended voyage, by Gods permittion in the Good Ship Warwick, Richard Shutter, Commander, bound to Bengall and from thence to Bombay. Began Dec. 29, 1738. Manuscript. En route, 29 December 1738 - 25 August 1741. W26
Ship's log to India and back, kept by the fourth mate. Good information on products and trade.

Wallace, Jaques, recipient. [Letters from his brother in Philadelphia]. Manuscript. Various places, 21 June 1751 to 10 December 1763. W27
Descriptive of colonial life in Pennsylvania, New York, New Jersey and Maryland, frequently involving concerns for the frontier war with French and Indians.

[Wallenberg, Jacob.] Min son pa Galejan, eller en Ostindisk resa, innehållande allahanda bläckhornskram samlade på skeppet Finland. Stockholm, Joh. Christ. Holmberg, 1781. W28
An account of a voyage to China in which the author uses life aboard ship and in foreign places to make observations on people in a humorous way, producing a work of major literary merit.

Waller, William, *Gent.* An essay on the value of the mines, late of Sir Carbery Price. London, 1698. W29

A promotion piece for raising capital to develop mines in Cardiganshire, with comparisons to the mines at Potosí in South America.

[Walpole, Horatio Walpole, Baron.] The grand question, whether war, or no war, with Spain. London, J. Roberts, 1739. W30
Favors continued negotiations despite Spanish infringement upon English West Indies trade.

[Walpole, Horatio Walpole, Baron, and Concanen, Matthew.] The rise and fall of the late excise, impartially consider'd. London, J. Peele, 1733. W31
A review of the excise proposal by two of its partisans, noting the misinterpretations placed upon it by its opponents in defeating it.

[Walpole, Robert, Earl of Orford.] A letter from a member of Parliament to his friends in the country. London, T. Cooper, 1733. W32
Points out the need to convert duties on tobacco and wine from customs to excise taxes to avoid frauds in the trade in these items.

[Walpole, Robert, Earl of Orford.] Observations upon the treaty between the crowns of Great-Britain, France, and Spain, concluded at Seville, on the ninth of November, 1729. n.s. London, J. Roberts, 1729. W33
A defense of the treaty, with respect to both Continental and West Indian interests of Great Britain.

[Walpole, Robert, Earl of Orford.] Observations upon the treaty between the crowns of Great-Britain, France, and Spain. Dublin, S. Powell, George Risk [etc.] 1730. W34
A reprint of the London edition of 1729.

[Walpole, Robert, Earl of Orford.] Some general considerations concerning alteration and improvement of publick revenues. London, J. Roberts, 1733. W35
A concise and lucid statement of the benefits to be derived from an excise tax, with answers to the opposition's arguments against it.

Walter, John. Autograph letter signed to M. Perrault l'Aine, dated Quebec 16 May 1789. W36
Concerns the settling of accounts between traders in the "Esquimaux country."

Walter, Richard. A voyage round the world, in the years MDCCXL, I, II, III, IV, by George Anson. London, For the Author by John and Paul Knapton, 1748. W37
The first edition, containing forty-two copper engravings depicting routes, harbors, islands, and other geographical features observed during Commodore Anson's circumnavigation of the earth. The author was chaplain of the fleet.

Walter, Richard. A voyage round the world in the years MDCCXL, I, II, III, IV. London, For the Author, 1749. W38
A reprint of the fifth English edition of 1748, adding a map of the route of the *Centurion* and including a slightly altered introduction.

Walter, Richard. Voyage autour du monde ... par George Anson. Amsterdam & Leipzig, Arkestee & Merkus, 1749. W39
The first French edition.

Walter, Richard. Reize rondsom de werreld ... door den Heere George Anson. Amsterdam, Isaak Tirion, 1749. W40
The first Dutch translation.

Walter, Richard. Des Herrn Admirals, Lord Ansons Reise um die Welt. Leipzig & Göttingen, Abraham Vandenhoeck, 1749. W41
The first German edition.

Walter, Richard. Ansons Reise um die Welt ... Tübingen, J.G. Cotta, 1795. W42
An abridgement, intended for young readers.

Walter, Richard. Viaggio attorno al mondo fatto negli anni MDCCXL. I. II. III. IV. dal signore Giorgio Anson ... Livorno, Gio. Paolo Fantechi, 1756. W43
The only Italian edition.

Walter, Richard. Amiralen Lord Ansons resa rundt omkring jorden åren 1740, 41, 42, 43, 44. Stockholm, Lor. Ludv. Grefing, 1761. W44
This Swedish edition has no illustrations. It includes an account of the *Wager*, derived from a French compilation of descriptions from Bulkeley and Cummins, Alexander Campbell, and Isaac Morris.

De walvischvangst, met veelbeyzonderheden daartoe betrekkelyk. Amsterdam, Petrus Conradi; Harlingen, Volkert van der Plaats, 1784. W45
A discussion of Dutch whaling in the Arctic from both the historical and technical point of view.

Wansey, Henry. The journal of an excursion to the United States of North America in the summer of 1794. Salisbury, Printed and sold by J. Easton, 1796. W46
An account of an English woolen manufacturer's visit to the United States.

Wansey, Henry. Dagbog paa en reise igjennem de forenede Nordamericanske stater. Copenhagen, A. Soldius [ca. 1797]. W47
The first and only Danish edition, with extensive notes by the translator.

[Wansleben, Johann Michael.] Nouvelle relation en forme de journal, d'un voyage fait en Egypte. Paris, Compagnie des Libraires Associés, 1698. W48

A survey of the geography, history, culture and economy of Egypt made at the request of Colbert. This appears to be a re-issue of the sheets of the first edition, Paris, 1677.

Ward, Bernardo. Proyecto economico, en que se proponen varias providencias, dirigidas á promover los intereses de España. Madrid, D.J. Ibarra, 1779. W49

Proposals to improve the Spanish economy, including plans to improve the volume of trade with Spanish America.

Ward, Sir Patience. London, 29. Nov. 1674. A scheme of the trade, as it is at present carried on between England and France. [London, 1674.] W50

A balance sheet showing England's unfavorable balance of trade with France.

Ware verthooning ende afbeeldinghe van eenen dooden ende meerst half verrotten vis ... Middelburg, A. van Vivere, 1608. W51

A propaganda tract in which a dead whale cast up on Dutch shores is interpreted as an omen that Philip of Spain's death is near, and that the proposed treaty limiting Dutch commercial activity will not have to be signed.

Warhafftige und gewise newe Zeytung, wie die Röm. Key. Mey. auff den xx. Octobris dess xli. Jars mit einer treffenlichen Armada, die Statt Algiero zü Erobern da selbst ankommen ... [n.p., ca. 1541.] W52

A newsletter account by Charles V to lay siege to Algiers.

Warren, George. An impartial description of Surinam upon the continent of Guiana in America. London, W. Godbid, 1667. W53

A well-balanced account of Surinam and its commercial opportunities, noting rivers, harbors, and products, as well as disadvantages to trade.

Warren, John. A sermon preached before the incorporated Society for the Propagation of the Gospel in Foreign Parts, at their anniversary meeting in the parish church of St. Mary-le-Bow, on Friday, February 16, 1787. London, T. Harrison and S. Brooke, 1787. W54

A pessimistic sermon, reflecting the decline in missionary work in North America, only thirty-three missionaries remaining, the result of the American Revolution.

Warren, Robert. Industry and diligence in our callings earnestly recommended: In a sermon preached before the honourable trustees for establishing the colony of Georgia. London, W. Meadows, 1737. W55

A religious exhortation to carry out the natural plan for mankind which is that all are capable of improvement for their own good and for the benefit of others and the glory of God. Colonial enterprises are seen as the fulfillment of this plan.

Warren, Thomas. A true and exact particular and inventory of all and singular the estate and effects whatsoever, of Thomas Warren ... London, S. Buckley, 1732. W56

Pertains to a scandal in the management of the Charitable Corporation for the Relief of Industrious Poor.

Wassenaer, Nicolaes van. Historisch verhael alder ghedenck-weerdichste geschiedenisse ... Amsterdam, Ian Everts Cloppenburgh, 1622-35. W57

A twenty-one volume set of news publications issued in April and October of each year, recording recent events. There are numerous items relating to the Dutch commercial and exploratory voyages to the East and West Indies.

Wassenberg, Eberhard. De gout-myn van Vranckryck. [n.p.] 1672. W58

A survey of French and German commerce, noting specific items exported to various countries.

Waterdrincker, Zibrant Barentsz. Journal ofte korte ende waerachtige beschryvinge van de voornaemste gheschiedenissen ter zee onder ... Marten H. Tromp. [Amsterdam] Crispijn der Pas, 1639. W59

An account by an eyewitness of the defeat of the second Spanish armada by Marten Tromp in 1639.

Watermeyer, Albrecht Anton. Statistisch-historisch-geographisches Handbuch, zur Grundlegung der Kentnis der Staten und Länder, und ihrer Geschichte. Hamburg, B.G. Hoffmann, 1786. W60

A comprehensive work providing descriptions of the major countries, with brief histories, factual information regarding religions, products, political situations, etc.

Watson, Richard. The principles of the Revolution vindicated in a sermon preached before the University of Cambridge on Wednesday, May 29, 1776. Cambridge, J. Archdeacon, 1776. W61

"The natural equality and independence of individuals here contended for, is ... the surest foundation of all just reasoning concerning the origin and extent of civil government in every part of the world."

Waugh, John. A sermon preached before the incorporated Society for the Propagation of the Gospel in Foreign Parts, at their anniversary meeting in the parish-church of St. Mary-le-Bow, on Friday, February 15, 1722 [i.e. 1723]. London, J. Downing, 1723. W62

The bishop notes among obstacles to the Society's success the prejudices against Christianity left among Indians by the Spaniards.

We have been all in the wrong; or, Thoughts upon the dissolution of the late, and conduct of the present Parliament. London, J. Debrett, 1785. W63

In addition to commenting on the parliamentary crisis, this tract contains a dispassionate discussion of the situation in India.

The wealth and commerce of Great-Britain consider'd. [n.p.] 1728. W64

A contradiction to those who were lamenting the decline of British commerce.

The wealth of Great Britain in the ocean. London, M. Cooper and W. Owen, 1749. W65

A review of the problems caused by Dutch fishing in English waters, together with a proposal for an Anglo-Dutch fishing company.

The weavers and clothiers complaint against the East-India-trade. London, A. Baldwin, 1699. W66

A broadside in verse which:

"Shews rise and progress of the trade
To India drove, and who 'twas made
The first steps to our wooll trades ruin,
And how it proved to folks undoing."

Webber, Samuel. An account of a scheme for preventing the exportation of our wool. London, T. Cooper, 1740. W67

The author, a woolen manufacturer, proposes a detailed system of accounting for all wool shorn in Great Britain, and other trade restrictions to guarantee protection of the woolen industry.

Webber, Samuel. A short account of the state of our woollen manufactures. London, T. Cooper, 1741. W68

A series of letters discussing the English wool trade and its decline in the face of French competition.

Weber, Friedrich Christian. Nouveaux memoires sur l'etat present de la grande Russie ou Moscovie. Paris, Pissot, 1725. W69

An account of recent events in Russia, including Lorenz Lange's embassy to Peking, 1715-17.

[Webster, W. (William).] The consequences of trade. London, T. Cooper, 1740. W70

England's unsatisfactory economic situation is attributed to the exporting of raw wool.

[Webster, W. (William).] The consequences of trade, as to the wealth and strength of any nation ... London, T. Cooper, 1740. W71

This third edition contains a postscript not in the previous editions, testifying to its popularity and to the arguments it raised.

[Webster, W. (William).] The draper confuted. London, T. Cooper, 1740. W72

The author here replies to his own pamphlet, *The consequences of trade*.

Webster, W. (William). The draper's reply to some Remarks on the consequences of trade. London, T. Cooper, 1741. W73

In large part a refutation of a pamphlet entitled *Remarks upon Mr. Webber's scheme and The draper's pamphlet*. Webber's "scheme" and the author's pamphlet had been published the previous year.

Weederwaardige te huis-reyze, van het Neederlandsche Oost-Indische-Compagniesch retourschip, gezegt de Gerechtigheid, ten dienste van de kamer Delft ... Amsterdam, Bernardus Mourik [1755?]. W74

An account of a homeward voyage from the East Indies, with adventures on the east coast of Africa.

Weidenfeld, Adam. Epistola ... ad Joannem Paulem Oliva praepositum generalem, Societatis Jesu. Tyrnau, Typis Academicis, 1689. W75

A brief history of the Jesuit mission in Japan, noting bishops, missionaries, martyrs, and mission stations.

Den wel-gedischten Olipodrigo t'Amsterdam. [n.p., 1674.] W76

A supposed discussion among persons of several nationalities in which the Englishman points out the high cost of goods because of war with the Netherlands and the advantages of peace with the English.

Weld, Isaac. Travels through the states of North America, and the provinces of Upper and Lower Canada, during the years 1795, 1796, and 1797. London, John Stockdale, 1799. W77

An account of travels from northern Virginia to Canada, with observations on social, economic, governmental and other aspects of life in North America with a view to advising potential immigrants.

Weld, Isaac. Voyage au Canada, pendant les années 1795, 1796, et 1797. Paris, Imprimerie de Munier, 1800. W78

The first French edition.

Weld, Isaac. Reizen door de staaten van Noord-Amerika, en de provintiën van Opper- en Neder-Canada. The Hague, J.C. Leeuwestijn, 1801-02. W79

The first Dutch edition.

Weld, Isaac. Viaggio nel Canadá negli anni 1795, 1796 e 1797. Milan, Giambattista Sonzogno, 1819. W80

The first Italian edition.

Welser, Marcus. Opera historica et philologica, sacra et profana. Nuremberg, Wolfgang Maurits [etc.] 1682. W81

Includes a reproduction of the Peutinger Table with an extensive commentary by the author.

Der Welt Kugel: Beschrybung der Welt und dess gantzen Ertreichs ... [Strassburg, Johanne Grüniger, 1509.] W82
The first edition of a geography describing newly discovered parts of the world. It is frequently attributed to Martin Waldseemüller.

Welwood, William. An abridgement of all sea-lawes; gathered forth of all writings and monuments, which are to be found among any people or nation, upon the coasts of the great ocean and Mediterranean Sea. London, Humfrey Lownes for Thomas Man, 1613. W83
A practical guide for persons involved in maritime affairs, taken from the codes of Oléron and Wisby as well as Roman law. It includes an anti-Dutch statement with respect to the *Mare liberum* of Grotius.

Wendelin, Marcus Friederich. Marci Friderici Wendelini Archi-Palatini, Admiranda Nili, commentatione philologica geographica, historica, physica & hieroglyphica, ex CCCXVIII autoribus, Graecis & Latinis vetustis & recentibus illustrata ... Frankfurt, Typis Wechelianis, 1623. W84
A description of the Nile River including its natural history, geography, history, and its importance in ancient times.

Werdenhagen, Johann Angelius. De rebuspublicis Hanseaticis. Frankfurt, M. Merian [1641]. W85
A source book for the history of the Hanseatic League and its relationship with other cities of Europe. Contains numerous documents relating to privileges granted to other commercial towns.

Wesley, John. A calm address to our American colonies. London, R. Hawes [1775]. W86
A warning to colonists contending for liberty that they are the dupes of scheming persons in England who are enemies of monarchy, a condensation of Samuel Johnson's *Taxation no tyranny*.

Wesley, John. Thoughts upon slavery. London [1774]. W87
An anti-slavery tract which was crucial in turning Methodists in Great Britain against slavery and also involving them in the beginning of missionary work among slaves in the West Indies.

West, John. The substance of a journal during a residence at the Red River Colony, British North America. London, L.B. Seeley and son, 1824. W88
An account of life at the Red River Colony by one of its early chaplains.

West India Planters and Merchants (London, England). Considerations on the present state of the intercourse between His Majesty's sugar colonies and the dominions of the United States of America. London, 1784. W89
An attempt to show that products from Canada could supplant those formerly sent to the West Indies by the mainland colonies.

West India Planters and Merchants (London, England). The legal claim of the British sugar-colonies to enjoy an exclusive right of supplying this kingdom with sugars ... London?, 1792. W90

[West Indian maritime and military records.] Manuscript in French. Various places, 1780-1783. W91
The collection consists primarily of correspondence relating to ships, cargoes, movement of troops, etc. in the French West Indies, some apparently pertaining to naval affairs connected with the American Revolution.

West Zanen, Willem Pietersz van. Derde voornaemste zee-getogt ... na de Oost-Indien. Sanderam, Hendrick J. Zoet, 1648; Amsterdam, Tymen Houthaak, 1648. W92
An account of the voyage of Heemskerck and Harmansz to the East Indies in 1601-03. The editor, H. Soete-Boom, inserted many descriptions of places visited.

West-Indisch discours; verhandelende de West-Indische saeken. [n.p.] 1653. W93
A discussion by two gentlemen who are "treating of West Indian affairs and how they may be improved for the good of the company."

West-Indische Compagnie (Netherlands). Accoord met de staten van Zeeland aangegaan, wegens de koop en overneminge van de colonie van Suriname. Amsterdam, J. Lescailje & D. Rank [1749]. W94
A collection of documents dealing with the colony at Surinam maintained by the Dutch West India Company.

West-Indische Compagnie (Netherlands). Artyckel-brief van de ... West-Indische Compagnie. The Hague, J. Scheltus, 1675. W95
A series of sixty-six articles and regulations set forth for the management of the West India Company, and concurred in by the States General.

West-Indische Compagnie (Netherlands). Consideratien ende redenen ... over den treves met den Konink van Hispangjen. Haarlem, Adrian Rooman, 1629. W96
A plea for the continuation of the war with Spain which had been advantageous to the Dutch West India Company.

West-Indische Compagnie (Netherlands). Consideratien ende redenen der e. heeren bewind-hebberen vande geoctroijeerde West-Indische Compagnie ... Haarlem, A. Rooman, 1629. W97

"Considerations and discussions of the high administrators of the chartered West India Company ... concerning the present deliberations of a treaty of peace with the King of Spain."

West-Indische Compagnie (Netherlands). Extract uit het Register der resolutien ... [n.p., ca. 1773.] W98
Regulations on the use of company ships by individuals.

West-Indische Compagnie (Netherlands). Extract uut de missive van den president ende raden aen de ... Staten Generael. The Hague, Ludolph Brekevelt, 1648. W99
A report on the critical situation of the West India Company's outpost at Recife where the Dutch were trying to hold out against the Portuguese.

West-Indische Compagnie (Netherlands). Extracten uyt de registers der resolutien van de ... Nederlandsche West-Indische Compagnie. [n.p., 1780.] W100
A series of nine shipping regulations.

West-Indische Compagnie (Netherlands). Lyste van 't ghene de Brasil jaerlijcks can opbrenghen. [n.p., 1648.] W101
A report on the profitability of the sugar trade in Brazil to the Dutch West India Company.

West-Indische Compagnie (Netherlands). Project en consideratien van bewinthebberen van de ... West Indische Compagnie. Amsterdam, Niclaas ten Hoorn [ca. 1715]. W102
Describes the commercial value of Curaçao, Surinam, the Gold Coast, and other Dutch holdings.

West-Indische Compagnie (Netherlands). Reglement byde West-Indische Compagnie, ter vergaderinge vande negentiene, met approbatie vande Ho: Mo: Heeren Staten Generael ... The Hague, Weduwe ende erfghenamen van wijlen H.J. van Wouw, 1638. W103
"Regulation of the West India Company provisionally decreed in the assembly of the nineteen with the approbation of the States General respecting the opening of trade with Brazil."

West-Indische Compagnie (Netherlands). Remonstrantie ... by de bewinthebberen van de ... West Indische Compagnie. Amsterdam, Pieter Jansz, 1664. W104
The company protests against inroads on their commerce being threatened by a newly formed Danish African Company.

West-Indische Compagnie (Netherlands). Kamer Zealand. Memorie van remarques van bewindhebberen der Generaale Ge-octroyeerde West-Indische Compagnie ter Kamer Zeeland, in dato 3 February 1773 ... [n.p., 1773.] W105
The Dutch West India Company's chamber from Zeeland questions the wisdom of making a canal between the Demerary and Essequebo rivers and of building a fort on the Essequebo.

[Westerveen, Abraham.] Dissertatio de jure, quod competit societati privilegiatae Faederati Belgii ad navigationem & commercia Indiarum Orientalum. Amsterdam, R. & G. Westenios, 1723. W106
An argument against the right of the Ostend Company to participate in the East Indian trade.

[Westerveen, Abraham.] Dissertation où l'on prouve le droit exclusif de la Compagnie Orientale des Provinces-Unies ... [The Hague, T. Johnson, 1724.] W107
This translation was made by Jean Barbeyrac.

Westerveen, Abraham. Dissertatio secunda de jure, quod competit societati privilegiatae Faederati Belgii ... Amsterdam, R. & G. Westenios, 1724. W108
An answer to the attack made by Patrick MacNeny upon an earlier tract by Westerveen.

Westerveen, Abraham. A second dissertation concerning the right of the Dutch East-India Company. The Hague, T. Johnson, 1724. W109
An English edition of the preceding work.

[Westerveen, Abraham.] Vertoog van het regt dat de Vereenigde Nederlandsche Oost-Indische Mattschappy heeft op de vaart en koophandel naar Oost-Indiën. Amsterdam, J. de Ruyter [1723]. W110
A translation from the Latin.

Westerveen, Abraham. Tweede vertoog van het recht, het welk de Vereenigde Nederlandsche Oost-Indische Maatschappy. Amsterdam, R. and G. Wetstein, 1724. W111
A translation from the Latin.

De wettelijcke verantwoordinge der Hollanders ... doorgaens aengewesen werdende de trouloose handeling van Vranckryck. Amsterdam, C. vander Gracht, 1674. W112
The Dutch charge France with fifty years of faithlessness in treaty obligations, and with innumerable acts of violence against the commerce of other nations.

Wexell, S. D. (Sven Didrik). Rolofs händelser Gastuvs sons, prinsens utaf Goa. Stockholm, Jacob Merckell, 1755. W113
A literary piece set in Asia, involving travel to India, Burma, and China.

Weyman, Daniel. Antwoorde en versoeck, vande heeren Weyman ende Copez ... Leiden, Jan Dyvoet, 1659. W114

A plea to the Dutch government to do all possible to maintain the alliance against Sweden after the closing of the Sound to Dutch trade.

[Whately, Thomas.] Considerations on the trade and finances of this kingdom ... London, J. Wilkie, 1766. W115

A review of Great Britain's commercial and financial situation following the Seven Years War.

[Whately, Thomas.] Mémoire sur l'administration des finances de l'Angleterre, depuis la paix. Mainz [Paris] Jean Faust & Jean Guttenberg, 1768. W116

This is not a translation of William Knox's *The Present State of the Nation*, as stated in many bibliographies and catalogs. It is a translation of the preceding work, with notes and an introduction by the French editor.

[Whately, Thomas.] The regulations lately made concerning the colonies, and the taxes imposed upon them, considered. London: Printed for J. Wilkie ... 1765. W117

A summary and optimistic view of the situation of the British colonies in North America and the West Indies following the defeat of France.

Wheeler, John. A treatise of commerce, wherein are shewed the commodities arising by a wel ordered, and ruled trade. Middelburg, Richard Schilders, 1601. W118

The secretary of the Company of Merchant Adventurers defends his organization against critics, citing specific advantages that come to England through the workings of the company.

Wheelock, Eleazar. A plain and faithful narrative of the original design, rise, progress and present state of the Indian charity-school at Lebanon, in Connecticut. Boston, Richard and Samuel Draper, 1763. W119

This is Wheelock's first description of the founding and early progress of his charity school, giving an account of the motives, methods, and early results in integrating Indian boys and girls with New England children.

Wheelock, Eleazar. A continuation of the narrative of the state, &c. of the Indian charity-school, at Lebanon, in Connecticut, from Nov. 27th 1762, to Sept. 3d, 1765. Boston, Richard and Samuel Draper, 1765. W120

A second report on the progress of the charity school, concerned with both financial support and progress being made by the teachers. The school had 127 students.

Wheelock, Eleazar. A continuation of the narrative of the Indian charity-school, in Lebanon, in Connecticut: from the year 1768, to the incorporation of it with Dartmouth-college ... [Hartford] 1771. W121

This report is concerned primarily with the financial and political aspects of the school which was being moved to Hanover, N.H. where it became a part of Dartmouth College.

Wheelock, Eleazar. A continuation of the narrative of the Indian Charity School, begun in Lebanon, in Connecticut, now incorporated with Dartmouth-College, in Hanover, in the province of New-Hampshire. New-Hampshire, 1772. W122

A description of the school's beginnings at Hanover, N.H. where it was necessary to construct buildings, clear land, plant and harvest crops in order to become self sufficient.

Wheelock, Eleazar. A continuation of the narrative of the Indian charity-school, begun in Lebanon, in Connecticut, now incorporated with Dartmouth-College, in Hanover, in the province of New-Hampshire. Hartford, 1773. W123

This report notes the arrival of Huron Indians at the school and contains descriptions of some western Indian tribes based on the report of one of them at the school.

Wheelock, Eleazar. A continuation of the narrative of the Indian charity school, begun in Lebanon, in Connecticut, now incorporated with Dartmouth-college, in Hanover, in the province of New-Hampshire ... Hartford, Ebenezer Watson, 1775. W124

The final report by Wheelock on the school's progress, presenting an optimistic plan to settle a largely Christian community of Indians among the Iroquois.

Whiston, James. The causes of our present calamities in reference to the trade of the nation fully discovered, with the most proper expedient to remedy the same. [London] Edw. Poole, 1695-1696. W125

A proposal to improve England's commercial position through the election by ballot of a committee of merchants charged with guiding the national economy.

Whiston, James. A discourse of the decay of trade ... [London, Samuel Crouch, 1693.] W126

A proposal to remedy England's lagging commerce by the establishment of a council of merchants, representing both geographic areas and specific industries, to recommend policies in the national interest.

Whiston, James. England's state-distempers, trac'd from their originals: with proper remedies and means to make her vertuous and prosperous. London, Samuel Crouch, Edward Poole, and Joseph Fox, 1704. W127

The author laments the decline in both morality and trade, and recommends the election of committees to advise and govern in matters of appointments and commerce.

Whitaker, Nathaniel, ed. A brief narrative of the Indian charity-school, in Lebanon in Connecticut, New England ... London, J. and W. Oliver, 1766. **W128**
A collection of testimonies on the importance of the school and its conformity to the intentions of the founders of New England.

Whitaker, Nathaniel. Appendix to the former narrative of the Indian charity-school in Lebanon in Connecticut, New England ... [London: Printed by J. and W. Oliver, 1767.] **W129**
This appendix contains a group of letters, mostly from Eleazar Wheelock, noting the progress of the school.

Whitbourne, Sir Richard. A discourse and discovery of New-found-land. London, F. Kyngston for William Barrett, 1620. **W130**
This description of Newfoundland was written in the hope of encouraging English colonists to settle there by one who had been there frequently. It contains a large section "shewing the commodities thereof."

Whitbourne, Sir Richard. A discourse and discovery of New-found-land. London, Felix Kingston, 1622. **W131**
The second edition, containing more than fifty pages of additional material.

White, George. An account of the trade to the East-Indies. London, 1691. **W132**
The East India Company is praised for its trade, but criticized for meddling in Indian politics.

White, George. Een verhael van den handel op Oost-Indien. Amsterdam, Aart Dirksz Oossaan, 1692. **W133**
A translation of the previous pamphlet.

[White, John.] The planters plea. Or The grounds of plantations examined, and usuall objections answered. London, William Jones, 1630. **W134**
A clear statement of a philosophy favoring English colonies in New England as well as a good history of the beginnings of the Massachusetts Bay Company by one who was instrumental in founding it.

White, John, surgeon. Journal of a voyage to New South Wales. London, J. Debrett, 1790. **W135**
A doctor's description of the first English settlement in Australia.

White, John, surgeon. Resa till Nya Holland, åren 1787 och 1788. I sammandrag af Samuel Ödmann. Upsala, J. Edmans enka, 1793. **W136**
A much abridged text, typical of the translations of Samuel Ödmann. Four illustrations from the original edition are included, and Ödmann introduces the work with an essay on the exploration of the Pacific.

White, John, surgeon. Voyage a la Nouvelle Galles du Sud, à Botany-Bay, au Port Jackson, en 1787, 1788, 1789. Paris, Pougin, 1795. **W137**
The first French edition.

White, John, surgeon. Voyage a la Nouvelle Galles du Sud, à Botany-Bay, au Port Jackson, en 1787, 1788, 1789. Paris, Guillaume, 1798. **W138**
The second French edition.

White, Peter. A memorable sea-fight penned and preserved. London, T. Forcet, 1649. **W139**
Compares English, Dutch, and Spanish fleets with special interest in the Dutch who were major commercial rivals of the English.

White, William. Journal of a voyage ... from Madras to Columbo, and Da Lagoa Bay. London, John Stockdale, 1800. **W140**
A description of Delagoa Bay and its potential usefulness to England as a possible base for commercial, whaling, and naval operations.

[Whitlocke, Bulstrode.] Free ports and the nature of them stated. London, W. Du-Gard, 1651. **W141**
The author looks toward England's capturing much of the carrying trade enjoyed by the Netherlands.

Whitworth, Sir Charles. Commerce de la Grande-Bretagne. Paris, Imprimerie Royal, 1777. **W142**
French translation of the preceding work.

Whitworth, Sir Charles. State of the trade of Great Britain in its imports and exports, progressively from the year 1697 [to 1773] also of the trade to each particular country, during the above period, distinguishing each year ... London, G. Robinson [etc.] 1776. **W143**
A statistical recording of British trade, with commentary on Britain's commerce with each nation included in the study.

Wichers, J.D. [Autograph letter signed.] The Hague, 6 April 1786. **W144**
The letter is addressed to a committee of finances for the province of Groningen, and concerns the Dutch colony in Surinam.

[Wichsell, Jöran.] Beskrifning om Rysslands belägenhet, gräntzor, landskaper, städer ... och andra beskaffenheter. Stockholm, Olao Enaeo, 1706. **W145**

A survey of Russia which includes a section on commerce and notes the commercial importance of some of the major cities.

Wicquefort, Abraham de. l'Ambassadeur et ses fonctions ... augmentée d'un Traité du juge competent des ambassadeurs, ecrit en Latin par M. de Bynkershoek ... et traduit en François par M.J. Barbeyrac. The Hague, T. Johnson, 1724. W146

In appending the work of Bijnkershoek the publisher is adding the impression of the 1723 edition of that work.

Wicquefort, Abraham de. The embassador and his functions. To which is added An historical discourse concerning the election of the emperor and the electors. Translated into English by Mr. Digby. London, Bernard Lintott [1716]. W147

The first English edition, translated from the French. It concerns a variety of ambassadorial functions including matters of mercantile concern.

Wiehe, Johan Heinrich. Ueber die dänischen Bankzettel, Handelsbalanz, und den ostindischen Handel. Copenhagen, Christian Gottlob Profts, 1788. W148

A survey of the financial aspects of Denmark's East Indian trade.

Wigglesworth, Edward. Calculations on American population. Boston, J. Boyle, 1775. W149

Argues for the reestablishment of good relations between the colonies and Great Britain, pointing out that the American population will continue to grow, becoming a large market for Great Britain.

Wijtloopige deductie van de ... Staten Generael ... Raekende de pretensien van de Engelsche. Rotterdam, Cornelis de la Tour, 1662. W150

A reply to English claims for compensation for two ships taken by the Dutch.

Wilcocks, Joseph. A sermon preached before the incorporated Society for the Propagation of the Gospel in Foreign Parts, at their anniversary meeting in the parish-church of St. Mary-le-Bow, on Friday the 18th of February, 1725 [i.e. 1726]. London, Joseph Downing, 1726. W151

This preacher expresses urgent concern for ministers to work with colonists and sees little hope for conversion of Indians.

Wild, Johann. Neue Reysbeschreibung eines gefangenen Christen. Nuremberg, B. Scherff, 1613. W152

An account of travels in the Near East from 1604 to 1611. The commerce of various eastern Mediterranean cities is described.

Wild, Johann. Neue Reysbeschreibung eines gefangenen Christen ... Nuremberg, Ludwig Lochner, 1623. W153

Another edition of the preceding book.

[Wilkins, Isaac.] Short advice to the counties of New-York, by a country gentleman. New York: Printed by James Rivington, 1774. W154

A Loyalist pamphlet calling attention to the excellence of British government and predicting that any government that might emerge from the independence movement would fall victim to tyrants and foreign powers.

Wilkinson, William. An answer to the book written by the Guiney Company in their own defence, for the management of their trade in Africa. [London, 1690.] W155

A tract hostile to the Royal African Company of England, contending it lacks sufficient establishments to control the slave trade and that its actions often alienate that trade into the hands of competitors.

Wilkinson, William. Systema Africanum: or, A treatise, discovering the intrigues ... of the Guiney Company. London, 1690. W156

A complaint that the monopoly of the Royal African Company is stifling British commerce with Africa, and depriving American plantations of slaves.

Willebrand, Johann Peter. Hansische Chronick, aus beglaubten Nachrichten. Lübeck, Auf Kosten des Autoris, 1748. W157

A history of the Hanseatic League from its beginnings to 1630, including numerous documents relating to the commerce of individual cities in the League.

William, of Conches. Philosophicarum et astronomicarum institutionum, Guilielmi Hirsaugiensis olim abbatis, libri tres ... Basel, Henric Petrus, 1531. W158

A treatise in astronomy by one of the more original medieval thinkers in that science.

[Williams, Edward.] Virginia's discovery of silke-worms, with their benefit, and the implanting of mulberry trees. London, T.H. for John Stephenson, 1650. W159

A promotion piece for Carolina with detailed instructions for developing silk culture, growing grapes and other fruits, and for constructing a saw mill for the production of lumber.

Williams, Edward. Virgo triumphans: or, Virginia richly and truly valued; more especially the south part thereof. London, T. Harper for J. Stephenson, 1650. W160

A description of Carolina, noting its commercial potentialities, and comparing them to those of Persia and China. Shows the strategic value of the region as a bulwark against the Spainiards and suggests a possibility that a river leading to the Pacific Ocean may be nearby.

Williams, Griffith. An account of the island of Newfoundland. [London] T. Cole, 1765.
W161
A clear and informative description of the Newfoundland fishing trade.

Williams, John. An enquiry into the truth of the tradition, concerning the discovery of America by Prince Madog ab Owen Gwynedd about the year 1170. London, J. Brown, 1791. W162
An essay attempting to prove that the Welshman Prince Madog ab Owen Gwynedd discovered America in 1170.

Williams, John. Farther observations on the discovery of America by Prince Madog ab Owen Gwynedd about the year 1170. London, J. Brown, 1792. W163
A series of agruments to prove the existence of tribes of Indians descended from Welsh settlers of the twelfth century.

Williams, John. The redeemed captive returning to Zion, a faithful history of remarkable occurrences, in the captivity and deliverance of Mr. John Williams. Boston, John Boyle, 1774.
W164
The fifth edition of a popular narrative, appending the sermon delivered upon the author's return and a report of others killed or captured at Deerfield, Massachusetts.

[Williams, Reeve.] A letter from a merchant to a member of Parliament, relating to the danger Great Britain is in of losing her trade. London, 1718. W165
The author's purpose is to show the danger that the growing naval power of Spain poses to English trade to the Levant. Illustrated by a map of the Mediterranean.

Williamson, Peter. The travels of Peter Williamson, among the different nations and tribes of savage Indians in America. Edinburgh, For the Author, 1768. W166
This work is closely patterned on the author's and adds some natural history material and a large section on Niagara Falls.

Wills, William, surgeon. A narrative of the very extraordinary adventures and sufferings of Mr. William Wills, late surgeon on board the Durrington Indiaman, Captain Richard Crabb, in her voyage to the East-Indies, under the convoy of Admiral Boscawen. London, W. Webb, 1750-51. W167
The narrative centers on the conflict between the author and the captain, illustrative of life aboard ship, and the administration of justice under East India Company jurisdiction.

Willyams, Cooper. An account of the campaign in the West Indies, in the year 1794, under the command of Their Excellencies Lieutenant General Sir Charles Grey K.B. and Vice Admiral Sir John Jervis, K.B. commanders in chief in the West Indies. London, T. Bentley for G. Nicol [etc.] 1796. W168
The chaplain of a ship in the British navy gives a highly personal account of the early victories and later defeats of the British West Indian expedition.

Wimmannus, Nicolaus. Navigationis Maris Arctoi, id est, Balthici, & Sinus Codani, descriptio. Basel [1753]. W169
The Baltic Sea, its navigation, and its port cities are described.

[Wimpffen, François Alexandre Stanislaus, baron de.] Lettres d'un voyageur. Amsterdam & Paris, De Bure, 1788. W170
A series of twenty-eight letters, supposedly written during a voyage down the west coast of Africa, containing observations on the people and trade of that area.

Wimpffen, François Alexandre Stanislaus, baron de. A voyage to Saint Domingo, in the years 1788, 1789, and 1790. London, T. Cadell [etc.] 1797. W171
A description of the island and of conditions that led to the slave rebellion there.

Windus, John. Reise nach Mequinesz. Hanover, Nicolaus Förster & Sohn, 1726. W172
An account of the expedition of Charles Stuart, who went to Morocco in 1721 to negotiate for the release of English prisoners being held there. Describes commercial relationships between Fez, Morocco, and other cities.

Winslow, Edward. The glorious progress of the gospel, amongst the Indians in New England ... London: Printed for Hannah Allen, 1649.
W173
The fourth in a series of eleven pamphlets published between 1643 and 1671 to report the progress of missions and to stimulate further interest in them. This one includes letters from John Eliot and Thomas Mayhew.

Winterbotham, William. An historical, geographical and philosophical view of the Chinese empire. London, The editor [etc.] 1795.
W174
A description of China inspired by Macartney's embassy, including an account of that embassy based on Aeneas Anderson's book.

Winterbottom, Thomas Masterman. An account of the native Africans in the neighbourhood of Sierra Leone: to which is added, an account of the present state of medicine among them. London, John Hatchard, 1803. W175
An account of life in the Sierra Leone colony which was a re-settlement of Blacks from England and the American colonies.

Wintergerst, Martin. Der durch Europam lauffende, durch Asiam fahrende, an Americam und

Africam anländende, und in Ost-Indien lange Zeit gebliebende ... Reissbeschreibung. [Memmingen] Anton Nepperschmid, 1713. W176

The first issue, with some differences in introductory matter from the second issue of the same sheets which appeared in 1713.

Wintergerst, Martin. Zwey und Zwantzig-Jährige Reysen durch Europam, Asiam, Africam, Americam und Ost-Indien. Frankfurt & Leipzig, Daniel Bartholomae, 1713. W177

Contains ten plates illustrating the author's travels.

Winterpraatje voorgefallen in een treffelijke herberge in den Hage ... The Hague, 1660. W178

Comments on the war in the Baltic.

Winther, Peder. Anviisning og underretning angaaende tobaks-plantning, grundet paa giorte forsøg. Copenhagen, Trykt hos Nicolaus Møller, 1773. W179

A treatise on the cultivation of tobacco, noting methods used in Virginia and elsewhere.

Wissenburg, Wolfgang. Erklärung der Tafel über das Heilig Land. Strassburg, Wendel Rihel, 1538. W180

A description of a seven-sheet map, no longer extant, of Palestine.

Wit, Frederik de. Atlas major. Amsterdam [ca. 1707]. W181

Includes 130 maps of Europe, Asia, Africa, and America.

Witsen, Nicolaas. Aeloude en hedendaegsche scheeps-bouw en bestier ... Amsterdam, Casparus Commelijn; Broer en Jan Appelaer, 1671. W182

The definitive work on shipbuilding in the seventeenth century, with numerous illustrations.

[**Witsen, Nicolaas.**] A letter ... containing a true description of Nova Zembla. [London, 1674.] W183

An extract from the *Philosophical Transactions*, consisting of a brief description of Novaya Zemlya with a map which shows it to be a peninsula.

[**Witsen, Nicolaas.**] Middelen om uit te vinden de ware ladinge der scheepen na hare groote. [Privately printed for the Dutch East India Company, ca. 1690.] W184

This treatise on ship loading was the Dutch East India Company's answer to the problem of controlling the amount of goods taken aboard by captain and crew for their own private adventuring abroad.

Witsen, Nicolaas. Nieuwe lantkaarte van het noorder en ooster deel van Asia en Europe ... [n.p.] 1687. W185

The earliest printed map to show the internal overland and river routes of central Asia, based on extensive experience and correspondence with Asian travelers.

Witsen, Nicolaas. Noord en oost Tartarye. Amsterdam, 1692. W186

A description of eastern and northern Russia and inner Asia, based on correspondence the author maintained with persons in those regions.

Witsen, Nicolaas. Noord en oost Tartaryen: behelzende eene beschryving van verscheidene Tartersche en nabuurige gewesten. Amsterdam, M. Schalekamp, 1785. W187

The most complete edition of Witsen's account of central and eastern Asia, a reissue of the 1705 sheets with new introductory matter.

[**Witt, Cornelis de.**] Een brief uyt Holland aangaande de vryheyd van conscientie. [n.p., 1688.] W188

A translation from the English which includes concern for a plot by English weavers in the Netherlands to mix Spanish, English, and Dutch wool in order to compete with Dutch weavers.

Wolder, Simon. New Türckenbüchlin, dergleichen vor diser Zeit nie getruckt worden, Rathschlag und christliches Bedencken, wie one sonderliche beschwerde der Obrigkeit, auch der Underthanen, der Christenheit Erbfeind, der Türck zu Wasser unnd Land zuüberziehen. [n.p.] 1558. W189

An exhortation to Europeans of all classes to resist the advances of the Turks, calling for levies of troops and taxes, and ridiculing the selfishness of clergy and nobility for not meeting this need.

Wolf, Jens Lauridsøn. Norrigia illustrata, eller Norges med sine underliggende lande og øers korte og sandfaerdige beskrifvelse. [Copenhagen] Jens Lauridsøn Wolff [1651]. W190

This account of Norway includes histories of the Faeroe Islands, Iceland, and Greenland under Norse dominion.

Wolf, Johann Christoph. Reise nach Zeilan. Nebst einem Berichte von der holländischen Regierung zu Jaffanapatnam. Berlin & Stettin, Friedrich Nicolai, 1782-84. W191

An account of an extended travel in Ceylon by a German who served the Dutch East India Company there.

Wolfshagen, Adolphus van. De schoole der princen. Ceulen, Hermanus Albedeuyt, 1673. W192

Contains references to the numerous areas in which the French were interfering with Dutch trade.

Wonderen des werelds. Amsterdam, M.W. Doornick, 1672. W193
   Extracts from numerous travel narratives with descriptions of plants, animals, and peoples of various regions.

Wood, John Philip. A sketch of the life and projects of John Law of Lauriston, comptroller general of the finances in France. Edinburgh, Peter Hill and George Kearsley; London, 1791. W194
   A brief, well-written biography including details of Law's banking activities and of the Mississippi Company under his management.

Wood, William. New England's prospect. London, Thomas Cotes, 1634. W195
   The first detailed description of Massachusetts, noting the harbors, towns, soil, weather, and products. The goods for which there was a ready market in Massachusetts are noted.

Woodfall, William. An account of the proceedings of the general quarterly court, held at the East India House. London, Chapman and Co., 1794. W196
   The proceedings deal with the shipping of the East India Company.

Woofe, Abraham. The tyranny of the Dutch against the English. London, John Crowch and Tho. Wilson, 1653. W197
   An account of Anglo-Dutch rivalry in the East Indies in the 1618-1620 period.

Woolley, Richard. A true, exact, and particular inventory of all and singular the lands, tenements, and hereditaments, goods, chattels, debts, and personal estate whatsoever, which Richard Woolley was seized and possessed of ... upon the first day of January ... one thousand seven hundred and thirty ... London, S. Buckley, 1732. W198
   Relates to Woolley's involvement in the management of the South Sea Company.

Worm, Johann Gottlieb. Ost-Indian-und persianische Reisen. Frankfurt & Leipzig, 1745. W199
   The second edition of an extensive description of the East Indies and Asia based upon ten years of travel.

Worshipful Company of Weavers (London, England). Reasons humbly offered by the Weavers of London, against a bill now depending in Parliament, entitled, A bill for the more effectual preventing the importation of foreign thrown-silk, &c. [London, 1726.] W200
   The silk-weavers of London object to the bill in Parliament which would restrict imports on foreign silk because they are dependent upon it for part of their work.

Worshipful Company of Weavers (London, England). The weavers reply to the linen-drapers, and other dealers in printed callicoes and linens. London, T. Warner, 1720. W201
   A reply to *The case of the linen drapers*, contending that the importing of calicoes was detrimental to the woolen industry of England.

Wright, Thomas. The use of the globes, or, The general doctrine of the sphere ... to which is added, A synopsis of the doctrine of eclipses. London, John Senex, 1740. W202
   An educational text with twenty-nine illustrations relating to globes and instruments produced by John Senex.

[Wtenbogaert, Johann.] Tsamen-spraeck over de twee slechte gesellen van Treveskrack ende bysonder van Capo de Grijp. [n.p.] 1630. W203
   A reply to the West India Company's advocates of continuing the war with Spain.

Wurffbain, Johann Sigmund. Reisz-beschreibung welche er in namen und wegen der hochlöblichen in Niderland angeordneten Ost-Indianischen Compagnie ... Nuremberg, M. Endter, 1646. W204
   This edition of Wurffbain's account of the East Indies was published by his father from his son's letters. Later, the son suppressed it because of its incorrect information.

Wurffbain, Johann Sigmund. Vierzehen Jährige ost-indianische Krieg und ober kaufmanns Dienste ... Journal und Tage-Buch. Nuremberg, A. Lichtenthaler, 1686. W205
   The authorized and more complete edition of an account of East Indian commerce and exploration by a German in the service of the Dutch East India Company.

Wurmb, Baron von. Briefe ... auf ihren Reisen nach Afrika und Ostindien. Gotha, Carl Willhelm Ettinger, 1794. W206
   A series of letters describing the Cape of Good Hope and Java.

Wurmb, Baron von. Merkwürdigkeiten aus Ostindien. Gotha, Carl Wilhelm Ettinger, 1797. W207
   Contains descriptions of Borneo, Sumatra, Celebes, and Timor.

Wyland, Jan Pieter. Journaal, of dags-aantekening van het voorgevallene in de colonie van Barbiecie. Amsterdam, Johannes Roos & Hendrik Holthuysen [1763]. W208
   An account of a slave revolt in the colony of Berbice, the chief slave-trading area of the Dutch West India region.

Wylde, Charles. Journall kept ... in shipp Bonito, beeing bound by God's assistance from England to the island Assada. Manuscript. February 4, 1650, to July 28, 1652. W209

The journal of a voyage from England to Java by way of Asada and other islands near Madagascar, Madras, Masulipatam, and the Persian Gulf. A number of charts and a description of the Asada settlement are included.

Wynne, John Huddlestone. A general history of the British Empire in America. London, W. Richardson and L. Urquhart, 1770. W210

A survey of the general history and development of the North American colonies, with an interesting discussion of the state of the colonies, especially with regard to agriculture and foreign trade.

Wynne, John. A sermon preached before the incorporated Society for the Propagation of the Gospel in Foreign Parts, at their anniversary meeting in the parish-church of St. Mary-le-Bow, on Friday the 19th of February, 1724 [i.e. 1725]. London, Joseph Downing, 1725. W211

The sermon calls attention to the opportunity afforded by British commerce to carry Christianity abroad, and notes the SPG's position to participate.

Wytfliet, Corneille. Descriptio Ptolemaicae augmentum ... Louvain, J. Bogardus, 1597. W212

This work actually contains nothing from Ptolemy, but is the first atlas to be devoted entirely to America. The text describes the geography, natural history, and ethnography of the New World.

Wytfliet, Corneille. Histoire universelle des Indes, Orientales et Occidentales. Douay, François Fabri, 1605. W213

The first translation of this important work, with additional material on the East Indies.

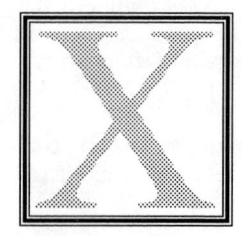

Xarque, Francisco. Insignes missioneros de la Compañia de Jesus en la provincia del Paraguay. Pamplona, Juan Micòn, 1687.   X1

An account of Jesuit missions in Paraguay, Tucuman, and Rio de la Plata, from a Jesuit point of view, with biographies of several of the missionaries.

Xavier, Manoel. Vitorias do governador da India Nuno Alvarez Botelho. Lisbon, Antonio Alvarez, 1633.   X2

An account of a Portuguese victory against the King of Achin at Malacca in 1629, and of subsequent actions against Dutch ships in the East Indian archipelago.

[Xerez, Francisco de.] Libro primo de la conquista del Peru & provincia del Cuzco de la Indie Occidentali. Venice, Stephano de Sabio, 1535.   X3

The first Italian edition of an account of Pizarro's conquests, written by the conquistador's secretary. It was first published in Spain in 1534.

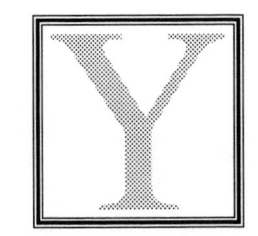

Yarranton, Andrew. England's improvement by sea and land. London, R. Everingham, For the Author, 1677. Y1
Contains a number of suggestions for the improvement of England's commerce, including improved river navigation, a public bank, and a court of merchants.

Yarranton, Andrew. England's improvement by sea and land. The second part. London, Tho. Parkhurst, 1698. Y2
Concerns the need for more capital to serve commerce, the fishing trade, and the tin, iron, linen, and woolen industries as well as inland navigation.

Yonge, Philip. A sermon preached before the incorporated Society for the Propagation of the Gospel in Foreign Parts: at their anniversary meeting in the parish-church of St. Mary-le-Bow, on Friday, February 15, 1765. London, E. Owen and T. Harrison, 1765. Y3
The accusation that colonial expansion was an invasion of Indian lands and rights is countered with the expressed need to make "moral virtue" available to them.

Yorke, James. A sermon preached before the incorporated Society for the Propagation of the Gospel in Foreign Parts ... in the parish church of St. Mary-le-Bow, on Friday, February 19, 1779. London, T. Harrison and S. Brooke, 1779. Y4
The sermon notes the impact of the American Revolution upon the work of the missions.

[Young, Arthur.] Observations on the present state of the waste lands of Great Britain. Published on occasion of the establishment of a new colony on the Ohio. London, W. Nicoll, 1773. Y5
A favorable view of the upper Ohio River valley as an area for settlement of English emigrants, together with a general discussion of the value and motives of emigration.

[Young, Arthur.] Political essays concerning the present state of the British Empire. London, W. Strahan and T. Cadell, 1772. Y6
These essays are largely concerned with the impact of colonial commerce and industry upon the economy of Great Britain.

[Young, Sir William, bart.] Corn trade. An examination of certain commercial principles, in their application to agriculture and the corn trade, as laid down in the fourth book of Mr. Adam Smith's treatise on the wealth of nations. London, John Stockdale, 1800. Y7
The author takes exception to Smith's free trade principles where agriculture is concerned, noting the practical necessity of protecting the food supply of a nation.

Z

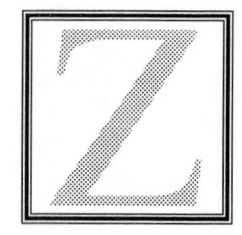

[Zaltieri, Bolognini.] Il desegno del discoperto della Nova Franza. [Venice, Lafreri, 1566.]   Z1
The earliest known printed map to contain the name of the Strait of Anian.

Zani, Valerio, conte. Il genio vagante. Parma, Giuseppe dall' Oglio & Ippolito Rosati; Ippolito & Francesco Maria Rosati, 1691-93.   Z2
This compilation of travels contains 123 items, including accounts of merchants, missionaries, and explorers to Asia, Africa, North and South America, and the Arctic regions.

Zappullo, Michele. Historie di quattro principali città del mondo, Gerusalemme, Roma, Napoli, e Venetia ... aggiuntoui un compendio dell'istorie dell'Indie. Vicenza, Giorgio Greco, 1603.   Z3
A history of Jerusalem, Rome, Naples, and Venice, with a history of Spanish conquest in the New World appended.

Zárate, Agustin de. Le historie ... dello scoprimento et conquista del Peru. Venice, Gabriel Giolito de' Ferrari, 1563.   Z4
The author of this history of the Spanish discovery and conquest of Peru was an official in the colonial government and an ardent champion of colonization.

Zárate, Agustin de. Historia del descubrimiento y conquista de las provincias del Peru. Seville, Alonso Escrivano, 1577.   Z5
The first Spanish edition.

Zárate, Agustin de. Histoire de la decouverte et de la conquete du Perou, traduite de l'Espagnol d'Augustin de Zarate, par S.D.C. Amsterdam, Chez J. Louis de Lorme, 1700.   Z6
The first French edition.

Zárate, Agustin de. Histoire de la decouverte et de la conquête du Perou. Paris, Michel Clousier, 1706.   Z7
One of four issues of this work from Paris in 1706, following the first French edition of 1700. The translation is by S. de Broë.

Zatta, Antonio. Atlante novissimo. Venice, Antonio Zatta, 1779-85.   Z8
This four-volume atlas is one of the outstanding map collections published in Italy in the eighteenth century. It contains 214 maps.

Zavala y Auñon, Miguel de. Representacion al Rey ... que florezca en nuestros dominios un comercio ... [Madrid?] 1732.   Z9
A study of the Spanish economy with emphasis on the colonial commerce.

Zavala y Auñon, Miguel de. Representacion al Rey ... que florezca en nuestros dominios un commercio ... [Madrid?] 1738.   Z10
A reprinting of the preceding work.

Zee praetien gehouden by een rentier, winckellier, zee-man, boer, heer, predikant, coopman, schrijver, bode. [n.p.] 1639.   Z11
An enthusiastic discussion of the defeat of the Spanish fleet by the Dutch.

Zeegevier, oststeken over de drie beroemde zeeslagen, voorgevallen den 7 en 17 juny, en den 21 augusti, dezes jaers 1673 ... Dordrecht, Simon Onder de Linde, 1673.   Z12
A rhymed description of naval actions against France, involving Admirals De Ruyter and Tromp.

Zeeland (Netherlands : Province). Staten. Missive, geschreven uyt Middelburg, in dato 23 Martii 1684. Mitsgaders een placaet, tot voortsettinge de negotie in die provintie. [n.p., 1684?]   Z13

Zeeland (Netherlands : Province). Staten. Resolutie vande ... Heeren Staten van Zeelant. Genomen den 22. September 1663. [n.p., 1663.]   Z14
A protest against Holland's import tax on salt and other commodities from Zeeland.

Zeeland (Netherlands : Province). Staten. Resolutie van de provintie van Zeelandt nopende t' afsonderlyck teyckenen van het tractaet van vrede met Spaengien. [n.p.] 1648. Z15
Concerns the Treaty of Westphalia.

Zeeland (Netherlands : Province). Staten. Verklaringe vande Ed: Mo: Heeren Staten van Zeelandt ende Utrecht, op de propositie gedaen in haere Ed: Mog: Vergaderingen by de gedeputeerde vande Ed: Groot Mog: Heeren Staten van Hollandt ende West-Vrieslandt. [n.p., 1650.] Z16

De Zeeusche verre-kyker. Vlissingen, 1649. Z17
Indicates a strong wish for peace in Brazil, even though it is opposed by the Dutch West India Company.

Zeiller, Martin. Neue Beschreibung der Königreiche Dennemarck unnd Norwegen. Ulm, Balthasar Kühnen, 1648. Z18
Includes descriptions of major Danish and Norwegian cities and their commerce.

Zeiller, Martin. Neue Beschreibung der Königreiche Schweden unnd Gothen ... Ulm, Balthasar Kühnen, 1650. Z19
Descriptions of the commerce of Sweden, particularly of its cities.

Zeiller, Martin. Newe Beschreibung dess Königreichs Polen und Grosz-Hertzogthumbs Lithauen. Ulm, Balthasar Kühnen, 1647. Z20
Includes descriptions of major cities and references to their commercial activities.

Zeitung, welcher Gestalt, im Martio dieses fünffundachtzigsten Jars, etlich König und Fürsten auss Japonia ihre Abgesandten, dess Glaubens halben, gen Rom geschicht haben: Mit angehefter kurtzer Beschreibung derselben jetztgemeldten Land unnd Inseln: Auch eines evangelischen Manns Censur und Urtheil, was von solcher Schickung zuhalten sey. [n.p.] 1585. Z21
An account of the mission of three Japanese envoys to Pope Gregory XIII, including a description of Japan and a commentary on the event from a Protestant point of view.

Zenner, Gottfried. New-Europa oder die Alte in der Neuen Welt, das ist: deutliche Vorstellung, wie Gott, nach seiner Güte und Weissheit, nicht allein das grosse Welt-Theil Americam ... dass alle christeliche See-Nationen ... Leipzig, Georg Christoph Wintzer, 1720. Z22
A description of the colonial establishments, present and past, of the Europeans in North and South America, with particular emphasis on British colonies.

Zeno, Niccolò. De i commentarii del viaggio in Persia ... Venice, F. Marcolini, 1558. Z23
This book, together with its accompanying map, was supposedly based on a narrative of Antonio and Niccolò Zeno the Elder, who allegedly explored the Greenland coasts in 1380 and later.

Zettersten, Erik. Om allmänna handels historien och wetenskapen. Stockholm, Kongl. Finska Boktryckeriet, 1769. Z24
A general survey of world commerce, including chapters on Asia and Africa.

Zettersten, Erik. Allmänna handels-historien och köpmanna-wetenskapen. Stockholm, Wennberg och Compagnie, 1779. Z25
An enlarged edition of the preceding, with specific reference to commerce between Europe and Asia, the trade of major European countries, and the history of Sweden's foreign commerce.

Zettersten, Erik. Allmänna handels-historien och köpmanna wetenskapen. Stockhom, Wennberg, 1779; Stolpiska, 1783. Z26
A re-issue of parts two and three of the 1779 edition. Part one adds fifty-six pages of information and analysis of the commerce of the New World and the Pacific Ocean.

Zettersten, Erik. Försök til en köpmanna-geographie. Stockholm, Wennberg & Nordström, 1770. Z27
A Swedish commercial handbook with a variety of information relative to shipping and to traveling abroad.

Ziegenbalg, Bartholomaeus. Königl. dänischen Missionarii in Trangebar, auf der Küste Coromandel ... Bericht. Halle, Waysenhauses, 1713-43. Z28
A chronicle of the Danish mission in India in 8 volumes with continuations by Heinrich Plütscho.

Ziegenbalg, Bartholomaeus. A letter to the Reverend Mr. Geo. Lewis ... giving an account of the method of instruction used in the charity-schools of the Church, call'd Jerusalem, in Tranquebar. London, J. Downing, 1715. Z29
A very specific description of the types of schools maintained by the Danish mission at Tranquebar for both boys and girls, along with an account of printing done for the mission on the premises.

Ziegenbalg, Bartholomaeus. Thirty four conferences between the Danish missionaries and the Malabarian Bramans ... in the East Indies, concerning the truth of the Christian religion ... London, H. Clements [etc.] 1719. Z30
A collection of exchanges of view between the head of Denmark's mission at Tranquebar and various spokesmen for Eastern religions.

Ziegler, Jacob. In C. Plinii De Naturali Historia librum secundum commentarius. Basel, Henric Petri, 1531. Z31

This commentary on the second book of Pliny's *Natural History* discusses problems of astronomy and meteorology relating to the earth's position among celestial bodies.

[Ziegler, Jacob.] Quae intus continentur ... Strassburg, P. Opilio, 1532. Z32

Chiefly concerned with the Near East, but also contains descriptions of northern Europe and a map showing a land connection between Scandinavia and North America.

Zierikzee (Netherlands). Gravamina, ofte, 17 pointen van bezwaernis, by de Heeren Regeerders der stadt Ziericzee; tegens de Heeren Staten en Steden respective van Zeelant gemoveert, op den 24. November 1668 ... Rotterdam, Johannis Redelijckhuysen, &c, 1669. Z33

Among the complaints of Zierickzee is the cost of the conquest and maintenance of the colony in Surinam.

Zimmermann, Heinrich, of Wiesloch. Dernier voyage du capitaine Cook autour du monde ... traduit avec un abrégé de la vie de ce navigateur célebre, & des notes. Berne, Nouvelle Société Typographique, 1782. Z34

The first French edition of Zimmermann's unauthorized account of Cook's third voyage, the first account of the voyage to be published in Europe.

Zorgdrager, Cornelis Gijsbertsz. Alte und neue grönländische Fischerei und Wallfischfang. Leipzig, Peter Conrad Monath, 1723. Z35

The first German edition of a history and description of the Arctic whaling industry, with maps of the principal islands used for whaling.

Zorgdrager, Cornelis Gijsbertsz. Beschreibung des grönländischen Wallfischfangs und Fischerey. Nuremberg, Georg Peter Monath, 1750. Z36

The second German edition.

Zorgdrager, Cornelis Gijsbertsz. Bloeijende opkomst der aloude en hedandaagsche Groenlandsche visschery ... met byvoeging van de walvischvangst, in haare hoedanigheden ... The Hague, P. van Thol en R.C. Alberts, 1727. Z37

The second Dutch edition. It includes much additional material on the natural history of the northern seas, and a section on the Newfoundland cod fishery.

Zorgdrager, Cornelis Gijsbertsz. Histoire des pêches, des découvertes et des établissemens des Hollandoise dans les mers du nord. Paris, Nyon, 1791-1801. Z38

A study of northern whaling based upon the work of Zorgdrager, ordered by the French government to promote French whaling.

Zucchelli, Antonio. Relazioni del viaggio, e missione di Congo nell' Etiopia inferiore occidentale ... Venice, Bartolameo Giavarina, 1712. Z39

Contains an account of the slave trade from Angola to South America.

Zurara, Gomes Eanes de. Começa a terceira parte da cronica del Rei dom João o primeiro ... na qual se cõtem a tomada na cidade de Seita ē Afriqua per ho cronista Gomez Enes de Zurara. Manuscript. [Portugal, early 16th century.] Z40

The Chronicle of John I, the earliest work of Zurara, is heavily concerned with the beginning of Portuguese interests in Africa with the conquest of Ceuta.